Treasures of Britain

W·W·NORTON

NEW YORK · LONDON

Contents

Contributors

Advisors

Alastair Laing: Advisor on pictures and sculpture to the National Trust.

Colin Amery: Special Advisor to the World Monuments Fund; Architectural Correspondent of the *Financial Times* for 20 years; recent publications include *Art and Architecture – The Story of the Sainsbury Wing at the National Gallery.*

Giles Waterfield: Director, Attingham Summer School and Royal Collection Studies; recent publications include *Art Treasures of England* and *The Hound in the Left-hand Corner.*

Neil Burton: Architectural Historian, director of the Architectural History Practice and formerly Secretary of the Georgian Group.

Simon Jenkins: *Times* columnist and author of *England's Thousand Best Churches.*

Penelope Hobhouse: Writer, designer and lecturer: author of many books, including *Garden Design.*

Dr David Walker: Professor Emeritus at the School of Art History, University of St Andrews; formerly Chief Inspector of Historic Buildings at Historic Scotland.

Authors

Development of the Landscape: Dr Richard Muir, Editor of *Landscapes* and honorary research fellow of Aberdeen University.

Architecture: Colin Amery, Hilary Macartney, Ann MacSween.

Art: Giles Waterfield, Hilary Macartney.

Gazetteer authors

London: Ian Collins, London correspondent of the *Eastern Daily Press* newspaper, whose books include *A Broad Canvas: Art in East Anglia since 1880*; and Paddy Kitchen, art reviewer and author, whose books include *Poets' London* and biographies of Patrick Geddes and Gerard Manley Hopkins.

South East: Ian Sutton, author of *Western Architecture* and David Lloyd, contributor to *Buildings of England.*

South West: Geoffrey Beard, author of 15 books, including *The National Trust Book of English House Interiors* and *Upholsterers and their Work in England, 1530–1840.*

West Country: Jeremy Pearson, Historian for the National Trust; previously worked in several museums.

South Midlands: Lucy Worsley, Inspector of Historic Buildings for English Heritage, specializing in great houses in the Midlands.

Home Counties: Emily Cole, Historian for English Heritage, researcher and writer on *Architecture of England and Ireland*; and Clare Campbell, Southern Caseworker at the Georgian Group.

East Anglia: Ian Collins and Peter Tolhurst, Historic Buildings Advisor, publisher and author of *East Anglia: A Literary Pilgrimage.*

North Midlands: Neil Burton (*see* details under advisors, left).

North East: Jane Hatcher, local and architectural historian and part-time lecturer at the University of Leeds; author of several books on Richmond, Richmondshire and Yorkshire.

North West: Frank Kelsall, Architectural Historian, previously inspector of historic buildings for English Heritage in the North West; now works as a consultant to the Ancient Monuments Society.

North and South Wales: Lindsay Evans, Trustee of the National Heritage Memorial Fund until 1999; author of several books including *Castles of Wales.*

Scotland: Callum Brines, Wendy Lee, Hilary Macartney, Ruth Noble, A. J. Paterson, Catherine Ianco, Nicola Taylor, Julia and John Keay, Mary McGrigor, Patrick Taylor, Martine Nouet, Richard Balharry, Syd Bangham, Greg Corbett, Joan Dobbie, Claudine Glot, Ann MacSween, Olwyn Owen.

Foreword by John Julius Norwich

 Nowhere in the world but in Britain – not in France, not in Germany or Spain, not even in Italy – will you find less than 90,000 square miles (233,000 square kilometres) containing such a profusion of medieval cathedrals and churches, of historic houses and castles spanning well over a thousand years, of dazzling museums and galleries, of glorious gardens and superb scenery. To describe it all between the covers of a single book is an impossible task. All we can hope to do is to give you some idea of the wonders awaiting you, to help you make your selection and to guide you on your way.

But there is an admission to be made: the sad fact is that a century ago our architectural heritage was considerably richer than it is today. Many of the losses – particularly in the City of London, in industrial areas like Coventry and in ports like Portsmouth – were the result of enemy action in World War II; but far, far more were due to the so-called planners of the decades immediately following. It was they who – in the name of progress – gutted one historic town after another, replacing the twisted street patterns with shopping malls and piazzas and 'recreational spaces'; and substituting, in the place of the old variety and character, a grim concrete uniformity that deadens the spirit. In several magnificent old cities – Gloucester and Worcester in particular spring to mind – they destroyed so much that one is mildly surprised to see the Cathedral still standing. Nor were they alone among the guilty. National governments, by refusing to give owners of historic houses any significant exemption from their crippling taxation, made the continuing maintenance of these buildings impossible. Between 1945 and 1974, over 250 historic houses were demolished. Here was official vandalism on a scale unparalleled since Henry VIII's Dissolution of the Monasteries over four centuries before.

Today, fortunately, things are a good deal better. Organizations such as English Heritage, the Historic Houses Association, Historic Scotland, Cadw, the National Trust and the National Trust for Scotland are doing a magnificent job; meanwhile the fact that almost everyone in the country owns or has access to a car has led to a huge increase in interest on the part of the general public, together with a new respect for architecture. All this means that if the present climate of opinion continues, it is difficult to imagine any further barbarities of the kind which were all too frequent half a century ago.

Where the countryside is concerned, on the other hand, the future looks a good deal less secure. Hedgerows, for example, are vital for many species of flowering plants, birds and insects, serving too as important corridors for animals to move from one place to another; yet the increase in the size of fields and the relentless spread of urban development has caused the disappearance of well over half of our hedgerows in the past 50 years, some 70,000 miles between 1984 and 1993. A degree of legal protection was secured in 1997, but this still protects only one in five of the hedges in England alone. Much the same is true of our flower-rich meadows and pastures, traditionally used for hay-making and the grazing of livestock; since 1945, 95 per cent of those meadows have gone and in the past decade alone, we have lost an area of permanent grassland the size of Bedfordshire, while what remains is still at risk.

What is to be done? One real contribution is to join English Heritage and the National Trust (see page 704). But the purpose of this introduction is not to hold out a begging bowl. The important thing is that you should make the most of your time in Britain, planning your itinerary in such a way as to see as many as possible of the things that interest you most. If this book helps you to do that, and if it succeeds in giving you some idea of the richness and variety of what our country has to offer, it will not have been written in vain.

John Julius Norwich

Introduction

People are increasingly recognising that their heritage is all around them. It is not just to be found in magnificent stately homes, the romantic ruins of medieval castles and abbeys, or beautifully arranged exhibits in museums. It is also the Victorian coalhole cover in their street, the 18th-century milestone that still points the way to their village, even the dusty and echoing remains of the mine or the mill in which their grandfathers toiled. The heritage is small and local as well as elegant and heroic; it lies in the model villages put up for their workers by philanthropic businessmen as well as in the great houses they built for themselves; it resonates in prehistoric land boundaries still in use in the uplands, and old cobbled streets.

English Heritage cares for all of this. Our historians, archaeologists and architects identify and research all aspects of the historic environment and recommend how it should be managed and protected. Listed buildings range from Blenheim Palace to a World War II prefab, and scheduled monuments from the Rollright Stones to coastal gun emplacements. Archaeological work includes traditional excavation as well as the analysis of standing buildings. Our grants go to cathedrals and churches as well as urban regeneration schemes. And this is only some of our work.

We also have over 400 properties directly in our care, ranging from World Heritage Sites such as Stonehenge and Hadrian s Wall to megaliths and ruined chapels in the middle of fields. Most of them are open to the public, many of them free of charge. Some are ruins, once home to kings and nobles, monks and prelates, while others are still habitable. The range is enormous, the variety boundless.

We are delighted to have worked with the publishers of this book to make one of the most ambitious and beautiful reference books to our extraordinarily rich architectural and artistic heritage.

Simon Thurley.

The National Trust plays an important part in the daily lives of millions of people: countryside in the Trust's care receives a conservative estimate of 50 million visits each year; and over 600,000 school children benefit from the formal educational opportunities offered by the Trust at its properties.

The Trust's fundamental purposes are as relevant today as they were in the vision of its three founders: Octavia Hill, Canon Hardwicke Rawnsley and Sir Robert Hunter in 1895. They wanted to provide people with opportunities for recreation, physical and mental, by preserving places of natural beauty or historic interest forever. This ambitious aim is founded upon a unique power vested in the Trust by Act of Parliament, to declare property inalienable. This means that it cannot be sold, mortgaged or compulsorily purchased against the Trust's wishes without the consent of Parliament.

This safeguard has encouraged tens of thousands of people to give and bequeath property and chattels (or furniture) as well as money for the purchase of land, in the knowledge that the Trust will look after them in perpetuity. Since the Trust's first acquisition, of a small area of cliffland above Barmouth, over 612,000 acres (248,000ha) of countryside farmed by some 2,000 agricultural tenants have been entrusted to its care, as well as 600 miles (960km) of coastline, 200 historic houses and a similar number of gardens.

The Trust is now responsible for a remarkable variety of sites, ranging in time from the largest prehistoric stone circle in Europe (Avebury, Wilts) to Sir Paul McCartney's teenage Liverpool home, and in size from TE Lawrence's cottage retreat (Clouds Hill, Dorset) to one of the largest private houses in England (Knole, Kent). The care of over 400 Sites of Special Scientific Interest and 31 National Nature Reserves requires active management to maintain their scientific value and promote wildlife conservation. New projects include the Victorian house Tyntesfield and a 19th-century workhouse near Southwell.

You will find descriptions of many National Trust properties in this magnificent book, and I hope it will inspire you to visit them and see the work that we are doing at first-hand.

Fiona Reynolds.

The 20 Best Country Houses

Selected by John Julius Norwich

From the staggering quantity and variety of the best country houses in England, Scotland and Wales, how can one possibly pick the best? Chatsworth and Blenheim, Holkham and Wilton and Knole would obviously feature on most lists, but at this point the selectors would go their own ways. What follows is therefore a personal selection, nothing more. It is based on a number of things: history, architecture, contents, and – by no means least – that indefinable quality that we know as charm. But it is only a start. The longer the time you have and the more widely you roam, the more treasures you will find.

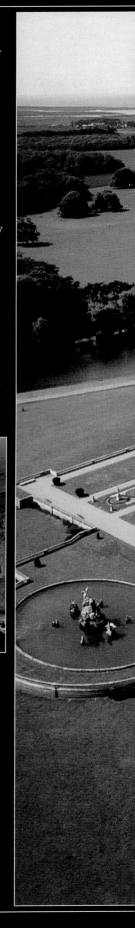

Alnwick, Nthumb
A romantic Border castle with an excellent art collection.

Blenheim Palace, Oxon
Built 1705-25 by a grateful government to designs by Vanbrugh, as a reward to the 1st Duke of Marlborough for his success in the wars against France.

Boughton House, Nhants
A magnificent early 18th-century house on Tudor foundations with superb interiors and glorious furniture and pictures.

Chatsworth, Derbys
The grandest house in England, seat of the Duke of Devonshire. Superb pictures, furniture, gardens and park.

Haddon Hall, Derbys
Perhaps the most romantic house in England, with the oldest kitchen in the country. originally Norman, last altered in Elizabethan times.

Harewood House, W R Yks
Magnificent 18th-century house with Adam interiors;

Hopetoun House, W Loth
A square classical-style building by William Bruce, extended by William Adam and sons. Good collections of paintings, furniture, porcelain and tapestries.

Houghton Hall, Norflk
Kent's Stone Hall is one of the great rooms of England. Superb pictures and plasterwork.

Knole, Kent
One of the largest houses in England – the size of a village and the most atmospheric. A world of its own. [NT]

Plas Newydd, Gwynnd
Built by Wyatt in Gothic Revival style in a spectacular position overlooking the Menai Strait between Anglesey and the mainland. Superb mural by Rex Whistler in the Dining Room. [NT]

St Michael's Mount, Cnwll
No house in England boasts a more spectacular site, on a great crag projecting into the sea , by which it is cut off from the mainland for 20 hours a day. [NT]

Castle Howard, N Yorks
The first work of Vanbrugh, featured in the *Brideshead Revisited* television series.

Claydon House, Bucks
A Jacobean manor house remodelled in the 1750s with some of the most spectacular plasterwork in England. [NT]

Cotehele House, Cnwll
A medieval fortified granite manor house with wonderful tapestries. Time stands still. [NT]

memorable collections of pictures, furniture and porcelain.

Hatfield House, Herts
Begun in 1607 by Robert Cecil, chief minister to James I, and still occupied by his descendants.

Holkham Hall, Norflk
A Palladian palace designed for Thomas Coke, 1st Earl of Leicester by William Kent, who was responsible for the interiors and much of the furniture.

Mellerstain House, Borders
A vast mansion built in the 18th century by William and Robert Adam. Magnificent plasterwork, furniture and picture collections.

Petworth House, E Susx
Late 17th-century house in French style. Don't miss the Grinling Gibbons carvings or the glorious landscapes by JMW Turner, who practically lived here in the 1830s. [NT]

Syon House, Gt Lon
Originally a monastery founded by Henry V, now the Thames-side house of the Duke of Northumberland. Spectacular series of rooms by Robert Adam.

Wilton House, Wilts
Mid-16th-century house partially rebuilt in the mid-17th century, possibly by Inigo Jones. Six dazzling state rooms; the Double Cube Room is among the finest in England.

Centre: Knole, Kent
Main picture: Holkham Hall, Norfolk

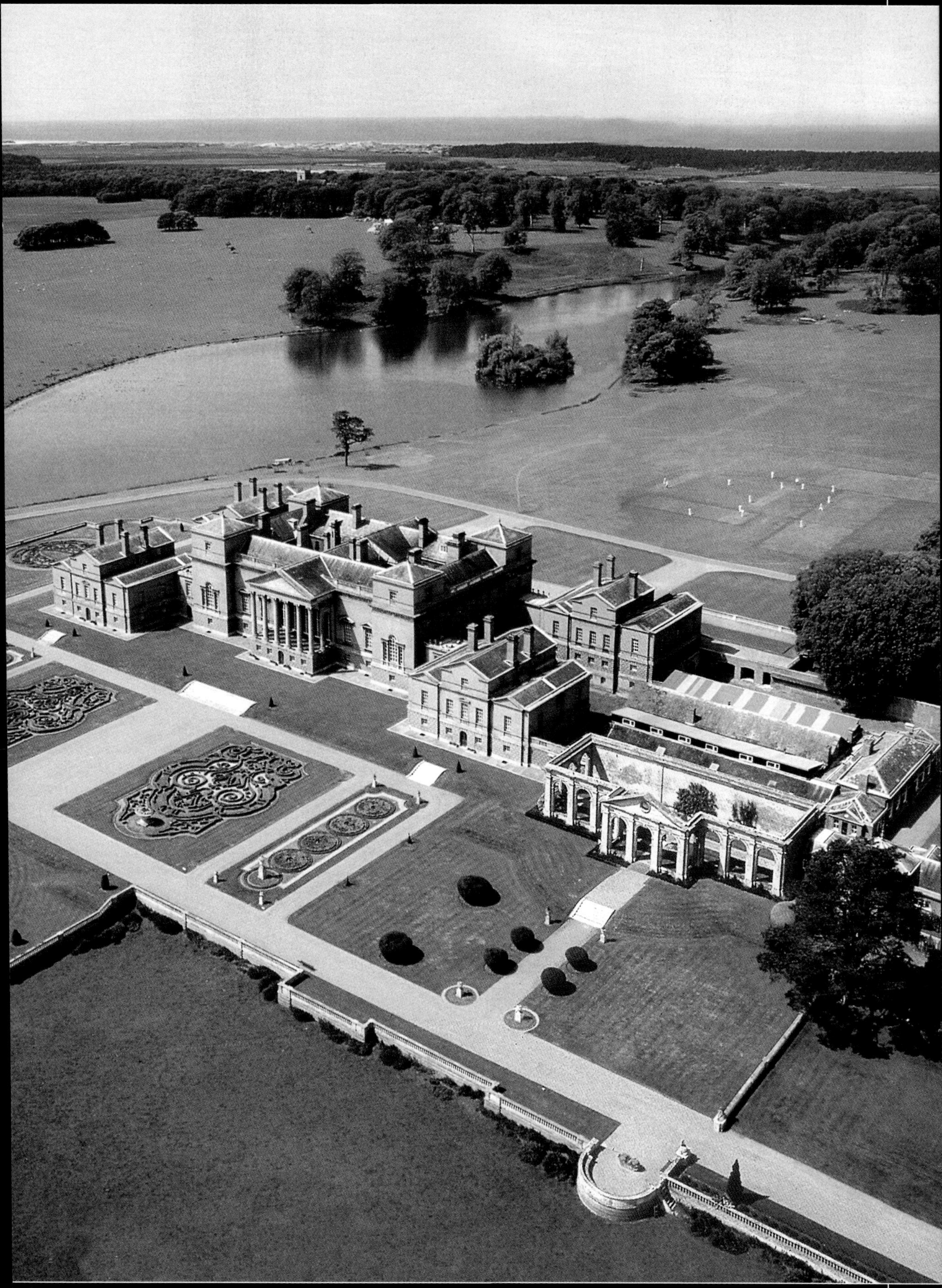

These are not the largest gardens, but the ones with the most exquisite designs and beautiful all-round planting. They date from the 17th through to the 20th century and include a mixture of formal gardens, landscape gardens and specialist plant gardens.

Barnsley House, Gloucs
Designed by Rosemary and David Verey since 1951. Strong framework of alleys, laburnum and pleached lime walk, matching period of 17th-century house. Shrub roses, mixed borders and superb French-style potager.

Biddulph Grange, Staffs
Extraordinary Victorian gardens, laid out from 1842 and recently restored. Themed Chinese and Egyptian gardens, conifer avenue, dahlia borders. [NT]

Buscot Park, Oxon
Superb Harold Peto water-garden design feeds into 18th-century lake. Border designs by Peter Coats and hop hornbeam tunnels by Tim Rees. [NT]

Chatsworth, Derbys
400 years of garden development: 1700s cascade, canals, orangery, sculpture, Capability Brown landscape, Victorian glasshouses, Paxton rockery and a yew maze.

Drummond Castle, P & K
Terraced gardens created in the 1630s with a St Andrew's Cross design from the 19th century. A dazzling formal display centred on a sundial.

Great Dixter, E Susx
Christopher Lloyd's famous garden around a house restored by Lutyens in 1910. Fine topiary, mixed borders, 'hot' tropical bedding, wild flowers and naturalized bulbs.

Hampton Court Palace, Surrey
Royal gardens from 16th century. 1691 maze, Fountain Garden and radiating lime tree avenues. William III's Privy Garden recently authentically restored. Vine planted in 1768. Jean Tijou gilded railings.

Hatfield House, Herts
Formal gardens, imaginatively restored by Lady Salisbury. 16th-century knot garden by old Tudor Palace with authentic planting. Victorian maze.

Hestercombe, Somset
Justly renowned for its Edwardian Lutyens/Jekyll garden, on different levels.

Lutyens for the stonework, Jekyll for the colour planting. Recently restored. Romantic landscape garden dates from 18th century designed by Copleston Warre Bampfylde.

Hidcote Manor, Gloucs
Designed as a compartmental garden by Lawrence Johnson in the early 20th century. Themed gardens, tapestry hedges, alleys, old roses, cottage-style planting. [NT]

Iford Manor, Wilts
Sir Harold Peto's early 20th-century garden. Italianate style on steep terraced slopes linked by steps. Pools, fountains, loggias, architectural fragments and evergreens.

Inverewe, Highld
Rare and delicate plants, including many from the southern hemisphere, flourish in this Scottish 'jungle'. Begun by Osgood Mackenzie in 1862.

Knightshayes Court, Devon
Borders and terraces by 19th-century house, with rare tender plants. Woodland garden since 1945, admirably maintained and imaginatively planted. [NT]

Levens Hall, Cumb
Late 17th-century topiary garden, extended by Victorians. Beech alleys and view to superlative countryside. Box-edged beds of impeccable massed annuals set off monumental yew sculpture.

Powis Castle, Powys
Formal 'hanging' terraces date to late 17th century. Decorated with clipped yews and fine lead urns. Spectacular border planting. [NT]

Rousham House, Oxon
William Kent's finest design between 1737 and 1741: a virtuoso arrangement of buildings, follies, serpentine woodland rill and views to countryside. Walled gardens near the house predate Kent but have modern planting.

Sissinghurst, Kent
Renowned 20th-century gardens designed and planted by Vita Sackville-West and Harold Nicolson. Yew hedges and pleached lime walks frame a white garden, 'hot' gardens, old roses, spring bulbs. [NT]

Stourhead, Wilts
Best-known English landscape garden begun in 1745. Valleys, lake, temples, grotto, hermitage. Victorian conifers and 20th-century rhododendrons. [NT]

Stowe Landscape Gardens, Bucks
Vast 18th-century landscape worked over by Bridgeman, Kent, and Brown. Grass, trees, temples and vistas make Stowe unforgettable.

Wakehurst Place, E Susx
Original Loder tree and shrub collection, now part of the Royal Botanic Gardens of Kew. Rhododendrons, Himalayan plants, water garden, walled garden, a rock walk and winter garden. [NT]

This selection does not include Britain's great cathedrals, all of which you will find described in the Gazetteer section. Instead, it highlights parish churches with remarkable architecture or interiors, wonderful settings and superlative carvings or stained glass. All are well worth a visit.

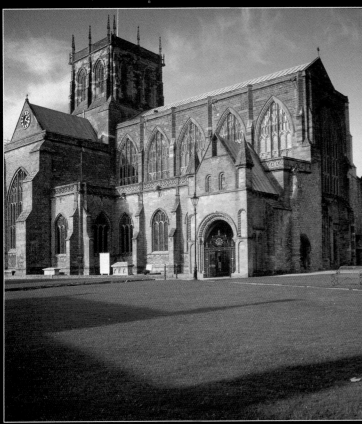

Patrington, St Patrick, E R Yk
Limestone jewel of early 14th-century gothic, lost in Holderness.

Rosslyn Chapel, Mdloth
The finest example of Scottish late gothic, founded in 1477.

Selby, N Yks
Abbey restored after fire; majestic east window.

Sherborne Abbey, Dorset
Superb fan vaults of Ham stone.

Tewkesbury, Gloucs
Massive Norman exterior encasing Despenser tombs.

Walpole St Peter, Nflk
Perfect East Anglian church; a study in light on stone.

Warwick, St Mary, Warwks
Home of the mighty Beauchamps, with monuments to match.

Beverley Minster, E R Yk 'Best' non-cathedral church in England; rich in building of all gothic ages.

Boston, Lincs
The 'Stump', the highest tower in England.

Bristol St Mary Redcliffe, Bristl
Seafarers' foundation, with 'oriental' porch and vaulted nave.

Burford, Oxon
Wealthy merchants' church of the upper Thames Valley, rich in tombs.

Cheadle, Staffs
Pugin's Roman Catholic masterpiece of early Victorian gothic.

Christchurch, Dorset
Norman core with dazzling Perpendicular chancel.

Cirencester, Gloucs
Cathedral of 'woolgothic'; superb marketplace porch.

Dunkeld, P & K
On the banks of the Tay, the best setting of any Scottish church.

Fairford St Mary, Gloucs
Unaltered medieval windows and woodwork.

Grantham, Lincs
Finest of all gothic steeples.

Long Melford, Sufflk
Perpendicular gallery of clothiers' wealth; Clopton chantry with lily crucifix.

Ludlow, Shrops
Cathedral of the Marches; Palmers Guild chapel and glass.

Ottery St Mary, Devon
Jumble of styles with vividly painted roof.

Top left: Sherborne Abbey, Dorset
Bottom: Cirencester, Gloucs
Main picture: Long Melford, Sufflk

The Development of the Landscape

The Framework of the Countryside

All the countrysides in England and Wales have been created by human activities such as farming, forestry and recreation. Most of the natural wildwood was cleared in prehistoric times and it now seems that the outlines of the farmed area were already well established by the Roman landings in AD 43. Timber was still essential for house-making, fencing, tool-making and fuel. The traditional woodland skills withered in Victorian times, but sometimes the traces of coppicing and pollarding can still be recognized. Much medieval woodland existed as coppice-with-standards, as the trees and shrubs of the underwood were cut at ground level every 10 to 20 years to produce light timber for fuel, wattle fencing and many other uses. Above the coppices towered oaks or elms grown as standards and felled when 70 or more years old for heavy, constructional timber.

Patterns of settlement varied. Particularly in the vales of the Midlands where ploughland was organized in vast, communally worked fields, population tended to be concentrated in large villages. Elsewhere, more ancient traditions survived and hamlets and farmsteads were common. The great majority of the villages of the Middle Ages were dormitories for the peasant households who formed an overwhelming majority of the population. Thousands disappeared when change affected farming patterns – as when farmlands were converted into depopulated sheep ranges in Tudor times, or when landscape parks were created in the 18th century. Binding fields, woodlands and settlements together were roads and tracks of many ages, some still bustling with traffic, others vanishing back into the countryside.

1. Farming was introduced to England from the Continent more than 6,000 years ago by the immediate forbears of the people who built megalithic tombs, like Pentre Ifan in Wales.

2. Like many others, this Roman road near Cambridge declined and became a minor lane after the legions withdrew.

3. A legacy of arched bridges remains from the days of packhorse trading, like this one, near Pateley Bridge.

4. The first lands to be farmed were the light, well-drained soils of the southern chalk uplands, like these downs near Shaftesbury.

5. In the uplands of England and Wales the collapse of mining, the decay of crafts and the vicissitudes of hill farming have led to the desertion of villages, as here in the Pennant Valley in Wales.

6. Until the industrial age the movement of goods over hilly country depended upon pack horses. Now the old pack horse roads, like this one in Nidderdale, are no more than footpaths.

7. Villages (this is Weobley) were the agricultural dormitories of the medieval realm, housing the peasant households that would be found working side by side during the day in the surrounding fields.

The Working Countryside

The working countryside is a mosaic of land uses, with fragments of ancient practices often showing through. Oldest of all may be the expanses of common land, sometimes surely inherited from prehistoric times. The commons provided grazing for the communal herds of cattle and sheep, peat for fuel, thatching and bedding material and much more. Most of the old commons were enclosed by straight walls and hedges in the century after 1750. The open field ploughlands, which sometimes survived for a thousand years following their appearance around AD 800, are now only recognizable as the corduroy-like patterns of ridge and furrow which mark the directions of peasant plough strips. This is an age of global trade in foodstuffs, but medieval communities were largely self-sufficient. Each one needed its ploughland, where wheat, barley, oats, rye, peas and beans grew, and pasture, commons and meadows where the hay needed to support the livestock through the bleak winter could be grown.

Just as the painted glass in a church window is set off by the leading, so the fieldscapes of England and Wales derive much of their charm from the walls and hedgerows that define the fields and properties and keep the animals apart from the crops. Walls are found where sources of stone are abundant and are features of the more exposed and rugged areas, where hedging shrubs do not flourish. Traditionally, hedges were rejuvenated by 'laying' about every 20 years. Hill farmers were, and usually still are, competent wallers, able to patch the gaps caused by winter gales.

1. The growing of cereals gave rise to a need for mills. Some grain was ground illegally in the peasant home, but most went to the manorial mill – a watermill if a water source was to hand, or otherwise a windmill perched on exposed ground, like this tower mill at Burwell in Cambridgeshire.

2. Mowing an upland meadow in Dyfed.

4. Field maple growing in a hedgerow: one of the trees, like oak or hazel, that are normally associated with older hedgerows. Hedgerows shelter wildlife and provide corridors for their movement.

5. Snow lingering in the furrows on this Wharfedale slope traces the outlines of ridge and furrow ploughland. The curves result from the oxen hauling the plough

The meadows of the old wetlands were cut later in the season than the modern meadows where the grass is cut soft and young for silage.

3. Golden buttercups in the hay meadows of Swaledale. Soon they will be over-topped by the grasses of the rising hay crop.

being swung into a turn as the headland was approached.

6. Gaps in these 18th-century field walls in the Yorkshire Dales reveal the destructive effects of winter gales.

Countrysides of the Powerful

Traditionally, the countrysides of England and Wales not only produced food but they also provided recreation for the powerful and privileged. After the Norman Conquest, the number and extents of royal hunting forests greatly increased, as did the severity of the laws enforced in the special Forest Courts. Medieval forests were not wooded areas, for most included a wide variety of countryside types, including plenty of farmland. Rather, they were areas subject to Forest Law, which conserved game. Gradually, the emphasis passed from the vast reserves controlled by the king to the much smaller deer parks of the aristocracy. Ringed by banks, ditches and palings, allowing animals to get in but not out, these parks confined the deer (normally fallow deer originally imported from southern Europe) until the day of the chase.

After the Middle Ages, the characteristic deer park landscape of wooded pasture and spinneys set amongst tree-studded lawns was adopted in the landscape parks of the gentry. As the monarchy became too powerful to challenge, so the baronial castle gave way to the stately home, standing alone amidst carefully contrived parkland. The Elizabethans built gardens of modest proportions with intricate beds and orderly lay-outs, often with ponds and canals. Later, immense lawns and plantations traversed by arrow-straight avenues were favoured, and their geometry seemed to assert the triumph of human rationality over Nature. During the 18th century, serpentine lakes and more naturalistic plantings came into favour. In the 19th century, a new aristocratic recreation developed as improvements in shotgun design and transport opened up the northern moors to grouse shooting parties.

1. The park gates at Castle Ashby, Northamptonshire. The Elizabethan and Jacobean mansion was approached by a main avenue some 3¾ miles (6km) long.

2. The Valley of Desolation near Bolton Priory was part of an ecclesiastical medieval deer park. The creation of multitudes of deer parks had a great impact on the English and Welsh landscape.

3. Deer parks and the later landscape parks had grazed lawns dotted with fine trees and they recalled the ancient wood pastures of the Domesday Book.

4. Boughs were cut from pollarded trees to provide browse for deer. In the New Forest this practice was outlawed in 1698, so this pollarded beech could be over 400 years old.

5. The last generation of parks and great houses included many which resulted from fortunes made in commerce and industry, like Lord Penrhyn's castle and park near Bangor; informal plantings of trees and rhododendrons grace the setting.

6. Sheep graze on the stepped terraces of an abandoned Elizabethan garden at Strixton in Northamptonshire. Traces of abandoned parks are common in the countrysides of England and Wales.

The Scottish Countryside

The Scottish Lowlands, with their open approaches and richer soils, were exposed to the spread of feudal influences from England in the 11th, 12th and 13th centuries. Countrysides with villages and plough strips developed, while small towns, the royal burghs and burghs of barony were founded by the kings and barons respectively. To the north and west of the Highland Boundary Fault, running from near Stonehaven in the east to the Firth of Clyde in the west, ancient Celtic customs persisted. In some places they held sway until the Jacobite defeat at Culloden at the dawn of the industrial age in 1746.

Countrysides in the Highlands were quite different from those in the Lowlands. Despite their beauty and desolation, Highland landscapes are very unnatural, being the products of former land hunger and overgrazing in a vulnerable environment. This was partly because the traditional chieftains were as much warlords as estate owners and they sought to retain more warriors than the harshly glaciated settings upland could easily sustain. By the time of Culloden, the ancient Caledonian Scots pine forest had dwindled and fragmented and iron masters and shipbuilders then removed much of what remained. The upland landscape was a place of impoverished clachans or hamlets, know in the English-speaking margins as 'fermtouns' – or 'milltouns' or 'kirktouns' if they had mills or churches.

Of the multitude of settlements, only ruins remain. Much of old rural Scotland vanished during the 'Improvements' of the 18th and 19th centuries, when estates were reorganized and modernized and countless tenants were evicted. In the Highlands the notorious 'Clearances', which saw families replaced by sheep and massive migration from the Clan homelands, were followed by further Victorian evictions to create deer forests for hunting.

1. Upland landscapes in Glen Nevis show a zoning of land use, from the riverside marshes and flood meadows, through the pastures and woodlands of the valley slopes to the unenclosed upland grazings and bare, heavily glaciated outcrops of the crest lines.

5

6

4. The spectacular monument at Callanish on Lewis was erected around the start of the Bronze Age, but afterwards the stones were almost engulfed by rising beds of peat when the climate turned cool and wet.

5. Despite its soulful beauty, the landscape of the Scottish Highlands is quite unnatural. The ancient Scots pine forest has almost vanished, replaced by sheep pastures and plantations of alien conifers. This is Loch Duich.

6. The traditional dwelling of the Highlands and Islands was the black house, with thick, windowless walls packed with peat and a roof of oat straw or heather anchored by a net weighted with stones. This restored example is at Colbost on Skye.

2. Survivors of the terrible Clearances emigrated or became established as crofters on the sea shore and islands, eventually gaining some security of tenure. These crofts, with their ribbon-like holdings, stand at the foot of Quiraing on Skye.

3. Ruined dwellings litter the upland landscape, many of them relics of the Clearances. This ruin, on the shore at Elgol on Skye, may have been home to crofters or a fisherman's family. The Cuillins are in the distance.

Architecture

Prehistoric/Anglo Saxon/Norman

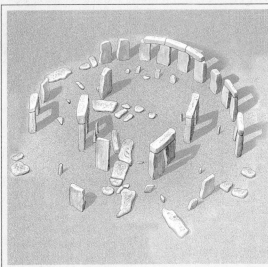

It could be misleading to call some of the earliest man-made artefacts that litter the soil of England and Wales 'architecture' – but they embody construction techniques that were subsequently developed and refined. Stonehenge today is very isolated and remote from any known building type but its great stones supporting lintels use a way of building that was well known in Mycenean Greece. Earthworks, tombs and rough stone walls evoke a way of life that was defensive and ruled by beliefs about unknown pre-Christian gods. The Anglo-Saxons who arrived in England in the 5th and 6th centuries did not achieve anything like the standards of the Roman colonizers. They were unable to comprehend the values of Roman life and either ignored the architecture of the Empire or pillaged it for building materials, while Danish raids may have assisted in the dismantling of much of the built inheritance of Rome.

Left: Stonehenge, Wiltshire
The great circle of giant upright stones on the Wiltshire plain dates from prehistory, probably 2nd or 3rd millennium BC. It is the annual focus of Druidic solstice rituals.

Below: Bradford-on-Avon church, Wiltshire
This church, founded by St Aldhelm, is dedicated to St Lawrence and was built in AD 700. For a long time it was in secular use but is now recognized as the most important Saxon church in England.

Left: Maiden Castle, Dorset
An Iron Age hill fort near Dorchester, which was captured by the Romans in a famous battle in AD 44 under Vespasian. Excavations in the 1930s uncovered Iron Age and Roman artefacts.

Right: Dover Castle, Kent
Built to defend the 'front door of England', what we admire today is mainly Henry I's 12th-century keep and curtain walls. The Constable's Tower and the chapel are spectacular remains of ancient English power.

Early Scottish Architecture

The earliest surviving examples of Scottish architecture are almost 6000 years old. Significant remains dating from the Stone Age (4000–2000 BC) to the Viking invasions (7th century AD), have survived in the north of Scotland, where stone was used as a building material. In the south, where wood was widely used, there are far fewer remains.

Left: Celtic cross, Iona, Argyll & Bute
The Scots, who came from northern Ireland *c*500 AD, introduced Irish Christianity and its decorative motifs. They erected crosses carved with a halo which combined biblical scenes and traditional Scottish images in bas-relief. A good example is the cross of St Martin (7th century) on the island of Iona.

Left: Maes Howe, Orkney
This impressive mound (*c*2700 BC) is 115 feet (35m) in diameter and 23 feet (7m) high, and stands on an artificial platform surrounded by a broad ditch. The central chamber has a remarkable sandstone dressing and incorporates what are probably three funerary niches. The entrance corridor is in line with the rising sun during the winter solstice.

Below right: Mousa, Shetland
Iron Age brochs were round defensive structures found only in Scotland, especially in the north and west. The double dry-stone walls sometimes enclosed a flight of steps, while a single entrance opened on to a central courtyard. Brochs were often associated with a group of buildings, like fortified farms, the central courtyard serving as a cattle pen and a place of refuge. The best preserved example is the 42-foot (13m) broch of Mousa dating from the 1st to 2nd century AD.

Far right: Pictish stone, Aberlemno, Angus
The Romans referred to the inhabitants of northern and eastern Scotland as the Pictii. The most remarkable monuments left by these people were stones decorated with symbolic motifs like those of Aberlemno. There has been much speculation about the function of these stones. They may have been used as boundary markers and their symbols may have represented the families or associated groups who occupied the marked territory.

Below: Skara Brae, Orkney
This remarkably well-preserved site in the Orkneys gives a good idea of what a Stone Age village must have looked like. The houses and workshops were built partially below ground and were linked by narrow passageways. Each dwelling had a central stone hearth, beds edged with stones and lined with moss, and a stone dresser. There were one or more underground larders and other storage spaces set into the walls. The roof, made of peat, heather or turf, was supported by slender poles. It served both as insulation and protection, and because it was fairly porous, it allowed the smoke to escape.

1 entrance to the village
2 main passageway
3 secondary passageway
4 doorway
5 hearth
6 dresser
7 beds
8 niches
9 cell
10 larder
11 outer corridor
12 other houses

Roman Architecture

Right: Hadrian's Wall, Northumberland
Long fragments of Roman walls and gates remain along the Northumberland borders, designed to keep out Picts and Scots. The most complete remaining Roman fortification in Europe.

Bath, St Albans, Chichester, Fishbourne, Hadrian's Wall, London and Colchester are all sites of important examples of the architecture of Roman Britain. But although England produces abundant evidence of the civilizing influence of Rome on the northernmost frontiers of the empire, the buildings are modest by the standards of other parts of the Roman world. Certain Romano-British cities like York, Lincoln, Canterbury and London survived in some form as Anglo-Saxon local capitals but what seems amazing to us today is the lack of understanding, which caused the collapse of Roman Britain in the 5th century. The most influential remaining element of Roman rule is the network of roads – like Watling Street and Fosse Way – that radiated in straight lines from the hub of London. Architecturally, England did not really become a classical nation again until after the Grand Tourists returned from their 18th-century visits to Rome itself.

Left: Lullingstone, Kent
A Roman middle-class villa, typical of many of the smaller Roman villas built in southern England. This reconstruction shows how it was built around its sheltered atrium garden.

Below: Temple of Mithras, London
One of London's most celebrated discoveries uncovered in 1954 during the post-war rebuilding of the City of London.
The cult temple was built in AD 245 and archeologists discovered a fine head of the bull slaying Mithras. The remains were left exposed on a raised site.

Below: Verulamium (St Albans), Hertfordshire
A very important Roman city; some of the brick and flint walls from AD 125 still stand. There is evidence of the forum, theatre, temples and good examples of the hypocaust system.

Above: Fishbourne, West Sussex
The most important villa in Britain – more of a palace, which suggests that it might have been one of the residences of a ruler. Grand mosaics and decoration evoke a sunnier world than damp Sussex.

Left: Bath, Somerset
The most splendid complex of pleasure buildings from the AD 60s, superbly excavated to show how the Romans enjoyed themselves in the spa dedicated to Aquae Sulis and the goddess Minerva.

Feudal Castles

Below: Tower of London, London
The Norman White Tower at the heart of the Tower of London, begun by William the Conqueror after the Battle of Hastings in 1066, once dominated London and is now the most important Norman fortified building in Britain. Successors each added their own features, Edward I building the outer curtain wall and moat in the late 13th century.

The introduction of the Anglo-Norman feudal system after the Norman Conquest of 1066 was accompanied by the construction of mottes or *motes* (a mound surmounted by a tower or castle) and baileys (the outer wall of a castle). In the late 12th and early 13th centuries the mottes were replaced by solid castles with a keep and a stone outer wall, and sometimes surrounded by moats.

Below: Bodiam Castle, East Sussex
Bodiam is a late example of a French type of castle, built in 1385. In plan it forms a perfect square, surrounded by a moat. Imposing gatehouses stand to the front and rear. It was saved and restored by Lord Curzon in 1919 and is now the property of the National Trust.

Above: White Tower, London
Built of Caen stone, its heavy Norman solidity contrasts with the charming pepper-pot cupolas, which are a later addition. The walls are 15 feet (4.5m) thick, 90 feet (27.5m) high and the building of the complex went on well into the reign of Henry I and the medieval kings. The chapel of St Peter ad Vincula is unchanged.

Below: Duffus Castle, Moray
Early castles were often old feudal mottes: a square wooden tower built on a mound, which dominated a courtyard, the whole structure fenced round, sometimes with a moat.
At Duffus Castle, the remains of a 14th-century stone keep stand on a 12th-century feudal motte.

Right: Drum Castle, Aberdeenshire
In the 14th and 15th centuries a number of stone keeps were transformed into tower-houses. Even if the enclosure wall contained outbuildings, the tower was still designed as a virtually autonomous unit. The only entrance was reached by means of a ladder or movable wooden staircase. The cellars and dungeons were in the basement, the kitchens occupied an entire floor or adjoined the banqueting hall, and the private apartments were above. There was often another reception room on the top floor. An easily defended spiral staircase linked the different levels.

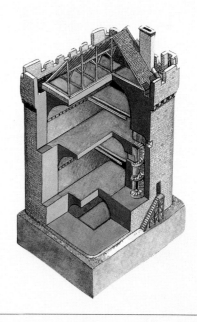

Medieval Churches and Cathedrals

The medieval period in England produced the finest masterpieces of ecclesiastical architecture – some cathedrals and parish churches are among the most impressive in Europe. The three phases of medieval architecture are known as Early English (roughly 1150 to 1275), Decorated (1275 to 1375) and Perpendicular (1375 to 1530). Their style is entirely gothic – i.e. the arches are pointed. There was a transitional period when round arches and pointed arches occur in the same building. Early English is seen at its purest in Salisbury Cathedral and the retro-choir of Southwark Cathedral. York Minster, Exeter Cathedral and St Mary Redcliffe in Bristol are all fine examples of the Decorated style, and King's College Chapel in Cambridge is the high point of Perpendicular, which is unique to England and Wales. In Scotland, a new type of late gothic which combined English and French influences.

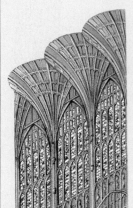

Top: Ely Cathedral, Cambridgeshire
The timber octagonal lantern at Ely Cathedral is unique. The star pattern vault has at its centre the figure of Christ looking down on the wonders beneath.

Above: King's College Chapel, Cambridgeshire
Founded by King Henry VI and begun in 1449. The walls of luminously coloured glass and a fan-vaulted roof make this one of the most advanced Perpendicular buildings in Britain.

Below: Jedburgh Abbey, Borders
This was one of the richest churches founded in the 12th century by the Scottish monarchy. It is a fine example of the transition from the Norman to the gothic architectural style with its characteristic pointed arches. Columns were no longer cylindrical (1) but composite (2). The Norman choir with its apse and apsidal chapels (3) was replaced by a choir with a square east end (4) and three horizontal levels: blind arches (5), triforium (6) and high bays (7). The cruciform layout was reinforced by the addition of a rectangular presbytery (8) to the crossing of the transept. On the original plan the side aisles were vaulted, but the nave and choir probably had an open-frame roof.

Above: Lincoln Cathedral, Lincolnshire
Spectacularly sited on a hill, the three slender towers give Lincoln a memorable silhouette. Note also the great screen across the front of the building.

Above: Canterbury, Kent
The premier See of England, where the story of the Church of England can be best understood. French gothic predominates, but the great central Bell Harry tower is by the English medieval master John Wastell.

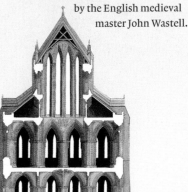

Above: Glasgow Cathedral, City of Glasgow
Glasgow Cathedral, begun c1240, is the only gothic cathedral in Scotland that is still virtually intact. It has an unusual stone roof screen and an impressive crypt, whose complex ribbed vault is echoed by the massive pillars with their leaf-work capitals. Above the crypt, the choir has a square east end with an ambulatory and a vaulted panelled ceiling. Two towers once stood on the cathedral's west façade.

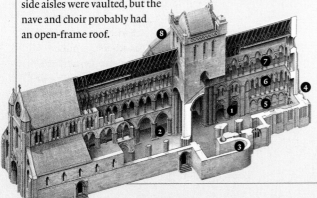

Scottish Renaissance Palaces

In the 15th and 16th centuries the Stuart kings, James IV and James V in particular, believed that culture increased the prestige of the monarchy. The renovation of royal castles and palaces – one of the chief forms of expression of the ideals of the Scottish Renaissance – reflected a growing interest in the artistic and intellectual trends in countries such as France, Italy and to a lesser degree England. Influenced by these new architectural ideas, the nobility followed suit and built magnificent castles and public buildings.

Below: Linlithgow Palace, West Lothian

Linlithgow Palace, begun by James I in 1425, was the first royal residence to meet the new requirements of the court. This involved providing apartments and privacy for the royal family and their entourage in a safe, modern castle built around a central courtyard. The west wing, added at the end of the 15th century, housed the king's apartments: the antechamber with the royal guard opened on to the throne room where ambassadors were received. Affairs of state were discussed in the bedchamber; the most private room was the study.

Right: Crathes Castle, Aberdeenshire

In the 16th century the emphasis was very much on outline. Roof decorations became more individual, with turrets, dormers, gables and corbelled chimneys crowning former parapet walks. Machicolations, cannons and crenellations lost their defensive function and became purely symbolic. This decorative exuberance created a link between the Scottish châteaux of the period and the Renaissance in western Europe.

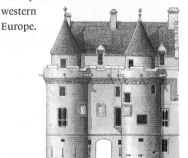

Above left: Falkland Palace, Fife

Like Holyroodhouse, Falkland Palace – a former hunting lodge redesigned in the 15th and 16th centuries by the Stuarts – had a fortified entrance. Although the palace retained some of its defensive features, the entrance became purely emblematic, evoking the medieval ideals of chivalry to symbolize the power of the Stuarts.

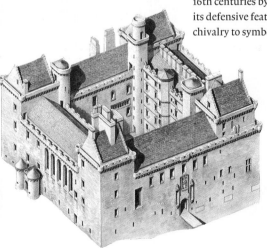

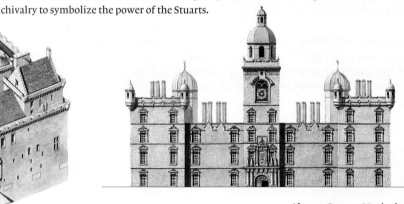

Above: George Heriot's School, City of Edinburgh

The school was built from 1628 onwards, on a palatial courtyard layout punctuated by towers. The pepper-pot turrets and window pediments may have been inspired by the north wing of Linlithgow.

Right: Stirling Castle, Stirling

The Great Hall of Stirling Castle combines medieval construction methods and Renaissance ideals of ceremony and grandeur. The most spectacular element is the hammerbeam roof (c1500) which attests to links with England. This complex wooden framework opens up a large amount of space, both vertically and horizontally.

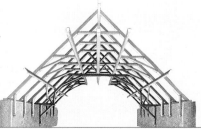

Tudor and Stuart

Tudor monarchs ruled in England from the accession of Henry VII in 1485 to the death of Queen Elizabeth in 1603. From c1520 we see Renaissance ideas gradually taking over from the gothic. The Tudor style thus shows the infusion of classical styles on to medieval plans. After the Dissolution of the Monasteries (1536–40), the newly enriched gentry built grand houses, often known as prodigy houses because of their extravagance. The Stuart period falls into two parts – James I and Charles I (1603–49), and Charles II and James II (1660–88) – separated by the Commonwealth. The second period was the age of Wren, Hawksmoor and Vanbrugh, and English Baroque. The Fire of London gave Wren the opportunity to rebuild the City of London; he left us St Paul's and 51 City churches.

Above: Queen's House, Greenwich, Greater London
Inigo Jones completed this early example of a Palladian House for Queen Henrietta Maria, 1616-18 and 1630-5. The entrance hall is a perfect cube and the ceiling was painted by Gentileschi.

Above: Bolsover Castle, Derbyshire
The interior of Bolsover is probably the work of John Smythson, who took over from his father Robert Smythson. The Pillar Chamber of 1616 is a mixture of gothic vaulting, Renaissance columns and a typically Jacobean fireplace.

Above: Hardwick Hall, Derbyshire
Built by the redoubtable Elizabeth, Countess of Shrewsbury – 'Bess of Hardwick'; her initials are in stone around the parapet. The High Great Chamber, approached by a long stone staircase, gives some idea of her feudal power. Built in a unified style between 1590 and 1597, the house has hardly been touched since.

Below: Hatfield House, Hertfordshire
This house was built in 1608–12 for Robert Cecil, 1st Earl of Salisbury, to the designs of Robert Lyminge. It is still inhabited by his descendants. The open loggia along the front was very fashionable. The porch is three storeys high, with paired columns of the Doric, Ionic and Corinthian orders. The gardens, too, are spectacular, with fountains and waterworks.

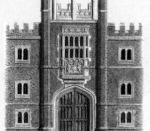

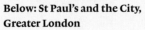

Above: Hampton Court, Surrey
Here is some of the finest Tudor architecture in England. Built for Cardinal Wolsey and later given to Henry VIII, the palace and its gardens rapidly became known as England's Versailles – especially after Wren expanded it for William and Mary. The gatehouse is shown here.

Below: St Paul's and the City, Greater London
After the Great Fire of 1666, Christopher Wren planned the new formal City. Although his plans were not accepted, his triumph was St Paul's Cathedral, surrounded by the spires of his city churches as recorded in this engraving of 1710.

Queen Anne to Georgian

The reign of Queen Anne (1702–14) was not really a complete architectural period, but her name became synonymous with a domestic classicism that characterizes some of the best small houses of the period. Her years also saw the high point of Baroque architecture in England. Under the four Georges, who reigned from 1714 to 1830, the Baroque was quickly supplanted by the Palladian, inspired by the foremost architect of 16th-century Europe, Andrea Palladio. This meant a return to cool, classical lines; to symmetry, harmony and proportion. This in turn gave rise to the neoclassical style of Robert Adam and Sir John Soane – although simultaneously from the mid-18th century we see the beginnings of the Gothic Revival.

Above: Fenton House, Hampstead, Greater London
Built in 1693 by an unknown architect, it is a near-perfect example of the architecture of its period.

Above: Mausoleum at Castle Howard, North Yorkshire
One of the most sublime classical temples in England, designed for Lord Carlisle by Nicholas Hawksmoor. The tight circle of columns seems determined to keep the dead inside.

Above: Belton House, Lincolnshire
A superb late 17th-century house, worked on by James Wyatt in 1777. Inside there are a great marble hall and beautiful chimneypieces.

Above: Queen Anne's Gate, Greater London
Eighteenth-century houses with lovely door canopies gather round the statue of the Queen to form one of the finest enclaves in Westminster.

Right: Georgian house, Bath, Somerset
In the Museum of the Building of Bath, this model shows exactly how a typical Georgian house, was constructed and used – note all the cellars under the built-up road.

Architects

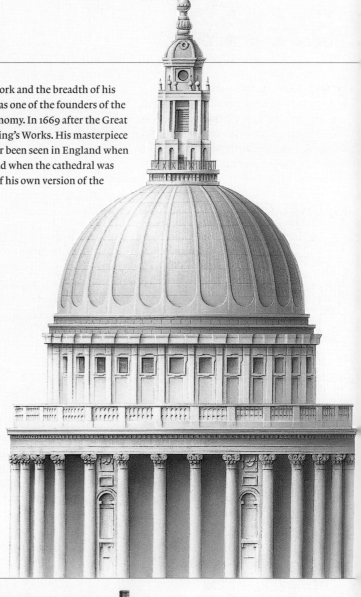

Sir Christopher Wren (1632–1723)

England's greatest architect because of the range of his work and the breadth of his intellectual and scientific interests and knowledge. He was one of the founders of the Royal Society and in 1657 he was made Professor of Astronomy. In 1669 after the Great Fire of London he became the Surveyor General for the King's Works. His masterpiece is the dome of St Paul's (right), the like of which had never been seen in England when it was built. He was scholarly and refined as a designer and when the cathedral was finished in 1709, the 77-year-old Wren saw the triumph of his own version of the Baroque style.

William Adam (1689–1748)

The influence of William Adam (left) and his sons John, Robert – the best known – and James extended to Europe and America. William Adam designed Duff House (below) in the baroque style, but the dimensions and quality demanded more massive financial investment than the client would countenance, so it was never finished and ended in acrimonious litigation. Façades were characterized by the use of different materials, architectural devices and finishes. Colonnades were to link the central body of the building to pavilions or outbuildings on the models of the villas of Andrea Palladio (1508–80).

Robert Adam (1728–92)

After studying classical and Renaissance architecture in Rome in 1755–7, Robert Adam developed a vast repertoire of classically inspired motifs which he used in the decorations and furnishings of the many mansions he was commissioned to design. Their fineness suited the rococo and neoclassical styles that were currently in vogue and made the 'Adam' style famous throughout Europe. In England, he designed interiors for Syon House (see the doorway, left), Harewood, Osterley and Kedleston; in Scotland, his work included Culzean Castle and Edinburgh's Charlotte Square.

Sir John Vanbrugh (1664–1726)

Not just an architect but a soldier, playwright, adventurer and possibly a spy. He worked alongside Wren as Comptroller at the Office of Works as a result of the patronage of Lord Carlisle, for whom he was building Castle Howard. Blenheim Palace, built for the Duke of Marlborough, is his triumph, where the interior and exterior demonstrate his theatrical as well as his architectural skills. Above is the bridge over the lake at Blenheim.

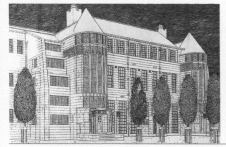

Charles Rennie Mackintosh (1868–1928)

The leading figure of the Glasgow Style, Mackintosh believed that architecture should meet people's spiritual and material needs. He completed only a relatively small number of architectural projects, of which Glasgow School of Art, Hill House and the Scotland Street School (above) are the most famous.

Sir John Soane (1753–1837)

One of the world's most original neoclassical architects, Soane has left us his own house as a museum which says more about the architectural creativity of his mind than any of his surviving buildings. He trained under George Dance and Henry Holland. His house and the Dulwich Picture Gallery are perfect examples of his very individual style. A section of his Breakfast Room is shown above.

Nicholas Hawksmoor (1661–1736)

From the age of 18, Hawksmoor was Wren's assistant and he worked closely with him at Greenwich. He designed Easton Neston on his own in 1702 and went on to design six major London churches as well as parts of All Souls at Oxford and the gothic west towers of Westminster Abbey. His spire for Christ Church (above), in London's Spitalfields, soars above the arched pediment of the portico and dominates the whole design of the church.

John Nash (1752–1837)

His famous classical designs include London's Regent Street, the houses around Regent's Park and Marble Arch. Grovelands (left) is a fine house that he built in 1797 with a room inside decorated to suggest a gilded birdcage. It is now a psychiatric hospital.

Alexander 'Greek' Thomson (1817–75)

Thomson spent all of his life in Scotland, bringing his individual neoclassical style to the churches, warehouses and tenements of Glasgow. Holmwood House (below) was built in 1857–8 for the paper-mill owners James and Robert Couper, using decorative elements borrowed from Ancient Greece.

Country Houses, Parks and Gardens

Britain's most original and valuable aesthetic contribution to the world is its country houses, especially when they are placed in a designed Arcadian setting. Landscape designers like Capability Brown and Humphry Repton made England the home of the 'picturesque' landscape, banishing the formality of French gardening, killing off the knot garden and pushing the parterre out of sight. The *jardin anglais* spread all over Europe, including Russia where it was adopted by Catherine the Great and her architect Charles Cameron. In Scotland, Robert Adam emphasized the relationship between architecture and the landscape by choosing spectacular settings for his houses which served to underline their neoclassical harmony.

Below: Chinese Pagoda at Kew, Greater London
Designed by Sir William Chambers in 1762, it is 163 feet (50m) high and was, on completion, very elaborately decorated. It is one of a series of ornamental buildings that Chambers scattered around the royal park at Kew.

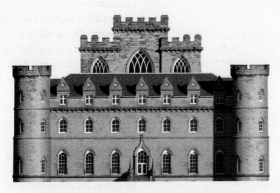

Above: Torosay Castle, Mull, Argyll & Bute
The Baronial style, which dominated the design of Scottish castles until the 20th century, is characterized by the marked asymmetry of the façades. Those of Torosay Castle, built in 1856 by David Bryce, appear even more asymmetrical when viewed from the gardens below: stepped gables, corbelled towers, split-level roofs and projections create an interplay of light and shadow.

Left: Inveraray Castle, Argyll & Bute
Although designed by William Morris, architects William Adam and his son John were involved in the design and construction of this huge, 1740s square castle punctuated by towers, which was among the first neo-gothic buildings in Britain to be built completely anew. The castle replaced a 15th-century tower-house as the residence of the Duke of Argyll, the powerful chief of the Campbell clan. The unusual combination of a symmetrical layout and neo-gothic architecture was more in keeping with the concept of feudal power than that of clan loyalties.

Left: Painshill Park, Surrey
The predecessor of Stourhead in Wiltshire, this recently restored garden was laid out by Charles Hamilton in the 1740s. It has a magnificent grotto and a Turkish Tent as well as lakes and follies.

Above left: Shugborough, Staffordshire
A perfect example of the designed landscape with some exotic elements like this Chinese house of 1747.

Left: Erddig, Wrexham
Palladian-style 'Venetian' windows brought the Adriatic to houses like Erddig in North Wales, as well as to Harewood House in Yorkshire.

Above: Culzean Castle, Dumfries & Galloway
Robert Adam was very much aware of the concepts of the 'picturesque' and the 'sublime'. In his architecture he made every effort to reconcile Scottish national tradition with his preference for classical design, and to integrate his creations into a Romantic vision of the surrounding landscape.

Below left: Attingham Park, Shropshire
One of the grandest houses of the mid-18th century, designed by George Steuart and altered later on by John Nash. Repton designed the park.

Below: Strawberry Hill, Greater London
Built for the aesthete and writer Horace Walpole from 1748, it is an exquisite exercise in the gothic taste with remarkable, lavishly decorated interiors. One room is inspired by the chapel of Henry VII in Westminster Abbey.

Victorian Architecture

The Victorian era is architecturally eclectic. All styles flourished; there was even a 'Battle of the Styles', which came to a head over the design of the Foreign Office when gothic and Classical designs fought it out. In the end Classicism won the day. Earlier in the reign of Queen Victoria (1837–1901) the Palace of Westminster was erected in a rich gothic style but on a classical plan, and the collaboration of Charles Barry and Augustus Welby Pugin seemed to predict the richness of the architecture of the reign. The Gothic Revival was probably the most distinctive feature of the period, and was a very serious undertaking by a whole range of architects. Historicism seemed to march alongside technological improvements and radical uses of newer materials like cast iron and glass. The Victorian clients were rich, the Empire flourished and architects were encouraged to create wonderful fantasy worlds in the most unlikely places. The reaction to Georgian reticence was extreme, but the seeds had already been planted during the Regency.

Above: Royal Courts of Justice, Greater London
Architect George Edmund Street was worn out by this huge project and died in 1881, before the completion of his masterly gothic design (1874–82). Its style is pure 13th century and it was the only major government-funded building erected in the gothic style other than the Houses of Parliament.

Above: Glasgow City Chambers, City of Glasgow
Glasgow's City Chambers were built in 1883–8 on George Square by William Young. The building embodies the wealth and pride of the once 'second largest city in the Empire'. With its impressive dimensions, classical composition, elaborate baroque façade and opulent interior decor, it is a fine example of the eclectic style that was currently in vogue.

Above right: Albert Memorial, Greater London
Completed in 1876 and restored in 1999, the gilded statue of the Prince Consort sits under the high gothic canopy designed by George Gilbert Scott; the prince is holding the catalogue of the Great Exhibition of 1851.

Right: St Bartholomew's, Brighton, East Sussex
Taller than Westminster Abbey, this church is quintessentially Victorian in its aspiring piety. Built by Edmund Scott in 1872–4, it has a silver altar by Harry Wilson and is overpowering in its hugeness.

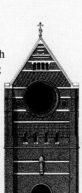

Above: National Gallery of Scotland, City of Edinburgh
To link the Old Town and New Town, a series of green spaces and monumental public buildings were designed and built, in the early 19th century, at the foot of the Castle. The 'Greek temples' designed by William Playfair – such as the National Gallery of Scotland (1850–8) – earned Edinburgh the epithet 'Athens of the North'.

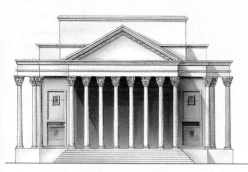

Left: St George's Hall, Merseyside
The new civic hall with a concert hall and law courts was completed in 1856. The classical design by Harvey Lonsdale Elmes won the architectural competition in 1839.

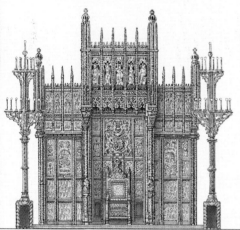

Above: Houses of Parliament, Greater London
AW Pugin's design for a throne in the House of Lords made the British sovereign appear like a medieval monarch. In 1836 Charles Barry won the competition for the contract to build a new Palace of Westminster (its predecessor having been destroyed by fire). The interior, by Pugin, everywhere shows his mastery of medieval gothic design.

Above: Truro Cathedral, Cornwall
John Loughborough Pearson's masterpiece was begun in 1880 and finished by his son in the Normandy gothic style.

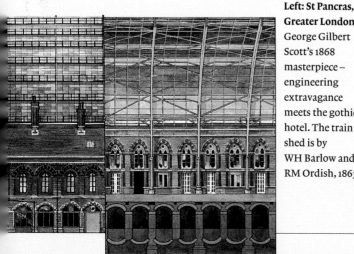

Left: St Pancras, Greater London
George Gilbert Scott's 1868 masterpiece – engineering extravagance meets the gothic hotel. The train shed is by WH Barlow and RM Ordish, 1863.

Below: Cardiff Castle, Cardiff
William Burges' dream home for the Marquess of Bute has some of the finest Victorian fantasy interiors in the country.

Edwardian Architecture

The era that followed the long reign of Queen Victoria was a kind of Imperial sunset before World War I. It was a time when large prosperous houses were built and public buildings were grand and pompous. The 'Battle of the Styles' ended in a draw: gothic was the style for churches, while secular buildings were usually 'classical'. It was a period when the apprenticeship system ensured that the standard of craftsmanship remained high. One architect dominates the period – Sir Edwin Lutyens (1869–1944), whose masterpiece was New Delhi, the Imperial capital of British India.

Above: Royal Geographical Society, Greater London
The London home of the society of geographers and explorers was built by Norma Shaw as a house for the Hon. William Lowther. Although it dates from 1874, it embodies the characteristics of many Edwardian houses.

Above: Lady Lever Art Gallery, Merseyside
The gallery is in the heart of Port Sunlight near Liverpool – a well-designed company town for the makers of soap. It is a classical centrepiece to the vernacular garden suburb, designed by William and Segar Owen (1914–22), who had designed much of the housing from 1889 onwards.

Left: Victoria Memorial, Greater London
The great Queen is commemorated in a vast memorial by Sir Aston Webb, in front of Buckingham Palace, under the shadow of an enormous winged Victory.

Above: Broadleys, Cartmel Fell, Cumbria
CF Voysey was an Edwardian domestic architect who built fine houses of great simplicity. This example is in the Lake District.

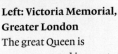

Below: Tigbourne Court, East Sussex
On the road to Brighton stands this beautifully built house by Lutyens, with his trademark giant chimneys.

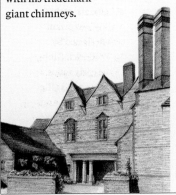

Right: Castle Drogo, Devon
The last castle built in Devon by Lutyens for the Drew family, who had made a fortune from 'Home and Colonial' grocery shops. Building was sadly interrupted by World War I.

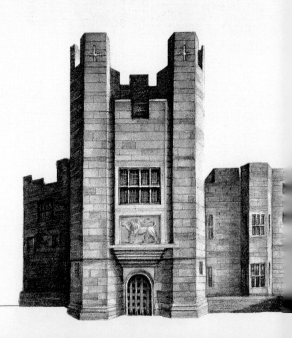

Modern Architecture

Britain had to rebuild itself after the devastation of World War II and the development of modern architecture both benefited and suffered from the scale of rebuilding. Before the war architecture looked promising, with garden cities, new underground railways for London and an occasional flourish of Art Deco. The war changed everything and rehousing became a priority; the cheap copies of Le Corbusier, with tower blocks and concrete town centres, proved an aesthetic and social disaster.

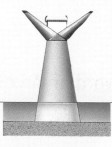

Above: Millennium Bridge, Greater London
A new bridge over the River Thames by the architect Sir Norman Foster and the sculptor Sir Anthony Caro, 2000.

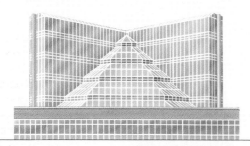

Below: Lloyd's, Greater London
The dynamic home of the insurance market in Leadenhall Street, EC3, was designed in the early 1980s by Richard Rogers. It houses the underwriting rooms and the old Lutine Bell in a spectacular modern atrium building with glass lifts.

Above: History Faculty, Cambridgeshire
James Stirling designed this striking but controversial greenhouse to house a library in 1964.

Above: Arnos Grove underground station, Greater London
Charles Holden designed the extension of the Piccadilly Line into the northern suburbs in the 1930s. His brick and concrete stations have lasted well and are now listed historic buildings.

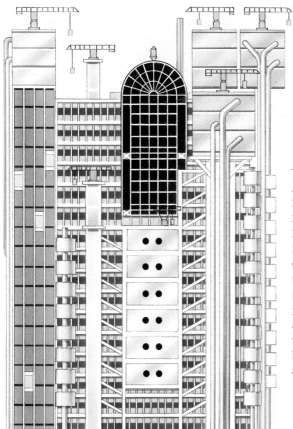

Above: Hoover Building, Greater London
Built in 1933 as a factory, it was designed by Wallis Gilbert and Partners on the Great West Road north of London as a potent Art Deco advertisement for the vaccuum cleaner. It now houses offices and a supermarket.

Below: Liverpool Roman Catholic Cathedral of Christ the King, Merseyside
Built on top of the crypt of Lutyens' cathedral, 'paddy's wigwam' was designed by Sir Frederick Gibberd in the early 1960s. Also in Liverpool is Giles Gilbert Scott's Anglican Cathedral, another great 20th-century building.

Art

From the Middle Ages

The flourishing art of medieval England survives primarily in churches. In the 16th century numerous continental artists, notably Hans Holbein, settled in England, while miniature painting developed through such native masters as Nicholas Hilliard.

Above: Hugo van der Goes, 'Holy Trinity Altarpiece' (1470s)
Until the early 17th century Scotland was known for mostly religious paintings and royal portraits by foreign – predominantly Flemish – artists. The two themes are combined in a magnificent portrait of James III, which forms one of the panels of the Holy Trinity Altarpiece. Van der Goes conveys the status of the central figure by the richness of his garments, and his identity by the presence of St Andrew, the patron saint of Scotland, and the lion on the coat of arms.

Above: Hans Holbein, 'The Ambassadors' (1533)
Hans Holbein brought international sophistication to England during his London stays in the 1520s and 1530s. His portrait of the French ambassador and a bishop is executed with meticulous realism and filled with symbolic detail, such as the lute with broken string and the anamorphic skull (shown in distorted perspective) in the foreground. Such works raised courtly portraiture to a new level of sophistication.

Top right: Nicholas Hilliard, 'Young Man against a Rose Tree' (1500s)
Trained as a jeweller, Hilliard became famous as a miniaturist and received the patronage of Queen Elizabeth I. Influenced by Holbein, he and his younger contemporary Isaac Oliver developed the art of the miniature, generally intended to be enjoyed only by those close to the sitter, into a powerful independent medium. In this study of a contemplative Young Man, he combines the clear outlines of the engraver with the fresh strong colours of his jewellery training in a stylized and poetic image.

Below: 'Sleeping Jesse' (1400s)
Many of the great works of medieval British art have been lost, but notable pieces survive such as this fragment of a 15th-century carving of the sleeping Jesse, once highly coloured and part of a larger sculpture. It comes from St Mary's Priory, Abergavenny.

Portraiture

Right: Allan Ramsay, 'The Painter's Wife, Margaret Lindsay' (1754–5)
The most remarkable Scottish portraitist of the 18th century, Ramsay was influenced by French pastel painting in his creation of beautifully executed and psychologically acute portraits. In this portrait, Margaret Lindsay, his second wife, is shown as though at home arranging flowers, which suggest the freshness and happiness of their love. She turns towards the artist as though interrupted in her task. This work reflects the growing interest in intimate expressions of affection in the mid-18th century, compared to the formality of earlier painting.

Above: William Hogarth, 'Portrait of Captain Coram' (1740)
Portraiture by British rather than foreign artists became a crucial aspect of British art in the 18th century, and found an increasing market in a generally prosperous society. Captain Coram was not a fashionable sitter: he was a naval captain, famous for his acts of charity. Moved by the plight of children abandoned by their mothers, he founded the Foundling Hospital in London, where they would be looked after. Hogarth, a supporter of the charity and champion of British art, painted Coram in the manner of a grand portrait, showing his strong unpolished individuality.

Above: Henry Raeburn, 'Neil Gow' (c1793)
Most Scots of the period would have recognized this portrait of the famous composer and violinist who revived local folklore. Raeburn rejected the academic tradition and drew straight on to the canvas with his brush without making a preliminary drawing. By depicting the musician lost in thought, he produced a fascinating study of the process of artistic creation. The dramatic contrast of light and shadow heralds the intense eloquence of the Romantic generation.

Left: Thomas Gainsborough, 'Countess Howe' (c1763–4)
Gainsborough was one of the most gifted of British artists, forced by financial need to paint portraits although it was landscapes he most enjoyed. Around 1753 he painted this dazzling portrait of Lady Mary, wife of a naval hero. The artist performs the difficult feat of suggesting that his sitter is moving through the landscape. The shimmering silks and lace of her costume, while extremely lavish, suggest clothing suitable for a country walk. She eyes the viewer confidently, at ease in the appealing English countryside, which Gainsborough studies with such affection.

Landscape and Romantic Art

Left: George Stubbs, 'Cheetah and Stag with Two Indians' (c1765)

The greatest of British animal painters, Stubbs painted this work around 1765. The year before, the Governor-General of Madras had given a cheetah to King George III, and it is shown here with its two Indian keepers on the point of being released to chase the stag. Stubbs was fascinated by the power of raw nature and by the challenge of depicting the strength and the anatomy of animals. Here he contrasts the graceful energy of the cheetah with the perturbed uncertainty of its likely victim. The picture, set against a brooding sky, creates a sense of uncanny aggression.

Below: John Constable, 'Golding Constable's Flower Garden' (1816)

Landscape painting has long been one of the major preoccupations of British artists, important to the definition of a national identity. Constable paints the garden from an upstairs window in his parents' house at East Bergholt, Suffolk. Apparently a small and unambitious painting, this is a highly innovative landscape, with hedges and shrubs arranged in a bold diagonal across the centre of the canvas, and foreground shadows creating distance.

Above: John Sell Cotman, 'Brignall Banks on the Greta' (1805)

The watercolour painter Cotman chooses a picturesque East Anglian landscape to create a highly individual view of the countryside. He seems emotionally engaged in his subject, expressing the character of this deep gorge and its surrounding trees with a sympathy for nature quite unlike the cheerful topographical approach of Italian artists.

Left: Canaletto, 'Old Walton Bridge over the Thames' (1754)

During his extended stays in England, the Venetian artist Canaletto reacted enthusiastically to the soft changing light, painting with a freshness, which in Venice he sometimes forgot. Here he paints an elaborate view of the bridge at Walton-on-Thames for his patron Thomas Hollis. Hollis, with a friend and his dog, stand in the foreground.

Right: William Blake, 'Ancient of Days' (1824)
One of the most inspired of mystical artists and writers, Blake created several illustrated poetic books. The watercolour print of *The Ancient of Days* was intended as the frontispiece to *Europe*, in which he prophesied the defeat of inhuman and cruel reason by what he regarded as the truer power of imagination. Urizen, creator of the universe and enforcer of reason, is shown imposing the compass on 'the face of the depth' as he creates the world. Inspired by Michelangelo, this is a powerful work of imagination and bold design, executed in a combination of etching and watercolour peculiar to Blake.

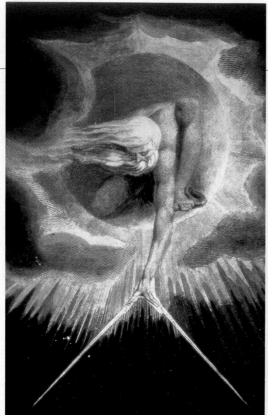

Left: Jacob More, 'Corra Linn' (1771)
Scottish landscapist Jacob More painted the upper fall on the River Clyde, a view that was very popular at the time. The work reflects the sense of the 'sublime' inspired by the power of nature, as suggested by the figures in the foreground.

Top right: Thomas Gainsborough, 'Harvest Wagon' (1767)
Gainsborough was passionate about painting landscapes. These were inspired by Dutch 17th-century painting but developed in works like *Harvest Wagon* a soft melting style in which vegetation and figures are suffused with light.

Above: Henry Fuseli, 'Lady Macbeth Seizing the Daggers' (1812)
A Swiss artist living in London for most of his life, Fuseli painted bold, sexually charged images in which traditional literary stories provided the vehicle for an exploration of human desire, cruelty and repression.

Right: Joseph Mallord William Turner, 'Loch Coruisk, Skye' (c1815)
In the early 19th century the wildness of Highland landscapes captured the imagination of the European Romantics. Thus painters and poets visited the isolated Loch Coruisk, on the Isle of Skye, described by Sir Walter Scott. Turner went there in 1831 to illustrate Scott's text and painted the loch under a stormy sky. The watercolour demonstrates the artist's ability to capture the nuances of light.

Victorian Painting

Right: Ford Madox Brown, 'Work' (c1863)
The Pre-Raphaelite Brotherhood, founded in 1848, had a powerful influence on 19th-century British painting. One of its members, Ford Madox Brown, executed this realistic and closely detailed study of a London street. The labourers symbolize the dignity of manual labour in contrast to the ragged children and the unemployed who have never been taught to work. On the right stand two intellectuals (Thomas Carlyle on the left), advocates of education for all, epitomizing the importance of labour for the health of society.

Below: William Powell Frith, 'The Railway Station' (1860–2)
One of the most successful Victorian painters, Frith was admired for his detailed studies of everyday life. At the Royal Academy, his works had to be protected by a barrier. In this study of Paddington Station he shows a crowd hurrying to catch a train. The figures include two boys saying goodbye to their mother before departing for school, a bride and groom leaving for their honeymoon, and (on the right) two detectives arresting an escaping criminal.

Left: William Holman Hunt, 'Isabella and the Pot of Basil' (1866–8)
The story, from a poem by Keats, tells how Isabella, whose lover has been murdered by her brothers, places his head in a pot planted with basil. She is shown adoring this grisly memento in a painting loaded with sinister eroticism. The careful, almost oppressive, detail is typical of Pre-Raphaelitism.

Left: Frederic Leighton, 'Mother and Child (Cherries)' (c1865)
Leighton was an academic late Victorian painter and President of the Royal Academy. His luxurious house survives in London and is open to the public. He was famous for his richly executed and sensuous studies of classical subjects. In this painting, exhibited in 1865, he shows a modern subject, maternal love, but gives it a strange inward-looking quality and a highly ornate pictorial style.

20th-century Art

Below: David Hockney, 'Mr and Mrs Clark and Percy' (1970–1)
This is one of the most famous paintings by an artist who in his early work epitomized the Swinging Sixties. He shows his friends Ozzie and Celia Clark in their London living room. In this cool sunlit space, painted in a hyper-realist style, they are spare and elegant, yet curiously self-conscious and detached.

Below: Lucian Freud, 'Man's Head (Self Portrait)' (1963)
Born in Berlin of a celebrated Austrian family, Freud moved to England at an early age. He is now recognized as one of the leading British painters of his generation. Highly aware of the art of the past, he brings to his work a powerful direct technique, confronting the fragility and sexuality of the human body while responding to men and women as social beings. His accomplished yet agonized portraits reflect the conflict between the social and the private human being, and a fascination with the peculiarities of human nature and the human body.

Right: Stanley Spencer, 'Furnaces' (1946)
The cycle known as *Shipbuilding on the Clyde*, commissioned by the War Artists' Advisory Committee from the English painter Stanley Spencer, depicts a completely different world: that of the Lithgow shipyards of Port Glasgow. The shipyard workers are painted almost as caricatures, but are transfigured by collective effort and the mysterious process of industrial transformation.

Above right: Francis Bacon, 'Figure Study II' (1945–6)
Still one of the most disturbing of artists, Bacon became prominent in the 1940s. His savage works are inspired by his feeling for traditional art, in particular Italian Renaissance painting (as here) and the work of Velasquez. In *The Magdalene*, he shows an ambiguous and disturbing figure, its mouth open in a scream of grief – a comment on the plight of humanity.

Henry Moore, 'King and Queen' (1952–3)
Moore was one of Britain's most internationally influential 20th-century sculptors and draughtsmen. Abandoning the classical ideal of beauty, he used his knowledge of ancient Mexican and African works, as well as classical art, to create a semi-abstract, highly energized style, reflecting his feeling for his materials. As he wrote, 'The human figure is what interests me most deeply.' In this work, he develops the theme of the linked king and queen (or family) which he had been exploring for years.

The Gazetteer

Gazetteer entries are arranged alphabetically by the name of the country house, garden, island, city, town or village. The city index on pages 681–2 lists properties that appear within an entry for a town or city rather than under their own name. After the heading of each entry, the county name is given (see list of abbreviations, below), then a reference to the map section at the back of the book (page number followed by grid reference). If there is a cross reference with a map grid reference at the end of an entry, it means that the property concerned does not have its own map entry but can be found near the entry to which it is cross-referenced. See also the list of symbols used, below.

Scotland

Aber C	Aberdeen City
Abers	Aberdeenshire
Ag & B	Argyll & Bute
Angus	Angus
Border	Borders (Scottish)
C Edin	City of Edinburgh
C Glas	City of Glasgow
Clacks	Clackmannanshire
D & G	Dumfries & Galloway
Dund C	Dundee City
E Ayrs	East Ayrshire
E Duns	East Dunbartonshire
E Loth	East Lothian
E Rens	East Renfrewshire
Falk	Falkirk
Fife	Fife
Highld	Highland
Inver	Inverclyde
Mdloth	Midlothian
Moray	Moray
N Ayrs	North Ayrshire
N Lans	North Lanarkshire
Ork	Orkney Islands
P & K	Perth & Kinross
Rens	Renfrewshire
Shet	Shetland Islands
S Ayrs	South Ayrshire
S Lans	South Lanarkshire
Stirlg	Stirling
W Isls	Western Isles
W Duns	West Dunbartonshire
W Loth	West Lothian

England

Beds	Bedfordshire
Berks	Berkshire
Bristl	Bristol
Bucks	Buckinghamshire
Cambs	Cambridgeshire
Ches	Cheshire
Cnwll	Cornwall
Cumb	Cumbria
Derbys	Derbyshire
Devon	Devon
Dorset	Dorset
Dur	Durham
E R YK	East Riding of Yorkshire
E Susx	East Sussex
Essex	Essex
Gloucs	Gloucestershire
Gt Lon	Greater London
Gt Man	Greater Manchester
Hants	Hampshire
Herefs	Herefordshire
Herts	Hertfordshire
IOW	Isle of Wight
IOS	Isles of Scilly
Kent	Kent
Lancs	Lancashire
Leics	Leicestershire
Lincs	Lincolnshire
Mersyd	Merseyside
Norflk	Norfolk
N York	North Yorkshire
Nhants	Northamptonshire
Nthumb	Northumberland
Notts	Nottinghamshire
Oxon	Oxfordshire
Rutlnd	Rutland
Shrops	Shropshire
Somset	Somerset
S York	South Yorkshire
Staffs	Staffordshire
Suffk	Suffolk
Surrey	Surrey
T & W	Tyne & Wear
Warwks	Warwickshire
W Mids	West Midlands
W Susx	West Sussex
W York	West Yorkshire
Wilts	Wiltshire
Worcs	Worcestershire

Wales

Blae G	Blaenau Gwent
Brgnd	Bridgend
Caerph	Caerphilly
Cardiff	Cardiff
Carmth	Carmarthenshire
Cerdgn	Ceredigion
Conwy	Conwy
Denbgs	Denbighshire
Flints	Flintshire
Gwynd	Gwynedd
IOA	Isle of Anglesey
Myr Td	Merthyr Tydfil
Mons	Monmouthshire
Neath	Neath Port Talbot
Newpt	Newport
Pembks	Pembrokeshire
Powys	Powys
Rhondd	Rhondda Cynon Taff
Swans	Swansea
Torfn	Torfaen
V Glam	Vale of Glamorgan
Wrexhm	Wrexham
IOM	Isle of Man

London entry map references

The locations of most of the London entries are referenced to 'London' on the mapping – 691 F5.

Symbols

* =	a cross reference to another entry in the Gazetteer
693 H5 =	a reference to the maps on pages 686–703
NT =	National Trust
EH =	English Heritage

Abberley, Worcs 693 H5, The Italianate clock tower of Abberley Hall (now a school) is known locally as 'Jones's Folly' and is visible from miles around. The foundation stone was laid on 4 May 1883 by its builder's wife Sarah Amelia Jones. Designed by the church architect JP St Aubyn, it originally contained 20 bells that could play 40 tunes.

Abbey Dore, Herefs 693 G6, The red-and-grey stump of the crossing and chancel of the Cistercian monks' church is now St Mary's parish church at Abbeydore, by the rushing stream which formerly drove the mill. Around the church lie the remains of Dore Abbey. Inside, the blocked door high in the north wall once led to the monks' dormitory. After they left, however, Lord Scudamore erected the hefty 1630s screen across the chancel and added handsome stalls, benches and a communion rail. The 17th-century wall-paintings include a fine and muscular Angel of Death with an enormous scythe. **Abbey Dore Court,** across the river, has pleasant gardens, with a large collection of herbs.

Abbotsbury, Dorset 689 H6, There are the remains of a Benedictine abbey here, while the sub-tropical gardens, 20 acres (8ha) of rare and exotic plants, lie a mile (1.6km) west of Abbotsbury village, and the Swannery is a few hundred yards to the south. The Swannery was established in the 14th century by the Benedictine monks, and every May hundreds of swans nest here.

Abbotsford, Borders 699 G5, Sir Walter Scott devoted the last 20 years of his life to extending a farmhouse into a romantic Scots baronial mansion to designs by William Atkinson. The house stands in a fine park and its remarkably well-preserved interiors house some 9,000 rare works, a collection of weapons and many personal souvenirs. When his publishers went bankrupt in 1826, Scott worked furiously to pay off his debts and keep his estate. He died, exhausted, on 21 September, 1832, in the dining room overlooking the River Tweed.

Aberaeron, Cerdgn 692 D5, A grid-patterned planned town of commodious, clean-cut and confident houses, the result of the entrepreneurial talents of the heiress of the local house of Tyglyn and her husband and cousin, the Reverend Alban Thomas. Her personal fortune was augmented by the legacy of another cousin, Lewis Gwynne of the neighbouring house of Monachty. The outcome was the construction of a harbour, the development of a highly successful shipbuilding company, and one of the most pleasingly integrated towns in Wales. The harbour is popular with yachtsmen. Nearby lived the internationally acclaimed and sadly lamented operatic baritone Sir Geraint Evans.

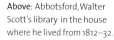

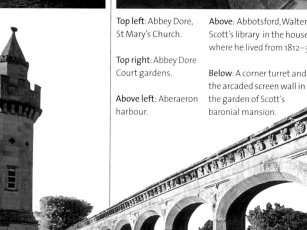

Top left: Abbey Dore, St Mary's Church.

Top right: Abbey Dore Court gardens.

Above left: Aberaeron harbour.

Above: Abbotsford, Walter Scott's library in the house where he lived from 1812–32.

Below: A corner turret and the arcaded screen wall in the garden of Scott's baronial mansion.

Aberdeen

Aberdeen, Aber C 702 E6, With a population of almost 200,000, the 'Granite City' is Scotland's third largest. The modern conurbation was created in 1891 by the amalgamation of two medieval villages: Aulton or Old Aberdeen, on the mouth of the River Don, and the port on the Dee estuary, 2 miles (3.2km) to the south. Aberdeen's economy was boosted in the 1970s when oil was discovered in the North Sea. The city became the capital of the European petroleum industry, acquiring a research centre and developing a vast infrastructure for the off-shore rigs. Although in decline since the 1980s, the industry financed the construction of many hotels, restaurants, shops and leisure facilities.

Brig o'Balgownie: A footpath leads from Seaton Park to this attractive bridge (1320s) whose gothic arch spans the River Don.

Harbour: Aberdeen has a modern fishing fleet whose catches are auctioned in the Albert Basin Fish Market between 7 and 8am, Mondays to Fridays. Ferries leave Jamieson's Quay for Orkney*, Shetland* and, in summer, Norway, Iceland and the Faeroes. The Harbour Board occupies a strange circular building on North Pier, built by John Smeaton in 1775–81 to prevent the port silting up. Between North Pier and the beach are the delightful cottages of Footdee (pronounced 'Fittie'), a fishing village built between 1808 and 1809.

King's College: Scotland's third largest university was founded in 1495 by Bishop Elphinstone. It was named in honour of James IV, whose coat of arms appears on the west façade, together with those of his wife, Margaret Tudor, and of his natural son Alexander, Bishop of St Andrews. The Round Tower, at the southeast corner of the courtyard, is a defensive tower built in 1525, while the Square Tower (Cromwell's Tower), at the northeast corner, was built as a student hall of residence in 1658. Of particular interest is the gothic Chapel (1500–5), whose tower is surmounted by a remarkable crown-shaped lantern which was restored in 1633. The chapel has a rood screen, canopied choir stalls and a beautifully carved pulpit from St Machar's Cathedral. The modern stained-glass windows are by Douglas Strachan. The area around the cathedral and university, with its cobbled streets bordered by old cottages and mansions, has been classified as a conservation area.

Marischal College: This Protestant university was founded in 1593 by George Keith, 5th Earl-Marischal of Scotland, and rebuilt to neo-Tudor designs by Archibald Simpson, 1837–44. In 1860 it merged with King's College to form Aberdeen University. The Franciscan church was replaced by the present neo-gothic façade designed by A Marshall Mackenzie (1905), unusually elaborate for a granite building. The Marischal Museum, on the far side of the courtyard, has interesting archeological and anthropological collections.

Mercat Cross (Castlegate): The market cross (rebuilt in 1821) was first erected on the market place of the medieval town in 1686. Its white marble unicorn

Above: Provost Skene's House on Guest Row. It is now a museum of local history with many items illustrating domestic and social life in the city over the centuries.

Above: Exhibits from the archeological collections at Marischal College.

Left: The tower and steeple of Aberdeen's Town Hall (by Peddie & Kinnear), on the corner of Castle Street and Broad Street.

(the emblem of the kingdom of Scotland), gargoyles and medallion heads of the Stuart kings make it one of the most beautiful market crosses in Scotland.

Provost Skene's House: For a time this vast 16th-century manor belonged to the rich merchant and Provost of Aberdeen, George Skene. It still has its 17th-century stucco ceilings and panelling. The paintings on the ceiling of the chapel (late 16th century) illustrate scenes from the New Testament, rare in post-Reformation Scotland.

St Machar's Cathedral: The cathedral was founded in 1131 and dedicated to a disciple of St Columba who had built a chapel on the site in AD 580. The present building dates from the 14th–15th centuries. The choir was demolished during the Reformation and the transept destroyed when the central tower collapsed in 1688. The two massive defensive towers on the west façade are a feature unique to Great Britain. Their slender spires are believed to have been added by Bishop Gavin Dunbar in 1519–21, as was the nave's panelled oak ceiling decorated with 48 shields. The shields, arranged in three rows, bear the coats of arms of Pope Leo X, the Holy Roman Emperor Charles V, St Margaret and Scottish bishops and nobles during the reign of James V. They serve to confirm the role of Scotland, and Aberdeen in particular, in 16th-century Europe.

Town Hall: The town hall, a Flemish-style granite building designed by Peddie & Kinnear on the corner of Castle Street and Broad Street, was built between 1868 and 1874. It incorporates the tower and spire of the Tolbooth (1615), a former prison which today houses a Civic History Museum.

Union Street: Aberdeen's main street was built in 1801 as part of a development programme undertaken by the municipal authorities. It is bordered by fine granite buildings whose stone is ideally suited to the neoclassical austerity of their Georgian architecture. The most impressive is the Music Hall (1820) designed by Archibald Simpson, a native of Aberdeen and the architect of many of its public and private buildings. His rival, John Smith, was responsible for the Ionic screen of St Nicholas Churchyard (adapted from a design by Decimus Burton, 1830); the Record Office in King Street (1832); the Town's Schools in Little Belmont Street (1841); the Blind Asylum in Huntly Street and the splendid North Church (City Arts Centre, 1830–1). The east end of Union Street gives way to Castle Street, named after the castle that stood behind the former church until 1337.

There are many good castles around Aberdeen: *see* **Balmoral***, **Braemar***, **Castle Fraser***, **Corgarff Castle***, **Craigievar Castle***, **Crathes Castle***, **Drum Castle***, **Fyvie Castle***, **Kildrummy Castle*** and **Tolquhon Castle***.

Above: Marischal College and New Greyfriars Church, built in the granite for which the city is famous.

Left: The area around the cathedral and university with its cobbled streets and old houses has been designated a conservation area. The view shows the spires of the cathedral and its gate lodges of c1820.

Top: Aberdulais Falls.

Centre: Aberfeldy, Castle Menzies.

Bottom: Aberfeldy's famous Bridge over the Tay, designed by William Adam in 1733 to carry General Wade's military road.

Aberdulais Falls, Neath 689 F3, This spectacular gorge in the Vale of Neath was acquired in 1981 by the National Trust of Scotland, which has interpreted the site's long industrial history in a fascinating interactive display. The gorge was much painted in the 18th and 19th centuries, most famously by JMW Turner.

Aberfeldy, P & K 699 F2, This little town was immortalized in a poem by Robert Burns, 'The Birks [silver birches] of Aberfeldy'. A walk starting on the central square (The Square) leads through woodland to the place where Burns was inspired to write his poem. The association with Burns is not the town's only claim to fame: its bridge across the Tay is one of the most photographed bridges in Scotland. Near this massive work of art, designed by William Adam and built in 1733 by General Wade, a statue of a kilted soldier commemorates the formation of the Black Watch Regiment at Aberfeldy, in 1739. Castle Menzies lies to the northwest of the town. It is a fine example of a 16th-century Z-shaped tower-house and is currently being restored. In Grandtully, to the southeast of Aberfeldy, St Mary's Church (16th

century) has a magnificent painted ceiling dating from the 1630s.

Aberfoyle, Stirlg 698 E3, This peaceful little town in the heart of the Trossachs* is almost unrecognizable in summer when it is inundated with tourists. The visitor centre at Queen Elizabeth Forest Park, to the north of Aberfoyle, is an ideal starting point from which to explore the park's 74,000 acres (30,000ha) of forests, lochs and mountains.

Abergavenny, Mons 693 F6, Its significance in the Middle Ages is reflected in the monuments in St Mary's Church, established as a Benedictine priory in 1090; for it was here that the great families associated with the castle were buried. The result is a collection of tombs and effigies of exceptional importance, raising the church to the rank of a major cathedral. Among the treasures is a 15th-century oak figure of Jesse, an immensely commanding carving (*see* page 40). A municipal park surrounds the Norman castle above the Usk, and although only fragments remain, one of the towers was rebuilt in the early 19th century by the Nevill family, owners of the property since the 17th century, for use as a hunting box. It now houses the Museum of Local History.

Aberglasney, Carmth 692 D6, This ancient country seat was once owned by Anthony Rudd, bishop of St David's from 1594 to 1615, and later became the property of the Dyer family. The house suffered severe neglect between the 1950s and the 1970s, but in the 1980s, thanks to the unfailing enthusiasm of a local artist, surveys revealed the extensive archeological challenges of this enigmatic estate. The Tudor gatehouse, the arched yew tunnel, arcaded court, parapet walk and cloister garden were all reinstated through sensitive and imaginative restoration, and the opening of the gardens to the public in 1999 was celebrated in a television series, *A Garden Lost in Time*. These projects, together with judicious planting, have resulted in the retrieval of an alluring piece of historical garden design. The nearby parish church of **Llangathen** has a handsome classical canopied tomb to the Rudd family. Five miles (8km) outside Aberglasney are the **National Botanical Gardens of Wales.** They occupy what was once the estate of Middleton Hall, designed at the end of the 18th century by SP Cockerell for Sir William Paxton. The house was gutted by fire in 1931 and demolished in 1954, and the present imaginative enterprise entailed the restoration or reconstruction of seven lakes, waterfalls, cascades, weirs, an ice-house and the stable block which is now the visitor centre. Near the site of the mansion stands Norman Foster's **Great Glasshouse,** the largest single-span greenhouse in the world, designed so that it seems an integral part of the surrounding hillsides. **Paxton's Tower,** a triangular belvedere also designed by Cockerell for Paxton at the beginning of the 19th century in honour of Admiral Nelson, rises up from these hills.

Above: Aberlemno, one of the standing stones with motifs that recur in Pictish art: a serpent, a double disc, a broken arrow and the mirror-comb.

Aberlemno, Angus 699 G2, The village has some magnificent Pictish stones (7th–9th century), one in the churchyard and three at the roadside. They may have been used to mark a boundary or burial site, or to celebrate a ritual. The stone in the churchyard shows a battle scene which may commemorate the victory of the Picts over the Angles at Nechtansmere in 1685.

Abernethy Forest RSPB Reserve, Highld 701 J6, This reserve covers an area of 30,000 acres (12,000ha) and provides sanctuary for such species as Scottish crossbills, capercaillies, whooper swans and especially the ospreys that nest on Loch Garten. The Royal Society for the Protection of Birds has built a hide from which, between late April and August, visitors can observe the nests through binoculars or on a video surveillance screen. The small Strathspey Steam Railway operates between Boat of Garten and Aviemore.

Aberystwyth

Aberystwyth, Cerdgn 692 D4, The west coast town of Aberystwyth, 'Aber' to older generations who have memories of it as a popular resort (until the 1960s), owes its rapid development to the extension of the railway from Shrewsbury in 1864. The history of the town dates back to the late 13th century with the construction of the castle by Edward I, and its satellite development whose military origins still survive in names like Eastgate Street and Great Darkgate Street. Its harbour, now relatively quiet, was built in order to export the lead of the Cardiganshire hills. Laura Place, with its fine houses and Assembly Rooms, illustrates the refinement of a fashionable seaside town of the 1820s.

University College: The High Victorian building by JP Seddon at the southern end of the promenade started life as a hotel, part of the ambitious scheme to make Aberystwyth a flourishing holiday centre. The pier, built in 1867 two years after the opening of the unfinished hotel, was part of the same enterprise, as was the funicular railway of 20 years later. The hotel failed within a year, and the building was put up for sale. Hugh Owen, a pioneer in the field of Welsh education, was instrumental in its purchase, and it became the first University College of Wales, opened in 1872 thanks to the support and subscriptions of a population anxious to have a national and non-sectarian university.

Rapid development in education after World War II resulted in the launch of a vast building programme on Penglais, above the town. Penglais already had another major institution: the National Library of Wales, which has been built in stages since 1911. The Library is divided into three principal departments: Printed Books, Manuscripts and Records, and Prints, Maps and Drawings. Nearby is the Arts Centre, a development of the 1970s, incorporating expansive exhibition areas, a concert hall and the Theatr y Werin (the People's Theatre). The town's Coliseum cinema (once a music-hall) now houses Ceredigion Museum, the museum of Cardiganshire life.

Aberystwyth's handsome railway station is the terminus of the Vale of Rheidol Railway to Devil's Bridge (12 miles/19km), crossing the River Mynach. The name relates to the legend of the devil who disguised himself as a monk in order to lure a girl across the bridge. The present structure surmounts two older bridges: one medieval, the other 18th century.

Centre: Aberystwyth Castle, one of the four built by Edward I in his first campaign to subject the Welsh in 1277.

Above left: Aberystwyth University College. The hotel designed by JP Seddon was converted before its completion into the University College of Wales.

Abingdon, Oxon 690 D4, The town, which abounds with sites of architectural interest, grew up around the Augustinian abbey founded in AD 675, of which only fragments now remain. Most impressive is the late 15th-century gatehouse, attached to the medieval church of St Nicholas. The mainly 15th- and 16th-century church of St Helen contains an exquisite painted ceiling of *c*1390 in the north aisle. In the churchyard can be

seen a small organ-blowing chamber and three sets of excellent almshouses. Abingdon's Town Hall was built in 1678–82 by Christopher Kempster. Its former courtroom now houses the Abingdon Museum, which provides a series of varied exhibitions focusing mainly on contemporary crafts and local history.

Accrington, Lancs 697 F6, The town is dominated by a railway viaduct that crosses the valley in which it lies. Its special contribution to the Lancashire textile industry was the manufacture of necessary machinery. It has a good town hall and one of Lancashire's best covered markets. To the south of the town Sir Charles Reilly's large war memorial in Oak Hill Park is a reminder of the 'Accrington Pals', who went to war together and suffered heavy losses. Not far away, in a small Arts and Crafts house designed by Walter Brierley in 1909 for a local factory owner, is the Howarth Art Gallery, noted above all for its outstanding collection of Tiffany glass sent from New York by an expatriate who had connections with the firm. Accrington is also the home of the hard red brick made by Nori ('iron' backwards), whose inability to weather gracefully has left its mark across much of the Northwest.

Achiltibuie, Highld 701 F3, This coastal village stands in the magnificent setting of the Coigach peninsula. The Hydroponicum is a 'futuristic garden' where all kinds of exotic plants, flowers and fruit are grown under glass without soil. A traditional smokehouse for fish and meat is open to the public at Altan Dubh, 2 miles (3km) to the south.

Top left: Achiltibuie on the Coigach peninsula in northwest Scotland.

Above and right: Ackworth Friends' School, originally a Foundling Hospital built in 1758. The classical architecture includes a pediment and a cupola with clock and bell.

Left: Acorn Bank, the gable end of the house seen from the gardens.

Ackworth, W York 697 H6, A pleasant village with many interesting features, including the **Friends' School,** which began as a Foundling Hospital in 1758, and still looks severely institutional. It was purchased in 1778 by John Fothergill, a medical doctor and member of an important Quaker family, who opened it as a school for the children of Quakers, or Friends, the following year. The Meeting House is nearby.

Acorn Bank, Cumb 696 E3, Just outside Penrith is a fine house of the mid-18th century set round a centre of *c*1600. The interior is rarely accessible but the outside can be seen from the splendid gardens [NT] with a huge collection of culinary and medicinal herbs, orchards and woodland walks, leading to a watermill.

Acton, Ches 693 G2, St Mary's Church is a mixture of medieval work and thorough Victorian restoration, but it contains some outstanding monuments to the Mainwaring family and also some carved Norman stonework.

Acton, Suffk 691 H3, All Saints Church contains the life-size brass to Sir Robert de Bures (d. 1302), in chainmail and surcoat, one of the earliest military brasses in existence, and probably the finest.

Acton Burnell, Shrops 693 G4, The village lies in deep country and the ruined castle stands in the grounds of an 18th-century house. The castle was built in 1284–93 for Bishop Robert Burnell, Lord Chancellor of England and a close friend of King Edward I. 'Castle' is a misleading term, because

Acton Burnell was intended principally as a house; its red sandstone walls still have battlements and square corner towers, but there was an ordinary front door on the ground floor and the main rooms on the first floor had large bay windows to the outside world. In fact, this is one of the earliest examples of a semi-fortified manor house in England. The building fell out of use in the 15th century and later became a barn, but three of the four sides and all four corner towers survive, as well as much of the window tracery. A short distance away are two big stone gables, the relics of a large barn built by Robert Nurnell at the same time as the house. The church is also the bishop's work and the chancel, in particular, bears testimony to 13th-century craftsmanship of the highest order.

Acton Round Hall, Shrops 693 G4, Built in the early 18th century by Sir Whitmore Acton as the dower house to Aldenham Park. It is a beautiful little building of red brick, with a high roof, and most of the rooms inside retain their original panelling and fireplaces. It is worth making a short detour to the parish church to see Sir Whitmore's handsome gothic monument.

Adcote, Shrops 693 G3, A mid-Victorian mansion by the architect Norman Shaw, built in the late 1870s for Mrs Darby, heir to an industrial fortune. It is a powerful interpretation of the 16th-century style with a varied skyline and some excellent tiled fireplaces by William de Morgan.

Adderbury, Oxon 690 D3, St Mary is one of several Oxfordshire churches (such as Hanwell*) with lively carving dating from the 14th century. Note the frieze of grotesques below the parapets. New

Top right: Acton, St Mary's Church from the northeast.

College, Oxford* endowed the building with the rather grand chancel and vestry. The head and arms of the college's founder, William of Wykeham, Bishop of Winchester*, can be seen over the east window, as well as on the roof corbels and window hoods. A good group of houses surrounds the church: the early Georgian Old Vicarage, the Manor House and the Grange with its tithe barn.

Adlington Hall, Ches 693 H1, An attractive mixture of brick and timber buildings grouped round a quadrangle. They are all the work of various members of the Legh family who have been at Adlington since 1315. Most spectacular is the Great Hall, completed in 1505 but improved with larger windows in 1581. The Hall has an elaborate hammerbeam roof, with a 'ceilure' (decorative canopy) at the high end and a fine 17th-century organ by 'Father' Smith. The grand stable block was added in 1749 as part of a range of improvements that included the 1757 south front with its tall Ionic portico.

Affpuddle, Dorset 690 B7, The church of St Laurence is entered through a fine 13th-century doorway, and there are good Renaissance benches and pulpit, probably of 1547.

Ailsa Craig, S Ayrs 698 C6, A volcanic island (1,114 feet/340m high) that lies midway between Belfast and Glasgow. Its Gaelic name means 'Fairy Rock'. Today it is a bird sanctuary.

Adlington Hall
Above right: The Great Hall with its fine 17th-century organ.
Above left: The courtyard.

Left: Acorn Bank, the gardens include a circular woodland walk that runs beside the Crowdundle Beck to Acorn Bank watermill.

Albury Park, Surrey, The appearance of this imposing country mansion is due mainly to AWN Pugin, who remodelled it in 1846–52. Its roof supports chimneys of 63 different designs, and it has good interiors, including a top-lit picture gallery. The gardens were laid out by diarist John Evelyn in the mid-17th century. The church of St Peter and St Paul stands alone on the estate, the village having moved in the 19th century. The church encompasses Saxon, Norman and 13th-century fabric, but the highlight is the decorative chapel by Pugin, designed for Henry Drummond, then owner of Albury Park. *See* **Shere* 691 F6.**

Alcester, Warwks 694 C6, A pleasant small market town, as it was in Roman times. Roman finds are still frequently made in the surrounding fields.

Aldborough Roman Town, N York 697 H5, Just off the York road out of Boroughbridge lies the site of Isurium Brigantum, the main settlement of Roman Britain's largest Iron-Age tribe, the Brigantes, and thus an unusual example of a high-status Roman civilian settlement [EH]. It had a grid-plan of streets and a central forum, near which were shops and offices. Only a small area of this large site is exposed, including parts of the town's defensive wall built of distinctively red sandstone, and two fine tessellated pavements, both from the same luxury town house. The site museum contains some very fine Roman artefacts, including sculptures, horse harnesses, household utensils and personal effects such as jewellery. In Aldborough Church, which stands near the site of the forum, is a Roman carving of the god Mercury.

Aldeburgh, Suffk 695 K7, With its wide High Street and heavily restored Tudor moot hall on the seafront, Aldeburgh is not all there. The moot hall was once in the central market place, but half the town has already been lost to the sea. To the south the Napoleonic Martello tower, now a Landmark

Aldeburgh
Top: Fishing boat on the beach.
Above: The seafront, looking south along Crag Path.
Below right: The Martello Tower at Slaughden, the most northerly Napoleonic defence along the Suffolk Coast.

Trust holiday home, marks the position of Slaughden, birthplace in 1755 of Aldeburgh's most famous son, the poet George Crabbe. This desolate spot was the setting for his *Peter Grimes*, the poem that inspired Lowestoft-born Benjamin Britten to write the opera that gave birth to the town's music festival in 1948. The bracing sea air and the genius of Crabbe have also attracted a succession of eminent literary figures – Thomas Hardy, Henry James and Virginia Woolf were all here and MR James' ghost story, *A Warning to the Curious* (1925), is set in the town.

Aldershot, Hants 690 E6, The chief base of the British Army since the 1850s; of interest to visitors are

several museums, including the Aldershot Military Museum and the Airborne Forces Museum.

Aldworth, Berks 690 D5, The 14th-century effigies to the de la Beche family in the church of St Mary form one of the best collections anywhere in the country. There are eight in total, six under two different sets of three canopies. Three are unusual in that they are not recumbent: two are turned to the side and one is semi-reclining.

Alfriston, E Susx 691 G7, A pretty village with a couple of picturesque old inns and the 14th-century timber-framed Clergy House, the first property to be bought by the National Trust (in 1896).

Alkerton, Oxon 690 D3, The 4-acre (1.6ha) hillside garden of Brook Cottage, Well Lane, has a wide variety of trees, shrubs and herbaceous plants, including over 200 roses.

Allerton Park, N York 697 H5, A Tudor baronial castle designed by George Martin for Lord Stourton (1848–51) with fairytale skyline visible from the A1 and A59, from which can also be seen the

Temple of Victory, a grand Georgian folly of classical form surviving from the earlier house on the site. The estate was owned briefly in the 1780s by the 'Grand Old Duke of York' – Prince Frederick, younger brother of the future King George IV – whose indecisiveness in military matters is commemorated in the nursery rhyme; the hill on which the Temple stands is said to be the one in the rhyme.

Allington Castle, Kent 691 H5, From the outside a well-preserved 13th-century castle, modernized inside and now owned by the Carmelites of Aylesford*.

Top right: Alfriston, the 14th-century Clergy House.

Centre: Allington Castle. Dating originally from 1281, it was remodelled in the early 16th century, when it was the home of the poet Sir Thomas Wyatt. In 1822 it became a ruin and was carefully restored by the architect W D Caröe from 1905 onwards, the work being completed by Philip Tilden from 1917.

Left: Alloway, the cottage where Robert Burns was born.

Centre right: A contemporary portrait of the bard.

Alloway, S Ayrs 698 D6, The village where Robert Burns was born is devoted to his memory. Several buildings and museums form the Burns National Heritage Park, with Burns Cottage and Museum occupying pride of place. The thatched cottage was built by William Burns in 1757 and his son Robert was born there on 25 January 1759. William Burns and his wife Agnes Broun are buried in the cemetery of the Auld Kirk, where Tam o'Shanter saw the 'warlocks and witches in a dance'. The Burns Monument, a neoclassical temple dedicated to the poet's memory (1823), stands in a nearby garden. Editions of his works in various languages can be seen on the ground floor, while the first floor offers an attractive view of the garden and, beyond, of the famous Brig o'Doon, the 13th-century bridge over which Tam o'Shanter made his escape from the witches. The Land o'Burns Centre has an exhibition on the life and works of Burns and the town of Ayr* in the 18th century.

Almondsbury, Gloucs 689 H3, On the edge of Bristol and bisected by motorways, but boasting the entrancing cruciform church of St Mary the Virgin. The church has an uncommonly beautiful interior where marble, stone and timber combine in graceful harmony. The church has Norman remains; its chancel, with fine shafts and foliage capitals, and its vaulted roof, with richly carved bosses, date back 700 years. There is a 16th-century tomb with two effigies, and a window in memory of Charles Richardson, originator and engineer of the Severn Tunnel. The church's broach spire is supported on a central tower.

Alnwick Castle
Top left: The Library.
Centre: Ebony veneer cabinet originally made for the apartment of Louis XIV at Versailles.

Top right: Exterior view of the medieval defensive walls.

Alnwick Castle, one of the largest inhabited castles in England, has been the Percy family home since 1309, and is still the Duke of Northumberland's main residence. Parts of the castle date from the 14th century, although some of the medieval effects, including the distinctive stone figures lining its defensive walls, are of the 18th century. An expensive restoration programme begun in 1854 by the architect Anthony Salvin was partly Victorian gothicization, but incorporated some Italian Renaissance state rooms by Luigi Canina. It removed, however, most of the 18th-century interiors created here by Robert Adam, one of whose most extravagant patrons was the 1st Duke of Northumberland. The present interiors are complemented by a sumptuous collection of paintings which includes works by Titian, Canaletto and Van Dyck.

Alnwick, Nthumb 699 J6, The castle has a dramatic outlook over the River Aln and a Capability Brown landscape. In its extensive parkland is the eye-catching Brizlee Tower, a gothic composition of 1781 by Robert Adam, and the ruins of Hulne Priory, one of the earliest Carmelite houses in England, partly converted into a gothic summerhouse. Both these picturesque effects were created for the 1st Duke of Northumberland, for whom John Adam designed in 1773 the imposing Lion Bridge, taking its name from the Percy emblem, on the parapet. For the new millennium the present Duchess has created in the former kitchen garden the Alnwick Garden, with grand cascade and fountains, topiary and sculptures.

Alnwick town is an assemblage of fine spaces, crouching like an extended barbican to its castle. It was walled in 1434, the unembattled Hotspur Gate surviving in Bondgate Without. Outside it the former railway station has found a sympathetic new use as a huge secondhand bookshop. Back within the walled town, in Bondgate Within, the White Swan Hotel has a panelled room from the First Class Smoking Lounge of SS *Olympic*, sister ship of the *Titanic*, launched in 1910 and broken up at Jarrow in 1935. The remainder of the fittings survive in the works canteen of AKZO Novel at Haltwhistle. Alnwick has many fine buildings of a variety of dates, styles and functions, but usually associated with the patronage of the Northumberland estate. In the Market Place, the Northumberland Hall of 1826 is a first-floor room above ground-floor shops behind arcades; and in Finkle Street the older Town Hall has a domed tower. The Pottergate Tower is a gothic folly of 1768, replacing a medieval gateway. On the last Sunday of July the annual Alnwick Summer Tournament, usually held in the castle grounds, provides all-day entertainment.

Althorp, Nhants 694 D6, The low and rambling house, whose external appearance owes much to the work of Henry Holland in the 1780s, consists of extra layers added on to a house originally begun in 1573. But the house is completely

Left: Alnwick Castle, a corner tower.

Bottom right: Althorp, the Painters' Passage, created during Henry Holland's 1788 enlargement.

outclassed by the stables with four corner towers, and an immense Tuscan portico copied from Inigo Jones' famous church of St Paul in Covent Garden, London*. The stables, with room for 100 horses, now contain a museum dedicated to Diana, Princess of Wales, whose childhood home this was. The exhibition is moving and well designed, and there is a woodland walk to the lake where she is buried.

Alton, Hants 690 E6, A market town with a long main street, it has some fine Georgian frontages, a medieval church with interesting Norman carvings, and the Curtis Museum, which displays local material of general interest and includes a small gallery devoted to toys. Nearby is the Allen Gallery, with a collection (not all on display) of works by the local artist WH Allen, an underrated painter of rural scenes around 1900, and a fine general display of ceramics.

Alton Towers, Staffs 694 C4, At the centre of the colossal leisure park is the ruined shell of the vast gothic mansion house of the Talbots, partly by AWN Pugin. The garden has survived more or less intact, with ornamental trees and garden buildings that include an elaborate glass conservatory. There is also a pagoda fountain.

Amberley Castle, W Susx 691 F7, From a distance, the castle looks more impressive than it turns out to be at close quarters as everything inside is a ruin. It is in fact the curtain wall of a castle built in 1377 but incorporating some earlier work. The twin-towered gatehouses have survived more or less intact.

Ambleside, Cumb 696 E4, This small town is essentially a creation of Lake District tourism. It grew in the 19th century after it gained a church by Sir George Gilbert Scott. The architectural curiosity that most visitors head for is Bridge House, a small, square one-room building sitting on a miniscule bridge over a river which, at that point, is little more than a stream. Nearby is Stagshaw Garden, a recent garden created by a former National Trust agent and containing fine camellias, rhododendrons and azaleas. South of the town, towards Windermere*, is the National Park's Lake District Visitor Centre, in a house built in 1895 for the Manchester silk merchant Henry Adolphus Gaddum and set in formal gardens laid out by the leading landscape gardener in northwest England, Thomas Mawson.

Amersham, Bucks 690 E4, Amersham has early origins and, like nearby High Wycombe*, grew up around a gap in the Chiltern Hills. Amersham-on-the-Hill to the north is a modern suburb built around the Metropolitan Line station; but Old Amersham remains charming with its fine Market Hall of 1682 and a church containing several noteworthy monuments. The Amersham Museum at 49 High Street, occupying part of a 15th-century hall-house, is thought to be the oldest building in the town.

Althorp
Top: Lady Kitty Spencer, by R Becket, 1994.
Above: The exterior, begun in 1573 and worked on by Henry Holland in the 1780s.

Bottom: Alton Towers, the Great Conservatory by Robert Abraham.

Amesbury, Wilts 690 C6, The church of St Mary and St Melor – an unusual dedication – was founded for Benedictine nuns in AD 980, and then re-founded as a priory in 1177. It is a flint church, partly Norman in date, with amendments of later centuries. There is a square Norman font, fashioned in Purbeck marble. The town, 10 miles (16km) north of Salisbury, is usually entered over the imposing, five-arched Queensberry Bridge of 1775. Amesbury Abbey, a successor to the priory, was then in the possession of the 3rd Duke of Queensberry. Though the gatehouses are of the early 17th century, the main house, built by John

Webb in 1661, was demolished in 1830, and a new one was built on the old lines by Thomas Hopper.

Ampthill, Beds 690 E3, A typical Bedfordshire town with a market dating back to 1219 and some attractive buildings, particularly in Church Street and Woburn Street. At the central crossroads stands the Moot Hall, built in 1852 with the shaped gables and the cupola of its predecessor, the obelisk pump of 1784, built to Sir William Chambers' design, and the White Hart, an early 18th-century coaching inn. Walking towards the church one passes Avenue House, built c1780 for John Morris, the Ampthill brewer, and enlarged by Henry Holland between

Above: Angel of the North, Antony Gormley's impressive iron sculpture benevolently dominating the A1.

Left: Anglesey Abbey. Four-tiered pagoda-shaped Regency clock by Henry Bovell (1795–1841) in the Living Room. The tapestry is a 17th-century Felletin.

Below: Antony House, *Hypercone* by Simon Thomas – a sculpture in the gardens.

1792 and 1795. The iron gates to No. 28 are reputedly from Houghton* in Norfolk. Church Square is rather attractive, with two large Georgian houses framing the ironstone church of St Andrew, set back from the road. It contains an unusual monument to Richard Nicolls (d. 1672) with the cannon ball that killed him embedded in a pediment. At Nos. 15 and 16 Woburn Street are pairs of thatched *cottages ornés* built in 1812. Further out of the town to the west, St Catherine's Cross was erected in 1773 to commemorate Ampthill Castle and Catherine of Aragon, who lived there while Henry VIII arranged their divorce. Outside the town, Oxford Hospital is a handsome almshouse, founded by John Cross of Oxford University in 1697. It is built of chequer brick, with a hipped roof and dormers; in the middle, beneath the wooden pediment, is a small chapel.

Angel of the North, T & W 697 G2, The A1 south from Gateshead is now dominated by this huge late 20th-century iron sculpture by Antony Gormley, a powerful symbol of protection with its very long outstretched arms.

Anglesey Abbey, Cambs 695 G6, The lodgings of a 12th-century Augustinian priory, converted into a private house after the Dissolution, just east of Cambridge on the edge of the Fens [NT]. Its most striking features were created by Huttleston Broughton, later the 1st Lord Fairhaven, from 1926. He adorned the house with fabulous art collections (jade, clocks, silver, Chinese lacquer, Chippendale desks, Claude Lorraine paintings) and surrounded it with spectacular grounds. Imported garden statuary includes Corinthian columns from Chesterfield House and female graces from Stowe*. Best is the Hellenistic Bacchus, formerly at Painshill* and Fonthill. The canon's fishponds, the original lode or waterway and the fully restored watermill are reminders of Anglesey's more prosaic origins.

Anglesey Column (Twr Marcwis), IOA, Built in 1816 to commemorate the first Marquess, second-in-command to the Duke of Wellington at Waterloo, it now lies just off the A5, not far from the Britannia Bridge. The Marquess' service on the battlefield cost him a limb, and gained him the nickname 'Old One-leg'. A climb of over 100 steps is rewarded by wonderful views of Snowdonia*. *See* **Llanfair PG* 692 D2.**

Anstey, Herts 691 G3, The church contains a wealth of carvings and a fine Norman font. The base is crudely fashioned into four columns which support the basin, into which mermen are naively carved.

Antony House, Cnwll 688 E7, Set within the extensive lawns and avenues of a landscape designed by Humphry Repton, this very early 18th-century house [NT] may have been designed by master-mason John Moyle after plans by James Gibbs. Within the pinkish granite walls is the most remarkable collection of family and other portraits, modern pictures, fine furniture and tapestries, formed by the Carews (whose seat this was), the Poles of Shute in east Devon, and now the Carew Poles. There are several pictures by Sir Joshua Reynolds, Thomas Hudson, Jan Wyck and John Wootton, and furniture attributed to John Channon. The woodland garden has miles of walks through groves of camellia, rhododendron, magnolia and other well-established shrubs, with glorious views across the Lynher and Tamar rivers.

Appleby-in-Westmorland, Cumb 697 F3, This town straddles the route across the Pennines. The main street, Boroughgate, leads from the church at the bottom to the castle at the top. There are several good houses, especially the White House, which has curious gothick detail, and the delightful almshouses, St Anne's Hospital, founded in 1651 by Lady Anne Clifford. This indomitable lady was an indefatigable builder; there is a monument to her in St Lawrence's Church, of which she rebuilt the chancel. Appleby Castle was her property until her death in 1676. Within the medieval castle curtain walls, there is a tall 12th-century keep and a late 17th-century range in up-to-date country house style, built by Lady Anne's son-in-law, the Earl of Thanet. The castle houses Lady Anne's extraordinary family triptych.

Appleby Magna, Leics 694 C5, At Moat House, the remains of the moat and the medieval manor house within it can be traced. Of the house itself only the gatehouse still survives, now joined to a 16th-century timber-framed house as part of a very picturesque group.

Antony House
Top left: South front of the early 18th-century house with its mid-19th-century *porte cochère*.
Top right: The entrance hall displaying a portrait of Richard Carew, author of the *Survey of Cornwall* (1602).

Above: Arbeia Roman Fort, view from the verandah towards the triclinium.

Left: Appleby Castle, the 12th-century keep.

At nearby Appleby Parva is the Old Grammar School, originally designed by Sir Christopher Wren and built in the 1690s.

Appledore, Devon 688 E5, A remarkably unspoiled maritime town hugging the western bank of the Torridge where it meets the Taw. From the 17th to the 19th century, trading ships left from here bound for North America, and this period is well documented in the excellent Maritime Museum in Odun Road.

Appuldurcombe House, *see* **Isle of Wight*.**

Arbeia Roman Fort, T & W 697 H2, South Shields marks the eastern end of the Roman frontier; here the fort of Arbeia controlled the mouth of the River Tyne, where a port, the precise location of which is as yet unknown, developed to supply the Roman armies with food and equipment.

Top right: Arbeia Roman Fort, the reconstructed West Gate, showing the impressive scale of Roman military architecture on Hadrian's Wall.

Left and above: Arbury Hall, seen from the lakeside. Sir Roger Newdigate's Saloon is in the centre of the south front of the Hall.

Below: Arbroath Abbey ruins. It was here that Robert the Bruce signed Scotland's famous declaration of independence from England in 1320.

Although a large site, Arbeia Roman Fort is surprisingly hard to find: the latter part of the route seems unlikely to be correct, and the signposting shows just a stylized Roman helmet – the only mention of a name is at the site itself. Excavations were begun in the late 19th century, and these uncovered evidence of the usual series of reconstructions and changes of use throughout the Roman period. The West Gate was somewhat controversially rebuilt in 1988, followed by the Commanding Officer's House and a barrack block. The plan of the fort can be best appreciated by climbing to the top of the West Gate, from which there are also panoramic views of the surrounding topography. The upper chambers contain useful interpretive material. The museum contains displays of the many important objects that have been found on the site, which has yielded an impressive collection of fine quality small artefacts.

Arbroath, Angus 699 H2, A former royal burgh, this 400-year-old fishing port and centre of light industry is renowned for its 'smokies' (haddock smoked over an oak fire) and its abbey. The red-sandstone abbey church was consecrated in 1178 but the present building dates from 1285. It was in this abbey, which once housed the relics of St Columba, that the Declaration of Scottish Independence was signed in April 1320. It was here, too, that the 'Stone of Destiny', stolen from Westminster in 1950, was found on the altar in 1951. The abbey ruins, which combine Norman and early gothic styles, include a decorated west doorway and the beautiful south transept, with its two rows of blind arches surmounted by a row of open arches, high gothic windows and a circular window (the 'Round O of Arbroath').

The 15th-century sacristy is very well-preserved, as is the Abbot's House (15th–early 16th century) which today houses a museum. A signal tower built in 1811 to communicate with the teams working on the Inchcape or Bell Rock lighthouse, 12 miles (19km) to the southeast, now houses a museum tracing the history of Arbroath and the lighthouse.

Arbury Hall, Warwks 694 C6, Arbury's interiors could be spun in sugar, so elaborate and delicate are the vaults and tracery of the early Gothic Revival remodelling for Sir Roger Newdigate (who appears in George Eliot's *Scenes of Clerical Life* – she was born on the estate). Sir Roger started work on the old house, based on the quadrangular plan of

the monastery, in the same year as Horace Walpole began Strawberry Hill*. A 17th-century stable survives from the earlier house.

Arbuthnott, Abers 702 D7, Arbuthnott House, a 15th- to 18th-century mansion renowned for its plasterwork and painted panelling, is open to the public only on certain days, while the gardens and 17th-century parterre are open throughout the year. St Ternan's Church was consecrated in 1242, but the bell tower and late-gothic Lady Chapel (or Arbuthnott Aisle) date from 1500. James Leslie Mitchell, better known as Lewis Grassic Gibbon (1901–35), is buried in the churchyard. An exhibition in the old schoolhouse is devoted to this novelist.

Ardchattan Priory, Ag & B 698 C2, The priory, founded in 1231 by Duncan MacDougall, Lord of Lorne, was bought after the Reformation by Alexander Campbell and is still occupied by his

Arley Hall
Top: The Drawing Room with its heavy Victorian strapwork ceiling.
Above: The main entrance front, built to the designs of George Latham, 1833–42, and partly remodelled in 1967.

descendants. The only parts of the priory (burned by Cromwell's troops) open to the public are the ruined cloister, which houses some monumental sculptures from the Iona* School, and the gardens.

Ardeley, Herts 691 F3, The Cromer Windmill is a 17th-century post-mill, restored to working order by the Hertfordshire Building Preservation Trust.

Ardington, Oxon 690 D4, This village, east of Wantage, is worth a visit for Ardington House, built in 1721 in the Vanbrughian style. The Hall contains an imperial staircase and there is a good plasterwork ceiling in the dining room. Also of note is the church, of Norman origin but richly decorated during the 1800s.

Ardnamurchan peninsula, Highld 700 D7, South of Lochailort, the A861 crosses the Moidart to the Ardnamurchan peninsula: 200,000 acres (81,000ha) of varied but equally rich landscapes. Against this backdrop stand the ruins of Castle Tioram (13th century), on the south shore of Loch Moidart, and those of Mingary Castle (14th century), near Kilchoan. The Point of Ardnamurchan is the most westerly headland on the British mainland.

Arley Hall, Ches 696 F8, Rowland Egerton-Warburton built the present house in the 1840s to replace the earlier Tudor building. The Victorian-Jacobean hall is built of red brick with blue brick patterning, curvy roof gables and mullion and transom windows. The chapel, designed by Anthony Salvin, was built during the same period. The attractive cobbled stable yard features a Grade 1 Cruck Barn dating from the medieval period, with a distinctive one-handed clock tower straddled

Arlington Court
Above centre: The Greek Doric porch.
Bottom: The reception rooms.

Left: Arley Hall gardens.

Right: Arran, the ruins of Lochranza Castle.

above, again built by Rowland Egerton-Warburton, and linked to the atmospheric Tudor Barn, dating from 1603, which is now a restaurant.

Arlington Court, Devon 689 F4, This commodious Regency house [NT] was built for Colonel JP Chichester by Thomas Lee of Barnstaple, whose family had lived here since the 16th century. The plain exterior, relieved only by a single-storey Doric porch, does not prepare one for the lavishness within. Along the south front are three

intercommunicating reception rooms with delicate plaster ceilings, divided by pairs of scagliola columns. Many of the rooms are filled with the idiosyncratic collections formed by Miss Rosalie Chichester, the last of her line, but it was probably her great-grandfather who purchased the important watercolour of 1821 by William Blake. Also commemorated here are the exploits of her step-nephew Sir Francis, who sailed single-handed around the world in 1967 in *Gipsy Moth IV*. The stable block has a fine collection of carriages.

Arran, N Ayrs 698 C5, The Isle of Arran lies between the mouth of the Firth of Clyde and the east coast of Kintyre. The southern part of the island is fertile and fairly flat, rather like the Scottish Lowlands, while the more austere and mountainous north evokes the Highlands. The fishing port and coastal resort of Brodick is also the 'capital' of Arran. It nestles in a bay dominated by Goatfell (2,867 feet/874m), the highest point on the island. There is a ferry service between Brodick and Ardrossan and, in summer, Rothesay on the island of Bute*. The Isle of Arran Heritage Museum at Rosaburn occupies an 18th-century farmhouse and presents the island's economic, social and natural history. **Brodick Castle** has lush gardens due to the fact that, like the rest of Scotland's west coast, Arran is subject to the influence of the warm Gulf Stream. The 13th-century castle, the home of the dukes of Hamilton between 1503 and 1895, has been enlarged several times, in particular by

Top: Arthur's Stone, the two pieces of the boulder capstone.

Bottom: Arundel Castle from the air. The medieval round keep is in the centre. The building in the foreground is a 19th-century reconstruction.

James Gillespie Graham in 1844. Napoleon III lived in Brodick while in exile. The collections include works by Gainsborough, Turner and Watteau, and some beautiful 18th- and 19th-century furniture. Lochranza, on the north coast, is a former herring port dominated by the ruins of its castle (14th–15th century). At Machrie Moor Stone Circles (near Tormore), pottery dating from the 2nd millennium BC has been found, but the function of the stones remains a mystery.

Arrochar, Ag & B 698 D3, This little village at the head of Loch Long is a favourite summer rendezvous for walkers and climbers, who come to pit themselves against the munros and other peaks of Arrochar: Ben Arthur (2,890 feet/880m), nicknamed The Cobbler because its outline resembles that of an upturned shoe; Beinn Ime (3,315 feet/1,010m); Beinn Narnain (3,040 feet/926m); Ben Vane (3,005 feet/916m); and Ben Donich (2,780 feet/847m).

Arthur's Stone, Swans 688 E3, On the minor road from Reynoldston over Cefn-y-Bryn, this dolmen is much visited, not only as a renowned prehistoric monument, but also because of the spectacular views from the site.

Arundel, W Susx 690 E7, From the south, presenting what seems to be a perfect medieval silhouette, this hill town is dominated by a castle on one side and a cathedral on the other. In fact, both are creations of the 19th century. Of the old castle, one of the seats of the Duke of Norfolk, the shell keep on a mound, the gatehouse and a few fragments remain. The rest was built by C A Buckler between 1890 and 1903, though it includes an interesting earlier room, the Library, in Regency gothic of 1801. There is a fine collection of furniture and paintings, including Daniel Mytens' pair of portraits of Thomas, Lord Arundel, and his wife. Genuinely medieval is the church of St Nicholas (1380), actually two churches in one: the nave, which is Protestant, belongs to the parish, and the Fitzalan Chapel, which is Catholic, to the Norfolk family. It has a spectacularly elaborate gothic pulpit and a splendid series of 15th- and 16th-century tombs, including one made famous by Philip Larkin. The cathedral-like church visible from a distance is the Catholic church of St Philip Neri, a successful pastiche of 13th-century French gothic by J A Hansom (1870) – very competent, very expensive, with plenty of carved capitals and a stone vault.

Ascot, Berks 690 E5, Ascot is known chiefly for its racecourse. Queen Anne moved the Windsor race meeting here in 1711, and in the mid-18th century the Duke of Cumberland established a stud at Windsor. The racecourse has been a popular haunt of royalty ever since. Most of the buildings seen today date from the 20th century, but the atmosphere remains traditional.

Ascott

Ascott, Bucks 690 E4, This is one of several houses in
Buckinghamshire built by members of the Rothschild family.
The original timber-framed house dating from 1606 is in the
centre of the front, but it has been all but engulfed by extensive
building programmes undertaken by Leopold de Rothschild
between 1873 and 1888. A total of eight different building phases
resulted in the picturesque house we see today. The works were
begun by Devey, who also designed the Main and Northeast
lodges, the Steward's and Agent's Houses, the cottages on Ascott
Green and the hunting and domestic stables for Leopold's
famous stud. The black-and-white appearance of the main

house and the interior date from 1937–8. Leopold also oversaw
the extensive creation of a new garden, essentially designed by
Devey; Veitch & Son advised on the planting. The result is an
excellent example of a 19th-century garden. Terraces offer fine
views across the parkland. The bronze fountain of Venus and
her cherubs in a chariot pulled by seahorses and the Cupid
Fountain are by Thomas Waldo Story. By the late 19th century
the gardens were famed for their topiary hedges, shaped into
tables, churches, birds and animals; today only a topiary
sundial survives. The house contains fine collections of
Oriental porcelain dating from 1400 to 1700, 18th-century
French furniture and a small but select collection of superb
paintings, including Cuyp's *View of Dordrecht* and Stubbs'
Five Brood Mares [NT].

Top: *Venus and Cherubs in
Chariot* in the Venus Garden,
a circular enclosure
surrounded by a yew hedge.
The figures are in two shades
of bronze and the basin is in
yellow Siena marble.

Above: *A Lady Receiving a
Letter,* by Ludolph de Jongh.
One of an outstanding series
of paintings by Dutch 17th-
century masters.

Left: *Peasants at an Inn* and **bottom right**, *Interior of an Inn*, both by Adriaen van Ostade.

Bottom left: A Riesener roll-top writing desk in the Common Room. Riesener was one of the leading 18th-century French cabinet makers in Paris. Above the desk is a portrait of Hélène Fourment, after Rubens.

Ashbourne, Derbys 694 C4, An attractive small town with a large and handsome medieval church. The north transept served as the Boothby family chapel and contains the famous monument by Thomas Banks to Penelope Boothby (d. 1793). The little girl lies as if asleep in a long frock; there is a moving inscription. The church is linked to the town centre by Church Street, which is among the best streets in Derbyshire (containing the grammar school, Owfield's almshouses and several handsome Georgian mansions). Church Street turns into St John Street, which is spanned by the sign of the Green Man and Black's Head Inn. Just off St John Street is the sloping triangular Market Place.

Ashby-de-la-Zouch, Leics 694 D5, A pleasant little town concentrated around the gently sloping Market Street. Hidden away at the top end of the street is St Helen's Church, a large 15th-century building with Victorian additions, which stands within the original enclosure of the castle, first built in the 12th century by the earls of Leicester but turned into a very comfortable mansion by Edward IV's friend Lord Hastings in the 1470s. Many of his buildings can still be seen, but they are roofless and ruined.

Ashdown House, Oxon 690 C5, South of Ashbury is this Dutch-style house [NT], built in *c*1660 for the first Earl of Craven and described by Pevsner as 'the perfect doll's house'. The building has a magnificent oak staircase (occupying a quarter of the house) with portraits, a roof platform which offers fine views of the surrounding area, and two flanking office ranges. It was built in honour of Elizabeth of Bohemia (known as 'The Winter Queen' because she was Queen for one winter only), sister of Charles I. There are plenty of walks to be had nearby, and attractions include Weathercock Hill and Alfred's Castle.

Ashover, Derbys 694 C3, The handsome church of All Saints has a pleasant setting. The latest part of the building is the west tower and spire built by the

Below left: Ashby-de-la-Zouch Castle, the keep built by Lord Hastings in the 1470s.

Below right: Ashdown House. Its extraordinary tall and narrow proportions are somewhat balanced by the pavilions (the corner of one is glimpsed in the photograph). The house contains important paintings contemporary with the house.

Babbington family in the early 15th century. Inside the church is a particularly good and highly ornamented Norman font made of lead, a reminder that Derbyshire was the centre of lead mining; there is also a fine early 16th-century alabaster tomb to Thomas Babbington.

Ashridge Estate, Herts 690 E4, An estate of over 4,000 acres (1,600ha) that runs across a ridge of the Chiltern Hills on the borders of Herts and Bucks [NT]. It offers extensive walks through woodland, downland and commons, affording visitors a chance to inspect Sir Jeffry Wyatville's monument to the Duke of Bridgwater (erected 1832). Ivinghoe Beacon has breathtaking views of the surrounding countryside.

Ashwell, Herts 691 F3, This large and well-preserved village contains the beautiful 14th- and 15th-century church of St Mary with its splendid west tower (176 feet/53.6m tall) and its light and spacious interior. There is a detailed scratching of the south side of Old St Paul's Cathedral* on the north wall.

Aske Hall, N York 697 G4, A house of many periods built around a 15th-century pele tower, extended

in the 1570s, 1680s, 1740s and 1760s. More recent alterations have included a reduction in size under the architect Claude Phillimore in 1963, and the addition of a family wing designed by the York architect Martin Stancliffe in the 1990s. Contents include some of the collection of paintings and furniture amassed by Sir Lawrence Dundas for his seven estates throughout the British Isles in the 1760s. Adjacent to the Hall is the handsome former stable block designed by John Carr of York in 1763, partly converted into an Italianate chapel in 1887. In the grounds is the Temple, a splendid gothic folly of 1745. The vast late 19th-century stable block was impressively converted into a complex of business units in 2000. High Lodge, a grand entrance to the estate, has a triumphal arch with splendid wrought-iron gates which commemorate the racing triumphs of the family's horse Voltigeur.

Astbury, Ches 693 H2, The approach to St Mary's Church is up a charming street and through a 17th-century gateway. Although much of the church dates from the 14th century (most of the south aisle windows and the north tower are of that period), of overriding interest is the Perpendicular rebuilding, which was probably carried out in the late 15th century. Among the most characteristic features of the Perpendicular style are tall, wide windows, and Astbury has plenty of them. The fittings inside the church are particularly fascinating; font cover, chancel screen pulpit and pews all date from the 17th century.

Astley Hall, Lancs 696 E6, The Hall is set in a landscaped park at Chorley. In appearance it is a mid-17th-century great house, the home of the Charnocks, though at its core is a timber-framed courtyard house. The hall seems old-fashioned in its asymmetrical composition and many details, especially the great areas of glazing, are reminiscent in quantity, if not in sophistication, of Hardwick Hall*. Inside is a fine scrolly staircase, panel paintings of heroes as varied as Tamburlaine, Elizabeth I and Christopher Columbus, and deeply undercut ceiling plasterwork of barbaric character. In the top floor Long Gallery is the longest shovelboard table in England.

Top left: Athelhampton House, Great Hall. A magnificent timber roof surmounts the towering oriel window at the left and the three-light window on the end wall. Athelhampton was built at the end of the 15th century.

Attingham Park
Below left: George Steuart's main front of 1784.
Below: His Round Room with its slim columns, domed ceiling and delicate arabesque decoration.

Aston Munslow, Shrops 693 G4, The White House is a small farmhouse that has evolved steadily since the 14th century. The farm outbuildings shelter an excellent collection of farm vehicles and implements from hay wains to billhooks.

Athelhampton House, Dorset 689 J6, Built for Sir William Martyn in 1485, this manor house is one of the finest examples of its time. It has the usual (Tudor) Great Hall, with a four-sided oriel window rising through its substantial height (terminating on the outside in battlements), a splendid timber roof, and a great deal of armorial stained glass. The east wing was restored after a fire in 1992. The house is surrounded by 20 acres (8ha) of grounds, laid out in 1891, including a

Great Court, with 12 giant pyramids of yew. There is also a 16th-century dovecote, originally designed for 1,200 birds, and three formal enclosed gardens, one with a crest of obelisks.

Atherington, Devon 689 F5, Set proudly on a high hill with panoramic views, the church of St Mary is renowned for its very fine and rare 15th-century rood screen and loft. The nimble can climb the rood loft stairs and stand close to the carved roof bosses. Stretching across one aisle, the nave altar stands behind a simpler, late medieval screen removed from the nearby Umberleigh Church. Opposite the lych gate stands an old cottage with the poignant inscription 'JM 1917 VERDUN'.

Attingham Park, Shrops 693 G4, An impressive house built for the 1st Lord Berwick in the

1780s and altered by John Nash in 1805 [NT]. The park was landscaped by Humphry Repton in the 1790s. The handsome main rooms, with excellent original neoclassical decoration by George Steuart, are arranged in two main apartments either side of the entrance hall. Beyond the hall is Nash's picture gallery with its iron and glass ceiling and good Old Masters, and his main staircase with reeded wooden walls meant to look like drapery.

Aubourn Hall, Lincs 694 E3, At one end of the village of Aubourn, 7 miles (11km) south of Lincoln*, stands Aubourn Hall, next to the old church. It is an L-shaped house, originally Tudor but rebuilt between 1587 and 1628. The interior has 16th- and 17th-century decoration, including a staircase with carvings of leaves and snakes.

Auckland Castle, Dur 697 G3, The palace of the Bishops of Durham is first approached through a whimsically gothic gatehouse of 1760 topped by a clock tower, and then a more seriously gothic entrance screen of c1795 by James Wyatt, who also extensively altered the state rooms of the palace itself for Bishop Shute Barrington. The elegant 12th-century aisled Great Hall of the early palace, its lofty piers with shafts of Frosterley marble from Weardale, was converted into a chapel by John Cosin, Bishop of Durham 1662–72, and it is his burial place. The fittings are mostly the black oak church furniture for which he is renowned. In the grounds is the Deer House [EH], a large and elaborate cloister-like structure designed by Thomas Wright, built c1760 to provide shelter for the parkland deer. The castle has given its name to the town of Bishop Auckland close by.

Top right: Auckland Castle exterior.
Below right: The Dining Room. In the year 2001 the decision was taken to sell the large portraits hanging in the Dining Room of Jacob and his Twelve Sons, collected by Bishop Trevor in 1760. Painted in 1640 by the Spanish artist Francisco Zurbarán, they had been captured by pirates on their way to South America.

Bottom: Aubourn Hall. The tall, early 17th-century south front with its cross-windows and asymmetrical porch.

Audley End, Essex 691 G3, Best approached through the park from Saffron Walden*. Transfixed by a golden reflection in its mirror-like lake, this glorious house [EH] seems untouched by time. Appearances can be deceptive.

The Benedictine abbey of Walden, dating from 1140, was suppressed by Henry VIII and the property handed to the Lord Chancellor Sir Thomas Audley (who helped dispatch Sir Thomas More and queens Anne Boleyn and Catherine Howard). His black marble sarcophagus in the town's church prompted the condemnation 'no blacker than the soul and no harder than the heart' of the man buried there. Remodelled as a great Jacobean 'prodigy' house, Audley End was relaunched in 1614 by the Lord Treasurer, the 1st Earl of Suffolk, to please a visiting king. Four years later the Earl was disgraced. Charles II later bought it as a base for Newmarket*. Like Hampton Court*, it was originally arranged around two inner courtyards, but was faced in Lincolnshire limestone, not brick. The grand Entrance Hall has an elaborately carved wooden screen at one end and a restrained stone arcade at the other. After decline and demolition – on Vanbrugh's advice it was reduced substantially – Sir John Griffin ordered a Georgian overhaul, with Capability Brown landscaping and a succession of neoclassical rooms by Robert Adam.

In the 1820s the 3rd Lord Braybrooke added an opulent 'Jacobean' suite with authentic plaster motifs, ousting the Adam plans, and a chapel in delicate Strawberry Hill* gothic. The park is dotted with Adam temples, an obelisk and bridges at either end of the lake, one incorporating a Palladian tea house and a kitchen garden, recently restored and run organically.

Top left: Theophilus Howard, 2nd Earl of Suffolk, inherited the burden of his father's profligacy. Portrait by Biagio Rebecca.

Above right: Audley End, the palatial west front, faced with creamy limestone, in Capability Brown's landscaped park.

Above: This *Still Life* by Dutch Old Master Pieter Claesz was recently returned to Audley End.

Right: Although dating from the early 17th century, the 'Jacobean' Great Hall was decorated and furnished by the 3rd Lord Braybrooke more than 200 years later.

Ault Hucknall, Derbys 694 D3, Isolated in countryside, the church of St John the Baptist is an interesting building, either Saxon or more probably very early Norman, with fine Victorian fittings by William Butterfield. There are also early Norman carvings, a wonderful monument of 1627 to Anne Keighley and a plain black slab that commemorates the philosopher Thomas Hobbes.

Avebury, Wilts 690 C5, Though less well known than Stonehenge*, the prehistoric site of Avebury is scattered over a much greater area. Its stone circles, enclosed by a ditch and external bank also encompassing an avenue of about 100 pairs of standing stones, extend over some 28 acres (11ha). The most thorough investigation of the circles was undertaken in the 1930s by Alexander Keiller, whose family had made their fortune in Dundee* from marmalade. His finds can be seen in the museum at Avebury bearing his name.

Avington, Berks 690 D5, The church of St Mark and St Luke is a fine example of a small and unspoilt

Above: Aydon Castle from the air, with the oldest buildings to the left.

Below: Avebury Stone Circle ranks as one of the most important works of prehistoric man. It is less well known than Stonehenge, and in consequence makes a greater impact.

Norman country church, which survives in a picturesque setting with a large cedar tree. Inside is a Norman font with finely carved figures.

Axbridge, Somset 689 H4, The church of St John the Baptist is the dominant building in this small town, and is thorough-going Perpendicular in style, dating to the middle of the 15th century. It contrasts sharply with the Town Hall of 1833, and the so-called King John's Hunting Lodge, owned by the National Trust. This is neither a hunting lodge nor anything to do with King John, but an early Tudor merchant's house, now run as a local history museum.

Axminster, Devon 689 H6, East Devon had prospered from its wool trade for several hundred years before Thomas Whitty began carpet manufacture in Axminster in the 18th century. After a long interval carpets are once again being made in the town. A few miles northeast is the Baptist Chapel at Loughwood: a thatched hall built in 1653 with box pews, an octagonal pulpit and a bath for total immersion. Nearby is a tribute to a former pastor, Isaac Hann (d. 1778), whose 'wit sparkled in his pleasing face'.

Aydon Castle, Nthumb 697 F2, A 13th-century manor house overlooking the precipitous valley of the Cor Burn, it was originally built without defences in a rare period of peace in the Borders, but soon had to be fortified [EH]. It survives as a remarkably complete example of a Northumberland fortified house, despite later alterations when it became a farmhouse (which it remained until 1966). Replica furniture is displayed in the medieval Great Hall.

Aylesbury, Bucks 690 E4, Since it replaced Buckingham* as the county town in the 18th century, Aylesbury expanded gradually until it experienced a period of very rapid growth in the 1960s culminating in the 1973 completion of the ring road. It thus presents a rather mixed appearance with few major attractions. There are,

Top left: Aynho Park House, the main entrance. It was destroyed by Royalists after the Battle of Naseby but restored and enlarged by Thomas Archer.

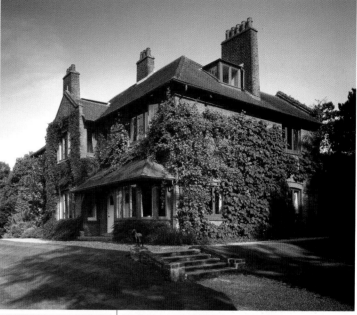

Top right: Ayot St Lawrence, Shaw's Corner, built in 1902. This was the house the playwright George Bernard Shaw intended to become a literary shrine.

however, the County Hall, started in 1722 and designed by Thomas Harris, and the medieval church of St Mary. The Buckinghamshire County Museum in Church Street is housed in well-restored buildings that include an 18th-century grammar school. It contains the magical Roald Dahl Children's Gallery and displays on the county's heritage.

Aylesford, Kent 691 G5, A house of Carmelite friars, which fell into ruin after the Dissolution and was turned into a large house (severely damaged by fire in 1930). In 1949 the Carmelites returned. A new church was built and became a flourishing centre of modern Catholicism.

Aylsham, Norfk 695 J4, A small, attractive 18th-century town with Dutch-gabled brick houses around the Market Place. These spill down Millgate to the River Bure and along the road to Blickling Hall*, the source of its agricultural wealth. The church has interesting monuments, including one outside to the landscape designer Humphry Repton (d. 1818), whose body gave 'form and colour to the Rose', according to his epitaph.

Aynho Park House, Nhants 690 D3, A great long barrack of a house, with rows of offices standing formidably to attention on each side of the drive. The original E-shaped 17th-century house has had many interesting additions and remodellings, including the baroque Entrance Hall by Thomas Archer, and Sir John Soane's delicate Garden Hall.

Ayot St Lawrence, Herts 691 F4, The church of New St Lawrence is an ambitious and unusual building of 1778–9 designed by Nicholas Revett (of *Antiquities of Athens* fame) in the Greek Revival style. Ayot St Lawrence was the home of George Bernard Shaw from 1906 until his death in 1950. His Edwardian house, **Shaw's Corner**, at the southwest end of the village, remains intact with interesting personal relics and the summerhouse in which he wrote [NT]. There is a pretty garden with fine views of the Hertfordshire countryside.

Ayot St Peter, Herts 691 F4, The church has a wonderfully colourful Arts and Crafts interior of 1874–5 by the architect JP Seddon. The chancel arch is ceramic and decorated with birds and

Above: Aynho Park House. This window is one of the baroque features by Thomas Archer.

Above right: Ayot St Lawrence, Shaw's writing desk at Shaw's Corner. The house is set out as it was in his lifetime.

Below: The door knocker given to Shaw by his friend, Rosie Banks Danecourt entitled, 'Shaw, Man and Superman'.

flora, the font is enlivened with a mosaic of fish and flowers, and the organ pipes, chancel floor tiles and roof panels are all painted with saints and angels.

Ayr, S Ayrs 698 D6, Its beautiful sandy beaches have made Ayr – a former royal burgh and busy port until the 18th century – the leading resort on the Firth of Clyde. Robert Burns is very much in evidence: he immortalized the Auld Brig, a 15th-century cobbled bridge across the River Ayr, and was christened in the Auld Kirk, built in 1650 and dedicated since 1957 to the memory of those killed in the two world wars. Also on the High Street, visitors can stop for a drink at the Tam o'Shanter Inn, from where Burns' hero Tam set off on his famous ride home. Wallace Tower, near the inn, was built in 1831 on the site of a tower from which William Wallace escaped after being imprisoned by the English.

Ayton Castle, Borders 699 J5, Guided tours enable visitors to view the beautiful interior of this red-sandstone castle, built in 1846 by James Gillespie Graham. It stands on an escarpment surrounded by mature woodlands and has often been used as a film location.

Baconsthorpe, Norfk 695 J4, Approached along a track from the village, the ruins of Sir Henry Heydon's fortified and moated manor of 1486 stand romantically in the fields; they comprise gatehouse, curtain walls, bastions and remains of the Great Hall. Robbed stone was reworked into the 18th-century gothic house nearby, also in ruins.

Badbury Rings, Dorset 690 B7, An Iron-Age hill fort near Kingston Lacy*. The earthworks are owned by the National Trust. The botanically rich rings are given over to grazing, and dogs are not permitted.

Baddesley Clinton, Warwks 694 C6, The moat surrounding the manor house was dug in the 13th century, and the cluster of buildings around the three-sided court has a venerable air [NT]. Two ranges date from the 15th century, while the third was added by the Elizabethan Henry Ferrers, whose descendants lived in the house until 1939. Family portraits and diaries describe quiet Victorian daily life in the house that was – and is still – venerated as a shrine to history.

Above: The courtyard.

Below: The house seen from the across its moat.

Above: Embossed leather hangings, mid-18th century, surrounded by religious paintings by Rebecca Dulcibella Orpen.

Above right: The Sacristy, showing the cross placed over the garderobe shaft, which became the only entry to the hiding place, c1590.

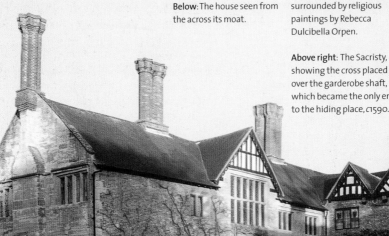

Bailiffscourt, W Susx, To all appearances a small medieval house, but in fact built in 1935. Architect Amyan Phillips retained a 13th-century chapel and injected many other genuinely medieval features, including timber roofs from Somerset. It is now a restaurant. *See* **Climping* 690 E7.**

Bakewell, Derbys 694 C3, A cheerful little town on the River Wye. Bakewell was clearly of importance in Saxon times because the parish churchyard contains the stump of a Saxon cross, and there are many fragments of Saxon carved stonework around the south porch. The church itself is quite ambitious, with a crossing tower and transepts. A fair amount of the Norman building survives, although it is partly submerged under a large number of Victorian restorations. In *c*1800 the Duke of Rutland, who was the principal landowner, decided to transform Bakewell from a modest market town into a spa resort to rival the Duke of Devonshire's new developments at Buxton*. The centre of the new town was to be Rutland Square, with its handsome Rutland Hotel. From the Square, Bridge Street runs down to the river and the medieval bridge, and King Street runs up towards the church. Both these main streets have a mixture of 17th-century and later houses and shops. Bakewell's riverside location is picturesque, and a number of spacious villas was built on the outskirts of the town centre in the 19th century.

Baldock, Herts 691 F3, The church of St Mary has a remarkably complete 14th-century interior.

Ballachulish, Highld 698 C2, Near the bridge that spans Loch Leven, a granite monument marks the spot where James Stewart of Aucharn was hanged in November 1752 for the murder of Colin Campbell of Glenure, a government officer, during the Highland Clearances. Robert Louis Stevenson based one of the characters in his novel *Kidnapped* (1886) on the main suspect, Alan Breck Stewart.

Balls Park, Herts, This charmingly idiosyncratic house of *c*1640, whose architect is unknown, is now part of the Hertfordshire College of Education. The most curious feature is the north entrance, where Tuscan pilasters of stone are superimposed on Ionic brick pilasters. Above the pilasters are two large corbels supporting a

Above: Balmoral, holiday home of the royal family since the 1850s.

Below and bottom: Bamburgh Castle, on a naturally fortified site, rising up above the sand dunes on an outcrop of the Whin Sill.

balcony. The balcony is linked to the door by a dwarf pilaster. The house contains excellent plaster ceilings. *See* **Hertford* 691 F4.**

Balmoral, Abers 702 C6, Queen Victoria had been looking for an estate in the Highlands for some time when she came across Balmoral. The royal couple bought the estate in 1852, and commissioned a new house, much larger than the existing 16th-century tower-house but with a similar tower (1854–6), designed by Aberdonian architect William Smith. The Queen helped to promote wider interest in the region when she published her travel journal: *Leaves from a Journal of our Life in the Highlands*, in 1867. The gardens and ballroom, which houses an exhibition tracing the estate's history, are open to the public in summer, except in August when the family is in residence. Nearby are Crathie Church (1895), attended by the Royal Family, and Royal Lochnagar Distillery, founded in 1845 and suppliers by Royal Appointment since the time of Queen Victoria. The royal estate stretches south to Lochnagar (3,786 feet/1,154m) and the magnificent Glen Muick (pronounced 'Mick'). It was here, on the shores of Loch Muick, that Queen Victoria had a modest retreat built in 1868, seven years after the death of Prince Albert. From the glen, footpaths lead up the slopes of Lochnagar, while others lead south across country to Glen Cova.

Bamburgh Castle, Nthumb 699 J5, Superbly set on a craggy promontory of the Whin Sill, the Norman castle was restored in the 1890s by the 1st Baron Armstrong, an engineer and munitions magnate, and appropriately contains a notable collection of armour. In the village, the church of **St Aidan** is mainly 13th century; the churchyard has an ornate monument to Grace Darling, an early Victorian example of a 'media' heroine. On 7 September 1838 she and her lighthouse-keeper father William launched a Northumbrian coble to rescue survivors of the steamship *Forfarshire*. The 400-ton vessel, shipwrecked during a storm in the Farne Islands* while sailing from Hull to Dundee, had

Above: Banbury Cross, 1859, designed in the style of an Eleanor Cross to commemorate the marriage of Victoria, Princess Royal.

Left : Bangor, the Cathedral, originally a monastery and founded by Deiniol. Its present structure dates from 1130.

Right: Barden Tower, the extensive ruins of a large medieval tower-house, set in the beautiful landscape of Wharfedale.

39 passengers, 24 crew, and a cargo of cloth and hardware on board. Two valiant journeys in their rowing boat saved eight men and one woman from the wreck. Queen Victoria supported a public subscription to Grace Darling, but she died in 1842 aged only 26.

Bampton, Oxon 690 C4, Bampton is a well-known centre of morris-dancing, which goes on along its village street. The important cruciform church, of Norman origin, has a double-tiered Easter Sepulchre. Its elegant spire dates from the 13th century; the transition from the square tower to the octagonal spire is aided by the miniature flying buttresses positioned at the corners, which are topped with statues. Three are original, the other is a Victorian replacement. The village has two dovecotes, one in Bushey Row, over the centre of a barn, and the second in the garden of the butcher's shop in Bridge Street. The Public Library was the grammar school, built in the mid-17th century – the ground floor was one large space, with the teachers' rooms above.

Banbury, Oxon 690 D3, The Banbury Cross from the well-known nursery rhyme was destroyed by Puritans in 1602; the present cross is an 1859 replacement. The striking church of St Mary was built to the design of SP Cockerell. The High Street has a 17th-century timber-framed house, with prominent jetties and elaborate carving in the gables. The shop front was inserted in the 19th century.

Banff, Abers 702 D4, This port and former royal burgh on the mouth of the Deveron is one of the most attractive towns in the northeast. It has beautiful 18th-century houses and some older buildings and monuments, like the market cross decorated with a Virgin and Child that has stood opposite the Town Hall since the 16th century. *See also* Duff House*, nearby.

Bangor, Gwynd 692 D2, Of the four colleges that established the town's reputation as a centre of learning, only two remain: the Normal College, a college of education, and the University College of North Wales, a handsome Jacobean-style building of the 1910s that dominates the town. Known as Lower Bangor, the commercial area consists of one long street with no features of distinction, and even the cathedral makes very little impact. However, Bangor claims the beginnings of what is thought to be the oldest religious foundation in Britain: St Deiniol's Monastery, founded in the first half of the 6th century. The saint enclosed it with a wattled fence, the Welsh word for which was *bangor*. Fragments of ornamental crosses and other monuments displayed at the west end of the north aisle are all that survive from the pre-Norman history of the foundation. The present building dates from 1130, but was substantially

altered between the 13th and 16th centuries and heavily restored by Sir George Gilbert Scott between 1868 and 1870. Its finest possession is the almost life-size figure of Christ, a woodcarving of great poignancy. Known as 'the Mostyn Christ' because it came into the possession of the Mostyn family, its origins remain a mystery. Near the cathedral, which also serves as the parish church of St Deiniol, is the peaceful enclave of the Biblical Garden in which is grown, climate permitting, every plant mentioned in the Bible. Bangor's 1,500-foot (457m) pier seems to stretch almost as far as Anglesey. A most attractive survivor of a peculiarly British invention, with domed shelters and kiosks, the pier has spectacular views of coast and mountains and of the towers of Penrhyn Castle*.

Banwell, Somset 689 H4, The church of St Andrew has a soaring tower 101 feet (31m) high with buttresses, pinnacles and a parapet. Here is the best of carved rood screens, dated 1522.

Barcaldine Castle, Ag & B 698 C2, This tower-house, built in 1609 by Duncan Campbell of Glenorchy, was re-roofed in the late 19th century. Its restored interiors and secret passages are open to the public; it is even possible to rent a room.

Barden Tower, N York 697 G5, Once the lodge of the verderer who controlled Wharfedale's ancient Forest of Barden, where wild boar were hunted, it was remodelled as a large tower-house in the reign of Henry VIII by the 'Shepherd' Lord Clifford. Barden Tower was restored again in 1658–9 by the remarkable Lady Anne Clifford, who also built the adjacent late-gothic former chapel and priest's house.

Barfrestone, Kent 691 J6, Famous for the church of

St Nicholas, one of the most sumptuous and best preserved Norman parish churches in England. On the tympanum of the south doorway is a relief of about 1160 showing Christ blessing, flanked by foliage scrolls containing a king and queen. The arch framing it is carved into three orders with many tiny figures in foliated circles and ovals: humans, animals, fabulous beasts and scenes of daily life. In the south wall of the chancel is a relief of St Michael slaying the Dragon, and there is further sculptural enrichment to the east wall.

Barham, Suffk 691 J3, The surprise here is Henry Moore's Madonna and Child in the church, designed originally as a war memorial. Nearby, Sir Charles Barry's enlarged Italianate Hall (c1850) emerges above the River Gipping's wooded flank. Now a health spa, Shrublands Hall has terraces

Above: Barnack, detail of the Saxon tower of St John's Church.

Left: Barfrestone, church of St Nicholas. The taller half is the nave, with its sculptured doorway, the smaller the chancel and its rose window and gable.

Below: Barnard Castle, the Bowes Museum, built in the style of an immense French château.

and cascading stone steps inspired by the Villa d'Este at Tivoli.

Barlaston Hall, Staffs 693 H3, An exquisite Georgian villa of the 1750s, probably designed by Sir Robert Taylor and spectacularly sited on the top of a steep rise. It was destabilized by coalmining and was left totally derelict by the 1960s, but it has now been restored and is lived in once more, a landmark in the history of building preservation.

Barming, Kent 691 G6, The church is worth a visit for the sake of the wooden stalls, which incorporate amazing carvings – thought to be German – of c1300. How they got there nobody knows. They show St Michael slaying the Dragon, Samson and the Lion, and Christ in Limbo.

Barnack, Cambs 695 F5, The source of limestone for Peterborough and Ely cathedrals and for many local churches. The quarry was exhausted in the 18th century, but the site survives as a picnic spot dubbed 'the Hills and Hollows'. The church of St John is fascinating, with work from all periods, notably the tower and seated Christ sculpture, both late Saxon, the north aisle c1200, Decorated chancel and medieval monuments.

Barnard Castle, Dur 697 G3, A grittily attractive market town on the steep bank of the River Tees,

here crossed by an old bridge. Near the bottom of The Bank, the main street, is a handsome market cross of 1747, octagonal in plan, with an open Tuscan colonnade where perishable commodities were sold. An upper chamber with Venetian windows and niches, surmounted by a cupola, was used as a town hall. The Castle [EH] was granted in 1095 to Guy de Baliol by William Rufus, whose son Barnard gave his name to the town. On the outskirts of the town is the enormous **Bowes Museum**, commissioned in 1869 by John Bowes and his French wife Joséphine from Parisian architect Jules Pellechet. It contains their outstanding collection of furniture, mainly French. The single most famous exhibit is a delightful 18th-century silver swan musical automaton, but the museum is also rich in paintings, especially French and Spanish.

Barnsley House Gardens, Gloucs 690 C4, The village manor house, built in 1697, has a beautiful new garden created by the late Rosemary Verey and her husband, the Gloucestershire historian David Verey. It contains two 18th-century summer-houses, one gothic and one neoclassical.

Barnstaple, Devon 689 F4, North Devon's main town, and like Bideford made rich through its trade with North America in the 17th and early 18th centuries. The River Taw is crossed by an ancient 14-arch bridge that leads into the heart of the town – which, despite the appearance of some tower blocks, is still dominated by the motte of the early castle. The narrow streets of the old town have many largely 17th-century merchants' houses with good plasterwork ceilings, several almshouses, the church of St Peter and St Paul with its numerous monuments, the famous Victorian Pannier Market and the adjacent Butchers' Row – outside the doors of which are to be found buckets of laver (an edible seaweed) when in season. The present town council is an enthusiastic supporter of the Britain in Bloom scheme, and the ancient streets (and not so ancient roundabouts) are ablaze with bedding flowers in the summer.

Above and below: Barnsley House Gardens. The 4½ acres (1.8ha) of gardens also contain features such as a fountain and a decorative vegetable patch.

Barra (Barraigh), Western Isles 700 B6, This tiny island is renowned for the beauty and diversity of its landscape. It has 1,000 different species of wild flowers. Planes from Glasgow*, Benbecula* and Lewis* land on the Cockle Strand airfield, the sandy bay of Traigh Mhor, tide and weather permitting. Castlebay (Bagh a Chaisteil), the island's only village, is also an active fishing port, although lobsters have replaced the herring catches of the past. The bay is dominated by Kisimul Castle (12th and 15th centuries), the ancestral seat of the MacNeil clan who owned Barra between 1427 and 1838. The Barra Heritage Centre traces its history. The cottage museum in Craigston, near Borve, is on the west coast, and Cille-Bharra, the burial place of the MacNeil chief, is near the village of Eoligarry (Eolaigearraidh), in the north. The tiny island of Vatersay (Bhatarsaigh) is linked to Barra by a causeway. A monument recalls the shipwreck in which 450 emigrants bound for Quebec lost their lives when the *Annie Jane* sank in West Bay in 1826. In summer boats link Castlebay to Sandray, Mingulay and

Pabbay, the most southerly of the Outer Hebrides*. Large colonies of seabirds nest on their cliffs.

Barrington Court, Somset 689 H5, A splendid garden, influenced in its planting by the ideas of Gertrude Jekyll. It surrounds the Tudor manor house, restored in the 1920s by the Lyle family. The house and estate are owned by the National Trust.

Barry, V Glam 689 G3, It was the 3rd Marquess of Bute who was indirectly instrumental in bringing about Barry Docks and the rapid expansion of Barry Town. His raising of the levy on coal exported from his father's docks in Cardiff*, now totally unable to cope with the trade and traffic, enraged David Davies, an energetic entrepreneur. The outcome was the construction of a rival port in 1880, which caused the transformation of a medieval settlement named after the de Barri, and its neighbour Cadoxton – which between them had only 500 inhabitants – into a sprawling town. The impressive Docks Office still looks over the waterfront (although there is now no activity). In front of it stands the statue of David Davies, with a map, surveying his properties and their prospects. A similar statue of him stands in his native village of Llandinam in Montgomeryshire. The municipal buildings in Holton Road reveal the once-assured optimism of the town.

Barton upon Irwell, Gt Man 697 F7, This area is much frequented because of the enormous Trafford Centre, a Middle American shopping mall, by

Right: Barrington Court, built a little after 1514.

Below: The main Ham stone block, symmetrical and in an 'E' formation. It sprawls across its site, with a stable block (c1670) and offices to the left. The house acts as a showroom, with antiques for sale.

Leach, Rhodes and Walker, 1999, set in the suburbs of south Manchester*. But Barton contains two monuments of major and contrasting interest. It was here that the Duke of Bridgewater's canal had to cross the River Irwell. In the 18th century it was forded by an aqueduct designed by James Brindley but with the coming of the Manchester Ship Canal larger shipping had to pass below the canal. The solution was the Barton Swing Bridge, which turns a whole section of the Bridgewater Canal. Close by is All Saints Church, EW Pugin's finest Roman Catholic church built for the de Trafford family, 1867; no expense was spared, especially when it came to their chapel. The church is high but has no tower or spire, just a small bellcote, not unlike EW Pugin's church at Gorton for the Franciscans who now serve Barton.

Barton-upon-Humber, Lincs 694 E1, Originally the southern end of the Humber ferry service, withdrawn in 1981 when the Humber Bridge opened. The bridge, by the engineers Freeman Fox & Ptnrs., was the world's longest suspension span. As a crossing point the little town was always important and there are relics of earlier prosperity, of which by far the most important is the church of St Peter. The first church on the site

Top: Barton-upon-Humber, the Humber Bridge.

Centre: Rudyard Kipling, *c*1910.

Bottom left: Basildon Park, beautiful gardens set in the Thames Valley.

Bottom right: Bateman's, home of Kipling.

was Anglo-Saxon, and the late 10th-century west porch and nave-cum-tower still survive. East of the tower the church was extended several times in a complex series of developments which has been documented by archaeological investigations over many years. The existing church is partly 13th but mostly 14th century.

Barton Turf, Norfk 695 J5, The church of St Michael is remote and picturesque. Inside, a marvellous late 15th-century Broadland screen features a rare depiction of the Nine Orders of Angels and three female saints with emblems of Martyrdom,

including Apollonia with tooth and Barbara with tower.

Basildon Park, Berks 690 D5, This elegant Georgian mansion [NT] was built by John Carr for Sir Francis Sykes in 1776–83. The interior retains fine plasterwork, a tall staircase and, in the centre of the garden front towards the Thames, the unusual Octagonal Room, probably by JB Papworth, with a fine set of paintings by Pompeo Batoni. The house is set among pleasure gardens in an area rich in downland and woodland walks.

Basing House, Hants 690 D6, The remains (mainly extensive earthworks) of a house at Old Basing, which began as a Norman castle, became a palatial Tudor mansion and was destroyed during and

after a memorable siege (with Oliver Cromwell personally in command) in 1645. A Tudor garden has recently been re-created and there is a fine, undamaged, Tudor barn.

Basingwerk Abbey, Flints 693 F2, Originally Savigniac, the Abbey [owned by CADW] had control over St Winefride's Well (*see* Holywell*) between the 13th and 15th centuries, but later became engulfed by industrial opportunism.

Bateman's, E Susx 691 G6, Rudyard Kipling's home in Burwash, part of a house of 1634 built by a Sussex ironmaster [NT]. Most of the rooms, including his book-lined study, are much as Kipling left them.

Bath

Left: The Roman Baths with the Abbey Church in the background. This celebrated view allows the visitor to see Roman and medieval architecture alongside each other.

Above: Lansdown Tower, built in 1825–6 for William Beckford, who lived at the end of his life in Lansdown Crescent, Bath.

Bath, Somset 690 B5, Bath Spa, the only city in England to be classified as a World Heritage Site, rises up the hillsides as a cluster of honey-coloured stone buildings. The Georgian terraces climb high, as if set around a giant bowl, with the River Avon flowing over a weir below. Bath is a city to walk in: to arrive by train is ideal; if you drive here, abandon your car in a 'Park and Ride' facility for the day. The car is an annoyance in this maze of one-way systems, restriction 'gates' and narrow streets, and parking is restricted and expensive.

It is said that the hot mineral spa that made Bath famous was discovered by Bladud, a Briton prince, who noted the waters' healing effects on his leprous swine as they wallowed joyously in the mud. Whatever the truth of this, 'Aquae Sulis' soon became the best-known of the Roman spa towns, and the legionaries enjoyed the torrent of healing springs, gushing forth thousands of gallons a day, at a constant temperature. The soldiers proved the forerunners of all those who believed in the curative properties of the waters. Charles II came in 1677, James II ten years later, and the wealthy and noble-born throughout the next 150 years. They bathed, wrapped themselves in cold sheets, and doubtless felt better for the effort. Their wealth increased or decreased by their success in the 'New' Assembly Rooms, at cards and games of chance.

Two architects, father and son, both named John Wood, profited from this affluence, and soon transformed the medieval city with its beautiful late 15th-century abbey. John Wood the elder (1704–54) proposed buildings and spaces based on Roman architecture, a Royal Forum, a grand Circus and an Imperial Gymnasium. Some of this he carried out, starting in 1728 with Queen Square, where he lived himself for a while.

Below: The Great Bath, some 110 feet (34m) long, is situated in its own hall, with steps leading down into the hot waters. Windows above allow a view from the Pump Room.

As the buildings rose they proved to be a twofold success, both in their proportions and in their undoubted commercial value. Many clients were attracted by the scheme, and even more to Wood's final effort, a walk uphill in a straight Roman line to the King's Circus.

Wood did not start this Circus until 1754, the year of his death. Approached by three streets, it is essentially a great circle of 30 houses. Their façades bear three tiers of columns, superimposed one above the other, Doric, Ionic and Corinthian. His concept was not based on the Colosseum, as thought at one time, but on stone circles at Stanton Drew* and Stonehenge*, and as such was a commemoration of the native culture that Wood believed to have flourished in pre-Roman Bath, and which he had studied and written about in 1747. Three months after laying the foundation stone of the first house, Wood died, and his son dealt with their actual construction. John Wood the younger (1727–81) became as well known as his father through his modification of the plans for the Royal Crescent (1767–75), perhaps the most famous such crescent in the world. At its head is No.1, headquarters of the Bath Preservation Trust, restored and furnished as a gentleman's town house. A cursory inspection of the houses in the impressive curving span, with their Victorian sashes and plate glass at first-floor level, will show the wisdom behind the careful restoration carried out at No. 1.

The younger Wood was also the architect of the **Assembly Rooms** of 1771, a mere stone's throw away along Brock Street (which, as if part of a giant question mark, connects the Royal Crescent and King's Circus), and another significant part of Bath's Georgian life of routs, dances and assemblies. The building, severe from the outside, is now owned by the National Trust. It was gutted in the Baedeker raid Bath suffered from the Luftwaffe in 1942, but has been beautifully restored. Within is a magnificent ballroom, at 106 feet (32.3m) the longest room in Bath, with five richly cut glass chandeliers by William Parker of Fleet Street, London. There is an adjacent tea room with a minstrels' gallery amid a two-tiered screen of columns, and in the basement is the celebrated Museum of Costume, with exhibits of international importance from 1580 to the present.

Refreshments are served in the **Pump Room**, designed by Thomas Baldwin (1750–1820) and built in 1786–92, which has provided facilities for visitors to the Spa since the late 18th century. The handsome room, set about with giant Corinthian columns, still echoes daily to the music of the resident trio, and the passing time is measured by the longcase clock Thomas Tompion, the celebrated London clockmaker, gave the city in 1709. The view from the window bay, where the spa water may be drunk, is to the steaming King's Bath. The various hot baths have altered over the centuries from their Roman appearance, and there are plans to gather them into a grand spa complex.

Outside is the towering west front of the **Abbey Church**, with its heavily carved doors of 1617, and stone angels climbing their ladders to heaven. Oliver King, who had been appointed bishop in 1495, had a dream in which he heard a voice telling him 'Let an Olive establish a Crown and let a King restore the Church'; and the ladders, olive tree and crown were put there by him in his rebuilding programme. They are now much restored. Within the church are fine fan-vaulted ceilings dating to 1499, comparatively early in the Perpendicular style. The nave ceiling, which looks medieval, was in fact erected in 1869 under the architectural direction of Sir George Gilbert Scott, when the Jacobean timber roof was demolished. The Abbey had ceased to exist by the time of the Dissolution, but became, in its rebuilt state, the grandest parish church in England. While the bishop of this diocese is called the

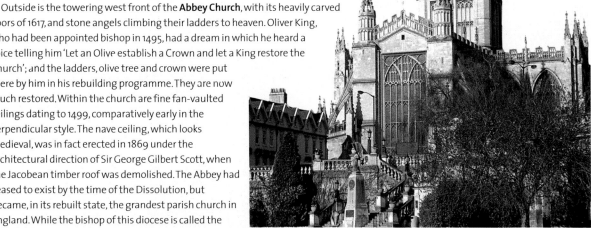

Top: The Pump Room, built in 1789–9 by Thomas Baldwin. The pedimented colonnade screens the Abbey Church. Its interior is presided over by a statue of Beau Nash, the 18th-century Master of Ceremonies.

Above, left and below: The Abbey Church was begun in 1499 by Bishop King, chief secretary to Henry VII. It impresses within, with the Bishop's mitre aloft, and its silhouette is a dominant feature from all around Bath, with the tall spire of the Catholic church of St John (1861–7) rising to the left.

Bishop of Bath and Wells, a double title confirmed by Pope Innocent IV in 1245, it is at Wells* that he has his cathedral, palace, dean and chapter.

There are two more surprises in Bath city centre. The Octagon Chapel by Thomas Lightoler (1765) in Milsom Street formerly housed the Royal Photographic Society's exhibitions. It has an eight-sided continuous gallery and shallow dome. Nearby is the Guildhall, designed by Thomas Baldwin in 1776 and containing, on its first floor, a grand ballroom. It is the most magnificent room in Bath, Adamesque in decoration, and an outstanding achievement for a young architect, then but 26 years old. Its lesser-known east side also has a fine façade, where there is the entrance to the covered 19th-century market. Pass by the bacon, biscuits, ground coffee and vegetables and emerge at the east side across from Robert Adam's **Pulteney Bridge**: there are tiny shops on either side, spanning the Avon. It was designed in 1769, to connect Lord Pulteney's Bathwick estates to the city. On the other corner is the **Victoria Art Gallery**, which has a fine collection of watercolours and engravings of the city. Walking across the bridge you see the grandest street in Bath, Great Pulteney Street, straight as a ruler, 1,100 feet (335m) long, 100 feet (30m) wide, and flanked on each side by Thomas Baldwin's pedimented terraces of 1788. They may

over-extend, but there is no denying the importance of their statement. The long vista is terminated by the classical façades of the **Holburne Museum**, built in 1796 as a hotel and now housing fine paintings, silver and ceramics.

Above: Prior Park, the colonnaded entrance front.

Left: *Rosamund Sargent*, by Allan Ramsay, 1749, in the Holburne Museum.

Further over the hill (on a Wednesday walk down steep Guinea Lane, with its antique market) is the Countess of Huntingdon's Chapel, now administered as a **'Building of Bath Museum'** by the Bath Preservation Trust, an essential stop for all those interested in how the Georgian city was built. Selina, Countess of Huntingdon (1707–91), having been converted to evangelical Methodism, built the chapel in 1765. Horace Walpole called her 'Queen of the Methodists' and John Wesley preached there within a few months of its opening.

A lesser-known crescent (but arguably more successful and elegant than the Royal Crescent) is **Lansdown Crescent**, designed and built by John Palmer in 1789–93. It still has its overthrow lamps across the porches leading to its fan-headed doors. No. 19, at its west end, was the home of the writer William Beckford from 1822. With some of his West Indian fortune still intact, he slung a bridge to incorporate the next house, and from the back of his property he could ride up across the hills to his folly, 'Beckford's Tower', built for him in 1823–7 by HE Goodridge. The thin, lantern-topped tower (restored from 1999 by the Bath Preservation Trust) has a small house at its base, decorated opulently by Beckford (although he never lived here). Alongside, through a heavy Romanesque doorway, is a consecrated cemetery in which Beckford's remains lie, along with those of his architect.

Below: The Holburne Museum contains an impressive array of ceramics, silver, furniture and paintings, and is wonderfully sited at the end of Great Pulteney Street.

High above Bath near the University is the American Museum in Britain, housed in Claverton Manor, a fine classical Bath stone building of 1819–20 by Sir Jeffry Wyatville. There are historic American interiors constructed to fit their new spaces, with quilts, and Pennsylvania German and Shaker artefacts, among many others.

From Bath, there are buses to the beautiful landscaped gardens of **Prior Park**, restored by the National Trust (there is no car park). The great house, now a school, was begun by the elder John Wood for Ralph Allen in 1735. Allen, whose lovely town house is tucked away behind buildings on the south side of the Abbey Church, was an energetic tycoon, not only quarrying Bath stone but also profiting from a countrywide system of cross-posts which he introduced when postmaster in Bath. In the park below the house is the wonderfully sited Palladian Bridge, a 1750 copy of the famous one at Wilton*. Across the hilltop is the sham castle built by Allen in 1762 as an 'eyecatcher' to be viewed from his Bath town house.

Top: Royal Crescent, 1767–75, by John Wood the younger. This is one of the great pieces of European architecture.

Bottom: King's Circus, 1754, by John Wood the elder (father of Wood the younger), with its imposing columns dominating the complete circle.

Battle Abbey, E Susx 691 G7, The Battle of Hastings (1066) was fought not at Hastings* but further inland at a site now appropriately called Battle. William the Conqueror built a monastery here as an offering of thanks; the altar of the church stood on the spot where the English King Harold was killed. The church has gone, but the gatehouse (1338) and the 13th-century dormitory survive [EH]. Other parts were incorporated into a Victorian mansion in 1857.

Bayham Abbey, E Susx 691 G6, Founded about 1210 by the Premonstratensian Order [EH]. There are substantial remains of the church and monastic buildings (the cloister, chapterhouse and undercroft of the dormitory). The grounds were landscaped in the picturesque style by Humphry Repton to harmonize with a later (Victorian) house.

Beaconsfield, Bucks 690 E4, The old town has been saved from unsightly modern developments by the new town, 1 mile (1.6km away). Four streets radiate from the Market Place and contain some good early to mid-18th-century houses.

Beamish Museum, Dur 697 G2, The scale of the North of England Open-Air Museum is so immense that visitors ride on trams and other historic vehicles between various sections, which represent the farm, the colliery village, the manor

Battle Abbey
Above left: The Gatehouse, built in 1338, two polygonal turrets flanking the gateway.
Above right: The undercroft of the Dormitory, late 13th or early 14th century.

Right: Bayham Abbey: a Premonstratensian abbey preserved as a romantic ruin. This is the south wall.

and the town, and other areas of daily life relating to the North. Visitors can venture into an underground drift mine, experience the discipline of an old school, and enter shops and houses of the past.

Bearwood, Berks 690 E5, Now the Royal Merchant Navy School, it was built for the owner of *The Times*, John Walter III, in

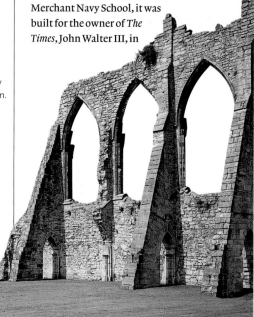

Beaulieu
Centre: Part of the medieval building transformed into a Victorian hall.
Bottom: The 19th-century mansion.

Beaumaris Castle
Top right: The masterpiece of James of St George at the eastern end of the Menai Strait.
Bottom, left and right: The castle seen from across the moat.

Beaumaris   **B**

the 1860s. It is a vast pile designed in the Jacobean style by Robert Kerr, Professor of Architecture at King's College and author of *The English Gentleman's House*, in which he set forth his ideas realized at Bearwood.

Beaulieu, Hants 690 D7, Officially in the Forest but has its own landscape – that of a private estate, centred on the site of a Cistercian abbey founded in 1204 at the head of a tidal estuary. After the Reformation the abbey lands passed to the ancestor of the present Lord Montagu of Beaulieu. The heartland of the estate has been developed since World War I as a showplace – one of the earliest and most successful of its kind. Palace House was enlarged out of the 14th-century abbey gatehouse. Of the abbey there are picturesque ruins of claustral buildings, and an intact range including a museum; the present parish church (accessible from the village) was the monks' refectory. The National Motor Museum grew from a private collection of early cars; the present

building, with its impressive interior, dates from 1972 and displays a remarkable series of vehicles. Beaulieu Village (completely separate from the Abbey and Museum complex) is very picturesque, set beside the beautiful tidal estuary. Here the well-wooded, winding foreshores have been preserved from indiscreet development, although it is a fashionable venue for yachting. Down the estuary is Buckler's Yard, with a wide grass-bordered street of Georgian houses and cottages ending at the waterside. This was the scene of an important shipbuilding industry in the last days of wooden ships, as depicted in the Maritime Museum.

Beaumaris, IOA 692 D2, It was at Beau Marreys, the Norman French for 'fine marsh', that Edward I chose to build a castle to guard the eastern extremity of the Menai Strait, whose western approach already had the stern sentinel of Caernarfon* as protection. This coastal plain was the ideal terrain for the King's military surveyor, Master James of St George, to fulfil his ambition to design a genuinely concentric castle. The result was an inner ward with four corner drum towers and one placed centrally on the west and east, an arrangement which dominated the octagonal outer ward, protected by 12 angle towers, and a northern and southern gatehouse. Both are out of alignment with their inner counterparts, not because of any lapse in the perfection of the symmetrical design, but because of James' mastery of defensive tactics. The scale of the northern range, which mirrors that of the incomplete south range, indicates that Beaumaris was intended to accommodate royal apartments. Building began in 1295 and work was still in progress for almost another 50 years, by which time techniques of warfare had rendered the castle an anachronism. The remains of the mill and the dock point to an unparalleled sophistication in military self-sufficiency.

Close to the castle is the **Court House**, a plain rectangular building of 1614, with additions and improvements of the early 19th century which indicate an increasing awareness of its dignity. Convicts of the last century would have had no inclination to admire the two fine, late 18th-century houses at the end of Castle Street on their way to the nearby prison, a suitably stern building of 1829 that retains many of its original features, including a treadmill. The architect was JA Hansom (of 'cab' fame) who was responsible for the fine Victorian terrace that characterizes Beaumaris as a fashionable resort. The adjacent Bulkeley Arms Hotel is named after the family whose seat, Baron Hill, is now a ruin among the trees on the slopes behind the castle. Memorials to this once highly influential dynasty grace the parish church, which includes among its relics from the Priory of Llanfaes the sarcophagus of King John's daughter Joan-Siwan, wife of Llywelyn Fawr (Llywclyn the Great).

Beaupre

Top left: Beaupre.

Centre: Beccles, Roos Hall.

Bottom left: Beckingham Hall.

Top right: Beddington, the roof of Carew Manor's Great Hall.

Bottom right: Bedford, St Paul's.

Lord Williams of Thame, close by the historic remains of three rectangular moats. The church contains fragments of an important series of late medieval stained-glass windows.

Beddington, Gt Lon 691 F5, The Great Hall at Carew Manor is over 60 feet (18m) long and 32 feet (9.7m) wide, with a fine hammerbeam and arch-braced roof. The octagonal dovecote dates from the 18th century. The church contains a charming organ with a case decorated by Morris & Co.

Bedford, Beds 690 E3, A 'large, populous and thriving town, and a pleasant well-built place' – or so Daniel Defoe described it in *A Tour Through the Whole Island of Great Britain*. The River Ouse flows lazily through the town's centre and is ideal for boating. The town has four medieval churches, the best of which is **St Paul's,** dating from the 14th and 15th centuries but heavily restored. It contains the

Beaupre, V Glam 689 G3
A trek through fields near St Hilary is an odd way to approach one of the Vale of Glamorgan's gems. Plain and uninteresting from a distance, this courtyard house, often called 'castle', has one of the finest Renaissance features in any Welsh house: a three-storey porch leading to the hall, each storey displaying a different architectural order. It was erected in 1600 by Richard Basset to celebrate his 65th birthday.

Beccles, Suffk 695 J6, This former wherry port and cabin cruiser centre with Dutch gabled Georgian streets (Ballygate, Puddingmoor, Northgate) was linked by 'score' alleys to the Waveney. Fires devastated the town in the 17th century, but Elizabethan Roos Hall, with its pedimented windows and step-gables, survives, as does Leman House (conspicuous with its fine brick and flint façade and Tudor-style windows of 1631), a museum and former school. The church, with double-storey porch and detached freestone tower occupying a commanding position above the river, is where Admiral Nelson's parents wed.

Beckingham Hall, Essex 691 H4, A small, partly 16th-century timber and brick house surrounded by a Tudor brick wall with a large turretted gatehouse and turrets at each corner. Some panelling from

the Hall, dated 1546, can be seen in the Victoria & Albert Museum*.

Beckley, Oxon 690 D4, The site of Beckley Park is ancient; in the 9th century it belonged to King Alfred. The handsome, unusually well-preserved brick house standing today was built in c1540, probably by

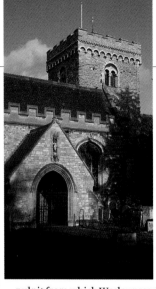

pulpit from which Wesley preached his Assize Sermon in 1758. The nave was almost entirely rebuilt by the Victorians. Evidence of the original Anglo-Saxon church of **St Peter de Merton** remains visible in the fabric today. The now central tower was originally the west tower of the church, and the present chancel would have been the nave. The chancel is just wider than the nave; long and short quoins can be seen inside on the west face. The Swan Hotel, built in 1794 by Henry Holland for the Duke of Bedford, contains a staircase from Ampthill's Houghton House. Behind the Victorian exterior of St John's Rectory is a medieval hall house, with an open timber roof and original hall dating from the late 14th century. Alfred Waterhouse designed the Shire Hall, *c*1880. The Town Hall is the result of two building phases. To the left is the beautiful Harpur's School (1756), with its old fashioned two-light windows. The right-hand side was designed by the local architect James Horsford in 1859–61. By the 1820s Harpur's School had become too small, and the Bedford Modern School was built. A symmetrical, neo-Tudor building, it was designed by John Wing, but finished after his death by Edward Blore. Perhaps the most notable school building is the Bedford High School for Girls, Bromham Road, a prettily detailed Tudor-style building of

Top left: Bedford, St Peter de Merton Church and the statue of John Bunyan in the High Street by Sir J E Boehm, 1874. After the Restoration, Bedford became a centre of religious conflict.

Top right: Belas Knap, the finest long barrow in the Cotswolds.

Below: Beeston Castle, the 13th-century gatehouse with an entrance bridge spanning the rock-bed ditch.

1878–82 by Basil Champneys, which led to his commission from Newnham College. In Castle Close is the **Cecil Higgins Art Gallery**, former home of Bedford brewers, the Higgins family. Furnished as a Victorian house, it contains furniture designed by the architect William Burges. Adjoining the 19th-century mansion is a modern gallery displaying a collection of watercolours, prints and ceramics. In the High Street is a statue of John Bunyan, 17th-century author of *Pilgrim's Progress*, who preached here.

Beech Court Gardens, Kent 691 H6, A small but attractive garden that flowers throughout the year, surrounding a medieval farmhouse.

Beeston Castle, Ches 693 G2, A royal castle until the Civil War, standing majestically on an isolated rocky crag that forms part of the defences. The inner parts of the castle, which was begun in the 1220s, are in a severe state of ruin [EH].

Beeston, Norfk 693 H5, The remote church of St Mary has the most atmospheric interior and beautiful 14th-century work: Decorated tracery, a hammerbeam roof with carved figures, benches and an exquisite parclose screen.

Beinn Eighe National Nature Reserve, Highld 701 F4, The oldest nature reserve in Britain covers an area of 11,860 acres (4,800ha) and provides sanctuary for red deer, roe deer, martens, golden eagles and peregrine falcons. Aultroy Visitor Centre presents information on flora and fauna, and there are two nature trails on the slopes of Beinn Eighe.

Belas Knap, Gloucs 690 C3, A steep climb up through the woods, with views over Sudeley Castle* in the

valley below, brings you to the long barrow of Belas Knap. It is the finest example of about 50 long barrows in the Cotswolds*, and is about 4,000 years old. Over 30 skeletons were found here in excavations in 1863–5, but since 1930 it has been presented as a 'restored' long barrow in Ministry of Works fashion. Three of the burial chambers have external entrances, but the north end has a 'false' entrance between two piers of earth. This massive central 'false' doorway was possibly to mislead tomb robbers.

Belmont, Kent 691 H5, A charming late 18th-century villa probably by Samuel Wyatt, complete with original decor and furniture. Below the upper windows of the south front is an image of a reclining woman in classical dress. Inside, the staircase hall is top-lit and has two balconies, the upper one reached by a separate staircase.

Belper, *see* **Cromford***.

Belsay Hall and Gardens, Nthumb 699 J7, In 1810, Sir Charles Monck (1779–1867) designed himself a new house. Having studied the architecture of ancient classical Greece, he created a temple-like house in the austere Greek Doric order, raised on a podium, with giant columns to the entrance and pilasters on the walls [EH]. Exactly 100 feet (30.5m) square in plan, the house has a central atrium around which the principal rooms are arranged. Monck then transformed the area from where the stone for the house had been taken into

Belsay Hall
Top: The central atrium, around which all the rooms are arranged.
Centre: Exterior view showing the giant entrace columns.
Bottom: The gardens are a mixture of formal and informal with mature woodland.

a magnificent quarry garden. This and the Cragwood Walk were planted with many fine and rare plant specimens. Further landscaping was carried out by Monck's grandson Sir Arthur Middleton (1838–1933). Ferns thrive in a green gorge, exotic plants hanging down its sheer walls, and there is a brilliant display of rhododendrons. The nearby **Belsay Castle** is a small medieval tower-house with a ruined Jacobean wing.

Belton House
Top left: The Saloon with its 17th-century panelling and 17th-century-style ceiling.
Bottom: Exterior view.

Top centre: A late 17th-century Italian lapis-lazuli cabinet.
Top right: Lord Leighton's portrait of Lady Adelaide Talbot, Countess Brownlow.

Belton House, Lincs 694 E4, Built for Sir John Brownlow between 1685 and 1688, it still gives an excellent impression of a great late 17th-century mansion. For many years it was believed that Christopher Wren was its architect but it now seems more likely that its design is by William Winde (d. 1722). The plan of the building is in the form of an 'H', with the central section two rooms deep. The walls of the house are of grey-gold Ancaster stone, and from the outside Belton looks much as it did in the 1680s, apart from the surround of the front door which was added by James Wyatt in 1777. A great deal of the original interior decoration has also survived. There are splendid plaster ceilings by Edward Goudge in the Saloon, the little Marble Hall and the Chapel. The Library and Boudoir have ceilings by James Wyatt, who gave the interior a face-lift in the 1770s. Many of the rooms have painted walls; in the Chapel Drawing Room the panels are painted dark green and gold in imitation of marble, making a rich background for some late 17th-century English tapestries. In the Chapel and Marble Hall there is also some excellent woodcarving, probably by Edward Carpenter and well up to the standard of Grinling Gibbons. The house was acquired by the National Trust after 300 years' continuous occupation by the Brownlows, and it still contains a large amount of fine period furniture. There is an exemplary collection of late 17th-century English portraits and a very early Boucher. The park was laid out in the 18th century by William Eames.

Belvoir Castle, Leics 694 E4, So named because it stands on a ridge with a magnificent view across the hunting country of Vale of Belvoir. The medieval castle has gone, and there is nothing to be seen of the great classical house of the 1650s designed by John Webb except for a model in the Ballroom of the present castle: a gothic fantasy, designed by James Wyatt. It was begun by the 5th Duke of Rutland in 1801 just after his coming of age, destroyed by fire in 1816 but immediately rebuilt. The reconstruction was carried out under the supervision of Wyatt's son Benjamin and was finished in 1830. The castle, with its array of towers, turrets and battlements, looks spectacular and romantic. Inside are the cold and cavernous Great Staircase and Ballroom, designed in a gothic style copied from Lincoln Cathedral* and decorated with suits of armour. The Elizabeth Saloon – named in honour of the 5th Duchess – is immensely opulent, with a gilded and painted ceiling, French gilt wall carvings and French furniture and carpet. The Dining Room is another cold sepulchre but the Picture Gallery contains several great treasures, including paintings by Holbein, Poussin and Gainsborough, miniatures by Hilliard and Oliver and a great 17th-century state bed with hangings of Venetian velvet. Beyond again are the King's Rooms, fitted out for George IV, and the Regent's Gallery, which is the principal room surviving from James Wyatt's house.

Above: The castle designed by James Wyatt.

Left: The Regent's Gallery includes some nationally important works. There are miniatures by Nicholas Hilliard, three Poussins, two good Gainsboroughs, some portrait busts by Nollekens and examples of work by many of the famous Dutch masters.

Right: 'Winter' by Caius Cibber (1620–1700) in the Rose Garden.

Ben Nevis, Highld 701 F7, Ben Nevis, the highest
point in the United Kingdom (4,410 feet/1,344m),
has an annual rainfall of around 157 inches
(398cm) and its summit is shrouded in mist for
most of the year. Some of its north-facing ravines
are covered with 'eternal snows'. According to
legend, if they melted, the Camerons of Glen
Nevis would lose their lands. In fine weather it is
possible to climb to the top of Ben Nevis in four or
five hours, following one of the two main routes.

Benbecula, W Isls 700 B5, This flat, marshy island is
linked to Stornoway, Barra* and Glasgow* by air.
Balivanich (Baile a Mhanaich), on the northwest
coast, is the administrative and commercial centre
of the Isles of Uist. Liniclate (Lionacleit) secondary
school houses a small museum. The ruins of
Nunton Church (mid-14th century) can be see at
Aird, and a ruined fortress at Borve.

Benenden, Kent 691 H6, A progressive public school
founded in 1859. The buildings, in Elizabethan
style, are by David Brandon.

Bengeo, Herts , On higher ground just north of
Hertford is one of the best-preserved Norman
churches in the county. St Leonard's has been little
altered since the 1100s and has a rare surviving
chancel with apse. *See* **Hertford* 691 F4.**

Beningbrough Hall, N York 697 H5, A handsome
house with long façades in orange-red brick with

Beningbrough Hall
Above left: The interior
contains exquisite
woodcarving. The
magnificent staircase has
richly carved balusters, plus
panels imitating elaborate
wrought-ironwork.
Above right: The panelled
Drawing Room.

Left: Bengeo, St Leonard's
Church showing the large
Norman apse with round-
headed windows set in
deep inner splays.

ashlar dressings, completed in c1716 for John
Bourchier, who also had a York town house in
Micklegate. The interior of the house has a
baroque look in terms of spatial effects and
decorative detail [NT]. Both the exterior and the
interior show a bias towards the woodcarver's
art, since the house was designed by the York
carpenter-architect William Thornton.
Particularly impressive is the main staircase,
which purports to be cantilevered but is
constructed in wood, not stone, with wide
marquetry treads and half-landings – the latter
inlaid with the date 1716 and John and Mary
Bourchier's initials. The balustrade has
exquisitely delicate wooden panels imitating
wrought-ironwork. Several rooms are panelled,
the bolection mouldings projecting into the room
below richly elaborate friezes. Splendid
collections of blue-and-white china adorn corner
fireplaces in small closets, and there are some
magnificent early 18th-century beds with ornate
testers. The house also provides an authentic
setting for a display of over 100 pictures of the
period from the National Portrait Gallery,
London*, including members of the Kit-Cat Club
in the dining room. Two cupola-topped pavilions
flank the main entrance; there is also a delightful
walled garden and children's playground.

Benington, Herts 691 F3, The most interesting
feature of this attractive village, about 4 miles
(6.4km) east of Stevenage*, is Benington Lordship,
a Queen Anne house reworked during the 19th
century in the neo-Norman style. The hilltop
gardens are open to the public and offer beautiful
herbaceous borders, lakes, castle ruins and
veranda teas. The neighbouring church of
St Peter, built mainly from the late 1200s to the
early 1300s, retains an important medieval tomb
chest with effigies.

Below: Benthall Hall, an oblique view of the gabled entrance front.

Bennachie, Abers 702 D6, The remains of a fort dating from the early centuries AD stand at the top of Mither Tap, the east summit of Bennachie (1,773 feet/540m). The traces of a Roman camp found at Durno, a little to the north, suggest that Bennachie was the site of Mons Graupius where the troops of the Roman commander Agricola defeated the Caledonians in AD 84.

Benthall Hall, Shrops 693 G4, A late Tudor mansion built between 1580 and 1618 for the Benthall family [NT]. It has pleasant panelled rooms, several of which contain the rare Caughley porcelain made locally in the late 18th century.

Bentley House, E Susx 691 G7, An 18th-century farmhouse in Halland, added to by the architect Raymond Erith and containing a motor museum.

Bentley Wood, E Susx 691 G7, One of the rare International Modern houses of the 1930s, by Serge Chermayeff. It uses large glazed walls. (There was once a statue by Henry Moore on the terrace.)

Bere Regis, Dorset 690 B7, The church of St John the Baptist has a Perpendicular tower, chequered in flint and stone, and the finest timber roof in Dorset (c1500), with carved central bosses and horizontal angels at the hammerbeams.

Berkeley Castle, Gloucs 689 J3, Pinkish Berkeley Castle is built of a stone 'rose red and grey... the colour of old brocade,' according to Vita Sackville-West. The 14th-century castle is hidden under layers of later use and the famous cell where Edward II was murdered for incompetence and

Benthall Hall
Left: A 17th-century chest.
Right: The fine, richly carved timber stair with its bold newel posts.

Below: Berkeley Castle, the Great Hall, 62 feet (19m) long, was built around 1330 by Thomas, 3rd Lord Berkeley.

perversion (with a red-hot poker, according to several sources – including the bloodthirsty playwright Christopher Marlowe) is a melancholy little room. It is within the keep, erected on the site of a Norman motte soon after 1067 by Fitz Osborn, Earl of Hereford. The castle's Hall features the unusual 'Berkeley' arches, which instead of being round, have four flat facets. The sleepy town of Berkeley has a spacious street lined by brick houses. Next door to the castle is the thatched hut, now part of a museum, where Edward Jenner (1749–1823), Berkeley's most famous inhabitant, began inoculating people against smallpox in 1796. Further afield is the incongruous Berkeley Nuclear Power Station built in the 1960s.

Berkhamsted Castle, Herts 690 E4, The remains of the substantial 11th-century motte-and-bailey castle lie outside the town centre, on the north bank of the River Bulbourne.

Berkley, Somset 690 B6, The small Georgian church of 1751 was probably designed by Thomas Prowse,

an amateur architect who owned the nearby manor house. It has a central octagonal dome with wondrous rococo plasterwork.

Berneray (Bearnaraigh), *see* **North Uist*.**

Berriew, Powys 693 F4, The name is a corruption of Aber (mouth) and Rhiw, the river which flows into the nearby Severn and comprises a delightfully peaceful enclave of half-timbered houses – of which the vicarage of 1616 is a particularly striking example – epitomizing the architecture of the Severn Valley. Many of the surrounding cottages were restored in the late 1800s by the squire of Vaynor, and have made a major contribution to the village's successes in the Best Kept Village competition. Though the house is not open, the splendid gardens of Vaynor offer incomparable views of this rich borderland.

Nearby **Glansevern Hall Gardens,** surrounding an early 19th-century Greek Revival house, are now resuming their former splendour after years of neglect. A shaded lakeside walk contrasts with the

generous open lawns and their rich borders, and the walk-in grotto is particularly attractive. Outhouses and walled gardens add enormously to the appeal of a remarkable restoration.

Berrington Hall, Herefs 693 G5, The fashionable architect Henry Holland was summoned to Herefordshire after Thomas Harley had made a fortune supplying uniforms and pay to the British Army in America. The site of Harley's new Hall [NT] was chosen by Capability Brown, whose undulating park and lake survive. On a knoll stands the extremely sleek and simple neo-Grecian house begun in 1778. Indoors is an astonishingly lavish neo-Grecian interior, full of ideas Holland had picked up in France. The complex staircase hall, where shafts of light fall unexpectedly from a skylight, has hints of the baroque fantasies of Piranesi.

Above left: Berrington Hall's complex neoclassical staircase.

Above right: Berwick-on-Tweed, with its bridges crossing the River Tweed.

Below: Berry Pomeroy Castle, begun in 1547 and abandoned in 1701. It is reputed to be haunted.

Berry Pomeroy Castle, Devon 689 F7, In the 18th century, the castle [EH] was much featured by Romantic artists seeking inspiring subjects, and indeed it would be hard to conceive of a more picturesque site, halfway up the beech woods on the hillside and overlooking the Gatcombe brook as it passes through a deep ravine. The oldest walls date from the second half of the 15th century, and beyond lie the ruins of the ambitious house built for Edward the Protector, Duke of Somerset. As the castle was begun in 1547, not much could have been completed by the time of his execution in 1552, but later descriptions tell of great grandeur: chimneypieces of marble and statues of alabaster. All, alas, was abandoned by 1701.

Berwick-upon-Tweed, Nthumb 699 J5, Situated on the 'Scottish side' of the River Tweed, the port passed back and forth between England and Scotland until 1482 – Berwick is rightly famous for its defences. It also has three significant bridge links with England – the 15-arched Old Bridge of 1610–34, Mouchel's New Bridge of 1925–8, and Robert Stephenson's Royal Border Railway Bridge of 1847, which has 14 arches on two tiers, like a Roman aqueduct. Despite its inevitably chequered history, the town has many handsome buildings, notably the Town Hall of 1754–60, with a giant Tuscan portico and a tall belfry reminiscent of the towers of London City churches. Berwick played a significant part in the Civil War, and its Holy Trinity (1648–52) is one of the very few churches that date from the Commonwealth period. It still has some Puritan fittings.

Berwick's medieval walls were frequently repaired and upgraded until in 1558, the first year of the reign of Queen Elizabeth I, they were given a more radical remodelling to take advantage of, and protect against, cannon fire. (The work was ultimately to cost

her £128,648 5s.9d.) These new artillery fortifications, unique in Britain and among the finest in Europe, consisted of flat-topped ramparts around the two landward sides of the town, with projecting bastions designed by Italian engineers using Renaissance principles of mathematics to calculate the fields of fire for the guns. The hour-long brisk walk along the fortifications provides a series of wonderful views of the town, river and sea. Soldiers, billeted in local alehouses and private houses, often caused a degree of disorder highly unpopular with the resident population. The Jacobite Rebellion of 1715 led to such a local outcry that the **Ravensdowne Barracks** [EH] were constructed between 1717 and 1721, at a cost of £4,937.10s.6d., to house 600 infantrymen and 36 officers. The grand design seems to have come from Nicholas Hawksmoor. The principal gate, above which is the coat of arms of King George I, is flanked by the 'black hole' or prison to the left, and the guard-house, now the public entrance, to the right. Three three-storey accommodation blocks are formally arranged around the parade square. The soldiers were crammed eight to a barrack room, while the 36 officers had 24 rooms between them. The central block, intended for stores but now called the Clock Block, houses the Borough Museum on the ground floor, and the Art Gallery on the first. This contains many treasures collected by Sir William Burrell (1861–1958), the shipping magnate better known as the founder of the Burrell Collection in Glasgow*. He took a particular interest in the small Victorian museum then in Berwick Town Hall, and in 1935 made the

Beverley Minster
Top: The west side showing double transepts.
Above: Early English architecture can be seen in the great transept.

Below: Berwick-upon-Tweed, Ravensdowne Barracks, the parade square looking towards the Clock Block, which houses the Borough Museum and Art Gallery.

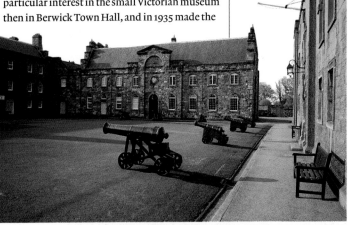

first of several substantial donations, which continued for the next 20 years. On his return from long spells abroad, he would pop in and leave brown paper packages containing what are now priceless exhibits. The collection includes his personal passions, Japanese Imari ware, medieval religious art, and paintings by his particular protégé, Joseph Crawhall.

Besford, Worcs 690 B3, On the way to Croome Park* lies an unusual tiny timber-framed church, constructed out of units 5 foot (1.5m) square, with diagonal beams for strength, and probably dating from the 14th century. Inside, the stone lip of the rood loft is an interesting pre-Reformation survival.

Beverley, E R Yk 697 J6, A delightful small town, with a wealth of medieval and Georgian architecture. There are several attractive streets, including a number of market spaces, the Tuesday Market square having a handsome market cross of 1714. The Guildhall is a 15th-century building with early Georgian alterations; its Court Room has a rich stucco ceiling by Giuseppe Cortese. **Beverley Minster,** with its twin-towered west front a perfect Perpendicular composition, was a collegiate church with double transepts begun in the 1220s. The Early English plan was continued when the nave was completed early in the 14th century, but with Decorated details, including delightful musician figures playing their instruments along the wall canopies. In the choir the ogee-canopied Percy tomb is a sumptuous example of Decorated intricacy, and the choir stalls of 1520, finely crafted by the Ripon* School of Woodcarvers, have misericord seats carved with intriguing scenes. The large 12th-century font is of black marble from Frosterley in County Durham; its immense cover of 1713 is worthy of a London City church. This date reflects a major repair programme, when the north wall of the north transept, then leaning badly, was pushed upright again by a timber frame with a screw mechanism which could be tightened as it succeeded in its task. This ingenious contraption was devised by the York carpenter-architect William Thornton (who designed Beningbrough Hall*) in conjunction with the more famous Nicholas Hawksmoor. The latter also designed the choir pavement, a dramatic geometric pattern in black and white marble. Another set of fascinating misericords can be found in **St Mary's Church,** rebuilt by the guilds of Beverley – one of medieval England's most prosperous towns – after damage caused by the central tower's collapse in 1520. The medieval town was defended by a rampart and ditch with gates. Only North Bar survives, dating from 1409–10. It is a very early example of brick construction, which was pioneered in the East Riding.

Biddulph Grange
Top: The exterior view.
Centre: The dog or lion
stands in the Chinese
section of the gardens.

Bottom: Bickleigh Castle, the
15th-century gatehouse
with the thatched
farmhouse wing to the left.

Bideford

B

Bexhill, E Susx 691 G7, Bexhill's claim to fame is the De La Warr Pavilion by Erich Mendelssohn and Serge Chermayeff (1933), one of the first examples of International Modern architecture in Britain. The best view is from the beach; go inside to see the graceful glazed spiral staircase.

Bexleyheath, Gt Lon 691 G5, In William Morris' time this was the beginning of rural Kent. Here in 1859 he decided to build a home for himself and his bride, designed by his friend Philip Webb. It was to be a milestone in domestic architecture, a rejection of the prevailing classical style and, for Morris, 'very medieval in spirit'. In the event, the **Red House** is a free adaptation of many periods, and full of individual details expressive of the characters of both men.

Bibury, Gloucs 690 C4, This ridiculously pretty village suffers a little from tourists drawn to its picturesque buildings, mill ponds, streams and little bridges. They come to see Arlington Row [NT], a haphazard terrace of early 17th-century cottages, built for the weavers whose cloth was 'fulled', or pounded, at the mill opposite. The mill itself has been converted into a museum of local and agricultural history. Some parts of the row of cottages date back to the 14th century; these were probably originally constructed for sheep, and converted later into dwellings. Bibury was also once the home of one of the earliest racing clubs. Charles II attended the races here.

Bickleigh, Devon 689 G5, A small village set in the rich farming valley of the Exe, with a crafts centre and two pubs. It was while staying at one of these pubs that Simon and Garfunkel were inspired to write 'Bridge Over Troubled Waters'. The *castle* was the home first of the Courtenays and then of the Carews. Although now much altered, it is still approached through a restored 15th-century gatehouse and charming gardens. In the 17th-century farmhouse wing is a remarkable overmantel carved with many small scenes that may refer to the Prayer Book Rebellion of 1549.

Bicton Park, Devon 689 G6, The extensive grounds were first created about 1730 for Henry Rolle, whose descendants built the vast Edwardian mansion (now the county agricultural college). In the early 19th century John, Lord Rolle and his wife created the arboretum and pinetum, planted a monkey puzzle avenue and built the bulbous Palm House. Bicton also boasts orangeries, a shell house, a hermitage, a china tower and an ice house. The mausoleum in the grounds was erected by the pious Lady Rolle to a design by Pugin, and has a colourful interior enlivened by Minton floor tiles.

Biddulph Grange, Staffs 693 H2, The gardens at Biddulph were laid out by John Bateman, starting in about 1845 [NT]. They include the long

Wellingtonia Avenue, the Egyptian Court, the Great Wall of China and the Chinese Pavilion. Mr Bateman's house, to which the gardens were attached, was almost completely destroyed by fire, and the present house (not open) was built by his son in the 1890s.

Bideford, Devon 688 E5, The main feature of the bustling port is the 24-arch medieval bridge over the River Torridge. Each arch is different, as the structure was paid for by a variety of donors and guilds. At one end, East-the-Water, is the Royal Hotel, whose later exterior conceals two of the finest 17th-century plasterwork ceilings in the

county. At the town end of the bridge are pleasant streets; Bridgeland Street boasts several handsome 17th-century brick houses with important door-cases. All these streets lead back to the quay from which, in the 17th century in particular, there were important trading links with North America in pottery, tobacco and Newfoundland fish. Some of these are commemorated in the church of St Mary, where a window engraved by Laurence Whistler commemorates one of Devon's great heroes, Sir Richard Grenville, whose family did much to expand the town.

Biggin Hill, Gt Lon 691 G5, The airfield is famous for the part it played in the Battle of Britain in 1940. A Spitfire and a Hurricane stand near the entrance.

Bignor, W Susx 690 E7, A large Roman villa consisting of a series of lavish rooms round a courtyard, some of them with mosaic pavements depicting Venus with a peacock and gladiator-cupids.

Binfield, Berks 690 E5, Inside the church is an interesting iron hourglass stand with the arms of the Farriers' Company in London (probably

Above: Binham Priory, the glorious early 13th-century west front built by Prior Richard de Parco predates Westminster Abbey as the first example of Early English architecture in the country.

Below: The ruins of the Norman priory chancel lie east of the parish church.

17th century). Also depicted are leaves, grapes, a lion, a pelican and a wolf.

Binham, Norfk 695 H4, Norfolk is rich in monastic remains tucked away in remote countryside. The small Augustinian house at North Creake in the Bure Valley, wiped out by the plague before the Dissolution, is a prime example. Sturdy Norman work from the great Benedictine Priory at Binham, founded by Peter de Valoines, is now the parish church in the centre of this tweedy flint village. Its chief glory is the west front, a noble early 13th-century composition and one of the first examples of Early English work.

Binley, W Mids 694 D6, The 1770s church of St Bartholomew is worth a visit. A spare interior with Tuscan columns contains decoration described by Julian Byng as being 'in the ballroom taste,' but it in fact shows the restraint and delicacy of the Adam style.

Binns, House of the, W Loth 699 F4, The House of The Binns is named after the twin hills to the east. The original house, which was probably 14th

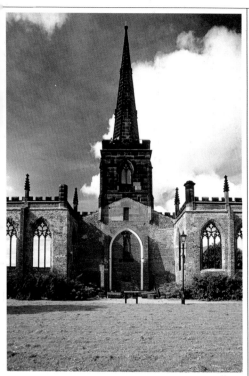

Above: Birkenhead Park, the bandstand overlooking the lake.

Left: Birkenhead, St Mary's Church.

century, was bought in 1612 by the merchant Thomas Dalyell, who built the present house. It was extended in 1630 and crenellated towers were added in the early 19th century. Today it houses a collection of paintings, furniture and porcelain, and boasts beautiful 17th-century stucco ceilings.

Birkenhead, Mersyd 696 E7, The ruined remains of a Benedictine Priory, with vaulted undercroft and chapter house, stand next to St Mary's Church of 1819 by Thomas Rickman. These are situated on a headland overlooking the Mersey and the shipbuilding yards where many great ships have been fitted out. The yards were the works of the Scot William Laird, to whom Birkenhead owes its growth. The architectural set piece is Hamilton Square, designed by James Gillespie Graham and therefore very Scottish in character, with similarities to Edinburgh* architecture. Three of the sides are grand, balanced Doric compositions with emphasized centres and end pavilions; the east side left a gap for the Town Hall, not built until the 1880s and then in a richer Corinthian style. Birkenhead Park south of the town centre was England's first public park, laid out by Sir Joseph Paxton. Money came in part from residential development around the edges and many of the villas remain but the most interesting buildings are the lodges and other structures within the park, including a boathouse and bandstand facing the lake. Birkenhead's outer areas include New Brighton, where Fort Perch is an early 19th-century artillery fort, and Perch Rock, a lighthouse designed by the Liverpool architect John Foster. The Wallasey Unitarian Church, with excellent interior decoration by the Birmingham Guild, has recently been acquired by the Historic Chapels Trust.

Birmingham

Birmingham, W Mids 694 C6, In 1948 the population of Birmingham overtook that of Glasgow* to make it Britain's second largest city. Although it suffered greatly in the 1970s with the decline of its traditional manufacturing industries, this enormous sprawling city now has a surprisingly vibrant and attractive centre, with plenty of café society and culture. Landmarks include the ponderous but archaeologically accurate and impressive classical temple of the Town Hall. Birmingham's Symphony Orchestra has an international standing, as does the National Exhibition Centre on the outskirts of the city and the New Concert Hall. Chamberlain Square contains a piece of frozen street theatre with its three noteworthy statues. Joseph Priestley is shown in the act of discovering oxygen and James Watt, inventor of the steam engine, is also commemorated. Politician Thomas Attward has descended from his plinth and sits reading on the steps beside it. **Birmingham Museum and Art Gallery** is deservedly the mecca of Pre-Raphaelite enthusiasts. Rossetti, Holman Hunt and Millais are

Left: *The Last of England* by Ford Madox Brown (1852–5) at Birmingham Museum and Art Gallery.

Below: Aston Hall. The entrance front, begun in 1618, is a fine example of Jacobean architecture.

represented. There is a whole room of Edward Burne-Jones' overwrought ladies in addition to a good 18th-century collection. The city has other exhibition halls and galleries of note. The **Ikon Gallery** is dedicated to modern art, providing an interesting use for the 19th-century school building which houses it. Regularly changing exhibitions of contemporary artists have given it its innovative reputation, and The Thinktank is the latest of Birmingham's museums, a new project dedicated to science and technology.

The Jewellery Quarter of Birmingham, traditionally home of the jewellery trade, has been restored to economic and cultural vibrancy. Historic houses and offices front the streets, while the jewellers' workshops, many still in their original use, are tucked away behind.

Soho House, a polite 18th-century mansion, is a surprising find in the middle of Birmingham. Its owner, industrialist Matthew Boulton, made his money in the nearby Jewellery Quarter where his factory – along with many others – made buckles, clocks and silver plate from the 1750s onwards. As his friends were the engineers and thinkers of the later 18th century, it is not surprising to find that his house had innovative central heating, and that he designed his own eccentric furniture.

Another unexpected pleasure in the middle of the city is **Aston Hall**, a typical brick Jacobean house complete with decorative gables, Long Gallery and motifs inspired by Renaissance prints and engravings. It was begun in 1618 by Sir Thomas Holte (1571–1654), one of the many knights who purchased the newly invented title of 'baronet' from James I in 1611. Two plans of the house survive in John Thorpe's collection of Elizabethan and Jacobean architectural drawings, but his designs were not followed accurately and he was probably only asked

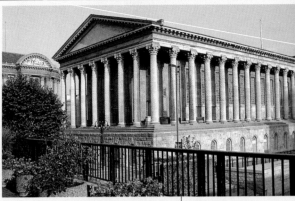

Above: Birmingham Town Hall, based on the Temple of Castor and Pollux in Rome, opened in 1834.

Left and below: Selly Manor, two half-timbered buildings in Bournville rescued by George Cadbury, which now house a museum.

to provide initial advice rather than to oversee the building process. Sir Thomas himself took a keen interest in architecture, and his house, although old-fashioned in plan, has dramatic massing and striking symmetry. One of the interesting features of the house's later history is the way that the 18th-century Holtes carried out sympathetic alterations and furnishings in the spirit of the Jacobean revival. The portrait on display of Sir Thomas Holte standing in front of the Hall, for example, was in fact made in the 18th century. Aston Hall's 19th-century owner, James Watt, also commissioned furniture 'in the antique style' in a further act of Jacobean nostalgia. Aston Hall's setting in the middle of the city meant that it was ripe for demolition until a working men's club purchased it for public enjoyment. Queen Victoria opened the building to visitors in 1858, and it was taken over in 1864 by the Birmingham Corporation as a very early example of a publicly owned country house run as a museum and place of entertainment. As such, it avoided the Victorian 'improvements' that many lived-in houses underwent, and is today furnished according to 17th- and 18th-century inventories. The Hall is still run by the city of Birmingham.

Bournville, the suburb which gives its name to its very own line of chocolate, is a famous planned settlement by the Quaker Cadbury family, owners of the confectionery company and much land in Birmingham. It was begun by George Cadbury in 1895 when he re-located his factory out of the city centre. The 8,000 houses of his workers were influenced by Arts and Crafts Utopian ideas, and timber-framed buildings, such as **Selly Manor**, were brought from elsewhere to create a bucolic atmosphere. Even today inhabitants have to keep their gardens tidy. Schools, an Art Institute, a Friends' Meeting House and churches were provided, but the Cadburys stopped short of supplying a pub. Marvellous smells waft through the factory museum of Cadbury World, which gives more information about the family and their philanthropic traditions, and it is easy to over-indulge on the numerous samples.

The **University of Birmingham**, with its enormous red-brick copy of the famous campanile from Siena, lies in a pleasant leafy campus.

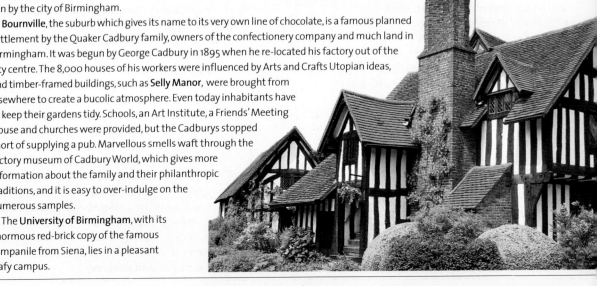

Bisham, Berks 690 E5, There are two buildings of particular interest in this delightful village by the Thames. **Bisham Abbey** started life as a preceptory of the Templars, was an Augustinian priory after 1337 and was an abbey for only three years before the Dissolution. Despite much that is medieval, what we see today is mainly the 16th-century work of the Hoby family. Note the impressive chimney-piece and overmantel in the hall.

All Saints Church has a Norman west tower but was over-restored by Benjamin Ferrey in 1849. It contains the exquisite alabaster monument to Lady Margaret Hoby (d. 1605) which carries four swans, the family's supporters.

Bishops Cannings, Wilts 690 C5, A large church, formerly part of the Bishop of Salisbury's estate. It is Early English in style. An oddity is the Penitential Seat, with its painted inscriptions of sin and death.

Bishop's Cleeve, Gloucs 690 B3, This overgrown village contains an interesting church, St Michael and All Angels, dating from several periods, including a Gothic Revival tower of 1700. The windows contain fragments of 14th- and 15th-century glass. In the upper room of the unusual two-storey south porch a series of peculiar animal paintings survives, the work of the village schoolmaster in the 1800s. Nearby is the splendid rectory, with a grand stone screen in the hall.

Bishop's Stortford, Herts 691 G4, A busy town presenting a real architectural mix. One of the earliest buildings is the Black Lion on Bridge Street, a 16th-century inn with exposed timber-framing. St Michael's is a good late medieval town church with an airy interior, original roofs,

Above and right: Bishop's Waltham Palace, the remains of the three-storey tower and Great Hall. It was the medieval seat of the Bishops of Winchester.

15th-century screen and chancel stalls, and a pulpit made locally in 1658. Also of interest is the neo-Grecian Corn Exchange, built in 1828 and designed by Lewis Vulliamy.

Bishop's Waltham, Hants 690 D7, The ruins of the palace of the Bishops of Winchester* overshadow this town of Georgian brick houses. The palace is Norman but was remodelled in the late Middle Ages and is still set in wooded grounds [EH].

Blackburn, Lancs 697 F6, The town is ancient but most of what the visitor sees is much more recent. The large parish church was rebuilt in the 1820s and then extended in 1926 when it became the cathedral of a newly created diocese. The most obvious sign of this change of status is the corona and thin spire added by Lawrence King in 1961. Most of the public buildings are seemly rather than outstanding, though there is a nice 18th-century church, St John the Evangelist, and a church by Sharpe, Holy Trinity, of 1837–46, with a highly decorated interior now cared for by the Churches Conservation Trust. Outer areas include St Gabriel's Church by the Liverpool* architect FX Velarde, an outstanding church of 1932–3 in blocky brickwork. Most astonishing, south of the town in Darwen is the India Mill Chimney, built some 300 feet (90m) high in the form of an Italianate campanile. The area is at the heart of the textile industry, and Blackburn has one of the best historical presentations in the Lewis Textile Museum. Nearby, the Blackburn Museum is in a delightful Arts and Crafts building decorated with sculpted panels representing various trades and industries.

Blackness Castle, Falkirk 699 F4, This castle overlooking the Firth of Forth is one of the four main Scottish castles – along with Edinburgh*, Stirling* and Dumbarton* – where the English maintained a garrison after the Act of Union in 1707. The central 15th-century tower-house served in turn as a royal castle, a Covenanters' prison and then a gunpowder store in the 1870s.

Blackmore, Essex 691 G4, Rising pagoda-like above the cornfields and capped by a slender shingle spire, St Laurence's 15th-century bell tower is the most beautiful of a unique group in south Essex. Its massive oak posts, reminiscent of Norwegian stave churches, complement the powerful Norman architecture of nave and choir, part of a former Augustinian priory.

Left: Blackburn Museum, the Arts and Crafts exterior.

Blackpool, Lancs 696 E6, Perhaps more than any other resort in England, Blackpool is a product of mass tourism brought by the railways. It was built as a holiday resort for the workers of industrial Lancashire when they were released from their factories for one or two weeks a year. An astonishing collection of buildings was provided to entertain them, most notably Blackpool Tower, a landmark building which identifies its home town. Opened in 1894, it was modelled on the Eiffel Tower; but whereas the Parisian prototype stands free, Blackpool Tower surmounts a seafront building housing an entertainment complex. Two of the interior spaces are among the theatre architect Frank Matcham's best: the Circus Arena, a Moorish fantasy; and the Ballroom, a rococo extravaganza of plasterwork and decorative painting carefully restored after a fire. Matcham produced another outstanding interior for the Grand Theatre. The Winter Gardens is another entertainment complex, based on a theatre of the 1870s but with many additions, each trying to

outdo its predecessor in exotic ostentation, ending with the Galleon Bar, Baronial Hall and Spanish Hall of 1931, decorated in fibrous plaster by Andrew Mazzei, art director of the Gaumont Film Company.

Blackwell, Cumb 696 E4, Blackwell was designed in 1897 for the Manchester brewer Sir Edward Holt by the Arts and Crafts architect MH Baillie Scott. Beautifully sited near Windermere*, the house has great views across the lake. The interior is beautifully crafted, informally planned and a model of what the architect described as true romance: 'a still, quiet earnestness which seems to lull and soothe the spirit with promises of peace.' Blackwell has recently been restored and opened

Left: Blackpool Tower and the Blackpool illuminations, symbol of Britain's most popular seaside resort.

Blackwell
Centre: Inglenook in the entrance hall.
Above: The entrance front.

to the public, and is the now the most accessible of a group of Arts and Crafts houses within a few miles of each other; this group includes two of CFA Voysey's most characteristic houses, Broadleys (now the motor boat club) and Moor Crag, both built in 1898.

Blaenau Ffestiniog, Gwynd 692 E2, This is one of Snowdonia's two major 'slate experience' complexes (the other is some distance away at Llanberis*), for most Welsh people a town suggesting not just slate, but rain as well. The Llechwedd (meaning 'slope') Slate Caverns date from the 1840s, and were opened to the public in 1972. Their success is owed entirely to the scope and detail of the presentation of a quarryman's life. The extensive underground tour offers some of the awesome fascination of Big Pit, Blaenavon*, in South Wales.

Blaenavon (Blaenafon), Torfn 689 H2, The B4246 from Llanfoist and the lush pastures of the River Usk climb steeply to the bleak wastes of Blaenavon; few journeys in Wales offer such a dramatic contrast between the rural and the industrial. This contrast was brought about when a small group of entrepreneurs opened an ironworks in the late 18th century and put into motion the revolution that was to give South Wales its industrial identity: furnaces, chimney stacks and winding gear. Blaenavon had all these in abundance; the vast furnaces of the ironworks were fed with coal from Big Pit, sunk in 1880. The decline of steel production in the 1930s and the dwindling demand for coal brought about unemployment on such a scale that the then Prince of Wales, on seeing the poverty-stricken community of Blaenavon, said 'Something must be done'.

A century after it was opened, Big Pit began functioning as a museum, with underground tours for the more courageous visitors who – divested of matches – don protective clothing before being lowered by steel cage into the coal 'roads' where ex-employees explain the collier's typical 'shift'. The popularity of such an enterprise partially revived the local economy, but the blast furnaces of the ironworks have only been recently appreciated for the great industrial creations they are, designed by the foremost engineers of the day. Often compared to cathedrals in their scale, they dominate an area where the geological history of Wales from the earliest times to the present can be discerned and interpreted. In 2000, Blaenavon, with its population of 6,000, was awarded UNESCO World Heritage Status, a distinction it shares with Stonehenge and the Taj Mahal.

Blair Castle
Top: The Drawing Room.
Centre: Exterior view
showing the wooded setting
with a backdrop of hills.

Blandford Forum

B

Blair Castle, P & K 701 H7, The impressive white castle, the home of the Dukes of Atholl, stands in a wooded hillside setting. The tower-house, built in 1269 to defend the Grampians and the road to Inverness*, has been attacked and rebuilt many times over the centuries. It was rebuilt in Georgian style in 1747–58 with sumptuous interiors by Abraham Swan and others, plasterwork by Thomas Clayton, and refurbished in Scots baronial style by the architect David Bryce c1870. The entrance hall is hung with ancient weapons, including muskets and shields from Culloden*, which evoke the castle's turbulent past. During the Jacobite Risings the Murray brothers of Atholl fought on opposite sides, with the result that one of them besieged his own castle in 1746. In addition to Jacobite memorabilia, collections of furniture, portraits, tapestries and porcelain, there are some remarkable papier-mâché objects made on the Isle of Man*, which was ruled by the family in the 18th century. The dukes are renowned for their intensive

reforestation programme: over the last hundred years they have planted 14 million larches in the region, firing the seeds from a cannon. The trees were all grown from seed taken from five trees on the lawns of Dunkeld* Cathedral.

Blaise Hamlet, Bristol 689 H3, To the west of the church in Henbury, one of Bristol's villages, is this picturesque – if artificial – layout of cottages (1811) designed by John Nash to accommodate Blaise Estate pensioners. There is a city-administered museum in Blaise Castle House, built originally by William Paty in 1796 for a Quaker banker.

Blakeney, Norfk 695 H4, Narrow streets lined with sparkling pebble cottages lead down to a quay animated by visitors and sailing dinghies. The old Guildhall's 15th-century vaulted undercroft is

Above: Blakeney Point, a great spit with mud flats and salt marshes, is an important sanctuary for migrant birds.

Right: Blaise Hamlet. John Nash designed this picturesque display of detached cottages in 1811, at once artificial, delightful and secluded, a tumble of thatch, slate and stone.

evidence of Blakeney's former prosperity on the Glaven estuary. Blakeney Point, a long shingle spit widening into sand dunes, has a resident colony of grey seals, thriving bird life, a rare and fragile eco-system and National Trust exhibition in the old corrugated-tin lifeboat station. The church is a mighty landmark on rising ground south of the village, whose turret was originally a lighthouse.

Blandford Forum, Dorset 690 B7, The elegant Georgian town of Blandford Forum is now mercifully bypassed by the constant flow of traffic to and from the south coast. A fire in 1731 destroyed most of the town, but enabled the two surveyors in charge of the rebuilding, William

Above: Blenheim Palace, looking out across the lake.

Left: Blantyre, David Livingstone painted by Charles Need, 19th century.

and John Bastard, to exercise their considerable talents. The parish church of **St Peter and St Paul** (with the Bastard family tomb in its churchyard) and the Town Hall (1734) are two examples. Within the church the panelled galleries are slung between giant Portland stone columns with Ionic capitals, and the box pews, font cover and mayor's chair (1748) are all finely crafted.

Blantyre, S Lans 698 E5, In Blantyre, the birthplace of David Livingstone, a museum traces the life and career of the intrepid 19th-century missionary and explorer who discovered the Victoria Falls and then went in search of the source of the Nile with Harry Morton Stanley.

Bledlow, Bucks 690 E4, The garden, laid out by the Carrington family, is open all year. Holy Trinity Church, with its chunky square tower, is a pretty flint building containing a good Aylesbury* font.

Blenheim Palace, Oxon, This magnificent baroque palace, built for John Churchill, 1st Duke of Marlborough, was largely paid for by a grateful nation in thanks for his victory over the French at the Battle of Blenheim in 1704. The building was sanctioned by Queen Anne and Parliament, and the Queen personally approved the initial plans. Blenheim was to be a national monument symbolizing the glory of the nation, a palace to rival Versailles itself.

It is the creation of the architectural partnership of Sir John Vanbrugh and Nicholas Hawksmoor, who had already begun work on their other baroque masterpiece, Castle Howard*. The scale and power of the architecture is breathtaking: the buildings and courts cover 7 acres (2.8ha). The house is designed around a *cour d'honneur*; the main block looks out across the lake, and the sides are framed by the kitchen and stable courts, linked to the house by short quadrants. The centrepiece is a giant Corinthian portico; the pediment, carved with the Marlborough coat of arms, appears to have split a second pediment, which is set above and behind it. At the four corners of the house stand four pavilions, topped with 30-foot (9m) finials. The sculpture is patriotic and theatrical; much of it was executed by Grinling Gibbons. Over the gates to the service courts the lion of England savages the cock of France. On the south front is a bust of Louis XIV, a trophy of the Duke's from Tournai. Britannia dominates the main entrance and the tower finials are cannon balls,

Top left: Blenheim Palace, Sir Winston Churchill's Birth Room. Churchill was born here on 30 November 1874. 'At Blenheim,' he was later to

declare, 'I took two very important decisions: to be born and to marry.'

Blickling Hall
Top right: Sir Henry Hobart, by Daniel Mytens, c1624.
Bottom: The main southwesterly prospect.

Blickling Hall

B

supporting reversed fleurs-de-lys and ducal coronets.

The construction of the palace was marred by conflict. In 1710 the Marlboroughs fell from favour and went into exile for two years (1712–14). On the death of Queen Anne they returned and the Duke resolved to finance the rest of the building himself. Vanbrugh and the Duchess never saw eye-to-eye; she was infuriated by Vanbrugh's extravagance, and in 1716 he left. When he returned in 1725 he was not admitted.

The grandeur of the setting is equal to that of the architecture. The sweeping landscape was designed by Capability Brown between 1764 and 1774. The Great Lake was created out of a small river and the parkland replanted. The 9th Duke laid out the two formal gardens to the east and west.

The interior is no less impressive than the exterior. The Great Hall, rising to 67 feet (20m), opens into the Saloon, on either side of which is a suite of three state rooms in the manner of a French *appartement*. The furnishings are sumptuous. The oval painting on the Great Hall ceiling is by Sir James Thornhill; it shows the duke dressed as a Roman general receiving a laurel wreath of victory from Britannia. There are portraits of the duke and duchess by Sir Godfrey Kneller and works by Reynolds and Sargent, among many other fine paintings, furniture and tapestries. There is also an exhibition dedicated to Sir Winston Churchill, who was born at Blenheim. The Chapel contains the tomb of the duke and duchess, designed by William Kent; the life-size figures were carved by Rysbrack.
See **Woodstock* 690 D4.**

Bletchingley, Surrey 691 F6, The church of St Mary, heavily restored by the Victorians, should not be missed for the memorial to Robert Claydon in the south chapel. The style is exuberant baroque; columns and a pediment frame Sir Robert and his wife, dressed in the robes of the Lord Mayor and Mayoress; beneath, in delicate lace, is their son who died in infancy. The 15th-century Brewer Street farmhouse has attractive timbering.

Bletchley Park, Bucks 690 E3, This house, outside Milton Keynes, offers visitors something a little out of the ordinary. Bletchley Park, built in the 19th and early 20th centuries, was made famous during World War II as the government's intelligence centre. It was here that Colossus, the world's first large electronic valve computer, helped to crack Nazi enigma codes.

Blickling Hall, Norfk 695 J4, The Hall, built for Lord Chief Justice Sir Henry Hobart between 1616 and 1627, is a jewel, a beautiful Jacobean house in warm red brick with stone dressings, more intimate and endearing than its Palladian successors at Houghton* and Holkham*. The architect, Robert Lyminge, whose initials appear over the entrance, was probably also at work on the south front of Felbrigg Hall*. He replaced a moated manor once owned by Sir John Fastolf of Caister Castle* near Great Yarmouth*, and the Boleyn family, whose brasses are in the church; but there is no truth in the rumour that Anne Boleyn was born here.

The main prospect of Blickling Hall [NT] is unforgettable, a perfectly symmetrical façade with a central clock tower rising gracefully above the main entrance and Dutch gables flanked by domed corner towers. The whole delightful composition is framed by servants' quarters and the most extraordinary undulations of yew hedge, over 16 feet (5m) high and as old as the house. Originally U-shaped, the far side was filled in by the Ivory brothers, Norwich architects, between 1767 and 1779 for the 2nd Earl of Buckinghamshire. According to the tablet placed there, the countess bequeathed her jewels towards the cost of rebuilding the west front. William Ivory was also responsible for the grand double staircase of 1767, built in the Jacobean style, that rises from the main entrance hall, and the life-size rococo relief figures of Elizabeth I and her mother Anne Boleyn. The chief glory of Blickling is its Long Gallery in the east wing, 127 feet (39m) long, lined with over 12,000 books, with a dazzling plaster ceiling full of abstract and naturalistic designs, and views over the parterre. Next is the no less opulent Peter the Great Room, redesigned for the 2nd Earl to display the tapestry depicting the Tsar in 1764 (a gift from Catherine the Great). Also captured for posterity here, the earl's own full-length ermine-clad figure by Gainsborough with his wife's portrait alongside, and in a room nearby, that of his aunt, the ravishing Countess of Suffolk, mistress of George II. The park, with its long sinuous lake and Bonomi's suitably austere pyramidal mausoleum for the earl and his two wives (1793) is, like the orangery of c1785, attributed to the local genius Humphry Repton, buried just down the road at Aylsham*. The Victorian parterre and sumptuous herbaceous borders are a 1930s conceit, but the fountain came from Oxnead Hall, home of the Pastons, demolished in 1731. The two symmetrical groves with their dissecting avenues and the central walk up to a pedimented temple are genuine 18th-century creations.

Left: Blythburgh Church, the nave with slender Perpendicular columns and a glorious angel roof.

Blisland, Cnwll 688 D6, Perhaps the only village in the county set around a large green, with Georgian and earlier cottages on two sides, and the Norman church of St Protus and St Hyacinth on the third. Built with massive granite blocks, the church itself is small; its interior is its chief delight. It has a particularly good, and very colourful rood screen of 1896–7, set somewhat incongruously between wildly leaning stone columns. Nearby, on the edge of Bodmin Moor is the Jubilee Rock at Pendrift, inscribed with the Royal Arms and other devices and the date 1809. The ancient Trippet Stones form a stone circle on Blisland Manor Common; eight of the 20 stones are still standing. The Stripple Stones henge on Hawksmoor Down is a large prehistoric enclosure which retains a strange, mystic atmosphere.

Blithefield Hall, Staffs 694 C4, This large house is a mixture of Georgian work and early 19th-century gothic grafted on to an earlier building still visible in places.

Bloxham, Oxon 690 D3, This lovely village is home to one of Oxfordshire's stateliest churches, St Mary's, built mainly in the 14th and 15th centuries. Its splendid spire is a prominent landmark and is probably by the same unknown masons who worked at Adderbury*. Note the elaborately painted 15th-century rood screen.

Blunham, Beds 691 F3, The church contains a 14th-century alabaster statue of the Virgin, beautiful despite her headless state.

Blyth, Notts 694 D3, Once a small town on the Great North Road, it is now a quiet, sprawling village bypassed by the A1. Blyth's origins can be traced back to a Benedictine priory, founded in 1088; the priory church, St Mary and St Martin, still survives as the parish church, though much altered. The

Above: Bloxham, St Mary's Church, the elegantly proportioned tower and spire. The church was under royal patronage until 1547 when it passed to Eton College.

chancel, transepts and part of the nave have all been pulled down, leaving a blank east end. The south aisle is of the early 1300s, and a large 15th-century tower has replaced the Norman west end. Even so, what survives is tall and grim enough to show that this was an austere early Norman building of some importance. Inside there are traces of a Doom painted on the otherwise blind east wall, and late medieval wooden screens in the nave and south aisle.

Blythburgh, Suffk 695 J6, There are stunning views across the estuary of this beautiful clerestoried church sailing gracefully above the reedbeds. It is equally impressive up close, with large Perpendicular windows, stone lacework parapets and flush-flint buttresses. The interior is full of light, limewash and pale stone columns with angels, wings outstretched, hovering above carved bench ends and scrubbed brick floors.

Boarstall, Bucks 690 D4, West of the beautiful hilltop village of Brill are two fascinating survivals. Boarstall Tower [NT] is an early 14th-century stone gatehouse altered in the late 1500s or early 1600s, all that remains of a fortified medieval manor house demolished in the later 18th century. On a nearby lake surrounded by woodland is Boarstall's more peculiar sight, a duck decoy of c1697 in complete working order [NT].

Bodelwyddan Castle, Denbgs 692 E2, A 19th-century building on much earlier foundations, now housing part of the Victorian section of the National Portrait Gallery. The highly elaborate 'Marble Church' nearby was built by a daughter of the house, in memory of her husband, Lord Willoughby de Broke.

Bodiam Castle, E Susx 691 H6, The perfect picture of a medieval castle, with towers and battlements reflected in the dark waters of a moat [NT]. It was built in 1383 as a secure place against French invaders (they had attacked Rye and Winchelsea in 1377 and 1380). Inside the walls not much remains, but the hall, living quarters, kitchen and chapel can all be traced.

Bodmin, Cnwll 688 D6, The former county town is now bypassed, and superseded by Truro*. The priory church of St Petroc is one of the largest churches in the county, and ruins of the monastic buildings are still to be seen in the nearby park. The County Assize on Mount Folly (1837–8) contains one of the last Grand Jury boxes in the country and is now a judicial museum. Malefactors tried here were often taken to Bodmin Jail (now in ruins) at the other end of the town. The third county institution was the County Lunatic Asylum at St Lawrence on the western edge of the town, while on the southern edge was the large barracks of the Duke of Cornwall's Light Infantry – a fascinating museum lies near the well-preserved steam-powered Bodmin and Wenford Railway.

Top: Bodiam Castle, one of the last great medieval castles, has kept its moat, walls and towers. It saw no fighting until besieged by the Parliamentarians during the Civil War.

High above the town is a 144-foot (44m) obelisk erected to the memory of Lt Gen Sir Walter Raleigh Gilbert in 1856–7, commemorating his exploits in India.

Bodnant Gardens, Conwy 692 E2, Although, like those at Powys Castle*, the gardens are of world distinction, they are much more recent, dating from the latter part of the 19th century when Henry Pochin purchased the property. His daughter, the 1st Lady Aberconway, continued her father's initial planting. The site has not only the pictorial advantages of a valley, but the

Left, right and below: Bodnant Gardens, the 'Pin Mill' transported from a country house in Gloucestershire to Bodnant in the 1930s.

Left: Bodrhyddan, the entrance front designed by WE Nesfield in 1873.

backcloth of the Snowdon* range. The 2nd Lord Aberconway gave the garden to the National Trust in 1949. It is famous for its rhododendrons and azaleas, and its laburnum arch but is worth visiting at any time of year.

Bodrhyddan, Denbgs 693 F1, The medieval core of the family house underwent many alterations

Top right: Bolton Priory, the pointed arches of the choir.

and additions through the centuries, most significantly in 1870 when WE Nesfield designed an elaborate west front. The original southern entrance became the garden front, with parterres consistent with the 1696 date on the doorway. A pair of gate piers adds to the impression of 17th-century formality.

Boduan (Gam Bodfean), Gwynd 692 D3, Part of the spine of hills that give Lleyn* its distinctiveness. Its importance as a hill fort suffers from comparison with the dramatic impact of Tre'r Ceiri*.

Bodysgallen, Conwy 696 C8, Prominent on the hill opposite Gloddaeth*, another Mostyn property, this house was purchased by Richard Broyd as the first of his Historic House Hotels.

Bognor Regis, W Susx 690 E7, Deliberately created as a seaside resort in the 1780s, Bognor is probably the model for Jane Austen's Sanditon. Of the original buildings the Dome (1787), an ambitious terrace of five houses, is the best. Butlin's Holiday Camp is (or will be, if it survives) an interesting relic of the 1960s.

Bolsover Castle, Derbys 694 D3, The fantastic house of the Cavendishes roughly follows the outline of the earlier castle, but the buildings date mostly from the 17th century and many are now ruined. The Little Castle is a pretend medieval castle; the architect was Robert Smythson who probably designed nearby Hardwick Hall*, which stands on the same ridge as Bolsover, but overlooks a country estate rather than an industrial landscape. Built between 1612 and 1620, Bolsover is full of small rooms whose rich ornamentation compensates for the lack of furniture. The main

Above centre: Bodysgallen's extensive gardens include terraces, formal ponds and woodland walks.

Above: Bolsover Castle, the keep and main range.

Right and below: Bolton Priory, the ruined choir and roofed nave with the west tower transformed into a porch.

living range stretching away from the castle is roofless, yet has some extraordinary decoration, and there is also a huge and handsome Riding House (the Cavendishes were passionate about horses and dressage) [EH].

Bolton Castle, N York 697 G4, The site so commands Wensleydale – the dale of the River Ure – that the castle can be seen from far and wide, especially when floodlit. An original building contract of 1378, written in French, survives for what was clearly another phase of a part-completed structure. The builder was John Lewyn, a master-mason of national reputation, and the client Richard Scrope, Lord High Chancellor in 1379 when licence was granted for crenellation. The castle's ingenious plan makes it of major importance in architectural

history, as it reconciles military strength with domestic comfort. A courtyard is surrounded and protected by four ranges of buildings containing, as well as the communal chapel, the Great Hall, kitchen and service rooms, and a large number of self-contained apartments of varying size but each with its own fireplace and garderobe. In this way, important rooms could have large windows facing the central courtyard, leaving the outside walls almost unbreached for defence. Because it was comfortable and well appointed as well as secure, Mary Queen of Scots was imprisoned here by Queen Elizabeth I in 1568. The adjacent village of **Castle Bolton** is a good example of medieval town planning. The surrounding estate contains many features of archeological interest. It also has a rabbit warren.

Bolton Priory, N York 697 G5, Founded by Augustinian canons in c1151. Their ruined choir has intersecting round arches creating pointed arches, typical of c1170. The nave subsequently became the parish church, and only in 1983 was the west tower, still unfinished when the priory was dissolved, transformed into its porch. The priory ruins, Bolton Abbey village and surrounding woods belong to the Duke of Devonshire, as the 4th Duke had married the daughter of that famous patron of the arts (and high priest of Palladian architecture) Richard Boyle, 3rd Earl of Burlington, who had inherited the property from the Wharfedale-based Clifford family.

Bolton

Bolton, Gt Man 697 F7, Bolton has the most metropolitan feel of all the cotton towns surrounding Manchester*. A 1930s town planning scheme, Le Mans Crescent, by local architects Bradshaw, Gass and Hope, provides a setting for the large classical Town Hall by William Hill of Leeds, 1866, which owes much to Brodrick's masterpiece there. There is a large covered market of the 1850s neatly combined with a modern shopping centre. The local Art Gallery and Museum contains work by Thomas Moran, the Bolton-born American artist. The parish church, St Peter, was largely rebuilt by EG Paley in 1867 in a spacious manner; earlier churches are the domestic-looking St George's, 1794, now in commercial use, and Holy Trinity, an expensive Commissioners' church by Philip Hardwick, 1823. The outskirts of the town contain some architectural gems, including one of Paley and Austin's best town churches, All Souls Astley Bridge, 1880, now in the care of the Churches Conservation Trust, and St Stephen and All Martyrs Lever Bridge, 1842, still in a villagey setting, which is the best surviving of Edmund Sharpe's early terracotta churches. A local coal-mine owner sought to promote terracotta as a material and this church uses it both structurally and decoratively, for all the extensive 'carving' in moulded work, including the rich organ case with ballflower ornament. The martyrs included Charles I, and one window has glass showing the execution of the king. Contrasting with these is the typically long and low late medieval church of St Mary Deane. The principal secular buildings, apart from some spectacular cotton mills, are two survivors from Bolton's pre-industrial past. **Hall i' th' Wood** is a very attractive timber-framed house, mainly 16th and 17th century, with nice detail, though good detective work is needed to separate the alterations made in 1899 when Lord Leverhulme bought the building and gave it to his native town. It is best known as the home of Samuel Crompton, inventor of the spinning mule which did so much to revolutionize the textile trade, and is now a museum. At **Smithills Hall** there is a clearer distinction between the old and new parts. It is centred on a late medieval Great Hall, with screens passage, service arrangements and tiers of quatrefoiled windbraces. Extensions were made in the 17th and again in the 19th century. The house is set in attractive woodland.

Left: Smithills Hall, 14th-century manor house with Tudor panelling. It contains displays of furniture and stained glass.

Above: Bolton Town Hall, by William Hill, 1866.

Left: Hall i' th' Wood, the timber-framed 16th-century range.

Boscastle, Cnwll 688 D6, One of the few harbours on this treacherous coast, where seatrading flourished until the arrival of the railways in the 1890s. The harbour was always difficult to enter; rowing boats and horses led along paths either side of the harbour entrance were used to help sailing boats berth. Above the clustered cottages of the port are the Forrabury Stitches, medieval field

Boscobel House
Above: A bedroom.
Left: The timber-framed exterior. King Charles I hid here after the Battle of Worcester.

Left: Boscastle harbour at high tide, a view of the curving breakwater, built in 1584 by Sir Richard Grenville.

Bottom: Boston Stump (the massive late 15th-century tower of St Botolph's church) rising behind the Assembly Rooms next to the River Witham.

strips still farmed in the traditional, communal way. Some way up the Valency Valley is the church of St Julitta, which was restored by the young Thomas Hardy, who worked for a London architect before he began his writing, in 1871–2; the rector's sister-in-law became his first wife.

Boscobel House, Shrops 693 H4, A small timber-framed house, which claims to be the refuge of King Charles I after the Battle of Worcester. For one day the King hid in a nearby oak tree. Although the original 'Royal Oak' has been carried away piecemeal by souvenir hunters, the house itself has been restored to tell the story [EH].

Bosham, W Susx 690 E7, It was here that King Canute conducted his experiment with the waves (the main street is still flooded at high tide), and from here that King Harold set off on his voyage to Normandy, which delivered him into the hands of William the Conqueror in 1064. The church appears in the Bayeux Tapestry, and its chancel arch survives, massive and rather crude.

Boston, Lincs 695 F4, Now evocative and remote, this town was once a wealthy seaport until the river silted up, and although ships still come in, the wealth seems to have evaporated. The town and the flat fenland for miles around are dominated by **Boston Stump,** the immensely tall tower of the great medieval church of St Bodolph which stands between the river and the broad market square. The Stump itself is 272 feet (83m) high – a monument to the daring medieval builders –

and the church is one of the largest in the country. Around the market square are streets full of Georgian houses; one of the best is **Fydell House,** a substantial town mansion built in 1726.

Bothwell Castle, S Lans 698 E5, Near Uddingston, the red-sandstone ruins of Bothwell Castle, one of the most impressive 13th-century fortresses, stand above the River Clyde. The castle was built by Walter de Moravia (later Moray, then Murray), in 1242, but work was interrupted by the Wars of Independence in the late 13th century and the castle was never completed. In 1301 it was besieged by Edward I, who demolished the ramparts using a machine made specially in Glasgow*. It changed hands repeatedly over the years and was rebuilt and demolished a number of times. Although partly ruined, its circular keep is a fine example of 13th-century defensive architecture.

Bottesford, Leics 694E4, A very attractive village in a loop of the river, which is spanned by an early 17th-century brick bridge. There are some pretty buildings, including two sets of almshouses. St Mary's Church is large and mostly Perpendicular, although earlier work can easily be detected in the chancel and north transept. The church's best feature is the splendid crocketed spire, which is one of the tallest in the county. The interior is handsome, and has a notable collection of family pieces in the chancel: medieval monuments to the Roos family and the tombs of eight successive earls of Rutland dating from the 1540s to the 1670s. The inscription on the 6th Earl's tomb refers to children killed by witchcraft; the tombs of the 7th and 8th Earls are by Grinling Gibbons.

Gallery. The 1st Duke's contributions to the park included water gardens and canals, laid out by a Dutchman, Van der Meulen. John Montagu, the 2nd Duke, known as 'John the Planter,' planted over 70 miles (112km) of avenue on the estate. Boughton's pretty estate village of Geddington has one of the three surviving gothic crosses which marked the resting places of Queen Eleanor's funeral cortège in 1290. The Geddington boundary of the Boughton park is constructed as a deer-leap, with a ditch on the inner side of a wall. Deer from the surrounding forest could therefore leap into the park, but the height was too great for them to escape again.

Boughton House, Nhants 694 E6, The 'English Versailles' has the most arrogant of loggias and Frenchified pavilions with mansard roofs, the work of the 1st Duke of Montagu at the end of the 17th century. Not surprisingly, Ralph Montagu was British ambassador to Louis XIV in Paris between 1669 and 1678, and brought home gifts of furniture from the king as well as architectural ideas from Paris. Behind the façade, though, the courtyards of the 15th-century monastery remain, and Montagu's work was never finished. This is made dramatically clear in his 'unfinished wing', which remains a shell and has never been fitted out. Its interesting features include the ingenious internal gutters and pipes designed to avoid visual intrusion into the external view. The visitors' entrance to the northwest pavilion today is via the *trompe l'oeil* painted Hall of 1695 by Louis Chéron. The adjoining Little Hall, also with a ceiling by Chéron, contains paintings by El Greco, Teniers, Taddeo Zucchero and Annibale Caracci. The nether regions of the house contain a collection of firebuckets and an interesting shuffleboard table in the Audit Room

Above: Elizabeth Vernon, Countess of Southampton, wife of Shakespeare's patron, by an unknown artist, c1600.

Top left: The Great Hall with its Mortlake tapestries of *The Four Elements*.

Left: Bureau attributed to Pierre Gole, c1672, oak veneered with pewter and brass. One of the pieces of superb French furniture at Boughton.

Boughton Monchelsea, Kent 691 H6, An Elizabethan house, built in 1567 and altered in the 19th century. It incorporates a charming mixture of styles, with decoration and furniture of all periods. There are two walled gardens.

Bournemouth, Dorset 690 C7, This sedate seaside town lies at the mouth of a valley flanked by 100-foot (30m) cliffs, where pine trees line the chines that lead through the chalk hills down to the long stretches of beach. It underwent its greatest period of expansion with the coming of the railways in the 19th century, when, with its superb sands and generally mild climate, it became a popular holiday destination. The erection of its grand stuccoed villas was soon

Above: Bournemouth, St Stephen's Church. Interior of JL Pearson's grandest church, built (1881–98) in memory of AM Bennett, the wealthy local vicar who railed against the Anglo-Catholics.

Right: Boughton Monchelsea, the 16th-century east range. The battlements were added in 1819.

Below: Bourton-on-the-Water, a footbridge across the River Windrush.

under way, along with even more impressive Italianate structures such as the Royal Bath Hotel. The private house (1894) of the hotel's original owner, Sir Merton Russell-Cotes, is now the **Russell-Cotes Art Gallery and Museum.** It contains a splendidly eclectic range of exhibits, which included oil-paintings, shells, former possessions of the actor Sir Henry Irving, and local and exotic butterflies and moths. The museum is instructive and well arranged within an Italian-style interior. The late 19th century saw the erection of about 25 new churches; their tall spires now share the skyline with blocks of flats. The best of these churches is **St Stephen's** (1881–98), by JL Pearson, which has a complete scheme of stained-glass windows by Clayton and Bell. Talbot Village, a model village of 1835 onwards, is an interesting curiosity.

Bourton-on-the-Water, Gloucs 690 C4, This is a picturesque village with a tame river running through it. It is famous for its miniature model

village, constructed from locally quarried stone – a copy, at a scale of one-ninth, of Bourton itself as it was before World War II.

Bovey Tracey, Devon 689 F6, On the slopes of Dartmoor* this charming and bustling small town is notable for its church, founded as an act of penance by William Tracey for his part in the murder of Thomas à Becket, with its richly carved interior. At the Riverside Mill centre for the Devon Guild of Craftsmen, visitors can see a wide range of crafts of the highest quality.

Bowhill, Border 699 G6, The sophisticated décor of this vast early 19th-century mansion, progressively enlarged from an 18th-century core by the Dukes of Buccleuch, provides the setting for beautiful French furniture, exceptional Mortlake tapestries (1670) and a collection of paintings by Leonardo da Vinci, Guardi, Canaletto, Ruysdael, Reynolds, Gainsborough and Claude Lorraine.

Bowood House, Wilts 690 B5, The house was begun about 1720, and was bought by the 2nd Earl of Shelburne in about 1754. Much of it was demolished in 1955, leaving a perfectly proportioned Georgian house. The Diocletian wing, designed by Robert Adam, contains the splendid Library, and the laboratory where Joseph Priestley discovered oxygen in 1774. The Sculpture Gallery exhibits some of the famous

Above, left and right: Bowood House terraces and the orangery, now a picture gallery. There are good collections of miniatures, watercolours and jewellery.

Right: Box Hill, roughly 988 acres (400ha) of countryside, with views south over the Weald.

Below: Boxgrove Priory, the Guest House of about 1300, part of the monastic buildings attached to the very fine church. It was originally two-storeyed.

Lansdowne marbles. The Park extends over 2,000 acres (800ha), and is the work of both Capability Brown and Humphry Repton. It has a Cascade, Grotto, a Pinetum, Arboretum, Temple and Mausoleum in the approved 18th- and 19th-century style, and famous Rhododendron Walks.

Boxgrove Priory, W Susx 690 E7, The nave is ruined, but the chancel, contemporary with the Early English work in Chichester* Cathedral, is of the highest quality. Inside, the De La Warr Chantry (1526) is an exquisitely extravagant tomb bringing together gothic angels and Renaissance cherubs.

Box Hill, Surrey 691 F6, This is a beautiful area of woodland and downland, 1 mile (1.6km) south of Dorking*, which also offers fine views.

Brackley, Nhants 690 D3, A pleasant small town with a wide main street and an excellent second-hand

bookshop. Many of the houses are a typical mixture of red and blue brick, laid in patterns.

Bradenham, Bucks 690 E4, A picturesque village set among fine beech woodland with a large, sloping green. The church of St Botolph has a Norman south doorway and a 19th-century font and cover by GE Street.

Bradfield, Suffk 695 H6, The novelist Angus Wilson lived for many years on the edge of a large area of primeval forest. Once owned by the monks of Bury St Edmunds*, it is now managed by Suffolk Wildlife Trust on a traditional coppice rotation. The wood, one of Britain's richest wildlife habitats, with over 350 species of flowering plants (including the rare oxlip, herb paris and wild service tree), is also home to many unusual fungi, small mammals and song birds. A visit is most enchanting in spring, when nightingales and butterflies perform in the sunlit rides.

This page: Bradford-on-Avon, church of St Lawrence, one of the most important structures of its original 8th-century date in Britain. Small though it is, this Anglo-Saxon church, altered in the 10th and 11th centuries, has a powerful dominance, as much due to the external pilasters as to the narrow openings and simple deep windows within.

Bradford, W York 697 G6, The parish church was raised to cathedral status in 1919. The exterior is typically West Riding Perpendicular, with a west tower of c1500 and many 20th-century additions. Inside there is a particularly splendid late Perpendicular font cover. The Industrial Revolution came late to Bradford, which then acquired many large and handsome Victorian buildings, notably the Gothic Revival Town Hall of 1873 and Venetian gothic former Wool Exchange of 1864–7, both by local architects Lockwood and Mawson. Little Germany is an area of erstwhile warehouses for expensive worsted cloth, much of which was exported, hence its name. The warehouses, like huge Italian palazzi, rise above narrow stone-setted streets. Lister's Manningham Mill of 1871–3 makes its huge presence felt on the skyline with its immense

Braemar Castle.
Left: Braemar Castle, the Dining Room.
Right: The crenellated parapets of the stair tower and turrets are Hanoverian additions (replacing the original conical roofs), as are the star-plan outer defences.

Left: Bradwell-juxta-Mare, St Cedd's Chapel (7th century) stands forlornly on the edge of the Essex Marshes.

Below and bottom: Bramall Hall, roof of the south range and garden front and terraces.

Climbing the hillsides all around it are the larger houses of the merchants and the crowded 18th- and 19th-century shops that served them. The church of Holy Trinity, with its nave of *c*1300, has two good monuments: Charles Steward (d. 1701) by John Nost and Anthony Methuen (d. 1737) by JM Rysbrack. The church of St Lawrence is one of the most important late Anglo-Saxon churches in Britain: the nave is only 23 feet (7m) long by 13 feet (4m) wide, yet over 25 feet (7.6m) high.

Brading, *see* **Isle of Wight***.

Bradwell-juxta-Mare, Essex 691 H4, The Latin tag is instructive. St Cedd's Chapel, a lonely outpost of Christianity at the mouth of the Blackwater, was founded by a missionary *c*654 close by Othona, a 3rd-century Roman shore fort. This nave of a larger building, one of the earliest and best-preserved Saxon churches, became a barn in the 17th century.

Braemar Castle, Abers 702 B6, The tower-house built

in 1628 by the Earl of Mar was burned in 1689 by John Farquharson. Fortified by John Adam, it housed a Hanoverian garrison after the Jacobite Risings of 1715 and 1745. It was subsequently bought and restored by the Farquharsons.

Italianate mill chimney. Large numbers of immigrants have come from the Indian subcontinent to work in the textile mills, making Bradford a multi-cultural society, and one of the country's best places for curries.

Bradford-on-Avon, Wilts 690 B5, The picturesque town, surrounded by steep hills, has many interesting features. In the centre of its nine-arched bridge is a 17th-century chapel, which replaced a medieval one. By the early 19th century Bradford-on-Avon had 32 cloth factories.

Bramall Hall, Gt Man 697 F7, A solidly impressive timber-framed house built over several centuries for the Davenport family. Dating the various parts is difficult, but most is probably 16th century. Originally there was an open courtyard in the centre, but one whole side of it was removed in the 18th century. A Victorian owner, Charles Nevill, repaired and restored the house, so quite a lot of 19th-century work is visible. There are some splendid rooms, including what is called the 'Ballroom' in the south wing, with its Elizabethan wall paintings, and the Drawing Room, which has a splendid Tudor plaster ceiling.

Bramber, W Susx, A village with a small Norman church and St Mary's House, one of the best timber-framed houses in Sussex, which contains interesting old furniture, an Elizabethan 'painted room' with *trompe l'oeil* murals and a display of costume dolls. *See* **Steyning* 691 F7.**

Bramfield, Suffk 695 J6, The church boasts several local specialities: a unique detached round tower opposite an 18th-century serpentine or crinkle-crankle wall, a reed thatch roof and a sumptuous rood screen with evangelists beneath a vaulted canopy. Don't miss the ledger slab to Bridget Applewhite in the floor of the nave.

Bramham Park, W York 697 H6, An early 18th-century country house, Bramham was probably designed by its owner, Robert Benson, later the 1st Lord Bingley. He was Lord Mayor and Member of Parliament for York, and a favourite of Queen Anne. It is a long, low house built of magnesian limestone, with dramatic flanking colonnades: the interiors date mainly from restoration after a major fire in 1828. The house is somewhat eclipsed by its magnificent and extensive early 18th-century

Above: Brantwood, John Ruskin's Lake District home at Coniston.

formal gardens, also laid out by Lord Bingley, in a manner much influenced by the French designer Le Nôtre. Despite a damaging storm in 1962, these gardens contain impressive beech hedges forming avenue vistas with statuary. A T-shaped canal feeds six ponds connected by cascades. Good garden buildings include a chapel, once an orangery designed by James Paine *c*1760, a gothic temple in the manner of Batty Langley, and an Ionic temple from which six avenues extend. Ten avenues radiate from an obelisk in an area known as Black Fen about a mile (1.6km) away from the house.

Branscombe, Devon 689 G6, Lying in a narrow combe that twists its way to the sea, the village houses – many of them thatched – form picturesque groups. The Manor Water Mill, the Old Bakery and the Smithy are all owned by the National Trust and frequent demonstrations of their workings are given.

Brant Broughton, Lincs 694 E4, The church of St Helen is late medieval, with exquisite stone carving. The chancel was rebuilt in the 1870s by George Bodley, a leading Gothic Revivalist, who refitted the rest of the interior.

Brantwood, Cumb 696 E4, Brantwood has an excellent site and attractive gardens overlooking Coniston Water. Like many Lake District houses, it is more important for its associations than its architecture. This was John Ruskin's home from 1872 to his death in 1900 and still retains many of his drawings, paintings and personal items from the period when he was England's most influential art critic. The most attractive way of reaching Brantwood is to take the steamboat *Gondola* [NT] across the lake. This was the Lake District's first tourist boat, built in 1859 when railway connections first made the area attractive to visitors in large numbers. After some years as a houseboat, *Gondola* was restored in 1980 and now provides a luxurious and eerily quiet cruise across the water.

Bratton, Wilts 690 B6, Salisbury Plain reaches its highest point – 755 feet (230m) – at its northwest edge. Here stands **Bratton Castle**, a fine Iron-Age fort, commanding breathtaking views. It is protected by a double row of earthworks rising 35 feet (10.6m) high in parts. The great **White Horse** cut into the turf is much older than that at Westbury: it is believed that it was carved out of the ground to celebrate Alfred's victory over the Danes. The horse measures 180 feet (55m) long, 107 feet (32.6m) high, and its eye has a circumference of 25 feet (7.6m). As well as its castle and its white horse, Bratton has one other unique feature: a 13th-century **church**, standing alone on

a hillside and reached by 180 steps. It is one of the most charming small churches in the country. Its 15th-century tower has a stair turret and is embattled like the aisles, and all have big gargoyles. Its chancel is severely true to 13th-century tradition, and the north transept has delightful corbel angels, either playing musical instruments or carrying shields.

Braunton, Devon 688 E4, The church is dedicated to St Brannock, a Welsh missionary who found a white sow with a litter of piglets in his cell. These are still remembered in many of the church carvings. South of the village lies the Great Field; here, some 140 strips of land are still farmed by five different families whose land is scattered all over the coastal plain. Divided by ditches or *rhines*, the landscape has hardly changed at all since Saxon times.

Breadsall, Derbys 694 D4, The west tower of All Saints Church has a spectacularly tall spire dating from the 14th century. The church itself, although medieval in origin, was largely rebuilt in 1915 after it had been set alight by suffragettes.

Breamore, Hants 690 C7, A combination of great house open to the public, associated museums, interesting church and picturesque village. The house is partly Elizabethan, particularly the main front of brick with stone dressings, but the centre section was rebuilt after a fire in 1856; it is full of interesting furnishings. The Georgian stables

Above and bottom centre: Breamore church, built around AD 1000.

Left: Bratton Castle ramparts.

Bottom left: *The Boy with the Bat*, c1760, in Breamore's great house.

house a collection of carriages; the Countryside Museum illustrates farming and farm-workers' lives through the ages. The church is exceptional – substantially of about AD 1000 with later alterations; one original arch has a message in Anglo-Saxon script, and there is a damaged Saxon crucifix, still impressive, within the porch. An enormous green lies to the west, loosely fringed with typical vernacular cottages, some timber-framed, others of old brickwork, many thatched; a second street of old houses lies further west.

Brechin, Angus 699 H2, This town on the South Esk is centred on its 13th-century cathedral. In the adjoining churchyard stands one of Scotland's two Irish-style Round Towers (the other is at Abernethy), a 110-foot (33m) building dating from the 11th century. The Pictavia Museum, which stands in the grounds of Brechin Castle, traces the history of the Picts.

Breckland, Norfk & Suffk 695 H6, An area of dry infertile soil covering 400 square miles (1036 sq km) of Norfolk and Suffolk, created from a mixture of wind-blown sands and glacial deposits. This and the combination of hot summers, cold winters and the lowest rainfall in Britain has produced a unique habitat supporting many rare Breckland plants and birdlife.

The heathland was first created by Stone-Age farmers, who cleared the light woodland using flint tools from Grimes Graves*. As the soil soon became exhausted, cultivated areas, or 'Brecks', became abandoned and new clearings opened up. Grazing soon created vast tracts of heath and Breckland became the main sheep-rearing area in medieval England. Rabbits, first introduced by the Normans, were farmed for their meat and fur in large enclosed warrens – a 15th-century warrener's lodge outside Thetford survives. Over-grazing often led to widespread soil erosion and sandstorms that partly buried Santon Downham in 1668. The agricultural depression of the late 19th century led to the creation of large shooting estates such as Elveden, Lynford and Merton, patronized by royalty and famous for the numbers of game birds slaughtered. Huge areas were also purchased by the Forestry Commission who planted up Britain's largest lowland pine forest, now managed as a Forest Park with picnic areas, woodland walks and a visitor centre at High Lodge. Elsewhere the distinctive Breck habitat is restricted to a few nature reserves – East Wretham Heath, Chippenham* and especially Weeting Heath where the rare stone curlew, the woodlark and the wheatear still breed. Here can be found the equally rare arable weeds – spiked speedwell, Spanish catchfly and bur medick, more typical of the Russian steppes.

Brecon (Aberhonddu), Powys 693 F6, The town takes its name from a Welsh chieftain, Brychan. One of its most impressive badges of pride is TH Wyatt's Shire Hall (1842), with its massive portico. Since the 1970s it has been the **Brecknock Museum**, the showpiece of the region's past. Although its central feature is the Assize Court, which was in use from 1843 until 1971, the collection is wide, varied and instructive, ranging from the county's earliest archaeological remains up to the earliest photographic images of town and country. Among the artefacts on display are those excavated at the Roman fort Y Gaer. **Y Gaer**, sometimes referred to as Brecon Gaer, west of the town, was probably built within 20 years of the Roman conquest, and

its site on the confluence of two rivers – the Usk and Yscir – was characteristic of the invaders' military tactics, as at Gobannium, later Abergavenny*. Set as it is amid farmland, only part of the fort excavated by Mortimer Wheeler in 1926 is accessible; but the remains of two towers and three gateways are displayed for visitors.

Bernard of Newmarch's castle was replaced in stone in the 13th century, and the remains of its Great Hall form a prominent feature of the castle's hotel. It was Newmarch who established the church of St John the Evangelist, contemporary with his castle in 1093 and probably built on the site of an earlier Celtic church. The austerity of the church, rebuilt from 1200 onward, is softened by an avenue of trees, and the uncluttered interior has a simple dignity. In 1923, the parish church, as it had become after the Dissolution, was chosen for the Cathedral of the Diocese of Swansea and Brecon after the disestablishment of the Welsh Church in 1920. The imaginative conversion of a 16th-century tithe barn in the 1990s encapsulates the rich heritage of this relatively unknown early Christian place of worship.

Brecon Beacons National Park, Powys 692 E6 & 693 F6 Inaugurated in 1957, the 520 square miles (1,346sq km) of this landlocked national park stretches into

Dyfed (Carmarthenshire) to the west, into Monmouthshire (Gwent) to the east, and beyond into the Herefordshire border. The Beacons themselves stand in the heart of the Park, with Pen-y-Fan, 'the Head of the Beacon', rising it to 2,906 feet (886m), making it the highest peak in South Wales. Although not as well known as the other two national parks in Wales (Snowdonia*, for the dramatic scale of its mountain ranges, and the Pembroke* Coast, for its spectacular coves, caves and beaches), the Brecon Beacons National Park's natural resources provide a wide range of interests for most ages. Llangorse Lake (Llyn Safaddan), the largest natural lake in South Wales, has excellent facilities for sailing and windsurfing. The Monmouthshire and Brecon Canal – the only canal to pass almost entirely through a national park – makes its way through rich agricultural countryside.

Above the small village of Libanus is the Brecon Beacons Mountain Centre. Opened in 1966, it is an attractive amenity, offering information, advice and refreshments. With magnificent views from a height of 1,100 feet (335m), it is an excellent place from which to get one's bearings.

Brede Place, E Susx 691 H7, Originally a 15th-century manor house. The Lord's Chamber and Chapel survive intact, the former with later panelling. The Hall was divided into two floors in the 16th century and given a new porch. The house belonged to the sculptor Clare Sheridan, and contains a selection of her work, including bronze busts of Lenin and Trotsky.

Brentor, Devon 688 E6, Visible for miles around, the church of St Michael de Rupe lies 1,130 feet (345m) above sea level on a volcanic outcrop and has been a place of pilgrimage for seven or more centuries. Built by the monks of Tavistock, it measures only 40 x 14 feet (12 x 4.3m) and the ancient tower is a mere 32 feet (9.8m) high, but it dominates a wide area of Dartmoor* and north Cornwall as well. There are also the remains of an Iron-Age hill fort.

Bridgnorth, Shrops 693 G4, The town enjoys a spectacular site on a tall sandstone cliff, honeycombed with caves, above the Severn. The broad High Street is lined with Georgian houses; at its centre stands the Town Hall of 1652.

Bridgwater, Somset 689 H4, This once-busy port was soon eclipsed by Bristol* to the northeast. Cromwell's troops savaged it, but its low-slung church of St Mary survived; it is a mixture of Decorated and Perpendicular styles, with a fine Jacobean screen in the south transept. Castle Street was begun in 1723 for the 1st Duke of Chandos, and The Lions on West Quay is a fine mansion of about 1730. There is plenty of other good early Georgian architecture, some by the London builder-architects Thomas Fort and Edward Shepherd (both of whom worked on

Above: Brecon Beacons. Their scale and character can be appreciated by driving from Merthyr Tydfil to Brecon along the A470.

Below: Bridgnorth, the bridge over the River Severn, seen from the upper town.

Cannons, the Duke's great Middlesex house, demolished in 1747).

Bridlington, E R Yk 697 K5, There are two distinct parts of Bridlington, the resort – or Quay – served by the railway, and with a harbour and north and south piers on the seafront, and the Old Town to the north. This consists mainly of one good Georgian street – where the exceptional late 20th-century conservation architect Francis Johnson had his practice – leading towards **Bridlington Priory.** Founded for Augustinian canons c1120, the nave now serves as a large and impressive parish church. The Bayle Gate was its gatehouse, crenellated in 1388.

Bridport, Dorset 689 H6, Fifteen miles (24km) northwest of Weymouth* is the best of Dorset's small towns, with three broad streets that form a junction where the late 18th-century Town Hall stands. The town is famous for its long history of rope-making (a 'Bridport dagger' is a hangman's halter). Its wide pavements were originally 'rope-walks' where the cord was laid out for twisting and drying. The wonderful views of the surrounding hills provide a superb backdrop to Bridport's elegant Georgian and Victorian façades, which sometimes conceal much earlier buildings. The Chantry in South Street is perhaps 14th century. The castle (now a Museum and Art Gallery) has a 16th-century stone façade. Bridport has a bevy of Non-Conformist chapels, with the 17th-century Meeting House of the Society of Friends taking pride of place opposite the 14th-century church of St Mary.

Right: Palace Pier with its
Art Deco ornament arcade.

Below: Brighton Pavilion,
a chandelier in the
Banqueting Room.

Brighton

Brighton, E Susx 691 F7, Brighthelmstone was a small fishing village until the mid-18th century, when its development as a seaside resort began. In 1786 the Prince of Wales (later George IV) chose it as a holiday home where he could be with Mrs Fitzherbert, whom he had secretly married, and began converting an old farmhouse into what is now the Royal Pavilion. His first architect was Henry Holland, who gave it two wings with bow windows linked by a central rotunda. In 1815 John Nash began transforming it into the wonderful Hindu-Chinese fantasy that we see today. It is equally amazing inside and out; the climax is the Banqueting Room, with a huge chandelier hanging from a silver dragon. Next to the Pavilion are the very large domed stables (1804) by William Porden, already Indian in style, which have been converted into a theatre. The very enterprising Brighton Museum can be found next door.

Top right: Gold dragon, detail from the Music Room.

Top left: Brighton Pavilion's exotic copper domes. On the right is the central Saloon, and on the left is the Music Room.

Below: The West Pier of 1863, partly demolished in a storm and now being restored at enormous cost.

The old fishing village of Brighthelmstone still exists: an area of tiny houses and alleys known as The Lanes, now mostly boutiques and antique shops. Outside this, to the east and west, there are still attractive areas of Regency houses. Kemp Town, on rising ground to the east, was developed in the 1820s, with squares and terraces on the model of Nash's Regent's Park in London*. To the west the ground also rises steeply. Here is the old parish church (the outstanding Norman font should not be missed, carved with reliefs showing the Last Supper and scenes from the life of St Nicholas) and more attractive terraces, merging into Hove*. On the

seafront itself insensitive modern development is compromising Brighton's old character. There are two piers, of which the older, the West Pier, is being restored at enormous cost.

Brighton is rich in interesting 19th-century churches. St Peter's, of 1824, is by Sir Charles Barry, architect of the Houses of Parliament*. St Bartholomew's, of 1872, by the local architect Edmund Scott, is a vast brick church, higher than Westminster Abbey*, with outstanding metalwork by the Arts and Crafts designer Henry Wilson. St Michael's is two churches, a small one by JF Bentley, architect of Westminster Cathedral*, which became the south chapel of a much larger one by William Burges (also responsible for additions to Cardiff Castle* and the remodelling of Castell Coch* in South Wales).

On the outskirts of Brighton is Preston Manor, an 18th-century house, now a rather unusual museum of 'upstairs' and 'downstairs' life in an Edwardian gentry home, with over 20 rooms, including a butler's pantry, servants' quarters, kitchens, attic bedrooms and a nursery.

Bottom: Brinkburn Priory, the Early English monastic church restored in 1858.

Brill, Bucks 690 D4, This hilltop village has excellent views of the surrounding countryside. The spot was chosen by Edward the Confessor for one of his palaces. The windmill dates from 1680.

Brinkburn Priory, Nthumb 699 J6, Occupying an idyllic wooded site beside a loop in the River

Coquet, the Priory [EH] was founded for Augustinian canons in 1135. The ruins of their church, a fine example of Early English architecture, were restored and re-roofed for use as a church again in 1858. There is a later manor house alongside.

B

Bristol

Left, centre left and far left:
The church of St Mary
Redcliffe, called by Queen
Elizabeth I 'the fairest,
goodliest, and most famous
parish church in England'.
Tapering spire, dramatic
outer door and the lofty
Perpendicular interior
conspire to warrant this
description.

Opposite page, top:
Clifton Suspension Bridge,
designed by Isambard
Kingdom Brunel in 1829.
But delay ensued: Brunel
died in 1858, and his daring,
graceful design was slung
across the Gorge and
completed in 1864.

Bristol, Bristol 689 H3, The Anglo-Saxon settlement at Bristol grew up around the bridge and harbour on the River Avon. With access to the sea, it increased in importance. From the flocks of sheep grazing on the local pastureland, most of it originally monastic, wool was sent out in the 14th century to the Baltic countries and Ireland. In 1497 John Cabot sailed from here to find the Americas, landing in Newfoundland (a replica ship accomplished the journey again in 1997), and in 1552 the Society of Merchant Venturers was founded here. The port did a flourishing trade, importing wines, tobacco and chocolate, and slaves bought in West Africa to be sold in the Indies. The emancipation of slaves in the 1820s, and the growing competition from Liverpool*, led to Bristol's decline. Further opportunities to develop came with the launching of Isambard Kingdom Brunel's steamships *Great Western* and *Great Britain*. The *Great Britain*, the first screw-propelled passenger ship, returned to Bristol in 1970 (for its restoration and an honoured place in the dock) after it had been abandoned in the Falkland Islands in 1886.

Brunel, whose London–Bristol railway line (1841) terminated in his gothic-style station of Temple Meads, had long been involved with Bristol. He had remodelled the docks in 1830, and six years later designed the **Clifton Suspension Bridge** over the 250-foot (76m) deep Avon Gorge. This, however, was delayed through inadequate funding, and not built until 1864 (five years after Brunel's death) by the Institute of Civil Engineers, as a tribute to their former colleague. Clifton, a residential suburb of Bristol, spreads from the downs above the city in Georgian and Regency terraces. Royal York Terrace, which looks out across the Avon Gorge, is the largest crescent in England.

Bottom left: The Wills Tower
of the University of Bristol,
built in 1925 in a bold display
of late gothic. One of Bristol's
landmarks, it stands at the
top of its principal street.

Bottom right: St Mark on
College Green, bought in 1541
as the official place of
worship for the Lord Mayor
and Corporation. The
dominant 15th-century west
window replaces that of
*c*1300 taken down in 1822.

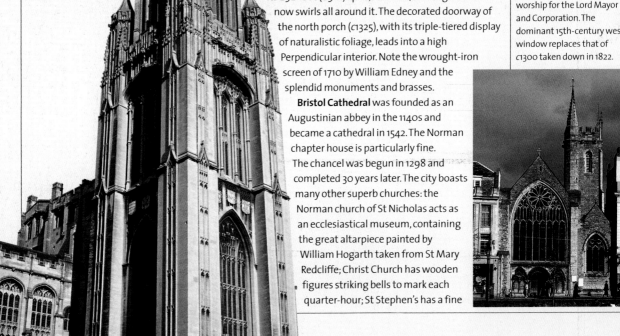

During the bombing raids of World War II many churches and historic houses were lost. Fortunately, the finest parish church in England, **St Mary Redcliffe**, with its 292-foot (89m) spire, survived, although traffic now swirls all around it. The decorated doorway of the north porch (*c*1325), with its triple-tiered display of naturalistic foliage, leads into a high Perpendicular interior. Note the wrought-iron screen of 1710 by William Edney and the splendid monuments and brasses.

Bristol Cathedral was founded as an Augustinian abbey in the 1140s and became a cathedral in 1542. The Norman chapter house is particularly fine. The chancel was begun in 1298 and completed 30 years later. The city boasts many other superb churches: the Norman church of St Nicholas acts as an ecclesiastical museum, containing the great altarpiece painted by William Hogarth taken from St Mary Redcliffe; Christ Church has wooden figures striking bells to mark each quarter-hour; St Stephen's has a fine

Perpendicular tower; and the Lord Mayor's chapel of St Mark on College Green is noted for its remarkable German, French and English stained glass (some bought by the Corporation at the 1823 sale of William Beckford's Fonthill). There are also some minor treasures – the wrought-iron sword rest of 1702 by William Edney, and the Poyntz chantry chapel of the 1530s with its Spanish floor tiles. Bristol has some interesting Georgian churches, too: Redland Chapel (1741–3) built by William Halfpenny for the London grocer John Cossins (his bust by Rysbrack is kept here), with its attractive woodcarving by Thomas Paty (1743); and the outstanding Christ Church of 1786 by William Paty. Regular concerts are given in St George's (on Brandon Hill, off steep Park Street), a church by Sir Robert Smirke of 1823, now transformed into a concert hall and used by the BBC for recordings.

At the top of Park Street, in Queen's Road, stands the imposing **Wills Tower** (1925) of the University, one of the landmarks of Bristol, designed by Sir George Oatley. Here also is the Museum and Art Gallery, with its collections of maritime effects, its blue Bristol glass, Cookworthy porcelain and paintings by the 'Bristol School' (Francis Danby and others) of the Avon Gorge and elsewhere. Pride of place should perhaps go to the two outstanding paintings by Sir Thomas Lawrence, PRA (1769–1830), a Bristol man; his portrait of Lady Caroline Lamb (1827) is particularly remarkable. Don't miss the houses maintained by Bristol's Museums Service, especially the 16th-century Red Lodge and the Georgian House, which contains 18th-century furniture and fittings.

There is almost too much to see in Bristol: other gems include John Wood's Corn Exchange of 1743, the Coopers' Hall by William Halfpenny, of the same year, the 1739 Grotto at Goldney House in Clifton, the long south façade (1635) of Ashton Court, and the 1669 Christmas Steps (off the beginning of Park Road). At the top is the tiny Perpendicular chapel of the Three Kings of Cologne (1504), with Foster's Almshouses of 1861 arranged around it.

King's Weston, on the city's outskirts, is a fine house, 1712–14, designed for Sir Edward Southwell, a lawyer, by Sir John Vanburgh. Like so many great houses, it has had a chequered history; now it is leased by the City of Bristol as a conference centre. The extensive grounds are open to the public, from which one can admire the exterior – the south entrance front, with its six Corinthian pilasters, and the amazing crenellated arcade of chimneys above the roofline.

Above: Bristol Cathedral. The lierne-vaulted Chancel, built at the end of the 13th century, has unusual cusps linking them together, and may have originated at Bristol. The aisles are the same height as the nave, a German device. Bristol was, however, only given Cathedral rank by Henry VIII in 1542.

Brixham, Devon 689 G7,
A bustling fishing port, as it was
in 1688 when William of Orange
landed here with 15,000 men
and 6,000 horses to claim
the English throne.
His statue stands
near the excellent
National Fisheries
Museum, which tells
the story of the
industry, and the
courage of the
Brixham men who
went forth to the
Newfoundland
fishing grounds
from the early 16th
century onwards.
Brixham also has literary
connections; Francis Brett
Young and Flora Thompson
lived in the town, and the
Reverend Henry Francis
Lyte, Vicar of All Souls,
wrote the hymn 'Abide
with Me'.

**Brixworth, Nhants
694 E6,** There is a
great barn
of a church
here, as
befitted the

Above: Broadlands, the
entrance side, by Henry
Holland, with a portico of
giant Ionic columns of
pink stone.

Left: Brixham, statue of
William of Orange.

Right: Broadlands, Sir Harold
Hillier Gardens.

former seat of a bishop, and not surprisingly as
it is essentially an early Christian basilica. Parts
of its fabric date probably from as early as the 7th
century AD. Pevsner claimed that, in size at least,
'it surpasses all other Anglo-Saxon churches
in England'. The crushingly heavy arches of
Roman bricks were once open and led to aisles,
which are now missing.

Broadclyst, Devon 689 G6, The estate village of the
Aclands of Killerton*, which lies a couple of miles
away. Assembled round the green are thatched
houses and shops; nearby, the church is large and
impressive. There are several grand tombs, but the
most elaborate is that of Sir John Acland (d. 1620),
the first of his line in Broadclyst, who had the
monument made during his lifetime.

Broadlands, Hants 690 D7, The Mountbatten family
home, just south of Romsey*, open to the public in
the summer; it was designed c1768 by Capability
Brown (who also remodelled the landscape) and
enlarged in 1788 by Henry Holland; there is an

WILLIAM
PRINCE of ORANGE.

exhibition on the life of Earl Mountbatten. In Victorian times this was the home of Lord Palmerston, Prime Minister. To the northeast are **Sir Harold Hillier Gardens** with a wonderful collection of trees and garden plants.

Broads, The, *see* **Norfolk Broads*.**

Broadway, Worcs 690 C3, Although crowded in the summer, the village is justly famous for its harmonious vernacular architecture and its association with the Pre-Raphaelite Brotherhood. The villages of the Vale of Evesham*, only a couple of miles away, are brick-built; Broadway is almost uniformly constructed of the local golden limestone. Its houses share the common Cotswold* features of ornamental chimneys, decorative high gables in the attic storey, and finely carved drip mouldings around their windows. William Morris began the 19th-century artistic influx while staying in Broadway Tower on the hill above. Henry James, John Singer Sargent and Frank Millet were all temporary residents. **Broadway Tower**, designed by James Wyatt in 1794, was built for Peggy, wife of the 6th Earl of Coventry, and is visible from their seat at Croome Court. Although the Tower has some of the fanciful and impractical elements of a folly, it was possibly built to celebrate the centenary of the Coventry earldom that was created in 1697. Certainly a huge bonfire and fireworks display were held at the Tower in 1797. It was sold in 1827 for use as a printing press, and later William Morris was the guest of Carmel Price, an Oxford don who repaired and redecorated it. On a clear

Above: Broadway Tower stands above the village of Broadway; it is a landmark that can be seen for miles around.

Below right: Brockhampton Manor House seen from across its moat. The building to the left is the unusual detached gatehouse.

day, 12 counties can be seen from the Tower, and it now forms the centrepiece of a country park.

Brockhampton, Herefs 693 G6, The lower house lies in a verdant valley, and survives because later owners chose the better views from the hillside above to build the 18th-century Brockhampton House. The 15th-century manor house [NT] is almost unrealistically picturesque with its moat and timbered gatehouse. Inside, the roof of the Great Hall is made of giant cruck blades supporting a festive quatrefoil decoration at the top.

Brocklesby Park, Lincs 697 K7, The mansion is of 1710 but has been much rebuilt and altered, most recently in the 1950s. Extending south is a 2-mile (3.2km) picturesque ride with a number of small garden structures, memorials and temples. At the end of the ride is the magnificent mausoleum commemorating Sophia Aufrere, designed by James Wyatt and built in 1792. Besides a statue of Sophia by the English sculptor Joseph Nollekens, it contains several other Pelham family monuments.

Brodick, *see* **Arran***.

Brodie Castle, Moray 701 J5, The Z-shaped tower-house built in 1567 and renovated in the 17th and 19th centuries is worth a visit for its collection of European paintings, French furniture and the remarkable ceiling of the dining room. In the gardens stands the Rodney Stone, a Pictish stone bearing an ogham inscription.

Brodsworth Hall, S York 697 H7, A starkly classical two-storey house of 1861–3 near Doncaster*, less

Brodsworth Hall
Above left: The ornate Drawing Room.
Above: A detail of the South Hall.

Right: Bronllys round keep. The accommodation of the keep comprised a room on each floor. It was declared beyond repair in 1521.

Italianate than Italian – designed by an architect from Lucca in Tuscany who never visited the site. The house [EH] was built from a £700,000 legacy, over which legal disputes lasted 60 years. They were eventually resolved by the House of Lords, and provided Charles Dickens with the idea for *Bleak House*. The will was that of London banker Peter Thellusson, and the house was built by his great-grandson, Charles Sabine Thellusson. It was intended for sumptuous Victorian entertaining, and the ground floor consists of a succession of grand and gracious spaces for the display of Thellusson's collection of fine Italian white marble statues, several of which are reflected in contemporary mirrors.

The house is particularly important as it retains most of its original furniture, fittings and decoration, including the wall-painting imitating red, green, grey and yellow marble, and silk wall-hangings and wallpaper, as well as carpets specially woven for their position, and the bright Minton tiles that match them. The Billiard Room is a true period treat, toplit and with padded leather, raised wall-benches and pictures of horses. Paintings of the Four Seasons by an unknown Flemish artist working c1600, based on concepts by the 16th-century Venetian painter Jacopo Bassano, returned to Brodsworth in 2001. Visitors can marvel at the large number of water closets in the house, and glimpse Victorian life below stairs.

The extensive gardens, which are still being restored, include the pleasure grounds near the house, with their formal lawns and colourful bedding, and a varied quarry garden.

Bromham, Beds 690 E3, The working watermill and Art Gallery are attractively sited by the River Ouse, where there is a bridge and causeway dating from the late 13th century. The church of St Owen contains a fine brass to Thomas Wideville (d. 1435) and his two wives.

Bromham, Wilts 690 B5, This church repays a visit if only for its Tocotes and Beauchamp Chapel, licensed in 1492. Inside it has a fine painted ceiling, and inside are monuments to Sir Richard Tocotes (1457) and Elizabeth Beauchamp (c1492). There are also good monumental brasses.

Bromley, Gt Lon 691 G5, In a town that has not been improved by modern developments, the most interesting building is Bromley College, built from 1670 onwards as a home for 20 widows of clergymen. It forms a quadrangle of brick cottages, each with four rooms and a kitchen, bounded by a cloister. A second quadrangle was added about 1800. One can normally walk round freely.

Bronllys, Powys 693 F6, Like Tretower*, Bronllys boasts a round keep. It is all that survives of the 13th-century stone reconstruction of a timber castle of the late 1080s, but the severe slope of the motte on which it stands gives some indication of its former defensive strength. It is an example of a first-floor entry stronghold, and the space beneath, reached by trap-door, would have been used for stores. First and second floors are accessible, and the view looks down on a private house and stables built within the castle's inner bailey.

Brookland, Kent 691 H6, The church of St Augustine is remarkable for its free-standing, octagonal wooden belfry with three diminishing stages of roof; the interior, with four vast vertical posts, is worth inspecting. Inside the church are 13th-century wall-paintings and a Norman lead font with reliefs illustrating the labours of the months and the signs of the zodiac.

Brough Castle, Cumb 697 F4, Brough is on a dramatic site in the Pennines, which was previously a Roman settlement. What is seen now is the result of a rebuilding by William the Lion, King of Scotland, after the Scots had burnt an earlier English castle, and some rebuilding and alterations in the 17th century by Lady Anne Clifford. Her medievalizing work merges with the original to form a handsome ruin that dominates the road across the hills.

Brougham Castle, Cumb 696 E3, This medieval castle with a keep and curtain wall [EH] is situated just outside Penrith*. As at Brough* and Appleby*, there was medievalizing work by Lady Anne Clifford in the 17th century. Her hand is less obvious in the castle than in the nearby churches of St Ninian and St Wilfrid, and the Countess Pillar, erected in 1656 to commemorate her mother's death 40 years earlier. Nearby, at Yanwath, is **King Arthur's Round Table,** a henge monument some 300 feet (90m) in diameter, now only traceable as an earthen bank – though standing stones, which still survive at Castlerigg*, were recorded in the 17th century.

Broughton Castle, Oxon 690 D3, One of the county's most complete medieval houses, begun c1308 and still surrounded by its impressive moat. The castle was remodelled during the late 1500s, but the original hall and a 14th-century domestic chapel both survive. The house is usually attributed to John de Broughton, a knight of Edward I, whose effigy can be seen in the church.

Broughton Castle
Right: View towards the gatehouse and church. The gatehouse dates from the late 14th century.
Below right: The Great Hall, incorporating part of the medieval hall of 1300. The pendant plaster ceiling dates from the 1760s.
Left: The Ladies Garden, established in the 1880s on the site of the 16th-century kitchens.

Bottom: Brough Castle, the keep and curtain wall.

Broughton Hall, N York 697 F5, This elegant classical mansion conceals within it an Elizabethan house, improved in the late 17th century, when water gardens were created. Further alterations were made in 1722, the building was re-fronted *c*1750, and pedimented flanking wings attached in 1809. George Webster of Kendal added a portico to the north front, an imposing chapel tower and porte-cochère in 1838–41. Handsome Regency rooms contain furniture by Gillow of Lancaster*. Since medieval times Broughton has been the home of the Tempest family, who have steadfastly retained their Roman Catholic tradition, and there is a gothic chapel here. The large conservatory of 1853 is by Andrews and Delaunay of Bradford, and the Italianate parterres of 1855 are a rare survival of the work of WA Nesfield.

Brownsea Island, Dorset 690 C8, The island, acquired by the National Trust in 1962, is now a haven for a rich variety of wildlife, including the threatened red squirrel. Boat trips to the island from Poole*,

Swanage* and Bournemouth* are popular. The island has a Henrican castle, a garrison in the Civil War. The church of St Mary (1853–4) is now a museum, but has impressive Dutch and Venetian sculptures, collected by AF Cavendish-Bentinck.

Browsholme Hall, Lancs 697 F6, For centuries this has been the home of the Parker family, who held the delightfully titled office of Bowbearer of the Forest of Bowland. The house is set in the remote countryside on the western slopes of the Pennines. A rather plain Elizabethan stone house was embellished in the 17th century with an elaborate frontispiece of three superimposed classical orders and there were subsequent alterations by Sir Jeffry Wyatville. The house has furniture and pictures, including family portraits by Arthur Devis, which emphasize the character of the family home. One of the watercolours is a view of the house by Turner, who did many local paintings and drawings under the patronage of Reverend TD Whitaker.

Broxbourne, Herts 691 F4, A lively village a little way south of Ware following the old road between

Above: Browsholme Hall, the entrance hall.

Left: Brownsea Island appears as a forest rising in the middle of Poole Harbour. The church and castle there vie for attention with the abundance of wildlife.

London and Hertford (the A1170), with its large, open green traversed by the New River. Broxbourne is a haven for commuters and has many charming spots, mostly centred around the extensive and wonderful Lea Valley Recreational Park, and the fine medieval church of St Augustine. For those feeling energetic there is the Lido, with rowing boats for hire.

Bruton, Somset 689 J4, The 14th-century church of St Mary is one of the best in the county. To the west of the church can be found remains of the Augustinian priory wall, and the buildings of King's School (16th–19th century). Not far from the main bridge over the River Brue is an early packhorse bridge. Gants Mill is a working watermill, surrounded by an attractive garden.

Brympton D'Evercy, Somset 689 H5, The house is not open, but with its garden, chantry house and church of St Andrew, it makes a very satisfying ensemble of Ham stone buildings. Within the church, lit by three brass chandeliers, is 14th- and 15th-century glass, a mid-15th-century bellcote and a Jacobean pulpit.

Buckden, Cambs 695 F6, A village of brick and timber houses a short distance southwest of Huntingdon* is distinguished by its spacious church with fine monuments and Tudor brick towers. Catherine of Aragon, discarded by Henry VIII, was sent to Buckden Towers – whose restored 15th-century gateway and massive Great Tower remain from the Bishop of Lincoln's palace and are now occupied by Catholic missionaries.

Buckfast, Devon 689 F6, Lying just east of the Devon Expressway (the A38), this was once a wealthy weaving town. Here the terminus of the Buckfastleigh Steam Railway leads down through the valley of the Dart to Totnes. To the north of the road, and well hidden from it, is Buckfast Abbey, the site of perhaps the richest medieval Cistercian monastery in the west of England. In 1882 it was acquired by the Benedictine Order, which began to erect a temporary church (now the chapterhouse) in the same year. Most of the

Top left and right: Buckfast Abbey was built on the 12th-century foundations and is on the same plan as the original Cistercian church.

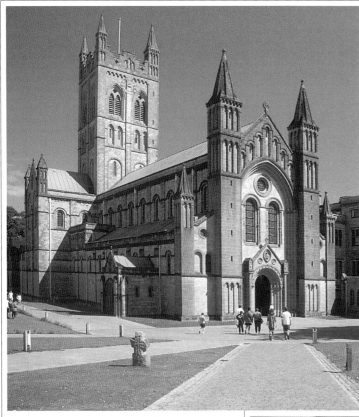

large church was built by the monks themselves of grey limestone with Ham stone dressings and an interior of Bath stone, and was dedicated in August 1932. More spectacular furnishings are by Bernhard Witte of Aachen and date from the late 1920s.

Buckingham, Bucks 690 D3, Thanks to the removal of court and administrative business to Aylesbury* by the 1700s, Buckingham has remained unspoilt and full of atmosphere. There are plenty of good buildings, constructed after a major fire of 1725. Of particular note are the Town Hall, finished in 1784, and the very handsome Old Gaol (Market Hill), built in 1748. This is now a museum with 'cell' shop and displays

Buckland Abbey
Above: The Drake Chamber.
Bottom left: Portrait of Sir Francis Drake, 1591, after Gheeraerts.
Bottom right: The Abbey exterior.

on the town's past. One important medieval building escaped the fire, the Buckingham Chantry Chapel. This was reconstructed in 1475, retaining a rich Norman doorway, and was rebuilt again in 1875 by Sir George Gilbert Scott.

Buckland Abbey, Devon 688 E7, To a greater degree than in many other abbeys converted into homes after the Dissolution, the form of the original Abbey church is easily discernible. After he became rich from his voyages and from royal patronage, Sir Francis Drake purchased the property from Sir Richard Grenville of *The Revenge*, and it is now largely a memorial to this great Devon seadog. His famous drum is kept here, together with many other mementoes and portraits. Fire ravaged the mansion in 1938; but

the nearby Tithe Barn, some 159 feet (48.5m) long remains a testimony to the wealth of the Cistercians who bred sheep on this part of Dartmoor* from 1278.

Bude, Cnwll 688 E5, A pleasant and traditional holiday resort, which is divided by the Bude Canal, built in the early 19th century for transporting sand to enrich the soil of the farms towards Launceston*. More ancient is the adjoining town of Stratton, on whose outskirts the Battle of Stamford Hill was fought in 1643, when the Royalist Sir Beville Grenville led his troops to victory.

Budleigh Salterton, Devon 689 G6, The pebble beach has perhaps preserved this little seaside town from the mass tourism that afflicts Exmouth* and Torquay*. Instead, a peaceful atmosphere pervades the pleasant streets and *cottages ornés*. John Everett Millais stayed in a house at the beginning of South Parade, and remembered its wall when he painted his *Boyhood of Raleigh*. Fairlynch, the town museum, is nearby and has a fine collection of costume and lace.

Buildwas Abbey, Shrops 693 G4, The abbey monks were of the Cistercian order, whose buildings were austere and without much ornament, though nearly always given beautiful and remote settings. Here the buildings nestle within a loop of the River Severn, with the cloisters between the church and the river. The massive nave walls and the crossing are well preserved [EH].

Bungay, Suffk 695 J5, Almost an island, surrounded by water-meadows in a huge loop of the Waveney. Home to Black Shuck, a ghostly dog that ran amok in the church during a storm in 1577, this delightful market town grew up around the

Top: Burford House was built in 1728 for William Bowles, who was then owner of a glassworks at Vauxhall.

Above: Buildwas Abbey, the vaulted ceiling of the Chapter House.

Bungay
Left: Remains of the medieval castle gatehouse.
Bottom left: Handsome Georgian buildings line the narrow streets of the market place.

massive keep of Roger Bigod's castle, notable today for its early 13th-century gatehouse. Also Norman was the Benedictine nunnery founded by Gundreda, and the round tower of Trinity Church, but more imposing is the landmark tower of St Mary's that, unlike the priory, escaped the disastrous fire of 1688. Another survivor (*c*1500) opposite has three carved cillboards: a sinuous Hercules wrestling two dragons, Samson and mermaids. The town's focal point is its domed Butter Cross, a charming octagonal structure on Tuscan columns erected just after the fire and surmounted, since 1754, by a handsome statue of Justice. Elaborate wrought-iron brackets nearby announce old coaching inns, just two signs of Bungay's Georgian prosperity that also supported the Fisher Theatre in Broad Street, one of England's oldest theatres, today undergoing restoration.

Bunny, Notts 694 D4, Bunny was the home of Sir Thomas Parkyns, 'the wrestling baronet', a lawyer and an enthusiast both for wrestling and for building. Sir Thomas died in 1741 and inside the large mostly 14th-century village church is his monument, on which his carved marble figure stands poised, ready for the next wrestling bout. A short distance from the church is **Bunny Hall**. The part designed by Sir Thomas himself and built in the 1720s is a slightly mad building with a square tower, a huge round pediment and stone decorations all jumbled together. In the village are the plain brick school and almshouses built by Sir Thomas in 1700.

Buntingford, Herts 691 F3, St Peter's is a remarkable building of 1614–26 with a Greek cross plan (the porch and apse were added in 1899). Wards Hospital is a handsome almshouse built in 1684 by Bishop Seth Ward, a friend of Christopher Wren.

Burford, Oxon 690 C4, Burford is the oldest of the small Oxfordshire medieval towns, with merchants' guilds established by the end of the 11th century. The town was a principal crossing point, as Witney Street was the main Oxford and London road and Sheep Street the route to Wales and the West. The museum with its pillared front was the collection point for toll charges and the focus of town business. The Old Vicarage at the bottom of the hill is a striking house of 1672, which has three Dutch gables and very large mullion and transom first-floor windows. The other Old Rectory in Church Street is attributed to Christopher Kempster, one of Wren's City masons who was born in Burford. His name, together with that of Smith of Warwick, has been associated with the Wesleyan in the High Street (only a chapel since 1849). It is an architectural gem with a rusticated façade, fluted giant Corinthian pilasters and a crowning balustrade. The Great Almshouses were founded in 1457 by Warwick the Kingmaker, although they were rebuilt in 1828. The fine 12th- and 15th-century church was a point of debate in the late 1800s when William Morris protested at its thorough restoration. The vicar is reputed to have responded: 'The church Sir is mine, and if I choose to I shall stand on my head in it.'

Burford House Gardens, Shrops 693 G5, The plain red-brick house originally had wings, now demolished. The 4-acre (1.6ha) gardens are home to the national clematis collection, and include a garden house with a Tuscan portico.

Burgh Castle, Norfk 695 K5, One of nine remaining Roman 'Forts of the Saxon Shore' and among the earliest survivals of East Anglian flint architecture. Burgh Castle [EH], known as Gariannonum in Roman times, was built in the late 3rd century and abandoned around AD 408. Now land-locked, it originally stood on a broad bay. Three sides of the fort's massive walls still

Top: Burford, a picturesque town with houses tumbling down the High Street towards the river.
Above: Tucked behind the High Street is Burford Church with its elegant spire.

Below: Burgh Island at low tide. At high tide a sea tractor transports visitors across to the island.

loom large, together with bastions built to hold catapults. St Fursey founded a monastery here in the early 7th century.

Burgh Island, Devon 689 F7, Joined to the mainland at Bigbury on Sea by a causeway, which is flooded at high tide. Burgh Island has ancient ruins, a pub devoted to the local smuggler Tom Crocker, and an Art Deco hotel built by Archibald Nettlefold, who had married the Princess Pearl, daughter of a Rajah of Sarawak, in 1929. He created a fashionable resort, which was much frequented by Agatha Christie and Noel Coward.

Burghead, Moray 702 B4, This coastal resort built on the site of a Pictish stronghold is famous for the 'Bulls of Burghead', six carved stones dating from the 7th–8th century. Two of these stones are housed in the town library, two in Elgin* Museum, one in the Museum of Scotland in Edinburgh* and one in the British Museum in London*.

Burghley House, Lincs 695 F5, Rising up majestically just outside Stamford*, this is one of four great houses by William Cecil, Secretary of State to Elizabeth I. 'God send us both long to enjoy Her, for whom we mean to exceed our purses in these', wrote Cecil to Sir Christopher Hatton, referring to the queen whom they both served and to the vast mansions they were building in her honour. Begun in the 1550s and finished by 1587, Burghley was intended as a showpiece, and certainly the enormous stone palace with its fantastic silhouette of towers and chimneys is an unforgettable sight. The house is built round a courtyard, with the Great Hall and kitchen on the east side and the other principal living rooms on the first floor of the other three sides. Little of the Elizabethan interior of survives. The Tudor state rooms were redecorated in the 1680s by the 5th Earl of Exeter and the ceilings covered with paintings by the fashionable Italian decorative painter Antonio Verrio, who lived at Burghley for ten years while the painting was in progress. His most spectacular work is in the Heaven Room. At the same time the Long Gallery on the west side was divided up into a series of smaller rooms. The redecoration was still unfinished in 1700 when the earl died, and the rooms were not completed until about 1800. The earl had been a great collector, and the treasures he brought back from his travels in Europe form the core of the Cecil family's huge collection of paintings, which covers most of the walls. The large park surrounding Burghley was landscaped in the mid-18th century by Capability Brown, who also designed the gothic stables and greenhouse. The grounds now host the famous Burghley horse trials.

Top: The west front, which was the original entrance front, with its tall gatehouse and exquisite iron gates by Tijou.

Above: The Third George Room with a ceiling by Verrio.

Right: The Great Hall with its tall hammerbeam roof and vast chimneypiece.

Burnham-on-Sea, Somset 689 H4, The white lighthouse draws visitors towards the resort's 7 miles (11km) of sandy beach, but many also come to see the marble remnants of the Whitehall Altar in the church. The altar was originally carved in 1687 by Grinling Gibbons and his partner, Arnold Quellin, for the chapel at Whitehall Palace. When the Catholic chapel was dismembered, the pieces were moved to Hampton Court* and then to Westminster Abbey*. There they remained until 1820, when George IV gave the kneeling angels and reliefs to the Vicar of Burnham.

Burnhams, The, Norfk 695 H4, A remarkable group of seven close-knit medieval parishes, once prosperous from water-borne trade on the River Burn. **Burnham Market** is the largest and most precious, with handsome Georgian houses and specialist shops (catering mainly for London weekenders) gathered around an elongated green. On the hill **Burnham Norton**'s round-towered church of St Margaret is a local landmark; its 15th-century pulpit depicts the four Doctors of the Church. Below it in the valley there is early 14th-century flint flushwork on the gateway to the remains of a small Carmelite friary. St Mary's Church at **Burnham Deepdale** on the coastal road has one of England's most spectacular Norman fonts, with vigorous high-relief carvings of the

Left and bottom left: Burnham Market. Rows of 18th-century red-brick houses, many now specialist shops, line the green.

Burnham Thorpe
Below: The church is a shrine to Nelson's memory and several members of his family are buried here.
Bottom right: Lord Nelson's medicine chest, on display in the church.

Labours of the Months. The National Trust has restored **Burnham Overy**'s watermill (1737) and windmill (1814), reminders of its Georgian agricultural prosperity. Horatio Nelson (1758–1805), who gave eye, arm and ultimately life for his country, was born in **Burnham Thorpe** rectory. His childhood home has gone, but the restored church (where the White Ensign flutters from the tower, and oak from the flagship *Victory* has been carved into the lectern and crucifix), Nelson Hall and time-warp local pub (without a bar) still pay homage to the naval hero.

Burnley, Lancs 697 F6, An old town more or less completely overlain by the effects of the Industrial Revolution; it was a centre for the weaving of cloth from yarn, which was mainly spun further south in Lancashire. Near the town centre is the Weavers' Triangle, a restored complex by the Leeds and Liverpool railway, which crosses Burnley on a spectacular embankment. Further out is Queen Street Mill, a weaving mill driven by a surviving steam engine. The engine has been preserved; the mill still works occasionally and gives an unrivalled experience of how noisy a 19th-century factory was.

Burston, Norfk 695 J6, Strike School (1900), on the green, is a museum and monument to the longest dispute in British labour history and stands alongside the Tolpuddle* martyrs in the annals of the Trade Union movement.

Burstow, Surrey 691 F6, The church has a striking timber tower, and its square base is weatherboarded, concealing aisles on three sides. The upper stages, the tower with corner pinnacles and the spire are shingled.

Burton Agnes

Burton Agnes, E R Yk 697 K5, Burton Agnes Hall was built 1601–10 for Sir Henry Griffiths, a member of the York-based Council of the North, knighted in 1603. Designed by the great northern Elizabethan architect Robert Smythson, the house is a symmetrical composition in East Riding brick. Standing guard at the roadside is the Gatehouse, with ogee-capped octagonal turrets and bearing the date 1610 on the coat of arms of James I. The drive is flanked by a yew avenue. The south front is totally symmetrical, even to the extent of having twin tower porches (the left one forms the entrance), and short wings projecting from each end have semicircular bow windows the full height of the house. The south front gives the impression of a three-storey building, but side views reveal that the top floor exists only to the south, where there is the handsome Long Gallery.

The ground- and first-floor windows in the centre of the south side light the amazing two-storeyed Great Hall. The left tower porch leads into a screens passage, the screen itself being one of the chief glories of the house, with more than 50 carved figures. The lower part, in oak, comprises two round arches, between paired Ionic columns, with Honour and Liberty, Peace and Concord carved on and above the keystones, and the Twelve Patriarchs of the Tribes of Israel on the entablature. It supports plaster bas-reliefs, in three tiers, of the Four Evangelists, Twelve Apostles and Theological Virtues. The immense chimneypiece has carved alabaster scenes depicting the parable of the Wise and Foolish Virgins. The Wise are on the left with trimmed lamps, dutifully spinning; the Foolish are on the right dancing the night away. The sumptuously panelled Drawing Room has another fascinating chimneypiece, this time of carved oak, showing –

somewhat incongruously to modern eyes – the Dance of Death, with a macabre skeleton trampling on symbols of earthly power. The remarkable staircase, with tall paired newel posts joined by short arches, leads to the handsome early 18th-century Upper Drawing Room, hung with excellent pictures, which include several Impressionist paintings, and two bedrooms with rich Jacobean panelling and plasterwork.

A short distance away stands the Hall's predecessor, **Burton Agnes Manor House** [EH], with a Norman vaulted undercroft with water-leaf capitals. On the first floor is the erstwhile Great Hall. Behind the building is the wheel of a donkey-engine that drew water from a well for drinking and washing. Nearby is the church of St Martin, which contains numerous fine monuments to the owners of both Manor House and Hall.

Above: a glimpse of the exciting modern gardens .

Left: Exterior view of the symmetrical house designed by Robert Smythson 1601–10.

Burton Constable

Right: The Staircase Hall of c1770 leading up to the Elizabethan Long Gallery, running south along the west front.

Burton Constable Hall, E R Yk 695 F1, Mainly of c1570 with 18th-century alterations, it was, as the name implies, the home of the Constable family [HH]. The east front gives an impression of length, despite its three-storey height and two almost symmetrical forward-projecting lower wings. The exterior is predominantly Elizabethan, of brick with stone dressings, and has ogee-topped turrets and large mullion and transom windows. Inside, most of the rooms have been Georgianized – with some decoration in an interesting Jacobean Revival style – but there is, as one would hope in so fine an Elizabethan house, a magnificent Long Gallery, which in the 18th century served the dual function of library and scientific laboratory. It still contains an interesting mixture of scientific instruments and souvenirs of the Grand Tour. This mix of curiosity and science is reflected in the Museum Room which contains 'the most important Cabinet of Curiosities still in private hands', with air-pressure equipment vying with collections of shells and mineral specimens. The collection was brought together by William Constable (1721–91).

The splendid craftsmanship obvious in furniture and fittings reflects Constable's practice of obtaining plans from leading designers and often having them made up locally, proving that at its best provincial craftsmanship could equal that of London. The recent restoration of three mirrors adds magnificence to the Great Drawing Room, which had marked the final phase of the 18th-century remodelling, and is a rare survival of a room designed by James Wyatt.

The former deer park was landscaped by Capability Brown, and interesting garden buildings include a menagerie designed by Thomas Knowlton, gardener to Lord Burlington from nearby Londesborough, and an orangery by Thomas Atkinson.

Centre right: The Great Drawing Room.
Below: The east front, with a grid of mullion and transom windows, flanked by turrets, castellated towers and lower wings.

Burwell, Cambs 695 G6, An elongated Fen-edge village with good vernacular buildings and the moat of a castle where Norman rebel Geoffrey de Mandeville died in a siege. An Ely*-style octagon crowns its spacious Perpendicular church; within, local clunch (chalk) ornamentation complements roofs adorned with allegorical subjects and musician angels. A churchyard headstone records the 1727 conflagration that killed 78 people during a barn puppet show.

Bury St Edmunds, Suffk 695 H6, Laid out on the banks of the River Lark by Abbot Baldwin in the 11th century, Bury is a fascinating mixture of monastic power and Georgian prosperity, and ranks among the best provincial towns in England. Elegant yellow-brick houses line the rectangular pattern of streets, some merely façades to buildings that survived the 1608 fire. Abbeygate Street has good period shop fronts, but stucco and pale limestone were reserved for more illustrious civic buildings. Local gentry flocked to the Adam-style ballroom in Francis Sandys' 1789 Athenaeum on Angel Hill, staying, like Dickens, at the Angel Hotel he immortalized in *The Pickwick Papers*. Cupola House had been newly built for apothecary Thomas Moore when travel writer Celia Fiennes admired the view from its belvedere in 1698. Angel Corner, completed four years later in warm red brick, houses an impressive collection of timepieces, and Moyse's Hall, Norman dwelling turned House of Correction, is another excellent local museum. Robert Adam's stately Market Cross on the Corn Hill served as the town's theatre until William Wilkins's balconied Theatre Royal of 1819 was built, both period-piece and working playhouse [NT]. The late Georgian Corn Exchange, now a library and art gallery, was also replaced soon after by the heavy porticoed structure of 1861, complete with a statue of Ceres. A small monastery founded in AD 630 won fame 250 years later when the body of Edmund, East Anglia's martyred king, arrived here, and the Benedictine abbey built to house his saintly relics grew to become one of Europe's greatest shrines. Rubble fragments in the Abbey Gardens mark its extent, but only the two precinct gatehouses suggest the abbey's former grandeur: the Norman Gate, a perfection of Romanesque decoration, and the Great Gate below Angel Hill, a more sophisticated design built soon after the riots of 1327. Great illuminated manuscripts now grace the world's top museums but Jocelyn of Brakeland's late 12th-century *Chronicle* provides a unique insight into monastic strife under its authoritarian Abbot Samson. Two large medieval churches remain beside the monastic site: Tudor St James, elevated to cathedral status in 1912 with central tower now under construction, and the more interesting St Mary's. Its wonderful

Above: Bury St Edmunds' Church of St Mary, dating from the 15th century.

Perpendicular roof, adorned with a menagerie of carved beasts, real and imaginary, looks down on the tomb of Mary, sister of Henry VIII. The Presbyterian chapel in Churchgate Street, restrained and classical in red brick, with an unspoilt interior to match its Ipswich cousin, was built in 1710, the latest religious house to grace the town.

Buscot, Oxon 690 C4, Buscot Park [NT] is a neoclassical house of *c*1770 best known for containing – in the Parlour – the series of 1890 paintings by Burne-Jones called the *Sleeping Beauty (Briar Rose)*. It also houses the Faringdon Collection of furniture and artwork, and has an early 20th-century water garden by Harold Peto. In the village is **Buscot Old Parsonage** [NT], a Cotswold stone house of *c*1700 on the banks of the Thames.

Bushmead Priory, Beds 695 F6, A rare surviving refectory range from an Augustinian priory founded in 1195. The building has a good timber roof and contains wall-paintings and fragments

Above: Buscot Park, home to the Faringdons. The serene exterior of the house hides a wealth of treasures from the Faringdon Collection.

of stained glass.

Bute, Ag & B 698 C4, This small island in the Firth of Clyde has been a popular destination for Glaswegians for over a century. There are ferry services between Rothesay and Wemyss Bay (Ayrshire), between Rhudobach, at the north end of the island, and Colintraive on the Cowal peninsula.

Ardencraig Gardens are renowned for their fuchsias, water garden and aviaries.

Mount Stuart: Robert Rowand Anderson undertook the construction of this extravagant neo-gothic mansion in 1879–85 at the request of the 3rd Marquess of Bute. The cathedral-like appearance of the vast marble hall, with its stained-glass windows and vaulted ceiling studded with glass stars, the white marble chapel lit by purple-glass windows and the 'Horoscope' study, reveal the mystical leanings of this art lover, who was the patron of a dozen architects and financed some 60 building projects. There is an exceptional collection of paintings. With its pinetum, Victorian vegetable garden and beautiful informal gardens, the vast estate offers many pleasant walks.

Rothesay, the only town on the island, is a popular coastal resort whose fountains, winter garden (1924) and extravagant public toilets (1899), now a listed building, give it a certain outdated charm. In the 13th century, after two Norse occupations, Rothesay Castle was surrounded by a circular curtain wall punctuated by four round towers.

It was rebuilt in 1406 and became the summer residence of the Stewarts, who added the Great Tower in the 16th century. It was burned by the Earl of Argyll in 1685 and has been partially restored since the 19th century. The Bute Museum, in the street next to the castle, presents the geology, fauna and history of the island, which was first occupied some 5500 years ago. Rothesay Creamery, the local cheese factory, presents a more up-to-date aspect of life on the island.

St Blane's Church: This ruined chapel at the sound end of the island, consecrated in the 12th century on the foundations of a 6th-century monastery, has kept its beautiful Norman vault.

Butley, Suffk 691 J3, Begun in 1171, Butley Priory became Suffolk's second richest medieval convent after Bury. Its early 14th-century gatehouse, whose carved stone and flint flushwork has been described as 'one of the noblest monuments of English monasticism', is preserved as a private house.

Buxton, Derbys 694 C3, There has been a spa here since Roman times and its water still provides a healthy income for the local council. The old part of Buxton straddles a hilltop (it is the highest market town in England), with its older buildings loosely grouped round the large main square. Some of the houses look 18th century and may be older, but they are all fairly modest in scale. It was at this time that the Duke of Devonshire, who owned most of the land, decided to turn Buxton into a fashionable spa resort that, he hoped, would rival Bath*. The mineral springs are at the foot of the hill on which the old town stands and here, over the foundations of the Roman spa, the Duke paid for the building of the extremely handsome **Buxton Crescent.** John Carr, the most highly regarded architect working in northern England at that time, was engaged to design it, and it was completed in 1780. The Crescent originally contained hotels and lodgings for those who had come to take the waters, and the very handsome, large **Assembly Room** in the style of Robert Adam for social gatherings. Next to the Crescent is the **Old Hall Hotel,** which is much earlier and stands

Top left: Buxton Crescent, John Carr's splendid architectural centrepiece for the new spa town.

Top right: Bushmead Priory, founded in 1195.

Right: Bute, Mount Stuart's east front, looking out to sea. The design of the house was refined over a 20-year period: the parapet was roofed over as an eaves gallery in the 1890s and the south wing (seen on left) was extended to include a gothic swimming pool in 1906.

Below: Butley Priory's gatehouse is a dazzling display of chequerwork decoration.

Above: Byland Abbey, view through the ruined church to the west front with its remarkable silhouette of half a rose window.

Right: Bute, Mount Stuart's Horoscope Study.

on the site of an even earlier building where Mary Queen of Scots stayed in 1573 when she came to take the waters. The slopes in front of the Crescent, which rise to the old town, were laid out as an ornamental pleasure ground in the early 19th century. Ten years after the Crescent was finished, Carr also designed for the duke a huge circular stable block to the north of it, which was converted into a hospital in the 1850s and then given a huge dome in the 1880s. This building is also empty. Nowadays, Buxton is best known for its summer festival, which centres round the Edwardian Opera House and the Glass Pavilion with its octagonal concert hall. **Poole's Cavern**, outside the town, is a spectacular succession of natural caves.

Byland Abbey, N York 697 H5, Cistercian monks finally began Byland in 1177, after various aborted attempts at a settlement nearby. The architecture is therefore transitional, between Romanesque and Early English, and the abbey has one of the most memorable west fronts of any monastic ruins, with one semicircular half of its rose window suspended from its flanking turret. But perhaps the greatest joy of Byland is its medieval pavements, in tiles of various colours and an amazing variety of geometric patterns [EH].

Cadhay, Devon 689 G6, Lying in lush pastures near Ottery St Mary, Cadhay was built in the mid-16th century, probably with stones from the demolished College of Secular Priests in Ottery. Notable features include the Central Court (dated 1617) of chequered sandstone and flint, with its four doors surmounted by statues of Henry VIII and his three sovereign children, the Great Hall with roof beams made of chestnut, and a Long Gallery. It stands in fine grounds with ponds and ancient trees.

Cae'r Berllan, Gwynd, A 17th-century miniature gentry house of unexpectedly sophisticated formality, in the middle of a hard-working farm. *See* **Castell y Bere* 692 E4.**

Caerhayes, Cnwll 688 D7, The gardens are world-famous as the home of Williamsii camellias. Descendants of JC Williams, the hybridizer, still live in the picturesque castellated mansion built by John Nash in 1808, which stands proudly overlooking the small lake and the open sea beyond.

Caerlaverock Castle, D & G 696 D2, The ruins of the castle built by the Maxwells on the northern shores of the Solway Firth are still an impressive sight. The castle, whose construction began *c*1270, was

captured by Edward I in 1300 and remained in English hands until 1312. It subsequently changed hands several times before being extended in the 15th and 16th centuries, and was finally abandoned in 1640. An impressive guardhouse and two 'drum' towers mark the corners of the triangular courtyard, which was surrounded by a defensive outer wall protected by a double moat. The 1st Earl of Nithsdale built the elegant Renaissance apartments overlooking the courtyard in 1621, before the castle was sacked in 1634 by the Covenanters.

Caerleon (Caerllion ar Wysg), Newpt 689 H3, The name is Welsh for 'legionary fortress', founded by the 2nd Augustan Legion in AD 75 as Isca, the Latin form of the River Usk or Wysg. It was one of three permanent legionary fortresses in Britain, and retains far more visible evidence than at Chester and York; indeed, it is in among the best-preserved Roman military sites in Europe, and includes the foundations of a legionary barrack-block (centuria) – the only example to survive. Such an establishment provided not only baths (thermae) and a swimming pool (natatio), but a

Above: Caernarfon Castle, Edward I's largest castle in Wales and remarkable not only for its scale but also for its polygonal towers and banded masonry.

Left: Caerlaverock Castle has water-filled moats, an unusual triangular layout and beautiful Renaisaance carvings. Three miles (5km) away is the Caerlaverock Wildfowl and Wetlands Centre, where some 12,000 geese over-winter.

sequence of rooms of varying temperatures from the cold (frigidarium) to the warm (tepidarium) and the hot (caldarium). The interpretation of this aspect of life in the fortress is fascinating in its reconstructive and illustrative detail. Outside the enclosure is the oval amphitheatre, used not only as a training-ground for the soldiers, but also for displays of physical and sporting prowess. Contemporary with the Colosseum in Rome, the arena had eight entrances, two for performers and six for spectators, of whom there could be as many as 6,000. In Welsh legend, it was identified as the site of King Arthur's Round Table; and, according to *The Mabinogion*, Arthur held court at Caerleon since it 'was the most accessible place in his dominions by sea and by land.' In 1867, Alfred Tennyson stayed at the local Hanbury Arms in order to absorb the atmosphere in preparation for *The Idylls of the King*.

The Legionary Museum in the High Street is housed in a handsome classical building and offers a comprehensive display of artefacts illustrating aspects of Roman life at the fortress. It is organized under the aegis of the National Galleries and Museums of Wales (*see* Cardiff*).

Caernarfon, Gwynd 692 D2, Probably the most visited of Edward I's castles; it was to Samuel Johnson 'an edifice of stupendous majesty and strength'. But the site was by no means new as a defensive strong point, as Romans, Normans and Welsh had all profited from the ample protection afforded by its position by the River Seiont and the Menai Strait. The Romans adapted the name of the river for their settlement of Segontium, which Agricola established in AD 78 as an auxiliary fort, with the symmetrical arrangement of four gates, a centrally placed administrative centre and rows of barracks and ancillary buildings. Fully excavated in the 1920s, it is now well interpreted in the site museum. Among the displays are coins depicting Magnus Maximus (late 4th century), better known to readers of the Welsh tales *The Mabinogion*, as the Roman emperor Macsen. Macsen saw in his dream a beautiful woman who lived at Caer Aber Seint, 'the fort on the mouth of the River Seiont' and set out to find her and to make her his empress. Edward I's fortress was more than a forceful means to overcome the Welsh. It was a statement of regal power through which he could relate to the glories of Constantinople, whose polygonal towers with their banded masonry Caernarfon emulated. The two-warded castle is dominated by the Eagle Tower – Magna Turis – with three turrets each displaying a stone eagle, the symbol of imperial Rome.

It was at Caernarfon Castle that Prince Charles was invested as Prince of Wales in 1969, in a ceremony designed by Lord Snowdon but largely based on that planned in 1911 for his great-uncle, who reigned briefly as the uncrowned Edward VIII. This had been the idea of David Lloyd George, the constable of the castle and MP for Caernarfon, to whom there is a statue in the Square (Y Maes). The ground floor of the Chamberlain Tower is used for displays and exhibitions. The Queen's Tower houses the museum of the Royal Welsh Fusiliers, and part of the East Tower offers an audio-visual interpretation of the castle's history. The layout of the original bastide town is clearly discernible, and although only one building, No. 6 Palace Street, evokes a pre-19th-century spirit of place, the Welsh identity of Caernarfon is well conveyed by the varied structures that constitute Pencadlys Gwynedd, the County Hall.

Top left and centre left: Caerphilly Castle, renowned for its leaning tower as much as for its size. The layout of the castle displays considerable defensive sophistication. The restored Great Hall is used for receptions.

The Cairngorms
Top right: Golden eagles hunt in the wild mountain regions.
Bottom and right: The Cairngorms were formed by the most recent Ice Age. At high altitude they are characterized by scree slopes and vast plateaus covered with Arctic-Alpine vegetation. The lower slopes are carpeted with heather or wooded with pines, and glacial depressions are filled with small lochs.

Rows of cars and a host of many-coloured leisure craft now occupy the harbour, once full of activity associated with the slate trade.

Caerphilly Castle, Caerph 689 G3, Gilbert de Clare, a powerful Marcher lord, built what was the largest non-royal castle in Britain at the end of the 13th century. It had a formidable structure and elaborate water defences.

Cairngorms, Highld 701 J6, The range of granite mountains known as the Cairngorms covers an area of 100 square miles (259sq km) in the heart of the Grampians, between Strath Spey and Braemar. It has around 50 summits over 3,000 feet (914m) high and reaches its highest point at Ben Macdui (4,925 feet/1,500m). Most of the Cairngorms have been classified as a nature reserve to protect their delicate plants and wildlife, which include species only found in Scotland.

Caister Castle, Norfk 695 K5, The moated 15th-century castle was built for Sir John Fastolf (model for Shakespeare's Falstaff), and allegedly funded by ransom money paid for a French knight captured at Agincourt. It was subsequently

besieged, as the Paston mercantile family and the Duke of Norfolk fought for ownership. Now a motor museum, the castle is said to be visited one midnight each year by a ghostly carriage pulled by four headless horses.

Caistor St Edmund, Norfk 695 J5, The site of the Roman garrison town of Venta Icenorum, built after Boudicca's defeat in AD 61 and abandoned in the 4th century, south of Norwich* in the Tas Valley. The large rectangular space grazed by sheep within raised banks has well-preserved sections of wall. The parish church in the southeast corner is built of reused Roman bricks.

Calder Abbey, Cumb 696 D4, Like Furness*, this was founded as a Savignac monastery but merged with the Cistercians in 1147. Significant remains of the abbey survive, some of them in an 18th-century house built on the site. The best upstanding part of the church is the north arcade of the nave, with

alternating quatrefoil and octagonal piers of the monastic buildings, the chapter house and dormitory. Not far away are the pioneer buildings of the British nuclear industry at Sellafield.

Caledonian Canal, 701 G6, The canal was built between 1803 and 1822 by Thomas Telford according to plans by James Watt. It was designed to link the North Sea and the Atlantic so that

Left: The Caledonian Canal links the North Sea with the Atlantic Ocean. It provided a useful route for 19th-century merchant shipping that avoided the hazards of the sea journey around Scotland's north coast.

Calke Abbey
Top: The flower garden
Bottom left: The south front
Bottom right: Tilly Kettle's portrait of Frances Harpur with her son Henry.

merchant ships did not have to make the long, dangerous journey round the north coast of Scotland. The lochs of Glen Mor make up a major part of this 60-mile (96km) waterway, so that only about 20 miles (32km) had to be constructed. Given the size of modern vessels and the small capacity of its locks, the canal is today used only by pleasure craft.

Caledonian Forest, Highld 701 F6, Written records left by the Romans refer to the 'great Caledonian forest', a huge forest of Scots pines that covered much of Scotland. At the time it was inhabited by bears, wild boars and wolves, animals that have today disappeared from the region. While it retains some pines that are over 400 years old,

only small stretches of this forest remain (1 percent of its original area).

Calke Abbey, Derbys 694 D5, Although the house is famous for being one of those that time forgot, it was not so much forgotten by time as owned by a succession of slightly eccentric Harpur-Crewes, many of whom lived as recluses, rejecting not only society but also such modern comforts as running water and electricity. They did not throw away possessions they did not want, but merely piled them up in one room after another and shut the doors. When the estate was acquired by the National Trust in 1975 all these accumulations came to light, and were then lovingly preserved. As its name suggests, Calke was originally a priory of Augustinian canons. The Harpur family first acquired the property in the 1570s, and embedded in the present house are the remains of a Tudor mansion built round an open courtyard; but the modern visitor sees a slightly clumsy baroque front of 1701 with a Greek Revival portico added in 1806. The architect responsible for the early 18th-century work is not known, and Sir John Harpur probably employed a local surveyor to build something adapted from more fashionable houses of the time. A handsome brick stable block was put up in 1712 by William Gilks, a local master builder, and in the 1760s a riding school was added. The house was given its present appearance in a long-lasting overhaul between 1789 and 1810 carried out for the 7th Baronet, first of the notable recluses. The interior is a muddle of incompetent planning but there are handsome rooms, particularly the Saloon (originally the Entrance Hall), the neoclassical Dining Room and the Georgian main staircase. A campaign of redecoration was carried out in the 1850s but nothing significant has been done since then. One of the chief pleasures of the interior, in both the grand rooms and the lesser spaces, is the rich and unusually varied mixture of paintings, furniture and other possessions.

Callaly Castle, Nthumb 699 J6, Once a typical Northumberland pele tower, it was improved during the 17th century – there is a sundial dated 1676 – and in the 18th century was transformed into a classical mansion of complex form. In about 1750 the interior was remodelled, and there is some fabulous plasterwork created by the same Italian *stuccatori* who worked on Wallington Hall*. The entrance hall and drawing room are particularly fine.

Callander, Stirlg 698 E3, This small town on the eastern edge of the Trossachs* is the region's main

Above: Callanish Standing Stones on the Hebridean Island of Lewis. They are thought to have been erected between 3000 and 1500 bc.

Right: Camber Castle was begun in 1511, but enlarged in 1539. It has a series of lobe-shaped platforms for cannons. The designer was probably an Austrian, Stefan von Haschenberg.

summer resort. Its many tea rooms and souvenir shops are part of a flourishing tourist industry which dates from the 19th century and owes much to the works of Walter Scott and William Wordsworth. The Rob Roy and Trossachs Visitor Centre, housed in a former church on Ancaster Square, presents a lively and romanticized version of the life of the famous outlaw. The slopes of Ben Ledi (2,885 feet/879m), to the northeast of Callander, offer some beautiful walks.

Callanish Standing Stones, W Isls 700 D2, This prehistoric site on the island of Lewis* consists of 50 standing stones erected in stages between 3000 and 1500 BC. Thirteen of the stones form a circle around a huge monolith and a small cairn which was probably a later addition. Two rows of standing stones form a cross within the circle, radiating out towards the four points of the compass. Together with Stonehenge*, it is one of the principal prehistoric sites in Britain.

Calne, Wilts 690 B5, This was once a clothiers' town, but apart from the church of St Mary, and some surrounding Georgian houses, little pre-19th-century building survives. In the church there is a fine organ case by CR Ashbee and the Campden Guild, c1905. There are two supermarkets, a new library and shops (in a style surely unsuited to the local vernacular), mostly on the central site of the now lamented Harris's Bacon Factory, founded about 1770. There is also a fine girls' public school (St Mary's).

Camber Castle, E Susx 691 H7, Built under Henry VIII on the model of Walmer* and Deal* castles, with six lobes surrounding a circular tower [EH]. Camber Sands, on the other side of Rye*, is a popular beach several miles long and still undeveloped. No esplanade, hotels or restaurants; only a lavatory and a fish-and-chip shop.

Cambridge

Cambridge, Cambs 695 G6, Situated on the southern edge of the Fens, this venerable university city of grand buildings and narrow streets continues to be both an educational centre of international repute and a backwater. It is an exhilarating blend of medieval courts and Tudor gatehouses, golden stone chapels and Renaissance libraries, green spaces, books, punts and bicycles where Town and Gown and tourists mingle more amicably than they have down the centuries.

Above: Emmanuel Chapel, built by Wren c1670.

Left: Mathematical Bridge, built in 1749 without the use of nails.

The original Celtic settlement had grown up on the north bank of the River Cam at the head of navigation before the Romans recognized its strategic importance and established the small town of Durovigutum at the junction of roads from London to Lynn and Chester to Colchester. Saxon occupation spread south of the river between Sidney and St Johns/Trinity streets where St Benet's, the oldest surviving church, has a Saxon tower. The Normans re-affirmed the defensive importance of the north bank with a castle, marked only by the motte in the grounds of Shire Hall. Two nearby churches have Romanesque remains, including St Peter's with its magnificent 12th-century triton font. In Bridge Street, despite drastic Victorian restoration, Holy Sepulchre Church (c1130), is the earliest of four surviving round churches in England. By this time Cambridge had become a prosperous town renowned throughout Europe for its annual fair held on Stourbridge Common under the auspices of St Mary Magdalen, whose Romanesque leper hospital, stranded between road and railway, remains unscathed.

Supposedly founded by unruly students expelled from Oxford in 1209 and from Paris 20 years later, Cambridge suspects it is an even older centre of learning – indeed the oldest in the land. Legend identifies St Amphibulus the Martyr as the first University Chancellor in AD 89. By the early 13th century several religious houses had been established and attracted sufficient students for Henry III to recognize Cambridge as a seat of learning in 1231. Peterhouse College, founded in 1284 by the Bishop of Ely, claims to be the oldest. Most of the 15 colleges in existence by the Reformation had grown out of the cloistered world of monastic scholarship. Remains of St Radegond's nunnery are incorporated in Jesus College; Sidney Sussex and Emmanuel colleges also occupy monastic sites east of the medieval city. By the 17th century the greatest concentration of colleges had developed outside the city gates, running south from Bridge Street between the Cam and the Trinity Street/Trumpington Street axis. A standard layout developed as student hostels attached to religious orders were replaced by more formal arrangements around a courtyard. Approached through its own impressive gatehouse, each college consisted of a master's house, accommodation for fellows and undergraduates, a great hall or refectory and a college chapel. Purpose-built libraries were often added later. Any tour of the old colleges should include:

Bottom left: King's College, begun in 1446.

Below: Christ's College courtyard.

Bottom right: Punting on the River Cam, with Clare College in the background.

Christ's College: Milton's college was founded in 1439 as 'God's House' and refounded by Lady Beaufort, Henry VII's mother, in 1505. The Fellows Building, three-storeyed with dormers, was added c1640 in the new classical style.

Clare College: Its three-storeyed court is a mixture of gothic and classical in Ketton stone. Thomas Grumbold's bridge c1640, gives access to the 'Backs'.

Corpus Christi College: Old Court is the oldest, most complete medieval quadrangle in Cambridge. The 1820s New Court is by Wilkins. The college owns a beautiful collection of silver plate and a library of illuminated manuscripts. Christopher Marlowe enrolled here.

Downing College: A relatively recent foundation of 1800. Monumental neoclassical buildings by William Wilkins round a spacious open quad.

Emmanuel College: Founded in 1584 on the site of a Dominican friary as a theological college. The graduate exodus to New England included John Harvard, founder of the American College. It has an exquisite Wren chapel of c1670.

Gonville and Caius College (pronounced 'keys'): Founded by Edmund Gonville in 1349 and re-endowed by Dr Caius in 1557 on his return from Italy. His increasingly monumental Gates of Humility, Virtue and Wisdom, and Honour, represent student progress.

Jesus College: Visitors are greeted by the statue of founder Bishop Alcock of Ely (1496), on his beautiful gate tower. The chapel is an impressive remnant of the original Romanesque nunnery church with a beautiful 13th-century chancel resurrected by Pugin in 1846. It also has important Pre-Raphaelite glass, and a painted ceiling. Coleridge studied here.

King's College: The Perpendicular chapel, begun in 1446 and financed by Henry VI and VIII, is one of Europe's great gothic buildings, a mixture of breathtaking fan vaulting, stained glass, carved screen and choir stalls. Its beautiful proportions are further emphasized by Gibbs' long and low classical Fellows Building of 1723. Former pupils include Maynard Keynes and EM Forster.

Above: Aerial view of Cambridge, with King's College Chapel prominent in the centre and the Backs curving round behind the colleges.

Magdalen College: The Abbot of Crowland built the first students' hostel here on the west bank of the Cam in 1428. The main attraction is Pepys' Library, a graceful colonnaded building erected to house the old boy's bequest, including the famous diaries that remained undeciphered and unpublished for over 200 years.

Pembroke College: Founded in 1347 by Mary, Countess of Pembroke. The original late 14th-century gatehouse has survived stone cladding of 1717. Wren's 1664 temple-style chapel, his earliest work in Cambridge and first clear statement of the new architecture, was a gift to the university from his uncle, the Bishop of Ely.

Peterhouse College: This earliest foundation has a splendid Dutch-gabled chapel begun in 1632, for Matthew Wren, and is transitional between the Perpendicular style of King's and his nephew's design for Pembroke.

Queen's College: The brick-built Front Court and Gatehouse date from its 1446 foundation. Refounded by Margaret of Anjou, wife of Henry VI, in 1465, the college has a picturesque President's Lodge with its long gallery in mellow brick. The Cloister Court was completed just before the arrival of Erasmus in 1510.

St John's College: The ostentatiously heraldic gatehouse and First Court, one of three interconnecting courtyards, are part of the 1511 foundation by Lady Beaufort. Grumbold's Old Bridge, 1712, with nautical panels, based on a Wren design, gives access to the late Georgian New Court. The Library of 1624 is unashamedly Perpendicular; the picturesque Bridge of Sighs (1831) is in the romantic spirit of Wordsworth, here from 1785, and Byron, at Trinity in 1805.

Sidney Sussex College: Founded in 1596 with extensive late Georgian remodelling by Wyatville. The head of Thomas Cromwell, its most famous pupil, was returned for burial here in 1960.

Trinity College: Founded in 1356 and re-established by Henry VIII in 1546. King Edward's Tower (1430), the oldest Cambridge gatehouse, and the original Perpendicular chapel were incorporated in Master Thomas Nevile's early 16th-century remodelling of the Great Court. Punctuated by a Renaissance fountain of 1602, it is the University's most spacious quadrangle.

Top: Girton College Chapel's red-brick flying buttresses.

Above: King's College Chapel seen from the Backs.

Left: The timber-framed gallery of the President's Lodge, Queen's College.

Below: The Bridge of Sighs, St John's College, built in 1831, links New Court with Third Court.

Top left: When Henry VI
founded King's College,
he intended it to dominate
the city.

Fitzwilliam Museum
Centre left: The exterior
Top right: Monet, *Les
Peupliers*.

Cambridge   **C**

Fitzwilliam Museum
Bottom left: Maiolica dish
from Cafaggiolo, 1514.

Bottom right: German
armour for horse and man,
c1520.

A procession of the nation's finest scholars have passed through its Great Gate; distinguished scientists from Newton to Rutherford and literary giants from Marvell and Dryden to Tennyson and Housman. Many are commemorated in Wren's Great Library of 1676, his gift to the college; among the tributes are Roubiliac's famous bust of Newton and Byron's statue.

Trinity Hall: Founded in 1350 by the Bishop of Norwich, and best known for its Elizabethan brick library, complete with original book cases. A visit to Cambridge should also take in:

Fitzwilliam Museum: Dominating the southern end of Trumpington Street, a monumental porticoed edifice designed by George Basevi, begun in 1834 to house the sumptuous collection of artefacts and paintings bequeathed by the 7th Viscount Fitzwilliam to his old university. This grandest of provincial museums, aptly described as a scaled-down British Museum, is crowded with Egyptian antiquities, ancient Greek pottery, Persian miniatures, illuminated manuscripts, Renaissance paintings, French Impressionists and work by East Anglia's own Constable and Gainsborough; a place to savour and revisit at leisure.

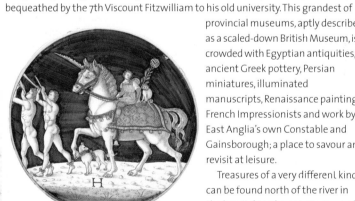

Treasures of a very different kind can be found north of the river in the bewitching house-museum of **Kettle's Yard.** You can doze in an armchair, read the art books or admire the eclectic taste of donor Jim Ede, a key collector of 20th-century British art. Prominent are works by Alfred Wallis, David Jones, Christopher Wood and the Nicholsons. Tales of the Fens are brought alive nearby in the **Cambridgeshire Folk Museum**.

Senate House: Gibbs' stately Palladian range in white Portland stone facing south down King's Parade was built to house the Bishop of Ely's bequest to the university. The **Backs** by the river and the **Botanic Gardens**, opened in 1846, are calm oases, even when Cambridge is teeming; or you can also punt upstream in the wake of Rupert Brooke for tea in The Orchard at **Grantchester**. The poet lived here in the Old Rectory between his time at King's until his death during World War.

Cambuskenneth Abbey, Stirlg, All that remains of the monastery founded by David I in 1147 is the 14th-century belltower and the foundations of the monastery buildings. This rich abbey hosted several meetings of the Scottish Parliament, including the first at which the royal burghs were represented (1326). A memorial erected by Queen Victoria marks the tomb of James II and his wife Margaret of Denmark. *See* **Stirling* 698 E4.**

Campbeltown, Ag & B 698 B6, This resort at the head of Campbeltown Loch is the peninsula's main town. Formerly Kinlochkilkerran, it acquired its present name in the 17th century when Archibald Campbell, 7th Earl of Argyll, gained control of the town after a long and bitter struggle with the Macdonalds of Kintyre. It became a royal burgh in 1700 and was a herring port until the 1920s. In the late 19th century it had

Above: Canons Ashby. The Landmark Trust runs a holiday flat in the tower.

Below left: The drawing room, which was originally the Elizabethan 'Great Chamber'.

34 distilleries, of which two are still active today. The fine Campbeltown Cross opposite the harbour dates from the 14th century.

Campton, Beds 691 F3, All Saints contains a fine monument to Sir Peter and Sir John Osborn (1655), consisting of two white altars and reredos.

Cannon Hall, S York 697 G7, A late 17th-century house with mid-18th century wings, which now contains a museum. Its internal alterations and redecoration were designed by the great York architect John Carr.

Canons Ashby, Nhants 690 D3, An unusual house of the 16th and 17th centuries [NT], which has escaped extensive later alterations. Its tower looks down on to a famous baroque garden, recently restored, with Italianate yews. Inside, the plasterwork of the Dryden family home is outstanding, and some early painted decoration survives on areas of panelling. A small room with early 18th-century painted pilasters cut out of card like stage scenery is unique, although the church across the road was decorated in a similar style by the same Mrs Creed, cousin of the owner.

Canterbury

Canterbury, Kent 691 J5, A flourishing town under the Romans, Canterbury became the capital of the kingdom of Kent under Aethelbert in the 6th century. Here St Augustine came in 597, sent by the Pope to christianize England, and here he built his first church. Ever since, its archbishop has been the senior churchman of Britain. After the Norman Conquest William I appointed Lanfranc as archbishop, and it was he who built the Norman cathedral, one tower of which survived into the 19th century. The murder of Thomas à Becket in 1170 and his subsequent canonization made his shrine one of the most popular in Europe, and Canterbury grew rich on the offerings of pilgrims. This source of wealth came to an end at the Reformation, when Henry VIII destroyed the shrine and appropriated all the treasures. Between then and the 20th century it remained a quiet cathedral city surrounded by its walls, largely untouched by the Industrial Revolution. In World War II it was severely damaged, the whole of the southeast quarter being reduced to rubble, but the cathedral itself largely escaped. Canterbury is now a major tourist centre, and the seat of the University of Kent.

After the cathedral, the other great ecclesiastical foundation of Canterbury was St Augustine's Abbey. This has now disappeared, apart from a lavish gateway, and only foundations are visible. These are not easy to interpret because several buildings are superimposed and have to be separated in the mind. There were originally two Saxon churches, linked to the middle by an 11th-century rotunda unique in England. This curious arrangement was swept away for a big new church built at the same time as the cathedral and equally impressive. It lasted until the Reformation, when it was completely demolished.

There are still several charming streets in Canterbury, and some buildings of more than local interest: the Westgate of 1375 with two sturdy round towers; Eastbridge Hospital, founded in the 12th century, with hall, undercroft and chapel, many picturesque half-timbered houses, and a number of medieval churches. A bizarre surprise is the former synagogue in King Street, now a church hall, a replica of an ancient Egyptian temple in cement. The Canterbury Museum and Art Gallery in the High Street exhibits an excellent collection of 19th- and 20th-century British art, notably strong in portraiture, along with a collection of military memorabilia.

Top left: The Beaney Institute, Royal Museum and Free Library, 1897–9, by AH Campbell. It is a Victorian pastiche with pseudo-medieval features.

Above: St Augustine's Abbey, the remains of the wall of the north aisle. The upper part is Tudor brickwork, constructed when the ruins were incorporated into Henry VIII's Manor Place.

Below: Christ Church Gate, completed in 1517, faces the town's war memorial in Buttermarket Square.

Top left: A detail of one of the capitals.

Bottom: The Norman crypt.

Top right: The east end of Canterbury Cathedral, with William of Sens' choir followed by William the Englishman's Trinity Chapel.

Canterbury Cathedral

Canterbury Cathedral is the most important medieval building in Britain, both architecturally and historically; but it does not reveal all its secrets at first glance. Between 1096 and 1130 the eastern part was lavishly rebuilt on a much larger scale under Archbishop Anselm, but four years later it was gutted by fire, leaving only a smoking shell. A French master-mason, William of Sens, was appointed to rebuild between 1175 and 1179 and his work introduced the new gothic style to England – with pointed arches, sexpartite vaulting and a system of buttressing concealed under the aisle roofs.

Like many English cathedrals, Canterbury was also a Benedictine monastery. Much of the monastic layout survives, all in the north side. There were two cloisters – the Great Cloister from which the Chapter House and Dormitory were reached, and the Infirmary Cloister, which retains some delicate arcading and an ornate tower from which water was distributed to the rest of the precinct. The partly surviving infirmary is to the east. Most remarkable of all is the covered stairway in the North Hall, where pilgrims stayed. On the south side of the cathedral entrance to the precinct is the spectacular Christ Church Gate of 1517, mostly refaced in the 1930s.

Trinity Chapel contains Becket's shrine, a marvel of mosaic and rich decoration. Around it the English nobility built their tombs; among them was Edward the Black Prince (d. 1371). The stained-glass windows, still largely intact, form the greatest collection of 13th-century glass in Britain, and repay careful examination through binoculars. They tell stories of miraculous cures at the shrine. Larger windows with larger-than-life-size figures of prophets were formerly in the clerestory but were later moved to the north transept, where they can be seen more easily.

Only in 1378 was it decided to demolish the old nave and rebuild in the new Perpendicular style. The architect was Henry Yevele; his work is higher, lighter and more rational than the old, making an immediate impact as one first enters the cathedral. A new west front was also begun, but only one tower was built. The other (on the north) did not replace the Norman tower until 1832. The cathedral's crowning glory, the tower over the crossing known as Bell Harry, was designed by John Wastell and built between 1496 and 1503.

Below: The cathedral from the northwest. In the foreground is the cloister, with the Chapter House on the left and nave on the right. In the centre is Harry Tower.

Right: Trinity Chapel, stained-glass window of St Thomas à Becket, the murdered archbishop. (The face is modern.)

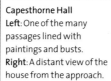

Capesthorne Hall
Left: One of the many passages lined with paintings and busts.
Right: A distant view of the house from the approach.

Cape Wrath, Highld 701 G1, The name of the northwest tip of Great Britain is derived from the Norse *hvarf* ('point of turning'). This windswept rocky promontory offers magnificent views. In fine weather the lighthouse (1828) offers views of Orkney* to the northeast and the Isle of Lewis* to the west. Visitors can observe the colonies of seabirds that nest on the Clo-Mor Cliffs.

Capel Garmon, Gwynd 692 E2, Two miles (3.2km) to the southeast of the popular small town of Betws-y-Coed is the village of Capel Garmon, which gives its name to a neolithic tomb consisting of three burial chambers. Only the one to the west, used as stables in the 19th century and which is now the means of entry, retains its capstone. It conforms to the Cotswold-Severn type of structure, the appearance of which, so much further to the north, is of particular interest. The site, within the acres of Tyn y Coed Farm, has magnificent views of the Conwy Valley.

Capesthorne Hall, Ches 693 H2, Its very striking spiky silhouette is the result of two phases of rebuilding in the 19th century. The main rooms inside are handsome, with high ceilings and a varied collection of furniture and paintings.

Cardiff

Left and above: Cardiff Castle's Norman keep and moat stand in extensive grounds in the town centre.

Opposite page, centre: Cardiff Castle interiors
Left: Marble interior of the Moorish Room.
Centre: The Arab Room in Herbert Tower.
Right: Gilded Islamic ceiling in the Arab Room, dating from 1881.

Opposite page, bottom:
The castle's ornate towers, added by William Burges from the 1870s.

Cardiff, Cardif 689 G3, The name describes the town's origins: 'the fort of the Taf'. The castle is one of the most fascinating in Wales, showing its architectural development from the 6th century BC up until the 1900s. The Norman keep is spectacular, not just for its scale but also for the height of the motte. Even so, by the second half of the 13th century the castle had been greatly strengthened in order to deter the attempts of Llywelyn ap Gruffudd (Llywelyn the Great) to deprive the owners, the de Clares, of their control over the area. Each successive generation added to the castle, some more considerably than others, but there were no significant changes after 1550 until the mid-18th century, when the property passed into the possession of the illustrious Scottish family, the Butes. The principal range was converted into a country house by the 1st Marquess in the

1770s, but it was the 3rd Marquess who gave the castle its unmistakable outline and its highly ornate interiors, through which he was able to express his love of the Middle Ages and display his knowledge of religions and history. His architect and mentor in the great programme that started in the early 1870s was William Burges; between them they succeeded in spending the fortune which the 2nd Marquess had acquired by making Cardiff the coal metropolis of the world. Summer and Winter Smoking rooms, an Arab Room, a Chaucer Room, a Moorish Roof Garden and a Banqueting Hall were all rich in iconographical detail.

Above: *Mountains at l'Estaque* (1878–80) by Cézanne, at the National Museum of Wales.

The National Museum of Wales is housed in one of the most distinguished buildings of the city's splendid Edwardian baroque Civic Centre. The site on which it was built was part of the Bute estate, sold to the corporation by the 3rd Marquess, whose grand scheme for the ceremonial outlay of Cathays Park was only partly realized before his death at the age of 53 in 1900. Over 20 years earlier, the idea of the museum – not then conceived as a national institution – was considered as part of the town's Free Library (a building reconditioned in 1999 to exhibit media arts). The museum was not opened until 1927; its galleries display aspects of the arts and the sciences, and it houses one of the finest collections of Impressionist paintings in the world. It also contains some medieval, baroque, 18th- and 19th-century works along with its Davis collection.

Carew Castle, Pembks 692 C7, Dating from the early 13th century, the castle is wonderfully situated on the tidal creek of the Carew River, where the water reflects the exuberance of the 16th-century additions made by Sir John Perrot: two rows of expansive mullion-and-transom windows and two large oriel windows. This ambitious building scheme was a continuation of the improvements made by Rhys ap Thomas to celebrate the knighthood granted him for his support of young Henry Tudor at Bosworth in 1485. When he was made a Knight of the Garter in 1505 he held an extravagant tournament to which he invited the leading noble families of Wales. The eloquent ruins are maintained by the Pembroke Coast National Park. The early Christian monument, the

Above: Carlisle Castle gun emplacement.

Right: Carew Castle. From the early-13th century until the 17th century, this splendid stronghold underwent a series of ambitious improvements.

Carew Cross, commemorates 'Maredudd the King, son of Edwin' who was killed in 1035.
Carisbrooke Castle, *see* **Isle of Wight*,**

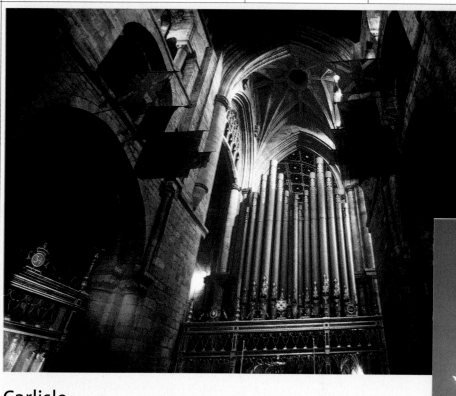

Carlisle

Carlisle, Cumb 696 E2, The city marks England's northwest frontier with Scotland and still has the atmosphere of a border town, though most of the city walls have gone. At the western end of Hadrian's Wall*, the Roman settlement was significant; its importance in Roman times is gradually being revealed by a a series of excavations, most recently on the open land in front of the castle. The centre of the city is reached from the south via the 16th-century citadel by Henry VIII's military engineer Stefan von Haschenperg, recast into Assize Courts by Sir Robert Smirke in 1810–11. The buildings form a group with the Citadel Railway Station by Sir William Tite and the County Hotel by Anthony Salvin. In the centre of the city a triangular market place contains the Market Cross (1682), the rather humble Old Town Hall of 1669, altered and extended in 1719, and the Guildhall, now a museum, the only survivor of Carlisle's medieval timber-framed architecture. The city has much pleasant 18th- and 19th-century townscape, reflecting its status as a county town and developing industrial city of which the most notable landmark is the chimney to Dixon's Mill, 300 feet (90m) high, designed by Richard Tattersall in 1836 with William Fairbairn as engineer.

Carlisle Castle marks the strategic importance of the city at a time when England and Scotland were often at war and it was sometimes occupied by the Scots. Indeed, it is the last English castle to have fallen to an enemy, as it was captured by Bonnie Prince Charlie's retreating army after the failure of the 1745 rebellion. The original

Above centre: Carlisle Cathedral, nave and crossing.

Above: A lion and sundial adorn the Market Cross (1682) outside the Town Hall.

castle consisted of its 12th-century keep and medieval curtain wall; the keep displays curious and somewhat inexplicable later carvings by prisoners. Apart from the inner ward and keep, the most impressive medieval part is the main gatehouse, De Ireby's Tower, built by the master-mason John Lewyn in 1378 according to a building contract which still survives. The castle was refortified for Henry VIII by Stefan von Haschenperg in the early 1540s, with a half-moon battery and gun platforms, and in 1568 became a place of imprisonment for Mary, Queen of Scots. In the 19th century the castle found a new lease of life as an army depot, partly so that troops would be on hand in case of industrial unrest, and the outer ward contains a series of regimental buildings of some distinction. The army is still there (as is the Border Regiment Museum) giving Carlisle Castle a history of some 900 years of continuous military use.

The **Cathedral** is the smallest in England, founded in 1102 as an Augustinian Priory. It became the centre of the diocese established by Henry I in 1133. Much of the 12th-century nave was destroyed by the invading Scottish army in 1645; what is left shows the Norman origins of the church. The chancel is gothic, 13th and 14th century, spectacular for the carvings on the capitals of the arcades which represent the months of the year. Among the cathedral's notable features are the very fine east window; flowing tracery now filled with Hardman glass; some excellent joinery in the medieval, richly canopied stalls; Prior Salkeld's screen of c1541, a fine example of the Renaissance fashion for placing profile heads in medallions; and a pulpit originally from Antwerp. The cathedral is not dominant in the city but sits comfortably with its precinct of canons' houses.

Tullie House takes its name from Thomas Tullie, Dean of the Cathedral, who built his house where the Roman city had its forum. The 1689 building has an impressive seven-bay classical front and good interiors, staircase and panelling. It became the city's art gallery and museum and has been given two major facelifts, the first in the 1890s by the local architect CJ Ferguson and then in the 1990s by the London practice of Stanton Williams. It has a very good collection of Pre-Raphaelite paintings.

Above: Carlisle, the citadel and entrance to the city from the south, designed by Robert Smirke, 1810–12.

Below: Carlisle Castle, curtain wall with De Ireby's Tower, and the keep beyond.

Carlton Towers, N York 697 H6, An early 17th-century house, heavily disguised within a Victorian gothic shell. Most of the remodelling was done by EW Pugin in 1873–6, and completed by JF Bentley – both leading Roman Catholic architects, for the owners stuck to their old religion. A sequence of several Victorian state rooms forms an impressive enfilade.

Carmarthen (Caerfyrddin), Carmth 692 D6, The English version of the name is derived from the Roman fort Moridunum, whereas the Welsh 'Caerfyrddin' links it fancifully with the birthplace of the wizard Myrddin, or Merlin. Much of the

Above and bottom:
Carreg Cennen Castle. Set on a rocky outcrop, it commands spectacular views of lush Carmarthenshire pastures.

Left: Carmarthen Guildhall, one of the most handsome 18th-century public buildings in Wales.

masonry of the Norman castle above the River Tywi was used in the late 18th century for a county gaol designed by John Nash (of which only part of the governor's house remains). A great deal of the medieval defensive site was taken up in the 20th century by the County Hall, its rounded corner towers surmounted by conical caps making it look like a château on the Loire. Recent removal of unsympathetic buildings has resulted in the greater prominence of the castle's gatehouse (similar to that at Kidwelly*), approached from Nott Square. Here stands a statue to General Sir William Nott, the hero of the Afghan wars, whose father was born in Carmarthen.

The plan of the medieval settlement is still discernible, even if much of its character has been eroded. The town can boast a handsome Guildhall of 1770s, probably designed Robert Taylor, two of whose pupils, SP Cockerell and John Nash, worked extensively in west Wales. It befitted the dignity of a town which was the largest in the country in the 18th century. As the centre of an agricultural area, the market has retained its Welsh vibrancy and the delightful clock tower survives (although many trading stalls and booths have disappeared).

The double nave parish church of St Peter's has many noteworthy monuments; foremost among them is the tomb of Sir Rhys ap Thomas and his wife. It was Sir Rhys who was the chief prop of Henry Richmond on his march from Dale in Pembrokeshire, gathering supporting troops until he reached Bosworth Field and ousted Richard III on the 22 August 1485, thereby becoming Henry VII and establishing the Tudor dynasty. Among the tablets is one 'Sacred to the memory of Robert Ferrar, DD Bishop of St. David's, burnt in the Market Place of Carmarthen 30 March, 1555, for adhering to the Protestant Religion.'

The County Museum, once housed in the town, is now 3 miles (5km) away at Abergwili, the site chosen for the bishop's palace when it moved from St David's* in the 16th century. The present building is an early 20th-century replacement, and makes a fitting home for a comprehensive display of artefacts from prehistory to the present day. The bishop's chapel on the first floor remains largely unaltered, and is open for private contemplation.

Carnassarie Castle, Ag & B 698 C3, This abandoned castle was built in the 16th century by John Carswell, the first Protestant Bishop of Argyll and the Isles, whose Gaelic translation of John Knox's liturgy was one of the first works published in Gaelic (1567). The castle still has some beautiful fireplaces and Renaissance details.

Above: Cartmel Priory from the south, showing carved stone tombs in the graveyard.

Carneddau Hengwm, Gwynd 692 D3, These two neolithic burial chambers are among the most interesting in Wales. They lie south of Harlech*, and are reached by a road offering expansive views of Tremadoc Bay. The area is rich in prehistoric remains.

Carreg Cennen Castle, Carmth 692 D6, A native Welsh castle, occupying one of the most awesome sites of any fortification in Wales. It was referred to in Dylan Thomas' *Under Milk Wood* as 'Carreg Cennen, King of Time', as if it had witnessed age after age of man coming to terms with his environment and his adversaries. It fell into English hands in 1277 and remained the property of the Crown almost without a break for the next 200 years, when its demolition was brought about by 500 men 'with bars, picks and cross-bars of iron and other instruments for the same purpose.' Visitors can still appreciate the remarkable defensive ingenuity of its layout even though it is in ruins.

Carreglwyd, IOA 692 C1, The 16th-century house of Carreglwyd was replaced in 1634 by Dr William Griffiths, Master of the Rolls to Charles I. His grandson's marriage to an heiress of two other Anglesey estates resulted in a major remodelling of the house in the 1760s. A long drive from the lodge outside the village of Llanfaethlu runs through high open grazed parkland with extensive views across Holyhead Bay, before dipping down into the heavy woodland which shelters the house and gardens, and the lake with its boathouse and delightful circumference pathway.

Carshalton, Surrey 691 F5, A picturesque town centre with a series of delightful bridges and ponds. Carshalton House in Pound Street, now a school for girls, is a Queen Anne mansion with good 18th-century interiors, the best of which is the Painted Parlour. The grounds were laid out by Charles Bridgeman in the early 1700s. Of particular note is the Water Tower, possibly by Vanbrugh, which pumped water from the river to supply the house. Little Holland House at 40 Beeches Avenue was built and furnished by the artist and craftsman Frank Dickinson from 1902 for his own use. For those interested in the town's history, a visit to Honeywood Heritage Centre should prove illuminating.

Cartmel, Cumb 696 E5, Cartmel is an attractive small town in Furness dominated by the great church, Cartmel Priory. It was formerly an Augustinian priory, founded in 1188, which survived the Dissolution because it was also the parish church. Its architecture has monastic size and richness. The exterior is distinctive in the way that the late medieval top stage of the tower sits diagonally on the square work of the late 12th century below. Inside there is excellent joinery, especially the 15th-century choir stalls with poppyheads and misericords and an unusual screen of c1620 (the

Above: Castell Coch, looking like a Rhenish Schloss, is a whimsical restoration by the 3rd Marquess of Bute and William Burges. The bird shown above is a detail from one of the decorated walls in the Drawing Room.

gift of George Preston of the nearby Holker Hall*) which seems to be Gothic Revival rather than survival. Best of all is the stone tomb of Sir John Harrington (d. 1347). It is richly carved, with a base frieze of almsmen and mourners and a painted wooden ceiling. In the town the priory gatehouse also survives.

Cassington, Oxon, An interesting amount of Norman work survives in the church, together with some good carving. *See* **Yarnton* 690 D4.**

Castell Coch, Cardif 689 G3, The name means 'red castle' because of the colour of its stone; it is set on the wooded slopes of the Taf, 5 miles (8km) north of Cardiff*. It was smaller, it was dramatically placed, and it had been neglected for four centuries. The decoration was based on genealogical, historical, religious and literary allusions. The most ornate room is the domed polygonal drawing room, with its colourfully playful figures drawn from Aesop's *Fables*. Above the drawing room, on the top two floors of the keep, is the Marchioness' Bedroom, with a Victorian Moorish-style bed centrally placed under the dome. In complete contrast, the Marquess' Bedroom is spartan in its simplicity and obvious lack of comfort. A working drawbridge and portcullis are playful aspects of Castell Coch and add to its considerable appeal.

Castell y Bere, Gwynd 692 E4, Llywelyn ap Iorwerth's Castell y Bere is probably the most remote and least known of the castles of Wales. It was once of enormous significance, since it guarded the mountainous route between the estuaries of the Dyfi and the Mawddach, not only against the English but also against attacks from ambitious

Left: Castell y Bere, one of the most remote castles in Wales.

Castle Ashby
Top right: The grand entrance is now through the screen (1625–35) which fills the fourth side of the earlier courtyard.
Below: The Dining Room has embroidered wall panels.

compatriots. The irregular plan of the castle was dictated by the natural rock defences which, however formidable, could not withstand King Edward I's eventual onslaught. The quality of the castle's decorative masonry can best be seen in the National Museum of Wales in Cardiff*.

Castle Acre, Norfk 695 H5, This pretty village of brick and flint cottages gathered about a tree-lined green, on the northern flank of the Nar Valley, lies between the substantial remains of two great centres of Norman authority. East of Bailey Street and approached through a 13th-century bastioned gatehouse are some of the finest castle earthworks in England. Beyond St James' Church, with its wine-glass pulpit depicting the four Doctors of the Church and contemporary apostolic rood screen (15th century), the largest and most beautiful monastic ruins in the region rise above the water-meadows. Here the early 16th-century gatehouse and well-preserved prior's house [EH] are offset by the noble west front of William de Warenne's Cluniac church of c1090. The whole Nar Valley is studded with monastic remains, from the impressive Augustinian gatehouses downstream at Pentney and West Acre to Priory Farmhouse at Litcham.

Castle Ashby, Nhants 694 E6, Northamptonshire certainly has more than its fair share of country houses, and Castle Ashby is another Elizabethan monster, standing boldly on a prominence. It once had endless terraces of gardens, now buried under Victorian replanting. Its roofline is crowded with turrets that have twisting staircases in the corners of the building, and is topped by a homily in letters 2 feet (0.6m) high about the importance of the home. The three-sided courtyard was completed by a flamboyant screen that is persistently attributed to Inigo Jones.

Bottom: Castle Acre, the Romanesque west front of the priory church.

The Italianate gardens (open to the public) were laid out in the 19th century and include a picturesque orangery. They climax in the kitchen garden with its decorative walls. The strange curved boxes on legs are bee-boles.

Castle Campbell, Clacks 699 F3, The castle stands above Dollar, famous for its school (Dollar Academy). Perched high on a rocky outcrop, it dominates the surrounding area as far as the Firth of Forth. The tower-house was built in the 15th century by the 1st Earl of Argyll, while the two wings and gardens were added in the 16th and 17th centuries. Unsuccessfully besieged by the Duke of Montrose in 1645, it was burned by Cromwell's troops in 1654.

Castle Combe, Wilts 690 B5, This Cotswold* village, set in a river valley, is of renowned beauty, though some consider it over-restored. It has a 15th-century stone-canopied market cross, mellowed stone houses and cottages. The church, mostly Perpendicular, was restored in 1851 but the original tower still stands. Inside lies the 13th-century effigy of Walter de Dunstanville, who built the original castle (of which only a few traces remain). The manor house, a short distance away, is now a hotel.

Castle Drogo, Devon 689 F6, Perhaps the last castle to be built in England. Castle Drogo [NT] was conceived on a grandiose scale by Julius Drewe, who had made a fortune early in life from the tea trade and then from his large chain of Home and Colonial grocery stores. In 1910 he bought a site overlooking the Teign Gorge near Drewsteignton, where he thought his ancestors might have once lived after the Norman Conquest. His architect was Sir Edwin Lutyens, who was charged with building a medieval-style castle with walls 6 feet (1.8m) wide. The first schemes were grand and costly, the finished design more economical but still monumental. To help his client conceive his idea, full-size mock-ups of parts of the building were built in wood and canvas. Work started in 1911–12 and finished in 1930, the year before Drewe's death. The plain exterior is of granite, with huge mullioned windows and a castellated parapet; the only relief is the large Drewe lion carved above the entrance door, which even has its own portcullis. The interior is notable for its cool, wonderfully controlled spaces, its long vaulted corridors and its wide, dramatic staircase that leads down to the panelled Dining Room. In

Left: Castle Fraser, the northwestern tower and the west range of the court; the corresponding southeastern tower is circular.

Castle Howard
Right: An aerial view showing the north front. On the right is Robinson's Palladian west wing, less baroque than Vanbrugh's domed centrepiece and east wing. Beyond is the axial vista.
Below right: Hawksmoor's Mausoleum.
Far right: The Great Hall.

contrast the Drawing Room above is lighter and has painted panelling, with a window looking out on to the staircase. The nearby Library is more masculine, with an oak-coffered ceiling, and a huge billiard table in the anteroom, from which it is divided by a massive granite arch. The basement complex of kitchen and other service rooms is also architecturally interesting, and Lutyens designed many of the fittings here, including the kitchen tables. The ornamental grounds lie some way from the house. Yew hedges surround the circular croquet lawn; beyond, along a shrub-lined path, is a large rectangular rose and herbaceous garden with corner pavilions of hornbeam.

Castle Fraser, Abers 702 D6, Mar's largest castle, built between 1575 and 1636, was the property of the Frasers until the early 20th century; since 1976 it has belonged to the National Trust for Scotland. The two towers that stand diagonally opposite on either side of the main of the building were built by Thomas Leiper. Another master-mason from

the region, John Bell, was responsible for the complex tiered corbelling, turrets, elaborately worked roofs and Renaissance-style chimneys.

Castle Hedingham, Essex 691 H3, The village below looks up to the castle, perched on a wooded hill. The de Veres, mighty war lords, acquired it after the Conquest, and in 1140 Aubrey de Vere built the Great Tower Keep which King John besieged in 1215. The great monolithic structure, one of the best preserved keeps in England, has two 100-foot (30m) corner turrets, a mighty Banqueting Hall and Minstrels' Gallery. The brick bridge over the moat may have been built to welcome Henry VII in 1498. The village, gathered about its triangular market site, has excellent Georgian houses in Queen Street. After its beautiful Tudor brick tower, the church's almost complete Norman interior is a revelation of arcading; there is also a sumptuous south doorway. Don't miss the carved misericords, the Earl of Orford's splendid monument (1539) and the 12th-century churchyard cross.

Castle Hill, Devon 689 F5, Built by Hugh Fortescue, Lord Clinton, in the late 1720s after consultations with Lord Burlington. It is a fine Palladian composition, but the interiors are much altered after devastating fires. The grounds contain a range of 18th-century buildings: an early sham castle, a menagerie, Spa Wood Cottage with its

arch, the Ugly Bridge and three temples. The sham village, a hermitage, a Chinese Temple and the Sybil's Cave have all disappeared.

Castle Howard, N York 697 J5, Familiar to many as the setting for the acclaimed television dramatization of *Brideshead Revisited*, this was, amazingly, the soldier and playwright Sir John Vanbrugh's first attempt at architectural design. Begun in 1699, it is a baroque masterpiece, and was the first English house to be crowned with a dome. The original plan was so enormous that it was not completed, the west wing being added by Sir Thomas Robinson. The full Vanbrughian theatricality is best appreciated in the monumental Great Hall. At the bottom of the staircase stands the marble altar from behind which the Oracle at Delphi prophesied; there are also some remarkable ancient classical sculptures and cinerary urns brought back from the Grand Tour. The grounds of Castle Howard are a particular delight. A visit in June is rewarded by the overpowering scent of old roses in the walled garden;

visitors can get married in the splendid setting of the Temple of Four Winds, glimpse eternity from afar in a vista of Nicholas Hawksmoor's mausoleum, or experience the Egyptian concept of the after-life with the pyramid and obelisk. John Carr's magnificent stable block has been given a new lease of life as the entrance facilities.

Castle Kennedy Gardens, D & G 698 C8, The grounds of Lochinch Castle include the ruins of Castle Kennedy and its 75-acre (30ha) gardens on the isthmus between the Black and White lochs. The gardens, designed by William Adam for the Earls of Stair in the 18th century, were restored in 1847. Rhododendrons, azaleas, magnolias and monkey-puzzle trees abound.

Castle Rising, Norfk 695 G4, An impressive Norman hall keep, one of the largest in England, with elaborate blind arcading not unlike Norwich Castle, is surrounded by immense earthworks and approached over the ditch through a 12th-century gatehouse [EH]. Access to the Great Hall is via a dramatic stone staircase. The castle once held Queen Isabella (dubbed the 'She-Wolf of France') who, having helped to murder her husband, Edward II, in 1327, was detained here (and elsewhere) by her son Edward III for 27 years. She wanted for nothing, save power, freedom and, ultimately, sanity. The picturesque, feudal village full of carstone estate cottages, has a heavily restored Norman church with a richly ornamental west front. Nearby the quadrangular almshouse Hospital of the Holy and Undivided Trinity, with its own chapel and some original furniture, seems little changed since 1614, when Lord Privy Seal Henry Howard endowed it as a home for needy and deserving spinsters. The residents still wear scarlet Jacobean capes with the Howard coat of arms to church each Sunday and pointed black hats on Founder's Day.

Castle Stalker, Ag & B 698 C2, This private castle, perched on a rocky outcrop at the entrance to Loch Laich, south of Portnacroish, is surrounded by an aura of romantic splendour. It was built c1520 by the Stewarts of Appin, abandoned c1800 and restored in the 1970s by Colonel Stewart Allwood.

Castle Sween, Ag & B 698 B4, From Bellanoch a minor road runs through Knapdale Forest and along the east shore of Loch Sween to its mouth. It passes the ruins of Castle Suibhne (or Castle Sween), a fine Norman castle, one of the earliest in Scotland,

Above: Castle Rising, the great Norman keep.

Below: Castle Stalker, on Loch Linnhe just where it joins Loch Laich.

built in the 11th or 12th century and dismantled in 1647. Today the castle is sadly surrounded by a caravan park.

The road also leads to **Kilmory Knap Chapel,** which houses some beautiful Celtic and medieval crosses. The 15th-century MacMillan Cross, which has a crucifixion carved on one side and a hunting scene on the other, evokes the memory of one of the keepers of the castle.

Castlerigg Stone Circle, Cumb 696 D3, A few miles outside Keswick* is the best remaining evidence for the extensive prehistoric settlement in the Lake District*. Most signs of this are in the earthworks and field systems, but at Castlerigg [EH] there is a circle of 38 standing stones which enclose a unique inner rectangle of 10 stones. Current opinion dates the circle perhaps as early as 3000BC, when the area was the centre of an extensive trade in stone axes.

Castor, Cambs 695 F5, This part of the Nene Valley has important Roman remains, notably the town of Durobrivae where Ermine Street crossed the river, and the complex of temple, baths and villas excavated near the church in 1822.

St Kyreburgha's Church, with its glorious central tower, its unique dedication to the daughter of Mercia's pagan King Peada and its consecration inscription of 1124 is the most complete Norman church in the county.

Cattistock, Dorset 689 H6, The village has an outstanding 19th-century church – St Peter and St Paul – by George Gilbert Scott, with contributions

Above: Castlerigg Stone Circle on its bleak Pennine site.

Cawdor Castle
Below: The tower-house, licensed in 1454 by William 6th Thane of Cawdor, rises above the courtyard built by the Campbells in the mid-17th century.
Left: A display of weaponry.

from his father, Sir George. It is in a Perpendicular style, with a tower that can be seen from far around, and a splendid stained-glass window of 1882 designed by William Morris.

Caverswall Castle, Staffs 693 H3, A medieval castle that was turned into a castle-like house in 1615 by Robert Smythson. His client was Matthew Cradock, one of the first generation to profit from the wool trade, who probably wanted to display his new wealth. The house was formerly moated.

Cawdor, Highld 701 H5, The delightful village of Cawdor, with its picturesque 17th-century church, nestles at the foot of Cawdor Castle. Macbeth, chief of Moray, who murdered Duncan I and was crowned King of Scotland at Scone in 1040, was also Thane (baron) of Cawdor and undoubtedly owned lands

nearby. Legend has it that the original tower, reached via a drawbridge, was built in the late 14th century by the Earl of Cawdor on the exact spot where he dreamed that his donkey was in the habit of spending the night. The hawthorn bush under which the animal sheltered has been reverently preserved in the basement of the building. The vast castle gardens are a blend of fantasy and formality and provide an attractive setting for the castle (enlarged in the 17th and 19th centuries).

Cawston, Norfk 695 J4, An attractive village presided over by the mighty freestone tower of St Agnes' church, largely rebuilt by the powerful de la Pole family in the early 15th century. Inside, a majestic angel roof has floral bosses and delicate spandrel

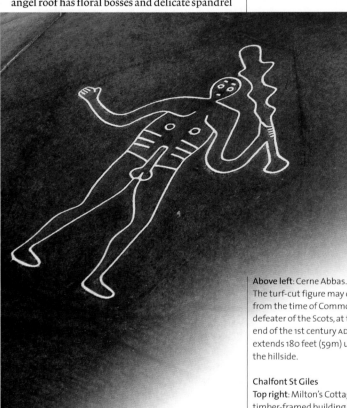

tracery; the early 16th-century chancel screen is complete with saintly panels.

Cerne Abbas, Dorset 689 J5, Once the site of a Benedictine abbey, which stood in what is now the graveyard of the church of St Mary. The porch to the Abbot's Hall, with its fan vault, deserves close inspection. A few hundred yards away is the wondrous but simple figure of the Cerne Abbas' Giant, cut in the turf through to chalk, with his long outstretched arms, erect phallus and club. The figure, thought to be associated with ancient fertility rites, may have been cut in the 2nd century AD, although many now believe it to be a 17th-century antiquarian joke.

Above left: Cerne Abbas. The turf-cut figure may date from the time of Commodus, defeater of the Scots, at the end of the 1st century AD. It extends 180 feet (59m) up the hillside.

Chalfont St Giles
Top right: Milton's Cottage, a timber-framed building with brick infill. Built in the early 17th century and extended in the 18th century.
Above right: A portrait thought to be Milton, aged ten, on display in the cottage.

Right: Chalgrave Church. It contains exceptional wall-paintings of c1310.

Chaddesley Corbett, Worcs 693 H5, A typical Worcestershire village, with early Georgian brick houses and many yeomen's timber-framed houses.

Chaldon, Surrey 691 F5, The church of St Peter and St Paul contains an important wall-painting of

c1200. The painting represents the Purgatorial Ladder; its devils and images of the Seven Deadly Sins are quite unnerving.

Chalfont St Giles, Bucks 691 E4, A large village with two noteworthy sights. The church of St Giles retains a cycle of wall-paintings of c1330 and a good hanging wall-monument to Sir George Fleetwood (d. 1620) and his wife.

Milton's Cottage, at 21 Deanway, is where John Milton fled to escape the plague in 1665 and where

he completed his epic *Paradise Lost*. The cottage and its garden are open to the public and there is a small museum.

Chalgrave, Beds The small unspoilt church, consecrated in 1219, is typical of the county. Worth a closer look are the wall-paintings of c1310 and two 14th-century monuments of knights. *See* **Toddington* 690 E3.**

Chanctonbury Ring, W Susx 691 F7, Within the parish of Steyning* is a circular prehistoric earthwork planted with beeches, around which many legends have accumulated: if you run round it seven times the Devil will appear and offer you a bowl of soup (don't accept); meanwhile, the ghost of Julius Caesar can be raised if you count the trees.

Chappel, Essex 691 H3, The Colne Valley is crossed by a 32-arch railway viaduct of 1847. Aping a Roman aqueduct, it celebrates the age of steam. The village station now hosts the East Anglian Railway Museum.

Charlecote Park
Top left: The Great Hall.
Bottom: The main entrance.

Right: Charleston
Farmhouse, two painted
interiors.

Charlwood

C

Charlecote Park, Warwks 694 C6, Considered for many years to be the ultimate Elizabethan manor house, Charlecote [NT] stands in low and luxuriant meadows next to the River Avon and its tributary the Hele, within a park where Shakespeare is said to have poached the deer. The story goes that he was caught and sentenced in the Great Hall at Charlecote by its then owner, Sir Thomas Lucy, and later had his revenge by depicting Lucy in his plays as the fussy and ridiculous Mr Justice Shallow. Once you have passed through the magnificent and genuinely Elizabethan Gatehouse (c1580), however, you enter the Victorian re-creation of Elizabethan times of George Hammond Lucy, who greatly extended the house. Lucy also fitted out the lavish and ponderous interiors which still survive today, including sumptuous furniture and objects from the Fonthill sale. The Great Hall, Library and Dining Room were decorated by Thomas Willement between 1830 and 1840. The house was originally E-shaped in plan, and retains its octagonal turrets in each corner. The original two-storeyed porch is now balanced by a huge oriel window inserted by George Hammond Lucy's wife, Mary Elizabeth, who made further alterations in her widowhood in the 1850s. James Lees-Milne, who was involved in negotiating the gift of the house from Sir Montgomerie Fairfax-Lucy to the National Trust in 1946, considered that these Victorian improvements were 'injudicious'. They should be presented to visitors with the caveat that they were not of artistic or historical importance, he argued, a view that has obviously since changed in favour of the 19th-century work. The outbuildings at Charlecote are particularly interesting, and the brew-house with its huge copper vats and wooden casks is a well-preserved example. The cellars beneath the house had the capacity to store 4,000 gallons of ale. The church of St Leonard, a short walk away across the park, was built in 1853 by Mary Elizabeth Lucy but still houses the magnificent Renaissance tombs of earlier Lucys. Nicholas Stone's tomb of Sir Thomas Lucy III (d. 1640), a friend of John Donne, is particularly noteworthy, and features his books.

Charleston Farmhouse, E Susx 691 G7, The home of Vanessa Bell and Duncan Grant, an 'outpost of Bloomsbury' (see under London*) from 1916 to 1958. It is full of paintings and ceramics by the couple and their friends.

Charlestown, Cnwll 688 D7, Charming colour-washed cottages fringe the large granite harbour established in the 1790s by the mining magnate Charles Rashleigh for the exportation of minerals and china clay from the St Austell area. In front of the Rashleigh Arms at the head of the harbour is a large cobbled area where the clay and ores were stored, ready to be loaded into the ships in the deep harbour. Four masted schooners and other vessels used for sail training and films are now moored here, encouraging all that see them to imagine how these ancient and bustling ports must once have looked.

Charlton-on-Otmoor, Oxon 690 D4, The church contains a remarkably complete rood screen of the early 16th century, richly carved and originally painted and gilded.

Charlwood, Surrey 691 F6, An attractive Weald village with tile-hung and timber-framed cottages. The screen in the church is elaborately carved in late Perpendicular style. Winged dragons hold the donor's initials in the cresting.

Charney Bassett, Oxon 690 D4, The church of
St Peter retains some Norman work, including
the carved south doorway with 11th-century
tympanum. The adjacent manor house,
remodelled in the 1800s, incorporates the late
13th-century solar wing of a hall-house.

Charterhouse, Surrey, Just north of Godalming,
an ancient cloth-making centre, rises the
impressive gothic skyline of Charterhouse School,
moved here in 1872 to buildings designed by
PC Hardwick. Later additions are the Great Hall
of 1885 by AW Blomfield and the detached Chapel
of 1922–7, built as a war memorial by Sir Giles
Gilbert Scott. *See* **Godalming* 690 E6.**

Left: Chartwell, a portrait of
Winston Churchill as a young
man, by Sir John Lavery.

Chartham, Kent 691 J5, A splendid church of about
1300, the windows displaying typical Kentish
tracery. The church boasts the famous life-size
military brass to Sir Robert de Septvans, 1306.
Chartwell, Kent 691 G6, Winston Churchill's house,
mostly rebuilt in 1923 [NT]. Here Churchill lived,

example, contains a 'chamber-horse' for bouncing up and down on when it was too wet to ride outside. The house was built in 1603 by Walter Jones, a wealthy wool stapler, and lived in by his descendants up until 1997. The grounds contain much Victorian topiary. On the lawn here the game of croquet was invented and codified by a 19th-century owner, Walter Whitmore Jones. In keeping with the time-capsule presentation, admission is strictly limited.

Chatham Dockyard, Kent 691 H5, The dockyard itself, on the east bank of the Medway, was founded by Henry VIII but most of the existing buildings date from the 18th and 19th centuries. Until recently closed to the public, these are now accessible. The main gate, of 1720, has a huge royal coat-of-arms over the entrance. Inside, the most interesting buildings are the Storehouse (1780s and 1790s) with original tackle; the Ropery (1785), nearly a third of a mile long (last used in the Falklands War), the Admiral's House (which has a ceiling painted by Sir James Thornhill) and Officer's Terrace, and the so-called 'Slips', Victorian boat-sheds roofed with iron.

Chatley Heath, Surrey 691 F5, The curious Chatley Heath Semaphore House is a five-storeyed tower built as part of an early 19th-century chain of semaphore stations. Messages could be sent from Whitehall to Portsmouth in less than a minute.

wrote and painted for more than 40 years. The rooms are preserved as they were in his time and there are good collections of memorabilia. The garden studio contains some of his paintings and the gardens have a rose walk planted on Sir Winston and Lady Churchill's golden anniversary by their children.

Charwelton, Nhants 694 D7, This Northamptonshire village on the road from Daventry to Banbury has a fine 14th-century pack-horse bridge. It remains in pedestrian use, and has twin pointed and chambered arches.

Chastleton, Oxon 690 C3, The glory of this pretty little village is Chastleton House, a magnificent early 17th-century building in golden stone. When the National Trust opened the house in 1997, it was trumpeted as a new approach in conservation. The works done to it went no further than minimal repairs, rather than restoration. This approach was carried through to keeping 1950s plastic light switches as well as the triumphant Jacobean textiles. Chastleton is an amazing marriage of exciting Jacobean architecture, including a Long Gallery with barrel plaster ceiling, with an accumulation of the curiosities of everyday life. The Gallery, for

Top right: Chartwell, the home of Winston Churchill from 1922 to 1964.

Top left: Chartham Church, the chancel with its amazing east window of about 1296. This is the epitome of the Decorated style in a particular local form. The top of the lights consists of cusped quatrefoil, with each cusp split, the so-called 'Kentish' tracery.

Right: Chatham Dockyard, founded in the 16th century, was developed as one of the main bases of the English fleet in the 1720s and continued to be enlarged into the early 20th century.

Chatsworth, Derbys 694 C3, The great classical house is impressive, its contents are outstanding and the grounds enormous. These attractions bring hordes of visitors, but there seems to be room for all of them. The first Chatsworth was an Elizabethan house planned round a courtyard. The court still remains, but each side of the house was rebuilt in turn between 1687 and 1707 by William Cavendish, 1st Duke of Devonshire. The south and east sides were designed by William Talman. The architect of the pedimented west side is unknown, but it was probably Thomas Archer, whose curving north front completed the building. The massive north wing was added a century later by the 6th Duke.

Many of the rooms in the main house retain their early Georgian character, with ceilings grandly painted by Verrio and Laguerre and first-rate carved decoration by Samuel Watson and others. Past the rather gloomy Entrance Hall, the visitor's route leads through the Painted Hall, the Oak Room, which has woodwork from a German monastery, and the Chapel, which was finished in 1694. Its alabaster altarpiece is wonderfully carved, the ceiling is painted by Verrio and the air is perfumed by the cedarwood panelling. The State Apartments on the second floor comprise a series of rooms of overpowering splendour occupying the whole south front. There are many other rooms to be seen on the tour, a good proportion of

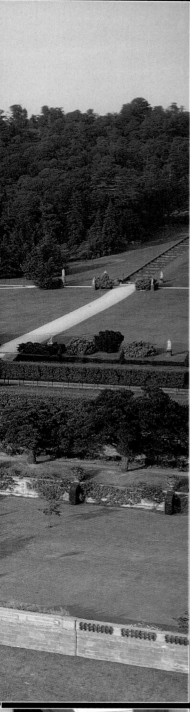

them containing decoration and furniture from the time of the 6th Duke in the 1830s. Chatsworth has exceptional collections of paintings and furniture, augmented by the contents of Devonshire House and Chiswick House*, the family's former London residences. A small part of the formal gardens to the south of the house is private but the spectacular cascade, the camellia houses and a number of formal walks are open, as is the whole of the enormous park. The handsome 18th-century stable block has been converted into a restaurant.

Left: View of Chatsworth set in its grounds, which were landscaped by Capability Brown and Joseph Paxton.

Below left: The Sculpture Gallery.

Above: A *trompe l'oeil* violin from the Music Room.

Below: The Library.

Chavenage, Gloucs 690 B4, A restrained, grey, Elizabethan house with the classic arrangement of a E-shaped plan with a porch opening into the screens passage and minstrels' gallery above. This leads into the Hall, which is distinguishable outside by its tall windows, still containing fragments of 17th-century heraldic glass; but this is now cut in two by a first floor rather than being open to the roof as originally. The date of 1576 and the initials of Sir Edward Seymour, its builder, appear over the front door. Inside, the tapestry from the Mortlake factory is interesting, hanging in the room supposed to have been slept in by Oliver Cromwell, who had come to harangue the then owner of Chavenage, a reluctant regicide.

Chawton, Hants 690 E6, At Chawton, Jane Austen's House is a modest Georgian house where she lived from 1809 to 1817. She is buried under a stone slab in the north aisle of Winchester* Cathedral.

Cheadle, Staffs 693 H3, St Giles Church, with its very tall, very thin spire, is the masterpiece of AWN Pugin, prophet of the Gothic Revival in England. He wanted to make Cheadle 'a perfect revival of an English parish church of the time of Edward I' and his client, Lord Shrewsbury, had the money to make this possible. Architecture and fittings are of the best and richest.

Cheam, Surrey 691 F5, Whitehall, on the corner of Park Lane, is an excellent example of a 16th-century timber-framed house, covered with weather-boarding in the 18th century.

Cheddar Gorge, Somset 689 H4, Around 15 miles (24km) from Bath* are the steep limestone rocks of the Cheddar Gorge. The caves are rich in remains left by prehistoric man, and full of stalactites and stalagmites. *See* **Wookey Hole***.

Top: Cheadle, sedilia in St Giles Church, of carved and painted stone, part of the immensely rich interior.

Top left: Chawton, Jane Austen's house, where she wrote her later novels.

Above left: Chedworth Roman Villa, mosaic from the dining-room floor.

Above right: Cheltenham, Regency terraces.

Chedworth Roman Villa, Gloucs 690 C4, In this remote valley, it is possible to imagine the villa's builders, with their baths, nymphaeum and hypocausts, seeing themselves as the last civilized outpost of a distant empire. Their dining-room floor mosaic includes the figure of a Briton, wearing the woolly cloak or 'birrus Britannicus' that the Romans considered to be British national dress. The two courts of the villa [NT] are now topped by a 19th-century hunting lodge, built on the spoil heap of the excavations, and paid for by the Earl of Eldon in 1864–6. It houses a museum and photographs of earnest Victorian visitors .

Chelmsford, Essex 691 G4, The county town boasts an ancient history: it was probably Julius Caesar's base during his 54 BC conquest of Britain, and

became the foremost town of Essex in the 13th century. Since the 1930s it has developed out of all recognition. It has an interesting museum, and **St Mary's Church**, with a 1749 needle-spire and lantern on a medieval tower, which won cathedral status in 1913.

Cheltenham, Gloucs 690 B3, A town full of flowers, the brighter the better, in which the local authority takes enormous pride. It still has a holiday air, having been a spa since the famous spring was discovered in 1718, reputedly by observation of the drinking habits of some very vigorous pigeons. Captain Henry Skillicorne, who owned the site, was keen to exploit the powers of the waters and constructed the first spa in 1738. A visit from the Royal Family for five whole weeks in 1788 confirmed the reputation of the purgative

powers of the waters, and Cheltenham has not been out of fashion since.

The **Pittville Pump Room** with its domed roof is the heart of this activity, built by John Forbes between 1825 and 1830 with an Ionic colonnade and set in a park. Today it houses a museum including a display of 18th-century costumes. Cheltenham flourished particularly in Regency times, when many neo-Grecian houses were laid out along carefully planned tree-lined avenues. Many of the elegant crescents and terraces survive, complete with their delicate filigree iron verandahs. JB Papworth's Lansdown estate is one of the earliest developments, rivalled by the Pittville Estate, built by the MP Joseph Pitt.

The town became particularly popular with those retiring from the colonies or India, and has become synonymous with prosperous respectability. The smart shops of Montpellier Walk are separated by elegant iron caryatids, and the wide Promenade is fringed with arcades, obelisks and trees. The town is periodically peppered with the green uniforms of girls from the exclusive Cheltenham Ladies' College. The College's reputation developed under Miss Dorothea Beale, who was headmistress from 1858 to 1898.

Above: Cheltenham, Pittville Pump Room, now a museum.

Right: Chepstow Castle. To the left of the twin towers of the gatehouse is Martyn Tower, named after Henry Martyn, one of the men who signed Charles I's death warrant. Martyn was a prisoner here for 20 years.

Below: Cherryburn, the family home of wood-engraver Thomas Bewick.

Chenies, Bucks 690 E4, The manor house is a handsome building of the 15th and 16th centuries, formerly owned by the Russells (later Dukes of Bedford) and visited by both Henry VIII and Elizabeth I. The house has much to offer: Tudor tapestries and furniture, hiding places, a sunken garden, two mazes and a medieval undercroft probably belonging to an earlier house. The Bedford Chapel of 1556, on the north side of the church of St Michael, contains a splendid series of monuments to the Russell family and is still in use.

Chepstow (Casgwent), Mons 693 G7, The best way to appreciate the genius of William Fitzosbern's choice of ground is to approach Chepstow along the old Gloucester road, when its siting as the first Norman stronghold – and in stone – in Wales (1067) is immediately obvious. Chepstow sits on the narrowest point of a promontory on the Wye*, with the protection of the river on one side and a deep ravine on the other. Subsequent additions were restricted to only two sides, accounting for the elongated character of the castle, with each building phase displaying an advance in sophisticated military design. Parts of the town wall still stand, and the Town Gate resolutely challenged motorized traffic until the building of the first Severn Bridge. The main street hurtles down a steep hill towards the river. Half way up or down is St Mary's Church, which has retained its handsome Norman west door.

Cherhill, Wilts 690 C5, Cut into the chalk in 1780, the white horse – one of several in the region – can be easily seen from the main road to Marlborough from Calne. Alongside it, and visible for many miles, is the **Lansdowne Obelisk**, erected in the 1840s by the 3rd Marquess of Lansdowne to commemorate his ancestor, the 17th-century economist Sir William Petty.

Cherryburn, Nthumb 697 G2, Thomas Bewick (1753–1828) was born in the small cottage forming part of a vernacular farmyard. He was possibly Northumberland's greatest artist, and was known as the 'father of wood engraving'. As the family became more prosperous, a 19th-century farmhouse was added; this now contains a museum of Bewick's work, much of which was devoted to the study of nature. The National Trust has added a collection of animals to help re-create the rural atmosphere.

C

Chester

Chester, Ches 693 G2, In Roman times Deva, as it was known then, was one of the most important towns in England, and the headquarters of the 20th Legion. It retained its prominence during the Middle Ages and has kept its medieval walls, nearly 2 miles (3.2km) in circumference. Within them are picturesque half-timbered houses and a splendid cathedral. It is a city of colours, red sandstone and black-and-white half timbering. In the centre many houses have covered galleries for pedestrians at first-floor level, known as the Rows, which make Chester unique in England. The cathedral is of red sandstone; although a whole series of Victorian restorations added spindly towers and pinnacles to the exterior, the inside is impressive, especially the choir of 1260–1320. An odd fact about the nave is that the north side was built almost a hundred years after the south side. Until 1540 the cathedral was a Benedictine abbey and many of the abbey buildings survive, although much altered and restored. The castle, founded by William

the Conqueror, was almost entirely replaced in the 1790s by a group of handsome public buildings designed by the architect Thomas Harrison. These are major monuments of the Greek Revival style, especially the Entrance Gate, which recalls Berlin's Brandenburg Gate, and the semicircular Shire Hall. The City Walls, studded at intervals by towers, are accessible to visitors and the wall gives excellent views of the city. The centre of Chester has a picturesque medieval appearance, with the Rows and many buildings remaining striking with their black-and-white timber-framed fronts (although the great majority of these buildings are Victorian rebuilds of the originals). There are also some handsome Georgian houses , Victorian public and commercial buildings and neoclassical buildings. The Grosvenor Museum has good displays on the Roman era in Chester, including some Roman tombstones.

Above: Watergate Street is typical, with its rich mixture of black-and-white buildings and brick and stone classical fronts.

Far left: Spectacular Victorian black-and-white work in the Rows.

Left: Chester Cathedral, the 15th-century nave with its elaborate timber roof.

Below: Eastgate Street at the turn of the century, with bold Victorian half-timbering and the jubilee clock tower on the bridge.

Top: Chesterfield, the famous twisted spire of St Mary's Church, which dominates the town.

Bottom: Chettle House standing at the head of its extensive gardens.

Chesterfield, Derbys 694 D3, In the centre of town is an enormous market place. The church of St Mary and All Saints is nationally famous because its lead and timber spire has warped into a comically twisted shape. The church beneath the spire is a large, handsome building.

Chesters Roman Fort, Nthumb 697 F2, The fort of Cilurnum [EH] housed a 500-strong cavalry regiment, and so is larger than many other forts. The surrounding wall contains particularly well-preserved examples of gateways. In the centre of the fort are the remains of barrack blocks, the 'principia' or headquarters building, and next to it the commanding officer's house, with his private bath-house and hypocaust heating system. Outside the fort, towards the North Tyne river, can be seen extensive remains of the soldiers' bath-house, an elaborate complex of rooms for hot and cold, dry and steamy conditions with changing facilities. Beside the river are the impressive stones of an abutment from the Roman bridge, several times rebuilt.

Chettle, Dorset 690 B7, This fine house, dating from about 1710–20, has a most unusual plan to commend it, and is of national importance as an illustration of English baroque. It is designed with unusual curved corners, and bears a curved projection with flat pilasters on its west front; these tricks were inspired by the Italian travels of its architect, Thomas Archer, at the end of the 17th century. Within, there is a fine double staircase which continues through an archway at the upper level, a spacial conceit beloved by artists versed, like Archer, in the Roman baroque. The staircase has a superb double flight, with three turned balusters to each tread and fluted Doric columns as newels.

Chetwode, Bucks 690 D3, A minor Augustinian priory was founded here in 1245, the church of

which was granted to the parish in 1480. This act ensured that not all of the building was lost at the Dissolution; the present St Mary and St Nicholas represents the long 13th-century chancel of the priory church.

Cheviot Hills, Nthumb 699 J6, Just south of the border, these hills were once a no-man's-land and war zone between Scotland and England, where lived the 'border reivers', feuding families who survived by raiding. The dangers of the area dictated the form of vernacular architecture found in these parts: the pele and bastle towers, miniature castles with few windows and a first-floor entrance, built of stone to resist attack by fire. Of much earlier date, set atop a 1,185-foot (361m), lightly wooded rounded hill in Glendale, is **Yeavering Bell**, a large Iron-Age fort of 13.5 acres (5.5ha), encircled by a stone rampart with three gateways and containing perhaps 130 hut circles. Beside the B6351 between Yeavering Farm and

Below: Chesters Roman Fort. The typical 'playing card' shape has gateways in each side. The regular pattern of barrack blocks is visible.

Kirknewton stands a monument marking the site of the Anglo-Saxon palace of Ad Gefrin ('the place of the goats'). This was one of the residences of the 7th-century Northumbrian King Edwin and his Queen Ethelberga, in which – according to the Venerable Bede – Paulinus gave them instruction in Christianity. The lower slopes of Yeavering Bell and the neighbouring Newton Tors are home to the Cheviot flock, shaggy brown animals descended from medieval domestic goats, the billies with large horns.

Chewton Mendip, Somset 689 H4, The church of St Mary Magdalene is Norman, but has an imposing 16th-century tower, one of the highest in Somerset. It contains fragments of medieval glass and 14th-century effigies.

Chicheley, Bucks 690 E3, A fine house built between 1719 and 1724. Its interiors bear testimony to some excellent workmanship, including a screen

possibly by Flitcroft, and there are pretty formal gardens. Previously the home of Admiral Lord Beatty, it contains a small naval museum but is privately owned and occupied.

Chichester, W Susx 690 E7, Sussex's only cathedral is small in scale but high in quality. It was begun c1090 and is still structurally a Norman building with thick walls, round arches and a minimum of ornament. In 1187 there was a great fire which destroyed the wooden roof. This was replaced by an Early English stone vault; the way in which the vaulting shafts were added to the old piers can easily be made out. At the same time the east end was extended in the same style, following Canterbury, with very refined piers surrounded by shafts of Purbeck marble with elegant crocket capitals. In 1861 the central tower and spire collapsed and were rebuilt in replica by Sir George Gilbert Scott. Inside are two very expressive sculptured reliefs showing the Raising of Lazarus and Christ in the House of Mary and Martha. Once thought to be Saxon, they are now dated about 1125. There is still a good deal of the monastic precinct left (the cloister and kitchen, for example). A very unusual, indeed unique, medieval survival is St Mary's Hospital, built c1290. It consists of a large aisled hall like the nave of a church, with a chapel at the end like a chancel; patients had beds along the walls. In the 17th century the space was divided by brick walls into tiny houses, each with a large chimney. This arrangement remains. It is normally

Left: Chichester Cathedral, the nave looking east, the walls of 1090, the vaults 1187. At the end of this view stands the Arundel Screen, a beautiful stone screen made c1460.

Below: Chillingham Castle, a mid-14th century quadrangular fortress with corner towers.

Bottom left: Chiddingstone Castle. The exterior dates from about 1830 and was designed by Henry Kendall.

private, but can be visited by appointment. The rest of Chichester is mainly Georgian, but still follows the Roman plan of two streets crossing at right-angles. At the intersection stands the octagonal market cross of 1501. Of later buildings the most notable are Pallant House, a mansion of 1712 with dodos on the gate-piers, St John's Church (1812) by James Elmes, with a huge three-decker pulpit on the focal point, and the Festival Theatre (1961) by Powell and Moya.

Chiddingstone Castle, Kent 691 G6, An exercise in Romantic Gothic, a 17th-century house with battlements added between 1808 and 1830, and a collection of Jacobite relics. The village is virtually unspoiled – 16th- and 17th-century houses, picturesquely tile-hung and timber-framed. The next village, Chiddingstone Causeway, has a notable church by JF Bentley (the architect of the Roman Catholic Westminster Cathedral), with attractive Arts and Crafts fittings.

Chilham, Kent 691 H6, A small village powerfully evocative of the past. The church (over-restored) contains three outstanding 17th-century monuments, one by Nicholas Stone, and several of the 19th century. Across the village square stand the remains of a 12th-century castle and an ambitious Jacobean house. The castle's unusual plan is laid out as five sides of a hexagon, one side

left open. Within the house, finished in 1616, not a great deal survives apart from the staircase and a few chimneypieces.

Chillingham Castle, Nthumb 699 J6, The licence for this courtyard-planned fortress, with four corner towers, was issued in 1344. An entrance range and elaborate frontispiece to the Great Hall were added in the 17th century. Unoccupied for many years, the castle is gradually being restored, and visitors can see craftsmanship in progress. The formal grounds were laid out in the Italian style by Sir Jeffry Wyatville in the early 19th century. In the enclosed park is a herd of undomesticated white cattle, descended from ancient wild oxen. The herd is dominated by a 'king bull', the fittest and

strongest of the males, which fathers all the herd's calves. There is a famous engraving of the 'Chillingham Bull' by Thomas Bewick, who was born near Stocksfield. Nearby Ros Castle is a hilltop earthwork with double ramparts.

Chillington Hall, Staffs 693 H4, The home of the Giffard family since the 12th century. The house is Georgian but its layout was dictated by an earlier incarnation. The main front with its Ionic portico is by Sir John Soane, who carried out major alterations in the 1780s and made a saloon by putting a domed roof over what had been the Great Hall of the Tudor house. The park was landscaped by Capability Brown and is an excellent example of his informal design.

Chiltern Open Air Museum, Bucks, This museum offers the visitor a unique chance to get to know the historic buildings of the region, not through photographs or drawings, but by exploring the re-erected structures themselves, many saved

from demolition. These include a furnished 1940s prefab house, a tin chapel, a 19th-century toll house and a blacksmith's forge. Look out for the tall cherry ladders in the barn. *See* **Chalfont St Giles 690 E4.**

Chilterns, The, Berks–Bucks, 690 E4, The beautiful Chiltern Hills, a long escarpment famous for its beech woods and walks, have many peaceful villages nestling within the

Top: Chillington Hall, the east front of the house, with its giant portico by Sir John Soane.

Right: The Chilterns, a scarp slope with beech woods, the classic landscape of the area.

Left: Chiltern Open Air Museum, one of the recreated interiors, complete with water pump and kitchen utensils.

Chipping Camden
Left: Monument in the church of St James.
Bottom: Mellow stone houses and the Market Hall (1627).

undulating landscape. One such example, **Abbots Langley,** has an unspoilt High Street and important church of Norman origin. Nicholas Breakspear, the only Englishman ever to become Pope of Rome (Adrian IV), was born here at the end of the first millennium.

Chippenham, Wilts 690 B5, In the northwestern reaches of the county is this railway town, with its high viaduct on the Brunel railway line from Paddington. Seek out (on foot, for it is surrounded by traffic), Ivy House and gaze through the gates at an English baroque façade of c1730, unexpected in a town which wanders in style from the 17th century to the present (and not always very inspiringly). The church of St Andrew contains a good ornate Perpendicular feature, the Hungerford Chapel, built in 1442 by Walter, Lord Hungerford, the Lord High Treasurer to Henry VI.

Chipping Camden, Gloucs 690 C3, The archetypal Cotswolds' wool merchants' town, full of lavish stone early Renaissance houses. 'Chipping' means 'market' and by 1246 the town had weekly markets and three annual fair days. William Grevell (d. 1401) was the greatest of its wool merchants, and his brass is set in the chancel floor of St James' Church. The nave, c1488, was probably built by the same masons as Northleach Church. The whole

town was revitalized in 1902 for a short while by CR Ashbee's 'Guild of Handicrafts,' which moved out of London's East End in search of a rustic idyll. Ashbee himself restored the house of William Grevel, 'flower of all wool merchants of England,' which is the prettiest house in the main street with a tall bay window, built in about 1380. His work was continued by the Campden Trust, which was formed in 1929 for architectural preservation. Annual events in Chipping Camden include the Scuttlebrook Wake and the sporting competition known as 'Dover's Games.' The games, which included leaping, wrestling and bull-baiting, lasted from 1612 to 1852 when they were stopped because of the noisy crowds. They were revived in a more sedate format at the time of the Festival of Britain, but still include shin-kicking.

Chipping Norton, Oxon 690 C3, An important market town made wealthy in the 1400s by its thriving wool trade. It retains plenty of good buildings, many re-fronted in the 1700s. Note the White Hart Hotel, and the Bunch of Grapes in Middle Row. Now converted into flats, the former King's Head is baroque with its giant fluted pilasters, possibly reflecting the influence of

Above: Chirk Castle. The yews seem to copy the shape of the battlements. The distinguished garden opens onto views of several counties across the English border.

Below: Cholmondeley Castle. The new house was begun in 1801 on a site some distance from the older mansion, with a view over the lake and the splendid park.

Vanbrugh (who was working nearby at Blenheim Palace*). Just outside the town is the Bliss Valley Tweed Mill, clearly visible from the Stow road with its tall chimney stack. It was built by Lancashire architect George Woodhouse in 1872.

Chirk Castle, Wrexhm 693 F3, Built a little south of Llangollen* by Roger Mortimer, a staunch ally of

Edward I, it was meant to have been a concentric stronghold, but only half of it was completed. Its evolution from medieval fortification to country house is a textbook study of the development of domestic architecture.

Chiselhampton, Oxon 690 D4, A wonderfully preserved and modest Georgian church of 1762. Apart from the Jacobean pulpit, all the fittings are original. Chislehampton House is 18th century; more interesting is Camoys Court, a moated manor house with 14th-century origins.

Chislehurst, Gt Lon 691 G5, A spacious village that avoids seeming suburban. In its midst is Chislehurst Common, a large expanse of green, and to one side Petts Wood, several hundred acres of untouched woodland. There are two good churches, one medieval, the other Victorian by James Brooks. Camden Place, an 18th-century house, now a golf club, was the home of Napoleon III after his exile from France. When he died a mortuary chapel by Henry Chilton was added to the Catholic church, but was later transferred to Farnborough*.

Chittlehampton, Devon 689 F5, This was the site of the martyrdom of St Urith, a local woman killed by the scythes of her neighbours in the 6th century. The pilgrimage riches this brought created an impressive church with a 115-feet (30m) high, four-stage tower rising above the important village square. Her shrine probably lay in the narrow space to the north of the chancel.

Cholmondeley Castle, Ches 693 G2, An early 19th-century house in the castle style by Robert Smirke, architect of the British Museum*, built in a good position with a view over the lake and fine landscaped grounds. There was an earlier house on the site, of which the chapel still survives, with a complete set of fittings, from the Civil War period.

Christchurch, Dorset 690 C7, This attractive old town, with its wide, shallow harbour and narrow outlet to the sea, is small and bustling. It takes its name from its impressive church (once part of an Augustinian priory), the longest parish church in the country. The towering stone reredos of c1350, with its crowded figures, tiers and niches, is awe-inspiring, rising to the height of the chancel. The carved wooden misericords afford a fascinating glimpse of medieval life and imagination: here are animals, jesters, even a fox wearing a cowl. Christchurch also has the remains of a Norman

house and castle, built originally of wood, on an artificial mound to dominate the surrounding countryside. By the late 13th century the castle had acquired walls 30 feet (9m) high and 10 feet (3m) thick, only to be reduced to ruins in the Civil War.

Christ's Hospital, W Susx 691 F6, A large Victorian public school near Horsham, which moved here from the City of London in the 1890s. The buildings were designed by Sir Aston Webb, architect of the Victoria and Albert Museum*. They consist of a large quadrangle giving access to halls and chapel. Some statues were transferred from the London site, including one by Grinling Gibbons.

Church Hanborough, Oxon 690 D4, The tall spire of the church is clearly visible in the surrounding countryside. Within, the church has a Norman tympanum over the north door and elegant arcades.

Chysauster Ancient Village, Cnwll 688 B7, Near Penzance*, this is a deserted Roman village with eight well-preserved houses [EH].

Cilgerran Castle, Pembks 692 C6, The view of the castle enjoyed by 19th-century 'tourists' as they came upstream from Cardigan is now seen only by coraclemen. Today visitors approach by way of the nondescript village of the same name, but the castle's remains still convey its importance as a Norman stronghold. It was substantially strengthened in the 13th century by William Marshall II, who showed much of the genius of his father, the builder of the great keep at Pembroke. Painters such as Richard Wilson, Turner and de Wint have left us memorable views of the rock-perched stronghold high above the Teifi.

Cirencester

Cirencester, Gloucs 690 C4, 'Ziren', as it is sometimes known locally, was for a while the second most important town in the Roman province of Britain. Founded in ad 75, the location was probably chosen because the local Dobonni tribe were well disposed towards the Romans. The Icknield Way, the Fosse Way and Ermine Street all meet here at a junction of Roman roads. The grassy remains of an amphitheatre survive to the west of the town, and many Roman finds can be seen in the Corinium Museum. The town is now agricultural and stagnating a little under the vicissitudes of British farming. However, its architectural heritage, paid for by the profits of wool-farming, is exceptionally rich. It includes St John's Hospital, built by Henry I, the Norman Abbey Gate, the Weavers' Hall, founded in 1425 to house poor weavers, and a fine Friends' Meeting House of 1673.

The church of St John the Baptist is one of the largest of the wool churches (the others are Chipping Camden*, Burford*, Northleach* and Fairford*). The scale of St John's is stupendous: the porch towards the market is three storeys high and the Perpendicular tower rises from stout battlements. This cathedral-like scale is explained, of course, by the fact that Cirencester was the largest wool market in England in the Middle Ages. The church was restored by Sir George Gilbert Scott in 1865–7. It has a peal of 12 bells.

Cirencester Park, a peculiar Palladian mansion built by the 1st Earl Bathurst, is eccentrically positioned close up to the town, sheltered by an enormous yew hedge. 'How comes it to look so oddly bad?' asked the writer, Alexander Pope. Meanwhile its park, with immensely long rides, spreads to the south. Cecily Hill leads you from the town past a mock-medieval folly into deep parkland in minutes, and on to a 5-mile (3km) avenue through the woods to Sapperton.

Top left: The Norman Abbey Gate, the only surviving feature of Cirencester Abbey.

Top: The Market Place.

Above left: Cirencester Park, built in the 18th century, is almost invisible behind its huge hedge.

Above: Many of the streets date from medieval times.

Left: Cirencester church of St John the Baptist. The west tower, as well as reaching a terrific height, contains the oldest peal of bells in the country.

Clandon Park, Surrey 690 E6, A beautiful Palladian house at West Clandon, rebuilt by Giacomo Leoni between 1713 and 1729 and little altered since [NT]. The plain brick exterior does nothing to prepare one for the stunning two-storeyed, stuccoed Marble Hall, which has fireplaces and overmantels by JM Rysbrack. Clandon Park contains good collections of 18th-century furniture and ceramics, and houses both the Ivo Forde Meissen collection of Commedia dell' arte figures and the Queen's Royal Surrey Regiment Museum. The 18th-century Maori Meeting House in the garden comes as quite a surprise.

Clare, Suffk 691 H3, A fascinating place with earthworks from an Iron-Age hill fort and a Norman motte. It also boasts the remains of England's first Austin Friars priory, founded in 1248. Beside the churchyard the 15th-century Ancient House Museum, once a priest's house, is pargeted with luxuriant foliage and dated 1473.

A wonderfully carved swan gives the pub its name in the High Street. The church is still interesting despite the attentions of 'Smasher' Dowsing, who 'brake down 1,000 superstitious images' during the Reformation.

Claremont Landscape Garden, Surrey, This beautiful garden on the south edge of Esher was created in

Clandon Park
Top: Leendert Knyff's painting showing Clandon in its early formal setting in 1708.
Above: The main entrance.

Left: Claremont Landscape Garden, the lake from across the ha-ha showing the cascade and island pavilion, Anon, c1740.

the 18th century and worked on by Vanbrugh, William Kent and Capability Brown. It has been well restored by the National Trust and includes a lake with an island, a turf amphitheatre and a grotto. The 18th- and 19th-century house is now a school but advertises opening times. *See* **Esher* 691 F5.**

Clava Cairns, Highld 701 H5, Clava Cairns, to the south of Nairn, are three burial mounds of a very particular type. Each of the mounds, which are at least 4000 years old, is surrounded by a circle of standing stones. Three stone pavements radiate out from the central cairn (ring-type but with no entrance) to its circle of stones. The other two are passage-type cairns. Funerary objects and human remains, some bearing evidence of cremation, were discovered on the site. The beliefs and rituals of the people who built these cairns have sunk into oblivion – the significance of the cup-like depressions in some of the stones is not known – and the site remains shrouded in mystery.

Claverley, Shrops 693 H4, The church of All Saints is a large building that forms a charming group with the 15th-century vicarage, the lych gate and the village cross, and dominates the village below. The history of the church is complex and begins in the late 11th century; the north aisle is early 12th century, the south aisle 13th century; the chancel was rebuilt in the 14th century and most of the rest is 15th and 16th century. But the justification for a trip to Claverley is to see the wonderful series of wall-paintings on the north wall of the nave. They date from about 1200 and show the battle between the virtues and the vices, with the characters dressed as mounted knights in armour.

C   Claydon House

Top left: Charles I, after Sir
Anthony Van Dyck, in the Saloon.

Bottom left: Overhead view of an
Octagonal Table in the Library,
showing a head of Bacchus.

Top right: The Chinese Room.

Centre: The west front.

Bottom right: Portrait of Sir Edward
Verney, 3rd Bt, by GB Canevari.

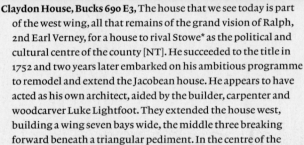

Claydon House, Bucks 690 E3, The house that we see today is part of the west wing, all that remains of the grand vision of Ralph, 2nd Earl Verney, for a house to rival Stowe* as the political and cultural centre of the county [NT]. He succeeded to the title in 1752 and two years later embarked on his ambitious programme to remodel and extend the Jacobean house. He appears to have acted as his own architect, aided by the builder, carpenter and woodcarver Luke Lightfoot. They extended the house west, building a wing seven bays wide, the middle three breaking forward beneath a triangular pediment. In the centre of the ground floor is a Venetian window, with a rusticated Gibbsian surround, set in a recessed arch. Above the pedimented ground-floor windows are roundels with false windows. It was not until 1768, when further works were planned, that Verney called for the aid of the gentleman architect, Sir Thomas Robinson. The main front was extended to an impressive 265 feet (80m) and a rotunda entrance hall constructed. But it soon turned sour;

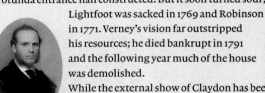

Lightfoot was sacked in 1769 and Robinson in 1771. Verney's vision far outstripped his resources; he died bankrupt in 1791 and the following year much of the house was demolished.

While the external show of Claydon has been curtailed, the interior remains an exuberant rococo fantasy, and one of the finest decorative schemes in the country. Much of the decoration is not, as it might appear, plasterwork, but in fact carved woodwork, or papier-mâché. The craftsman was Lightfoot, and the work is an astonishing testament to his skill and imagination. In the Pink Parlour, the scenes are taken from Francis Barlow's illustrations of Aesop's *Fables*, a popular source for rococo decoration. The double-cubed Hall contains carved swans, wyverns, *putti*, trophies and garlands. Upstairs the decoration continues, most spectacularly in the Chinese and Rococo rooms, the latter with a pagoda-like alcove and *chinoiserie* decoration.

The staircase is a beautiful piece of design, with parquetry steps and a wrought-iron balustrade of scrolls with gilded husks of corn. Florence Nightingale was a relation of the Verneys and a frequent visitor to the house; her room can be seen upstairs. The church contains a handsome monument to Edmund Verney, who died at the Battle of Edgehill.

Clayton, W Susx 691 F7, A small, unassuming church, but containing what is probably the best collection of Romanesque wall-paintings in England. They cover most of the chancel arch and north wall (and originally the south and west walls as well). What survives shows the Last Judgement with Christ as judge and the blessed being received into Heaven. They were painted about 1140 and discovered under layers of whitewash in 1895. Also at Clayton is the gothic entrance to a railway tunnel built in 1840 and two windmills called Jack and Jill.

Clearwell Caves, Gloucs 693 G7, A 'scowle hole' is a surface mine used casually by the old coal-miners of the Forest of Dean*, but at Clearwell they burrowed deeper into a natural cave system in search of iron and the minerals used in cosmetics. The long chambers are littered with debris and mining equipment, often knocked together by the miners from unlikely materials. In the furthest cave an iron ladder leads enticingly down to deeper levels not open to the public.

Cleeve Abbey, Somset 689 G4, Extensive remains of an abbey, founded as a Cistercian house in 1198. Best preserved is the complete grouping of cloister buildings. The refectory was rebuilt in the 16th century, and has one of the finest timber wagon

Top right: Clevedon Court manor house was once partly fortified.

Cley next the Sea
Above: A windmill on the edge of Cley marshes
Below: The Norfolk Wildlife Trust nature reserve.

roofs in Somerset, with carved angels supporting the principal beams. Cleeve was saved from destruction at the Dissolution by being turned into a house and then a farm.

Cleeve Hill, Gloucs 693 H6, An archeological as well as a geological oddity, and the highest point of the Cotswolds. The Iron-Age fort of Cleeve Cloud provides stunning views [EH].

Clevedon Court, Somset 689 H3, Here is a town that is still predominantly Victorian, although Clevedon Court manor house, 2 miles (3km) from the centre, is mainly 14th century [NT]. Once partly fortified, it has a 12th-century tower and 13th-century Hall, but it is the splendid collection of Nailsea glass and pottery by the English art potter, Sir Edmund Elton (1846–1920), that attracts most visitors. Clevedon Court was the Elton family home from 1709.

Cley next the Sea, Norfk 695 H4, Forsaken by the sea, Cley (pronounced to rhyme with 'fly') was once a prosperous port on the Glaven estuary. An elegant

18th-century Customs House, photogenic windmill by the old quay and curious 'knucklebone' house (so called because of its distinctive cornice of animal vertebrae) adorn the congested main street. St Margaret's Church, an ambitious 14th-century structure with magnificent clerestoried nave and 15th-century porch, peers out over Newgate Green towards Wiveton church on the opposite bank. The church has an atmospheric interior and tabletomb in the churchyard to James Greeve (d. 1686), 'who was Assistant of Sir Cloudesly Shovel [another Norfolk sea captain] in ye burning ye Shipps in ye Port of Tripoly in Barbary Jan. 14th 1676'. Cley marshes, with its mixture of reedbeds, grazing marshes and shallow pools, is one of the best bird sanctuaries in the country. Established in 1936, it is Norfolk Wildlife Trust's oldest reserve, with waterfowl, rare migrants, breeding avocets and bittern, hides and a visitor centre.

Cliffe, Kent 691 G5, A fine medieval church, the nave 13th century, the chancel added soon after 1300, with especially inventive window-tracery.

Clifton Reynes, Bucks , St Mary contains interesting 14th-century tombs to the Reynes family, with wooden effigies. The carving on the font is also worth noting. *See* **Olney* 690 E3.**

Climping, W Susx 690 E7, A remarkable Norman church. The tower has a flat buttress on each side, and in the buttress a narrow window with deeply carved zig-zag ornamentation all round, not just top and sides, an extraordinary effect.

Clitheroe, Lancs 697 F6, This is the chief town of the valleys of the upper Ribble and its tributaries. The town is compact, its chief monument a castle now in a municipal park and said to have the smallest keep in England; it houses a tiny museum. Damage to the eastern wall was probably due to its neglect after being held for the Crown in the Civil War, though local legend attributes it to a stone thrown by a giant from Pendle Hill. The surrounding countryside has some delightful villages, such as Downham and Slaidburn, the latter with St Andrew's Church, especially notable for its joinery including a Jacobean screen and a three-decker pulpit.

Cliveden, Bucks 690 E5, The estate comprises 375 acres (115ha) of beautiful gardens and woodland set around an Italianate country house, built in 1850–1 and designed by Charles Barry [NT]. It offers spectacular views along the Thames Valley and includes a parterre, rose garden and water garden, with a Chinese pavilion made for the Paris Exhibition of 1867. The Octagon Temple of 1735, designed by Giacomo Leoni, was converted into a chapel during the 1800s and has a lovely Byzantine-style mosaic interior. Three rooms of the house (a hotel since 1985) are currently open to the public.

Cliveden
Opposite page: The Fountain of Love, made by Thomas Waldo Story in Rome in 1897.
Right: Charles Barry's Italianate exterior.
Bottom: Portrait of Nancy Astor, by John Singer Sargent, 1906.

Below: Clumber Chapel, a superb building of the 1880s.

Below centre: Clovelly harbour, one of the few safe anchorages on the North Devon coast.

Below right: Clun Castle.

Clovelly, Devon 688 E5, Best approached along the 3-mile (5km) Hobby Drive through hanging woods above the precipitous coast, the village is justly famed for its beauty. The steep cobbled main street with its donkey-drawn sledges leads down to a tiny harbour and curved pier. Much of the character of the place dates from between the wars, so would not have been known by Charles Kingsley, whose father was the rector here, and who describes the village in *Westward Ho!* (1855).

Clumber Park, Notts 694 D3, A mansion of the Dukeries (*see* Sherwood Forest*), built by the Duke of Newcastle in the 1760s. It was enlarged in the 19th century but pulled down in 1938 when the future of such great houses seemed bleaker than it does now. There is a large and splendid park, with a serpentine lake, Victorian walled garden and apiary [NT].

Clun, Shrops 693 F4, A little town, rising steeply from the medieval bridge over the river Clun, with a spectacular ruined castle looking out over open country [EH].

Clynnog-fawr, Gwynd 692 D2, Very much part of the Pilgrims' Way was the *clas* (monastery) at Clynnog Fawr, the principal shrine of St Beuno. The importance of the site resulted in major rebuilding between the 15th and 16th centuries, making it one of the finest perpendicular churches in North Wales. The saint himself is, by tradition, buried here, and the chapel built in his memory was visited by pilgrims who sought the healing powers of nearby St Beuno's Well on their way to Bardsey Island (*see* Lleyn*). Nearby, in a field overlooking the sea, is the neolithic burial chamber of Bachwen, distinguished by its ornate capstone.

Cobham, Kent 691 G5, A small village with three buildings of outstanding interest, St Mary's Church, the College and the Hall. The church was built in the 13th century and in the 14th received a lavish piscina and sedilia. Its claim to fame, however, is its exceptionally rich collection of monumental brasses, unmatched in the whole country for quantity and quality. They mostly commemorate the lords of Cobham and their wives, and the masters of the College, ranging in date from 1310 to 1529. All are worth close examination for the details of the men's armour and the women's costumes.

The College was founded in 1362 by Sir John de Cobham for a master and four priests to say masses in perpetuity for his soul. In 1598, after Henry VIII had abolished masses for the dead, it was turned into an almshouse. There were originally two courtyards, of which only one remains, containing the Hall. Twenty elderly people live here; it is a place of calm beauty where anyone would be happy to end their days.

Cobham Hall is one of England's major Elizabethan houses – very large, very ornate, and in its time very modern. It consists of three wings, the two at

the sides (north and south) of the 1580s and 1590s, the middle one later, of the 1660s. The north and south wings are impressively long, of brick, with bay windows, prominent chimneys and turrets at the ends. The house is now a school and has been a good deal altered but it retains many original features, notably a series of huge extravagant chimneypieces. The Long Gallery is on the upper floor of the north wing. In the central wing the best room is the Gilt Hall, with its original ceiling of 1672 and walls decorated by James Wyatt in the 1790s. In the grounds is a mausoleum by Wyatt (1783), a severely classical design of Doric columns surmounted by a pyramid. It has been walled up because of vandalism, but is currently being restored.

Cobham, Surrey 691 F5, A large and busy village in two parts, Street Cobham and Church Cobham. There are some good buildings in the area including 18th-century Cedar House (Mill Road), which incorporates medieval work.

Cochwillan, Gwynd 692 D2, Situated near Tal-y-bont, and arguably one of the first gentry houses to be built after the

Cockermouth
Above: Wordsworth's House, where the poet was born in 1770.
Right: Portrait of Wordsworth by an unknown artist.

Cobham Hall
Left: View showing the central block of the 1660s, with two earlier wings on either side.
Below: The Gilt Hall, combining a ceiling of 1672, galleries of 1779 and wall decoration by James Wyatt of 1791.

Tudor accession. Having served as a barn for centuries, it was restored in the 1960s to reveal the splendid craftsmanship of its roof timbers.

Cockayne Hatley, Beds 691 F3, The baroque woodwork in St John the Baptist makes it unique in Bedfordshire. It was mostly brought from Belgium in the 1820s by the then lord of the manor, Henry Cust. The heavily ornate stalls and stall-backs with their Catholic saints came from Aulne Abbey near Charleroi, and are dated 1689. The Yorkshire stained glass in the north aisle is also worth a look.

Cockburnspath, Border 699 H4, Cockburnspath has a 14th-century church surmounted by a 16th-century round beacon-tower and a market cross erected in 1503. About a mile to the northwest the beautiful Dunglass Collegiate Church (15th century) stands in the Dunglass House estate.

Cockermouth, Cumb 696 D3, A small market town with the remains of a medieval castle on a dramatic site at the junction of the Derwent and Cocker rivers. Wordsworth House, the birthplace of the poet [NT] is the best Georgian building in the town. This is a large nine-bay fronted town house in Main Street, now housing a collection of Wordsworthiana.

Cockington, Devon 689 F7, A popular stop just west of Torquay*, this pretty hamlet has a 16th-century court, a forge, and a fine inn designed in the 1930s by Sir Edwin Lutyens.

Cogges, Oxon 690 D4, Immediately south of Witney*, an L-shaped house incorporating work of c1250, with its Manor Farm Museum. The rooms have been furnished to depict life in the 1800s.

The manor was recorded in the Domesday Book and the moats are still visible, although dry. The church tower is unusual, having a square base that becomes octagonal in the upper stages and is capped by a conical roof. To the east of the village was a small Benedictine priory established by the monks of Fécamp in Normandy, and French influence can be seen in the church, particularly in the carving of the north chapel. *See* **Witney***.

Coggeshall, Essex 691 H3, This village of pargetted plaster houses was the home of Thomas Paycocke, wealthiest cloth merchant in Tudor Coggeshall, who built a fine timber-framed house in 1505. Paycocke's [NT] contains exquisite wood carving and linenfold panelling, plus a display of Coggeshall lace. A Cistercian abbey, founded around 1140, has disappeared, save for an early gothic gate-chapel. The idyllic setting of a weather-boarded water-mill on the Blackwater remains unchanged since monastic times. Coggeshall Grange Barn, Europe's earliest timber-framed barn, with nave and side aisles, was where the monks stored their tithe-tax, a tenth of farm production.

Coity Castle, V Glam 689 G3, A Norman castle, now in ruins but still extensive and magnificent. The 12th-century keep is surrounded by curtain walls. A round tower was added in the 13th century and the eastern gatehouse in the 14th century.

Top: Coggeshall, Thomas Paycocke's sumptuous medieval merchant's house.

Above: Coggeshall Grange Barn, timber-framed and weatherboarded with a great peg tile roof sweeping down over the nave and side aisles.

Right: Colby Woodland Garden has delightful walks through secluded valleys.

Colby Woodland Garden, Pembks 692 C7, The property takes its name from the family who built a new residence in the early 19th century on an old estate near Amroth. The work was supervised by John Nash, who had been responsible for the principal Colby house, Ffynone (now the home of the Earl Lloyd George of Dwyfor). Colby Lodge,

described in 1834 as 'an elegant mansion beautifully situated in a romantic dell opening at one extremity towards the sea, of which it commands a fine and interesting view', is privately occupied, but the gardens were bequeathed to the National Trust in 1979 by the owner at the time, who had been responsible for creating an early 20th-century rhododendron

Above: Colby Woodland Garden, a view showing Colby Lodge.

plantation with extensive woodland walks. The walled garden is enhanced by a raised polygonal gothic gazebo with decorated cornices. The peace and serenity of this outstanding horticultural enclave give little indication of the shallow coal-mining activity in the area which persisted until the 18th century. Part of the estate has been designated a Site of Special Scientific Interest.

Colchester

Colchester, Essex 691 H3, On a ridge above the Colne valley, Colchester's Victorian brick skyline announces Britain's oldest recorded town. The 'painfully assertive' (according to Pevsner) water-tower looks decidedly Italianate and the civic tower is crowned by a statue of Constantine the Great's mother, St Helena, born here in the garrison town. Before surrendering to Claudius the British king Cunobelin (Shakespeare's Cymbeline) ruled southeast England from here (at that time known as 'Camulodunum'). The western edge of this capital of the Trinovantes tribe is marked by the Lexden dykes, still partly intact, that ran from the Colne south to the Roman River.

The *colonia* established by Claudius and stormed by Boudicca was resurrected with grand public buildings within mighty, still-visible walls that include the great Balkerne Gate. Using Roman brick and local stone, the Normans built Europe's largest castle keep directly over the Claudian temple. It now houses the greatest collection of Roman artefacts found in Britain. Re-used brick is also evident in the colonnaded remains of St Botolph's Priory, founded nearby, c1100, as the Augustinianss first English base, and wrecked in a Civil War siege. St John's Benedictine Abbey, south of the

Left: Bourne Mill, an ornate Elizabethan fishing lodge that was later converted into a working mill. Much of the machinery is intact, including the waterwheel.

Top: Colchester Castle.

Below left: St Botolph's Priory.

Right: St John's Abbey, the Gate House.

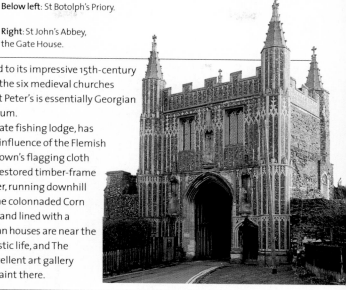

centre across a congested relief road, was reduced to its impressive 15th-century flint-panelled gatehouse in the same conflict. Of the six medieval churches within the walls, Holy Trinity has a Saxon tower, St Peter's is essentially Georgian and All Saints has become a natural history museum.

Bourne Mill, built a mile south in 1591 as an ornate fishing lodge, has elaborately shaped gables that demonstrate the influence of the Flemish weavers invited by Queen Elizabeth to revive the town's flagging cloth industry with their 'New Draperies'. Delightfully restored timber-frame houses rub shoulders with Georgian brickwork in the old Dutch Quarter, running downhill from the High Street, where the late 15th-century Red Lion Hotel and the colonnaded Corn Hall (1820) are most impressive. North and East hills are both dramatic and lined with a series of good buildings from the 16th century onwards. The best Georgian houses are near the Castle and include Holly Trees (1716), now the town's museum of domestic life, and The Minories, 1776, built for cloth merchant Thomas Boggis and now an excellent art gallery with charming garden, linked to the Pissarro family as Lucien used to paint there.

Cold Knap, V Glam 689 G4, Beyond the causeway leading to Barry Island and its funfair is Cold Knap, its Roman foundations submerged by a 20th-century development of prim houses, a boating lake, and a 1920s lido, the only one of its kind in Wales.

Coleridge Cottage, Somset 689 G4, The little village of Nether Stowey lies 8 miles (13km) west of Bridgwater*, on the A39. In Lime Street is Coleridge Cottage [NT], where Samuel Taylor Coleridge lived from 1797 to 1800. Here he wrote part of 'Christabel', as well as 'The Rime of the Ancient Mariner', and there are mementoes of the poet on display. Wordsworth lived just 2 miles (3.2km) away, at Alfoxden.

Coleton Fishacre, Devon 689 F7, Between Brixham and Kingswear lies a property first acquired by the National Trust for its magnificent coastline, but now both the house and garden, created 1923–26 by Oswald Milne for Richard and Lady Dorothy D'Oyly Carte (of the Gilbert and Sullivan operas and the Savoy Hotel), are open to the public as well. The cool, spacious interiors and loggia look out across the colourful and luxuriant grounds that run down the small valley to the sea.

Coll, Ag & B 698 A2, The port of Arinagour is the island's only village. Breacachadh Castle, a

Below centre: Coleridge Cottage. This simple house was home to the poet Samuel Taylor Coleridge for three years at the end of the 18th century.

Below right: Colne, St Bartholemew's Church.

Bottom: Coll, the tower-house of Breacachadh Castle.

15th-century tower-house, stands at the head of a loch on the southwest coast. The castle has been restored and is now a training centre for humanitarian aid workers. It stands in the middle of a bird sanctuary which stretches to the southern tip of the island and is frequented by the red-throated diver and greylag goose. The most beautiful beaches are found on the northwest coast, once the most populated part of the island.

Colmworth, Beds 695 F6, The church, St Denis, contains a commanding monument of excellent quality to Sir William Dyer and family (1641).

Colne, Lancs 697 F6, A gritty town high on the western side of the Pennines. Its best building, St Bartholomew's Church, is a good example of the long low late medieval churches of the northwest.

Colonsay, Ag & B 698 A4, The island has beautiful beaches, rich plant life and a number of megaliths. To the north of Scalasaig, the island's only village, Colonsay House is open to the public. The magnificent gardens of this 18th-century mansion have many varieties of exotic plants, introduced by Lord Strathcona, who bought the island in 1904. At low tide, Colonsay is linked to the island of Oronsay by a causeway. On Oronsay stand the fine ruins of an Augustinian priory built in the 14th century on the site of a Celtic monastery. An Irish stonemason from Iona, by the name of O'Cuinn, is said to have carved the beautiful cross (1510) to the west of St Oran's Chapel.

Colyton, Devon 689 G6, A pleasant town still run by its elected feoffees. Despite the ravages of a fire in 1933, the church of St Andrew is worth visiting for the much-restored tomb of Margaret, Countess of Devon and grand-daughter of John of Gaunt, and the 17th-century monument to Sir John Pole and his wife Elizabeth.

Combe, Berks 690 D5, A remote hamlet south of Walbury Hill, with the remarkable Combe Gibbet, a tall gallows on a Neolithic barrow. Its isolation and aspect is disturbing even today.

Combe Martin, Devon 689 F4, Combe Martin is said to have the longest High Street in Britain, running for 3 miles (4.8km) through the village. It also boasts the extraordinary 18th-century white-painted Pack of Cards Inn, a four-storey house on a cruciform plan with 52 windows and eight chimneys. In the 16th and in the 19th centuries there were small silver mines in the parish. From this Devonshire silver, a shawl pin fashioned in the form of Dartmouth and Kingswear castles , was made by Henry Ellis of Exeter and presented to Queen Victoria.

Above: Compton Castle, the Great Hall, originally built c1340 and restored in 1955.

Left: Colyton, the church of St Andrew with its octagonal top storey to the crossing tower.

Combe Sydenham, Somset 689 G4, This deer park and woodland walks are set on the site of a monastic settlement near Taunton; the house is mainly of c1580. Guided tours are available.

Come-to-Good, Cnwll 688 C7, In a secret valley, with its Quaker Meeting House of whitewashed cob and thatch and adjoining stable (1709).

Compton, Surrey 690 E6, The rural village of Compton is remarkable for two things: its ancient church and the Watts Gallery. The church of **St Nicholas** was originally built in the 11th century, but its most memorable work dates from the later 1100s. This period is represented mainly by the impressive two-storeyed sanctuary separated from the chancel by a late-12th-century guard rail, one of the country's earliest pieces of church woodwork. The well-known Victorian painter and sculptor George Frederic Watts lived at Compton for much of his life. Over 350 of his works are displayed in the fascinating **Watts Gallery**, purpose-built in 1903 near his country house, Limnerslease. Also open to the public is the extraordinary Cemetery Chapel, designed by Watts' wife Mary. The circular interior is completely covered in ornate Celtic and Art Nouveau decoration.

Compton Acres Gardens, Dorset 690 C7, The famous gardens near Poole* surround a neo-Tudor villa of 1914. They were laid out from 1919 and include

Above: Compton Wynyates, the west front.

Left: Compton Acres Gardens, near Poole.

Right: Compton Castle, Devon.

Below: Compton, the 19th-century red-brick Mission Cottage.

rock and water gardens, Japanese and Italian gardens, a Heather Dell, a Woodland Walk and a subtropical Glen. There is attractive bronze and marble statuary.

Compton Beauchamp, Oxon 690 C5, Compton House dates originally from the early 16th century but was much altered in the Georgian period. It has a tall centre and lower wings. Near the moat of the house is the little church of St Swithin, probably built in the 13th century, with transepts and a slender west tower. The paintings in the chancel (c1900) are by Lydia Lawrence.

Compton Castle, Devon 689 F7, The Gilbert family built this fortified manor house with curtain walls in three periods: 1340, 1450 and 1520 [NT].

Compton Verney, Warwks 690 C3, The mansion has recently opened to visitors as an excellent and unusual museum with widely varied art collections from unexpected traditions. It is built in the bleak

Vanbrughian style, standing in a serene and rolling park.

Compton Wynyates, Warwks 690 C3, Once known as 'Compton-in-the-Hole' because of its position in a dip among the surrounding hills, about 10 miles (16km) west of Banbury*, it is one of the most visually satisfying of early Tudor houses. Gabled, turretted and rambling, surrounded today by clipped yews, it was visited in its time by Henry VIII, Elizabeth I and Charles I. Its later name, 'Wyn Yates,' refers to the vineyards that once thrived here.

C

Left: Conisbrough Castle was commissioned by Henry II in the late 12th century.

Left: Congresbury Church spire and a stone carving of a parishioner with toothache, who was miraculously cured by Bishop Button in the 13th century.

Condover, Shrops 693 G4, Although the north transept of Condover church is late Norman, the south transept, nave and tower were all rebuilt in 1662, just after the restoration of King Charles II. The nave is unusually wide, almost certainly because it replaces both the nave and aisles of the older church. Over it all rises a handsome late 17th-century timber hammerbeam roof. The church contains an excellent collection of monuments to the Owen and Cholmondeley families, of which the most striking are Roubliac's mid-18th-century statues of Roger Owen and his wife, and the monuments to Reginald Cholmondeley and his wife Alice, both by the great Victorian painter and sculptor George Frederick Watts. Near the church

Right: Conishead Priory in its new incarnation as a Buddhist Centre.

Below: Conisbrough Castle's six canted buttresses are remarkably well preserved.

stands Condover Hall, the grand late-Elizabethan mansion built of stone in the 1590s by Thomas Owen (d. 1598). The interior contains some good 18th-century decoration.

Congresbury, Somset 689 H4, A village of beautiful doorways, not least that of the 13th-century church, boasting one of the most graceful of Somerset's few spires. Inside is a font with a bucket-shaped Norman bowl on a 13th-century pedestal, and with a Jacobean cover. Between the clerestory windows is a collection of little people in red and green, many of whom are obviously suffering from toothache. They are believed to commemorate Bishop Button, whose wonderful cures are remembered in his cathedral at Wells*.

Conisbrough Castle, S York 694 D2, The inspiration for Sir Walter Scott's Rotherwood in *Ivanhoe*, the Castle [EH] has a superb late 12th-century keep, a fine example of Norman military architecture which is, unusually, circular in plan. The battered base ingeniously merges into six buttresses which project deeply and are also canted. The extraordinarily thick walls contain staircases and passages, but could not easily be pierced for

windows; the interior must therefore have been extremely dark when originally roofed, despite the high quality of the internal architectural details. On the top floor is the private oratory with rib vaulting and richly carved bosses. The ground-floor chamber could be accessed only from above by means of a central eye in its stone vault, through which water could be drawn up from a well.

Conishead Priory, Cumbria 696 E5, The priory was built in 1821–6 by Philip Wyatt for Colonel Bradyll. It is a folly of Fonthill*-like ambition but fortunately it has not fallen down. A huge example of pre-archeological Gothic Revival, it has neither the earnestness nor the quality of materials that marked the later stages of the movement. The interior contains some good woodwork – some of it imported from Samlesbury* – and its new use as a Buddhist centre has wrought some unlikely changes: Wyatt's magnificent staircase now frames a majestic statue of the Buddha.

Conwy

Conwy, Conwy 692 E2, The character of this 13th-century fortified town with its 21 towers could have been completely destroyed had not Nicholas Edwards (Secretary of State for Wales, 1979–87) and the Marquess of Anglesey insisted that a tunnel rather than a new road was the solution to the town's notorious traffic congestion. Edward I's castle took full advantage of a rock that controlled mountain and estuary. Access from the east was possible only by ferry until Thomas Telford's elegant suspension bridge was erected in 1825, a precursor of his other masterpiece that crosses the Menai Strait to Anglesey*. That bridge carried all the traffic until the present one was built in 1958. Like Caernarfon*, Conwy is a two-warded castle of eight drum towers, four of which are surmounted by turrets and mark the second ward as the independently defensible royal quarters. The disjointed shape of the Great Hall indicates how the fortress was built to obey the contours of the rock. From the ramparts, the two humps of the ancient defensive site that Henry III adapted for his own castle at Deganwy are a prominent landmark. Edward abandoned his father's stronghold in order to gain easier access to tidal water, a major consideration of defence. Queen Eleanor's Chapel is one of the best preserved rooms in the castle.

A hundred years before Edward completed his enterprise at Conwy, work had just finished on the church of the Cistercian Abbey of Conwy, founded by Llywelyn ap Iorwerth as part of the Llys (court) of the Welsh princes, but transferred by Edward to a new site at Maenan in the Conwy Valley. The Abbey was put to parochial use as the church of St Mary and All Saints. A fine rood screen and a late 15th-century font have avoided zealous 19th-century restoration. A handsome bust celebrates the achievements of John Gibson, the distinguished early Victorian sculptor and native of the town.

The town's oldest domestic building is **Aberconwy House**, on the corner of Castle Street and High Street; the timber jetties make a striking contrast with the rest of the house, which is of stone [NT]. Since 1990 the upper floors have been furnished to illustrate the use of the building from its origins as a merchant's house to the period when, between 1850 and 1910, it was a temperance hotel.

In the High Street, and extending almost to Chapel Street, is **Plas Mawr**, the display-case of Robert Wynn, a go-getting Elizabethan gentleman with all the right connections. Its refurbishment by CADW in the mid-1990s has highlighted the social as well as the architectural importance of Wynn's house, probably the best surviving example of its period in Britain. Behind Plas Mawr, in an imaginatively converted chapel, is the gallery of the Royal Cambrian Academy of Art.

Above: Aberconwy House was built around 1490 for a local timber merchant, but has been much altered over the years.

Below: Conwy Castle. Stephenson's railway bridge on the left was an attempt to blend with the mighty castellations of Edward I's great fortress of the 1280s.

Cookham, Berks 690 E5, In 1891 the well-loved artist Stanley Spencer was born in this pretty village by the Thames, a place that inspired him throughout his life. The **Stanley Spencer Gallery**, opened in 1962 in a converted chapel in the heart of Cookham, contains an important collection of his work, including *The Last Supper* of 1920 and *Beatitudes of Love: Contemplation* of 1937. The atmosphere is kept alive by staff and Friends, whose enthusiasm for Spencer's work is infectious.

Combe Bank, Kent 691 G5, A Palladian mansion near Sundridge, designed for the Duke of Argyll by Roger Morris, a follower of Lord Burlington, whose influence is very apparent here. In 1879 Walter Crane redecorated the Saloon, where a frieze of 16th-century Florentine paintings runs round the top of the wall. Crane made elaborate carved doorcases and fireplaces, and a spectacular ceiling representing the signs of the zodiac in relief.

Copford, Essex 691 H3, Impressive Romanesque frescoes in this atmospheric Norman church were probably part of the original 1140s building plans. The best, in the apse, shows Christ encircled by angels and a rainbow, preceded by the signs of the zodiac around the entrance.

Corbridge Roman Site and Museum, Nthumb, 697 F2 The site of Roman Corstopitum lies just south of Hadrian's Wall*. The town [EH] was established in the 80s AD and was occupied – longer than any other site in the area – until the Romans withdrew from Britain early in the 5th century. Initially a fort, its strategic location at the

junction of Dere Street and the Stanegate, two major Roman roads, meant that it developed into an important supply depot; the remains of extensive granaries, with their ingenious ventilation system, can still be seen. Fine artefacts in the site museum include the well-known Corbridge Lion, originally part of a fountain. In Corbridge itself, the market town half a mile (0.8km) away, Roman stones were used to build the Vicar's Pele, a fortified vicarage dating from *c*1300. The church of St Andrew was an important Saxon monastery.

Corfe Castle, Dorset 690 B8, One of Britain's most majestic ruins, the castle has a bloody history,

Above and bottom: Corfe Castle was a powerful castle at the head of the Purbeck Valley from the 11th century, until it was ruined by Parliamentary forces in 1646.

Below left: Corbridge Roman Site Museum, a bronze jug and a glass flask used to carry oil, both found on the site.

having been the scene, in AD 978, of the murder of the 18-year-old King Edward ('The Martyr'). It once controlled the gateway to the Isle of Purbeck, and had been an important fortification until it was besieged by Cromwell in 1646. Lady Bankes defended it valiantly against an army of more than 500 Parliamentarians for six weeks, until she was eventually betrayed. Much of its stone was later used in local buildings. Although it is now little more than a jumble of walls, ramparts and steep ditches, it is still impressive on its hilltop site, and has a fine array of Norman and Early English features to tell its long story [NT].

Corgarff Castle, Abers 702 C6, This 16th-century castle was converted into a barracks for Hanoverian troops after the Battle of Culloden* in 1746. Its star-shaped loopholed wall was built in 1748. During the 1830s the garrison played a key role in the suppression of smuggling, especially of whisky.

Cornwell, Oxon 690 C3, This village, nestling in a little valley, was completely gone over in 1938–9 by Clough Williams-Ellis, the architect responsible for Portmeirion* in Wales. He enclosed the Green with a stone wall and there is now no entry except for access.

Top left: Corsham Court's unified, symmetrical front elevation. It was added to in the 18th and 19th centuries.

Below: The State Rooms contain an outstanding collection of over 150 paintings, many housed in the celebrated Picture Gallery of the 1760s.

Cornworthy, Devon 689 F7, Nestling in the hills above the River Dart, the medieval church has interesting monuments, and a pulpit surmounted with a trumpeting angel given by John Seale of Dartmouth* (d. 1777).

Corsham Court, Wilts 690 B5, A celebrated Elizabethan house of 1582, halfway between Bath* and Chippenham*. It was bought by Paul Methuen in the mid-18th century and now houses an outstanding collection of about 150 paintings, including some fine Italian Renaissance pieces and works by Van Dyck. The design includes Capability Brown's Picture Gallery of the 1760s (he also worked in the surrounding park), in which paintings are set over crimson damask. This damask also covers the large suite of Chippendale-style settees and chairs, all set below a plaster ceiling by Thomas Stocking of Bristol*.

Cotehele, Cnwll 688 E6, This ancient estate was the home of the Edgcumbes from the 15th century. The present house [NT] became their secondary residence after the construction of Mount Edgcumbe*, and therefore slumbered until renovations in 1862 transformed the old service range into a dower house. The original state

Cotehele
Centre left: The fortified entrance front.
Centre: The Great Hall hung with ancient armour and unchanged since 1840.
Bottom right: An Italian cabinet in the old Drawing Room.

rooms survive in a remarkable way; filled with Flemish and English tapestries and curious and ancient furniture, they have not changed since Nicholas Condy recorded them in c1840. Four four-poster beds have survived with a variety of elaborate, rare and early hangings, and chairs in the Punch Room still possess their early 18th-century covering of 'Queen Anne's tatting'. Beyond the delightful gardens is the Prospect Tower, the Chapel in the Woods and the manorial Mill. The last of the Tamar barges, *The Shamrock*, is moored at the once-busy quay. This was a famous market-gardening and mining area in the 19th century, but it is now difficult to imagine the teeming traffic of sailing vessels and paddle steamers that once plied the narrow channel of the Tamar.

Cothay Manor, Somset 689 G5, At Greenham stands the finest example of a small medieval manor house in England; it has remained virtually untouched since it was built in c1480. It gazes out over lake waters and its gardens (first laid out in the 1920s) have been revised and extended.

Cotswolds, The, Gloucs–Wilts 690 C4, Not true hills, but uplands or 'wolds', full of sheep enclosures or 'cots'. They stretch for 100 miles (160km) from Chipping Campden* to Bath*. The character of the villages comes from the stone – Jurassic limestone, originally formed in a warm and shallow sea. Plentiful and easily worked, it was the obvious material for the increasingly prosperous sheep farmers and wool merchants to use for their churches and manors from the 14th century onwards. Renaissance and baroque ideas arrived slowly, and with many intriguing and distinct local variations as Cotswolds craftsmen adapted them. Cotswold stone was used in many other places: for Oxford* colleges, for St George's Chapel, Windsor*, and for Christopher Wren's version of St Paul's Cathedral*. The bare slopes of the Cotswolds were once cropped by thousands of sheep. 'Upon these hills are fed large flocks of sheep with the whitest wool,' wrote William Camden in the 1580s, 'having long necks and square bodies.' Unfortunately, now that grazing the unimproved limestone grasslands is no longer economic, many

are reverting to scrub, and habitats for orchids and butterflies are being lost. Villages such as Painswick*, Northleach* and Stanway* can be more rewarding than the more famous attractions, such as Broadway* and Bourton-in-the-Water*.

Top: The village of Minchinhampton, not far from Stroud*.

Above: Stone cottages, in Stanton.

Left: Vineyard Street in Winchcombe.

Top left: The village of Slad. Dry stone walls, built without cement, are a feature of the area.

Top right: The River Coln, flowing through the Slad Valley, inspired Laurie Lee's 1959 novel *Cider with Rosie*.

Bottom: The River Eye flows through the village of Upper Slaughter.

Cottesbrooke Hall
Top left: The gardens.
Below left: The red-brick exterior.

Top right: Coughton Court.

Cottesbrooke Hall, Nhants 694 E6, The Anglo-Saxon church at Brixworth* stands firmly in the centre of the great axial prospect from the front of Cottesbrooke Hall.

Right: Covehithe Church's perpendicular tower seen through the chancel's ruined east window.

The Hall, begun in 1702, is in red brick, with white pilasters and two curving wings stretched out towards the outbuildings. Double-height bow windows added movement to the reception rooms at the back in an Adam-style remodelling of the 1780s. The whole is impeccably maintained, as is the garden. Inside is an exceptional art collection featuring horses and hunting: this is the country of the Pytchley hunt, and each village around here contains a pub called 'The Fox and Hounds'. The Hall is also a possible model for Jane Austen's *Mansfield Park*, as she knew the family. The village of Cottesbrooke contains a fine Victorian postbox, with its 'VR' monogram, saved by public outcry when the Post Office closed in the 1970s.

Cottingham, E R Yk 697 J6, Said to be the largest village in England, now a dormitory for Hull*, particularly for the universities. It has a fine Perpendicular church.

Coughton Court, Warwks 694 C6, The Catholic Throckmortons still live at Coughton Court [NT] and enjoy the magnificent central gatehouse tower, built around 1530, which rises to four turrets on the fourth storey. From there, stunning views over the hunting park would once have made it an excellent place to watch the chase. Visitors today can look down over the timber-framed, gabled wings added slightly later, and the Georgian remodelling of the main block to either side. Home to some of the Gunpowder Plotters in 1605,

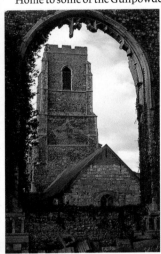

Coughton Court's Catholic past is also represented by the dress worn by Mary Queen of Scots at her execution, and by two superb portraits by Largillièrre.

Courts, The, Wilts 690 B5, The garden at Holt is Wiltshire's best kept secret. Archetypically English, it has water features, plantings, topiary, spring flowers – something for each day, spring to autumn. It is immaculately maintained by the National Trust.

Covehithe, Suffk 695 K6, Like Walberswick*, this became a church within a church after the older edifice was dismantled and a new one built within.

Below and bottom: The Courts is famous for its topiary and fine specimen trees.

C

Coventry

Coventry, W Mids 694 C6, On Thursday 14 November 1940 an air-raid destroyed much of medieval Coventry, and 554 people were killed. 'We seemed to sit and wait for death,' wrote one local teacher. The targets were the city's engineering plants, including those of the Daimler company, then churning out aircraft and armoured vehicles. (In the late 19th century the city's many bicycle factories began to adapt themselves for car production. The Daimler company was the longest-lived, while others included Triumph, Hillman and Humber. By 1910, a tenth of the city's population worked in car plants.) After the bombings, more than 2,000 homes were made uninhabitable and only 30 buildings survived in the central area of 40 acres (16ha). A great amount of rebuilding followed. While car plants and some inhumane urban planning have since characterized the city, some of the redevelopment was very successful, including a now-listed shopping arcade, and of course, the Cathedral. The Garden of International Friendship and the new Priory Visitor Centre, set in a grove of pleached limes, have been the most recent developments. Coventry was also a prosperous city in the Middle Ages, when its most famous inhabitant was Lady Godiva, popularly believed to have been wife of Leofric, Earl of Mercia. She rode naked through the town, fulfilling a condition set by her husband in return for which he agreed to her request that he reduce punitive taxes. Lady Godiva ordered all the inhabitants to stay indoors while she passed through the streets naked, and the only one to break the injunction, Peeping Tom, went blind. The story first appears in 1188, although her husband Leofric was a genuine figure and built the priory in Coventry. The Coventry mystery plays, held until 1589, were also famous. Each guild of the city sponsored the acting-out of a biblical story on portable stages. One man who habitually played Herod put on a particularly convincing impression of madness that was referred to by Shakespeare.

Top left: Jacob Epstein's *St Michael Vanquishing the Devil* outside Coventry Cathedral. St Michael was modelled on Epstein's son-in-law.

Above: The entrance to Coventry Cathedral with the ruined church to the left and Basil Spence's work of 1962 to the right.

Coventry Cathedral, designed by Basil Spence, was built in 1962. It incorporates the ruins of the old church as a forecourt, linked by a glass screen to the new work. Benjamin Britten's *War Requiem* was first performed here. The cathedral contains Spence's sculptural *Crown of Thorns*, John Piper's Baptistery window and Graham Sutherland's enormous tapestry of Christ, with a minuscule man standing between his feet. The other high point is outside: Jacob Epstein's *St Michael Vanquishing the Devil* from mid-air near the main entrance.

The **Herbert Read Art Gallery** contains much more than the average local history museum. 'Godiva City' is an interactive exhibition on the ground floor. Upstairs are further interesting pictures, with many variations on the Godiva theme, including Collier's famous pre-Raphaelite version.

Left: Coxwold, Shandy Hall, Laurence Sterne's study from 1760 to 1768, where he wrote *Tristram Shandy*.

Coxwold, N Yorks 697 H5, An attractive village with interesting buildings flanking the main street, which climbs up to its parish church of St Michael. The church is a splendid Perpendicular building of c1430 with an unusual octagonal tower at its western – uphill – end, and medieval roof timbers inside. Outside the south side can be seen the tombstone of Laurence Sterne, perpetual curate here from 1760 to 1768. He was buried in Bayswater, but the stone was moved in 1969 when that churchyard was redeveloped. Inside the church are Georgian furnishings installed in Sterne's time. Of particular note is the unusual U-shaped 18th-century altar rail, made to fit the particularly narrow space in the chancel encroached upon by the huge monuments to various owners of nearby Newburgh Priory (whose estate village Coxwold still is). A short distance from the church is **Shandy Hall,** the 15th-century house where Sterne lived when in residence at Coxwold Church, and where he did some of his writing. **Newburgh Priory** became an Elizabethan country house after the Augustinian canons' religious house was dissolved in the 16th century, and later alterations include chimneypieces, panelling and Italian plasterwork. In the attic is said to be the tomb containing the headless body of Oliver Cromwell.

Cragside House, Nthumb 699 J6, On a rugged hillside above Rothbury, this is the best northern example of Norman Shaw's 'Old English' style [NT]. It has beautifully decorated rooms and the Drawing Room, which doubles as a picture gallery, has a carved marble fireplace weighing 10 tons. The house was designed for the 1st Lord Armstrong, the munitions magnate, and was technically very advanced, having as early as the 1880s hot and cold running water, and even a Turkish bath suite, central heating, fire alarms, telephones and a passenger lift. It was the first private house to be lit by hydro-electricity, and the kitchen was powered by hydraulics. On the slopes around and below the house are terraced rock gardens, and across the valley can be seen glasshouses and terraces where exotic fruits were grown, even at this altitude.

Craig yr Aderyn, Gwynd 692 D4, The valley is dominated by the dramatic 'bird rock', the haunt of cormorants that nest further inland here than anywhere else in mainland Britain.

Craigievar Castle, Abers 702 D6, This tall L-shaped fairytale castle has pink rough-rendered walls surmounted by turrets and gables. It was built in 1626 for William Forbes, a merchant who made his fortune through trade with the Baltic, and is a fine example of 17th-century Scots baronial style.

Craigmillar Castle, C Edin, It was in this castle that the Preston family received Mary Queen of Scots

Cragside

Above: The spectacularly craggy woodland setting.
Left: Portrait of Lord Armstrong sitting in the inglenook fireplace of the Dining Room, painted by Henry Hetherington Emerson.

Below: Craigievar Castle seen from the southwest. Its interiors have splendid plasterwork.

after the murder of David Rizzio in September 1563. It was here, too, in 1566, that the Queen's advisers urged her to divorce her second husband, Lord Darnley. The 14th-century castle was surrounded by an early 15th-century crenellated curtain wall, while the apartments were added in the 16th and 17th centuries. Abandoned in the 1750s, the castle fell into ruins. The Banqueting Hall on the second floor still has its beautiful canopied fireplace. *See* **Edinburgh* 699 G4.**

Craignethan Castle, S Lans 698 E5, The castle, one of the strongholds of the Hamiltons, was built in the 15th century to resist artillery attacks. The steep outcrop on which it stands made it impregnable on three sides, while the only vulnerable side was defended by a fortified outer courtyard and a dry moat with a *caponier* (a large vaulted chamber set across the floor of a broad, dry moat from which the enemy could be fired upon), one of the first of its kind in Britain. A 17th-century manor house stands in one corner of the outer courtyard.

Craig-y-Nos Castle, Powys 692 E6, The romantic name (meaning 'rock of the night') is most suitable for such a romantic place, built in the 1840s for a local landowner. Its previous name, Bryn Melin ('Millhill'), was more in keeping with the baronial sturdiness that TH Wyatt thought appropriate for the mountainous terrain. It was the diva Adelina Patti who transformed the property after 1885, by quadrupling its size with castellated additions and creating an exquisite private opera house where she could sing her favourite roles with her husband, Ernesto Nicolini. The 200-seat theatre is used during the summer by a local operatic company. Her splendid

Top left and right: Crail harbour. Among the 16th- to 19th-century houses there is a medieval church and tollbooth.

Winter Garden now forms the framework of the Patti Pavilion in Swansea's Victoria Park. Below the 'castle', regularly used for antiques fairs, the riverside grounds, still showing signs of opulent country-house taste, are part of the Craig-y-Nos Country Park.

Crail, Fife 699 H3, This former royal burgh, with its 200-year-old golf course, is the most delightful port on this stretch of coast. A small museum occupies one of the elegant 16th- to 19th-century houses that stand on the market place at the top of the town. Other old houses border the narrow streets leading down to the harbour and quays.

Cramond, C Edin 699 G4, In the 17th and 18th centuries this delightful village on the mouth of the River Almond had a number of small ironworks. Near the church (1656) are the foundations of a fort built by the Romans in AD 142 to defend the harbour.

Cranborne Manor, Dorset 690 C7, A fine Jacobean manor house 16 miles (25km) south of Salisbury, created as a hunting lodge for Robert Cecil, 1st Earl of Salisbury. Only the historic walled garden is open to the public, one day a week and occasional weekends, but it alone is well worth the trip. It may be difficult to trace the origins of the first plants, many supplied to the 1st Earl by John Tradescant, an intrepid traveller who visited Russia in 1618 and north Africa in 1620–1; but Cranborne still delights, particularly with its outstanding display of spring bulbs.

Cranbrook, Kent 691 H6, The church embodies a grand unified design of the 14th and 15th centuries. Inside is a curious monument to the Roberts family (1740) consisting only of a long family tree, a vivid example of the 18th-century obsession with pedigree. The town is picturesque; one particularly notices Cranbrook School, begun in 1727, several Georgian houses in the High Street and a very tall windmill (1814) that is still in working order.

Crantock, Cnwll 688 C7, Although Newquay* is visible on the horizon, Crantock seems a remote place, quaintly disposed around its ancient circular Round Garden, or village pound. The Church of St Carantocus was restored by Edmund Sedding. Its stained-glass windows by CE Kempe are of 1902, yet manage to convey a good idea of what dark, rich and mysterious places Cornish medieval churches must have been.

Crathes Castle, Abers 702 D6, The castle is an L-shaped tower-house whose roof positively bristles with corbelled turrets, dormers and chimneys. It was built between 1553 and 1594 by the Burnett family, on lands granted to their

Crathes Castle
Above: The remains of a classical garden laid out in the early 18th century lie alongside a series of gardens designed in the 1930s by Sir James Burnett of Leys.
Above right: Detail of a 17th-century painted ceiling.

ancestor by Robert Bruce after the Battle of Bannockburn in 1314, and enlarged in the 17th and 19th centuries. The interior has some beautiful old furniture, including an impressive carved oak bed (1594), and some magnificent 17th-century painted ceilings. People, animals, plants, mottoes and heraldic motifs decorate the ceilings of the Nine Nobles Room, the Green Lady's Room (named after the resident ghost) and the Muses' Room. The Long Gallery has a remarkable oak-panelled ceiling, while the ivory horn inlaid with precious stones (Horn of Leys) that hangs above the fireplace of the main hall is said to have been a gift from Robert Bruce. Eight magnificent walled gardens designed in the 1930s set off this castle steeped in tradition.

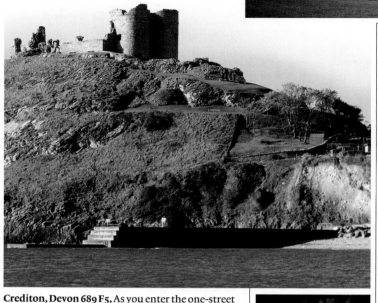

Crediton, Devon 689 F5, As you enter the one-street town from the east you cannot fail to be impressed by the large former collegiate church of Holy Cross. The birthplace of St Boniface and the seat of the western bishopric from 909 until 1050, Crediton has long been a religious centre in the folds of the lush mid-Devon hills. Much rebuilt in the early 15th century, the church has a largely Perpendicular air and a good range of monuments, including one to General Sir Redvers Buller, VC of the Boer War, who lived locally. The wide main street has a handsome collection of 18th- and 19th-century houses, their predecessors destroyed in a series of disastrous fires. The burghers of the town also removed the centrally placed market as part of a road improvement scheme in 1836. The railway station (probably designed by Brunel) is the first stop on the peaceful and verdant North Devon line.

Cressing, Essex 691 H4, The Temple is the earliest Knights Templar building in England, and the two extraordinary barns are a measure of the considerable wealth and power of this unique order of warrior-monks. Each has a huge nave and side aisles incorporating over 500 oaks, covered by a great sweep of peg-tile roof. The Wheat Barn with brick nogging infill is 50 years later than the weather-boarded Barley Barn of c1200.

Crewkerne, Somset 689 H5, This is a prosperous town with an important church, castellated with polygonal turrets at the west front. Inside there is a chapel behind a chapel in the northwest corner, and a rare Norman font of Purbeck marble. The town comprises a good mixture of buildings, dating from the 17th to the 20th centuries.

Criccieth Castle, Gwynd 692 D3, This 13th-century Welsh castle, eloquent on its high promontory overlooking Tremadog Bay, rivals Harlech* for its views. Equally eloquent was a local boy, David Lloyd George – later to be Liberal prime minister – to whom is dedicated a comprehensive museum at

Top right: Croft Castle's 14th-century round towers positioned in an 18th-century front.

Top left: Criccieth Castle. LLywelyn ap Iorwerth chose the form and size of his castle to take full advantage of the naturally defensive position of the site.

Centre: Croft Castle, *The Children of Richard Croft, 6th Baronet,* by Sir William Beechey, 1803.

Above: Cromarty, Hugh Miller's house, built in 1711 with a thatched roof.

Llanystumdwy, where he was brought up from an early age at Highgate House. He retired to Ty Mawr*, which is within walking distance and is now used for writers' residential courses. His memorial on the nearest banks of the River Dwyfor was designed by Clough Williams-Ellis.

Crichel House, Dorset 690 B7, This important house in More Crichel has one of the most outstanding 18th-century rooms, designed in neoclassical style in about 1773 by James Wyatt. The church of St Mary adjoins the house, near the lake. It has an ambitious interior, with a high hammerbeam roof to the nave (1886).

Crichton Castle, Mdloth 699 G5, These impressive ruins stand on a small hill above the River Tyne. The original tower-house was built in the 15th century by William Crichton, chancellor to James II. One hundred years later it passed to the Earls of Bothwell, who transformed it into an elegant Italianate mansion around a central courtyard. The remarkable diamond bosses that decorate the interior façade of the north wing were commissioned (1581–91) by Francis Hepburn, the 5th Earl of Bothwell. James VI, outraged by the Earl's insolence in displaying such magnificence, ordered the castle to be destroyed, but the order was never carried out and Crichton Castle was left to fall slowly into decline.

Cricklade, Wilts 690 C4, The Duke of Northumberland and the Hungerford family built the heavy tower of the church of St Sampson in the early 16th century. The dedication, however, denotes a Celtic origin, and the south wall of the nave is Anglo-Saxon. Look for the embattled Hungerford Chapel, built in the 15th century. A small school was built at Cricklade in 1651, the gift of a London goldsmith, Robert Jenner, and there is the usual mix of later buildings. The town itself was once fortified, probably by King Alfred, and a square enclosure can still be seen.

Crieff, P & K 699 F3, Before the advent of the railway made it a fashionable Victorian spa town, Crieff was famous for its cattle markets. Today its principal attraction is Glenturret Distillery, one of the oldest distilleries in Scotland (1775). South of the town are the formal gardens of Drummond Castle* – built in the late 15th and rebuilt in the 19th century – and the remains of Ardoch Roman Camp (1st–2nd century), near Braco. Tullibardine, to the southwest of Crieff, has one of Scotland's best-preserved medieval churches. The red-sandstone church, built in 1446 and enlarged c1500, houses the tombs of the earls of Perth.

Croft Castle, Herefs 693 G5, A pleasant mixture of castle and country house [NT]. Fourteenth-century round corner towers sandwich an 18th-century front with mock-medieval battlements, and nostalgic Gothic Revival windows hint at the exuberant Georgian gothic staircase inside.

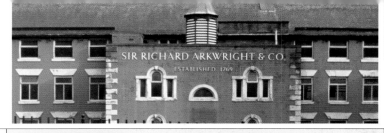

Avenues traverse the huge park, one of 350-year-old Spanish chestnuts and another of silver birches leading to Cock Gate. The Iron-Age fort of Croft Ambrey is a steep 40-minute walk away.

Cromarty, Highld 701 H4, Situated on the tip of Black Isle, the fertile peninsula that lies between the Firths of Cromarty, Moray and Beauly, Cromarty was once a prosperous port. It was passed over by the development of overland communication links in the 19th century, since when it appears to have lapsed into inactivity. It still has its medieval market cross, beautiful merchants' houses, East Church with 18th-century galleries, and the house where the geologist Hugh Miller was born. The house, along with the neighbouring court house (1782), has been converted into a museum.

Cromer, Norfk 695 J4, Like its neighbour and rival Sheringham*, Cromer grew from fishing village perched on a crumbling cliffline to genteel Regency resort mentioned by Jane Austen. Bow-fronted Brunswick Terrace and The Crescent on East Cliff date from this period, but the real expansion came with the railway; streets of château-style tenements with corner turrets and ostentatious clifftop hotels. Most have gone, but Edward Skipper's exuberant red-faced Hôtel de Paris, once the haunt of aristocrats and foreign royals, still towers above the pier. Taller still, the 160-foot (50m) tower of St Peter and St Paul rears up in the centre of town, the focal point of narrow streets running through to the clifftop, once a lighthouse and beacon of faith to those in peril on the sea. More reliable perhaps was Cromer's heroic coxswain Henry Blogg whose lifeboat, now in the museum, saved hundreds of lives between 1909 and 1945. The lifeboat is now launched from the end of Cromer's delightful pier, but was once horse-drawn up the granite causeway below East Cliff. Sir Arthur Conan Doyle, one of many distinguished visitors, got his idea for *The Hound of the Baskervilles* from the local Black Shuck legend he learned while on the golf links.

Cromford, Derbys 694 C3, The first successful cotton-spinning mill worked by water-power was started here by Richard Arkwright in 1771. His mill still survives and is gradually being restored. Arkwright, who was responsible for several other large mills along the valley, built Cromford village for his workers. His partner was Jedediah Strutt, who developed another great industrial centre at Belper, where the great sluices that channelled the water for the mills can still be seen. He was also responsible for the North Mill of 1804, which now contains a small museum.

Cromford
Top: Masson Mill of 1783.
Above: Belper East Mill, built in 1912.
Inset: A waterwheel.

Bottom left: Cromer seafront.

Bottom right: Croome d'Abitot Park, one of the many features and follies to be seen here.

Crondall, Hants 690 E6, Crondall, west of Farnham* in Surrey, has a particularly fine 12th- to 13th-century church (especially inside), with a 17th-century tower.

Cronkhill, Shrops 693 G4, A small and quite delightfully Italianate villa by Nash, which can be glimpsed from Atcham village. It was built for the estate steward at Attingham Park*.

Croome d'Abitot Park, Worcs 690 B3, The current Croome Court was begun in 1751, and is a typical house of its time with a stern Palladian façade and a park landscaped by Capability Brown [NT]. Unusually, in this case, Brown also seems to have had a hand in the design of the house as well. His patron was the 6th Earl of Coventry, whose

Above: Croscombe church of St Mary contains one of the most complete examples of Jacobean woodcarving in Somerset, with arches and mask-faces set round with carved foliage.

friends, such as Sanderson Miller, also pitched in with ideas. The park still contains many of its temples and ornaments, which are being gradually restored by the National Trust. They include a gothic ruin, Adam's panorama tower, and a Tuscan temple or 'greenhouse'. Croome d'Abitot Church is itself an eye-catcher on a rolling hill, designed in a perfect early Gothic Revival style outside. It, too, is possibly by Capability Brown, with an interior by Robert Adam including a crisp and elegant font and pulpit with fanciful ogee curves.

Croscombe, Somset 689 H4, Two miles (3.2km) southeast of Wells* is the church of St Mary. Its high Jacobean rood screen with obelisks is of about 1620; the pulpit is dated 1616 and has a large tester with similar obelisks on top.

Cross Bucks Way, Bucks 690 E3, A 24-mile (38km) walk linking the Grand Union Canal near Linslade on the Bedfordshire border to the Oxfordshire border near Marsh Gibbon.

Crossraguel Abbey, S Ayrs 698 D6, The monastery was founded in 1244 by Duncan, Earl of Carrick, for Cluniac monks who occupied it until 1592. It was largely rebuilt after the Scottish wars of independence. Today its extensive ruins include the choir of the church with its three-sided apse, an elegant chapter house and fortified guard room (15th century), and a 16th-century tower house. The abbey's name is derived from the cross of Riaghail (an Irish saint sometimes associated with St Rule) which once stood on the site.

Crowland, Lincs 695 F5, A strange, remote place on the flat edge of the fens. In the centre of the little town is the extraordinary triangular bridge – a medieval, probably 14th-century structure replacing an even earlier bridge of the same form at the junction of the rivers Nene and Welland. Dominating the area is the stumpy shape of the tower of **Croyland Abbey**, founded in 716 on the site of St Guthlac's cell. The abbey had a complicated building history and is now much ruined and reduced in size. The visitor is confronted by the west wall of the nave dating from the mid-13th century, with tiers of figures and a handsome twin doorway. The rest of the nave has gone. Next to this front is a massive tower with a two-storey porch and a great window, which was added to the north aisle in the 1460s. The north aisle now serves as the parish church.

Croxteth Hall, Mersyd 696 E7, This was the home of the Molyneux family, Earls of Sefton, and is now owned by the City of Liverpool*. The house is large and rambling, on a 16th-century core. The best front is to the west, built 1702; the rest is largely the result of a recasting by McVicar Anderson in 1902. He did much of the interior at the same time, and those parts not damaged by fire in 1952 are now presented as an Edwardian country house. The grounds at Croxteth are perhaps more rewarding than the house and contain some excellent buildings, especially a dairy of 1861 by WE Nesfield and a laundry and kennels by John Douglas. The home farm has a good series of Victorian and Edwardian model buildings, and the kitchen gardens retain such curiosities as a heated wall and a mushroom house.

Cullen, Moray 702 C4, This coastal resort, famous for 'Cullen Skink', a kind of smoked-haddock soup, has an elegant Georgian upper town. Its Auld Kirk, where the internal organs of Elizabeth de Burgh, the wife of Robert Bruce, are said to have been buried in 1327, was extensively renovated in the 16th century when it became a collegiate church. It is well worth a visit to see the Sacrament House, the elaborately carved baroque tomb of Alexander Ogilvie and the impressive Seafield Loft (1602) in the upper gallery.

Culloden, Highld 701 H5, This vast moor, 5 miles (8km) south of Inverness*, is haunted by the bloody massacre of the Jacobites. The Battle of Culloden, on 16 April 1746, marked the end of the epic adventure of Bonnie Prince Charlie and the failure of the attempt to restore the Stuarts to the throne of Scotland. The Jacobite Risings not only divided clans and families but precipitated the disintegration of traditional Highland society. It took less than an hour for the 9,000 troops of the Duke of Cumberland, the son of George II, to crush the 5,000 exhausted and demoralized Highlanders. Prisoners and wounded were not spared in the massacre, which earned Cumberland the nickname of 'Butcher'. Following the battle, the Young Pretender became a fugitive, leaving Scotland for ever five months later. The visitor centre has a reconstruction of the battle, while Old Leonach Cottage shows the interior of a cottage of the time. Flags mark the position of the two armies during the battle and monuments mark the spots where the clan chiefs fell. Every April a service is held in front of the Memorial Cairn in memory of those who died.

Cullompton, Devon 689 G5, One of the many West Country towns made prosperous by the wool trade. The result of this wealth is evident in the church of St Andrew, whose 100-foot (30m) tower built just before the Reformation dominates the town. Justly famous is the Lane aisle of *c*1526, begun by John Lane, a cloth merchant. Heavily decorated both inside and out with symbols of his trade (ships,

cloth shears, merchant's mark and teasels, which were using for brushing the cloth) the fan-vaulted space is a testament to the ostentation of the late Middle Ages. Cullompton's single street is lined with houses dating from the 16th to the 18th century, and has many charming courtyards off it.

Culross, Fife 699 F4, This old port on the Firth of Forth is one of the gems of Scottish vernacular architecture, dating from the 16th–17th century. Its cobbled streets and white houses with red-tiled roofs have been carefully restored. A flourishing coal and salt

Top: Croxteth Hall, the west front built in 1702.

Above: Culloden Memorial Cairn, where a remembrance service is held every April.

Left: *The Battle of Culloden*, by David Morier (1746).

Below: *Prince Charles Edward Stuart*, by Antonio David.

Bottom right: Culross Market Place has buildings dating from the 16th and 17th centuries.

trade with the Netherlands and the Baltic countries enabled Culross to obtain a charter in 1588. However, the development of trade with the American colonies marked the beginning of its decline in the late 17th century. The visitor centre, housed in the stone and slate town hall or tolbooth (1626) overlooking the River Forth, has an audiovisual presentation on Culross. **Culross Palace** is a beautiful town house with its ochre-coloured rough-rendering, standing on the banks of the River Forth. It was built for Sir George Bruce in 1597 and enlarged in 1611. The pine-panelled walls, decorative paintings, numerous chimneys, fire-proof strong room and period furniture reflect the lifestyle of a rich merchant of the time. On the market place stand the oldest house in Culross (1577) and the study of Bishop Leighton (1610), a corbelled out-turret with beautiful painted ceilings. Visitors can also admire the restored façades of the residence of Bishop Robert Leighton, in Mid Causeway, and a convent and a hostel (The Ark), in Wee Causeway. At the top of the town stand the remains of a Cistercian abbey founded in 1215 by Malcolm, Earl of Fife. The parish church occupies the choir of the 14th-century abbey church and houses the beautiful funeral memorial of Sir George Bruce (d. 1625) and his family. The monastic buildings were demolished and their stone used to build nearby Abbey House, begun in 1608.

Culzean Castle, S Ayrs 698 D6, This castle (pronounced 'cullane'), which dominates the Ayrshire coast, is an architectural masterpiece by Robert Adam. Commissioned by David Kennedy, the 10th Earl of Cassillis, Adam transformed the ancestral tower-house into an elegant castellated mansion between 1777 and 1792. Two outstanding features of the castle are the Oval Staircase and the Round Drawing Room. The castle houses collections of 18th- and 19th-century weapons, furniture, tapestries, silverware, porcelain and paintings. When he gave the castle to the National Trust for Scotland in 1945, the 5th Marquess of Ailsa requested that General Eisenhower, Supreme Commander of the Allied forces in Western Europe during World War II, be presented with an apartment for use during his lifetime. The 560-acre (227ha) park includes, in particular, a walled garden, an orangery, a small lake and a deer park. On a clear day the terrace overlooking the garden offers a magnificent view of the Isle of Arran*, the Mull of Kintyre*, Ailsa Craig* and even the Irish coast.

Cwm Du, Carmth 692 D6, No more than a strip of
sleepy cottages and a Baptist chapel of 1839,
Cwmdu (meaning 'dark valley') had all the
essentials: a shop-cum-post-office, a pub and a
pair of two-seater lavatories, with an evergreen
hedge dividing the *Dynion* from the *Merched*. Rural
depopulation had brought with it neglect and
decay, until in the 1980s the National Trust
revitalized this minute community by restoring
the buildings to their original purpose for the use
of local people and holiday-makers. The cottage
gardens on the banks of the stream are an ideal
place for lunch.

Cyfarthfa Castle, V Glam 689 G2, Built in 1825, at a
cost of £30,000, by William Crawshay, one of the
great iron-masters of South Wales; the house's
towers and battlements were a manifestation not

only of his vast new wealth, but also of his
hankering after an ancient pedigree. Its architect,
Robert Lugar, chose a style 'designed for the
situation, standing alone in the midst of rising
ground in a bold country. Thus placed, no other
character of mansion would appear with equal
effect'. With its close proximity to the ironworks,
the 'Castle' was constantly lit by the glare and flare
of the furnaces, seen at their most awesomely
spectacular at night.

The Crawshay world at Cyfarthfa lasted for less
than a century. In 1909, it was acquired by Merthyr
Borough Council to serve as a grammar school, a
municipal museum and an art gallery, surrounded
by a public park. The galleries, accommodated in
the formal ground-floor rooms, contain a mixture
of Crawshay memorabilia, Welsh porcelain and
pottery, and a small but interesting collection of
19th- and 20th-century pictures relating to aspects
of Welsh life. The cellar is devoted to the history of
Merthyr from the earliest times to the present day.
Plans are afoot to give visitors direct access to the
site of the former ironworks.

Cyfartha Castle
Right: *Salome* (1938) by Alfred
Janes (1911–99) hangs in the
Art Gallery along with the
works of other Welsh artists.
Centre left: The castle was
the status symbol par
excellence of a South Wales
industrial entrepreneur.

Below: Cymer Abbey near
the small village of
LLanelltyd, north of Dolgellan
on the A487. The three arches
are the most prominent
remains of the Cistercian
foundation.

Not far from the
'Castle' is the
start of the
Glamorganshire
Canal, which until
the building of the
Taff Vale Railway
in 1840 was the
only method of
transporting iron
from Merthyr to
the docks at
Cardiff*. Nearby,
No. 4 Chapel Row
was the birthplace of Joseph Parry (1841–1903),
Wales's most prolific 19th-century composer, best
known by his compatriots for his opera *Blodwen*
and his hymn-tune *Aberystwyth*. It is now a small
museum honouring him. A pit-boy at the age of
ten, he moved to the ironworks two years later,
and by the time he was 13, he was working with
his father in the rolling mills at Dannville,
Pennsylvania. From 1888 he was a lecturer in
music at the University of Cardiff.

Cymer Abbey, Gwynd 692 E3, The Cistercian abbey,
which was founded in 1198, takes its name from
the Welsh word for 'confluence', that of the river
Mawddach (Abermawddach, gave rise to Abermo
or Bermo, and the English version, Barmouth) and
the lesser-known Wnion. The remains of the early
13th-century buildings are sparse, and it is
unlikely that the establishment, smaller than
most other abbeys in Wales, was ever completed.
The monastic ruins stand comfortably side by side
with a farmhouse, but the pastoral setting is
marred by a caravan site.

Dale Abbey, Derbys 694 D4, The ruins benefit from a delightful site below sandstone cliffs, but in fact there is little left of the medieval abbey, founded here in c1200, other than the footings of the walls and the great arch of the chancel east window.

Dalemain, Cumb 696 E3, One of the more traditional country houses of the Lake District*, this lies between Penrith and Ullswater. From the road the visitor sees the restrained nine-bay front of 1747 built by Edward Hasell. An earlier Edward Hasell was steward to Lady Anne Clifford and bought the estate in 1679. His descendants still live there. The classical front disguises a more complex building, with a medieval pele tower and a small internal courtyard. The enfilade of rooms behind the classical front has excellent interiors including a room with Chinese wallpaper and a 'Chinese Chippendale' rococo chimneypiece.

Dalmeny, C Edin, The small Norman church of Saint Cuthbert (12th century) is well worth a visit, in

Above: Darlington, clock tower on Alfred Waterhouse's Old Town Hall and Market Hall.

Above right: Dalton-in-Furness, Dalton Castle.

particular for the heads and silhouettes of mythical animals that decorate the romanesque south door. Since 1662 Dalmeny House on the shores of the Firth of Forth has belonged to the Primrose (Rosebery) family. The house, by Willian Wilkins, was the first to be built (1817) in neo-Tudor style. The drawing room houses a fine collection of 18th-century French tapestries, porcelain and furniture, much of it from the Rothschild collections at Mentmore*. The dining room has paintings by Gainsborough, Raeburn, Reynolds and Lawrence, while the former billiard room has furniture and objects that once belonged to Napoleon. The medieval keep of Barnbougle, on the Firth of Forth, was restored as a library in 1881. *See* **South Queensferry* 699 F4.**

Dalton-in-Furness, Cumb 696 D5, An attractive small town dominated by its church and castle [NT]. St Mary's Church is one of Paley and Austin's bigger efforts, with a square tower and unusual detail in chequerwork that seems to have strayed from elsewhere. The churchyard has a monument to the

Above: Dalemain, the east front with its nine bays, built in 1747 by Edward Hasell.

Right: Dalmeny House, the Napoleon Room contains furniture and effects that once belonged to the French emperor.

painter George Romney who was born in Dalton. Next to the church, in an unusual urban setting for the building type, is Dalton Castle, a 14th-century pele tower.

Danbury, Essex 691 H4, Rising above its wooded hill just east of Chelmsford, St John's spire is a local landmark. The church, set within ancient earthworks, has three life-size wooden effigies of unidentified knights c1300. There are attractive walks on Lingwood and Danbury commons (both National Trust), and through Danbury Park.

Danny Park, W Susx 691 F7, A large Tudor house built 1582–93. The east front has a centre of five bays, a porch in the middle and the tall widows of the hall to the left. At the ends two-bay wings project. In the 18th century the hall was remodelled and a Georgian façade built on the south.

Darlington, Dur 697 G4, Known for its Quaker industrial and banking families, and famous as the birthplace of railways. The Stockton and Darlington Railway opened in 1825, thanks to the efforts of the local businessmen Edward Pease and George Stephenson (*see* Wylam*). The parish church of St Cuthbert is a grand example of an Early English edifice, with a spire. There is also a spire on the clock tower of the Old Town Hall and Market Hall of 1861–4 by Alfred Waterhouse. The town's erstwhile major industry, locomotive engineering, is commemorated in the brick train sculpture built in 1997 alongside the A66 bypass. The work of the Scottish artist David Mach, it uses 180,000 bricks.

Dartington, Devon 689 F7, The extensive medieval house of John Holland, Duke of Exeter, half-brother of Richard II and stepson of the Black Prince, is set within glorious gardens and includes his tiltyard. It is a huge residence set around a great courtyard. The Great Hall was built between

Dartington Hall
Top left: The Great Hall seen from across the Tiltyard.
Left: The interior of the Great Hall, one of the finest of the period in England, restored by William Weir, 1926–38.

Dartmoor
Below right: St Michael's Church at Brent Tor.
Bottom: Remains of a Bronze Age hut, one of 24 found at Grimspound.

1388 and 1399. Holland's symbol, the ear of wheat, surrounds the white hart of Richard II on the boss in the entrance porch. The property has had a chequered history, variously the home of Margaret Beaufort, mother of Henry VII, Henry Courtenay, Earl of Devon, and then the Champernownes, some of whom were notable musicians. The imaginative revival of the buildings and the grounds in the 1920s and 1930s is owed to Leonard and Dorothy Elmhirst. Dorothy's American fortune financed the creation of Dartington College, a large, liberal school and college of the arts; High Cross was built for the headmaster in 1931–2 by William Lescaze in the International Modern style. The sharp geometric light-filled rooms house a fine contemporary collection of art and craftwork. The Cider Press Gallery at Shinner's Bridge is also part of the Dartington empire, and the many well-designed goods sold there help to continue the pioneering work of the Dartington Trust in developing rural communities in Devon.

Dartmoor, Devon 689 F6, Dartmoor covers an area of over 200 square miles (518 sq km) extending between Okehampton*, Tavistock*, Ivybridge and Moretonhampstead*. The central granite plateau is wild and remote, with the small depressions filled with treacherous bogs and morasses. The tors – granite outcrops of contorted forms – dominate the skyline, and are sometimes surrounded by great clusters of granite slabs and boulders of extraordinary shapes. The mist can descend at unexpected times, and then it is easy to recall the hound of the Baskervilles, who haunted these lonely slopes in Conan-Doyle's famous story. The foothills are softer, characterized by deep ravines and gentle, sparsely wooded green valleys with charming villages such as North Bovey* or Widecombe-in-the-Moor*.

Dartmouth, Devon 689 F7, In the 14th century Dartmouth was one of the four great towns of the county. It is thought that Chaucer visited it, for he immortalized one of the shipmen of 'Dert-e-mouth' in *The Canterbury Tales*. A richly decorated church and the timbered Butterwalk are testament to the early wealth of the little port, as are the later houses around Bayard's Cove. It was from this quay, near a little fortress, that the *Mayflower* and the *Speedwell* were repaired in 1620 before setting out for Plymouth* and the New World with the Pilgrim Fathers. At the mouth of the river lies the small church of St Petroc beside the Castle of 1481, which looks across to its neighbour at Kingswear; in times of war a chain could be raised between them, thus protecting the anchorage. At the other end of the town stands the imperial mass of the Royal Naval College, designed by the architect of the Victoria and Albert Museum*, Sir Aston Webb, and opened by Edward VII.

Dawlish, Devon 689 G6, The main railway line from Plymouth to Exeter (opened in 1846) cuts this charming little watering place off from its beach. The oldest part of the town, with Regency houses, lies about a mile (1.6km) inland and can be approached through a little park surrounding the Dawlish Water, on which black swans glide. Red sandstone cliffs flank the town and have produced two rocks, the Parson and the Clerk, off the coast.

Deal, Kent 691 J6, Deal Castle [EH], the largest of Henry VIII's forts on the south coast, built in 1536-40, is well preserved, though some of its battlements were rebuilt during World War II. Inside one can see the living quarters of the garrison, the rooms nearly all segments of circles.

It has a circular centre surrounded by six semi-circular battlements, giving it a distinctly geometrical appearance.

Deddington, Oxon, An early market town built of golden stone, with several good old houses. Leadenporch House on New Street, the main Oxford* to Banbury* Road, dates from *c*1315. Southeast of Deddington are the substantial earthworks of the castle where Piers Gaveston, the unfortunate favourite of Edward II, lodged in 1312. *See* **Adderbury*** **690 D3.**

Above: Deene Park and, below centre, an obelisk in the grounds.

Below left: Deal Castle's shape may have been designed to symbolize the Tudor rose.

Dedham, Essex 691 H3, The Dedham Vale stretch of the Stour is lovingly preserved much as John Constable knew and painted it. Retrace the artist's boyhood path from his school downstream to his father's Flatford Mill*, lined with pollarded willows. Dedham, another wool town, has timber-framed and Georgian houses and a 16th-century church with interesting commemorative pews. John Webbe's 16th-century house opposite, now Sherman's Hall, has a beautiful little Queen Anne façade in brick. Outside the village Castle House was the home of the equestrian painter Sir Alfred Munnings, and is now a museum.

Deene Park, Nhants 694 E5, The Brudenell family of Deene Park slowly built their conservative yet harmonious house over the centuries. It has a medieval core, a 16th-century porch (probably made by the same masons working at nearby Kirby Hall*), a 17th-century wing and tower, and interesting pictures. One of the Brudenells, the 7th Earl of Cardigan, led the charge of the Light Brigade at Balaclava in the Crimean War.

Deerhurst, Gloucs 690 B3, The priory church of St Mary's, close by the River Severn, has a narrow, 8th-century nave, patches of herring-bone construction in the walls, small and savage triangular windows and other Anglo-Saxon features. But the real surprise here is **Odda's Chapel,** an almost complete Anglo Saxon church, which was only discovered during the chance repair of an ordinary-looking half-timbered house in 1885. Dedicated by the Earl of Odda in 1056, it was a pre-Conquest place of pilgrimage. In later times, the nave became a tall kitchen. The chapel has now been uncovered and forms the western end of the farmhouse 650 feet (200m) southwest of the church.

Denbies Wine Estate, Surrey, This vineyard with 300,000 vines is open to the public. There are footpaths through the vines. *See* **Dorking*** **691 F6.**

Deerhurst
Top: The church of St Mary.
Below: Odda's Chapel,
dedicated in 1056.

Denbigh (Dinbych), Denbgs 693 F2, The 'little fort' of the Welsh name is in fact one of the biggest castles in Wales, built by Henry de Lacy from 1282, possibly under the supervision of Master James of St George, the brilliant military surveyor of Edward I. The complex defensive ingenuity of the gatehouse is most certainly the work of a master. The panoramic views from the ramparts are unsurpassed in their splendour. The area surrounding the stronghold was originally walled, and although only fragments of these outer defences remain, the formidable Burgess Gate indicates their strength. On the hillside below the castle stand the outer walls of the chapel started by Robert Dudley, Earl of Leicester, who came into possession of the castle in 1563. Its aim was to serve the devotional needs of a growing population, and reputedly to replace St Asaph as the diocesan see.

The mother church of Denbigh, St Marcella (Yr Eglwys Wen) – at Whitchurch, 2 miles (3 km) from the town on the Llandyrnog road, is of considerable interest. Double-naved, with hammerbeam roofs, it contains some of the best Renaissance monuments in any North Wales church. The exquisite alabaster tomb of Sir John Salusbury (d. 1578) and his wife, of the nearby great house of Llewenni (demolished), features their eight sons and four daughters in the panel below. A brass to Richard Myddelton, Governor of Denbigh Castle, and his wife Jane depicts the couple facing one another, with seven daughters behind their mother and nine sons behind their father. There is a wall monument to Humphrey Llwyd (1527–68) antiquary and cartographer, whose contact with another native of Denbigh, Sir Richard Clough, agent to Sir Thomas Gresham in Antwerp, put him at the centre of Renaissance thought and ideas.

Below: Denbigh's hilltop castle commands magnificent views of the Vale of Clwyd and the northeast coastline.

The town is a pleasing mixture of sturdy vernacular and refined Georgian. In one of its many narrow streets is Gwasg Gee, the printing press established in the early 19th century for publishing literary and devotional periodicals and, until the 1970s, a weekly newspaper.

Denham, Bucks 691 F4, Denham has retained its quaint village appeal. A string of 17th- and 18th-century houses lines the main street between the church and the beautifully proportioned, late 17th-century Denham Place. The house is famous for its plasterwork.

Denmans Garden, W Susx 690 E7, The modern garden designer John Brookes' own garden. The different areas include a walled gravel garden, architectural and foliage plants, dry stream beds with self-seeders, a water garden and examples of native planting. There is a school of garden design in the Clock House.

Dennington, Suffk 695 J6, Lord Bardolf (d.1441), who fought at Agincourt and was probably the original for Shakespeare's character in *Henry IV*, lies beneath a splendid alabaster tomb in St Mary's, one of Suffolk's great medieval churches. Lovely decorated tracery in the chancel windows, magnificent parclose screens with delicately carved lofts, a triple-decker pulpit (1625), surrounded by box pews and a glorious menagerie of real and mythical bench-end beasts adorn the interior. Do not miss the unique and fabulous Sciapod, a desert creature in the shade of Lord Bardolf's enormous foot.

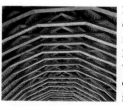

Denny Abbey, Cambs 695 G6, The stone-built remains of 12th-century Denny Abbey [EH] at Waterbeach, north of Cambridge*, are incorporated in a post-Dissolution farmhouse – fittingly so, in view of the now-adjoining Farmland Museum. Former residents include Knights Templar, Franciscan nuns and the Countess of Pembroke.

Denston, Suffk 691 H3, This complete late Perpendicular church, used as a college for chantry priests in 1475, is adorned with an extraordinary collection of carved beasts, both real and

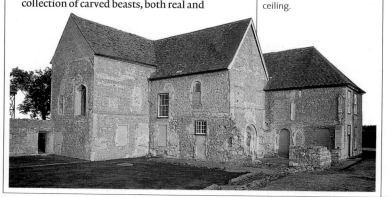
Left and below: Denny Abbey, built in the 12th century, has a remarkable timber-framed ceiling.

Denston church
Below: The Elizabethan 'wineglass' pulpit.
Right: A hound at bay, one of the many carved bench ends depicting animals.

imaginary. Hares, hounds and harts pursue each other along the wall-plates between foliated spandrels. There are many more animals in miniature on the bench ends and the figure of a crane on a misericord.

Derby, Derbys 694 C4, Derby is still a large and thriving city, although it is no longer the great centre of railway building it once was, and many of its Georgian buildings have gone. All Saints Church, now a cathedral, has a large 16th-century west tower, but the rest of the building is a handsome Georgian structure by James Gibbs. Sloping down from the cathedral is St Mary's Gate, which has some fine Georgian houses, and the massive Court House (1660s) at the bottom.

Derwentcote Steel Furnace, Dur 697 G2, The earliest and most intact steel furnace surviving [EH]. Probably dating from the 1720s, it was one of a series in the Derwent Valley. It used a new manufacturing process known as cementation, which produced high-quality steel particularly suited to making springs and tools with sharp cutting edges. When technology moved on to making steel in crucibles, manufacture moved to Sheffield*.

Devil's Arrows, N York 697 H5, Three megaliths from a large late-neolithic or early Bronze-Age monument stand alongside the minor road between Boroughbridge and Roecliffe, and can be glimpsed from the A168.

Devil's Ditch, Cambs 695 G6, The open chalk prairies east of Cambridge* are rich in archeological sites, notably Devil's Ditch, the longest of several Saxon defensive ditches, stretching 7 miles (11km) from Reach to Woodditton. It cut across the most accessible prehistoric corridor between the Fens and the wooded chalk hills transversed by the Icknield Way.

Devil's Punchbowl, Surrey, A dramatically deep valley [NT]. *See* **Hindhead*** **690 E6.**

Devizes, Wilts 690 C5, A busy market town, pervaded by the hops and malt smell from Wadsworth's Brewery. Its church of St John has a splendid Norman chancel (*c*1125) with elaborate and interlocking zig-zag arches. There is also the ornate Beauchamp Chapel with its riot of heraldry. The Town Hall of 1806 is a five-bay building by the Bath architect Thomas Baldwin, with restrained Adamesque plasterwork within. The Devizes Museum in Long Street houses a large collection of prehistoric, Roman, Saxon and medieval artefacts. Its library offers excellent facilities for the study of local history. On a hillside near the town is a flight of 29 locks, the longest in Britain, which carry the Kennet and Avon Canal over the 230-foot (70m) Caen Hill.

Top: Devil's Arrows, two of three remaining impressive megaliths.

Bottom left and right: Devil's Ditch. This great Saxon defensive earthwork cuts straight across the prairie landscape of south Cambridgeshire in a northwest/southeast line. Much of the bank is traversed by a public footpath.

Devonport

D

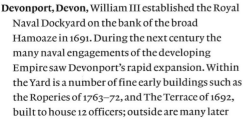

Devonport, Devon, William III established the Royal Naval Dockyard on the bank of the broad Hamoaze in 1691. During the next century the many naval engagements of the developing Empire saw Devonport's rapid expansion. Within the Yard is a number of fine early buildings such as the Roperies of 1763–72, and The Terrace of 1692, built to house 12 officers; outside are many later naval residences, such as Hamoaze House (1795, built for the Duke of Richmond) and the Port Admiral's House of 1808–10. In the civilian part of the town, Ker Street is terminated by a curious composition: a Greek town hall (1821), a remarkable Egyptian-style institution (1823) and a Doric column commemorating the creation of the borough in 1824. All are by John Foulston.

This civic complex originally included a 'Hindoo'-style church and was approached through classical terraces. Both these and the church were damaged in World War II and have been replaced by unsympathetic modern blocks of flats. Bound for Plymouth, the visitor might see two of the great naval compositions of the town, the Royal Naval Hospital of 1758–62 – a series of small pavilions, built separately to prevent diseases from spreading but connected by a colonnade – and the great Royal William Victualling Yard. This was

Dinefwr, Newton House
Top right: The east front.
Above: Venetian gothic detail on the west front.

Left: Devonport, the appropriately severe Greek Town Hall by John Foulston, 1821.

Bottom left: Dinefwr Castle.

Bottom right: A view over Dinefwr Park to the sea on the horizon.

built by Sir John Rennie between 1825 and 1833, following the triumphs of the Napoleonic wars, and has a supremely self-confident air – conceived on a massive scale, the buildings contained a bakery, a brewery and a butchery with numerous other support buildings, all facing the water to allow for easy access to the many vessels lying at anchor nearby. The impressive gateway off Durnford Street is surmounted by a 13-foot (4m) statue of William IV (r. 1830–7), aptly known as 'The Sailor King'. *See* **Plymouth* 688 E7**.

Dinas Bran, Denbgs, Just north of Llangollen, enough remains of Castell Dinas Bran ('Fortress of the Crow') to suggest its stature as a stronghold of the lords of Powys Fadog, who maximized the advantage of this originally Iron-Age fort in order to repel Edward I's encroachment. One of the most prominently defensive sites in Wales, it commands tremendous views. *See* **Llangollen* 693 F3.**

Dinefwr, Carmth 692 D6, One of the three royal seats of Wales, Dinefwr Castle was the stronghold of Rhys ap Gruffudd, the Lord Rhys, 'Prince of South Wales' (d. 1197), who was a great patron of the arts and of the monastic foundations of Ystrad Fflur (Strata Florida*) and Tal-y-Llychau (Talley). He is probably responsible for the stone refortification of the castle, which stands on an elevated rock commanding magnificent views of the Tywi Valley between Llandeilo* and Carmarthen*. Major conservation work on the early fortifications was completed by CADW in 1998. After the Battle of Bosworth in 1485, Henry VII presented Dinefwr to one of his staunchest supporters, Rhys ap Thomas, in gratitude for his allegiance. A descendant abandoned the castle in

Top left: Ditchley Park, the curved corridors linking the pavilions to the main house.

Dolwyddelan Castle

D

represent Doddershall's medieval village, which was depopulated in c1500.

Doddington Hall, Lincs 694 E3, A late Tudor mansion set back from the main road behind its pretty brick gatehouse. The perfect balance achieved in its main front suggests a good architect, and Doddington is probably the work of Robert Smythson, who also designed Hardwick Hall* in Derbyshire. Although the outside of the house has hardly changed since it was finished in 1600, most of the interior was redone in the 1760s for Sir John Hussey Delaval.

Doddington Place Gardens, Kent 691 H5, A 10-acre (4ha) landscape garden comprising different

favour of Newton House, a more convenient and comfortable residence on lower ground. This, with its medieval backdrop, became the focal point of a landscaped park by Capability Brown in the 18th century. The house, which was Victorianized by R K Penson, was acquired by the National Trust in 1990. The visual effect of the juxtaposition of such contrasting properties in an incomparably beautiful setting is a rare delight.

Dinton, Bucks 690 E4, The church of St Peter and St Paul appears to be standard work of the 13th, 15th and early 16th centuries. Until, that is, one walks around to the south side and finds the amazingly sumptuous, reset Norman doorway.

Dirleton, E Loth 699 G4, Old cottages and trim little gardens make this a truly picturesque village. The castle, built in the early 13th century and badly damaged by Cromwell's troops in 1660, still has its original massive keep and Great Hall (15th century). Within its walls are a garden, bowling green and dovecote (17th century).

Diserth, Powys 693 F5, St Cewydd, standing on the River Ithon, a mile east of Newbridge-on-Wye, dates to the 14th century. Its furnishings include a three-decker pulpit of 1687 and box pews bearing dates from 1666 to 1722 as well as the initials of their owners. The church owes its beguiling simplicity to the fact that it escaped the zeal of Victorian restorers.

Ditchley Park, Oxon 690 D4, Ditchley Park, completed in 1722, is one of James Gibbs's best and most significant buildings. The house has a typical Palladian plan and features interiors worked on by William Kent and Henry Flitcroft.

Doddershall Park, Bucks 690 E4, The house, near Quainton, forms three sides of a courtyard, with timber-framed ranges of c1520 to the east and north, and a brick addition of 1689 to the south. Of particular interest are the Tudor Hall and Great Chamber. The earthworks close to the moat

Doddington Hall
Above right: The handsome symmetrical entrance front.
Below: The Drawing Room.

Left: Ditchley Park, the Ionic Temple.

areas, including Edwardian rock garden, formal terraces, woodland garden and a folly.

Dolaucothi, Carmth 692 D6, In the village of Pumpsaint ('Five saints') on the A482 between Llanwrda and Lampeter*, the cottages with their lattice windows and the name of the hostelry are a reminder of the Dolaucothi estate, now without its house, which was given to the National Trust in 1941 as a memorial to the Johnes family, its owners since Tudor times. The gold mine nearby was worked as an open-cast quarry with tunnels and shafts by the Romans, and intermittently since then, particularly during the 19th century, and up until the 1930s. The site is expertly interpreted by the National Trust by means of guided tours and a visitor centre opened in 1986.

Dolbadarn Castle, Conwy 692 D2, One of two stone castles built for the Princes of Gwynedd near Snowdonia* by Llywelyn ap Iorwerth. The tower, painted by both Richard Wilson and JMW Turner, dominates the lakes of Padarn and Peris. *See also* **Dolwyddelan***.

Dolwyddelan Castle, Conwy 692 E2, Together with Dolbadarn*, this castle (1210–40) represents Llywelyn ap Iorwerth's achievements as a castle builder. The remarkable state of preservation of the keep is the result of improvements undertaken in the middle of the 19th century by Lord Willoughby de Eresby, to whom the property had passed through his marriage to a Wynn of Gwydir*.

D

Doncaster

Doncaster, S York 697 H7, Hallowed in the minds of racing enthusiasts as the home of the famous St Leger horse race, Doncaster may be imprinted in the memories of older drivers as an infamous bottleneck at this ancient bridging point over the River Don. The A1 now bypasses the town. Of the Roman town of Danum there is no visible evidence, although some artefacts are on display in Doncaster Museum and Art Gallery. The museum also has good displays of glassware, ceramics and Yorkshire pottery, horse-racing exhibits and Dutch paintings.

St George's Church is extremely large, and looks medieval in style, but its immense scale points to the fact that it was rebuilt in 1854–8 by Sir George Gilbert Scott. It is one of his most successful churches. Another Victorian architect who had a hand in the design was Sir Edmund Beckett, later Lord Grimthorpe, a scion of Doncaster who also designed clocks – most famously that in the tower of Big Ben*.

Present-day Doncaster is generally rather nondescript, but it has one exceptionally fine Georgian building, the **Mansion House** of 1748, designed by James Paine as a place for the mayor to entertain on a lavish scale, and indeed to reside for his year of office. It is a handsome Palladian villa, albeit surrounded by other lesser buildings. Among its features is a fine Venetian window flanked by pedimented windows lighting the first-floor Banqueting Hall, which has exquisite Italianate plasterwork. **Cusworth Hall** is a spacious Palladian country house of 1740, altered by James Paine and illustrated in Volume IV of *Vitruvius Britannicus* (1767). The main block is flanked by two wings which project forward to enclose a front court. Now used as a museum, the building has excellent rococo interiors, most notably in the chapel situated in one of the side pavilions, decorated in Palladian style with sumptuous Italianate plasterwork.

See also **Conisbrough Castle***, 5miles (8km) southwest of Doncaster.

Left: Paine's Mansion House, designed for sumptuous entertaining.

Below: Doncaster Museum and Art Gallery.

Bottom: Cusworth Hall, the front entrance court with quadrant link between main block and service wing.

Left: Donnington Castle, built in the 14th century.

supported on cast-iron columns and a Thomas Hardy Memorial Room. Close by is St Peter's Church, a wonderful example of Perpendicular architecture, the Town Hall of 1855 by Benjamin Ferrey, and his church of Holy Trinity, 1875.

Dorchester, Oxon 690 D4, One of England's earliest Christian centres, and a cathedral city from 634 to 707. Although nothing from that period survives, there is one important Norman building, the huge late 12th-century Abbey Church. This was remodelled in the later Middle Ages, when the most impressive alterations were lavished upon the east end from the late 1200s to the early 1300s. The famed sculpture includes the carved Jesse window and the immense east window, of a

Donnington Castle, Berks 690 D5, Most of the Castle was destroyed during one of the longest sieges of the Civil War, but the earthworks and remains are unexpectedly impressive [EH]. It was originally licensed in 1386 and the imposing twin-towered gatehouse is the most impressive of the time.

Dorchester, Dorset 689 J6, The lines of Dorchester's main roads were laid down by the Romans, and the remains of a Roman villa can be seen in Colliton Park near the County Hall. Dorset's county town is more famous, however, for the years spent there by Thomas Hardy. Very little has changed since Hardy's day, and the character of the town may be absorbed merely by walking the length of the High Street. In High Street West is the excellent County Museum, whose collections cover all aspects of Dorset's history, geology and natural history. It has an interior exhibition hall

Left: Dorchester, Oxon, Abbey Church stained glass.

Dorchester, Dorset
Right: Thomas Hardy exhibits in the County Museum.
Below: In the town is Eric Kennington's statue (1931), showing Hardy as an old man, hat on knee.

fantasy and elaboration unparalleled in England. Also of note are the very well-preserved lead font of c1170, medieval stained glass and several fine monuments.

Dorfold Hall, Ches, A Jacobean house built for Ralph Wilbraham in 1616, of smoky red brick with the diamond-shaped patterning known as diaperwork. Although the builders made an effort to produce a symmetrical main front, the rest of the house looks a bit jumbled, and some of the interior rooms were redone in the later 18th century. *See* **Acton* 693 G2.**

Dorking, Surrey 691 F6, Dorking, once known for its edible snails, is a good place from which to explore the surrounding countryside. **Leith Hill** [NT] rises to the southwest of the town and reaches – with the help of an 18th-century gothic tower – exactly 1,000 feet (304m). It is the highest point in the southeast of England and offers magnificent views, especially southwards to the Weald. One mile north of Dorking is Box Hill*, a beautiful area of woodland and downland which also offers fine views.

Dorney, Bucks, In a peaceful setting beside the church stands Dorney Court. Dating from 1440, the older parts are timber-framed with brick nogging. Inside the house retains much of its 16th-century appeal. *See* **Windsor* 690 E5.**

Dornoch, Highld 701 H4, This pleasant family resort, renowned for its spacious beaches and golf links, stands on the north shore of Dornoch Firth. This

Top right: Dorney Court, home to the Palmer family since 1642.

Centre right: Dovedale's spectacular narrow limestone ravine.

Centre: Dorking, the gothic tower on Leith Hill.

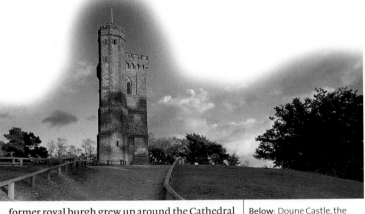

branch of the Stewart family, who still own it today. The curtain wall and the massive 100-foot (30m) extremely well-restored keep, with its huge state room and vast kitchens, give some idea of the past power of this castle.

Dovedale, Derbys 694 C3, A narrow and wooded limestone ravine, one of the most famous of the beautiful dales that make Derbyshire so popular with walkers.

former royal burgh grew up around the Cathedral built in the 13th century by the bishops of Caithness on the site of a 6th-century chapel. The Cathedral, destroyed by fire in 1570, was redesigned in the 17th century, almost entirely rebuilt in 1835–7 and restored in 1924. The tower of the former bishop's palace (16th century), opposite the Cathedral, today forms part of a luxury hotel.

Doune Castle, Stirlg 698 E3, This impressive castle, which stands above a bend in the River Teith, was built in the late 14th–early 15th century by Robert Stewart, Duke of Albany (d. 1419) and his son Murdoch, both regents of Scotland under James I. The king had Murdoch executed on his release from captivity in 1424, and the castle passed to the Earls of Moray, another

Below: Doune Castle, the court with the Great Hall on the right.

Dover, Kent 691 J6, It is here, in the closest English town to the Continent, that the history of fortifications can best be studied, although the fact that Dover has been in continuous military occupation from Norman times to 1958 has meant that little has survived unaltered. The oldest building on the site is the tower of the church, which was a Roman lighthouse. In *c*1000 it was incorporated in, but not physically joined to, a Saxon church, St Mary sub Castra. Much of the original structure survives, and the interior was given mosaic decoration by William Butterfield in 1888. Dover's Norman keep was begun about 1180, a square tower with corner turrets. It is surrounded by a double circuit of walls, the first close to the keep, the second further out and extending as far as the cliff edge. Such a system was extremely up-to-date for the late-12th and early-13th centuries. Inside the keep one can still see the upper and lower chapels, and the Hall, where the ceiling was lowered in about 1800 to support guns on the roof. The same thing happened to the tops of the towers in the outer wall.

Underneath the castle is a vast system of tunnels, begun in the Middle Ages, extended in the 18th and 19th centuries and again in the 1940s, when they were used by Winston Churchill and his staff in the defence of Britain. They are now all open to the public and form one of the most vivid evocations of life during World War II [EH].

The **Western Heights**, on the other side of the town, was turned into a fortress between 1793 and 1814 as a defence against Napoleonic invasion. It contains the amazing double spiral staircase called the Grand Shaft, occasionally open to the public. The town of Dover has so suffered from shelling and bombing that not much of interest remains, but the Victorian Dover College incorporates parts of a 12th-century monastery, including its refectory, gatehouse and guest hall (near the chapel).

Down House, Gt Lon 691 G5, The home of Charles Darwin, where he wrote *The Origin of Species* and *The Descent of Man* – works that put forward the theory of natural selection, one of the cornerstones of modern thought. The house, restored by English Heritage, is now maintained as it was in his time, vividly conveying the great scientist's personality.

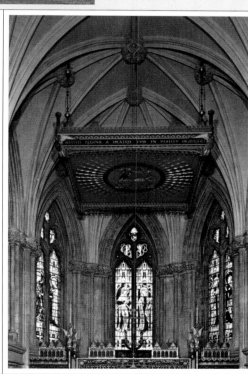

Left: Down House.
Above: Charles Darwin, who lived there for most of his life and died there in 1882. Knowing that his theory of natural selection would scandalize conventional Christians, he waited many years before publishing.

Right: Downside Abbey. The medieval-style rib-vaults, are actually of the 20th century. They are more than suitable for a premier example of buildings of English Catholicism.

Downside Abbey, Somset 689 J4, The buildings of this Benedictine community in Stratton-on-the-Fosse now house a Roman Catholic boarding-school. The Abbey Church itself is longer (328 feet/100m) internally than many cathedrals.

Doyden Castle, Cnwll 688 D6, Given a dramatic setting above Port Quin and the crashing waves of the Atlantic, it was probably built by the Wadebridge merchant Samuel Symons about 1830 as a gambling den, with an extensive wine cellar. A former Governor of Chatham Prison built the nearby Doyden House, which is a National Trust holiday cottage, about 1830.

Drayton Beauchamp, Bucks 690 E4, The church contains a large monument to Lord and Lady Newhaven (c1730). The figures are seen against a pyramid within an architectural frame; she is seated at her husband's feet.

Droitwich, Worcs 693 H5, A small town 7 miles (11km) north of Worcester*, which was once an important spa. The remains of its brine baths survive. Just outside the settlement to the north stands the dramatic Château Impney, now a hotel, which was built in the style of Louis XIII for Droitwich's 'salt king', John Corbett.

Drum Castle, Abers 702 D6, The splendid square, red-granite tower that dominates the castle is the oldest in the region (1296). It is attributed to Richard Cementarius, a master mason by appointment to the king, who was also the first Provost of Aberdeen. In the 14th century the castle passed into the hands of William Irvine, standard and armour bearer to Robert Bruce, and remained in the Irvine family until it was bequeathed to the National Trust for Scotland in 1976. The wing built in the early 17th century, during the reign of James IV, houses old furniture and a collection of family souvenirs.

Drumlanrig Castle, D & G 699 F6, The impressive residence of the Dukes of Buccleuch and Queensberry stands on the site of a 15th-century Douglas stronghold. The castle was built (1679–91) from local pink sandstone for the 3rd Earl of Queensberry. It houses exceptional paintings by Holbein, Rembrandt, Murillo, Ruisdael, Ramsay, Reynolds and Gainsborough, and some beautiful 17th- and 18th-century French furniture. Charles Edward Stuart spent a night in the castle as he retreated from Derby in 1745.

Drummond Castle, P & K 699 F3, South of Crieff*, the formal, French-style terraced gardens of Drummond Castle were created in the 1630s, but

Left: Drumlanrig Castle. The gardens have been restored to the plan of 1738.

Below: Drum Castle, owned for 653 years by the Irvine family.

Bottom: Drummond Castle gardens, with the famous sundial designed by John Milne, master-mason to Charles I.

the St Andrews Cross design dates from the 19th century. Neatly clipped trees and shrubs, elegantly planted beds and carefully designed borders form a dazzling display centred on a sundial.

Dryburgh Abbey, Borders 699 H5, The ruins of Dryburgh Abbey, founded in 1150 by the Constable of Scotland under David I for Premonstratensians from Alnwick*, stand in a beautiful park on the banks of the Tweed. The Abbey suffered at the hands of the English on several occasions and was never rebuilt after being destroyed in 1544 by the troops of Henry VIII. The family of Walter Scott owned the abbey lands for a short time in the early 18th century and retained the right to be buried ('stretch their bones') there. Today visitors can still admire the semicircular doorway in the church's west façade (15th century) and the transept (late 12th–13th century) whose north arm contains the tombs of Walter Scott and Earl Haig, the commander of the British forces during World War I. The romanesque monastic buildings are the best preserved in Scotland. To the east of the ruined cloister are the old vestry, the parlour, the magnificent chapter house, the warming room and the novices' day room (the dormitory occupied the entire floor above these buildings). The refectory lay to the south, above the crypt, while the kitchens, set apart to reduce the risk of fire, would have occupied the southwest corner of the building.

Duckpool, Cnwll 688 E5, A charming hamlet set beneath the blasted woods of Stowe*, which lies on the hill to the west. It clusters around a small stream which flows into the Atlantic past a point on the beach where a Roman outpost lies buried. By the ford in the centre of Duckpool stand a range of picturesque thatched cottages, a mill and the pair of cottages where the Reverend RS Hawker,

Top: Duffus Castle, view from the southeast showing the projecting forework containing the entrance and stair.

poet and scholar, lived for a while before the Rectory was built at Morwenstow*. The house is instantly recognizable by the curious cruciform window on the first floor, which lit his study. Most of the cottages and buildings in the village are now let as holiday homes by the Landmark Trust.

Dudmaston Hall, Shrops 693 H4, Built c1700, this substantial red-brick house was modernized in the Regency period when a new main stair was inserted. The house contains period furniture and good collections of Dutch flowerpieces and 20th-century Spanish art. There is also a dramatic garden, laid out in a steep dingle falling down to a large lake [NT].

Duff House, Abers 702 D4, In 1735 William Adam laid the first stone of this magnificent mansion near Banff* designed for the 1st Earl of Fife. Only the main building was finished, the architect having been taken to court over the cost of the work.

Right: Duff House, the main front. See page 32 for an illustration of the original scheme of colonnades and flanking wings.

Bottom left: Dudmaston Hall, built around 1700.

Bottom centre: Dumbarton Castle and Rock, a view showing the Governor's House.

Adam had shipped top-quality stone from his own quarry at South Queensferry* for the Corinthian pilasters and elaborately carved pediment of the façade. Today the restored building houses paintings by El Greco, Ramsay, Raeburn and Boucher, and some superb furniture from Scottish national collections.

Duffus Castle, Moray 702 B4, These ruins of a 14th-century stone keep stand on a 12th-century feudal motte. The castle belonged to the Moravia family (whose name became Moray and then Murray).

Duloe, Cnwll 688 E7, Near the pedestrian main street of this village is a stone circle, some 38 feet (11.5m) in diameter. The medieval church, dedicated to St Cuby and St Leonard, has an unusual plan with a tower attached to the south transept.

Dumbarton, W Duns 698 D4, This industrial town was formerly the capital of Strathclyde, the kingdom of the Britons which became part of Scotland in 1034. It is also said to be the birthplace of St Patrick, kidnapped by pirates as a young man and sold into slavery in Ireland where he became a Christian and began to convert the people of Ireland in 432. Dumbarton is also the port from which Mary Stuart secretly set sail for France in 1548. Dumbarton Castle dominates the Firth of Clyde from the top of a 240-foot (73m) rock.

The castle was fortified in the 13th century when it became a royal residence. In 1305 its governor used treachery to capture William Wallace and hand him over to Edward I of England. The castle, badly damaged in the wars between England and Scotland, was rebuilt after 1707, when the Act of Union stipulated that it must house a garrison. From the former Governor's House (1735–1832) steps cut out of the rock climb to the Wallace Guardhouse where two more flights of steps lead east to the magazine and west to the orientation table on the site of the White Tower. The panorama over the Clyde from this viewpoint is well worth the effort.

Dumfries, D & G 699 F7, This peaceful market town with its pink-sandstone houses is the capital of Galloway. Founded on the River Nith in 1186, it suffered a number of English invasions during the 15th and 16th centuries. It was here in the Franciscan monastery that Robert Bruce murdered his rival, Sir John Comyn, in 1306, before being crowned at Scone. The event is commemorated by a plaque on the wall of Greyfriars Church. But Dumfries's most famous son is Robert Burns, who spent the last five years of his life here.

Burns' House: The poet-farmer lived in this ordinary house at the south end of High Street. It has been well preserved and today houses a collection of personal items, letters and original manuscripts, as well as the famous editions of his works published in Kilmarnock and Edinburgh. The window pane of his room, on the second floor, still bears a signature that he is said to have inscribed with his diamond ring.

Burns Mausoleum: Robert Burns was buried in the cemetery of St Michael's Church, to the south of his house. In 1815 his remains were transferred to the neoclassical mausoleum overlooking the cemetery. His wife, Jean Armour, and several of their children are also buried there.

Dumfries Museum: The museum is housed in an 18th-century windmill and its annexes, which stand on a hill above the Robert Burns Heritage Centre. The exhibits in its mineralogical,

Above: Dunadd Fort, a footprint carved in the stone.

Left: Dumfries, Burns' House, and, top centre, Tam o'Shanter figurines.

Below: Duncansby Head cliffs, home to colonies of seabirds.

archeological and historical collections range from early Christian stones to domestic, agricultural and industrial objects from the Victorian age. A Camera Obscura on the top floor of the museum presents panoramic views of the town and surrounding area.

Robert Burns Heritage Centre: This small museum occupies an 18th-century mill on the bank of the River Nith. It traces the life of Burns in Dumfries and at Ellisland Farm.

Dun, House of, Angus 699 H2, This impressive Georgian mansion, designed in 1730 by William Adam and refurbished in the 19th century, still has its magnificent plasterwork and Victorian gardens. It is owned by National Trust for Scotland.

Dunadd, Ag & B 698 C4, The isolated hilltop that dominates the River Add, to the northwest of Bridgend, was fortified during the Iron Age. Around 500 it became the site of the capital of Fergus, the first king of Dalriada. Its remains include carved stones – an inscription in the ogham alphabet, the image of a boar, a footprint and a shallow basin – which were probably associated with the coronation ceremony of the Scottish kings. The stones act as a reminder that Dunadd was the first site of the 'Stone of Destiny'.

Dunbar, E Loth 699 H4, The town has had a turbulent history, as evidenced by its ruined castle above the old harbour. This strategic fortress on the road to the South was successfully attacked by Edward I of England in 1295, but valiantly withstood a six-week English siege in 1339. Mary Stuart and the Earl of Bothwell sought refuge here after the murder of David Rizzio in 1566. The castle was demolished on the orders of the Scottish Parliament following the Queen's defeat in 1567, and the stones were used by Cromwell to improve the harbour in 1650. The High Street has several interesting buildings: the 17th-century Town House (no. 126) where the naturalist John Muir was born, which is now a museum dedicated to his life, and Lauderdale House, a classical-style mansion built by Robert Adam in 1790.

Dunblane, Stirlg 698 E3, This delightful little town has a Cathedral founded in 1150 on the site of a 6th-century church. All that remains of the original cathedral are the first two floors of the tower; the rest was built between 1233 and 1258 by Bishop Clement. Extended in the 15th century and restored in the 19th and 20th centuries, the Cathedral has a magnificent gothic façade and beautiful 15th-century carved choir stalls. Dean's House (1624) is occupied by a small cathedral museum and an exhibition of local history.

Duncansby Head, Highld 702 C1, The northeastern tip of Scotland is worth visiting for its cliffs (213 feet/65ms) with their colonies of seabirds and the caves, ridges, arches and bridges sculpted by thousands of years of erosion.

Duncombe Park
Top right: The Withdrawing
Room.

Centre: The Hall, which is
40 feet (12m) high.

Bottom left: Father Time,
with sundial in the grounds.

Bottom right: Vista from the
Ionic Temple in the grounds.

Duncombe Park, N York 697 H5, On the edge of
Helmsley*, a Vanbrughian composition of c1713
by Yorkshire gentleman-architect William
Wakefield. Much of the interior dates from
rebuilding after a major fire in 1895, but the
landscaped garden is largely a survival of the
early 18th century – the Stephen Switzer/Charles
Bridgeman period. On one side is a serpentine
bastion and yew walk, on another a large lawn and
a curving terrace flanked at each end by a temple,
with splendid views down into the valley of the
River Rye. From here one can survey the
outstanding arboreal specimens and glimpse
Rievaulx Abbey* in the distance [EH].

Left: Dundee, the McManus Galleries, formerly the Albert Institute, which was built by Sir George Gilbert Scott in 1865–7.

Below left: The external staircase to the Albert Institute.

Dundee, Dund C 699 G2, Scotland's fourth largest city, situated on the Firth of Tay at the foot of the Sidlaw Hills, is a port, an industrial centre and a dynamic university town. It was elevated to the status of royal burgh in 1190 and soon became one of the principal towns in the kingdom, as well as one of the hardest hit

by internal divisions and the wars between England and Scotland. It prospered in the 18th century and enjoyed its golden age during the Victorian era owing to its flourishing textile (especially jute) and jam industries (including the famous orange marmalade invented by Mrs Keiller in 1797) and journalism. Today, modern industries have replaced the more traditional forms of production, but Dundee remains the seat of the Thomson newspaper group which publishes Scotland's best-known Sunday paper, the *Sunday Post*.

City churches (Nethergate): These three churches occupy a single building dominated by St Mary's Tower. The tower – all that remains of the 15th-century parish church – houses a small museum of religious history.

Dundee Contemporary Arts Centre: In 1999 Scotland's largest modern art centre moved into the building designed by Richard Murphy at 152 Nethergate. It offers visitors the opportunity to explore all areas of artistic creation – plastic arts, decorative arts, music, dance, cinema – through exhibitions, workshops and meetings with the artists.

McManus Galleries: This beautiful Victorian gothic building in Albert Square, designed by George Gilbert Scott in 1867, houses a museum of local history and archaeology and an interesting collection of works by 19th- and 20th-century European and Scottish artists.

Above right: Dunfermline Abbey, the nave showing the chevroned cylindrical piers similar to those at Durham*.

Verdant Works: This old factory, founded in 1833, traces the history of Dundee's jute industry.

Dundrennan Abbey, D & G 696 C3, The mother-house of Sweetheart Abbey (*see* New Abbey*) was founded (1142) for the Cistercian order by David I or Fergus, Lord of Galloway. The early gothic ruins of the 12th-century church and 13th-century chapter house can still be seen today.

Dunfermline, Fife 699 F4, The development of this royal burgh, a favourite town of Scottish

sovereigns from the late 11th to the 14th century, was closely linked to its religious influence. After marrying Malcom III in 1070, the pious Queen Margaret founded a priory which her son David I made a Benedictine abbey in 1128. Several Scottish kings and queens are buried there, the Abbey having superseded Iona* as a royal place of burial in the 12th century. Dunfermline was one of the principal centres of the linen industry from the 16th to the early 20th century, and the birthplace of Andrew Carnegie (1835–1919), the steel magnate and philanthropist to whom it owes its annual festival of music and drama.

Abbot House: This delightful 15th-century abbot's house in Maygate, with its walled garden, houses an introduction to the town's history.

The Andrew Carnegie Museum (Moodie Street), housed in the weaver's cottage where Carnegie was born, traces his life and work.

Dunfermline Abbey: The Abbey Church stands on the site of a church founded by David I. Over the centuries it has been ruined and rebuilt many times. By contrast the interior of the nave, inspired by that of Durham* Cathedral and skillfully restored in the 16th century by William Shaw, has retained all its Norman grandeur: its semicircular arches are supported by tall, cylindrical piers, four of which are carved with Norman motifs. Today the only part of the abbey used for worship is the gothic choir, rebuilt in 1817–22, where Robert Bruce is buried. Beyond the apse of the sanctuary are the foundations of the 13th-century chapel which housed the remains of Malcolm III and the relics of St Margaret and was for a long time a place of pilgrimage. To the south of the church are the ruined monastery buildings (13th-century refectory) and the kitchens of the abbey guest house, transformed in the 14th century into a royal palace where several Scottish kings were born.

Pittencrieff House: West of the abbey in the lush setting of Pittencrieff Park stands a 17th-century manor now a museum of local history and costume. There are also the ruins of Malcolm's Tower where, in 1068, Malcolm III received his future wife and her brother, Edgar Atheling, who fought against William the Conqueror.

Dungeness, Kent 691 H7, At the tip of the peninsula of Romney* Marsh is Dungeness, with its stylish new lighthouse of 1959 and its nuclear power station of 1960. More appealing, however, is the garden that the writer and film-maker Derek Jarman created round his tiny cottage on the bleak, stony, east-facing beach. Here, where it seemed that nothing would grow, he lovingly assembled flowering plants and bushes that could live among pebbles and sand, interspersed with pieces of old timber and iron rescued from the sea – a unique and poetic landscape.

Dunham Massey Hall, Gt Man 697 F7, A large, plain red-brick Georgian house of 1732 [NT], built on the site of the Tudor house by George Booth, 2nd Earl of Warrington. The Hall contains an excellent collection of Georgian paintings, Stuart and early Georgian furniture, fine Huguenot silver, and a famous carving of the Crucifixion by Grinling Gibbons. Most of the state rooms were renovated in the early years of the 20th century under the direction of Percy Macquoid, a furniture expert who took care to provide appropriate decorations.

Dunkeld, P & K 699 F2, The seven-arched bridge, built across the River Tay by Thomas Telford in 1809, offers a sweeping view of the

Above: Dunham Massey, the Great Hall of 1740, with the original panelling and chimneypiece.

Below: Dunnottar Castle seen from the mainland, painted by the eminent portrait painter George Reid. Some of the buildings have since been re-roofed.

charming town nestling on the banks of the river below wooded mountains. This Pictish stronghold became a principal place of pilgrimage when Celtic monks, driven from Iona by the Vikings, brought the relics of St Columba to Dunkeld in 850. The Cathedral, built between 1260 and 1501, evokes the town's golden age. It was twice destroyed: in 1600 by the Reformers and, in August 1689, during a battle which ended with the defeat of the Jacobites, who only a month before had defeated the English at the battle of Killiecrankie. The roofless nave stands open to the sky, its grassy floor paved with tombs. The choir has been restored several times and is now used as the parish church. It has a carved oak screen which conceals the tomb of the 'Wolf of Badenoch', the natural son of Robert II who, amongst other evil deeds, burned the Cathedral of Elgin* in 1390. The cathedral, which stands on lawns planted with trees on the banks of the River Tay, occupies a truly idyllic setting. Beyond its monumental gate, the white façades of Cathedral Street and High Street provide a striking contrast with the severity of some Scottish villages. These 'Little Houses' were built on the ruins of old Dunkeld, which was burned in 1689 along with the Cathedral.

Dunnottar Castle, Abers 702 D7, The Castle stands on a steep rocky outcrop separated from the mainland by a deep ravine. A Pictish fort was the first building to be erected on this isolated rock. It was followed by a chapel in the 5th century, and later a castle and church which were destroyed by William Wallace in 1297. The present ruins are those of a tower-house built after 1392 by William Keith, hereditary Earl-Marischal of Scotland and, as such, guardian of the royal insignia. His descendants transformed it into what was virtually a fortified town. It was badly damaged by Cromwell's troops in 1651–2, confiscated following the 10th Earl's involvement in the Jacobite Rising of 1715, and remained abandoned

until the 20th century. The oldest ruins are those of the 14th-century chapel and L-shaped tower-house. The fortified guardroom (1575) and elegant apartments built around a square courtyard (14th–17th centuries) are attributed to the 5th Earl-Marischal and founder of Marischal College in Aberdeen*. A complex of domestic buildings – kitchen, bakery, brewery, wine vault, forge and stables – is also open to the public.

Dunoon, Ag & B 698 D4, Dunoon, the 'capital' of Cowal, stands on the bend of the Firth of Clyde. The village became a fashionable spa town in the 19th century when a ferry service was established between Dunoon and Gourock. Its Victorian villas are dominated by the ruins of a 13th-century castle, destroyed in 1685. According to tradition James III made the Earls of Argyll the castle's

Above: Dunstanburgh Castle, sited spectacularly close to the North Sea.

Left: Dunoon's ferry pier, in mock-Tudor style, juts out into the Firth of Clyde.

Below: Dunster Castle.

Bottom: Dunrobin Castle, surrounded by formal gardens.

keepers, on condition that they presented him with a red rose whenever he asked for one.

Dunrobin Castle, Highld 701 H3, This impressive castle, the seat of the Sutherlands since the 13th century, stands on a natural terrace overlooking the sea. The foundations (1275) and keep

(14th century) were incorporated into subsequent additions to the Castle. The present building, in Scots Jacobean style, was designed in 1845–51 by Sir Charles Barry. The interior was restored in 1915–21 by Sir Robert Lorimer after a fire. It houses a fine collection of paintings, including family portraits by Ramsay and Reynolds, and two Canalettos. A small Victorian museum, containing hunting trophies, family souvenirs and some good examples of Pictish stones, stands on the edge of the beautiful formal gardens below the castle.

Dunsfold, Surrey 690 E6, This village in the Weald close to Sussex boasts the unusually complete church of St Mary and All Saints, built in c1270. Inside, the later medieval bell turret is supported by a four-post cage and there are some good 13th-century pews.

Dunstable, Beds 690 E3, A modern town that retains one building of outstanding interest, the 12th-century Dunstable Priory. This church represents the principal surviving part of an Augustinian priory founded in 1131 by Henry I. The west front is impressive, and inside is an excellent Norman font, probably recut during the 1800s.

Dunstaffnage Castle, Ag & B 698 C2, In the 13th century the MacDougalls of Lorne built a stronghold on a promontory above the entrance to Loch Etive, said to have been the site of the court of Kenneth MacAlpin before he moved to Scone. In the 15th century the 1st Earl of Argyll bought the castle and appointed the Campbells of Dunstaffnage as its hereditary captains. The three round towers and towerhouse built above the entrance date from the 16th century.

Dunstanburgh Castle, Nthumb 699 K6, Accessible only on foot, this romantic castle [EH and NT] stands spectacularly above the North Sea on a promontory of dolerite rocks. It was built in 1313–16 to defend this lonely stretch of the Northumberland coast against the Scots around the time of the English loss at Bannockburn. Dunstanburgh is therefore almost contemporary with Edward I's great Welsh castles, and it too has a large gatehouse, with semi-circular towers, containing living accommodation. The castle's defences were upgraded in 1380–4 by John of Gaunt, Duke of Lancaster and Lieutenant of the

trophies, even coins, carved flowers and foliage, all in elm, dating to about 1683.

Duntrune Castle, Ag & B 698 C3, The north entrance to the bay at Crinan is guarded by this Castle, built in the 13th century to counter Viking attacks. The Castle is closed to the public but its lovely gardens are well worth a visit.

Dunwich, Suffk 695 K6, Surrounded by marshes, forest and heath and at the mercy of the sea, this village was the sixth greatest town in England in the early 13th century. The ruins of Greyfriars' Priory, built on the western outskirts of the medieval town, is now near the cliff edge. The story of Dunwich – the terrible storm of 1328 and its subsequent demise – is told in the excellent local museum. The melancholy sight of All Saints' Church toppling over the cliff at the turn of the 19th and 20th centuries attracted a succession of literary tourists from Swinburne to Henry James and Edward Thomas, who stayed in the coastguard cottages on Dunwich Heath, the setting for PD James' thriller *Unnatural Causes* (1967).

Durdle Door, Dorset 690 B8, West of Lulworth* Cove is the famous spot where impermeable folded strata were forced up on end to produce a huge natural arch of Purbeck limestone jutting out into the sea. From Durdle Door, a spectacular chalk cliff walk stretches 5 miles (8km) west towards Weymouth*, with magnificent views of wild landscape, jagged rocks and sea. (Be warned, however, that the walk may be closed in places, owing to landslips.)

Scottish Marches, but it was severely damaged during the Wars of the Roses and was sold by the Crown into private hands in 1604. The path from Craster skirts the silted-up harbour where Henry VIII's fleet was found, having been lost for three weeks on a voyage from Scotland.

Dunster Castle, Somset 689 G4, At the west side of the county, 3 miles (4.8km) southeast of Minehead, this little town is dominated by the Luttrell Arms (the Dunster residence of the abbots of Cleeve), by the octagonal Market Cross, and by the Castle, which is set dramatically on a wooded hilltop, above the River Tor. Although there has been a castle on the site since Norman times, the present building was largely rebuilt in 1868–72 under the direction of Anthony Salvin. Salvin was working for George Luttrell, whose family had lived at Dunster for over 600 years. Within the house [NT], there are fine plasterwork ceilings. The Dining Room ceiling, dated to 1681, is attributed to the leading London master, Edward Goudge. There is also a splendid staircase with an oak handrail and panels of hunting and military

Top and above: Dunwich seafront.

Above right: Durdle Door, the dramatic rock archway.

Right: Dunster Castle, looking through to the Hall, which has an early 17th-century ceiling. Over the entrance front is the ancient motto 'Gained by strength, held by skill', appropriate perhaps for a structure which has known much fighting.

Durham

Durham, Durham 697 G3, One of the country's most spectacular views from a train is that from the railway viaduct, towards the cathedral and castle perched on their narrow promontory in a loop of the River Wear. **Durham Cathedral**, epitomized by Sir Walter Scott as 'Half church of God, half castle 'gainst the Scot', was built to house and protect the body of St Cuthbert, brought here via Chester-le-Street from Lindisfarne on Holy Island*. The present building was begun in 1093 as a Benedictine priory under a prince bishop who enjoyed

extensive temporal powers (including his own parliament, coinage and right to grant licences to crenellate), and to whom military service was due.

Externally the cathedral is powerful, whether viewed from level ground on Palace Green to the north, with the full lengthwise elevation demonstrating the satisfying dominance of the late-15th century central tower, or from the River Wear below, looking up to the early-13th-century west towers. On the main north door is a replica of the famous 12th-century sanctuary knocker. Internally, the cathedral is awesome, with its rhythm of stout piers, some cylindrical and incised with template patterns, others of composite form, carrying round arches which support England's earliest exercise in high-level rib vaulting. The choir vault was completed by about 1104, the nave vault about 1130 – the first phase of building had been completed by 1133. Beyond Sir George Gilbert Scott's choir screen of 1870–6, the delicate Neville screen behind the High Altar of c1380 in Caen stone, is a fine gothic work (despite the loss of 107 alabaster statues at the Reformation), and may have been designed by the royal master-mason Henry Yevele. Behind it on a raised platform is St Cuthbert's tomb, now marked by a plain slab simply inscribed 'Cuthbertus'. Nearby is the tomb of Bishop Hatfield who died in 1381, surmounted by the slightly earlier Bishop's throne – the loftiest in Christendom.

The choir stalls, erected by Bishop John Cosin in 1665 to replace those burnt by the Scots during the Civil War, are an exercise in exuberant gothic, with fretted canopies. The Norman apsidal east end was replaced between 1242 and 1280 by an eastern transept, the Chapel of the Nine Altars, based on that at Fountains Abbey* but with local Frosterley marble-like shafts. At the west end of the nave stands the font, surmounted by a splendidly lofty cover, erected by Bishop Cosin in 1663, then the Galilee Chapel, added in Transitional style and finished c1189 with an enthusiastic zig-zag motif on the arches. Since 1370 it has contained the tomb of the Venerable Bede, whose bones were brought to Durham in 1020. Around the cloister to the east is the Chapterhouse with intersecting wall arcading, to the south the octagonal Prior's Kitchen (now the shop) of 1366–74 by the leading master-mason John Lewyn, and to the west the Monks' Dormitory of c1400. Beyond the cathedral the close, or College, is an area of many attractive historic buildings.

Top left: The Neville Screen has delicate gothic carving.

Top right: Durham Cathedral, the choir aisles containing some of the earliest rib vaulting.

Left: The early-Norman piers have incised carving achieved by ingenious template design.

Below: The famous Sanctuary Knocker.

Durham Castle became the University of Durham in 1836. It was originally built as the palace of Durham's prince bishops, in motte-and-bailey form but with a later shell keep. An exquisite early Romanesque vaulted chapel dates from c1080, and another splendid chapel from the 1540s. A Norman gallery has a richly sculpted round-arched entrance, and Bishop Cosin constructed the Black Oak Staircase as part of post-Civil War repairs in the 1660s. The large Great Hall of 1284, with screen passage, buttery and kitchen, dated 1499, is now used as a student dining hall. Durham is very much a seat of learning: many buildings near the cathedral, particularly on Palace Green, in Old Elvet and inevitably now on the outskirts of the city, belong to the university. In the Market Place stands an equestrian statue of the 3rd Marquess of Londonderry.

Durham has several old bridges, including the medieval Framwellgate and Elvet bridges and Prebends' Bridge of 1772–8, from which there are impressive views. The Kingsgate footbridge (1961–2) is by Ove Arup & Partners.

Above: Durham Cathedral from the River Wear.

Left: The medieval Framwellgate Bridge.

Dyrham Park
Top right: The Diogenes Room.
Centre right: State Bed in the Queen Anne Room.
Bottom left: Exterior view.

Dyffryn, V Glam 689 G3, This late Victorian mansion, occupying the site of an earlier house, is Wales' best surviving example of the work of Thomas Mawson, the great Edwardian garden designer. The man who commissioned the ambitious undertaking was Reginald Cory, whose wealth as the son of a Cardiff ship-owner and coal exporter allowed him to travel widely and to indulge in one of his favourite pursuits, collecting rare plants. The allure of the garden is the product not only of Cory's horticultural enthusiasm, but also of its thematic layout, resulting in a series of highly individual compartments such as the Moorish Court, the Pompeiian Garden, the Lavender Court, the Cloister, and – best known of them all – the Theatre Garden, extensively used for productions of Shakespeare. Dyffryn House, by EA Lansdowne (1893) contains much important German and Netherlandish interior work. Since Cory's death in 1934, it has been used for educational purposes. A programme of repair work and restoration of ornamental buildings and structures, as well as the clearing of vistas and the replanting of borders, is safeguarding the future of Cory and Mawson's outstanding achievement.

Dymchurch, Kent 691 J6, There are two Martello towers, built in 1806, one of them owned by English Heritage.

Dyrham Park, Gloucs 689 J3, Designed by William Talman, this country mansion, crowned with a balustrade affording fine views of the surrounding parkland, was built in c1698 for William Blathwayt, politician and Secretary of State for William III. Its rooms, panelled with oak, walnut and cedar, have changed little since then. The house has a fine collection of portraits, tapestries and blue-and-white delftware, reflecting the contemporary taste for Dutch fashion. There are furniture and illusionistic pictures by Samual van Hoogstraten, that had belonged to Thomas Percy, friend of Pepys and Evelyn.

Below: Dymchurch Martello tower.

Below centre: Earls Barton Church.

Bottom right: Easby Abbey, the impressive refectory.

Earlham Park, Norfk 695 J5, South of Norwich*, East Anglia's lakeside university is a showpiece of post-war architecture where Denys Lasdun's 1960s concrete ziggurats are linked by elevated walkways to Norman Foster's hangar-like Sainsbury Centre. Here works by Moore, Bacon and Degas stand alongside Benin bronzes and other ethnic wonders in a minimalist masterpiece embraced by the smooth, sinuous form of Rick Mather's 1990s Constable Terrace.

Earls Barton Church, Nhants 694 E6, All Saints Church appears in all the standard introductions to ecclesiastical architecture because of its late Saxon tower. Unbuttressed and massive, it is latticed with decorative long and short stones to make blind arcades and bizarre stripes, possibly in imitation of the timber towers that must have just preceded it in architectural development.

Easby Abbey, N York 697 G4, From the top of the keep of Richmond Castle* can be seen the ruins of the

East Grinstead, Standen
Above: The aerial view brings out Philip Webb's informal planning.
Left: Apprentice Seat in the porch by TH Kendall of Warwick.
Below: Elaborately inlaid rosewood cabinet in the Drawing Room, designed by Stephen Webb and made by Collinson & Lock.

Premonstratensian house founded in 1155 by Roald, constable of the castle [EH]. The site lies beside the River Swale, and was neither quite large nor level enough to accommodate a conventional monastic plan; consequently variants have emerged, including a three-storey block for the prior's quarters, guest hall and canons' dormitory. Little remains of the abbey church, but the impressive Refectory, with fine geometric-traceried windows, is well preserved, as is the Gatehouse, standing roofless but otherwise complete, even to its stone vaulting. A chimney stands incongruously above the abbot's suite to the north. Easby's church of St Agatha stood here before the abbey, which enclosed it within its precinct. This little building contains some surprises – the chancel has mid-13th century

wall-paintings, depicting on the north side scenes from the Garden of Eden and four of the Labours of the Months, and New Testament scenes on the south side. There is also a cast of a very fine Northumbrian cross shaft, dating from c800, carved not only with interlace and vine scrolls with birds and beasts, but also the Risen Christ and the Twelve Apostles. The original is in the Victoria & Albert Museum*.

East Budleigh, Devon 689 G6, Much visited for its pretty thatched cottages that nestle by the church, and for Hayes Barton, the large farmstead where Sir Walter Raleigh was born in 1552.

East Grinstead, W Susx 691 F6, An unassuming country town, but with several exceptionally interesting buildings: Cromwell House, 15th century; Sackville College (almshouses) of 1617; St Margaret's Convent, by GE Street (1865–83), now remodelled as housing; and Saint Hill, c1830, the headquarters of the Scientologists. Outstripping them all is Standen [NT], Philip Webb's best house, of 1891, an informal Arts and Crafts composition reflecting a mixture of periods and preserved complete with all its furniture and William Morris wallpaper.

East Harling, Norfk 695 H6, The church of St Peter and St Paul has a delicate spire rising

from clustered flying buttresses to dominate the skyline. The spacious interior has an angel roof and light streaming through beautiful 15th-century glass in the east window. Kneeling figures include Sir William Chamberlain, who rebuilt the church and whose richly carved tomb of 1462 is in the chancel. Equally impressive is the Lady Chapel, with a splendid screen and Sir Thomas Lovell's magnificent tomb (1604).

East Lambrook, Somset, The cottage-style gardens at this house were designed by Margery Fish, who was almost as celebrated in her day as Gertrude Jekyll. There is a profusion of rare plants. *See* **Kingsbury Episcopi* 689 H5.**

East Riddlesden Hall, W York 697 G6, This 17th-century yeoman-clothier's home [NT], with mullioned windows, decorative plasterwork and oak panelling, is complemented by solidly constructed, and typically Yorkshire, oak furniture, textiles and pewter of the period. There are attractive gardens, and nearby is a magnificent 17th-century oak-framed barn.

East Shefford, Berks 690 D5, St Thomas's has been restored by the Churches Conservation Trust and contains good tombs to the Fettiplace family, who once held the manor.

Eastbourne, E Susx 691 G7, A popular seaside resort, whose main attraction is the high white cliffs of Beachy Head, parts of which occasionally fall into the sea. There was a medieval town here, of which the church remains.

Eastnor Castle, Herefs 693 H6, Begun in 1812 for the newly created Earl Somers, this is Sir Robert Smirke's striking interpretation of a Marcher baron's castle from about the time of Edward I. The porte-cochère and bay windows are more modern features protruding from between the

four massive battlemented and machicolated towers. The interiors contain a Drawing Room designed and furnished by Pugin, with a splendid gothic chandelier that was shown at the Great Exhibition in 1851. The grounds include an arboretum planted by Lord Somers between 1840 and 1860.

Eaton Bishop, Herefs 693 G6, St Michael's Church with its Norman tower has interesting stained glass. This has the special colour scheme of the 'Decorated' period: mainly green and yellow

rather than red and blue. One window, probably dating from the 1330s, shows Adam de Murimonth, the patron, with a row of saints above him in tall canopies and a distinctive trellis pattern behind them.

Eaton Bray, Beds 690 E4, The exterior of the church of St Mary may not look like much, but inside are exquisite 13th-century arcades and a font of c1235–40. Note the ironwork of the south door.

Ebberston Hall, N York 697 J5, A stately home in miniature, built in 1718 and designed by Palladian architect Colen Campbell for William Thompson, MP for Scarborough. Behind the house is an Italianate water garden of similarly early date, now somewhat overgrown but nevertheless a great joy.

Eccleston, Ches 693 G2, One of the villages on the Eaton Hall estate belonging to the Grosvenors. The church, built in 1899, displays a high standard of workmanship; its architect was GF Bodley, one of the great names of the English Gothic Revival. It is of red sandstone, in 14th-century style with a fine cathedral-like interior enhanced by the richly decorated reredoses and chancel screens and elaborate carved pews. All the stained glass is by Burlison and Grylls, one of the better late Victorian firms. The 1st Duke of Westminster, who commissioned Bodley, has a handsome canopied monument.

Eden Project, Cnwall 688 D7, Two great biomes set on the slopes of a 50-foot (15m) deep former china clay pit at Bodleva near St Austell. Billed as the eighth wonder of the world – and certainly one of the largest greenhouses in existence – the Project houses a wide range of productive plants from the humid tropics (Malaysia, West Africa, South America and Oceania) and the warm temperate zone (the Mediterranean, California and South

Above: Ebberston Hall, a Palladian stately home in miniature.

Africa). Its mission is to show human dependence on plants and their produce, such as cotton, vines, teak and mahogany. Planted in the outside areas are species that grow well in Cornwall, but which originate in the Himalayas, Chile and India. As well as a research centre the Eden Project has a large arena for a wide range of exciting events.

Edensor Village, Derbys 694 C3, One of the estate villages of Chatsworth* House. Edensor (pronouced 'Ensor') was built from new in the mid-19th century to replace the original village, which was too close to the house for the taste of the 6th Duke. The layout and many of the houses were designed by the Duke's gardener Joseph Paxton, and the mixture of architectural styles and leafy spaces is most agreeable. The church was added by Sir George Gilbert Scott in the 1860s; it contains a grand but slightly gruesome monument to the 1st Duke, who died in 1625.

Edgcote House, Northants 690 D3, The plain, restrained 18th-century manor house is sandwiched between gargantuan stables and the church, which together make a pleasant prospect. The latter contains several beautiful alabaster figures reclining on chests, all 16th-century members of the Chauncey family.

Above and right: Eden Project the humid biome opened in 2001 to demonstrate our dependence on plants.

Edinburgh

Edinburgh, C Edin 699 G4, Edinburgh stands in a natural setting of volcanic hills and lochs. From an architectural point of view it is in fact two cities in one, with the winding alleys (vennels) of the old medieval centre (Old Town) offering a striking contrast to the elegant, neoclassical façades and geometric layout of the Georgian New Town, which opens on to the countryside of Lothian and the Firth of Forth.

Calton Hill: This volcanic hill at the east end of Waterloo Place offers panoramic views of the city. It is surmounted by the National Monument, the 'Scottish Parthenon' designed by Charles Robert Cockerell and William Playfair in 1823, in memory of the victims of the Napoleonic Wars. The monument was never finished owing to lack of funds. To the south stands the Nelson Monument (1807), a tower in the form of an inverted telescope, erected in honour of the victorious commander of the Battle of Trafalgar. To the southwest are the Old Observatory, designed by James Craig in 1776, and the City Observatory, designed by Playfair in 1818. Calton Old Burial Ground has some beautiful classical-style tombs.

Canongate: The Canongate Tolbooth (1591) also served as law courts and later a prison. Today it houses The People's Story, a museum devoted to the lives of the ordinary people of Edinburgh from the late 18th century to the present day. The Kirk was built in Caroline baroque style in 1688, next to the Tolbooth.

Castle: This most visited of Scottish tourist sites has dominated Edinburgh since the 11th century. Occupied alternately by the Scots and the English, it was a royal palace and then a military fortress until the 20th century. The vast 18th-century esplanade offers some magnificent views of the city. In the northwest corner stands the Witches' Well, erected in 1894 on the spot where 300 women accused of 'witchcraft' were burned alive between 1479 and 1722. A moat dug in 1650 by Cromwell's troops separates the esplanade from the 19th-century guard house. The Half Moon Battery (16th–17th century) runs beneath the 16th-century Portcullis Gate from where visitors can climb to Argyll's Tower (19th century) and Mills Mount Battery. Since 1861 a cannon, which originally indicated the time to ships on the Firth of Forth, is fired from the upper battery every day at 1pm. St Margaret's Chapel is a little romanseque chapel said to have been built on top of Castle Rock by Saint Margaret, the pious wife of Malcolm III, just before her death, in 1093. The construction of Queen Mary's Apartments, in the southeast

Top: The view from Calton Hill, with Dugald Stewart's monument (Playfair, 1831) in the foreground; behind are the Bank of Scotland, the Castle, the tower of the Balmoral Hotel and the Scott Monument.

Above: *The Monuments of Edinburgh*, by D. Rhind.

Left: Canongate, the 17th-century White Horse Inn, which was the departure point for the London coach.

Bottom: Arthur's Seat in Queen's Park, Holyroodhouse.

Left: Edinburgh Castle, perched on a rock 400 feet (134m) high, offers magnificent views over the city.

Far left: Greyfriars Bobby, the bronze by sculptor William Brodie. It was commissioned by the Baroness Burdett-Coutts, 1872.

corner of Crown Square, was begun c1430. Mary Stuart gave birth to the future James VI of Scotland (James I of England) in a first-floor room in 1566. In 1617 the apartments were specially refurbished for a visit by the King, their last royal guest. Old Parliament Hall, a large, 15th-century banqueting hall, occupies the south side of Crown Square. It was restored in the early 16th century and was used to hold the sessions of the Scottish Parliament until 1639, when it was converted into a barracks and then a hospital. Its beautiful open-timber roof was restored in 1887–91. One of the vaulted cellars of the castle houses Mons Meg, the cannon, 13 feet (4m) long and weighing 5 tonnes, made at Mons in Belgium in 1449. Early 17th-century buildings house the National War Museum of Scotland, with a collection of uniforms, weapons, flags and medals that traces the history of various Scottish regiments.

Castle Hill: Housed in a 17th-century house reconstructed as an observatory in 1853, an ingenious Camera Obscura, installed by Patrick Geddes, projects moving images of Edinburgh. There are also telescopes on the roof terrace. The Hub, a neo-gothic building surmounted by the tallest spire in the city (275 feet/84m), was built in 1842–4 by James Gillespie Graham and Augustus Pugin to house the General Assembly of the Church of Scotland.

Greyfriars Kirk: As its name suggests, the church was built (1612) on the site of a Franciscan friary. It was here that the National Covenant was signed in February 1638. The kirkyard (cemetery) has a 'mort safe', an iron device designed to prevent graves from being violated, at a time when selling bodies to the medical school was one way of earning a living. Among the beautiful 17th- and 18th-century funerary monuments is the memorial, on the northeast wall of the kirkyard, dedicated to the 1,200 Covenanters imprisoned here for five months in 1679 before being executed. At the end of Candlemaker Row, a bronze statue of Greyfriars Bobby pays tribute to the faithful little Skye terrier which spent the last 14 years of its life watching over its master's tomb in Greyfriars Kirkyard.

High Street: Lined with closes and inner courts, this runs from Lawnmarket to Netherbow. Its beautiful houses act as a reminder that, from 1677, the use of building materials other than stone, slate and tiles made the owner liable to a fine. At 249 High Street are the City Chambers, originally built between 1753 and 1761 as a Royal Exchange, according to plans by John Adam. But merchants preferred to do business in the street, so it was bought by the city authorities in 1811 and is today the meeting place of the town council. The west wing, added in 1904, has 11 storeys. Mary King's Close, walled up after the plague of 1645 and subsequently incorporated into 18th-century buildings, is said to be haunted by former occupants.

Holyrood: The abbey and palace of Holyroodhouse, dominated by the steeply sloping Arthur's Seat, have long played a major role in Scotland's history. James II was born, married and buried at Holyrood, while the palace became the favourite residence of Scotland's Renaissance King James IV, killed at Flodden. It was here that Mary Stuart married Bothwell in 1567, Charles I was crowned in 1633, and Charles Edward Stuart briefly established his court in 1745. Although the Abbey and Royal Chapel today lie in ruins, since the reign of Queen Victoria the palace has been the official residence of the Royal Family when they visit Edinburgh. Having decided to transform Holyrood Abbey's guest house into a royal palace, James IV built the new quadrangular palace with a south tower and gatehouse (1498–1505). His son, James V, added the northwest tower and rebuilt the west range (1528–32). Although Charles II never resided at Holyrood, in the 1670s he gave the architect William Bruce and his master stonemason Robert Mylne the task of reconstructing the Palace, which had been devastated by fire 20 years earlier. A southwest tower was added and linked to the northwest tower by a new quadrangle. Beyond the main entrance, decorated with the arms of Scotland, a small vestibule leads to the central courtyard, the buildings of which are in the purest renaissance style (with superimposed classical orders). Inside the palace the Grand Stair leads to the State Apartments, occupied by the Royal Family when they visit Edinburgh. The Picture Gallery presents

Left: City Chambers, the Corinthian pilastered centrepiece seen over the arcaded screen wall facing onto High Street. Within the court is the bronze of Alexander and Bucephalus by Sir John Steell, finally cast in 1883.

Centre: The west front of Holyroodhouse. James V's tower is on the left. The fountain dates from 1858–9, modelled on the 1628 Cross Well at Linlithgow*.

Bottom: The palace and Queen's Park seen from the northwest, with the ruins of the abbey church on the left. In the foreground is the former Holyrood Church, currently being converted as a royal picture gallery.

the portraits of 89 Scottish sovereigns painted between 1684 and 1686 by the Dutch artist Jacob de Wet the Younger. The other rooms, with their magnificent plaster ceilings, are hung with Flemish and Gobelin tapestries (16th–17th century) and furnished in 18th-century style. The Historical Apartments occupy two floors of the northwest tower, refurbished in 1672. They are closely associated with the memory of Mary Stuart, whose apartments include the antechamber where her secretary and favourite David Rizzio was murdered in front of her in 1566.

Huntly House: The building was formed in 1570 by combining three houses (142–146 Canongate) and extended in the 17th and 18th centuries. Today it houses the City Museum, Edinburgh's principal museum of local history.

John Knox House: There is some disagreement as to whether John Knox, one of the leading figures of the Scottish Reformation, actually spent the last years of his life in this house at 45 High Street. It is in fact two

15th-century houses combined, with an external staircase built in 1556 by John Mosman, Mary Stuart's gold- and silversmith. The building has some beautiful panelling and oak parquet floors, a 16th-century fireplace and an interesting painted ceiling (early 17th century). Today the museum houses a collection of bibles and rare books, and a reconstruction of a goldsmith's workbench.

Lawnmarket: The vaulted passageways (closes) that open off the Lawnmarket lead to small courtyards (courts) surrounded by fine buildings. The most interesting from an historical and architectural point of view are Milne's Court (no. 517), whose buildings date from 1690, and James Court (no. 493), built 1725–27 and renovated by Patrick Geddes in 1895. Riddle's Close (nos. 322–328) has a beautiful late 16th-century house, while the 16th–17th-century Brodie's Close (nos. 306–310) was the home of Deacon William Brodie, a respected town councillor and cabinet-maker by day and a thief by night. He was hanged in 1788, on a gallows whose mechanism he had designed himself. He is said to have inspired Robert Louis Stevenson's novel *The Strange Case of Dr Jekyll and Mr Hyde* (1886). At no. 477B Lawnmarket is Gladstone's Land, a five-storey tenement building acquired in 1617 by the wealthy merchant Thomas Gledstanes. During restoration work the frontage of a booth was discovered beneath the first-floor arcades, and its interior was reconstructed. The apartments, with the original painted ceilings and period furniture, evoke perfectly the comfortable 17th-century interior.

Museum of Childhood: The collection includes toys, games and books as well as artefacts and documents relating to children's clothing and education since the Victorian era.

Museum of Scotland: The museum, designed by Benson and Forsyth (1998) as an extension of the Royal Museum, houses more than 10,000 works of art, everyday objects, costumes and machines which illustrate the history of Scotland. The basement gallery presents the formation of the country's landscapes and the various stages of its settlement from 8000 BC to AD 1100. The six upper galleries trace Scotland's political, economic, social, cultural and religious development. The 20th century is represented by some 300 objects, chosen by the Scottish people.

National Gallery of Scotland: The Gallery comprises two buildings, the Royal Institution, later Royal Scottish Academy (1822–6, 1831–6) and the National Gallery (1848–53), both designed by William Playfair. It houses one of the finest collections of paintings in Great Britain. Scottish artists (Ramsay, Raeburn, Wilkie, Nasmyth,

Top left: Detail of the gates at Holyroodhouse.

Far left: John Knox's House, now a museum.

Left: Gladstone's Land, acquired and restored by Thomas Gledstanes in 1617.

Below: Sign outside Gladstone's Land in Lawnmarket.

Bottom left: The Hunterston brooch (8th century), one of the exhibits in the Museum of Scotland.

McTaggart) are well represented, as well as Italians (Raphael, Titian, Tintoretto, Lotto, Veronese, Tiepolo), Dutch (Rembrandt, Vermeer, Hals), Flemish (Rubens, Van Dyck), Germans (Cranach, Holbein), Spanish (El Greco, Velázquez, Goya), English (Hogarth, Reynolds, Gainsborough, Constable, Turner) and French (Poussin, Watteau, Corot, Courbet, Degas, Renoir, Monet, Cézanne, Gauguin).

National Library of Scotland: Founded in 1682, this has one of the richest and most impressive collections in Great Britain. It has over 4.5 million works – illuminated manuscripts, ancient and modern books, maps, music scores, letters – which are often the subject of literary and historical exhibitions.

New Town: In 1752 the Lord Provost, George Drummond, published his 'proposals for public works', a visionary project for the creation of a 'new town' to the north of the city and a major architectural competition was won by James Craig in 1767. The young architect's plans incorporated squares and gardens into a grid of elegant streets whose names symbolized the union of the Scottish and English parliaments, while glorifying George III and the House of Hanover. George Street, the main thoroughfare, runs parallel to Queen Street (to the north) and Princes Street (to the south), and links two squares named after the patron saints of Scotland and England: St Andrew Square (to the east) and St George Square (to the west). St George Square was soon renamed Charlotte Square in honour of Queen Charlotte, wife of George III. North Bridge was completed in 1772, while an artificial hill, the Mound, was created from the material excavated between Princes Street and the Old Town. The New Town, with its elegant, terraced façades, became very fashionable from 1796 onwards. So much so, in fact, that after 1802 it was extended northwards to Fettes Row. It has retained its residential character and classical elegance, especially Great King Street and Royal Circus, designed by William Playfair. Between 1817 and 1860 the New Town spread eastward to Calton Hill (Playfairs's Royal, Carlton and Regent Terraces) and westward around Melville Street. James Gillespie Graham

Left: New Town, Charlotte Square, designed by Robert Adam, 1791. This is the Georgian House Museum at no. 7, open to the public; no. 6, Bute House, is the house of the First Minister of the Scottish Parliament; no. 5 is the offices of the World Heritage Trust. The greater part of the south side of the square is occupied by Wemyss House, the offices of the National Trust for Scotland.

Below: The dome of St George's Church (now West Register House) designed by Robert Reid in 1811 (in Charlotte Square).

Left: Bronze statue of Prince Albert in Field Marshall's uniform by Sir John Steell, designed 1865, completed 1876, in Charlotte Square.

designed the network of crescents of the Moray Estate, to the north of Charlotte Square, in the 1820s and 30s. Charlotte Square, designed by Robert Adam in 1791 and completed in 1820, is the most beautiful square in the New Town. Its symmetrical façades look onto a private garden dominated by an equestrian statue of Prince Albert. The official residence of the First Minister of the Scottish Parliament stands on the north side of the square, at no. 6, while no. 7 houses the Georgian House Museum, an elegant Georgian residence that has been restored and furnished in late 18th-century style.

Parliament House: On the south side of Parliament Square, this was the meeting place of the Scottish Parliament from 1639 until its dissolution under the Act of Union in 1707. Today it is occupied by the Court of Session and the High Court. Built in 1632–40, it was extended and given a classical façade between 1808 and 1814. It is open to the public during the week and visitors can admire the roof by John Scott (1637), the portraits of eminent jurists from past centuries and the huge 19th-century stained-glass window in Parliament Hall. On the west side of Parliament Square are the neoclassical façades of various libraries and law courts, built between 1816 and 1833 by Robert Reid.

Left: Interior of the Georgian House Museum in Charlotte Square.

Below: Princes Street Gardens, view up to the Castle with the bronzed cast-iron fountain made by A Durenne of Paris for the International Exhibition of 1862 and presented to the city by Daniel Ross in 1869. The sculptor was Jean-Baptiste Klagmann.

Princes Street and Gardens: This residential street, which marked the southern boundary of the New Town, became a commercial street with the advent of the railway in the 1840s. Although its Georgian façades have disappeared behind hotel signs and department-store windows, Princes Street is still one of the most attractive shopping streets in Europe, with its beautiful gardens at the foot of Castle Hill. Usher Hall (a concert hall), Saltire Court (a complex comprising restaurants, offices and the Traverse Theatre which stages modern plays) and the Exchange (a new business and conference centre) can be glimpsed above the trees to the right of the castle.

Royal Botanic Gardens: The Gardens created at the Physic Garden, Calton, in 1670 were transferred to Leith Walk in 1822–4. The collections cover an area of 70 acres (28ha) and include 34,000 plant species from all over the world. They are presented in themed gardens (rockery garden, heather garden, Chinese garden, arboretum) and glasshouses (alpines, winter garden, cacti and succulents, palms). Inverleith House, at the centre of the park, houses temporary exhibitions.

Royal Mile: This consists of a series of four streets – Castle Hill, the Lawnmarket (the site of the medieval market), the High Street and Canongate – that run between the Castle Esplanade and Holyroodhouse.

Royal Museum: The museum's exhibits range from natural history (fossils and minerals) to technology (machines from the Victorian era and scientific instruments) and arts throughout the world (sculpture, costumes, decorative arts). It is housed in a beautiful Victorian building by Captain Francis Fowke of Victoria & Albert Museum* fame (1861–88), which includes a vast cast-iron-framed hall with a glass roof. The façade is in Venetian Renaissance style.

St Giles' Cathedral: The gothic cathedral, which stands on the site of a Norman parish church, has many commemorative monuments. All that remains of the cruciform Norman church (*c*1120) are the four pillars supporting the square 15th-century tower and its elegant spire, the 'Crown of St Giles'. The church acquired lateral chapels in the 14th century, was extended in the 15th, and renovated a number of times after the Reformation. John Knox was minister there (1559–72) and his statue, which once stood in the parish enclosure near his tomb, today stands near the west door. In 1829–33 William Burn gave the exterior a uniform gothic ashlar face but retained the surviving tracery in re-cut form. Some of the stained-glass windows are by the pre-Raphaelite Edward Burne-Jones. The Thistle Chapel, built in flamboyant gothic style (1911) by Robert Lorimer, has magnificent stalls bearing the arms of James VII/II, founder of the Most Ancient and Most Noble Order of the Thistle (1687), his original twelve knights and their successors. A cobblestone heart (the 'Heart of Midlothian') in front of the cathedral's west door marks the site of the Old Tolbooth, the town hall and law courts in medieval times. It was converted into a prison in 1639 and demolished in 1817.

Scottish National Gallery of Modern Art: This modern art gallery, which occupies the Greek Doric John Watson's School designed by William Burn in 1825, gives pride of place to 20th-century Scottish painters: Peploe, Fergusson, Cadell. It also presents a general overview of the major international trends, from the Nabis to Pop Art. Sculptures by Moore, Epstein and Hepworth are exhibited in the grounds, remodelled as a landform by Charles Jencks in 2001–2. Opposite is the towered Dean Gallery (originally Orphanage) designed by Thomas Hamilton in 1831–3, which houses the Paolozzi and Penrose collections.

Scottish National Portrait Gallery: From its location at no. 1 Queen Street the gallery offers unrestricted views of the Firth of Forth. A generous donation by the then owner of the Scottish daily, the *Scotsman*, financed the construction of this huge, gothic-style building, built in red sandstone in 1885–90. Its walls are a portrait gallery of historical figures by all the leading Scottish sculptors of that time.

Tron Kirk: This former church in Hunter Square, built near a public weighbeam (tron) by John Mylne in 1637–63, is now an information centre for the Old Town. The south wing was lost when South Bridge was built in 1785–8. Its spire, destroyed by fire in 1824, was rebuilt in 1828, while the stained-glass windows date from the Victorian era. Excavations revealed the remains of Marlin's Wynd, an alley (vennel) that lay beneath the church and was named after the French stonemason responsible for cobbling the High Street in 1532.

Above: The Royal Mile, the two-storey late Georgian shopfront at 160-164 High Street.

Left: The cathedral's west front. The statues are the Duke of Buccleuch (by JE Boehm, 1887) in front of the cathedral and the recent bronze of David Hume by Alexander Stoddart in the foreground.

Below: Stained glass in St Giles' Cathedral.

Exhibits in the National Gallery of Scotland
Above: Lorenzo Bartolini's *Campbell Sisters* in front of Benjamin West's *Colin Fitzgerald rescuing King Alexander III of Scotland from the fury of a stag*.
Left: *The Vision after the Sermon* by Paul Gauguin (1888).

Edington, Wilts 690 B6, The village has an important church, dedicated to St Mary, St Katharine and All Saints. Completed by 1361, it is the survivor of a priory built for the rare Bonshommes canons. The church is a remarkable example of how the linear Perpendicular style replaced the ornate Decorated style, and looks like a small fortified citadel,

Above: Egglestone Abbey, the romantic ruins with the choir to the left.

Below: Edlingham Castle ruins.

castellated, with square-headed windows and a dominant square tower.

Edlesborough, Berks 690 E4, The village adjoins Easton Bray in neighbouring Bedfordshire. The church contains a rare and elaborate four-tier pulpit canopy.

Edlingham Castle, Nthumb 699 J6, A ruined fortified house occupying a surprisingly low-lying site – access is often waterlogged in winter [EH]. The main feature is the handsome three-storey tower of about 1340, which was erected on top of a mid-13th-century first-floor hall-house set in a moated enclosure. The castle is approached past the Norman church of St John the Baptist, long and low, with a stumpy west tower seemingly added to provide refuge for the parishioners during the turbulent period of 14th-century border warfare.

Edmondsham House and Gardens, Dorset 690 C7, The house, in Cranborne, is characterized by a good blend of Tudor and Georgian architecture. Surrounding it is a walled garden and 6 acres (2ha) given over to unusual trees and flowers.

Eggesford, Devon 689 F5, Set in a quiet valley, above the River Taw, the church of All Saints can barely accommodate its congregation, stuffed as it is with 17th- and 18th-century monuments to members of the Chichester and Fellowes families. Standing silent above the church are the remains

Top left: Egham, Royal Holloway College, an aerial view showing the rectangular plan enclosing two courtyards.

Victorian architect WH Crossland. The silhouette is particularly impressive, especially from a distance, with its numerous tourelles and cupolas. It was built for Sir Thomas Holloway between 1879 and 1887 as one of the first colleges for women in the country. The style is that of the French Renaissance (it was modelled on the Château de Chambord, and Crossland and his assistant Taylor spent two years visiting the Loire and drawing the elevations). The plan is 550 feet (167m) by 376 feet (115m) with two courts. Open to the public is the fine Art Gallery; its collection, amassed mainly in 1881–3, includes work by Landseer, Luke Fildes and Frank Holl. Crossland's lesser-known Holloway Sanatorium, opened in 1884, is the companion building to the College and has a good front in the Continental gothic style.

of Eggesford House, former home of the Earls of Portsmouth, built in the 1820s and ruined in 1917.

Egglestone Abbey, Durham 697 G4, Founded as an off-shoot of the Premonstratensian Easby Abbey* by Ralph de Malton, c1196, it is situated close to the River Tees and now offers a ruin of romantic profile. The substantial church remains [EH] have been largely rebuilt from the original scheme. The east window is without tracery, and is a particular enigma. In the crossing there is a large tomb-chest to Sir Ralph Bowes. The north range of monastic buildings became an Elizabethan house (now also a ruin) after the Dissolution.

Egham, Surrey 690 E5, The home of the Denham family, including the 17th-century poet Sir John, whose father's monument (d. 1639) can be seen in the church of St John the Baptist. This shows a figure rising from the grave above a well-carved charnel house and is possibly by Maximilian Colt. **Royal Holloway College** is the *magnum opus* of the

Above: Egham, Mr and Mrs Holloway, by Count Gleichen, outside Royal Holloway College.

Below: Eilean Donan Castle, built c1220.

Eilean Donan Castle, Highld 700 E5, Eilean Donan Castle near Dornie* is one of the most photographed castles in Scotland. The islet located between Lochs Long, Alsh and Duich is named after a 6th-century Celtic hermit. The castle, built c1220 by Alexander II to give advance warning of Viking raids, became the stronghold of the Mackenzies in the 14th century. In 1719 these fervent supporters of the Stuarts entrenched themselves in the castle with 300 Spanish soldiers who had come to support the Jacobite cause. Two months later the castle was bombarded by three English frigates. It was nothing but ruins when, in the 1920s, Farquhar Macrae and John Macrae-Gilstrap began the task of restoring it to its former glory.

Electric Brae, S Ayrs 698 D6, Electric Brae or Croy Brae is famous for an amazing optical illusion: the road seems to go down when it is in fact climbing. An information board on the parking area explains how best to observe this phenomenon.

Top left and top centre: Elgin Cathedral, the presbytery and west entrance.

Top right: Elstow Moot Hall, red-bricked and half-timbered, was built c1500.

12th-century church with a stone-vaulted chancel. The now-blocked north door and narrow windows were designed for slender Normans. Visitors can creep up the spiral staircase leading to an unusual dovecote with 40 nesting-places over the chancel. If you find the stairs are too narrow, you can still see the blocked doves' entrances in the east wall outside.

Elmstead, Essex 691 H3, Just east of Colchester* is a small and isolated church with a memorable interior; west gallery, box pews, a two decker pulpit and the recumbent wooden effigy of Sir Roger de Tany (1301).

Elsham Hall, Lincs 697 J7, Although essentially an 18th-century house, it was very much altered in the 1930s by Guy Elwes, who added an extra storey

Elgar's Birthplace Museum, Worcs 690 B2, This tiny red-brick cottage in the village of Lower Broadheath is now adjoined by a splendid new visitor centre. It contains a display of Elgar's letters in his spidery handwriting; his musical manuscripts still lie scattered on his desk. A statue of the composer stands outside Worcester* Cathedral, and the celebratory Three Choirs and Malvern Festivals continue to reinforce the musical associations of this part of the country.

Elgin, Moray 702 C4, The attractive county town of Moray is built in the local sandstone. The medieval town and cathedral were burned in 1390 by Alexander Stewart, 'Wolf of Badenoch', after he had been excommunicated by the Bishop of Moray. The Cathedral (1244), the 'glory of the kingdom', which had already been rebuilt after a fire in 1270, was rebuilt once again before being plundered and abandoned after the Reformation. Although the nave no longer exists, the elaborately carved entrance flanked by two 14th-century towers, and the two 13th-century transepts and choir have survived. To the north stands the octagonal Chapter House with its finely carved vaults. A museum of local history, which has a large collection of fossils, stands at the end of the High Street, bordered by elegant arcaded houses (17th century). Also worthy of note are St Giles' Church (1828), built by Archibald Simpson, and Thunderton House, the 17th-century mansion where Bonnie Prince Charlie stayed on the eve of the Battle of Culloden (1746). At the end of the street, a statue of the 5th Duke of Gordon dominates Lady Hill, the former site of the medieval castle and chapel.

Elkstone, Gloucs 690 B4, Hidden away beneath the tall trees in the churchyard is an extraordinary

Centre: Elkstone Church. The dovecote is over the chancel and the doves entered through holes in the eastern wall.

added in places and brought the house to a more unified form. The Orangery dates from the 1760s. There is a theatre, craft workshops, mini zoo and clocktower museum set in lakeside gardens.

Elsing, Norfk 695 H5, The church has one of the great English military brasses to Sir Hugh Hastings (d. 1347), surrounded by angels and mourning relatives. The family lived at Elsing Hall, a 15th-century moated manor house.

Elstow, Beds 691 F3, A Benedictine nunnery was founded here in c1075, and its beautiful 12th- and 13th-century nave survives in the church of St Mary and St Helen, the pride of the village. Also of note are the so-called Chapterhouse near the building's west front and the detached 15th-century campanile. The remains of early 17th-century Hillersdon Hall are nearby, as is the fine Moot Hall of c1500 where John Bunyan and his adherents often met.

Bottom: Interior of Elstow Moot Hall. John Bunyan was born in Elstow in 1628 but his cottage has now been demolished.

Elton, Cambs 695 F5, Stone and thatch cottages spread between river and park in the Nene valley. Most of **Elton Hall** was pulled down by Sir Thomas Proby, who left only the gatehouse and chapel undercroft, and it was rebult in a mix of medieval, gothic and classical styles. His family have lived here ever since. The library is one of the finest in private hands, with more than 12,000 books – including Henry VIII's prayer book, inscribed by the Tudor king and two of his wives – and a collection of Victorian pictures. The Sapcotes, original owners of the Hall, have monuments in the church.

Ely, Cambs 695 G6, Best known for its Cathedral (*see over*). Within the cathedral precincts are substantial remains of the late 12th-century Infirmary and Prior Crauden's Chapel, another jewel in the Decorated style. The King's School, founded by Alfred the Great, now occupies a range of medieval buildings beside the Gallery.

Elton Hall
Above: Fine furniture and paintings are displayed in every room.
Below: The gardens have been restored.

Left: Ely, the Oliver Cromwell Museum, in the house where he used to live.

Further along is the southern gatehouse, or Ely Porta, begun in 1397. The Bishop's Palace with Tudor brick towers, begun for Bishop Alcock, occupies an attractive corner site on Palace Green; nearby is the Oliver Cromwell Museum in the house he once occupied. Elsewhere in this little yellow-brick town there is little of distinction, but St Mary's church has the communal grave of those hanged in the Littleport food riot of 1816. The High Street is redeemed by more precinct buildings, and below Back Hill are the converted waterfront warehouses of Ely's inland marina.

Ely Cathedral

Ely Cathedral, Cambs, Looming over the city of Ely – and the flat landscape for miles around – is one of England's most glorious cathedrals, dubbed 'the Ship of the Fens'. Its unique octagonal lantern, offset by a cluster of cylindrical turrets on the west tower, is a memorable sight, especially from Stuntney to the southeast. The original minster was founded by St Etheldreda in 673 but sacked by the Danes two centuries later. A new monastery became the last stronghold of Saxon resistance to the Normans as Hereward the Wake exploited the watery defences of Eel Island.

In 1081 Abbot Simeon began the transformation of a modest abbey into a Norman masterpiece, carved out of creamy limestone shipped across the Fens from Barnack*. The richly arcaded west front, 'intricate and monumental', is an impressive transition from Romanesque to gothic. Inside, the eye is drawn down the nave between massive Norman columns and up into Alan de Walsingham's apparently gravity-defying successor to the central tower that collapsed in 1322. His ingenious starburst lantern is the supreme act of faith, held aloft by wonderful fan vaulting. The Lady Chapel, started a year earlier, is a jewel of Decorated stonework. Beyond the central crossing, Bishop Hugh de Northwold's 13th-century chancel – where St Etheldreda's remains were finally laid to rest in 1253 – is a triumph of pure Early English architecture. Hugh, like the other medieval bishops buried here, would have walked to daily service through the early-12th-century prior's doorway which, like the monk's doorway, is alive with beautiful late Romanesque carving, dominated by Christ in Majesty flanked by winged archangels. *See* **Ely* 695 G6.**

Above: The beautiful fan-vaulted Lady Chapel (early 14th century).

Right: The great 12th-century west tower complete with its 14th-century top.

Above and left:
Ely's crowning glory is
Alan de Walsingham's
breathtaking central
lantern, a spectacular
display of medieval
engineering and
architecture. The painted
ceiling of the nave is by
HS Le Strange and
T Gambier Parry (1858–65).

Far left: The central crossing
point of the Cathedral seen
from the dizzy height of the
lantern.

Emmetts Garden
Top left: A bluebell wood
Centre left: A fountain
outside the main house.

Top right: Erddig, a view
of the formal gardens of
the east front from beyond
the canal.

London, where Dick Turpin practised the art of surprise on unsuspecting travellers. William Morris, whose stylized designs were inspired by childhood rides through the dense foliage, led the campaign that saved the Forest in 1882. Elizabeth I's heavily restored hunting lodge just outside Chingford is now its museum.

Erddig, Wrexhm 693 F2, There are more impressive country houses in Wales, but few National Trust properties have attracted as much interest and affection as Erddig, opened to the public by the Prince of Wales in 1977. Its remarkable state rooms still retain their 18th- and 19th-century furniture and fittings, including some beautiful Chinese wallpaper. Most rooms have no electric light.

A range of 'servant portraits' give an extraordinary evocation of backstairs life 100 years ago. Kitchens, laundry, stables and sawmill, bakehouse, smithy and joiner's shop make up a fascinating range of outbuildings.

Eriskay (Eiriosgaigh), W Isls 700 B6, This undulating little island, linked by a causeway to Ludag (South Uist*), is renowned for its patterned knitwear and ponies. In 1941 a cargo ship bound for Jamaica sank off the coast with 264,000 bottles of whisky on board. The event gave (Sir Edward Montague) Compton Mackenzie the idea for his novel *Whisky Galore,* which was made into a film (shot on the island) in 1948.

Escomb, Dur 697 G3, St John's is a complete church dating from the Early Christian period of Bede. It is tiny, with a tall, narrow nave and chancel. Much of the fabric consists of re-used Roman stones from the

Emmetts Garden, Kent 691 G6, A garden influenced by William Robinson – natural and informal in style – in Ide Hill [NT]. Laid out in the 19th century, it contains many rare exotic trees and shrubs. There are spectacular displays in spring.

Englefield House, Berks 690 D5, Only the gardens of this attractive house, mainly 19th-century but Elizabethan in origin, are open to the public. They feature woodland, rose and herbaceous borders, and are set in an extensive deer park. Among the grounds stands Englefield's typical High Victorian church by George Gilbert Scott.

Epping Forest, Essex 691 G4, This remnant of a vast medieval forest, administered by the monks of Waltham Abbey* and drastically reduced to supply generations of naval shipbuilders, still covers over 6,000 acres (1,800ha) of oak, pasture and ancient pollarded hornbeams on the edge of

Erddig
Above right: The Saloon contains fine 18th-century mirrors and chairs.
Far right: The State Bed dates from the 1720s.
Bottom right: *Portrait of Thomas Pritchard, gardener,* by William Jones (1830s), one of the range of servant portraits on display.

having handsome two-light transomed windows and fireplaces. An impressive gate tower, added to the southeast corner slightly later in the 14th century, had a portcullis and drawbridge; an upper chamber was probably used as a chapel. A former Presbyterian chapel on the site houses an exhibition on border warfare. Etal Castle was suddenly plunged into the forefront of national history when the Battle of Flodden was fought nearby in 1513.

Eton, Berks, Eton College was founded in 1440 by Henry VI and is one of England's most prestigious public schools. The college buildings incorporate much important medieval work, such as Lupton's Range with a gatehouse of 1517–c1520. The chapel was built c1449–75 and has an impressive interior

Above: Etal Castle, the Gatehouse from the outside. It once had a drawbridge, portcullis and guardrooms. The first-floor chamber seems to have been used as a chapel.

Right: Eton College, Lupton Gatehouse (added 1517–c1520) facing the school yard.

nearby fort at Binchester. The chancel arch is a particularly good example of the Roman technique of constructing arches. On the outside south wall of the nave is an Anglo-Saxon sundial.

Esher, Surrey 691 F5, A pleasant if busy town with an interesting history. Bishop Waynflete of Winchester once lived in the 15th-century Esher Palace, of which only the fine gatehouse survives, gothicized by William Kent in c1730. In the church of St George is the handsome Newcastle Pew, built in 1725–6, possibly by Vanbrugh.

Essendon, Herts 691 F4, St Mary's contains an elegantly detailed Wedgwood black basalt font, one of only two in the country; the other is in Cardington, Bedfordshire.

Etal Castle, Nthumb 699 J5, A short but very pretty village street with rebuilt thatched cottages – looking rather like a film set – leads to the castle [EH], which guarded the crossing of the River Till. The original manor house was superseded by a simple tower house, heightened and crenellated in 1341. Curtain walls defined a rectangular enclosure with towers at each corner; the northeast tower has been lost, and the southwest tower survives only partially. The four-storey Great Tower in the northwest corner is the main feature of the site, still impressive despite its roofless state, its first- and second-storey rooms

with some accomplished 15th-century wall-paintings. Eton is one of the few non-enclosed English parishes and is still surrounded by pretty open fields. *See* **Windsor* 690 E5.**

Ettington, Warwks 690 C3, Ettington Park, by John Pritchard and John Pollard Seddon, 1858–62, is one of the major Victorian gothic mansions in England. The Norman church of St Nicholas has a coloured marble monument by the London sculptor John Francis Moore (c1775).

Etwall, Derbys 694 C4, Chiefly notable for the quadrangle of almshouses founded by Sir John Port and rebuilt in the 1680s.

Euston Hall, Suffk 695 H6, Set in a park landscaped by William Kent beside the Black Bourn river, the

house rose in the 1660s, was renovated along Palladian lines in 1902 and much reduced in 1951. It was built by Lord Arlington, Secretary of State to Charles II, whose only daughter married the 1st Duke of Grafton (the king's son by Lady Castlemaine). Dukes of Grafton have lived here ever since, surrounded by family portraits by Van Dyck, Kneller and Lely. Kent's temple (1746) is on rising ground in the park beyond St Genevieve's church, rebuilt in 1676, and with good Gibbons-style wood carving. The surrounding landscape is described in 'The Farmer's Boy' (1800) by peasant poet Robert Bloomfield, brought up on the estate.

Evesham, Worcs 690 C3, The market town for the fruit-growing Vale of Evesham, snowed under with white apple blossom in the spring. The town is on the bank of the River Avon, and its nub is the Benedictine Abbey. Though largely ruined, several of its buildings survive, including the Almonry, which contains a museum, and two churches.

Above and top: Euston Hall, two copies of Van Dyck, *The children of Charles I* and *Charles I as a country gentleman.*

Right: Ewelme almshouses, built by Chaucer's grand-daughter.

Quite why the two were built so close together is unclear; perhaps so that the monks were not disturbed by the parishioners. There is also the Perpendicular bell tower, 100 feet (30m) tall, which was only finished in 1539, the very year of the Dissolution of the Monasteries. Finally, the Norman gateway with its 15th-century timbered upper storey leads into the town. Simon de Montfort, killed at the Battle of Evesham in 1265, is buried in the Abbey. An obelisk on Green Hill to the north of the town commemorates the spot.

Ewelme, Oxon 690 D4, This village, set in a charming valley and formerly the home of the Chaucer family, was once favoured by Henry VIII and Elizabeth I. Alice, Duchess of Suffolk, grand-daughter of Geoffrey Chaucer, lived here during the 1400s and the handsome group of church, school and almshouses that she built still survives. Alice's finely carved monument, depicting her both as in life (the top part) and as a worm-eaten corpse (below), can be seen in the church, as can 15th-

century screens, a font and a spectacular font cover.

Ewenny Priory, V Glam 689 G3, Founded in 1141 as a Benedictine community for a prior and 12 monks. After the Dissolution the nave at Ewenny continued as a parish church, and much of the rest of this strikingly simple

early Norman building is still roofed and full of atmosphere. There are medieval sepulchre slabs.
Ewloe, Flints 693 F2, A Welsh castle, neither Norman nor medieval, and one of the least known in Wales. Much of the fascination of Llywelyn ap Gruffudd's

13th-century stronghold, 'built in the corner of the woods', is its unlikely defensive situation – it is certainly a last-minute surprise. It contains a remarkably intact mural staircase. *See also* **Flint***.
Exbury Gardens, Hants 690 D7, The gardens on the east side of the Beaulieu estuary were created after 1920 by Lionel de Rothschild. Famous principally for rhododendrons and azaleas, the enormous gardens, open through the summer, contain a great variety of other plants.

Top right and centre right: Exbury Gardens, one of the most remarkable gardens in England, owned by Edmund de Rothschild. They are especially notable for rare trees and for the Rothschild plant collection.

Left: Ewenny Priory, a remarkable survival of Norman architecture, combining strength and siimplicity.

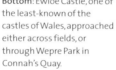

Bottom: Ewloe Castle, one of the least-known of the castles of Wales, approached either across fields, or through Wepre Park in Connah's Quay.

Exeter

Exeter, Devon 689G6, Devon's county town bestrides the River Exe at its lowest bridging point, and has been the crossing place since Roman legions established a fortress here in ad 55–60. The remains of the Roman Bath House, with its mosaic floor, now lie buried under the Green, near the west front of the cathedral. The foundations of the Roman city walls can still be seen, as well as the route of the main street, which bisects the city. In Saxon times it maintained its importance, and the Normans continued to develop it. By the 13th century there were over 20 churches within the walls, together with St Nicholas's Priory (now a museum) and the cathedral.

Exeter Cathedral, low and grey, is hidden from the main shopping streets and is visible among the city rooftops only from across the river. The present site is close to an earlier monastery and Saxon cathedral, and all that remains of a major Norman church are the towers, which were completed about 1200. After the ravages of the wars between Stephen and Matilda work was begun on a larger church, with Bishop Bronescombe adding the Lady Chapel and Chapterhouse in c1230. By 1300 Bishop Quinil added the transepts – from the extremities of which, most unusually, spring the twin towers – and the whole Decorated interior was finished by the middle of the 14th century in the time of the great Bishop Grandisson. The satisfied Bishop was able to inform the Pope that his church 'is marvellous in beauty and when completed will surpass every church of its kind in England and Wales'. The west front bears ranks of medieval kings and saints in niches, surmounted by St Peter – to whom the Cathedral is dedicated. But it is the interior that is its chief glory. The 300-foot (91m) nave is resplendent with Purbeck marble columns. The bosses, recently restored and repainted, are also breathtaking in their scale and detail. The choir has a range of unusual misericords, carved between 1230 and 1270, but the outstanding feature of this part of the church is the Bishop's Throne, built in 1316 for Bishop Stapledon. It is 60 feet (18m) high, and is constructed without nails. In the north transept is the Exeter Clock, installed in 1376. The Cathedral Library has many medieval books, including the famous Exeter Book given by Bishop Leofric (who was appointed by Edward the Confessor), and the Exeter copy of the Domesday Book.

On Exeter's northern flank stood the castle, with its imposing gateway at Rougemont, protecting and dominating a city that was already prosperous through its cloth trade. This developing wealth is evident in the late medieval clergy houses overlooking the cathedral, in the

Above: The Exeter Clock of 1376 in the north transept of the cathedral. It shows the Earth at the centre of the Universe and also records the phases of the Moon.

Left: The tomb of Bishop Edmund Strafford.

Below: The north tower of Exeter Cathedral. The earliest surviving parts of the building date from around 1200 but most is from the 14th century.

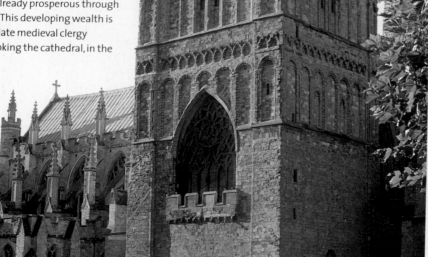

several half-timbered merchants' houses that survive in the High Street and in the **Guildhall**. The front of the present building, with its four massive granite Tuscan columns, was added to the earlier hall in about 1592–5. The elaborate strapwork around the windows of the first-floor Mayor's Parlour was once painted and gilded. The surviving building accounts suggest that the Hall was constructed between 1468 and 1470; it has a particularly fine seven-bay arch-braced roof. There are some good paintings on display, including a portrait of the Princess Henrietta Maria, a daughter of Charles I, born in the city during the Civil War. The collection of civic plate is outstanding, and includes a rare Hat of Maintenance and State Sword.

Further down the main street is **Tucker's Hall**, the sole surviving livery hall in the city and still the home of the Guild of Tuckers, Weavers and Shearmen. Their livelihood – the production and finishing of cloth, which was then exported to the Continent or taken to other parts of the country – was the source of the city's wealth. On the quay, the Customs House of 1681, with its first-floor rooms decorated with extravagant plasterwork ceilings in high relief, is also a symbol of the thriving wool trade. The warehouses and other buildings in this area now make a popular port of call for the many visitors to the city.

As its textile industry was eclipsed by developments elsewhere, Exeter became the centre of society for the Devon gentry and the seat of the all-powerful Bishop. Assembly rooms, banks, hotels and a new Palladian Sessions House in the castle precinct all came in the 18th century, as did fine terraces such as Southernhay (1792) just outside the city walls. Queen Street has fine 19th-century architecture: the façade of the Higher Market by George Dymond and Charles Fowler (1834); the Rougemont (railway) Hotel; and the **Royal Albert Memorial Museum and Art Gallery**, with a college, art school, library and museum, paid for by the gentlemen of Devon as a memorial to Prince Albert, and designed by John Hayward. Built with several varieties of local stone, it was completed in 1866. Many of the exhibits date back to the early days of the museum, and are by locally born artists of the Devon School. Decorative arts include good displays of Exeter-made silver (some from Devon-mined ore); pottery from north and south Devon; the finest of laces from east Devon; and an exceptionally fine and comprehensive collection of costume. Ethnographic collections encompass items from Alaska, the Niger and the Pacific, and the large natural history department displays examples of flora, fauna and geology from all over the world. The new displays devoted to the history of Exeter only confirm its early prosperity.

Nearby to the west is the cast-iron bridge, built in 1834–5 to ease the work of horses toiling out of the city across a deep valley. The nearby **church of St Michael** with its tall spire is often mistaken for the cathedral. It was built in 1865–8 by Rhode Hawkins and paid for by William Gibbs, whose considerable fortune came from guano. The city suffered from bomb damage during World War II, and from redevelopment afterwards.

One success story, however, is the establishment of the University of Exeter in the grounds of several large houses on the northern edge of the city. Although many of the buildings are of little merit, the planting of the gardens is exceptional, and takes full advantage of the previous planting and the mild south-coast climate.

Far left: Exeter Cathedral, the west front begun in 1329, with its famous image screen.

Left: The effigy of Lady Dodderidge (d. 1614) from the joint tomb of her and her husband in the Lady Chapel.

Below: The splendid vaulted nave roof, looking east (built 1310–40).

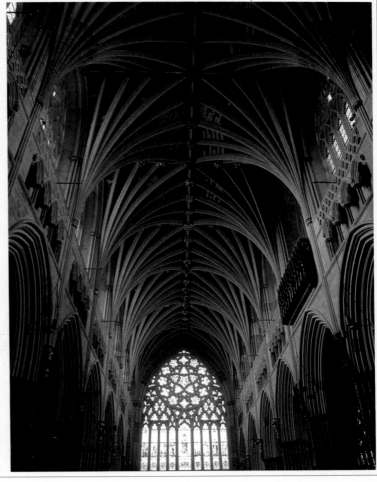

Exmoor National Park, Somset 689 F4, Extending to the northern coastline from Minehead in Somerset to Ilfracombe* and Combe Martin* in Devon, Exmoor covers about 170,000 acres (68,800ha), a plateau of moorland and upland farms with deep wooded combes along the main rivers, the Exe, the Barle and the Lyn. Most of the land is owned by the National Trust. The

coastline, stretching about 30 miles (48km), is beautiful and dramatic; key tourist centres are located at Minehead, Porlock and Lynmouth*. Exmoor has a proliferation of ling, bellheather and gorse, and the climate is often wet, with sea breezes. The moor is a haven for an enormous variety of flora and fauna. Sheep amble nonchalantly across the roads, and red deer can often be spotted. Pony trekking and riding are well catered for, and the sturdy Exmoor pony is bred here.

Exmouth, Devon 689 G6, Broad sandy beaches encouraged the development of this still charming resort in the 19th century. Among the bungaloid sprawl that fringes the town are several

Eyam Hall
Top: The manor house is dated 1676 on a rainwater pipe.
Above centre: The Tapestry Room.
Above right: The Dining Room.

Above left: Exmouth, A La Ronde. The 16-sided house was originally thatched.

Below: Eyam churchyard, a rare example of a Saxon cross with the cross-head surviving.

houses of note, including (at Foxholes) The Barn, the splendid Arts and Crafts house by ES Prior, and on another hill at the other end of the town, the gloriously dotty **A La Ronde** [NT]. This 16-sided *cottage orné* was built by Miss Jane Parminter and her cousin Mary in 1798. All the wedge-shaped rooms open out of the central hall (said to be based on the Church of San Vitale in Ravenna), with its extraordinary shellwork grotto on the top floor. The Parminters were keen on intricate handicrafts – other examples of their work include bizarre featherwork friezes in the Drawing Room. Nearby at Point in View, where Jane Parminter is buried, is a Congregational chapel and four small almshouses built in 1811.

Exton, Rutland 694 E5, A pretty village with thatched cottages. The church of St Peter and St Paul has a rather unusual tower with an octagonal lantern, topped by a miniature spire. Although the building is essentially medieval it was thoroughly rebuilt in the mid-19th century after lightning damage. The architects responsible were RC Carpenter and JL Pearson, who between them replaced much of the original medieval stonework. Among the chief points of interest are the tombs of the Haringtons and the Noels, later viscounts Campden and earls of Gainsborough. The most striking is the massive monument to the 3rd Viscount, completed in 1686 by Grinling Gibbons with a total of 25 figures of wives and children, as well as the Viscount himself. Simpler and more moving is the shrouded white marble effigy of Anne, 1st Lady Harrington, who died in 1627. A short distance from the church are the ruins of Exton Old Hall, burnt down in 1810, and the present Exton Hall beyond.

Eyam, Derbys 694 C3, Famous as the village that nobly shut itself off from the rest of the world in 1666 when the plague had been brought here from London. There are some pretty houses round the

churchyard. Set back from the main street behind a formal garden is Eyam Hall, built in 1676.

Eye, Suffk 695 J6, A quiet town on the banks of the Dove, shaped by William Malet's 11th-century castle into a medieval borough with its own weekly market and Benedictine priory. The castle mound, capped by a Victorian mock ruin, still presides, but the town's chief landmark is one of East Anglia's great flushwork church towers lording it over the early 16th-century Guildhall. Inside is a richly decorated rood screen with doll-like saints, mainly female, but also the boy martyr William of Norwich; above it Ninian Comper's gilded crucifixion, 1929. Medieval streets full of good vernacular buildings converge on a market place dominated by Eye's crudely Italianate Town Hall. Lambeth Street has cottages with carved cillboards and a long rippling serpentine wall, another Suffolk speciality.

Faenol Fawr, Denbgs, Cross-stepped gables, such as can be seen on this 1597 house, now a hotel, are very much a feature of the Vale of Clwyd, and were introduced by the Denbigh-born Richard Clough, who had formerly been the agent of Sir Thomas Gresham. *See* **Bodelwyddan Castle* 692 E2.**

Fair Isle, Shet 703 K5, The island, owned by the National Trust for Scotland, lies midway between Shetland* and Orkney* and is linked by plane to Sumburgh and Tingwall and by ferry to Grutness, on Mainland. It has an ornithological observatory: it lies on a major migratory route and 34 of the 350 species recorded nest regularly on the island. The George Waterston Centre and Museum (named after the island's former owner) traces its history. The Fair Isle Crafts cooperative exports sweaters whose patterns date from the time of the Vikings.

Fairford, Gloucs 690 C4, This is perhaps the best known of the 'wool' churches (the others are at Chipping Camden*, Burford*, Northleach* and Cirencester*), and has the best stained glass. The Late Perpendicular church contains windows painted by Henry VII's master glass painter, Barnard Flower, from Flanders; the town scenes show his typical Dutch gables and Flemish towers on the houses. John Tame, the patron, intended to present the story of the whole Bible on glass, beginning with Adam and Eve and ending with Judgement Day at the west end. In addition, the carved oak screens around the chancel are carved with humorous figures: a woman pulling a man's hair, for example, and a dog stealing some food. John Tame's tomb is in the Lady Chapel.

Fairstead, Essex 691 H4, The small Norman church has remarkable frescoes with scenes from the Passion above the

Top: Fairford church, rebuilt by John Tame between 1491 and 1497, and completed by his son after his death in 1500.

Above: Eye church, its grand flint tower rising above the medieval Guildhall.

Below centre: *The Fair Isle Jumper* by Stanley Curister, first half 20th century.

Below right: Falkland Palace, the gatehouse.

chancel arch, notably Christ on a horse, and the Last Supper.

Falkland, Fife 699 G3, This medieval village, raised to the status of a royal burgh in 1458, has carefully maintained its old weavers' cottages and beautiful 17th- and 18th-century houses with their carved lintels. **Falkland Palace** on the High Street is a former Stewart hunting lodge, which was transformed into a magnificent palace in the 15th and 16th centuries. The building, abandoned after 1650, has been the subject of several restoration programmes since the late 19th century. The south wing, the best preserved, has a magnificent renaissance façade (1537–42) and houses a collection of 17th-century Flemish tapestries with a royal chapel dating from the 16th century. James V died in 1542 in the royal apartments of the east wing, only a few days after the birth of his daughter Mary. In the gardens are the foundations of the north wing and a wall court, dating from 1539, for real (or royal) tennis.

Falmer, E Susx 691 F7, The site of the University of Sussex, one of the first new universities to be built after World War II, designed by Sir Basil Spence and built fairly rapidly in the 1960s. Spence saw himself as a Modernist, of the school of Le Corbusier; but he was not a revolutionary, and the human scale and informal grouping of his campus are now more appreciated than they were at the time. His favourite elements, red-brick

walls and flat-arched concrete vaults, give consistency to the ensemble.

Falmouth, Cnwll 688 C8, A bustling port on the western bank of the Fal and overlooking a large natural harbour, but perhaps not as busy as it was in the 18th century, when it was a packet station from which up to 40 vessels regularly left for Spain, North and South America and the West Indies. The neoclassical Customs House in Arwenack Street and the brick-built shipping agent's office opposite are relics from this time. *See also* **Pendennis Castle*.**

Faringdon, Oxon 690 C4, The remote town can be recognized for miles around by the 140-foot (42.7m) Lord Berners's Folly of 1936, possibly the last

Top: Falmouth, headland with Pendennis Castle guarding the approach.

Above and left: Farleigh Hungerford. The ruins of this once-imposing castle, now concentrated on its two towers, date to the 14th century, and show how impressive it must have been: strength and architecture in equal measure.

building of its type completed in England, in the grounds of late-18th-century Faringdon House. The medieval church of All Saints retains shafted crossing arches of *c*1200, a beautiful 13th-century south door and good monuments.

Farleigh Hungerford Castle, Somset, The late 14th-century castle [EH] has extensive ruins, the chapel of which contains the tomb of its builder, Sir Thomas Hungerford. The little church of 1443, dedicated to St Leonard, has a portrait of a knight in stained glass, with Sir Thomas's initials. *See* **Westwood Manor* 689 J4.**

Farley, Wilts 690 C6, The church of All Saints was built for Sir Stephen Fox by Alexander Fort, joiner to the Office of Works, and was completed by 1690. Inside, there is a fine monument to Sir Stephen and his wife of 1716. The nearby Almshouses of 1681 were also erected by Fort.

Farnborough, Hants 690 E6, St Michael's Abbey was established in 1886 by the exiled Empress Eugénie, together with an elaborate mausoleum for her husband, Napoleon III, and their son, killed in the Zulu War of 1879.

Top left and right:
Farne Islands, the dolerite
cliffs which provide bleak
shelter for puffins, eider
ducks and tern.

Fawsley Court   **F**

Farne Islands, Nthumb 699 K5, A few miles off the Northumberland coast, the 28 Farne Islands [NT] form one of Britain's most important bird sanctuaries; access – by boat, sailing from Seahouses when weather permits – may be limited during the breeding season. The puffins, eider ducks and four species of tern that make their home here are generally fearless of humans, and can sometimes be observed at close quarters. There is also a large colony of seals. The name 'Farne' is derived from a word for pilgrims, for Saint Aidan came here to meditate in solitude in AD 640, and Saint Cuthbert retired to a cell on Inner Farne, where he died in AD 687. The spot is commemorated by St Cuthbert's Church, a small chapel built about 1370 and restored in the 1840s when some of Bishop Cosin's furnishings from Durham Cathedral* were brought here. West of the church stands Prior Castell's Tower, erected about 1500, with a first-floor chapel that offers spectacular views of the dolerite cliffs of the other islands, and across to Bamburgh*. *See also* **Holy Island***.

Farnham, Surrey 690 E6, A fascinating town, with fine buildings from a range of periods and pretty scenery. Most imposing is Farnham Castle [EH], occupied by the Bishops of Winchester for over 800 years. Special features are the Norman shell keep, which encloses a motte with foundations of an earlier 12th-century structure, and the so-called Fox's Tower built by Bishop Waynflete in 1470–5. Farnham is well known for its handsome Georgian architecture, which can be seen at its best in West Street and Castle Street. Willmer House (38 West Street) of 1718 is especially impressive, with its noble

Bottom left: Farnham Castle, begun in 1138 and added to over the centuries. The red-brick tower dates from 1470.

Bottom right: Fawsley. The church of St Mary contains many monuments to the Knightly family who lived at Fawsley Court.

cut-brick façade. It now serves as the Museum of Farnham, and has displays on various subjects including local history. Next door is the equally good Sandford House. In Bridge Square is the house where William Cobbett was born, now a pub bearing his name. Cobbett's tomb can be seen in the 15th-century church of St Andrew. A good way to explore the town is to follow the excellent Farnham Heritage Trail. Maps are available from the town council.

Faversham, Kent 691 H5, A small town of great atmosphere, well worth exploring. The streets are lined with 16th-, 17th- and 18th-century houses, including that of Arden of Faversham, murdered by his wife's lover and the subject of a famous Elizabethan play.

Fawley, Bucks 690 E5, A mile north of Henley* is Fawley Court, begun in 1684 for Colonel William Freeman and attributed to Sir Christopher Wren. Despite alterations of the 18th and 19th centuries, including work by James Wyatt, the house retains its late 17th-century plan and some exquisite original plasterwork. It also contains a museum with a collection of sabres and documents of the Polish kings. The attractive gardens were laid out in 1731 by John Freeman, who also altered the village church and built the Freeman Mausoleum in the churchyard.

Fawsley Court, Nhants 694 D6, The house at Fawsley is now a luxurious hotel, but many public footpaths traverse its rolling 18th-century park

and weed-choked lakes. The parish church stands alone on a hilltop and contains the interesting alabaster tombs of the Knightly family.

Felbrigg, Norfk 695 J4, The Hall has a park by Repton, with a fine lake and woodland walks,

adorning a celebrated 17th-century house remodelled by Palladian architect James Paine around 1750. Compare the south and west fronts if you want to see the revolution that took place in English architecture between the 1620s and the 1670s – the former is in cool Jacobean stone, the latter in brick with sash windows. The Hall contains original 18th-century furniture, William Windham's Grand Tour paintings and a gothic library. An 18th-century octagonal dovecote in the kitchen garden and stable courtyard complete the picture. The parkland church, crammed with family monuments, once served a vanished village. The estate was willed to the National Trust.

Felixstowe, Suffk 691 J3, An Edwardian resort with elegant hanging gardens along the promenade and elaborate, no-longer-grand hotels and villas. To the south, alongside a sprawling container port, the Landguard Point nature reserve has rare coastal plants and a fort of 1718 built to guard the entrance to Harwich* harbour.

Felmersham, Beds 694 E6, The church of St Mary, one of the finest Early English buildings in the Home Counties, comes as quite a surprise in the quiet setting of Felmersham. It was built between c1220 and 1240 and has a noble west front, fine interior and screen.

Fenny Stratford, Bucks 690 E3, The interior of St Martin at Fenny Stratford is vibrant with polychrome brickwork of 1865 by William White.

Fens, Norfk 695 G5, An area of fertile farmland north of Cambridge that used to be covered by water but has been drained via a series of sluices. Work on

Top right: Fens, Walpole St Peter.

Felbrigg Hall
Left: *Old London Bridge*, by Samuel Scott, is among the works of art on display.
Centre left: The Drawing Room.
Bottom: The 18th-century library, designed by James Paine.

Below: Felmersham, the harmonious west front of the Church of St Mary.

the drainage was begun in the 17th century by Cornelius Vermuyden, a Dutch engineer. *See* **Flag Fen*, Wicken Fen*.**

A magnificent concentration of richly endowed marshland churches, much loved by John Betjeman and the Prince of Wales, can be found between the Great Ouse and Nene rivers. Here Norfolk flint yields place to Lincolnshire limestone shipped down the rivers from Barnack* quarries. The whole group is a moving testament in wood and stone to the medieval prosperity of this area and the faith of those who drained the Fens.

Terrington St Clement is a handsome Perpendicular church to rival Walpole (*below*). Known as the 'Cathedral of the Marshes' and dressed in grey freestone, it is heavily buttressed and sprouts a forest of turrets and pinnacles. A magnificent 17th-century font cover, the most memorable of many good fittings, opens to display scenes from the Life of Christ.

Walpole St Peter, known as the 'Queen of the Marshes', is all Perpendicular – light and spacious. The 15th-century pews have pierced backs and carved arm rests, notably with camels (not common in the Fens) and a wolf with the head of East Anglia's martyred King Edmund in its mouth.

Pride of place must go to **West Walton** just north of Wisbech, with its detached early-14th-century bell tower. For purity of form it ranks among the finest Early English churches anywhere. The interior has graceful nave columns with foliate capitals and slim, detached shafts of Purbeck marble. The **Wiggenhall** churches strung out beside the Ouse have a remarkable selection of carved bench ends. The intensely medieval interior of **St Germaine's** has the Vices and an exquisitely carved pulpit of 1631, with its original hourglass. **St Mary the Virgin** has a set of elaborate

Above and top: The Fens.

Below: Fetlar's rare birds include the great skua.

poppy-head pews and attendant figures, a brass eagle lectern (1518), a pelican font cover (1625), and stylish armorial tomb to Sir Henry Kervil (1624), with his wife in fashionable farthingale.

Fetlar, Shet 703 J2, This island, linked by car ferry to Gutcher (Yell*), is the most fertile in Shetland*. It was occupied in prehistoric times, as shown by the many remains, including the circle of standing stones at Haltadans, to the south of Vord Hill, and the neolithic mound at Finnigert that once divided the island in two. In addition to these sites, the RSPB North Fetlar Reserve protects such rare moorland species as the whimbrel and the red-necked phalarope, and is visited by the snowy owl. Houbie, Fetlar's main village has a small interpretation centre which presents the island's natural and social history.

Ffestiniog railway, Gwynd 692 E3, This was built to transport slate from Blaenau Ffestiniog* to Porthmadog*, but now operates as a picturesque private railway.

Ffynnon Gybi, Gwynd 692 D3, A building, now ruined, testifies to the faith people had in the healing powers of the well that it protected; but even in 1813, Richard Fenton, the Pembrokeshire scholar-traveller, noted that 'faith in such saintly wells is daily diminishing'.

Fiddleford Manor, Dorset 690 B7, Northwest of Blandford and near the small town of Sturminster Newton*, this has been called 'the most spectacular medieval manor house interior in Dorset'. Its late-14th-century roof structures are wonderfully shaped, into great ogee curves and trefoils and quatrefoils [EH].

Filkins, Oxon 690 C4, A pleasing village of large houses and picturesque cottages, with an elegant church by GE Street in the French gothic style. The apse is decorated with gold stars on a blue ground. The limestone slab fencing pre-dates many of the houses and is evidence of the abundance of stone in the locality.

Finchale Priory, Dur 697 G3, This ancient monument shares an idyllic riverside site, in a bend of the River Wear, with a caravan site and picnic area. There are substantial remains of the religious house first established by the colourful hymn-writing hermit Godric, who lived to the remarkable age of 105. The priory church [EH], instead of demonstrating continual enlargement up to the Dissolution, was actually reduced in size in the mid-14th century when Finchale (pronounced 'finkle') became a 'holiday home' for the monks of its parent monastery at Durham. The cloistral buildings are particularly well preserved. There is a square chapterhouse, with benches that step up to the equivalent of the chairman's chair, and a first-floor refectory, which sits over a rib-vaulted undercroft with a central row of piers; some of the old iron grilles survive in the window openings. The prior enjoyed particularly luxurious accommodation, part of which has become known as the Douglas Tower. High up on the outside north wall of this is the 'wishing chair', actually the base of a first-floor projecting oriel window; according to local folklore, it would cure infertility and procure issue for any woman who 'having performed certain ceremonies sat down

Above: Fingal's Cave on the island of Staffa, just to the west of Mull*. It inspired Mendelssohn's famous overture, written in 1832.

Finchale Priory
Left: Seen from across the River Wear.
Below: Looking east through the large window above the altar of St Mary in the south transept. The pinnacle is on the east end of the choir arm of the church.

therein' (history does not record how they were supposed to climb up to it).

Finchcocks, Kent, An interesting baroque house of 1725 in the style of Vanbrugh, chiefly notable for its collection of over 90 historic keyboard instruments, which are often played when the house is open. *See* **Scotney Castle* 691 G6.**

Finchingfield, Essex 691 G3, A picture-postcard village with a white post windmill on the road to Steeple Bumpstead and a squat church tower at the top, from where thatched and tiled cottages slope down around the green to the pond. The 15th-century Guildhall is now a museum. Here too is Spains Hall, an Elizabethan manor house, with a 300-year-old cedar of Lebanon in its garden.

Fingal's Cave, Ag & B 698 A2, The islands that lie to the west of Mull* include the fertile Inch Kenneth, the former 'granary' of Iona*, with its 13th-century church, Ulva (whose Gaelic name means 'island of wolves') and Staffa, an uninhabited island famous for its basalt rock formations. Staffa's huge Fingal's Cave became a place of romantic pilgrimage in the late-18th century and inspired Mendelssohn to write the overture known as *Fingal's Cave (The Hebrides)*. Further west the Treshnish Islands, fortified in the Middle Ages by the Lords of the Isles, are today a bird sanctuary. Seals bask on the rocks at the foot of the basalt cliffs that provide a nesting site for petrels and puffins.

Fingest, Bucks 690 E4, The church is renowned for its Norman tower, and is surrounded by a good group of houses.

Fingringhoe, Essex 691 H4, Overlooking the Colne estuary is a 14th-century church with a square-topped tower striped with flint and limestone, and chequered flushwork and brickwork decorating a battlemented porch and parapet.

Firle Place, E Susx 691 G7, The home of the Gage family since the 15th century, reconstructed in Georgian style in the 1730s. There are attractive period rooms with good collections of Old Masters, fine furniture and Sèvres porcelain.

Fishbourne Palace, W Susx 690 E7, The remains of a spectacular Roman palace were discovered in the

unaided. The bicentenary was commemorated by the Fishguard Arts Society, who commissioned a 100-foot (30m) tapestry narrating the event in the tradition of the Bayeux Tapestry's depiction of the Norman Conquest. This remarkable work, created with the expertise of 70 stitchers, is displayed in the Tourist Information Centre.

The road to Cardigan dives steeply into Lower Fishguard, which has retained much of its quaintness, before climbing up towards Dinas. A wide parking area on the summit offers uninterrupted views towards Fishguard Harbour and the Irish Ferry Terminal. It was designed at the beginning of the 20th century as a trans-Atlantic port but never made the grade.

Flag Fen, Cambs 695 F5, A unique survival in England, where peat has preserved some of the million timbers used to build a causeway and fortified island 3,000 years ago. Marks from Bronze-Age axes are still visible [EH].

Flamstead, Herts 691 F4, The church of St Leonard has a very important series of wall paintings (13th–15th century), including scenes from the Passion. Flaxman's monument to Sir Edward Sebright depicting Hope and Faith is particularly elegant.

Flatford Mill, Suffk 691 H3, Forever linked with John Constable, who drew and painted it and whose father owned it, this is now a Field Study Centre. Footpaths fringing the meadows follow the banks

1960s and large parts of it are now open to the public. It was very large, with probably about 100 rooms, many with mosaic floors and painted plaster walls. It seems to have been abandoned about AD 300. Part of the Roman garden has been reconstructed [EH].

Fishguard (Abergwaun), Pembks 692 B6, Perched on a high hilltop, with a small town square. On one corner stands the diminutive Royal Oak Inn, where the treaty between the British and the French ended 'the last foreign invasion of Britain, 22 February 1797' at nearby Carreg Wastad. Associated with this abortive attempt is Jemima Nicholas, a cobbler from the town, who has passed into national legend for capturing 12 Frenchmen

Firle Place
Top: The downstairs Drawing Room, with portraits of General Thomas Gage and his American wife, Margaret Kemble; over the fireplace is Teresa, daughter of the First Viscount Gage.
Above: The garden front.

Below: Fishguard, the picturesque harbour, a dramatic contrast with the Irish Ferry Terminal at Fishguard Harbour.

of the Stour with views to farmer Willy Lott's cottage, depicted in *The Hay Wain*, and upstream to Dedham. Bridge Cottage has been opened as a Constable Museum, with tea-garden, information centre and boat hire – allowing visitors to meander in the wake of Constable family barges. In **East Bergholt**, the painter's birthplace has been replaced by a house called 'Constables', but his

Above and below: Flatford Mill, made famous by John Constable.

parents lie undisturbed in the village churchyard. The church has a memorable bell-tower built like a dovecote.

Fleetwood, Lancs 696 E6, This new town was the creation of Sir Peter Hesketh Fleetwood of Rossall. A little to the south the family house is now part of Rossall School, founded in 1844 and comprising a rather miscellaneous collection of buildings of all dates, the best by Paley and Austin. The idea behind the new town was that trains to the north should terminate there, passengers continuing their journey by coastal steamer to Glasgow* and elsewhere. But the Cumbrian hills proved less of an obstacle to steam power than had been thought and Fleetwood had a short life as a passenger terminal, becoming instead a major trawler port. It is now the northern end of the tram journey from Blackpool*. The architectural relics of the enterprise are most interesting. Decimus Burton provided the North Euston Hotel, the Queen's Terrace (Queen Victoria used Fleetwood on her way from Scotland in 1847), two lighthouses and a

rather thin gothic church. The story of the town is told in the Fleetwood Museum in Dock Street.

Flint Castle, Flints 693 F2, Flint was the first of Edward I's castles, built during his first Welsh campaign in 1277. It is known for its Great Tower offering independent defence from the rest of the stronghold.

Flitton, Beds 691 F3, The entire east end of the 15th-century church of St John the Baptist is taken up by the de Grey Mausoleum, a remarkable series of rooms containing the 16th- to 19th-century monuments of the de Grey family. It is an impressive statement of family pride.

Floors Castle, Border 699 H5, The castle, which stands in a magnificent park overlooking the Tweed, was built in 1721–5 by William Adam for the 1st Duke of Roxburghe. Between 1837 and 1845

it was transformed by William Playfair into a huge neo-Jacobean mansion. It houses a good collection of English, Italian and French furniture, Chinese porcelain, 17th-century Brussels and Gobelin tapestries, and paintings by Raeburn, Hogarth, Hoppner, Gainsborough, Reynolds, Matisse and Bonnard. In the park a holly tree marks the spot where James II of Scotland was killed by a cannon during the siege of Roxburgh*, in 1460.

Folkestone, Kent 691 J6, The old centre has little of historic interest, but the Leas, a steep pine-clad slope to the west developed as a promenade in the 19th century, retains its charm. Rows of stucco villas and hotels at the top are reminders of past glory. Just north of the town is the entrance to the Channel Tunnel.

Fonmon Castle, V Glam 689 G3, Although the Castle today bears all the characteristics of a country house, its origins are those of a genuine fortification, built by Oliver St John. As one of the twelve knights who helped Robert Fitzhamon in the Norman conquest of Glamorgan, he was

Top: Floors Castle, the southwestern end of the main house, as extended and remodelled by Playfair.

Above centre: Flitton church of St John the Baptist, some of the numerous monuments to the de Grey family of Wrest Park*.

Above right: Fonthill Abbey, the north wing of the house built by Wyatt for William Beckford, 1796–1812; the remainder was demolished after the collapse of 1825.

Left: Flint Castle, dominated by the Great Tower, stands on the Dee estuary, with views of the Wirral.

Bottom right: Ford, Lady Waterford Hall, a wall-painting of *Joseph and his Brethren*.

granted the manor of Fonmon, near Barry – not far from where the River Thaw flows into the Bristol Channel. The site he chose for his stronghold was naturally defended by a ravine on the east and northeast sides. The core of the house belongs to the late 12th and early 13th centuries, and it is the only castle in Glamorgan that has been lived in continuously. During all this time, it has changed hands only once – the descendants of Oliver St John were forced to sell the property in 1656 because of vast debts. The purchaser was Colonel Philip Jones, Controller of Oliver Cromwell's Household and the leading Parliamentarian in South Wales. He added the substantial block to the north of the house, but the main transformation of the castle into a country house of considerable refinement was the work of a descendant, Robert Jones III. From the first-floor hall of the original keep, he created one of the best rococo rooms in Wales.

Fonthill Abbey, Wilts 690 B6, This fragment of the north range of the Abbey is the only remnant left of the massive structure where William Beckford (*see* Bath*) used to live. The dramatic building, with its great central tower, all designed by James Wyatt, collapsed in 1825. Lord Nelson was one of many earlier visitors: he had Christmas dinner there in 1800.

Ford, Nthumb 699 J5, Lady Waterford Hall is the name now given to the village school built in 1860 by Louisa, Marchioness of Waterford, who in 1862–83 painted on its inside walls a remarkable series of biblical scenes – Old Testament on the north wall and New Testament on the other three. Local schoolchildren and villagers acted as models for the figures. The Hall is situated in the short street of the model village also built by Lady Waterford, where rows of neat cottages with well-tended gardens facing onto immaculately mown grass lead away from a polished Aberdeen granite column (1859) with a fountain, a memorial to her

husband, the Marquess of Waterford. Close to the quadrilateral 14th-century castle is the early 13th-century church of St Michael, with an unembellished bellcote. It is altogether a remarkable settlement, with a nearby industrial suburb at Heatherslaw complete with corn water-mill, forge complex and light railway, which runs to Etal Castle*.

Forde Abbey, Somset 689 H5, Just into Somerset and near Chard, the beautiful remains of a Cistercian abbey founded in 1138 have developed into this impressive house dating largely from the middle of the 17th century. It has wonderful plaster ceilings, Mortlake tapestries woven from Raphael cartoons and splendid woodwork. Its award-winning gardens stretch over some 30 acres (12ha), with five lakes, an arboretum, a bog garden and magnificent trees and shrubs.

Forest of Dean, Gloucs 693 G6, The trees of the Forest of Dean are not all ancient; 30 million acorns were planted in the 1800s. This was after centuries of depredations to the Royal Hunting Forest, designated by the Normans in the early 11th

Left: Forde Abbey, the Saloon of 1657, showing one of the tapestries woven at Mortlake from the original cartoons of the Acts of the Apostles by Raphael. The original tapestries were woven in Flanders for the Sistine Chapel in Rome. Charles I subsequently acquired the cartoons, which are now in the Victoria & Albert Museum* in London.

Forres
Centre right: The Falconer Museum, built to the designs of A & W Reid in 1869 with a bequest from the nabob Alexander Falconer and his scientist brother Hugh, and embellished with busts of scientists and engineers.
Far right: Sueno's Stone is shown in its modern protective glass case.

Bottom: Forest of Dean. King John hunted here from his lodge at St Briavels*.

century. Surprisingly, the Forest was important as an industrial area for mining coal and minerals. The foresters have always had a kind of special regional autonomy: they enacted forest law at the Speech House, now a pub, in the middle of the Forest. Anyone born within 100 miles (160km) of St Briavels still has the right, as a 'free-miner' of the Forest, to mine their own coal.

Forncett St Peter, Norfk 695 J5, Approached down an avenue of limes, this Saxon round-towered church has fascinating bench-end figures. The church contributes to a picturesque grouping that includes the Queen Anne rectory where Dorothy Wordsworth established a school in 1789. Rare flower-rich water meadows survive beside the River Tas, where she walked with brother William.

Forres, Moray 701 J4, On the outskirts of the town stands Sueno's Stone, a remarkable 20-foot (6m) sandstone block carved in the 9th–10th century. One side is decorated with a huge Celtic cross and the other with a series of panels depicting a battle, possibly between the Picts and the Vikings or Scots. The Falconer Museum, in Tolbooth Street, traces the history of this former royal burgh.

Although no longer active, the Dallas Dhu Distillery is open to the public and presents the various stages involved in the production of the national drink.

Fort Augustus, Highld 701 G6, In 1729 General Wade, governor of the 'North of Great Britain', built a fort at the south end of Loch Ness* near the mouth of the Oich. It was named after the second son of George II, William Augustus, Duke of Cumberland. Lord Lovat donated it to an English Benedictine order in 1876. The Benedictine monks from Bavaria, who occupied Fort Augustus Abbey until recently, built the East Cloister, the Chapter House and St Andrew's Chapel shortly afterwards. Today the town of Fort Augustus is crossed by the Caledonian Canal* and six of its locks.

Left: Fort George. The engineer was Colonel William Skinner and the contractors were architect brothers, John Robert and James Adam.

Fort George, Highld 701 H5, The fort was built by the government in 1747–69 after the Battle of Culloden*, to guard the Moray Firth, but it has never been attacked in its entire history. It was designed to resist storms and Highland attacks and has barely changed since it was built. This symbol of the power of the House of Hanover remains one of the most impressive forts in Europe. Certain buildings are open to the public and give an insight into the living conditions of soldiers in the 18th century.

Fort William, Highld 701 F7, The capital of the Lochaber district stands on Loch Linnhe, at the foot of Ben Nevis and to the north of the famous 95-mile (152-km) footpath known as the West Highland Way*. The region has given its name to the 'Lochaber axe', an axe with a long, slender blade and a yew handle ending in a hook, designed to unseat riders. The town was named after the earthwork fort built in 1655 by General Monck and rebuilt in stone in 1690 under William III (William of Orange). The fort withstood the Jacobite attacks of 1715 and 1745, but was demolished in 1866 to make way for the railway. The West Highland Museum presents the region's natural history, popular traditions, its role in the Jacobite Risings and the wave of emigration provoked by the repression that followed. Old Inverlochy Castle, near the bridge across the River Lochy, is the impressive ruins of a tower-house that was probably built by the Comyns in the 13th century. The Ben Nevis Distillery has produced the whisky known as 'The Dew of Ben Nevis' since 1825.

Above: Fotheringhay, pulpit of St Mary and All Saints Church.

Fort William
Centre: Ben Nevis whisky distillery.
Bottom: Neptune's Staircase Walk follows the route of the Caledonian Canal.

Foston Old Rectory, N York 697 H5, Built by the Georgian divine and wit Sydney Smith while incumbent (1806–29) of Foston-le-Clay, between York and Malton, before he returned to London as a canon of St Paul's Cathedral*. 'My living in Yorkshire,' he wrote, 'was so far out of the way that it was actually twelve mile from a lemon. When I began to thump the pulpit cushion on my first coming to Foston, the accumulated dust of 150 years made such a cloud that for some minutes I lost sight of my congregation.'

Fotheringhay, Nhants 695 F5, This village has one of east Northamptonshire's most beautiful churches, founded in 1411, with bold but slender flying buttresses. It was originally built as a college with cloisters and other facilities. An earlier chancel, now pulled down and replaced, was intended to house the 12 fellows and 13 choristers. Instead of a spire it has battlements and pinnacles.

A low mound by the Nene marks the remains of **Fotheringhay Castle**, dating from about 1100. This was where Mary Queen of Scots was beheaded on 8 February 1587. Scottish thistles, known locally as Queen Mary's Tears, grow in the slopes of the mound. Her executioner, Bull, is said to have stayed in the New Inn (now a private house with a 15th-century gateway) in the main street.

Fountains Abbey, N York 697 G5, On Boxing Day 1132, after an uncomfortable interview in Ripon* with Thurstan, the Archbishop of York, 13 disaffected Benedictine monks from St Mary's Abbey in York* headed towards the wild, secluded valley of Skelldale. Adopting the Cistercian Rule, they began to build what became that Order's wealthiest monastery. The movingly beautiful ruins of Fountains Abbey [NT & EH], now a World Heritage Site, epitomize medieval monasticism. The stone has breathtaking hues of purple, pink and blue as well as yellow and brown.

Much of the church survives – the 12th-century Transitional nave, used by the lay brothers and never upgraded; the Early English choir (extended by an eastern transept), where the fully professed monks sang their nine daily services; and the Chapel of the Nine Altars (similar to that at Durham Cathedral*). Abbot Huby's impressive tower, added to the north transept c1500, was built in open defiance of earlier Cistercian principles, which had eschewed ostentation.

The claustral buildings also remain largely intact. Of particular note is the west range, which has an immensely long vaulted undercroft of simple monumentality for storage and the use of

the lay brothers, below what was the monks' dormitory. On the south side can be found the monks' refectory and kitchen, and the warming house with its complete fireplace and chimney, carried on a lintel that takes the form of a flat arch constructed of joggled voussoirs. The abbey's name comes from the ample supply of water here (the River Skell runs through the domestic buildings). The lay-brothers' reredorter is worth seeing, a long row of round-arched cubicles, reminiscent of large seaside public conveniences, flushed by the stream. The monastic watermill was restored and reopened in 2001. After the Dissolution, a handsome Jacobean mansion, Fountains Hall, was built (1611) next to the ruins, which eventually became a feature of Studley Royal* landcaped garden.

Above: The undercroft in the west claustral range, used for storage and as a dining room for the large numbers of lay brothers who tended the Cistercians' sheep flocks. The immensely long vault, with ribs continuing down the piers without capitals, is spatially very impressive.

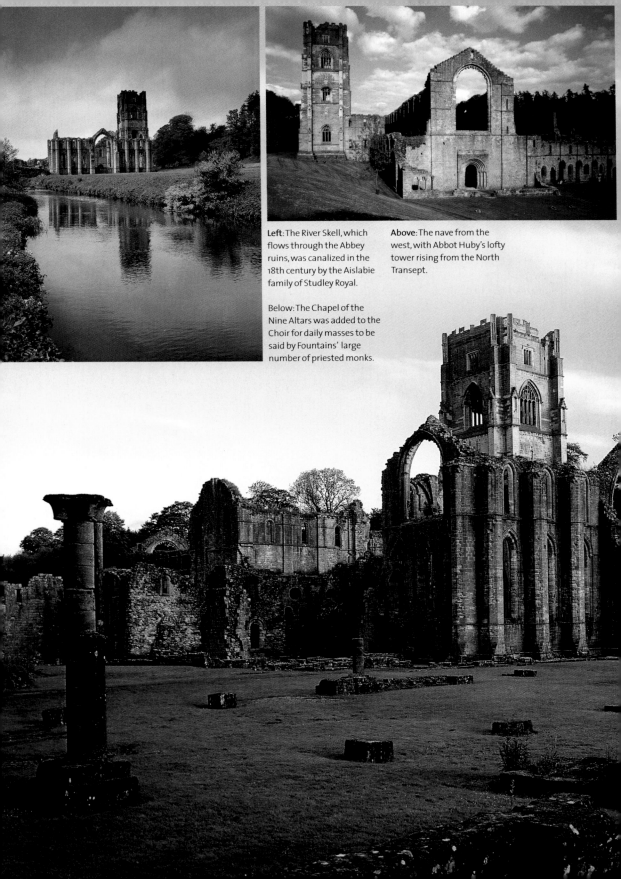

Left: The River Skell, which flows through the Abbey ruins, was canalized in the 18th century by the Aislabie family of Studley Royal.

Above: The nave from the west, with Abbot Huby's lofty tower rising from the North Transept.

Below: The Chapel of the Nine Altars was added to the Choir for daily masses to be said by Fountains' large number of priested monks.

succession was secure. From Wall Walk there are views over The Mere to Framlingham College, founded in memory of Prince Albert in 1865. In addition to the Howard tombs within the impressive church are superb Renaissance alabaster tombs, including the those of the early dukes of Norfolk. Note the helmet in the chancel

belonging to the 2nd Duke, who led the English a Flodden in 1513. The poet Henry, Earl of Surrey, has his coronet by his side because he was beheaded in 1547. The Market Place is an attractiv triangular space with raised tree-lined walkway and good vernacular buildings.

Frampton, Dorset 689 J6, The church of St Mary has interesting monuments, some to the memory of the Brownes of Frampton Court. The principal of these is that of Robert Browne (d. 1734), its long inscription informing us that he embellished the church tower (1695) with two tiers of Tuscan columns, and built the court (now demolished).

Frampton-on-Severn, Gloucs 693 H7, This low, damp village by the ship canal claims to have the largest village green in England. The shaggy meadow covers 4 acres (1.6m) and is surrounded by some pretty houses. Facing each other across the pond are the old manor house and its replacement, a timbered manor farmhouse, and the provincial baroque of Frampton Court. The farmhouse is the reputed birthplace of Fair Rosamund, mistress of

Fowey, Cnwll 688 D7, On the western bank of a fine natural harbour the serried terraces of this ancient port are dominated by the twin towers of the church of St Fimbarrus (14th century, with many

Fowey
Left: The town Quay and the King of Prussia Inn.
Below left: Looking from Polruan across the safe anchorage to Fowey.

Below: Frampton, church of St Mary.

Bottom: Frampton Court, Gloucs, the entrance front.

tombs of the Rashleigh family) and Place, the nearby seat of the ancient family of Treffry. Their home is an Elizabethan house much extended by the mining magnate JT (Austin) Treffry in the second quarter of the 19th century, who used alabaster, porphyry and other minerals in its internal decoration.

Framlingham, Suffk 695 J6, Built and rebuilt by the rebellious Bigods Earls of Norfolk in the 12th century, Framlingham's first castle was surrendered to Henry II in 1157; the second was seized by John in 1216. Thirteen outer towers survive, linked by a curtain wall and topped with the fake chimneys by which the Howards disguised a clapped-out castle as a Tudor mansion [EH]. Mary Tudor waited here in 1553 until her

Henry II. The Court has an interesting Dutch-style ornamental canal in the garden, topped by a gothic orangery which is now an unusual house.

Fraserburgh, Abers 702 E4, This major 19th-century herring port still has its fishing fleet and fish market. The Museum of Scottish Lighthouses evokes the history of the 'northern lighthouses' the first of which (1787) was built on the top floor of an old towerhouse, Kinnaird Castle, on nearby Kinnaird Head. The mysterious 16th-century Wine Tower is decorated with coats of arms in bas-relief. The Fraserburgh Heritage Centre has an exhibition devoted to Thomas Glover (1838–1911), who created the modern Japanese navy and inspired Puccini's hero in *Madama Butterfly*.

Freeland, Oxon, The church of St Mary is an excellent High Victorian building of 1869–71 by JL Pearson, with perfectly preserved fittings. *See* **Church Hanborough* 690 D4.**

Frinton-on-Sea, Essex 691 J4, An elegant Edwardian coastal resort with low cliffs and a view of the 1830 pier of rival Walton-on-the-Naze*. Its greatest monument is The Homestead, CF Voysey's model villa of 1905. There is William Morris glass designed by Burne-Jones in Old St Mary's church. To the north, Hamford Water's mud creeks and Horsey Island's causeway were the setting for Arthur Ransome's children's story *Secret Waters*.

Froncysyllte, Denbgs 693 F3, Thomas Telford's Pontcysyllte Aqueduct (1794–1805), carrying the Shropshire canal across the Dee at a vertiginous height, is half a mile (0.8km) north of the village.

Fulbeck Hall, Lincs 694 E4, Quite a modest, mainly 18th-century mansion, obviously a first cousin to many of the houses in the streets of nearby Stamford*. There is a museum dedicated to the 1st Airborne Division, who were stationed here during World War II.

Furness, Cumb 696 D5, The southern part of Cumbria is Furness, formerly Lancashire over the Sands and separated from the County Palatine by the flat expanse of Morecambe Bay. The area was dominated in the Middle Ages by Furness Abbey [EH], founded by the Savignacs in 1127 and Cistercian from 1147. Set in a steep valley, the abbey site still gives some impression of the remoteness sought by the Cistercians. The impressive ruins of the church, with a short chancel and long nave, retain much 12th-century detail such as waterleaf capitals, and good examples of later alteration such as the elaborately canopied 15th-century sedilia. There are important remains of the convent buildings, especially the Chapter House,

Top: Furness Abbey, the cloister and crossing.

Fyvie Castle
Above: The John Bryce drawing room.
Below: The superstructure of the Seton Tower on the south front, showing the arch linking the heightened drum towers flanking the entrance of the 13th-century royal castle.

entered from the cloister through beautifully moulded arches, the Dormitory and the Infirmary. Above the abbey is the Abbey House Hotel, built by Sir Edwin Lutyens for the managing director of the Barrow shipyard; not Lutyens at his most inspiring but the best example of his domestic work in the region. Beyond is the town of **Barrow-in-Furness,** almost entirely a mid-19th-century town built round steel and shipbuilding yards (in 1876 Barrow had the largest steelworks in the world). There are wide tree-lined streets that are more impressive than the buildings which face them. Best buildings are the Town Hall by W H Lynn of Belfast, and Devonshire Buildings, a set of working-class lodgings now being converted into a hotel. There is an interesting Dock Museum.

Fyvie Castle, Abers 702 D5, When he bought the estate in 1596 Alexander Seton, the loyal manservant of Mary Stuart and future Chancellor of Scotland, decided to remodel the quadrangular 13th-century Royal Castle. He built up its gatehouse as the Seton Tower and remodelled the remainder in conformity with it, bristling with turrets and dormers, creating the great 'wheel staircase', one of the most beautiful circular staircases in Scotland. The northeast tower was built in the 18th century by the Gordons. Alexander Forbes-Leith, a native of Aberdeen who made his fortune in the American iron industry, acquired the estate in 1889. He added the northwest tower and gave the castle its opulent Edwardian interiors, which house an art collection that includes works by Ramsay, Gainsborough, some magnificent paintings by Raeburn, the splendid portrait of Colonel William Gordon of Fyvie by Pompeo Batoni and works by French and Dutch masters.

Gaddesby, Leics 694 D5, The large and stately parish church of St Luke is chiefly remarkable for the exceptionally rich carved stone decoration of the south aisle, which probably dates from the 1330s. Presumably there was a private chantry in this part of the church, for which the benefactor required something special. The church contains a dramatic marble monument to Colonel Cheyney, on one of the four horses killed under him at the Battle of Waterloo.

Gadshill, Kent 691 G5, Literary pilgrims will want to see Gadshill, the last home of Charles Dickens, where he died. Dickens lived as a boy in Rochester* (*Great Expectations* is set there and in the marshes nearby), and buying this house was the fulfilment of a childhood dream. It is now a school, and the only room with any atmosphere is Dickens' study, the door of which is lined with fake book-spines with titles such as *The Life of the Cat, in Nine Volumes,* among others of a similar vein.

Gainsborough, Lincs 694 E2, The tall medieval tower of All Saints Church still survives, but the rest was rebuilt in the 1730s, probably by Francis Smith of Warwick. Gainsborough Old Hall [EH] rises up grandly out of very ordinary urban surroundings, and proclaims itself a late medieval house of the first importance. Sir Thomas Burgh's enormous Great Hall with its elaborate timber roof survives, along with the Great Kitchen – possibly the most complete medieval kitchen in England – and other catering rooms. In 1484 Sir Thomas entertained King Richard III here. Other parts of the mansion were rebuilt in the 1590s.

Gairloch, Highld 700 E4, This former fishing port on the shores of Loch Gairloch has been a summer resort since the Victorian era. It has fine sandy beaches, a lighthouse built by Stevenson – the engineer and grandfather of the writer, Robert Louis Stevenson – and a Heritage Museum

Top: Gants Mill, surrounded by its beautiful colour-themed designer garden. This working watermill is within a few hundred yards of the centre of Bruton.

Right: Gardens of the Rose, one of the best collections of roses in the world.

Bottom left: Gainsborough Old Hall, the east wing, containing the Great Chamber and the northeast tower of about 1460.

Bottom right: Gaulden Manor, one of a pair of paintings of servants of the Starkie family, c1840. The initials LGS on the buckets stand for Le Gendre Starkie.

which presents the region's maritime and agricultural traditions.

Galashiels, Border 699 G5, For 700 years this town has been a flourishing textile centre whose history is traced in Old Gala House (16th century) and the Lochcarron Cashmere Wool Centre.

Gants Mill, Somset, John le Gaunt built a fulling mill here, in the valley of the River Brue, c1290. The present building, a four-storey watermill, was built by Lord Berkeley c1740. It has been fully restored and visitors can watch it in operation, grinding corn. *See* **Bruton* 689 J4.**

Gardens of the Rose, Herts, Two miles (3.2km) south of St Albans at Chiswell Green are these glorious gardens, arranged around an attractive house, run by the Royal National Rose Society. They feature over 30,000 roses with companion plants, including over 100 varieties of clematis – an important collection. *See* **St Albans* 691 F4.**

Garendon, Leics 694 D5, The mansion was pulled down in the 1960s but the park still contains a number of fine and interesting structures, most notably a stone triumphal arch built in the 1730s by the landowner Ambrose Philips in loose imitation of the Arch of Titus in Rome, and the Temple of Venus, a circular building on a hill overlooking the drive.

Gatton Park, Surrey 691 F6, North of the ancient town of Reigate*, an area on the North Downs escarpment that offers walks through lovely woodland, parkland and downland with breathtaking views all around. The owner of Gatton Park, Lord Monson, commissioned the neo-gothic church of St Andrew in 1834. The interior is full of the French and Flemish woodwork and glass he collected. The family pew, complete with fireplace, has a side entrance, and there is a covered walkway to the house.

Gaulden Manor, Somset 689 G5, Once the seat of the Turberville family, this charming small manor house in

made up of timber-framed mansions and large pools. The chancel contains tombs of the Fitton family, who lived in the Hall until the 17th century.

Gawthorpe Hall, Lancs 697 F6, Just outside Padiham, the Hall [NT] was built in 1600 and is the best example in the northwest of that compact Elizabethan planning associated with the designs of Robert Smythson. Of its original interiors the best is the spendid Long Gallery. Gawthorpe was restored and improved in 1850 by Sir Charles Barry and is now as much a monument to him as to its first builder, Lawrence Shuttleworth. Barry worked for the Kay-Shuttleworths, whose family collection of needlework, together with 17th-century portraits from the National Portrait Gallery*, make Gawthorpe treasured for its contents as well as its architecture.

Tolland was often referred to in the writings of Thomas Hardy. It has interesting gardens with old-fashioned roses and herbs.

Gawsworth Old Hall, Ches 693 H2, A picturesque, rambling timber-framed house mostly built in the 15th century, when it was twice the size it is now. There is one long show front with a splendid three-storey bay window, and the house contains a fine collection of paintings and sculpture. The village church is set in picturesque surroundings,

Above: Gaulden Manor, past seat of the Turberville family, immortalized in Thomas Hardy's *Tess of the D'Urbervilles*.

Right and below: Gawsworth Old Hall. The 16th-century timber-framed house has a superb setting next to a lake.

Gayhurst, Bucks 690 E3, The church of 1727 is wonderfully idiosyncratic, with giant Ionic half-columns supporting a small pediment on the south elevation, and two superimposed on the north. Inside is an outstanding monument (1720s) to George and Sir Nathan Wrighte; Sir Nathan was the Keeper of the Seal to Queen Anne. The two figures stand in contemporary dress, framed by pilasters and pediment, beneath a baldacchino. Note also the plasterwork.

Georgeham, Devon 688 E4, Henry Williamson lived here and wrote *Tarka the Otter* (1927) and many other books while at Ox's Cross.

Germoe, Cnwll 688 C8, In the upper churchyard is the Chair of St Germoe (probably medieval), with its two pointed arches and triple seat. It is thought that it played an important part in the Palm

Above and top: Gibside Chapel has a Greek cross plan surmounted by a central dome.

Sunday processions around the ancient (but now much restored) medieval church.

Gerrards Cross, Bucks 690 E5, All Saints is a bright and charming Arts and Crafts church by Temple Moore (1912–13). St James was designed by Sir William Tite, architect of the Royal Exchange, in neo-Byzantine style.

Gibside, T & W 697 G2, An important 18th-century landscaped garden, once grand, then derelict, now being restored [NT]. There is an immense Column of Liberty, which forms the focal point of many vistas; the ruined Orangery; the gothic Banqueting House (now a Landmark Trust holiday cottage); and the Palladian-style **Gibside Chapel,** designed by James Paine, a Greek cross in plan and an exquisite exercise in centralized design. It was begun in 1760 as a mausoleum for

Gilling Castle, N York 697 H5, Now a preparatory school, the castle has the country's finest Elizabethan Great Chamber, complete with heraldic glass windows dated 1585, pendant rib ceiling, lozenge wall panelling, and a painted frieze depicting the family trees of the Yorkshire gentry, as well as the Fairfax family's musicians. In origin a 14th-century tower-house, it also has early Georgian wings with rococo plasterwork by the Italian Giuseppe Cortese.

Gilston, Herts 691 G4, Within the church is an amazing survival of a 13th-century screen.

Gipping, Suffk 695 H6, This remote chantry chapel to the Tyrell family is a small and perfectly formed Perpendicular church. Exquisite flint flush motifs, among the best in East Anglia, include the Tyrell knot and interlaced Arundel hearts.

Gisborough Priory, N Yorks 697 H4, Founded for Augustinian canons by Robert de Brus early in the 12th century, it was rebuilt after a fire in 1289 [EH]. The Decorated east window beautifully frames a

view of the Cleveland Hills. Nearby is an early dovecote, and in Guisborough parish church, a richly carved chest tomb from the priory.

Glamis, Angus 699 G2, Glamis Castle, a former royal hunting lodge and home of the Bowes-Lyon family, earls of Strathmore and Kinghorn, was the childhood home of the late Queen Elizabeth The Queen Mother, daughter of the 14th Earl. The tower-house, built in the 15th and 16th centuries, was enlarged in the 17th and 19th centuries. Some of the richly furnished apartments and a chapel decorated with panels painted by the Dutch artist Jacob de Wet in 1688 are open to the public. The collections of the Angus Folk Museum housed in a number of old cottages in the village, are worth a visit.

the Bowes family, who owned the Gibside estate. Inside, it offers an unfamiliar concept of a church interior, the main feature being a splendid three-decker pulpit centrally placed below the dome.

Gigha, Ag & B 698 B5, The island of Gigha (pronounced 'Gear'), whose name means 'island of the gods' in Gaelic, lies 3 miles (5km) west of Kintyre. It is a tiny, fertile island bordered by beautiful beaches. The trees and shrubs of Achamore Gardens provide shelter for such delicate species as magnolias and camellias.

Gilling Castle
Above: Italianate plasterwork in the entrance hall.
Left: A 16th-century overmantel in the Great Chamber.

Glasgow

Glasgow, C Glas 698 E4, With some 740,000 inhabitants, Glasgow is Scotland's most densely populated city. The city centre stands on a series of small hills on the north bank of the River Clyde. It has a great many Victorian monuments, museums and art galleries centred on George Square. To the east of the square lies the redeveloped commercial district of Merchant City and the East End. To the west the city's main shopping streets climb towards the terraced houses of the wealthy residential district of Blythswood Hill.

The Barras: With its old stores, open-air stalls, cafés and little restaurants, this flea market (between Gallowgate and London Road) – whose name is a distortion of 'barrows' – is one of the East End's main attractions. Voluble stallholders sell all kinds of new and second-hand goods at bargain prices.

Botanic Gardens: The gardens, which occupy a 50-acre (20ha) site on the banks of the River Kelvin, are renowned for their collection of ferns, begonias and orchids. They also contain the Kibble Palace, one of the largest Victorian glasshouses in Britain. This huge metal-and-glass structure was originally built in 1864 on the shores of Loch Long by the engineer John Kibble. It was transferred to its present site in 1874 and served as a conference venue and concert hall before being used to house plant specimens from all over the world, including a remarkable collection of tree ferns from Australia and New Zealand. Other glasshouses contain amazing species of tropical plants.

Burrell Collection: In 1944 the wealthy Glasgow shipowner William Burrell donated his art collection to the city. The collection, remarkable for its size and diversity, was the fruit of a lifetime of research and acquisition. The building designed by Barry Gasson to house the collection was opened in 1983. Some 3,000 of the 8,000 pieces are on permanent display, while the others are displayed in rotation. The courtyard is dominated by the Warwick Vase, an 18th-century reconstruction of a 2nd-century marble vase from Hadrian's villa at Tivoli. The Hutton Castle Rooms, a reconstruction of the hall, drawing room and dining room of Hutton Castle, which Burrell owned, are filled with tapestries, oriental carpets and antique furniture. There are fine galleries of Ancient and Oriental Art. The collection of Medieval and Post-Medieval European Art brings together more than 150 tapestries, 600 stained-glass windows and 300 stone and wood statues. Three Period Galleries house works by 17th- and 18th-century British masters, while the paintings, drawings and bronzes on display on the mezzanine floor include works by 19th-century French artists Géricault, Boudin, Sisley, Cézanne and especially Degas.

Above left: Detail of a panel in the White Bedroom of the Mackintosh House, a reconstruction of Mackintosh's Glasgow home.

Far left and left: Buddha and a Rodin sculpture in the Burrell Collection, in Pollok Park.

Below: *The Trongate of Glasgow,* painted in 1826.

Right: Botanic Gardens, interior of the Kibble Palace.

Clyde: A walkway along the River Clyde follows the quays past Victoria Bridge, a granite structure built in 1854 to replace a medieval bridge, and the pedestrian Suspension Bridge (1851–71). The Scottish Exhibition and Conference Centre (SECC) has hosted exhibitions, conferences and concerts since 1985. The nearby Clyde Auditorium, also a conference centre, was designed by Sir Norman Foster in 1997. The Pumphouse, which once supplied the electricity for the hydraulic cranes and swing bridges of the docks, has been converted into a museum tracing the history of the Clyde shipyards.

Gallery of Modern Art: Since 1996 this rich collection of modern art has been housed in the Royal Exchange, a magnificent neoclassical building designed by David Hamilton in 1827, which incorporated the 1780 mansion of the tobacco tycoon William Cunninghame. Four themed galleries present works by Scottish artists such as Peter Howson, Stephen Campbell and Ken Curry, and foreign artists such as Niki de Saint Phalle, Andy Warhol and Eduard Bersudsky.

George Square: The square, dedicated to George III, was built in 1781. Originally a residential area, with the advent of the railway it was surrounded by hotels before becoming the centre of Merchant City c1850 and then the administrative centre in the Victorian era. The statues of well-known celebrities that line the esplanade are dominated by an 80-foot (24m) column surmounted by a statue of Walter Scott. At the northwest corner of the square a gilded merchant vessel adorns the Italianate façade of Merchants' House, built by John Burnet Senior in 1874 and today occupied by the Glasgow Chamber of Commerce. On the south side of the square the

Far left: The Clyde Auditorium, designed by Sir Norman Foster, 1997.

Above: The Suspension Bridge over the River Clyde, built 1851–71.

Tourist Information Centre occupies the former General Post Office building (1876). The entire east side of George Square is taken up by the impressive Glasgow City Chambers, designed by William Young and opened in 1888 by Queen Victoria. Beyond the grandiose neoclassical façade lie magnificent interiors in Italian renaissance style, with majestic marble staircases and vaulted ceilings decorated with gold leaf.

Glasgow Cathedral: This impressive gothic cathedral enjoys the unusual distinction of having been built on two levels. It is also one of the few gothic churches in Scotland to have been spared during the Reformation, following the intervention of the trade guilds in 1578. The first cathedral, consecrated in 1136, was destroyed by fire; work began on the present edifice in 1197. The choir was built between 1233 and 1258 in early gothic style. The sacristy, central tower and stone spire date from the first half of the 15th century, while the nave was completed in 1480. Archbishop Blacadar added the flight of steps leading to the Lower Church, the remarkable stone rood screen (whose carvings represent the Seven Deadly Sins) and the flamboyant gothic side aisle named after him. The Lower Church, designed to house the tomb of St Mungo, dates from the first half of the 13th century, although its chapter house was renovated in the early 15th century. The cathedral's balanced proportions and delicate ornamentation make it a fine example of Scottish early gothic architecture.

Glasgow Green: This vast park on the banks of the River Clyde has been the centre of Glasgow's public life since at least the 12th century. Glasgow's Fair Fortnight is held here in July and it is the venue for a number of processions, including the May Day procession, and public events. It also boasts Britain's first Nelson memorial, a 145-foot (44m) monument erected in 1806 to commemorate the victory of Trafalgar. On the north side of the Green, the renaissance-style People's Palace (1898) was originally a cultural centre for the workers of the East End. Today it houses an interesting museum which traces the history of Glasgow from its official foundation in 1175, placing the emphasis on the economic and social transformations of the 19th and 20th centuries.

Glasgow School of Art: Charles Rennie Mackintosh was only 28 when he won the competition to design the school (167 Renfrew Street). The building, which was constructed in two stages (1896–9 and 1907–9), is regarded as the architect's greatest work. It is both elegant and functional and combines traditional Scottish architecture with modern techniques and materials. The Mackintosh touch is applied to the slightest decorative detail, as illustrated by the geometric and floral motifs that appear on the fireplaces, wall lamps, carpets, enamelling and furniture. The Mackintosh Room and the Furniture Gallery house collections of the architect's furniture, designs and watercolours. The oak-panelled

Top: A Rangers football club supporter.

Above: Flags in George Square.

Left and below: Glasgow Cathedral, begun in the 12th century.

Opposite page
Top left: Princes Square shopping centre.

Top centre: Templeton's Carpet Factory, designed by William Leiper, an extravagant combination of coloured mosaics and bricks, inspired by the Doge's Palace in Venice.

Main picture: A marble staircase in Glasgow City Chambers.

Library is particularly impressive with its suspended ceiling, its positively vertiginous windows, its mezzanine gallery with carved and painted balusters, and the metal and glass light fittings in the Reading Room.

Glasgow University: The university was founded in 1451 by Bishop William Turnbull. Lectures were initially held in the cathedral and then in various buildings in the High Street. In 1870 it was transferred to the Gilmorehill campus. The main building (Gilmorehill Building), designed by Sir George Gilbert Scott in 1866, was partly inspired by the Cathedral but the main inspiration was Flemish, particularly for the tower. Scott's son, John Oldrid, built Bute Hall in 1882 and the tower in 1887. Part of the 17th-century university was rebuilt as Pearce Lodge in 1887. There is a magnificent chapel by Sir John Burnet, designed 1913 and built 1923–7. Inside the Gilmorehill Building, the Hunterian Museum, Glasgow's oldest museum, is centred on the eclectic collection bequeathed to the university by a former student, Dr William Hunter (1718–83). This famous doctor of medicine, professor of anatomy and royal physician was also a keen collector of paintings, an archeologist, zoologist and mineralogist. The numismatics collection (30,000 coins and medals) constitutes its main attraction. The **Hunterian Art Gallery** houses the largest European collection of paintings and personal items belonging to James McNeill Whistler. The **Mackintosh House** is a reconstruction of the Glasgow home of Charles Rennie Mackintosh, with some 60 pieces of furniture and numerous drawings, sketches and watercolours by the famous architect and designer. Several galleries are devoted to 19th- and 20th-century Scottish painting. The collections also include some remarkable prints and engravings belonging to the University, paintings by Rembrandt, Rubens, Stubbs and Chardin, a number of French Impressionist paintings and a collection of modern sculpture.

The Hat Rack: With its lead roof and finely carved ridgepole, the tall building at 144 St Vincent Street, designed in 1902 by James Salmon Junior, does indeed look like a hat rack. Its narrow façade pierced by numerous windows and the delicate Glasgow Style details are reminiscent of the work of the Catalan architect Antonio Gaudí.

'House for an Art Lover': The 'Haus eines Kunstfreundes' is owned by the Glasgow School of Art and is within Bellahouston Park. It was inspired by the plans designed in 1901 by Charles Rennie Mackintosh and his wife Margaret Macdonald for a competition in a German design magazine. The entrance hall, dining room, music

Left: The Library of the Glasgow School of Art, within the 1907–9 western wing.

Centre: Tenement House, the first-floor flat of Miss Agnes Toward, still furnished as in 1911, within a late 19th-century red sandstone tenement. It is owned by the National Trust for Scotland.

Bottom left: Glasgow University, the main building from the southwest, showing the pavilion containing the Humanity Classroom, which has been preserved in its original form.

Left: The Kelvingrove Art Gallery was designed by Sir John W Simpson, who won the competition in 1891. It is one of the great examples of 'the New Sculpture'.

Below: The Connal Building, 34 West George Street, by James Thomson, 1898–1900, with sculptures of Glasgow notables and locomotives by James Young.

room and oval room enable visitors to compare the design project, which greatly contributed to establishing the architect's international reputation. The work was carried out (1989–96) by Graham Roxburgh and a team of modern interior designers.

Kelvingrove Art Gallery and Museum: The city's Art Gallery and Museum, opened in 1902, has one of the richest collections in Britain: 3,000 paintings, 12,500 drawings and engravings and 300 sculptures. The architect, Sir John W Simpson, designed it as a shrine of 'the New Sculpture', with major items by Sir George Frampton and Derwent Wood which form part of the structure of the building. The ground floor presents Scotland's natural history and archaeology, as well as weapons and armour from Europe and the East. The first-floor balconies are devoted to the decorative arts (gold and silverware, jewellery, glass and ceramics) while its galleries present a remarkable collection of paintings. The Continental (west) Wing gives pride of place to the Italians (Bellini, Botticelli, Giorgione, Caravaggio), Dutch (Rembrandt, Ruisdael), Flemish (Brueghel the Elder, Rubens) and French (the Barbizon School, Impressionism, Fauvism, Cubism). Scottish painting from the 16th century to the present day is particularly well represented in the British (east) Wing by Ramsay, Raeburn, Wilkie, McTaggart, the Glasgow Boys and the Scottish Colourists.

McLellan Galleries: The building at 270 Sauchiehall Street was constructed in 1855 by James Smith to house the private collection of Archibald McLellan (1797–1854), which mainly consisted of paintings by Italian, Dutch and Flemish masters. These works are now in the Kelvingrove Art Gallery and Museum, and the McLellan Galleries hold major temporary exhibitions.

Merchant City: After a long period of neglect this district east of George Square was the subject of an extensive redevelopment programme in the 20th century. The warehouses and 18th-century merchants' houses were renovated to provide residential and commercial accommodation. Many of the street names, such as Jamaica Street and Virginia Street, evoke the golden age of trade with the British colonies, or pay tribute to famous merchants. Within this area is **Hutchesons' Hall**, where a slender white tower marks the office of the National Trust for Scotland (158 Ingram Street). This former business centre was built (1802–5) by

Bottom left: Mackintosh designs for the reception and music room in the House for an Art Lover.
Below: Chair design for the Willow Tea Rooms.
Bottom right: Chair in the Argyle Tea Rooms.

DER WETTBEWERB FUR EIN HERRSCHAFTLICHES WOHNHAUS EINES KUNST-FREUNDES

EMPFANGS-RAUM U. MUSIK-ZIMMER PANELS VON MARGARET MACDONALD MACKINTOSH

David Hamilton on the site of a hospice founded 1639–41 by the Hutcheson brothers. All that remains of the original building are the statues of the two philanthropists decorating the façade. The elegant interior was designed by John Baird II (1876). See also Clarke and Bell's magnificent City and County Buildings of 1844

and Trades House, a charitable institution in Glassford Street, built by Robert Adam in 1791, worth visiting for the Venetian windows and Ionic columns of the façade.

Mitchell Library: South of Charing Cross is the green dome of the Mitchell Library (1906–11), which was designed by WB Whitie to house the public library founded in 1874 by Stephen Mitchell, a rich tobacco merchant. Today the library has over one million volumes and, unsurprisingly, gives pride of place to Scottish literature and the history of Glasgow.

Necropolis: Although the cemetery adjacent to Glasgow Cathedral is as old as the church, it was designed in the 1830s along the lines of the Père-Lachaise cemetery in Paris. It contains a profusion of abandoned tombs and neoclassical monuments erected in memory of great 19th-century industrialists and financiers. There is a statue of John Knox by William Warren and Robert Forrest, 1825, on top of a Doric column.

Pollok House: This beautiful Georgian house was built c1750 for the Maxwell family, owners of the vast Pollok Park estate since the 13th century. William Adam was involved in the design, but the extent to which his scheme was used is uncertain. The elegantly furnished rooms provide the ideal setting for Britain's finest private collection of Spanish paintings (El Greco, Velázquez, Murillo, Goya) as well as paintings by Italian, Flemish and English masters. The collection was assembled by William Stirling Maxwell (1818–78). Sir John Stirling Maxwell added the Entrance Hall and the formal French-style gardens in 1890–1908.

Provand's Lordship: The oldest house in Glasgow (3 Castle Street) was probably built in 1471 for the priest in charge of St Nicholas Hospice, which has since disappeared. Today it houses a reconstruction of an early 16th-century parlour, as well as various objects and furniture evoking the building's long history. The Garden of St Nicholas, at the back of the building, is filled with medieval medicinal plants.

St Mungo Museum of Religious Life and Art: This fascinating museum (2 Castle Street) compares the world's major religions and traces the religious history of Scotland. The many religious works of art include Salvador Dali's famous *Christ of St John of the Cross* (1951). Its tall 16th-century-style building was designed by Ian Begg, 1989–90.

St Vincent Street Church: This colonnaded church, built on monumental foundations and surmounted by a slender tower, is one of the few surviving churches by Alexander Thomson. It was built in 1857–9 and combines Egyptian, Greco-Roman and Indian architectural styles. Behind its austere façade lies an interior bathed in light from the spectacular windows and richly coloured by the reds, greens and blues of its walls,

cornices, friezes and cast-iron columns. It has recently been restored by the World Monuments Fund in Britain.

Scotland Street School Museum of Education: The school was designed by Charles Rennie Mackintosh, 1904–6. It is now a museum that traces the development of the Scottish education system from the Victorian age to the present day.

Trongate: The Tolbooth Steeple, a solid, square tower was added to St Mary's Church in 1625–7. The 15th-century church was accidentally burned down in 1793 by members of the Hell Fire Club after an evening's drinking. It was replaced with a building designed by James Adam and is today occupied by the Tron Theatre. Glasgow Cross, to the east of Merchant City, has a market cross (1929), a replica of the

Top: Portrait of the Glasgow
tobacco merchant John
Glasford and his family, by
Archibald McLauchlin (c1767),
in the Kelvingrove Art Gallery.

**Bottom left, centre and
below**: Provand's Lordship.
Built in 1471 as an almshouse,
it has also served as an
alehouse, and is now a
museum of domestic
interiors and artefacts
reflecting its long history.

original. It was the heart of the medieval city and remained a nerve centre
until the end of the Victorian age. Tolbooth Steeple is all that remains of the
17th-century building that served as a town hall, prison and law court. In front
stood the public weighbridge (tron), which determined the amount of tax to
be paid on merchandise entering the city.

Willow Tea Rooms: Like the three other tea rooms owned by Miss Kate
Cranston, the Willow Tea Rooms (217 Sauchiehall Street) were entirely
designed and decorated by Charles Rennie Mackintosh. Kate Cranston was
one of the architect's fervent admirers and a member of a temperance society.
She decided to fight drunkenness by opening sophisticated establishments
that would attract regulars away from the pubs. The Tea Rooms, open
between 1904 and 1926, were restored in 1980.

Above and top: Glastonbury. The remains of the monastic buildings, c1185, lie near to the small market town, whilst only the tower is left of the late-13th-century Church of St Michael (Glastonbury Tor).

Top left and left: Glen Coe, site of the infamous massacre.

Below: Glendurgan Garden, renowned for its spring flowers and glimpses of the Helford River.

Bottom: Glenfinnan. The West Highland Railway, opened in 1901, crosses a 98-feet (30m) high viaduct before arriving at Glenfinnan station.

Glastonbury, Somset 689 H4, There are two great legends linked to this bustling town, with its Victorian market cross at the centre. Joseph of Arimathea is said to have journeyed to Glastonbury from the Holy Land, intent on converting the British, and to have buried the Holy Grail (the cup used by Christ at the Last Supper) beneath a spring at Tor Hill, to the east of the present town. He is also supposed to have built a chapel where the Abbey was later constructed. A few remains are left, some merely foundations in the grass. The transept side of the Abbey Church (1184) rears up symmetrically, the masonry remains of doors and arches cut off against the sky. There are also claims that Tor Hill is the legendary Avalon, the burial-place of King Arthur.

Glen Coe, Highld 698 D2, This deep, narrow valley is bounded by barren mountains, including Bidean nam Bian (3743 feet/1140m), the highest point in Argyll, and its foothills, the Three Sisters of Glen Coe: Beinn Fhada, Gearr Aonach and Aonach Dubh. In addition to its harsh beauty and Highland flora and fauna, the infamous massacre that took place in the glen in 1692 has made it a site of historic interest. The Glencoe Centre at Clachaig has a presentation on the geology and history the valley. Further along the valley the Glencoe Ski Centre has a chair-lift that climbs to 2,300 feet (701m) and

offers a spectacular view of the village of Glencoe and Rannoch Moor. From the eastern end of Glen Coe, a minor road runs southwest along the glacial valley of Glen Etive to Loch Etive.

Glendurgan Garden, Cnwll 688 C8, Strung out along the Helford River are some exceptional gardens created by the Fox family. Members of this Quaker shipping-agent dynasty made holiday homes for themselves at Glendurgan and Trebah*, both deep valleys protected from the prevailing winds, where magnolias, tree ferns and camellias all flourish. Glendurgan [NT] also has an unusual laurel maze created in 1837.

Glenelg Bay, Highld 700 E6, From Shiel Bridge a small road crosses Mam Ratagan Pass and passes to the west of the village of Glenelg whose name ('Glen of the Irish') may be an indication of its first inhabitants. The region has a number of brochs (round forts), including Dun Telve, the best-preserved broch on the Scottish mainland, and Dun Troddan. Near Glenelg are the remains of Bernera Barracks (built in 1723 and abandoned in 1790), the most westerly outpost built by the Redcoats to counter the Jacobite threat.

Glenfinnan, Highld 700 E7, This little village is steeped in Jacobite history. It was here, at the north end of Loch Shiel, that Charles Edward Stuart rallied the Highland clans to support his cause on 19 August 1745 and from here that he set out, at the head of an army of 1,300 men, on the epic adventure that was to end so tragically at Culloden* on 16 April 1746. The event is commemorated by a column surmounted by the statue of a kilted Highlander (1815), and each year a Highland Gathering is held in a nearby field on the Saturday nearest 19 August .

Gloddaeth Hall, Conwy, The Tudor house, now St David's College, has retained its principal feature: the 16th-century Great Hall, with its intricate painted plaster canopy at the dais end. The fireplace bears the Mostyn family motto: 'Heb Dduw heb ddim; Duw a digon' ('Without God, nothing; With God, an abundance').
See **Llandudno*** 692 E1.

Gloucester

Gloucester, Gloucs 690 B4, Surprisingly, the city has its own harbour master although it has always been an inland port. The cathedral rises up above the lowest crossing point of the Severn, and looks down on a recently excavated 2-acre (0.8ha) Roman forum. The two main streets crossing nearby run on Roman lines. The city's museum contains the oldest-known backgammon set, along with paintings by Turner. Despite its heritage, Gloucester remains a down-to-earth place with a twice-weekly influx of cattle farmers going to the livestock market.

The **cathedral** has something in common with the 'wool' churches of the county, although there are plenty of hints of its previous use as the church of a Benedictine monastery dating from c679. The cloister contains 20 perfect carrels, or stone seats, where the monks studied in silence outside their library, and also a long lavatorium for communal washing. The nave, dominated by heavy Norman pillars, forms the first chapter of the textbook collection of architectural styles from different periods that makes up the rest of the fabric. The cathedral has several superb Renaissance tombs, including Thomas Machen's in the north aisle. He and his wife are shown with their four small sons and four small daughters, and their three tiny dead children. Round the corner, John and Ann Bower inhabit a battlemented castle with their 16 painted offspring. But the best-known tomb here is Edward II's, with its alabaster figure. His body was brought over after his murder at Berkeley Castle* in 1327, and his final resting-place drew pilgrims from afar. The other notable feature of the cathedral is the great east window, filled with some scenes from daily life as well as saints, and the devices of those who fought at the Battle of Crécy in 1346.

Above: The docks, begun in the 18th century, were finally superseded by those at Bristol.

Gloucester began to suffer in the early-19th century as bigger ships found Bristol a more convenient entrance to England; but in 1827 the Sharpness Canal was opened to make ship traffic less dependent on the Severn, and the area of warehouses around the docks was the result of the revived business of importing grain. Fourteen warehouses still stand, and now form a vibrant tourist and shopping centre. The Robert Opie Museum of Packaging, the National Waterways Museum, the Regiments of Gloucestershire Museum and the pleasure boats moored at the quay are all interesting.

Above: Gloucester Cathedral. The massive Norman piers of the nave were built between 1089 and 1260.

Above right: The cloister. The cathedral was used as a setting for the film *Harry Potter and the Philosopher's Stone* (2001).

Right: Romano-Celtic head from the Bon Marché, on display in the City Museum and Art Gallery.

Glynde Place, E Susx 691 G7, An Elizabethan mansion, much altered; it is worth visiting for the works of art that it contains, especially the portraits and 18th-century Italian masterpieces. The gate piers have appealing lead wyverns by John Cheere.

Glyndebourne, E Susx 691 G7, Famous for its opera house, founded in the 1930s by John Christie, a music-loving millionaire, and in 1995 rebuilt on a much larger scale; the summer opera season, with champagne-and-strawberry picnics during the interval and ladies and gentlemen in evening dress, is now rather less exclusive than it once was.

Glynllifon, Conwy 692 D2, On the A499 Caernarfon* to Pwllheli road stands the proudly imperial screen surmounted by a lion and eagles that proclaims the entrance to the estate of a once-powerful Welsh family. The red-brick home that Sir Thomas Wynn (the 1st Lord Newborough) built in 1757 went up in flames in 1836, and was replaced during the next ten years by a vast neoclassical stucco mansion. Alas, this has now been insensitively institutionalized. The grounds, open to the public, are worth exploring, and have a grotto, a rustic cottage, a mausoleum and, intriguingly, Fort Williamsburg (1761), built in case of a French invasion. Wynne also built Fort Belan, at the entrance to the Menai Strait.

Above: Godalming towpath runs for 20 miles (32km) along the River Wey.

Right: Glynllifon, the handsome front. It was built by the 3rd Lord Newborough to replace a mid-18th-century house destroyed by fire in 1836.

Gobions, Herts 691 F4, All that survives of the house that belonged to Sir Thomas More and his family is the Folly Arch, a castellated gateway of c1750.

Godalming Navigations, Surrey 690 E6, The River Wey opened to barge traffic in 1653 and offered a valuable new trade route between Guildford and London. In 1764, the Godalming Navigation opened, enabling barges to move a further 4 miles (6.4km) upriver. The whole section of water is now maintained by the National Trust, and the pretty 20-mile (32km) towpath is open to walkers. *Reliance*, a restored Wey barge moored at the historic Dapdune Wharf in Guildford, contains an interesting display on the waterway's past. Exploration of the area can be done on foot, by canoe, rowing boat, or even by horsedrawn barge.

Top left: Godinton Park, the east façade (1628), in an up-to-date style with much emphasis on shaped gables. The wide bay windows flanking the entrance were added in 1631–2. This whole brick front conceals a much older house behind (14th century).

Goddards, Surrey 691 F6, An imposing house built by Sir Edwin Lutyens in 1898–1900 and reworked by him in 1909–10. It started life as a ladies' hostel and has a delightful garden laid out by Gertrude Jekyll.

Godinton Park, Kent 691 H6, A sumptuous 17th-century house near Ashford, concealing a 14th-century core. It has an ambitious staircase and a fine Great Chamber with a vast Jacobean chimneypiece. It also houses an impressive collection of pictures, Chippendale and other furniture, and English and continental porcelain. The formal garden was laid out by Sir Reginald Blomfield in 1900.

Godolphin House, Cnwll 688 C8, The ancient seat of the Godolphins, whose most illustrious member was the 1st Earl, Lord Treasurer to Queen Anne and great friend and financier of the great Duke of Marlborough. The colonnaded façade with its

massive Tuscan columns dates to the 1630s and fronts an earlier 15th-century wing and later apartments, which include the King's Room. This handsome and brightly lit apartment contains part of the elaborately carved wooden screen that once

Godolphin Park
Left: The second courtyard looking to the first-floor King's Room.
Right: The panelled Dining Room in the 15th-century wing.

Bottom left: Goddards, now run by the Landmark Trust.

Bottom right: Goodnestone Park. The circular vestibule, with niches and delicately painted floral decoration, was probably designed by Robert Mylne in 1770.

stood in the Great Hall, demolished in the time of the Earl's descendants, who had become the dukes of Leeds. During their tenure, it declined to the level of a large farm, which proved its saving: its tenants allowed the garden layout of the early 1600s, the many ancient hut circles, medieval rabbit warrens and mining remains on the hill to lie undisturbed. Although the house is still occupied, it is regularly open to the public.

Golden Cap, Dorset 689 H6, The highest cliff in southwestern England, at 617 feet (188m), affording breathtaking views along the coastal path to Portland Bill* [NT].

Golden Valley, Herefs and Worcs 693 F6, The valley of the River Dore in Hereford and Worcestershire reaches into the eastern foothills of the Black Mountains; its network of lanes provides beautiful drives and mountain views. Of its

villages, Rowlstone Church has Norman carving, and Abbeydore* has substantial monastic remains.

Goodnestone Park Gardens, Kent 691 J5, An 18th-century house, surrounded by 14-acre (6 ha) grounds, including a woodland area and walled garden. Jane Austen stayed here after her brother Edward married a daughter of the owners.

Goodrich Castle, Herefs 693 G6, Much of the fabric of Goodrich has survived, including a flimsy bridge over a moat, leading to the monumental D-shaped barbican. The white Norman keep stands surrounded by later ranges of apartments and a curtain wall in red sandstone. These include two suites of grand rooms as well as a substantial

Goodrich Castle
Left: The 12th-century keep still stands three storeys high.
Below right: The entrance is through the barbican to the right.

Goodwood
Below: The Egyptian State Dining Room, designed by James Wyatt in 1802, was one of the earliest and most scholarly exercises in the Egyptian Revival, using yellow scagliola and bronze. In 1906 it was dismantled and was entirely reconstructed between 1996 and 1998.
Bottom right: The house seen from the park.

and largely intact suite for the castellan in the gatehouse. The wide dry moat was cut deep into the bedrock, and out of it rise four round towers, each with Goodrich's distinctive corner bastioning. The towers have stunning views over the Wye below, and the ferry crossing where 18th-century steamers moored and disgorged tourists visiting the castle. The views are also shared by the sad remains of Edward Blore's fantastic 19th-century counterpart to the Castle, the mock-medieval Goodrich Court. Estate buildings in the same arch-gothic style survive in the village, including 'Ye Olde Hostelrie', which nevertheless dates from about 1830 [EH].

Goodwood, W Susx 690 E7, A house by James Wyatt of about 1790. It was intended to be much bigger, on a highly original octagonal plan, but only three of the eight wings were built. Inside are some impressive neoclassical rooms, including the Tapestry Room and the Library, containing a number of fine paintings (with works by Stubbs and Canaletto). Goodwood is best known for its racecourse; the monumental stables (1757–63) are by Sir William Chambers.

Top left: Gorhambury, as rebuilt 1777–84, painted by Felix Kelly, 1983.

Below left: Sir Francis Bacon, Viscount St Albans, by Paul van Somer.

Below centre: Mary Grimston (1657–c1695), daughter of the 3rd Baronet, by William Wissing.

Below right: The remains of the courtyard house built 1563–8 by Sir Nicholas Bacon, Lord Keeper of the Great Seal of Elizabeth I.

Gorhambury House, Herts,

This was once the seat of Sir Nicholas Bacon, Lord Keeper of the Great Seal under Elizabeth I, and elder brother to Francis. All that now remains of the 16th-century house is the fine early-Renaissance porch; the rest was demolished in 1787. It was replaced by the Palladian house we see today, commissioned by the 3rd Viscount Grimston in 1777–84. The architect was Sir Robert Taylor, who designed the villa along the standard Palladian format of a central block joined to two side wings by low-level links, but on a vast scale. In the early-19th century the north wing and link were raised and enlarged, but the south wing and link suffered the same fate as the Elizabethan house and were demolished. Despite this the house remains impressive, with a commanding giant

Corinthian portico on the entrance front. It was re-faced with Portland stone in 1957–67. When the Grimston family bought the Bacon house in 1651, they also acquired the furniture, which is on display inside. The large entrance hall contains two screens of enamelled glass from the old house. There are portraits and busts of both the Bacon and Grimston families. Other works of art include three beautiful paintings by Sir Nathaniel Bacon, one of the most talented English 17th-century painters. The house also boasts two stunning fireplaces by Piranesi. See **St Albans* 691 F4.**

Goring-by-Sea, W Susx 691 F7, The Catholic church looks unprepossessing, but those who enter are in for a surprise. It is covered by a complete replica (on a reduced scale) of Michelangelo's ceiling of the Sistine Chapel in Rome. The work is skilfully done, and gives a better idea of the original than any reproduction in a book. Nearby is Highdown Gardens, laid out in 1909 in a disused chalk pit.

Goring Heath, Oxon 690 D5, The charming almshouses were built in 1724 by the then Mayor of London, Henry Alnutt. The central chapel contains the original pulpit, altar rails and some of the pews.

Gorsey Bigbury, Somset 689 H4, A Bronze Age sanctuary near Cheddar Gorge*; on view is the earthwork, a circular enclosure 160 feet (48m) across.

Gosfield Hall, Essex 691 H3, Sir James Thornhill's ceiling fresco in the entrance of an Elizabethan and Palladian mansion – at one time the Courtaulds' country seat, now a retirement home – remains intact. A footpath through the park leads to St Katherine's Church and Rysbrack's baroque sculpture of Sir John Knight and his wife.

Gower Peninsula (Penrhyn Gŵyr), 688 E3, One of the most remarkable promontories in Wales, stretching from between Swansea* Bay and Carmarthen* Bay, and reaching its most western point at Worm's Head. Accessible for only two hours either side of low tide, Worm's Head attracts walkers and naturalists; the less active can still admire its primeval shape at the end of the broad grassy cliff-top walk from the tiny village of

Below: Gower Peninsula, the wide sweep of Rhosili Bay.

Rhosili, with its scattered white cottages and grey church with saddleback tower. The enormous sweeping beach stretches northward. Untouched by modern development, it is accessible only on foot, with one solitary white house standing between the sand and Rhosili Downs. On the northern side of the beach near Llangennith are the remains of an Iron-Age hill fort occupying a site on Burry Holms, a tidal island like Worm's Head. Excavations in the 1960s disclosed the remains of a 12th-century chapel, probably attached to a medieval hermitage. The Gower Peninsula was designated an Area of Outstanding Natural Beauty in 1957, the first in Britain.

Gowthorpe Manor, Norfk 695 J5, A Tudor manor acquired by the grandfather of Anne Boleyn between 1494 and 1505, and much altered over the centuries. There is an oak-framed spiral staircase, added c1550. It can be visited by appointment.

Goxhill Priory, Lincs 697 K6, Sometimes called Goxhill Hall, a 14th-century moated house with a vaulted undercroft.

Grantham, Lincs 694 E4, Clearly a highway town, which takes much of its character from the fact that the Great North Road passed through the centre (it is now bypassed). There are countless inns, notably the Angel and Royal Hotel, where King Richard III signed the Duke of Buckingham's death warrant. Its carved stone front is 15th century. The other conspicuous

building, a monument to the medieval wealth accumulated from the wool trade, is the church of St Wulfram, which has a staggeringly tall spire.

Grantown-on-Spey, Highld 701 J5, This elegant little town on the banks of the River Spey was laid out in 1776 by the then laird, Sir James Grant. It became a famous health spa whose popularity was further boosted by Queen Victoria's visit in 1860. As well as a winter-sports resort and salmon-fishing centre, it is the departure point for walks along Strath Spey. It also has its own museum. On the northern edge of the town is Castle Grant, built in 1563 and refurbished by John Adam in 1753–6 and 1765.

Above: Gravesend, Milton Chantry has been used as the chapel of a leper hospital, a tavern and, in 1780, part of a fort.

Right and below left: Grasmere, Dove Cottage, where Wordsworth lived from 1799 to 1808.

Grasmere, Cumb 696 E4, More than any other part of the Lake District*, Grasmere is associated with Wordsworth. **Dove Cottage** [NT], an attractive piece of Lakeland vernacular architecture, was where the poet lived a romantic, simple life from 1799 to 1808, a period that is meticulously recorded in his sister Dorothy's journal. He then moved to larger and more formal premises at Rydal Mount* nearby, where he stayed until his death in 1850 – just long enough for him to campaign against the threat that he thought the railways would bring to his beloved Lake District. Both houses now display Wordsworth memorabilia and furnishings from his day.

Graveney, Kent 691 H5, A very attractive, unspoiled church, mostly of the 14th century: it contains notable brasses (1381 and 1436).

Gravesend, Kent 691 G5, Milton Chantry is the chapel of a 14th-century leper hospital at Gravesend, later used as an inn.

Great Altcar, Lancs 696 E7, On the flat lands between Liverpool* and Southport*, this village has an exquisite timber-framed church by John Douglas, built 1879 and following the Cheshire tradition from villages such as Peover*.

Great Amwell, Herts 691 F4, A place which, despite its importance, has managed to stay secluded and utterly unspoilt. As the name suggests, the village houses a great well, which was tapped by Sir Hugh Myddelton for the creation of his New River (1609–13), a successful scheme to provide better drinking water for London. The river makes a beautiful sight in the centre of the village; it has two islands bearing monuments to Myddelton, one of them an urn (1800) erected by the architect Robert Mylne. Towering high above this delightful spot is the medieval church of St John the Baptist, with its Norman apse and pretty graveyard.

Great Bookham, Surrey 691 F6, The church contains various monuments. The best is that to Cornet Geary of 1776, with Britannia mourning over a portrait medallion.

Great Brington, Nhants 694 D6, Business has boomed at Great Brington post office, near Althorp*, since the death of Diana, Princess of Wales brought the village to the world's attention, and many of its customers are now Japanese. It is a typically pretty Northamptonshire village in a dirty-yellow stone, and the church contains the outstanding fan-vaulted Spencer chapel with Renaissance effigies, including that of William, Lord Spencer, by Nicholas Stone, and the extraordinary figure of Sir Edward Spencer in the process of being resurrected from his funerary urn.

Great Canfield, Essex 691 G4, Hidden away in the upper Roding valley are well-preserved earthworks, vestiges of de Vere's Norman castle, and a nearby Romanesque church with an elaborate south doorway and a lovingly depicted Virgin and Child mural (c1250).

Great Chalfield Manor, Wilts 690 B5, Between Bradford-on-Avon* and Melksham is this superb

Great Chalfield
Above: The manor house is surrounded by a moat and defensive wall.
Below: The Great Hall.

Top right: Great Brington church, the monument to John, 1st Earl Spencer (d. 1783), designed by Cipriani and carved by Nollekens.

Right: Great Comp Garden hosts a festival of chamber music in the summer.

late-15th-century manor house [NT] enclosed by a moat and a defensive wall. The Great Hall has a dais for the high table, and there are good oriel windows – the window of the Great Chamber, on the first floor of the east wing, has a lierne-vaulted ceiling with three pendants. In the adjacent church of All Saints, the wagon-roofed Tropenell Chapel was completed about 1480.

Great Comp Garden, Kent 691 G5, A large and very impressive garden with a varied collection of trees, walks, ruins and lawns laid out round a 17th-century manor house near West Malling. A festival of chamber music is held in the summer.

Great Coxwell, Oxon 690 C4, The manor of Great Coxwell once belonged to Beaulieu Abbey* in Hampshire, which explains the magnificent 13th-century tithe barn [NT] that survives here, divided by posts into nave and aisles. The stone-built barn was considered by William Morris to be 'as noble as a cathedral'.

Great Cressingham Manor, Norfk 695 H5, The remains of a brick house built in 1545, with a decorative frieze carved on the south front featuring a hawk, wreaths and leaves.

Great Linford, Bucks 690 E3, Great Linford retains its attractive ensemble of church, manor house and almshouses. The almshouses flank a two-storey, Dutch-gabled school house of 1696–7.

Great Malvern, Worcs 693 H5, Once compared to an Indian hill station, the town does have something of the same air of genteel retirement as it creeps up the sides of the Malvern Hills. The best hotels are higher up, with astounding views over the Vale of Evesham. When Elgar lived in Malvern his house faced this way, and his works are often considered anthems to this stretch of English countryside. Queen Victoria added greatly to the town's prestige by coming to take the waters, which have a remarkably low mineral content as they filter quickly through the granite to over 60 springs. The remains of the Priory form the nucleus of a

splendid collection of 19th-century hotels and villas. There is also the Winter Garden Concert Hall, where George Bernard Shaw promoted the annual Malvern Festival.

Great Maytham Hall, Kent, 691 H6, A 1909 house by Sir Edwin Lutyens in his most classical style. The centre block incorporates a house of 1721.

Great Tew, Oxon 690 D3, A beautiful and memorable little village, created mainly in the early 19th century. It is the epitome of English picturesque,

Centre left: Great Malvern Priory Church of Saints Mary and Michael.

Centre and centre right: Great Warley church, crowned by a typical Essex spire. The interior is bedecked with fabulous Art Nouveau fittings.

Left: Great Maytham, one of Edwin Lutyens' largest and most classical houses.

Below: Great Tew, a charming thatched cottage.

with thatched cottages and gardens bursting with delphiniums, hollyhocks and lupins.

Great Torrington, Devon 688 E5, Sometimes known as the 'English Jerusalem' – because of its position on a high escarpment, clustering around the castle and protected by a horseshoe bend in the River Torridge – the town is visited principally by those interested in its large glassworks. Its centre, however, possesses some attractive buildings that include the Market House (1842) and the nearby

Town Hall (of 1861, but still Georgian in style). The church of St Michael was rebuilt after it was largely destroyed by an explosion during the Civil War, whose other casualties are said to be buried in the large mound in the churchyard.

Great Warley, Essex 691 G4, St Mary's, designed by Charles Harrison Townsend, is a temple to Art Nouveau: a dove-crowned spire, silvery apse and banded, barrel-vaulted nave festooned with lilies and a screen of espaliered brass trees with bunches of red pomegranates.

Great Witcombe, Gloucs 690 B4, There is a Roman villa here in a very quiet spot by a stream. The mosaics are in a roofed building that is only occasionally open, but the remains of the villa's walls and octagonal dining room are always accessible [EH].

Great Yarmouth

Great Yarmouth, Norfk 695 K5, The River Yare, from which Yarmouth takes its name, eventually reaches the sea 3 miles (4.8km) south, deflected in its purpose by a long sand spit that has shaped the town's growth. A settlement was well established when Yarmouth received its royal charter in 1208 and began the system of fortification – 10 gates and 16 towers, 3 of which survive. The main religious orders were quickly established and there are considerable remains of the Franciscan Friary in no. 91 Middlegate; but it was the closely packed alleyways called The Rows that gave the medieval town its distinctive character. Of these – there were over 200 until the last war, hung with nets and thronged with children – little remains. Restored 17th-century merchants' houses only hint of old glory days, but the bombs and bulldozers have done their worst.

Among notable survivals are the birthplace of Anna Sewell, author of *Black Beauty*, and nearby the charming early-18th-century Fisherman's Hospital. The church of St Nicholas, despite a direct hit and some unimaginative restoration, remains England's largest parish church. In the churchyard the young George Belloe's headstone vividly records an earlier disaster in 1845 when the town's suspension bridge collapsed in a storm. St George's survives unscathed, an impressive and unusual Georgian design by John Price of 1714, complete with galleries. Other maritime monuments include William Pilkington's huge quadrangular

Above left: The 1720 Customs House.

Above: The royal coat-of-arms on the side wall of the South Quay Customs House.

Left: Exterior and interior of the medieval Merchant's House, in the care of English Heritage.

Top left: John Price's early 18th-century brick church, complete with delicate two-stage lantern, crouches beside St George's Plain.

Top right: A house in the famous Rows.

Royal Hospital of 1810, in pale yellow brick; further south the crumbling Norfolk Pillar of 1819, a 144-foot (44m) column to Nelson by William Wilkins, stands forlornly in a wasteland of factories.

South Quay, deemed by Daniel Defoe the loveliest in England, is where the wealthy merchants built their houses; notably the Customs House (1720) for John Andrews, said to have been the greatest herring merchant in Europe, and the refronted Elizabethan House Museum with its remarkable plaster ceiling and Conspiracy Room where Charles I's trial was allegedly plotted. The Maritime Museum for East Anglia, in a former refuge for shipwrecked sailors, is a joy.

The Dutch ran much of the herring industry, and their contribution to life on Yarmouth beach was captured by several Norwich School artists, especially the brilliant watercolourist JS Cotman, who lived in the town 1812–23. The beach was immortalized in *David Copperfield* with Peggotty's upturned boat on South Denes.

The neon-lit town that gave us the bloater, kipper and fish finger is now more gaudy than great. The transformation from fishing port to seaside resort began when the railways brought the first train-loads of holidaymakers from the industrial north to bask on its golden sands. Britannia Pier and The Pavilion, though much altered, are the two great examples of seaside fantasy architecture. The Winter Gardens, a Torquay Crystal Palace re-created here in 1903, is now a beer garden in a resort inclined to the surreal, where day trippers from the Lancashire mill towns still mingle with Texan oil-rig engineers to the sound of Dolly Parton records.

Greathed Manor, Surrey 691 G6, A little south of Lingford is an imposing example of Victorian eccentricity built in 1868 by the architect Robert Kerr (see Bearwood*). Kerr appears to have included something of everything in the long frontage: a Dutch gable, an English gable, a French pavilion roof and an Italianate tower.

Below: Gregynog. The brick house built by Charles Hanbury-Tracy in 1837 was recast (in painted concrete) as a half-timbered house c1870.

Greenfield Valley, Flints, A walk through the Greenfield Valley, now effectively interpreted through displays and signs, admirably illustrates the economic history of this part of Wales. Agriculture, lead and copper smelting, and the making of brass and wire were all dependent on hydraulic power, which, according to Dr Johnson

and Mrs Thrale's account of their Welsh journey of 1774, 'turns 19 mills…and an opportunity of seeing the cutting of a bar of iron at a stroke.' See **Basingwerk Abbey* 693 F2.**

Greensted-juxta-Ongar, Essex 691 G4, The romantic stave church of St Andrew's has a weather-boarded late-medieval tower and cottage-like dormer windows in the nave roof. Norman flint, Tudor brick and Victorian glass complement 9th-century Saxon carpentry, which includes nave walls of cleft oak trees.

Gregynog, Powys 693 F4, Located near the village of Tregynan, this house was bought by Miss Gwendolen and Miss Margaret Davies after World War I, and is very much part of 20th-century Welsh cultural history. It was the home

of the Gregynog private press (1923–40), which produced 42 books as well as programmes for the festivals held at the house. The former billiards room was extended to make a Music Room, where Gustav Holst and Ralph Vaughan Williams played their compositions. The sisters were avid collectors, and their bequest of Impressionist and Post-Impressionist paintings is now one of the major attractions of the National Museum of Wales in Cardiff*. The mock-Tudor house of 1837, built on a much older site, was bequeathed to the University of Wales as a conference centre. The Gregynog Press was restarted here in 1975; more recently the festival tradition has also been revived, under the directorship of the tenor Anthony Rolfe-Johnson.

Gresford, Wrexhm 693 F2, All Saints Church, along with St Giles at Wrexham*, is one of the 'Seven Wonders of Wales'. It was built under the patronage of Margaret Beaufort, the mother of Henry VII. Opposite is an ensemble of early 18th-century almshouses and a charity school. The interior is joyfully light, and rich in monuments. A recent addition is the depiction of the Gresford Disaster, an underground explosion in which over 250 died, and which is also commemorated in the local park. The Trevor Chapel is dedicated to the life of John Trevor of Trefalun, whose family seat, Trefalun Hall*, can be seen from the main road between Gresford and Rossett.

Gressenhall, Norfk 695 H5, An excellent rural life museum in the old Georgian workhouse with fascinating insights into 18th- and 19th-century country life in Norfolk. Home Farm is a 1920s working unit with traditional breeds.

Gretna Green, D & G 696 E2, In the 18th century this village on the English–Scottish border specialized in elopements, the law at that time being more liberal in Scotland than in England. Until 1940 many of these marriages were held in the Old Smithy, now a museum. Some couples still choose to take their marriage vows here.

Grime's Graves, Norfk 695 H5, The mounds and hollows of Grime's Graves, in a forest clearing, form Britain's largest group of neolithic flint mines [EH]. There is a new exhibition centre and one of the 360 pits is open to the public: a ladder descends into low tunnels where the flint was dug out with antlers before it was fashioned into tools and weapons. The name may have been coined by Anglo-Saxons who perceived 'graves' (here meaning depressions) as being created by 'Grime', a nickname for Woden, god of war and magic. This most powerful Saxon deity was later linked to Satan and to many eerie earthworks in the country (such as Devil's Ditch*).

Grimspound, Devon 689 F6, High on Dartmoor lies a Late Bronze Age enclosure with a river running through it. Sixteen circular huts are found within, the homes of farmers whose stock grazed these fields. There are also remains of store huts and cattle pens [EH].

Grimsthorpe Hall
Above: Sir John Vanburgh's Stone Hall of the 1720s.
Left: One side of the old house can be seen behind.

Right: Guildford House Gallery, portrait of Mr Seaton by John Russell.

and most happy-looking town that I ever saw in my life'. It is now the busy centre of Surrey, but still has picturesque qualities and some excellent buildings. In the steep main street is the elegant Guildhall, refronted in 1683, the Tudor Grammar School founded in 1509, and the adjoining red-brick Abbot's Hospital built in 1619–22 by George Abbot, Archbishop of Canterbury. Guildford House Museum at 115 High Street features a range of changing exhibitions, some on the history of the town, and is contained in a superb town house of 1660. Note the carved staircase, wrought-iron work and plaster ceilings. To one side of the main street are the remains of the ancient castle, with its 11th-century motte and impressive 12th-century tower keep. In cobbled Castle Arch is the pretty, tile-hung front of the Guildford Museum, founded in 1898, behind

Grimsthorpe Hall, Lincs 694 E5, A magnificent muddle. The great north entrance front and the cavernous stone Great Hall behind it are the work of Sir John Vanbrugh, architect of Blenheim Palace* and Castle Howard*. Vanbrugh was employed to rebuild the whole house, but he died in 1726 and the Tudor house, built round a courtyard, with parts of a medieval castle still embedded in it, was left more or less untouched. The gardens are still partly formal, in a way that complements Vanbrugh's work.

Groombridge, E Susx 691 G6, This has two of Norman Shaw's best and most characteristic houses – Glen Aldred of 1867 and Leyswood of 1869. Both were crucial in the development of his relaxed, asymmetrical, brick and tile-hung vernacular houses. Leyswood was once much bigger – now only one range and a gatehouse remain. Across the county border in Kent, **Groombridge Place** is a well-preserved brick house of about 1600, surrounded by a moat, with classical features such as Ionic columns and gate-piers surmounted by pineapples. Inside are some Wren-period plaster ceilings.

Grosmont Castle, *see* **Three Castles*.**

Guildford, Surrey 690 E6, The essayist and politician William Cobbett described Guildford as 'the prettiest, and taken altogether the most agreeable

Right: Groombridge Place. The aerial view shows clearly how the 17th-century house was buit inside the courtyard of a (now demolished) medieval house surrounded by a square moat.

Gunby is said to be the 'haunt of ancient peace' mentioned in his poem 'The Palace of Arfi'.

Gunwalloe, Cnwll 688 C8, Behind the beach of powdered shells lies the half-submerged church of St Winwaloe, with its isolated tower looking out to sea. It was restored by Father Sandys Watson, the slightly eccentric incumbent, at whose rectory

which is assembled Surrey's largest collection of archeology, local history and needlework, with relics of local figures such as Gertrude Jekyll and Lewis Carroll. There is no historic cathedral at Guildford – the present building was started in 1936 to designs by Sir Edward Maufe – but there is the fine, mainly Norman church of St Mary. The River Wey was opened to barge traffic in 1653, creating an important new trade route between Guildford and London. Moored at the historic Dapdune Wharf is the *Reliance*, a restored Wey barge, which hosts an interesting display on the waterway's past.

Gunby Hall, Lincs 695 G3, A building of 1700, with wood-panelled interiors typical of that date and an attractive garden [NT]. Gunby was the home of the Massingberds since the 18th century, and has strong associations with the poet Alfred, Lord Tennyson who was born in the area.

Top left: Gunwalloe, Dollar Cove.

Gunby Hall
Top right: The box-like main house.
Below centre: One of the principal rooms.

Bottom: Groombridge Place, the entrance front with its Ionic columned porch sheltering the front doors.

Compton Mackenzie stayed when he was first married. The name of the nearby Dollar Cove commemorates the many coins that were washed up there from wrecked Spanish and Portuguese treasure ships. Sir John Betjeman frequented the Mullion golf links that overlook the church. He was so distracted by the beauty of the spot that he often hit balls into the sea.

Gwennap, Cnwll 688 C7, An oval auditorium formed by fallen mine workings, first visited by John Wesley, founder of Methodism, in 1762. It was here that he spoke to huge congregations, although the pit that we see today was remodelled in 1806 and is circular and smaller than the one that accommodated the 32,000 people recorded by Wesley. There has been an annual service of commemoration here since 1807. Gwennap parish is said to have provided more wealth from its tin and copper than any equivalent spot in the world.

Left: Gwydir Castle, though never fortified, gained its title 'Castle' in the 18th century, possibly because of the tower-like appearance of the wing.

Gwydir Castle, Gwynd, This was the seat of the illustrious Wynn family. Although much mutilated, first by fire and then by vandalism, this enigmatic house and its gardens are now being restored by its current owners. On the nearby thickly wooded hillside is Gwydir Uchaf Chapel, attached to the second and smaller of the two Wynn houses (now demolished). The ceiling, with its naively painted angels, the handsomely decorated gallery (1673) at the west end, and the Oxbridge inward-looking pews display the family pride. This is also evident in the Gwydir Chapel (1633) in the south transept of the parish church of St Grwst. This handsome, well-lit extension not only houses monuments to the family, but also reputedly the sarcophagus of Llywelyn Fawr (Llywelyn the Great) from nearby Maenan Abbey, where it had been originally brought from Aberconwy after Edward I's victory. On the way to the church are the Wynn alms-houses, now refurbished after years of neglect, and put again to community use. One of the last known Welsh harp-makers, for whom Llanrwst was a renowned centre, spent his final days here at the end of the 18th century. *See* **Llanrwst* 692 E2.**

Gyrn Castle, Flints 693 F1, The house owes its grand title to the castellations added in 1820 by John Douglas, a Lancashire cotton magnate, to a much older house – the front door porch is dated 1700. It was bought in the early 1850s by Edward Bates, the owner of a shipping fleet in Liverpool, which he was able to survey through binoculars from the tower of his Welsh estate with its magnificent views over the Dee and Mersey estuaries. The

Above: Haddo House, the Library, decorated and furnished in pioneer Adam revival by the London decorators Wright and Mansfield in 1880.

Below: Hackfall, the man-made Alum Springs, fed from a reservoir to fall over tufa. They were once viewed from a grotto known as Kent's Seat, now lost beneath the undergrowth.

house has a large purpose-built, top-lit picture gallery, a rare example of its kind in a Welsh country house.

Hackfall, N York 697 G5, This mid-18th century garden, created by William Aislabie of Studley Royal*, was a pioneering example of what was to become known as the 'sublime' style. Awe-inspiring and dramatic, with follies and waterfalls dotted among hanging woods, it became a place of pilgrimage for sightseers. The Banqueting House was designed to appear as a classical Roman bath-house on one side and a gothic folly on the other, looking out across the valley to a sham gothic castle. But Hackfall's isolated site eventually led to its decline in popularity, and in the mid-20th century the trees were sold for timber. Amazingly, however, the hanging woods have now regenerated. Rescued by the Woodland Trust, it is once again a wild and mysterious place, with stunning views of the River Ure, and has regained much of the atmosphere that prompted Wordsworth to recommend that tourists call here en route to the Lakes.

Haddington, E Loth 699 G4, The regional capital of East Lothian was granted a royal charter in 1147 and built its prosperity on a flourishing cloth, wool and cereal trade. John Knox was born here in 1505. In spite of repeated sieges and plundering raids, by the 16th century Haddington was Scotland's fourth largest town and went on to enjoy its golden age in the 18th century. It is still extremely attractive, with footpaths along the River Tyne and a great many listed buildings: the coloured façades of the High Street and Lodge Street (including the home of Jane Welsh, 1801–66, wife of the writer Thomas Carlyle), the Town House (town hall) built in the market place by William Adam in 1748, the 17th-century architecture of Mitchell's Close, in Market Street, and the private houses in Court Street. Near the river stands 14th–15th-century St Mary's Church, restored in the 19th and 20th centuries. It has some beautiful stained-glass windows, some of which are based on sketches by Edward Burne-Jones. In the Lauderdale aisle is the tomb of the Maitland family with its beautiful 17th-century alabaster recumbent statues.

Haddo House, Abers 702 D5, William Adam designed this symmetrical Palladian-style mansion just north of Pitmedden* for William Gordon, 2nd Earl of Aberdeen. In 1879–81 the 7th Earl and 1st Marquess of Aberdeen carried out some radical renovations: a hayloft was converted into an elegant library, and the architect GE Street designed the neo-gothic chapel (1876–81), whose huge stained-glass window is signed by Edward Burne-Jones. The private apartments house a fine collection of portraits.

Haddon Hall, Derbys 694 C3, This medieval, grey stone house is a wonderfully romantic jumble of battlemented walls, towers and chimneys, built round two small courtyards and standing on a wooded slope above the River Wye. It was abandoned by the Manners family in 1700 and at first sight remains pretty much as they left it, although in fact the house was superbly and sensitively restored by the 9th Duke of Rutland in the 1920s and 1930s. The house originally had one large central courtyard but in c1370 a range containing the Great Hall, kitchen and parlour was built across the middle, forming two smaller courts. A steep path leads to the gatehouse and then into the lower court. Here is the Chapel, with its medieval wall paintings and woodwork dating from the 1620s. The main living range is particularly interesting. The kitchens still have the medieval bread cupboards and wooden troughs for salting meat, all massive and highly insanitary. The Great Hall roof was replaced in the 1920s but the screen at one end dates from 1450.

The parlour beyond the hall is now essentially a Tudor room with a ceiling of about 1500 and panelling of the 1540s, both rare examples of the period. Upstairs are the Great Chamber, and the Long Gallery, with its beautifully carved panelling of about 1600. The room is made doubly attractive by the light streaming in through the large bay windows with their myriad diamond-shaped panes, or quarries, set at slight angles to each other so that they sparkle in the sunshine. The rooms at Haddon are sparsely furnished, but in some ways this is an advantage, being far more typical of early interiors than overfurnished rooms would be. The garden was laid out in the 17th century in a series of terraces, and now contains a fine collection of roses.

Top left: The Long Gallery.
Top right: The Tudor parlour.
Below: The courtyard.

Hadleigh, Suffk 691 H3, One of Suffolk's most pleasing small towns, nestling in the Brett Valley. Here, eclectic vernacular spanning six centuries is lovingly preserved, a delightful mix of gabled colourwash, pargeting and red brick. The church's broach spire rises for 135 feet (41m) above a 14th-century tower. The red-brick Deanery gatehouse is all that remains of Archdeacon Pykenham's palace, built in 1495, more than half a century after the timber-framed Guildhall, with its two overhanging upper storeys. The latter building, little altered and still used for local functions, abuts the 1851 Town Hall and the 1813 Corn Exchange. Toppesfield Hall now houses the Tourist Information Centre.

Hadrian's Wall, Nthumb 697 F2, Now a World Heritage Site and the most important Roman monument in Britain [EH & NT]. For 250 years Hadrian's Wall marked the northern edge of the Roman Empire. It ran westward from Wallsend on the Tyne to Bowness on the Solway. Ordered by the Emperor Hadrian in the 120s AD, the boundary structure consisted of a substantial stone wall with a ditch facing the 'barbarians' and an earthwork called the *vallum* on the southern side.

Above: Hadleigh, Archdeacon Pykenham's Tudor gatehouse.

Right and above right: Hagley Hall, the rich interiors contrast with the restraint of the exterior.

Below left: Hadrian's Wall, with the ditch facing the 'barbarians' and an earthwork on the south side.

The Wall climbed up hill and down dale, quite precipitously in places. In addition to forts, spaced about a day's march apart, there was a milecastle every Roman mile and, between each, two turrets. The turrets served as watchtowers, while the milecastles formed sheltered look-out positions and had a gateway through the border. Providing accommodation for Roman troops and their supplies, the forts were the shape of playing cards in plan, their surrounding walls forming a rectangle with rounded corners, and with imposing gateways in the sides from which roads intersected at right angles. At the main junction in the centre of each fort was its headquarters building, with the house for the commandant alongside. Around these were barrack blocks, storage buildings and other facilities, perhaps a hospital. Temples to various deities were

established in and around the forts, and altars and votive statues are to be found in many of the site museums. At Carrowburgh there is a *mithraeum*, or temple to the god Mithras, and nearby is Coventina's well, a shrine in which 13,490 coins were found in 1876. A civilian settlement, or *vicus*, grew up near most forts, so not all the archaeological discoveries made on the sites along Hadrian's Wall are military. *See also* **Arbeia Roman Fort*, Chesters Roman Fort*, Corbridge Roman Site*, Housesteads Roman Fort*** and **Vindolanda***.

Hadspen House, Somset 689 J5, A lovely walled nursery garden attached to Castle Cary.

Hagley Hall, Worcs 693 H4, A fine, early example of a picturesque landscape garden. It was created from

the undulating park in the Clent Hills that belonged to the 1st Lord Lyttelton (1709–73), and featured a ruined castle, temples and columns. Lyttelton, cruelly satirized by Tobias Smollett as 'a long, lean and misshapen Spectre' with 'a Neck of prodigious Extension,' retired to Hagley and its landscape improvements after disappointments in his political life. His picturesque projects included Sanderson Miller's famous gothic ruin of 1747, praised by Horace Walpole as possessing 'the true rust of the Barons' Wars,' and James 'Athenian' Stuart's Greek temple of 1758. The house itself, also designed by Sanderson Miller, has some similarities with Houghton*. The stark exterior contrasts with the rich rococo decoration inside; the White Hall, with a chimneypiece actually signed by the great plasterworker Francesco Vassalli, is a highlight, as is the Rococo Drawing Room. There are fine Soho Arabesque tapestries and portraits by Batoni, Ramsay and Van Dyck.

Hailes Abbey, Gloucs 690 C3, The peaceful country setting is the attraction here, made all the more allluring by the melancholy remains of the cloister [EH & NT]. Vigorous excavation in the 1960s revealed the footings of the east range and chapterhouse of a monastery founded in 1246 by Richard, Earl of Cornwall. Its most famous artefact was the Relic of the Holy Blood, a gift from the founder's son in 1270, which was a great attraction for pilgrims. It even merited an oath from Chaucer: 'By the blode of Crist that is in Hayles.' Although the Abbey formerly owned 13,000 acres of land, only 20 monks were left by the time of its dissolution in 1539. The Holy Blood, described at the time as 'an unctuous gum, discoloured', was thrown away.

Hailes Castle, E Loth 699 H4, The castle of the Hepburn family, a fine example of 13th- and 14th-century defensive architecture, was demolished by Cromwell in 1650. James Hepburn, the 4th Earl of Bothwell and third husband of Mary Stuart, stayed here with the Queen in 1567.

Haileybury College, Herts , The college was built as the training school for the East India Company in 1806–8 by William Wilkins. It is 42 bays long with a central portico and chapel. *See* **Hertford*** 691 F4.

Haldon Belvedere, Devon 689 F6, This triangular tower near Dunchideock, with corner turrets and gothic windows, was built in 1788 by Sir Robert Palk, a local landowner, in memory of his friend General Stringer Lawrence. An over-lifesize statue of the General in classical garb, modelled from Coade stone, stands on the ground floor. The upstairs rooms command magnificent views.

Hales, Norfk 695 J5, St Margaret's is the perfect Norman village church, with a round tower, thatched roof and apse, one of several near Loddon

Right: Hales, St Margaret's Church, a perfect little Norman church with a distinctive East Anglian round tower and curved apse.

that have Romanesque carving of the highest quality. The decorative panache of the door surrounds, with their rare Norman sculpture of a seated priest, suggests a single craftsman. At the end of a long green, Sir James Hobart, Attorney General to Henry VII, built a moated mansion. The Tudor gatehouse and 14-bay step-gabled barn at Hales Court form an impressive group belonging to the outer courtyard.

Right: Halifax Piece Hall, detail of cast-iron gates.

Below: Hall Place, a house of two periods, one chequered grey and white, the other red brick.

Halifax, W York 697 G6, Of the medieval town, the only remnant is the splendid church of St John, a large Perpendicular wool church. It has an intriguing poor box (1701) in the shape of 'Old Tristram', a life-size wooden figure of a man holding an alms box. **Shibden Hall,** a late-medieval timber-framed house later encased in stone, was once the home of the remarkable lesbian diarist Anne Lister (d. 1840), but now houses a museum. The **Piece Hall** is a monumental expression of the importance of the town's former cloth industry, built on an enormous scale in 1779 to provide individual rooms for the hundreds of merchants who traded in the 'pieces', or lengths of woollen cloth, produced in local cottages. Sir Charles Barry designed the magnificent town hall, 1859–62, with its tower and cortile-like central hall. George Gilbert Scott's All Souls Haley Hill, 1856–9, one of the country's finest, has a tall spire and is rich in sculpture.

Hall Place, Gt Lon 691 G5, A 16th-century house in Bexley, of which the hall and one range survive, with a 17th-century addition at the back. It has been much altered over the years and is now run as a museum by the local council. In front are some splendid 18th-century iron gates.

Halstead, Essex 691 H3, The long white weather-boarded Townsford Mill straddles the River Colne.

Originally a corn-mill, it was converted by Samuel Courtauld in the early-19th century for silk manufacture. The medieval church contains monuments to the Bourchier family of Stanstead Hall.

Halton, Bucks 690 E4, A Rothschild village, with many buildings displaying the five arrows of the family crest. Halton House was built for Baron Alfred de Rothschild in 1884 to designs by WR Rogers.

Hambledon, Surrey 690 E6, One of the best buildings in this picturesque Surrey village is Oakhurst Cottage [NT], a small timber-framed house of the 16th century with a typical cottage garden.

Hammerwood House, E Susx 691 G6, Virtually the only English work of Benjamin Latrobe, who emigrated to America in 1795 and became famous as the architect of Baltimore Catholic Cathedral and the porticos of the White House in Washington, DC. Hammerwood was built as a hunting lodge and demonstrates mastery of perspective and symbolism. The mirrored drawing room is unique.

Hampstead Norrey's, Berks 690 D5, In St Mary's Church is wonderful 13th-century relief sculpture, over 2 feet (60cm) high, of a knight on his charger.

Hamptworth Lodge, Wilts 690 C7, The architect Sir Guy Dawber rebuilt this Jacobean manor house at Landford, on the edge of the New Forest*, in 1910–12. Some of the Elizabethan and Jacobean overmantels came from Goodrich Court* in Herefordshire. The gardens are open to the public.

Hamstead Marshall, Berks 690 D5, The medieval church was remodelled in the 18th century, but retains excellent 17th-century furnishings, including box pews and a pulpit with tester.

Top left: Hamptworth Lodge. The house, with its picturesque elevations, is in the Tudor style, but mainly of 1910–12.

Top, centre and right, and above: Hammerwood House, built by Benjamin Latrobe as a hunting lodge.

Left: Hambledon, Oakhurst Cottage, one of several National Trust-owned cottages in the village. The garden has 16th-century plant species.

Hanbury Hall, Worcs 693 H5, The Hall, completed in 1701 (according to a date over the door), is the perfect substantial country home of a squire at the turn of the 18th century [NT]. The Vernon family used a local architect to build the red-brick pile with its rudimentary pedimented front, but the fashionable Sir James Thornhill himself painted the dramatic staircase. Outside is the curious detached Long Gallery, perhaps inspired by the Water Gallery at Hampton Court* which William III had recently demolished. The grounds hold an ice house capable of holding 24 tons of ice, which was cut from a pool in front of the building then taken along the 28-foot (8.5m) entrance passage.

Hanslope, Berks 690 E3, The elegant spire of St James soars towards the clouds. It was built with funds left by the rector Thomas Knight in 1414, and was 200 feet (60m) high before 20 feet (6m) were removed after lightning struck. The parapet is embattled with polygonal pinnacles, linked to the spire by pierced flying buttresses. The spire is octagonal and decorated with crockets.

Hanwell, Oxon 690 D3, The church was largely rebuilt in the 14th century and contains some fascinating carvings of figures and monsters. They were executed by a group of local masons whose work can be seen in other parishes of north Oxfordshire. East of the church is Hanwell Castle, a late 18th-century house that incorporates the remains of a medieval fortified house.

Harberton, Devon 689 F7, In a county famous for its elaborately carved medieval church screens, here is one of the best, but with paintings added during the restoration of 1870. Twenty-five years later Robert 'Tito' Harvey, scion of the family who lived at Dundridge, died at the age of ten. His memorial by the Exeter-based Harry Hems is very poignant. A life-like figure in marble, he lies there with his hands clasped with a lily across him. He is immortalized again in the family mausoleum in the churchyard, lying between his father and his mother with her 3-foot (0.9m) plaits.

Hardham, W Susx 690 E7, The church is renowned for its 12th-century wall-paintings. There are more of them than at Clayton* but they are less well preserved: most are now so faded that the subjects are unrecognizable. Over the chancel arch were Christ and the Doctors, the Annunciation and the Visitation. Even in their present state, they remind us that the interiors of medieval churches were covered in plaster and painted, in complete contrast to their present stony appearance.

Hardingstone, Nhants 694 E6, In this village to the south of Northampton* lies Delapré Park. It still follows the boundary of the meadow or 'pre' that gave its name to the Cluniac nunnery of Delapré Abbey, now absorbed into a later country house. At the park's edge stands the elaborate canopied 13th-century **Queen Eleanor's Cross.** Queen Eleanor died in Northamptonshire in 1290, and her forlorn husband Edward I set up crosses at each place where the procession carrying her body back to London stopped for the night. The final one was Charing Cross in London. This is one of only three original crosses still surviving.

Hardknott Roman Fort, Cumb 696 D4, Perhaps more spectacular for its setting among the Lakeland hills, and the twisting approach via Hardknott and Wrynose Passes, than for the ruined remains of the fort. Nevertheless the ruins, the plans partly set out in the grass, include the square enclosure, the commandant's house, the granaries and a bath-house [EH].

Hardwick Hall, Derbys 694 D3, Elizabeth, Countess of Shrewsbury, better known as Bess of Hardwick, married four times and rose further up the social ladder with each marriage. When she parted from her last husband (the Earl of Shrewsbury) and left his house at Chatsworth* she set about enlarging her family manor house at Hardwick. After the Earl's death in 1590 she began a completely new mansion a short distance from the old one. It was finished in seven years. Her architect was probably Robert Smythson, the best man of his day. The house is very tall, and built to an H plan with a tower at each end and two towers on either side. The buff stone walls, recently repaired, are pierced by huge mullioned windows which gave rise to the rhyme 'Hardwick Hall, more glass than wall'. Few Elizabethan houses look so crisp and modern. The central entrance door leads into the hall, which runs from the front to the back of the house, not across as is more usual. The rest of the ground floor was used mainly by the servants. The family living rooms are on the first floor and the state rooms, which were used only on great occasions, are on the top floor.

Many of these rooms still have their original furniture and wall-hangings. Embroideries, some of which were made by or for Mary Queen of Scots when in captivity in the Earl of Shrewsbury's other houses, contribute powerfully to the legend of her 'presence' at Hardwick. At the back of the hall the Great Staircase rises past the Private Drawing Room, which has 18th- and 19th-century furniture belonging to the late Duchess of Devonshire as well as Flemish tapestries belonging to Bess of Hardwick. The stairs are also hung with tapestries. At the top of the stair is the High Great Chamber, the main State Room, with a huge painted plaster frieze by Abraham Smith, who did a lot of the decorative work at Hardwick. The room was designed to fit the tapestry, which still lines the walls. Behind the chamber is the Long Gallery, running the full length of the house, its own tapestry-lined walls hung with portraits and lit by the enormous bay windows.

The two huge fireplaces were carved by Thomas Accres. A back staircase, hung with examples of the stitchwork for which the house is famous, leads down to the family living rooms and chapel on the first floor, then down to the kitchen, now the tea room, but still with a fine display of copper saucepans.

Outside the house the original garden wall survives, though the planting is later. The gaunt ruins of Hardwick Old Hall also remain, amazingly, with some surviving plasterwork, and are now in the care of English Heritage.

Top: The enormous Long Gallery, with its distinctive hang of pictures over the Gideon tapestries.

Above: The High Great Chamber with its painted plaster frieze of the Court of Diana, the huntress goddess.

Above right: Lucretia, the centrepiece of one of a set of patchwork hangings, originally made for Chatsworth in the 1570s.

Right: The Blue Room, with a bed of 1629 and 16th-century Brussels tapestries.

carved in 1939. There is a fine collection of old masters acquired in the 1920s, including works by Bellini, Titian, Tintoretto, Veronese and El Greco, as well as magnificient Sèvres porcelain and Chippendale furniture made for the house. Across the park is the redundant All Saints' Church, which contains six outstandingly good medieval alabaster recumbent effigies of the owners of the parish manors – they provide detailed insight into the costume and jewellery of their period.

Hardy's Cottage, Dorset 689 J6, The small cob and thatch cottage was built at Higher Brockhampton by Thomas Hardy's great-grandfather, and has been altered little since then [NT]. Hardy was born here in 1840, and it was from here that he would make the daily trek to school in Dorchester.
Hare Hill, Ches 693 H2, A woodland garden [EH] set around a walled garden with stunning rhodendrons and azaleas.

Harewood House, W York 697 G6, Edwin Lascelles' mansion was financed from the proceeds of West Indian sugar plantations. It was built of beautiful honey-coloured ashlar sandstone to a design by John Carr of York, with later alterations by Sir Charles Barry, and has outstanding interiors by Robert Adam. Standing somewhat pugnaciously in the entrance hall, which is lined with Doric half-columns in a dark red imitation of porphyry, is Jacob Epstein's great marble statue of Adam – punning the name of the architect-decorator –

Top: Harewood House, the sandstone pediment on the north front.

Left: Hare Hill woodland garden.

Hardy's Cottage
Bottom left: Low-slung vernacular with its cob and thatch.
Right: An interior furnished by the National Trust.

Right: Harlaxton Manor, the south front.

Harlaxton Manor, Lincs 694 E4, Southwest of Grantham* lies the wildest and most fanciful 1830s mansion in the whole of England. The

architects – first Anthony Salvin then William Burn – copied parts of all the major Jacobean houses they could think of and combined them with an eye to theatrical effect. There are continental baroque interiors in the Music Room and South Gallery and an exceptional Cedar Staircase, making the interiors just as wild as the outside.

Harlech

Harlech, Gwynd 692 D3, In *The Mabinogion* there is a reference to Harddlech, 'the High Rock', where Bendigeidfran had his court in the 12th century; yet there is no archeological evidence of a defensive building here before Edward I chose this lofty site for the third castle of his second Welsh campaign in 1283. Harlech is renowned for the rugged architecture of its fort, as well as for its views of Snowdonia and the switchback outlines of the Lleyn Peninsula. The most significant military feature of the castle is the innovative use of the gatehouse made by the King's engineer Master James of St George (1235–1308), not only for defence and storage but also for domestic accommodation of relative comfort. This was feasible because of the depth of the rock-cut ditch in front of it. On another two sides, nature provided its own craggily precipitous protection,

while allowing enough level space on the rock itself for James to attempt a concentric design similar to that which he was to achieve at Beaumaris*. Unlike Beaumaris, however, Harlech did not have its own dock; but it did have access to the sea, which in the 13th century would have come up to the base of the rock. Despite all this, the defences proved inadequate when confronted with Owain Glyndwr's attack of 1404, which resulted in his establishing Harlech as a Welsh royal court. Owain was crowned Prince of Wales in the presence of witnesses from Scotland, Spain and his ally in his fight for Welsh independence, France. During the Wars of the Roses, the castle was the last to surrender to the Yorkists, and this chapter in its history inspired the marching song, 'Men of Harlech'. A similar determination was shown during the Civil War, when it was the last of the King's castles to surrender.

Coleg Harlech, a residential college, otherwise known as the 'College of the Second Chance', was founded in 1927 as an enlightened experiment offering opportunities to rural and industrial manual workers who would otherwise have had little formal education. It was the brain-child of Thomas Jones, of humble Rhymney Valley origins, who became Deputy Secretary to the Cabinet. The building chosen for the College was Wern Fawr, constructed between 1907 and 1910 by George Walton for George Davison, head of European Kodak Sales. Solid and stolid, it owes much to the vernacular buildings of these parts. The wonderful westward views over sand dunes and the golf course can also be enjoyed from the bar of the adjoining Theatr Ardudwy, built in the 1970s. Independent of the college, it offers a wide range of popular bilingual entertainment.

Above: Harrogate, the Stray.

Harris, *see* **Lewis and Harris*.**

Harrogate, N York 697 G5, An attractive and bracing town. The beneficial properties of its waters were first observed in 1652, and it became an important spa with many grand hotels. There were several wells with mineral characteristics (magnesia, chalybeate, etc.) dotted in and around the town, a few marked by ornamental well-heads. Spa treatments have now been discontinued, and the Victorian and Edwardian Royal Pump Room has been converted into a museum commemorating Harrogate's spa heritage. The town has exceptional floral displays, particularly splendid in spring when the large open spaces which characterize the town, including the Stray, are edged with crocuses. Also of note, for plant enthusiasts and others, are the Valley Gardens and Harlow Carr Gardens. Shops have an Art Nouveau look, with coloured and curving glass windows and cast-iron canopies, most famously on Betty's Tea Shop.

Hartland, Devon 689 E5, Set in a remote triangle off the A39, this corner of Devon is still criss-crossed with quiet roads, green lanes and mysterious foot paths. On the coast at Hartland Quay the menacing and jagged rocks face the Atlantic swell, but tucked away inland is Hartland Abbey, a former Augustinian abbey acquired by the Sergeant of the Royal Wine Cellars at the Dissolution, through whose family it has passed to the present day. The entrance and hall were designed by Sir George Gilbert Scott and have notable murals.

Right: Hartland Abbey, the Drawing Room, showing linenfold panelling and murals painted 1852–9 by Alfred Beer.

Below: Hartlebury Castle, the exterior of the Great Hall.

Hartlebury Castle, Worcs 693 H5, For centuries this has been the official residence of the Bishop of Worcester. Most of the house was demolished during the Civil War, when the castle was taken after a two-day siege and slighted by Colonel Thomas Morgan. Bishop Fleetwood began the reconstruction process in 1675, but the old moat of the castle was retained, along with some other elements of the earlier building. The interior of the Great Hall is more obviously 15th-century than its delicate 18th-century exterior suggests. One of the hip-roofed wings contains the pretty fan-vaulted chapel. The servants' quarters in the north wing now contain the Worcestershire County Museum. It includes a number of vacuum cleaners, part of the Tickenhill Collection that illustrates 19th- and 20th-century domestic life. Outside there is a collection of horse-drawn vehicles, including gypsy caravans or 'living waggons', used by migrant farm labourers to travel about Worcestershire and each custom-built for its owner. There is also a cider mill, dating from c1700, with a stone crushing-pan and press ready to receive a load of apples.

Hartlepool, Dur 697 H3,
The de Brus lords of the
older manor of Hart
developed a medieval
port, which supplied
the English army
during Edward I's
campaigns against
Scotland, and was
therefore heavily
defended (as can be

seen from the Sandwell Gate). Also impressive is
the Early English church of St Hilda, dedicated to
the famous abbess of Whitby* and of the Early
Christian monastery here.

Hartwell, Northants 690 E3, St Mary's is one of
England's most perfect 18th-century churches,
built in 1753–5 to gothic designs by Henry Keene.
This superb little building (now disused and in
ruins) sits on a mound near Hartwell House, an
important country house of the early 17th and
18th centuries, remodelled as a hotel in 1986–9.

Harvington Hall, Worcs 690 C3, A medieval house
owned by the Roman Catholic Church, inside an
irregular Elizabethan brick carapace encircled by
a moat. It is famous for its priest-holes, secret
passages, trapdoors and false stairway, used to
hide the priests sheltered by its Catholic owners
from potential Protestant persecutors. The most
elaborate priest-hole is off the library: a visit
involves passing through a secret door in the
fireplace into a small room with a removable floor.
The hiding place beneath has an escape chute to
the moat below. John Wall, its 17th-century owner,
was a Catholic priest and in 1679 was the last man
in England to be executed for his faith. The hall
has fine monochrome late 16th-century wall
paintings uncovered during restoration.

Harwich, Essex 691 J3, A key port on a peninsula at
the mouth of the Stour and Orwell estuaries for
over 1,000 years. Bound up in its history are
seafarers Drake, Raleigh, Nelson and Christopher
Jones, master of the *Mayflower*, which carried the

Top left: Harvington Hall,
where priests used to hide
from their Protestant
persecutors.

Left: Harwich, the early 19th-
century Low Light, one of two
lighthouses in the town.

Right: Hastings, crypt of
St-Mary-in-the-Castle. It is
now a concert hall.

Pilgrim Fathers to America. Samuel Pepys was its
MP when the town was the main base of the King's
Navy. Note a treadwheel crane of 1667. Narrow
streets lead to a Napoleonic fort, the slim brick
octagonal High Lighthouse (now a maritime
museum) and Low Light, a curious pagoda-like
lighthouse of 1818. A core of old buildings is
gathered around Halfpenny Pier, its charming
entrance kiosk now an information centre, where
the Great Eastern Hotel has become the Town
Hall. Light here is the order of the day – don't miss
the delightful Electric Palace Cinema (1911), fully
restored and operational.

Hascombe, Surrey 690 E6, The church of St Peter
(1864) is one of the most accomplished buildings
produced by the architect Henry Woodyer.

Haslemere, Surrey 690 E6, This small town set
among wooded hills near the Sussex border
became popular in the late 1800s. Many good Arts
and Crafts houses are to be seen, including some
by Voysey and E J May.

Hastings, E Susx 691 H7, One of the Cinque Ports,
dating back to Saxon times; it had an important
castle which has now mostly fallen into the sea.
It began to decline early and remained small until
the 19th century. It is now a town of dual character:
on the one hand, it is a brash modern holiday
resort and on the other a picturesque old port of
narrow streets and a seafront specially notable for
its strange collection of net-stores, tall black
timber structures like towers, used to haul in the
fishermen's nets. One of them houses a museum of
the fishing industry that is well worth a visit. In
Pelham Crescent is the curious church of St-Mary-
in-the-Castle, a rotunda dug into the cliff behind.
The church of St Thomas of Canterbury, of 1889, is
not notable architecturally, but has a complete
scheme of Victorian frescoes and stencilling.

Hatchlands Park

Top: The south and west elevations of two and three storeys respectively.
Left: The understated exterior conceals a series of rich interiors.
Right: Caryatid figure, a detail of the Adam fireplace in the Drawing Room.

Hatchlands Park, Surrey 691 F6, Between East Clandon and West Horsley is this impressive country house built in 1756–7 for Admiral Boscawen, hero of the Battle of Louisburg. Hatchlands is set in a delightful park landscaped by Humphry Repton and with interiors by Robert Adam [NT]. In the house are the Cobbe Collection of early keyboard instruments associated with composers such as Bach, Mozart, Chopin and Purcell (the world's largest), as well as pictures.

Hatfield, Essex 691 G4, Hatfield Forest is a rare medieval survival: a royal hunting forest of ancient oak and pollarded hornbeam extending over 1,000 acres (405ha) with great rides and woodland glades presided over by Stansted* jets and the National Trust. Laetitia Houblon's 1759 Shell House now serves tea beside her husband's ornamental lake. Broad Oak Church, the surviving late 14th-century nave of a Benedictine priory, has atmospheric fittings, including carved pews, a chandelier and Georgian railings.

Hatfield Forest

Right: A clearing.
Far right: Shell House, Laetitia Houblon's 18th-century house.

Bottom left: Hatfield House, the Long Gallery, running the entire length of the south front, 180 feet (55m).

Hatfield House, Herts 691 F4, The finest Jacobean house in the country was built 1607–12 by Robert Cecil, 1st Earl of Salisbury, after he exchanged the nearby Theobalds* with James I for the old Bishop's Palace. As chief minister to Elizabeth I, and now to James, and newly created the Earl of Salisbury, Cecil immediately set about demolishing the old Bishop's Palace and erecting a mansion that reflected his status. Five years later the house was finished, having cost a grand total of £40,000.

It was probably designed by the carpenter and builder Robert Lyminge, who later went to work at Blickling Hall*, Norfolk. Cecil himself also seems to have been closely involved, advised by friends and by the Surveyor to the King's Works, Simon Basyll. Basyll was succeeded by Inigo Jones, to whom the stone central portion and clock tower may be attributed.

The house is built in a U-shape, and on an exceptionally large scale. The state rooms were arranged in the centre and the wings contained separate apartments. The original entrance was on the south front, between the wings that faced the London road. Along the front was a highly fashionably open loggia (there were other notable examples at Theobalds* and at Trinity College, Cambridge*) enclosed by the 2nd Marquis of Salisbury in 1846, to form an armoury. Round-headed arches were supported on Doric pilasters. The porch is three storeys high, with paired superimposed columns of the Doric, Ionic and Corinthian orders. The design is enlivened by strapwork. Inside, the screen in the Great Hall and the grand staircase are wonderful examples of Jacobean carving by John Bucke. The newel posts of the staircase are decorated with figures and

Top left: Part of the surviving range of the Bishop's Palace, 15th century.

Bottom: An aerial view showing the palatial scale of the house and gardens at Hatfield.

Top right: The grand staircase with its highly decorative details and carved figures, and the surviving dog gate at the bottom.

Hatfield House   **H**

strapwork. King James' Drawing Room takes its name from the life-size statue of the King in Maximilian Colt's chimneypiece. The house contains many other treasures such as the famous Rainbow Portrait of Elizabeth I, Hilliard's Ermine Portrait, rare tapestries, furniture, and paintings by Sir Joshua Reynolds. The surviving range of the Bishop's Palace stands in the grounds to the west of the house. The palace was acquired by Henry VIII from the Bishops of Ely, and it was here that Mary Tudor and Elizabeth I spent their childhoods. It was built between 1480 and 1490 and is ranked among the finest examples of medieval brickwork. The timber roof is equally impressive.

Cecil designed the gardens on a similarly grand scale to the house, with fountains and waterworks by Solomon de Caus, and designs produced and plants procured by John Tradescant. The vineyard was stocked with 30,000 vines. The numerous gardens, designed by the present Lady Salisbury, are exceptional. The church of St Etheldreda is also well worth a visit and contains (in the Salisbury Chapel) the splendid monument to Robert Cecil (d. 1612), with sculpture by Maximilian Colt.

Haughley, Suffk 695 H6, Haughley Park is a well-restored red-brick Jacobean hall set in wooded parkland. Its gables were removed in 1824 but returned in the 1960s after fire gutted much of the interior. The village church stands beside Suffolk's biggest Norman motte-and-bailey castle at the end of a green lined with attractive timber houses.

Haughmond Abbey, Shrops 693 G3, An abbey of Augustinian canons founded in about 1135. It lies with its east boundary against Haughmond Hill, and some of the walls have their lower parts cut out of the solid rock. The Abbey church has almost completely disappeared, but other parts of the monastery complex survive to a good height [EH].

Haverfordwest, Pembks 692 B6, St Mary's Church, which occupies a commanding position on the High Street, dates to the mid-13th century, and was considerably enlarged and improved during the early years of the 16th century. Its spaciousness, together with the quality and exuberance of its decoration and fittings, make it one of the most impressive parish churches in South Wales.

Hawkshead, Cumb 696 E4, A village between Windermere and Coniston, set round an informal square with a long, low church and a war memorial in the form of an Anglo-Saxon cross, designed by the Lakeland scholar and antiquary WG Collingwood. The Grammar School, dating

back to the 16th century, much altered but with a fine doorway of 1675, is a place of pilgrimage because Wordsworth was educated there from 1773 to 1783 [NT].

Hawkstone Park, Shrops 693 G3, The park surrounds Hawkstone House, an interesting Georgian building. Created by Sir Richard Hill, mostly in the 1790s, it is a wonderful example of late Georgian landscaping, making use of dramatic natural features and the ruins of a medieval castle to produce something thrilling and romantic.

Haworth, W York 697 G6, On a hilltop reached by a narrow stone-setted road is Haworth parish church of 1879 and, across its chilling graveyard, the older Parsonage of 1778. This was the home, from 1820 until 1861, of the Reverend Patrick Brontë, his three novelist daughters and drunken son Bramwell. Inspired by the area's bleak moors, winter winds and damp mists, the sisters produced their novels, using male pseudonyms so that their writing would be taken seriously. Containing much of the furniture added when Charlotte became famous, the Parsonage Museum is now a Brontë shrine with a large collection of manuscripts, paintings and personal family treasures. The Brontë children were not born here but in a still-surviving house in Thornton, near Bradford.

Haxted, Surrey 691 G6, The watermill is weather-boarded with a two-gabled mansard roof.

Hay-on-Wye (Y Gelli), Powys 693 F6, The largest centre for second-hand bookshops in Britain, with its own self-styled 'king', Richard Booth, selling books in the castle (which was made into a mansion in the 17th century). There are books on every conceivable topic laid out on improvised

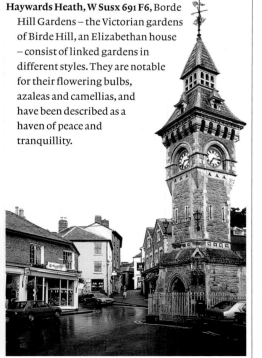

stands in lanes and alleyways, as well as in the shops themselves. The character of this idyllic market town was enhanced in the 1980s by the foundation of an annual Literary Festival held in late May, attracting exceptional speakers and writers. Hay stands at the head of what is known as 'The Golden Valley', surrounded by glorious walking country.

Haywards Heath, W Susx 691 F6, Borde Hill Gardens – the Victorian gardens of Birde Hill, an Elizabethan house – consist of linked gardens in different styles. They are notable for their flowering bulbs, azaleas and camellias, and have been described as a haven of peace and tranquillity.

Right: Heaton Hall, the park front with the typical Wyatt bow and shallow dome, and the fine Coade stone decoration.

Hay-on-Wye
Left: One of the many shops now serving the international market for books.
Below left: The Clock Tower of 1881 is ornate enough to grace a much larger town.

Heath Chapel, Shrops 693 G4, Quite alone in a field stands this perfect example of a small Norman church. It is just a nave and chancel with tiny slit windows and an elaborate but decayed south doorway. Inside, the font is Norman but almost all the rest of the fittings are Jacobean. There are traces of a wall-painting of St George on the south wall of the nave.

Heath Hall, W York 697 H6, A Queen Anne house at its core, but extended and given handsome rococo interiors by the great John Carr of York, who was born at Horbury on the other side of Wakefield.

Heaton Hall, Gt Man 697 F7, Manchester's major contribution to the classical country house is set on rising ground to the north of the city with fine views across to the Pennines. In more than 600 acres (244ha) of landscaped grounds, Heaton is a

major work by James Wyatt, with additions by others of the Wyatt family – Samuel and Lewis. The client was Sir Thomas Egerton, later 1st Earl of Wilton. Heaton, a 1772 rebuilding of an earlier villa, is the finest neoclassical house in the northwest. The long south front, facing the open landscape, centres on a typical Wyatt shallow-domed bow with the service wing to the left and a conservatory ending the range to the right. The quality of the workmanship is excellent, mainly in fine sandstone with early Coade stone details. The house is entered from the rather gloomier north and offers a series of state rooms with fine chimneypieces and plasterwork. These include a splendid library and a music room with a contemporary organ. The highlight of the whole plan is the circular first-floor Cupola Room, in the bow facing south, which has exquisite painted 'Etruscan' decoration by Biagio Rebecca. Heaton became a public park at the beginning of the 20th century and some of the historic parkland is now municipalized with flower beds, a boating lake and a golf course; but these have not destroyed the setting of the house, and the landscape still retains a number of fine garden buildings – Smithy Lodge is now the main entrance, though Grand Lodge was perhaps nearer Manchester and the source of the Egertons' wealth. Near the house is a small round temple on a knoll, an excellent viewing platform, and further away there is a dower house in the form of another temple. All these buildings are more or less contemporary with the house. Lower down is an imported landscape feature – the façade of the former Manchester* Town Hall, built in King Street by Francis Goodwin and removed by the city to Heaton after the building of Waterhouse's town hall had made it redundant. The park also contains the home farm and stable buildings and a rockwork tunnel, probably early 19th century, so that the cows could cross the path from the house to the shrubberies.

Hebrides, *see* **Arran*, Barra*, Benbecula*, Bute*, Coll*, Colonsay*, Eriskay*, Gigha*, Iona*, Islay*, Jura*, Lewis and Harris*, Mull*, North Uist*, South Uist*, Tiree***.

Heckington, Lincs 695 F4, The church at Heckington figures in every book of English gothic church architecture because of its splendid and elaborate chancel fittings. It is a large church, built of

Above: Heligan, the romantic Italian garden.

Helmingham Hall
Centre left: Moated home to the Tollemache family since 1485.
Centre right: A herbaceous border in the walled garden.

Ancaster stone, with a broach spire. The windows are filled with flowing tracery, and the east window in particular is one of the best examples of such tracery in England. The splendidly carved and buttressed south porch gives a foretaste of what lies inside. Beyond the nave is a long chancel, which was almost certainly built or rebuilt in the 1330s when Richard de Potesgrove was rector and also chaplain to King Edward III. His tomb, richly

Helensburgh, Hill House
Below: The original decor is retained.
Bottom: View from the southeast.

carved, is one of the important fittings of the chancel. The others are the sedilia, with delicate little vaults over the seats and carved domestic scenes, the piscina and, richest of all, the Easter Sepulchre.

Helensburgh, Ag & B 698 D4, This coastal resort stands on a hillside on the north bank of the Firth of

Clyde. At the top of Colquhoun Street stands **Hill House,** the house designed and decorated (1902–4) by Charles Rennie Mackintosh and Margaret Macdonald for the Glaswegian publisher Walter W Blackie. The house combines several different styles – Arts and Crafts, Glasgow Style and Scots Baronial. White and dark wood-panelled walls punctuated by stencilled motifs, stuccoed panels and stained-glass insets attest to an attention to detail that is echoed by the furniture and lighting designed by the architect.

Heligan, The Lost Gardens of, Cnwll 688 D7, The extensive walled gardens surround the large 18th-century house once home to the Tremaynes. In recent years the gardens have been authentically and painstakingly restored, and include such rarities as a pineapple pit. The rhododendron garden, the valley garden with its tree ferns and the Italian garden are among Heligan's most memorable features. The largest garden restoration scheme in Europe, it has been the subject of a number of books and a television series.

Helmingham, Suffk 695 J6, A quadrangular moated mansion raised in the reign of Henry VIII, and made to look more castle-like by the Nash battlements added to its Georgian façade. Since 1485 the hall has been the home of the Tollemache family, who founded Ipswich*'s Tolly Cobbold brewery in 1886 and whose monuments adorn the church. Only the grounds are open, but the glorious gardens and 400-acre (160ha) deer park, with its 900-year-old oaks, are well worth the trip. Constable's *Helmingham Dell* was painted here.

Helmshore, Lancs 697 F6, The town has one of the oldest textile mills in Lancashire: Higher Mill,

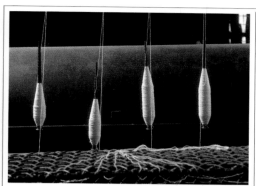

Left: Helmshore Textile Museum, where cotton spinning on the cotton mule is one of the attractions.

Right: Helpston, John Clare's tomb.

Bottom: Helmsley Castle, the west face of the west range from across the moat.

built as a water-powered fulling mill in 1789. Next to it is Whitaker's Mill, rebuilt after a fire in 1860. The two buildings now form the Helmshore Textile Museum, where the processes as well as the products of the Lancashire cotton industry can be understood. The museum stands in the shadow of the viaduct of the former East Lancashire Railway, leading north to Rawtenstall, beyond which is the old Baptist Goodshaw Chapel, showing the simple arrangements of the 18th-century nonconformist church.

Helmsley, N York 697 H4, An attractive market town of white stone buildings with red pantile roofs dominated by **Helmsley Castle** [EH], which is surrounded by two very impressive rock-cut ditches. As well as medieval structures, there is an Elizabethan range with carved woodwork and fireplaces. The castle's living accommodation was eventually superseded by that of Duncombe Park*.

The walled gardens have recently been restored on historic principles.

Helpston, Cambs 695 F5, On the edge of the Welland Valley is the birthplace of 'peasant poet' John Clare (1793–1846), who raged against enclosure while we weep for lost hedges. The poet's tomb at Helpston draws literary pilgrims. An odd monument erected to his memory on the green is eclipsed by the battlemented and gabled medieval village cross. In the nearby nature reserve of Castor Hanglands, where Clare wandered, nightingales still sing.

Helston, Cnwll 688 C8, The wide Coinagehall Street

testifies to the town's past as a marketing centre for the Lizard peninsula and its gateway. It is now best known for its Furry Dance on 8 May, its name taken from *fer*, the Cornish for 'fair'; the three dances of the day – for children, the gentry and their servants – welcome the summer. Any fragile windows are covered with grills decorated lavishly with bluebells, and the dancers weave their way through the streets and in and out of some of the shops and houses. At the midday dance the men wear morning suits and the ladies long dresses, elbow-length gloves and wide-brimmed hats.

Hengrave Hall, Suffk 695 H6, Built of limestone and yellow brick by Sir Thomas Kytson in the 1530s, the house has a magnificent triple bay window over the main entrance adorned with Renaissance cherubs. Now a religious retreat, it was home to the great Elizabethan madrigalist John Wilbye and stands in parkland, alongside a small church with an early Norman round tower and a crowd of Kytson and Gage family memorials.

Henley-on-Thames, Oxon 690 E5, Henley is set on a broad stretch of the Thames that constitutes the finest regatta course in the country. The River and Rowing Museum has good displays relating the history of the town's association with rowing, since 1829 when the first Oxford and Cambridge boat race took place here. Architecture from a range of periods is represented with special sights, including the attractive bridge rebuilt in 1786 by William Hayward and the Kenton Theatre of 1805. The medieval church has a prominent tower supposedly built by John Longland, Bishop of Lincoln in 1521–47. Facing the churchyard is the timber-framed Chantry House of c1400.

Hemel Hempstead, Herts 690 E4, Although it is often thought of as a new town – and, indeed, was designated as such in 1947 – the old town is unexpectedly attractive, with a mixture of timber-framed and Georgian house fronts lining the High Street. The large Norman church of St Mary remains exceptionally complete, with a rib-vaulted chancel of c1150 and a late 12th-century nave and transepts. Piccott's End is a group of cottages on the boundary of the town. No. 68, originally a late medieval pilgrims' hostel or hall-house, contains fine wall-paintings of c1500.

Hemingford Grey, Cambs 695 F6, The moated manor, dating from 1130, is said to be the oldest continuously inhabited house in England. Restored and opened to the public by Lucy Boston, it was the setting for her 'Green Knowe' childrens' books. She laid out the garden with irises, roses and topiary. St James's red brick tower beside the Great Ouse is a memorable set-piece.

Hereford

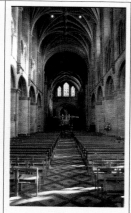

Hereford, Herefs 693 G6, The restored early 14th-century tower of the red sandstone cathedral dominates the low-lying town of Hereford, which is set in a bend of the River Wye. It was at its most important in the 13th century after Edward I conquered Wales, when it was in the powerful grip of the Mortimer family who controlled much of the border territory. Most people will approach the cathedral along the generous Broad Street, which also contains the City Museum and Art Gallery with its façade of carved monkeys. Highlights of the collection include Roman pavements from Kentchester, a garrison town nearby. The town also has a Museum of Water Works and the Bulmer Railway Centre.

The cathedral's west tower and part of the nave fell down on Easter Monday, 1786. James Wyatt – whose commissions on several cathedrals have earned him the nickname of 'Wyatt the Destroyer' – was appointed as architect for the restoration work. Here he did try to retain and unite all the surviving works of previous periods, but without managing to create a harmonious whole. The Norman arches survive at the east end of the aisle, each with its own unique chevron design, but the best parts of the cathedral are the pointed windows, arches and blind arcades in the Early English north transept. Twentieth-century hands have also touched Hereford Cathedral. Tapestries designed by John Piper hang in the south transept, and Sir William Whitfield was responsible for the new library building for the famous Mappa Mundi, which was voted 'Building of the Year' in 1997. This famous 'map of the world', made c1300, was nearly sold by the cash-starved cathedral in the 1980s. After considerable panic, it was saved for Hereford thanks chiefly to Sir Paul Getty, who paid for its new building. The map, now shown in subdued light, shows Jerusalem at the centre and Britain at the extreme edge of the known world. It is covered with pictures of places, people and real and mythical creatures, and a man up among the fjords is skiing. Next to the map is the Chained Library, the Cathedral's historic reference collection containing books on subjects from theology to botany. Each book is chained to the shelves to stop it from being removed. The bishop and the dean each have private gardens in the town, and the dean's has a 17th-century plaque at its entrance, showing the hand of God holding a watering-can. Both gardens can be seen from the walks along the River Wye.

Top left: Windows in the cathedral's north transept.

Top centre: The tower, recently restored, with ballflower decoration.

Top right: The Norman nave, looking up towards the 19th-century high altar and arch at its eastern end.

Below: Hereford has had a cathedral for as long as the city has existed. Many piligrims were drawn by the shrine of its patron, St Ethelbert.

Hergest Croft Gardens, Herefs 693 F5, This is a plantsman's garden, created by the Banks family from the mid-19th century onwards. Over 200 species of rhododendrons can be found here, especially on the sloping bank known as the Flower Fall.

Herstmonceux, E Susx 691 G7, A fairy-tale castle surrounded by a moat, built in 1440. It was a ruin by the 18th century, and was restored only in 1933, along with its fine Elizabethan garden. In 1948 it was taken over by the Royal Observatory when it moved from smog-polluted Greenwich* (London).

Hertford, Herts 691 F4, The county town remains a homely, surprisingly compact place with a mixture of historic and modern buildings. Not much survives of the once important medieval castle, but what there is (parts of curtain walls and a 15th-century gatehouse, gothicized during the 1700s) lies in tranquil parkland in the centre of town by the river. Hertford is renowned for its excellent – though not cheap – antique shops, its riverside pubs and its busy shopping areas. Of particular note are the Friends' Meeting House of 1670 in Railway Street (said to be the oldest still in use) and the 19th-century buildings of McMullen's Brewery. The local museum is housed in a 17th-century house, re-fronted by a Georgian architect.

Hestercombe Gardens, Somset 689 G5, In the 1750s Coplestone Warre Bampfylde laid out 40 acres (16ha) of Georgian pleasure gardens

Above: Hergest Croft Gardens contain the National Collection of birches, maples and zelkovas.

Below: Herstmonceux Caste. The shell is that of a real 15th-century castle, but the interior has been entirely rebuilt.

complete with lakes, temples and woodland walks; these grew over, but are currently being restored. There are also formal gardens designed by Sir Edwin Lutyens and Gertrude Jekyll.

Heveningham Hall, Suffk 695 J6, The Palladian house, once the loveliest in Suffolk, has suffered drastically since 1949 from fire, sales, thefts and dispersals. Sir Robert Taylor built it in the 1780s for Sir Gerald Vanneck, and James Wyatt did the interior (complete with its celebrated neoclassical entrance hall and orangery). Capability Brown laid out the recently restored park. There is a stunning prospect of the principal elevation above the lake, from the roadside or the footpath through the park. Although not open at present, it is an important, clearly visible landmark.

Hever Castle, Kent 691 G6, Famous as the home of Anne Boleyn's family. With its ivy-covered walls, moat and drawbridge, from the outside it looks the perfect medieval fortified manor; the interior, however, is a disappointment. By the 19th century it was a ruin and was bought in 1903 by Lord Astor, who restored it with some fine Edwardian woodwork. For extra guest accommodation, rather than compromise the old building, he built a convincing 'Tudor' village next door.

Hever Castle
Above: One of the bedrooms with its magnificent four-poster bed.
Left: Portrait of Henry VIII, who wooed Anne Boleyn here.

Hexham, Nthumb 697 F2, An attractive market town. The Moot Hall is a rather dour 15th-century fortified gatehouse, and the Shambles of 1766 have Tuscan columns around the open selling space. **Hexham Abbey,** a medieval Augustinian priory which became the parish church after the Dissolution, has handsome Early English architecture, some good medieval fittings and well-preserved Roman altars. In the chancel, the 7th-century bishop's throne serves as a reminder of the church established here 675–80 by Saint

Wilfrid, Abbot of Ripon and Bishop of Northumbria from 669. The only part of the building that survived sacking by the Danes in 876 is the Anglo-Saxon crypt, built of re-used Roman stone (there is a similar crypt at Ripon*). Some original wall plaster still adheres to the stonework of the relic chamber.

Heydon, Norfk 695 J4, The Bulwer Long family have been based at Heydon for 600 years. Their Elizabethan hall borders an idyllic estate village: church, pub, post office, blacksmith's forge and 18th-century brick cottages gathered around a green at the end of a lane.

Hidcote Manor Garden
Centre left: The garden created by the botanist and plant-hunter Lawrence Johnston, who had a yellow rose named after him.
Centre right: The 'White Garden'.

Bottom: Highcliffe Castle. The oriel on the left was rescued from the demolition of the Grande Maison des Andelys in Normandy.

High Beeches Garden, W Susx, A natural garden in a picturesque setting, with wildflowers and rare plants. *See* **Nymans Garden* 691 F6.**

High Wycombe, Bucks 690 E4, This large, sprawling town built around a steep valley was an important point on the main Oxford to London road (now bypassed by the M40). The most significant sights include the fine Palladian Guildhall of 1757 by Henry Keene and the spacious church of All Saints. The church contains an excellent monument to Henry Petty, Earl of Shelburne (d. 1751) by Peter Scheemakers. The Wycombe Museum (Priory Avenue) is housed in the mainly 18th-century Castle Hill House. It has displays on the history of the district and is surrounded by pretty grounds.

Highclere Castle, Hants 690 D5, Home of successive earls of Carnarvon, a sumptuous mansion reconstructed by Sir Charles Barry, 1842–9. Among its treasures are relics from the Tomb of Tutankhamun, which the 5th Earl, with Howard Carter, discovered in 1922. The park was landscaped by Capability Brown.

Highcliffe, Dorset 690 C7, This small seaside village has been enlivened by the opening of Highcliffe Castle, built in 1830 for Charles Stuart of the family of the marquesses of Bute, later Lord Stuart de Rothesay. (It is sometimes known as Rothesay Castle, after him.) His architect, WJ Donthorne, gave him a gothic mansion, with French interiors to honour his important collection of French medieval stonework and stained glass. The once ruinous house has now been transformed by Christchurch Borough Council into a successful and popular attraction.

Hidcote Manor, Gloucs 690 C3, After the Boer War, the American Major Lawrence Johnston retired with his pack of tiny dachshunds to Hidcote, to garden. His creation has been described as 'a cottage garden on the most glorified scale' [NT]. Small enclosures crammed with plants lead one into another over 10 acres (4ha) in a kind of 'haphazard luxuriance', presided over by two little gazebos. Johnston returned from trips to China and South Africa with new plants, and the gardens' camellias and rhododendrons are famous. Hidcote Manor and the nearby Kiftsgate Court Gardens* are open mostly on the same days and the two visits can be pleasantly combined.

Hill Hall, Essex 691 G4, The house has a monumental mural cycle from 1570; its Italian and Flemish gardens were laid out from 1883 by Charles Eamer Kempe [EH].

Hill Top, Cumb 696 E4, Between Coniston and Windermere*, there is a small cottage [NT] much visited because for many years it was the home of Beatrix Potter; the staircase appears as a drawing in *The Adventures of Tom Kitten*. Its literary associations have kept a good example of Lakeland vernacular architecture from too much modernization.

Hillesden, Bucks 690 D3, A tiny village, worth visiting for the extraordinarily rich decoration of its late medieval church of All Saints. George Gilbert Scott drew the church when aged only 15 and came back to restore it in 1873–5.

Hilton, Cambs 695 F6, The turf maze on the green was cut in 1660 by William Sparrow; his stone memorial is now at the centre. But a maze may have existed here in earlier times – possibly to thwart the devil, who was thought capable of travelling only in a straight line.

Hinchingbrooke House, Cambs 695 F6, Henry VIII gave the ruined Benedictine priory at Hinchin Brook to Richard Cromwell, Oliver's great-grandfather, for help in closing Fenland monasteries. Hinchingbrooke House (now a school) emerged from the rubble. Oliver's uncle raised it to ever greater heights – prompting the king to pay many visits – until the expense ruined him.

Hindhead, Surrey 690 E6, Described by William Cobbett as 'the most villainous spot God ever made', probably because of its notorious highwaymen. Nowadays it is known as an excellent place from which to view the surrounding landscape, and has lovely walks among heath and woodland.

Hingham, Norfk 695 H5, Robert Peck left here in the early 17th century to escape religious persecution and founded Hingham, Massachusetts. He was joined by Samuel Lincoln, whose descendant, Abraham, was one of America's greatest presidents

Above: Hinton Ampner, scene from *The Winter's Tale* by Henry Fuseli.

Left: Hill Hall.

Below: Hinwick House was built 1709–14 but adjacent buildings date from 1430.

Above: Hinchingbrooke House; the site was given to the Cromwell family by Henry VIII.

Bottom left: Hill Top, where Beatrix Potter, creator of Peter Rabbit, lived for many years.

(there is a bust of him in the church). Hingham's role as a small 18th-century watering-hole for local gentry explains the elegant Georgian houses around Market Square. The large church of St Andrew has an outstanding mid-15th-century monument to Lord Morley.

Hintlesham Hall, Suffk 691 H3, A restored Elizabethan mansion, whose fine plasterwork ceilings can be viewed by guests at what is now a prized hotel and restaurant (opened by Robert Carrier in 1972). A Palladian façade added from 1725 is visible from a public footpath passing through the park.

Hinton Ampner, Hants 690 D6, The house is good 20th-century neo-Georgian, built as a replica of its predecessor, which burnt down in 1960. It has fine Regency furnishings and mainly Baroque features. The garden is superb – a mixture of formal and informal.

Hinton St George, Somset 689 H5, The church of St George contains the Poulett chapel and important monuments and brasses to that family, who lived at nearby Hinton House.

Hinwick, Beds 694 E6, This village has two memorable manor houses: Tudor Hinwick Hall with its early 18th-century east front, and the classical Hinwick House, built 1709–14 at a cost of £3,848.4s.9d. Hinwick is a handsome mansion, if a little awkward with its weighty attic storey and prominent string course appearing to squash the giant Corinthian pilasters. The carving of Diana in the pediment is by John Hunt of Northampton. The treatment of Hinwick Hall is slightly vernacular in comparison.

Hitchin, Herts 691 F3, An interesting town, its wealth during the late medieval period proudly demonstrated by the spacious church of St Mary. A visit is well rewarded by the series of excellent roofs, screens and monuments. Also worth viewing are the early 17th-century Biggins Almshouses by the river; Hitchin Priory, incorporating fragments of the medieval Carmelite house, and with a south front of 1770–7 by Robert Adam; and William Butterfield's church of the Holy Saviour (1863–5, Radcliffe Road). Hitchin British Schools is a unique complex of school buildings dating from 1837 to 1905. The Lancasterian School room is thought to be the only surviving example of a galleried classroom.

Hoar Cross, Staffs 694 C5, Holy Angels Church is one of the best churches of George Bodley, a leading Victorian church architect. It was built between

1872 and 1876 to commemorate Hugo Ingram of Hoar Cross Hall. The church is all of stone, in the Decorated style. The interior, with its soaring chancel, is richly furnished.

Hoarwithy, Herefs 693 G6, St Catherine's Church is a 19th-century Romanesque-style masterpiece. Paid for by the vicar of the parish, William Poole, who described the earlier church as 'an ugly brick building with no pretensions to architecture', it was designed by his friend the architect JP Seddon. The interior is astonishingly colourful, with mosaics and semi-precious stones such as lapis lazuli and tiger eye used to create the effect of rich Byzantine profusion.

Hodnet Hall Gardens, Shrops 693 G3, Sixty acres (25.5ha) of woodland shrubs and flowers, which have been carefully planted to emphasize the garden's changing character from early spring to late autumn.

Hoghton Tower, Lancs 696 E6, The Tower, between Preston and Blackburn, looks earlier than its Tudor date, its gatehouse and battlements giving

Above and top, left and right: Hodnett Hall Gardens, with lakeside and woodland walks.

Right: Hoghton Tower; three houses have occupied the site since 1100. The present one was built by Thomas Hoghton in 1560–5. This view shows the imposing approach to what is a romantic family house, despite its military aspect.

it a medieval military air. Set round two courtyards, it was carefully restored by Paley and Austin in the 19th century for owners very conscious of their family's long lineage. The de Hoghtons, who still live there, claim descent from a companion of William the Conqueror and Lady Godiva. The house, well maintained on its hilltop setting and in admirable gardens, has an almost unreal quality and has often been used as a film set. The interiors have Gillow furnishings and in the hall is the oak table on which James I is reputed to have dubbed his joint of beef 'Sir Loin'.

Holcombe Rogus, Devon 689 G5, With Holcombe Wood as their backdrop, the 15th-century church, buttressed church house and Tudor great house of the Bluetts form a very fine group. All Saints is notable for its rare Jacobean family pew, with 15 medallions of Old Testament scenes in the cornice and the many fine memorials to the extensive Bluett family. The two-storey **Priest House** with a single large room on the first floor may have been used as a village hall or inn below, with a large kitchen and brewery (for important feast days), before it became the home of the local priest in the 16th century. **Holcombe Court** is built on a courtyard plan with a tower and three oriel windows at the entrance. The long gallery on the first floor has ten small rooms opening off it in

Holdenby House
Top: Known as the Boudoir, this is, in fact, the family sitting room. The gilded decoration dates from 1913.

Bottom left: The former service wing of Holdenby House, later made into a mansion in its own right.

which Spanish prisoners were reputedly imprisoned after the Armada.

Holdenby House, Nhants 694 E6, Today only a tiny fragment of the prodigious Elizabethan mansion built by Sir Christopher Hatton remains. Hatton has always had a lightweight reputation, as a 'mere vegetable of the court who sprung up at night and sank again at his noon', who won Queen Elizabeth I's favour by his excellent dancing. Holdenby was one of the handful of huge houses

built to welcome the Queen on her summer pilgrimages, and was staggeringly vast, built around two courts. The outline of the gardens can be seen as earthworks, and the gateways into the lower court still stand, although bereft of their walls.

Holker Hall, Cumb 696 E5, Near Cartmel, this old house was Victorianized for the 7th Duke of Devonshire by George Webster of Kendal in 1840 and again by Paley and Austin of Lancaster in 1873, so presenting a textbook example of two stages of 19th-century domestic design. Still occupied by the Cavendish family, the house has very fine gardens, which have been worked on by Sir Joseph Paxton and Thomas Mawson and more recently by the present owners.

Below: Holker Hall is a Victorian house whose character is much enhanced by its setting in an Italian/English garden with formal and woodland areas.

Holkham Hall, Norfk 695 H4, In 1718, having spent five years on the Grand Tour, young Thomas Coke returned from Europe and decided to build a mansion sufficiently opulent to house his huge new art collection. In doing so he transformed this bleak, rabbit-infested outpost overlooking the marshes into a great treasure house set in an enormous park planted with long avenues of ilex, beech and oak. His complaint, or boast, that his nearest neighbour was the King of Denmark, may have been a deliberate snub to Robert Walpole, whose own mansion was already taking shape a few miles away at Houghton*. Coke soon engaged the services of William Kent (who was working at Houghton) and commissioned an even grander house in the latest Palladian style.

Kent's masterpiece, begun in 1734 and completed 27 years later, has an elaborate H-shaped plan and a raised entrance to the main south elevation within a pedimented portico flanked by corner towers and elaborate side wings. The sheer scale of it puts Houghton in the shade but the staccato composition and choice of yellow brick gives Holkham an

austerity that has led some to murmur that 'it has never been much admired by the neighbours'.

The unadorned exterior is, however, no preparation for the inside. The great, unsurpassed entrance hall in pink Derbyshire marble was devised by Coke himself in collaboration with the chief Palladian exponent, Lord Burlington. It leads up to the first floor and a series of richly ornamented state rooms: a glittering array of gold plaster ceilings, walls hung with tapestries and Old Masters, and Kent furniture. The Landscape Room has an unrivalled collection of Claude Lorraine and Poussin paintings while the Long Gallery was designed to display Coke's ancient Greek and Roman statues.

Among the family portraits is one of Sir Edward Coke, Lord Chief Justice and founder of the Coke fortune, who lies buried at Tittleshall*, and Gainsborough's famous study of the 1st Earl of Leicester (1782), represented not in ermine but as a gentleman farmer and sportsman in a wooded landscape. This is Coke of Norfolk, the great agricultural improver, far more interested in his annual sheep-shearings held in the Great Barn and attended by the aristocracy than in his ancestral treasure-house. On his death in 1842 grateful tenants commissioned a 120-foot (36.5m) high column to his memory.

The enormous park was laid out by Capability Brown in 1762 with a long sinuous lake to the north flanked by Coke's monument on one side and St Withburga's church – heavily restored in 1870 and with family monuments – on the other. Due south of the hall the view across the parterre is terminated by an 80-foot (24m) obelisk. Nearby and also of 1729 is a Palladian temple, and at the far end of the South Avenue, the main entrance gate, c1850. Beyond it, some 3 miles (4.8km) from the hall, stands the Triumphal Arch. Holkham estate village beside the north gates has neat Victorian Tudor cottages, reading room and thatched pump cover.

Left and top: William Kent's plans for the design of Holkham were faithfully realized.

Above: The North Tribune, with Greek and Roman statuary.

Below: The entrance hall in local marble and alabaster leads up to the first-floor state rooms.

Holme by Langford, Notts 694 E3, A couple of miles north of Newark*, across the River Trent, the remote church of St Giles is worth a visit. It was rebuilt in 1491 by John Barton out of profits from the wool trade, and is a perfect and moving example of a Tudor church.

Holme Cultram Abbey, Cumb 696 D2, In the far northwest of England, this abbey survives as St Mary, Abbey Town. It was a Cistercian house founded by the son of the Scottish king in 1150. The church retains the nave without the aisles, and the arcade is filled curiously with 18th-century windows. The best surviving medieval feature is the west door, which has four orders of columns with waterleaf capitals.

Holme Pierrepont, Notts 694 D4, Now tucked away behind the Water Sports Centre is a curious house – part Tudor, part Jacobean and part Victorian – the remains of a much larger building.

Holy Island, Nthumb 699 J5, Just off the Northumberland coast, not far from the Bernician kings' principal palace at Bamburgh*, the island is accessible at low tide by a causeway. This is where Saint Aidan came in 635, from Iona* in the Inner Hebrides, invited by King Oswald to establish a monastery. Saint Cuthbert was prior, later bishop, and when he died on the Farne Islands* in 687, he was buried here. The corpse,

Top left: Holme Pierrepont Hall, the gatehouse range dating from the early 16th century.

Holy Island
Top right: Lindisfarne Castle, interior view of Lutyens' blend of medieval and Arts and Crafts Movement architecture.
Below and bottom: The castle's dramatic setting.

when dug up 11 years later, was found to be undecayed – a sign of his holiness – and so this became known as Holy Island, one of the holiest sites of Northumbrian Christianity and still a place of pilgrimage. In this monastery, in about 698, the famous Lindisfarne Gospels were written, very beautifully, on the skins of 160 calves, by the Celtic monk Eadfrith. The capital letters were magnificently illuminated using 45 different colours and pure gold leaf. A touchscreen electronic version of these, with 'turning the pages' facility, can be seen in the Lindisfarne Heritage Centre.

Destructive Danish raids beginning in 793 forced the early monks to begin their prolonged wanderings with Saint Cuthbert's body, which were eventually to end in 995 at Durham*. Durham monks re-established a religious house here, at Lindisfarne Priory [EH], architecturally very similar to Durham Cathedral but on a smaller scale. Lindisfarne Castle [NT], a 16th-century fort, was bought in 1902 by Edward Hudson, owner of Country Life magazine, who commissioned Edwin Lutyens to convert the ruins into a small country house. Lutyens created a most attractive series of living spaces while successfully retaining the atmosphere of a castle. Typically, he also designed most of the furniture and even such details as door catches. Nearby is a tiny walled garden laid out by Gertrude Jekyll, whose design for it was lost for many years until a Durham professor of astronomy discovered it in a library in California. This site well illustrates the successful partnership of Lutyens and Jekyll. She had become his mentor after they met, while he was still a talented young architect working on an early commission in Surrey. Her knowledge of materials, together with her network of friends and contacts, helped Lutyens to design numerous country houses, usually in the Arts and Crafts style.

Holyhead, IOA 692 C1, Although a packet service from here to Dublin existed in the 17th century, Holyhead grew considerably at the beginning of the 19th century with the construction of a new harbour and with Telford's turnpike road (now the A5), the last toll road to be built in Britain. The project started with the Admiralty Pier (1821) and a year later the problem of crossing the straits was solved by an embankment, named after its principal sponsor, Lord Stanley. Later buildings in the scheme included Thomas Harrison's Doric Arch (1824) to commemorate the visit of George IV in 1821 and to celebrate the completion of Telford's enterprise.

Top: Honington Hall, the magnificent Octagonal Saloon, completed in 1751.

Holywell, Flints 693 F2, The town owes its identity to a well whose curative properties were said to stem from the miraculous recovery of the 7th-century Saint Gwenfrewi (Saint Winefride) who, having escaped an attempted rape, was beheaded by her pursuer, Caradog, a chieftain, but brought back to life by her uncle, Saint Beuno. Above the shrine is a handsome chapel, which owes its existence to the patronage of Margaret Beaufort, mother of Henry VII.

Honington Hall, Warwk 690 C3, A perfect house of the 1680s with rosy brickwork, chunky stone quoins, high chimneys and unusual decorative busts of the caesars in niches across its front. It was built by the Parker family, but the elaborate plasterwork is thought to date from the 1740s refurbishment by Joseph Townsend, the *nouveau-riche* brewer's son who bought the Hall from the Parkers in 1751. He used a friend who was an

Above: Honiton lace.
Bottom right: All Hallows Museum, Honiton.

Left: Honington Hall, the south front, believed to have been built *c*1682.

amateur architect to design the magnificent octagonal Saloon on the site of the original staircase.

Honiton, Devon 689 G5, Renowned for the hand-made lace industry based here from the 16th century, this pleasant market town flourished from the patronage of Queen Victoria, whose wedding dress was decorated with the local lace. The small All Hallows Museum contains some very fine examples of 19th-century bobbin-made Honiton lace.

Hook Norton, Oxon 690 D3, The hilltop church of St Peter retains an imposing Norman chancel. It has another Norman relic, its font, which is carved with primitive figures.

Hopetoun House, W Loth 699 F4, This huge,
    impressive palace built by the earls of Hopetoun
    stands in a vast, formally landscaped park which
    has two deer herds. The square, classical-style
    building was built by William Bruce in 1699–1704.
    It was extended between 1721 and 1754 by William
    Adam, who built the baroque east façade with its
    curved colonnade, and his sons, Robert and John,
    who completed their father's work by adding the
    main entrance and redecorating the state
    apartments, including the famous Yellow
    Drawing Room. There are exceptional furniture,
    tapestries, Meissen porcelain and paintings by
    Ramsay, Raeburn, Gainsborough, Titian, Rubens
    and Canaletto. A roof terrace offers a magnificent
    view of the park and the Firth of Forth.

Above: Hopetoun House, the west front with the Bruce house in the centre. The circular pool was once the centre of a great parterre with statuary.

Horley, Oxon 690 D3, The late Norman church of
    St Etheldreda still contains work of this date,
    but the real highlight is the 15th-century wall-
    painting of Saint Christopher crossing the river.
    It is beautifully preserved and depicts fishermen
    and fish, with a background of flowers.

Horton Court
Right: The ambulatory is detached from the house.
Below: Exterior of the Cotswold manor house.

Horn Park Gardens, Dorset 689 H5, This garden,
    lying close to Beaminster, with its views of the sea,
    appeals as much by its position as by its unusual
    trees, shrubs and plants. It has a bluebell wood,
    woodland garden and a wildflower meadow.

Hornby Castle, Lancs 696 E5, Probably 12th-century
    in origin, the castle has undergone frequent
alterations at the hands of a series of owners –
among them Lord Monteagle, who discovered the
Gunpowder Plot. What is seen now is essentially a
romantic castle, like Wray* but better detailed.
It gains most from its situation above the River
Lune. It is the most picturesque of a series of small
manor houses along the river; the finest is Burrow
Hall of 1740 by Westby Gill.

Horton Court, Gloucs 689 J3, This Cotswold house
    is probably the oldest rectory in England [NT].
    It was much altered in the 19th century, but the
    magnificent 12th-century Great Hall survives,
    and elsewhere in the house there remain early
    Renaissance features, including stucco caricatures
    of classical figures. There is an exceptionally fine
    detached loggia and an unusual late Perpendicular
    ambulatory in the garden.

Houghton Conquest, Beds 691 F3, Within the 14th-
    and 15th-century church of All Saints are the
    excellent brasses of Isabel Conquest (d. 1493),
    her husband and her son.

Below left: The Marchioness of Cholmondeley, painted by John Singer Sargent, 1919.

Below centre: Sir Robert Walpole, by John Wootton.

Right: Chinese export dinner service with Sir Robert's coat-of-arms.

Far right: The sumptuously furnished Saloon.

Bottom: The west front of Sir Robert Walpole's Palladian 'house of State and Convenience'.

Houghton Hall, NorfK 695 H4, In the open, rolling landscape of northwest Norfolk stands Houghton Hall, one of England's most beautiful Palladian houses. Set in a huge deer park and filled with major stately treasures, Houghton is the creation of the Walpole family. This house of State and Convenience, originally built to hold Sir Robert Walpole's picture collection, remains a grand expression of 18th-century wealth and power. Walpole, who was to become England's first prime minister, began to modernize the old Elizabethan hall in 1700, but it remained cold, draughty and overrun with vermin; 20 years later he abandoned the project for a more ambitious scheme. His decision to build a new mansion nearby was probably determined by the formal landscaping of perimeter belts and radial avenues already established. This decision ushered in a period of frenzied activity.

Walpole commissioned James Gibbs to design the Hall in 1720–2, with work supervised by Thomas Ripley, who ordered the pale ashlared sandstone from Whitby. In 1723, Gibbs was replaced by Colen Campbell. He did not make significant changes to the main elevations but substituted pedimented towers on the model of those at Wilton House* for Gibbs's domes. By 1725, Walpole had changed his mind and preferred the original design. Gibbs was brought back and constructed the domes as originally planned in 1725–7.

Inside, William Kent was given his first big job. The lavish ceilings and furnishings are mostly his work although there are overmantels by Grinling Gibbons and Rysbrack, and Mortlake tapestries. The magnificent collection of paintings, sold to the Empress of Russia in 1779 to pay off debts, has since been well replenished. Campbell's mansion stands at the centrepiece of an ambitious design flanked by pavilions, and to the south by a huge quadrangular stable block faced with rich brown carstone and by the glorious walled garden. The pedimented and porticoed west front that originally overlooked an elaborate parterre now gazes out across open parkland dramatically enlarged to enhance Sir Robert's grand new house. This involved rebuilding the parish church as a gothic eyecatcher and relocating medieval Houghton village at the southern end of the park where pairs of neat late 18th-century brick cottages now lead up to Lord Cholmondeley's elaborate wrought-iron entrance gates. New Houghton remains one of the earliest and best-preserved estate villages in the country and the whole composition of village, park and hall, lovingly preserved by generations of the Walpole and Cholmondeley families, remains true to Sir Robert's original concept.

Houghton House, Beds 690 E3, The home of the Countess of Pembroke, sister of the poet Sir Philip Sidney, believed to have been started *c*1615. Impressive remains are now all that are left [EH], for the house was dismantled in 1794. The Jacobean elevations are adorned with splendid frontispieces of *c*1635–45, which have been attributed (on no evidence) to Inigo Jones.

Houghton Mill, Cambs 695 F6, A 17th-century working mill on the Great Ouse, massively tarred and weather-boarded, on a site where corn has been ground for over a millennium. There are also attractive riverside walks.

Housesteads Roman Fort, Nthumb 697 F2, Visitors to the fort [NT & EH] first walk through its extensive *vicus* (civilian settlement) past a few excavated buildings (one of which was found to have a murder victim buried beneath its floor), and enter by the south gate. Nearby is a vast latrine for the troops, its larger drain once covered by wooden seats, the smaller one for rinsing the sponges used instead of lavatory paper, which were mounted on sticks. At the east gate the ground is scored with the marks of cart-wheels, the ruts almosts exactly the same width apart as modern railway tracks. Other buildings excavated include the headquarters building, the commandant's house, with the rooms arranged around a central courtyard, barrack blocks, granaries and a hospital consisting of wards and a large space that perhaps served as an operating theatre. *See* **Hadrian's Wall*.**

Above: Housesteads Roman Fort, one of the best-preserved and most dramatic sites on Hadrian's Wall.
Below: The gateway of the Wall's Milecastle 37.

Hove, E Susx 691 F7, The westward extension of Brighton* is marked by much grander terraces and squares, some of them opening towards the sea on their fourth side. Embassy Court, of 1934, by Wells Coates, is an intruder but very accomplished in its own style, a mixture of modernist and art deco. It has one of JL Pearson's best churches, All Saints (1890), and the British Engineerium, a museum of engineering with a superb Victorian beam-engine.

Hovingham Hall, N York 697 H5, A mid-18th century house, most unusual in that the best rooms are situated on the first floor above the vaulted riding school and stables, which were clearly of greater importance to the owner-architect, Sir Thomas Worsley.

Hoxne, Suffk 695 J6, A Benedictine priory was founded on the site where St Edmund is said to have been killed in 869, a local legend disputed by archeologists. Undisputed is the spectacular Roman treasure discovered in the parish in 1992 and now in the British Museum. The village itself has a pretty triangular green with the Swan Inn at the bottom – an impressive timber-frame building – and the church at the top, with interesting 15th-century murals (including the Seven Deadly Sins) and a grand west tower.

Hoy, Ork 703 G7, Ward Hill (1,570 feet/478m), the highest point on this island, is also the highest point on Orkney*. At the foot of the cliffs on the northwest coast stands the Old Man of Hoy, a 450-foot (137m) red sandstone stack. In the north is Dwarfie Stane, a neolithic rock tomb, where a passageway and two long cells have been carved out of a colossal, red sandstone monolith. To explain the role of Scapa Flow during the two world wars, Lyness Naval Base, on the southeast coast, has been converted into a museum.

Huddersfield, W York 697 G7, A former textile town with some handsome buildings, notably the railway station of 1847, with an impressive portico worthy of a Roman temple. The re-opened Huddersfield Narrow Canal has 74 navigable locks and includes the Standedge Tunnel, driven through three-quarters of a mile (1.2km) of rock.

Hughenden Manor, Bucks 690 E4, The private retreat of prime minister, statesman and writer

Right: The Old Man of Hoy, a landmark on Orkney.

Below: Huddersfield Railway Station's 1847 portico.

Hughenden Manor
Above right: The inner hall.
Above: Portrait of Benjamin Disraeli by Sir Francis Grant.

Bottom: Hovingham Hall is set in extensive grounds, with what is said to be the oldest cricket ground in England.

Benjamin Disraeli, who lived here from 1848 until his death in 1881 [NT]. It has a dramatic red-brick exterior as remodelled in 1862–3 by EB Lamb. The gothic-style interior contains Disraeli's study and mementoes of his life, and the attractive gardens have been recreated following the designs of his wife, Mary Anne. Disraeli's insignia as Knight of the Garter can be seen in Hughenden Church, where he is buried.

Huish Episcopi, Somset, The Perpendicular-style west tower of **St Mary** is divided by decorated friezes and well supported by corner pilasters. It rises in three stages to battlements and two-tier pinnacles. *See* **Langport*** 689 H5.

Hull

Hull, E R Yk 697 K6, Properly Kingston-upon-Hull (from King Edward I's acquisition of the town in 1293), the town has seen many changes in recent years as its magnificent docks eventually declined. There remain, however, hints of a noble past: its maritime history is epitomized by the handsome Trinity House complex, catering for the young and the old with a school and almshouse. **Holy Trinity Church**, perhaps the largest parish church in England, is a rare example of medieval brick construction. **Wilberforce House**, a merchant's house of c1626, was the birthplace of the anti-slavery campaigner William Wilberforce (1759–1833). Together with adjacent Georgian houses, it now contains the Museum of Slavery, holding exhibitions on the history of the slave trade and the campaign for its abolition. It is the only museum of its kind in Britain. **Maister House** [NT] is a Georgian merchant's residence of 1743, and behind the restrained street frontage is a fine staircase, with a wrought-iron balustrade by Robert Bakewell, and spectacular plasterwork. The **Ferens Art Gallery** contains an important collection of Dutch old masters and marine paintings, British portraits and contemporary art, which now includes video art.

Top left: The Ferens Art Gallery.

Bottom: The spire of Holy Trinity Church, behind terraced houses in the old town.

Humber Bridge, *see* **Barton-upon-Humber***.

Hunstanton, Norfk 695 G4, North of Heacham, with
its aromatic fields of blue Norfolk lavender, lies
this Victorian resort, laid out for the Le Strange
family at the height of the railway boom. The place
is famous for its banded cliffs of red and white
chalk and brown carrstone, beneath which Eustace
and Hilda played in LP Hartley's novel, *The Shrimp
and the Anemone.* The moated Hall and park at Old
Hunstanton, home until recently to generations
of the Le Strange family, also feature in the novel,
and there are family monuments in the church.

Huntingdon, Cambs 695 F6, The town is famous for
two of its MPs: former prime minister John Major
and Oliver Cromwell, the only commoner to head
the British state, who was born into local gentry in
1599. His baptismal font is in All Saints' Church,
having been moved from another church
destroyed by a Royalist raiding party after the
Battle of Naseby. Cromwell's birthplace is lost but
the grammar school he and Pepys attended – once
part of the 12th-century Hospital of St John – has a
museum in his honour (admire the Lord Protector's
felt hat, gaiters and death mask). As a rising force
in Puritan politics, he rallied Parliamentary forces
during the Civil War from the Falcon Inn.
Huntingdon also has a stately red-brick Town
Hall of 1745, Norman castle earthworks and a
medieval stone bridge across the Ouse.

Huntly Castle, Abers 702 C5, Two standing stones
mark the main square of this former royal burgh,
whose history is traced by the Brander Museum.
The remains of Huntly Castle, at the confluence
of the rivers Deveron and Bogie, reflect the
development of Scottish castles. The castle motte,
built in the 12th century by the Duncans, earls of
Fife, can still be seen. So, too, can the foundations
of the keep built by the Gordons in the 14th
century. As fervent Catholics and key players in the
Counter-Reformation, the castle of the earls of
Huntly was destroyed in 1549. In 1602 George
Gordon, 6th Earl of Huntly, began to restore the
magnificent castle; it was, however, abandoned
shortly afterward and fell slowly into ruin. Even so
the south façade is still one of the most beautiful
in Britain, with its oriel windows (possibly
inspired by the Château of Blois) and stone friezes
bearing the names of the 1st Marquess and his wife
Henrietta Stewart.

Hurst Castle, Hants 690 C7, Built as a fortress by
Henry VIII at the entrance to the Solent. Two
38-ton guns form the armaments [EH].

Hutton-in-the-Forest, Cumb 696 E3, A romantic and
complex house, acquired by Richard Fletcher of
Cockermouth and still in the hands of his
descendants. The earliest fabric is a 14th-century
pele tower. Additions include a further tower,
a Long Gallery of the 1640s by Alexander Pogmire
and a baroque frontispiece by the mason

Above: Huntly Castle, the
magnificent heraldic
entrance of 1602.

Top right: Hutton-in-the-
Forest grounds have terraces,
a woodland walk and walled
garden.

Right and bottom right:
Hyde Hall garden has the
National Collections of
viburnums and ornamental
crab apples.

Edward Addison. An extensive remodelling by
George Webster of Kendal in the 1820s did not
detract from this fascinating variety. The inside is
equally varied, with work of almost all periods
including a fine carved staircase of 1680, 18th-
century decoration with plasterwork by Joseph
Rose, Gothic Revival work by Webster and some
original William Morris fabrics and wallpaper.

Hyde Hall, Essex 691 H4, A beautiful hilltop garden
run by the Royal Horticultural Society. Attractions
include a large rose collection, ornamental ponds
and a Farmhouse Garden.

Hythe, Kent 691 J6, Once a major port but now, like
the other Cinque Ports, a picturesque backwater.
The church reflects its medieval importance. Its
13th-century chancel is built on a grand scale and,
unusually for a parish church, was intended to be
vaulted (though the actual vault was not
constructed until 1886). Underneath, accessible
from the outside, is a rare 'bone house' containing,
for those with a taste for the macabre, rows of
skulls on shelves.

Ickworth, Suffk 695 H6, The house is set in a beautiful Capability Brown park southwest of Bury St Edmunds* [NT]. With its central rotunda and curving wings, it is unique and oddly unsettling, haunted by the ghosts of the Hervey family who lived here in varying degrees of unhappiness. Frederick, 4th Earl of Bristol and Bishop of Derry, began the site with Francis Sandys in 1795 as a gallery for Grand Tour acquisitions, most of which were later seized by Napoleon. John Flaxman sculpted *The Fury of Athamas* and modelled terracotta friezes around the outside of the rotunda. Major paintings and grand furnishings chiefly reflect the late Regency taste of the 4th Earl's son and heir. His successor, the 3rd Marquess of Bristol, added the Pompeian Room frescoes (actually copied from murals in Rome's Villa Negroni).

The Victorian gardens are planted in formal, evergreen, Italian style. The church, on its own near the lake, has Flemish glass and Hervey monuments. Nearby are the early 18th-century walled garden and greenhouse.

Above: Don Balthasar Carlos, by Velázquez.

Above centre: The Pompeian Room.

Right: The rotunda and its wings were designed by Francis Sandys in 1795 at the insistence of the eccentric 4th Earl of Bristol, to house his collection of Old Masters. Sandys worked from a design prepared in Rome by Mario Asprucci.

Left: Ightham Mote, the south side, showing the mixture of periods and materials making up the house. In the centre, half-timbering takes over from stone.

Left and above: Iffley St Mary's, the elaborate late-12th-century carving.

Below: Ilkley, White Wells, a survival from the fashionable days of the 19th-century spa.

The oldest part is a 13th-century crypt; the Hall dates from the 14th century [NT].

Ilchester, Somset 689 H5, Originally the Roman town of Lendiniae, Ilchester was always important, and in the Middle Ages had four parish churches. Today it is the massive 13th-century tower of St Mary Major which attracts attention. Inside there is much of a later date – the south aisle is of 1880. There is a triangular green near the church, with Georgian buildings and an 18th-century cross. The Town Hall possesses the oldest mace, or staff of office, in England.

Ile Abbots, Somset 689 H5, Within the church of St Mary, honey-coloured stone contrasts strikingly but harmoniously with darker Ham stone. There is a unique piscina (a basin for washing Communion vessels), framed by two panels and surmounted by five more. The niches on the church tower still retain most of the original statuary.

Ilfracombe, Devon 688 E4, The wild and romantic scenery of the north Devon coast where it meets Exmoor greatly appealed to the Victorians, who flocked to this new resort either by narrow-gauge railway from Barnstaple or by paddle-steamer from the ports of the Bristol Channel. Terraces of boarding houses and yellow-brick hotels hug the conical hills and look out toward Lundy*.

Ilkley, W York 697 G6, Nestling below the moor, the town most famous for the song 'On Ilkla Moor Baht At' was a fashionable 19th-century spa – the whitewashed White Wells on the moorside, still containing the spa bath, can be visited. An exhibition on the spa town can be seen in the Manor House Museum, in a 16th- and 17th-century building on the site of Olicana Roman fort. Wealthy West Riding businessmen like to retire to Ilkley, and in 1906 a villa was commissioned by such a gentleman from Sir Edwin Lutyens. **Heathcote,** visible from Grove Road and King's Road, was the turning point for Lutyens, marking his graduation from the Arts and Crafts style to classical design, and forming a miniature prototype for his great buildings in

Iffley, Oxon 690 D4, St Mary's is one of the country's most beautiful Norman churches. It was built c1170–80 and is lavishly decorated with zig-zag and beakhead motifs. Northwest of the church is the Old Parsonage, built mainly in c1500 but of Norman origin. From here there is a fine prospect of both the nearby church and the distant skyline of Oxford.

Iford Manor Garden, Wilts, The Tudor manor is surrounded by a garden designed by Harold Peto (early 20th century). It has pools, statues and a cloister. *See* **Westwood Manor* 690 B5.**

Ightham Mote, Kent 691 G6, A medieval house, more modest than Knole* nearby, but older and exceptionally picturesque. It consists of four wings round a courtyard, surrounded by a moat.

New Delhi. **Rombald's Moor** is a wild open space over 1,300 feet (400m) above sea-level, rich in prehistoric remains. There are rock engravings here, but the fanciful shapes of the Cow and Calf are the work of nature, not of cavemen.

Image Garden, Cumb 696 E3, The garden in Reaghyll was created by a self-taught local man, Thomas Bland, to celebrate the coronation of Queen Victoria. Some 50 pieces of garden sculpture are arranged in 'rooms' with specific themes such as 'Shakespeare's plays' or 'mythical characters'.

Impington, Cambs 695 G6, The Village College is one of several education centres around Cambridge promoted by pioneer Henry Morris. It is a brilliant building designed in 1938 by Walter Gropius (with Maxwell Fry) after his rescue from Nazi Germany. Sadly, other commissions were not forthcoming and the Bauhaus giant moved on to America.

Inchcolm, Fife 699 G4, This island in the Firth of Forth is the site of St Colm's Abbey, founded in 1123. The well-preserved buildings include a late-13th-century octagonal chapter house with a stone roof and a 14th-century cloister with a dormitory .

Ingatestone Hall, Essex 691 G4, A red-brick, step-gabled mansion begun in 1540 for Sir William Petre, minister under Henry VIII and Edward VI, with a gatehouse and clocktower added in the late 18th century. Rewarded for organizing the Dissolution of the Monasteries, he now lies elaborately entombed in St Edmund's Church.

Ingestre Hall, Staffs 693 H3, A brick Jacobean house that has suffered many alterations, especially in the 19th century. St Mary's Church, standing close to the Hall, is dated 1676 and is almost certainly by Sir Christopher Wren – it is very like a City church, with elaborate plaster ceilings.

Inveraray, Ag & B 698 C3, With its whitewashed two-storey houses and classical public buildings, this

Top left: Ingatestone Hall's distinctive styling of tall Tudor chimneys and crow-stepped gables.

Inveraray Castle
Top right: The castle was designed by Roger Morris with assistance from William Adam and sons.
Left: Morris's galleried central hall with its displays of weaponry.

Above: Inverewe Gardens have many rare and delicate plants from the southern hemisphere, and several varieties of rhododendron from the Himalayas.

former royal burgh (1648) and seat of the Campbell clan since the 15th century is an exceptional example of 18th-century urban planning. When Archibald Campbell, 3rd Duke of Argyll, decided to rebuild his ancestral castle in 1744, he moved the surrounding village to Gallows Foreland on the shores of Loch Fyne. The public buildings were designed by John Adam and Robert Mylne. Inveraray Courthouse and Jail by Gillespie Graham (1816–20, closed in 1889), is now a museum with courtroom and prison cells. The Bell Tower of the Episcopal church, erected by the 10th Duke of Argyll in memory of the Campbells killed during World War I, offers panoramic views of the town and Loch Fyne. The castle, designed by Roger Morris assisted by William Adam and his sons John and Robert, was built between 1746 and 1758. The interior decor was renovated (1772–82) by Robert Mylne. The painted panels by the French artists Guinand and Girard, who worked for the Prince Regent at Carlton House, are among the finest examples of neoclassical decor in Britain. There is an impressive collection of weaponry, family portraits (Gainsborough, Ramsay, Raeburn, Batoni), furniture, gold- and silverware, and Beauvais tapestries.

and the prison, now the district court, by Thomas Brown, 1846–8.

Inverness Museum and Art Gallery: The well-stocked museum on Castle Wynd covers history, natural history, archeology, ethnography and Jacobite relics.

Balnain House: The Georgian mansion in Huntly Street, built by a wealthy merchant in 1762, today houses a research centre on the music of the Highlands and Islands.

Inverpolly National Nature Reserve, Highld 701 F3, This 27,000-acre (10,926ha) nature reserve incorporates the vast Loch Sionacaig and Cul Mor (2,875 feet/876m). As in the Torridon* region, the sandstone relief rises from a plateau of Lewisian gneiss that is 3 billion years old. The reserve has some of the last remains of the Caledonian Forest* and abundant wildlife: golden eagles, deer and wild cats.

Inverurie, Abers 702 D6, The county town of Garioch is also the main cattle market in the northeast. The region is of great archeological interest. Three Pictish stones stand in the churchyard at the southeast end of the village. Nearby is The Bass, a feudal motte built in 1160 by David, Lord of Garioch and brother of Malcolm II. Another Pictish stone, the Brandsbutt Stone, stands on the northwest edge of Inverurie. It is decorated with symbols and an ogham inscription, and is thought to be a funeral stone from the 6th–7th century.

Inverewe Gardens, Highld 700 E4, In 1862 Osgood Mackenzie (1842–1922) began to create a garden on the barren, windswept and previously uncultivated Kernsary peninsula, east of Poolewe. Taking advantage of the influence of the warm Gulf Stream, he patiently put together a remarkable botanical collection. Today the collection comprises over 2,500 species of mainly exotic plants, forming a lush garden that lies on the same latitude as St Petersburg.

Inverness, Highld 701 H5, Inverness, capital of the Highlands, stands at the mouth of the Ness, occupying a strategic site between the North Highlands and the Grampians. Early in its history St Columba came to convert the Pictish king Brude (Brudei) to Christianity. In the 11th century Macbeth built a castle here, which was later destroyed by Malcolm III to avenge the murder of his father, Duncan I. The town was made a royal burgh by David I c1140 and subsequently suffered a number of sieges. It was occupied by the English during the wars of independence, recaptured by Robert Bruce in 1307, then passed into the hands of the Highland clans, supporting Mary Stuart in 1562 and the Jacobites in 1715 and 1745. Few ancient buildings have therefore survived.

Church Street is lined with old buildings: High Church (13th century, restored 1722), Dunbar's Hospital (1688) and Abertarff House (1593), regional office of the National Trust for Scotland.

Inverness Castle: In 1746 the Jacobites destroyed the last fortress on Castle Hill. The site was cleared in 1833 to build the present castle, comprising the Sheriff Court designed by William Burn in 1833–5

Top: Inverness from the River Ness, by JMW Turner (1779–1851).

Above: Inverness Castle.

Below and bottom: Inverurie, Pictish stones.

Iona

Iona, Ag & B 698 A3, This tiny island off the southwest tip of the Isle of Mull*, played a key role in Scotland's conversion to Christianity. An Augustinian nunnery was founded in the early 13th century by Reginald, whose sister, Beatrice, became the first prioress. Today its ruins stand behind the post office, to the left of the path running from the ferry to the cathedral. The church still has its choir, nave and part of its vaulted roof. To the south lie the remains of the cloister, today a garden, and those of the chapter-house and refectory. The 13th–14th century church of St Ronan, built on the foundations of an 8th-century chapel to the north of the nunnery, houses a small museum.

MacLean's Cross: The Celtic motifs decorating this 15th-century cross beside the footpath are a fine example of the work of the Iona School.

St Oran's Cemetery (Reilig Odhrain): St Oran's Chapel stands in the centre of one of Scotland's oldest Christian cemeteries. Many clan chiefs from the Hebrides, 8 Norse kings, 4 Irish kings and 48 Scottish kings (including Kenneth MacAlpin and Duncan I) are buried here.

Street of the Dead: A section of the Street of the Dead, the paved road that led from the ferry and was used for funeral processions, still links the cemetery and cathedral.

The cathedral: This former 13th-century Benedictine church, built on a cruciform plan, has been extensively renovated. In the 15th century the south side was extended, a square bell tower built on the crossing of the transept, the north aisle transformed into a sacristy and St Columba's Chapel (said to be the saint's first burial place) incorporated into the complex, to the west of the cloister. The beautiful carved capitals of the south arch of the choir date from the same period. The door in the north wall of the nave opens onto the cloister in the centre of which stands a group by Jacques Lipchitz: *The Descent of the Spirit* (1960). The chapter house was restored in 1955 and the refectory in 1949. In front of the Cathedral's west façade stand a beautiful St Martin's Cross (8th century), a copy of the St John's Cross in the Infirmary Museum, which dates from the same period, and the broken shaft of a St Matthew's Cross (11th century).

Infirmary Museum. The former infirmary, to the northeast of the abbey, houses a beautiful collection of carved stones from the Celtic and medieval periods, including the original St John's Cross (8th century) and the most beautiful tombstones from St Oran's cemetery.

Left: Relics of St Columba.

Below: St Martin's Cross in front of the west façade.

Centre left: A fragment of the Book of Kells.

Bottom: The whole site was roofless until 1899 when restoration of the church began.

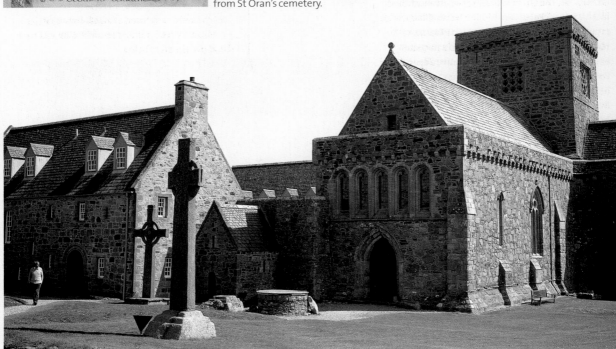

Ipswich, Suffk 691 J3, Between muscular dockland warehouses and one of England's most beautiful town parks, impressive fragments of the town's golden age lurk behind invasive office blocks – but much has gone completely. Tower Ramparts is a ghostly reminder of medieval walls; gone too are extensive monastic remains, notably Cardinal College founded by local boy Thomas Wolsey in 1528 when he was Henry VIII's Chancellor. The site today is marked by a modest brick gateway. Anchored at the head of the Orwell estuary, Ipswich was a rich cloth-exporting port by the

17th century, much praised by Defoe. Twelve medieval churches remain, but apart from St Margaret's, with its splendid painted roof, none is large or lavish. Isolated gems include St Peter's rare Tournai marble front with feline frieze. Richly carved timber buildings survive in St Margaret's Street and Northgate Street, and there are some good merchant's houses near the docks. Others, like the Great White Horse, immortalized in *The Pickwick Papers*, are hidden behind later brick façades. Most lavish is the **Ancient House**, with 16th-century moulded ceilings and a pargeted extravaganza of *c*1670 featuring naïve allegories of the four known continents. You may trace the demise of late medieval Ipswich in **Christchurch Mansion**'s graveyard collection of panelling and carved corner posts. The Mansion, on the site of an Augustinian priory, was built to an Elizabethan E-plan for Withipole merchants, with porch and Dutch gables added in 1675. Saved for the town by wealthy Cobbold brewers, it is now a marvellous museum and art gallery with works by Gainsborough, Constable and other local artists. There are good Georgian terraces in Lower Brook Street, and the heavily classical quayside Custom House of 1844 should not be missed, but Joseph Friar's Meeting House of 1699, a bold statement of religious tolerance with huge shipmast pillars and carved pulpit, is the most atmospheric. Its face is now reflected in the black glass screen of Ipswich's only outstanding modern building, Norman Foster's 1975 insurance office.

Above: Ipswich, St Margaret's Church, the most impressive of the town's dozen medieval churches.

Below: Ironbridge Gorge, *View of the Iron Bridge*, by William Williams, 1780, on display at the Ironbridge Gorge Museum.

Ironbridge Gorge, Shrops 693 G4, A dramatic narrowing of the River Severn where it joins Coalbrookdale valley. From the early 18th century an ironmaster named Abraham Darby made this a famous centre of the British iron industry, first by introducing coke instead of wood for smelting and then by adopting a new process for making cast iron malleable. For the first half of the 20th century the area suffered slow decline, but then, fortunately, its historical importance was recognized. Ironbridge has now been designated a World Heritage Site and the whole area is a collection of museums devoted to industry, ceramics, decorative arts and living history. There was never a proper town here, just a random collection of furnaces, factories and houses. The nearest thing to a centre is the Market Square, which lies at the north end of the Iron Bridge itself, designed for Abraham Darby by the Shrewsbury architect Thomas Farnolls Pritchard and built in 1778 [EH]. It was the first large bridge in the world to be built wholly of iron and at once became a tourist attraction, which it has remained ever since. The bridge has a span of 120 feet (36.5m) and the arch, composed of an elaborate lattice of cast-iron struts, is almost semicircular and rises far above the river below.

Islay, Ag & B 698 A5, Islay, the most southerly of the Inner Hebrides, is also the largest and most fertile. For centuries its whisky was produced and sold illegally. Today the island has six legal distilleries, a cheese factory and tweed mill. It is linked to Kennacraig (Kintyre), Colonsay* and Jura* by ferry. **Port Ellen,** Islay's largest town, on the southeast coast, was rebuilt in 1821 according to plans by Walter Frederick Campbell. The road leading to Kildalton, to the northeast of Port Ellen, services several of the island's distilleries. It also passes beneath Dunyvaig Castle, built in the 14th century by the Macdonalds, Lords of the Isles. The 13th-century church of Kidalton houses one of Scotland's most beautiful Celtic crosses, probably carved on Iona in the 8th or 9th century. The churchyard has some fine tombstones. **Bowmore:** Islay's administrative centre, also has its oldest legal distillery (1779). The island was bought by Donald Campbell of Shawfield in 1725. His grandson, Donald the Younger, inspired by the architecture seen on a visit to Italy, designed this model village in 1768 with its circular Kilarow Church. Gruinart Flats RSPB Nature Reserve (south of Loch Gruinart) is mainly for barnacle geese. **Port Charlotte** is a delightful little harbour, founded in 1828 by Walter Frederick Campbell on the west bank of Loch Indaal, with an interesting Museum of Islay Life. The 'Friends of Finlaggan' have opened a small museum to the northeast of Loch Finlaggan. They also provide a boat to enable visitors to reach the ruined castle, a former Macdonald stronghold, that stands on an island in the middle. Together with Port Ellen, Port Askraig is one of the island's two ferry ports for Kintyre and the only ferry port for Jura and Colonsay.

Isle of Man

Isle of Man IOM 696 B5, The sovereign of the Isle of Man is the sovereign of the United Kingdom but the island is practically independent and feels it. Green and hilly, it is attractive more for its isolation than for its architecture. There are the many stone crosses, relics of early Christianity, the best at Braddan, Onchan (the church where Captain Bligh was married in 1781), Kirk Andreas (where mixed pagan and Christian scenes include Sigurd roasting the heart of the dragon he had slain), and Kirk Michael. At Castletown there are the remains of the Cistercian Rushen Abbey and Castle Rushen, one of the most complete medieval castles in Britain. Castletown has a good townscape, as do Peel and Port St Mary, but the island's capital, Douglas, has more of the atmosphere of a Victorian seaside resort, somewhat blemished by new replacement buildings designed for offshore financial institutions. The island's most spectacular monument is undoubtedly the water-wheel at **Laxey,** the largest of its kind in the world. The wheel, 72 feet (22m) in diameter, is still turning – though now to no purpose as the lead mines it once drained no longer function. It is known as 'Lady Isabella', after the wife of the island's governor in 1854 when the wheel was commissioned.

Above: Castle Rushen in Castletown dates from the 13th century.

Below: Port Erin, on the island's southwest coast.

Isle of Wight

Isle of Wight, Hants 690 D8, Diamond-shaped, 23 miles (37km) from east to west and 13 miles (21km) north to south, the island is full of variety. A chalk range marks the east–west axis, ending in the Needles peninsula, the dramatic series of detached rocks at the western extremity, and Alum Bay, famous for its many-coloured sands.

On the northern side the country is fairly flat, with tidal inlets and estuaries; to the south it is hillier, with outcrops of sandstone used in many of the older buildings. The coast is varied; there are good beaches at the main resorts of Ryde, Sandown, Shanklin and Ventnor, some impressive chalk cliffs to both east and west and, in the far south and southeast (the area called the Undercliff), an uneven coastline backed by steep, broken hillsides where the topography was formed by landslips millennia ago. Newport is the main central town, and Cowes an estuarine port famous as a base for yachting; Yarmouth is much smaller. Much of the island, particularly inland, is very rural. Freshwater is a sprawling place, but Freshwater Bay is an attractive cove. Nearby is Dimbola Lodge, the former home of Julia Margaret Cameron, pioneer of photography, now a museum in her honour. Westward, Tennyson Down is a chalk ridge with sheer white cliffs on its edge, seen in distant views along the coast to the southeast. Nearer at hand, the Down offers superb walking along its crest. Tennyson lived nearby at Farringford House, now a hotel. Further westward still is the Needles peninsula.

Appuldurcombe: The preserved shell of a great house of 1701–13, by John James (with alterations c1805–10) in a beautiful setting; the main façade has been completely restored.

Top left: Brading Villa, east front and formal garden.

Top right: The Library in Nunwell House, Brading.

Main picture: Compton Bay, looking southeast.

Left: Appuldurcombe House, a palatial 18th-century house, now a ruin but in the process of restoration.

Below: 4th-century mosaic of Medusa at Brading Villa.

It and its predecessor were the home of the Worsleys, the leading Isle of Wight family from Tudor to late Georgian times. Members of the family are commemorated in a fine series of tombs in Godshill Church, set on a hill behind picturesque cottages. Shorwell Church is also interesting.

Brading: Here stands a fine 13th-century church with monuments to the Oglander family, who lived at Nunwell, to the west, a 17th- and 18th-century house and garden. The Roman villa at Brading (exposed foundations with mosaics) is interesting and well laid out. Near Ventnor, in the romantic scenery of the Undercliff, is a Botanic Garden.

Carisbrooke Castle: One of the most interesting castles in southern England. It has a keep on a Norman motte; a former Great Hall, altered in the 19th century and now a museum; Norman and later curtain walls, and a 14th-century Great Gateway; outer defences added in the Elizabethan period; and a treadwheel over a well, regularly operated by a donkey. Charles I was imprisoned here, tried unsuccessfully to escape, and was brought hence to his execution in London in 1648.

Mottistone: The 16th-century manor house was rescued from near-ruin in the 1920s.

Newport: The island's capital, 'new' in the late 12th century, has some fine Georgian and earlier buildings constructed on a medieval street pattern. The Guildhall (1816), now a museum, is by John Nash, with a Jubilee tower commemorating Queen Victoria. (Both the Queen and Nash had their favourite residences on the island.)

Above: The Needles, a row of sharp rocks at the extreme west end of the island. One of them collapsed into the sea within living memory.

Left: The interior of St Nicholas Chapel at Carisbrooke Castle was restored from a ruin in the 1920s.

Newtown: The 18th-century Old Town Hall (now a museum) was built after the town had largely disappeared – because Newtown still 'elected' two members of Parliament (with a handful of voters) and there was still a town corporation [NT].

Osborne House: Built from 1845 on an estate bought by Queen Victoria in that year, designed essentially by Prince Albert in partnership with Thomas Cubitt, the successful builder of much of Belgravia*. It is an Italianate, classical palace of many parts, dominated by two towers of different heights. The main domestic section is open to the public, furnished as in the Queen's time; the formal gardens have been restored, and the extensive grounds have, among other attractions, the Swiss Cottage built for the royal children, with a toy fort nearby. It was Victoria's favourite home; she spent most of her time there after Prince Albert's death in 1861, and died there herself in 1901. There is a major art collection on display, reflecting the personal tastes of Victoria and Albert. The Indian-inspired Durbar Room is of particular interest.

Quarr Abbey: The remains of the medieval abbey are fragmentary but the present abbey, built from 1908 for Benedictine monks originally from France to the design of Dom Paul Bellot, has a magnificent church in a style inspired by southern European buildings but highly original, all in plain bricks from Belgium.

Ryde: Developed from the 1820s, the town preserves a late-Georgian to mid-Victorian character; its best building is the Royal Victoria Arcade (1836) with a splendid classical interior by William Westmacott, behind an altered façade.

Yarmouth: A miniature town with ferries to Lymington, a small harbour used by yachts, and attractive older streets. The Castle is one of the coastal forts built by Henry VIII (1547).

Top left and centre left: Quarr Abbey, a unique and powerful example of brick Expressionism in English architecture.

Top right: Freshwater, Isle of Wight.

Below: Osborne House, the garden front. This was Queen Victoria's favourite home. She died here in 1901.

Isleham, Cambs 695 G6, The remains of an 11th-century Benedictine priory in the shape of a well-preserved early Norman chapel are complemented by a great Fen-edge church with a glorious hammerbeam roof (*see* Mildenhall*). Note Thomas Peyton's canopied brass of 1487, with fashionably dressed wives; his family financed St Andrew's ambitious Perpendicular make-over [EH].

Iver, Bucks, Iver Grove is a very handsome baroque house of 1722. The west front has a pediment supported on giant Doric pilasters. On the north and south elevations, the centrepiece continues up to an attic section with a pediment and two flanking chimneys. The vertical emphasis is typical of the style of the Royal Office of Works, and the house has been attributed to John James. *See* **Slough* 690 E5.**

Ivinghoe, Bucks 690 E4, Ford End Watermill, Station Road, is the county's only working watermill to survive with its original machinery. The building was first recorded in the 1700s, but has been restored as a museum. Not far away is the church of St Mary, with 13th-century arcades, an early 14th-century crossing tower and late medieval roofs. The **Ridgeway National Trail** runs from Ivinghoe Beacon, one of the earliest hillfort sites, to Avebury* in Wiltshire. Covering 90 miles (144km), it is part of an old prehistoric route from the Dorset coast to the Wash.

Jarlshof, *see* **Shetland*.**

Jarrow, T & W 697 G2, The town was made famous by the Jarrow March in 1936, a protest against the closure of its shipyard, but its origins are much more ancient. Here, Benedict Biscop, Abbot of Wearmouth, founded a sister house to his Monkwearmouth monastery at Sunderland*. Above the chancel arch in St Paul's Church is the inscribed stone recording the dedication of Benedict Biscop's monastery in 685. Jarrow was

Above: Ivinghoe, Ford End Farm Watermill, brick with a timber-framed and weatherboarded upper floor.

Below: Jarrow, St Paul's Church with Anglo-Saxon tower, and ruins of the later medieval monastery.

the home of the Venerable Bede, the scholar and early historian, who wrote his *History of the English Church and People* here. Bede also died here, in 735, and was buried in the church, but his bones were later taken to the cathedral at Durham*. Jarrow's Anglo-Saxon monastery was abandoned in the 9th century after Danish raids, but was refounded after the Norman Conquest: the ruins of St Paul's Monastery [EH] can be seen around the old church. The Bede's World Museum is a short walk north of the church.

Jedburgh, Border 699 H6, Above the river stand the impressive ruins of Jedburgh Abbey, founded in 1138 by David I for Augustinian monks from Beauvais. His son Malcolm IV was crowned in the Abbey in 1153. Henry VIII's campaign of 'rough wooing' left the building in ruins in 1544–5, although part of the church was used for Protestant worship between 1560 and 1875. The crossing of the transept and the choir (mid-12th century) are the oldest part of the church. Even without a roof, the nave with its nine bays is still impressive, while its three perfectly balanced levels are a fine illustration of the transition between

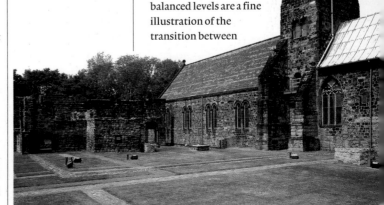

Romanesque and gothic architecture. The north transept was rebuilt in the 15th century and the square tower above the crossing in the early 16th century. At the top of Castlegate stands Castle Jail Museum, a former prison built (1823) on the site of the castle razed in 1409 to prevent it falling to the English. Mary Queen of Scots' House in Queen Street is a late 16th-century house where Mary Stuart spent several weeks in 1566 after riding to Hermitage Castle to visit the wounded Bothwell.

Jervaulx Abbey, N York 697 G4, One of North Yorkshire's many ruined Cistercian abbeys. As it is privately owned, it still retains something of the character of a cherished feature in an 18th-century park. In addition to the intrinsic historic interest of the buildings, there is added value in that the site is a habitat for a treasure-trove of wildflowers.

John o' Groats, Highld 702 C1, John o' Groats was named after Jan de Groot, the Dutchman who established a regular boat service between the port and Orkney* at the request of James IV. This is still the shortest link with the islands.

Jordans, Bucks 690 E4, The village of Jordans was designed by Fred Rowntree and begun in 1919 on the model of a garden suburb built exclusively for Quakers. In Welders Lane survives a Friends Meeting House of 1688. This is a modest structure of considerable historic interest, as it was built by Isaac Penington immediately after the Toleration Act. The gravestone of William Penn (d. 1718), founder of Pennsylvania, can be seen in the burial ground.

Jura, Ag & B 698 B4, This wild island, dominated by the three summits of the Paps of Jura (the highest is 2,576 feet/785m), was named after the deer that inhabit it (*Dyroe* in Norse). The Strait of Corryvreckan, between the northwestern tip of Jura and the uninhabited island of Scarba, is renowned for the whirlpools created by counter currents from the Atlantic and the Sound of Jura above a submerged reef. The noise can be heard for up to 10 miles (16km) away. The strait, in the past thought to be a witch's cauldron, is an extremely dangerous stretch of water.

Kedington, Suffk 691 G3, The church here displays a long tradition of fine wood carving: the 15th-century rood screen used to make up the Barnardiston pew, the triple-decker pulpit and Georgian musicians' gallery, and the wonderful sequence of 16th- and 17th-century alabaster tombs to the Barnardiston family, which must take pride of place.

Kedleston Hall, Derbys 694 C4, The parkland sweeps up from the lake to the long main front of the house, built for Sir Nathaniel Curzon, 1st Lord Scarsdale, between 1759 and 1765. The first architect was Matthew Brettingham, and James 'Athenian' Stuart designed the great Marble Hall. Before the house was finished, however, Robert Adam took over. He designed a completely new and highly original south front based on a Roman triumphal arch, and reorganized the interior, with a view to showing off Lord Scarsdale's important collection of pictures, many of which are set into the walls. Behind the south front is the Rotunda, a huge

circular room originally intended for the display of classical sculpture. Most of the other rooms have Adam ceilings and many have furniture designed by him as well. The park is enormous and contains a variety of garden buildings (including a delightful Fishing Pavilion and Boat House), again mostly by Robert Adam. Both house and park are the property of the National Trust.

Keiss, Highld 702 C1, The remains of two brochs can be seen beside the coastal path leading to the medieval ruins of Keiss Castle. Like the white castle (private property) set back from the coast, built in Scots Baronial style in the 18th century, Keiss Castle is the property of the Sinclairs, earls of Caithness.

Top centre: Kedington church wood carving.

Kedleston Hall
Top right: A fireplace in the Marble Hall.
Left: Robert Adam's unexecuted design for the mirrored chimneypiece wall of a Book Room.
Bottom: Adam's south front of the 1760s.

Right: Kellie Castle, with furniture by Robert Lorimer.

Kelham Hall, Notts 694 E4, Now local council offices, the Hall was built as a private mansion in the 1850s to the design of Sir George Gilbert Scott after the old house burnt down. It was at Kelham that Scott first tried out his ideas for modern secular

buildings in the gothic style, ten years before he designed St Pancras Station in London*. Just across the lawn from the Hall is the medieval church of St Wilfrid. The Lexington chapel contains an elaborate monument to Lord Lexington (d. 1723) and his wife.

Kellie Castle, Fife 699 G3, This 16th-century castle perched on a wooded hillside was restored and given a Victorian garden by the Lorimer family in the 1880s. It has a T-shaped layout, some distinctive stuccoed ceilings and painted wall

panels (17th century), and furniture designed by Robert Lorimer [National Trust for Scotland].

Kelmarsh Hall, Nhants 694 E6, The bland red-brick façade of Kelmarsh Hall, designed by James Gibbs in the early 18th century, hides exceptional stuccowork inside. The little lodges follow Gibbs' designs, but were commissioned by Sir Albert Richardson in the 1960s.

Kelmscot, Gloucs 690 C4, The great 19th-century artist and designer William Morris made his country home here, near the Gloucestershire border, and the Manor House in which he lived from 1871 until 1896 remains an eminently picturesque and tranquil place. The house was built in c1570 and has a north wing added in the late 17th century. It contains a fascinating collection of works by Morris and his equally talented associates, including Sir Edward Burne-Jones and William de Morgan, from tiles around fireplaces to carpets on the floor, as well Morris's own possessions. Morris's printing press at Hammersmith was named after Kelmscott. The small Norman village church is also worth a visit, both for itself and for Morris' grave in the churchyard, designed by Philip Webb. Commemorative buildings to Morris include the Morris Cottages of 1902 and the Village Hall, built between 1928 and 1934.

Kelso, Border 699 H5, With old cobbled streets bordered by elegant 18th-century houses and a French-style square dominated by the Town Hall (1819), Kelso is a picturesque market town. Situated at the confluence of the rivers Tweed and Teviot, the town grew up around the nearby Reformed Benedictine abbey, founded in 1128 by David I near the town and royal castle of Roxburgh*. It suffered a number of raids at the hands of the English, the most disastrous of which was led by Edward Seymour, Earl of Hertford in 1544–5, on the orders of Henry VIII. The ruins of the Borders' most powerful abbey stand near the five-arched bridge built between 1799 and 1808 by John Rennie. The Abbey Church was built according to an original plan comprising a narthex, two transepts separated by a short nave and a choir that probably formed an apse. All that can be seen today are the narthex, the first transept and the first two bays of the nave. The projecting doorway of the north transept, with its reticulated pediment, is the only one of its kind in Scotland. The small cloister (1933) to the south of the church houses the tomb of the Kerr family (the family name of the Dukes of Roxburghe).

Above: Kendal, a view over the townscape that is the key to the southern part of the Lake District*.

Above: Kempley, the Norman church of St Mary.

Below: Kenilworth Castle. In 1266 it resisted a siege for nearly nine months.

Kempley, Gloucs 693 G6, Visit remote St Mary's Church to see the 'Wheel of Life' on the north wall of the nave, one of the many medieval wall-paintings here dating from the 13th century onward. Spreading across the tunnel vault is a picture of Christ seated uncomfortably on a rainbow, which was only discovered from beneath Reformation whitewash in 1872. Unfortunately, as was often the case, early preservative treatments caused more damage that they prevented.

Kendal, Cumb 696 E4, The most important building is Abbot Hall, 1759, built by John Carr for Colonel Wilson, so close to the town centre and the church that it is a town house but with its own grounds and outbuildings that give it a sense of space. It is a late Palladian villa with a central block and lower wings with Venetian windows. The house is now an excellent museum and art gallery while the outbuildings house the Museum of Lakeland Life.

Kenilworth, Warwks 694 C6, After 250 years of royal warfare and sieges, John of Gaunt had converted the almost impregnable Kenilworth Castle into a pleasure palace [EH]. The huge bulk of the tower glows pink, and once must have been wonderfully reflected in the Mere, the lake that surrounded it until the Civil War. The Mere was created by a 17th-century dam, and at one time extended for just over a mile to the castle's south and west. Henry V was responsible for creating a moated garden known as the 'pleasance', a mile (1.6km) away across the lake. The castle was slighted in the Civil War and the causeway dam was breached, but plans are afoot to re-flood the Mere. Today, a good deal of 16th-century fabric survives, including the new lodgings, a more convenient gatehouse entrance and stables added by Robert Dudley, Earl of Leicester, who turned the castle into a comfortable Tudor mansion.

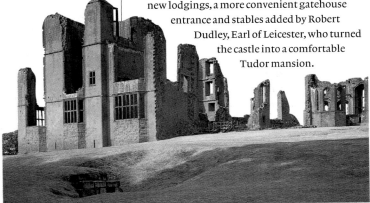

Sir Walter Scott stayed at the King's Arms and Castle Hotel, Kenilworth, while writing his stirring tale of the Elizabethan court set at the castle. Published in 1821, it fired the imagination of many a Victorian visitor. His novel was so topographically accurate that he provided a plan for readers to locate their position among the ruins. In his book he retold the true tale of the 19-day entertainment staged in 1575 for Queen Elizabeth by the Earl of Leicester as his last bid to persuade her to marry him. William Camden, describing the castle at this time, noted that 'if you regard the magnificence of the buildings, and nobleness of the Chase and Parks lying round and belonging to it, it may claim a second place among the Stateliest Castles in England.' The Earl of Leicester also added the rectangular garden outside the keep, an innovative feature designed to be looked down upon from the vantage point of a high bank. The older part of the town northeast of the castle has pleasant streets and pubs.

Kerrera, Ag & B 698 C3, The island of Kerrera, a walkers' paradise, protects the entrance to Oban* harbour and is linked to the town by ferry.

Below: Keswick, at the head of Derwentwater, centre of the northern Lake District.

Top: Kidwelly, a castle of unusual design, in an outstandingly good state of preservation.

Alexander II was killed here in 1249 when he fought Duncan, Lord of the Isles, who refused to take an oath of allegiance. Gylen Castle, at the southwest tip of the island, was built by Duncan MacDougall in 1582. Because his clan had supported the royal cause during the war (1642–8) between Charles I and the Covenanters, the latter burned the castle, which was subsequently abandoned.

Kersey, Suffk 691 H3, Built across a valley, medieval Kersey made good use of the water splash at the bottom of the main street and gave its name to a type of cloth. Half-timbered and colour-washed weavers' cottages and a fine 15th-century church with a beautiful south porch roof on top of the hill, make this one of Suffolk's prettiest, most photogenic villages.

Keswick, Cumb 696 D3, A small but busy town at the head of Derwentwater, this is the centre of the northern Lake District*. It has a good early 19th-century Town Hall that now serves as an information centre, and a church by Anthony Salvin. Derwentwater has a single large inhabited island with a villa of the 1840s. A few miles to the west, by Bassenthwaite, is **Mirehouse,** a late Georgian house owned by the Spedding family, who maintained contacts with many literary and artistic families; Tennyson is said to have written *Morte d'Arthur* in the garden.

Kettles, Nthumb 699 J6, A promontory hill fort, with somewhat complex defences but lacking visible hut circles.

Kidderminster, Worcs 693 H5, Historically a carpet-making town, but worth visiting today in order to board the Severn Valley Railway. It winds up the magnificent valley to Bridgnorth.

Kidlington, Oxon 690 D4, The church contains early misericords from the 13th century and a beautiful

east window, made from stained glass taken from the other windows.

Kidwelly (Cydweli), Carmth 692 D7, A Norman borough developed around the magnificent castle which, after falling in and out of Welsh hands, was refortified in masonry in the second half of the 13th century. It followed the original bow-shaped plan dictated by the naturally defended ridge above the River Gwendraeth, and had an impressive twin-towered south gatehouse which was a self-contained defensive unit, still in a remarkable state of repair. The parish church of St Mary was originally a Benedictine priory and a cell of Sherborne Abbey. Its spacious dignity and numerous architectural details make it one of the most interesting churches in Carmarthenshire. From the mid-18th century until the 1940s, Kidwelly was a major centre for the manufacture of tin plate; the Industrial Museum offers a unique demonstration of the processes involved in its production.

Above: Kerrera, at the entrance to Oban harbour.

Below, left and right: Kiftsgate Court is famous for its superb views as well as for the gardens themselves.

Kiftsgate Court Gardens, Gloucs 690 C3, Home of the famous rose. The gardens lie on the edge of the Cotswold escarpment close by Hidcote Manor* (they are open on the same days), and enjoy views towards Malvern. They were the creation of Heather Muir, a friend as well as a neighbour of Lawrence Johnston at Hidcote. Shrubs and trees border the terraced path that slowly descends the steep hillside to a lawn and swimming pool below.

Kilchurn Castle, Ag & B 698 D3, At the north end of Loch Awe*, the ruins of Kilchurn Castle are said to be haunted by a mythical monster. The tower-house was built by Sir Colin Campbell of Glenorchy in 1440, extended in 1693 and abandoned in the 1740s.

Kildrummy Castle, Abers 702 C6, The ruins of the most powerful fortress in the Highlands are still impressive. The first castle, built during the reign of Alexander II (1214–49), was a keep protected by a curtain wall and a broad ditch. The impressive

guardhouse and six round towers were probably added by Edward I, who occupied the castle between 1296 and 1303. The Scots recaptured Kildrummy shortly afterwards and, in 1306, Robert Bruce considered it a safe place for his family. The English, however, obtained Bruce's surrender through the treachery of a blacksmith to whom they had promised as much gold as he could carry. The castle was besieged again in 1335, before

Top: Kilchurn Castle on the shore of Loch Awe.

Centre left: Kildrummy Castle, the lancets of the chapel.

Centre right: Kilpeck Church, the fantastic south door.

Bottom left: Killerton, Museum of Costume, part of the ever-changing displays of the Paulise de Bush collection of costume.

Bottom right: Kimbolton Castle, remodelled by Vanbrugh and Hawksmoor, 1707–10. The Galilei portico is on the right.

becoming the residence of the Earls of Mar. It was confiscated following the Earl of Mar's involvement in the Jacobite Rising of 1715 and dismantled shortly afterwards.

Killerton, Devon 689 G5, The grounds that surround the plain house of 1778–9 are full of rare and tender shrubs, some of them early introductions from the nursery firm of Veitch in Exeter [NT]. The rustic Bear Hut, probably dating from the early 19th century, has in its central chamber a ceiling of deer skins and a floor of knuckle bones. The splendid herbaceous borders in front of the mansion command views across the valleys of the Culm, and lead on to a fine viewpoint overlooking the valley of the Exe where the Aclands, who have lived here since the early 17th century, were planning a large and elaborate house by James Wyatt. It was never built, and their 'temporary' home now accommodates the

Paulise de Bush collection of costume, charmingly displayed in period room settings, and a rich collection of family portraits. The chapel in the grounds by CR Cockerell is austerely neo-Norman, and inspired by the Lady Chapel at Glastonbury*.

Killiecrankie Pass, P & K 701 H7, This wooded pass, which forms a strategic link between the Highlands and Lowlands, was the scene of the first great encounter between the Jacobite and government forces. On 27 July 1678 John Graham of Claverhouse, 'Bonnie Dundee', routed the army of William III of Orange before dying of his wounds. He is buried in the ruined church of Old Blair, behind Blair Castle*. A footpath leads to Soldier's Leap, where a redcoat is said to have jumped 20 feet (6m) to escape from his Jacobite pursuers. The pass is inhabited by a wide range of wildlife and has been declared a site of scientific interest. The most elusive species is the nocturnal wildcat, while the most sought-after is the salmon, once so abundant that peasants used to hang baskets in the River Garry and wait for the fish to get caught in them as they swam upriver.

Kilmartin Glen, Ag & B 698 C3, Late Stone Age (c3000 BC) and Bronze Age remains abound in this glen between Lochgilphead* and Kilmartin. The most interesting are the cup-and-ring markings carved on two flat rock surfaces at Achinabreck Farm, and the two Templewood Stone Circles and the three burial mounds at Nether Largie. See also the excellent small museum in Kilmartin House and the 14th- to 16th-century tombstones in the neighbouring kirk.

Kilpeck Church, Herefs 693 G6, It is astonishing that the carving at the church of St Mary and St David has survived so well, with so little weathering, since Norman carvers made it. The corbels around the outside show a sequence of staggeringly concise and characterful animals, motifs and figures, and a rude *sheila-na-gig*, a female fertility symbol. Around the door elongated men grapple with decorative spirals while over it birds' faces look down with the huge sad eyes of cartoon characters. Behind the church stand the remains of the local castle, and there are dramatic views of the Black Mountains including the Sugarloaf and Skirrid peaks.

Kilravock Castle, Highld 701 H5, The castle is the seat of the Roses of Kilravock (pronounced 'Kilrock'). The keep of the present castle was built in the 15th century and extended in the 17th to 18th centuries. Mary Stuart was received here in 1562 and Bonnie Prince Charlie stayed two days before the Battle of Culloden in 1746. Later guests included Robert Burns and Charles Dickens.

Kimbolton, Cambs 695 F6, A delightful little stone town with a wide High Street in the Kim Valley on the edge of Kimbolton Park. It has the only

Above: Kilmartin Glen churchyard has an interesting collection of 14th–16th-century tombstones.

Below: Kings Langley church of All Saints, heraldic stained-glass window.

Moravian church in England, built in 1823, and a medieval broach-spired church with a painted screen. The castle, a school since 1950 and Catherine of Aragon's last residence, was remodelled by Sir John Vanbrugh and assistant Nicholas Hawksmoor 1707–10; a huge porticoed front was added by Alessandro Galilei in 1718–19. Other delights are the 1690s Great Hall, Robert Adam Gatehouse and Pellegrini panels in the Chapel and on the staircase.

Kingham, Oxon 690 C3, The village is on the main line between London and Worcester and has a number of attractive houses. These include cottages of banded limestone – alternate courses of oölite (light grey) and ironstone (tawny brown). It was used either to save money by making the expensive stone go further or for decorative effect, and became something of a local fashion. Further evidence of the plentiful stone can be seen in the church, where stone pew-ends and backs were added as part of the Victorian restoration. The Old Rectory is a handsome early 18th-century house, beautifully proportioned.

Kings Langley, Bucks 691 F4, A royal palace once stood to the west of the High Street, from which the name derives; the site is now occupied by school buildings. The medieval church of All Saints contains a monument to Edmund of Langley, fifth son of Edward III, born here in 1341. The effigy rests on a rich tomb chest of c1393–8.

King's Lynn

King's Lynn, Norfk 695 G5, In the 18th century Daniel Defoe thought Lynn had 'more gentry and gaiety than either Norwich or Yarmouth', and perhaps because of its isolated position on the edge of the Fens* it remains an enchanting little town, touched by royalty. 'More worth seeing than any other town of equal size in England,' was the opinion of one commentator writing in the 1950s when, mercifully, Lynn was too poor to wreck its illustrious past. Since then the High Street has been scarred by brash new shop fronts but, thanks partly to the efforts of the town's Preservation Trust, it retains an impressive legacy of historic buildings.

Lynn owes its prosperity to the river; a settlement was already in existence here, on the banks of the Ouse, when Bishop de Losinga built **St Margaret's Church** beside what is now the Saturday Market. Monastic houses took up valuable space, so that by the mid-12th century Bishop William Turbus decided to lay out a more spacious market between Purfleet and Fisher Fleet on Terra Nova, with its own church dedicated to St Nicholas. The town remained Lynn Episcopi until the Dissolution, when it became King's Lynn. True to its name it remained one of the few Royalist towns in the region during the Civil War.

Often hidden behind later façades in Lynn's distinctive purple/brown brickwork is a remarkable sequence of medieval buildings where the great merchant dynasties orchestrated a lucrative trade with the continent. The early 15th-century Guildhall of St George, one of the best-preserved merchant guilds in the country, and once a theatre where Shakespeare probably acted, is now the Lynn Arts Centre. Nearby at no. 32 King Street is the oldest house, late Norman, and then further south in Queen Street, behind the Georgian façade of Clifton House with its barley-twist entrance columns, is another courtyard complex complete with Elizabeth tower. Thoresby College, built c1500 for 13 chaplains of Trinity Guild, now has a beautiful Dutch-gabled front; and the great Hansiatic warehouse, 1428, in St Margaret's Lane, one of the four established in England, is a monument to Lynn's trade with the Baltic, where German merchants conducted their business.

St Margaret's, largely 13th-century in Barnack* stone, has an unusual arrangement of twin west towers and two magnificent life-size Flemish brasses to prominent local merchants: one to Adam de Walsokne and his wife, surrounded by scenes of rural life, and the other to Robert Braunche and his two wives, depicting the famous peacock feast held in honour of Edward III's visit in 1349. The church, its leaning pillars set deep in the Ouse mud, has survived many acts of God and the great fire of 1421 when Lynn's own mystic and daughter of the mayor, Margery Kempe, prayed so fervently that the snowstorm which extinguished the fire was attributed to her. This remarkable woman also travelled widely in Europe and dictated the earliest autobiography in English, *The Book of Margery Kempe*.

Opposite St Margaret's stands the **Guildhall of the Holy Trinity** (1421), a dazzling chequerwork display in stone and knapped flint on this, the richest of Lynn's 51 medieval guilds, a pattern repeated next door on the 1895 Town Hall. Here among the stupendous collection of civic regalia is one of the great treasures of medieval art. King John's enamel and gold cup, made in 1340, more than 100 years after his treasure-laden baggage train was engulfed by a Wash tide, is adorned with minute scenes of courtly life. More authentic is the sword given by the monarch in recognition of the hospitality he received in 1204 when granting Lynn its royal charter.

The most unusual and least visited of the town's medieval monuments is the **Red Mount Chapel of Our Lady** (1485), in The Walks. Fan-vaulted and octagonal in red brick, it was a reception centre for pilgrims on their way to

Left: The Great Ouse river has brought prosperity to the town of King's Lynn through the centuries.

Below: A street lined with medieval merchant's houses

Top: Purfleet Quay, Henry Bell's Dutch-style Custom House, 1683, set among waterfront houses and converted warehouses.

Above: The clock on St Margaret's Church.

Left: The town's strikingly decorated medieval Guildhall.

Far left: One of St Margaret's twin towers with the Guildhall beyond.

Walsingham*. The 13th-century Greyfriars' tower, also octagonal, is the most substantial monastic ruin in Lynn and the South Gate of 1520 is the last surviving fortified entrance into the town.

Of Lynn's outstanding secular buildings pride of place must go to the Custom House (1683), alone on Purfleet Quay, designed by Henry Bell for Sir John Turner, a wealthy wine merchant and benefactor. Its niche statue to Charles II signalled the town's Royalist sympathies. Bell, twice mayor and a local architect of some distinction, was also commissioned by Turner to build the Duke's Head in the Tuesday Market Place, a vast rectangular space defined by a cheerful mixture of architectural styles that includes the 'jolly and vulgar' Victorian corn exchange. Just north in St Anne's Street stands St Nicholas' Chapel, with its splendid 15th-century south porch and angel roof. This part of town has suffered rather more from redevelopment, but the fishermen's cottages in Pilot Street are another National Trust success story.

King's Norton, Leics 694 D5, Built in 1760, St John's is one of the earliest churches of the Gothic Revival. The interior is one of the very few in the whole country that still has all its original fittings in their original position, with the pulpit in the middle of the nave.

Kings Sutton, Oxon 690 D3, The church of St Peter and St Paul is described by Pevsner as having 'one of the finest, if not the finest, spire in this county of spires'. Gaily crocketed and decorated, it dates from the 14th century, although it was rebuilt in the 19th. Outside, on the village green, the stocks still await miscreants.

Kingsbridge, Devon 689 F7, Situated at the head of the Salcombe* estuary, this old market town rises up the main street to the Italianate Town Hall, with its four-sided clock of 1875; the Shambles nearby is raised on pillars dating from 1585. Towards the top of the street is the Old Grammar School, founded by Thomas Crispin in 1670. It is now a museum dedicated to William Cookworthy, a local man who found china clay and began to manufacture porcelain in Plymouth in 1768. The first-floor schoolroom houses a master's desk with a canopy and a royal coat of arms dated 1671. The church steeple was used as a landmark by ships coming up the river.

Kingsbury Epicopi, Somset 689 H5, The church of St Martin has a dominant west tower, built of Ham stone, and is similar to that at Huish Episcopi*, 5 miles (8km) north. The chancel is lit by finely

Above: King's Norton, church of St John, the south side of the Georgian gothic nave.

Below right: Kingston Lacy, originally designed by Sir Roger Pratt in 1663–5, then remodelled 1835–41 by Sir Charles Barry.

detailed windows, and should ideally be visited on a bright summer morning.

Kingston, Dorset 690 B8, Near to Swanage is GE Street's magnificent church of St James, the result of a building programme devised by the 3rd Earl of Eldon to keep his estate labourers in employment during the agricultural recession of the 1870s. Construction took six years (1874–80), and there were no restrictions on form or cost. Born out of this is a church of rare perfection, with an interior of cathedral-like splendour. The central tower is visible for miles.

Kingston Bagpuize House, Oxon 690 D4, This dignified, tall brick house was built c1720 and retains its original cantilevered staircase, panelled rooms, and some good pictures and furniture. The attractive gardens contain some fine trees and shrubs. The curious name of house and village derives from the de Bagpuize family who held the manor from 1086.

Kingston Lacy, Dorset 690 B7, Not far from Wimborne* and the great Iron-Age hill fort of Badbury Rings* is this fine 17th-century house [NT]. It was built for Sir Ralph Bankes in 1663–5 to

Top left: Kinross House, built in the 1680s by William Bruce.

Kiplin Hall **K**

Kingston Lacy
Above: Portrait of Marchesa Maria Serra Pallavicino by Rubens.
Far left: The Saloon ceiling.
Left: Cardinal Camillo Massimi, by Velázquez.

Bottom: Kinross House gardens.

replace the ruined Corfe Castle*, 12 miles (19km) to the south, which had been defended in the Civil War by Ralph's mother, Dame Mary. The original design for Kingston Lacy was the work of architect Sir Roger Pratt, but the house was remodelled in 1835–41 by Sir Charles Barry for the traveller, collector, and exile, William Bankes. There is an important collection of some 150 oil paintings, including fine Spanish works by Velázquez, Murillo and Zurbarán, displayed on the gilded leather-lined walls of the Spanish Room.

The room also has a ceiling from one of the Contarini palaces in Venice, acquired by William Bankes on the London market in 1838.

Kingston Lisle, Oxon 690 C5, In the village can be seen the Blowing Stone, formerly on the Ridgeway, a perforated sarsen that produces a loud sound when blown. According to legend, Alfred the Great used it to muster his armies against the Danes. Kingston Lisle Park has a complicated architectural history, but was probably built in c1677. It is a fine Palladian house set in 140 acres (56.7ha) of attractive parkland with three spring-fed lakes. The *pièce de résistance* of the house is its interior, dating mainly from c1825–30, with a remarkable series of vaulted rooms and an extraordinary flying staircase.

Kingston Maurward Gardens, Dorset 689 J6, Eighteenth-century gardens near Dorchester*, which surround the classical Georgian house of 1717–20 and spread over some 35 acres (14ha). There is also a restored Edwardian garden, a walled demonstration garden and national collections of pentstemons and salvias.

Kinnersley Castle, Herefs 693 F5, A wild and woolly Elizabethan manor house on the Welsh borders, with unusual stepped brick gables. The 16th-century battlements on the older tower hint that this is a remodelling of a medieval border castle. Inside are interesting plaster ceilings, and the arms of the builder, Roger Vaughan, set in a spreading oak tree in the overmantel of the Great Chamber.

Kinross, P & K 699 F3, This small town stands on the shores of Loch Leven, popular with trout fishermen. Kinross House, built and owned by the architect William Bruce in the 1680s, and its gardens are open to the public. On an island in the loch are the ruins of the castle where Mary Stuart was imprisoned in June 1567 and from which she escaped in May 1568 with the help of her jailer's son. Vane Farm Nature Reserve, south of Kinross, offers an opportunity to observe the waterfowl that nest and winter on the loch.

Kintbury, Berks, Standing guard over the road is Halfway House, a delightful late 18th-century tollhouse. Built in the castle style, it has battlements, four corner turrets, gothic glazing bars and mock arrow slits. *See* **Avington*** **690 D5.**

Kiplin Hall, N York 697 G4, A house with a Greek cross plan, in brick with stone dressings, the turrets topped by lead-covered ogee domes. Entry by the tower porch leads into a panelled hall, a long gallery crosses from turret to turret on the top floor, and there is an Elizabethan-style Victorian library. The house was built c1620 by Sir George Calvert, Secretary of State to James I, who in 1625 was created 1st Lord Baltimore in the Irish peerage, and in 1632 was granted land by Charles I to found a colony in America named Maryland after his queen, Henrietta Maria.

Kirby Hall, Nhants 694 E5, The peaceful ruin echoes with the screams of peacocks. The courtyard house is nostalgic in plan, but has the most flamboyant of Renaissance decoration, including giant pilasters marching around the inner courtyard. The masons here used contemporary pattern books for their ideas but in an innovative way. The little boys and dolphins that flank the doorway leading into the main courtyard, for example, were copied from the frontispiece, not the plates, of John Shute's book *The First and Chief Grounds of Architecture*, published in 1563. The house was begun by Sir Humphrey Stafford, but later bought and completed by Sir Christopher Hatton (*see* Holdenby House*). He added a state suite in expectation of a visit by Elizabeth I that never materialized. James I, however, paid several

Kirkby Lonsdale, St Mary's Church
Right: A 19th-century stained-glass window of the Crucifixion.
Bottom: The Norman church, set in a churchyard from which there are great views of the Lune Valley.

Kirby Hall
Left: The restored 'Great Garden', possibly designed by George London.
Below left: One of the great bay windows of the State Suite.

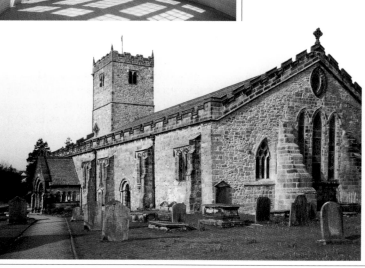

visits, and the now-empty rooms contain drawings of how they may have appeared at that time, based on the furnishings listed in an inventory dating from 1619. Outside, an approximation of the 1680s parterre garden – made by Hatton's gardening descendants – has been recreated by English Heritage with cut-work grass platts, conical yews and box trees in tubs. These gardens, and the extensive wilderness of rare trees, became known as 'ye finest in England,' but they fell into decay in the 18th century. Kirby Hall was abandoned in the 19th, but its isolation and ruinous state is part of its melancholy charm. Sir John Summerson described how for him 'the beauty of Kirby's decline is that it was private and without violence. The house was never burnt, ravaged, used as a quarry or assaulted by mobs. It simply lapsed… today the masonry is still unsullied, sharp and clear, so that if roofs, windows and doors suddenly reassembled themselves, the stones would take it as an unsurprising compliment.'

Kirkby Lonsdale, Cumb 696 E5, High up the Lune Valley, the town guards the approaches to the Lake District* from Yorkshire. It has good stone houses and a fine church, near which is Church Brow Cottage, a picturesque garden pavilion. The view over the Lune from Kirkby Lonsdale was painted by Turner and was described by Ruskin as one of the loveliest scenes in England.

Kirkcudbright, D & G 696 C2, This delightful former royal burgh on the banks of the River Dee has some beautiful old houses and a picturesque harbour. The harbour is dominated from the end of High Street by the ruins of Maclellan's Castle,

a turreted mansion built in 1582 by the Provost Thomas Maclellan. The artist Edward Hornel occupied Broughton House between 1901 and 1933. Today the 18th-century mansion houses a collection of his works and a vast library of

Scottish books and manuscripts, and has a Japanese garden [National Trust for Scotland]. The old Tolbooth (1629), now a museum, traces the history of this artists' colony and displays paintings by Hornel and his friends. The Stewartry Museum, in St Mary Street, traces the natural and social history of east Galloway – the last Scottish region still administered by a steward (the Duke of Rothesay) – and the history of the Solway coast.

Kirkham Priory, N York 697 J5, In an idyllic setting beside the River Derwent, the main joy of this site is the very impressive late 13th-century gatehouse, with crocketed gables and much carving [EH].

Kirkstall Abbey, W Yorks 697 G6, Once a remote and typically Cistercian site in the valley of the River Aire, now only 3 miles (5km) west of Leeds' vibrant city centre. Founded in 1152, this was a large monastery, as can be seen from the extensive remains – particularly of the church, with its massive crossing tower and vaulted chapter house. The public have access to the cloister. The Abbey House Museum in the former gatehouse is a lively folk museum.

Kirkwall, see **Orkney*.**

Kirtling Towers, Cambs 695 G6, South of Newmarket, London lawyer Edward North turned Kirtling Castle into a major Tudor house, with a gateway built to rival those of St John's and Trinity colleges in Cambridge*. This imposing

Kirkham Priory
Top left: The vaulted front entrance to the cloister with the remains of the southwest tower behind.
Top right: The eastern section of the church.

Left: Kirkstall Abbey, the north transept.

Right: Kit's Coty House, all that is left of a megalithic burial chamber. Up to the 18th century it was covered by a long barrow nearly 200 feet (60m) long.

brick entrance survives as Kirtling Towers; its founder and his son have elaborate Renaissance tombs in the nearby Norman church.

Kirtlington, Oxon 690 D4, The church contains very fine early 18th-century gates, with scroll cresting

from Northbrook House, home of the Dashwood family. Northbrook was demolished and Kirtlington built between 1742–6 to a Gibbsian design. It contains fabulous rococo interiors, including a 'Monkey Room' by Clermont. This rococo theme was popular in France and Germany but rare here. The only other surviving example in Britain is on Monkey Island in the River Thames.

Kit's Coty House, Kent 691 G5, A megalithic burial chamber near Aylesford*, consisting of four big stones [EH].

Knap Hill, Wilts 690 C5, This high point at Alton Barnes, with its neolithic and Romano-British camps, overlooks Pewsey* Vale.

Knaresborough, N Yorks 697 H5, An attractive and historic market town, with some handsome Georgian buildings and a tucked-away market place. Knaresborough's many curiosities include a shrine and a house cut into the cliff. The ruined medieval castle overlooks the steep gorge of the River Nidd, and the gothic church of St John contains impressive monuments to the Slingsby family of Scriven Hall. From High Bridge there is a riverside walk through woodland planted by Sir Henry Slingsby in the 18th century, before Harrogate* took over as the leading local spa town. It passes underneath the railway viaduct and beside the weir which powered Castle Mills. This half-mile (1km) 'Long Walk' leads to the Dropping Well, an attraction since 1630, and perhaps the only petrifying well of its kind in England. The constant flow of water – 700 gallons per hour – containing calcium carbonate and sodium sulphate, down a stone rock face overhanging a grotto-like cave, calcifies objects hung over the edge. Close by is Mother Shipton's Cave, associated with the prophetess Ursula Sontheil (1488–1561). The riverside woodland path

continues through the Beech Avenue. An early guide to the 'Dripping Well', as it was first called, was a young 'Blind Jack' Metcalf (1717–1810), who became a noted builder of turnpike roads despite his disability.

Knebworth, Herts 691 F4, Knebworth House, the home of the Lytton family since 1490, is approached through a large and impressive park. The battlemented, gothic appearance of the house dates mainly from the 19th century but there is much evidence of earlier work, as this is the sole surviving range of a great early Tudor courtyard mansion which stood substantially intact until 1811. The interior includes the Banqueting Hall

Knebworth
Top: The battlemented exterior, mainly of the 19th century.
Above: The Jacobean Banqueting Hall.
Below left: The formal garden designed by Lutyens.

Below: Knightshayes Court, a dramatic view of Burges' edifice.

with an early 17th-century screen and panelling, a fine staircase and armoury, and the sumptuous early Victorian State Drawing Room. The gardens were worked on by Edwin Lutyens (who had family connections with the Lyttons) and Gertrude Jekyll. The medieval church of St Mary within the grounds contains the Lytton Chapel with excellent early 18th-century monuments. In the village of Knebworth, the church of St Martin is essentially the design of Lutyens, who gave it prominent eaves and playful interior; but it was unfinished at his death, and was completed in 1964 by Sir Albert Richardson.

Knightshayes Court, Devon 689 G5, In 1869 William Burges was commissioned to build a gothic house for the Heathcoat Amorys, whose lace- and net-making factory in Tiverton* is visible from the main rooms. Built of local stone, the three-storey house has several extravagant and colourful interiors, some provided by the more economical JD Crace. The collection of pictures includes old masters, and a charming watercolour of the works outing to Teignmouth in 1854. The outstanding garden has a wide range of tender and exotic shrubs. Near the house are formal terraces, with topiary foxes and hounds in full flight [NT].

Top left: The ballroom with its splendid chimneypiece of 1607.

Below left: The Great Staircase, 1605–8.

Below centre: Lady Frances Cranfield, by Van Dyck.

Bottom: The Venetian Ambassador's Room, 1688.

Top right: The 16th-century front, a semi-fortified gatehouse flanked by a gabled range.

Knole

K

Knole, Kent 691 G6, Seat of the Sackville family, and one of the most atmospheric late medieval houses in England, and also one of the largest, with 365 rooms, 4 long galleries and 7 courtyards [NT]. Entry is via a gatehouse into the Green Court, added in the 16th century to an earlier house begun in 1456 by Thomas Bourchier, Archbishop of Canterbury. This consists of four ranges round a courtyard, the one facing the entrance containing the hall and kitchen. Further smaller courts lie behind. The interiors were largely remodelled in the 16th century, and the prevailing style remains Tudor and Jacobean (the Sackvilles arrived in 1566). The most notable features are the hall screen (a large, crudely carved affair), the painted Great Staircase of 1605 and Cartoon Gallery, and the series of 17th-century panelled rooms. The Ballroom has a chimneypiece reaching to the ceiling, the overmantel delicately carved with flowers and musical instruments. Knole is especially famous for retaining so much of its original furniture. One of its owners, the 6th Earl of Dorset, held the position of Lord Chamberlain of the Household to William III, and this gave him the right to help himself to any of the royal furnishings that were deemed to be in need of replacement. This perquisite brought to Knole a whole set of chairs of state covered in purple velvet, and walnut chairs upholstered in blue silk damask made for Charles II (marked 'WP' for Whitehall Palace). There is also a famous suite of 17th-century silver furniture, some splendid four-poster beds with their original hangings, superb tapestries and a roomful of paintings by Reynolds. Knole 'slept' during the late 17th and 18th centuries, leaving its contents miraculously undisturbed.

Lacock
Top left: The ideal English village.
Centre left: The Perpendicular cloisters of the Abbey, dating from the late-14th to 15th century.

See individual entries on **Ambleside***, **Blackwell***, **Brantwood***, **Castlerigg***, **Cockermouth***, **Dalemain***, **Grasmere***, **Hawkshead***, **Hill Top***, **Kendal***, **Keswick***, **Rydal Mount***, **Sizergh Castle***, **Windermere***.

Lampeter, Cerdgn 692 D5, A market town with a great deal of charm. The College became a constituent of the University of Wales in 1971. It was founded in 1822 as St David's, a theological college to enable young Welshmen to have a university education, without the expense of an Oxford or Cambridge degree. This aim was clearly reflected in the unmistakably Oxbridge layout and character of CR Cockerell's designs.

Lamphey, Pembks 692 C7, Similar to nearby Manorbier*, with its vineyard, orchards and fishponds, was the Bishop's Palace at Lamphey, of which the arcaded parapet resembles that at the

Knutsford, Ches 697 F8, An attractive town, with a Georgian parish church and a nicely winding main street, whose most conspicuous building – looking like some kind of mad fugitive from Gaudi's Barcelona – is the King's Coffee House of 1907.

Kymin, The, Mons 693 G6, A Round Tower built in 1794 by the local dining club. They also built a Naval Temple (1802) to commemorate the victories of Nelson and other admirals. It stands on a hill overlooking the Wye* and Monnow valleys.

Lacock, Wilts 690 B5, The village, owned by the National Trust, has at its core an abbey founded in 1232 but converted about 1540 into a Tudor country house, now with later 18th-century Gothic façades. The medieval cloisters and chapterhouse survive. Nearby is the Fox Talbot Museum [NT] commemorating the pioneering photography of William Henry Fox Talbot (1800–77), whose family lived here. Thanks to his calotype process, he is generally credited with the invention of photography. The lovely village has often featured in television productions.

Ladham House Gardens, Kent 691 G6, The gardens, at Goudhurst, go back to the 18th century, when the house was built. They include several interesting features, including a bog-garden.

Lake District, Cumb 696 D4, This corner of northwest England measures only about 35 miles (56km) across and comprises 16 lakes amongst stunning fells and valleys that attract hordes of tourists. It is characterized by its small houses rather than mansions, some of them shrines to famous literary figures who have lived there.

Above: *The Three Eldest Children of King Charles I,* a copy of the portrait by Van Dyck in Lacock Abbey.

Above: Lamphey, Bishop's Palace.

palace at St David's*. Beautifully landscaped to show off the handsome ruins, the spot manages to convey the serenity as well as the grandeur of episcopal life.

Lamport Hall, Nhants 694 E6, With a central block of the 1650s by John Webb and the wings added 80 years later by Francis Smith of Warwick, the main façade is like a encyclopaedia of Palladian styles. Built by the Isham family, whose witty motto is 'I sham not', it contains Royalist paintings, as well as the original fireplaces and other features that are to be found in Webb's own drawings. Sir Charles Isham, the 10th baronet, who did much work in the gardens in the mid-19th century, holds the dubious honour of being the man who introduced garden gnomes to England. St Peter's Church, in the village of Isham, has a tower with a *sheila-na-gig* – a female fertility symbol – as a gargoyle.

Lanark, S Lans 699 F5, This market town, a royal burgh since 1140, has a long history. Kenneth II convened the Scottish Parliament here in 978, and the town also witnessed the beginning of William Wallace's rebellion against the English. Outlawed for the murder of the Sheriff of Lanark, Wallace gathered a small army and returned to massacre the English garrison in May 1297. His statue (1822) on the façade of St Nicholas' Church shows him, unusually, with a beard. *See also* **New Lanark***.

Lancaster

Lancaster, Lancs 696 E5, This is the county town of Lancashire, though the County Council's headquarters are now at Preston. The historic core of the city centres upon the hilltop medieval castle and priory church. There are a number of good Georgian houses, including the Judges' Lodging, a 17th-century house adapted for the visiting assize judges and now a museum containing an outstanding collection of Gillow furniture. The Gillows were a local family whose business started in Lancaster and whose country house was Leighton Hall*. The former Lancaster Town Hall, now the City Museum, was designed in 1781 by Major Thomas Jarratt; he was given the freedom of the city for his trouble.

Lancaster has a strategic position at the first crossing point of the Lune. This is now marked by two notable examples of the engineer's art. **Skerton Bridge** was designed in 1783 by Thomas Harrison; its five semi-elliptical arches spring from piers decorated with aedicules and carry a level roadway from bank to bank. Further

Below: Lancaster Maritime Museum is housed in a former Customs House designed in 1764 by Richard Gillow. Displays explain the era when Lancaster was a flourishing port and an important centre for the slave trade.

upstream the Lancaster Canal is carried across the river by John Rennie's almost equally splendid **Lune Aqueduct** of 1797.

In the 19th century Lancaster was the home of the northwest's principal architectural practice, founded by Edmund Sharpe in the 1840s, but best known for its most creative years as Paley and Austin. Never succumbing to the temptation to move the practice to London or another bigger base, Paley and Austin scattered northwest England with churches and secular buildings, both new and restored, in which the quantity (over 500 commissions) never drove down the quality and of which the creative inspiration, especially after Austin's arrival in the practice in 1870, was of the very highest. Their principal monument in Lancaster itself is probably St John's Roman Catholic Cathedral – by Paley, 1859 – with a reordering by Giles Gilbert Scott of 1909, once condemned but now carefully reinstated by Frank Roberts.

Lancaster Castle is now a prison. The square stone keep of the 12th century rises visibly above the medieval curtain wall which has towers, including one where the Witches of Pendle are said to have been imprisoned. An imposing early-15th-century battlemented gatehouse is called John of Gaunt's Tower, though it was built by his son, Henry IV. Inside the purpose-built prison buildings are some of the best surviving from the period just after John Howard's reforms and they include a Women's Prison of 1818, designed by Joseph Gandy on the panopticon principle. Other parts of the prison were by Thomas Harrison, a local architect until he moved to Chester; some of his other additions to the castle are more easily accessible. The Shire Hall of 1796 is semi-circular, plaster-vaulted and timber-furnished (by Gillows) in a beautifully detailed gothic manner, decorated with hundreds of shields as a genealogical guide to Lancashire's history; this

Above: Lancaster Castle, view with Gatehouse

Left: Skerton Bridge, designed by Thomas Harrison in 1783, was the first level road bridge in England.

Below: Houses and warehouses on St George's Quay, on the banks of the River Lune. This was once the centre of a busy port.

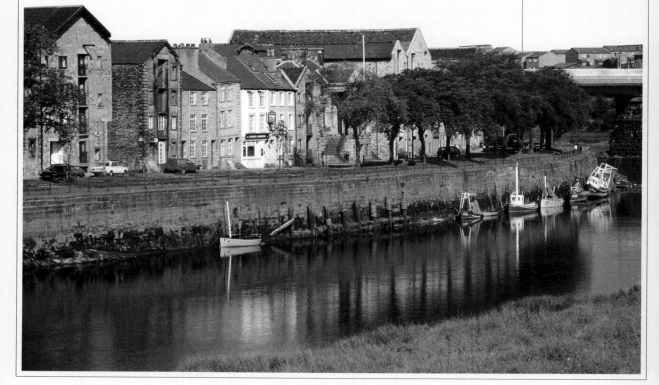

was originally the civil court. Adjacent is the rather cooler criminal court, and between them the Grand Jury Room with a complete set of Gillow furniture.

Lancaster Priory is one of Lancashire's finest parish churches. Now mainly 15th century, the name comes from its location on the site of the former Benedictine monastery. The west tower, rebuilt 1753, is a notable example of conscious gothic revivalism. Inside, the glory of the church is the set of 14 canopied choir stalls, among the oldest and finest in England. They date from the mid-14th century and have carving of almost unbelievable richness and intricacy, concealing little heads and faces. The chapel of the Kings Own Royal Regiment, added in 1903, contains some Coptic crosses brought from Abyssinia by the regiment in 1868.

The **Custom House** on St George's Quay demonstrates Lancaster's importance as a port in the 18th century. The quay was the product of an Act of Parliament in 1749 and still retains a number of houses and warehouses (mostly converted to housing). The Custom House was built in 1764 to the design of Richard Gillow in an accomplished Palladian manner but by then furniture rather than architecture was the basis of the Gillow

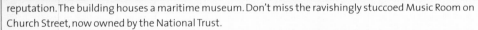

reputation. The building houses a maritime museum. Don't miss the ravishingly stuccoed Music Room on Church Street, now owned by the National Trust.

The **Ashton Memorial,** on rising ground to the east of Lancaster, is the City's most visible monument. In the 19th century Lancaster became the national centre for the manufacture of linoleum and the leading maker was James Ashton, later Lord Williamson. In a park above the city, with magnificent views across the city, Morecambe Bay and towards the fells of the Lake District, Ashton built a memorial to his wife, an enormous baroque confection designed by John Belcher. The architect was not local and the materials – white Portland stone and a green copper dome – seem alien, but the panache of the design, with the dome standing on a square base and lesser domes at the corners, the whole raised on a rusticated substructure, can be appreciated in any context.

Lancaster University, one of the new campus universities, was established in 1964, but its layout and architecture, by Shepheard and Epstein, has not received as much acclaim as some of its rivals. The most notable individual building was perhaps the chaplaincy, with clover-leaf plan and central spire, an inspiring effort at ecumenical planning. South of the city the buildings were set in a carefully designed landscape; the designs can now be better appreciated as the landscape matures. The university has continued to grow and its latest addition is perhaps its most dramatic – the new Ruskin Centre by Richard MacCormac, opened in 1999 to house the books, manuscripts and drawings that belonged to John Ruskin. The oval plan is deliberately ecclesiastical with the entrance, archive and reading room standing for narthex, choir and sanctuary. The exterior is white concrete with sparkly marble aggregate and green polished bands, the main doors sheathed in bronze. For those who associate Ruskin with gothic, especially Venetian gothic, the building may be a surprise, but its care for colour and texture, and decoration with individual works of art, is entirely within the Ruskinian ideal.

Above left: James Ashton's Memorial to his wife, a piece of Edwardian baroque extravaganza.

Above: The Ruskin Centre by Richard MacCormac, 1999, the most recent addition to the University campus.

Far left: Lancaster's Norman Castle has imposing battlements. Over the years it has been a prison, a judge's lodging and a court house. George Fox, founder of the Quakers, was imprisoned here in 1663–5.

Left: Judges' Lodging, a 17th-century house for visiting judges, is now a museum with a good collection of Gillow furniture.

Bottom: John Ruskin, painted by William Gershom Collingwood, 1897.

Lancing College, W Susx 691 F7, The giant chapel of Lancing College stands proudly on the slope of the Downs. Designed by RC Carpenter, who died in 1855, only a year after building had begun, it is of cathedral proportions but was never properly completed. The west front is a modern compromise.

Land's End, Cnwll 688 B8, This remote, largely level peninsula that rises northward to the Penwith Moors is windswept and mysterious; neolithic, Bronze-Age and Iron-Age remains are scattered all around. At Land's End itself is a sizeable, largely modern tourist complex that includes restaurants, exhibitions (one concentrates on the many travellers who trek from here to John O'Groats*) and a stimulating high-tech Lost Labyrinth visitor experience.

Laneast, Cnwll 688 E6, The Church of St Sativola and St Gulval was built between 1450 and 1500, of Polyphant stone. It has intriguing fragments of early glass, and stands close by an early schoolroom and a Gothic vicarage. This lovely parish, half on Bodmin Moor, also possesses one of Cornwall's many holy wells.

Above: Lanercost Priory, a substantial monastic survival on the English/Scottish border, was built partly of stones from the nearby Hadrian's Wall.

Lanercost Priory, Cumb 696 E2, In a secluded site near Hadrian's Wall*, a house of Augustinian canons was founded in the 1160s. The nave of the church survives because it became the parish church; the chancel, although unroofed, presents a substantial ruin. Of the claustral buildings part survive as a house, which includes the pele tower, the prior's lodging. Most of the church is of the early 13th century and there is a profusion of shafts with shaft-rings and simple mouldings such as nailhead and dog-tooth [EH].

Langdon Cliffs, Kent 691 J6, The lighthouse is open to the public, and the nearby Gateway to Dover*'s famous White Cliffs is a visitor centre with views across the English Channel.

Langford, Oxon 690 C4, The most important Saxon remains in Oxfordshire can be seen at the church of St Matthew. In 1086 it was recorded in the Domesday survey as one of the royal estates, and this may explain the exceptional quality of the work, which is far above the standard of local craftsmen. The squat tower is Saxon, as is the relief of the Crucifixion, which has been reset over the south porch door. On the east wall of the porch Christ is shown triumphant with arms outstretched; the figure is life-size, although sadly now headless. It is thought to be of *c*1000.

Langley Chapel, Shrops 693 G4, A perfect early-17th-century small chapel with its original fittings – pulpit, benches, pews and a musicians' pew at the back. Nearby is a gatehouse, the sole reminder of Langley Hall, the mansion of the Lee family.

Langport, Somset 689 H5, All Saints Church, with a splendid array of stained glass in its east window, is set on a hilltop looking towards Muchelney Abbey* and the town. Within, there are very tall chancel windows, with rich tracery. The east window has good stained glass. Langport's Guildhall is dated 1733, and is faced in brown Ham stone on the ground floor. The Guildhall and other surrounding Georgian buildings indicate a rebuilding at this time.

Lanhydrock, Cnwll 688 D7, Nestling under the protective lee of a hill, the ancient home of the Robartes was largely destroyed by fire in 1881. All that survived this conflagration was the gatehouse

Lanhydrock House
Right: The house, with the Church of St Hydroc nestling behind.
Below: A ground-floor corridor decorated in High Victorian style – carved oak furniture, antlers and colourful floor tiles.

and the Long Gallery, with its outstanding 17th-century plasterwork ceiling depicting Old Testament scenes; both were built soon after Sir Richard Robartes purchased the property in 1620 [NT]. The Victorian parts of the house are remarkable for their well-planned state and service rooms. Especially notable is the large kitchen, with a whole range of attendant larders, dairies, a bakehouse and a scullery. The ancient parish church lies beyond the formal gardens, embraced by groves of magnolias, rhododendrons, camellias and azaleas. The long avenue leading to the house was originally laid out in the 1640s, and has fine views of Restormel Castle*.

Lanteglos by Fowey, Cnwll 688 D7, In contrast to the crowded western bank of the Fowey* estuary, this parish is still quiet and remote. At its centre, in a sequestered valley, lies the ancient Church of St Wyllow, seemingly in a farmyard. Daphne du Maurier was married here, having travelled by boat from her home at Bodinnick to Pont Creek below the church.

Lanyon Quoit, Cnwll 688 B7, There are many Bronze- and Iron-Age remains in the parish of Madron, north of Penzance. The Quoit is composed of three man-size boulders supporting an 18-foot (5.5m) stone that formed the core of an ancient tomb. Men an Tol, a circular stone with a hole in it set between two other upright stones, lies not far away. This is an ancient and atmospheric place. Legend has it that a woman will conceive a child if she passes through the hole.

Largs, N Ayrs 698 D5, Largs is the most attractive family seaside resort on the Firth of Clyde. It is also the principal ferry port for Great Cumbrae Island where, in 1263, Alexander III routed the fleet of King Haakon of Norway. The Vikingar Centre on the seafront commemorates the battle that resulted in the Vikings of Norway ceding the Hebrides to Scotland. In the old cemetery, just off the High Street, Skelmorlie Aisle, originally the north transept of the parish church, was converted into a mausoleum by Sir Robert Montgomerie of Skelmorlie in 1623. His splendid tomb lies beneath a richly decorated barrel-vault. Nardinis restaurant and ice-cream parlour (by Charles Davidson, 1936) is a quintessential Scottish seaside café with a superb Art Deco setting.

Larmer Tree Gardens, Wilts 690 B7, The historical gardens of General Pitt-Rivers, high on Cranborne Chase at Tollard Royal. Created in 1880, the gardens are of national importance and are surrounded by an unusual set of buildings – a Roman temple, an open-air theatre, and colonial and oriental buildings.

Lastingham, N York 697 J4, A village beautifully set in a slight hollow of the North York Moors*. An air of sanctity pervades it, and it is no surprise that this was the site chosen for a 7th-century monastery. Bede records that it was founded by King Oswald's son Ethelward. Clear water still flows from St Cedd's Well, named after one of the remarkable family of four brothers who, having attended St Aidan's school at Lindisfarne on Holy Island*, became monks here. Between them they produced three bishops and two saints, the other being Chad. An attempt was made to re-found the monastery in 1078, but this was abandoned when the monks moved to St Mary's Abbey in York*. Lastingham's church of St Mary is a remnant of that early Norman monastic church, with a particularly memorable crypt.

Laugharne (Talacham), Carmth 692 C7, Best remembered as the haunt of Dylan Thomas,

Above: Larmer Tree Gardens, a folly designed by General Pitt-Rivers in 1880.

Left: Laugharne Castle, built in the 13th century to command the estuary flowing into Carmarthen Bay.

Bottom right: Launceston Castle's motte rises dramatically over the ancient market town.

whose village of Llareggub in *Under Milk Wood* was probably based on this sleepy estuary town. He lived with his wife Caitlin in the Boat House overlooking 'the heron-priested shore'. The rooms are now set out as a small museum of Thomasiana, with audio-visual presentations and recordings of the poet's unmistakable tones declaiming his verse. On the cliff walk above is his writing shed.

Launcells, Cnwll 688 E5, St Andrew's is one of the great churches of the county, right by the Devon border. It lies in a wooded valley by St Swithin's holy well. It has fragments of medieval wall paintings and medieval bench ends in the nave, 18th-century box pews in the north aisle, a splendid gothic pulpit, altarpiece and rails (the latter set behind one of the finest surviving 15th-century tiled floors). Also of note are the arms of Charles II sculpted by Michael Chute of nearby Kilkhampton. Launcells is a light and airy church, with a quiet and unsophisticated atmosphere, that has obviously been cherished for centuries.

Launceston, Cnwll 688 E6, One of the most impressive townscapes in the county. Dominated by the ruins of the motte-and-bailey Norman castle [EH], the town is the gateway to Cornwall on the northern route; any invader would have been intimidated by the strength of the defences on the high outcrop overlooking the River Tamar.
The castle also acted as a prison and at different times housed St Cuthbert Mayne and George Fox. Nearby the carved granite church of St Mary Magdalene is notable for the work to the south aisle undertaken by Sir Henry Trecarrel between 1511 and 1524. The palm leaves, roses, thistles and pomegranates that adorn the exterior do nothing to prepare the visitor for the somewhat plain interior. The jumbled streets of the town are worth exploring for the medieval South Gate, the grand Georgian houses in Castle Street and the picturesque mixture of 18th- and 19th-century houses in the Square.

Lauriston Castle, C Edin 699 G4, The towerhouse, built c1590 by Sir Archibald Napier (father of John Napier, who invented logarithms), was the birthplace of the Scottish financier John Law, who founded the first bank in France (1716). It was extended in 1827 by William Burn, then bought in the early 20th century by William Robert Reid, a famous cabinet-maker who put together an attractive collection of engravings, paintings, furniture, tapestry, porcelain and 'bluejohn' china (named after a *bleu-jaune* – blueish-yellow – amethyst mined in Derbyshire).

Lavenham, Suffk 691 H3, A picturesque medieval town, with undulating streets full of remarkable half-timbered houses still flaunting 15th-century wool wealth. The Guildhall has dominated the Market Place since 1529, when the Guild of Corpus Christi received its charter to regulate the wool trade (after weaving begun by Flemish migrants had actually peaked). The timbering of the Swan

Top left: Lavenham Guildhall, carved cornerpost of one of the town's best buildings.

Centre right: Lavenham church of St Peter and St Paul, one of East Anglia's greatest medieval wool churches.

tombs in the local church they endowed (not least with a lively fresco of St Christopher). The gatehouse is flanked by two octagonal towers, with eight tiers of large windows designed for display rather than defence. Topping the red and blue-glazed brick structure in place of battlements are scallop-shaped terracotta gables with dolphins.

Leafield, Oxon 690 C4, Sir George Gilbert Scott was responsible for the rectory and the austere church of 1860 with its tall central spire.

Leamington Spa, Warwks 694 C6, A pleasant town just south of Kenilworth*, with good late-Georgian terraces and solid Victorian villas. A string orchestra occasionally plays in the still-functioning Pump Room.

Ledbury, Herefs 693 G6, The parish church is crammed with monuments, including the five little sons and five kneeling daughters of the famous Renaissance Skynner Tomb. The narrow cobbled street called Church Lane is lined by excellent Herefordshire timbered houses jutting towards each other; the best example is the

Inn and Wool Hall behind it is particularly fine. Fittingly, Little Hall is now home to the Suffolk Preservation Society, and a former Benedictine priory-turned-rectory contains Elizabethan wall-paintings. But the main showpiece is the huge church of St Peter and St Paul, with its 140-foot (43m) tower, superbly carved screens and soaring artistry in knapped flint and dressed stone, a monument to the Springs, the Branches and the other merchant families who financed it.

Laxton, Notts 694 E3, Situated a few miles north of Newark*, this is the only village left in the country that still uses the medieval open field system of cultivation, with all the land surrounding the village divided into long strips.

Layer Marney Tower, Essex 691 H4, The highest and most lavish Tudor gatehouse in England arose out of the fields southeast of Colchester around 1520 as the entrance to a planned palace worthy of the 1st Lord Marney, Henry VIII's Keeper of the Privy Seal. His death in 1523, followed by that of his son in 1525, ended not just the male line but the building project as well. Both lords have exquisite terracotta

Right: Lavenham, half-timbered buildings

Bottom: Layer Marney Tower, the most glorious Tudor brick gatehouse in the country.

Market House with its timber columns and herringbone-patterned walls. Like the Hall at Leominster*, it is thought to be the work of carpenter John Abel, whose masterpiece was the now-lost Town Hall at Hereford*. The black-and-white colour scheme of these houses is usually a Victorian innovation: the beams were originally left unpainted and silvery. John Masefield and Elizabeth Barrett Browning were from Ledbury.

Leeds

Leeds, W York 697 G6, A large city with a long history. At its heart, Kirkgate boasts Chantrell's fine early Victorian parish church where an Anglo-Saxon cross can be seen, while Briggate disguises a medieval town plan. St John's Church in New Briggate, externally Perpendicular Gothic Survival, internally magically Laudian, reflects 17th-century cloth prosperity, and Holy Trinity, Boar Lane has resulted from early Georgian expansion. Continuing 19th-century success has bequeathed Cuthbert Brodrick's splendidly towered Town Hall of 1853–8 and his elliptical Corn Exchange of 1861–3. There are several important industrial monuments, including Temple Mills, an Egyptian-Revival delight of the 1830s for flax-processing, and the Hispano-Moorish St Paul's House, which was a warehouse of 1878 for the pioneer of ready-made clothing, Sir John Barran. Noteworthy also is the primly Victorian Thornton's Arcade of 1878. Later arcades in exuberantly Art Nouveau style by theatre architect Frank Matcham have become part of the Victoria Quarter, in which can be found the famous northern branch of Harvey Nichols. This is typical of the late 20th-century reinvention of itself which has seen Leeds again become a vibrant city and a northern shopping mecca.

Other attractions include Leeds City Art Gallery, with major 19th- and 20th-century British paintings; the Henry Moore Institute, with top-class sculpture collections; the Royal Armouries Museum, which houses one of the world's greatest collections of arms and armour; Roundhay Park, an exceptionally large public open space to find within a large city; and the nearby Tropical World, with its butterflies, exotic birds and animals. *See also* **Kirkstall Abbey*** and **Temple Newsam***.

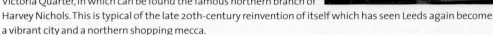

Top: One of the stone lions on the steps of the Town Hall, reputedly a reject from Trafalgar Square in London.

Above: A clock on the Civic Hall.

Left: Leeds Town Hall, Cuthbert Brodrick's impressive building, opened by Queen Victoria in 1858.

Leeds Castle, Kent 691 H6, An enchanting sight from a distance, several stone buildings on an island in a lake. Parts of it indeed go back to the 13th century, but mostly it is Victorian pastiche.

Leicester, Leics 694 D5, A thriving city with a long history dating back to Roman times. In the Middle Ages Leicester was a prosperous market town; in the 18th century it became the centre of the stocking industry, which began as a domestic concern, with weaving looms in private houses, but developed enormously in the early 19th century with the arrival of mechanization. Leicester today is still prosperous; it has a large Asian population, and boasts two universities. The best preserved reminder of Roman Leicester is the **Jewry Wall**, a stone and tile wall over 20 feet (6m) high which is now thought to have been part of a Roman public bath-house. The Saxons incorporated the wall into the porch of the church of St Nicholas, but it now stands by itself. The church also survives and its Anglo-Saxon nave is Leicester's oldest building. **St Martin's Church**, originally the medieval parish church, has been a cathedral since 1927. Immediately opposite the west front is the medieval Guildhall with its enormous Great Hall.

Leicester Castle is worth a visit for the church of St Mary de Castro and the former Court House, built within the Norman Great Hall. Just outside the castle enclosure is the Newarke (an extension to the castle enclosure built by Henry, Earl of Lancaster about 1330), and the Newarke Houses Museum, formed out of two early buildings. In the city centre are several good public buildings, including the County Rooms, built in the late 1790s as a hotel and ballroom for those attending Leicester Races, and the handsome but florid 1870s Town Hall in Town Hall Square. Leicestershire Museum and Art Gallery in New Walk has good

British paintings from the 18th to the 20th century. There is also a fine collection of German Expressionist art, and the remains of the famous Rutland dinosaur. On the northern edge of Leicester is **Belgrave Hall**, a small country house built about 1710 for Anne and Edmund Cradock. There are handsome iron entrance gates and the rooms are furnished to illustrate life in a moderately well-to-do 18th-century family.

Leighton Buzzard, Beds 690 E3, This town on the River Ouse has an interesting market cross of the 15th century. The cross is pentagonal, with a vaulted lower stage, a recessed upper stage, and a particularly well-preserved statue. The church of All Saints was consecrated in 1288 and contains some medieval stalls and misericords. The west door is decorated with attractive ironwork, mostly scrolls, possibly by Thomas of Leighton (*see* Turvey* and Easton Bray*).

Leighton Hall, Lancs 696 E5, North of Lancaster*, this was the home of the Gillows from 1822 and remains in their family. Richard Gillow gothicized an existing Georgian house in typical romantic fashion and Paley and Austin made more scholarly additions in the 1870s. Notable inside are the Hall, with a delightful cast-iron gothic arcade and a top-lit billiard room (Gillows were among the first to make billiard tables). Not surprisingly, the house is full of outstanding Gillow furniture and the chapel has a very early altarpiece (1750), a symbol of the family's consistent Catholic faith. Near Leighton is Warton Old Rectory, a somewhat puzzling medieval stone house, domestic in character in an area where so many early stone buildings are defensive.

Leiston, Suffk 695 J6, Originally a remote monastic cell in Minsmere marshes, the late-13th-century priory relocated in fields north of Leiston is now Suffolk's largest religious ruin [EH]. Six hundred years later Garrett's ironworks transformed this unlikely place into a small industrial town producing agricultural

Above: Leith, the quaysides of the old harbour preceding John Rennie's now-infilled docks of 1799 onwards.

Left: Leighton Hall, set in a fold in the hills, is especially notable for its fine Gillow furniture.

Below: Leith, the former royal yacht *Britannia*, taken out of commission in 1997, is moored at North Leith where it is open to the public. The yacht, launched from the Clyde shipyards in 1953, sailed over 1 million miles (1.6 million km) on its 968 official voyages throughout the world.

machinery. The original Long Shop is now a fascinating industrial steam museum.

Leith, C Edin 699 G4, For a long time this was Scotland's busiest commercial port and it is still a splendid Georgian town, with a magnificent Greek Doric Customs House (Robert Reid, 1820), Assembly Rooms (Thomas Brown, 1809) and Leith Bank (John Paterson, 1806). In Kirkgate, Trinity House (by Thomas Brown, 1816) has a fine collection of navigational instruments.

Lenham, Kent 691 H6, An attractive and picturesque village, with a medieval church, a square surrounded by old houses, and in the High Street rows of chequer-brick cottages with a raised pavement on one side. Honyward is a half-timbered house dated 1621.

Leominster, Herefs 693 G5, The agricultural town of Leominster (pronounced 'Lemster') is famous today for its antique trade, which finds an appropriate home among old coaching inns and picturesque black-and-white buildings. It was an important medieval centre with its Priory and weekly market, but was frequently attacked by the Welsh. The town later lost trade to Hereford* and Worcester*, and the Priory was closed in 1539 when the prior, John Glover, was hanged outside his own gates.

The **Priory Church**, in swarthy red brick, survives from the Priory of St Peter and St Paul that originally provided a focus for the town. After the Dissolution the nave was retained as a parish church, but it was damaged in a great fire in 1699. Repairs took place and it was in use again by 1705; Sir George Gilbert Scott undertook a further restoration between 1866 and 1891. Close by the west door is an interesting carving of a hairy 'Green Man' or medieval fertility symbol. Outside stands a ducking stool, apparently still in use as late as 1809 when one Jenny Pipes was paraded through the streets and then ducked in the river. The **Town Hall**, dated 1633, has been moved from its original position and is now used as offices. Built by John Abel, later the King's Carpenter, it is decorated with male and female busts, and in an interesting parallel between the hierarchies of architecture and society the frieze says that the columns below support the building as 'noble gentry... support the honour of a kingdom.' **Eye Manor**, 4 miles (6.4km) outside town to the north, was erected in 1680 by Ferdinando Gorges

from the profits of his trading in sugar and slaves. The interiors contain fine Carolean plasterwork.

Leonard Stanley, Gloucs 690 B4, The pretty village once contained an Augustinian priory, of which the church of St Swithin remains with its good Norman carving. The capitals of the shafts in the chancel – most unusually for Norman work – show excellent figures: a Nativity on one side, and a woman wiping Christ's feet on the other.

Leonardslee Gardens, W Susx 691 F6, A very large woodland garden in Horsham, and one of the most spectacular in the country, with exotic trees, azaleas and rhododendrons. Laid out in 1889, its special features include a spectacular rock garden, a lake, a collection of bonsai and an Alpine house. Wallabies roam, and there is a herd of deer. There is also a collection of pre-1900 motor cars.

Above: Leonardslee Gardens, an exotic experience in the Sussex countryside, with plants brought from all over the world.

Lerwick, *see* **Shetland*.**

Lesnes Abbey, Gt Lon 691 G5, At Belvedere stand the spare ruins of a 12th-century Augustinian monastery. The foundations are clearly laid out among pleasant green lawns.

Letchworth, Herts 691 F3, This is the original garden city inspired by the urban theorist Ebenezer Howard's book, *Tomorrow: the Peaceful Path to Real Reform*. The idea was to control the social and architectural structure together with population growth with the aim of self-sufficiency and, beginning in 1904, Barry Parker & Raymond Urwin attempted to realize it at Letchworth. St George, 1961–4 by Peter Bosanquet, is an impressive building designed for a corner site. A most original building is the Cloisters, 1905–7, built as a School of Philosophy.

Levens Hall, Cumb 696 E4, The Hall has remained in the hands of the Bagot family for some 300 years, and they can claim descent, by convoluted routes, from earlier owners, the Bellinghams and the Grahmes. Levens, like its near neighbour Sizergh*, is built round a medieval pele. Important additions were made in the 16th and 17th centuries, including much oak woodwork and rich plaster ceilings. At the end of the 17th century the owner, Col James Grahme, added a major staircase and a room exquisitely lined with Spanish leather and he filled the house with William and Mary furniture. His most notable achievement, however, was to commission England's greatest topiary garden from Guillaume Beaumont, formerly gardener to James II, for whom Grahme had been Keeper of the Privy Purse.

Lewes, E Susx 691 G7, The county town of Sussex, with a castle [EH], a prison and a rewarding High Street, lined with harmoniously blending houses

Levens Hall
Above: The interiors have fine panelling and plasterwork, with good period furniture.
Right: The Topiary Gardens, laid out by Beaumont from 1694, are internationally famous. There are over 90 pieces of topiary, some of them over 30 feet (9 metres) high.

of all periods. In Castle Place is a house by Amon Wilds, with his distinctive amante capitals to giant pilasters. An Elizabethan house, misleadingly called 'Anne of Cleves's House', is now a museum and has an interesting furniture collection. Priory Crescent of 1835–45 is but one example of Lewes' fine Georgian and Regency building.

Lewis (Leodhais) and Harris (Hearadh), W Isls 700 D3, This barren island, scattered with lochs and beautiful beaches, is the largest and most northerly of the Outer Hebrides. It is divided in two, both by the mountainous isthmus of Tarbert whose highest point, An Clisham (2,620 feet/798m) is also the highest point on the Outer Hebrides, and by an ancient schism in the MacLeod clan. It is an island of contrasting landscapes, with the moorlands and peat bogs of Lewis to the north, and the more pronounced, rocky terrain of Harris to the south.

Arnol Blackhouse Museum: This cottage-museum on the outskirts of Arnol on the west coast was built in the 1870s and occupied until 1964. Its living room, hearth with no smoke outlet, box beds and outbuildings are typical of the island's traditional dwellings.

Clach An Truiseil: An 18-foot (5.5m) standing stone, near the village of Balantrushal (Baile an Truiseil) on the northwest coast of the island.

Dun Carloway Broch: The broch was built just before the 1st century AD on a hill near Carloway (Carlabhagh), which offers a spectacular view of East Loch Roag and Harris.

Eye Peninsula (An Rubha): This peninsula, bordered by high cliffs and a number of lovely beaches, lies to the east of Stornoway and offers some magnificent views of the Minch. At Aignish (Aiginis), on the A866, stand the ruins of the 13th-century church of St Columba, the first church built on Lewis by the MacLeods. Its churchyard contains some beautiful carved crosses.

Garenin (Gearrannan): The village has been classified as a site of historic interest. Its dry-stone cottages are attractively restored.

Leverburgh (An T-ob): Ferries leave the port for North Uist*. The An Clachan Centre has a small exhibition on the islands of St Kilda*.

Rodel (Roghadal): It is well worth a visit to St Clement's Church, built c1500 and restored in 1787 and 1873. It houses the tombstones of a number of Macleods from Harris and Dunvegan, including the beautiful recumbent statue commissioned by Alasdair Crotach, Macleod of Macleod (d. 1546), 19 years before his death.

Scalpay (Scalpaigh): This boat-shaped island has an active fishing community and is linked to the east coast of Harris by a bridge.

Shawbost (Siabost): The village has a museum of local history, and a restored Norse watermill and drying kiln.

Stornoway (Steornabhagh): This once-active fishing port was founded in the late 16th century on the east coast of Lewis. Today it is the largest town in the Outer Hebrides

Above: Lewis and Harris, Luskintyre beach, seen from Nisabost on Harris's west coast.

Right: Lilleshall Abbey, remains of the façade with Norman arch and some early English arcading.

Below: Lichfield Cathedral, the west front begun in 1280.

Bottom: The Lewis Chessmen, Viking walrus-ivory pieces found in 1831.

(population 8,000). The wooded park at the foot of the neo-gothic Lews Castle, built by Sir James Matheson in 1856–63, offers beautiful views of the port and in July hosts the Hebridean Celtic Festival. The Nan Eilean Museum in Francis Street traces the history of the Outer Hebrides from prehistoric times. It sometimes exhibits pieces from the collection of Viking walrus-ivory chessmen found in 1831 by a farmer from Ardroil. The town hall houses an art gallery, the An Lanntair Arts Centre.

Tarbert (An Tairbeart): The principal port of Harris, where ferries leave for Lochmaddy (North Uist*) and Uig (Skye*), stands at the head of a fjord, on the narrow isthmus between North and South Harris.

Lewtrenchard, Devon 688 E6, Sabine Baring Gould was squarson here for many years. He was one of the first to collect folk songs, and also wrote hymns, among them 'Onward Christian Soldiers'. He may also have designed some of the houses in the village, such as the Old Rectory, The Ramps and the Blue Lion.

Lichfield, Staffs 694 C5, A city with a long history and a medieval street pattern, although it looks Georgian – which is appropriate for the home of Dr Johnson. The red sandstone Cathedral of St Mary and St Chad, with its three conspicuous spires, has its origins in Bishop Hedda's church of 700, but nothing is left of that, nor of the Norman cathedral. Most of the present building belongs to the period 1220–80, except for the easternmost parts, which were added before 1350. The west front is richly carved, although all the figures were replaced in the 19th century. The cathedral, the smallest but perhaps the most graceful in England, and its precinct are separated from the rest of Lichfield by two pools, or meres, which make a very picturesque setting. **Tamworth Castle**, in the centre of this much rebuilt city, is remarkably well preserved. It still has a stone keep on top of the tall castle mound, and several other castle buildings, including the Jacobean Great Hall, remain intact.

Lilleshall Abbey, Shrops 693 H3, The ruins of this abbey of Arroasian canons, founded in 1148, are evocative and extensive [EH]. The chancel is Norman, the crossing and nave Transitional.

Lincoln

Lincoln, Lincs 694 E3, As a Roman legionary fortress and town Lindum, as it was then known, had a large and prosperous community, and many remains of the Roman city walls and gates survive. The continuing importance of the town was recognized by William the Conqueror, who built a major castle here and also made Lincoln the centre of the old Saxon bishopric of Dorchester on Thames. Lincoln rivals Durham* in having the best site of any English cathedral city. The cathedral itself, together with the castle, stands on the edge of a dramatic ridge, down which the cobbled streets of the medieval town run to meet the more modern part built on the banks of the river and extending to the railway station. The cathedral dominates the countryside for miles. It is quite simply one of the most stunning medieval buildings in England and is full of experiments in construction of every kind, in vaulting and in ornament. The building is essentially of three periods: the Norman west front; the Early English transepts, choir and nave; and the Perpendicular towers. It seems that the west front originally looked much more like a castle than a church, but it was ornamented and extended by Bishop Alexander in the 1130s and 1140s with a spectacular screen of sculpture. In 1185 much of the cathedral fell down and it was rebuilt by Bishop Hugo ('Little St Hugh'). Work began in 1192 with the eastern transepts and the nave was roofed in 1233. In the 1260s the Angel Choir was added at the east end: a brilliant early example of English High Gothic, with exceptionally rich carved stonework, amongst which are the carved figures that give the choir its name.

Around the cathedral is the greensward of Minster Yard, fringed by the Deanery and the large houses of the cathedral canons. The Yard was once enclosed by a fortified wall, which can still be seen in many places. Just outside the walls on the steep south slope was built a magnificent Bishop's Palace, with three great halls [EH]. The buildings, now ruined, are worth exploring both for their own interest and for the magnificent panorama of the city below. The main gate through the wall was the Exchequer Gate, opposite the west front of the cathedral.

Beyond the gate lies **Lincoln Castle,** still enclosed by its wall, which was begun by William the Conqueror in 1068. It occupies almost a quarter of the enclosure of Roman Lincoln. Within the medieval fortifications are the late Georgian Gaol and the Assize Courts. South of the castle lies the old town, which is at its most picturesque in Steep Hill. Here are several very early buildings, including **The Jew's House,** a rare survival of a domestic building of the 12th century. At the bottom of the slope the buildings are largely late-18th and 19th century.

Below the cathedral and entered from Lindum Road is the **Usher Art Gallery**, built in 1927 with money left by James Ward Usher, whose watches, portrait miniatures, blue and white china and antique silver were the foundation of the present collection. There is a good group of paintings by the watercolourist Peter de Wint, who was associated with the town; and Tennyson's cloak and large-brimmed hat are also on display. To the north of the cathedral lies the Newport Arch, part of the Roman wall, which is probably the only Roman arch in England still used by modern motor traffic.

Top left: Lincoln Cathedral's towers rising above Exchequergate.

Centre left: The Usher Art Gallery, built in 1927 by Sir Reginald Blomfield with a bequest from James Ward Usher.

Above and below: Decorated watches, c1800 by William Libery, from the Usher Art Gallery.

Bottom left: *Lincoln from the South West*, by Peter de Wint.

Left: The Angel Choir.

Below: A view of the cathedral's great central tower, seen from the Bishop's Palace.

Above: Little Gidding. St John's Church is largely unchanged since it was built by Nicholas Ferrar's Puritan community in the early 17th century.

Lindisfarne, *see* **Holy Island*.**

Lingfield, Surrey 691 F6, The large Perpendicular church of St Peter and St Paul contains the tombs of Sir Reginald Cobham and his wife, who re-built much of the church and founded the college for secular chaplains here in 1431. The figures are beautifully executed. The Saracen crest on Sir Robert's helmet is a Crusader symbol. Elsewhere in the church another Cobham effigy rests his feet on a Saracen.

Linlithgow, W Loth 699 F4, This peaceful town on the shores of a small loch was the birthplace of James V (1512) and his daughter Mary Stuart (1542). The impressive 16th- and early 17th-century façades on the High Street evoke the former prosperity of this royal burgh chartered by David I. In 1302 Edward I of England built a tower-house here, which David II and his successors incorporated into a royal palace. An impressive gateway, built *c*1535, opens on to the park, which provides the setting for Linlithgow Palace and the Church of St Michael. In 1424 the palace was devastated by fire and only the walls of the original house (the square southwest tower) were left standing. The reconstruction of the residence, begun by James I in 1425, included the construction of the west wing which housed the royal apartments. In the 16th century James IV and James V added the south (the

Chapel) and east (the 90-foot/27m Great Hall) wings, architecturally the finest parts of the palace. The palace was abandoned after the Union of the Crowns (1603) and the transfer of the court of James VI to London. The north wing, which collapsed in 1607, was rebuilt in 1618–30. Cromwell occupied the palace in the 1650s, and Bonnie Prince Charlie stayed there briefly in 1745, shortly before the troops of the Duke of Cumberland set fire to it and left it in ruins. In the interior courtyard (the Quadrangle) stands the beautiful stone fountain (c1530) said to have flowed with wine on the occasion of James V's marriage to Mary of Guise in 1538.

The Church of St Michael, consecrated in 1242 and rebuilt (1425–1531) in Flamboyant style, is one of the largest churches built in Scotland before the Reformation. Supporters of John Knox stripped it of its statues, and Cromwell's soldiers stabled their horses in it. The original openwork crown of the tower, demolished in 1820 for safety reasons, was replaced in 1964 by a 'crown of thorns' made of aluminium and laminated wood. Of particular note is the finely carved window of the chapel, where a ghost is said to have warned James IV of the fatal outcome of the Battle of Flodden.

Liskeard, Cnwll 688 E7, A pleasant market town beneath the southern slopes of Bodmin Moor. Nearby are The Hurlers, three enigmatic stone circles arranged in a row, each one over 100 feet (30m) in diameter, with stones about 6 feet (1.8m) high.

Lismore, Ag & B 698 C2, There are a number of monuments on this small island in Loch Linnhe, the seat of the bishopric of Argyll from the late 12th to the early 16th century. The parish church of Clachan (1749) is all that remains of St Moluag's Cathedral, built c1183. The ruins of Tirefour Broch (100 BC–AD 100) stand on the southeast coast, while those of Achaduin Castle (13th century), the bishop's palace, are on its southwestern tip.

Little Easton, Essex 691 G3, The church, just north of Stane Street Roman road, is full of splendid memorials to the Bourchiers, 1365–1549, Earls of Essex, and the Maynards, their successors at Easton Lodge, which has now disappeared. Equally important is the late Romanesque mural of a seated prophet and 15th-century scenes from the Passion.

Top left and above: Little Moreton Hall, the gatehouse range with the long gallery and the bay window of the Great Hall.

Bottom right: Linlithgow Palace and the Church of St Michael.

Little Gaddesden, Herts, James Wyatt and Sir Jeffry Wyatville added the south chancel chapel to the church. There is a good range of monuments, notably from the late 17th century, and a tender one to the 7th Earl of Bridgwater by Westmacott. *See* **Ashridge Estate* 690 E4.**

Little Gidding, Cambs 695 F6, The inspiration for one of TS Eliot's 'Four Quartets' was itself inspired by Nicholas Ferrar's religious community founded here in 1626. The pinnacled stone façade of diminutive St John's was added in 1714, but its simple Puritan interior is persuasively contemporary and oddly moving.

Little Hormead, Herts 691 G3, This church should not be overlooked: it has wonderfully lively ironwork on the north door, depicting dragons, birds and flowers among arabesques.

Little Kimble, Bucks 690 E4, The small church of All Saints contains the most extensive wall paintings in Berkshire. They date from the 14th century and portray several saints and a depiction of Hell.

Little Maplestead, Essex 691 H3, One of five round churches of the Knights Templars left in England. This one is early 14th century but ravaged by Victorian restorers; the others are Norman.

Little Missenden, Bucks 690 E4, The church stands beside the manor, and contains an Aylesbury font and traces of wall-paintings. There is some controversy over whether it dates from the Saxon or Norman period.

Little Moreton Hall, Ches 693 H2, Perhaps the best-known timber-framed building in England: the elaborate patterns of its walls appear on National Trust tea towels in thousands of homes. The higgledy-piggledy parts of the house are grouped round a courtyard. Across from the entrance is the Great Hall, with rooms either side, completed about 1480. Two bulging bay windows were added in 1559, as a carved inscription records. The rest of the house, including the front range with its Long Gallery crazily perched on top, was finished by 1580. Since then little has been changed.

Littlewick Green, Berks, Not to be missed in St John the Evangelist is the early 15th-century painting of the Adoration of the Magi. The panel is 10 feet (3m) long and now set in the reredos. *See* **Shottesbrooke* 690 E5.**

Liverpool

Liverpool, Mersyd 696 E7, The city has some wonderful buildings, especially from its years of prosperity as a port. Its skyline is dominated by two 20th-century cathedrals.

Castle Street area: The historic centre of Liverpool is by Castle Street, though nothing old now survives. Facing along the street, at its north end, is the **Town Hall**, first designed as an exchange by John Wood of Bath in 1749, then altered by Wyatt and the Liverpool architect John Foster after a fire in 1795. The principal suite of rooms, in enfilade on the main floor, is reached by a fine staircase with a statue of George Canning by Francis Chantrey. The rooms are handsomely decorated and among the finest of their type in England; they retain much of their original furniture. Castle Street mainly comprises offices in a variety of styles; the best is undoubtedly CR Cockerell's Bank of England, 1848. It is a bold composition and typically Cockerell in its adventurous but scholarly use of the orders, monumental in scale but quite small in size. Across the face of the Town Hall runs Dale Street, which is also mainly commercial. The highlight is the exuberant **Royal Insurance** building on the corner of John Street, 1896, by JF Doyle with assistance from Norman Shaw; its Edwardian baroque front conceals an early steel frame. Lower down, in Water Street, are two examples of work by Liverpool's leading inter-war architect, Herbert Rowse: the former Martins Bank headquarters with a splendid banking hall, and India Buildings with an arcade running through the middle. Rowse was the star pupil of Sir Charles Reilly's Liverpool School of Architecture. Oriel Chambers, 1864, by Peter Ellis, astonished its contemporaries with its five-storey elevations, almost totally glazed with the oriel windows, which give the building its name.

Cathedrals: Sir Giles Gilbert Scott's **Anglican Cathedral**, started 1903, is one of the last and most beautiful expressions of the Gothic Revival, and took three generations to complete. Built in a warm red sandstone, the nave and chancel seem short because of the dominating central part, twin transepts flanking north and south portals and between them the huge 330-foot (100m) tower. Inside the spaces are breathtaking. The short nave has a bridge flying across it and at the southeast the Lady Chapel is almost hidden away and approached at gallery level from the south chancel aisle. This was the first part of the cathedral to be built, before Scott made a significant redesign in 1909. To the east of the cathedral, in a former quarry, is St James's Cemetery, established 1825, one of the most attractive in England with many fine monuments. The best is perhaps that to William Huskisson, the Liverpool MP who was killed by a train at the opening of the Liverpool and Manchester Railway in 1830. It is a small domed rotunda designed by Liverpool's best-known architect, John Foster, who also provided the mortuary chapel which is on the lip of the cemetery's edge just outside the cathedral's front. At the other end of Hope Street, Frederick Gibberd's **Roman Catholic Metropolitan Cathedral** took less than a decade from design in 1959 to completion. Built on the crypt of Lutyens' abandoned cathedral, designed in 1932, which would surely have been his finest work, Gibberd's design puts the altar in the middle of a round plan and directly under the spiky lantern that crowns the 16 concrete trusses that form the structure; inside these is a vast airy space and, at their feet, enclosed side chapels. Already it looks dated – in a way that Scott's Cathedral never will.

Docks: Liverpool's first dock, built in the early 18th century, is now filled in. From the early 19th century docks spread north and south from the Pier Head facing the river. Here the 'Three Sisters', buildings of radically different character, have become symbols of the city. The Mersey Docks and Harbour Board building, 1907, at the south, is by Arnold Thorneley;

Far left and left: The Anglican Cathedral of St John's great central tower and the lofty crossing beneath it, completed in 1978 after 75 years of work. Scott was only 22 when he won the competition to design it. The plans had been modified several times before his death in 1960.

Below: A puzzle jug, probably made between 1740–60, from the National Museums and Galleries on Merseyside

Left: St James's Cemetery, established in 1825.

Above and below: interior and exterior of the Roman Catholic Cathedral of Christ the King, a radically new design for English cathedral architecture in the 1950s. Pugin presented a design in 1853, of which only the Lady Chapel was built. Lutyens' plans were abandoned after the building of the crypt and Gibberd was appointed to design the current building. The altar stands in the centre of the circular cathedral.

L

Left: Liverpool Museum was built in 1860 to designs by John Weightman. All but the façade was rebuilt after a fire in 1941.

Below: The Royal Liver Building's towers are topped by the liver birds from which the city is said to have derived its name.

it is in Edwardian baroque style with a lofty domed and galleried hall in the centre. The Cunard Building, 1913, by Willink and Thicknesse, is square and squat compared to its neighbours; and the Royal Liver Building, an American-influenced skyscraper of 1908 by W Aubrey Thomas, has twin domes bearing sculptures of the mythical Liver birds. Behind them is the stone-clad ventilation tower of the Mersey Tunnel by Herbert Rowse with a nice relief sculpture of a begoggled motorcyclist by Tyson Smith. Albert Dock, opened in 1845, is the best-known and by the far the most important architecturally of Liverpool's enclosed docks. Philip Hardwick designed the monumental dock office with its huge cast-iron columns and pediment. The dock buildings extend right to the water's edge to save carriage across the quays, as pioneered at St Katharine's in London, and the ground floor has an open arcade supported on cast-iron columns. The dock walls themselves are in Hardwick's favourite cyclopean masonry.

St George's Hall: The civic centre of Liverpool is St George's Hall, begun in 1839 by Harvey Lonsdale Elmes. It was designed as a monumental Greek temple raised on a podium and described by Norman Shaw as 'the finest building in the world'. The east side, facing the station and St George's Plateau, has a giant portico of

13 columns supporting an attic; the south end has a pedimented portico of eight columns. The structure as well as the design is breathtaking: the main hall is raised on vaults of Piranesian splendour and the enormous Great Hall is ceiled in hollow blocks to lighten the load. Elmes died young and the principal interiors were designed by Cockerell. The Great Hall is a vast barrel-vaulted space, with five bays articulated by red granite columns, a richly plastered ceiling, much commemorative sculpture, enormous chandeliers and an immense floor of Minton tiles. At either end are two law courts, no longer in use, and to the north there is a great staircase leading to Cockerell's delicate small concert room, with a fine plaster ceiling, an undulating gallery front supported by draped ladies with their arms raised and another wonderful chandelier. St George's Hall is undergoing a thorough restoration with the help of the World Monuments Fund in Britain, who aim to improve the exit staircase to the concert room to satisfy fire regulations; until this is achieved, audiences have to be limited in number.

St George's Hall
Top: Corinthian columns on the south and east façades. providing classical grandeur at its most inspiring.
Left: The Great Hall, finished by CR Cockerell, with its Minton tile floor.

Above: Albert Docks, with arcades opening onto the water at ground-floor level. Now pleasure boats rule, but the fireproof warehouses contain Tate North and the Maritime Museum.

Below: Rodney Street, the birthplace of William Gladstone.

Museums and Galleries: To the north of St George's Hall is the centre of Liverpool's cultural quarter, with a fine range of buildings along William Brown Street, now mostly part of the National Museums and Galleries on Merseyside. These are for the most part not by front-rank architects but most are in a restrained classical form which is exactly right for the setting. These comprise, from the east and upper end, the former Sessions House, 1884, The Walker Art Gallery, 1874, the round Picton Reading Room, 1875, the William Brown Library and Museum, 1857, and, at the bottom, the only non-classical item, EW Mountford's former College of Technology, 1896, now incorporated with the Museum. The Walker Art Gallery in particular has a remarkable range of old masters and more recent paintings. In addition to those by St George's Hall, the National Museums and Galleries on Merseyside include the recently opened Conservation Centre in the former Midland Goods Warehouse, where the entrance is dominated by an enormous statue of the Spirit of Liverpool, removed from the pediment of the Walker. At Port Sunlight* is the Lady Lever Gallery; and at Sudley House, in south Liverpool, the Holt family collections are housed in an 1830s villa, extended in the 1880s, by which time the profits of shipping had led to substantial acquisitions. At the Albert Dock there is a more locally focused Museum of Liverpool Life, and in one of the former warehouses a Maritime Museum demonstrates Liverpool's role in world shipping and presents a poignant reminder of its part in the slave trade. Also housed in one of the Albert Dock warehouses is Tate Gallery North, especially noted for its temporary exhibitions but now expanded to give it more permanent display space.

Georgian buildings: Liverpool claims to have more Georgian buildings than Bath* though, regrettably, they are being depleted at a faster rate than anywhere else in England. These are mainly of the late Georgian period, as the city's wealth grew and its influence expanded remarkably in the early 19th century. A few remnants of the earlier City survive in the centre, such as the former Bluecoat School, 1716, with a delightful garden, exemplar of the urban oasis, at the back; it is now an arts centre. The finest and earliest of the streets of good housing is Rodney Street, with a mixed collection of later 18th-century houses. The earlier 19th century produced more

Walker Art Gallery
Far left: The Sculpture gallery.
Left: The 17th-century
Landscape gallery.

Below: *The Ashes of Phocion
Collected by his Widow*, by
Nicolas Poussin, at the
Walker Art Gallery

Above left: *Pietà* by Ercole
de'Roberti, at the Walker Art
Gallery.

Above: *Woman Ironing*, by
Degas, at the Walker Art
Gallery.

Left: Vase made at
Herculaneum Pottery, *c*1815,
at Liverpool Museum.

Above: *Mr Fleetwood
Hesketh*, by Joseph Wright of
Derby, at the Walker Art
Gallery.

regular rows, the best perhaps in Percy Street (stone and Greek); Canning Street (long and brick); and, among the latest, Falkner Square (stucco and leafy).

University: Liverpool University, based on an original building of 1887 by Waterhouse, has now expanded into a residential area, especially around Abercromby Square, where the Senate House of 1966 contrasts sharply with the early houses on the other sides. Nearby are the Philharmonic Hall, 1937, and the Philharmonic Hotel of 1898, in the freest of free styles outside and housing a gin-palace interior with riotously rich decoration.

Suburbs: Liverpool's outer suburbs are much more rewarding than Manchester's. This is partly because Liverpool had a much larger commercial middle class but also because the city's boundaries spread further. Around Princes Park and Sefton Park there were substantial terraces and villas. Sefton Park is a very fine public park with a magnificent Palm House of 1896, comprising three tiers of glass domes on a slender iron structure. On the approach, at Princes Road, is a remarkable group of religious buildings: St Margaret's Toxteth, 1868,

one of Street's finest Anglican churches; the Synagogue of 1874, vaguely Moorish, by W and G Audsley, with a rich interior in marble and gold and more easily accessible than most because of local pride and the support of the Open Churches Trust; the Welsh Presbyterian Church, 1865, also by the Audsley, though this is not evident from the Early English Gothic style; and a Greek Orthodox Church, 1865, by Henry Sumner, which is suitably domed. At Sefton Park there are also some remarkable churches: St Agnes, 1883, is one of JL Pearson's best, plain brick on the outside but ashlar and vaulted on the inside; the vicarage is by Norman Shaw; the Roman Catholic St Clare, by Leonard Stokes, 1888; and the Unitarian Church, 1896, by Percy Worthington, liturgically laid out in Anglican manner and beautifully detailed. Other suburban highlights include Rickman's St George Everton, built on Cragg's patented cast-iron system in 1812, not so obvious from the outside but very prettily so on the inside. Opposite is the best of Thomas Shelmerdine's Liverpool public libraries, built in 1895. Everton is approached along Shaw Street, where most of the early terraces have gone, but Elmes' Liverpool Collegiate School remains. Tudor Gothic and most unlike St George's Hall, it was recently rescued after dereliction and fire and converted into flats. Opposite is St Francis Xavier, 1845, by JJ Scoles, with a fine Lady Chapel of 1888 by Edmund Kirby.

Above: Interiors at 20 Forthlin Road, childhood home of Sir Paul McCartney – a celebrity from a council house.

Left: St George Everton, built in 1812.

Bottom: Bluecoat School, built in 1716–17 and acquired in 1927 as a centre for artists and musicians. It is the best surviving bit of Georgian Liverpool.

Council estates: Liverpool's slums were notorious and city council efforts to deal with them commendable. Many areas of council estate were planned with wide boulevards laid out under the direction of Sir Lancelot Keay, city architect and President of the Royal Institute of British Architects, a little-known but influential figure in the development of public architecture in Britain. These estates contain a number of good churches of the 1930s, especially two by Bernard Miller: St Christopher Norris Green, which makes a dramatic use of parabolic arches, and St Columba Anfield, dramatically lit from high windows. Even the council houses themselves have more interest than many – and one, 20 Forthlin Road [NT], is now visited for its status as the childhood home of Sir Paul McCartney and accessible as a shrine to Beatlemania. Other attractions for Beatles fans include Cavern Walks, with a reproduction of the old Cavern Club in its basement, and The Beatles Story at Albert Dock.

Lizard, Cnwll 688 C8, A geologically fascinating area, with cliffs of serpentine and slate and a plateau in the hinterland. It is renowned for its unusual flora, both on the central heathland and along the coastal fringe. St Keverne, Cadgwith and Coverack are all charming villages on the eastern side; Lizard Town with its famous lighthouse is the most southerly point of Great Britain. Overlooking Mount's Bay is Kynance Cove, immortalized by Lord Tennyson, and the sheltered harbour of Mullion.

Llananno, Powys 693 F5, Those looking for Llananno Church could easily miss it, since it lies well below the road on the banks of the Ithon, just north of Llanbister. Nothing in its unprepossessing Victorian exterior prepares one for the uplifting experience of confronting the early 16th-century screen. Christ occupies the central niche, with the Twelve Apostles on the right and twelve patriarchs and prophets on the left. The 19th-century restoration of the church fortunately spared the churchwarden's box pew of the late 17th century.

Llanberis, Gwynd, Across the waters from Dolbadarn are the steep slopes of the Dinorwic Quarries, idle

since 1969. The National Museums and Galleries of Wales (NMGW) are responsible for the admirable Llanberis Slate Museum. *See* **Dolbadarn Castle* 692 D2.**

Llandaff, Cardiff 689 G3, Although only a few miles away from Cardiff* city centre, a village atmosphere still prevails.

Top inset: Lizard Town lighthouse, now open to the public, contains beautifully kept Victorian machinery
Top: Lizard Point is the most southerly point in England.

Above: Llandovery Town Hall.

Left: Llandaff, the restored southwest tower, and on its left the Jasper Tower, named after Jasper Tudor, uncle of Henry VII.

Its cathedral, dedicated to St Teilo, sits in a hollow, a situation similar to St David's* and Bangor*, and an indication of its early Celtic origin. The Green, with its preaching cross, conveys the atmosphere of a medieval settlement, although most of the houses are 19th century and later. Nearby is the twin-towered gatehouse that once led to the ruined Bishop's Castle. The cathedral itself was much restored in the 19th century by John Prichard, whose other diocesan work is evident in Llandaff. The most significant post-war addition was Sir Jacob Epstein's aluminium figure, *Christ, Majestas.*

Llandegwning, Gwynd 692 C3, Diminutive and charming, this church of 1840, designed by the Denbighshire architect John Welch, has the appearance of a Staffordshire ornament, with the tower and its conical tower accommodating a pastille burner.

Llandovery, Carmth 692 E6, In spite of its small size, the village is rich in historical, literary and cultural associations. The Normans followed the Romans here, but favoured a river position for their stronghold, of which very little remains. The earlier hillside fort became the site of Llanfair-ar-y-Bryn (The Church of Mary on the Hill), a 13th- and 14th-century building of austere simplicity, partly built with the Roman bricks. Llandovery College was founded in 1847 by Thomas Phillips, a native of the neighbouring county of Radnorshire and surgeon of the East India Company, to provide 'a good, sound classical and liberal education', and to give encouragement to the Welsh language and the study of Welsh history and literature. That aim is still fulfilled. The stables opposite the Castle Hotel, a former coaching inn, have been converted into an attractive Heritage Centre, giving comprehensive coverage of the town and surrounding area, including the 19th-century printing press that published Lady Charlotte Guest's English translations of the medieval Welsh tales, *The Mabinogion,* the exploits of Twm Shon Cati (*c*1530–1609), popularly referred to as the Welsh Robin Hood or Rob Roy, and descriptions of the local habitat of rare birds of prey.

Llandrindod Wells, Powys 693 F5, The renown of Llandrindod Wells as a spa stems back to the 17th century. Most of the present buildings date to the late 19th century. The gentility of a once popular health resort – with boating lake, ornate Pump Room and thickly wooded Rock Park – remain evident, and surprisingly unchanged. The relatively unmodernized railway station serves the Heart of Wales line, between Shrewsbury and Swansea, through ravishing countryside.

Llandudno, Conwy 696 C8, Known as the 'Queen of the Welsh Resorts', it owes this distinction not only to the promenade which follows the generous arc of the bay, but to the spacious grid-planning of the town itself, with many of the shops retaining late-Victorian and Edwardian canopies and verandas. Its unmistakable landmark is the Gogarth, the 'Great Orme', which can be encircled by car, allowing spectacular views of the coast. Another means of appreciating the early geological history of the area, with its copper mines, is by the Great Orme Tramway, a street funicular similar to those of San Francisco.

Llanegryn, Gwynd, Dedicated to saints Mary and Egryn, the church is renowned for its delicately wrought rood screen. Prominent also are the memorials to the owners of the main estate in these parts. *See* **Peniarth* 692 D4.**

Llaneilian, IOA 692 D1, The church of St Eilian, with its 12th-century tower, owes the fascination which it has held for visitors as much to its remoteness as to its antiquity. The nave and chancel were rebuilt in the late 15th century, the period of many of the church's most interesting features, including the musicians carved on the corbels of the roof beams,

Right: Llandovery, where several rivers merge to flow into the Towy.

Above: Llanelli, Parc Howard, an Italianate mansion of the 1880s on the outskirts of the town, houses a museum and art gallery.

Below: Llandudno, a vista of one of the finest promenades in Wales.

and the rood screen with its primitive painting of a skeleton and scythe, bearing the words *Colyn Angau yw Pechod,* 'The Sting of Death is Sin'. A covered passage connects the church to St Eilian's Chapel.

Llanelli, Carmth 692 D7, Like Kidwelly*, the town was associated with the production of tin-plate until World War II, and was often referred to as Tinopolis. The most distinguished building is **Llanelly House,** the early 18th-century town house of the Stepney family, landowners and later industrial entrepreneurs who became linked through marriage with the Howard family. **Parc Howard** is now a museum and art gallery just outside the town. Among its exhibits are examples of Llanelly pottery; there are also landscapes by John Dickinson Innes, born in the town in 1887.

Llanengan, Gwynd 692 C3, The double-aisled church of St Einion is rich in 16th- and 17th-century

features, among them a rood screen across both aisles surmounted by a gallery, and fine Communion rail.

Llanerchaeron, Cerdgn 692 D5, One of the small country houses that John Nash designed in western Wales in the 1820s. The property has a remarkable collection of estate buildings that have remained unaltered [NT].

Llanfair, IOA 692 D2, Celebrated as having the longest name in Britain, if not in the world: Llanfairpwllgwyngyllgogerychwyrndrobwllllan-dysiliogogogoch (the fabrication of a 19th-century local tailor) – shortened to Llanfair or Llanfairpwll. The only attractive building

Llanerchaeron

Left: The entrance front before the National Trust restored its symmetry.

Right: One of the many farm buildings on the unspoilt estate.

Below: The name Llanerchaeron means 'the glade on the River Acron'.

is Telford's octagonal toll-house, which is less altered than other buildings in the town.

Llanfihangel Court, Mons 693 F6, A fascinating late 16th-century house in the village of Llanfihangel Crucorney, whose original medieval hall plan is still evident, and whose roof line and chimneys indicate later additions. The entrance front, once enhanced by radiating avenues, contrasts with the informality of the back quarters, with its pond and small courtyard. There is a particularly good timber-framed barn, and handsomely proportioned stables.

Llangollen, Denbgs 693 F3, Straddling the River Dee is a mid-14th-century bridge built by John Trevor (d. 1357), Bishop of St Asaph. The riverside railway station at Llangollen is once again in use, thanks to the determination of voluntary enthusiasts who have opened the track as far as Carrog (a journey of 20 minutes).

Llanidloes, Powys 692 E4, The church of St Idloes owes much of its distinction to an early 13th-century five-bay arcade, and a handsome hammerbeam roof, with winged angels holding shields decorating each beam. Both structures were removed from the Cistercian Abbey of Cwm Hir* in Radnorshire after the Dissolution. The

building spans many structural and decorative styles, from the late 14th-century tower to the Lady Chapel Screen of 1956, and in many ways reflects the development of the town itself, whose early 13th-century origins are still discernible in the grid-plan. Among the other attractions is the

much photographed early 17th-century timber-framed Market Hall, taking pride of place on the medieval cross-roads, and the Town Hall, built 300 years later, but like the Market Hall, having a lantern and an open ground floor. *See also* **Plas Newydd, Denbgs***.

Llanrhaeadr-yng-Nghinmeirch, Denbgs 693 F2, Also known as Pentre Llanrhaeadr. The church of St Dyfnog is renowned for its Tree of Jesse east window in the north nave, dated 1533 and considered to be the most beautiful in North Wales. Among the church's other remarkable features is the highly theatrical early 18th-century monument to Maurice Jones, of nearby Llanrhaeadr Hall, since architecturally much altered, and now serving as a residential home.

Llanrwst, Conwy 692 E2, This charmingly situated market town in the Conwy Valley has suffered several onslaughts in its history, notably during the Owain Glyndwr rebellion and later during the Wars of the Roses. The steeply humped bridge of 1636, fancifully attributed to Inigo Jones, is one of the town's endearing and enduring features, matched by the perilously placed but aptly named Tu Hwnt I'r Bont ('Beyond the Bridge'), once a court house.

Llanthony Priory (Llanddewi Nant Honddu), Mons 693 F6, Begun towards the end of the 12th century, the priory stands in the pastoral serenity of the Vale of Ewyas. Although it was partially restored at the end of the 18th century, the priory gained a brief new lease of life when the poet, Walter Savage Landor, bought it in 1807, with grandiose plans. He left, however, before fulfilling any of his ambitions.

Llantrithyd, V Glam 689 G3, Llantrithyd Place is now a ruin, but its former status is reflected in the handsome family memorials, which give the nearby Church of St Illtyd such unexpected distinction. These include early-17th-century monuments and tablets to the Basset family, one of whose members built the mansion in the mid-16th century, and those of the late-18th century to

Top left and centre: Llanfihangel Court, Dining Room and exterior.

Below: Llanthony Priory. Its incomparable situation breathes tranquillity.

Sir Thomas Aubrey and his wife, descendants of the Aubrey who embellished Llantrithyd Place in the early 17th century.

Lleyn (Ynys Enili), Gwynd 692 C3, The most far-flung of the settlements of the Lleyn Peninsula, Aberdaron* was the last place on the pilgrims' way to the Island of Bardsey. The parish church of St Hywyn was challenged by the sea to such an extent that it was abandoned at the beginning of the 19th century. The design for its replacement caused so much wrath that the earlier building was restored. Two miles (3.2km) across the Sound (Y Swnt) lies 'The Island of 20,000 Saints', the final resting place of pilgrims and holy men who came to its 6th-century monastery. The tower is all that remains of the 13th-century Augustinian abbey, whose stones were put to more secular use. In 1870 Lord Newborough, the owner, built farmhouses and cottages with the aim of revitalizing the island, which is now administered by the Bardsey Island Trust.

Loch Awe, Ag & B 698 C3, Scotland's longest inland loch (25 miles/40km) and a fisherman's paradise. The neo-gothic St Conan's Kirk stands on the shores, to the west of Lochawe village. It is an idiosyncratic building incorporating medieval fragments with a cloister that was built 1881–1930. The fine 15th- and 17th-century ruins of Kilchurn Castle* stand at the head of Kinloch Awe.

Loch Katrine, Stirlg 698 D3, The reservoir for the city of Glasgow* since 1859. There is a footpath along the north shore and the loch can be crossed in the *Sir Walter Scott*, which stops at Stronachlachar on the west shore. Experienced climbers and hikers will enjoy climbing Ben Venue (2,360 feet/719m) and Ben A'an (1,520 feet/463m) on the loch's shore.

Loch Lomond, Stirlg 698 D4, Loch Lomond (23 miles/37km long) is the largest freshwater area

in Great Britain, overlooked by stunning hills and forest. The road that runs along the east shore, more wooded and less busy than the west shore, comes to an end at Rowardennan Lodge. This is a popular destination for hikers following the West Highland Way* toward Queen Elizabeth Forest Park or climbing Ben Lomond (3,195 feet/974m).

Loch Morar, Highld 700 E7, With a depth of 1,000 feet (304m), this is Scotland's deepest inland loch. It is said to be haunted by Morag, a monster which appears when a Macdonald of Clanranald is about to die.

Loch Ness, Highld 701 G5, Although no more than a mile (1.6km) wide, Loch Ness is one of the longest lochs in Scotland (23¼ miles/38km) and also the most famous, due to Nessie, the mysterious monster that is supposed to haunt its waters. It has a depth of up to 820 feet (250m) in places and an average temperature of 41°F (5°C) which means it never freezes over. The old road built by General Wade lies along the loch's east shore between Fort George* and Fort Augustus*.

Loch Tay, P & K 698 E2, This beautiful loch, famous for its salmon, stretches for 13 miles (21km) along the foot of Ben Lawyers (1,980 feet/603m). One of the artificial islands (crannogs) built on the loch by the ancient Celts has been reconstructed at the Scottish Crannog Centre of Kenmore. The charming unspoilt 19th-century village of Kenmore and Taymouth Castle lie at the west end.

Loch Tummel, P & K 698 E2, To the northwest of Pitlochry* a series of hairpin bends climbs to the Queen's View viewpoint, from where Queen Victoria enjoyed the breathtaking view of Loch Tummel. The loch stretches majestically between the mountains, dominated by the conical outline of Schiehallion (3,545 feet/1080m), while the summits of Glen Coecan be seen in the distance.

Opposite page
Top: Loch Maree.

Centre left: Loch Ness.

Centre right: *On the Shores of Loch Katrine*, by John Knox (1778–1845).

Main picture: *Loch Lomond*, by Horatio McCulloch, 1861.

This page, below: Loch Lomond.

Above: Lochaber and Ben Nevis, overlooking Loch Linnhe.

Below: Loch Earn.

Lochgilphead, Ag & B 698 C4, The early 19th-century town of Lochgilphead, at the head of Loch Gilp, is the administrative centre of Argyll and Bute.

Lochindorb, Highld 701 J5, On an island in the loch stand the ruins of a castle built by the Comyns in the 13th century and fortified by Edward I of England in 1303. It was demolished in 1458 on the order of James II after it was used as a stronghold by the 'Wolf of Badenoch'. This was the nickname given to Alexander Stewart, Lord of Badenoch and brother of Robert III of Scotland (1390–1406), after he had plundered several villages and churches.

London

Admiralty Arch, SW1, 691 F5, Designed by Sir Aston Webb, and finished in 1911, this triple triumphal arch marks the start of the processional route (conceived as part of the national memorial to Queen Victoria) from Trafalgar Square, along the Mall, to the Victoria Monument outside Buckingham Palace*. The central gate is opened only for ceremonial processions.

Albert Hall, SW7, 691 F5, Francis Fowke's 1867–71 oval building with a 135-foot-high (41m) glass-and-iron dome is reminscent of a Roman

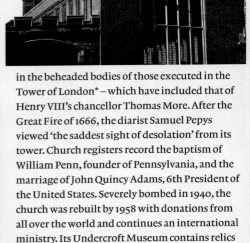
Right: All Hallows by-the-Tower, where Richard I's heart was traditionally said to be buried.

amphitheatre. It was to have been called the Hall of Arts and Science until Queen Victoria demanded another tribute to her husband. The magnificent high frieze around the outside is by Armitage, Pickersgill, Marks and Poynter and illustrates 'The Triumph of Arts and Letters'. The 150-ton organ has 9,779 pipes measuring a total of 9 miles (14.4km). It now hosts concerts (notably the annual 'Proms' series), with very occasional conferences, conventions and sporting contests.

Albert Memorial, SW7, 691 F5, Lately restored, Sir George Gilbert Scott's Albert Memorial [EH] in Kensington Gardens* now glitters as it did when completed in 1876, 15 years after Queen Victoria was cast into a desolate widowhood. Near the site of the 1851 Great Exhibition, which the capable and progressive Prince helped to plan, the

monumental hero sits beneath a gilded spire and coloured marble canopy facing the Albert Hall*, amid mosaics, enamels, polished stone, wrought iron and nearly 200 sculpted figures.

All Hallows by-the-Tower, EC3, 691 F5, The oldest church in the City, on Byward Street, it used to take

in the beheaded bodies of those executed in the Tower of London* – which have included that of Henry VIII's chancellor Thomas More. After the Great Fire of 1666, the diarist Samuel Pepys viewed 'the saddest sight of desolation' from its tower. Church registers record the baptism of William Penn, founder of Pennsylvania, and the marriage of John Quincy Adams, 6th President of the United States. Severely bombed in 1940, the church was rebuilt by 1958 with donations from all over the world and continues an international ministry. Its Undercroft Museum contains relics from Saxon and Roman times.

Above: Albert Hall, whose foundation stone was laid by Queen Victoria in 1868.

Apsley House
Right: The Corinthian portico.
Bottom centre: *The Waterseller of Seville* by Velázquez.
Bottom right: A candelabrum from the Wellington collection.

Bottom left: Albert Memorial, with a 14-foot-high (4m) gilt bronze statue of Prince Albert by John Foley.

Apsley House, W1, 691 F5, Now the Wellington Museum, this was once the grand home of the 1st Duke of Wellington, bought two years after his victory at Waterloo in 1815. Today it is stranded on a traffic island at Hyde Park Corner, but in its time it had a parkland setting and the splendid address 'Number One London', as it was the first house encountered past the toll-gate into London from the countryside. The Iron Duke had the Adam house remodelled by Benjamin and Philip Wyatt and filled it with victor's spoils, including the huge and almost nude

Canova statue of the vanquished Napoleon that dominates the ornate staircase. The picture collection in the 90-foot (27m) Waterloo Gallery includes works by Rubens, Goya, Murillo and Velázquez, looted by Napoleon and presented by the King of Spain, grateful for his restoration. Wellington's opulent dinner and dessert services are displayed – including one commissioned by Napoleon for his Empress Joséphine. It is the last remaining great London town house, with collections largely intact and family still in residence. The gates behind it were designed by Giuseppe Lund, with lion and unicorn panels sculpted by David Wynne, to celebrate the 93rd birthday of Queen Elizabeth the Queen Mother.

Bank of England Museum, EC2, 691 F5, Housed within the mighty Bank itself in Bartholomew Lane, the Museum traces its history from 1694 when it was founded to raise a public loan to fund William III's war against France. Rebuilding schemes have reduced Sir John Soane's magnificent late 18th-century reconstruction of the Bank to an outer wall; but a fragment of his fine neoclassical interior has been recreated for a display of bank notes and gold bars, and there are the pikes and muskets once used to defend the Bank against rioters. The 1930s figures on the façade by Charles Wheeler include 'The Old Lady of Threadneedle Street' – the Bank's traditional nickname, deriving from a satirical reference by Richard Brinsley Sheridan and a subsequent cartoon by the caricaturist James Gillray.

Banqueting House, sw1, 691 F5, Inigo Jones' masterpiece, commissioned as an addition to the old Whitehall Palace by James I to provide a grand setting for formal banquets and court masques. Jones was the self-taught son of a London clothmaker who steeped himself in the architecture of Renaissance Italy and especially admired Andrea Palladio. The Banqueting House

Bank of England
Above left: The building seen from Threadneedle Street, rebuilt by Herbert Baker in the 1930s.
Above right: The sculpted figures from the façade are by Charles Wheeler, president of the Royal Academy 1956–60.

Right: Banqueting House, with Rubens' painted ceiling depicting the benefits of the wise rule of James VI and I.

opened in 1622 with a masque by Ben Jonson, for whose theatricals Jones had long designed increasingly elaborate sets and lighting effects. After the death of James I, his son Charles I commissioned the magnificent ceiling paintings by Rubens to celebrate his father's life. It is the only Rubens scheme to remain intact in its original position. Masques were performed elsewhere after its installation so that the paintings would not be damaged by lamp smoke. But it was here that the King was to meet his death. On 30 January 1649, before a crowd of thousands, Charles walked through the third window onto a scaffold erected against the Banqueting House walls. Eleven years later, Charles II celebrated his restoration here. Fire destroyed much of the surrounding Whitehall Palace in 1698 and the Banqueting Hall was converted into a Chapel Royal. In 1893 it was granted to the Royal United Services for use as a museum, but in 1962 it was restored as one of the finest banqueting venues in London. The vaulted basement, which James I used as a drinking den, has been thoroughly refurbished.

Barbican Centre, EC2, 691 F5, Part of a major high-rise development conceived in 1955 by the architects Chamberlin, Powell & Bon to replace acres laid waste by bombs in World War II. The somewhat unwieldy Centre, on Silk Street, completed in 1981, contains a rich array of facilities for the arts – concert hall, theatre, cinema, art galleries and sculpture court. The City's largest public library is also housed here. Beyond the ornamental lake and fountains outside, the church of **St Giles without Cripplegate** seems marooned within this modernity. It was reduced to ruins in an air raid and rebuilt as the parish church of the Barbican development. Oliver Cromwell was married here, and the poet John Milton buried.

Battersea Park, SW11, 691 F5, A beautiful, large (200-acre/81ha) riverside park full of surprises. The lake is home to herons, cormorants and grebes, as well as ubiquitous ducks; there is a children's zoo, and a deerpark with peacocks. Marvellous trees and flower gardens give solace from urban stress, as does the Japanese Peace Pavilion built by Buddhist monks in 1985. Jazz concerts at the lakeside café and exhibitions in the Pump House gallery provide entertainment, while the energetic can play scratch football or use the tennis courts.

Bedford Square, WC1, 691 F5, Begun in 1775, this is the only complete Georgian square left in Bloomsbury. The whole square is Grade I listed to guarantee its survival. The Paul Mellon Centre is at No. 16, the Architectural Association at No. 19.

Top left: The Barbican has twenty blocks in all, containing a total of 2,014 flats.

Above: Bedford Square, a surviving, and now protected, pocket of Georgian London.

Right: Bethnal Green Museum of Childhood is decorated with 19th-century *sgraffito* panels depicting the arts, sciences and agriculture. It was designed by FW Moody and executed by students of the National Art Training School.

Belgravia, SW1, 691 F5, Once the marshy haunt of robbers, this area was developed as an opulent residential area to rival Mayfair* between 1820 and 1850. The entrepreneur builder Thomas Cubitt used earth from the St Katharine's Dock* excavation as a foundation for the elegant squares and terraces, and bricks were made on site from clay dug from the ground. Fashionable from the start, Belgravia is favoured now for embassies and diplomats' residences. Its centrepiece, Belgrave Square, was designed by George Basevi, cousin of prime minister Disraeli – who loftily condemned the development as 'so contrived as to be at the same time insipid and tawdry'.

Benjamin Franklin's House, WC2, 691 F5, The great American statesman and scientist lived at No. 36 Craven Street from 1757 until 1762. It has recently been refurbished and will open as a museum dedicated to his life and work.

Bethnal Green Museum of Childhood, E2, 691 F5, An outpost of the Victoria and Albert Museum* in the East End (Cambridge Heath Road), this has one of the largest collections of childhood items in the world. Baby equipment, nursery furniture, children's clothes and teenage fashions all feature. But the strongest focus is on toys, with charming displays of puppets, automata, dolls and dolls' houses. A Nuremberg house dates from 1673, and there is a model of Queen Victoria in coronation robes made in the 1840s. Each

month a selection of new items is shown. The Museum was officially dedicated to childhood in 1974. Its prefabricated iron frame had been transported from temporary museum buildings in South Kensington to the deprived East End in 1872 and encased in its distinctive red brick. Then its displays included what is now the separate Wallace Collection* and the beginnings of the National Portrait Gallery*. It started to focus on children

and to collect childhood material in the 1920s under its keeper Arthur Sabin, who pursued an unusually enlightened education policy for his day.

Bevis Marks, EC3, 691 F5, The Spanish and Portuguese Synagogue in Heneage Lane. Jews were expelled from England in 1290 but allowed back by Cromwell. This, the oldest surviving English synagogue, a handsome red-brick box with galleried interior, Tuscan columns and carved woodwork, was built for Sephardic worship in 1699–1701 by the Quaker carpenter Joseph Avis.

Big Ben, SW1, 691 F5, The clock's deep chimes, broadcast daily around the world, became operational on 31 May 1859 and soon became a symbol of Britain. The name 'Big Ben' originally referred just to the huge 14-ton bell (whose manufacture encountered controversial technical problems), and whether it derived from the large Chief Commissioner of Works, Benjamin Hall, or

Left: Bevis Marks Synagogue has possibly the best preserved original ecclesiastical interior of any religious building in London.

a popular 18-stone boxer, Benjamin Caut, is still undecided. The light above the four-faced clock in the Palace of Westminster's 320-foot (97.5m) tower is switched on when Parliament is sitting.

Bishop's Park, SW6, 691 F5, Formerly the grounds of Fulham Palace football club. A handsome avenue of mature plane trees shades the riverside walk. Yachts often sail the river here, and the annual University Boat Race between Oxford and Cambridge starts at nearby Putney Bridge.

Blewcoat School Gift Shop, SW1, 691 F5, Built in 1709 by a local brewer to teach poor children to 'read, write, cast accounts and the catechism', and in use as a school until 1939, this red-brick building in Caxton Street is now a National Trust shop.

Bloomsbury, WC1, 691 F5, Dominated now by the University of London and the British Museum*, and with traffic hurtling towards the rail termini on the Euston Road, this area still has pockets of calm amid the squares and terraces that characterized its development in the 18th century. Once a favourite area for writers, painters and musicians, it gave its name to the influential group who began to meet in 1905 at Gordon Square, and included Virginia Woolf, Vanessa Bell, EM Forster, Lytton Strachey and Roger Fry.

British Library, NW1, 691 F5, The British Library, on the Euston Road at St Pancras*, was the largest

Right: The British Library's open portico gates reveal Paolozzi's courtyard sculpture of Sir Isaac Newton.

20th-century public building in Britain. Fully opened in 1999, it cost £511 million, provides seats for 1,200 readers and stores 12 million books in deep basements. The architect Colin St John Wilson has housed a state-of-the-art storage, retrieval and display system in a building that some consider is a work of art in itself. A celebration of human knowledge begins in the piazza, with Eduardo Paolozzi's statue of Isaac Newton plotting the immensity of the universe with a pair of dividers.

Different reading rooms allow researchers to study manuscripts, maps, rare books and musical scores, the humanities, the sciences, and the Oriental and India Office collections. The 65,000-volume King's Library, collected by George III and given to the nation by George IV, is held in a six-storey glass tower. Public exhibitions focus on the scope of the library, on postage stamps, and on the history of communication. Best of all are the treasures in the John Ritblat Gallery: the *Codex Sinaiticus* (c350), the Lindisfarne Gospels (c700), Magna Carta (1215), the Gutenberg Bible (1455) and Shakespeare's First Folio (1623). The Gallery also displays samples of the handwriting of Leonardo da Vinci, Lewis Carroll and many others.

British Museum, WC1, 691 F5, Exciting developments are taking place as 'the world's greatest storehouse of priceless treasures' approaches the 250th anniversary of its foundation in 1753. The Great Court (designed by Norman Foster and opened in 2000), which surrounds the restored Reading Room, has transformed the British Museum. Its vast area, previously hidden from the public, used to be filled with bookstacks from the British Library*. The domed Reading Room designed by Sydney Smirke in the 1850s still retains the long desks where such luminaries as John Ruskin, Dante Gabriel Rossetti, Karl Marx, WB Yeats and George Bernard Shaw studied and wrote.

The Museum first opened to the public in 1759, in a house on its present site. Its foundation was prompted by the physician Hans Sloane offering to Parliament, for under half their value, his

Over 6 million objects reveal the awesome prodigality of human history and artistry. Some of the most magnificent displays highlight the ancient civilizations of Egypt, Greece and Rome. The Rosetta Stone – inscribed in 196 BC but not unearthed until 1799 – laid the foundation of our knowledge of ancient Egyptian language. In 1804 Lord Elgin brought back marble sculptures from the Parthenon – having purchased them from the occupying Turks, who were using them for target practice – and when he sold them to the Museum in 1816 (for £35,000) he supplied it with its most famous exhibit and its longest controversy, for Greece still presses for their return.

The cultures of Africa, the Americas, Asia, Europe, Japan, the Near East and the Pacific are unfolded through recovered relics dating from prehistory to the products of recent times. Some of the

tremendous collections of art, antiquities and natural history. Purchases and gifts of other collections followed, including the 10,500-volume Royal Library presented by George II in 1757. The Museum soon outgrew its premises, and in 1823 work began on the present neoclassical building, with its imposing portico of Ionic columns, designed by Robert Smirke (brother of Sydney). Congestion was further relieved in 1881 when the natural history collections were removed to the new Natural History Museum*, leaving the British Museum to concentrate on illuminating world cultures.

earliest northern Native American artefacts were brought to England by Captain Cook for Hans Sloane; from modern America come metalwork, jewellery, ceramics and glass. The Mayan and Aztec cultures are well represented and include carved lintels from the Mayan city of Yaxchilan and a famous collection of Mixtec-Aztec turquoise mosaics. Especially prized among the British exhibits are the treasures from Sutton Hoo. This was the site of a Saxon ship-burial mound, excavated in 1939 and found to contain the remnants of a 38-oar boat plus an astounding hoard of precious objects. There were no signs of a body so it was at first assumed to

Centre of page
Top left: Sutton Hoo buckle (7th century AD).
Below left: Painted wooden anthropoid coffin of the Libyan Pasenhor who lived in Thebes c700 BC.
Centre left: The Rosetta Stone.
Right: Study of Adam by Michelangelo.

Right: Bas-relief of a hunted lioness found in the Assyrian palace at Nineveh. One of several carvings depicting the feats of King Assurbanipal (ruled 669–627 BC).

Below: *The Three Crosses,*
drypoint and burin printed
on vellum, by Rembrandt.

Far left: Basalt statue from
Easter Island.
Left: The Portland Vase
(perhaps from Rome, c5–25 BC)
– the most famous cameo-
glass vessel from antiquity.
Right: Human-headed bull and
attendant genie, Khorsabad,
Assyria, c710 BC.

be a memorial to a king. Later analyses have however suggested
that the corpse may have totally decayed; it may therefore be the
sumptuous grave of either King Raedwald (590–625) or King
Sigebert (d. 637). The gilt bronze helmet, jewelled sword, royal
sceptre, silver dishes, drinking vessels and jewellery allow the visitor
a glimpse of the life of a warrior king, both barbaric and
sophisticated.

In 1970 the Museum's Department of Ethnography removed to
the **Museum of Mankind** in Burlington Gardens, near Piccadilly*, to
gain more space; but now its collections representing the cultures
of indigenous peoples throughout the world are returning to the
main, expanded, site where in 2003 the new Wellcome Gallery
opens for their display. The impact of carvings from these
collections, particularly their directness, humour and honesty, had a
profound influence on 20th-century sculptors such as Jacob Epstein
and Henry Moore.

The Museum's collection of prints and drawings – approximately
3 million – covers the history of the graphic arts from the 15th
century to the present. Containing the etched rural idylls of Samuel
Palmer, scenes by those Japanese masters of the colour-print,
Hokusai and Hiroshige, satirical prints from the 18th and 19th
centuries, wonderful watercolours by Turner, bright ephemeral
posters – it boasts infinite riches.

Brompton Oratory, sw7, 691 F5, An Italianate monument to the late 19th-century English Catholic revival. Established by Cardinal John Henry Newman and designed by the young Herbert Gribble, the church was finished in 1884 but is enriched by earlier treasures: the marble figures of the Apostles, for example, were carved by Giuseppe Mazzuoli for Siena Cathedral in the late 17th century. The statue of Newman by Chevalliaud stands outside.

Brown's Hotel, w1, 691 F5, Opened in Dover Street in 1837 by former manservant James Brown and his wife Sarah, who had been Lady Byron's personal maidservant. Cecil Rhodes and Rudyard Kipling were among many distinguished patrons, as was Theodore Roosevelt, who walked from here to his wedding in Hanover Square. In 1905 Franklin and Eleanor Roosevelt honeymooned at Brown's.

Buckingham Palace, sw1, 691 F5, Built in 1703 by the Duke of Buckingham and bought by George III as a private town dwelling for Queen Charlotte in 1762, this house-turned-palace has been the London home of British monarchs since the accession of Queen Victoria in1837. When the sovereign is in residence the Royal Standard flies above it. The present 300-room palace, which retains the shell of the original, was built over three decades to 1825 designs by John Nash with many additions by other architects. (When Queen Victoria moved in, the drains were unreliable and many of the 1,000 windows would not open.) The east front, facing the Mall, was given its present design by Sir Aston Webb in 1913.

The 18 State Rooms are open to the public in August and September. Chambers in crimson and gold contain vast chandeliers, Sèvres porcelain, Gobelins tapestries, mirrors, inlaid furniture and portraits of kings and queens. The Queen's Gallery, first opened to the public in 1962, holds

Above and below: Brompton Oratory, church of a community of priests called the Oratorians, whose Italian founder, St Philip Neri, bid his followers 'be devoted to the Madonna'.

Left: Buckingham Palace, the White Drawing Room.

changing exhibitions drawn from the spectacular Royal Collection amassed over 500 years. Redeveloped by John Simpson and Partners, 1998–2000, to more than treble the display space, the expanded gallery's grand neoclassical design, complete with entrance portico, pays homage to John Nash and John Soane. The palace forecourt is patrolled by sentries in full dress uniform.

Bunhill Fields, EC1, 691 F5, Designated a cemetery after the Great Plague of 1665, Bunhill Fields off City Road was soon allocated to Nonconformists (who were banned from churchyard burial). John Bunyan, Daniel Defoe and William Blake lie here. Since the last burial in 1854, it has been preserved as a public garden. John Milton wrote *Paradise Lost* while living in adjacent Bunhill Row.

Burgh House, NW3, 691 F5, Built in 1703 and dubbed 'the finest Queen Anne house in London', this became the home of famous spa physician Dr William Gibbons. The house, in New End Square, now hosts the Hampstead Museum, and music-room recitals and lectures.

Burlington Arcade, w1, 691 F5, One of three 19th-century arcades off Piccadilly selling traditional British luxury goods, Burlington Arcade was built for Lord Cavendish in 1819 to stop passers-by throwing garbage into his garden. Beadles still patrol to ensure that suitable standards prevail. Almost as splendid and much less crowded is John Nash's Royal Opera Arcade off the Haymarket, completed in 1818.

Burlington House, w1, 691 F5, A great stone gateway designed by Charles Barry Junior (1868–73) leads off Piccadilly to the courtyard of what was once the mansion of Lord Burlington, great patron of the arts (*see* Chiswick House*). The house (1717–20)

Left and below: Canary Wharf, the office cityscape which has replaced the East End docks.

has been much altered and enlarged over the years and in 1854 was bought by the Government. It is now the home of the Royal Academy of Arts* and various learned societies.

Cabinet War Rooms, sw1, 691 F5, Below the Government offices in King Charles Street is a warren of 21 spartan bomb-proofed rooms from which Winston Churchill's government often operated during World War II. They are preserved almost exactly as they were: visitors can see the table where the War Cabinet met during air raids, and the map room where information from all the fronts was co-ordinated. A tiny anteroom housed a direct line to Washington, so that Churchill could speak privately to President Roosevelt.

Canary Wharf, E14, 691 F5, Pinnacle of the Docklands development on land left derelict when the docks shifted down-river to Tilbury's modern container port, Canary Wharf was planned as a mini-city of 21 office blocks, with shops, flats and leisure facilities. Cesar Pelli's 800-foot (350m) office block at One Canada Square (1992), which originally towered from a distance like a giant

Above: Cenotaph, national memorial to the 'Glorious Dead'.

Bottom left: Carlyle's House, Robert Tait's *A Chelsea Interior*, 1857, showing Thomas and Jane Carlyle and their dog Nero in their parlour.

white pencil, has had its splendid isolation destroyed by two more tower blocks. The best view of the whole area is from the overhead Docklands Light Railway.

Carlyle's House, sw3, 691 F5, This plain Queen Anne house in Cheyne Row was the home of writer and historian Thomas Carlyle (1795–1881) – known as 'The Sage of Chelsea' – for 47 years. Original furnishings, books, pictures and personal items of Carlyle and his wife Jane evoke their life, and the walled garden continues the Victorian memory. Dickens, Chopin, Tennyson, George Eliot and many other luminaries called here.

Cenotaph, sw1, 691 F5, The austere Whitehall memorial, created in 1921 by Sir Edwin Lutyens, commemorates the dead of World War I; the name means 'empty tomb'. It is devoid of decoration, save for the flags of the three services and the Merchant Navy. An annual service to honour the dead from both world wars, attended by the Royal Family and leading politicians, is held at the eleventh hour on the Sunday nearest to the eleventh day of the eleventh month.

Channel 4 Headquarters, sw1, 691 F5, Tucked amid the dark buildings of Horseferry Road in the heart of Westminster, this vigorous 1994 glass and metal building by Richard Rogers springs an architectural surprise.

L

Charterhouse, EC1, 691 F5, A 14th-century gateway leads to the remains of a Carthusian monastery dissolved by Henry VIII. In 1611 the buildings were converted into a hospital for needy pensioners and the Charterhouse charity school, whose pupils included the writer William Makepeace Thackeray and the founder of the Boy Scouts, Robert Baden-Powell. The school moved to Surrey in 1872, but apartments for the genteel old remain.

Chelsea, SW3, 691 F3, Once a riverside village, Chelsea has been fashionable since Henry VIII's day – fine Tudor monuments (including one to Thomas More) line Chelsea Old Church, rebuilt after wartime bombing. A Bohemian reputation established by the Chelsea Set of writers and

artists in the 19th century – when Turner, Whistler and Rossetti were drawn to the Thames views from Cheyne Walk – survives in Carlyle's House* and the Chelsea Arts Club. A raffish tradition continued in the King's Road from the hippy 1960s to the punk 1970s, but this shopping street is now sedately chic. Antique shops and galleries proliferate, the high rents having forced artists from their studios and writers from their garrets. Sloane Square, laid out in the late 18th century, contains the well-designed 1936 Peter Jones department store by William Crabtree.

Chelsea, Royal Hospital, SW3, 691 F5, Some 400 veterans live in this noble establishment in Royal Hospital Road, which Charles II commissioned from Christopher Wren in 1682 as a retirement home for old and wounded soldiers. With their scarlet coats and black tricorn hats, the residents have been known as Chelsea Pensioners since the late 17th century. Wren's chapel remains; his panelled Great Hall is still used as a dining room. It was here that the Duke of Wellington lay in state in 1852; so many people filed past that two were crushed to death. Every May, the spacious grounds host the spectacular Chelsea Flower Show.

Chelsea Physic Garden, SW3, 691 F5, Founded by the Society of Apothecaries in 1673 for the study of medicinal plants, the garden, on Swan Walk, was saved from closure in 1722 by the wealthy physician and collector Hans Sloane. The benefactor's statue survives, as does one of London's most fascinating cultivated spaces – which now has a collection of 6,000 species. Stones from the Tower of London were brought to form the foundation of the 1771 pond and rock

Top: Chelsea's Royal Hospital, with a granite obelisk to the memory of 255 soldiers who fell at Chilianwalla in the 2nd British-Sikh war, 1849.

Above: Charterhouse Square, a fine ironwork gateway.

Left: Chelsea Physic Garden's gateway.

Right: Chiswick House is the finest surviving example of Palladian architecture in Britain and has beautiful gardens rich in architectural features, including a gateway by Inigo Jones, acquired by Lord Burlington from Beaufort House, Chelsea. The magnificent cast-iron gates on the axis of the forecourt were those of Grosvenor House, Park Lane, re-erected in 1934.

garden, the oldest on public view. Current interest in plant-based medicine has inspired the Garden of World Medicine – Britain's first garden of ethnobotany – and also a new Pharmaceutical Garden.

Chiswick, W4, 691 F5, Between the Thames and the A4, a stretch of fine houses runs from Upper Mall to Chiswick Mall via Hammersmith Terrace. Façades date from the 17th century; interiors may be older. Artists, writers and actors have lived here. Built around 1780, **Kelmscott House** (No. 26 Upper Mall) was where Sir Francis Ronalds invented the electric telegraph in 1816 (he planted miles of cable in the garden). The great designer and social idealist William Morris established his printing and design works here, and the house still has his wallpaper and the fireplace designed by Philip Webb as a wedding gift. Morris died here in 1896. St Nicholas, Chiswick's parish church, retains its medieval tower; the rest was rebuilt by the Victorian architect John Loughborough Pearson. William Hogarth (who lived nearby in Hogarth House*) is commemorated in the churchyard by an urn on a large pedestal.

Chiswick House, W4, 691 F5, A splendid 1729 Palladian villa in Burlington Lane, designed by the 3rd Earl of Burlington for the express purpose of entertaining his friends and displaying his works of art. (He actually lived in an adjacent Jacobean mansion, demolished in 1758.) As a young man Burlington was inspired by Palladio's published designs and twice travelled to Italy to see the master's works at first hand; the design of Chiswick House is based on the Villa Rotonda near Vicenza. After Burlington's death, the 4th Duke of Devonshire inherited the house, and it remained in that family until the 8th Duke moved to

Chatsworth* in 1892, when it became a private mental home. Fortunately it was publicly purchased in 1928 and careful restoration began. Two wings by James Wyatt which had been added in 1788 were demolished in 1952.

The original front façade has a portico flanked by a double stair, and at the back are three large recessed Venetian windows overlooking the garden. The dome, which rises at the centre of the building, tops the grand octagonal Saloon, now restored, which was designed to house Lord Burlington's art collection. The sumptuous interiors, with their spectacular plaster ceilings, and most notably the gilded Blue Velvet Room, are by Burlington's friend and protégé William Kent. The gardens of Chiswick House were revolutionary in their day, as they sought to harmonize with nature rather than exercise absolute control over it. (The fashion until then was for strict architectural symmetry, with plants clipped to conform.) At first the garden was quite formal, a simple Renaissance knot-garden preceding the completion of the house itself. In 1730 the Palladian villa was complemented by a 'Roman' garden of avenues, obelisks, geometrical pools and a maze, all ornamented with statuary – some of which remains – and small pavilions. But a few years later William Kent began to introduce 'the natural taste in gardening' by means of a rustic cascade and a meandering canal bordered

Above: Chiswick House, the Blue Velvet Room ceiling by William Kent.

Below: Christ Church, Spitalfields, was built under the Fifty New Churches Act (1711) from money raised by a tax on coal.

with informal planting. Kent was celebrated in his time as the first landscape designer to have 'leap'd the fence and seen that all nature is a garden'. In 1753, the year Burlington died, an orangery was built and some of the geometrical pools filled in to create more space for planting. Among the friends he had entertained in this carefully contrived idyllic setting were Handel, Swift and Pope. Pope's verses on 'The Use of Riches' stipulate that the rich man, when laying out his garden, must 'let Nature never be forgot' and should 'Consult the Genius of the Place in all' – comments said to have been inspired by Chiswick House.

English Heritage and the Borough of Hounslow have carefully restored both house and garden to recreate the style Lord Burlington originally planned for the delight of his celebrated friends.

Christ Church, E1, 691 F5, The most impressive of Nicholas Hawksmoor's six London churches. Built between 1714 and 1729, but later disfigured by Victorian alterations and 20th-century vandalism, the exterior was restored and the building reopened in 1987. The soaring spire and arched portico on four pedimented Tuscan columns dominate the surrounding streets as they were always intended to do, since the church was designed to combat the spread of Nonconformism in the Huguenot stronghold around Spitalfields*.

City of London, EC2/EC4, 391 F5, For 800 years the Square Mile (as the City is known) has been governed by a Lord Mayor and Corporation. Livery Companies have played a key role in its administration and commerce since medieval times, and 100 of these trade guilds survive today – Mercers, Goldsmiths, Salters and Vintners among them. In November the Lord Mayor's Show is staged, when the Mayor rides in procession to pledge allegiance to the Crown at the Law Courts – just as Richard ('Dick') Whittington did in 1397.

The 1666 Great Fire destroyed or damaged 87 of the City's 100

churches, but that calamity gave Christopher Wren scope to design a new capital. Grand plans for thoroughfares radiating from St Paul's* and the Royal Exchange* were rejected as too expensive – to be picked up over a century later for Washington, D.C. The great cathedral and 51 churches were rebuilt, however. The bomb devastation of World War II rivalled that of the Great Fire, but again churches were gradually rebuilt and the Barbican* development achieved. The Museum of London* tells the story of the City of London from pre-Roman times.

Far left: Thomas Gresham's grasshopper sign outside Martin's Bank.

Left: Detail of the capitals outside Leadenhall Market, designed by Sir Horace Jones, 1881.

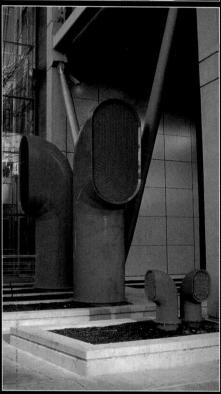

Opposite page, main picture: St Mary-le-Bow retains much of its ancient fabric, though it has been restored many times since Wren designed it after the Great Fire. It is from here that the famous 'Bow bells' sound.

Above left: Ventilation feature at 88 Wood Street, designed by Richard Rogers, 1999.

Above: St Mary-at-Hill has one of the best interiors of all the City churches (Wren, 1677). Its fine vaulted ceiling soars above box pews and a magnificent organ case and pulpit.

Cleopatra's Needle, WC2, 391 F5, This granite monument on Victoria Embankment, whose inscriptions praise the pharaohs, was raised in Heliopolis around 1500 BC and presented to Britain by Mohammed Ali, Viceroy of Egypt, in 1819. Erected on the newly completed Embankment along with Victorian bronze sphinxes in 1878, it had a time capsule (including photos of 12 fleshy beauties and a train timetable) placed in its base. A twin stands in New York's Central Park. The designer of the Embankment (and of the London main drainage system), the great Victorian engineer Joseph Bazalgette, is commemorated nearby with a bronze bust by George Simonds.

Clink Prison Museum, SE1, 691 F5, Close to the faked historical horrors of the London Dungeon, this museum in Clink Street recreates the real thing. Once a jail for prostitutes, debtors, drunkards and religious dissenters – and long run by the Bishops of Winchester, a remnant of whose palace is visible in a 14th-century rose-window – the original building was burned down by rioters in 1780.

Above: Crystal Palace's Italianate terraces. Local residents have fought to preserve their park from development as a multiplex.

Left: The College of Arms was saved from flames in a 1941 air raid by a change in the wind direction.

Below: *Covent Garden Piazza and Market,* by John Collett.

Cloth Fair, EC1/SE1, 691 F5, This quiet backwater is named after boisterous Bartholomew Fair – the main cloth fair in medieval and Tudor England, held annually until 1855. The Poet Laureate Sir John Betjeman lived at No. 43.

College of Arms, EC4/SE1, 691 F5, The home of the royal heralds in Queen Victoria Street, rebuilt after the Great Fire by Maurice Emmett (records dating from medieval times were rescued). Still recording pedigrees and examining armorial bearings, the College was presented with wrought-iron gates and railings from Goodrich Court in Hertfordshire by an American benefactor in 1956.

Columbia Road, E2, 691 F5, A street of small Victorian shops which erupts with colour each Sunday when the flower market opens.

Commonwealth Institute, W8/SE1 691 F5, The Institute, at the bottom of Kensington High Street* (next to Holland Park) aims to promote communication and understanding between young

people across the British Commonwealth of Nations. The striking 1962 building has a hyperboloid roof of Zambian copper.

Covent Garden Piazza, WC2/SE1, 691 F5, Although most buildings are Victorian, Inigo Jones's original plan can be glimpsed in colonnaded Bedford Chambers, rebuilt in 1879. Charles Fowler's 1833 glass-and-iron-roofed central market has held chic small shops and craft stalls since the fruit and vegetable wholesalers moved to Battersea in 1973.

St Paul's Church was built in 1631–33 by Inigo Jones for the Earl of Bedford, a low churchman. Fearful of too much decoration and expense, Bedford purportedly said: 'I would not have it much better than a barn.' 'You shall have the handsomest barn in England,' replied Jones. It is all that remains of the architect's plan for a residential square based on the piazza at Livorno in Tuscany. The impressive portico was never used as the main entrance since it faces east and the Bishop of London insisted the altar should be placed on the east wall. The portico is now completely closed and has become a stage for street entertainers. A plaque records that Pepys once watched an Italian puppet play from here. Known as 'the Actors' Church', St Paul has an interior lined with

Left: Design Museum aims to increase awareness of design standards in everything from kettles to cars.

Right: Dickens House, an engraving of the author as a young man, after a drawing by Samuel Laurence.

Dr Johnson's House, EC4, 691 F5, Scholar and lexicographer Dr Samuel Johnson – responsible for the much-quoted line 'When a man is tired of London, he is tired of life'– lived at many addresses in his beloved city, but only No. 17 Gough Square has survived. This fine 1700 house alone was saved when alleys off Fleet Street were blitzed and then bulldozed for offices. Living here from 1746 to 1759, Dr Johnson – with the aid of six clerks – wrote his *Dictionary of the English Language* in an austere garret which can now be seen in this poignant museum to his memory.

Downing Street, SW1, 691 F5, George II gave No. 10 to the first prime minister, Sir Robert Walpole, in 1732, and it has been the official residence and workplace of British prime ministers ever since. No. 11 in this modest little cul-de-sac is the Chancellor of the Exchequer's official base, and No. 12 is the Whips' Office. The street was closed to the public by Margaret Thatcher and can now be seen only through wrought-iron gates.

Dulwich Picture Gallery, SE21, 691 F5, Britain's first public art gallery stands in a village setting 4 miles (6.4km) south of Trafalgar Square, in College Road. Designed by Sir John Soane and opened in 1814, the building contains 12 galleries and a mausoleum (with sarcophagi of the original donors). A stupendous collection of old masters includes works by Rembrandt planned on the Marsh Royal Collection, Rubens, Van Dyck, Canaletto, Claude, Poussin and Watteau. Here you can see Gainsborough's sublime double portrait of the Linley Sisters, with Elizabeth evidently all set to elope to France with Richard Brinsley Sheridan.

memorials to the great actors of the past – Ellen Terry among them. Leading artists and writers lie in the crypt. JMW Turner, whose father was a barber in Maiden Lane nearby, was baptized here.

Crystal Palace Park, SE19, 691 F5, Named after Joseph Paxton's huge glass conservatory, the setting for the 1851 Great Exhibition in Hyde Park, which was removed here to be the centrepiece of an amusement park. In 1936 it burned down, but Paxton's surreal menagerie of 29 painted bronze prehistoric monsters has survived. There is an attractive modern open-air concert site.

Design Museum, SE1, 691 F5, Once a banana warehouse, this was the first centre in the world to celebrate the history, theory and practice of design in mass-produced consumer goods. The imprint of style guru Terence Conran spills across the trendy restaurants of Butler's Wharf.

Dickens House, WC1, 691 F5, Charles Dickens lived at No. 48 Doughty Street for only two years (1837–9) but made his literary name here, working on *The Pickwick Papers*, *Oliver Twist* and *Nicholas Nickleby*. Saved from demolition in 1923, the house is the only surviving London home of the author. It is filled with personal memorabilia such as his desk, chair and writing quills. The Dickens Library is in the basement.

Dulwich Picture Gallery
Below: *The Triumph of David*, by Nicolas Poussin c1631–3.
Bottom right: View of the galleries, which were designed by Sir John Soane.

Left: Dickens House, where the young author's family gathered for convivial evenings while he wrote with his feather pen in the corner.

Top, above left and above: Eltham Palace, where the medieval Great Hall is linked to an extravagant 1930s residence inspired by Wren's Hampton Court*. Its interiors are a treasure trove of 1930s luxury, from the decorative features in exotic woods and precious metals to the sunken baths and centralized vacuum cleaner system.

Eltham Palace, SE9, 691 G5, This moated medieval palace in Court Yard, extended by Edward IV, was a childhood home of Henry VII. The building crumbled over the centuries, and the Great Hall was used as a barn before it was renovated as a grand music room in the 1930s for an adjoining Art Deco fantasy house. The home of socialites Stephen and Virginia Courtauld until 1945, and now restored with reproduction furnishings, it crosses Hollywood film-set with Cunard liner. The gardens created by the Courtaulds are an attractive mixture of formal and informal – the ideal setting for a picnic.

Fitzrovia, W1, 691 F5, The name Fitzrovia was coined between the world wars for the Fitzroy Square and Charlotte Street area – whose pubs (such as the Fitzroy Tavern and the Wheatsheaf) were favoured by poets and painters including Dylan Thomas and Augustus John. Its skyline is now dominated by the 580-foot (177m) Telecom Tower built in 1964.

Fleet Street, EC4, 691 F5, The flight of newspapers from Fleet Street in the 1980s has seen the 'street of shame' redeveloped for City offices. Even the Wig and Pen Club, which survived the Great Fire, has closed – although Prince Henry's Room of 1610, with a richly decorated plaster ceiling and the display about diarist Samuel Pepys, remains open. Elderly journalists still totter into El Vino's Wine Bar after memorial services at St Bride's Church, but Ye Olde Cheshire Cheese (where scribes like Pepys, Johnson, Dickens and Mark Twain once slaked their thirst) is nowadays for tourists. The black glass building at Nos. 121–8 designed by Owen Williams and built for the *Daily Express* in 1931 – the first curtain-wall construction in London – has recently been renovated by its new owners and there is public access to its Art Deco foyer.

Florence Nightingale Museum, SE1, 691 F5, The hospital reformer was known as the 'Lady of the Lamp' after working among Crimean War casualties. Her life is recalled in a museum within St Thomas's Hospital on Lambeth Palace Road, where she set up the first school of nursing after returning to England in 1856.

Fortnum and Mason, W1, 691 F5, Founded in the 18th century by royal footman William Fortnum and grocer Hugh Mason, this famous store on Piccadilly* is now a mecca for those seeking exotic foods. It once sent special provisions to officers fighting far-flung wars, and still specializes in hampers for all occasions. It was completely rebuilt in 1925, and the clock over the entrance, on which the figures of Mr Fortnum and Mr Mason bow to each other on the hour, was added in 1964.

Freud Museum, NW3, 691 F5, Old and ill, Sigmund Freud fled Nazi Austria for London in 1938. To this house in Maresfield Gardens he moved his furniture (including the celebrated desk and couch), together with his books and antiquities,

Top: Freud Museum, the home where Freud worked surrounded by objects from ancient civilizations.

and recreated Vienna in Hampstead*. He died the following year. His house, bequeathed by his analyst daughter Anna, is now a museum, which includes a research archive, educational resource and cultural centre.

Geffrye Museum, E2, 691 F5, Originally 18th-century almshouses built on land bequeathed by the Lord Mayor Robert Geffrye, it was converted to a museum in 1914 to display furniture of a 'fine standard of technical and artistic excellence'. Today the Museum, on Kingsland Road, has expanded premises with a chronological series of period rooms spanning 400 years, from 17th-century oak furniture and panelling to a contemporary warehouse loft conversion. At Christmas the rooms are decorated according to the traditions of their period. A series of period garden rooms are in summer.

Globe Theatre, SE1, 691 F5, In the late Elizabethan period the Bankside area of Southwark saw London's first fixed theatres – the Swan, the Hope, the Rose and, most famously, the Globe. The great 'Wooden O' in which Shakespeare acted and invested was gutted in 1613 when a cannon fired

during a performance of *Henry VIII* set the thatched roof ablaze. Puritanism felled the replacement. Now, thanks to the herculean efforts of the late American actor and director Sam Wanamaker, a marvellous replica of the original building runs annual summer seasons. There is also a Shakespeare museum.

Above: Geffrye Museum's vivid Regency Period Room.

Left: Globe Theatre. Modern audiences can stand in the pit for an authentic Elizabethan experience.

Right: Gray's Inn Hall, where Winston Churchill first met Franklin Roosevelt in 1918, dining at the high table.

Gray's Inn, WC1, 691 F5, One of the four surviving Inns of Court*, built on the site of Chief Justice Reginald le Grey's 13th-century manor house. The restored Elizabethan Hall, destroyed by bombs in 1941, contains a screen said to be made from the wood of a captured Spanish Armada galleon. Shakespeare's *A Comedy of Errors* was first performed here in 1594.

Green Park, SW1, 691 F5, The peace of Green Park, planned by Charles II, was often disturbed by the sound of pistol shots in the 18th century, when it was a favourite site for duels. It was also popular for early balloon ascents and elaborate firework displays.

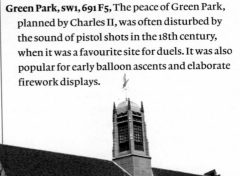

Greenwich

Greenwich, SE10, 691 F5, Best approached by river bus from Tower Bridge, via the foot tunnel under the Thames from Island Gardens (opened for dockworkers in 1902), or on the speedier Docklands Light Rail. Cutty Sark station is named after the 1869 tea clipper in a dry dock nearby. This fine vessel was carrying cargoes until 1922; now it is a nautical museum with the best extant collection of carved figureheads. Next to the *Cutty Sark,* and dwarfed by it, is *Gipsy Moth IV,* the tiny yacht in which Sir Francis Chichester sailed single-handedly around the world in 1966–7.

A short walk away lies **Greenwich Park**, 190 green acres (80ha) crammed with history. Henry V's brother the Duke of Gloucester first enclosed the space, where in 1437 he rebuilt an existing palace. It became a favourite residence of the Tudors: Henry VIII, Mary I and Elizabeth I were all born here.

The twin royal and naval traditions that governed the evolution of Greenwich are now manifest in the **National Maritime Museum** with the Queen's House as its central portion. This Palladian-style house by Inigo Jones was commissioned by Queen Anne of Denmark, wife of James I, in 1616. Among the surviving original features are

the 'tulip staircase' (the first centrally unsupported spiral stair in Britain) and the painted ceiling in the Queen's bedchamber.

In 1692, during the reign of William and Mary, the Queen was so affected by the sight of so many wounded after a sea battle that she ordered a naval hospital to be built around the house. Christopher Wren and his illustrious assistant Nicholas Hawksmoor designed it without charge. The decoration of the great Painted Hall, begun by James Thornhill in 1708, took 19 years to complete, and has a ceiling representing the joint sovereigns handing Liberty and Peace to Europe. This grand building was not very suitable for a hospital, and in 1873 it became the Royal Naval College. The Painted Hall and the nearby Chapel (rebuilt to the neoclassical design of James 'Athenian' Stuart after Wren's burnt down in 1779) are open to the public in the afternoons.

The National Maritime Museum harbours all aspects of the history of Britain at sea, including maritime art, naval portraits, globes, early charts, ship models and plans, scientific and navigational instruments, and 100,000 books dating from the 15th century. In 1999 new galleries, grouped around the vast glass-roofed Neptune Court, were added. Admiral Horatio Nelson lay in state in the Painted Hall in 1805, and the Nelson Collection was begun in 1823. Most breathtaking among its many items is JMW Turner's huge painting *The Battle of Trafalgar;* most poignant is Nelson's blood-stained uniform, the fatal bullet-hole visible in the left shoulder.

Top: Greenwich Park, with Flamsteed House, Queen's House, National Maritime Museum and Royal Naval College.

Left: The Maritime Museum's Neptune Court, designed by Rick Mather Architects and the Building Design Partnership.

Below: Flamsteed House – the old Royal Observatory – designed by Wren.

Above and left: Cutty Sark, whose name comes from the distinctive chemise – or 'cutty sark' – worn by the figurehead, the heroine of Robert Burns' poem 'Tam o' Shanter'.

Above and left: Queen's House underwent considerable refurbishment in the 1990s and now contains works from the Maritime Museum's fine art collection.

Below: The Old Royal Naval College – formerly Greenwich Hospital – has been described as 'one of the most sublime sights English architecture affords'.

At the centre of Greenwich Park stands **Flamsteed House**, once the Royal Observatory and now an addition to the National Maritime Museum. The original house, designed by Wren, is named after John Flamsteed, the first Astronomer Royal, who was appointed by Charles II in 1675 'to find out the so much-desired longitude of places for perfecting the art of navigation'. Various buildings were added as the science of astronomy developed, and in 1848 an International Meridian Conference agreed that the Prime Meridian of the world – Zero Meridian – would be fixed at Greenwich. The **Greenwich Time Ball**, erected in 1833 on a turret of Wren's Octagon Room, drops daily at 1pm precisely.

At the southwestern edge of the park a handsome 18th-century red-brick villa, **Ranger's House**, contains the Suffolk Collection of portraits – including nine full-length Stuart portraits displaying Jacobean power, costume and style. In adjacent Croom's Hill, a steep and winding ancient road, is the **Fan Museum**, housing around 3,000 fans from all over the world, some dating back to Tudor times. **St Alfege's Church**, at the north end of Greenwich High Road, is dedicated to an archbishop of Canterbury murdered by Danes in Greenwich in 1012. Henry VIII was baptized here, and Thomas Tallis, 'Father of English Church Music', was buried here in 1585. The church was remodelled by Hawksmoor in 1712–18, and was beautifully restored after World War II bomb damage – a Thornhill altarpiece was repainted by Glyn Jones. Following in the Tallis tradition, the church maintains a fine reputation for music-making.

Almost five centuries after Henry VIII surveyed his fleet from Greenwich Park, the views across London remain stunning. Of all the additions to the landscape since then, none is so instantly recognizable to the contemporary eye as the Millennium Dome. The huge circular shape, with its translucent fabric roof and upholding steel structure – like a tremendous mushroom sporting giant quills – makes an impressive landmark.

Guards' Museum, SW1, 691 F5, Part of the Wellington Barracks, this museum in Birdcage Walk tells the story of five regiments of Foot Guards (Grenadier, Coldstream, Scots, Irish and Welch) over the 350 years to the Gulf War.

family by Sydney Smirke in the 1830s, is now a local museum. In the grounds there is a surviving bath-house from an earlier Palladian building used by Princess Amelia, daughter of George II, in the summers of 1763–86.

Ham House, Surrey 691 F5, On the south bank of the River Thames*, this fine red-brick Stuart mansion, with its restored formal 17th-century garden, appears grand yet restrained [NT]. Inside, however, the luxurious furnishings and collections of the Duke and Duchess of Lauderdale, leading participants in Restoration court life and intrigue, are anything but sober. As the diarist John Evelyn remarked after he visited the house in 1678, it is 'inferior to few of the best Villas in Italy itself; the House furnished like a great Prince's'. The court painter Antonio Verrio adorned the ground-floor apartments.

The ambitious Duchess had inherited the original house, built in 1610, from her father. After she married the Duke – a member of Charles II's 'Cabal' Ministry – in 1672, they set about greatly enlarging it, intending to impress. In the Long Gallery hang Stuart portraits in heavy gold frames, and elsewhere a Peter Lely portrait of the Lauderdales themselves depicts them as haughty and unappealing. Enough has survived of their trappings and furniture to recreate a vivid impression of their life of splendour, and the

Guildhall, EC2, 691 F5, Focal point of the City of London's government since the first mayor was installed in 1192, the present structure in Gresham Street was begun in 1411, but was ravaged by both the Great Fire and the Blitz. The surviving 15th-century fabric comprises the porch, crypts and walls of the Great Hall. After the roof of the latter was bombed, a temporary one was constructed in steel. The present roof was restructured by Giles Gilbert Scott who added stone arches to what was previously a purely timber roof. Each November, soon after the Lord Mayor's Show, the Prime Minister addresses a banquet here. A magnificent library, founded with a bequest by Richard ('Dick') Whittington, Lord Mayor in the late 14th and early 15th centuries, was seized by the Duke of Somerset in 1549 – possibly to furnish his new palace, Somerset House*. In 1828 a new library was begun, and is now one of the finest sources of information on London.

Gunnersbury Park Museum, W3, 691 F5, This neoclassical mansion, altered for the Rothschild

Top right: Guards Memorial in St James's Park, by HC Bradshaw with figures by Gilbert Ledward, 1926.

Above: Guildhall was the site of the trial of Lady Jane Grey in 1553.

Right and below: Ham House has survived relatively unaltered from the 17th century.

interiors have been faithfully restored. Most attractive are the bright-hued little closets, ideal for private plotting and gossip. In one of them the Duchess's miniature cabinet for storing sweetmeats and tea can be seen. Another small room displays their fine collection of miniatures. The garden is a rarity since most historical formal gardens have long since disappeared. Full restoration began in 1975, using an old 17th-century plan. Gradually the features which John Evelyn

Top left: Ham House, the Great Hall. The art collection includes paintings by Lely and Van Dyck, works from the Roman and Flemish schools, and a fine collection of miniatures.

Fenton House
Bottom left: A 16th-century painted harpsichord in the North Room.
Bottom right: The 1693 house in its walled garden.

with hornbeam hedges, clipped yews, little summer-houses, a border of seasonal flowers for cutting, the orangery and tea garden (open April–October), and a wildflower meadow all contribute to the timeless atmosphere. A foot-passenger ferry runs on certain days in summer across the river to Marble Hill House*.

Hampstead, NW3, 691 F5, One of London's best villages. Dotted with blue plaques recording once-resident writers and artists, its leafy streets of Georgian houses ascend to the 800 acres (325ha) of Hampstead Heath, Parliament Hill Fields and Kenwood. Woods, meadows and bathing ponds (male, female and mixed) abound with wildlife and strolling celebrities. In the early 19th century the poet Shelley could have been seen sailing paper boats on the Vale of Health pond for a friend's young son. A blue plaque on the wall of 16 Phillimore Place recalls Kenneth Grahame, author of the children's classic *The Wind in the Willows*, who lived here from 1901 to 1908.

At the top of the Heath is Jack Straw's Castle, a historic wooden pub visited by Charles Dickens. The novelist also frequented the Spaniard's Inn, the Spanish ambassador's residence during the reign of James II. It was here, in 1780, that the landlord got the Gordon Rioters drunk to stop them burning Kenwood House*.

Fenton House [NT] in Windmill Hill is a splendid house of 1693, named after the Baltic merchant Philip Fenton, who bought it a century later.

noted – 'Parterres, Flower Gardens, Orangeries, Groves...' – reappeared, and the flowers and shrubs of the period were reinstated. Box-edged beds of lavender in the knot-garden, grassy walks

Outside is a walled garden with roses, vegetables and orchard, but the main delights lie inside: 18th-century furniture and porcelain, a dozen William Nicholson paintings and, best of all, the Benton Fletcher Collection of Keyboard Instruments. It includes a 1612 harpsichord probably used by Handel, lent by the Queen. *See also* **Keats's House***, **2 Willow Road***.

Hampton Court

Hampton Court Palace, Surrey 691 F5, The favourite 'country home, hunting lodge and pleasure palace' of English monarchs for two centuries, starting with Henry VIII. Set on the River Thames* 15 miles (24km) from central London, this weathered red-brick palace with tall decorative chimneys used to be approached by royal barge and saw court life at its most lavish.

Cardinal Wolsey, Henry VIII's imperious Lord Chancellor, acquired the site in 1514 and built himself a palace which was royal in all but name – it had no less than 280 guest rooms. Wolsey fell from favour when he failed to expedite Henry's divorce from Catherine of Aragon, and to save his position he presented the palace to the King – who promptly confiscated all the rest of his goods and land. For three years Wolsey stayed on in one of his own guest apartments, which, with its original fine linenfold wall-panelling, still survives, as does his gatehouse at the western entrance. Henry then embarked on an ambitious programme of new building, most notably the Great Hall with its wonderfully carved hammerbeam roof. He honeymooned at Hampton Court with five of his six wives and had his own rooms refashioned several times. Today all that remains of the Tudor royal apartments is the Great Watching Chamber with its bow window. But the vast kitchens are still there and have been laid out as though a Tudor feast is in preparation.

For royal recreation there were the hunting park, the famous enclosed tennis court, tiltyards for jousting and bowling alleys. Henry also took a keen interest in the gardens – an involvement which his daughter, Elizabeth I, inherited. She liked to work in the gardens herself, 'briskly when alone' according to a contemporary, though in a more leisurely regal style when accompanied.

Charles I, England's greatest royal patron of the arts, brought many treasures to Hampton Court. Now displayed in the Lower Orangery are the imposing nine canvases by Andrea Mantegna, *The Triumph of Caesar*, purchased from Mantua's ruling Gonzaga family. After the Civil War Oliver Cromwell lived at Hampton Court, disposing of much of the royal collection and destroying 'popish and superstitious pictures and images'; he approved of the severe Mantegnas, and hung them prominently. Following the Restoration in 1660, Charles II recovered many of the royal treasures and set about repairing the palace.

When William and Mary came to the throne in 1689, they decided to make Hampton Court their principal residence. Christopher Wren was appointed architect, and at first intended to demolish everything except the Great Hall in order to build 'a new Versailles'. The King and Queen took an interest in every detail and wanted quick results, but with Mary's premature death from smallpox in 1694, a devastated – and cash-strapped – William abandoned the project for four years. Only Henry VIII's state apartments had actually been demolished, their bricks being used for the new Banqueting House. The grand French Renaissance buildings surrounding the new Fountain Court were still little more than shells when at last their magnificent interior decoration was resumed. The appearance of Hampton Court today owes more to William than to any other monarch, but before he could enjoy it he too died – of complications following a bad fall from his horse in the palace park.

Queen Anne continued the unfinished work, most notably the completion of the Queen's apartments and the refitting of the Chapel, with its great classical reredos by Grinling Gibbons.

George II spent summers there with his family and engaged William Kent and Sir John Vanbrugh to make alterations. By 1760 there were only 40 staff (Wolsey had had 500), one of whom was landscape gardener Capability Brown. It was he who planted the Great Vine in 1769, which still produces up to 500lbs (227kg) of grapes each year. Meanwhile antiquarians and architects were becoming increasingly interested in the Tudor origins of the palace, and in 1796 the King's Surveyor, James Wyatt, restored the Great Hall.

Restoration of Tudor features continued throughout the 19th century, and in 1838 Queen Victoria declared that the palace should be open to the public, 'free and without restriction', on certain days.

Parts were divided up for grace-and-favour residences, and it passed
from royal to government administration. During the 1970s and 1980s
the on-going task of making its complex history more accessible to
visitors began; but in 1986 a terrible fire swept through the King's
Apartments, sending tons of timbers and molten lead crashing down,
and the palace had to be closed. Repairs started immediately, and the
apartments are now much as they were when completed for
William III in 1700.

Hampton Court Palace contains unsurpassed evidence of the lives
of English kings and queens during the centuries when royal
patronage of the arts and architecture was paramount.

Handel House Museum, W1, 691 F5, London's first composer museum, this modest house at 25 Brook Street was where George Frideric Handel lived and composed prolifically from 1723 to his death in 1759. It has been expertly restored and furnished to approximate its original state, and the walls are hung with portraits of Handel, his colleagues and patrons. In the small back room on the first floor, German-born Handel composed such works as *Zadok the Priest*, *Music for the Royal Fireworks*, and *Messiah*, which immediately became, and remained, an indispensable part of England's musical culture.

Harrods, SW1, 691 F5, In 1849 Henry Charles Harrod, formerly a tea-dealer in Eastcheap, took over a small grocer's shop on the Brompton Road and diversified into stationery, perfumes and patent medicines. The increasing splendour of Harrods – with 100 assistants by 1880 – matched that of the surrounding Knightsbridge district. Completed in 1939, the present department store is ablaze with lightbulbs at night, like a seaside pavilion.

Hatton Garden, EC1, 691 F5, Close to the London Silver Vaults in Chancery Lane, this is the capital's diamond and jewellery centre. A pawnbroker still trades here.

Highgate, N6/N19, 691 F5, A mainly Georgian village with a few modernist flourishes, notably the 1930s apartment blocks Highpoint 1 and 2 by Lubetkin and Tecton, which Le Corbusier hailed as 'a vertical garden city'. On Highgate Hill, Lauderdale House (Tudor remains behind a late Georgian façade) is said to have been the residence of Nell Gwynne and her baby son by Charles II; it is now a museum and cultural centre. Nearby Cromwell House (not open) is a rare, Inigo Jones-influenced survival from 1637. At the bottom of Highgate Hill the statue of a black cat marks the legendary spot where a penniless apprentice and his feline companion heard the bells of St Mary-le-Bow urging him to return and become Lord Mayor of London. Sir Richard Whittington, thrice mayor, bequeathed a 1423 fortune to endow the Guildhall* and inspired a perennial pantomime.

Highgate Cemetery, an overgrown and wildly romantic burial ground off Swain's Lane, was designed in 1838 by Stephen Geary and now holds almost 170,000 bodies in 51,000 graves. The Victorian fascination with death is reflected in startling architecture, ranging from gothic follies

Top: Highgate Cemetery, where this sleeping stone lion lies on the tomb of George Wombwell, a menagerie proprietor.

Above: Hoover Building, which inspired Elvis Costello's song 'Hoover Factory', containing the line 'Must have been a wonder when it was brand new'.

Right: Horniman Museum and clock tower, designed by Charles Harrison Townsend, with mosaics by Robert Anning Bell. The museum's ethnographic and musical instrument collections are among the finest in Britain, numbering some 70,000 and 7,000 items respectively.

to the Egyptian Avenue and the Cedar of Lebanon Catacombs. No wonder Hammer House of Horror filmed here. Eminent Victorian residents include Christina and Dante Gabriel Rossetti, Michael Faraday, George Eliot and John Galsworthy. Atheists make pilgrimages to the monumental tomb of Karl Marx; agnostic evolutionist Herbert Spencer lies opposite.

Hogarth's House W4, 691 F5, In 1749 William Hogarth chose this 'little country box by the Thames' for its tranquil location; now an endless stream of traffic flows alongside. The artist spent much time here, leaving the night before he died for his town house in Leicester Square*. A museum since 1909, the retreat celebrates Hogarth's life and work, displaying the engravings taken from his hard-hitting picture series lampooning the vices and follies of society – *A Harlot's Progress* and *The Rake's Progress* among them. A mulberry tree in the garden dates from his day.

Hoover Factory, Perivale 691 F5, West London has two surviving gems of industrial Art Deco, both from 1932. The Hoover building on Western Avenue was designed by Wallis, Gilbert and Partners with green windows and red-and-blue striped faience as a 'palace of work', but is now a supermarket. The other is the Coty Factory on the Great West Road, with a majestic doorway.

Horniman Museum and Gardens, SE23, 691 F5, The Art Nouveau building on London Road, surrounded by elegant gardens (with a Victorian conservatory) was given by tea merchant Frederick J. Horniman to Londoners in 1901. A mosaic panel on the façade shows an allegory of life's journey, and the exhibits include natural history specimens (with Living Waters Aquarium), musical instruments, and ethnographic art from the donor's travels.

Top: Houses of Parliament –
the 19th century palace –
seen from the Thames just
above Westminster Bridge.

London – Houses of Parliament   **L**

Horse Guards, sw1, 691 F5, William Kent's noble Whitehall buildings were completed in 1755 on Henry VIII's former tournament ground. Mounted sentries stand outside from 10am to 4pm, changing every hour.
Houses of Parliament, sw1, 691 F5, Work began on the first Palace of Westminster for Edward the Confessor in 1042, and the building remained a royal residence until a fire in 1512. It then developed as the seat of a two-chamber Parliament – the House of Lords, with a large hereditary element (until the recent reforms enacted under Tony Blair), and the elected House of Commons. Westminster Hall, dating from 1199, with Europe's biggest hammerbeam roof added under Richard II in the late 14th century, has been a debating chamber, law court, banqueting hall, shopping arcade and place of lyings-in-state of monarchs, their consorts and – rarely – very distinguished statesmen; but it is now usually closed to the public. Along with the cloisters, crypt chapel and Jewel Tower, the Hall survived the 1834 fire that made way for the great gothic building by Charles Barry and Augustus Pugin which – with the clock tower that houses Big Ben* – we

Above left: *Interior of the House of Commons*, by Joseph Nash, 1858, 11 years after that part of Pugin's and Barry's architectural masterpiece was completed.

Above: Westminster Hall, the only surviving part of the original 11th-century Palace of Westminster.

know today as the Houses of Parliament. They were bombed 11 times during World War II, the last raid reducing the House of Commons to rubble. Giles Gilbert Scott rebuilt it to Barry's plan, though sadly modifying Pugin's ornamental decoration. The nearby Jewel Tower was built of Kentish ragstone around 1365 as a moated three-storey safe for Edward III, and used for royal treasures until the reign of Henry VIII. This outpost of the Palace of Westminster later held parliamentary records.

Hyde Park, Central London 691 F5, This, the largest of the royal parks, has been a prized public space since James I opened it in the early 17th century. Henry VIII had seized the ancient manor from Westminster Abbey* at the Dissolution of the Monasteries in 1536, retaining it as a private hunting ground. The Serpentine, an artificial boating and bathing lake, was created when Queen Caroline, wife of George II, ordered the damming of the River Westbourne in 1730; it was here that Harriet, the pregnant and abandoned wife of the poet Percy Bysshe Shelley, drowned herself in 1816. Down the centuries the park has hidden highwaymen and duellists, and hosted fairs, firework displays, balloon ascents, concerts and the 1851 Great Exhibition. Since 1872 the northeast ('Speakers') Corner has attracted Sunday orators and ranters who compete with hecklers and each other. John Nash's **Marble Arch,** moved from Buckingham Palace in 1851 because it was too narrow for stately coaches, stands close to the site of Tyburn gallows, where public hangings took place until 1783.

Imperial War Museum, SE1, 691 F5, Formerly the old Bedlam lunatic asylum built in 1815, the huge building on the Lambeth Road now displays a collection relating to conflicts involving British or Commonwealth troops since 1914. A huge central hall holds military hardware, from planes (Sopwith Camel, Spitfire, Mustang) and tanks (Churchill, Sherman, Grant) to submarines and Polaris missiles. Elsewhere medals, firearms, artworks, photographs, ephemera, books, films and recordings recall land, sea and air warfare, and

Top: Hyde Park, where horses and riders can exercise along designated routes.

Above: The Imperial War Museum covers all aspects of life in wartime, at home and on the battlefield. Its collections range from armoured fighting vehicles to fine art – including works by official war artists of the two world wars.

life on the home front. Recreated 'experiences' simulate trauma in a Flanders trench and in the London Blitz.

Inner Temple, EC4, 691 F5, The name derives from the Knights Templar, who resided in the vicinity in the 12th century and built the Temple Church*. Among the luminaries who had chambers in this Inn of Court* were James Boswell and John Galsworthy. Many buildings suffered during the Blitz; the Library and Hall by Hubert Worthington date from the 1950s. Between 1888 and 1913 the Royal Horticultural Society's spring show was held in the Gardens.

Inns of Court, EC4/WC1/WC2, 691 F5, Lawyers have been based around Temple Bar since the Middle Ages – at first coming to London for sessions of the

Royal Courts of Justice and lodging in taverns, the ancestors of the Inns of Court. Law schools also arose here. Compared with ten Inns in the 14th century, there are now only Lincoln's Inn*, Middle Temple*, Inner Temple* and Gray's Inn*. Each has its own hall, church, library, cloister and gardens – a tranquil and timeless world (although much rebuilt after Hitler's bombs).

Temple Church is a religious castle built in the 12th and 13th centuries for the Knights Templar. It is one of the few circular churches to survive in England. A military order protecting pilgrims to the Holy Land, the Knights Templar were based here from 1185 until suppressed by the Pope in 1312. Stone effigies of the knights, which had lain in the church for centuries, were severely damaged in the Blitz. They were skilfully restored, as was the fabric of the church.

Institute of Contemporary Arts, SW1, 691 E5, Part of John Nash's Classical Carlton House Terrace (1833) on The Mall, constructed

on the site of the residence he built for George IV. The building is now given over to contemporary art, with a cinema, gallery and auditorium, and hosts exhibitions, films, concerts, talks and plays.

Keats House, NW3, 691 F5, Much of John Keats' best work was written here – including his 'Ode to a Nightingale', penned under a plum tree. He died in Rome in 1821 (at only 25), just before his planned marriage. The house in Keats Grove is now a museum dedicated to his life and work. It

originated as a pair of attached cottages built in 1816 in a shared garden but combined in Victorian times. Keats lodged in one house and fell in love with Fanny Brawne, who lived next door. A heart-rending display includes his love letters and the engagement ring Fanny wore until her death.

Kensington Gardens, W8, 691 F5, These were the grounds of Kensington Palace* until they were turned into a public park in 1841. In contrast to prairie-like Hyde Park*, with which they merge to the east, the gardens are packed with charming features. The Sunken Garden was laid out next to the Palace in 1909, and can be glimpsed through the gates and hedges. The Diana, Princess of Wales children's playground was built as a memorial to the Princess, who lived in the Palace. It is based on a Peter Pan theme, with pirate ship, seaside path, wigwam village, tree house encampment and 'movement and musical' garden, complete with wooden xylophone and water piano. A 1912 bronze by George Frampton of Peter Pan, the boy who never grew up and who forever plays his pipe to the animals and fairies in a column below his feet, is among London's best-loved statues. Also popular is the Elfin Oak, a tree-trunk carved with woodland figures by Ivor Innes. Children pay their respects to both sculptures, then sail model boats on the Round Pond created in 1728. Nearby, George Frederick Watts' powerful statue of a primly gelded horse and rider symbolizes *Physical Energy*. Dead animals get their own tribute close to Lancaster Gate in a dogs' cemetery, started in 1880 by the pet-loving Duke of Cambridge. The Serpentine Gallery, a former tea pavilion of 1912, holds temporary exhibitions of contemporary art.

Kensington High Street, W8, 691 F5, A busy shopping street, but until the onset of the Victorian era a village lane among market gardens and mansions

Top left: Inns of Court. The Inner and Middle Temples adjoin each other between Fleet Street and the Embankment.

Above: Keats House and a likeness of the poet from a miniature by Joseph Severn.

Kensington Gardens Top right: The marble statue of Queen Victoria by her daughter Princess Louise, outside Kensington Palace.
Left: *Physical Energy* by G.F. Watts.

– most notably the rambling Jacobean Holland House, largely demolished in the 1950s after wartime bombing. A remnant survives in lovely **Holland Park**, with a 1630s Orangery and the old Garden Ballroom (the former now a gallery, the latter a restaurant). Kensington Church Street, off the High Street, has many antique shops.

Kensington Palace, W8, 691 F5, In 1689 William and Mary bought a Jacobean mansion away from the stink of Whitehall and commissioned Christopher Wren to convert it into Kensington Palace. The Orangery was built in 1704 for Queen Anne, to Hawksmoor's designs as modified by Vanbrugh. Born in the palace in 1819, Victoria was awoken here on 20 June 1837 with news that her

uncle William IV was dead and she was now Queen. Visitors can tour a series of ornate state rooms and a display of court dress since 1760. The rest of the palace is a warren of royal apartments. Diana, Princess of Wales lived here with the two princes from 1981 until her death in 1997 and some of her clothes are on show. The regal female figure carved in stone outside the palace represents the young Victoria; it is the work of her daughter, Princess Louise.

Kenwood House, NW3, 691 F5, Its lake-centred parkland merging into Hampstead Heath*, Kenwood has

outstanding neoclassical interiors, containing an even more impressive art collection – with works by Vermeer, Turner, Gainsborough and Reynolds, together with the Rembrandt self-portrait voted the most prized painting in Britain. An opulent Robert Adam library, with Corinthian columns

Kew Gardens
Opposite page, top:
The 1987 Princess of Wales
Conservatory.
This page, top left: The
classic Victorian Palm House.

Top right: Leicester Square,
Art Deco carvings by
Bainbridge Copnall on the
façade of the Warner cinema,
designed by Stone and
Somerford, 1937–8.

and enriched ceiling of 1764, remains intact. This house of the earls of Mansfield was bought by the brewing magnate, the 1st Earl of Iveagh, who bequeathed it and his picture collection to London in 1927. There is a lovely café in the old stables and a walled garden, and summer concerts are held beside the lake.

Kew Bridge Steam Museum, Brentford 691 F5, A 19th-century pumping station on Green Dragon Lane, which used to supply Londoners with water, is now a museum of steam pumping engines. The earliest of five giant ones dates from 1820 and once pumped water out of Cornish tin and copper mines. All the major engines are in action at the weekends.

Kew Gardens, Brentford 691 F5, The Gardens evolved from a small garden established at Kew in 1759 by Princess Augusta, George III's mother, with William Chambers adding the Orangery and Chinese Pagoda. Subsequently combining his Richmond* and Kew estates, George III employed Capability Brown and encouraged naturalist Joseph Banks to oversee a botanic garden to which specimens could be sent from all over the globe. He and his wife summered at Kew, latterly at Kew Palace – dubbed the 'Dutch House' because of its 1631 gabling. Queen Charlotte's 1771 Cottage echoes Marie Antoinette's Petit Trianon at Versailles. Acquired by the state in 1840, the Royal Botanic Gardens grew apace under their first director William Hooker and today cover 300 acres (91ha), with 30,000 different plants and a great horticultural and botanical research centre. There are three glorious glasshouses: Decimus Burton's 1840s Palm House, the Temperate House of 1899 and the recent Princess of Wales Conservatory with its ten climatic zones, each one a haven on a cold day. The Marianne North Gallery, with 832 vivid botanical oils by that valiant Victorian traveller, is a hothouse of colour.

Lambeth Palace, SE1, 691 F5, This Thames-side palace has been the London base of the Archbishop of Canterbury, senior cleric of the Church of England,

Above: Lambeth Palace, the last survivor of the great London seats of bishops along the south bank of the Thames.

Opposite page: Kenwood House
Bottom left: The south front with orangery (left) and library (far right).
Centre: Interior of the Robert Adam library.
Below centre: *The Guitar Player* by Jan Vermeer.
Bottom right: Design for a pillar by Robert Adam. Lord Mansfield gave him full scope to implement his elegant ideas.

Above: Leighton House, the fantastic Arab Hall added in 1877–9.

for 800 years. Although the building is much restored, the chapel and undercroft date from the 13th century and a fine Tudor gatehouse from 1486. The large library (entry by prior request) began with Archbishop Bancroft's 1610 bequest: treasures include the 1150 Lambeth Bible and Sir Thomas More's *Utopia*. (In 1534 More had been interrogated in the Guard Room for refusing to endorse Henry VIII's break with the Church of Rome.)

Leadenhall Market, EC2, 691 F5, A food market has existed here (on the site of a Roman forum) since medieval times. The market, in Gracechurch Street, takes its name from a 14th-century mansion with a lead roof. The present ornate covered shopping precinct of 1881 was designed by Horace Jones, who also built Smithfield* and Billingsgate (the Thames-side fish market that moved to the Isle of Dogs in 1982).

Leicester Square, WC2, 691 F5, In the 17th and 18th centuries this was an elegant square built around a formal, railed garden. Joshua Reynolds, first president of the Royal Academy, lived here in style for 32 years. The square's character changed as private residents moved out in the 19th century, and now it is a hurly-burly of fast-food cafés, cinemas, amusement arcades, souvenir shops and street entertainers. Scores of West End theatres are concentrated nearby – especially in Shaftesbury Avenue. The Shakespeare fountain was placed at the centre of the square in 1874, and the bronze statue of Charlie Chaplin by John Doubleday was unveiled by Ralph Richardson in 1981.

Leighton House, W14, 691 F5, The house, in Holland Park Road, was built in 1865 for Frederic Leighton, lionized leader of the Victorian classical school of painters, to his own designs and those of his friend George Aitchison. Red-brick outside; inside, a startling Moorish palace with red marble columns (capitals by Randolph Caldecott), 16th- and 17th-century floral tiles from

Top: Lloyd's of London, a spectacular modern atrium building with glass lifts at the heart of the City.

Bottom: Lincoln's Inn, the gate. Among its famous members have been John Donne, Disraeli, Gladstone and John Galsworthy.

Rhodes, Cairo and Damascus (these collected by Richard Burton), a dazzling gilt mosaic frieze by Walter Crane, and a resplendent fountain. Paintings by Leighton (whose studio has a gilded dome), Burne-Jones, Millais and other contemporaries are hung throughout the house.

Lincoln's Inn, WC2, 691 F5, The oldest of the four Inns of Court*, its records go back to 1422. The great oak doors of the Gate House on Chancery Lane, which was largely rebuilt and restored in the 1960s, date from 1564. Dickens used the Old Hall for the opening court scene of *Bleak House*. The Chapel Bell tolls a curfew of 60 strokes each night at 9pm, and from 12.45 to 1.15pm on days when news of the death of a member of the Inn is received.

Linley Sambourne House, W8, 691 F5, A fascinating survival of a late Victorian town house in Stafford Terrace, Kensington. The decorations, fittings and furniture are preserved as they were when book illustrator and *Punch* political cartoonist Edward Linley Sambourne lived here from 1874 to his death in 1910. His own work is displayed with that of artist friends – Kate Greenaway, Walter Crane and Sir John Tenniel among them.

Lloyd's of London, EC3, 691 F5, Founded in the late 17th century and

Top left: London Eye slowly revolves to reveal to its passengers the panorama of the capital.

Top right: Marble Hill House, the Great Room, with its immaculately restored lavish gilding.

named after the coffee house where ships and marine insurance were traded. It soon became the world's main stock exchange for insurance contracts, with the Lutine bell tolling for good or bad news. Since 1986 it has been based on Lime Street in a brilliant glass and steel building by Richard Rogers, co-designer of the Pompidou Centre in Paris. With an arch-roofed central atrium, satellite towers and external lifts and piping, the assembly looks most effective when floodlit in blue at night.

London Central Mosque, NW8, 691 F5, A copper dome gleams among the white and cream classicist sweeps of Nash terraces partly ringing Regent's Park. The Mosque, on Park Road, was designed by Frederick Gibberd and completed in 1977.

London Coliseum, WC2, 691 F5, Frank Matcham's exuberant 1904 building in St Martin's Lane, topped with an illuminated globe, boasts an unaltered Edwardian interior. It is the largest theatre in London and now the home of English National Opera. A four-year refurbishment programme – notably installing better air-conditioning and restoring decorative splendour – will not interrupt opera seasons and is due for completion in 2004.

London Eye, SE1, 691 F5, The British Airways London Eye on the South Bank, designed by architects David Marks and Julia Barfield, was the success of the millennium. The world's largest observation wheel at 443 feet (135m) high has become both a favourite landmark and a popular ride: a half-hour, slow-moving 'flight' over London, with fabulous views. On a very clear day you can see Windsor Castle* some 25 miles (40km) away.

London Transport Museum, WC2, 691 F5, The old Victorian Flower Market in Covent Garden* has been converted into a giant tram, train, bus and carriage shed, tracking past and present public transport. Children may sit in the drivers' seats and a gift shop sells copies of many exhibits.

Lord's Cricket Ground, NW8, 691 F5, The home of the MCC (Marylebone Cricket Club) and the headquarters of Britain's chief summer sport since

1787. A museum display outlines the history of the site, off St John's Wood Road, and the sport. Exhibits include an urn containing burned wood, known as the Ashes, which is the object of fierce annual competition between the English and Australian national teams. The 1987 Mound Stand by Michael Hopkins, with its floating fabric roof, has managed to please architectural critics and cricket-lovers alike.

Madame Tussaud's, NW1, 691 F5, Wax-modeller Madame Tussaud made death masks of famous figures beheaded in the French Revolution, and displayed her macabre work in Baker Street from 1835. The large building on the Marylebone Road frequently updates a cast of characters that now spans celebrities in Garden Party and Grand Hall settings together with villains in the Chamber of Horrors. A Spirit of London finale takes visitors in stylized taxis on an historical journey from the 1666 Great Fire to the Swinging Sixties. Part of the same complex is the London Planetarium, with its star show and interactive Space Trail exhibition.

Mansion House, EC2, 691 F5, A Palladian portico with six Corinthian columns gives a suitably grand appearance to the Lord Mayor's official residence in Bank. The building, completed to the design of George Dance the Elder in 1753, boasts splendid state rooms – including the spectacular Egyptian Hall – and the excellent Samuel Collection of Dutch 17th-century paintings. It also includes 11 holding cells, for the Mayor is the City's chief magistrate and his residence doubles as a court.

Marble Hill House, Gt Lon 691 F5, This Thames-side Palladian villa, set in a 66-acre (26ha) park off the

Below: Mansion House, the Palladian Banqueting Room – known as the Egyptian Hall – with Victorian stained-glass window by Alexander Gibbs.

Richmond Road, was built in the 1720s for Henrietta Howard, Countess of Suffolk and mistress of George II. The house contains important early Georgian furniture and pictures, and the Lazenby Bequest of Chinoiserie. A popular venue for riverside concerts.

Mayfair, W1, 691 F5, Mayfair was laid out in the area between Hyde Park*, Oxford Street, Regent Street* and Piccadilly* by the earls of Grosvenor.

Grosvenor Square (1720–5) has been associated with the United States since 'minister plenipotentiary' John Adams (later President) moved into No. 9 in 1785. During World War II, when General Eisenhower's headquarters was located there, it became known as 'Little America'. The present embassy, designed by Eero Saarinen, was completed in 1960; its gilded eagle atop the front façade is by Theodore Roszak. The cost of the square's memorial statue to Franklin D. Roosevelt was raised in a day from British subjects by 200,000 donations of not more than 5 shillings (25p) each.

No. 44 **Berkeley Square**, built by William Kent in 1744, has been called 'the finest terrace house in London'. The square's plane trees, planted in 1789, are among the oldest of their kind; the nymph fountain is by the Pre-Raphaelite sculptor Alexander Munro. Besides grand residences

Above: Middle Temple Great Hall where senior members dine at a table made from an oak tree given by Queen Elizabeth I.

Above: Museum of Garden History, the Tradescant Garden, a replica 17th-century knot garden designed by Lady Salisbury.

(Queen Elizabeth II was born at 17 Bruton Street), Mayfair's expensive enclave embraces Bond Street shops and art galleries, Savile Row tailors, and Claridge's hotel.

Middle Temple, EC4, 691 F5, This Inn of Court* has, in its Hall (completed 1573), a glorious example of Tudor architecture. The exterior suffered Victorian 'improvement', but inside the Hall's double hammerbeam roof and enormous, elaborately carved screen are the finest of their kind. Scene of many revels, banquets and plays, Shakespeare's *Twelfth Night* was produced here on 2 February 1602. Golden carp inhabit the pool in Fountain Court, where ancient mulberry trees are crutched for support.

Monument, EC2, 691 F5, Wren's memorial to the Great Fire of 1666 is the tallest free-standing stone column in the world (205 feet/62m high). Reliefs show Charles II restoring the ruined capital. There is a viewing platform at the top of the 311 steps.

Museum in Docklands, E14, 691 F5, This offshoot of the Museum of London* in West India Quay tells the story of London's river, port and people.

Museum of Garden History, SE1, 691 F5, Housed in and around the 14th-century tower of St Mary-at-Lambeth Church, Lambeth Palace Road, the museum and garden honour the pioneer plantsmen of the 17th century, John and John Tradescant – father and son – who lie in the charming churchyard beside Captain Bligh of the *Bounty*.

Museum of London, EC2, 691 F5, A showcase for life in London since prehistoric times, housed in a modern building on the edge of the Barbican* at London Wall. Its wonderfully rich resources (it is the world's largest urban history museum and Europe's largest archeological archive) are employed to make London's whole history come alive. The collections are divided into two main sections: Early London History covers prehistoric, Roman (over 47,000 objects), Saxon and Medieval, and Tudor and Stuart; Later London History deals with Costume and Decorative Arts, Oral History (4,000 hours of interviews) and Contemporary Collecting, Painting, Prints and Drawings, Photographs (280,000), and Social and Working History. There are animations, recreated interiors and street scenes, including an animated model of the 1666 Great Fire accompanied by Samuel Pepys' eyewitness report. Objects range from caddy spoons to the Lord Mayor's magnificent State Coach. Galleries are

Top: The Monument. After many previous suicides, the death of a maidservant in 1842 led to the enclosure of the viewing gallery.

Museum of London Centre: Tobacconist's shop, part of the Victorian Walk in the World City gallery.

Bottom: *The Great Fire of London 1666*, by Lieve Verschuler.

also devoted to the early 20th century, World War II and London Now. World City, a recently added gallery, concentrates on London's entrepreneurial role during the fast-development years 1789–1914. The Museum's Archeology Service (MoLAS) carries out many excavations each year and undertakes continuous research.

Musical Museum, Middlesex 691 F5, This former church in Brentford High Street houses an amazing assembly of automatic musical instruments. There's the Steinway Duo Art grand

piano that reproduces the playing of such as Myra Hess and George Gershwin, a mighty self-playing Wurlitzer cinema organ, miniature pianos, and a collection of over 30,000 music rolls.

National Army Museum, sw3, 691 F5, The history of British land forces over almost six centuries since Agincourt is charted here, in a building in Royal Hospital Road. Personal experiences as well as strategies of campaigns and battles are chronicled with relics, paintings, dioramas, archive film clips and life-size uniformed models.

National Gallery

Above: The National Gallery, facing Trafalgar Square, provides a coherent overview of Western European painting from its beginnings in medieval Italy to the early years of the 20th century. There is also a continuous programme of special exhibitions.

Left: George Stubbs' study of a half-rearing, half-wild racehorse, *Whistlejacket*, 1762. The artist published a monumental *Anatomy of the Horse* illustrated by his own engravings.

National Gallery, wc2, 691 F5, Founded in 1824, when prime minister Lord Liverpool helped to secure the public purchase of 38 paintings – including works by Titian, Raphael, Rembrandt and Rubens – from the estate of the merchant and philanthropist John Julius Angerstein. The campaign for a national gallery had been spearheaded by King George IV, the portrait painter Thomas Lawrence, and the leading patron Sir George Beaumont, who donated his own collection. A site was found in newly developing Trafalgar Square*, and William Wilkins' neoclassical building was commissioned in 1833 and built in 1834–8 – at first only one-room deep, but since very much enlarged.

The gallery's first director, Charles Eastlake (also president of the Royal Academy*), travelled yearly to Italy for a decade, buying pictures by such as Duccio and Piero della Francesca, which were still regarded as 'curiosities' by most Victorian collectors. His inspired purchases form the basis of the glorious early Renaissance collection which can be seen in the Sainsbury Wing, opened in 1991.

Not the largest, but certainly one of the very finest collections of European paintings in the world, the permanent collection of over 2,300 works represents Western European painting from 1250 to 1900 and includes Leonardo da Vinci's *Virgin of the Rocks*, Holbein's *Ambassadors*, the *Rokeby Venus* by Velázquez, Vermeer's *Young Woman Standing at a Virginal*, and Seurat's *Bathers at Asnières*. There are also major works by British artists such as Gainsborough, Constable and Stubbs, though when the Tate Gallery (now Tate Britain*) opened in 1897, much of the British collection – including Turner's estate – moved there.

During World War II all the pictures were evacuated from Trafalgar Square and stored in a slate mine in Wales, safe from bombs under 200 feet (60m) of solid rock. The gallery itself was damaged in raids, but that did not stop the lunchtime concerts – instigated by the pianist Myra Hess and held in the empty galleries – which ran uninterrupted from October 1939 until April 1946.

Above: *A Cup of Water and a Rose*, by Francisco de Zurbarán; one of his exceptionally rare but classically serene still lifes.

Left: *A Lady with a Squirrel and a Starling* by Hans Holbein the Younger, probably painted during his first visit to England c1526–8. Also in the collection is his very popular *The Ambassadors* (*see* page 40).

Far left: *The Baptism of Christ* by Piero della Francesca, c1439. It was painted as an altarpiece for a priory in the artist's native town of Sansepolcro in Umbria – which can be seen in the background.

National Portrait Gallery, WC2, 691 F5, Behind the National Gallery*, in St Martin's Place, the making of British history can be seen in more than 9,000 famous faces and figures from Tudor times to the present day. Established in 1856, it was 40 years before the Portrait Gallery had its permanent home, a Florentine Renaissance-style building by Ewan Christian with carved portraits of eminent men on the exterior. Its policy has always been to consider the status of the sitter rather than just the artistic quality of any portrait, which has not prevented many fine pictures (including artists' self-portraits) being collected among the more mundane and eccentric. There are portraits of monarchs, courtiers, writers (including the only known likeness of Shakespeare taken from life – the first picture to enter the collection), scientists, statesmen, heroes and villains. The 20th-century galleries are crowded with paintings and photographs of household names, from politicians and princes to pop musicians, film stars and sports personalities. Since the 1970s, the Gallery has pursued an active policy of encouraging the art of portrait-painting and photography by commissioning works and holding an annual Portrait Award scheme and exhibition.

Natural History Museum, SW7, 691 F5, Alfred Waterhouse's cathedral-like building on the Cromwell Road opened in 1881 as a Victorian showcase for the glories of creation. Now divided into Earth and Life galleries, it holds more than 68 million specimens, over a million books and manuscripts, and a series of dramatic displays. Impressive exhibits range from robotic dinosaurs to creepy-crawlies, and from a walk-through rotating globe to

Right: Natural History Museum, for which the design brief from Richard Owen, a celebrated paleontologist, was to provide a building suitable 'for housing the works of the Creator'. Owen coined the word 'dinosaur'.

Below: Old Bailey, EW Mountford's building, opened by King Edward VII, has been the setting for the trials of the traitor William Joyce ('Lord Haw-Haw') and the murderer Peter Sutcliffe (the 'Yorkshire Ripper').

a simulated earthquake and volcano. The Ecology Gallery explores the network of the natural world and humankind's power to save or destroy. There are recreations of British country habitats such as an oak and bluebell wood, hedgerows, ponds and a wildflower meadow. Don't miss the astonishing detailing, in the entrance and elsewhere.

Notting Hill, W11, 691 F5, Notting Hill is best known as the scene of Europe's biggest street carnival, with costumed parades flooding the streets and gyrating to a Caribbean beat every August bank holiday weekend since 1966. The area has also given its name to a film starring Hugh Grant and Julia Roberts and has become one of the trendiest and costliest parts of London, with specialist small shops, celebrity residents and fashionable cafés. But the locality's greatest abiding glory is **Portobello Road,** where a market has been held since 1837. Antiques, bric-a-brac and junk are traded from 2,000 stalls each Saturday (a must for collectors and souvenir hunters who might also venture to Camden Passage on Wednesday, Bermondsey on Friday and Greenwich on Sunday – but only the earliest market birds catch the bargain worms). The Electric Cinema, one of the oldest cinemas in Britain, has recently been beautifully restored and is showing films once again.

Old Bailey, EC4, 691 F5, Topped by the famous dome of a bronze statue of blind Justice brandishing her sword and scales, the new Central Criminal Courts have tried major cases since 1907. But a Sessions House operated from 1539, and Judge Jeffreys dispensed injustice here in the 1670s. Part of the site was also occupied by the notorious Newgate prison.

Old Operating Theatre Museum, SE1, 691 F5, Rediscovered in 1957 in the bricked-up loft of what was once the parish church of St Thomas's

Top right: Osterley Park, the Tapestry Room, with Gobelins wall-hangings and seat-covers woven by Jacques Neilson to designs by François Boucher and Maurice Jacques.

Hospital (which moved to Lambeth in 1862 to make room for London Bridge Station) in St Thomas's Street. This was the women's operating theatre, used before the development of antiseptic surgery and anaesthetics. Restored to its original form, it has five steep tiers on which medical students once crammed to watch surgeons carve into gagged and bound women. Old instruments for childbirth, surgery, cupping, bleeding and trepanning are on display.

Orleans House, Gt Lon 691 F5, Only the Octagon, with its fine interior plasterwork, survives of this 1720 James Gibbs building in Twickenham. It was named after the Duke of Orleans, who lived in exile here from 1800 to 1817 before becoming King Louis-Philippe of France in 1830. Exhibitions are held in the adjacent gallery.

Osterley Park, Gt Lon 691 F5, This imposing red-brick house in Isleworth, with steps rising to a pedimented portico on Ionic columns and corner turrets topped with cupolas, is a mid-18th century design that has absorbed the plan of its Tudor forebear. The turrets once marked the corners of the courtyard of the country mansion completed

Below and bottom right: Osterley Park, exterior and the entrance hall, one of Robert Adams' idealized interiors. In 1773 Horace Walpole described it as 'the palace of palaces ... so improved and enriched'.

rooms, designed to impress the Childs' high-ranking visitors. The antechamber to the State Bedroom has a French air, its pastoral Gobelins tapestries and carpet echoed all around in the wall decorations and upholstery. The dressing-room – known as the Etruscan Room – reverts to a classical theme, with finely detailed wall decorations of figures and fancy urns set under arches.

for Thomas Gresham, founder of the Royal Exchange*, in 1575. Francis Child, who founded one of the first English banks, bought the property in 1711 but never lived here, and when his grandson and namesake inherited it, the young man set about transforming Osterley into a neo-classical palace. After Francis's early death at 28, his brother Robert continued the work.

The designs were begun by William Chambers and taken over by Robert Adam – they both became appointed architects to King George III in 1760. The work took 19 years to complete, and Adam was able to indulge to the utmost his genius for interior decoration, considering every detail with meticulous care. The entrance hall, cool in grey and white, epitomizes his love of classical grace and beauty, with its plasterwork ceiling, ornamental pilasters, and Greek deities set in niches. More of his delicate plasterwork can be seen throughout the house, especially in the state

Above: Orleans House, the Octagon, added in 1730 so the owner, James Johnston, could entertain Caroline, Princess of Wales, wife of George II.

Osterley remained in the Child family until it was given to the National Trust in 1949. The landscaped park, with its serpentine lakes and ancient cedars, is still as Chambers and Adam intended, except that the M4 has severed the northern section. The Tudor stables of Thomas Gresham survive, as do Adam's semicircular greenhouse and Chambers' Doric Temple of Pan.

Pall Mall, sw1, 691 F5, Named after the croquet-cum-golf game played here in the 17th century, this has been the elegant heart of London clubland for almost 200 years – from Nash's 1827 United Services Club (No. 116, now the Institute of Directors) and Decimus Burton's Athenaeum (1830), to Barry's Travellers' (1832) and Reform (1837) clubs. But the pride of Pall Mall is Wren's Marlborough House, commissioned by Queen Anne for the Duke of Marlborough and completed in 1711. Enlarged for use by 19th-century royalty – and the social centre of London when home to the

future Edward VII – it now houses the Commonwealth Secretariat.

Parliament Square, sw1, 691 F5, Laid out in the 1840s to show off the new Houses of Parliament*, today it is a traffic island containing statues of soldiers and statesmen – including the best bulldog image of Winston Churchill, by Ivor Roberts-Jones. The mock-gothic Middlesex Guildhall of 1913 stands behind a seated Abraham Lincoln. In a sculpture by Thomas Thorneycroft, the English Queen Boudicca appears to be aiming her chariot at the Palace of Westminster. Founded in the 12th century, **St Margaret's** has been Parliament's parish church since 1614. The stained-glass east window marking Prince Arthur's engagement to Catherine of Aragon was intended for adjacent Westminster Abbey* but sickly young Arthur died just after the wedding. (His younger brother Henry VIII succeeded to bride and later throne.) Pepys, Milton and Churchill were all wed at St Margaret's. There is a memorial window – donated by Americans in 1882 – to Sir Walter Raleigh, who was buried here after his 1618 execution in nearby Old Palace Yard. In the south aisle there are windows, installed in 1967, by John Piper.

Percival David Foundation of Chinese Art, wc1, 691 F5, Exceptional Chinese ceramics, dating from the 10th century and left to London University by scholar and collector Percival David, are now displayed in a Georgian town house at 53 Gordon Square. Many are the finest outside China, from the Sung, Yuan, Ming and Ch'ing dynasties. There is a gallery for special exhibitions of East Asian art and a reference library.

Petrie Museum, wc1, 691 F5, In Malet Place, University College London exhibits antiquities assembled by its first professor of Egyptology, Sir Flinders Petrie (1853–1942), who excavated dozens of major sites, continuing his diggings well into old age. His discoveries in Egypt included King Akhenaton's palace, the Greek city of Naucratis and pieces of a huge statue of Rameses II. The collection today houses around 80,000 objects.

Petticoat Lane, E1, 691 F5, This teeming Sunday street market of over 1,000 stalls still has sections devoted to cut-price clothes. Leather jackets are a speciality, but literally any domestic or novelty object may be found and bargained for.

Above: Petrie Museum, image of a Shabti.

Left: Pall Mall, the Athenaeum Club by Decimus Burton, 1828-30.

Above right: Pitshanger Manor.

Right: Postman's Park

Below: Piccadilly Circus, Eros, whose surrounding steps provide a traditional meeting place at the very hub of London.

Piccadilly, w1, 691 F5, Piccadilly Circus, now a blaze of gaudy neon signs above a chaotic roundabout, was once part of John Nash's grand plan for Regent Street*. The central 'Eros' statue, surmounting a large fountain pedestal, was unveiled in 1893 and is by Alfred Gilbert. It was originally named the *Angel of Christian Charity* and dedicated to the philanthropic 7th Earl of Shaftesbury. Piccadilly itself extends from the Circus to Hyde Park Corner, and is lined with London landmarks such as Fortnum and Mason*, the Royal Academy of Arts*, and the colonnaded château-style Ritz. The Hotel, which oozes Edwardian opulence, still preserves period charm in its institution of afternoon tea. Wren believed his church of **St James**, finished in 1684, one of his finest. Even bomb damage and alterations have not ruined its effect. Note the tall windows and slim spire (a cunning fibreglass replica of 1966). The altar screen and marble font are by the 17th-century master carver Grinling Gibbons. Just off Piccadilly, in Dover Street, Elisabeth Frink's 1975 sculpture *Horse and Rider* creates a pocket of calm.

Pitshanger Manor and Gallery, w5, 691 F5, For the first ten years of the 19th century this was the country villa of Sir John Soane. Long ago engulfed

Queen Anne's Gate
Top left and top centre: Queen Anne's Gate, a neo-Queen Anne doorcase and the statue of the queen that originally stood in a square at the west section.

Centre: Regent's Park, the central block of Cumberland Terrace, with pediment sculpture by George Bubb representing Britannia with the arts, sciences and trades of her empire.

Bottom: Primrose Hill provides views from Canary Wharf in the east to the Post Office Tower and beyond in the west.

park never received most of its intended villas, nor the pleasure palace conceived for the Prince Regent. But delights include the summer Open Air Theatre, Queen Mary's Rose Garden, a boating lake teeming with native and ornamental waterfowl and, in the northwest corner, the **London Zoo**. Opened in 1828, the menagerie is both tourist attraction and conservation centre. Two features are of architectural interest – Berthold Lubetkin's Penguin Pool of 1936 and Lord Snowdon's 1964 Aviary.

Regent Street, W1, 691 F5, Regent Street was first built between 1813 and 1823 to designs by John Nash as a majestic route of stucco-fronted houses and shops linking the Prince Regent's Carlton House home in St James's Park to Regent's Park. Rebuilt from 1898, the street now houses luxury shops, most notably Liberty's department store, founded in 1875, behind a mock-Tudor façade on Great Marlborough Street. Crossing Regent Street at Oxford Circus, **Oxford Street** is London's longest shopping street, running 1¼ miles (2km).

in the suburb of Ealing (Mattock Lane), it has been restored, partly filled with bizarre Martinware pottery and Soane's own decorative schemes recreated in the library, breakfast room and bedchamber. The 1940s extension houses the largest contemporary art gallery in west London.

Postman's Park, EC1, 691 F5, Created from three adjacent churchyards in 1880, the green was much used by staff from the nearby General Post Office (where there is now a National Postal Museum). The Victorian artist GF Watts dedicated one wall to plaques hailing the bravery of ordinary people.

Primrose Hill, NW3/NW8, 691 F5, Once a medieval forest, now a grassy hill offering wonderful views over London. An indicator board marks the position of famous buildings. There is a Druid ceremony every year on the autumn equinox, and a spectacular firework display on the Saturday nearest 5 November.

Queen Anne's Gate, SW1, 691 F5, Terraced houses in this elegant enclave date from 1704, the earliest with ornate front door canopies.

Queen Elizabeth's Hunting Lodge, Greater London 691 F4, Built for her father, Henry VIII, in 1543, as a grandstand for blood sports in the royal forest of Epping. At what is now 6 Rangers Road, Chingford, Gloriana shot her crossbow from the first-floor room in which a hunt breakfast has now been re-created.

Regent's Canal, W9/NW1, 691 F5, Opened in 1820 to link the Grand Junction Canal at Paddington with the London docks at Limehouse, this is now a leisure amenity. The paved towpath is a popular walkway and boat trips meander between London Zoo, Little Venice and Camden Lock.

Regent's Park, NW1, 691 F5, Designed as a garden suburb by John Nash and enclosed in 1812, the

Richmond, sw15/Surrey 691 F5, Lovely Richmond was the summer residence of the Plantagenet kings. Elizabeth I and her grandfather Henry VII died here: his coat of arms adorns the gatehouse of the otherwise vanished palace, just off what some think is England's finest green. Jousting and pageants once took place upon its turf, and, being common land, Richmond Green was also a sheep pasture for the villagers. Early 18th-century houses stand on the site of the palace – the ones in Maids of Honour Row were built for the future Queen Caroline's ladies-in-waiting. The Wardrobe, in Old Palace Yard, was where soft furnishings were stored, and Trumpeter's House beyond is a fine early 17th-century house, its classical façade looking out on to the river. Prince Metternich, the Austrian statesman, lived here from 1848 and 1851, when he was fleeing revolution in Vienna; Disraeli came to visit him and called it 'the most charming house in the world'.

Left: Richmond Theatre, opened in 1899, whose sumptuous original interiors were refurbished in the 1990s.

Opposite page
Centre: White Lodge, by Roger Morris, 1727.

Bottom: *Richmond Hill* by JMW Turner, showing the lovely 18th-century bridge over the Thames.

The Richmond Theatre on Little Green, late Victorian in red brick and shiny terracotta, has an interior designed by Frank Matcham. Models of the old royal palace may be seen in the Museum of Richmond in Whittaker Avenue. From there the riverside walk leads to James Paine's beautiful five-arched Richmond Bridge of 1777, widened in 1937. At the top of Richmond Hill there is a celebrated view (protected by Act of Parliament) of the Thames meandering in the valley below that has inspired artists such as Richard Wilson, Turner and Constable. Joshua Reynolds had Wick House built for

him by William Chambers in 1772 and lived here until his death 20 years later.

Richmond Gate, designed by Capability Brown in 1798, leads into the 2,470 acres (1,000ha) of Richmond Park – the largest open space in Greater London. Once a royal hunting ground, the park was first enclosed by Charles I. Ladderstile Gate from Kingston Hill indicates John Lewis's method of entry when he determined

Above left and right: Richmond Park, home of wild deer and ancient oak trees.

to win back pedestrian rights of way for the public – a case he successfully defended against the Crown in the reign of George II. Within the park there are lakes, deer-grazed grassland, and trees that include several splendid medieval oaks. Its highest spot is Henry VIII's Mound – which may once have been a Bronze-Age barrow. Here, with its views from Windsor Castle* to the Tower of London*, Henry is said to have stood awaiting the signal to inform him that Anne Boleyn had been executed.

Across the park is White Lodge, a Palladian villa – with many additions – commissioned by George II and a favoured residence of Queen Caroline. The future Edward VIII (later Duke of Windsor) was born here in 1894, and his brother and sister-in-law (later George VI and Queen Elizabeth the Queen Mother) lived here after their marriage. It is now home to the younger members of the Royal Ballet School. Richmond was given its name by Henry VII after his earldom in Richmond, Yorkshire. For Londoners Richmond Park is their nearest approximation to open country. Riders trot along the bracken-fringed rides, and wildlife flourishes.

Left: *View of the Thames from Richmond Hill* by John Constable.

Roman Bath, WC2, 691 F5, Beside a large window in Surrey Street, a light switch illuminates an antique bathing pool. Popular for cold plunges in the 19th century, the bath probably began as part of Arundel House – one of several Strand palaces commissioned in the Tudor era.

Rotten Row, SW7/SW1, 691 F5, Its name deriving from the French *route du roi*, it links Kensington Palace* to St James's*. It was the first road in England to have street lighting when William III ordered hundreds of lanterns to be hung from the trees as a defence against highwaymen. Today, riders on this route – ranging from children on ponies to Horse Guards – pose less threat.

Royal Academy of Arts, W1, 691 F5, The Academy was founded in 1768 by 34 painters, sculptors and architects, with George III as its patron and Joshua Reynolds its president, to promote art and design and to train artists. A century later the RA moved into Burlington House*, Piccadilly – England's first Palladian town house – building galleries over the gardens. Displays staged throughout the year include the Summer Exhibition (held annually since 1769; all artists can submit work for possible inclusion). Sir Norman Foster's 1991 Sackler Galleries host smaller shows. The RA permanent collection holds diploma works given by artists on election as Royal Academicians. But its greatest treasure, given by Sir George Beaumont, is Michelangelo's *Taddei Tondo* – one of only four sculptures by the artist kept outside Italy, depicting the Virgin and Christ with the infant John the Baptist.

Royal Courts of Justice, WC2, 691 F5, With 1,000 rooms, over 3 miles (4.8km) of corridors, and 35 million bricks faced with Portland stone, this warren houses the nation's main civil courts. Completed in 1882, GE Street's neo-gothic building on the Strand deals with such matters as divorce, libel, civil liability and appeals. The courts are open to all – justice must not only be done but be seen to be done – and about 32,000 tourists a year avail themselves of this right. 'Lists' in the high central hall give the names of parties in cases being heard, but no other details.

Royal Exchange, EC3, 691 F5, The City's oldest mercantile institution was founded in 1567 by

Top: The Royal Academy owns this unfinished Carrara marble tondo of *The Holy Family with the Infant St John*, by Michelangelo.

Right and below left: Royal Courts of Justice, opened by Queen Victoria a year after the architect died, probably due to stress caused by building delays.

Below: Royal Geographical Society, built by Norman Shaw as Lowther Lodge in 1872–5. It became the society's headquarters in 1913.

Right: Royal Exchange. The pediment was sculptured by Richard Westmacott Junior.

Opposite page
Top left: Royal Opera House.

Centre left: Royal Institution.

Centre right: Royal Mews pediment, *Hercules Capturing the Thracian Horses* by William Theed the Elder.

Bottom: Royal Mews entrance, built in the grand manner for George IV.

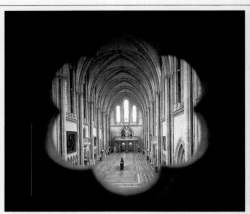

Thomas Gresham – remembered still for the dictum 'bad money drives out good', which in his day meant that currencies with coins of low metal content would remain in circulation while the rest were hoarded or melted. William Tite's lofty neo-classical building, dating from 1844, is the third on this site, at the junction of Threadneedle Street and Cornhill. Outside stands Francis Chantrey's equestrian statue of the Duke of Wellington – cast in bronze from French cannons captured at Waterloo.

Royal Geographical Society, SW7, 691 F5, The Society, based in a building on Kensington Gore has supported intrepid explorers since it was founded in 1830. The Library and Map Room have more than 900,000 maps and charts, plus atlases, globes and gazetteers. They are undergoing major reorganization and will reopen in 2003.

Royal Institution, W1, 691 F5, Founded in 1799 for teaching 'the application of science to the common purposes of life', Michael Faraday conducted pioneering work into electricity and

travelling. There is a fine collection of harness dating back to the 18th century.

Royal Opera House, wc2, 691 F5, Much of the song and dance associated with this celebrated Covent Garden landmark has centred on the building rather than the stage. It was built originally in 1732, but fires raged here in 1808 and 1856. EM Barry's design of 1858 – incorporating John Flaxman's earlier portico frieze of tragedy and comedy – has been lately enlarged and redesigned to create a better home for the Royal Opera and Royal Ballet companies. The barrel-vault roof and ironwork of the Floral Hall have been restored to provide the grand foyer. During redevelopment, excavations revealed extensive Saxon remains, including what was probably the 'King's Highway' – a solid road, made of gravel 3 feet (1m) thick, which once had flimsy houses of wattle and daub on either side.

magnetism here in Albemarle Street. His laboratory has been recreated in a basement museum. The building's classical façade by Lewis Vulliamy was added in 1838. Today, programmes of lectures and activities continue to encourage an understanding of science and appreciation of the contributions of scientists.

Royal Mews, sw1, 691 F5, A quadrangle of stables and coach houses for Buckingham Palace* was built to John Nash's design in 1825 and holds the stateliest examples of horse-drawn transport. Here are landaus, barouches and phaetons, and the Glass Coach used at royal weddings. The Gold State Coach, which conveyed George III to the 1762 State Opening of Parliament, weighs 4 tons and needs eight horses to pull it. It has decorative panels painted by the Florentine artist Giovanni Battista Cipriani. Two breeds of harness horses are used – Cleveland Bays and Windsor Greys. By tradition, the latter always draw the carriage in which the monarch is

became in turn a skating rink, a pickle factory and a boxing arena. Rebuilt in 1927 by the redoubtable Lilian Baylis, it became the home of ballet and opera companies. It reopened, after a costly update, as a high-tech dance centre in 1999.

St Anne, W1, 691 F5, The church, in Wardour Street, is 17th century, but the remaining tower was added in 1717 and rebuilt in 1803. It survived an air raid of 1940 when all else was destroyed. The essayist William Hazlitt is buried here; also the ashes of detective-story writer Dorothy L Sayers. The church gardens are raised to cover the remains of over 10,000 parishioners.

St Bartholomew the Great, EC1, 691 F5, The oldest parish church in the City. Once part of a monastery founded in 1123 by Henry I's jester, Rahere, after St Bartholomew had saved him from a winged

Sadler's Wells Theatre, E1, 691 F5, Built as a 'musick house' by Thomas Sadler in 1683, then rebuilt in 1765 as a theatre. Sarah Siddons and Edmund Kean performed here, and Joseph Grimaldi, the great comic actor who developed English pantomime, was a star performer. In the late 19th century the building, on Rosebery Avenue,

Bottom left: Interior of St Bartholomew the Great.

Below: St Clement Dane's, another of Wren's London churches, now the church of the Royal Air Force.

monster in a vision. Following the Dissolution the building, in West Smithfield, had diverse uses – in 1725 there was a printer's office in the Lady Chapel where Benjamin Franklin worked. It was restored to its original purpose by Aston Webb 1863–85. The choir screen of 1932 is by Frank Beresford and depicts the daily life of monks.

St Bartholomew the Less, EC1, 691 F5, Inside the gates of Bart's Hospital in West Smithfield, this church has served patients and their families, doctors and nurses, for five centuries. Architect Inigo Jones was baptized here; the post-Wren octagonal dome was constructed in 1789 and has twice been rebuilt. Badly damaged in the Blitz, the church re-opened in 1956. The hospital itself, designed by James Gibbs (1730–59) like an Oxbridge college, is simple and monumental. Inside there is a stunning series of murals by Hogarth.

St Bride, EC4, 691 F5, The Great Fire of 1666 destroyed the seventh church to occupy this Fleet Street site – the first having being established by the 6th-century Irish saint, Bridget. Wren designed the eighth, creating his tallest and most celebrated spire of successively diminishing octagonal tiers.

Left: St Bride, Fleet Street, the journalists' church with Wren's tallest and most celebrated spire (226 feet/70m).

A baker of the time copied it for a wedding cake and established a tradition. In 1501, Caxton's apprentice, Wynkyn de Worde, brought Fleet Street's first printing press here, and St Bride has ever since been associated with writers and journalists. National newspapers paid for much of its 17-year restoration after the Blitz. A crypt museum encapsulates its rich history.

St Clement Danes, WC2, 691 F5, Designed by Christopher Wren and now isolated on a traffic island in the Strand, it became the church of the Royal Air Force, who contributed to its reconstruction after World War II and whose dead are remembered here, as are the 1,900 American airmen killed while based in Britain. Once a year the bells ring out the nursery rhyme 'Oranges and lemons, Say the bells of St Clement's'.

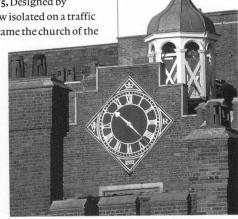

Right and below: St James's Palace. The gatehouse is the only substantial remaining part of the original Tudor palace.

St Dunstan in the West, EC4, 691 F5, The poet John Donne was rector at this Fleet Street church for ten years. His biographer, Isaak Walton – author of *The Compleat Angler* – was the church's 'Scavenger, Questman and Sidesman' and is commemorated by a tablet and stained-glass window.

St Giles-in-the-Fields, WC2, 691 F5, In 1101 this was the site of a leper hospital, built in fields outside the city wall. The Great Plague began in this parish and, in a church built in 1623, 1,391 burials were recorded in a single month. So much grave-digging brought about structural damage, causing the present church by Henry Flitcroft to be erected in 1733. In 1818, two of Shelley's children and Lord Byron's daughter Allegra were baptized here together.

St James's Palace, SW1, 691 F5, Built by Henry VIII in the 1530s on the site of a hospital for leper women, it has always been primarily a royal residence. Foreign ambassadors are still officially accredited to the Court of St James, although they are

nowadays received at Buckingham Palace*. The gatehouse is a distinctive Tudor landmark. Now separated from St James's Palace by Marlborough Gate, the Queen's Chapel was built by Inigo Jones for Charles I's wife, Henrietta Maria, in 1627. England's first classical church has a Carracci altarpiece. George III married Charlotte of Mecklenburg-Strelitz here in 1761. The exquisite interior is open only for regular Sunday worshippers.

St James's Park, SW1, 691 F5, Enclosed by Henry VIII as part of a string of hunting grounds (along with Green Park* and Hyde Park*), this was originally a marsh. Charles II landscaped it with avenues and a canal, and added an aviary along what is now Birdcage Walk. The Mall was converted into a processional route from Trafalgar Square* to Buckingham Palace* in the late 19th century.

St James's Square, SW1, 691 F5, Lined with exclusive houses as early as the 1670s, this square was intended for members of the nobility who wanted to live close to St James's Palace*, then the monarch's official residence. The London Library at No. 14 was founded in 1841 by Thomas Carlyle.

Below: St Katharine Dock, where visiting yachts may berth and historical craft are kept on display.

Below: St Katharine Dock, where visiting yachts may berth and historical craft are kept on display.

St John, NW3, 691 F5, This proprietary chapel with a wooden bell-turret was completed in 1823 as a place of worship for the residents of the new houses on Downshire Hill. Its white-painted late Georgian interior is airy and pretty, with box pews and a gallery. The young Gerard Manley Hopkins

Above: St Martin-in-the-Fields. Several royal babies have been christened here.

Left: St Katharine Dock, statue of Boy with Dolphin.

worshipped here – his father was churchwarden. A marble memorial bust of Keats was erected in 1894 by American admirers.

St John's, Smith Square, SW1, 691 F5, Thomas Archer's 1728 glorious feat of English baroque, concealed in a quiet leafy square, is known as Queen Anne's footstool. On being consulted over the design, the impatient queen is purported to have kicked over her footstool and ordered: 'Like that!' Over the centuries it has been struck by fire, lightning and aerial bombing; it was reopened after restoration in 1969 as a concert venue with superb acoustics.

St John's Gate, EC1, 691 F5, A museum in St John's Lane, telling the story of the Order of St John (Malta), a body founded during the Crusades, but once the entrance to the Priory of the Knights of St John of Jerusalem in Clerkenwell.

St Katharine Dock, E1, 691 F5, Built in the 1820s – razing a medieval district and displacing 11,000 people – it was the first of the London docks to close, in 1969. It has been revived as a leisure and residential centre, with the 1854 Ivory House now flats and a three-storey warehouse the Dickens Inn. One basin is a marina and another holds the Historic Ship collection, with tugs, traders, lightships and Captain Scott's HMS *Discovery* recalling the ages of sail and steam.

St Martin-in-the-Fields, WC2, 691 F5, This church by James Gibbs, the most influential London church architect of the early 18th century, upset many a zealous Protestant in the 1720s with its catholic use of ornament. Famous people buried here

church. William Blake married Catherine Boucher, the daughter of a local market gardener, here in 1782. The elderly JMW Turner was rowed across the river from his house in Chelsea to paint from the church tower.

St Mary Woolnoth, EC4, 691 F5, Rebuilt 1716–27 by Nicholas Hawksmoor; this is his most unusual church. Compressed into a small City site on Lombard Street, it is nevertheless imposing. The interior plan of a square within a square creates an illusion of spaciousness that makes the jewel-like interior seem oddly larger than the outside walls. Twelve mighty Corinthian columns support a clerestory with large lunettes, bathing the church in light. The west gallery is adorned with a 17th-century organ. In 1900 the crypt was sold to the Underground Railway and now contains the Northern Line booking hall.

St Pancras Parish Church, WC1, 691 F5, Designed in 1822 by William Inwood and his son Henry in uncompromising Greek Revival style, this was the most expensive church of its day. The caryatids on the side are in terracotta over cast-iron; they are casts of those on the Erechtheum in Athens, and are now better preserved than the originals. The church, in Upper Woburn Place, provides a venue for free lunchtime concerts.

include Charles II's mistress Nell Gwynne, the artists Joshua Reynolds and William Hogarth, the cabinet-maker Thomas Chippendale and the highwayman Jack Sheppard. After World War I the vicar, Dick Sheppard, opened the crypt for homeless soldiers, and the church has continued to provide help and shelter for those in need ever since. It is also noted for its fine concerts.

St Mary, SW11, 691 F5, William I gave the Saxon church on this site in Battersea Church Road to the monks of Westminster Abbey* after the Norman conquest. It was extended and developed over the centuries, and in 1777 rebuilt as a simple village

Top left and above: St Pancras Station and Hotel, a superb example of Victorian Gothic architecture.

Below: St Mary Woolnoth, whose twinned tower makes an appearance in TS Eliot's *The Waste Land.*

St Pancras Station, NW1, 691 F5, George Gilbert Scott's 250-bedroom Midland Grand Hotel opened in 1874 as the last word in comfort and modernity. The gingerbread gothic fantasy, best of the three rail termini along Euston Road, was used for offices from 1935, until restored as a hotel in recent years. The train shed behind is a miracle of Victorian engineering: its roof stretches for 700 feet (213m) and soars 100 feet (30m) high. The columns of the cloister-style entrance to the station are decorated with pairs of dragons, each different: eagle-clawed, crocodile-tailed and beaked. There is more carved decoration inside, including small sculptures of 19th-century railwaymen atop the four centre pillars in the booking hall.

St Paul's Cathedral, ec4, 691 E5, When the Great Fire of 1666 swept the City, it was the fourth time a church on this site – which had once contained a Roman temple to Diana – had been destroyed. A wooden structure, dedicated to St Paul in 604 by St Ethelbert, King of Kent, burned down 70 years later. A second cathedral, built in stone in 675–85, was laid waste by the Vikings in 961. A third burned down in 1087, and the Norman cathedral – larger than the present one – was begun straight away. Stone was brought by sea from the quarries of Caen, and the spire (to be struck by lightning in 1447 and destroyed by fire in 1561) was the tallest yet built.

After the Fire, Sir Christopher Wren was commissioned to rebuild not only St Paul's but another 51 churches throughout the City as well. His design, with a traditional cruciform gothic groundplan and a tall steeple, was finally accepted in 1675 and building began immediately. But the cathedral that was officially declared finished – after many rows and delays – in 1711 did not bear very much resemblance to those original plans. Gone was the steeple reaching for the sky; instead there was the great classical dome, ingeniously constructed so that the imposing outer roof is 60 feet (20m) taller than the inner ceiling. The lantern tower that crowns the dome is – together with the two fantastic western towers designed as late as 1707 – distinctly baroque.

James Thornhill painted the frescoes of the life of St Paul which adorn the inner dome. These are best seen from the Whispering Gallery, 100 feet (30m) high and famed for its acoustics. The Golden Gallery at the top of the dome offers spectacular views but entails a climb of 530 steps. Among the great craftsmen employed by Wren was the master-ironworker Jean Tijou, who made the gates to the north and south chancel aisles plus the balustrade to the elegant geometrical staircase by master-mason William Kempster. Grinling Gibbons, at his most inspired, carved the choir-stalls, bishop's throne and organ case. (The organ itself was played by both Handel and Mendelssohn.)

Wren died in 1723 aged 91, and appropriately was one of the first to be buried in the whitewashed crypt. An inscription in Latin above his modest marble slab, composed by his son, reads: 'Reader, if you seek his memorial, look about you.' Positioned immediately beneath the dome is Nelson's impressive black sarcophagus. Wellington's sarcophagus is towards the east of the crypt, while his massive memorial almost fills the north aisle above.

Below: View of the Cathedral from St Bride's.

St Stephen Walbrook, EC4, 691 F5, The first of Wren's churches to combine a cross-in-square plan with a large central dome – a marvellous practice piece for St Paul's Cathedral*. Controversially the 20th-century altar – an austere stone carving by Henry Moore – has been repositioned under the dome, emphasizing the approachable aspects of modern worship. The Reverend Chad Varah founded the Samaritans in the crypt.

St Vedast-alias-Foster (Foster Lane, EC2) 691 F5, Curiously named – Foster is an anglicization of Vedast. Standing in the shadow of St Paul's*, this was once a humble medieval church, remodelled by Wren. It boasts a unique baroque spire, an intricate beacon in the manner of Borromini, added from 1709 (probably by Hawksmoor).

Savoy Hotel, WC2, 691 F5, Opening on the site of the medieval Savoy Palace in 1889, this hotel is so grand that its forecourt off the Strand is the only street in Britain where traffic keeps to the right. The Savoy Theatre, built for the D'Oyly Carte operas by Gilbert and Sullivan, is a restored Art Deco delight by Basil Ionides, 1929.

Science Museum, SW7, 691 F5, Part of the legacy of the Great Exhibition of 1851, the present building on Exhibition Road was opened by George V in 1929. Seven floors of exhibits provide a panorama of scientific advances through the ages, with an especially rich record of inventions spurred by the Industrial Revolution. The basement has two state-of-the-art interactive galleries for children, and a nostalgic but comic look at things domestic in the Secret Life of the Home. Higher levels take in everything from transport, navigation and space exploration to meteorology, oceanography, computing, food, farming and medical history.

Seven Dials, WC2, 691 F5, This buzzing area might be termed the 'real' Covent Garden*. The local community fought for its survival from

Above: St Vedast-alias-Foster, where Poet Laureate John Betjeman was once a churchwarden.

Left: Science Museum mock-up of a Moon landing.

Below and bottom right: Sir John Soane's Museum, where the architect Soane lived and amassed extraordinary collections of precious and curious objects, including statues, casts and antique fragments.

developers in the 1970s, and continues to implement an imaginative programme of urban renaissance. A replica of Edward Pierce's 1694 Sundial Pillar (removed in 1882) now stands proudly at the hub of seven roads – the first monumental column to be built in London since Nelson's. Pubs, delis, boutiques and bookshops abound.

Sherlock Holmes Museum, NW1, 691 F5, Arthur Conan Doyle's fictional detective lived at 221b Baker Street. The Museum honours that imaginary address, though it actually sits between Nos. 237 and 239.

Sir John Soane's Museum, WC2, 691 F5, An Aladdin's cave of treasures and architectural tricks left to the nation by maverick John Soane in 1837. Architect son of a bricklayer who wed a wealthy builder's daughter, he completely reconstructed a 17th-century house at No. 13 Lincoln's Inn Fields, adorning it with domes, mirrors and lantern lights. His taste in rooms ran to Catacombs, a Monk's Parlour and a Sepuchral Chamber containing the sarcophagus of Pharaoh Seti I. The house is crammed with ancient artefacts, paintings (Hogarth's *Rake's Progress*, Canaletto, Turner, Watteau), books, fine furnishings and architectural drawings. A joy.

Smithfield Market, EC1, 691 F5, Anyone with a taste for full English breakfasts washed down with beer should pay an early morning call to Smithfield Market, where there is catering for (much diminished) meat-market traders from dawn. Horace Jones's Victorian market buildings still please the eye, but live cattle were last seen here almost 150 years ago.

Soho, W1, 691 F5, This cosmopolitan district between Regent Street* and Charing Cross Road, with its smart restaurants and cafés, strip clubs, pornographic bookshops and bars of all kinds, has long mixed sleaze and glamour. Wardour Street hosts the British film industry. Old Compton Street is London's latest gay mecca. Speciality food stores and Berwick Street market lure gourmets. Pubs proliferate: General de Gaulle drank at The French House in Dean Street and bohemians have been trying to drain the Coach and Horses in

Romilly Street since the 1940s. Carnaby Street, favourite haunt of dedicated followers of fashion in the Swinging Sixties, is now a precinct of tourist shops and unexciting boutiques. Three Chinese arches straddle Gerrard

Street, where the Chinese New Year is marked in late January with a vibrant festival.

Somerset House, WC2, 691 F5, This is a classical 1770s quadrangle by William Chambers. Built on the Strand, on the site of a Renaissance palace, it was Britain's first purpose-built government office block. The fabulous Courtauld art galleries occupy the former Fine Rooms of the Royal Academy of Arts* (based here 1771–1836). Impressionist and Post-Impressionist masterpieces amassed by textile magnate Samuel Courtauld have been augmented by other superb gifts, particularly of Italian and Flemish old master paintings. A fine collection of 20th-century British art is not entirely eclipsed. Another section displays masterpieces on loan from the Hermitage

and memorials – including the 1408 tomb of poet John Gower, friend of Geoffrey Chaucer. But Shakespeare is the poet who seems most in residence: his memorial in the south aisle was carved by Henry McCarthy in 1912, and an annual birthday service is held in his honour. A library extension by Richard Griffiths, inspired by the Arts and Crafts tradition, was opened in 2000 by Nelson Mandela.

Museum in St Petersburg; yet another, the Gilbert Collection of European gold, English silver and mosaics. William Chambers' great courtyard is now enhanced by a deceptively simple fountain – lines of orchestrated water jets that spring straight from the granite flagstones and act like magnets to small children on hot days. It is illuminated at night.

South Bank, SE1, 691 F5, The site of the 1951 Festival of Britain, celebrating the Great Exhibition's centenary, now hosts London's main centre for the visual and performing arts in concrete buildings: the Royal National Theatre, Queen Elizabeth Hall, Hayward Gallery, Royal Festival Hall and the National Film Theatre. There are continual plans afoot to make the whole complex greener and more welcoming. The arrival of the London Eye* to mark the millennium has proved popular.

Southwark Cathedral, SE1, 691 F5, A few traces remain of the 1106 Norman church – the third church to be built on this site and destroyed by fire in 1212. Its replacement is now the oldest gothic building in London, very much repaired, restored, altered and extended over the centuries. Originally the church of St Mary Overie ('over the water'), then the parish church of St Saviour, it became the cathedral of the new diocese of Southwark in 1905. It is rich in medieval features

Above: Somerset House has undergone comprehensive restoration and provides a palatial centre of culture just off the Strand.

Right: Southwark Cathedral, a view showing the entrance to its new library extension.

Spencer House, SW1, 691 F5, Said by some to be London's most beautiful building, Spencer House in St James's Place is the former home of the family of Diana, Princess of Wales. It is a Palladian palace, completed in 1766 – chiefly to designs by John Vardy – for the 1st Earl Spencer. With interiors now restored, the house is open by appointment as a museum, art gallery and centre for formal entertaining.

Spitalfields, E1, 691 F5, Just north of the City walls, this area has given refuge to waves of migrants – Huguenot weavers from the 17th century, then Jews, now Bangladeshis. Workshops, small factories, ethnic restaurants and places of worship have succeeded one another. Petticoat Lane*, a clothing market since the 16th century, is packed on Sunday mornings as crowds flow to the Bengali food shops in Brick Lane. Around Fournier Street, where 18th-century houses have light attics for silk-weaving, beautiful buildings have only lately been saved from demolition. The Spitalfields Historic Buildings Trust headquarters has a Victorian synagogue in its garden. *See also* **Christ Church*.**

Staple Inn Buildings, WC1 691 F5, In High Holborn, this is the last remnant of Elizabethan half-timbering left in central London. It was once the wool staple, where wool was weighed and taxed.

Stock Exchange, EC2, 691 F5, The Exchange has moved from 17th-century coffee houses to a base in Threadneedle Street, and now has a new home – a 26-storey office block in Old Broad Street, opened by Queen Elizabeth II in 1972. (Women members were not admitted until a year later.) The 23,000 sq ft (7,000 sq m) trading floor has calmed down since computerization.

Strand on the Green, W4, 691 F5, A riverside pocket of handsome 18th-century houses. Painter John

Spencer House
Top left: The west façade.
Above: The Palm Room (palm trees were a symbol of marital fidelity).

Left: Strand on the Green, where private gardens run down to the river walk.

Right: Syon House. The Great Conservatory, designed by Charles Fowler, said to have been the inspiration for Crystal Palace.

Zoffany, famed for his detailed conversation pieces, lived at No. 65 for the last 20 years of his life (1790–1810). Nancy Mitford lived at Rose Cottage and Dylan Thomas at Ship House Cottage.

Strawberry Hill, Gt Lon 691 F5, Horace Walpole – who wrote the first gothic novel, *The Castle of Otranto* – created, with the aid of five architects, his own miniature Gothic Revival castle between 1749

coffin was rested at Syon on its way to Windsor for burial, it is said to have burst open in the night – dogs were discovered licking at the remains.

In the 1760s, the existing house, built from a 15th-century convent, was considered by the Duke to be 'ruinous and inconvenient'; he engaged Robert Adam to remodel the interiors, and Capability Brown to landscape the grounds. Their achievements can still be admired. The lavish neoclassical rooms include a Great Hall with Doric columns, a Roman ante-room, dining room with ornamented half-domes, and a red drawing room with crimson silk walls and fine Stuart portraits. The entrance gates with colonnades and lodges are also by Adam.

Within the 200 acres (80ha) of parkland, Brown created two lakes – one now a trout fishery. There are over 3,000 trees, many of them rare. As early as 1837, the botanical gardens were opened to the public, and in 1965 the 10th Duke started the first national centre of gardening. Over 400 varieties of rose are grown. Today parts of the grounds are owned by a trust, including the magnificent Victorian conservatory built by Charles Fowler of gun-metal and Bath stone – inspiration to Joseph Paxton for his Crystal Palace at the Great Exhibition. The Butterfly House creates a tropical environment for exotic species, while the Aquatic Centre has self-contained ecosystems for all kinds of fish, reptiles and amphibians. Out in the protected wild of the riverside meadows, the rare German hairy back snail has its home.

and 1776. Eclectic rather than scholarly, its details were taken from illustrations in topographical books and adapted: a fireplace is modelled on Edward the Confessor's tomb, a staircase balustrade copied from Rouen Cathedral. Although it has been used since the 1920s by a college, efforts are now being made to conserve and restore its intricate, fragile interiors and to recover some of Walpole's famous collection, sold in 1842. Guided tours are by arrangement.

Sutton House, E9, 691 F5, With original brickwork, large fireplaces and linenfold panelling still intact, this Tudor merchant's house in Homerton High Street is a unique East End survival (though when it was built, in 1535, Hackney was a village). An exhibition traces the history of the house and its occupants – successively merchants, Huguenot silk-weavers, Victorian schoolmistresses and Edwardian clergy.

Syon House, Gt Lon 691 F5, The only large mansion in Greater London still in its hereditary ownership, Syon has been the home of the earls and dukes of Northumberland for 400 years. Earlier, Henry VIII's 5th wife, Catherine Howard, was imprisoned here before her execution, and when the King's

Top left: Strawberry Hill. 'The prettiest bauble you ever did see,' according to its creator and owner Horace Walpole.

Top centre: Sutton House, dining room with linenfold panelling.

Top right: Syon House, dining room. The statues represent gods and goddesses of food and wine.

Centre right: Strawberry Hill's gothic-style chimneys.

Tate Britain (Millbank), SW1, 691 F5, The sugar magnate Henry Tate funded the neo-baroque building by Sidney JR Smith that opened as a gallery of British art in 1897. He gave his own collection of 67 paintings, mainly Victorian and including John Millais' popular portrait of the drowned Ophelia (modelled by Rossetti's mistress Lizzie Siddall). In 1851, JMW Turner, Britain's greatest Romantic painter, had left 300 oils and 20,000 watercolours and drawings to the nation with the request that they be stored and shown in a home of their own. The art dealer Joseph Duveen funded a wing of the new gallery to meet – in part – this request. In 1916 it was decided the Tate should also form the national collection of foreign modern art; Duveen's son endowed a new wing plus, in 1937, the long sculpture gallery.

The addition, in 1987, of the immediately adjacent Clore Gallery, designed by James Stirling, meant there was at last an appropriate home for the complete Turner bequest. Then in 2000, Tate Modern* opened as London's centre for international modern art, leaving Tate Britain to revert to Henry Tate's vision of it as a showcase for British art. Annual rehangings have put many more of the nation's treasures on public view. Here are masterpieces by Gainsborough, Constable, Stubbs, Hogarth and Joseph Wright of Derby. Four very different brands of idiosyncratic English vision can be seen in the fine William Blake collection, in John Martin's huge, apocalyptic landscapes, in the lustrous narratives of the Pre-Raphaelites, and in the biblical Cookham* paintings of Stanley Spencer.

The Centenary Development, which opened in 2001, created several major new galleries and other resources – including a grand top-lit staircase. The new Millbank Pier provides a river link to Tate Modern.

Above: The Lady of Shalott, by John William Waterhouse, 1888.

Left: Miss Cicely Alexander: Harmony in Grey and Green, by James McNeill Whistler, c1872–4.

Below: Peace – Burial at Sea, JMW Turner, 1842.

Tate Modern (Bankside), SE1, 691 F5, Opened in May 2000, within a year this had become the world's most popular museum of modern art. Purists were not too sure – juxtapositions such as Claude Monet with Richard Long, or Georges Braque with Michael Craig-Martin did not, they felt, reveal enough about the chronological development and context of international modernism – but the public loved it. The huge building at Bankside – half vast, echoing space, half 50-or-so intricately connected galleries and reading spaces – became an instant, giant, object of affection. A one-time power station, it is a beacon example of recycling.

Giles Gilbert Scott designed the oil-fired Bankside Power Station in 1947. It was completed in 1963 and opened by Queen Elizabeth II. The great central chimney was limited to a height of 325 feet (100m) so as not to exceed the dome of St Paul's Cathedral* immediately across the river. The colossal turbine hall, 500 feet (150m) long and 115 feet (35m) high, ran right through the building. The power station was decommissioned in 1981 and in 1994 the building was acquired by the Tate. Swiss architects Herzog and de Meuron were appointed to design a conversion that respected Gilbert Scott's original design. The only major addition to the severely refined brick exterior is the discreet two-storey glass structure (known as the 'light beam') on the roof, while inside, the turbine hall retains its length and vastness. The displays are organized in four themed groups, each spanning a century and occupying a suite of galleries. Four traditional art categories – landscape, still life, the nude, and history painting – are expanded into four portmanteau headings: Landscape/Matter/ Environment, Still Life/Object/Real Life, History/Memory/Society and Nude/Action/Body.

Below left: *Death Hope Life Fear*, by Gilbert and George, 1984.

Below: *The Snail*, by Henri Matisse. In old age, when he was too ill to paint, Matisse assembled large-scale wor by cutting or tearing shape from painted paper.

The Thames

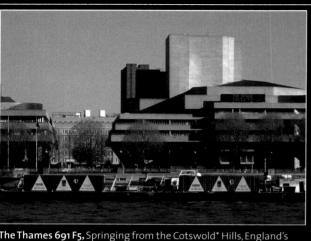

The Thames 691 F5, Springing from the Cotswold* Hills, England's longest river has flowed past Oxford*, Henley*, Eton* and Windsor* by the time it reaches London. From Hampton Court* the river curves to Kingston which, until 1750, boasted the first bridge up-river from London Bridge. After Teddington, a long bend leads to Eel Pie Island, hedonistic home of jazz and rock gigs in the beatnik 1950s and hippy 1960s. Past Marble Hill House*, under the bridges of Richmond* and Twickenham, the river reaches Syon Park*, the Royal Botanic Gardens at Kew* then Chiswick* bridge, the finishing point of the Oxford and Cambridge boat race. After Hammersmith's decorative suspension bridge, it approaches the Wetland Centre* at Barnes, then Putney Bridge, start of the Boat Race. An earlier wooden Battersea Bridge – mistily painted and etched by Whistler – was replaced by the present cast-iron structure in 1890. Albert Bridge, just beyond, with its beautiful web-like design by Rowland Ordish, was opened in 1873 and at night is one of London's most brilliant pieces of illumination. Then the river reaches the clean lines of Chelsea Bridge (opened 1934).

Vauxhall Bridge of 1906 has heroic bronze statues on its piers, representing the Arts and Sciences. Lambeth Bridge is on the site of an old horse ferry – closed in 1750. Before the embankments were built, this was one of the few places shallow enough for a coach and horses to cross.

The present Westminster Bridge, cast iron with seven arches, was opened in 1862, replacing a masonry one of 1750 on which no dogs had been allowed and graffiti culprits were threatened with death.

In several Claude Monet paintings, John Rennie's classical Waterloo Bridge (opened on the second anniversary of the Battle of Waterloo) gleams against a murky riverscape; he worked from a suite in the nearby Savoy Hotel*. The present bridge, built 1937–42, was designed by Giles Gilbert Scott and is of less noble design, but it offers wonderful views of Westminster and the City. Blackfriars Bridge, with its five cast-iron arches, and the immediately adjacent railway bridge (demolished except for its magnificent pillars and insignia) were built by Joseph Cubitt in the 1860s; the second, operative, railway bridge was erected in the 1880s.

The elegant low-dip suspension Millennium Bridge by architect Norman Foster and sculptor Anthony Caro, which links St Paul's* and the City to the Tate Modern*, is the first new span across the Thames in central London for 100 years.

From 1422 to 1856 the Lord Mayor's Show was partly staged on water, and fantastically ornate barges – some gilded and with silver oars – staged dramas and musical pageants as they sailed up-river from the City to Westminster*.

After Southwark Bridge comes London Bridge, until 1729 the city's only span across the Thames. It has been rebuilt many times, the first stone bridge having 19 arches and from 1201 a narrow street of over-hanging shops and houses – removed after 1758 for a widening scheme. John Rennie's 1820s bridge now crosses Lake Havasu in Arizona. The present (1972) bridge is the dullest to date. HMS *Belfast* built in 1939 and the largest Royal Naval cruiser ever, is moored opposite the Tower of London* and has been a floating museum since 1971.

Tower Bridge was opened in 1894; its gothic profile, looking like two Scottish castles, is nowadays more famous than the ancient Tower it echoes and overshadows. Described by architect Horace Jones as 'steel skeletons clothed in stone', the turrets house equipment to lift two 1,200-ton bascules (French for 'seesaw') and let ships into the Pool of London. The high-level footbridge, now glassed-in as part of the Tower Bridge Experience museum, gives superb views across London and beyond.

The river now begins its great S-sweep through the docklands, once the heart of London's trading. Rounding the northern part of Greenwich* the mighty Thames Barrier lies ahead. Best seen by boat, this exciting engineering feat, completed in 1984, freed Londoners from the fear of flooding. When perilous tides threaten, the barrier's 10 gates, pivoting from their normal position flat on the river bed, swing up to 6 feet (1.8m) above the level reached by the great surge of 1953. Thus the River Thames remains safely within its banks, and continues to be London's greatest resource.

Top left: The South Bank, part of the arts complex including the Royal National Theatre.

Top right: Westminster Bridge, built by Victorian architect-engineer Thomas Page.

Above: The Millennium Bridge, opened in 2002, runs from Tate Modern to St Paul's Cathedral.

Opposite page: Tower Bridge, whose design was chosen from over 50 submissions. Since 1976 it has been operated by oil and electricity rather than steam.

Theatre Museum, WC2, 691 F5, The Russell Street museum in Covent Garden* focuses on the history of all the performing arts – drama, opera, ballet, music hall, rock, pop, pantomime and circus – through playbills, programmes, props, costumes and fragments of lost venues. Productions are staged in a small theatre, and there are performance-related demonstrations and temporary exhibitions.

Theatre Royal Drury Lane, WC2, 691 F5, Nell Gwynne, mistress of Charles II, acted in the first theatre on this Drury Lane site when it was one of only two London venues where drama could legally be staged. Three successive buildings burned down, including one designed by Christopher Wren. The present theatre, by Benjamin Wyatt, opened in 1812.

Theatre Royal Haymarket, SW1, 691 F5, Oscar Wilde's *A Woman of No Importance* and *An Ideal Husband* had their premières here. The exterior is as designed by John Nash in 1821 though the interior has been refashioned several times. It was completely refurbished in 1994, with the application of much gold leaf.

Tower of London, EC3, 691 F5, The 900-year-old Tower has been a fortress, jail, torture chamber and place of execution for those who entered by boat through Traitors' Gate. Although a medieval palace was founded by Henry III in 1220, and high-ranking prisoners enjoyed comfortable confinement in Beachamp Tower, most inmates suffered terribly. Even royal status was no guarantee of protection – the Bloody Tower is linked to two boy princes, Edward V and his brother, who vanished in 1483

Top left and bottom: The Tower of London has 20 towers in all, the oldest being the White Tower – the first stone keep in England. The last state prisoner held in the Tower – for five days in 1941 – was Rudolf Hess, Hitler's deputy.

Top right: Theatre Royal, Haymarket, said to be haunted by the ghost of its Victorian manager, JB Buckstone.

(skeletons were found nearby in 1674). The Crown Jewels were first moved here for safety in 1303. They were sold or melted down by Cromwell, and the present ones are the priceless regalia used at royal coronations and other state occasions since 1661. A moving walkway takes visitors around cases of swords, rings, orbs, sceptres and 12 crowns. St Edward's Crown is the oldest, and the Imperial State Crown made for Queen Victoria the most opulent (with 2,800 diamonds, the Black Prince's Ruby, the Stuart Sapphire, and pearls worn by Elizabeth I). The legendary Koh-i-Noor or Mountain of Light diamond, set in the Queen Mother's crown, is said to bring bad luck to men. The ancient security drill of the Ceremony of the Keys still takes place each night (an attempt to

steal the Crown Jewels was made by Colonel Blood in 1671, but Charles II, instead of imprisoning the culprit, was so taken by his Irish charm that he gave him estates and a pension).

Legend has it that if the ravens ever desert the Tower the kingdom will fall – so a small colony of wing-clipped birds is tended by one of the 40 resident Yeoman Warders (dressed in distinctive uniforms and dubbed 'Beefeaters'). The cliff-like White Tower of 1097 was London's tallest building. This displays a selection of sporting and tournament equipment, suits of armour, cannons, swords, pistols and early machine guns from the Royal Armouries.

Trafalgar Square, wc2/sw1, 691 F5, Conceived by John Nash and constructed by Charles Barry between 1829 and 1841, the Square recalls the 1805 battle and its hero and casualty Admiral Lord Nelson. He gazes with one good eye from a 165-foot (50m) column, guarded by four 1860s lions by Edwin Landseer. The square is popular with protesters, New Year's Eve revellers and pigeons and is overlooked by the National Gallery*.

Twinings Shop, wc2, 691 F5, Tea has been sold at this shop on the Strand (No. 216) since 1706 – the doorway with two Chinese figures and a golden lion dates from 1787. A museum at the back of the shop outlines the Twining Company's history.

Trafalgar Square

Right: A 17-foot (5m) statue of Nelson by EH Baily stands on top of William Railton's monument.

Bottom: The fountains were installed as an afterthought by Barry in 1845 and later remodelled by Lutyens as memorials to World War I admirals, Jellicoe and Beatty.

Below: Twinings Shop on the Strand.

successfully transformed the presentation of the most comprehensive collection of British art and design. The Spiral, a daring extension by architect Daniel Libeskind and engineer Cecil Balmond, is planned to display contemporary work. The V&A has the national collections of furniture, sculpture, glass, ceramics, watercolours (including many lovely Constables), portrait miniatures and photography, and houses the National Art Library. There are fabulous holdings of artefacts and art from all over the world, given by the French widow of Sir Richard Wallace, including the Far East, India and Southeast Asia, together with the finest collection of Italian Renaissance sculpture outside Italy.

Victoria Tower Gardens, sw1, 691 F5, A green breathing space overlooking the river at Millbank, between the Houses of Parliament* and Lambeth Bridge. A marvellous Rodin bronze, *The Burghers of Calais,*

Victoria and Albert Museum, sw7, 691 F5, Built from the profits of the 1851 Great Exhibition, the Museum of Manufactures was renamed by Queen Victoria in memory of Prince Albert in 1899. Laying the foundation stone of Sir Aston Webb's building was her last public appearance. Controlling the compass and size of the V&A's collections was not initially a priority, and for some time the museum has battled to select and present its almost infinite cornucopia of riches appropriately for a modern audience. The 2001 redesign of the British Galleries (1500–1900) has

Above: Victoria and Albert Museum, the Italian Cast Court.

Right: Wallace Collection, *The Laughing Cavalier,* by Frans Hals, 1624.

stands here; also a statue of the militant suffragette Emmeline Pankhurst, by AG Walker. **Vincent Square, SW1, 691 F5,** Built on the old bear gardens of Tothill Fields, a few of the original 18th-century houses remain. The Royal Horticultural Society's headquarters is here in the Old Hall (1904), which houses the Lindley Library, arguably the most impressive collection of horticultural books in the world.

Wallace Collection, W1, 691 F5, This sublime collection, now in Manchester Square, was amassed by four generations of the Hertford family and given to the nation in 1897. Exceptional Sèvres porcelain, clocks, furniture, armour, sculpture and paintings spill through 25 galleries. Old Master highlights include Frans Hals' *Laughing Cavalier*, Rembrandt's poignant portrait of his son Titus and Nicolas Poussin's *Dance to the Music of Time*. The range of 18th-century French pictures (by Watteau, Boucher, Fragonard and others) rivals that in the Louvre. The central courtyard has recently been covered, creating one of the most elegant restaurants in London.

Wellcome Library, NW1, 691 F5, Founded on the collections of manufacturing chemist Henry Wellcome (1853–1936), the immensely wide-ranging medical library housed at 183 Euston Road has around 600,000 volumes – 70,000 of which are on open access – and 7,000 journals. The most ancient document in its Oriental archive is a papyrus prescription of c11,000 BC. Prints, drawings, photographs, films and paintings charting the history of medicine and related fields are also kept here.

Wesley's Chapel, SE1 691 F5, The 'Methodists' Cathedral' in City Road, with ship-mast columns and a beautiful austerity, was consecrated by its founder John Wesley in 1778. He lived next door for his last 11 years – many of his personal effects are now on display – and is buried behind the chapel. A crypt museum outlines the history of Methodism (note the electric-shock machine which Wesley used to treat cases of depression).

Westminster Abbey, sw1, 691 F5, Since William the Conqueror's coronation in the new abbey church on Christmas Day 1066, every monarch (apart from Edwards V and VIII, who were never crowned at all) has been crowned at Westminster. Edward the Confessor, last of the Anglo-Saxon kings, restored the already substantial Benedictine monastery at Westminster but on 28 December 1065 he was too sick to attend the consecration of his new church, and died eight days later. Nothing remains of that church (though traces were uncovered in the 19th century), but it is depicted in the Bayeux Tapestry as a cruciform structure with central tower and lead roof.

Edward was canonized in 1161, and in 1245 Henry III decided to honour the saintly king by demolishing his church and building a much grander one. It was the age of great gothic cathedrals, and the king and his master mason, Henry of Reyns, drew on examples in France, making the nave 103 feet (31m) high, far the loftiest in England. Edward's body was moved to a magnificent shrine in the chapel behind the high altar, and the Abbey became the favoured resting place for royalty.

Great commoners were first buried here during the reign of Richard II. When Henry III died in 1272, one bay of the nave, the transepts, the choir, rose windows, parts of the cloisters and the Chapterhouse had been completed at his expense. He was buried before the high altar, and building did not fully recommence for 100 years, when Richard II provided funds. His master-mason, Henry de Yevele, followed the original design, but the great nave was not finally completed until the early 16th century during the reign of Henry VII. He endowed the glorious Lady Chapel, which bears his name and houses his tomb – a magnificent work designed by Pietro Torrigiano. The exquisite fan vaulting in the chapel has been described as having 'the airy security of a cobweb'.

Left: West front, Lady Chapel.
Top right: Henry VII Chapel.
Below: Tomb of Queen Elizabeth I.

north transept are early 18th century, and the rest dates from the 19th and 20th centuries. Among the queens buried here are Edward I's Queen Eleanor of Castile, Catherine de Valois (Henry V's wife) whose embalmed body lay in an open tomb for 300 years, and Elizabeth I.

Following the Dissolution of the Monasteries and the Reformation, Elizabeth I re-founded the Abbey as a Collegiate Church, a Royal Peculiar not subject to the rule of any bishop. Oliver Cromwell was buried here, but at the Restoration his body was disinterred and hanged at Tyburn. Christopher Wren undertook renovation work between 1698 and 1723, and Nicholas Hawksmoor designed the two splendid west front towers, built from 1734 to 1745.

Unfortunately very little remains of the Abbey's glorious medieval stained glass. The great west window and the rose window in the

Poets' Corner began as a corner containing Chaucer's tomb, but then spread throughout the south transept and includes memorials to countless writers, including Dryden, Samuel Johnson, Tennyson, Dickens, Browning, Thomas Hardy, Henry James and TS Eliot. Byron's white marble tablet was not installed until 145 years after his death because 'the open profligacy of his life proved an obstacle to his commemoration'. Others remembered include Isaac Newton, Robert Adam, David Livingstone and Henry Irving. The last person buried in the Abbey was the philanthropist Angela Burdett-Coutts in 1906, since when only ashes have been allowed. The most visited tomb is that of the Unknown Warrior, whose body was brought back from France after World War I.

English Heritage runs the Abbey's octagonal 13th-century Chapterhouse, with original sculpture and floor tiles still intact, and the Pyx Chamber museum, with amazing wood and wax effigies of notable figures from medieval monarchs to Nelson. An arch near the Abbey's west door leads into the peaceful square of Dean's Yard and the entrance to Westminster School, whose old boys include Ben Jonson and Christopher Wren.

Westminster Cathedral, sw1, 691 F5, John Francis Bentley's neo-Byzantine building for the Catholic diocese of Westminster was completed on this former prison site in 1903. Constructed in brick with contrasting bands of Portland stone, it has a striking campanile, 273 feet (83m) high, dedicated to Edward the Confessor. The single bell is inscribed 'St Edward, pray for England'. The rich interior is decorated with over 100 different kinds of marble and brilliant mosaics. On the piers of the nave are Eric Gill's bas-reliefs of the Fourteen Stations of the Cross, completed by the controversial sculptor during World War I.

Westminster Central Hall, sw1, 691 F5, A flamboyant example of Beaux-Arts style by Lanchester and Rickards, belying its 1911 origins as Storey Gate's Methodist hall. The first General Assembly of the United Nations was held here in 1946.

Wetland Centre, sw13, 691 F5, Obsolete Victorian reservoirs were removed to create this 150-acre (60ha) wildlife habitat off Elisabeth Walk, opened in 2000 and designed to make nature accessible

Above: Westminster Cathedral, where Mass is sung daily by an outstanding choir.
Right: A carved entrance.

Far right: Whitechapel Art Gallery recently celebrated its centenary as a centre for modern art.

Below: Whitehall, Dover House, the seat of the Scottish Office. Originally designed for Sir Matthew Fetherstonhaugh, the circular entrance hall and portico were added by Henry Holland for the Duke of York.

(easy pathways and instructional viewing spots) without disturbing creatures or plants. There are examples of wetland habitats from tundra to billabong, and a deep-water lagoon for fish-eating birds. Indoor facilities include CCTV for a closer look at the secret worlds of waterfowl.

Whitechapel Art Gallery, E1, 691 F5, Founded to bring good art to the East End, the gallery has always specialized in contemporary work and enjoys an international reputation. Built in 1897–9, C Harrison Townsend's Art Nouveau design provides a very sympathetic, airy exhibiting space. The mosaic over the door is by Walter Crane.

Whitehall, sw1, 691 F5, This route from Charing Cross to Westminster is now principally occupied by ministries and other government offices. The Banqueting House* is all that survives of the old Whitehall Palace. The 1844 Treasury building by Charles Barry retains the columns and frieze of its predecessor by John Soane. Its interior was reconstructed in the 1960s, uncovering remains of the old Palace, including the walls of Henry VIII's tennis courts. Any road rage caused by traffic jams in this thoroughfare is nothing new: Samuel Pepys, writing in his diary in 1660, recorded that a 'great stop of coaches' caused 'a falling out between a drayman and my Lord Chesterfield's

coachman, and one of his footmen killed'. The Cenotaph* and Horse Guards Parade* are here.

Wigmore Hall, W1, 691 F5, This much-loved, Renaissance-style concert venue in Wigmore Street was built in 1901 by the German piano firm Bechstein, whose showroom was next door. Designed by Thomas Collcutt, using alabaster and marble in the interior, its celebrated acoustics have attracted great artists and composers such as Schnabel, Schwarzkopf, Segovia, Poulenc, Britten and du Pré. World War I caused the closure of the Bechstein business and the Hall was sold. It reopened in 1917, and became a favourite venue for debuts as well as major recitals. It now presents 400 concerts a year. In the cupola over the stage, a highly symbolic painting by Frank Lynn Jenkins depicts the Soul of Music gazing at the Genius of Harmony, while mere mortals strive to grasp the abstract elusiveness of music's beauty.

William Morris Museum, E17, 691 F5, In its extensive garden setting (now Lloyd Park), this 18th-century Water House in Forest Road was the elegant early home of the artist, writer, designer, craftsman and social reformer William Morris (1834–96). (He died, it was said, 'having done more work than most ten men'.) The fields in which he found inspiration have been engulfed by Walthamstow (whose old church is well worth visiting for its monuments), but the house cherishes his achievements and those of the Arts and Crafts movement. Exhibits include the Kelmscott Chaucer, the Woodpecker Tapestry, the medieval 'props' for the Pre-Raphaelite murals at the Oxford Union, plus Mackmurdo furniture, tiles

Above: View of Whitehall from Richmond House, by Canaletto.

Below left: William Morris's Woodpecker Tapestry, woven by Morris & Co in 1885.

Below: 2 Willow Road, a rare surviving example of modern movement domestic architecture complete with contemporary furnishings.

by de Morgan, Burne-Jones stained glass, and pottery by the Martin brothers. The Frank Brangwyn Collection adds 19th- and early-20th-century paintings. The Museum was appropriately opened by Prime Minister Clement Attlee in 1950 – the satchel in which Morris carried his Socialist pamphlets is one of the exhibits.

2 Willow Road, NW3, 691 F5, Modernist architect and high-rise enthusiast Ernö Goldfinger (1902–87) built a set of three terrace houses in 1939, and he and his artist wife, Ursula Blackwell, lived in this, the centre one. After their deaths the house was acquired by the National Trust in order to preserve an excellent example of intact domestic Modernism, with original fitted furniture (such as the dining-table supported on an industrial-lathe base) and personal effects. An engaging video establishes the history of the house and its occupants. There are artworks by Henry Moore and Max Ernst (Hungarian-born Goldfinger trained in Paris and associated with the Surrealists).

Wimbledon, SW19, 691 F5, Synonymous worldwide with 'tennis'. The Wimbledon Championships take up only a fortnight each summer, but the Wimbledon Lawn Tennis Museum is open during the rest of the year. Situated in the All England Lawn Tennis Club in Church Road, it has views over Centre Court and traces the history of tennis from the 1860s to the present day. Exhibits include tennis clothing, equipment, trophies and videos of 'tennis greats' in action. Wimbledon Village was a settlement in medieval times. On the High Street, Eagle House – built by Robert Bell, one of the founders of the East India Company – and the adjacent Rose & Crown date from the 17th century. The 1,140 acres (460ha) of Wimbledon Common are unfenced and contain much varied wildlife, as well as sports facilities, horse rides and a handsome, restored 1817 windmill.

Top left : Long Melford, the magnificent 15th-century interior of Holy Trinity Church, paid for by wealthy wool merchants.

Long Melford, Melford Hall Top right: The Library added by Thomas Hopper.

Centre right: The ambitious Elizabethan mansion built by Sir William Cordell, Master of the Rolls, with a distinctive skyline of pepperpot corner turrets.

London Colney, Herts 691 F4, All Saints Pastoral Centre is a rambling neo-Tudor building of 1899 by Leonard Stokes, of a similar style to his later work at Emmanuel College, Cambridge*.

Long Crendon, Bucks 690 D4, A large and attractive village, formerly known for its needle-making, which retains a number of good medieval buildings, many of cruck construction. The 15th-century Court House [NT] in the High Street is particularly impressive, with a jettied upper floor over a stone base. The upper chamber was used as a manorial courtroom from the reign of Henry V until the 19th century.

Above: Long Crendon.

Below: Longleat, with its park stretching away around the house.

Long Meg, Cumb 696 E3, At Glassonby, on the way up the high Pennines from Penrith*, is a single standing stone known as Long Meg, related to a larger oval of 59 stones, known as 'her daughters'. Not far away, Little Meg is a circle of 11 standing stones.

Long Melford, Suffk 691 H3, The medieval cloth trade paid for two great Tudor mansions and another majestic wool church. A 3-mile (4.8km) long Georgian and Tudor main street, now crammed with antique shops, gives way to a broad northern green leading to the hilltop church and Elizabethan almshouses. Holy Trinity is a Suffolk Perpendicular gem – with majestic walls of stone and flint flushwork and beautiful 15th-century stained glass featuring pious kneeling figures of Suffolk worthies and its chief benefactors, the Cloptons of Kentwell Hall. Melford Hall looks much as it did when William Cordell moved here in 1578. Six octagonal towers with pepperpot roofs rise above the roadside wall to preside over the green and a beautiful octagonal Tudor pavilion. Inside, visitors can admire the panelled Banqueting Hall, Regency Library and a display of watercolours by former guest Beatrix Potter. Moated red-brick Kentwell Hall, begun in the 1550s, and more modestly placed at the end of a long lime avenue, has a brickwork maze

in the form of a Tudor rose and regular 'historical re-creations' are staged.

Long Mynd, Shrops 693 G4, A ridge that rises abruptly to the southwest of Shrewsbury: open, wild and barren, with rocks and mountain pasture but with rich and fertile valleys folded away among the hills. Tucked into the western side of the Mynd is Church Stretton*, very much a Victorian hillside resort, from where a lane leads to Carding Mill Valley with its spectacular scenery and challenging walks.

Long Wittenham, Oxon 690 D4, A Norman church with Jacobean fittings, font case and cover, pulpit, stalls and screen in the south transept, the latter two from Exeter College, Oxford*. A curious detail is the miniature effigy of a knight, which forms the front of the basin of the piscina.

Longleat, Wilts 690 B6, In the west of the county, as it borders Somerset, is both the great Elizabethan house of Longleat, seat of the Marquess of Bath, and the landscaped park created at Stourhead* for Henry Hoare. Longleat, the first stately home to be opened on a commercial basis (in 1949), is set in a park of 900 acres (365ha) landscaped by Capability Brown. The house was built for Sir John Thynne and was more or less complete by 1580. In the Entrance Hall the standard is set by the great canvases of hunting scenes by John Wootton; the rest of the house is largely Victorianized, the work of JD Crace and Co. in the 1860s.

Longthorpe Tower, Cambs 695 F5, The remains of a fortified manor house, almost lost in Peterborough's suburban overspill. Its Great Chamber contains the finest 14th-century domestic wall-paintings in northern Europe, depicting the Labours of the

Above: Longthorpe Tower.

Top right: Longtown Castle has an impressive display of secular murals depicting popular medieval morality subjects.

Below: Long Mynd, one of the steep-sided valleys.

Months and popular morality subjects – the Five Senses and Seven Ages of Man [EH].

Longtown Castle, Herefs 693 F6, One of several lonely border castles in this area, but this is unusual in having a perfectly cylindrical keep. The walls are an impressive 15 feet (4.5m) thick [EH].

Longworth, Oxon 690 D4, The church of St Mary contains good Arts and Crafts fittings. The reredos paintings are by Kate Bunce and the metal frames by her sister. Most striking is the stained-glass window by Heywood Summer, 1900, showing Christ on the Cross.

Looe, Cnwll 688 E7, East and West Looe are joined by a 13-arched bridge, built in 1856. Now a popular holiday resort, this former fishing port rose in prosperity when copper from mines on Caradon Hill was brought down to the Buller, or Copper, Quay on the east bank. The grist mill opposite was established by Thomas Arundell of Trerice* who took a 600-year lease on the site in 1614. The earliest house in the town was built in 1456; most of the old fishermen's houses are approached up steps, with the basements used as a storage area for their nets. The Banjo Pier, now a favourite promenade, was built about 1850, with the circular end added in 1898 to prevent sand from entering the tidal Looe River.

Loose, Kent 691 H6, A picturesque village, with old cottages and numerous little streams. (Its Women's Institute is a favourite English joke, almost as old as the village.)

Lopen, Somset 689 H5, About 2 to 3 miles (3 to 5km) from Barrington, in a little village called Lopen, they have just announced the discovery of a Roman villa with a mosaic floor of international importance (very rare in its use of red, black and white, in its state of preservation, and in its depiction of dolphins).

Loseley House, Surrey, Just south of Guildford is this outstanding house, built for Sir William More in 1561–9. The setting is magnificent, with parkland, a walled garden and a huge cedar of Lebanon. The Great Hall contains the so-called Nonesuch Fittings, supposedly taken from the great Tudor palace demolished in the 1680s. Other treasures include King George IV's coronation chair and an overmantel dated 1570, traditionally made from one of Elizabeth I's travelling cases. *See* **Guildford* 690 E6.**

Lostwithiel, Cnwll 688 D7, A delightful small market town, with the remains of the medieval Duchy Palace down by the river, which was navigable to this point in the Middle Ages. Across the road is the Church of St Bartholomew, patron saint of tanners and of the sick. Its unusual Breton-style spire is inspired by Cornwall's close links with its Celtic neighbour across the Channel. Lostwithiel is one of the ancient Stannary towns; here an independent body or 'parliament' regulated the important tin trade and the activities of the numerous tinners in the area.

Lotherton Hall, W York 697 H6, This Victorian country house at Aberford is now a museum, containing fine collections of oriental art, fashion, 19th-century decorative art and modern craft and design. There is also an Edwardian garden.

Louth, Lincs 695 F3, An utterly delightful small town, tucked away beyond the Lincolnshire Wolds. This range of low wooded hills provides welcome relief from the flat fields of sugar beet that are typical of east Lincolnshire. Louth is mainly Georgian in character, but the church of St James dates principally from the 15th century. Its tall slender spire was completed in 1515.

Lower Kingswood, Surrey 691 F6, In 1892 two archeologists, Edwin Freshfield and Sir Henry Bonsor, endowed their parish with a highly original Byzantine-style church designed by Sidney Barnsley. The inspiration for the tower came from an example in Bulgaria. The chancel apse of coloured marbles and a gold-leaf mosaic dominates the interior.

Above: Loseley House, the picturesque Tudor north front with its many gables.

Left and bottom: Lotherton Hall, the former home of the Gascoigne family, contains fine paintings and furniture.

Right: Lowther Castle, built 1806–11 and deliberately unroofed in 1957.

Lowfield Heath, W Susx 691 F6, The charming church of 1867 is by William Burges.

Lowther Castle, Cumb 696 E3, Outside Penrith*, this was the work of Sir Robert Smirke for the first Earl of Lonsdale in 1806-11. The huge castellated palace is classical in composition but gothic in detail,

with battlements and turrets. In 1957 the house was deliberately unroofed to avoid tax and now stands as one of England's most impressive ruins, a landscape feature tended by grazing sheep. Nearby Lowther Village is an interesting estate village, planned by the Adam brothers in 1766 for Sir James Lowther, and only partly carried out. There are two rectangular closes of houses and at one end a crescent of workers' cottages, following in layout if not in detail the ideas of fashionable Bath*. This had been intended to be a full circus of houses but only half was completed.

Luddesdown Court, Kent 691 G5, A very early, almost unique, house, possibly dating from the 12th century. It has a first-floor hall which contains a fireplace, another rarity for the period. The windows are very small.

Ludham, Norfk 695 J5, An attractive Broadland village with its own dragon legend and a notable church. An eye-catching tympanum in the chancel arch has a 15th-century painted crucifixion and below it the rood screen, another East Anglian masterpiece of medieval woodwork and religious art, with 12 beautifully painted saints and kings wrapped in ermine, and a rare depiction of St Walstan, the Norfolk farmer-saint. Three miles (4.8m) south beside the Bure are the remains of St Benet's Abbey with a ruined windmill rising from the gatehouse, once a favourite subject for Norwich School artists. How Hill, local architect Boardman's Edwardian residence, now a Field Study Centre, stands above the River Ant. It has restored wind pumps, a marshman's cottage museum and extensive reed beds, demonstrating traditionally managed Norfolk Broads* landscape at its most evocative.

Ludlow

Ludlow, Shrops 693 G5, For years an unspoilt little market town which, despite new-found popularity, still retains its charm. Its 20th-century reputation was established through AE Housman's volume of poems, *A Shropshire Lad,* and more recently the town has become known for its cultural events and excellent restaurants. All this belies the fact that Ludlow in the Middle Ages was a place of enormous importance, with a massively strong castle which was the seat of government for the Marches, the lawless country along the border of England and Wales.

Left: Ludlow Castle, with its large outer courtyard. Much of the building still stands.

Below: Feathers Inn, one of the finest Jacobean buildings in the country.

The town's hilltop site ensured that the castle and the red sandstone tower of the church of **St Lawrence** could be seen for miles. The great height of the church tower and the large size of the church itself are a clear demonstration that medieval Ludlow was rich as well as powerful; the wealth came mostly from the wool trade. While there was certainly a church on the site in Norman times, the present building is largely 15th-century. Housman is commemorated in the churchyard.

Near the church and the pretty market place are the impressive ruins of **Ludlow Castle** which was built by Roger de Lacy c1090 to control the Welsh. In the 14th century, Roger Mortimer converted it into a palace and in the 15th century it became the seat of the Lord President of Wales. Most of the walls survive, including those of a highly unusual circular chapel which probably dates from about 1140. It has a large outer courtyard where townspeople could take shelter in the event of an attack. In summer, it is used as an open-air theatre.

The town outside the castle walls was laid out with the main streets, connected by narrow cross lanes, running down the hill to the River Teme. The best of the wider streets is Broad Street, lined with attractive houses and closed at the bottom end by Broad Gaters. There are many examples in Ludlow of black-and-white timber-framed buildings, notably the famous Feathers Inn in Bull Ring. Altogether, there are almost 500 listed buildings in the town.

Lullingstone Castle, Kent 691 G5, Tudor in origin, with its two-storeyed Hall and a lavish state Drawing Room, the house was largely rebuilt under Queen Anne. The charming little parish church in the grounds is medieval, but was 'beautified' in the 18th century; it has some outstanding monuments. The **Roman Villa** of Lullingstone [EH], excavated in the 1950s, dates from the 1st to the 4th centuries AD and is chiefly notable for its mosaic floor depicting the Rape of Europa. It also includes a Christian chapel, virtually the only surviving evidence of Christianity in Britain during the Roman period.

Lulworth Castle, Dorset 690 B8, Close to the coast is this castellated country house. After a long history of in-fighting among the Howard family, Thomas Howard, the 3rd Lord Bindon, acquired the estate of Lulworth in 1600. Lord Salisbury at Cranborne* gave him the idea of building a house there, and by 1610 it was habitable. But Bindon's death and subsequent problems led to its sale in 1641 to Humphrey Weld. This amazing house, with its compact plan and four corner towers, still remains in the family's possession. It is open to the public although still undergoing restoration by English Heritage after

Above: Lullingstone Roman Villa mosaic floor, detail showing Autumn, a mature woman with corn and straw in her hair.

Right: Lundy Island lighthouse. The old light built in 1819 stands 567 feet (173m) above sea level. Its role was taken over by other lighthouses at either tip of the island in 1897.

Left, above and below: Lulworth Castle.

Below: Lundy Island seen from Hartland Point, about 12 miles (19km) across the Bristol Channel.

a fire in 1929. In the grounds are two churches: the serene Catholic chapel (St Mary) of the Weld family, and the parish church of East Lulworth (St Andrew).

Lundy Island, Devon 688 D4, This 3-mile-long (4.8km) island has a remote and windswept character. There are lighthouses at either end, and a church built in 1896 by the owner and aptly named incumbent, the Reverend HG Heaven, near the Castle at the southern end. In the middle of the 18th century Thomas Benson, the notorious

MP for Barnstaple, illegally landed convicts bound for Virginia here, and made them build walls across the island in an attempt to establish agriculture. This venture failed, and the island is now home to large flocks of Soay sheep, Sika deer and black rabbits. It is administered by the Landmark Trust.

Luton, Beds 691 F3, The county's largest town was once known for its straw-plait and hat-making. Its main church, St Mary's, has Norman origins, although its setting is now quite modern. Note the font of c1330–40 with fine canopy, the Easter Sepulchre, and Hoo and Wenlock chapels. In George Street West are the last remaining handsome town houses of the 19th-century plait masters. One of the best buildings is the Union Chapel, 1836–44, with its Greek Doric portico, now sadly divided into flats. The Luton Museum and Art Gallery is housed in a Victorian mansion of 1875 set in Wardown Park. Also run by the Council are Stockwood Period Gardens on Farley Hill. The town has two water-towers, one of which – the West Hill Road Water Tower – was designed in the Arts and Crafts style.

Luxulyan, Cnwll 688 D7, Developed by Joseph Treffry of Place, Fowey*. The monumental 100-foot (30m) high Treffry aqueduct bridges this narrow and luxuriant valley; designed by James Palmer and built in 1839 at a cost of £7,000, it also has a track for a mineral railway. It is 660 feet (200m) long and has ten arches, each 40 feet (12m) across. The railway connected the north and south coasts of the county and the water from the aqueduct, which lay beneath the railway track, flowed towards the south where it powered machinery to crush the china clay from Treffry's quarries. Built of superb granite, it has the family arms at its centre. This finely grained pink and black spotted

Top: Luton, the flint and stone chequerwork at St Mary's Church.

Above left: Lydford Gorge, now under the ownership of the National Trust.

Above right: Luxulyan, the Tretty viaduct built in 1839.

Bottom: Lyddington Bede House, originally a medieval palace and now an almshouse.

stone, quarried in the parish and known as Luxulyanite, was used for the sarcophagus of the Duke of Wellington in St Paul's Cathedral*.

Lydd, Kent 691 H7, The church is grand in scale, reflecting the importance of the area when Romney was one of the Cinque Ports (along with Hastings, Hythe, Dover and Sandwich). The nave is of the 13th century, the chancel rebuilt in 1958 after war damage. Inside there are traces of the earlier Anglo-Saxon church. The tower, unusually splendid for Kent, dates from 1442–6.

Lyddington, Rutlnd 694 E5, In this village just south of Uppingham* is the Bede House, built in the 15th

century as a palace for the Bishop of Lincoln and then converted into an almshouse, or bedehouse, for old men [EH].

Lydford, Devon 688 E6, One of the four Dartmoor Stannary towns (where tin was mined and worked). Lynford has a castle [EH] whose keep was built in 1195 and for centuries afterwards was feared as a prison for those who transgressed the harsh laws of the Royal Forest of Dartmoor*. The little village lies above the rushing waters of the River Lyd, which passes through a very dramatic 80-foot (24m) gorge viewed from narrow precipitous paths cut into the cliffs.

Lydiard Tregoze, Wilts 690 C5, Four miles (6.4km) west of Swindon* is Wiltshire's best-kept secret: the ancestral home of the Bolingbrokes, built in the late 1740s. The house has interior decoration partly in the style of William Kent, and partly 1750s rococo. Immediately behind it is the church of St Mary, rich with monuments; it has a wonderful chancel ceiling of about 1633, painted

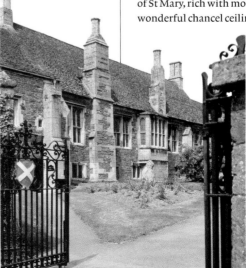

blue with stars, and a rich wrought-iron communion rail. On the monument of Sir Giles and Lady Mompesson of 1633, the stone figures sit facing one another under arches, apparently in conversation. She has a skull on her lap. There is also the tomb by Rysbrack of the Viscount St John (d. 1749) for whom the house was built. The park, with its rolling acres, is Swindon's lung.

Lyme Park, Ches 693 H1, A large and splendid stone
building, partly 16th-, partly 18th-century, with
some impressive rooms [NT]. The Tudor house of
Sir Piers Legh is still standing, but is hardly visible
because it was all refaced in stone by the architect
Giacomo Leoni in 1725 when he was called in to
modernize it. He added the west side and refaced
the courtyard walls to look like an Italian palace.
The square tower was built in 1816 to house the
servants. Some of the rooms inside are Tudor, some
early Georgian, and there are important collections
of portraits (many lent by the National Portrait
Gallery*) and English clocks. The garden has a
splendid conservatory and the deer park is
enormous, with a windswept tower called The Cage,
also rebuilt by Leoni, from which to observe them.

Lyme Regis, Dorset 689 H6, At the western end of
Dorset sits this ancient seaside town, its steep and
narrow streets leading down to Lyme Bay. Jane
Austen had a cottage on the sea front and set parts
of *Persuasion* here. It is a quiet haven, clustering
around the 14th-century breakwater, The Cobb,
with five small beaches beloved of fossil collectors.
The little Philpot Museum contains prints,
documents, lace and even an old Sun Fire
Insurance engine of 1710. It also houses the
fossilized remains of an ichthyosaurus, a 30-foot
(9m) long aquatic reptile living some 140 million
years ago. St Michael's Church occupies a superb
position, with its chancel turned towards the sea,
and incorporates an older church within its
puzzling architecture: it is really two churches in
one, giving a confusing assemblage of motifs, such
as a Norman crossing tower grafted onto a
spacious Perpendicular stone church.

Lymington, Hants 690 C7, A market and maritime
town with a handsome High Street, partly

Lyme Park
Top left: The Entrance Hall,
with carved decoration.
Above: Giacomo Leoni's
Georgian west front.

Below right: Lytes Cary
Manor; its 14th-century
chapel protrudes to the left
of the main entrance.

sloping, lined with largely Georgian frontages
over prosperous shops; the church, of several
periods, has an unexpected classical interior, and
there is a small museum. The Quay is approached
along narrow streets; the estuary is intensively
used as a base for yachting.

Lympne, Kent 691 J6, Lympne Castle (pronounced
'Lim') is a 15th-century manor house, restored
from a ruin and made habitable around 1910. Near
it is a private zoo begun by the late John Aspinall,
well worth a visit to see a variety of wild animals in
something like their natural surroundings. The
property included **Port Lympne**, a house built
before World War I by Sir Herbert Baker and
decorated after it by Philip Tilden. Its Art Deco
interior features a garden room painted by Rex
Whistler in 1933.

Lyndhurst, Hants 690 C7, St Michael and All Angels is
one of the finest Victorian churches in England, by

William White, in brick and varied stones, with
outstanding glass by William Morris and Burne-
Jones; Mrs Alice Hargraves, who as a girl proved
the inspiration for *Alice in Wonderland*, is buried in
the churchyard.

Lynmouth and Lynton, Devon 689 F4, The twin
villages are still remembered for the devastating
flood of August 1952 that destroyed nearly 100
houses and killed 31 people. They had become
popular resorts in the 19th century, largely because

This page: Lyveden New Bield, begun in 1595 by Sir Thomas Tresham.

of the splendid walks in the area, either along the banks of the East Lyn through rocky gorges to Watersmeet, or along the Valley of the Rocks towards Lee Bay – a wild and romantic spot known to Coleridge (who may have conceived 'The Rime of the Ancient Mariner' while walking here with William and Dorothy Wordsworth). It is also an area commemorated by RD Blackmore in *Lorna Doone*. Shelley stayed here, in a cottage which still stands by the rushing waters of the Lyn.

Lytes Cary Manor, Somset 689 H5, Northeast of Ilminster, near Charlton Mackrell, this house blends its parts effortlessly [NT]. Its 14th-century chapel protrudes forward and left of the entrance; its Tudor Great Hall, added to in the 18th century, was rescued from decay this century by Sir Walter Jenner. The south wing contains the Great Parlour, dated 1533, and above this is the Great Chamber with an early plaster ceiling decorated with stars and diapers. The arms of Henry VIII appear in the plasterwork.

Lytham Hall, Lancs 696 E6, The ancestral home of the Cliftons until extravagance brought it and most of the estate into the hands of corporate mortgagees, the Guardian Royal Exchange Insurance Company, who have now sold the Hall on to a local trust [EH]. An earlier house was given a new rectangular front block in the late 1750s by John Carr of York. Brick with stone dressings, the nine-bay front has a pedimented central feature with columns through first and second floors, a broad band course and Gibbs surrounds to the ground-floor windows, which at first give the impression of a typical Palladian country house. But Lytham's planning defies its exterior. There is no *piano nobile* for the best rooms and all the principal state rooms are on the ground floor. Nonetheless, there is a very fine staircase and several rooms with exquisite plasterwork, showing the transitional stage of mid-18th-century country house design, with earlier work in a free rococo manner and later in the restrained neoclassicism of the Adam style.

Lyveden New Bield, Nhants 694 E6, The 'new building' stands on the hill above the 'old building' amid spectacular Elizabethan water-gardens that incorporate canals, orchard and high earth pyramids, newly researched and restored by the National Trust. It is now possible to ascend the stately pyramids by their winding shallow ramps, and to look down, as planned, on to the canals and garden pavilion below. The tall New Bield was an intriguing destination for a garden stroll or period of secluded study. It is full of references to its builder Thomas Tresham's Catholicism.

Machynlleth, Powys 692 E4, This homely Welsh town has a clock tower, erected to celebrate the coming-of-age in 1873 of Lord Castlereagh, heir of the Marquess of Londonderry who had married the heiress of the Plas ('great house' in Welsh). Directly opposite the ornate gates of the Plas in the main broad street is the late-15th- to early-16th-century building known as Parliament House, now a brass-rubbing centre. An annual arts festival was established in the 1980s in Y Tabernacl, a former Wesleyan chapel converted into a concert hall. The ancillary buildings have become spacious areas for the display of contemporary Welsh art. Three miles (4.8km) away the Centre for Alternative Technology reveals the powerful potential of solar and wind energy.

Madingley Hall, Cambs 695 F6, The red-brick Madingley Hall, near the American Military Cemetery, is chiefly Tudor but its gothic gateway is a 15th-century relic from the Old Schools in

Above and below centre: Madresfield Court.

Below right and bottom: Maesyronnen Chapel. The design is one of austere simplicity.

Cambridge*, moved in 1754. Now a college conference centre, the Hall saw the final confrontation between Prince Albert and his wayward son, the future Edward VII, who lodged here when a student.

Madresfield Court, Worcs 690 B3, Between Worcester* and Great Malvern* is the small village of Madresfield with its moated manor house. Originally Elizabethan, most of the current fabric dates from the 1860s when PC Hardwick added wings, storeys and bell-turret in carefully studied 'haphazard' profusion for the earls of Beauchamp. This recreation of the 'olden time' is particularly picturesque in the inner courtyard, where elaborate brick patterns fill in the timberwork. The chapel is an interesting Arts and Crafts ensemble made by Birmingham craftsmen in 1902. The gardens were once famous for the purple-black Madresfield Court grape, and still contain a garden of artificial 'rocks' made of cement, signed by the names of the workmen who constructed it in the 1870s. This was the home of Evelyn Waugh's friends the Lygons, said to be

partial models for the Flytes in *Brideshead Revisited*.

Maes Howe, *see* **Orkney*.**

Maesmawr Hall, Powys 693 F4, One of the best timber-framed gentry houses in a region of Wales renowned for such structures. Although now a hotel, Maesmawr Hall, with its principal rooms built around a central stack, has kept its integrity.

Maesyronnen Chapel, Powys 693 F6, On a hillside a few miles outside Hay-on-Wye* stands Maesyronnen ('field of the ash tree') Chapel. It epitomizes the spirit of religious dissent, which could only be shown in remote farms and barns. Founded in 1696, it is the oldest independent meeting house in Wales. Nearby Clyro is associated with the Reverend Francis Kilvert, curate from 1865 to 1872, whose diaries evoke the feel of place and time so strongly that the area has become known as Kilvert Country.

Left: Maiden Castle, Dorset, a large and complex early hill-fort, at least 4,000 years old, which spreads its tall ramparts and ditches in a series of defensive ovals across 5 miles (8km).

Maiden Castle, Ches 693 G2, An Iron Age hill fort at Broxton, built on a promontory of land and defended by two massive earth ramparts, 7 feet (2m) high in places.

Maiden Castle, Dorset 689 J6, One of the most impressive earthwork fortifications in Europe [EH]. The site was first occupied some 4,000 years ago by a thriving community. The great oval ramparts, enclosing an area about half a mile (0.8km) long and half as wide, were erected several centuries before Christ, and when the Romans arrived in AD 44 under Vespasian, they constructed a temple within its confines. In places the ramparts (60 to 90 feet/18.2–27.4m high) were faced with stone and timber, but only the lower courses remain, and these are buried beneath the turf-covered slopes of the earthen mounds they once strengthened. Three or four lines of them encircle the hill, making 5 miles (8km) of trenches in all. Such a colossal defensive structure would probably not have been necessary at that time, and was more likely a chieftain's display of power. In about AD 70, occupation ceased and the inhabitants moved to nearby Dorchester.

Maids' Moreton, Bucks 690 E3, St Edmund's is an attractive church said to have been built in the mid-1400s by two maiden sisters. The wide, well-lit nave and chancel retain much of their original roof, and there is an elaborate sedilia.

Maidstone, Kent 691 H5, The county town of Kent has suffered from over-development, but the group of buildings by the river – the college, the archbishop's palace and stables (which contain a museum of carriages) and the large parish church – still merits inspection. The last is worth a visit if only for the extraordinary monument to Sir John Astley (1639) by Edward Marshall. It shows Sir John and three other figures all standing in their shrouds. Maidstone Museum and Art Gallery, in the 16th-century Chillington Manor, has Dutch and Italian paintings and items of local history.

Maldon, Essex 691 H4, This picturesque Blackwater port witnessed a 991 skirmish with the Vikings celebrated in the contemporary epic poem 'The Song of the Battle of Malden' (elderberries are still called 'Danes' Blood' locally). The site is opposite the causeway to Northey Island, now a bird sanctuary. The home of Maldon Sea Salt has two medieval churches: gothic All Saints, with a unique triangular tower and window saluting George Washington's great-great-grandfather; and St Mary's, which once served as a lighthouse. A third, St Peter's, is but a tower attached to an amazing 5,000-volume library, the second oldest public library in England, bequeathed by religious scholar Dr Thomas Plume in 1704. The 15th-century Moot Hall has a red-brick tower, stair-turret and amusing bell-cage. Maldon still retains the atmosphere of a small fishing harbour, with quayside inns, Thames barges and handsome Georgian buildings throughout.

Mallaig, Highld 700 E6, A busy fishing port that is linked by car ferry to Armadale (Skye*) and Castlebay (Barra*) and by boat to the Knoydart peninsula and the islands of Rhum*, Eigg, Muck and Canna. Marine World, near the station, traces the history of the fisheries while aquariums present the local marine life.

Malmesbury, Wilts 690 B5, A charter of 924 supports its claim to be the oldest borough in England. Pride of place goes to the magnificent nave of a 12th-century Benedictine abbey church. This survived the Dissolution in 1539 to become the great parish church of Malmesbury. Don't miss the chance to climb up inside to its small library, or to scrutinize the figure sculptures on the Norman south porch. In the 11th century a monk called Oliver broke both legs when attempting to fly from the abbey roof, using home-made wings. The event is portrayed in a stained-glass window in the church. The church of St John the Baptist, originally 13th-century, has been restored. It contains the monument to Sir Henry Knyvett (d. 1598) and his family.

Malvern Hills, Worcs 693 H6, It is possible to walk along the length of the humpy spine of the Malvern Hills in a day, rising and falling to three passes; one of them, Hollybush Pass, is an ancient route used by packhorses travelling from Droitwich to South Wales. The Hills extend south towards Malvern Links, Malvern Wells and Little Malvern. Above them on the hilltop is the British Camp, one of England's best Iron-Age hill forts, built in about 300 BC. The natural slope has been extended with ditches and banks and it is thought that about 2,000 people lived within its 32 acres (10ha). The beacon at its highest point later became the motte of a Norman castle. *See also* **Great Malvern***.

Below left and right: Malmesbury Abbey. The South Porch contains some of the best pieces of Norman decoration in England, with figure sculpture, albeit badly defaced, set out in the arch in eight continuous bands.

Manchester

Manchester, Gt Man 697 F7, If England was the world's first industrial nation, then Manchester has every claim to be the world's first industrial city. Its history stretches back long before its remarkable industrial growth (*c*1800) brought foreign visitors such as the German architect Schinkel to inspect and sketch the multi-storey mills, and Friedrich Engels to survey the condition of the working classes on which Marx based so much of his belief in the workers' revolution. Though much of Manchester's industrial heritage remains, the city's appearance is now due more to the commercial buildings of the later 19th and early 20th centuries and the remarkable flourishing of new buildings in the 1990s.

Albert Square is a piece of 19th-century town planning, intended to form a open space in front of the Town Hall. It contains Manchester's Albert Memorial by local architect Thomas Worthington and a fountain, recently brought back to the square from Heaton Park. The Town Hall, by local-architect-made-good Alfred Waterhouse, was started in 1867; he had already established a local reputation with the Assize Courts and Strangeways Prison. The completion of the Town Hall took him the rest of the century and has produced one of the masterpieces of 19th-century architecture, grand in its overall conception and refined in its detail. It occupies a large triangular site and its plan, to make use of this awkward shape, is masterly. The front to the square is dominated by a tall tower and spire, still a landmark despite the competition of more recent tall buildings, and the main ceremonial rooms overlook the square at first-floor level. The Great Hall fills the middle. From the low vaulted entrance hall the first-floor landing is reached by two monumental staircases, their subtle placement and composition smoothing the transition between the different axes of the entrance and the Great Hall. The building is beautifully decorated throughout, with details ranging from Puginian polychromy to aesthetic movement sunflowers. The highlight is a series of 12 murals by Ford Madox Brown in the Great Hall, representing scenes from the history of Manchester.

Ancoats, to the east of the city centre, shows how the industrialization of the city was made possible by the canals, first Bridgewater, then Rochdale. Coal could be brought along them to steam-powered mills, meaning they were no longer dependent on water power as the earliest textile mills had been. The range of mills along Redhill Street, facing the canal, is the most impressive, and these were drawn by Schinkel on his visit. The earlier mills are plainer but the internal fireproof structure is more interesting. Some mills were rebuilt, especially as mule spinning turned to ring spinning, and those built *c*1900 are more architecturally elaborate with turrets and terracotta decoration. Apart from the mills, the most impressive building in Ancoats is Victoria Square, a huge council housing scheme of 1889 filling a whole block and round a central square; it is well composed and has good brick and terracotta detailing. Opposite, early cottage dwellings were then proudly named Sanitary Street but 20th-century sensibility led to the dropping of the 's' and the 'ry', leaving the visitor wondering who Anita was.

Above left: Detail of the stonework on the Town Hall court.

Above: Albert Memorial, Thomas Worthington's tribute to the Prince Consort with a statue by Matthew Noble.

Opposite page: Manchester Town Hall, Albert Waterhouse's finest building, fills one side of Albert Square.

Banks and trade are most widely represented in King Street, a textbook of architecture of the last 150 years. Here are Cockerell's Greco-Roman Bank of England, 1845; Edward Salomon's Venetian gothic Reform Club, 1870; and Waterhouse's hard red-brick Prudential Assurance, 1881. From the 20th century there is Charles Heathcote's Edwardian baroque Lloyds Bank and Lutyens' magnificent Midland Bank, 1929, with all the subtle proportion and detail of Lutyens at his best. Nearby and of the same date is Ship Canal House, which when finished was the tallest building in Manchester; it was designed by Harry Fairhurst, perhaps Manchester's leading architect in the early part of the century. Post-war architecture includes Casson and Conder's National Westminster Bank, 1966, clad in Swedish granite; the merits of its modern form now seem greater when contrasted with the overpowering post-modern presence of Friends Provident House, set back behind King Street, with Cockerell's Bank of England as its footstool.

In **Castlefield** the Rochdale Canal comes off the Bridgewater Canal and a few of the early warehouses remain around the basin, now converted into flats and offices; a dramatic cast-iron viaduct flies across at high

level and ends up at G-Mex. Smaller scale is a fine new bridge by Whitby and Bird. The most significant buildings now comprise the Museum of Science and Industry and are based round the former terminal of Stephenson's Liverpool and Manchester Railway. Liverpool Road Station, 1830, is the oldest surviving railway station in the world; it looks surprisingly domestic. Behind it is a massive gabled warehouse of the same date, dominating the gentle curve of the railway track; it is built of brick on the outside but, unlike contemporary iron-framed textile mills, has a mighty timber-framed structure.

Cathedral: The parish church is a dramatic survivor from the medieval town and its setting now includes the remains of Manchester's only remaining timber-framed town house, The Old Shambles, carefully moved to its present position after the bomb attack on the city centre in 1997. The parish church became the cathedral when Manchester became a diocese in 1847. It had been re-founded in 1421 as a collegiate church by Thomas de la Warre, and the old building was progressively rebuilt to fulfil this function during the 15th and early 16th centuries. It has a six-bay nave with double aisles and a six-bay chancel, built in sandstone with rich Perpendicular decoration inside and out, though much of the present appearance is due to successive restorations by JP Holden, JS Crowther and Sir Hubert Worthington and additions by Basic Champneys. The most notable fittings are the chancel stalls of the early 16th century, among the best in England, with elaborate spiky canopies and cresting and a full set of misericords, carved with the usual popular subjects such as men playing backgammon and dancing pigs.

Chetham's Hospital: The Collegiate Church was served by a college of priests who lived in quarters which now form the base of Chetham's Hospital and School, just to the north of the Cathedral. The buildings had a Gatehouse, rebuilt in 1816, a Great Hall and lodgings round a small quadrangle. This arrangement is wonderfully preserved. After the Dissolution the buildings became the town house of the earls of Derby and for some time the home of the mathematician and astrologer John Dee. In 1653 the Earl of Derby sold the buildings to trustees appointed under the will of Humphrey Chetham to establish a school and free public library. These institutions remain on the site, the school mainly in later buildings and the library in the

converted priests' lodgings. The first floor contains the 17th-century bookcases and, in the former warden's chamber, a reading room with a splendid late-17th-century tympanum reminiscent of the woodwork of London's City churches; the moulded bases of the columns take the form, appropriately, of piles of books, as on Sir Thomas Bodley's monument in Merton College Chapel. This room also has one of the chained library chests that Chetham provided for several parishes near Manchester.

The **City Art Gallery and Museum**, at the corner of Mosley Street and Princess Street, has especially good collections of pre-Raphaelite paintings and 20th-century British art; it is also noted for its collections of the applied arts. The buildings which now comprise the museum are an oustanding complex of the new and the old. The Mosley Street front is Sir Charles Barry's former Royal Manchester Institution, 1824, in a severe and scholarly Greek manner. This is now joined with Barry's former Athenaeum, 1837; the top storey was altered after a fire in 1873. By 1837 Barry was in Italianate mode and the building is a trial run for the Reform Club in London's Pall Mall. The link between Barry's buildings and the filling in of the grid square is now occupied by Michael Hopkins' extension of 1999, its smooth surfaces contrasting with the elaboration of the Chinese Arch which marks the city's Chinese quarter just behind.

Free Trade Hall: The western part of the city centre lies along and behind Peter Street, where Manchester's second great civic building, the Free Trade Hall, awaits conversion into a hotel. The Hall was a celebration of

Manchester's role in the achievement of free trade. It is a monumental palazzo of one principal storey above an arcaded ground floor, the whole sumptuously decorated with carvings representing the arts, commerce, manufacture and agriculture, and the four continents with which the city did business; the architect was Edward Walters and the sculptor John Thomas. Immediately behind is Stephenson Bell's new Manchester Convention Centre, the former Central Station, Manchester's rival to St Pancras and now the G-Mex Exhibition Centre, and the former Great Northern Goods Warehouse. The Free Trade Hall has ceased to be a concert hall, since it was replaced by the Bridgewater Hall, 1996, by Renton Howard Wood Levin; this is marked externally by fashionable *brise-soleils* and internally by a spacious and cool entrance. A short distance away is Oxford Road Station, 1960, an ingenious exercise in shell construction in laminated timber, looking like a miniature Sydney Opera House.

St Ann's Church: The best city-centre fragment of early 18th-century Manchester is St Ann's Church, 1709–12, standing at the head of the city's first formal square, sometimes wrongly attributed to Wren but almost certainly by the Derbyshire builder/architect John Barker. It still retains its galleried interior and has interesting later glass, some by Peckett of York. A curious result of a reordering in 1890 by Alfred Waterhouse is the lowering of the pulpit into a small pit so that the fine structure could survive intact but not interfere with the sight-lines in a more ecclesiologically arranged church.

St Ann's Square: The square is very much at the heart of the commercial district. One side is dominated by the Royal Exchange, Manchester's fourth. This grand classical pile by Bradshaw, Gass and Hope (1914–21) contains the Royal Exchange Theatre built in a pod by Levitt Bernstein on the trading floor where cotton used to be bought and sold; the entrance to the square now has a dramatic new lift by the same architects. On the other side is the Barton Arcade (by Corbett, Raby and Sawyer, 1871), running through to Deansgate; it is a remarkable structure with highly ornate iron and glass domes and tiers of balconies.

Far left: Free Trade Hall in Peter Street, designed by Edward Walters, 1833–6.

Left: St Ann's Church, 1709–12, probably by John Barker. It is the city's best surviving 18th-century church.

Below: Detail of the stonework on Dalton Hall, Victoria Park.

University: South of the city centre is the University precinct. The older buildings were designed by Waterhouse between 1870 and 1900; the Manchester Museum is part of the Oxford Road frontage. Just opposite is JA Hansom's mighty Church of the Holy Name, 1869, with stone on the outside and terracotta within; the high and wide vaults are supported on piers so slender that they appear to be built on faith rather than calculation. Further along Oxford Road is the university's Whitworth Art Gallery of 1895, by JW Beaumont, specializing in works on paper with good watercolours and one of the country's finest collections of historic wallpaper.

Victoria Park: Beyond the university, there is a leafier area around Victoria Park where the principal monument is Edgar Wood's First Church of Christ Scientist, 1903, on which Pevsner's comment was that 'One can hardly drive originality and wilfulness farther, unless one is called Gaudí'. At Fallowfield is Platt Hall, by Timothy Lightoler, c1763, on the outside an exquisite small Georgian country house; the inside is now much altered but houses a splendid Museum of Costume. There is another of Edmund Sharpe's early terracotta churches, at Holy Trinity, 1845, and the local landmark of Hollings College, 1957, by city architect LC Howitt, nicknamed the 'toast-rack' because of the expressed structural form of its parabolic arches.

Warehouses: Manchester was laid out on a grid, but evidence of early houses is now hard to find. In the 19th century the houses were replaced by Manchester's distinctive contribution to English building types, the textile distribution warehouses; the earliest of these have Italianate fronts, and later ones have elaborate terracotta decoration. The first warehouse, built for Richard Cobden, is in Mosley Street; it is now largely rebuilt but retains the Portico Library, 1802, of which the upstairs remains as it was designed by Thomas Harrison while the downstairs has been converted into a pub. The most typical warehouses are probably those in Princess Street and Charlotte Street (for the earlier forms) and in Whitworth Street (for the later ones). The most dramatic is Watts's warehouse, now the Britannia Hotel, in Portland Street, by Travis and Mangnall, 1855, a huge five-storeyed building, each storey in a different style and with four rose-windowed pavilions.

Far left: The Manchester Science and Industry Museum

Below: The John Rylands University Library, named after a 19th-century cotton merchant and built 1890–9 for his widow by Basil Champneys. Originally an independent institution, it merged with the University Library in 1972.

Manderston House
Top left: The Drawing Room.
Centre left: Kinross' main
stair with its Petit Trianon-
style handrail.

It was in Manderston that the
very successful television
series 'The Edwardian Country
House' was filmed, in which
participants lived out
Edwardian roles.

Below right: Mapperton, an
urn in the Fountain Court.

Bottom left: Manorbier
Castle, the birthplace of
Gerald of Wales in 1145 who
thought it 'the pleasantest
spot in Wales'.

Manorbier Castle, Pembks 692 C7, A moated Norman
castle begun in the 12th century, which was never
attacked. The outer walls have crumbled but the
inner quarters remain intact, with a gatehouse,
Great Hall and chapel.

Mansfield, Notts 694 D3, The town became a focus for
industry (coal and stockings) in the 19th century,
but its pleasant centre recalls its Georgian past.

Mapledurham, Oxon 690 D5, A well-preserved
village near the Thames which contains the large

**Manderston House, Border
699 H5,** One of Scotland's
most remarkable
Edwardian mansions,
by the architect John
Kinross, 1903. The
soberness of the classical
façade contrasts with the
exuberance of the
interior – exotic woods,
expensive fabrics, precious metals, marble and
alabaster. The silver balustrade of the staircase
leading to the first floor is a replica of the
wrought-iron balustrade in the Petit Trianon at
Versailles. There are 60 acres (24ha) of gardens and
a number of exceptional outbuildings, including
a dairy lined with marble and a stable block of
unrivalled luxury: teak ceilings, teak stalls with
copper uprights, tiled drinking troughs and a
harness room in rosewood, marble and copper.

Elizabethan Mapledurham House begun in c1585
by Sir Richard Blount, whose monument can be
seen in the adjacent church. The house has a pretty
red-brick exterior and fine Tudor and Jacobean
staircases and ceilings. It was reworked in the late
18th century, which was when the private chapel was
built. Nearby is a lovely, fully restored watermill.

Mapperton, Dorset 689 H5, A Jacobean and Carolean
manor house with Tudor features and a classical
north front. It has fine Italianate gardens, created
in 1926, with an orangery, summer-house and
topiary, and formal borders which descend the
valley to fish ponds and shrub gardens. The
gardens are open to the public, the house can be
visited by appointment only. The undulating
Dorset hills and dark woodlands that surround
the house give it a dramatic setting. It has been
much featured in film and television adaptations
of classics such as Henry Fielding's *Tom Jones*
and Jane Austen's *Emma*. The L-shaped house
is the centre of an attractive manorial group,
which includes All Saints Church and stable
blocks. Its golden-brown carved stone dressings
come from the Ham Hill quarries near
Montacute* in Somerset.

March, Cambs 695 G5, Approached across the Levels
through orchards and market gardens, this
Fenland railway hub is memorable for missed
connections and the magnificent roof of its church,

uniquely dedicated to St Wendreda. A double hammerbeam structure built between 1470 and 1520 appears to be held aloft only by the efforts of some 200 winged angels, saints and apostles. **Marford, Wrexhm 693 F2,** A descendant of John Trevor was responsible at the beginning of the 19th century for the 14 enchanting gothic cottages and the Trevor Arms that formed the estate village of Marford.

Margam Park, Neath 689 F3, A vast Tudor gothic house by Thomas Hopper, 1830–5, separated from the chapterhouse of a medieval abbey and the remains of an earlier 16th-century mansion by a

Left: March, the extraordinary angel roof of St Wendreda's Church.

Below: Mapperton, with its topiary-decked gardens set out in a valley to the east, before the L-shaped Jacobean and Caroline manor house.

wide allée and an 18th-century orangery. The extensive grounds and woodland contain a sculpture park. Of interest also is the re-erected façade of the late-17th century, and the summer Banqueting House, or 'Temple of the Four Seasons', decorated with Ionic columns and pilasters and swagged capitals. The 12th-century abbey church, remodelled at the beginning of the 1800s and now the parish church, contains ornate tombs. A museum nearby displays inscribed stone crosses dating from the 6th to the 17th century.

Margaretting, Essex 691 G4, St Margaret's Church has one of the great Essex timber bell-towers – a heavily braced 10-post oak structure (there are similar splendours at Blackmore*, Bulpham, Navestock and Mountnessing). Glass in the east window depicts a complete 15th-century Jesse tree.

Margate, Kent 691 J5, Salmerstone Grange, on the edge of Margate, is a fascinating survival of a 14th-century monastic establishment, sympathetically restored and normally accessible to the public.

The chapel has interesting modern stained glass by John Trinick.

Markenfield Hall, N York 697 G5, A magical, moated, medieval manor house, built in 1310 but still inhabited and little altered except for the addition of an Elizabethan gatehouse. The main buildings lie in one corner of a fortified courtyard, the first-floor Great Hall over an undercroft. There is a solar tower which is vaulted on the ground floor and has a first-floor chapel.

Marlborough, Wilts 690 C5, Well known for its celebrated boys' public school, founded in 1845, which stands at the southern end of a very long and wide High Street – the result, it is said, of a great fire in 1653 that wiped out all that stood in its way. Everything worth seeing is ranged either side of this street, an assemblage of 17th- to 19th-century properties, with some later insertions, and a church at either end. St Peter and St Paul at the west end is a crafts centre, but the parish church of St Mary to the east has an interesting south arcade of five bays with dominant Tuscan columns. To the east of the town lie the reaches of Savernake Forest, a royal forest since the days of the Norman Conquest. Here can be seen, from the road and across the Capability Brown park, the imposing bulk of Tottenham House, built in 1825 by Thomas Cundy.

Marlow, Bucks 690 E5, Despite industrial growth around its edges, the town retains a historic character, with the River Thames as its central focus. The impressive Marlow Suspension Bridge, built in 1829–31, provides an interesting contrast to the nearby church of All Saints, rebuilt in 1832–5 by CF Inwood. In Station Road is the excellent Marlow Place of c1720, ascribed to Thomas Archer, with a commanding façade and Borromini motif; and in West Street Albion House, where Mary Shelley worked on the story of Frankenstein.

Martock, Somset 689 H5, The church of All Saints stands at a bend in the main street. The interior roof has 768 panels, in six repeated patterns. It dates to 1513 and is the best of its type in Somerset. The 13th-century Treasurer's House [NT] is a small medieval building.

Matlock, Derbys 694 C3, A curious town, as it is made up of a series of almost separate villages. One of these villages, Matlock Bath, became quite popular in the 18th and 19th centuries as a spa. The landscape, with its tall cliffs, is spectacular and from many parts of the town the Victorian folly of Riber Castle dominates the skyline.

Maunsel House, Somset 689 H5, A 13th-century manor house at North Newton, now popular for wedding receptions and other private functions.

Mawley Hall, Shrops 693 G5, A large, handsome early Georgian house built in about 1730 and probably designed by Francis Smith of Warwick. The exterior is restrained, like most of Smith's houses, but the interior is extremely handsome with a grand entrance hall, a main stair with a wonderful serpentine handrail, and lavish plasterwork in most of the principal rooms.

Medmenham, Bucks, A name recognized by collectors of Medmenham Ware pottery, founded in 1897 by Robert Hudson of Danesfield. Better known, however, is Medmenham Abbey, built mainly in the 16th, 18th and 19th centuries, where the Hell-Fire Club met from 1755 to 1763 (*see* West Wycombe*). See **Marlow* 690 E5.**

Below: Matlock, with the River Derwent in front and the Heights of Abraham behind.

Melbourne Hall
Top left: The East Front.
Top right: Robert Bakewell's
arbour, known as the
Birdcage.

Above: Mellerstain House,
worked on by William and
Robert Adam.

Below: Melrose Abbey

Meigle, P & K 699 G2, Twenty-five outstanding
Pictish stones (7th–10th century), all found in
the surrounding area, can be viewed in Meigle's
former schoolhouse.

Melbourne, Derbys 694 D4, A pleasant little town
with a very fine Norman church. Melbourne Hall
nearby is not a large house, but it has a handsome
front of 1725 which looks down over the sloping
formal garden, flanked by great yew hedges, to a
formal pond. Beyond the water is a small wrought-
iron arbour or summer seat, made in the early 18th
century by the famous smith Robert Bakewell.

Meldon Park, Nthumb 699 J7, An ashlar villa
designed by John Dobson in 1832, with an Ionic
porch and a grand staircase.

Mellerstain House, Border 699 H5, The two wings
were built by William Adam in 1725, and the
central body of the building added in the 1770s by
his son Robert, who also designed its magnificent
ceilings, friezes and other plasterwork as well as
some of the furnishings. The library is one of
Robert Adam's masterpieces, with its wall
decorations and delicately coloured ceilings with
medallions painted by Antonio Zucchi. There are
fine paintings by Van Dyck, Gainsborough,
Ramsay, Aikman and Nasmyth.

Melrose Abbey, Border 699 H5, Walter Scott's efforts
to preserve the ruins of Scotland's first Cistercian
abbey made the site a place of literary pilgrimage
during the 19th century. Founded in 1136 by
David I for monks from Rievaulx Abbey* in
Yorkshire, it was plundered and destroyed by
the troops of Edward II in 1322 and Richard II in
1385. It was rebuilt in the late 15th and early 16th
century, but was again reduced to ruins during the
campaign of terror
led by the Earl of
Hertford in 1544–5.
Today the
foundations are all
that remain of the
monastic buildings
but the Abbey
Church has some
interesting gothic
ruins: the south nave
aisle and its eight
chapels; the east part of the nave with its stone
rood screen separating the central aisle from
the monks' choir (which served as a Presbyterian
church between 1618 and 1810); the transept and
remains of the tower and the main choir (which
houses the tomb of Alexander II), beneath whose
high window the heart of Robert Bruce was
said to have been buried. Today the restored
Commendator's House, built in 1590, is occupied
by the Abbey Museum with its collections of
religious architecture and archeological remains
from the Roman camp of Trimontium, built by
Agricola near Melrose. The abbey is also the
departure point for St Cuthbert's Way, a footpath
that runs through the Borders for 56 miles (90km).

Melverley, Shrops 693 F3, In a county famous for its
black-and-white timber-framed houses, St Peter is

Above and left: Mentmore Towers, built for Baron Meyer Amschel de Rothschild.

Top right: Mereworth Castle, a close copy of Palladio's Villa Rotonda and a key building in the English Palladian movement. The dome is higher and more Baroque than the Italian original.

portraits and memorabilia. The home farm has a Palladian cow-house designed by the owner in 1951, which is now a listed building.

Meon Valley, Hants 690 D7, The River Meon is tiny, but its valley surrounded by rolling chalkland is distinctive. East Meon and Hambledon have fine churches in picturesque villages; Corhampton church is a little gem, hardly altered (except the eastern wall) since Saxon times, with remains of fine early wall-paintings depicting, *inter alia*, the life of Saint Swithin.

Mereworth Castle, Kent 691 G6, A very notable Palladian house built in 1723 with a classical portico on each of its four sides, designed by Lord Burlington's protégé Colen Campbell and a close copy of the Villa Rotonda outside Vicenza. The house is not open to the public but can be seen from the road. The church of St Lawrence next to it, built in 1744 by an unknown architect, is an exceptionally fine example of British neoclassicism. In the nave, two rows of Tuscan columns support a flat entablature and a barrel vault.

one of only two timber-framed churches. It dates from the late 15th or early 16th century and inside, with the quantity of timber bracing everywhere, it feels more like a barn than a church. It has a west gallery, probably put up 1588.

Mendip Hills, Somset 689 H4, A long range of hills stretching from the crags of Cheddar Gorge* and running south towards the Quantock Hills* to the north side of the cathedral city of Wells*.

Mentmore Towers, Bucks, Mentmore's architect, Sir Joseph Paxton, is best known for his mid-19th-century Crystal Palace*, but this remarkable Elizabethan Revival house (1850–5), designed in partnership with GH Stokes, has the same grandeur and magnitude. The enormous central hall carries a glass roof built on Paxton's ridge-and-furrow principle. *See* **Ascott* 690 E4.**

Meols Hall, Mersyd 696 E6, The Hall, just outside Southport*, has been a property of the Hesketh family since the 16th century but for many years was little more than a farmhouse on an estate whose owners' principal residence was at Rossall or Rufford*. The house was recolonized by the family in the 19th century but its present character is largely due to a recent owner, Roger Fleetwood-Hesketh, who maintained the 18th-century tradition of the gentleman architect. His careful reconstruction in the 1960s added a dignified Georgian block to the surviving earlier fabric, which at first sight could pass for a house by Leoni (one of whose doorways, from the demolished Lathom House, is in fact now the main entrance). The house contains other relics from demolished Lancashire houses and a good collection of family

Below: Merrivale. Bronze Age and other early remains such as this menhir abound on this part of Dartmoor.

Top right: Michelham Priory,
a 16th-century house built
from the ruin of a medieval
abbey.

Middleham   **M**

Merriments Gardens, E Susx, 691 G6, A large garden
at Hurst Green, planted on the naturalistic
principles of William Robinson, using local plants
carefully blended for their colours.

Merrivale, Devon 688 E6, The Rows are among
the most accessible of Dartmoor's early remains
[EH]. Two rows of small stones, one 850 feet
(259m) and the other 590 feet (180m) in length,
lead to a large circle of upright stones. Associated
with the avenue is a fine *kistvaen* and nearby there

are cairns, hut circles and a menhir (a single
standing stone). Here also is the King's Tor quarry,
among the most important on the moor; below it,
the railway track constructed by the French

Above and top: Merriments
Gardens, pulsatilla, originally
an import from Sweden.

Below: Mevagissey, the inner
harbour, looking to the
seaward wall; the haunt of
many artists.

prisoners of war to take the granite down to
Plymouth* is still visible.

Mevagissey, Cnwll 688 D7, Now a day-trippers'
paradise, the harbour was once one of the centres
of the enormous pilchard industry; at its height it
exported 35 million each year to Spain or Italy.
The old lifeboat house is now an aquarium.

Michelham Priory, E Susx 691 G7, Originally an
Augustinian monastery, founded in 1229 and
surrounded by a moat in the 14th century. It was
adapted as a private house in the 16th century.
There are some medieval remains. It contains a
collection of furniture, stained glass, tapestries,
farm implements, and other curiosities [EH].

Middleham, N York 697 G4, The Castle [EH] has an
exceptionally large Norman keep, and medieval
curtain walls. It was a Neville stronghold, and
became the home of Richard, Duke of Gloucester,
later Richard III, through his wife Anne Neville.
The Middleham Jewel, discovered near the Castle

by a metal detector in 1985 and now on display in the Yorkshire Museum in York*, is an exquisite example of the medieval goldsmith's art, minutely engraved with a Nativity scene on the back and the Holy Trinity on the front, set with a sapphire. It probably contained religious relics, and hung around the neck of a wealthy man, possibly King Richard himself.

Middlesbrough, N York 697 H3, A town that developed only from the 1830s, prospering from iron, steel and later from chemicals: despite decline the distant skyline still looks industrial. A major feature is the Transporter Bridge, a marvel of steel engineering opened in 1911 to carry workers across the River Tees without obstructing the busy shipping lanes below. The former Bell Brothers Offices in Zetland Road are a rare example of an office block designed by Philip Webb, the Arts and Crafts architect.

Middleton Cheney, Nhants 690 D3, The medieval church was heavily restored in the 1860s, and visitors come here to see the famous stained glass by William Morris's company of decorators. The vicar in the 1860s was a friend of Burne-Jones, whose designs here include the young men in the fiery furnace in the north aisle.

Midhurst, W Susx 690 E7, An old market town on the River Rother, with attractive houses and several fine inns. Just outside lie the ruins of **Cowdray Park,**

Above: Middleham Castle, the large Norman keep set within the later medieval curtain walls.

Milton Abbas
Centre right: The abbey church flows into the classical house (once the monastic buildings) and since 1954 a public school. The abbey consists of tower, crossing, choir and transepts only – the fragments of an original greater whole. It lies at the end of the attractive village of Milton Abbas.
Below right: St Catherine's Chapel, 12th century.

Bottom left: Middlesbrough Transporter Bridge, dominating the River Tees.

once one of the grandest Elizabethan houses in England, but largely destroyed by fire in 1793. Enough remains of the gatehouse, hall and chapel to show that it combined elegant Perpendicular Gothic with Italian Renaissance ornament.

Mildenhall, Suffk 695 G6, The stupendous treasure of Roman silver unearthed in the 1950s, notably the great Neptune dish, is now in the British Museum, London*. More accessible and equally wondrous is the angel roof of St Mary's with inspired biblical scenes and mythical beasts in the north aisle. The village centre has a 16th-century hexagonal market cross.

Mildenhall, Wilts 690 C5, The small village church, dedicated to St John the Baptist, has a Norman tower, a 12th-century chancel and north arcade, surviving box pews, good glass and a Jacobean roof. Gothic fittings were added in 1815.

Milton Abbas, Dorset 690 B7, Situated in breathtaking countryside, the little village has a beautiful street lined with thatched cottages. Its old abbey is one of the jewels of Dorset. Founded in 933, destroyed in a storm in 1309 and rebuilt in the 14th and 15th centuries, it remains a noble place characterized by exquisite architectural detail, such as the vaulting of the tower. With an internal length of 136 feet (41m) it is like a large Oxford college chapel, rich in furnishings. The reredos of 1510 has three tiers of niches; the font, although much later (1883), is supported by two life-size white angels. The rich south transept window was designed by Pugin with stained glass (1847) by John Hardman. The adjoining house is a public school, with extensive work by Sir William Chambers. The abbey church contains a white marble monument of the wife of the house's builder, Lady Milton, designed in 1775 by Chambers's rival, Robert Adam.

Milton Abbot, Devon 688 E6, A somewhat dull
church delights in the dedication of St Constantine
and St Aegidius. But the estate village of the Dukes
of Bedford, who lived nearby at Endsleigh, has
produced many attractive house and cottages,
most notably in the fine terrace around an open
court by Sir Edwin Lutyens. Built on the side of the
hill, the lowest house has a small shop tucked
under it at street level. The vicarage was designed
by Edward Blore; the Tudor gothic-style school
and the large house some way out of the village
were both designed by Sir Jeffry Wyatville.

Milton Ernest, Beds 694 E7, The Hall was designed by
William Butterfield in 1856 for his brother-in-law
and is typical of his style of work. Noteworthy is
the use of contrasting materials and pointing for
the exterior. Inside the church is a striking bread
cupboard of 1729 with three tiers of four arched
holes and a pediment. The brass chandelier made
a year earlier is also interesting.

Milton Keynes, Bucks 690 E3, The new town was
designed in 1967 with a view to accommodating
250,000 people by the end of the century; it
incorporated three towns and 15 villages. Various
historic buildings coexist with the new town
architecture and town planning. At the centre of
Middleton lies the village of Milton Keynes, which
gave its name to the new town. The Decorated
church of All Saints is a fine example of its kind
and should not be missed.

Above: Milton Lodge
Gardens, the view towards
Wells Cathedral*.

Right: Milton Lodge has fine
trees and old established
yew hedges.

Milton Lodge Gardens, Somset 689 H4, High up on
the slopes of the Mendip Hills* this terraced
garden, originally dating from 1909, was
replanned in 1962. It has all a good garden should
have, together with a 7-acre (2.8ha) arboretum.

Milton Manor House, Oxon, An uncommonly good
building of its period, with a tall, plain 17th-
century centre and short matching wings added
in 1776. The house has been attributed (on no
evidence) to Inigo Jones, but Milton was certainly

built in the Jonesian tradition. The gothic library and Roman Catholic chapel are particularly fine. The park has lakes and mature trees and there are also rare breeds of animals, including llamas, and shire horse cart rides. *See* **Steventon* 690 D4.**

Minack Theatre, Cnwll 688 B8, The open-air theatre has a regular series of week-long productions during the summer months.

Minsmere, Sufflk 695 K6, Flooded during World War II, this is now the RSPB's premier reserve, a haven for rare migrants including avocet and bittern.

Minstead, Hants 690 C7, The church, unrestored by the Victorians, is a jumble of medieval to Georgian features, including a

Top right: Minster Lovell, the remains of the Hall.

Above: Minack Theatre was largely built of concrete by its founder Rowena Cade, in the 1950s.

Below: Mistley Towers, 1776, by Robert Adam, are all that survive of St Mary's Church.

'three-decker' pulpit. Sir Arthur Conan Doyle is buried in the churchyard. Nearby are the attractive Furzwy Gardens.

Minster Lovell, Oxon 690 C4, On an enchanting spot by the River Windrush stand the remains of Minster Lovell Hall, an important 15th-century house built by William, Lord Lovell [EH]. The church is a 15th-century survivor with a spacious interior containing a good effigy of a Lovell knight.

Minterne Gardens, Dorset 689 J5, This is the perfect woodland garden, spreading over some 20 acres (8ha) just outside Dorchester*. Formality is banished in favour of vistas, plants and lakes in profusion. The gardens gather protectively around the large house, built in 1904 for Lord Digby and now open by appointment to special-interest groups.

Mistley, Essex 691 J3, The old quayside malting office and swan-adorned pond are, like Robert Adam's twin towers with their colonnades and domed caps [EH], striking reminders of Richard Rigby's attempt to upgrade the collection of Stourside granaries and warehouses into a fashionable late 18th-century spa.

Moccas Court, Herefs 693 F6, The house was built in the 1770s for the Cornewall family, and repays visiting on the one day a week when it is open in the summer. Robert Adam's strictly classical exterior in stark red brick belies the opulent interiors, which include a circular Etruscan room. It has an expansive Capability Brown park bounded by a meander of the Wye. Nearby, the church of St Michael, built in pink stone, contains 14th-century glass.

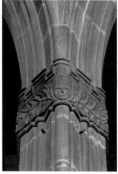

Left: Moccas Court, the Staircase Hall.

Monk Bretton Priory
Above: Detail of the stonework.
Right: View of the east wall of the Prior's Chambers, showing the fireplace.

Below centre: Mold, stained glass in the church of St Mary.

Bottom: Monmouth, Monmow Gate, the daunting fortified bridge of 1272 once guarding the River Monnow.

Mogerhanger, Beds 691 F3, The house dates from 1791. Sir John Soane worked on the first phase of the building, and then again for Godfrey Thornton, director of the Bank of England, in 1801. The Park is by Humphry Repton.

Mold (Yr Wyddgrug), Flints 693 F2, A market town based on a crossroads which rises to provide an elevated position for the town's most distinguished building, the parish church of St Mary, one of the foundations of Margaret Beaufort, mother of Henry VII. 'Mold' is probably a corruption of the name of Norman de Montalt or de Mohaut, who established a stronghold here. On the hillside, as part of a civic complex built in the 1970s, stands Theatr Clwyd, a highly innovative community arts centre, with a large auditorium, a theatre studio, a display gallery and a film theatre. Today it has a vibrant Welsh identity, giving it the status almost of a national theatre.

Monk Bretton Priory, S Yorks 697 H7, Founded in 1154 as a Cluniac house; this Order is uncommon in Yorkshire, a fact which may explain why, after many disputes, it became Benedictine in the late 13th century. The most interesting parts of the coal-blackened ruins are the 15th-century gatehouse and the prior's quarters, which show evidence of frequent upgrading and embellishment [EH].

Monkey Island, Berks 690 E5, Now a hotel, the fishing lodge and house were built for the Duke of Marlborough in 1774. A room within the lodge is decorated with grotesques of monkeys engaged in such activities as fishing and shooting by the *singerie* painter Clermont. There is another 'Monkey Room' at Kirtlington*, Oxfordshire.

Monmouth, Mons 693 G6, The town has a unique fortified gatehouse guarding entry from across the Monnow. Its origins go back to the Romans, who built the fort of Blestium on the land where the Monnow flowed into the Wye. William Fitzosbern built his second castle in Wales here in 1070. Little remains of the stone castle that replaced the original earthen stronghold, but the daunting appearance of Monnow Gate (1272) indicates that it would have been just as formidable. It was the birthplace in 1387 of 'Harry of Monmouth', who became Henry V in 1413. After the Civil War, Castle House – a fine residence – was built on the site of the former tower by the Marquess of Worcester. Monmouth has more fine 18th-century houses than any other town in Wales, and modern development has done little to spoil it.

Montacute, Somset 689 H5, Another great country house in this part of Somerset, situated not far from the formal gardens of Tintinhull*. Built in Ham stone, a warm biscuit tan in colour, Montacute [NT] was built about 1590 for Sir Edward Phelips, Speaker of the House of Commons; the date 1599 appears on one of the interior chimneypieces. The imposing Long Gallery (189 feet/58m) has been covered in rush-matting since the 1970s, when it and the chambers off it were hung with a wonderful display of Tudor and Jacobean portraits, on loan from the National Portrait Gallery* in London. Redecoration, and a new display of the portraits, was undertaken in 1998–9. Montacute suffered badly during the Civil War, and Colonel Edward Phelips (c1613–80) was impoverished by the conflict and by his debts. Most items were sold in 1651 by a commission of sequestration. The debts remained, uneasily, across the 18th century, but bequests to another Edward Phelips (1725–97) enabled him to improve the west front by incorporating shafts and panels from the demolished Tudor house of Clifton Maybank. In 1915 Montacute was leased to Lord Curzon, who then entrusted its redecoration to his friend, the novelist Elinor Glyn. Other bequests and gifts, as well as the Phelips acquisition, have succeeded in reanimating a glorious house.

Top left: The Elizabethan Interior Porch, c1565.

Below: This great mansion was built to an H-shaped plan and completed about 1600.

Above: The Library, formerly the Great Chamber.

Opposite page: The Library stained glass, featuring the arms of the Phelips family, their allies and neighbours.

Left: Elizabeth Knollys, Lady Layton, 1577, attributed to George Gower.

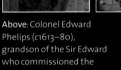

Above: Colonel Edward Phelips (c1613–80), grandson of the Sir Edward who commissioned the house.

Moor Park, Herts 691 F4, This is the county's most important 18th-century country house. The 17th-century brick mansion was heavily remodelled in the 1720s for Benjamin Styles, a merchant who made a fortune out of the South Sea Bubble in 1720. The architect he employed was Sir James Thornhill, more famous for his work as a painter. The giant Corinthian portico, soaring upwards for two and a half storeys, is a tremendous sight. Originally this was balanced by two pavilions

Montgomery (Trefaldwyn), Powys 693 F4, The town owes its name to Roger de Montgomery, Earl of Shrewsbury, who built the original motte-and-bailey castle. This was abandoned in the 13th century, when Hubert de Burgh built his fortress, with its formidable gatehouse, on a steep narrow ridge. The 18th-century town hall is proudly placed at the end of Broad Street, and the parish church of St Nicholas has among its many splendid monuments an effigy of Owain Glyndwr's grandson and the ornate canopied tomb of Richard Herbert and his wife, with their eight children. Among them were the poet George Herbert, and his brother Lord Herbert of

Above and right: Moorlands is set in a valley adjoining Ashdown Forest.

Below left: Montgomery church of St Nicholas. The 15th-century double-oak screen is one of the many splendours.

Cherbury, whose exquisite portrait by Isaac Oliver is one of the treasures at Powis Castle*.

Montrose, Angus 699 H2, This ancient royal burgh is a busy commercial centre and active port. It has some beautiful old gabled houses and a small neoclassical museum (1837) of local history. The Montrose Basin Nature Reserve Centre has a presentation on the 740-acre (299ha) nature reserve on the south shore of the tidal Basin.

Monymusk, Abers 702 D6, For a long time the Priory, founded on the ruins of a Celtic chapel, housed the Brec Bennoch, the reliquary containing the relics of St Columba, which is now in the Museum of Scotland in Edinburgh*. Near the 12th-century church, restored in the 20th century, stands a Pictish stone.

linked to the body of the house by curving colonnades, but these were demolished at the end of the 18th century. The interior is particularly grand, with an entrance hall occupying the full height of the building and a gallery running round all four sides at first-floor level. Four painted canvases by the Venetian Jacopo Amigoni depict the story of Io, and the central ceiling roundel is a *trompe l'oeil* of a view up to a lantern. The house is now a golf club. The park was worked on by Capability Brown and Humphry Repton.

Moorlands, E Susx 691 G6, A pleasant 4-acre (1.6ha) garden near Cranborough, with a river walk.

Morecambe, Lancs 696 E5, A somewhat forlorn seaside resort of which the finest building is the Midland Hotel, one of the modern movement classics, designed by Oliver Hill for the Midland Railway, and given some unique internal decoration by Eric Gill. A little further south, near a nuclear power station at Heysham, is clear evidence of early settlement: St Peter's Church and

St Patrick's Chapel. Is this evidence of the battle between Roman and Celtic Christianity? The best part of the early work is a hogback tombstone, formerly in the churchyard and now in the church.

Moreton, Dorset 690 B7, The church, 10 miles (16km) west of Wareham*, is dedicated to St Nicholas. It is Georgian Gothic in style (1776) and quite beautiful. There is a splendid apse with five traceried windows, which incorporate Laurence Whistler's engraved glass of 1958 representing the symbols of Christ's Passion amid candles and ribbons. TE Lawrence is buried in the churchyard.

Moreton Corbet Castle, Shrops 693 G3, The ruined keep of a 13th-century castle with the remains of a house built in 1579 [EH]. It was captured in 1644 by Parliamentarians.

Moretonhampstead, Devon 689 F6, Once a thriving wool town, it still remains one of the main centres for touring Dartmoor*. Little survives from those early days of prosperity, however, apart from the church and the colonnaded almshouses of 1637. The Manor House (now a hotel) was built in 1906–7 on a grand scale by Detmar Blow, as a summer residence for the son of WH Smith. There are many prehistoric remains in the area; cairns, hut circles and stone circles at Butterdon and Mardon Downs and hill forts at Wooston, Cranbrook and Prestonbury.

Mortimer's Cross, Herefs 693 G5, The Battle of Mortimer's Cross took place in February 1461

Moreton Corbet
Above: A detail of the ornamental stone carving.
Below: A view of the Elizabethan south range.

during the Wars of the Roses, and the village contains a monument commemorating it. Erected by public subscription in 1799, it stands near the site of the Lancastrian camp. The Lancastrians lost the battle to the future Edward IV, and many of their casualties lie buried in a field known as the 'Clamp', south of the road towards Lucton. There is also a working watermill, originally used for grinding animal feed and today in the care of English Heritage.

Morville Hall, Shrops 693 G4, A small Elizabethan house which is so similar to Wilderhope Manor* and Shipton Hall* that it must be by the same builder. The interior was made more comfortable in the 18th century [NT].

Morwellham Quay, Devon 688 E6, Developed by the Dukes of Bedford to serve the rapidly expanding and very prosperous mines of the upper Tamar valley, and in particular the copper mines of Gunnislake. Tavistock, some 4½ miles (7km) distant, is connected by canal to the inclined plane railway that leads down to the port on the River Tamar 250 feet (75m) below. Vessels of up to 200 tons could moor in the dock, which was serviced by an overhead railway. Arsenic and other minerals were also found here, and the wealth of the area is visible in the terraces of the estate cottages, the workshops, the chapel, and the Ship Inn. Costumed figures and horse-drawn wagons now enliven the scene and make this a very popular tourist destination.

Morwenstow, Cnwll 688 E5, Robert Stephen Hawker, the son of a Plymouth doctor, was one of the great eccentrics of the Victorian age. Born in 1803, he studied at Oxford before becoming Vicar of the remote parish of Morwenstow, to which he devoted his life – rebuilding the ancient church of St Morwenna and constructing a handsome new vicarage, whose five chimneys were modelled on the towers of the churches with which he had been connected. The kitchen chimney was based on his mother's tomb. He also built himself a hut on the vicarage cliffs, using timbers dragged up from a shipwreck on the beach below. Here he looked out across the treacherous Atlantic shore and if any vessel should founder he was always ready to lend assistance, or provide a decent Christian burial place for the victims in the churchyard. In 1842 the Arbroath brig *Caledonian* ran aground with great loss of life. The grave of the captain and some of the crew is marked by the ship's figurehead.

Moseley Old Hall, Shrops 693 H4, After his defeat at the Battle of Worcester in 1651 King Charles I took refuge in this small timber-framed manor house.

Above: Mount Edgcumbe looks over the safe waters of Plymouth Sound.

Moseley Old Hall
Top right: The Victorian exterior with a re-created parterre.
Below, left and right: Jacobean furniture in the kitchen and bedroom.

between 1547 and 1554 with four corner towers and a great central hall rising above the roof line. Greatly extended during the 19th century, the mansion suffered fire damage during World War II, and was then rebuilt in a reduced form. But there is much to see in the grounds: the earl's garden near the house; the formal French, Italian and English gardens at the foot of the hill; and the temples, ruins and other features scattered through the very extensive, largely early 19th-century park, with its carriage drives which hug the contours round to the delightful small coastal villages of Kingsand and Cawsand.

Mount Ephraim Gardens, Kent 691 H5, Eight acres (3.2ha) of gardens next to a family-run orchard. There is a Japanese rock garden, a water garden, topiary and rose terraces.

It looks rather different now because it was encased in purple brick in the 1870s, but the interior has altered little and the rooms have been furnished in an appropriate manner [NT].

Mottisfont Abbey, Hants 690 C6, A mainly Georgian house with remains of a medieval abbey, a room with *trompe-l'oeil* paintings of 1939 by Rex Whistler and part of the late Derek Hill's collection of pictures, set in a garden with a famous collection of old varieties of roses [NT].

Mount Edgcumbe, Cnwll 688 E7, The main house of the Edgcumbes was built

Bottom left: The arms of the Edgcumbe family.

Top right: Mottisfont Abbey is set in attractive gardens, through which flows a tributary of the River Test.

Much Hadham

M

Mount Grace Priory, N York 697 H4, The most complete Carthusian house in England. Unlike other religious orders which lived communally, here each monk enjoyed splendid isolation in his own two-storey cottage-like cell, to which most meals were brought and passed to him through a hatch designed to prevent him from seeing the servant. The church and other communal areas are relatively compact, since numbers in Carthusian monasteries were necessarily small. The cells are arranged around an extensive courtyard, and each has an ingeniously contrived water supply and drainage system.

Although a National Trust property, Mount Grace is administered by English Heritage, which has very impressively re-created the interior of one of the cells and the monastic garden, and has provided a useful interpretation of medieval monasticism in the 17th-century entrance range.

Mount St Bernard Abbey, Leics 694 D5, In 1835 Ambrose Phillips of Garendon bought 200 acres (80ha) of land for the foundation of a modest Cistercian abbey, the first in England since the 16th-century Reformation. The Earl of Shrewsbury gave money for more elaborate buildings, which were designed by Pugin. Construction began in 1839, and the monastery has been enlarged several times since then. The church itself is half by Pugin (1840s) and half by FJ Bradford (1930s). The whole complex is built of local Charnwood stone, giving it a dark and rugged appearance.

Mount Stuart, *see* **Bute*.**

Mousa, Shet 703 H4, The tiny island of Mousa, which lies off Leebooten (Leebitton) on the southeast coast of Mainland in Shetland*, is famous for its exceptionally well-preserved broch. The impressive dry-stone round tower (over 42 feet/13m high and with a diameter of almost 50 feet/15m at the base) probably dates from the 1st century AD. Its hollow walls conceal a narrow staircase which services six galleries and leads to the rampart walk.

Above left: Mount Grace Priory, with its cells arranged round a central courtyard.

Below: Much Hadham, a Henry Moore sculpture. The Henry Moore Foundation own and maintain his studio and workshop where examples of his work can be seen.

Mousehole, Cnwll 688 B8, St Clement's Isle shelters the narrow approach to the harbour, which has now been immortalized in the children's story, *The Mousehole Cat*. In 1595 the Spaniards invaded the village and sacked it, together with neighbouring Newlyn* and Penzance*. Only two houses survived. During the Christmas season Mousehole's famous Christmas lights decorate the harbour, and on 23 December, the villagers celebrate Tom Bowcock's Eve, commemorating the skilful fisherman who caught seven types of fish to feed a starving village.

Much Hadham, Herts 691 G4, This charming little village – a world away from busy Bishop's Stortford* nearby – still has an unspoilt main street which, with several good cottages and large 18th-century houses, is typical of the county. The mainly 14th-century church of St Andrew has two uncharacteristically modern head-stops to its west door: a king and a queen by the famous sculptor Henry Moore, who lived and worked at nearby Perry Green*. A working blacksmith's forge and garden with 19th-century plants and bee shelter can be seen at the Forge Museum and Victorian Cottage Garden.

Much Wenlock Priory
Top: The 13th-century transept.
Centre left: A 12th-century carving of Christ and St Peter at the Sea of Galilee.

Muchelney Abbey
Centre right: The remains of the Cloister.
Bottom left: The Refectory wall, with its tall blank five-light panelling.

Much Marcle, Herefs 693 G6, Hellen's House, a brick manor house, is a mellow fusion of different periods, although Jacobean plaster ceilings and fireplaces dominate the interior. The neighbouring churchyard boasts the Marcle Yew, with a hollow trunk in which seven people can sit. It also contains a mound to the north, the remains of yet another of the Mortimer family's border castles.

Much Wenlock, Shrops 693 G4, A pleasant little town with a large and picturesque medieval dwelling house – the Prior's Lodge – dwarfed by the ruined remains of a Cluniac priory [EH].

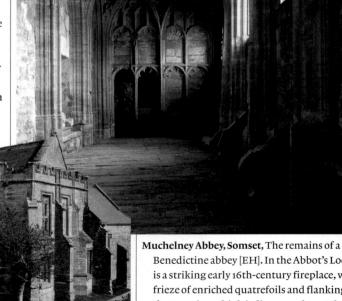

Muchelney Abbey, Somset, The remains of a Benedictine abbey [EH]. In the Abbot's Lodgings is a striking early 16th-century fireplace, with a frieze of enriched quatrefoils and flanking shafts that terminate high in lions couchant. The adjoining church of St Peter and St Paul has a painted wagon roof. *See* **Langport* 689 H5.**

Top left: Mull, Torosay Castle's Statue Walk, with marble statues by Antonio Bonazza.

Nairn   **N**

Mull, Ag & B 698 B2, This volcanic island is wilder than the Isle of Skye* but, like Skye, is renowned for the diversity of landscapes. Its highest point is Ben More (3,170 feet/966m). **Torosay Castle** was

built in Scots Baronial style (1858) by the architect David Bryce for the Campbells. It stands above Duart Bay and enjoys a sweeping view of Lock Linnhe, which stretches away to the Appin and Lorne mountains on the Scottish mainland. Its magnificent gardens were designed by Robert Lorimer at the request of the Guthries, who bought the estate in 1868, and decorated with marble statues by the Italian sculptor Antonio Bonazza (1698–1763).

Duart Castle, built *c*1250 to protect the major navigation route of the Sound of Mull, is the ancestral home of the chiefs of the MacLean clan. After a chequered history it was extensively restored 1911–16: the keep is all that remains of the original building. Various relics of the clan's history can be seen inside the castle.

Tobermory, the administrative centre of Mull, is also one of the most beautiful natural harbours on the west coast of Scotland. There are tiers of gaily coloured houses built on the hillside around the harbour. Founded in 1788 by the British Society for Encouraging Fisheries, it welcomed many of the farmers evicted during the Highland Clearances. At the harbour are a small museum of regional history, an art and craft gallery and a distillery founded in 1795.

Dervaig, the principal village on the west coast of Mull, founded in 1799, has the smallest professional theater in Britain, the Mull Little Theatre. Its museum, the Old Byre, has displays of the island's everyday life and natural history.

Above: Muncaster Castle, Victorian Gothic by Salvin. It contains fine furniture, porcelain, tapestries and oriental rugs.

Above left: Mull, Duart Castle, a Maclean stronghold since the 13th century and still home to the chief of the Clan MacLean.

Left: Muncaster Castle has grown from a medieval pele tower to the large structure seen today. It has been owned by the Pennington family since 1208.

Mullion, Cnwll 688 C8, The large harbour, generously provided by Lord Robartes of Lanhydrock* in 1893 and 1896, lies on the eastern flank of the Lizard. Shell fishermen still ply out of the harbour, using the old windlass at the top of the slip to pull their vessels out of the water.

Muncaster Castle, Cumb 696 D4, Set on rather bleak coast with a superb view inland to the Lake District* that was much praised by Ruskin. The house has been owned by the Penningtons for centuries and has a medieval core but most of what is now seen is the result of a major reconstruction by Anthony Salvin in 1862. His High Victorian interiors became even more opulent when the castle acquired the collections of the Ramsden family in the 1920s. At the same time the gardens were extended with plants brought back from the Himalayas by expeditions financed by Sir John Ramsden [EH].

Munstead, Surrey, This is an interesting region, in the hills over Godalming, famous for the number of country houses that were built here in the late 19th century by Lutyens – at the instigation of Gertrude Jekyll. She lived first at Munstead House, built for her parents (Col. and Mrs Jekyll) by Stevenson and altered by Lutyens, and later at Munstead Wood, built by Lutyens in 1896. *See* **Godalming* 690 E6.**

Mynydd Preseli, Pembks 692 C6, The highest ridge in Pembrokeshire, and the source of the 'blue stones', reputedly transported from here along the Irish trade route to Stonehenge*. With the status of a National Park, Presely Mountain protects the ancient settlements of Trefdraeth (Newport*), Dinas and the Gwaun Valley. The area is rich in prehistoric sites, among them **Parc y Meirw**, near Llanychaer, consisting of a row of upright stones dating from the 2nd millennium BC, four of which are still standing. On the Fishguard* road from Newport are the neolithic **Cerrig y Gof** ('The Smith's Stones') with five burial chambers of the 4th–3rd millennium BC.

Nairn, Highld 701 H5, The first records of the old town of Invernairne date from 1214. In the late 12th century William the Lion granted it a royal charter and built a castle which was destroyed in the 16th century. The town, situated on the south bank of the Moray Firth, was almost entirely rebuilt in the 19th century when it became a fashionable coastal resort. The 'Brighton* of the North' owed much of its success to Dr John Grigor, who recommended its invigorating air and sunny climate to his patients. In 1890 the town expressed its gratitude by erecting the statue that stands on the lawns of Viewfield House, the Georgian mansion occupied by the Nairn Museum and Literary Institute. For a long time Nairn had an

active fishing community, the Nairn Fishermen's Society, founded in 1767 and believed to be the oldest co-operative in Scotland. Although the narrow streets and modest cottages of the Fishertown district have changed little since the 19th century, the fishing and the herring industry declined in the 1920s and 1930s. Fishertown Museum, in King Street, traces the history and traditions of the town's fishing industry.

Nanhoron, Gwynd 692 C3, Capel Newydd (New Chapel) is a misnomer; a former barn, it is the oldest Independent Chapel in North Wales (1769). Alterations in the early 19th century have preserved its original simplicity.

Nant Gwrtheyrn, Gwynd 692 D2, Although associated with the 5th-century Vortigern, traditionally hated for his betrayal of his people, the place has a far more positive ring for the thousands of students of Welsh who have benefited from residential courses in the quarrymen's village of Porth-y-Nant, rehabilitated by a local trust after decades of disuse.

Nanteos, Cerdgn 692 D4, A handsome mid-18th-century house, whose name means the 'brook of the nightingale'. It once housed a wooden cup whose healing powers were traditionally attributed to its origins as the Holy Grail, supposedly brought here from the Cistercian monastery Ystrad Fflur (Strata Florida*). It was

Above: Nanteos, in its woodland setting outside Aberystwyth. Built in 1739, its architect has yet to be discovered.

Below: Naworth Castle still retains its medieval exterior.

Left: Nether Alderley Mill, the vast expanse of slate roof with tiny dormers.

fancifully believed to be the inspiration for Wagner's *Parsifal*, as the composer once stayed in the house. Nanteos is now a hotel.

Nantgarw, Rhondd 689 G3, Almost in the shadow of the wooded hillside of Castell Coch*, the village of Nantgarw ('wild brook') gave its name to a type of early 19th-century porcelain which rivalled some of the finest in Europe. The small museum was once the home of William Billingsley who came to the area in 1813 from the Derby Porcelain factory, where he was an accomplished flower decorator, and began producing a soft-paste porcelain of exceptional translucency. The venture was beset by technical difficulties, and incurred the loss not only of much of the product itself, but considerable sums of money as well, resulting in the closure of the factory in 1814. Exquisite examples of Nantgarw porcelain can be seen in the National Museum of Wales in Cardiff*.

Nantwich, Ches 693 G2, Together with Middlewich and Northwich, it grew rich from the salt industry that flourished here in Roman times, but salt-making had ceased by the 19th century. St Mary's Church is an impressive building with an unusual octagonal crossing tower and a very elaborate vaulted ceiling in the chancel. The church stands in the middle of the town, with pleasant streets radiating from the churchyard. An inscription carved on the outside of Churche's Mansion in Hospital Street reads 'Rychard Churche and Margerye Churche his wife Mai IIII Thomas Clease made this worke, anno dni MCCCCLXXVII in the XVIII yeare of the reane of our noble queene elesabeth.' The timber house that Mr Clease built for Richard Church in 1577 is an excellent example of a Tudor merchant's house, adorned with the elaborate timber patterns that were popular in the West Midlands.

Naworth Castle, Cumb 696 E2, The Castle's anagrammatic nickname 'War to the Clans' identifies its key position at the border. It is owned by one of the branches of the Howard family. The medieval form of the Castle survives but most the interior was a medieval re-creation by Anthony Salvin after a major fire in 1840. Contents include a number of imported items, including a screen from Lanercost*.

Nayland, Suffk 691 H3, In this pastel-shaded village by the Stour (navigable by Constable family barges until the 1930s), stands Alston Court, dating from 1480, with a hooded doorcase and beautifully carved bargeboards. The village is ranged around a church with exquisite linenfold carving on its doors. Constable's 1809 painting of Christ blessing bread and wine still hangs over the altar. His only other religious work has been taken from Brantham church to Ipswich*'s Christchurch Mansion Museum. Just south of Nayland,

Wissington has a perfect little Norman church next to the moated hall, with 13th-century frescoes that include a contemporary St Francis preaching to the birds. The hall was enlarged by Sir John Soane in 1791 for Samuel Beachcroft, Governor of the Bank of England (Soane also built Tendring Hall at Stoke-by-Nayland*, now demolished save for a gaunt doorway).

Neath Abbey, Neath 689 F3, What John Leland, Henry VIII's antiquary, described shortly before 1536 as 'the fairest Abbey in all Wales' is now the only Welsh monastery whose remains are surrounded by industrial expansion. It was founded in 1130 as a house of the order of Sevigny, but became Cistercian in 1147, although the ruins we see today belong to the building which was raised 150 years later. After the Dissolution, much of the monastic construction was used to create a grand house. This, too, is now in ruins, but suggests how members of the Tudor ascendancy asserted themselves through robust and outward-looking optimism. Neath Abbey has a strange fascination because of the circumstances which have reduced its former monastic and domestic stature to a forlorn piece of masonry in a blighted landscape.

Nether Alderley Mill, Ches 693 H2, A large watermill dating from the 15th century, with two overshot waterwheels. The Victorian machinery has been fully restored to working order by the National Trust, and the mill is in regular operation.

New Abbey
Above: View of Sweetheart Abbey from the north.
Left: View from the south, showing the nave and central tower.

Nether Winchendon House, Bucks, A very interesting medieval and Tudor manor house, remodelled between 1798 and 1803 in the gothic style. The fine quality of the frieze and linenfold panelling in the drawing room suggests royal connections, and indeed the early 16th-century owner, Sir John Daunce, was one of Henry VIII's privy councillors. *See* **Long Crendon* 690 E4.**

Netley Abbey, Hants 690 D7, The magnificent ruin of a 13th–14th century Cistercian monastery [EH].

Nevern (Nanhyfer), Pembks 692 C6, In the churchyard of St Brynach are a number of early Christian inscribed stones, and a majestic Celtic cross with intricately carved panels, of the same period as the one at Carew. Inside the church is a brass plate commemorating George Own of Henilys, Lord of Cemais (1552–1613), known for his invaluable *History of Pembrokeshire*. One of the yews that form an avenue to the church is known as the 'Bleeding Yew' because of the blood-red sap that drips from it. To the west of the church, cut into the rock, is the Pilgrim's Cross, so called because it was probably a shrine on the route to St David's.

New Abbey, D & G 696 D2, To the north of the village stands Shambellie House, a mildly baronial built in 1850 by David Bryce. Its Victorian and Edwardian interior houses a collection of costumes dating from the late 18th to the early 20th century. New Abbey Corn Mill is an 18th-century mill in perfect working order, famous for the ruins of Sweetheart Abbey, a Cistercian monastery founded in 1273 by Lady Devorguilla Balliol in memory of her husband, John Balliol, who died in 1269. His inconsolable widow never went anywhere without the reliquary containing her husband's embalmed heart. When she was buried, along with the casket, in front of the high altar in the abbey church in 1290, the monks renamed the abbey Dulce Cor ('sweet heart').

New Buckenham, Norfk 695 H5, A unique medieval planned borough 15 miles (24km) southwest of Norwich*, still confined by the line of its original town ditch. In 1145 William D'Albini II abandoned his fortification in Old Buckenham for a better site on the Norwich–Thetford road. Here he built another castle and laid out a new settlement with its own market on a grid of intersecting streets. The keep, now a romantic ruin encircled by a moat and steeply wooded ramparts, is the earliest and largest circular keep in England. The castle chapel, converted into a barn at the Dissolution, stands beside the road. The centrepiece of a village full of attractive houses is the Market House (1559), on the green, later raised on wooden Tuscan columns; beneath it is a whipping post complete with arm clamps. St Martin's, 'an uncommonly sumptuous Perpendicular church', has a rare 16th-century sill-board carved with the gatehouse of a walled town. One of the largest commons in Norfolk stretches away east of the village. Grazing-right owners still employ a 'pinder' to tend the cattle. The northern half, a nature reserve, has rare meadow flowers and crested newts in Spittle Mere.

Centre and bottom: New Forest, two views, one with newly planted trees, the other with trees that are centuries old. The New Forest ponies, which roam wild, are one of its main attractions.

New Forest, Hants 690 C7, Historically, a forest was an area given over to hunting by the monarch, not necessarily all wooded. What is now called the New Forest was already largely wild when King William II declared it a royal forest in 1079. Then, as now, more than half the area was probably heathland, grassland or bog, the rest woodland. Local people were permitted, under supervision, to graze certain animals there, but the requirements of royal hunting were paramount. Later, its timber came to be valued as a reserve for the Royal Navy. In the last 150 years many conifers were planted, but now the emphasis is on maintaining the forest for its wildlife and for recreation. Today there are three main types of New Forest landscape: open land (mainly heath); wild woodland with deciduous trees; and plantations, largely of conifers (which have to be fenced, for protection against grazing, until the trees are mature). Commoners (those having rights of grazing) are allowed to turn cattle, and the half-wild forest ponies, into the open forest under the supervision of the local Court of Verderers.

New Lanark, S Lans 699 F5, This 19th-century workers' village was one of the first to provide decent working and living conditions for a large workforce. In 1783 Richard Arkwright, who invented the water frame, was commissioned by the industrialist David Dale to design a cotton mill powered by the Falls of Clyde. The mill soon became the largest in Scotland and by 1799 was supporting 2500 people living and working on the site. Some of the workers' dwellings and the co-operative store have been restored to their original state and are open to the public. The village has been classified as a World Heritage Site. Robert Owen House contains personal posssessions of the mill owner and documents relating to his utopian philosophy. *See also* **Lanark*.**

Newark-on-Trent, Notts 694 E4, A handsome town which became rich from the wool and coal shipped up the River Trent. It was defended by a strong

castle, which incurred damage to its walls during the Civil War when it was besieged by Parliamentary forces. The town was important as a staging place on the Great North Road and as a centre of agriculture. Some of the great sheds built for malting still survive at its edge. At its heart is the broad and busy market square, where stands the splendid medieval church of St Mary Magdalen, one of the grandest parish churches in England. The building has the height and large windows typical of the late 15th century. Also in the square is the Palladian Market Hall of 1774 by John Carr. All around are streets of Georgian houses.

Above: New Lanark, view showing The Clyde and Double Row in the foreground and Braxfield Row behind.

Below centre: Newark-on-Trent, church of St Mary Magdalen, the spire seen across the market place.

Above right: Newbury, the River Kennet.

Left: Newark-on-Trent, the castle commanding the River Trent.

Bottom: Newby Hall, viewed from its glorious gardens.

Newbury, Berks 690 D5, A pleasant town on the River Kennet. Its good 16th- to 18th-century buildings reflect its former prosperity, since it was once the centre of a booming cloth-making trade. This industry was established by John Smallwood (also known by the names Jack O'Newbury and John Winchcombe) who lived in the early 16th century and was responsible for the nave of the fine church of St Nicholas built in *c*1500–32. In Wharf Road is the fascinating timber-framed Cloth Hall, built in 1626–7, now a museum.

Newby Hall, N York 697 H5, Externally a house of the very late 17th century, in brick with stone dressings and just a hint of baroque in its segmental pediments, but internally one of Robert Adam's masterpieces. The fine entrance hall exudes a profound sense of symmetry, with regularly spaced mahogany doors and an interesting contemporary organ. The *pièce de résistance* is the Tapestry Room, with a set of breathtaking tapestries specially commissioned from the Gobelins factory by the house's young owner William Weddell while on his Grand Tour in 1765–6. How did he know the measurements of the room for ordering the tapestries? The room was being built in his absence, yet the tapestries fit accurately around the doors, windows and

fireplace; even the shadows are woven into the tapestries, which give the impression of Georgian party decorations, with garlands of florists' blooms. Weddell's Grand Tour portrait by Pompeo Batoni hangs on the stairs. Weddell also brought home an outstanding collection of Roman sculpture, for which he built a new gallery based on the Tribune of the Uffizi Gallery in Florence. Newby Hall has extensive and attractive gardens, and within the grounds in the village of Skelton-on-Ure is the Church of Christ the Consoler, designed by William Burges as a memorial to Frederick Grantham Vyner, murdered by Greek brigands in 1870 (*see* **Studley Royal***).

N

Newcastle upon Tyne

Newcastle upon Tyne, T & W 697 G2, A handsome and vibrant city. Its architectural character is predominantly early 19th century; but there are some notable medieval buildings, Georgian churches, a fine railway station by John Dobson, and several good bridges over the Tyne, including the Millennium Blinking Eye Bridge. The Romans bridged the Tyne here at Pons Aelius. The Castle is an impressive 12th-century example built for Henry II. There are two cathedrals: the medieval St Nicholas with its stone 'crown' (an open lantern, supported by flying buttresses, on its west tower), and the Roman Catholic St Mary, designed by AWN Pugin, with fine Victorian stained glass. Elegant Grey Street has been described as the finest curved street in Europe. It was part of a new town centre development

resulting from the successful interaction of three remarkable men, the builder-cum-entrepreneur Richard Grainger, the architect John Dobson and the town clerk John Clayton. The Grey Monument is a huge Doric column surmounted by a statue of Earl Grey, the prime minister responsible for the passing of the Reform Act of 1832. The Laing Art Gallery has new exterior sculptures, *The Blue Carpet* and *Winding Steps* by Thomas Heatherwick. Intended as a unified design, they form an interactive sculptural piazza for visitors to walk on. Museums include the Discovery Museum, where the focal point of the display is the Turbina, the world's first steam-turbine-driven ship. Bessie Surtees House [EH] is a Jacobean merchant's house.

Above left: Bessie Surtees House, originally two merchants' houses.

Above: Grey Street and the Grey Monument.

Bottom left: The keep of the Castle that gives the city its name.

Newhouse, Wilts 690 C6, A brick house of c1609 in the village of Redlynch near the New Forest*, said to have been built as a hunting lodge for Sir Thomas Gorges of Longford Castle. It has two Georgian wings and a largely Georgian interior. Its three bays are intended to represent the Trinity.

Newland, Gloucs 693 G7, The giant church of All Saints in the Forest of Dean* is sometimes called 'The Cathedral of the Forest'. It dominates the village from its huge square churchyard, surrounded by almshouses and the old grammar school. Inside are two important pieces of forest history: the stone monument of the 'Forester of Fee' shows his 15th-century huntsman's outfit, and a brass in the south aisle (of unknown date) depicts a medieval miner with his pick, holding a candlestick in his mouth.

Newlyn, Cnwll 688 B8, Despite the recent problems of the local fishing industry, Newlyn is still the largest fishing port of the southwest. Dozens of vessels still regularly leave its large sheltered

harbour; and the narrow streets of the village still smell of fish and echo to the cries of the gulls (the Pilchard Museum is well worth a visit). A

bronze line at the entrance to the harbour denotes sea-level throughout the world. Newlyn Orion Art Gallery has an adventurous contemporary art exhibition programme. For this we must thank the Newlyn School and its leader Stanhope Forbes, whose *plein air* painting style attracted a number of other artists and craftsmen to the quaint village, bathed in brilliant light reflected off the sea.

Newmarket, Suffk 695 G6, The centre of British horse-racing since the 17th century. The National Horse Racing Museum is housed in the former Regency Subscription Rooms. It boasts a bronze figure of the most famous racehorse of all, Hyperion, and stands next to the Jockey Club. Everywhere the equestrian theme prevails. Newmarket Heath, where James I hunted hares, became a pleasure ground under Charles II and George Stubbs painted several scenes here. Rowley Mile Course is the world's longest and widest racecourse, and stables and stud farms stretch for miles in a landscape quartered by beech belts into gallops on the short, springy turf.

Newport, Essex 691 G3, A pretty thoroughfare village in the Cam valley just south of Saffron Walden. Notable buildings include the Crown House, impressively pargeted in 1692; the former House

Above: Newlyn's sheltered harbour. The fishermen of this busy port live in terraces of houses overlooking Mount's Bay.

Left: Newmarket, the National Horse Racing Museum and the statue of Hyperion.

of Correction, 1775, in white brick; the Charles II-style grammar school; and Monks Barn, with a Virgin and Angels oriel window. The church, large and formerly collegiate, has a 15th-century porch and clerestory.

Newport (Casnewydd-ar-Wysg), Blae G 689 H3, The remains of a motte-and-bailey castle were cleared in order to make way for Brunel's Great Western Railway in the 1840s. The Norman church of St Woolos has an impressive arch leading into a five-bay nave, supported by round pillars bearing sturdy scalloped capitals. The east end of the church was replaced by a chancel built by ADR Caröe between 1960 and 1964.

Newport Market Hall (1887–9) is a survivor of the town's Victorian spirit, its arched iron and glass reminiscent of a good provincial railway station. The Museum and Art Gallery, together with the municipal library, are housed in the same modern building in John Frost Square, named after the Chartist leader who instigated the uprising of November 1839. The incident is commemorated in a mural in the Square, as well as in the building itself, which displays a good collection of artefacts ranging from prehistoric relics and the Roman finds at Caerwent to the work of contemporary artists. More art can be seen in the Civic Centre (started in 1937, by Cecil Hewitt), where the murals in the central hall, commissioned in 1960, depict events affecting the history and development of the town. The hillside **Bellevue Park** was designed by TH Mawson, the great Edwardian landscape

Below: Newport Transporter Bridge, the extraordinary structure designed to carry vehicles and pedestrians on a galleried platform.

Left: Newquay. Fistral is just one of the beaches renowned for fine surf.

Right: Newstead Abbey, the late 13th-century façade of the former priory church.

artist, at the expense of the Morgan family of Tredegar House*. Their entrepreneurial acumen was a major contributory factor to the opening of Newport Docks, developed to export bituminous coal and iron (of which there were rich deposits in the hinterland). It was an attempt to cope with the almost insatiable overseas demand for coal at the end of the 19th century that accounted for the sudden growth not only of Newport, but also Cardiff*, Penarth* and Barry* as port towns.
A reminder of the heyday of this frenzied trade is the **Transporter Bridge** crossing the Usk, which has the greatest tidal rise and fall of any river in the United Kingdom. The bridge was built between 1902 and 1906 to the designs of François Arnodin, who was responsible for a similar one at Marseilles; it consists of two towers supporting a track from which is suspended a galleried platform which can ply back and forth from bank to bank, high enough over the river so as not to impede shipping. The platform, with a pair of canopied shelters for foot passengers and a navigator's cabin, can carry six cars.

Newquay, Cnwll 688 C7, One of the country's main holiday resorts, it is famed for its fine surfing beaches and has become the scene of many championships. One of the oldest buildings in the sprawling, largely Victorian town is the white-painted Huer's Hut below the magisterial Atlantic Hotel, where the huer kept look-out for the pilchards. When he spotted them he raised the cry of 'hera, hera, hera'. In 1863 £20,000 worth of pilchards were caught in one week, so large were the shoals. The small port built by Joseph Treffry of Fowey*, for the export of china clay, tin, lead and copper, also provided employment in the 19th century.

Newstead Abbey, Notts 694 D4, The west front is all that survives of the abbey church, but the cloister was turned into a large house by the Byron family, who acquired Newstead in 1540. By the time the 6th Lord Byron (the poet) inherited in 1798, the house was in a bad way; one of his friends called it 'a heap of rubbish'. But Byron loved the place; the house now contains many of the poet's effects, and his dog Bosun is buried in the abbey ruins (Byron himself is buried in Hacknall Church). In 1818 the house was sold to the Wildman family, who restored it in a neo-Tudor style with Norman

Above: Newtimber Place, an attractive 17th-century house, which is built of flint with rose-coloured brick surrounds to the windows.

Below: Newtown, statue of Robert Owen (1771–1858), the Utopian Socialist who lived there until the age of 10.

elements in 1828. Newstead is surrounded by large and elaborate gardens; the huge lake was used in the 1770s to stage miniature sea battles. Pretty mock 18th-century forts still survive on the edge of the lake.

Newtimber Place, W Susx 691 F7, A moated house of the 17th century, with a contemporary dovecote. There are late-18th-century Etruscan wall paintings in the hall.

Newtown (Y Drenewydd), Powys 693 F4, This pleasant Severn-side settlement owes its name to a charter given by Edward I to Roger Mortimer in 1279 to hold a weekly market and two annual fairs in Llanfair yng Nghedewain, which was to develop as the 'new town', with an urban plan that can be discerned to this day in the Broad and High streets. In the late 18th century it was known, somewhat optimistically, as the 'Leeds of Wales' because of its booming woollen trade, greatly aided by the Montgomeryshire Canal which reached it in 1819. During its heyday, a local businessman Sir Pryce Pryce-Jones started the first mail-order business in the world in 1861. Queen Victoria was one of the clients.
The town's most renowned son, the educational pioneer Robert Owen (1771–1858), often called 'the father of British socialism', left Newtown as a boy with vivid memories of the poor conditions of the weavers, and in time established the co-operative community at New Lanark*. Owen is buried in the graveyard of the old St Mary's Church, Newtown, abandoned in 1840 because of flooding. A monument of 1902 depicts labourers receiving justice at his hands. There is a small museum to him in the Robert Owen Institute, which stands on the site of his birthplace. In the High Street, WH Smith – reputedly the only branch to have retained its original façade and fittings, including wooden floors – has a small museum above the shop. In New Road is the High classic exuberance of Zion, a Baptist Tabernacle designed in 1881 at a cost of £8,000.

Left: A traditional thatched wind-pump on Horsey Mere, a quiet backwater away from the main cruiser centres.

Below: This intricate network of rivers and shallow lakes is a delicate eco-system of national importance.

Norfolk Broads, Norfk 695 J5, This strange watery landscape, the largest wetland in England, is a unique network of rivers, shallow lakes and drainage marshes. Today it is both a popular holiday destination with a lucrative boat hire industry and a fragile eco-system that is the home of many endangered species. The Broads Authority has been created to manage this conflict in what is now effectively a national park.

Until quite recently it had been assumed that the Broads were the natural remnant of a large inland lake, but documentary evidence now shows that in the Middle Ages the Benedictine monks of St Benet's Abbey acquired peat-digging rights across a wide area and a pool of peasant labour. Their enterprise created big profits and huge holes which, when sea-level and rainfall rose in the 14th century, filled with water. Fed by the rivers Bure, Yare and Waveney, and their tributaries the Ant, Thurne and Chet, the Broads came to cover 220 square miles (570 sq km) of wetland northeast of Norwich*. The terrain ranges from the vast reed-fringed lake at Hickling and the viciously tidal Breydon Water, to dykes, water-meadows and impenetrable marshes. The old reed cutters, wildfowlers, eel catchers and boat builders who inhabited this harsh and beautiful domain were captured by the pioneering photographer P H Emerson in several collections, notably *Life and Landscape on the Norfolk Broads* (1886), and by a clutch of romantic watercolourists. But even then the railway had reached Wroxham, and the Victorians soon discovered the pleasures of boating. Sailing, for the select few, was immortalized for children in Arthur Ransome's *Coot Club* (1934), a Broads' idyll threatened by motor launch noise and pollution. Thousands of trading wherries, those distinctive flat-bottomed barges finally sunk by competition from rail and road carriers, are now remembered in the form of the restored vessel *Albion*, which with several wherry yachts sails on serenely through the congestion of summer cruisers.

A century ago hundreds of wind-pumps drained this watery wilderness, of which dozens of stumps and shells, and several well-preserved examples (Horsey, Thurne Dyke, Boardman's, Strachey Arms) remain. The flat expanse of Halvergate Marshes, saved from the plough in the 1980s after a national campaign, is dotted with semi-derelict drainage pumps – now the subject of an ambitious restoration programme. Train journeys from Norwich to Yarmouth* and Lowestoft* are the best way to appreciate this Dutch landscape. Alight at the remote Berney Arms halt and walk across the meadows to the tallest wind-pump on the Broads beside the River Yare.

Rare flora and fauna include marsh orchids, swallowtail butterflies and the elusive, booming bittern. The native otter has been welcomed back after the ravages of pollution and the escaped coypu exterminated. Conservation measures have transformed the waters of Cockshoot Broad and Barton Broad, allowing water lilies and dragonflies to return. Elsewhere some of the most beautiful Broads have become important nature reserves. At Hickling Broad [Norfolk Wildlife Trust] and Horsey Mere [NT], home to the bearded tit, the osprey is an occasional visitor, marsh harriers hunt over the reed beds at Strumpshaw Fen [RSPB] and there is a large colony of cormorants on Ranworth Broad [NWT].

Top: Norham Castle, looking towards the distant Great Tower or keep.

Normanby Hall
Below centre: The library with a mid-Georgian chimneypiece.
Bottom: The severe late-Georgian entrance front.

later defences incorporated gun embrasures and provision for cannon.

Normanby Hall, Lincs 697 J7, Once the site of a grand Tudor house and then of a rather more ordinary mid-Georgian house, both built by the Sheffield family, and both now gone. The present house was built in 1820 to the designs of Robert Smirke. He was a serious-minded architect and Normanby was one of his attempts to introduce a stripped-down version of the classical style, which one contemporary called 'Mr Smirke's new cubical style'. The house is designed as a series of intersecting cubes with Greek ornament. The rear wing, which is in the baroque style and was added by Walter Brierley in 1906, is more immediately attractive. The Sheffields left Normanby in 1963, and it has become a rather good house museum.

Norham Castle, Nthumb 699 J5, On a magnificent site high above a bend of the River Tweed, the castle [EH] lay within the jurisdiction of the Bishops of Durham, who ruled this distant part of the country on behalf of the Crown. The buildings were thus of exceptional quality. The pink sandstone Great Tower or keep is of the 12th century and later, its romantic profile having inspired many artists, notably JMW Turner. There is an impressively photogenic view back from the gatehouse, towards the west gate and the village. The inner ward is separated from the outer by a deep moat, in the base of which, near the site of the bridge, are washing floors, constructed of stone paving and probably used for washing the wool that provided the bishops with revenue for the maintenance of this expensive border stronghold. Norham Castle continued to feature in the story of disputes with Scotland into Tudor times, resulting in repairs which reflected new developments in gunpowder artillery, and the

Normanton, W York 697 H6, Once a typical colliery town. The large Perpendicular church of All Saints has an interesting font and some good monuments.

Norrington Manor, Wilts 690 B6, The manor at Alvediston was built in 1377, but has been frequently altered. The hall and undercroft are of the original house. This is a family house, open only by appointment following written application.

North Berwick, E Loth 699 H4, This small fishing port and former royal burgh is today a pleasant coastal resort. Near the harbour are the ruins of a 12th-century church, the Auld Kirk, and the newly opened Scottish Seabird Centre. About a mile (1.6km) south of the town centre, the hill known as Berwick Law (610 feet/186m) offers some magnificent views of the surrounding countryside. It is surmounted by a strange archway made from the jawbone of a whale.

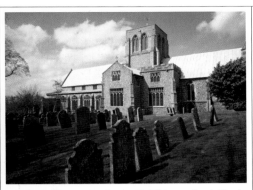

North Bucks Way, Bucks 690 E3, Thirty miles (48km) of footpath leading from the Ridgeway at Chequers Knap to Grafton Way on the Northamptonshire border.

North Cerney, Gloucs 690 C4, This pretty village contains the remarkable church of All Saints, of many periods, with a number of interesting galleries, eyries and changes in level. You enter from the south, down steps cut into the hillside. You can climb up to the rood loft, sneak through the man-sized squint into the chancel, climb again to the nave balcony, or even to the organ loft in the corner. The rood loft was designed by FC Eden, a friend of the church's benefactor William Iveson Croome. The windows contain 15th-century glass, and there are three 15th-century painted statues, of the Virgin Mary and two bishops, in the south transept. On the outer south wall of the south transept is a famous doodle of a 'manticore', top half man and lower half lion, probably carved by an idle mason.

North Crawley, Bucks 690 E3, The church of St Firmin, a saint from Pamplona, contains wonderfully carved woodwork. The wall posts of the tie-beam roof have apostles that appear to be standing on partridges. The complete, painted 15th-century screen is the only surviving one in the county.

North Elmham, Norfk 695 H5, Near the church are the remains of a Norman episcopal chapel set in

beautiful sylvan earthworks [EH]. Elmham had been centre of Norfolk's first Saxon bishopric until Bishop de Losinga replaced the small wooden cathedral with a stone chapel shortly after

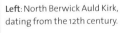

the see had moved to Thetford in 1071. It was converted into a 'des res' shooting box by Henry le Despenser, who was attracted by the deer park. This hunting bishop had helped crush the Peasants' Revolt of 1381 and, fearing reprisals, surrounded his Hall with massive earthworks. St Mary's Church, largely Perpendicular, has an impressive tower with a richly decorated west entrance, saintly rood-screen and pulpit carved in 1626 by the parish clerk at a cost of £5.3s.4d. A mile (1.6km) north, beside the River Wensum, stands the perfect Victorian rural station built in 1886 on the Wymondham–Wells line, to serve County School that once crowned nearby Bintree Hills.

North Leigh, Oxon 690 D4, A hilltop village which has the remains of a large Roman villa [EH]. The church of St Mary was originally built in c1000–50. Of note are the impressive mid-15th-century Wilcote Chapel and the early 18th-century Perrot Chapel built by Christopher Kempster. The latter contains a collection of brass plaques, supposedly coffin plates.

North Marston, Bucks 690 E3, The church of St Mary was restored with money donated by Queen Victoria – she had been left £250,000 by a local landowner, which enabled her to buy Balmoral. The other interesting fact about the church concerns the 14th-century rector, John Schorne, who claimed to have imprisoned the Devil in a boot, thus curing gout. The church became such a popular shrine that in 1478 the canons of Windsor removed his remains to Windsor in an attempt to raise funds for St George's Chapel.

North Molton, Devon 689 F5, One of the largest parishes in the county. The church occupies a magnificent site looking down upon the village square and across to Exmoor. The tower is over 100 feet (30m) high and dominates the adjacent Court House, the home of the Parkers, who were very prosperous wool merchants from the 15th century onwards. Oak panelling from the house now lines the chancel; many coats of arms show their alliances, and in the centre are those of James I. In the south aisle is the monument to Sir Amias and Lady Elizabeth Bampfylde with their twelve sons and five daughters depicted beneath them, erected in 1626 by their son John.

North Uist
Top: Scolpaig Tower, a folly built in the 1830s in the centre of a loch.
Centre: A croft house on the island of Berneray, just off the northwest coast.

Bottom: North York Moors, a typical landscape.

North Moreton, Oxon 690 D4, High-quality stained glass, dating from *c*1300, can be seen in the east window of the south chapel of the church of All Saints. It depicts 15 scenes from the lives of Christ, the Virgin, Saint Nicholas and saints Peter and Paul.

North Uist (Uibhist a Tuath), W Isls 700 C4, The Isles of Uist (Berneray, North Uist, Benbecula* and South Uist*) are linked by causeways and there is also a causeway to Eriskay*. The lochs and inlets of North Uist are a fly-fisherman's paradise, and the west coast beaches are stunning. Newton Ferry (Port nan Long), the island's most northerly point is a port of call for ferries from Lewis and Harris*. Nearby Dun an Sticar is a fortified Iron Age site that was occupied until the early 17th century. Lochmaddy (Loch Na Madadh), the tiny 'capital' of North Uist is linked by ferry to Leverburgh (Harris) and Uig (Skye*). A small museum and gallery, Taigh Chearsabhagh, occupies an 18th-century merchant's house. The bays and lochs here are a paradise for otters, seals and seabirds. Scolpaig Tower, a folly built in the 1830s on the site of a broch, stands on an island in Loch Scolpaig, in the northwest of the island. Balranald Nature Reserve on the west coast attracts almost 200 species of birds, including the endangered corncrake. The impressive cairn of Barpa Langass, a tumulus (burial mound) on the slopes of Ben Langass, can be seen about 7 miles (11km)

southwest of Lochmaddy. A little further on an unclassified road turns off to Pobull Fhinn, a small circle of standing stones to the southwest. Also worth a visit are the three standing stones of Na Fir Bhreige, northwest of Lochmaddy. At Carinish (Caranais), ruins are all that remain of Trinity Temple (Teampull na Trionaid), a religious foundation built in the 13th century by the daughter of Somerled, Lord of the Isles. The temple was a major centre of learning during the Middle Ages.

North York Moors, N Yorks, 697 J4 A National Park upland landscape, the moors heather-covered in late summer, with many pretty villages (*see* **Lastingham***, for example).

Northampton, Nhants 694 E6, The town centre boasts some good buildings. They include the sumptuous Sessions House by Henry Bell, built shortly after Northampton's terrible fire of 1674, and Godwin's fantastical Venetian Town Hall. A small terraced house in Derngate has a remarkable interior by Charles Rennie Mackintosh, and is shortly to open as a museum. The town Museum and Art Gallery has an enormous collection of shoes, not surprising given the town's former

Northiam, Great Dixter
Left: The original house was built in the last quarter of the 15th century and still retains its historic character. Lutyens restored it in 1910 and added another half-timbered house from Benenden in Kent. The two houses and garden now form a convincing and charming unity.
Above: View through to the gardens.

Bottom left: Norton Conyers.
Below: A view within the enormous walled garden.

main industry of bootmaking. Even the football team is known as 'The Cobblers'.

Northbourne Court Gardens, Kent 691 J6, The 17th-century garden of a demolished house of 1616. There are terraces on three sides and a 'mount', a common feature of Jacobean gardens but one that rarely survives: a raised vantage point from which to survey the whole view.

Northiam, E Susx 691 H6, There are two houses of interest, both with gardens. Brickwall House is Jacobean with some very rich stucco-work inside. Great Dixter is a splendid example of a 15th-century half-timbered cottage. It owes much to its restoration in 1910 by Sir Edwin Lutyens, who used his own imagination when evidence was lacking. By Lutyens too is the garden, which displays an ingenious use of architectural features.

Northill, Beds 691 F3, The much restored medieval church of St Mary has one outstanding feature: its rich stained glass of 1664 by John Oliver.

Northleach, Gloucs 690 C4, A silvery stone town as picturesque as any in the Cotswolds*, but with relatively few visitors. Rising above the small triangular Market Place, the great 'wool' church of St Peter and St Paul contains brasses depicting the wool merchants who built it. The best known is John Fortey's, showing him with one foot on a wool pack and the other on a sheep. John (d. 1459) and his father Thomas rebuilt the church, and their house stills stands in the town. The south porch is particularly well carved; one of its corbels shows a cat playing the violin.

Northumberland National Park, Nthumb 699 J6, Stretching 40 miles (64km) north from Hadrian's Wall* to the Cheviot Hills*, this – the least-populated of the country's national parks – contains some of the most spectacular scenery in England. There are National Park Centres at Rothbury and Ingram, and some delightful towns and villages. Among the many attractions of the area are Bremenium Roman Fort at High Rochester in Upper Redesdale, an outpost on Dere Street between Hadrian's Wall and the Antonine Wall in Scotland.

Norton Conyers, N York 697 G5, A charming house, medieval in origin but externally of 17th-century appearance, with eye-catching Dutch gables, and mullion and transom windows. Since 1624 it has belonged to the Graham family, who hosted various 17th-century royal visits. Charlotte Brontë came here in 1839 – it is thought she was given the idea for Mrs Rochester in *Jane Eyre* from the legend of a mad woman once confined to its attics. There is an enormous 18th-century walled garden which is still cultivated, and a very early example of a ha-ha.

N

Norwich

Norwich, Norfk 695 J5, Norwich is a thriving regional capital with a medieval heart as big as the City of London*, crowned by the equally magnificent Norman castle and cathedral. At night, thanks to superb civic lighting, the centre becomes a gigantic theatre set. Around the edges are remnants of its 2-mile (3.2km) medieval walls from its era as England's second city. Cow Tower, 1378, is most picturesque beside the River Wensum, and downstream the best preserved section runs from the Boom Towers uphill to Black Tower. None of the gateways survives but Bishops' Bridge, c1340, marks the position of the eastern entrance.

Norwich boasts the greatest concentration of medieval churches in Europe. No less than 33 survive, visible at every twist and turn of its narrow and mercifully pedestrianized streets. Many are redundant but well cared for and converted to arts and social centres, a hands-on science centre and even a puppet theatre. St Peter Hungate is a museum of church art. Among the others St Stephen's tower and St Michael Coslany have exuberant East Anglian flush flintwork. Norwich School painter John Crome (d. 1821) is buried alongside civic worthies in nearby St George Colegate, and St Gregory's has a splendid St George and the Dragon mural. The church of St Julian, where the medieval mystic wrote her *Revelations of Divine Love*, was rebuilt as a shrine after wartime bombing. St Andrews Hall, the former nave of a Dominican Priory, has been a public hall since the Reformation, with undercroft café and cloisters now part of the Art College.

Boosted by Huguenot immigrants, Norwich was an important centre of the cloth trade; wealthy merchants' houses, some with early brick-vaulted undercrofts, are dotted throughout the city. The mid-15th century Strangers Hall is now a costume museum; in Bridewell Alley a 14th-century house-cum-lockup is another local museum. King Street, once

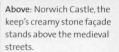

Above: Norwich Castle, the keep's creamy stone façade stands above the medieval streets.

Above left: City Hall, by CH James and SR Pierce, 1937–8, one of the best inter-war public buildings in Britain, dominates the covered market.

Centre left: St Peter Mancroft. The ornate stone tower is the largest and most impressive of the city's 33 surviving medieval churches.

Bottom: Norwich Cathedral. The slender spire rising from the banks of the River Wensum is a focal point at the end of many narrow streets.

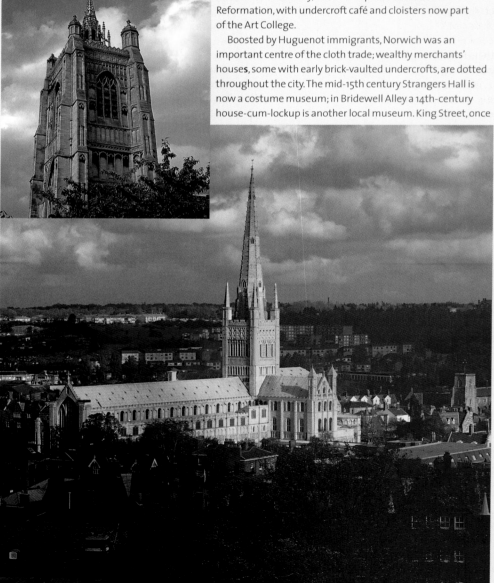

lined with wharfs, retains isolated treasures, notably a 12th-century Jewish merchant's house (Wensum Lodge) with contemporary undercroft and 14th-century Dragon Hall with an impressive crown post roof.

Colegate, north of the river, was the other main commercial quarter and has some of the finest Georgian houses among earlier merchants' dwellings, such as Bacon's House and the remarkable King of Hearts centre with Jacobean plastered ceiling. Nonconformist Norwich has bequeathed two gems here. The 17th-century Old Meeting House founded by Protestant refugees from Holland, and John Ivory's impressive Octagon Chapel of 1784 (the same date as Thomas Ivory's Assembly House, where farmers' wives still enjoy tea in the splendour of its banqueting hall). The Octagon, or 'devil's cucumber frame' became the centre for

early 19th-century dissent, attended by the poet Robert Southey and Harriet Martineau who, like Quaker Elizabeth Fry, was born in nearby Gurney Court. Occupying the high ground is the Catholic cathedral designed by George Gilbert Scott Junior, 1884; work was taken over by his brother, John Oldrid Scott, when he died in 1897. The cathedral was completed in 1910 as a huge ashlar edifice in studied Early English style and was the city's last religious building of note.

Squat and square on its huge mound, a Norman castle watches over the city, its unusually elaborate blind arcading faithfully renewed in the 1830s. Now the city's flagship museum, its keep holds hideous death masks and sumptuous civic regalia and its galleries display refined Lowestoft* porcelain, teapots galore and ravishing early 19th-century local landscapes by John Crome, John Sell Cotman and their Norwich School followers. At the base of the mound, below the former site of fairs and cattle markets, the Castle Mall shopping centre has been cleverly submerged. Nor has this sunken retail shrine eclipsed the ancient market, a perfect quadrangular space between the 15th-century Guildhall, enlivened by diaper flushwork, and majestic St Peter Mancroft Church, enriched by wonderful 15th-century Norwich School glass, its lavish west face now reflected in the

Above left: Stranger's Hall, the central courtyard. This is one of several medieval merchant's houses in the city.

Above: Octagon Chapel in Colegate was a centre of political dissent in late Georgian Norwich. John Wesley called it the most elegant meeting house in Europe.

Left: St Peter Mancroft, the sundial over the doorway.

crystal-ball gaze of a 21st-century library. Asserting itself above the coloured canvas stalls is the Stockholm-inspired 1930s City Hall with its slender portico, its 200-foot (60m) high campanile and guardian lions whose shadows rear up in the illuminated evenings. Pause in George Skipper's Art Nouveau Royal Arcade and peep into the opulent marble and mahogany interior of his Norwich Union building.

At every turn along antique lanes – Princes Street or hung-over and cobbled Elm Hill – Bishop Goldwell's cathedral spire provides a pointer. Tombland, an ancient word for market, is the spacious tree-lined café/club centre camped outside the precinct. Once through the graceful Erpingham Gate (1420), with the Norwich School chapel on the left (founded 1553; star old boy, Horatio Nelson), handsome houses around The Close head down to picturesque Pull's Ferry or the remarkable Great Hospital of 1249 complete with painted eagle roof. Soaring higher still is one of England's great Romanesque cathedrals, much of it built by Bishop Herbert de Losinga c1100 in pale limestone. The unique Norman plan survives, complete with bishop's throne in the apse behind the altar. The massive Norman nave and chancel, raised with glorious bursts of ribbed vaulting in 1490 and held aloft externally by a flurry of flying buttresses, are among its memorable architectural delights. But, more than anywhere, the cathedral is a monument in wood and stone to anonymous medieval craftsmen. Scenes from the Apocalypse, the Life of Christ and benign green men peer down from over 800 brightly painted bosses in the nave and more accessible cloister roofs. The witty carvings on 60 misericords in the choir and the Dispenser Reredos (1380) are a masterpiece of medieval art.

Norwood Park, Notts 694 D4, Outside Southwell is a mid-18th century gentleman's residence – a five-bay brick house in the manner of John Carr, said to date from 1763. Originally there were detached blocks on either side linked to the main house.

Nostell Priory, W York 697 H6, A Palladian house of two architectural periods, only a generation apart, in the early to mid-18th century [NT]. It was begun in 1735 by the amateur architect Colonel James Moyser, with modifications by the young James Paine, who created some sumptuous rococo interiors for Sir Rowland Winn. His son Rowland, the 5th Baronet, succeeded in 1765 and to extend the house brought in Robert Adam, who created one of his most unified classical design schemes. The Library has recently been restored. Most of the work created by the Otley-born cabinet-maker Thomas Chippendale survives in the rooms for which it was designed, along with some very good pictures, including Angelica Kauffman's *Self-Portrait of the Artist Hesitating Between Music and Painting.* He furnished the house completely, providing everything from the magnificent desk in the library to the chopping block in the kitchen, which is now open to the public.

Just within the grounds stands Wragby parish church, an embattled Perpendicular building with a chancel dated by inscription to 1533. The church windows contain several hundred small panels of Swiss stained glass, forming one of the finest such collections outside Switzerland. They were collected in the 19th century, and some date from as early as 1514.

Nostell Priory
Top: A late 16th-century copy of Holbein's celebrated lost conversation piece representing Sir Thomas More and his family.
Centre: Central pediment with the Winn family's coat of arms.

Bottom left: Nottingham Castle, the 14th-century gatehouse and bridge over the dry moat.

Nottingham, Notts 694 D4, In 1697 the traveller Celia Fiennes declared Nottingham 'The neatest town I have seen, built of stone and delicate large and long streets much like London and the houses lofty and well-built, the Market Place very broad...' Her town has mostly disappeared, but the place still has the feel of a large, bustling city. For centuries Nottingham was famous for its lace-making, and large red-brick Victorian lace factories still dominate a part of the town known as the Lacemarket. Nowadays, however, Nottingham is more famous as the home of Boots the Chemists. The ground is hilly, and the changing levels and unexpected views make it an exhilarating place to walk in.

From Saxon times it was recognized as the ideal location for a stronghold. Its highest point is **Castle Rock**, now dominated by the long low outline of the Duke of Newcastle's 17th-century mansion, built on the site of the castle keep and burnt out in 1831 by rioters who resented the Duke's opposition to parliamentary reform. In 1878 the building was restored as the **City Museum and Art Gallery**. From the castle terrace there is a magnificent view of the lower town, with the railway and Sir Michel Hopkins's new Inland Revenue headquarters. The rock beneath the castle is honeycombed with caves. The centre of the town is still the market place, where the large stone Council House was built in the late 1920s. Behind it is High Pavement, which contains two excellent museums and the great medieval parish church. High Pavement Chapel has been converted into a lace museum; the old Shire Hall with its late Georgian front now houses the

Centre left and bottom left: Nunnington Hall, the staircase and the main front with some of the earliest sash windows in the country.

Top right and centre right: Nymans Garden. The house, a convincing 1920s pastiche of an old manor house, is by Walter Tapper. Only a portion survives but the garden remains.

Bottom right: Oakham Castle, the Great Hall walls covered in horseshoes.

Oakham O

Museum of Law, with court rooms, cells and gallows. St Mary's Church is the second largest parish church in the county after Newark, built on a cruciform plan with the tower over the crossing. Like Newark*, it is mostly 15th century, and its tall, wide windows give the church the appearance of a glass house with a soaring interior.

Nunney Castle, Somset 689 J4, A small 14th-century moated castle, built on a symmetrical plan with oblong towers at the angles [EH].

Nunnington Hall, N York 697 H5, This small stone country house [NT] beside the River Rye is mainly 17th century; it has some of the earliest-known sash windows, installed in 1687. The Carlisle collection of miniature rooms is fascinating to study. There are exuberantly baroque gate piers and attractive gardens.

Nymans Garden, W Susx 691 F6, Created by the Messel family and home of the later Lady Rosse, founder of the Victorian society. It has an historic collection of trees, shrubs and flowers from 1895, arranged in formal vistas and natural woodland planning. There is yew and box tree topiary, of plump birds and geometric shapes [NT].

Oakham, Rutlnd 694 E5, Now once again the county town of Rutland, England's smallest county. It is

an attractive place, standing near the huge man-made lake known as Rutland Water, and possesses one nationally important building. The main walls of Oakham Castle have now been reduced to grassy banks but at its centre survives the best preserved early Great Hall of any English

castle, dating from about 1190. Both inside and out the form is very like that of a church nave. This is most evident in the interior, with its stone arcades, except for the curious fact that the walls are covered with horseshoes. (Since the late Middle Ages the Lord of the Manor of Oakham required every nobleman to forfeit a horseshoe on his first visit to the town. To judge by the shoes, some of the horses must have been larger than elephants.) On the edge of the castle enclosure are All Saints

Above: Oban, with McCaig's Folly looming over the harbour.

Church, whose tall spire dominates the town, and the Old Grammar School building of 1584. A mile or so outside Leicester on a ridge overlooking Rutland Water is Burley on the Hill, an enormous 18th-century mansion built for Daniel Finch, Earl of Nottingham.

Oakley Hall, Shrops 693 G3, Oakley is a fairly modest early-18th-century house, whose interest lies principally in the alterations made in the early 1820s to the designs of the architect CR Cockerell. His most notable alteration was the tall and splendid staircase hall, with its decorations copied from authentic Greek models.

Oakwell Hall, W York 697 G6, An Elizabethan manor house, with Civil War and Brontë connections, furnished as a 1690s family home. As well as a period garden and arboretum, there is a country park.

Oban, Ag & B 698 C2, One of the principal ports for the Hebrides*. The fishing port founded in the 18th century, on a bay sheltered by the island of Kerrera*, became a fashionable resort with the advent of the railway and the development of steam navigation in the 1850s. McCaig's Folly (begun in 1897 and never finished) in the style of the Colosseum in Rome, stands above the town. The distillery on Stafford Street dates from 1794.

Ockham, Surrey 691 F5, All Saints Church boasts one of only two surviving seven-lancet windows in England. There is much to interest the observer within the church, including a monument by Rysbrack to Lord King.

Ockwells Manor House, Berks 690 E5, A wonderfully elaborate timber-framed house of 1446–66, built a short distance from the village of Bray for the Master of the Wardrobe to Henry VI.

Oddington, Gloucs 690 C3, Well worth the trip south from the village, the desolate church of St Nicholas seems too narrow to contain the huge and overbearing 14th-century wall-painting known as a 'Doom.' The church was built in the 13th century to serve the nearby residence of the Archbishop of York, who was visited by Henry III on occasion and therefore needed impressive facilities. The wall-painting shows God sitting on a throne while angels sound the last trumpet. The thin white naked bodies of the sinners pass into hell, where a big black devil with paws, tail, horns and a prodding stick awaits them. Other later paintings in the church include allegories such as 'Magnificence'. It is at least possible that their subjects arrived here, via a travelling court painter, from a well-known Tudor mortality play satirizing Cardinal Wolsey. The reclining lady in the churchyard is the interesting late-17th-century effigy of Margaret Parsons. In the village of Upper Oddington nearby, the Old Stone House is the work of Arts-and-Crafts architect Guy Dawber, converted out of some 16th-century cottages.

Odiham, Hants 690 E6, A delightful small town with a long street full of Georgian-fronted houses (some are much older behind their façades). In nearby North Warnborough are some striking timber-framed houses and, along a side road, the prettily set ruin of Odiham Castle.

Offa's Dyke 693 G6, This massive earthwork, partly in the care of English Heritage, runs from the Welsh coast to the Severn at Sedbury. It was built in the 8th century by the Saxon king Offa of Mercia as he extended his kingdom westwards into what is now Herefordshire and made a treaty with the South Welsh. Offa brought all the southern English kingdoms under his power and was influential enough to be known of by Charlemagne and the Pope. The Dyke probably dates from the comparatively peaceful latter part of his reign between 784 and his death in 796. (He is believed to have been killed at Rhuddlan during a final battle against the Welsh, while he was trying to establish the final course of the Dyke to

this border area. The dyke begins at Sedbury Cliffs on the Severn near Chepstow*. A particularly good section survives at Lyonshall, south of Moccas*, and the most dramatic part is the length following the Wye gorge from Redbrook to the Devil's Pulpit. Some natural features such as the forests of Herefordshire and the gorges of the Wye were incorporated into the boundary of Offa's kingdom to save work. There is now an Offa's Dyke long-distance footpath, 170 miles (272km) long and marked by signposts bearing white acorns.

Ogmore (Ogwr), V Glam 689 F3, The castle, originally of earth and timber, was built by William de Londres in the early 12th century and was refortified in stone by his son, Maurice.

Okehampton, Devon 689 F6, Some way from the now bypassed market town lies the

the sea – it still remains unfinished at its northern end.) It is thought to have marked a political boundary, agreed by negotiation between the two sides, rather than a post-conquest military barrier. Although it was like Hadrian's Wall* in concept, parts of it are indefensible; some parts, however, probably served as a military feature on occasion, a continuing reminder of the turbulent character of

Right: Okehampton Castle, one of the largest in Devon.

Below: Ogmore Castle, built by William de Londres in the early 12th century as he forged his way west in the Norman attempt to overcome the Welsh.

Castle begun by Baldwin de Brionne, Sheriff of Devon after the Conquest. In about 1170 it passed into the hands of the Courtenays, who held it until 1538. It lies above the rushing waters of the West Okement on a natural spur; the square Norman keep is a reminder of its original defensive purpose. The later 14th-century building (largely by Hugh Courtenay II) was of a more ceremonial nature and incorporated the large Great Hall and several lodgings [EH].

Old Oswestry, Shrops 693 F3, On the edge of the town is a magnificent Iron Age hill fort [EH], nearly 40 acres (16ha) in extent, with three huge earthen banks later enclosed by a double rampart.

Old Sarum, Wilts 690 C6, Built around 500 BC, Old Sarum is the site not only of the ancient city of Salisbury* but also of the first cathedral. Evolving

Top: Old Sarum, with its earthworks of Early Iron Age, Roman and 11th- and 12th-century dates.

Bottom left and centre: Old Soar Manor, one of the parts of the house left intact though now much restored.

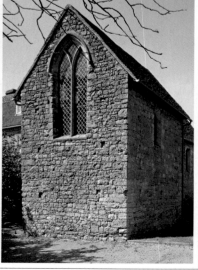

from a prehistoric hill fort, it was occupied in succession by the Romans, the Saxons and finally the Normans. Today it is a fine earthwork with a deep ditch and steep ramparts, spreading over 50 acres (20ha) [EH].

Old Soar Manor, Kent 691 G6, Part of a Wealden house of *c*1290. The hall range has gone, replaced by a Georgian brick house, but the solar, opening off the hall, and the chapel remain [NT + EH].

Old Warden, Beds 691 F3, The church is interesting for its interior, which brims over with fine woodwork, mainly Belgian, collected from 1841 by Lord Ongley. One mile (1.6km) away is Warden Abbey, a small and odd-looking remnant of an early Tudor house built on the site of an abbey founded in 1135. For those who like a walk in picturesque surroundings there is the Swiss Garden (Biggleswade Road), laid out in the early 1800s.

Old Wardour Castle, Wilts 690 B6, Near to Shaftesbury* is the majestic Old Castle – hexagonal ruins, set on a wooded bank above an 18th-century lake [EH]. Unusually, its courtyard is enclosed on six sides; its battlements date back to 1393, when it was licensed to crenellate. Interesting Elizabethan features were added in the 1570s for Sir Matthew Arundell, the new owner; the main staircase to the hall dates from this period. A mile (1.6km) across the landscaped park is the new house of **Wardour Castle,** designed in 1769–74 by James Paine for the 8th Lord Arundell. A wing of this great classical house contains a splendid chapel, which continues its function as the parish church and survives as one of the most impressive of the small but fascinating group of 18th-century Roman Catholic chapels. Paine conceived it and Sir John Soane enlarged it in about 1790. Their work had the support of Father John Thorpe, a Jesuit settled in Rome. He coped with Lord Arundell's perfectionist ways for over 20 years, arranging for an altar to be made in Rome by Giacomo Quarenghi. Thorpe's further offering was a relief panel of the Virgin and Child (1703) by the Roman Baroque sculptor, Pierre Monnot.

Top: Old Wardour Castle, the hexagonal ruins.

Oldham, Gt Man 697 F7, Northeast of Manchester*, this was the greatest spinning centre in the world, at one time producing some four-fifths of the world's yarn. The remnants of this extraordinary concentration can still be seen in places such as Chadderton, which is dominated by mill chimneys, many with the mill name picked out in white brick. The town centre is disappointing though the parish church has a richly decorated interior; the local architect Richard Lane defeated Charles Barry in a competition in the 1820s. At Chadderton too is Foxdenton Hall, a fine early 18th-century house now set in a municipal park. Not far away, in Middleton, is an excellent medieval church, St Lawrence's, but architectural pilgrims visit more for the works of Edgar Wood and JH Sellars. This remarkable local practice combined elements of Arts and Crafts with modern architecture. The Methodist Church in Long Street, 1899, is beautifully planned and detailed. The Elm Street School is a formal composition planned to face a garden and approached by arcaded passages.

Olney, Bucks 690 E3, A delightful small town, once known for its lace-making, with some good Georgian architecture. Of special note is the Cowper and Newton Museum on the Orchard Side of the Market Place, where displays on the town's history are shown in the former house of poet William Cowper alongside many personal relics. The 18th-century pulpit, used by Cowper's friend John Newton, is preserved in the 14th-century church, where he was curate. Olney has a Pancake Race every Shrove Tuesday.

Ombersley, Worcs 693 H5, This pretty Worcestershire village has a variety of inns and houses of interest, including two cruck-roofed houses.

Orchard Wyndham, Somset 689 G4, An English manor house that has been a family home for over

Above: Orford Castle. The revolutionary new design of Henry II's castle keep dominates the little market town of Orford.

700 years. Space is limited within, however, and the Wyndham Estate Office should be approached before a visit.

Orchardleigh, Somset 689 J4, It is worth persevering to get to the church of St Mary, surrounded by a lake, and in the middle of the extensive grounds of the house (1855). The church is of the late 13th century, restored sympathetically in 1879 by George Gilbert Scott, and with some good, mainly mid-15th century stained glass.

Orford, Suffk 691 J3, Another decayed borough and silted-up port on the Alde River with a pretty market place, a mythical merman, the Butly Oysterage (a renowned 1950s seafood cafe), a church with ruined Norman chancel and Henry II's formidable fortress. The castle [EH] is mainly reduced to defensive earthworks but retains a near-perfect central keep almost 100 feet (30m) tall incorporating the latest circular plan. There are commanding views from the top. The tower's 18 sides and three square turrets contain a labyrinth of rooms and passages constructed in 1165–7. The castle was captured by the French in 1217, during fighting after the death of King John. Orford Ness, Europe's largest vegetated shingle spit, has diverted the river 10 miles (16km) south to Shingle Street. A secret military site for 70 years from 1913, it is now a wildlife haven, particularly for rare plants and birds, managed by the National Trust; adjacent Havergate Island is an RSPB reserve. A ferry leads to a 5-mile (8km) walk through an eerie, desolate landscape to the lighthouse, past surreal pagoda-shaped bunkers once used to test nuclear components.

O

Orkney

Orkney 703 G7, The Orkney Islands lie 12 miles (19km) off the north coast of Scotland across the Pentland Firth, a dangerous stretch of water scattered with reefs and swept by storms. The 67 islands and islets in the group were worn flat by glaciers. Although the most northerly are situated on the same latitude as St Petersburg, the influence of the Gulf Stream means they have a particularly mild climate throughout the year. Today only about 20 are inhabited and of the 19,000 inhabitants, three-quarters live on the large central island, Mainland. Orkney has some remarkable prehistoric remains dating from the 4th millennium bc, including underground dwellings (earth houses), tombs and stone circles. *See also* **Hoy***.

Birsay: In this small village stand the ruins of the palace built *c*1580 by Earl Patrick Stewart. At low tide you can walk from Birsay to the neighbouring island of Brough of Birsay, where excavations revealed the remains of a Pictish settlement, including houses, a well and a bronze workshop, dating from the 7th–8th centuries. Between the 9th and 12th centuries there was an important Viking settlement on the island. Alongside the foundations of longhouses and a forge dating from the 10th–11th century are the remains of the Earl's Palace and the first Bishop's Palace built by Earl Thorfinn (d. 1064) in the 11th century. There are also the remains of a beautiful early 12th-century church which may well have housed the remains of St Magnus, the murdered uncle of Rognvald III. The Brough entered its period of decline when the saint's relics were transferred to Kirkwall and it was no longer a place of pilgrimage. The Kirbuster Farm Museum, 2 miles (3.2km) southeast of Birsay, traces the development of farming life on Orkney over the past 200 years.

Grain Earth House: An underground chamber near Kirkwall which was probably used as a storehouse and place of refuge for Stone Age farmers. Some 4 miles (6.4km) further on, another well-preserved structure of the same type (reached via a trapdoor and ladder) is in a farmyard at Rennibster, to the right of the road.

Holm of Papa: The island is the site of Diss o' the Holm, a huge burial cairn consisting of a 65-foot (20m) central chamber, subdivided into three smaller chambers, and twelve lateral cells.

Left: Italian Chapel on the island of Lamb Holm, built and decorated with bits and pieces of wood and iron by Italian prisoners of war.

Below: St Magnus Cathedral, Kirkwall, view from the southeast. The central tower dates from the 14th century.

Far left: One of the group of endearingly naive 17th-century tombs in St Magnus Cathedral.

Left: The mid 12th-century western section of the choir with the eastern arch of the crossing on the left.

Kirkwall: The principal town on Mainland stands at the head of Kirkwall Bay, on the site of a former Viking trading post, founded *c*1035 by Rognvald III. Its name is derived from the Norse *Kirkjugavar* ('Church Place'), a reference to the church dedicated to St Olaf, the patron saint of Norway. The old town, where most of the houses date from the 16th–18th centuries, still lies within the area occupied by the original Viking settlement. The port expanded when the cathedral was built in the 12th century, and became a royal burgh of Scotland in the 16th century.

In 1137 Rognvald III decided to build St Magnus Cathedral in honour of his uncle, Magnus, who was canonized shortly after being assassinated by his cousin and rival Haakon, in 1116. The construction of the cathedral lasted until the mid-13th century. The central spire was destroyed by lightning in 1671 but replaced in copper in the 1911–30 restoration. The height of the church, built in red and yellow sandstone in a harmonious blend of Norman and gothic styles, makes up for its relatively modest dimensions. It houses the remains of St Magnus and St Rognvald.

Left: Ring of Brodgar, a perfect circle, 340 feet (103.7m) in diameter. Of the 27 surviving stones, 13 were re-erected in the 19th century.

The Bishop's Palace was built near the cathedral *c*1150 by Bishop William the Old and refurbished in the 16th and 17th centuries. All that remains today are the walls of the great reception hall and the angle tower, Moosie Too'r. Haakon IV of Norway, fatally wounded at the Battle of Largs, died here in 1263. The Earl's Palace was built (1600–7) opposite the Bishop's Palace by Earl Patrick Stewart, an infamous tyrant who was executed in Edinburgh in 1615. Although roofless, the building is still a fine example of Renaissance architecture, with its monumental staircase, corbelled windows and finely carved fireplaces. Tankerness House, a beautiful 16th-century mansion, houses a museum of Orkney life and a collection of objects brought back by John Rae from his Arctic expeditions.

Maes Howe: This magnificent tomb, built almost 5,000 years ago, is covered by a mound – 24 feet (7m) high and with a diameter of 115 feet (33m) – surrounded by a ditch. A narrow passageway leads to a burial chamber, which is aligned with the rising sun of the winter solstice. The chamber, built with huge, perfectly cut and positioned sandstone blocks, opens on to three burial cells. The tomb was plundered by Norsemen in the 12th century, as shown by the carved runic inscriptions and images (including the famous Maes Howe lion).

Above: Marwick Head, with its memorial to Lord Kitchener.

Marwick Head: The headland, which is both a bird sanctuary and viewpoint, has a memorial to Horatio Herbert Kitchener (b.1850), the British Field Marshal and secretary of state for war, and the crew of HMS *Hampshire*, which went down off the coast of Mainland when it hit a mine in June 1916.

Papa Westray: This small, wild island – the birthplace of Christianity in Orkney – was inhabited by hermits in the early Middle Ages and was a place of pilgrimage until the 18th century. It also has two of the oldest stone houses that can still be seen in Western Europe (*c*2500 BC) at Knap of Howar.

Ring of Brodgar: A stone circle that stands on the narrow strip of land between Lochs Stenness and Harray. Only 27 of the original 60 megaliths are still standing. Like Stenness, Brodgar is surrounded by a broad ditch, but the earth bank that once formed the circle's outer limit has disappeared.

Rousay: This round island has a number of prehistoric remains, including the two-storey burial cairn of Taversoe Tuick and the cairns of Blackhammer and Knowe of Yarso. But the most impressive of these sites is the chambered cairn of Midhowe (98 feet/30m long), which was hollowed out in 3500 BC. Nearby are the remains of an Iron-Age broch.

St Margaret's Hope: This village on Mainland has some delightful 17th- and 18th-century cottages, while the Old Smiddy Museum, which occupies the old forge, pays homage to blacksmiths and farriers of the past.

Scapa Flow: In June 1919, 74 German ships, laid up in the roadstead since the armistice of 1918, were scuttled in Kirkwall Bay. The *Royal Oak* was sunk there in 1939 and when he came to office the following year prime minister Winston Churchill ordered four concrete dykes to be built between the islands of Mainland, Lamb Holm, Glimps Holm, Burray and South Ronaldsay, designed to strengthen the defences of Scapa Flow. They were not finished until the spring of 1945. These causeways still link the islands today, making communications much easier and giving motorists the impression of driving across the water. The experience is even eerier at night when the ebb tide reveals the ghostly shapes of the rusting wrecks.

Skara Brae: In 1850 eyewitness accounts spoke of 'flying sheep' when a hurricane devastated west Mainland. When the storm died down the islanders discovered that the gale-force winds had uncovered the remains of a group of prehistoric dwellings at Skara Brae on the Bay of Skaill. The houses were linked by narrow passages, originally covered, and were all – except one, possibly a workshop – designed according to the same layout, with a central hearth, larder and stone seats and beds. They were built on a layer of clay and buried up to the

Top: St Margaret's Hope, Mainland, developed from the 18th century onwards at the bay of the same name.

Bottom: Stromness, the 18th- and early 19th-century harbour with its warehouse of 1760.

roof in a compost of clay and household waste, which would have provided good insulation. The site, occupied between 3100 and 2500 BC, provided much new information about Stone Age life on the island. Near the site is Skaill House, a 17th-century manor house.

Standing Stones of Stenness: Only three of the twelve large standing stones that formed the original circle remain. Two smaller stones have recently been re-erected and four stones (possibly a hearth) excavated at the centre of the circle.

Stromness: The largest port on Mainland is also the ferry port for Shetland* and Scotland, which the islanders refer to as 'The Sooth' (South). Before becoming a whaling and herring port in the 19th century, Stromness flourished in the 17th century as the last supply port for the ships of the Hudson Bay Company en route to Canada, and as a port of call for English ships trading with Scandinavia and Russia. The Stromness Museum, at the end of Main Street, presents the natural and maritime history of Orkney.

Tomb of the Eagles: The tomb is named after the sea eagles' claws found alongside the bones of 342 people buried here in the 3rd millennium BC. The small private museum of Liddle Farm presents objects found on the site.

Westray: Apart from the ruins of two medieval churches and Noltland Castle (1560), the island is also renowned for Noup Head bird sanctuary.

Left: Prehistoric earth house at Skara Brae.

Below: A farm on the island of Westray.

Ormesby Hall, N York 697 H3, A mid-18th-century Palladian house, the ancestral home of the Pennyman family [NT]. The handsome stable block built by John Carr of York houses the Cleveland police horses.

Oronsay, *see* **Colonsay*.**

Osborne House, *see* **Isle of Wight*.**

Ospringe, Kent 691 H5, The 13th-century Maison Dieu was built as a leper hospital. The ground floor is of flint, the upper half-timbered.

Ossington, Notts 694 E3, The mansion house at Ossington (pulled down in the 1960s) was the home of the Cartwrights and then the Denisons,

Above and centre: Ormesby Hall, the garden front and the handsome first-floor gallery.

both heavily involved in the wool business. The church of the Holy Rood, which stood near the house, is a handsome classical box with a west tower topped by a dome rotunda. It was designed in the 1780s by John Carr, the leading Palladian architect in the north of England. Inside the church are several good monuments, including one to the Denisons with figures by Joseph Nollekens and scenes from the wool trade.

Otham, Kent 691 H6, The church contains a notable monument by Maximilian Colt, who made the

effigy of Queen Elizabeth in Westminster Abbey*. It has Corinthian columns and busts in sunken roundels. Stoneacre, nearby, is a 16th-century Wealden house, incorporating material from another house when it was restored in 1920 [NT].

Otley, Suffolk 695 J7,  The timber-framed and moated Hall, with beautiful linenfold panelling, emerged in the reign of Henry VII and expanded under James I. It was once the home of explorer Bartholomew Gosnold (d. 1607), who discovered Cape Cod and founded Jamestown, Virginia.

Ottery St Mary, Devon 689 G6, The important church of St Mary was founded by John de Grandisson, Bishop of Exeter in 1337, to serve a college, and was based on the design of Exeter* Cathedral. Elaborate vaults, exceptional roof bosses, fine bench ends and corbels embellish the interior – among the most charming figures are elephants and a 'green man'. The Bishop's brother Otho and his wife Lady Beatrix have fine Decorated monuments. Samuel Taylor Coleridge's father was vicar and schoolmaster here, and the poet lived here from 1772 until after his father's death, when he was sent to Christ's Hospital (then in London) at the age of nine. Coleridge never lost his affection for the little market town, about which he wrote several poems.

Outwood, Surrey 691 F6, Outwood Common Windmill was built in 1665. It is a post-mill, with a brick round-house base and weather-boarded top.

Overbecks, Devon 689 F7, An Edwardian house full of curiosities, set in terraced grounds with a wide range of unusual plants and a spectacular large magnolia [NT].

Otley Hall
Above: One of the most interesting and picturesque late medieval timber-framed halls in Suffolk.
Left: The main hall has beautiful linenfold panelling and heavily moulded ceiling beams.

Right: Ottery St Mary, the nave looking up to the varied 14th-century vaults.

Below: Overbecks, the sub-tropical garden with a view over the Salcombe* estuary.

Owl House Gardens, Kent 691 G6, These romantic gardens near Lamberhurst have large trees, rhododendrons and sunken pools.

Owlpen Manor, Gloucs 690 B4, Frequently hailed as one of the most picturesque manor houses in England. Seen from across the brook, its three gables are all different but 'illogically satisfactory', according to James Lees-Milne. The Hall and Great Chamber were added to the medieval house in about 1540, and further additions followed on. The house stood empty from 1850 but was rescued

Top right: Owlpen Manor. The separate Court House can be seen behind the 'room' made of yew trees.

in 1926 by Norman Jewson. The terraced garden, largely 19th-century in form, was influential on Gertrude Jekyll and Vita Sackville-West and their idea of gardens as outdoor chambers. 'Owlpen, that tiny grey manor-house' was described by Sackville-West as 'cowering amongst its enormous yew trees, yews that make rooms in the garden with walls taller than any rooms in the house: dark, secret rooms of yew…'. Indoors, the 16th-century painted cloths in the Great Chamber over the Hall are the most interesting furnishings. These are a rare survival of the oilcloths which used to cover most domestic walls and show Joseph and his brothers in a forest of gargantuan trees. The opening of the house is a jolly family concern, apparently run by the children. The Church of the Holy Cross, just behind the house, is a magnificent piece of Victoriana with late Pre-Raphaelite mosaics and tiles. The ceilings and organ pipes are all richly painted as well.

Above: The late 17th-century staircase, with portraits hung on the painted leather introduced in the 19th century.
Centre: The King's Room.
Below: The moated Tudor manor house built for the Bedingfelds in 1482.

Oxburgh Hall, Norfk 695 G5, The Hall [NT] is a romantic moated manor of mellow red brick built in 1482 for the Bedingfelds, who still live in one wing. Its centrepiece is the great gatehouse with octagonal turrets, rising 80 feet (24m) above the moat. Henry VII visited, and the house contains rare and exquisite embroideries worked by Mary Queen of Scots with Bess of Hardwick, wife of her custodian at Tutbury. The rooms progress from medieval to Victorian. The gardens contain an 1835 Catholic chapel by Pugin and a Victorian French parterre. Spectacular early Renaissance terracotta Bedingfeld tombs are housed in a chapel attached to the ruined parish church.

Oxford

Oxford, Oxon 690 D4, The larger and busier of England's two oldest university towns, but still retaining all its character and picturesque qualities. The first records date from *c*900, and two of the earliest surviving buildings are the towers of St Michael and St George, dating from the 11th century. St George's was part of the Norman castle; the remains of the motte can also be seen opposite Nuffield College. Like Cambridge*, the University has early origins: Merton, University and Balliol colleges were all founded during the 13th century. Nearly all the colleges are built around spacious green quadrangles and have a chapel and hall, but their design is by no means repetitive. Many of the country's finest architects have left their mark here, including Wren at Christ Church, Hawksmoor at All Souls, Wyatt at Oriel and Butterfield at Keble. Even the 1960s architecture of St Catherine's College is outstanding. But it is the older colleges such as Magdalen that stay in one's mind, and any one of them would make a trip to Oxford worthwhile. It is also these colleges that give Oxford its most distinctive characteristic, a remarkable skyline of spires, pinnacles and towers. The lovely River Cherwell that runs through the city provides a good means of exploration; punts may be hired at Magdalen Bridge.

All Souls College: Founded in 1414 in memory of those killed in the Hundred Years War. The Chapel contains a magnificent carved reredos covering the entire east wall and composed of 36 freestanding statues in canopied niches. (The figures are in fact Victorian replacements of the originals smashed in Edward VI's reign.) The north quad is by Hawksmoor.

Ashmolean Museum: The Greek Revival masterpiece of CR Cockerell, 1841–5. Its collections range from Egyptian antiquities to 20th-century art, and are of worldwide importance, especially the Arundel Marbles and the Old Master drawings, its Pissarros and pre-Raphaelites.

Top left: Bodleian Library, the entrance tower.

Centre left: Christ Church Cathedral's vaulted interior.

Below centre:The University Museum, by Benjamin Wood Ward, 1855–60.

Below: CR Cockerell's Ashmolean Museum of 1841–5.

Bottom: All Souls College, the pinnacled North Quad by Nicholas Hawksmoor, 1716.

Bodleian Library: This was opened in 1602. It holds an enormous collection of books, which is growing steadily, as the Library is required by law to receive a copy of every book published in England. Note particularly the five-tiered and five-ordered entrance tower of 1613–24.

Even the University's **Botanic Garden** boasts important architecture. Its three classical gateways were built in 1632–3 by Nicholas Stone. The garden was established in 1621 as the Physic Garden, part of the expansion of scientific research at the University.

Christ Church Cathedral: This began in the late 1100s as the priory church of St Frideswide and doubles as a college chapel. Roughly contemporary with the building of Canterbury Cathedral*, it bears traces of the new gothic style which can be discerned amongst the essentially Romanesque architecture of giant orders of arches. The contrast with the Early English gothic of the 13th-century Lady Chapel and Chapterhouse is a revealing one. Also of note are St Frideswide's shrine and watching loft, the monuments, and the other monastic remains. The beautifully elaborate stone vault over the chancel dates from c1500.

Christ Church College: Founded by that most famous of clergymen, Cardinal Wolsey, who obtained permission from the Pope for the dissolution of St Frideswide's Priory. After Wolsey's fall it was taken over by

Top left: Botanic Garden, the oldest in Britain.

Top right: Christ Church College, Tom Quad, a view showing the statue of Mercury immortalized by Evelyn Waugh, Bell Tower and part of the Hall.

Left: Tom Tower, by Sir Christopher Wren, in the gothic style.

Henry VIII. The 16th-century Tom Tower was designed in the gothic style by Sir Christopher Wren 'to agree' with the existing architecture. Also note the Peckwater Quad, 1707–14, designed in restrained classical style by Dean Aldrich. Christ Church is unique in having a Picture Gallery, a crisp 1960s building by Powell and Moya containing the College's fine collection of old master paintings and drawings, including Trecento panels; canvases by Carracci, Tintoretto and Van Dyck; sketches by Leonardo da Vinci, Michelangelo and Raphael; and the exceptional survival of a tempera painting on linen by Hugo van der Goes.

Clarendon Building: Built 1712–13, by Hawksmoor, for the University Press. The monumental qualities of Hawksmoor's design are seen in the giant Doric portico and heavy frieze.

Divinity School: The impressive school was begun in c1420 for the teaching of theology and contains a marvellous vault finished in 1483 by William Orchard. The publication of the Examination Statutes in 1849–50 finally replaced the old oral examinations with written papers, creating the need for the Examination School. The architect who won the competition of 1875 was Thomas Graham Jackson, who was to become the most prominent turn-of-the-century architect working in the city. Inspired by English, Italian and Flemish architecture, he later referred to this style as 'Anglo-Jackson'.

Keble College: Built between 1868 and 1882, this is a radical departure from the Oxford tradition in that it is constructed of brick and not stone. It famously drove John Ruskin to abandon his morning walk because he

O

found it so offensive. The architect was William Butterfield, who fully indulged his fondness of polychrome brickwork. A riot of colourful patterns dances across a background of red brick, reaching a climax in the soaring façade of the chapel. The effect inside is equally dazzling. The excellent 1970s extension was built by Ahrends, Burton and Koralek.

Magdalen College: Magdalen (pronounced 'maudlin') was founded by another great ecclesiastical magnate, William Waynflete, Bishop of Winchester and Chancellor of England, in 1458. Together with All Souls, this was the great foundation of the 15th century. The cloister, which has retained all its gothic buildings, is one of the most important and moving examples of late medieval architecture in the country. Set against the River Cherwell and the deer park, it is undoubtedly one of the most beautiful of the colleges.

Manchester College: By Thomas Worthington, 1891–93, this college is famous for the Burne-Jones stained glass in the Chapel.

Merton College: Founded with an endowment from Walter de Merton, a priest who became Lord Chancellor to Henry III. For over seven centuries after his death the chapel bell was rung every Friday morning. From 1380 the College supported a number of external students on a portion of the fellows' commons, the *portionistiae*, a term that was corrupted to Postmasters, by which Merton scholars are still known. The Chapel, begun in the late 13th century and famous for its ornate tracery, was intended to be of a similar length to St Frideswide's; its stained glass is some of the oldest in Oxford. The gatehouse is of 1418, the statues represent its founder Henry III and the relief sculpture shows de Merton and Saint John the Baptist; the college arms are above. The Mob Quad, dating from the 14th century, is the oldest of the quadrangles and retains much of its medieval character. The Fellows Quad of 1610 is the oldest three-storey quad.

Museums: Until the 19th century, the Ashmolean (the first English museum to be open to the public) was housed in a fine 17th-century building in Broad Street which now contains the city's Museum of the History of Science. Bringing the city right up to date is the Museum of Modern Art (MOMA) in Pembroke Street, which holds enjoyable, constantly changing exhibitions and events.

New College: Founded in 1379 by William of Wykeham, Bishop of Winchester and, like Walter de Merton, Chancellor of England. The most architecturally ambitious

Top: Magdalen College, founded in the 15th century.

Left: The colourful brickwork of Keble College and Chapel.

Below: Merton College viewed from Christ Church Meadow.

Bottom: New College. Its foundation stone was laid in 1380.

college, it has served as a model for collegiate architecture to the present day. Unlike the earlier colleges, whose growth was piecemeal, here the buildings were conceived as an architectural unit, and on a grand scale – the quad was four times the size of the Mob Quad at Merton. The Garden Quadrangle was built in 1682–1707 and was open on one side, establishing an alternative model for colleges. Do not miss the colourful borders of the garden.

Queen's College: Although Queen's was founded in 1341, none of the medieval buildings survives; they were demolished between 1670 and 1760 to make way for a grand scheme of classical building. Hawksmoor was responsible for the impressive screen wall and gatehouse that face the High Street. The rusticated wall

Above: Queen's College, the front quad, centrepiece of the Hall and Chapel.

Left: The Oxford Museum, the symmetrical main front. The Pitt Rivers Museum, added in 1885-6, is behind.

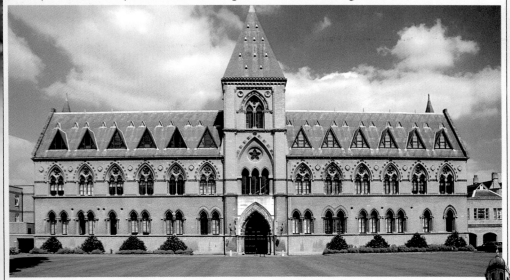

and pedimented end ranges contrast with the elegantly playful cupola over the gatehouse, beneath which is the statue of Queen Caroline. Hawksmoor also produced designs for the front quad.

Radcliffe Camera: A powerful baroque rotunda, this was built with a legacy of £40,000 left by Dr Radcliffe for the founding of a new library. The idea of a rotunda building came from Hawksmoor, but the architect who was chosen to realize the building, started in 1737, was James Gibbs. The base is rusticated; above are paired Corinthian columns, supporting a large entablature and balustrade, with the drum and dome rising behind. The interior has beautiful stone carving and stuccowork by the renowned plasters Joseph Artari and Charles Stanley.

Radcliffe Observatory: A delightful neoclassical building by James Wyatt, whose inspiration came from the Hellenistic Tower of the Winds in Athens, as illustrated in Stuart and Revett's *Antiquities of Athens*.

St Catherine's Cottage: Entirely the work of one architect, the Danish Arne Jacobsen, who worked here between 1960 and 1964; this makes it unique amongst the colleges. All the communal rooms were designed as 'total works of art', with Jacobsen designing the furniture, door handles and cutlery. The logical symmetry of the architecture is broken by the delightful planting in the garden.

St John's College: The architectural gem of St John's is Canterbury Quad, endowed by Archbishop Laud, President of the College from 1611 until 1621. The Old Library was already on the site and the north range was built in a similar style, but it is the west and east ranges that are remarkable. These illustrate the influence of the Renaissance, with their round-arched loggias. Within the elaborate centrepieces are bronze statues of King Charles I and Queen Henrietta Maria. Also note the Sir Thomas White Building by Arup Associates of 1975, an L-shaped block broken up by the staircase turrets.

St Mary's Church: A stately church with impressive spire, dating mainly from the 14th and 15th centuries.

Sheldonian Theatre: The University's ceremonial hall of 1663–9 is Wren's first work of architecture. The curved rear of the building faces on the Broad, screened behind a wall with piers displaying heads of Roman emperors. The model Wren used was the Theatre of Marcellus in Rome, which was, however, open to the sky; so here Wren hid the roof beneath an allegory set in the sky, painted by Robert Streater.

University Museum: The large and imposing museum was built in the gothic style by Benjamin Woodward and opened in 1860. Collections are displayed in the glass-roofed Museum Court, and aim to assemble 'all the

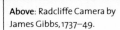

Above: Radcliffe Camera by James Gibbs, 1737–49.

O

materials explanatory of the organic beings placed upon the globe.' It is one of the earliest buildings in the country to exploit the properties of cast iron: tall piers with foliated capitals support wrought iron spandrels to form alternating naves and aisles. There is a profusion of carving, mostly executed by two Irish brothers, the O'Sheas; they were dismissed when they began to carve caricatures of the dons. The Pitt Rivers Museum was added to the Oxford Museum in 1885–6. It houses many wonders, including shrunken heads and painted masks.

Wolfson College: In north Oxford, this was one of two colleges founded in the 1960s (the other was St Catherine's). The architects were Powell and Moya, who were responsible for a number of college buildings in the 1960s and 1970s. Here they used an exposed reinforced concrete frame with large plate glass windows.

Left: The Sheldonian Theatre, with the heads of the Caesars, replacements of those made famous by Max Beerbohm's *Zuleika Dobson*.

Below: An aerial view of the 'dreaming spires', with the Radcliffe Camera a prominent landmark in the centre of the college quadrangles.

Left: Oxwich Castle, with the dovecote on the left, the late 16th-century range in the centre and the early 16th-century range to the right.

Packwood House
Right: The main gateway.
Below: The Long Gallery. The house was furnished by Graham Baron Ash in the 1920s and 1930s.

collection of furniture and paintings put together by Graham Baron Ash enlivens the old manor house. He also added a medieval hall. Immediately to the south of the house is a garden with four corner gazebos, the oldest dating from the 1680s. Beyond it is the famous garden crammed with yews, sometimes supposed to represent the audience of the Sermon on the Mount. The mount

Oxwich, Swans 688 E3, A generous beach on the south of the Gower Peninsula*, overlooked by the 'castle', the second building on the site. A fortified manor house rather than a purely defensive building, it owes much to the standing of its owner, Sir Rhys (or Rice) Mansel, whose name is closely associated with the early history of Glamorgan. After the Dissolution, he bought Margam Abbey and applied himself to making it into a grand residence. His son, Sir Edward, added the east range, an ambitious project showing considerable Renaissance verve, but within 50 years of completion the property was leased and went into decline. CADW undertook a programme of repair and conservation in the 1980s.

Packwood House, Warwks 694 c6, A semi-rural creation of the 1930s [NT]. A careful and beautiful

itself was in existence by 1756, though the planting of the yews appears to have taken place in the 19th century. Today a spiral brick path between box hedges leads up it.

Padstow, Cnwll 688 D6, Spreading out from the picturesque harbour, the ancient and proud town climbs the surrounding hills, affording fine views of the Camel estuary. On May Day the town is alive from an early hour with its annual 'Obby 'Oss celebrations – in which large black leather horses dance through the narrow streets.

Paignton, Devon 689 F7, A bustling seaside town dating from Saxon times, overlooking Tor Bay. Its chief point of interest is Oldway Mansion, the remarkable home of Isaac Singer (of the sewing-machine company). Finished by his third son, Paris, in 1907, it is modelled on Versailles. Up the

grand imperial staircase with its marble walls, visitors can see the extravagant first-floor rooms where Isadora Duncan once danced. The connected circular Riding School is but one of the features of the extensive grounds.

Painshill Park and Landscape Garden, Surrey, One of Europe's finest 18th-century landscape gardens, created by the Hon. Charles Hamilton 1738–73. It is the Europa Nostra medal winner for 'exemplary restoration'. The 14-acre (5.6ha) lake, filled by a massive waterwheel, gives a perfect setting for a ruined abbey, Turkish tent, Chinese bridge, crystal grotto and a working vineyard.

See **Cobham* 691 F5.**

Painswick, Gloucs 690 B4, A town built 5 miles (8km) south of Gloucester* of a silvery-grey stone, which appears to wonderful effect in the grandiose houses of its prosperous main street. Two of the best are opposite the lychgate of the church: Hazelbury House with an 18th-century Palladian front, and its neighbour Packers. The Falcon Hotel is another attractive building, dating from 1711, and the post office is half-timbered. The National Trust owns a 17th-century building in a side street called Little Fleece, once part of The Fleece Inn and restored in Arts and Crafts style in 1935, and there are many fulling mills straddling Painswick Brook down below the town. The town is the home of an annual exhibition held by the Gloucestershire Guild of Craftsmen. This part of the countryside, especially the valley to the east and the village of Sheepscombe, was made the ideal of bucolic wartime rural life by Laurie Lee in his book *Cider with Rosie*.

St Mary's Church and its churchyard, containing 99 beautifully groomed yew trees and marvellous tombs, sits in the middle of the town. It is a wool church, with nave and tower dating from the 1480s. The famous 'clypping' service each September has nothing to do with the manicuring

Top: Paignton, Oldway Mansion. The imposing east front, designed in 1904–7, looks out over the bay.

Painshill Park
Above left: The gothic temple.
Below centre: The Chinese bridge.

of the yews; the word in fact means encircling or embracing, and the custom is for children to link hands to encircle the whole church. The church endured a Royalist siege during the Civil War, and the chips in the tower and walls are supposed to date from the shots fired. One Parliamentarian soldier trapped in the church inscribed a pillar to the north of the nave with a quotation from Spencer: 'Be bold, be bold, but not too bold.' He was correct in his misgivings: the church was finally taken by the Royalists, and Charles I made his headquarters in the manor house just to the

Above: Painswick St Mary's Church.

Right: Painswick House Rococo Gardens, the exedra.

south for a while. **Painswick Beacon**, just north of Painswick, is an earthwork with marvellous views westward across to the Forest of Dean. The Cotswold Way footpath leads up to the top. Benjamin Hyett, who built the mellow 18th-century Painswick House, changed the course of garden history in the 1740s when he created **Painswick House Rococo Gardens**. Instead of overwhelming visitors with a grand axial front garden, he used a combe behind the house to make a garden with some vistas but with many winding paths. As you walk around the garden, you unexpectedly come across Gothic temples, seats, lodges and exedras arranged with the charming informality of the rococo style. The garden buildings have been restored with the help of a painting of a bird's-eye view made in 1748 by Thomas Tobins. Recent work includes the decorative geometric kitchen garden.

Paisley, Rens 698 E4, The town grew up around a 12th-century priory built by Walter Fitzalan, steward of David I and an ancestor of the first Stuart king of Scotland. It enjoyed its golden age in the 17th century when it became a centre for the textile industry, which copied the much sought-after cashmere shawls. 'Paisley' shawls became so popular that the term was used to refer to both the garment and the design. The church opposite the town hall is all that remains of the priory of Pasletum which housed the Cluniac monks of Wenlock (c1163) and the relics of St Mirren before becoming an abbey in 1249. Rebuilt c1450 and restored several times, it has a beautiful early-gothic porch dating from the 13th century, while the nave, long used as the parish church, still has its rich 15th-century decoration. In St Mirren's Chapel (1499) a series of 12th- and 13th-century panels depict the life of the saint, who was a friend of St Columba. The rebuilt choir houses the tombs of six High Stewards of Scotland, Robert III, the two wives of Robert II and possibly Marjory Bruce, the daughter of Robert Bruce and mother of Robert II. The Thomas Coats Memorial Church built by Hippolyte Blanc in 1894 is an amazing Gothic Revival building with a crown tower and an interior decor overloaded with marble and alabaster. Paisley Museum and Art Gallery, a very handsome neo-Greek building by John Honeyman, 1868, at the end of the High Street, traces the town's history and, in

Right: Pakenham, the 15th-century watermill restored to working order.

particular, the history of the famous Paisley shawls. Its small collection of paintings includes works by the 'Glasgow Boys' Hornel, Guthrie and Lavery. The interior of the Sma' Shot Cottages (George Place) evokes the everyday life of the 18th-century weavers and 19th-century mill workers.

Pakenham, Suffk 695 H6, Two working mills: an 18th-century water-mill on the Black Bourn, where the production of stone-ground flour can be observed on summer weekends; and a brick tower windmill c1820, set amid undrained marsh where reed is still harvested for thatching.

Pangbourne, Berks 690 D5, The town is notable for its naval college and the house where Kenneth Grahame wrote *The Wind in the Willows*, 1908.

Parc le Breos, Swans 688 E3, Otherwise known as Parc Cwm, a neolithic chambered cairn near Parkmill, 4th–3rd millennium BC, partially restored in the early 1960s. Another neolithic chambered cairn

Parham

Above: *Henry Frederick, Prince of Wales*, attributed to Robert Peake, c1611.
Right: The Great Hall.
Bottom left: A 17th-century needlework and walnut armchair in the Great Parlour.

stands off the minor road from Reynoldston over Cefn Bryn. There are spectacular views from the site.

Parham, W Susx 691 F7, Parham is an Elizabethan house of understated charm, although now it is a good deal restored. It has a nearly symmetrical grey stone front begun in 1577, and the hall has a typical Elizabethan screen. The Long Gallery is at the top of the house and has a Victorian ceiling. The house has an excellent collection of portraits.

consisting of a skeleton holding an hour glass,
a scythe and a spade.

Pashley Manor Gardens, E Susx 691 G6, A
'quintessentially English garden' designed by
Antony du Gard Pashley in the late 20th century.
It was deliberately composed to reflect the history
of the country house garden, picturesquely laid
out amid large trees, streams and fountains.
The early timber-framed house dates from 1550
and was enlarged in 1720.

Passenham, Nhants 690 E3,
St Guthlac's Church, in this
little village just outside
Milton Keynes*, has
remarkable joinery within.
The stalls have misericords
of various beasts, but these
supposedly medieval
features were probably no
more than nostalgic as they
were carved in the early 17th
century. Above is a similarly
gorgeous gallery, once part
of a rood screen.

Paston, Norfk 695 J4, The
village gave its name to a
great Norfolk dynasty,
whose famous *Letters* offer a
unique insight into family
aspirations in 15th-century
England. There is an
impressive thatched tithe barn, near the church.

Patrington, E R Yk 695 F2, St Patrick's Church is the
finest Decorated church in the area; its tall spire
can be seen from large tracts of Holderness.

Patrixbourne, Kent 691 J5, The church of St Mary
belongs to the same school as Barfreston*, with a
similarly carved south doorway. The subject is
Christ in a mandorla held by angels.

Parnham House, Dorset 689 H5, The large Tudor
manor house at Beaminster, enlarged by John
Nash in 1810, was restored by John and Jennie
Makepeace, and exciting contemporary
craftwork, particularly in wood, was exhibited
here, testament to the standard of training given
in the Makepeace furniture workshops. The
surrounding 14 acres (5.6ha) of gardens are
also impressive.

Parracombe, Devon 689 F4, The building of a new
church in a more convenient part of the parish was
the saving of the church of St Petrock. An early
medieval church, its 16th-century pews were
augmented in the 18th century by large box pews,
a pulpit with sounding board, and the painting of
the Commandments, the Lord's Prayer and Royal
Arms on the tympanum in 1758. Ruskin led the
protest to prevent its demolition in the 1870s,
recognizing that it was a rare survival of a simple
rural parish church of exceptional charm.

Partrishow (Partrisio), Powys 693 F6, The small
church of St Issui in its mountainous setting has a
seclusion, simplicity and serenity unmatched by
any other in Wales. Its most renowned feature is
the delicately wrought rood screen and loft of the
early years of the 16th century, but there are many
other points of interest, including a pre-Norman
Conquest font, and a *Memento Mori* mural,

Pattyndenne Manor, Kent, A timber house, built in 1472 with oak trees from the surrounding forests. Upturned oaks form corner posts and there are dragon beams, a king post and tie beams. It was a hunting lodge of Henry VIII's, and is said to be haunted. *See* **Ladham House Gardens* 691 G6.**

Paviland Cave, Swans 688 E3, The headless skeleton of the 'Red Lady of Paviland' was discovered in this prehistoric cave, between Rhosili and Oxwich*, in 1823, along with the bones of mammoth, woolly rhino and bison. (The 'lady', stained with powdered red ochre, was later discovered to be a young man.) The cave is accessible only at low tide.

Paxton House, Border 699 J5, This Palladian mansion was built in 1758 by John and James Adam and the interior designed by their brother Robert at the request of Patrick Home. It houses the largest collection of Chippendale furniture in Scotland, all of it comparatively plain, as Home specifically requested. In the 1810s Robert Reid designed the Art Gallery – whose collection belongs to the National Galleries of Scotland – and the Regency library furnished by William Trotter.

Peak District National Park, Derbys 694 C3, A large area of hillscapes that stretches from the beautiful town of Ashbourne* in the south to the craggy and remote High Peak District west of Sheffield*. Characteristic of the area are the buildings and field walls made of local grey limestone.

Above: Peebles, view from the bridge over the River Tweed with the crown tower of the parish church (1885) and one of the dolphin lamp standards which formed part of the 1900 widening of the bridge.

Right: Peckforton Castle, the splendid outline of the main hall range.

Above: Paxton House, the north front with its recessed Roman Doric portico, modelled on that of Palladio's Villa Emo.

Bottom left and below: Peak District, typical limestone country with rolling hills.

Peakirk, Cambs 695 F5, A little village just north of Peterborough*. The church is uniquely dedicated to St Pega, sister of Croyland's St Guthlac, who founded a cell here in 716. Impressive Norman work includes an ornate south doorway. There is a rare medieval lectern, and extensive murals include a 'Warning to Gossips' and a macabre reminder of mortality.

Peckforton Castle, Ches 693 G2, The Castle enjoys a splendid site challenging the medieval Beeston Castle*, but is wholly Victorian – a romantic fortress designed by Anthony Salvin and built by Lord Tollemache in the late 1840s as the centrepiece of his huge estate. Everything about the building is convincing: massive stonework, winding stairways, vaulted ceilings and huge stone chimneypieces. The wonder is that it was ever intended to be a comfortable gentleman's residence.

Peddar's Way, Norfk 695 H4, An 88-mile-long (140km) walk, following the route of an old Roman road to meet the path along the Norfolk coast.

Peebles, Border 699 G5, This small town on the banks of the River Tweed contains the ruins of its 12th-century church (Cross Kirk) and a small museum housed in the 17th-century Chambers Institute. West of the town on the Tweed stands Neidpath Castle, built in the 14th and extended in the 17th century.

P

Pembroke

Pembroke, Pembks 692 C7, The town of Pembroke, whose name is a corruption of the Welsh 'Penfro' ('Land's End') stands on a narrow rocky ridge above the river, which provided a natural defence. Man-made protection took the form of a town wall, parts of which still survive. It was in 1093 that Arnulf de Montgomery laid claim to the area by building 'a slender fortress of stakes and earth', and 100 years later a new castle was built by William Marshall, who came from a family remarkable for their castle-building ardour. Forsaking the traditional rectangular shape, he introduced a formidable cylindrical keep with a domed roof, which still dominates the town and its surroundings and is on a scale unrivalled in Wales. After the tenure of the Marshalls the castle was occupied by William de Valence, who added the outer defences and the gatehouse. In 1457, in one of the towers, Margaret Beaufort, a 15-year-old girl already three months a widow, gave birth to a son. His father Edmund, Earl of Richmond, had died while imprisoned by Yorkists in Carmarthen Castle. The baby was Henry Tudor. Twenty-eight years later, he was to become King Henry VII, the founder of the Tudor dynasty.

The origins of **Pembroke Dock**, 2 miles (3km) north of the tower, date back to 1814, when the Royal Naval Dockyard was established here. Its closure in 1926 was only temporary: during World War II it took on a new identity as a Sunderland flying-boat base for the Royal Air Force. The original grid-iron layout of the town remains intact, and a Martello tower (1849–57) still stands at either end of the dockyard.

Left and top: Pembroke Castle, the birthplace of Henry Tudor who was to become Henry VII. Its principal feature is the formidable circular keep built by William Marshall in the late 12th century. The towers and the gatehouse of the outer defences were added later by William de Valence.

Below: Pencarrow, the Dining Room with notable family portraits.

Pembrokeshire Coastal Path, Pembks 692 C7, Opened in its entirety in 1970, it was the first long-distance path in Wales, starting in the southeast near Amroth, and ending near St Dogmael's (Llandudoch) in the north west, a distance of almost of almost 180 miles (288km), skirting fine beaches such as Marloes, and commanding spectacular views of the cliffs in their wide diversity of awesome outlines, many of them the habitat or rare flora and fauna. To follow the entire trail will challenge the hardiest enthusiasts, but there are a number of short options, all immensely rewarding.

514

Pencarrow
Above: The Library.
Right: The house, built
1765–75, is set in extensive
grounds.

Left: Pendennis Castle.
The 16th-century keep
dominates the headland.

Pen Dinas, Cerdgn 692 D4, The name conveys its
origins as a hill fort, dating from the Iron Age.

Penarth, V Glam 689 G3, Once a small village, it was
developed for the local bourgeoisie, with wide
roads, wooded walks through parks, and an
esplanade and pier with an Anglo-Indian style
pavilion. Windsor arcade is a reminder of the early
patronage of a town that still conveys its genteel
aspirations of a hundred years ago. South of
Penarth is Lavernock Point, where in 1897 Marconi
received the first-ever radio message transmitted
across water from Flatholm.

Pencarrow, Cnwll 688 D6, One of the best later 18th-
century houses in the county, with fine contents,
including a remarkable portrait by Arthur Devis
of the four daughters of Sir John St Aubyn (4th
Baronet) of St Michael's Mount. Notable rooms
include the maple-grained Entrance Hall and the
Music Room with its fine rococo plasterwork. The
extensive grounds include a very large rockery
constructed in the 1830s. Sir Arthur Sullivan wrote
the music for *Iolanthe* during his stay with Sir
William Molesworth St Aubyn in July 1882.

Pendennis Castle, Cnwll 688 C8, Perched on a
headland and commanding the Carrick roads,

the castle dates back to the 16th
century [EH]. It was besieged during
the Civil War but bravely defended by
Sir John Arundell of Trerice*. With
many later additions, it is excitingly
and exceptionally well presented.
The National Maritime Museum of
Cornwall near Port Pendennis houses
a small boat collection and galleries
explaining the tides and the ways in
which sailing vessels respond to the
winds. *See also* **Falmouth*.**

Peniarth, Gwynd 692 D4, A name
associated immediately with Welsh
history and literature thanks to the
beneficence of WWE Wynne
(1801–80), who inherited the
incomparably important collection
of Welsh manuscripts of Hengwrt
collected by Robert Vaughan
(1592?–1667). These now form what
is possibly the most prized collection
of the National Library of Wales at
Aberystwyth*.

Penmon, IOA 692 D1, As one nears Penmon ('end of
Mon') one becomes increasingly aware of its
isolation. It was here that Seiriol, a 6th-century
saint, established his cell, later to become an
Augustinian priory. Rebuilt in the 12th century, it
is a remarkable survival; part of it now serves as a
parish church. Few places of worship in Wales
impart such a sense of historical and spiritual
continuity. Nearby is Ynys Seiriol, or Puffin Island;
sadly, the puffins have been threatened by rat

infestation. The mournful
sound of the bell of an
unmanned lighthouse
intensifies the sense of
remoteness.

Right: Penmon, a sacred spot,
with St Seiriol's Well, one of
the 'holy wells' of Wales.

Pennines 697 F3–5,
A loosely linked chain of hills forming the
'backbone' of England. They stretch from the Peak
District* to the River Tyne in Northumberland.
The highest peak is Cross Fell (2,930 feet/893m).

Penrhyn Castle
Top left: stained glass by
Thomas Willement in the
Grand Hall.

Top right: One of the many
impressive principal rooms
decorated in the neo-Norman
style, using timber from the
estate.

Penrhyn Castle, Conwy 692 D2, The gargantuan 19th-century display of wealth realized from the local slate, which roofed the ever-growing towns and villages of the Industrial Revolution. The medieval origins of Penrhyn [NT], refined in the 18th century, were swallowed up by Thomas Hopper's neo-Norman 'stately, massive and stupendous creation' which was built between 1827 and 1847. The fascination of the building is more than matched by the outstanding collection of old masters displayed in the dining and breakfast rooms. Along the estate walls are the remains of the tramway that brought the slate to Port Penrhyn, with its dignified port office and circular multi-seater privy, from the quarries that had created 'the biggest man-made hole in the world'. The quarrymen found their only release in their Sunday worship, formalized by the Bethseda Chapel. This gave its name to the rapidly growing community, which resulted in an increasing number of similar chapels. Some of these are quite grandiose, but all now suffer from neglect brought about by declining congregations.

Penrith, Cumb 696 E3, A good townscape with some excellent 18th- and 19th-century buildings, including the Mansion House, 1750, whose main five-bay house is linked to wings with Venetian windows bearing gothick motifs. The town is centred on St Andrew's Church, which was rebuilt in 1720, with internal galleries set on Tuscan columns. Penrith Castle [EH] is mainly of the 15th

Penrhyn Castle
Above: The so-called
'Burgomaster of Delft', by Jan
Havicksz Steen, from the
picture collection.
Below: The castle, built by
Thomas Hopper, 1827–47.

century, and was built as much for domestic comfort as for defence. The adjacent railway station (by Sir William Tite, who also built the station in Carlisle*) was designed in a gothic fashion to avoid competition. South of the town, in Reaghyll, is the Image Garden, created by a self-taught local man, Thomas Bland, to celebrate the coronation of Queen Victoria. Some fifty pieces of garden sculpture are arranged in 'rooms' with specific themes such as 'Shakespeare's plays' or 'mythical characters'.

Penrose Estate, Cnwll 688 C8, Extensive walks encircle the Loe Pool, the largest

freshwater lake in the county, separated from the sea only by the treacherous Bar.

Penshaw Monument, T & W 697 G2, Set near the A19, but visible on an exposed hilltop from many miles around, is this Doric temple, roofless like a miniature Parthenon [NT]. It was erected in 1844, by public subscription, to the 1st Lord Durham, Captain-General and Governor-in-Chief of Canada, and a champion of Parliamentary Reform with Lord Grey.

Penshurst Place, Kent 691 G6, One of the great medieval houses of Kent. The oldest part (1341) was built by Sir John de Pulteney, Lord Mayor of London. Of this house the Great Hall survives virtually intact with its timber roof and panelled screen, and the central hearth and (restored) louvre. By this date it had become customary for the lord to take his meals not with the retainers in the Great Hall but in a private room (the solar) reached by a staircase at one end. That at Penshurst is among the earliest of such rooms. The rest of Penshurst Place ranges of buildings forming three courtyards, dates from the 15th and 16th centuries. The Sidney family acquired it in 1552, and it was the home of the poet Sir Philip Sidney. The long gallery was built by his brother, Sir Robert, in about 1600. In 1818 Sir John Shelly Sidney employed JB Rebecca to restore the house fairly drastically, and many of the Tudor-gothic details are his. The gardens were restored in the 19th century to their appearance in the 17th. At the same time the village of Penshurst was rebuilt in a Tudor style that can easily deceive the visitor. In the local church, under the tower, is an extraordinary 13th-century coffin lid carved with the half-figure of a woman with raised hands, turning to one side, behind a foliated cross like the bars of a cage.

Pentre Ifan, Pembks 692 C6, One of the finest

neolithic burial chambers in Britain. Pentre Ifan ('Ifan's settlement') is remarkable not only for the enormous size of the capstone, but also for the ability of the four sidestones to support such a weight – a phenomenon that appealed to 19th-century sketching travellers as it does now to photographers. Excavated in 1936 and again in 1956, it is the most popular of all this area's numerous megalithic monuments.

Pen-y-Gwyrd, Gwynd 692 D2, From Llanberis* toward Capel Curig, the number of climbers on the rock faces of Llanberis Pass partly explains the importance of Pen-y-Gwryd Hotel. In the early 1950s it was the haunt of many of the world's finest climbers, among them Sir Edmund Hillary,

Penshurst Place
Top: View from the east.
Centre: The south front. The oldest part (1338–49) is in the centre – the Great Hall, octagonal stair turret and 'solar' to the left.

Left: Pentre Ifan, one of the most impressive ancient monuments in Wales.

Sir John Hunt and Sherpa Tensing, who wrote their signatures on the ceiling of the public bar.

Penzance, Cnwll 688 B8, The principal town of western Cornwall is dominated by the dome of a bank. This was a prosperous town thanks to its mining, maritime and tourist industries, and its wealth is reflected in the elegant terraces and squares of Regency houses, the Egyptian House in Chapel Street and the many grand houses on its outskirts. The Penlee House Museum and Art Gallery, set in lovely subtropical gardens, has a superb collection of pictures by members of the Newlyn School, and examples of copper and other wares produced by the local fishermen and their sons at the School of Art. There are also galleries devoted to the rich archeology of the area, together with its flora and fauna. The region's geology is best described at the Royal Geological Museum in St John's Hall, one of the largest granite buildings in the world.

Peover Hall, Ches 693 H2, Built in 1585 for Sir Ralph Mainwaring. Large later additions were removed in the mid-1960s and much of the interior of the old house was repanelled. The rooms are quite small, except for the huge kitchen, which has an unusual heavy timbered ceiling. The stables of 1654 are at least as fine as the house and have all their original fittings, while the nearby parish church has a collection of alabaster family tombs.

Perry Green, Wilts 690 B4, Henry Moore's studios, workshops, and now a new gallery (Sheep Field Barn) are owned and maintained by the Henry Moore Foundation in Perry Green, and are open for visits by appointment only. In this lovely, secluded part of the countryside Moore's sculptures can be seen at their best, dotted haphazardly around the garden and fields.

Pershore Abbey, Worcs 690 B3, Pershore is a pocket-sized Georgian town. Entering from the southeast, you pass the six-arched medieval bridge over the Avon. Climbing the hill, you reach the long main street of little red brick houses, mainly 18th century. Off the market place is the yellow stone Abbey, of which only the stump of the nave, the crossing, transepts and chancel survive. Its bulk seems out of scale with the town; originally the nave was nearly as long as those at Gloucester* or Tewkesbury*. The townsmen purchased the surviving section to use as their church at the time of the Dissolution.

Perth, P & K 699 F3, After 846 Perth, which may have been built on the site of a Roman camp, was overshadowed by Scone*, capital of the kingdom of Dalriada. In the 12th century the town obtained a charter, due to its port on the River Tay which linked it to the east coast, and became the principal residence of the Scottish monarchy. After James I was assassinated in one of the town's monasteries in 1437, James II transferred the royal residence to Edinburgh*. Perth's political eclipse did nothing to protect it: in 1559 rioters destroyed its monasteries; it was occupied by the troops of the Duke of Montrose in 1644, by Cromwell's troops in 1651, and by the Jacobites in 1689, 1715 and again in 1745. Fine Georgian buildings remain, notably Sir Robert Smirke's Greek Doric County Buildings of 1819.

Perth owes its original name of 'St John's Toun' to St John's Kirk, founded in 1126 by David I and renovated in the 15th century. On 11 May 1559 John Knox preached a sermon in the church which denounced papist idolatry. In North Port stands the Fair Maid's House on which Walter Scott modelled the house of the Fair Maid of Perth. Perth Art Gallery and Museum houses a museum of natural history, archeology and local history, the whisky and glass industries, in a classical-style building of 1824 and 1931. Also noteworthy is the JD Fergusson gallery in the neoclassical waterworks of 1832.

Peterborough, Cambs 695 F5, The only ancient city to become a New Town, it is a peculiar place. Amid a vast modern sprawl its old name of Gildenburgh ('Golden Borough') is still reflected in a

Top left: Pershore Abbey was already established by 972, when it became Benedictine. Part was knocked down at the Dissolution, leaving a lopsided fragment, which is still impressive.

Top centre: Perth, St John's Kirk, the medieval timber and lead spire.

Centre: Perth, Fair Maid's House, the meeting hall of the Glover Incorporation from 1629, restored in 1893–94.

Bottom: Peterborough, the Guildhall in Cathedral Square.

stupendous cathedral, but elsewhere in the city centre good historic buildings are hard to find. Cathedral Square is graced by a 17th-century Guildhall on Tuscan columns (note the arms of Charles II under the clock) which replaced a Tudor butter cross. The best Georgian buildings are in Priestgate, where the ashlar-faced museum and art gallery (1816) is rich in Roman relics from the Nene Valley. There is also embroidery by Mary Queen of Scots who had time on her hands before her execution at nearby Fotheringhay* Castle. The bone models and straw marquetry are also the product of enforced recreation, the work of Napoleonic prisoners of war held at Norman Cross beside the Great North Road. The old governor's house and a stone column,

eagle-topped until recently, salute the 1770 Frenchmen who died here between 1796 and 1816. The cathedral precinct, which has served as Trollope's Barchester in television adaptations, is approached from the Market Place through an outer gate flanked by more medieval buildings: the King's Lodgings and Abbot's Prison on the south side, and St Thomas's Chapel opposite. Straight ahead is the pinnacled west front of this glorious Norman building, built from local Barnack stone, to which the retrochoir with its superb fan vaulting was added by Abbot Kirkton at the eastern end, c1500. The site itself has a chequered history: a Benedictine monastery was founded here by King Paeda of Mercia in 654, sacked by the Danes, refounded by King Edgar, plundered by Hereward the Wake in c1070 and reduced to ashes in 1116. The present late Norman building was begun shortly after and took 80 years to complete. The long nave with its massive arcading is typically 12th century, but much rarer is the original painted wooden ceiling, a wonderful pattern of lozenges enlivened with figures saintly and royal and with Romanesque grotesques. The Hedda stone in the retrochoir, an exceptional piece of Saxon sculpture, is another of the cathedral's prize exhibits.

Peterborough was elevated to cathedral status at the Dissolution of the Monasteries – thanks to the tomb of Catherine of Aragon in the north choir. Mary Queen of Scots lay in the south aisle for 25 years after her execution, until her son James I removed her remains to Westminster Abbey.

Peterborough Cathedral
Top left: The west front of local Barnack Stone.
Top right: The choir.

Right: Peterhead, view of the harbour.

A portrait of Old Scarlett, gravedigger for both queens, hangs on the west wall.

Peterhead, Abers 702 E5, The port, founded in 1539, was built using the local pink granite. The Young Pretender landed here in 1715 with the help of the 10th Earl-Marischal of Scotland and his brother, James Keith, who later became a Field Marshal in the army of Frederick the Great of Prussia. He is commemorated by a statue presented to the town by William I of Prussia in 1868, which stands in front of the town hall. The vast port, begun in 1773, enabled Peterhead to become Britain's leading whaling port, and later one of its main herring ports, in the 19th century. Today it is a supply base for the North Sea oil rigs and Europe's leading whitefish port with a busy fish market. The Peterhead Maritime Heritage Museum traces the history of the port, while the Arbuthnott Museum presents a collection of Inuit artefacts brought back by whalers. Peterhead also has the oldest packing plant in Scotland (1585): the Ugie Salmon Fish House, which is still active today.

Petworth

Petworth, W Susx 690 E7, Sussex's major country house [NT]. Apart from a few earlier fragments in the chapel, what we see today dates from 1688–90. It is very large – the front of 21 bays – but very plain, although it did originally have a central dome. The architect is unknown. Ostentation is reserved for the interiors: the Marble Hall, solemn but austere; the Grand Staircase, with painted decoration by Laguerre, the staircase itself rebuilt in the 19th century; and the Carved Room, with Grinling Gibbons at his most brilliant. The chapel is basically 13th-century but filled with 17th-century woodwork, including some highly diverting and unholy cherubs by John Selden. In the early 19th century a gallery was added to the house for the 3rd Earl of Egremont's art collection. One of the main reasons for visiting Petworth, in fact, is to see its outstanding paintings and sculpture, including many works by Turner (whose most generous patron was the Earl, who let him use the Old Library as his studio), Van Dyck and numerous others, as well as Greek, Roman and Renaissance pieces. The park of Petworth, with its herd of deer, was laid out by Capability Brown, and the little town outside the gates is one of the most attractive in Sussex, full of 17th- and 18th-century houses. The fantastic lamp standard at the corner of East and North streets is by Sir Charles Barry.

Above: The North Gallery was added in 1824–7 and contains major early 19th-century British sculpture.

Bottom left: The wrought-iron gates screening the west front are copies of Tijon's work at Hampton Court*. They date from 1872.

Top: Page from a 15th-century version of *Canterbury Tales*.

Centre right: Thomas Wentworth, 1st Earl of Strafford, by Anthony Van Dyck.

Bottom right: The bust has long been called William III but there are reasons for thinking it may be a broken-nosed James II.

Above: *The Card Players,* by
Jan Matsys, c1510–75. The
painting has also been
identified as *The Prodigal Son*
gambling away his
inheritance, and as a
disguised portrait of
man and wife.

Above: *Bucks Fighting at
Sunset* by JMW Turner.

Left: *Dewy Morning at
Petworth,* by JMW Turner.

Pevensey, E Susx 691 G7, Here William the Conqueror landed in 1066. The Normans incorporated long stretches of 4th-century Roman walling on the outer building of their own castle of c1100 [EH].

Peveril Castle, Derbys 694 C3, Begun by William Peveril, William the Conqueror's bailiff for the locality, and paid for with revenue from the local lead mines, the castle was immensely strong [EH]. Although ruined in the 17th century, it is still spectacular: the walls of the keep survive at their original height, and the building dominates the village of Castleton below it.

Pewsey, Wilts 690 C5, One of several white horses in the region, cut in the chalk a mile or so south of the small town in 1785 but re-cut in 1937 (see also

Above: Peveril Castle, in a superb elevated position with natural defences.

Left: Pevensey Castle, the entrance to the Norman castle, incorporating parts of the Roman wall.

Bottom right: Pickering Castle, the steeply profiled motte.

Westbury* and Preshute*). The horse measures 66 by 45 feet (20.1 by 13.7m).

Pickering, N York 697 J4, A busy market town. The church of St Peter and St Paul has late medieval wall-paintings depicting a number of saints, many of them suffering gruesome deaths; interesting memorials to two Pickering surveyors who drew plans for Washington, DC; and the brothers John and William Marshall, agricultural reformers. Pickering Castle [EH] is a fine example of a motte-and-bailey castle.

Picton Castle, Pembks 692 C6, The nucleus was built between 1295 and 1308 by Sir John Wogan, justiciar of Ireland and described in 1302 as 'Lord of Pykton'. The male line came to an end early in the 15th century, and an heiress subsequently married

Thomas ap Philip, a prosperous landowner. Since 1491 Picton has remained the property of that family, which adopted the surname of Philipps. Unusually, the castle has never had a courtyard, but consists of a rectangular block, with drum towers at each end of the long sides. The two towers on the east side are so closely placed that they almost form a gatehouse. The single tower on the west side was dismantled in the early 19th century and replaced with a large four-storeyed block, which accommodates on the principal floor the beautifully proportioned Drawing Room and Dining Room. Much of the interior of the medieval castle was remodelled in the mid-18th century, when the Great Hall was given a balustraded gallery as an elegant setting for the Snitzler organ of 1750. Next to the castle is a woodland garden, much of it created by the late Lady Marion Philipps after World War II.

Pinmill, Suffk 691 J3, The Mill on the Orwell estuary produced wooden pegs for boat-building and inspired Arthur Ransome to write *Swallows and Amazons*. Many artists have painted the sail-rife scene of Thames barges, houseboats and the glorious view of Nacton Hall's wooded slopes and observatory. The Butt and Oyster pub, lapped by the tide, has a timeless interior.

Pitchford Hall, Shrops, Built in about 1570, a fine example of a large Elizabethan timber-framed gabled house. In the grounds, a huge lime tree bears an extraordinary tree house, built in about 1750. *See* **Acton Burnell* 693 G4.**

Pitlochry, P & K 699 F2, This town in the Tummel Valley enjoyed its golden age in the late 19th century, when it became a fashionable spa town. Set in magnificent surroundings, it has two distilleries, a salmon ladder and a popular summer drama festival.

Pitmedden Garden, Abers 702 D5, This huge garden created by Alexander Seton in 1675 reflects the influence of the French landscape designer Le Nôtre (1613–1700). The borders of the

Picton Castle
Top left: The medieval Great Hall transformed in the 18th century with the elegance of that period.
Top right: The castle is set in a woodland garden.

Bottom: Pitmedden Garden, the parterre. The garden boasts two fine square-plan pavilions at the corners.

lower terrace were redesigned in the 1950s and those of the upper terrace in the 1990s.

Plas Brondanw, Gwynd 692 D3, Clough Williams-Ellis' home, above Penrhyndeudraeth. The gardens only are open, but plainly testify to his originality, as do various buildings in the nearby village of Rhyd. *See also* **Portmeirion*.**

Plas Newydd, Denbgs, Although many large Welsh houses bear the name of Plas Newydd, this building – just south of Llangollen – is distinguished by its exuberant black-and-white decoration. For this we have to thank 'The Ladies of Llangollen', two friends of Irish extraction, Lady Eleanor Butler and the Honourable Sarah Ponsonby, who arrived there in 1780. They rented Pen-y-Maes, then no more than a rustic cottage, which they transformed into a *cottage orné*, renaming it Plas Newydd ('New Mansion'). The women, who became known as 'the two most celebrated virgins in Europe' lived here for almost 50 years, Eleanor dying in 1829 at the age of 90, and Sarah, 15 years her junior, two years later. During this time they received the untiring devotion of their servant, Mary Carryll, who shares their three-sided memorial in the graveyard of the parish church.

It is easy to understand the attraction Pen-y-Maes held for them. It was not only perched above a wooded stream, but also had as a backcloth the remains of the castle of Dinas Bran*, one of the highest in Wales, looking like an ossified primeval quadruped. The stream was given rustic bridges; gazebos and arbours were created, and a font from the nearby Vale Crucis Abbey* was given a suitably reverential setting. The gothicizing of Plas Newydd and its gardens embodied notions of the picturesque, and although much of the ladies' work has disappeared, enough remained to be sensitively restored by an enlightened local authority. There were enough county houses in the vicinity to provide the women with a lively social circle, and they were sufficiently well known to receive visits from the foremost celebrities of the day – among them Sir Walter Scott, Richard Brinsley Sheridan and William Wordsworth (who referred to Plas Newydd as a 'low-roofed cot'). Plas Newydd was later further extended by General Yorke, a relation of the Yorkes of Erddig*. Successive owners also made alterations until 1932, when it was bought by the district council. *See* **Llangollen* 693 F3.**

Plas Newydd, IOA
Top: View from the gardens over the Menai Strait.
Left: The stables.
Below left: Rex Whistler's mural in the dining room is rich in pictorial allusions to the Paget family.
Bottom: The cromlech, one of Anglesey's many neolithic monuments, stands in a prominent position above the stables.

Plas Newydd, IOA 692 D2, Overlooking the Menai Strait between Anglesey and the mainland is this classic 18th-century country house. The best view can be enjoyed by those sailing along the Strait between Caernarfon* and Beaumaris*, passing under two of Wales' most famous bridges, Stephenson's Britannia and Telford's Suspension.

The house, which itself boasts one of the best views in Wales (of the Snowdonian mountains) owes much of its present appearance to James Wyatt, who enlarged it to a style and scale suitable for its owner Lord Paget's new title, Earl of Uxbridge. His son, second-in-command to the Duke of Wellington at Waterloo, where he suffered the loss of a leg, acquired the title of 1st Marquess of Anglesey; and the elegance of his father's transformation of Plas Newydd proved admirably in keeping with his elevated status. With grounds laid out by Humphry Repton, Plas Newydd is probably Wales's most elegant 18th-century house, although its foundations are Tudor. The 7th Marquess of Anglesey, the distinguished military historian, gave Plas Newydd to the National Trust in 1976. It is now known principally for the vast mural in the Dining Room by Rex Whistler, probably the largest canvas – and certainly the most romantic – in the British Isles.

Plas Teg, Flints 693 F2, If John Trevor's Trefalun (*see* Gresford*) was an indication of his important social connections, this house (1610), built by his son, Sir John Trevor, was an even greater proclamation of success. Each of the four corner towers is topped with an ogival cupola, and the scrolled gables of the entrance front add further liveliness to what is the only Jacobean courtier house in Wales. A dual carriageway between Wrexham* and Mold* has destroyed the formality once surrounding this architectural eccentricity; but its oddities were never copied by the local

Plas Newydd, IOA
Top left: Rex Whistler painted himself into his mural; he can just be seen leaning on a broom halfway back.
Top right: Lady Caroline (Paget) Capel, eldest sister of the 1st Marquess, with infant asleep on her lap, by John Hoppner, 1794.

Right: Plas yn Rhiw, donated to the National Trust in 1949 by three remarkable sisters in honour of their parents.

gentry, who preferred the more regional style of Fferm, a quarter of a mile (0.4km) toward Mold. Further along the old Wrexham–Mold road, a pair of sadly neglected 18th-century lodges once formed part of the Leeswood estate. The magnificent white iron screen was wrought by the Davies brothers of Croes Foel.

Plas-yn-Rhiw, Gwynd 692 C3, The smallest of the National Trust houses in North Wales, and also one of the most charming – partly because this old manor house and garden in their wooded setting, rising above Cardigan Bay, was saved from oblivion by the Keatings – a widow and her three daughters – just before World War II. Its semi-fortified medieval origins were added to in the 16th and 18th centuries, and in the 20th were restored by the Welsh architect Clough Williams-Ellis (*see* Portmeirion*).

Pleshey, Essex 691 G4, A strange and atmospheric place, the entire village encircled by ramparts of

Geoffrey de Mandeville's massive Norman baronial earthworks, approached across a dramatic 15th-century brick bridge.

Plompton Rocks, N York 697 H5, Daniel Lascelles of nearby Harewood* started to develop the Plompton estate near Spofforth in 1760 but never completed the mansion, concentrating instead on the grounds. The architect John Carr designed a dam that created a much larger lake out of 15th-century fishponds, and Lascelles planted more than 2,000 trees to enhance the dramatic rocky scenery of the site. The resulting landscape was to become the haunt of many 18th-century artists such as Turner, Girtin and Hodges. When at Harewood, Queen Mary visited Plompton frequently, describing it as 'the nearest place on earth to heaven'.

Pluscarden Abbey, Moray 702 B5, The priory founded in 1230 became a Benedictine abbey between 1454 and the Reformation. In 1948 it was reoccupied by Benedictines, whose members re-roofed the Gothic church which has lost its nave, but has some striking modern stained-glass windows.

Plymouth

Top left: The Grand Hotel on Plymouth Hoe, mid 19th century, one of many built to accommodate early trans-Atlantic travellers.

Below centre: War memorial on the Hoe, erected 1920–4 to honour men lost in the Navy. It was designed by Sir Robert Lorimer and the sculpture was by WC Storr Barber.

Bottom left: An 1884 statue by Boehm of Sir Francis Drake on the Hoe, close to the spot where he played his famous game of bowls.

Plymouth, Devon 688 E7, Few towns in Britain are blessed with such a fine location – at the confluence of two rivers, with a lovely natural harbour overlooked by hills. An important fishing and trading port from early times, Plymouth had its nucleus at Sutton Pool; small Elizabethan houses are still to be found in the winding streets around the former Fish Market. Nearby is a row of commemorative stones recording many of the perilous voyages that have started from here, including that of the *Mayflower* in September 1620. Across a modern bridge is the National Marine Aquarium, the latest and one of the most successful tourist attractions in this bustling part of the port. The hill behind is crowned by the protective walls of the Citadel. Setting it high above the Sutton Pool and the Hoe, Charles II began the construction of a massive fortress in 1666 approached through a magnificent and fashionable baroque stone gatehouse or Portal. The elaborate trophies and statues were originally gilded. Guided tours around the Citadel, which is still in military use, take in St Katherine's Chapel and a range of messes, barrack blocks and other types of accommodation. Below the high walls of the fortress in New Street on the Barbican is the Elizabethan House [NT], one of the last Tudor jettied houses of the type that Sir Francis Drake and the other sea dogs would have known so well. It is furnished as it might have been during the reign of Elizabeth I.

The Hoe, famous as the place where Sir Francis Drake was playing bowls as the Spanish Armada approached, is still the favourite Plymouth promenade. The panoramic backdrop of the Sound to the Breakwater (finished 1841) and out to the Eddystone Lighthouse is still animated by marine traffic: naval vessels, ferries and pleasure craft. All are visible from the **Dome**, a modern interpretation centre describing the development of the port. The nearby top section of John Smeaton's lighthouse of 1756–9 was moved here from the treacherous Eddystone reefs in 1882. There are also many public monuments, chief among them the massive naval memorial of 1920–4 by Sir Robert Lorimer.

Plymouth's commercial heart lies to the northwest near the church of St Andrew, but it was badly damaged by bombs in World War II. The post-war reconstruction, under the direction of Professor Abercrombie, takes the form of three parallel shopping streets dissected by Armada Way. One of his ideas was to concentrate the same trades in one place, and they largely remain so to this day. A rare modern intrusion into this area is the Theatre Royal, which was completed in 1982. The Edwardian **Museum and Art Gallery**, at Drake Circus, opposite the recently founded University of Plymouth, has large and notable collections. Chief among these must be the Cottonian Collection of early drawings, prints and bronzes inherited and then amplified by the local 19th-century antiquary William Cotton. He also collected items belonging to local artists, such as Sir Joshua Reynolds, born at Plympton St Maurice* where his father was the schoolmaster. The work of later West Country artists is well represented and includes one of the greatest of the Newlyn School works, *The Fish Sale on a Cornish Beach*, by Stanhope Forbes. Plymouth was the home of William Cookworthy, who developed the first English hard-paste porcelain from Cornish china clays in the mid-18th century. His factory on Sutton Pool opened in 1768 but remained there for only two years before moving to the better established pottery town of Bristol. There are, however, many examples of the Cookworthy wares in the Museum, together with an outstanding range of pottery and porcelain from around the world. There are also galleries devoted to local history (including exceptional watercolours of the many buildings designed by the Plymouth architect John Foulston in the early 19th century) and natural history, especially geological specimens assembled by Sir John St Aubyn of St Michael's Mount, who had considerable interests in Devonport*.

Sadly there is little of note in the rapidly expanding suburbs of this, the largest town in the West Country. Relentless grey terraces climb across the valleys that once contained small hamlets or villages. In **Stoke**, however, convenient for both the Dockyard and Plymouth, there are handsome houses by Foulston at Albemarle Villas, at Belmont (now the Youth Hostel – very neo-Grecian with fine interiors), and in Wyndham Square. Other terraces and mansions here testify to the wealth of the area in the days of the expanding Empire.

Top left: Looking across Sutton Pool to the Customs House of 1810.

Top right: Smeaton's Eddystone lighthouse of 1756–9 was moved to the Hoe in 1882.

Below: The Duke of Cornwall Hotel by C Forster Hayward, 1865. The details are in terracotta.

Polesden Lacey
Top: The Regency villa.
Left: Large porcelain *famille rose* vases of *c*1760 in the corridor.

Above: *The Hon. Mrs Ronald Greville*, by Carolus-Duran, at Polesden Lacey.

Bottom: Poole's extensive harbour.

Plympton St Maurice, Devon 689 F7, Ancient streets cluster round the ruined motte-and-bailey castle, largely rebuilt in the 1140s by Baldwin de Redvers, Earl of Devon. The former Guildhall of 1696 stands on an open arcade, bearing the arms of the local families of Treby and Trevor on its façade. In George Street the grammar school founded in 1658, with a schoolroom built over a picturesque cloister, has become a place of pilgrimage: the Reverend Samuel Reynolds, father of Sir Joshua Reynolds, first President of the Royal Academy, was master here for many years, and local families – the Parkers of Saltram* and the Edgcumbes of Mount Edgcumbe* – encouraged Joshua's early talent. Curiously, the school produced another three famous artists, James Northcote, Benjamin Robert Haydon and Sir Charles Eastlake. A small Parliamentary borough, it once had as its MP Sir Christopher Wren.

Polesden Lacey, Surrey 691 F6, Polesden Lacey is a charming Regency villa remodelled in 1906 [NT]. It is beautifully set amid unspoilt gardens and grounds, with views south toward the North Downs. The house contains the fine collections of William McEwan and his daughter, The Hon. Mrs Ronald Greville ,which include silver, porcelain, furniture and very good paintings. The hall overmantel was formerly the reredos at Wren's City Church of St Matthew Friday Street, demolished in 1881. *See* **Great Bookham***.

Polstead, Suffk 691 H3, The church has rare Romanesque brick arcading. Nearby is the site of Maria Marten's infamous murder in the Red Barn in 1827, later the subject of a popular Victorian melodrama. Coincidentally, perhaps, Polstead has also been home to thriller writer Ruth Rendell.

Pontefract, W York 697 H6, A small town with a surprisingly large number of good Georgian buildings. Little remains of Pontefract Castle, although it played a major role in medieval history – it was here that Richard II died or, more probably, was murdered. It was besieged during the Civil War.

Poole, Dorset 690 C7, Famous for its great harbour, the town enjoyed a long history of prosperity until the early 19th century, when it was gradually eclipsed by the attractions of Bournemouth*. Down at the Quay one can still appreciate the scale of the harbour. The Custom House, reconstructed after a fire in 1813, has an open lower storey on Tuscan columns. It is flanked by fine warehouse groupings. Poole has a number of fine merchant houses, notably Poole House of 1730 and the Mansion House of *c*1790. The best, however, is Sir Peter Thompson's House of 1749 (now part of Poole College), with John Bastard of Blandford as its architect. The church of St James (1820) has fine arcades, said to be formed of pine trunks from Newfoundland, a 1736 reredos and several interesting monuments, including one with a good cartouche to George Lewen (1718). Just outside Poole, at Parkstone, is St Osmund's Church in Bournemouth Road. It is an amazing church, built in 1913–16 in the Byzantine style by ES Prior and Arthur Grove, with a great rose window and intricate façades. The altar inscriptions in the Incarnation Chapel are by Eric Gill. The famous **Compton Acres Gardens** surround a neo-Tudor villa of 1914. They were laid out from 1919 and include rock and water gardens, Japanese and Italian gardens, Heather Dell, Woodland Walk and the subtropical Glen. There is attractive bronze and marble statuary.

Port Penrhyn, Conwy, Built by Richard Pennant, the 1st Baron Penrhyn of Llandegai in the 1790s, its purpose was to export the slate from the Penrhyn

Quarries, a distance of 6 miles (9.6km), by an iron tramway falling through 500 feet (152m), and whose track is still discernible outside the walls of Penrhyn Castle on the outskirts of Bangor. The architect was Benjamin Wyatt, who was responsible for many estate buildings in the vicinity of Bangor, but few more attractive than the Port or Harbour Office. Less classical, but a surviving oddity, is the circular six-seater privy on the quayside. *See* **Penrhyn Castle* 692 D2.**

Port Sunlight, Mersyd 696 E7, This village is the major architectural achievement of the first Lord Leverhulme, a businessman with such an obsession for building that his wife complained that she never lived in a house where the builders weren't in. It takes its name from the soap that made his fortune. The idea of a factory with model village attached was in the tradition of Saltaire* or Bournville (*see* Birmingham*) but nowhere has the consistent quality of architecture and landscape been excelled. The factory opened in 1888 and the housing followed, at first on a rather picturesque plan and then with a more formal Beaux Arts layout. Leverhulme used many architects, who adopted a variety of neo-vernacular styles in brick, terracotta, timber-framing, roughcast and weatherboarding. The blocks are broken up into long and short runs and planned with ingenuity so that there is no sense of monotony. The best of the early housing is round The Dell, one of the inlets from the river which was turned into a sunken garden; there is now a visitor centre nearby. Christ Church (undenominational) has a vaulted loggia that houses monuments to Leverhulme and his wife. The most significant public building, of the later formal layout, is the **Lady Lever Art Gallery** of 1914, by William and Segar Owen; it is long and low, stone and classical, in contrast with the vernacular housing around.

Top left and top right: Port Sunlight, Lady Lever Gallery, classical formality among vernacular houses for the workers.
Right: Dressing table by Thomas Chippendale, rosewood and gilt, *c*1760.

Bottom: Portchester Castle, which is entered by a drawbridge over the moat.

It was built to house some of Leverhulme's extraordinary art collection and is now part of the National Museums and Galleries on Merseyside, with especially fine French 18th-century furniture and 19th-century British painting and sculpture. Outside the gallery is a noble war memorial by W Goscombe John.

Portchester Castle, Hants 690 D7, The oldest military monument in southern England [EH]. A fort was built by the Romans in *c*280 on the north shore of the harbour – the most westerly of several built to resist raids by Anglo-Saxons and others. Most of the external walls survive (the most substantial Roman structural remains north of the Alps). They were adapted for a Norman castle, of which the shell of the impressive keep is intact. Within the castle enclosure is the mid-12th-century St Mary's, originally part of a priory and now the parish church; the west front is particularly impressive.

Porthcurno, Cnwll 688 B8, Home of the fascinating Museum of Submarine Telegraphy. The cables that left Porthcurno beach in the late 19th century helped to form the British Empire.

Porthleven, Cnwll 688 B8, The 465-foot (141m) long pier stands at the end of the 4-mile (6km) beach that stretches down to the Loe Pool. It protects the elongated, narrow harbour from which copper from the Godolphin mines was exported and a large trade carried out in slate, limestone, coal, clay and tin. Nearby on the inland side of the road to Penzance* lies Tregonning Hill, where William Cookworthy first discovered china clay in Cornwall. He experimented with it at his Plymouth* porcelain works between 1768 and 1770 before moving his business to Bristol*.

Porthmadog, Gwynd 692 D3, Tremadog's* neighbour is always busy. In summer its popularity is owed to the marina, once the point of export for the slate brought from Blaenau Ffestiniog* on the narrow gauge railway, but now used purely for pleasure.

Portland Bill, Dorset 689 J6, The fine white limestone of Portland was chosen in the 1680s by Sir Christopher Wren to face St Paul's Cathedral, London*, and has often been used for important buildings. Portland itself is a remote, treeless spot, scarred with quarries, with three lighthouses (two of c1867 and one of 1905), and the lonely but splendid church of St George at Easton (1754–66). There is a mid-19th-century prison, built when convicts were engaged in the stone quarries, and two castles: Rufus Castle stands on the cliff edge and is largely of the late 15th century; Portland Castle is mid-16th century and made of crisp Portland stone ashlar, with an octagonal central space of two storeys.

Portmeirion
Above: The magical concoction set up by Clough Williams-Ellis.
Below: The Hotel, which was opened in 1926.

Portmeirion, Gwynd 692 D3, South of Porthmadog*, across the 'Cob', lies Clough Williams-Ellis' light-opera approach to architecture, the Italianate village of Portmeirion. Much of it is embellished by buildings rescued from demolition from as far afield as Liverpool* and Bristol*, all of them showing the architect's unmistakable eye for the picturesque. The village is best known nowadays as the setting for the cult television series, *The Prisoner*.

Portsdown Hill, Hants 690 D7, In the mid-19th century fears of a serious French invasion had again taken hold, and France was developing, perhaps more rapidly than Britain, new forms of armament and ironclad warships. A landing on the Solent shores was believed a possibility, followed by an attack on Portsmouth* from the landward sides, so a series of forts (called 'Palmerston's Folly' after the prime minister) was constructed along Portsdown Hill, a chalk ridge to the north of the city, and across the Gosport peninsula to the west. They are huge constructions of brick and earth, strong enough to withstand shells and surrounded by moats, which on Portsdown Hill had to be dry. They were made as inconspicuous as possible from the landward sides, but on the sides facing the sea they are prominent, with massive brick walls and stone- (or granite-) lined entrances and gun openings. One, Fort Nelson on Portsdown Hill, is now a branch of the Royal Armouries, with armaments on display; another, Fort Widley, is also sometimes open.

Portsmouth

Portsmouth, Hants 690 D7, The harbour is a broad inlet of the sea with a narrow mouth to the Solent; the Dockyard has been a base for the British navy for 500 years. Now partly open to the public, it has impressive 18th- and 19th-century buildings, mainly in local red brick and generally classical in style; some are now museums. The centrepiece is HMS *Victory*, one of the finest surviving wooden ships anywhere, restored as she was when commanded by Lord Nelson at the Battle of Trafalgar in 1805, and set in a stone-sided dry dock which itself dates from 1802. In a nearby dock, protected by a moisture-conditioned roof structure, are the reassembled remains of the *Mary Rose*, one of Henry VIII's ships, which sank off Portsmouth during a skirmish with the French in 1545 and was dramatically recovered from the sea bed in 1982. To complete this trio of historic ships open to the public, HMS *Warrior*, dating from 1861 and recently restored, was once a pioneer iron ship with steam engines and powerful guns (but still equipped with sails).

The original town of **Old Portsmouth**, still an entity, grew up beside the harbour entrance. It was badly bombed in 1940–1 but there remain fine Georgian or earlier houses fronting the long High Street and streets leading off, such as Lombard Street. The old parish church became the cathedral in 1927; the remarkable eastern end of c1200 survives, and the present choir dates from 1692–3. Extension westward began in 1935 under the architect Sir Charles Nicholson but was stopped by the war; the new west end was completed in 1991 under Michael Drury.

The furthest part of Old Portsmouth, on a narrow peninsula, is called Point, with well-known pubs and views into the harbour. Fronting the shore, beginning with the Round Tower, are the remains of defences (16th to mid-19th century), with splendid views over the Solent. The far stretch, the Long Curtain, is a grassy rampart with old gun emplacements, separated from the actual shoreline by a moat; a small bridge across this is a replacement of the one on which Lord Nelson crossed the last time he left land, to join the *Victory* anchored offshore.

The present city centre developed, away from Old Portsmouth, in the 19th century. At its heart is Guildhall Square, redeveloped in the 1970s to a successful traffic-free layout, centred on the Guildhall of 1886–90 (reconstructed after bombing). Southward is the two-storey iron frontispiece of the former Theatre Royal, which has a fine interior of 1900 by Frank Matcham. Park Building (1903–8) behind the Guildhall was built for the college that grew into the University of Portsmouth – now occupying scattered buildings. (One of the best, appropriately, is the School of Architecture in Portland Street well to the west, designed by the Professor of Architecture, Sir Colin Stansfield-Smith).

Charles Dickens was born in 1812 in one of a pleasant group of Georgian houses built a few years earlier, and now a museum in Old Commercial Road. His father, who held a post in the pay office of the Dockyard, moved on in 1814. At this time, Marc Isambard Brunel was working on the installation of machinery for mass-producing ships' pulley blocks. The machinery he invented – the first of its kind in mass production – provided an important step forward in the Industrial Revolution. His son Isambard Kingdom Brunel (1806–59) was born here, and grew up to become the flamboyant engineering genius of history.

Top: HMS *Victory*, Nelson's flagship at the Battle of Trafalgar, and the only great wooden ship to be so meticulously preserved.

Centre: Portsmouth Guildhall, built in an imposing classical style in 1886–90 and designed by William Hill of Leeds.

Left: Victorian boathouses 5, 6 and 7, built in the Royal Dockyard in 1843. This was originally a mast house. The interior has a remarkable cast-iron contruction.

Potteries, The, Staffs 693 H2, A group of five towns: Stoke-on-Trent*, Burslem, Hanley, Longton and Tunstall. Once distinct, they now all run together in a jumble of buildings. As the name suggests, they were once the centre of the pottery industry, characterized by hundreds of smoking kilns. Wedgwood opened his Etruria factory here in 1769. Now the kilns are mostly gone, but a fine assortment of museums remains: the Gladstone Pottery Museum at Longton, the Hanley City Museum and the Wedgwood Visitor Centre at Barlaston* are among the most rewarding.

Powderham Castle
Top: The exterior, built 1390–1420 by Sir Philip Courtenay. It was badly damaged during the Civil War. The buildings were transformed by the 10th Earl of Devon in the 1840s.
Left: The library.
Bottom right: The Great staircase has excellent plasterwork by John Jenkins, 1750s.

Powderham Castle, Devon 689 G6, This ancient home of the Courtenays, Earls of Devon, was reordered by Charles Fowler in the mid-1840s. The silhouette was embellished and made more romantic, and the rooms inside, some dating from the Middle Ages, were reorganized. The visitor enters through the gloomy 1860s Dining Hall before reaching the adjoining Ante-room. Within, the two magnificent bookcases of the 1740s with great baroque pediments are by John Channon of Exeter. In contrast, the apsidal-ended Music Room by James Wyatt of 1794–6 is a masterpiece of delicate neoclassical work, commissioned by the 3rd Viscount, who decorated some roundels in the room with the help of his 13 sisters. The Great Staircase has notable plasterwork by John Jenkins dating from the 1750s, and includes exuberant trophies and great garlands of fruit and flowers. The deer park stretches in front of the castle down to the River Exe, while behind the house is the mid-18th-century triangular Belvedere.

Powerstock, Dorset 689 H6, The road northeast from Bridport* leads to the church of St Mary at Powerstock, high on a knoll amid Victorian houses. It has a most elaborate Norman chancel arch, but the chancel itself is of 1854–9, albeit with good stained glass.

Powis Castle, Powys 693 F4, The great gardens [NT], descending in terraces from the pink medieval castle, were the creation of the nephew of William III, William van Nassau-Zuylestein, created Earl of Rochford. Among their most memorable features are the enormous clipped yews contemporary with the terraces, forming a line of umbrellas over the niches below them. Balustrading, ornamental urns,

statuary and wrought-iron gates all add to the fascination of the walk from the castle to the formal gardens at the base of the terraces. The heavily wooded hillside walks above the lawns reveal views of the castle and terraces at their most dramatic.

Prebendal Manor House, Nhants 694 E5, The oldest manor house in Northamptonshire, dating from the early 13th century. Many medieval features are retained, and the gardens have been recreated in medieval style, with fish ponds and a dovecote.

Preshute, Wilts 690 C5, One of several white horses in the region, cut in the chalk in 1804 (*see also* Westbury* and Pewsey*). The horse measures 62 by 47 feet (19 by 14m).

Presteigne (Llanandras), Powys 693 F5, A spacious and pleasing market town on the border-river Lugg. Its situation places it in the diocese of Hereford rather than in a Welsh see and from this it derived much of its wealth. This is evident in the striking quality of the church furnishings and building (dedicated to Saint Andrew, or Andras,

Powis Castle
Left: Powis Castle, a view of the lush Severn Valley from the ornate 'hanging gardens'.
Below: *Clive of India*, by Nathaniel Dance. His son married the Herbert heiress.

Above: Powis Castle, a miniature of the 1st Lord Herbert of Chirbury, by Isaac Oliver.

Bottom right: Preston, the Harris Museum and Library.

Bottom centre: Preston Tower, a well-preserved example of a Border tower-house.

from which the town's name derives), which incorporates work dating back to Saxon and Norman times. Among its prized possessions is a 16th-century Flemish tapestry depicting Christ's entry into Jerusalem. In recent years it has been a most inspirational setting for a prestigious annual music festival. Presteigne's former county-town status is still evident in the modestly classical building known as the **Shire Hall**, converted into a museum in the 1990s. It once accommodated the Judge's Lodging, whose history and function are effectively interpreted and juxtaposed with images of a man in his cell waiting to appear in the dock before facing his future. The town has some striking black-and-white buildings, notably the Radnorshire Arms, converted from a house in 1616.

Preston, Lancs 696 E6, The town stands in a loop of the River Ribble, its hilltop site marking its strategic position between the industrial south and more rural north of the northwest. It has two buildings remarkable for their uncompromising architecture. St Walburge's Church is the most impressive of a notable group of Roman Catholic churches in the town. It was built for the Jesuits by Joseph Aloysius Hansom and has all the structural grandeur of his Holy Name Church in Manchester*. The height of the spire (the highest non-cathedral spire in England) makes the church looks small; but once inside, the aisleless nave and steep hammerbeam roof provide a vast internal space, lit entirely by patterned rather than pictorial glass, on a cavernous and almost inhuman scale. In the town centre the Harris Museum and Library is the work of James Hibbert; it is a monumental classical building of the 1880s that would seem more at home in a German city than in the north of England. It stands on a high podium, its front to the Market Place, inscribed with the words 'To Literature, Arts and Sciences'; its pediment is filled to overflowing with sculpture. Inside there is a

square lantern lighting a central hall and staircase with sculpture by Thorwaldsen. The galleries contain work by the Preston artist Arthur Devis, including his self-portrait. Besides these monuments, the parish church of St John, by EH Shellard, 1855, seems modest, but it stands proudly above Church Street and contains a notable wall-painting by Hans Feibusch of 1956. By the prison, with its castellated gatehouse, is the former Court House, by Rickman, 1825, now the County Museum.

Preston on Stour, Warwks 690 C3, This is a village with so many 17th-century timber-framed houses that it takes on the look of a film-set. Several have elaborately decorated gables. Sadly, the church does not fit in with the Shakespearian atmosphere: much of the chancel and interior is an archeologically accurate gothic remodelling of the 18th century.

Preston Tower, Nthumb 699 J6, A privately owned ruined tower-house in a beautifully kept, idyllically wild site. Admission by honesty box! Small vaulted chambers contain interesting little displays on medieval living, and there are splendid views from the top. The prominent clock, with mechanical affinities to Big Ben*, has a surprisingly large, and loud, bell. The building has a secondary use as a water tower.

Prestonpans, E Loth 699 G4, The town has some well-preserved 15th to 17th-century houses and a magnificent sandstone market cross surmounted by a unicorn. To the east of the town is the site of the Battle of Prestonpans (September 1745) in which the Jacobites under Bonnie Prince Charlie defeated the Hanoverian government troops.

Prestwold Hall, Leics 694 D5, A telling reminder of the particular character of English early Victorian architecture. Although the house is essentially a mid-Georgian reconstruction of a Jacobean building, it was altered in 1805 by William Wilkins and again in 1842 by William Burn, one of most competent of country-house architects. Burn used a version of the Italianate style fashionable in the 1840s, and also built a large conservatory into one side of the house. In many of the internal spaces the ceilings have painted decoration in the manner of Raphael and walls painted in imitation of coloured marbles.

Priddy Circles, Somset 689 H4, Four miles (6.4km) north of Wells* are prehistoric remains, with long barrows, and the four Priddy Circles, large earthen rings each some 550 feet (168m) in diameter, placed side by side in the Bronze Age.

Prideaux Place, Cnwll, Above Padstow, and set in its own deer park, is the house where the Prideaux family has lived since the 1530s. There is a fine 17th-century plasterwork ceiling with biblical scenes in the Great Chamber. It was much renovated in the gothic style took place about 1810, resulting in a memorable staircase hall and library. The reading room is decorated with late 17th-century panelling taken from the Earl of Bath's great house at Stowe*. *See* **Padstow* 688 D6.**

Priest House, W Susx 691 F6, A 15th-century yeoman's house in West Hoathly, with furnished rooms and a herb garden [EH].

Above: Prideaux Place, the gothic south front. It is surrounded by woods and overlooks a deer park.

Centre: Priest House stands in a traditional cottage garden on the edge of Ashdown Forest.

Bottom: Priddy Circles consists of four large earthern rings, placed side by side. It is not known what they are, but they could be some form of early sanctuary.

Princes Risborough, Bucks 690 E4, Like Kings Langley*, the town took its name from a royal manor, which remained the property of the crown until 1628 when it was presented to the City of London by Charles I. The main feature of the town is its stately red-brick manor house, built probably *c*1630–50 and much reworked by the Rothschild family from 1886. The chalk-cut Whiteleaf Cross which dominates a hill to the east is probably a copy of a prehistoric original, as it was not noted until 1742.

Princetown, Devon 689 F6, Dartmoor Prison was built about 1806 as barracks for French (and then American) prisoners of war by Sir Charles Tyrwhitt, Lord Warden of the Stannaries, who had built himself a house at Tor Royal as part of his scheme to improve Dartmoor*. The barracks became a convict prison in 1850; the radial plan with seven blocks is clearly visible across the bleak fields. Princetown is dominated by the prison, which is entered from the town through a cyclopean granite arch. The sight of it must have struck terror into the heart of many a convicted felon.

Prinknash Abbey, Gloucs 690 B4, The site of the old house at Prinknash was described by Horace Walpole as 'a glorious but impracticable hill, in the midst of the little forest of beech, and commanding Elysium'. The hill now commands the sprawl of Gloucester*, but the view is still staggering. Prinknash Abbey is an unprepossessing yellow building built after designs by Goodhart-Rendel and Broadbent that took from 1939 to 1972 to complete. The chapel, with its chunky coloured glass, can be visited, as

can the monks' pottery in the grounds. The monastery houses about 25 Benedictine monks.

Probus Garden, Cnwll 688 D7, Cornwall's Demonstration Garden shows local gardeners how to plant in the county's many varied soils and conditions.

Prudhoe Castle, Nthumb 697 G2, This well-presented monument commanding a strategic crossing of the River Tyne epitomizes the border castle, having played a significant part in many English–Scottish conflicts [EH]. Prudhoe was built by the d'Umfraville family, later passing into the ownership of Percys, earls and later dukes of Northumberland. The castle is first seen across the millpond that served its corn watermill. Entry through the barbican leads under the Norman gatehouse, above which is a 13th-century chapel with a small sanctuary projecting out from its east wall as an oriel. The small keep is tucked away behind the early 19th-century manor house, which has Regency architectural details; its date reflects the castle's long period of occupation. There is a pleasant circular walk below the ramparts.

Purse Caundle Manor, Dorset 689 J5, A 15th- and 16th-century manor house with a Great Hall and Minstrels' Gallery. The upper Great Chamber has a barrel ceiling and an oriel window. The house has been described as a stimulating archeological puzzle, having been re-orientated by William Hannam in the 1570s.

Pyt House, Wilts 690 B6, This country house was designed in 1805 by its owner, John Benett. In two

Above: Prudhoe Castle viewed from across the mill pond.

Below: Prinknash Abbey, a Benedictine house set on a hill looking over Gloucester.

of the principal rooms are imposing Italian chimneypieces, one dated 1553 – an example of the curious and unexpected treasures that adorn so many English country houses.

Quainton, Bucks 690 E4, The church has some excellent 17th- and 18th-century monuments, including a powerfully modelled one by Rysbrack of 1728.

Quantock Hills, Somset 689 G4, Red sandstone hills extending from Bridgwater and Taunton towards the sea. The highest point is Will's Neck (1,261 feet/384m).

Quex Park, Kent 691 J5, A curiosity. Quex, in Birchington, was the home of Major Percy Powell-Cotton, who between 1887 and 1938 spent much of his time in Africa killing wild animals. The whole house is full of these animals, stuffed, and arranged in vivid dioramas imitating the jungle. One show-case exhibits the bloodstained shirt in which the Major was mauled by a lion, as well as the lion itself. In the garden stands an extraordinary bell-tower, built in 1819 to commemorate the Battle of Waterloo. It is crowned by an openwork spire made of cast iron, a bit like a miniature Eiffel Tower.

Raasay, Highld 700 E5, An island to the east of Skye*, with the wooded estate of Raasay House offering pleasant walks. There is a good view of the Outer Hebrides* and Skye from the top of Dun Caan, the extinct volcano that dominates the island (1,456 feet/444m).

Raby Castle, Dur 697 G3, Set in a deep park, this large quadrangular castle, built c1378 for John, Lord Neville, has four corner towers, one of which contains an impressive medieval kitchen. Some of the main rooms are the creation of the prolific 19th-century Scottish architect William Burn. Fine effigies of the medieval owners of Raby can be seen in Staindrop parish church.

Radburne Hall, Derbys 694 C4, A plain but handsome brick house of the 1740s designed by one of the Smith family of Warwick, who made a speciality of such gentry houses. The church standing in the grounds of the house is medieval. It contains some fine medieval benches brought from Dale Abbey and a good monument to German Pole, the Hall's builder, by Grinling Gibbons.

Raby Castle
Left: The small drawing room.
Centre right: The Neville coat of arms.
Centre far right: The late-14th-century stronghold.

Below: Raglan Castle, one of the last – and grandest – castles in Wales.

Radley, Oxon 690 D4, The church has an unusual wooden arcade, a Norman font and 16th-century stained glass.

Raglan Castle, Mons 693 G7, Enough remains to suggest its palatial concept. Had it not been a victim of the Civil War, it would have been more spectacular than either Powis* or Chirk*. Everything about Raglan makes it different from other castles in Wales. It was begun as late as 1435 by William ap Thomas, with a five-storeyed hexagonal tower. His son, William Herbert, eventually the Earl of Pembroke, launched a grand scheme of embellishing the castle; and the marriage of his granddaughter to Charles Somerset, later Earl of Worcester, consolidated its social prestige. The 3rd Earl continued the building tradition by creating terraces, formal gardens and a moat walk. Following its post-Civil War restoration, the family turned their sights towards Gloucestershire and the rebuilding of an inherited property: Badminton*.

Ragley Hall, Warwks 694 C7, Designed in 1680 and still lived in by the same family, the house is an early and earthy forerunner of the Palladian piles which were to dominate the 18th century. The first architect was Robert Hooke, James Gibbs carried out important work in the 1750s, and an Ionic portico was added by Wyatt in 1780. Hooke's plan originally provided for four separate two-room apartments, one in each of the four corners of the house, with four common reception rooms in the centre in which their occupants could meet. Today, however, the ground floor appears to consist of a great number of sitting rooms, as the bedrooms have of course moved upstairs. The scale of Gibbs' double-height Great Hall is overwhelming; it is complemented

by Gibbsian baroque decoration and furniture made especially for the room in 1750. The 8th Marquess of Hertford's 20th-century tastes can be seen in Graham Rust's murals on the subject of the Temptation in the south Staircase Hall. The figures include portraits of the Marquess's four children and their godparents. The park and lake, designed by Capability Brown, are now as popular an attraction as the house. Its most notable features are the semicircular stables designed by Gibbs, and the 17th-century gates, possibly by Tijou, in the kitchen garden wall.

Ragley Hall
Top: The exterior, with Wyatt's portico of 1780.
Above: The Red Saloon has some good English and French furniture.

Ramsbury, Wilts 690 C5, The church of Holy Cross has a rich store of monuments and unusual furnishings – the monument to Mary Burdett, with a long, pious poem, the gothic organ and the stone carvings on the font. There are 17th-century and Georgian houses.

Ramsey, Cambs 695 F6, The important Benedictine abbey at Ramsey, founded in 969 on an island in the Fen wilderness, was acquired by Richard Cromwell, Oliver's great-grandfather. Its stones were used to refurbish several Cambridge* colleges and to construct the village church tower (now with William Morris stained glass). The Cromwells built a great house, destined in later years to become a school, on the plundered site. A substantial fragment of the abbey's richly carved 15th-century gateway survives on the edge of Abbey Green, a large attractive space with pretty Victorian estate cottages opposite, flanked by the church. Originally the abbey's hospice, the church's 1672 tower is also monastic stone. The central portion of the gatehouse was removed by Cromwell to the family seat at Hinchingbrooke Hall*, near Huntingdon.

Ramsgate, Kent 691 J5, Here AWN Pugin built himself a house, the Grange, and next to it his own Catholic church, St Augustine's, where he is buried. It is small but spatially satisfying, serious and personal. The town, at the end of the so-called Isle of Thanet (not an island), retains something of its Victorian character, particularly evident in the steeply ascending Madeira Walk lined with massive artificial rocks made in Putney.

Ramster, Surrey 690 E6, Ramster Gardens offer 20 acres (8ha) of woodland and shrub garden.

Ranworth, Norfk 695 J5, St Helen's Church is a treasure-house of medieval art. Its vaulted screen is one of the great showpieces, with a celestial congregation of apostles flanked by winged and feathered dragon-slaying saints. St Michael dispatches a seven-headed monster with nonchalant ease. There is a rare painted cantor's desk, c1500, and a beautiful Sarum antiphonary, c1400, illuminated by the monks of nearby Langley abbey. Jonah and the Whale, King David and the Fool and courtly musicians are among 20 biblical subjects. The tower offers extensive views over surrounding wetlands, including Ranworth Broad, a Norfolk Wildlife Trust reserve of national

Left: Reculver. The 12th-century towers were allowed to remain as a landmark for shipping when the rest of the church – one of the most complete Anglo-Saxon buildings in the country – was demolished in the early 19th century.

Below: Redruth and Cambourne are the centre of Cornwall's rich mining heritage. Chimneys of old tin and copper mines are ubiquitous, like these, the Crown Consuls at Botallack.

importance with boardwalk, floating visitor centre and resident wildfowl.

Ravensburgh Castle, Herts 691 F3, This vast, oval Iron-Age hill fort survives on the summit of Barton Hills beyond Hitchin*, close to the Bedfordshire county boundary.

Ravenstone, Bucks 690 E3, The south chapel of All Saints was built to house the monument to the 1st Earl of Nottingham and Lord Chancellor. He is half seated under a canopy supported on four black marble columns, draped with white curtains.

Reading, Berks 690 E5, A Cluniac abbey was founded at Reading in the year 1121, and the town was well loved by English monarchy. Today, despite the remaining fragments of the abbey (the Church of St Lawrence was originally the abbey's 'chapel without the gates'), Reading is a modern university town centred around the rivers Kennet and Thames. Blakes Lock Museum (Gasworks Road) serves as a good introduction to Reading's industrial history with displays on the once-thriving wharves, canals and mills, and the fishing and boat-building trades. The Museum of Reading, contained in the 19th-century town hall, has displays on the town's earlier origins, with Roman life depicted in the Silchester Gallery. The museum also features the world's only full-size replica of the Bayeux Tapestry, painstakingly stitched by 35 Victorian ladies.

Reculver, Kent 691 J5, Until the early 19th century, here stood one of the most complete Saxon churches in

the country. It was demolished in 1809 leaving only the towers [EH], which were added in the 12th century. They now stand isolated amid caravans.

Red House Museum, W York 697 G6, The 1830s house at Gomersal where Joshua Taylor's family played host to Charlotte Brontë and inspired the fictional Yorke family in *Shirley*.

Redruth and Camborne, Cnwll 688 C7, The towns, whose fortunes are intertwined with the tin and copper industries, represent Cornwall's industrial heartland. The last mine, South Crofty, still lingers on, but its future is still very uncertain. In all directions the chimneys of the mines litter the landscape, the roofs of the Methodist chapels rise over the terraces of miners' houses and above both towns the monument to Lord de Dunstanville of Tehidy on Carn Brea is an ever-present reminder of the importance of the industry. The inventor William Murdoch lived in Redruth for a while; his house in Cross Street was the first in the world to be lit by gas, in 1792. Another inventor, Richard Trevithick, was born at Illogan, between the two towns, in 1771; he invented an early road vehicle and a steam threshing machine, and made many improvements to the steam engines that were essential to the mining industry. The **Camborne School of Mines** has an outstanding geological museum; some of its specimens have been presented by students (who come from all over the world).

Reepham, Norfolk 695 J5, A small and pretty town, its Market Place lined with good Georgian houses, most notably Dial House. Two medieval churches share a common churchyard with the remains of a third, Hackford church. St Mary's has an impressive armorial tomb to Sir Roger de Kerdiston (d. 1337), on a bed of pebbles.

Reigate, Surrey 691 F6, The church has good arcades inspired by the new choir at Canterbury, 1175–80, and Canterbury School. Also noteworthy is the fine baroque monument to Richard Ladbroke and the Victorian tomb of Rebecca Waterlow, with its four copper urns.

Top left: Repton, St Wystan's Church, a medieval building with a Saxon crypt.

Top right: Repton Priory. The priory buildings now house Repton School.

Right: Restormel Castle, the huge circular shell keep.

Renishaw Hall, Derbys 694 D3, Best known to many people as the family home of the Sitwells. The Jacobean house built by George Sitwell in the 1620s still survives, but has been much extended and altered so that the building is now a long, rambling structure – a mixture of Georgian sash windows and Gothic battlements. The rooms inside are almost all Georgian in character. The elaborate gardens near the house were laid out at the end of the 19th century, and the estate also has a large number of late Georgian picturesque buildings, such as the dairy, kennels, various cottages and an aviary.

Repton, Derbys 694 C4, The school dominates the small town, and incorporates many of the buildings of the priory, which was turned over to educational use in 1557 by Sir John Port; but long before that Repton was the capital of the kingdom of South Mercia. A monastery was founded here in the 7th century, and the present parish church of St Wystan probably incorporates some of the monastery church; the small crypt at the east end, now partly sunken underground, was built around 800.

Restormel Castle, Cnwll 688 D7, Now a ruined shell keep on top of a conical hill, the castle [EH] forms a perfect circle 110 feet (33m) in diameter, with the domestic apartments sheltering within the curtain wall. It dates largely from the 13th century.

Rhondda Valley, Rhondd 689 G3, The famous industrial valley in fact consists of two valleys: Rhondda Fawr and Rhondda Fach – the Greater and Lesser. There was extensive sinking of mineshafts in the middle of the 19th century but all traces of the winding gear, the pithead baths, the offices and the colliers' canteens have now disappeared, and the hillsides are returning to green. The Rhondda Heritage Park, based at the Lewis Merthyr Colliery, Trehafod, which closed in 1980, gives a penetrating insight into the working conditions of the coal miners. The guided tour includes a simulated descent to the underground 'roadways', and is recommended as an alternative to those too nervous to undergo the actual experience at Big Pit, Blaenavon*.

Rhuddlan Castle, Denbgs, The building dates from Edward I's Welsh campaign of 1277, although it was a site that had seen constant tussle between the Welsh and Anglo-Saxons until the Norman Conquest. The man entrusted with control of the area in 1073 threw up a motte-and-bailey castle, known as Twt-hill. Only a short walk away, the mound still appears a daunting challenge. Rhuddlan was the first of the three concentric castles designed by the King's military engineer, Master James of St George (c1235–1308). Unlike Harlech*, and the superlative Beaumaris*, Rhuddlan's inner ward is diamond-shaped, with formidable western and eastern four-storied

Richborough Castle
Left: Part of the Roman wall, built around AD 285 when Britain was threatened by the Saxons.
Below: Steelyard weight in the form of a satyr.

Bottom: Rhuddlan Castle, the formidable two-towered west gatehouse reflected in the River Clwyd.

gatehouses. Rhuddlan had the disadvantage of not being near tidal waters, a drawback overcome by the construction of a canal up to the castle. *See* **Bodhryddan* 693 F1.**

Rhum, Eigg, Canna and Muck, Ag & B 700 D6, Rhum (also known as Rum) is the largest of this group of islands across the Cuillin Sound south of Skye*. Scottish Natural Heritage has made it a National Nature Reserve and Biosphere Reserve. Footpaths start from the hotel, a castle built by the Bulloughs in 1901. Eigg is inhabited by a small farming community. Canna, the prettiest of the islands, is owned by the National Trust for Scotland and is a favourite haunt of seabirds. Muck is the smallest island in the group. It is named after the porpoises or 'seahogs' that frequent its waters.

Rhyl, Denbgs 692 E1, Its wide beaches and sea breezes made Rhyl – and, to a lesser extent, the neighbouring seaside town of Prestatyn – a great attraction for Liverpudlians, as well as for local people. It set out to be, and became, a popular resort. The view to the west of the promenade towards Snowdonia* is hard to rival.

Ribchester, Lancs 696 E6, Lies up the Ribble Valley and has Lancashire's best surviving Roman remains: part of a fort established by Agricola in AD 79 and a 2nd-century bath-house.

Richborough, Kent 691 J5, The site of the Emperor Claudius's landing in AD 43, which marks the beginning of the Roman occupation. Not much is to be seen except ruined walls and ditches, and the foundation of a huge monument in the form of a two-way triumphal arch (two arches crossing at right angles). A model in the museum on the site helps visitors to visualize it [EH].

Richmond

Richmond, N York 697 G4,
A market town that grew up on a steep hillside above the River Swale, around the castle built after William the Conqueror granted the 'Honour' of Richmond to his kinsman Alan Rufus of Brittany.

Richmond Castle [EH] is one of the country's oldest castles to be started in stone rather than beginning as a typically Norman motte-and-bailey castle rebuilt later. The curtain walls date from c1071, as does the Great Hall – 'Scolland's Hall', named after Alan's steward, Scolland, Lord of Bedale. In the mid-12th century Conan, Earl of Richmond and Duke of Brittany, built the magnificent keep which still dominates the town. The castle's outer bailey became the town's huge horseshoe-shaped Market Place, walled against the Scots in c1312. From the town wall two postern gates survive, on Cornforth Hill and in Friars Wynd. Greyfriars Tower is a reminder of the several religious houses established in medieval Richmond. At the Dissolution the choir stalls from nearby Easby Abbey* were moved into St Mary's Parish Church. The ancient house called St Nicholas was a medieval hospital, but is now better known for its remarkable early 20th-century gardens, which inspired those at Hidcote Manor* in Gloucestershire.

Richmond prospered in the 18th century, partly from the wool and lead-mining industries in Swaledale. With new-found wealth came fashionable horse races, military musters, assemblies and balls, and a notable grammar school. It is, however, the famous and well-preserved Georgian Theatre Royal that provides the best testimony to this epoch. Originally seating an audience of 400, since its 1960s restoration it holds fewer than 200, in an unforgettable atmosphere of intimacy with the stage – and one's neighbours. The eye-catching Culloden Tower is a gothic Georgian folly, originally part of a now-lost landscaped garden.

Richmond's hillside location affords remarkably fine views of green countryside, particularly Billy Bank Woods [NT], where there are attractive riverside walks. Castle Walk is a Georgian promenade which provides a smooth-surfaced level walk – something rare in this hilly town with its cobbled streets; from it there are breathtaking views down into the Swale Valley, and of the Green Bridge, rebuilt in 1788 to a design by John Carr of York, who was also bridgemaster for the North Riding of Yorkshire. Its medieval predecessor had been severely damaged by floods, to which the Swale is particularly prone. It is a treacherous river despite the seemingly idyllic spectacle it makes, flowing picturesquely over the Richmond Falls.

Above: The Fleece Hotel, a Scottish Baronial fantasy of 1897.

Left: Richmond Castle, looking south from the keep along the east curtain wall towards Scolland's Hall.

Bottom: Culloden Tower, a folly surviving from a lost 18th-century landscaped garden, now a Landmark Trust holiday cottage.

Rievaulx Abbey, N York 697 H4, Founded in 1131 directly from Clairvaux, it is a large complex, of which there are substantial remains [EH]. The Early English choir and refectory are particularly complete. The landscape quality of the site and the beauty of the ruins were instrumental in the development of Rievaulx Terrace [NT], from which there are breathtaking views of the abbey. *See also* **Duncombe Park*.**

Ring of Brodgar, *see* **Orkney*.**

Ringmore, Devon 689 F7, The rich and fertile South Hams have many villages beloved of the holiday-

Above and left: Rievaulx Abbey, an impressive Cistercian site with extensive remains.

maker. Such is Ringmore, with its thatched cottages and their gardens full of towering echiums. It was while staying here that RC Sherriff wrote *Journey's End*, which has given its name to the local pub.

Ripley Castle, N York 697 G5, A fortified manor house owned by the Ingilby family for nearly 700 years, with a 15th-century gatehouse, 16th-century pele tower with priest-hole, and some good Georgian interiors. Ripley village is a charming exercise in 1820s gothic town planning, inspired by places in Alsace-Lorraine. Its parish church is much older, with monuments to the Ingilby family going back to medieval times.

Ripon

Ripon, N York 697 G5, A small cathedral city with a handsome square Market Place set around a stone obelisk, designed by architect Nicholas Hawksmoor in 1702. The oldest such obelisk in the country, it was repaired in 1781, the date on its inscription. The town's patron saint is Wilfrid, who was abbot of a monastery founded here in c660 and who built a church destroyed by the Vikings in 950. The Saxon crypt of this church (see Hexham*) survives below **Ripon Cathedral**, which was refounded as a collegiate church. A rebuilding programme begun in the late 12th century produced fine Norman transepts, and completion of the west front in the 1220s has resulted in one of the country's finest Early English compositions, almost classical in its symmetry. The choir was altered early in the 14th century, the large east window having Geometric tracery of c1300, and the sedilia and piscina typically Decorated motifs. The nave was enlarged with fine Perpendicular arcades in the early 16th century, but this rebuilding was interrupted by the Reformation, hence the lopsided and only partly rebuilt central crossing arch. The church became a cathedral again in 1836.

Inside are choir stalls of 1489–94, carved in Ripon by William Bromflet, whose work appears in other Yorkshire churches. The seats have canopies above and misericords below, carved with intriguing scenes, some humorous, others of medieval life or biblical stories (Jonah leaving the whale, pigs dancing and making music, a pelican, a mermaid, a fox preaching and an angel with a shield bearing the date 1489). Some of the carvings are thought to have inspired Charles Lutwidge Dodgson (Lewis Carroll) with fanciful ideas for his *Alice in Wonderland* stories, while his father was a canon of Ripon.

Left: Ripon Market Place.

Ripon Cathedral
Top left: A pulpit.
Top right: The classically
symmetrical west front.

Roche Abbey

R

Rivenhall, Essex 691 H4, The church has the best medieval glass in Essex, appropriated by the rector from Tours in 1840. The collection includes roundels of the Entombment of the Virgin, figures of Abbots, and – famously – the mounted figure of Robert Lemaire of c1200, resplendent in full armour.

Rochdale, Gt Man 697 F7, The town is dominated by its Town Hall, one of the finest in England, and a high point in the secular Gothic Revival. It was designed by WH Crossland and the tower was finished by Waterhouse. The gabled and traceried exterior is complemented by a vaulted Entrance Hall and staircase leading to a public Great Hall dominated by a huge wall-painting of Runnymede by Henry Holiday. The old church of St Chad, on the hill above the town, seems rather isolated; nearer the commercial centre is St Mary's Church, an 18th-century box altered and extended by Sir Ninian Comper. The external form seems simple but the interior is complex, stonefaced and with much exquisite Comper joinery. Opposite, in Toad Lane, is a museum celebrating the establishment of the Co-operative Movement in Rochdale.

Roche, Cnwll 688 D7, St Michael's Chapel, set above a hermit's cell, is precariously perched on a massive granite outcrop. With the Cornish Alps, or china clay tips, as its backdrop, it makes a dramatic

Left: Roche Abbey, the white magnesian limestone ruins.

Rochdale Town Hall
Above: The gabled exterior, 1866; civic pride in Victorian gothic.
Right: The vaulted Great Hall, with a painted hammerbeam roof. Henry Holiday's *Runnymede*, 1870, is on the opposite wall.

sight. The tortuous climb, partly by ladder, reminds modern pilgrims of the trials undergone by their predecessors.

Roche Abbey, S York 694 D3, A Cistercian monastery founded in 1147 [EH]. The transepts of the abbey church, standing to roof height, are an interesting early example of Early English style. The design of the water-courses forms a fascinating aspect of the ruins. These are so spectacular in their almost dazzlingly white magnesian limestone that they were incorporated into Capability Brown's 18th-century landscaping scheme for the nearby splendid house of Sandbeck Park, designed by James Paine.

Rochester

Rochester, Kent 691 G5, In Roman times this was an important Roman town defending the mouth of the Medway and the bridge across the river. In Anglo-Saxon times it became the second Christian see in Britain, St Augustine ordaining Justus as its bishop in 604. William the Conqueror built the first castle. It remained prosperous during the Middle Ages and into the 19th century – but time has not been kind to Rochester. The cathedral has been cruelly restored, the castle half demolished, while the railway and the modern bypass have left the old High Street cut off and isolated. It remains a rewarding town to visit.

The castle and cathedral bear witness to Rochester's importance in Norman times. The castle keep, guarding the crossing of the Medway, is the tallest in England. Begun in 1123, it is square, with corner turrets. Inside it is a ruin without floors, but one can still identify the Great Hall, occupying the third and fourth storeys and divided by an arcade [EH].

The cathedral was begun even earlier, but of the original church only the stump of a tower (Gandulf's Tower, next to the north transept) survives. The rest belongs to the 12th and early 13th centuries. The exterior has been so restored that most of what one sees is Victorian: in 1825, the central tower was rebuilt (and again in 1905); in 1870, the east gables; and in 1888 the west front. The main west door, however, was allowed to remain – a rare example of Norman sculpture (but compare Barfreston* and Patrixborne*). The tympanum shows Christ in Majesty and the door is flanked by column-figures of Solomon and the Queen of Sheba. The better-preserved interior has its nave arcade of round arches, its choir (unusually between solid walls, not an arcade) and its Early English east end, the most architecturally sophisticated part of the building, with sexpartite vaults and graceful Purbeck marble shafts. The cathedral is rich in monuments of all periods, from the 13th-century tomb of a bishop in the presbytery to that of Lady Ann Henreken of 1792 in the north aisle, with its life-size figure by Thomas Banks.

Rochester High Street is lined with pleasant Georgian and Regency shops (many cashing in on the Dickens association – *see* Gadshill*); at the west end is a second-hand bookshop that claims to be the largest in England. The Guildhall of 1687 has a room with a good plaster ceiling. Eastgate House, of the 17th century, is as picturesque inside as out; it is now a Dickens museum. The best house in Rochester is Restoration House (16th and 17th centuries), with a splendid display of cut and moulded brickwork. It is thought to be the inspiration for Miss Havisham's house in *Great Expectations*.

Left: Rochester Cathedral, seen from the southwest. The nave, west front and crossing tower are essentially Norman, although drastically restored in the 19th century.

Below: Rochester Castle's 11th-century keep is the tallest in England. The entrance was via a forebuilding (projecting from the left in the photograph), making it easy to defend. The castle protected the crossing of the Medway by the Roman Watling Street, running from London to Dover.

Rock, Cnwll 688 D6, Now surrounded by the golf links, the small Norman church of St Enodoc, with its 13th-century tower and spire, lay buried by sand for over 150 years until it was uncovered in 1864. In the graveyard and near the lych gate lies Sir John Betjeman (1906–84). He set many of his poems in this area, where he spent holidays for almost all his life.

Rockingham Castle, Nhants 694 E5, Now descended from its Norman motte – today a

Above: Rockingham Castle, built by William the Conqueror and used by early kings of England until Henry VIII gave it to Edward Watson in 1530. The semicircular gatehouse towers were added by Edward I.

Rokeby Park, Dur 697 G4, Pronounced 'Rookby', the house is an early example of English Palladianism designed by the owner, gentleman-architect Sir Thomas Robinson, in 1725–30. Always extravagant, Robinson became increasingly involved as Master of Ceremonies in the Ranelagh Pleasure Gardens in London, which led to the sale of the house in 1769 to JS Morritt (it remains the property of his descendants). His elder sister Anne Morritt sewed many needlework pictures, which are displayed in the house. The finest room is the classically proportioned Saloon; among the paintings there is a copy of the famous Rokeby Venus, Velázquez's only female nude, whose face is visible in a mirror. Sir Walter Scott frequently visited Rokeby, and wrote a famous poem of that name.

Rollright Stones, Oxon 690 C3, Close to Great Rollright is this fascinating prehistoric site [EH], with extensive views toward Warwickshire. The main stone circle is known as the King's Men; set

garden feature – the castle sprawls along a bluff with views of the Welland Valley and Rutland spreading below. The royal castle, which King John visited no less than 14 times, later became a hotch-potch of Tudor accommodation including a Long Gallery, updated by Salvin in the early 19th century. He accentuated the medieval character of the castle with castellations and a tower.

Rode Hall, Ches 693 H2, The first house at Rode was built in 1708 by Randle Wilbraham. In the 1750s it became the kitchen range to a much larger new house built by Randle Wilbraham II. Sixty years later this house was stuccoed and given a big portico, while most of the interior rooms, apart from the main stair hall with its richly carved stair and rococo decoration, were fitted out in a stripped-down Regency manner that recalls the work of Sir John Soane.

Centre: Rokeby Park, an early Palladian house designed by the owner, architect Sir Thomas Robinson.

Above: Rokeby Park, Palladian gatepier with pediment, drape, Greek key motif and handsome rustication.

Right: Rollright Stones, the King's Men.

slightly apart are the huge King Stone and a group known as the Whispering Knights (probably a neolithic burial chamber). The stones are well known for the folklore that attaches to them. Most famous is the petrification legend, according to which the stones were once a king and his army; if the king had taken a few more steps forward, he would have seen Long Compton and become King of England, but he and his men were petrified by a witch's spell before he had a chance to do so.

Rolvenden, Kent 691 H6, Sir Edwin Lutyens built Great Maytham*

in 1909, incorporating an early Georgian house. Lutyens accordingly adopted a Georgian style himself, looking forward to his late classical manner. The lodge is also by him. In fine countryside outside the town is Hole Park, an attractive garden.

Romney, Kent 691 H6, Old and New Romney both have interesting churches, the first with 18th-century furnishings, the second with a sturdy Norman arcade and three spectacular east windows of reticulated tracery. The flat landscape of Romney Marsh has the lonely but impressive church of St Mary-in-the-Marsh; it has a Norman tower, and an Early English nave and chancel, and is virtually unrestored.

Romsey, Hants 690 D7, This interesting market town is dominated by the cathedral-like 12th-century Abbey Church which the townspeople bought for the value of its building materials to be their outsize parish church when the nunnery was closed at the Reformation. It is, internally, the most complete major Norman church in England, although the western part is early gothic. Two Saxon representations of Christ on the Cross survive, one external – on a wall of the south transept – the other internal. Earl Mountbatten of Burma is buried under a stone slab in the Abbey.

Roseland Peninsula, Cnwll, A soft, tranquil part of the county, with quiet sandy beaches, attractive villages such as Veryan, with its entrances guarded by early 19th-century circular cottages to keep out the Devil, and the ancient fishing ports of Mevagissey*, Gorran Haven and Portloe. *See* **St-Just-in-Roseland* 688 C7.**

Rosemoor, Devon 688 E5, Set either side of the B3220, Rosemoor is based on a fine shrub and tree garden established by Colonel JE and Lady Anne Palmer, but now supplemented by other gardens (notably a rose garden, magnificent in June) and other demonstration grounds full of rare plants that are suited to the balmy climate.

Rosslyn Chapel, Mdloth 699 G4, This magnificent 15th-century chapel nestles in the lush valley of the River Esk, near Roslin (Rosslyn). It is a masterpiece of decorative sculpture collected by William Sinclair, 3rd Earl of Orkney. The chapel of St Matthew, in late gothic style (1446–86), is in fact the choir of a cruciform collegiate church that was

Above: Rosslyn Chapel, the interior with its ribbed and patterned barrel vault.

Above: Romsey Abbey Church.

Left: Rothwell Market Hall. An agreement survives from 1578 when the mason William Grumbold was commissioned to build it by Sir Thomas Tresham.

never finished. Its barrel vaults are entirely sculpted, while the walls and pillars are decorated with biblical scenes, and floral and animal motifs. One of the most remarkable is the 'Prentice Pillar' at the east end of the south aisle. According to tradition an apprentice carved the pillar in his master's absence. On his return the mason, jealous of the exquisite handiwork, beat the young man to death with a mallet. The exterior decoration of the chapel – damaged in 1592 and 1688, and restored in 1862 – is just as lavish and intricate. Nearby Roslin Castle was built by the Sinclairs in the 14th century, and rebuilt in the 16th and 17th centuries.

Ross-on-Wye, Herefs 693 G6, Set upon a high hill, the town has something Italian about its situation that appealed to the 18th-century tourists who travelled up the Wye* in steamers as a cheaper substitute for the Grand Tour. On the way they admired the picturesque ruins of Goodrich* and Monmouth* castles, and visited natural features such as the rocky spire of Symonds Yat*. The Prospect Garden is the best place from which to admire the 'sublime' sweep of the river and to imagine the lakes of the Alps. This park, along with other amenities, was donated to the town by its benefactor John Kyrle (1637–1734). He also built the Market Hall with its massive squat columns; its south wall contains an unusual carving, the letters 'FC' and a heart. This medallion, visible from John Kyrle's house opposite, stands for 'faithful to Charles (II) in heart'. On his death, Kyrle lay in state for nine days at the church of St Mary's. Outside the church is an interesting Plague Cross from 1637, recording the death of 323 people (a third of the population of the town) in that year.

Rostherne, Ches 697 F7, The church is beautifully situated, above Rostherne Mere. The building is mostly medieval but the Georgian west tower dates from 1742 and the chancel was added in 1888. There is a splendid collection of late Georgian and early Victorian funeral monuments to various members of the Egerton family, notably that to Lady Charlotte Egerton, who is shown being woken from sleep by an angel.

Rotherfield Greys, Oxon, 690 E5, The main attraction of the village is Greys Court [NT], a mansion built probably in the early 1500s among the interesting ruins of a semi-fortified 14th-century manor house. It was altered in the 17th to 19th centuries and features some splendid rococo plasterwork. Outbuildings include a well-house, wheel-house

with a rare surviving donkey wheel, and the so-called Cromwellian Stables. The Bachelor's Hall takes its name from a Latin inscription reading 'Nothing is better than the celibate life'. The village church contains an excellent brass to Lord Robert de Grey (d. 1387) and the immense tomb of William Knollys, Earl of Banbury (d. 1632).

Rotherham, S York 694 D2, All Saints Church is one of the most impressive parish churches in West Yorkshire, mainly Perpendicular in style and of cruciform plan, with a graceful spire soaring above the crossing. The grand concept is partly attributable to a local man, Thomas Rotherham, who became Bishop of Lincoln and later Archbishop of York. The River Don is still crossed by a four-arched medieval bridge, which retains its chantry chapel – one of only a handful of bridge chapels surviving in the country – with vaulted sacristy below. The master of the grammar school bequeathed an endowment for the chapel in 1483.

Rothesay, *see* **Bute*.**

Rothwell Market Hall, Nhants 694 E6, Sir Thomas Tresham's Market House in Rothwell was never completed. With its elaborate plan of a cross and its decoration of religious mottoes and heraldic devices, it bears the hallmarks of his several 16th-century buildings. The Church of the Holy Trinity in Rothwell is also worth visiting for its remarkable crypt, occasionally opened to the public. Beneath the nave lie the remains of

Rousham House
Above: The splendid Palladian parlour designed by Kent.
Below: Kent's pioneering landscape gardens have escaped alteration.

1,500 bodies, thought to date from the 13th century. This charnel house was discovered by a grave-digger in 1700. The Jesus Hospital, founded 1591 for 26 blue-coated old men and a housekeeper, is another notable historic building.

Rousham House, Oxon 690 D3, Built in c1635, but much remodelled by William Kent in 1738–40. It is not Kent's architectural work that is of special interest here, however, but rather his garden design, a beautiful and little-altered 18th-century landscape. The idyllic gardens open out like a series of paintings and include the seven-arched Praeneste, the Temple of Echo or Townesend's Building, and Venus's Vale.

Roxburgh, Border 699 H5, This royal burgh, now a village, grew up, together with its 12th-century abbey, around Marchmont Castle. The town and castle fell to the English in the early 14th century. They were recaptured in 1460 but razed to the ground in reprisal for the death of James II. All that remains of the castle are a few wall sections on a massive earthwork. There is a superb railway viaduct by John Miller, 1847.

Roxton, Beds 691 F3, The charming Congregational Chapel, founded in 1808, is thatched, with a tree-trunk veranda.

Rudding Park, N York 697 G5, An early 19th-century house with a Grecian-inspired atmosphere. The entrance portico and several two-storey segmental bays, with deep ground-floor windows, emphasize the Regency date. The interior, clearly much influenced by the Wyatts, includes an imperial staircase. Close by is the gothic Roman Catholic chapel of 1874, formerly of the Radcliffe family. The house has been converted into a hotel.

Top left: Rufford Abbey, exterior stone carving.

Rufford Old Hall
Centre left: The Great Hall with hammerbeam trusses.
Bottom left: The black and white timbered exterior.

Centre right: Rug Chapel, the highly decorated ceiling and gallery of William Salusbury's Chapel.

Rufford Abbey, Notts, 694 D3, In the 17th century the Savile family constructed a mansion out of the old abbey church, but left in the 1950s and part of the house was demolished. English Heritage now cares for the abbey remains, and the outbuildings and grounds have been made into a country park.

Rufford Old Hall, Lancs 696 E7, The finest of Lancashire's black-and-white houses [NT], comparable to Cheshire's Little Moreton Hall* or Adlington*. Its 15th-century Great Hall is open to the roof, which has wonderfully decorated hammerbeam trusses. Between the spere posts at the service end stands a unique survivor, a movable screen, elaborately carved in as barbaric a fashion as the plasterwork at Astley Hall* and so exotic in its forms that it reminded Sir Nikolaus Pevsner more of Indonesia than of Lancashire.

Rug, Denbgs 693 F3, The leaden Victorian exterior does not prepare the visitor for the highly ornamental and colourful interior of the private chapel of Holy Trinity in the park of Rug, the 17th-century estate of the powerful North Wales family of Salusbury. It was built in 1637 by Colonel William Salusbury (1580–1660). The great joy of the interior of the Chapel is that the contemporary fittings and the decorative and symbolic *motifs* have survived interference by later hands and taste. There is a particularly graphic representation

of Everyman's fate, rendered all the more gruesome because of its formally classical setting.

Rugby School, Warwks 694 D6, Dr Arnold, poet and essayist, was the most famous headmaster of Rugby, but it was after his time that Butterfield designed the school's striking buildings. His polychromatic quadrangle and the marvellously garish chapel are masterpieces of boarding-school architecture. The school, home of the famous game, is occasionally open to visitors. The town was a 19th-century railway hub, and has a large station and various good examples of railway engineering. It is claimed that the best rugby balls in the world are still made here.

Runnymede, Berks 690 E5, In the famous riverside meadows King John granted the Magna Carta to the English people in 1215. The area, given to the National Trust in 1931, has pretty woodland and grassland, and there are memorial buildings, including some by Lutyens. Here too is a memorial to John F Kennedy. On a high escarpment above Runnymede is Cooper's Hill Memorial, built in 1953 by Sir Edward Maufe to commemorate the many members of the Allied air forces killed in in World War II. The spot offers magnificent views of the surrounding countryside.

Ruscombe, Berks 690 E5, Interesting details in the church of St James include the three light brick windows and bell openings, dating from 1638–9. Inside is a monument to Sir James Eyre by Westmacott of a female figure beside a weeping willow and an urn.

Rushton Hall, Nhants 694 E6, Sir Thomas Tresham – landowner, recusant and builder – is one of Northamptonshire's famous characters (*see also* Lyveden New Bield*). His Roman Catholicism put him into prison during the reign of Elizabeth I, but he amused himself there by sketching out the endless Christian symbols that obsessed him and

Runnymede
Above: The Magna Carta Memorial on Cooper's Hill.
Bottom left: The famous riverside meadows where King John granted the Magna Carta.

Right: Rushton Triangular Lodge, begun in 1594 and completed in 1597, reflects Sir Thomas Tresham's arcane enthusiasm for symbols of the Trinity.

decorate his buildings. His house at Rushton is full of triangular symbols of the Trinity, and garden walks led to his unusual warrener's lodge built on the plan of a triangle [EH]. The warrener (or rabbit-breeder) lived in a house covered with decorative Christian symbolism that is difficult but fascinating to decipher today.

Ruthin (Rhuthun), Denbgs 693 F2, A hilltop settlement that grew around its castle, which survived the Owain Glyndŵr rebellion of the early 15th century but was slighted by Cromwellian forces after the Civil War. The hotel now occupying the castle site was a 19th-century mansion, traces of which can still be seen in some of the decoration in the principal rooms. The most interesting house is Nantclwyd, a 15th-century cruck hall-house with a jettied porch. St Peter's was founded as a collegiate church in 1284 and became a parish church in 1310. It is entered through handsome 1720 wrought-iron gates made by the Davies brothers of Bersham, who were also responsible for those at Chirk* and Leeswood. The church is double naved, a characteristic of the principal churches of the Vale of Clwyd, and has a strikingly ornate panelled ceiling over the north nave.

Ruthven Barracks, Highld 701 H6, This fine ruined barracks is perched on an outcrop on the east bank of the Spey, near Ruthven, the birthplace of the

poet of Ossian, James Macpherson (1736–96). It was built by Hanoverian troops after the Jacobite Rising of 1715 and extended in 1734 by General Wade. It was defended by only a dozen or so men when the Jacobites attempted to capture it in 1745. The survivors of the Battle of Culloden* gathered at the barracks and blew it up before they dispersed.

Ruthwell, D & G 696 D2, The parish church houses the remarkable Ruthwell Cross, dating from the 8th century. The 17-foot (5m) cross, which

originally stood on the shores of the Solway Firth, was demolished by the Covenanters in 1642 and restored in the 19th century. The runic motifs carved on the base are inspired by one of the first works written in Old English: *The Dream of the Rood* (*c*700). Biblical scenes illustrating Christ's life and Passion are carved on each side.

Rycote, Oxon 690 D4, The small and lovely Chapel of St Michael was founded in 1449, furnished in the 1600s and has altered little since [EH]. The

Right: Rycote. The Chapel of St Michael has a two-decker Norreys' family pew, and another pew that is believed to have been erected for Charles I in 1625.

Left: Ruthwell Cross stands in an apse that was specially built for it.

Right: Rydal Mount, the Dining Room.

interior features a musicians' gallery and two beautiful early 17th-century roofed pews, the south pew supposedly set up for Charles I's visit of 1625. The great house of Rycote burnt down in the 18th century.

Rydal Mount, Cumb 696 E4, Wordsworth lived here from 1813 until his death in 1850, and was responsible for laying out the garden, with its terraces, trees and shrubs, and the summerhouse overlooking Rydal Water. The house contains family portraits and possessions.

Rye, E Susx 691 H7, A small picturesque hill town – once a busy port now abandoned by the sea – with cobbled streets sloping down from the medieval church. Henry James chose to live here, in Lamb House [NT]; EF Benson lived there 1918–40. Much of the town, including the Town Hall of 1743, is Georgian, but Rye preserves several interesting buildings of earlier times: the Ypres Tower, all that

is left of the medieval fortification; the 15th- and 16th-century Old Hospital (timber-framed); and Peacock's School of 1636 (brick).

Ryton Gardens, Warwks 694 D6, The Henry Doubleday Research Association, a membership organization that promotes organic gardening, began work on a garden at Ryton in 1985. The gardens are now well established and include areas for herbs, a demonstration allotment garden and plants belonging to the Henry Doubleday Research Association Seed Library. This is a bank of old varieties that are no longer grown commercially, but which are important for

Rydal Mount
Above: The gardens were landscaped by Wordworth and include the poet's summerhouse overlooking Rydal Water.
Right: Wordsworth and his sister Dorothy, by an unknown artist.

maintaining diversity. As it is illegal to sell unregistered varieties, the Henry Doubleday Research Association gives away its seeds for nothing. Unusual or forgotten vegetables grown here include cardoons (relations of the globe artichoke), skirret (an old root vegetable), and salsify (a long, thin, carrot-shaped root, sometimes called the 'vegetable oyster').

Saddell, Ag & B 698 C5, The Cistercian Abbey, where its founder Somerled (d. 1164) is said to be buried, stands in ruins. The many 14th–15th-century tombstones in its churchyard and those of the surrounding area attest to the talent of local medieval stone masons. The fine castle built in 1508 belongs to Landmark Trust.

Saffron Walden, Essex 691 G3, This delightful market town has a switchback High Street full of handsome brick houses and a small market place with a Tudorized Town Hall of 1879. Saffron Walden is named after the saffron crocus that yielded a dye and a herb, and brought the town

Top right: Ryton Gardens, run organically by the Henry Doubleday Research Association.

Centre left: Rye, Ypres Tower, a medieval defence post.

medieval prosperity. A Norman keep survives in the ruins of the castle. Around the Perpendicular church – the largest in Essex, with a soaring 1831 spire – many timber-framed houses are beautifully preserved, with colour washes and 17th-century plasterwork pargeting. Bridge End Gardens contain a Georgian domed summerhouse and Victorian planting; its rare lawn maze may pre-date the Reformation. The Victorian museum of the Quaker banker and arts patron Francis Gibson reopened in 1987 as the Fry Art Gallery. It features mid-20th century painters and craftspeople who clustered around Edward Bawden and Eric Ravilious in Great Bardfield.

St Albans

St Albans, Herts 691 F4, The picturesque market and cathedral town lying just beyond the suburban reaches of London started life as Verulamium, a large and important centre of Roman activity. It was founded around ad 43 in the valley of the River Ver (now a pretty park) and was occupied until the late 4th or 5th centuries. Only fragments of the original buildings are left standing, but excavations begun in the 1920s have uncovered – among other things – a mid-2nd-century theatre and foundations of the Basilica. Verulamium Museum contains many fascinating finds, including wall paintings and mosaics from Roman houses.

The church of St Michael is of great interest structurally, retaining a Saxon nave, chancel walls and Norman aisles. It is famous for its monument to Sir Francis Bacon (d. 1626). The Clock Tower is an unusual survivor of 1403–12 and stands conspicuously at the centre of the old market square. One of the most attractive roads in St Albans is Fishpool Street, which runs down to Kingsbury Mill, of 16th-century origin and now a museum.

Above and left: The excavated remains of the Roman town of Verulamium. The finds are displayed in the Verulamium Museum.

St Albans Cathedral

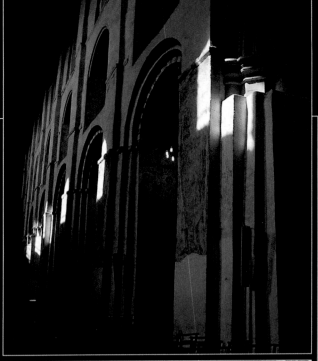

St Albans Cathedral, Herts The long, low form, with its squat tower, stands on the hill where St Alban was murdered in AD 209. The first church on the site was built in the 4th century, and the Benedictine monastery was founded in 793. Now all that remains of the monastic buildings is the big gatehouse of the 1360s (next to St Albans Grammar School) and, of course, the abbey church (a cathedral since 1877). St Albans Cathedral was built in a number of campaigns from the late 11th century through to the 1400s. It was started by Paul of Caen, the 14th abbot, who was no doubt inspired by Saint Étienne, where he was a monk under his uncle Lanfranc. Following his uncle's appointment as Archbishop of Canterbury after the Conquest, Paul of Caen rose to become the Abbot of St Albans. After 11 years' work, 1077–88, the church – built of scavenged Roman brick and flint – was complete, and a splendid 360 feet (110m) in length. A hundred years later the nave was lengthened in the

Early English manner. When some of the piers collapsed in the Norman nave in 1323, they were rebuilt in this later style. Between 1257 and c1320 the east end was also rebuilt. This rather unhappy mixture of architectural styles was exacerbated in 1879 when Lord Grimthorpe designed and paid for a new west front. The interior is impressive though gloomy, mainly because a series of fine screens cuts off the vista from the west end to the beautiful early 14th-century Lady Chapel at the east. Here, much of the impressive window tracery is original. Important surviving features are the numerous medieval wall paintings and the three chantry chapels. The Gloucester Chantry, late 13th century, has a fine iron grille and traceried vault. The Ramryge Chapel is the most ornate. The shrine of St Alban, which attracted countless pilgrims, originally erected c1302–8, was found in 2,000 pieces in 1872 and reassembled. It is still overlooked by the rare early 15th-century timber watching loft.

Top: The massive piers are austere in their lack of decoration. Much of the stone was raided from nearby Verulamium.

Centre left: Looking east from the choir with the Great Reredos of c1485, erected by Abbot Wallingford at a cost of 1,100 marks. It is filled with later figures by Harry Hems of 1884–90. The painted wooden vault of the Presbytery is beyond.

Centre right: View of the nave (late 11th-century and 1220–30), with its flat ceiling of the 1400s.

St Andrews

St Andrews, Fife 699 G3, St Andrews, the former ecclesiastical capital of Scotland, a renowned university town and the birthplace of golf, is also a delightful coastal resort. Traditionally its history dates from the 4th century when St Regulus (St Rule) was shipwrecked here and buried the relics of St Andrew which he was bringing back from Patras.

St Andrews Castle: The Scores, the promenade that borders St Andrew's Bay, links the cathedral and castle, a fortified bishop's home that was founded in 1200. They include the bottle-shaped dungeon in the northwest tower (Sea Tower), where the Protestant George Wishart was imprisoned before being burnt at the stake on the order of Cardinal Beaton, in January 1546. In May 1546 Wishart's friends captured the castle and killed the cardinal. They were joined by other Reformers, one of whom may have been John Knox, and held the castle for a year before being ousted by a French fleet and sent to the galleys. A tunnel dug by the attackers to undermine the foundations can still be seen in the courtyard.

St Andrews Cathedral: The town's three main streets (South Street, Market Street and North Street) converge on the ruins of the cathedral precinct and The Pends, its main entrance. In 1559 Reformers pillaged the cathedral, throwing its statues and paintings into the sea, while the stones were used for building materials. The least damaged sections are the east gable (12th century), the façade (1273–9) and the south wall of the nave (12th–13th century). To the south of the cathedral are the foundations of the monastic buildings and, to the southeast, all

The first faculty, St Salvator's College, which opened in North Street in 1450, united with St Leonard's College in 1747 as United College. St Leonard's was a centre of Reformation thought under Gavin Logie, Provost from 1523 to 1534: Patrick Hamilton, Andrew Melville, George Buchanan and Alexander Alane are among the best-known reformers who studied there and 'drank at St Leonard's Well'; some think John Knox may have attended, but there is no record of it. All that remains of United College today is the gothic chapel with its elaborately carved tomb (1460) of its founder, Bishop James Kennedy. The initials carved on the paving stones in front of the entrance are those of Patrick Hamilton, who was burnt at the stake on this very spot in 1528.

The United College was rebuilt in 1828–9 and 1844–6 in a neo-Jacobean manner. Also worthy of mention is the old

that remains of the Church of St Rule (11th or 12th century): the choir and a large square tower (108 feet/33m) which offers a splendid view of the town from the top of its 159 steps. The Cathedral Museum has a rich collection of sculpted crosses (8th–10th century) and a magnificent early 9th-century tomb.
The University: St Andrews University was founded in 1412 by Bishop Henry Wardlaw and recognized by papal bull in 1413.

University Library, in a 16th-century building reconstructed by the wright John Gardner in 1764 with an excellent Roman Doric columned interior.

St Leonard's School now occupies Queen Mary's House, a beautiful 16th-century house on South Street. A little further on stands St Mary's College (1537) which has housed the theological faculty since 1579.

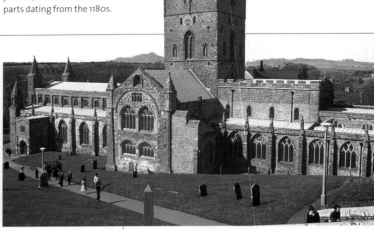

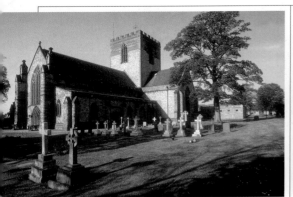

St Asaph's Cathedral, Denbgs 693 F2, A music festival is held here every September, the brain-child of the Welsh composer William Mathias (d. 1992). In the churchyard stands the Translators' Memorial to Bishop William Morgan and his collaborators in the Welsh translation of the Bible.

St Austell, Cnwll 688 D7, A town still dominated by the production of china clay, now largely used as a glaze in paper-making. To the north are the great biodomes of the Eden Project*. This, the largest town in the county, is the gateway to the Roseland Peninsula*.

St Briavels Castle, Herefs 689 H2, The 'castle' in the Forest of Dean is really a hunting lodge formerly used by King John, and his royal apartments have now become a youth hostel [EH]. The massive gatehouse was built in the 1290s by skilful royal masons, and acted like a keep in that it could be defended from the back entrance as well as the front. There were mini-portcullises defending even the entrances to the porters' lodges off the

Top left: St Asaph's, Britain's smallest cathedral, stands on the highest spot of the city's single main street.

Bottom left: St Briavels' Castle, the gatehouse.

Bottom right: St David's Cathedral, a decorative round window.

cathedral – which caused a speculative Bishop's Palace to be built by William White in 1850.

St David's (Ty Ddewi), Pembks 692 B6, The cathedral dedicated to Wales's patron saint is unexpected. Its site, Glyn Rhosyn ('The Vale of the Rose') was vital for the protection of this early Celtic foundation from marauders as well as from the elements. On entering the Tower Gate leading to the cathedral, the building itself is not visible, only the roofs, and even then the tower seems stunted. Only after reaching the base of the 'rose' bowl can the simple majesty of the building be appreciated. The cathedral, dating from the 1180s, has undergone additions and alterations until well into the 20th century. None of them has distracted from its serenity and spirituality, which gain much from the light flowing into the nave, highlighting the colour of the stone and putting the ornamentation of the arcading and capitals into deep relief, as well as showing off the tones of the 16th-century oak roof. A unique feature of the

entrance passage. In later times it became a debtor's prison, and the debtors' scribbled complaints on the walls provide gloomy decoration in some of the youth hostel bedrooms.

St Columb Major, Cnwll 688 D7, 'Town or country do your best/For in this Parish I must rest': the cry is raised on Shrove Tuesday, and again on the Saturday of the following week, as a silver-coloured ball is thrown into the air for the townsmen and countrymen to snatch and propel towards the goals, which are 2 miles (3.2km) apart. This small market town has a fine, large church, thought at one time to be suitable for the county's

Top left: St David's, Bishop's Palace, the magnificent ruins.

St Fagan's Castle   **S**

cathedral is that it is built on a slope: one literally walks *up* the aisle. The shrine of St David is in the north side of the presbytery, in the centre of which is the tomb of Edmund, Earl of Richmond, father of Henry VII, brought here from the Grey Friars' Church in Carmarthen* after the Dissolution. A casket in a niche in the wall behind the high altar was believed to hold the bones of the patron saint until tests undertaken in 1996 revealed the contents to belong to the 13th century rather than the 6th. Among the cathedral's splendid misericords is one of St Govan visibly suffering from his sea journey to Rome to ascertain the correct form of the Mass. To the west of the cathedral is the Bishop's Palace (late 12th–15th centuries). Enough remains to convey an idea of the sumptuous formality of the building as well as of its need for defence, exemplified by first-floor principal rooms built over a vaulted undercroft. The scale and magnificence of the palace is owed to the flair and

St Fagan's Castle
Top right: The Museum of Welsh Life.
Centre: Interior of an iron-worker's house of about 1800, from Merthyr Tydfil.
Right: A quarryman's cottage of 1762 from Rhostryfan in Gwynedd, re-erected at St Fagan's.

Left: St Donat's Castle, now Atlantic College, and the church of St Donat's overlook the Bristol Channel.

originality of Henry de Gower, who became bishop in 1328 and added a second and much larger hall on the south range, approached by an external ceremonial staircase. The splendour of the Great Hall is still conveyed by the rose window on the east wall, but the building's most memorable feature is the arcaded parapet on the east and south range. Everything fell into a sad decline when the episcopal residence was moved to Carmarthen in 1536. Signposts in the town indicate the way to the chapel of St Non, St David's mother. The holy well close by, with its 18th-century stone vault, retained its reputation for healing powers until after the Reformation.

St Donat's Castle, V Glam 689 G3, The 12th-century castle became, in the late 13th century, the property of the Stradling family, who retained it for over 400 years, transforming it from a fortified building into an impressive residence. In the 20th century it changed hands at least three times; one of the last private owners was William Randolph Hearst, the American newspaper tycoon. In the 1960s the castle became a school, known as St Donat's College, which was later changed to Atlantic College. Its wooded grounds above the Glamorgan coast, together with the 13th-century church of St Donat's (Sain Dunawd), are well worth a visit.

St Fagan's Castle, V Glam 689 G3, It was the 3rd Earl of Plymouth who presented his Elizabethan country house, together with 18 acres (7.2ha) of gardens and parkland, to the National Museum of Wales in 1946, with a view to making it a folk museum, the first of its kind in Britain. By the 1990s the extent of land had increased to well over 100 acres (40ha), allowing for a continuing programme of acquisition from all over Wales. This policy resulted in the Folk Museum being renamed the **Museum of Welsh Life**; it now exhibits not only agricultural buildings and rural homesteads, but also industrial cottages and a Miners' Welfare Hall. The range is all-embracing, from the reconstruction of man's earliest habitat to the sophistication of the castle itself, with its fine furniture acquired by bequests and legacies since the 1940s, its ponds, parterres and rose garden. From the start, the policy was to furnish each building in a way that was appropriate to its period, region and social class.

St Germans, Cnwll 688 E7, The well-kept estate village clusters around the greatest Norman church in the county. Built about 1050, the west front with its two towers and great portal is most impressive. There are also some interesting internal features, despite extensive renovation in Victorian times. A powerful monument to Edward Eliot (1722) by Rysbrack is dramatically located in a dark aisle, while most of the church is flooded with light, some from the east window designed by Sir Edward Burne-Jones. Adjacent, but largely hidden from view, is Port Eliot, the great house formed by Sir John Soane between 1802 and 1806 from earlier buildings, including the Priory of St Germans. It stands within a park designed by Repton in 1792–3.

St Govan's Chapel, Pembks 692 B7, This simple cell must have sorely tested the endurance of early Christians as they tried to reach it; St Govan's

Above: St Germans, the Anglo-Saxon cathedral of Cornwall, rebuilt *c*1050.

Right and bottom left: St Ives Tate Gallery opened in 1993 in a building designed by Evans and Shalev, on the site of an old gasworks. The wide central windows frame a view of Porthmeor beach below. It is famous for its paintings of the St Ives School and Bernard Leach pottery.

Bottom right: St Ives harbour is surrounded by steeply sloping narrow alleyways and the lichen-covered roofs of the fishermen's houses.

appears to have dropped out of the sky and found itself at the bottom of a cliff, reached by uneven steps whose total number, traditionally, differs between descent and ascent.

St Ives, Cambs 695 F6, The Easter Fair, granted in 1110 and one of the greatest in England, brought early prosperity and a stone bridge across the Great Ouse. Complete with rare cantilevered chapel, it remains the town's most famous monument, but All Saints' spire just upstream is equally picturesque. Cromwell's 1901 statue in the Market Place commemorates the great Parliamentarian's

1975) are places of pilgrimage for many of the town's visitors.

St Just-in-Roseland, Cnwll 688 C7, Standing at the head of a small tidal creek, this 14th-century church is now famous for its luxuriantly planted subtropical churchyard.

St Kilda, W Isls 700 A3, This little group of islands, 25 miles (40km) west of Benbecula*, is owned by the National Trust for Scotland and is also a UNESCO World Heritage Site. Its spectacular cliffs are colonized by thousands of seabirds, especially fulmers. For centuries these birds

humble years here as a farmer. The splendid Norris Museum is more interested in the Fenland sport of ice skating.

St Ives, Cnwll 688 C7, White beaches and one of the most picturesque roofscapes in the county have long attracted artists to the cobbled streets of Porthminster and Porthmeor St Ives. Many of the fishermen's cottages, often reached by exterior staircases spread out from the harbour, have now been converted into craft galleries or restaurants. The **Tate St Ives** (with a small but interesting

collection featuring works by Ben Nicholson, Barbara Hepworth, Naum Gabo, Terry Frost and prominent local artists) and the **Barbara Hepworth Museum and Sculpture Garden** (occupying the house and garden where she lived from 1949 to

Top left: St Kilda, Boreray, one of the islands in the archipelago.

Centre: St Mawes Castle, erected by Henry VIII on the other side of the River Fal estuary from Pendennis Castle*.

Bottom left: St Margaret's-at-Cliffe: one of the Norman piers of the nave, with elaborate carving on the arches.

constituted the islanders' main source of food and fuel before they emigrated en masse in 1930. The abandoned cottages of Village Bay can still be seen on Hirta, the main island.

St Leonards, E Susx 691 H7, A stylish, neoclassical planned suburb of Hastings designed by Decimus Burton (1828). Marian Court, a 13-storey Art Deco apartment block by the sea, was built in 1937–8 and has the attractive air of an ocean liner.

St Margaret's at Cliffe, Kent 691 J6, A very large and impressive Norman church. Its west doorway, arcade, wide chancel arch and four-bay chancel are typical of about 1150 and not too drastically restored, although the aisle windows are Victorian.

St Mawes, Cnwll 688 D8, At the far end of this pleasant resort and sailing haven, with its gracious between-the-wars marine residences and small hotels, lies the trefoil-shaped castle built on the orders of Henry VIII between 1540 and 1543 [EH]. It commands the eastern banks of the Carrick Roads and looks toward its sister-fortress at Pendennis*.

Top left: The Blue Drawing Room, decorated and furnished by Sir John St Aubyn in the 1740s, has pictures by Gainsborough, Hudson and John Opie.

Top centre: The Victorian wing grows from living rock.

Centre right: Cornwall's ancient granite crosses either marked pilgrimage routes or were used as meeting places by preachers.

St Michael's Mount, Cnwll 688 C8, Rising dramatically from the sands of Marazion, the Mount is an ancient place; it may have been the prehistoric Ictis, visited by early tin traders from the Mediterranean, and it has certainly been a place of pilgrimage for many centuries. The church on the summit is dedicated to the Archangel Michael, who according to legend appeared to some fishermen here in 495 AD. In 1135 a Benedictine community came from Mont St Michel, a similar tall rocky island off the coast of Brittany. The church they built was destroyed by an earthquake in 1275; what we see now dates from the 14th century. Following wars with France, the ownership of the Mount passed to Syon Abbey, which still owned it at the Reformation. During these centuries the Mount was also fortified to protect both its own bay and the western approaches.

During the Civil War the Mount was held for the Crown until the troops surrendered to the Parliamentarian Colonel John St Aubyn in 1647. Twelve years later he bought the island and his descendants continue to live in the castle today, although it is now the property of the National Trust. Visitors can see the church, the Chevy Chase Room, created in the 17th century from the monks' refectory, and the mid 18th-century Blue Drawing Rooms made within the walls of the Lady Chapel. Piers St Aubyn, a cousin of the then owner, made major additions to the castle in the 1870s. The views from the terraces are magnificent.

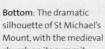

Bottom: The dramatic silhouette of St Michael's Mount, with the medieval church on its summit.

St Neot, Cnwll 688 D6, The village is famed for its church, with its outstanding early 16th-century windows depicting saints, biblical scenes, and the life of the local St Neot; beneath them are portraits of the donors.

St Osyth, Essex 691 J4, The Augustinian priory was founded in 1118, beside a creek just west of Clacton where Saxon princess and sainted nun Osytha was beheaded by the Danes. She is said to have walked for 3 miles (5km) with her head under her arm. The 15th-century flint and stone flushwork gatehouse with side wings is a magnificent sight – the most gracious lacework patterning of finely cut stone and knapped flint in existence. After the Dissolution the priory was turned into a country house by Lord D'Arcy (the noble family memorials can be seen in the village church), repeating flushwork in two towers, the whole shimmering grey complex offset by evergreen topiary. It was remodelled in the 18th century.

St Paul's Walden, Herts 691 F3, All Saint's Church boasts a remarkable classical screen separating the chancel (remodelled in 1727) from the medieval nave. Edward Gilbert, the man responsible for this wonderful 18th-century work, lived at The Bury nearby, which has a north wing of 1767, possibly by James Paine.

Salcombe, Devon 689 F7, Set in a spectacular position at the mouth of the great sailing waters of the River Salcombe, this is largely a late 19th- and early 20th-century resort with charming villas (some Arts and Crafts) set in subtropical gardens overlooking the water. One of these, at the far end of the town past Fort Charles, is Overbecks*.

Salford, Gt Man 697 F7, Its historic centre is close to Manchester, just over the River Irwell, but the city retains a proud independence. The most outstanding monument of the early borough is **Ordsall Hall**, one of the best examples of the local black-and-white tradition of timber framing, now a local museum. There is a Great Hall and much

Top left: St Osyth, the 15th-century gatehouse.

Centre right: Salcombe, subtropical gardens overlooking the River Salcombe.

Centre left: St Osyth, the priory gatehouse, a delicate pattern of distinctive East Anglian flush flintwork.

Bottom: Salford, The Lowry, *Coming from the Mill*, by LS Lowry.

good carved decoration, with quatrefoil panels inside and out. There are many good churches. Sacred Trinity is a nice mid-Georgian box of 1752 and St Philip an early classical Commissioners' church of 1825 by Sir Robert Smirke, a near-exact copy of his church of St Mary, Wyndham Place, in London. The Roman Catholic Cathedral, 1855, by Weightman and Hadfield, has a lofty spire which dominates the inner city. Here, facing a good shallow crescent of late Georgian houses, is the City Museum and Library; its paintings by LS Lowry have been taken to The Lowry but it still has a good local collection. The museum stands in Peel Park, one of the earliest municipal parks in England, and the library has every claim to be the

earliest free library supported by public funds anywhere in Britain. Further out is the former Buile Hill Museum of Mining, housed in a villa designed by Sir Charles Barry.

Recent development in Salford has concentrated on the former docks, at the end of the Manchester Ship Canal, where **The Lowry**, designed by Michael Wilford, is designated a National Landmark Millennium Project. It houses the city's collection of works by its most famous son, as well as other galleries and two outstanding theatres. Across the canal and connected to The Lowry by a new lifting footbridge is the site of the new Imperial War Museum North, designed by Daniel Libeskind.

Further north in the city is one of England's most sublime Victorian churches, **St Augustine Pendlebury**, 1874, by GF Bodley. The church is approached by a small gatehouse; the outside is brick and plainly detailed, while the inside is a lofty and majestic space with passage aisles through internal buttresses and windows high in the walls, the whole derived from Albi. Also in the outer parts of the city is George Gilbert Scott's St Mark, Worsley, one of his better churches, with skilled workmanship and a lavish use of materials.

Salisbury

Above: The Chapter House, of about 1280, with its slender central pier, and a circular centre with detached Purbeck marble shafts holding the eight-arched vault.

Below: The cathedral spire, added in 1334.

Salisbury, Wilts 690 C6, The cathedral city has its origins at Old Sarum, 2 miles (3.2km) north. It is a favourite spot for picnickers, who enjoy wonderful views, not least of the distant 404-foot (123m) cathedral spire, immortalized by John Constable's painting of 1823. The cathedral lies at the centre of one of the loveliest walled closes in England; the gates are still locked at night. Covering at least 1,000 square feet (300sq.m), green lawns stretch away to its perimeter. There are trees to give summer shade and cars are banished to the distant fringes.

Salisbury Cathedral was built in one phase (1220–58) with Chilmark stone, quarried 12 miles (19km) from the site. The octagonal Chapterhouse, begun in the 1260s and completed about 1300, contains an interesting medieval frieze depicting scenes from Genesis and the finest surviving copy of Magna Carta. The spire, on a heightened tower, was added later. Note the wide use of Purbeck marble in the shafting, and the enormous brass in the northeast transept, honouring Bishop Wyville (d.1375).

On the west side of the Close is the King's House (No. 65), a Grade I listed building, containing the internationally renowned collections of the Salisbury and South Wiltshire Museum. The Museum also houses fascinating displays on Stonehenge* and Old Sarum* as well as Salisbury, and is itself a fine building in a gracious setting. On the east end of the north side of the Close is **Malmesbury House**, originally a 13th-century canonry, but leased to the Harris family, whose descendant became in 1660 the first Earl of Malmesbury. There is wonderful rococo plasterwork within. At the west end of the north side is **Mompesson House**, a fine Queen Anne town house. It is owned by the National Trust, which has equipped it with excellent furniture and the renowned Turnbull collection of 18th-century drinking glasses. It has a small walled garden to enclose it, and was featured in a television production of Jane Austen's *Sense and Sensibility*.

Salisbury, tight within its original walls, is surrounded by four rivers, the Avon, Nadder, Bourne and Wylie, which in former times often flooded the city. Two of its churches, St Martin's and St Thomas of Canterbury, are particularly interesting: St Martin's for its wagon roof, St Thomas's for the angels on the beams of a much more low-pitched roof. Outside is the alluring oblong space of the Market, with the porticoed Guildhall (1788) in the southeast corner, and other varied and interesting buildings all around, dating mainly from the early years of the 18th century.

Malmesbury House Centre: A stone sundial. **Below centre**: Fine rococo plasterwork, c1750, on the staircase walls and ceiling.

Far right: Salisbury Cathedral, the nave, begun in 1220.

Bottom right: Mompesson House, 1701, the doorway with its segmental pediment filled with stone garlands.

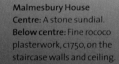

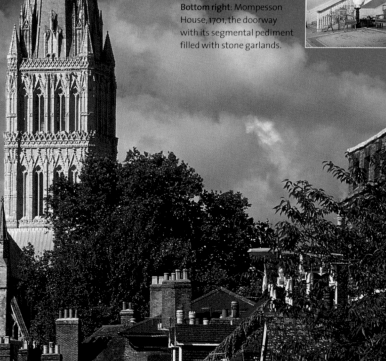

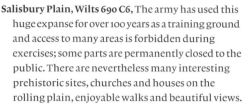

Salisbury Plain, Wilts 690 C6, The army has used this huge expanse for over 100 years as a training ground and access to many areas is forbidden during exercises; some parts are permanently closed to the public. There are nevertheless many interesting prehistoric sites, churches and houses on the rolling plain, enjoyable walks and beautiful views.

Salle, Norfk 695 J4, The village, shrunk to a few cottages, has the grandest Perpendicular church in Norfolk, 'the Cathedral of the Fields', financed by the wealth of three local families, the Briggs, Fountaynes and Boleyns. The lofty interior has beautiful fittings: bench-end monsters and misericords in the chancel, carved roof bosses, Norwich School glass, a wonderful font cover, Jacobean pulpit and that East Anglian speciality, the Seven Sacrament font.

Salt Island, IOA, A peninsula east of Holyhead harbour where salt was extracted from sea-water in the 18th century. *See* **Holyhead* 692 C1.**

Saltaire, W York 697 G6, An Italianate model village designed by Lockwood and Mawson for Sir Titus Salt, whose fortune was made from alpaca. His former mill of 1853 now houses an exciting art gallery dedicated to the works of David Hockney.

Saltash, Cnwll 688 E7, The railway bridge was completed to revolutionary designs by Isambard Kingdom Brunel in 1859 when it was opened by the Prince Consort. At this point, the Tamar is 1,100 feet (335m) wide and 70 feet (21m) deep. The Royal Navy demanded that the bridge should be at least 100 feet (30m) above the water, a requirement that Brunel ingeniously succeeded in meeting with only one deep-water pillar. The adjacent road suspension bridge was opened in 1961.

Saltram, Devon 688 E7, The finest surviving 18th-century house in the county, with much work by Robert Adam (between 1768 and 1782), built for the Parker family who became the Earls of Morley. George Parker acquired a Tudor house in 1712; subsequent generations clothed this with more fashionable and convenient apartments and furnished the rooms, although the old house is

Saltram
Above: Theresa Robinson, Mrs Parker, and her son, later 1st Earl of Morley, by Sir Joshua Reynolds.
Right: The Dining Room, 1780–1, with inset paintings by Antonio Zucchi.

Salle, church of Saints Peter and Paul
Below centre: A decorative window.
Bottom: The Perpendicular church, built in the 15th century.

still visible in the central core. The Parkers were also noted patrons of the arts, particularly of the locally born Sir Joshua Reynolds (*see* Plympton St Maurice*), and there are many pictures by him in the house. Also represented is the work of James Northcote, another Devonian, together with Rubens, Stubbs, de Hooch and Angelica Kauffmann. The main room of the house is the great Saloon, with its huge Venetian window, massive mirrors designed by Adam and a carpet echoing the tripartite panels of the ceiling, made by Thomas Whitty of Axminster in 1770. The velvet-hung Morning Room, the pillared Drawing Room, the apsidal-ended Dining Room and the masculine Library are other notable ground-floor rooms, while on the first floor some of the rooms are decorated with 18th-century Chinese wallpapers of the finest quality. The view from the grounds is no longer as idyllic as it once was, thanks to a council tip and a cement works, but there are still interesting buildings to visit: an orangery, a chapel (now an art gallery), an amphitheatre and grottos.

Saltwood Castle, Kent 691 J6, This was the seat of the art historian Sir Kenneth (later Lord) Clark, who achieved great public fame with his television series *Civilization*. Inner and outer baileys, with their walls and towers, are well preserved. The domestic range is not accessible, but the grounds are often open.

Samlesbury Hall, Lancs 696 E6, The most northerly of Lancashire's black-and-white houses, this has elaborate timber patterning on the outside panels. Inside the most dramatic space is the Great Hall, with arch-braced roof; the internal planning was

Top: Sandon Park, the Orangery. The extensive landscaped gardens feature some magnificent trees.

Samlesbury Hall
Above: The black and white patterned exterior.
Left: The Dining Room.

Below: Sandham Memorial Chapel, built in the 1920s.

changed in the 19th century so that a screen at the service end now supports a minstrels's gallery at the dais end. The hall houses furniture for sale.

Sand, Devon 689 G6, A small stone Tudor manor house, the home of the Huyshes from the late 16th century, with a fine screens passage and panelled hall. The garden has a pretty thatched summerhouse, with Tuscan columns and the arms of Rowland and Anne Huyshe of about 1600.

Sandford Orcas, Dorset 689 J5, North of Sherborne* stands this Tudor manor house, complete and very little altered. Later work includes the hall screen, which is Jacobean, and the left gable of the east entrance front, which was not added until 1873. There is armorial glass of the 16th century in the south window, and in an upper northeast room an elaborate rendering of the arms of James I, said to have been brought in from the Joiners' Hall in Salisbury*. Lovely gardens surround this fine architectural statement, with terraces, topiary and herbs in profusion.

Sandham Memorial Chapel, Hants 690 D5, The plain exterior contains some remarkable wall paintings by Stanley Spencer depicting scenes of army life in World War I, culminating in a scene of a battlefield, with soldiers with white crosses rising towards a figure of Christ. It commemorates Henry Sandham, who died after war service [NT].

Sandhurst, Berks 690 E5, The vast Royal Military Academy was built by John Sanders in 1807–12. The centrepiece, and saving grace of the building, is the commanding Greek Doric portico. The brick Byzantine Chapel dates from 1879; it was designed by Henry Cole.

Sandon Park, Staffs 693 H3, A large mid-Victorian mansion in the Jacobean style, designed in 1851 by William Burn for the Earl of Harrowby, with a splendid Victorian conservatory. The village has a good collection of Arts and Crafts houses.

Sandridge, Herts, The ancient St Leonard's Church has a Roman brick chancel arch above a 14th-century rood screen. *See* **St Albans* 691 F4.**

Sandringham, Norfk 695 G4, The Queen's country retreat in Norfolk, a Victorian pile built of local carrstone by the Prince of Wales (later Edward VII) in 1870. The heavily restored church in the park is furnished with various royal gifts; its ornate wrought-iron park gates were made in Norwich*. Several miles west stands Wolferton station, complete with sumptuous regal fittings, where a succession of European kings, princes and heads of state alighted en route to HM.

Sandwich, Kent 691 J5, In the Middle Ages one of the Cinque Ports, now a mile from the sea. Its commercial decline has had the advantage of preserving much of its medieval fabric and many houses of the 16th and 17th centuries. The timber-framed King's Arms is dated 1592. Manwood Court, nearby, of brick, was a free grammar school built in the 1570s. The only later building of note is 'The Salutation' by Sir Edwin Lutyens, of 1911, in his Queen Anne style.

Savill Garden, Berks 690 E5, A 35-acre (20ha) woodland garden within Windsor* Great Park.

Above: Sandringham House, designed by AJ Humbert to replace an earlier house of 1771.

Below: Savill Garden, planted for all-year-round colour.

Sawbridgeworth, Herts 691 G4, The church has a good range of monuments and brasses.

Saxby, Leics 694 E5, The church of St Peter is a gem, designed by George Richardson and built in 1789. The church itself is modest, but the tower and spire put on an architectural show reminiscent of Wren's City churches. Sadly the interior has lost its Georgian character.

Saxtead Green, Suffk 695 J6, A beautifully preserved white beacon of a post-mill, complete with machinery and dating from 1796, rises gracefully from a large Suffolk green [EH].

Scarborough, N York 697 J4, Enjoying a spectacular location, this is one of the country's oldest seaside resorts, having become famous as a spa in the 17th century. The sea front is divided into three parts, each of very different character. In the centre is the harbour and the heart of the old fishing town, with piers, cafés, gift shops and amusement arcades; to the south the grandiose evidence of genteel Victorian days; and to the north 20th-century developments, nevertheless mainly relatively tasteful. There is an Art-Deco feel to Peasholm Park, where a flotilla of model warships re-fight ocean battles. All three parts are linked by the Marine Drive, an impressive coastal road running round the base of the castle headland, with rocks and waves below. The town centre, still partially Regency and Victorian in character, is on the cliff top, with hydraulic cliff-lifts connecting the two levels.

Scarborough Castle [EH] occupies a precipitous headland site which has been in use since the Bronze Age. Only half the castle's handsome 12th-century keep survived the Civil War, and the North Sea has reclaimed a similar proportion of the site of a Roman signal station. Anne Brontë lies buried near the north wall of the graveyard of the church of St Mary, which once had a double-aisled cruciform layout before it lost its two west towers, north transept and chancel during the Civil War. Of greater architectural interest is GF Bodley's church of St-Martin-on-the-Hill, in Albion Road among the genteel terraces and squares of the South Cliff. Externally somewhat plain, internally

Top right: Saxtead Green post-mill, restored by English Heritage.

Top left: Saxby St Peter, the delicate 18th-century spire.

Scarborough Castle
Below centre: The surviving half of the Norman keep.
Bottom: North Bay seen from the Castle.

it is nevertheless a gem for Pre-Raphaelite devotees, with work by Bodley, Morris, Burne-Jones, Rossetti and Ford Madox Brown. Due east, far below at sea level, lies the rather baroque cast-iron and glass spa complex, the oldest part of it dating from 1877–80, with an open-air platform where concerts still take place daily in the summer season. Medicinal springs were discovered about 1620; there are several, including one visible in the roadside wall nearby.

The Grand Hotel, a vast Victorian concoction of the 1860s by Cuthbert Brodrick, is so enormous that its 13 storeys seem to stretch from the seafront to the town-centre level of St Nicholas Cliff. Nearby the steeply terraced St Nicholas Gardens have recently been revamped. St Nicholas Street was once Long Room Street, named after the 'long room' or assembly room of the Royal Hotel, which has a splendid staircase hall. The Town Hall, a little further along, was built in 1870 as a house in somewhat debased Jacobean style. There are also some two-storeyed Art-Nouveau cast-iron shop fronts. In nearby streets, such as Bar Street, are surviving terraces with segmental bow windows typical of the Regency period, and in Vernon Street there is a splendid library, built as the Oddfellows' Hall in 1840, with elegant Ionic columns on the first floor above squatter Tuscan ones.

Between the town centre and the spa is the valley, landscaped by Joseph Paxton to form the Valley Gardens, and crossed by the Valley Bridge – a structure of cast-iron lattice girders originally intended to form a new bridge across the River Ouse in York – designed by engineer William Dredge. Additional fencing has recently been added to the parapets because the Valley Bridge had become a well-known spot for suicide attempts. In the valley is the Rotunda, an early example of a purpose-built museum: the circular space has original curved cabinets. Lower down, hidden below the roundabout beside the Spa Bridge, is the original spa spring.

Above the valley is the Crescent, a Regency development of elegant curving terraces with cast-iron first-floor balconies, and several handsome villas: Wood End, a villa of 1835, later the summer home of the Sitwell family, which now houses the Natural History Museum; Crescent House, the home of the solicitor and town clerk John Uppleby who was one of the leading figures behind the Regency/early Victorian development of Scarborough, now the Art Gallery; and Londesborough Lodge, the Earl of Londesborough's seaside home, now the offices of the tourism department. Many thousands of visitors have come to Scarborough via the railway station, which has a splendidly baroque domed clock tower added in 1882. Inside is a ceramic map of the North Eastern Railway. Opposite the station is the former Odeon Cinema (1936) by Harry Weedon, in brown brick and white terracotta with black tiles and red strips, now the Stephen Joseph Theatre, the home of Alan Ayckbourn's plays, founded in 1955 as a 'theatre-in-the-round' by the son of actress Hermione Gingold. In front of the theatre is a suitably Art-Deco vertical shaft with blue neon lights. A few hundred yards to the west is Westborough of 1862, with a giant order of Corinthian columns in front of a recessed portico, shell niches and side turrets.

Scarisbrick Hall, Lancs 696 E7, Perhaps AWN Pugin's finest house, a recasting of an earlier house already partly gothicized in the 1820s in an unenterprising manner. Pugin's patron, Charles Scarisbrick, was short of neither imagination nor money, and he let his architect indulge some of his wildest ideas in planning and decoration so that both spatial arrangements and decoration are arresting. Moreover, he encouraged Pugin's antiquarian enthusiasm and trading instincts so that the fabric is liberally interspersed with Flemish woodwork, including a 16th-century panel from Antwerp Cathedral. The King's Room has a series of historical panels painted by Edmund Parris. Scarisbrick's children were illegitimate and on his death in 1860 the contents were sold for their benefit. The house was inherited by his sister but with a rent roll of £60,000 a year she was soon able to refill the house and extend it to designs by Pugin's son, EW Pugin, providing a further suite

Top: Scarborough Railway Station, the distinctive clock tower.

Above centre: Scilly Isles, Tresco Abbey Garden has plants from Australia, South Africa, Mexico and the Mediterranean, which thrive in the mild maritime climate.

Scone Palace
Right: The 141-foot (43m) long Royal Gallery with its 17th-century oak floor, diaper-patterned in bog oak. The vaulted ceiling is part of Atkinson's rebuilding of 1803–12.
Bottom: The south front, with the eastern entrance front on the right. The palace stands within a low crenellated wall and fosse enclosing the garden from the park.

of rooms for herself and extensive service accommodation. The new work is marked by a slender tower and spire, visible for miles in the flat landscape of southwest Lancashire.

Scilly Isles, IOS 688 A8, This archipelago lies some 28 miles (45km) off Land's End. Of the hundred or so islands, only five are inhabited, of which the largest is St Mary's. From here, boats leave regularly for the other islands, with their white sandy beaches, glorious sea views and flower fields protected from the boisterous winds by thick hedges. Tresco , with its Abbey garden, is one of the most popular destinations. Founded in the grounds of a former Benedictine abbey by Augustus John Smith, Lord Proprietor of the Isles in the mid-19th century, it is now famous for its subtropical grounds where exotic plants such as aloes, mimosa and palm trees line the terraced pathways. There is a variety of sculpture and the Valhalla collection of ships' figureheads.

Scone Palace, P & K 699 F3, In 1808 the town of Scone was relocated a few miles from its original site and renamed New Scone to make way for the palace built by William Atkinson for the earls of Mansfield. The style of the palace was designed to evoke the long history of the town as the capital of the kingdom of Dalriada, the capital of Kenneth MacAlpin (AD 835), the seat of the Scottish Parliament (1284–1402) and see of a great abbey (1114–1559). Scone owed much of its prestige to the 'Stone of Destiny' associated with the crowning of Scottish kings until the 13th century. The ceremony took place on top of Moot Hill which, according to legend, was formed from the earth brought to Scone on the soles of the shoes of foreign ambassadors. The stone was transported to London by Edward I in 1275, but this did not deter Scottish sovereigns from being crowned at Scone, and the tradition continued for almost 400 years, ending with Charles II in 1651. The stone was returned to Scotland at the end of the 20th century. The red-sandstone palace, a fine example of late Georgian gothic style, houses some beautiful collections of ivory, porcelain and 18th-century French furniture. It stands in a vast park inhabited by peacocks, sheep, donkeys and Highland cattle.

Left: Scotney Castle, the ruins of a 14th-century fortified house modernized in the 17th century. It is now simply a feature in a picturesque park.

Seaton Delaval Hall, Nthumb 697 G2, The mature Vanbrugh's masterpiece of 1718–19, for Admiral George Delaval, is more restrained than his earlier works. It has a dominant central block flanked by lower arcades and end pavilions, which break forward to enclose on three sides a deep court facing the chilly North Sea. The central block is very theatrical, heavily rusticated and turreted. The once-grand interior now gauntly bears the scars of a disastrous fire in 1822 – the two-storeyed Great Hall still has damaged statues in its niches, and the Saloon beyond has cast-iron columns where once there were Corinthian arcaded

Scotney Castle, Kent 691 G6, A combination of medieval ruin and Victorian mansion [NT]. The remains of the old castle, lying low beside a lake, were made into a romantic landscape in the 1870s to offset a neo-gothic house by Anthony Salvin.

Scrivelsby Court, Lincs 695 F3, All that survives of the house of the Dymokes is the great 14th-century gatehouse that formed one side of the courtyard.

Seaton, Devon 689 G6, This utilitarian town is the coastal resort for the area. It has a very early concrete bridge (1877) and an electric tramway that takes you to Colyton*.

Seaton Delaval Hall
Above centre: The south garden front and the west wing.
Above: The formal gardens.

screens. Two very fine cantilevered stone staircases lead down to the basement and the vaulted service spaces, wine cellar, steward's and housekeeper's offices. There is also a tradesmen's entrance large enough to admit horse-drawn carts. Upstairs, one room is still partly panelled in Honduras mahogany; it houses a display of impressive muniments, including letters patent with various royal great seals, including one of the Commonwealth period, and beautifully written account books and correspondence.

The west wing is still occupied. The east wing contains stables of almost cathedral-like splendour, where the stone stalls, divided by ball-topped columns, have huge mangers and water-troughs. Above each manger niche is the name of the horse resident there in 1822 – Prince, Hercules *et al* must have been terrified as the awful fire took hold on the night of 3 January. Outside to the east can be seen a handsome Tuscan orangery, and to the west is an impressive parterre designed by Jim Russell in 1950, with sculpture and a formal rose garden beyond.

Seend, Wilts 690 B5, This village is full of fine Georgian houses, several of which flank the church of Holy Cross. This has a good number of tablet monuments, one carved in coloured marbles by Thomas Paty of Bristol.

Selborne, Hants 690 E6, Home of Gilbert White (d. 1793), one of the best early writers on natural history; he studied the varied wildlife of the district. At his house, The Wakes, the garden is being restored as he knew it; behind rises the Hanger, one of a series of wooded hillsides that characterize the delightful countryside.

Selby, N York 697 H6, A market town at a crossing point of the River Ouse, dominated by its parish church, Selby Abbey, once the church of the earliest Benedictine abbey in England (founded in 1069). Much of the building is Romanesque, but some windows have very fine Decorated tracery.

Selkirk, Border 699 G6, From the 17th to the early 20th century this was a prosperous textile and glass-manufacturing centre. In the old Town Hall an audiovisual display traces the life of Walter Scott, who was Selkirk's county sheriff for 33 years. Near Market Square, Halliwell's House Museum and Gallery – a former ironmonger's store – houses the museum of local history.

Sempringham, Lincs 695 F4, The site of the largest monastery of the Gilbertine order, founded in the 1130s. The Gilbertines were the only monastic

Above: Sempringham parish church.

Sezincote
Bottom left: The traditional Moghul 'Paradise Garden' laid out in 1965 by Lady Kleinwort after a trip to India.
Below right: Thomas Daniell's Snake Pool and Bridge.

order of English origin; nuns and monks lived side by side, though in separate quarters. Nothing visible remains of the huge abbey church, which was quarried in the 16th century to build a mansion that is now only a grassy mound. Nor is there anything left of the village. What does survive is a handsome parish church with a massive Norman nave and tower.

Sevenoaks, Kent 691 G5, The most interesting building is Sevenoaks School, initiated, though not designed in detail, by Lord Burlington and William Kent. It was intended to combine almshouses with the provision of education for the poor. The High Street runs further downhill and the prevailing character is that of the early 19th century. Near the bottom is Lime Tree Walk, an estate of small houses built by the architect TG Jackson and his father in 1878–82 as a social experiment, mixing middle- and working-class accommodation. Just outside the town is **River Hill House** (1714), with an old hillside garden, and the magnificent Knole*.

Sezincote, Gloucs 690 C3, Sezincote is a remarkable house to find in this most English of landscapes: a Regency version of an Indian Moghul palace. Designed by Samuel Pepys Cockerell for his brother after a trip to India, its copper onion dome and 'peacock tail' arches, typical of Rajasthan, contrast oddly with a landscape park designed by Repton and the painter Thomas Daniell. Sir Charles Cockerell, the builder, made his fortune with the East India Company. His own bedroom, in a separate wing, is built like a tent supported by wooden spears. It is not surprising that the Prince Regent visited Sezincote in 1806 when he was thinking of building the Pavilion at Brighton*, although he was to use a different architect. The pleasure grounds, hidden among trees, continue the Indian theme with a bridge incorporating Brahmin bulls, designed by Daniell, who had lived many years in India. The stream descends through a series of pools to an Indian shrine before entering Repton's lake.

Shaftesbury, Dorset 690 B6, This Saxon hilltop town, close to the northern Dorset and Wiltshire border, once had the richest Benedictine nunnery in the county. The church survives in excavated form with its floor tiles still visible: more are on display in the adjacent museum in Park Walk. Down the very steep cobbled slopes of Gold Hill is a local history museum, and beyond lie the vast green reaches of Dorset. The Town Hall in the High Street was built in 1826, and has an arcaded ground floor. The Grosvenor Hotel nearby was also built in 1826: again the ground floor is open,

Above: Shalford Mill.

under Tuscan columns. But much of what can be seen (including the churches) is Victorian.

Shalford, Surrey 690 E6, This small village has a lovely 18th-century mill, which stands on the banks of the River Tillingbourne.

Shaw, Berks 690 D5, Shaw House is the largest surviving Elizabethan house in Berkshire. The rather imposing look of the gabled façade is echoed in the engraved mottos: 'Let no jealous enter' (Greek) and 'The toothless envies the eater's teeth, and the mole despises the eye of the goat' (Latin).

Sheffield

Left: *A Convalescent*, by James Jacques Joseph Tissot, c1876, at Sheffield's Mappin Art Gallery.

Below: Cutler's Hall dining room.

Sheffield, S York 694 D3, One of Yorkshire's largest cities, famous for cutlery, which takes its name from the River Sheaf. There is still a Cutler's Hall; the company was regulated from 1565, and by 1578 Sheffield already had about 60 silver hallmarks. The Shepherd Wheel is a water-powered cutlery-grinding workshop dating back to 1584, taking its name from a Mr Shepherd, who in 1784 was employing ten knife-grinders. Steel was made in small clay crucibles from c1740, and silver plating was invented about ten years later. The factory age came late, and most historically important developments took place in small workshops and forges. Sheffield lies within a cradle of hills, which provided many good sites for the harnessing of water power. The Abbeydale Industrial Hamlet contains four water-wheels that powered scythe-making machines, and also has an 18th-century crucible steel furnace. The Kelham Island Museum illustrates local skills of cutlery- and steel-making, and houses Britain's largest working steam engine.

The Graves Art Gallery concentrates on British and European paintings from the 16th century to the present day, but specializes in modern art, and also houses the Grice Collection of Chinese ivories. The City Museum and Mappin Art Gallery houses major historic collections of applied and fine art, archeology and ethnography, and natural history. A new Millennium Gallery has recently opened in the city centre, displaying local metalwork and with a gallery devoted to the works of Ruskin.

Set on a steep hill overlooking the city, Park Hill Flats is a vast concrete complex housing about 3,500 people in 'streets in the sky', designed 1956–61 by the city architect of the time, JL Womersley. It has been such an outstandingly successful example of 20th-century public housing that it has now become the country's largest Grade II* listed building.

South of Sheffield, Beauchief Abbey was a house of Premonstratensian canons. The west wall of the abbey church still survives, incorporated – somewhat incongruously – into a chapel of ease added c1660. This is quite a period piece, still containing its original 17th-century furnishings, including box pews and squire's pew, pulpit, reading desk and clerk's pew. High on a moorland summit on the Derbyshire border is Carl Wark, a large and magnificent example of a hill fort, probably Iron Age.

Bottom: *A Corner of the Artist's Room, Paris*, by Gwen John, at the Graves Art Gallery.

Sheffield Park, E Susx 691 G6, The house is closed but the magnificent garden (120 acres/48ha) is among the most exotic in the southeast [NT]. It was designed in the 18th century by Capability Brown and Humphrey Repton, it has a fine early 20th-century tree and shrub collection, and lake and woodland walks.

Shelton, Norfk 695 J5, St Mary is one of Norfolk's most beautiful Perpendicular churches, built by Sir Ralph Shelton in warm red brick, in 1487. A glowing light interior has fine monuments and lovely 15th-century stained glass with kneeling donors and angel musicians, one of them playing the bagpipes.

Left: Sheffield Park Gardens were laid out by Repton before 1794 but continuously added to during the 19th century.

Centre: Sherborne Abbey. The Perpendicular south side, begun about 1420, shows the clerestory soaring above the aisle. This continues to the left of the central tower.

Non-conformity is a presence here, with a Unitarian Chapel and Methodist and Congregational chapels. They are not as interesting as the church of St Peter and St Paul, dating from the end of the 14th century. It has a splendid Perpendicular wagon-roof, perhaps the best in England, with 350 panels and over 300 bosses.

Sherborne, Dorset 689 J5, The Abbey is imposing, with the historic boys' public school in its shadow. It has a fine monument to John Digby, Earl of Bristol, cut in 1698 by John Nost. In the complex of surrounding buildings there is much that is medieval, mixed in with good 19th-century work in the same style.

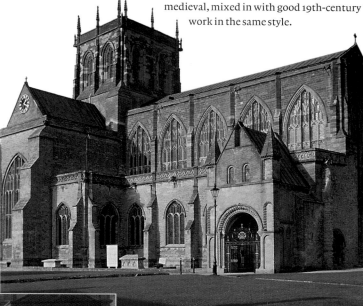

Shepton Mallet, Somset 689 J4, This is a busy market town. At its centre stands a Market Cross, off which the streets radiate downhill. There is a good mixture of buildings dating from the 17th century onwards; the most dominant is the railway viaduct of c1855, with 27 large arches.

Above: Sherborne Castle's historic collection includes *Elizabeth I in Procession*, British School.

Sherborne Castle, a little further south, was built by Sir Walter Raleigh in 1594, but has been home of the Digbys since 1617. Some of its rooms were redone in a Jacobean style in 1859–60 by the architect PC Hardwick, although notable older features still remain: the 17th-century ceiling and chimneypiece in the Red Drawing Room, the panelled interior of the Oak Room in the northeast wing (c1620), and the gothic Library (c1760) in the southeast wing. The rooms house fine collections of paintings, furniture and ceramics. The grounds surrounding the castle roll away to a 50-acre (20ha) serpentine lake at the north of Capability Brown's landscaped park of 1753. The 12th-century **Old Castle**, built by Bishop Roger of Salisbury between 1107 and 1135, was captured by the Parliamentarians in 1645, but still stands as a ruin 400 yards (366m) across the water, away from the later castle. The gatehouse has graceful arcading and evidence of Norman windows below the square ones of Raleigh's rebuilding in the 1590s [EH].

Shere, Surrey 691 F6, The church contains a good late Norman font, 15th-century brass and the remains of an anchorite's cell. Anchorites were hermits who, at the Bishop's discretion, incarcerated themselves to contemplate an impending death. The Well Head in the village, an arched recess with seats (1868), has Art Nouveau rails in the form of irises.

Sheringham Park, Norfk 695 J4, The park was laid out among wooded hills by the masterly East Anglian gardener-architect Humphry Repton. Born at Bury St Edmunds* and buried at Aylsham*, he executed over 220 landscape designs across England, around 30 of them in Norfolk and Suffolk. Sheringham, with its superb walks, viewing towers and dazzling rhododendron and azalea displays, is among his best [NT].

Sherwood Forest, Notts 694 D4, Robin Hood has become the best-known outlaw hero of the English Middle Ages. It is not certain whether he was a historical figure or whether the various ballads about him that appeared in the 14th and 15th centuries were romantic or political fiction.

Above: Sherwood Forest, statue of Robin Hood and Little John at the Visitor Centre.

In either case his portrayal as the people's hero, robbing the rich to give to the poor, has proved enduring. The democratic good fellowship of Robin Hood and his merry men, contrasted with the grasping and inhuman ways of the Sheriff of Nottingham, has been taken up countless times in books, films and dramas as a classic commentary on oppressive government. In reality, life in Sherwood Forest was sadly different. The soil was so poor it was not worth cultivating, and was left to go wild as scrubby wood and heath, useful only for hunting. The Norman kings made Sherwood a royal forest. After the monasteries of Rufford*, Newstead*, Welbeck and Worksop* were dissolved by Henry VIII, their lands reverted to the aristocracy. This part of Nottinghamshire became known as 'The Dukeries' because of the large number of great ducal estates and mansion houses nearby, including Clumber Park*, Welbeck Abbey* and Thoresby Hall*.

Shetland, Shet 703 H3, The Shetland Islands stretch for a distance of 68 miles (109km), rather like giant stepping stones in the sea between Great Britain and Scandinavia. These 100 or so islands and islets are bounded by the Atlantic to the west and the North Sea to the east. Their coastline is deeply indented by fjords (voes) formed by glacial erosion, which means that no point on the islands is very far from the sea. Today less than 20 of the islands are inhabited, but their many archeological sites attest to the fact that they were occupied as much as 5500 years ago. Like Orkney*, Shetland was colonized by the Vikings in the 7th century and annexed by the kingdom of Norway in the 9th century. Although it became part of Scotland in 1472, the Shetlanders did not break with their Scandinavian culture and traditions. Shetland's only towns – Lerwick, the modern capital, and Scalloway, the former capital – are both situated on the principal island of Mainland.

Bridge of Walls (Brig of Wass): The peatbogs in the west of Mainland have preserved a remarkable archeological heritage dating from 3000 BC: the remains of a farm at Scord of Brouster, eight well-preserved oval houses and their cairns surrounded by enclosed fields at Pinhoulland, and the foundations of two oval houses at Gruting School.

Busta: Beyond Brae is Busta House, a manor built in 1714 which enjoys a magnificent view of Busta Voe. Busta is one of the few sheltered sites in the Shetlands; rowans, planes and elders flourish in its delightful terraced gardens.

Catpund Quarries: These vast soapstone (steatite) quarries on South Mainland were exploited from the Stone Age to the Middle Ages, and the utensils and jewellery carved out of the soft stone by the Vikings were exported to the rest of Europe.

Far left: The Up Helly-Aa fire festival on the last Tuesday in January is designed to hasten the return of the sun and fertility.

Below: Voe, on North Mainland.

Clickhimin Broch: The remains of this round tower (16 feet/5m high) stand on a vast circular platform that was once an island in Loch Clickhimin, southwest of Lerwick. The farm that occupied the site c700 BC was transformed, 600 years later, into a fortified camp which remained inhabited until the 5th or 6th century.

Culswick: In a magnificent setting, between Loch Sotersta and Gruting Voe on the Sandsting peninsula, a remarkable broch built of huge blocks of pink and white granite rises to a height of

Top left: Clickhimin Broch, a fortified farmstead built *c*700 BC.

Top centre and top right: Jarlshof; its various periods of occupation span 3,000 years of history.

13 feet (4m). Stanydale Temple is almost 4,500 years old and was probably used for communal or ceremonial activities. Its dimensions (130 by 65 feet/40 x 20m) are twice those of the standard oval houses and its walls are up to 13 feet (4m) thick in places. Still visible in the centre are two holes into which the poles supporting the framework were slotted.

Eshaness peninsula: Tangwick Haa, a beautiful late 17th-century manor, has been restored and converted into an interesting museum. To the north of the former fishing station of Stenness, the lighthouse (1929) that stands on the northwestern tip of Mainland offers a magnificent view of the stacks known as the Drongs and the west coast of Papa Stour. The ruins of Houlland Broch stand on a peninsula in Loch Eshaness.

Giant's Grave: On the shore of the Loch of Housetter stand two pink granite standing stones and the remains of two megalithic tombs.

Hillswick: This fishing village is dominated by the St Magnus Bay Hotel, a wooden building prefabricated in Norway for the International Exhibition held in Glasgow in 1896 and erected on its present site in 1901. Booth is the oldest inn in Shetland (1684).

Jarlshof: This is the most famous archeological site in Shetland. It boasts the well-preserved remains of Bronze Age oval houses (3rd millennium BC), a broch and earth houses from the late Iron Age (2nd–1st century BC), large circular houses with a central hearth and radiating chambers (wheel houses) dating from the 3rd–8th century, the foundations of Norwegian long houses (9th–14th century), several walls from a medieval farm and the ruins of a manor built in the 16th century by Earl Patrick Stewart. Recent excavations have uncovered the Parliament of the Last King of the Isles.

Lerwick: The administrative capital (7,500 inhabitants) of Shetland lies on the east coast of Mainland. At the top of the town the neo-gothic Town Hall (1884), whose stained-glass windows celebrate the islands' cultural links with Scandinavia, stands opposite the Shetland Museum, which traces Shetland's natural and maritime history from prehistoric times to the

Left: Stained-glass window from Lerwick Town Hall, inscribed 'Landing in Zetland AD 870'.

Bottom: The rugged coastline at Eshaness.

Above: Salmon nets on Out Skerries.

Top: Lerwick, Albert Wharf, with the tower of the 1881 town hall on the skyline. Fort Charlotte is seen rising over the houses on the right.

Centre: Scalloway, the harbour, built from 1832 onwards and Scalloway Castle.

Bottom: The large L-plan castle, built for Earl Patrick by Andrew Crawford, here seen from the southeast.

remains of a chapel dating from the 7th century and a remarkable cache of Pictish silver, probably buried by the monks to save it from Viking pirates. Today these 28 objects are on display in the Museum of Scotland in Edinburgh* and replicas can be seen in the Shetland Museum in Lerwick.

Scalloway: This fishing port dates from the Viking period, when the court of justice and the assembly (*thing*) were held on Law Ting Holm peninsula, at the northern end of the Loch of Tingwall. Those involved set up camp at the mouth of the fertile Tingwall valley, on Huts Bay, from whose Norse name *Skalrvagr*

present day. Below the Town Hall stands Fort Charlotte, built in 1665–7 by John Mylne, the master-mason of Charles II. It was burned in 1673 by the Dutch and finally restored in 1782. Commercial Street, the town's main street, runs the length of the port. It is bordered by beautiful 19th-century merchants' houses and craft shops selling, among other things, the famous Shetland knitwear.

Ness of Burgi: At the end of this islet stand the ruins of an Iron Age fort defended by two rock-cut moats on either side of the massive ramparts.

Ness of Garth: Near Melby, a prehistoric fort defended by ramparts stands on an eroded promontory. From Melby there is a clear view of the coast of Papa Stour.

North Mainland: At the south end of Sullom Voe are the well-preserved megalithic tombs of Isleburgh and Punds Water. The landscapes of the district of Northmavine, to the north of Mavis Grind, are undoubtedly the most beautiful in Shetland.

Old Scatness: Not far from Sumburgh Airport, archeologists are excavating an Iron Age broch and village, subsequently occupied by the Vikings.

Ronas Hill: At the top of this hill (1,490 feet/454m), the highest point in Shetland, is a well-preserved Stone Age or Bronze Age burial chamber.

St Ninian's Isle: This delightful island is linked by a sandy isthmus to the west coast of Mainland. Excavations carried out in 1958 in the isolated ruins of a medieval church revealed the

Scalloway is derived. The resulting village remained the capital of Shetland until the early 18th century and enjoyed renewed prosperity due to fishing in the 19th century. In 1600 Earl Patrick Stewart built a magnificent castle whose tower-house can still be seen today. The Scalloway Museum, in Main Street, traces the history of the local fishing industry and tells the story of the 'Shetland Bus', an operation mounted jointly with Norwegian fishermen and which, between 1942 and 1945, transported resistance fighters, weapons and explosives from Shetland to occupied Norway and returned with fugitives from the Gestapo.

Shetland Croft Museum: With its outbuilding and small water mill, this restored and furnished farm on the hamlet of Voe recreates an image of farm life in Shetland in the 19th century.

Sumburgh Head: The southeast tip of Mainland is an excellent place for watching whales. Its high cliffs, surmounted by a lighthouse (1821) designed by Robert Stevenson, provide sanctuary for large colonies of seabirds.

See also separate entries on **Fair Isle*, Fetlar*, Mousa*, Unst*, Whalsay*, Yell*.**

Shipley, W Susx 691 F6, A large early Norman church, built about 1125 by the Knights Templar. It has a central tower, full of interest for its carved ornaments (chevron, zig-zag and foliate capitals). Nearby in Newbuildings Place, there is an intriguing house of 1687 with shaped gables.

Shipton Hall, Shrops 693 G4, A cousin to nearby Wilderhope Manor*, dating from the 1580s. It has a pretty setting at the top of a rise, with the stables on one side and the parish church on the other. The house was 'modernized' in the mid-18th century and given a handsome Georgian hall and staircase.

Shipton-under-Wychwood, Oxon 690 C4, The name Wychwood comes from the large forest named Hwicce after the people who lived here 1,500 years ago. The Shaven Crown Inn was built as an inn in the 15th century, reputedly by monks (hence the name). Shipton Court is a wonderfully grand Jacobean house of eleven bays under five gables.

Shobdon, Herefs 693 G5, The village church of St John is a fine example of 18th-century gothic designed by Richard Bentley. Some of the remains of the original Norman church were re-erected in the grounds of Shobden (*sic*) Hall nearby as a picturesque eye-catcher. The chancel arch and two doorways, suffering badly now from erosion, create a fine prospect at the end of an avenue.

Shoreham, Kent 691 G5, The village lies in a wooded valley, which still looks as it did in the early 19th century when Samuel Palmer and his friends – known as the Ancients – drew and painted it.

Shoreham-by-Sea, W Susx 691 F7, Old Shoreham has a fine Norman church, much restored in 1839, while New Shoreham can boast the still grander church of St Mary de Haura. It was originally much larger (the nave disappeared in the 17th century) but what remains is the transitional choir and crossing of about 1180, with a three-storey

Below: Shoreham-by-Sea, the surprisingly grand church of St Mary de Haura, New Shoreham, with its crossing tower of about 1180. The demolished nave, of which one bay can be seen on the right, once extended much further.

elevation (arcade, gallery, clerestory), all lavishly decorated, and a quadripartite stone vault. Curiously, the piers of the north and south arcades do not match.

Shottesbrooke, Berks 690 E5, The church of St John the Baptist is unexpectedly large, now that the college, established by Sir William Trussell in 1337, has largely disappeared. Inside are several brasses and two interesting tombs, one a double tomb, probably to Trussell and his wife, and one to a college warden, William Throckmorton.

Shrewsbury, Shrops 693 G3, Like many of the best English towns, it stands on a hill, which gives it a

memorable skyline of spires and towers. The heart of the town was built within a large loop of the River Severn, and here a great deal of Tudor Shrewsbury still remains: an area of small twisting streets known as 'shuts', with intriguing names such as Dogpole, Wyle Cop and Grope Lane. At the neck of the loop are the ruins of the castle with its Norman walls. Among Shrewsbury's highlights are the great church of St Mary, the circular Georgian church of St Chad, the old buildings of Shrewsbury School (now the Library) and the great brick and timber-framed Rowley's House, built at the end of the 1500s for the richest family in town.

Shugborough, Staffs 693 H3 Famous for its house, 18th-century park and fine collection of garden buildings [NT]. The house, which belonged to the Anson family, dates back to the 1690s but was enlarged in the 1750s with money from Admiral George Anson (who had captured a Spanish treasure galleon) and again in the 1790s by Samuel Wyatt. He added the giant colonnade across the main front and cased the whole house in slate painted to look like stone. The interior decoration is mostly by his plasterer, Joseph Rose. In the park is a host of garden buildings: the Chinese Pavilion dates from Admiral Anson's time, but the Tower of the Winds, the Doric Temple and Lantern of Demosthenes are all by the connoisseur architect James 'Athenian' Stuart, and are among the very first buildings in England to be designed in the Greek Revival style.

Shute Barton, Devon 689 H6, The handsome gatehouse, with its corner turrets and battlements, was built by William Pole about 1560 when he bought the estate. At the time of its construction it led to a large medieval and Tudor house, now much reduced and altered. The gatehouse was greatly extended

Shugborough
Top left: The west front, with Samuel Wyatt's extended pavilions and central bow.
Above: The Red Drawing Room, designed by Wyatt, plasterwork by Joseph Rose.

Top right: Shute Barton, the ancient home of the Bonvilles, then the Poles.

Bottom: Sidmouth, a view looking past shoreside cottages to Peak Hill.

at a later date to form an impressive entrance to Shute Barton, the seat of this important east Devon family. This now belongs to the National Trust, as does Antony* in Cornwall, where many of the family portraits of the Poles were transferred in the 1920s from the Palladian Shute House built in 1787.

Sidmouth, Devon 689 G6, Set between red cliffs, the largely Regency town has spread up the little valley of the Sid, beside which there are charming walks. Sidmouth became a fashionable resort in the early years of the 19th century and still retains a genteel air. The pleasant jumble of small shopping streets around the church of St Nicholas with St Giles is encircled by small parks, in one of

which stands the Chantry, created from remains of earlier church buildings by the local antiquary Peter Orlando Hutchison. Dominating the central seafront and sandwiched between later Victorian and Edwardian hotels is Fortfield Terrace, which was occupied by the Grand Duchess Helena of Russia (hence the Russian eagle above the two houses where she lived with her retinue).

Afterwards one of the houses was occupied by

Elizabeth Barrett, whose father thought that the warm climate would improve her health. Other visitors included the Duke and Duchess of Kent, who came in 1819–20 with their daughter, the young Princess Victoria, to stay at one of the charming *cottages ornés* (now the Royal Glen Hotel) that cluster at the western end of the Esplanade. In the church there is a memorial to the Duke, who died here in 1820. Throughout the town there are

thatched Regency cottages, mostly with elaborate dripping bargeboards and good ironwork, and often with gothic windows. A little inland are the aptly named Elysian Fields, where a

particularly fine group of such villas includes Sidholme (now a Methodist hotel), with its spectacular Music Room built for the Duke of Buckingham. The preservation of this charming town is partly thanks to the efforts of the Sid Vale Association – founded in 1846, it is not only one of the earliest but also one of the largest amenity societies in the country.

Silbury Hill, Wilts 690 C5, Immediately beside the Bath–Marlborough road is this giant man-made earthen mound, 130 feet (40m) high, presumed to be pre-Roman. Its purpose is uncertain. It may have been a giant burial mound, but 18th-century excavations revealed nothing, and have destabilized the setting [EH].

Silchester, Hants 690 D5, A scattered village [EH] containing the site of Calleva Atrebatum, abandoned following the Roman withdrawal after 400 and, unlike many Roman cities in England (such as Winchester*), not re-established

Sizergh Castle
Above: Roger Strickland in Polish costume, by A-S Belle, c1697.
Right: Margaret Messenger, Mrs Strickland, by George Romney.

later. Most of the town wall, in flint with rough stone, survives to varying heights, and the circuit of a 1¼ miles (2km) can be followed on foot. Many of the archeological finds made here are displayed in the Museum of Reading*. In a corner of the town site, bringing a feel of continuity, is the still-used medieval church of St Mary, of considerable charm and interest. Nearby, outside the walled area, are the remains of the rounded earthen amphitheatre.

Sissinghurst, Kent 691 H6, The remains of a big Elizabethan courtyard house which Harold Nicolson and Vita Sackville-West transformed with a garden in the 1920s and 1930s [NT]. Divided into sections by hedges and walls, this garden is a combination of sophisticated planting and charming informality.

Sizergh Castle, Cumb 696 E4, A typical accretive house of the northwest: the earliest part is a mid-14th-century pele tower, and the whole a mixture of additions given unity by the continuous ownership of the Strickland family, who are still there, though the freehold has passed to the National Trust. Like its near neighbour Levens Hall*, Sizergh has excellent gardens and

Top left and top right: Skipton Castle, the courtyard and round towers. It is one of the most complete and best preserved medieval castles in England, but quite bare within.

wonderful interiors of the 16th and 17th centuries with much carved oak, including a fine series of chimneypieces. The glory of the house is the Inlaid Room, just returned after a century at the Victoria and Albert Museum*. The house also has a notable collection of early paintings by George Romney, born not far away at Dalton-in-Furness*, and an excellent set of portraits of the exiled Stuarts.

Skara Brae, *see* **Orkney***.

Skenfrith Castle, *see* **Three Castles***.

Skipness Castle, Ag & B 698 C5, This impressive fortress once guarded the confluence of Loch Fyne, the Kilbrannan Sound and the Sound of Bute. The castle was built in the first half of the 13th century by a vassal of the Macdonalds of Islay and Kintyre. It was surrounded by a curtain wall c1300 and enlarged in the 16th century. Nearby stand the ruins of the 14th-century gothic church of St Brendan.

Skipton Castle, N York 697 F5, Partly 13th-century, with early 14th-century round towers and later

Below: Armadale Castle, the ruins of the large Gothic Revival house designed by James Gillespie Graham in 1815–20.

additions, damaged in the Civil War then restored by the famously formidable Lady Anne Clifford. Inside the gatehouse, carved on the parapet with the Cliffords' motto 'Desormais', is an early example of a shell grotto.

Skomer, Pembks 692 B7, The names of the islands off the Pembrokeshire coast show their Norse origins: Skokholm, Grassholm, and the largest and best known of them, Skomer, a National Nature Reserve. In addition to being one of the largest sea-bird colonies in northwest Europe, it has a number of prehistoric remains, including the footings of Iron-Age round houses and enclosures. This aspect of the island's history is now interpreted by an archeological trail.

Skye, Highld 700 D5, With an area of 60 square miles (155 sq km), this is the largest island in the Inner Hebrides. Its name is derived either from the Norse *ski* ('misty island') or *sgaith* ('winged island'), a reference to its shape. Its impressive landscapes – the result of intense volcanic activity during the Tertiary Period and glacial erosion during the Ice Age – attract geologists, climbers and walkers, making Skye one of Scotland's major tourist destinations. The island's economy is based on sheep and cattle, fishing and fish farming. Like the other islands of the Inner Hebrides, Skye was annexed by Norway in the 8th century and returned to Scotland in 1266. It was the theatre of bloody disputes between the principal local clans – the Macdonalds, Mackinnons and MacLeods – until the 17th century and became part of the Jacobite legend when a local young woman, Flora Macdonald, helped Bonnie Prince Charlie to escape dressed as her maid after the Battle of Culloden in 1746.

Armadale: In summer car ferries operate between Mallaig* and this tiny port on the Sleat peninsula, the sunniest, most fertile and most densely wooded peninsula on the island. The neo-gothic Armadale Castle (1815) stands in pleasant

Top: Duntulm Castle, built by the Macdonalds in the 15th century.

Centre: The Cuillins, a view from across the loch at Sligachan.

Bottom right: Dunvegan Castle, the towered and crenellated profile as remodelled by Robert Brown between 1840 and 1850.

Skye   **S**

to have invited a Scottish king to a nocturnal banquet. The peninsula's main attractions are the Croft Museum at Colbost, and the old watermill at Glendale. In fine weather, visitors can continue to Neist Point and climb to the top of the lighthouse.

Duntulm Castle: On the northwest coast of the peninsula north of Portree stand the ruins of the 15th-century castle built by the Macdonalds to guard the maritime route to the Outer Hebrides.

Dunvegan: Dunvegan Castle has been the seat of the chiefs of the MacLeods since the 12th century. The keep dates from the 15th century, while the 17th-century façade of the main building was rendered in the 19th century. The castle houses collections of paintings by famous artists and family souvenirs, including the Fairy Flag, a fragment of a silk flag probably woven in Rhodes in the 7th century and brought back from the Crusades by a MacLeod. According to legend a fairy, who fell in love with the 4th MacLeod chief, gave him the flag as a farewell gift, promising it would protect him and his clan.

Elgol: In fine weather this little port on the Strathaird peninsula enjoys a spectacular view of the Cuillins. Visitors can see the cave where Bonnie Prince Charlie was invited to a farewell banquet by the Mackinnons before leaving for Mallaig.

Kilmuir: In the local churchyard a tall Celtic cross marks the tomb of Flora Macdonald. On the edge of the village the traditional cottages (blackhouses) of the Skye Museum of Island Life evoke the rural life of yesteryear.

Kyleakin: Above this little port, linked to the Kyle of Lochalsh by a toll bridge, stands the ruined keep of Castle Moil, built by the Mackinnons in the 12th–15th century.

Luib: A cottage in the village of Luib, halfway between Broadford and Sligachan, has been converted into a Croft Museum.

Portree: Founded in the 1730s, the island's 'capital' is situated at the head of Portree Bay with its picturesque harbour, craft shops and modern art gallery, the An Tuireann Arts Centre. Visitors can find out more about the island's history in the Aros Centre and, in August, attend a traditional Highland gathering, the Skye Highland Games, held on the Meall, a promontory above the harbour.

Trotternish mountains: The peninsula to the north of Portree is famous for its spectacular rock formations. As you head northward the Storr, an impressive escarpment (2,360 feet/719m) formed from volcanic basalt above sedimentary rocks, stretches for 10 miles (16km). Over the centuries the

gardens and houses the Clan Donald Centre and a Museum of the Isles, which traces the history of the powerful Macdonald clan, Lords of the Isles during the Middle Ages. On the west coast of the peninsula, to the north of Tarskavaig, are the ruins of Dunsgaith Castle, the stronghold of the Macdonalds of Sleat until the 16th century.

Broadford: This resort nestles at the head of Broadford Bay. Its main attractions are the Vivarium and Skye Environmental Centre, which organizes walks and provides information on its natural heritage.

Brochs: Near Struan stands the dry-stone Iron Age fort (2nd century BC–1st century AD) of Dun Beag Broch. A long walk from Glen Brittle leads to Rudh an Dunain, the site of a Bronze Age broch and neolithic tumulus.

Cuillin Mountains: These spectacular mountains, carved out of the former magma chamber of a volcano, reach their highest point at Sgurr Alasdair (3,310 feet/1,009m). The Black Cuillins are formed from gabbro, an extremely hard igneous rock, and their main summit describes a semicircle of sharp peaks around the glacial depression of Loch Coruisk. The other side of Glen Sligachan is dominated by the rounded crests of the Red Cuillins, whose red sandstone has been more uniformly eroded by wind and water. Most excursions in the Cuillin Mountains are for experienced climbers only.

Duirinish peninsula: The peninsula is dominated by MacLeod's Tables, two flat-topped mountains on which a clan chief is said

Top: Portree, Victorianized early 19th-century houses, built in association with Thomas Telford's harbour of 1818–20.
Centre left: The harbour.

Centre right: Staffin Bay, a village with the Trotternish Mountains behind and the Minch in front.

Bottom: The Old Man of Storr, a famous landmark in the Trotternish Mountains.

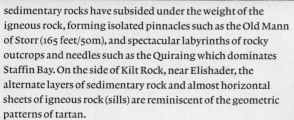

sedimentary rocks have subsided under the weight of the igneous rock, forming isolated pinnacles such as the Old Mann of Storr (165 feet/50m), and spectacular labyrinths of rocky outcrops and needles such as the Quiraing which dominates Staffin Bay. On the side of Kilt Rock, near Elishader, the alternate layers of sedimentary rock and almost horizontal sheets of igneous rock (sills) are reminiscent of the geometric patterns of tartan.

See **Hebrides*** for a list of entries on other islands in the group.

Sleaford, Lincs 695 F4, Perhaps because of its position on the edge of the Fens*, the town always feels somewhat remote. The arrival of the railway in the mid-19th century enhanced its importance as a centre of agriculture and by the end of the century produced the spectacular Maltings, a huge group of industrial buildings nearly 1,000 feet (305m) long which stand by the railway, now sadly neglected. The other building of note is the parish

church of St Denys in the Market Place, a large and complex church best known for its elaborate window tracery (one element in the mid-13th century refurbishment of the existing 12th-century church).

Sledmere House, E R Yk 697 J5 Representing many generations of building by the Sykes family, starting with a 1751 reconstruction, followed by additions of the 1780s, and rehabilitation after a serious fire in 1911. The interior decoration looks convincingly Georgian, as the original plaster moulds were used. There is a particularly grand staircase, a splendid library gallery (recently regilded) and an amazing Turkish bathroom.

Slimbridge, Gloucs 689 J2, The Wildfowl and Wetland Trust runs a centre for bird-watching at Slimbridge among the marshes of the River Severn. There is a 19th-century decoy house for catching ducks, but the centre is now used for studying them rather than shooting them.

Slough, Berks 690 E5, 'Come friendly bombs and fall on Slough, It isn't fit for humans now,' wrote Betjeman in 1937, in response to the buildings that sprang up after the founding of the Slough Trading Estate in 1920. Today it boasts a number of important 20th-century factory buildings. There are two more historic treasures in Slough, **Baylis House,** a handsome late 17th-century house with service wing, stables and coach house, now sadly surrounded by a sea of housing, and **St Mary's Church,** in the village of Langley Marish. The church has Norman origins, but its most interesting feature is the extensive work of the

Top left: Sledmere House, the drawing room with a plaster-moulded ceiling by Joseph Rose.

Centre: Slimbridge Wildfowl and Wetland Trust. Flamingos are among the 150 species that can be seen.

Bottom: Snowdon, the most visited mountain top in Britain, and Lake Glaslyn.

17th century, facilitated by Sir John Kedermister, superintendent of royal estate at Langley Park. From this period date the tower, Kedermister Chapel and the exquisite library, an extremely rare survival. The library is decorated with paintings of bears, saints and landscapes, one of them depicting Windsor Castle*.

Sma' Glen, P & K 699 F2, Ossian, the 3rd-century Scottish bard, is said to lie buried beneath the steep slopes of Sma' Glen, the 'narrow glen' immortalized by William Wordsworth. A huge stone surmounts the bard's supposed tomb, at the north end of the valley, once guarded by a Roman camp.

Smedmore House, Dorset 690 B8, A family home for nearly 400 years, lying close to the sea in Kimmeridge Bay, at the foot of the Purbeck hills. Little remains of the 17th-century building, and Smedmore is now mainly 18th century, with an entrance range dated 1761 on its rainwater heads. The house has a fine rococo chimeypiece in an upper room and also contains marquetry furniture, paintings and a collection of antique dolls. There is a beautiful walled garden.

Snowdon (Yr Wyddfa), Gwynd 692 D2, The highest mountain in Wales (3,560 feet/1,085m) was purchased by the National Trust in 1998. In the late 18th century the cragginess of the whole Snowdonia range (Eryri) appealed to travellers whose journeys to the continent were made impossible by the Napoleonic wars, and since then its popularity has never waned. After World War II it provided popular practice slopes for serious climbers who aspired to higher conquests elsewhere. For other visitors, the easiest of the ascents is the Llanberis Pass, which follows the track of the Snowdon Mountain Railway. This, the only rack railway in Britain, dates from 1896. Its base station is at Llanberis, near which the substantial Victoria Hotel testifies to the importance of the town as a tourist centre in the 19th century.

Snowshill Manor, Gloucs 690 C3, A beautiful manor house [NT] containing the remarkable collections of Charles Paget Wade, who lived alone for many years in the small cottage next door while using the house to amuse guests with costumed entertainments and his collections of curiosities. 'I have not bought things because they were rare or valuable,' he wrote, 'but of interest as records of various vanished handicrafts.' There is a room in the roof full of 'boneshaker' bicycles, for example, and another containing 26 suits of Japanese samurai armour displayed on mannikins in a terrifying array. One of Wade's masques was called 'Plague Year', and 'nothing could be heard but the distant footfall… as he paced the extremities of the house with swinging lantern, knocking on doors, and intoning menacingly "Bring out your dead! Bring out your dead!"'

Somerleyton Hall, Suffk 695 K5, Lowestoft* became a seaside resort thanks to railway speculator Samuel Morton Peto, who commissioned the future Somerleyton Hall (a spirited mock-Jacobean affair with Italian campanile) from architect John Thomas in the 1840s. He added a model village before going bust and selling to forebears of the current Lord Somerleyton.

Sompting, W Susx 691 F7, A notable Anglo-Saxon church with a tower ending in a gabled pyramid, the so-called 'Rhenish helm', unique in England.

Sonning, Berks 690 E5, The church contains a 17th-century monument by Stone, and one (c1800) by

Westmacott after his return from Rome (more carefully executed than some of his later work).

South Bucks Way, Bucks 690 E4, A 23-mile (37km) walk from Coombe Hill to Denham*.

South Elmhams, Suffk 695 J6, This isolated group of seven parishes south of Bungay* finds itself in a strange, lonely landscape of large commons, moated halls and small medieval churches. In the meadows near South Elmham Hall are remains of a Saxon minster, replaced c750 by the cathedral at North Elmham* in Norfolk. St Peter's Hall, looking very ecclesiastical among the beet fields, with gothic windows from Flixton nunnery, has its own brewery and a restaurant in the Great Hall.

South Lopham, Norfk 695 H6, The church has a magnificent central tower with blind arcading, quite the best Norman work in the county outside Norwich*. South Lopham and Redgrave Fen in the upper Waveney Valley together comprise the

flagship reserve of the Suffolk Wildlife Trust, home to the rare great raft spider. There are interesting exhibitions in the new visitor centre.

South Mimms, Herts 691 F4, The church of St Giles, essentially medieval but much restored in 1877–8, contains two splendid canopied monuments to members of the Frowyk family, wealthy city merchants. Both are 16th century and show the richness of early Renaissance sculpture.

South Molton, Devon 689 F5, An important stop on the coach route to Barnstaple*, this is still the principal market town for the scattered villages of north Devon. This prosperity is exemplified by the brick-built Town Hall of 1740. The previous year, members of the Corporation attended the sale of the Grenville house at Stowe* and purchased sash windows for half a guinea each, four Corinthian capitals for 8 guineas, and a range of interior fittings of the highest quality.

South Newington, Oxon 690 D3, The church has very fine medieval wall-paintings, most notably one of the murder of Thomas à Becket and the Virgin and Child.

Above: South Queensferry, the Forth Road Bridge on the left and Forth Rail Bridge on the right.

Left: South Newington, the medieval wall-painting of *The Murder of St Thomas à Becket*.

Right: South Uist, *Our Lady of the Isles*, by Hew Lorimer.

South Queensferry, C Edin 699 F4, This port lies between two huge bridges across the Firth of Forth. The Road Bridge, a toll bridge opened in 1964, replaced the ferry service ('the Queen's ferry') established by Queen Margaret, the pious wife of Malcolm III Canmore (1058–93), for pilgrims traveling to Dunfermline* and St Andrews*. The cantilever Rail Bridge, built in 1883–90 by Sir John Fowler and Benjamin Baker, is a fine example of Victorian civil engineering. In the town's well-preserved main street is the Carmelite Church of St Mary, built in the 1440s. The 17th-century Hawes Inn, where Robert Louis Stevenson set one of the scenes in *Kidnapped* (1886), stands at the ferry pier; ferries sail from here to Inchcolm*.

South Ronaldsay, *see* Orkneys*.

South Uist (Uibhist a Deas), W Isls 700 B5, Like North Uist* this is an island of contrasting landscapes. The east coast is mountainous and indented by deep fjords, while the west coast – the most densely populated – has beautiful white sandy beaches bordered by dunes, and meadows filled with flowers in summer. On the slopes of Ben Rueval, to the south of Loch Bee, stands *Our Lady of the Isles*, a remarkable statue of the Madonna and Child by Hew Lorimer, erected in 1957 by the island's Catholic population. Loch Druidibeg National Nature Reserve provides sanctuary for the birds which nest on the islands of Loch Druidibeg. Howmore (Tabha Mor) on the west coast is the burial place of the Macdonalds of Ranald. It also has two ruined medieval chapels and some attractive cottages. There is a memorial cairn at Milton (Gearraidh Bhailteas) near the ruins of the house where Flora Macdonald was born. Lochboisdale (Loch Baghasdail), the island's principal village is also the departure point for ferries to Mallaig*, Oban* and Castlebay (Barra*).

Southampton

Southampton, Hants 690 D7, Saxon 'Hamwic' was one of the few important trading towns in northern Europe at the end of the Dark Ages. In the Middle Ages the town was strongly walled and developed a rich trade with France (importing wine) and Italy. In the 15th century convoys of ships sailed from Venice and Genoa carrying expensive goods from the East, such as silks and spices, and landing them at Southampton for conveyance to London (this was then safer than the long exposed voyage round southeast England); on the return journey they carried English wool and cloth. Trade declined from Tudor times, to be revived after the opening of the railway in 1840 and the building of docks, especially from the 1880s to the 1930s when much land was reclaimed. With its open quays and almost perpetual deep water (owing to double tides), Southampton proved more practicable than Liverpool for the great transatlantic liners; the *Titanic* was one of the first to sail, in 1912. In the 1930s an aircraft industry developed that was to prove crucial in World War II: the Spitfire was the most notable local product. Although wartime bombing caused devastation, a surprising number of historic buildings were left intact, especially the walls. Now Southampton is very much a student city, as well as being a container port.

The Bargate, the northern gate of the walled town, is late 12th century at its core; the impressive north face is largely 13th–14th; the south side is more restored. The wall survives intermittently east of the Bargate till, at ruined Arundel Tower it meets the original shoreline, long since lost behind reclamation and subsequent development. Here, on either side of the 15th-century semicircular Catchcold Tower, is an impressive stretch of wall, actually built against an original low cliff so that the ground behind nearly comes to the wall's upper level. Further south there is a proper stone wall, not a retaining wall, with a series of gothic arches (called the Arcades) on its outward face. These were originally wide enough for a wall-walk on top. At one point there are the clear remains – with window and blocked openings – of a Norman merchant's house ('King John's House'), framed by two of the arches. This stone-built structure, with living accommodation above and storage below, originally faced an open quay but was taken over as part of the defences in the 14th century. The wall continues past the Westgate – the old town gate, quite small, which opened onto the quay – and now ends near a monument, erected in 1913 to commemorate the sailing of the Pilgrim Fathers in 1620. (They sailed originally from here, but pulled into Dartmouth* for repairs, and again into Plymouth*, from which they finally crossed the Atlantic.)

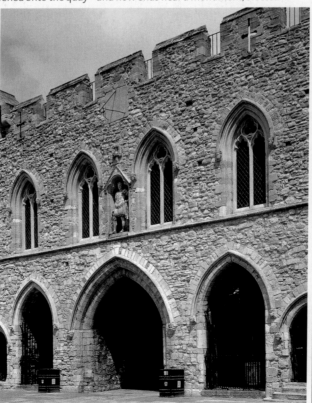

The Wool House, a 14th-century warehouse, is now the excellent Maritime Museum. Beside it Bugle Street, the best historic street in Southampton, leads to the heart of the Old Town. Tudor House Museum is a basically 15th-century house with a striking, much altered, timber-framed front. At the back is a modern replica of a typical Tudor garden and the entrance to the so-called King John's House – a stone-built shell with its original fireplace and window openings, and a rare example of a medieval chimney, re-erected here from a bombed site elsewhere. Opposite is St Michael's, a survivor of several medieval churches, with a needle-like spire on its central tower (which is supported internally on simple, impressive 11th-century arches). God's House Tower and Gate, 14th-15th

Top left: God's House Tower, part of the defensive wall built in the 15th century. It is now an archeological museum.

Bottom: The Bargate. The inner face was built in the 14th century and is not defensive in character, as is evident from the big windows. The two flanking arches date from the 10th century.

Top left: The Tudor House Museum, a timber-framed house, built between 1491 and 1518 and much restored in 1911 as a museum – 'as authentic as the restorers could make it'.

century and now an archeological museum, are at the southeastern corner of the walled town.

Southampton grew eastward after the arrival of the railway, and much fine Victorian building survives, such as the bow-windowed houses of Queen's Terrace and Oxford Street, the handsome stuccoed façade of the old railway station by Sir William Tite, 1839, and South-Western House, built as a hotel by John Norton, 1872. In Royal Crescent Road is the Hall of Aviation, celebrating early aircraft, including the Spitfire. Part of the early dockland has been transformed into Ocean Village centred on an old dock, now a marina, with shops and cafés, waterside housing, offices, and – a distinguished piece of modern architecture – the Harbour Lights Cinema. Crossing the estuary a little to the north, with five graceful spans, is the Itchen Bridge of 1977. The Civic Centre, including council offices, law courts, public hall, art gallery and library, built in 1930–9 by E Berry Webber in a modernized classical style, symbolizes the past importance of the town as Europe's leading passenger port; when the *Queen Mary* first left for New York in 1936, it was the largest liner among many that sailed from Southampton all over the world. The art gallery has a collection of national importance, especially of 20th-century works. Every four hours the tall, slender tower plays the tune of 'O God our Help in Ages Past', the best-known of many hymns by Isaac Watts, born locally in 1674. To the north, on the edge of Watts Park (where there is a statue of him) is the impressive Cenotaph by Sir Edwin Lutyens. Across the road is a baroque memorial to the engineer officers of the *Titanic*.

Above: *SS St Louis*, by Antonio Jacobsen, 1908, at the Southampton Maritime Museum.

Southport, Mersyd 696 E6, A cross between seaside resort and middle-class residential suburb, this has no great buildings but a memorable main road, Lord Street, built as a wide straight boulevard. It was subsequently landscaped by Thomas Mawson and dignified by a war memorial of 1923 by Grayson and Barnish, which takes the form of an obelisk flanked by two colonnades. North of the town centre is Hesketh Park, laid out by Edward Kemp on the principles of Birkenhead* Park.

Southsea, Hants 690 D7, Partly a suburb of Portsmouth* and partly a resort in its own right, Southsea has a fine beach and promenade with views across to the Isle of Wight*; South Parade Pier dates from 1908, rebuilt in places after a fire. Southsea Castle, built 1543–4 as one of a series of forts from Kent to Cornwall to ward off invasion threatened by Spain and France, is on the shoreside, its profile – deliberately – hardly rising above the beach. It was altered several times, particularly in the early- and mid-19th century and is now a museum of local military history. Nearby is the D-Day museum, and further east along the coast are the former Eastney Barracks of 1862–7, with the ornate Officers' Mess converted into the Royal Marines Museum.

Southwell, Notts 694 D4, A quiet little town, completely dominated by the superb Minster Church. Begun in about 1108, the nave of the Minster with its small windows and blunt pyramid-roofed west towers conveys better than anywhere else the typical character of the larger

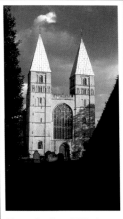

Above: Southwell Minster, the 12th-century nave and west towers with their pyramid caps. It has been a cathedral since 1884 and is one of the most glorious churches in England.

12th-century churches, as does the interior with its massive columns. The eastern parts of the Minster were rebuilt in the 13th century: first the chancel and then, after 1288, the octagonal chapterhouse, with exquisite stone carving of international importance. Dotted round the edge of the Close are the ruins of the Archbishop of York's Palace and a series of prebendal houses for senior clergy; many of these are medieval but have Georgian fronts. The present Bishop's Palace was by WD Caröe, 1907. Charles I spent his last hours at liberty at the Saracen's Head. Southwell Workhouse, 1824, is maintained by the National Trust.

Southwold, Suffk 695 K6, A genteel resort with a new pier, an old lighthouse and beach huts in every colour, a place derided by George Orwell (whose parents lived here in the 1930s), and feted by Real Ale enthusiasts: the home of Adnam's brewery is packed with pubs and hotels, to which the beer is still delivered by horse-drawn drays. Cottages and Regency villas are grouped around a network of greens, a more spacious layout adopted after the 1659 inferno, with St Edmund's great Perpendicular church towering above the rooftops. Don't miss the fine flushwork porch or the painted screens and pre-reformation pulpit. There is also a town museum and a delightful maritime museum in the Sailors' Reading Room, donated by a sea captain's widow in 1864.

Sparsholt, Oxon 690 C5, The church contains three larger-than-life, 14th-century oak effigies, very rare examples of wooden funerary sculpture.

Speke Hall, Mersyd 696 E8, South of Liverpool*, the Hall [NT] is surrounded by land that forms part of Liverpool Airport; the older buildings, terminal and hangars were pioneers of their building type in the 1930s. The Hall itself is well defended from visual intrusion (but less well from the noise) by its attractive grounds and landscaping, including the home farm buildings. Speke was built for the Norris family round a small courtyard and is approached by a narrow stone bridge across a moat. The development of the house is an exercise in deciphering the timber-work of several stages from the late 15th to the 17th centuries. The exterior is characterized by much decorative timber in herringbone and quatrefoil panels. There are outstandingly good atmospheric interiors – both original, with plasterwork, moulded beams and panelling, and later, including rooms with William Morris wallpaper.

Speldhurst, Kent 691 G6, The attraction of St Mary's Church in Speldhurst, on a hillside outside Tunbridge Wells*, is the stained glass by Morris and Co. There are ten windows by the firm, made in the 1870s and 1880s, and designed by Morris (six angels in the west window) and Burne-Jones (most of the rest) illustrating the range of his style from Pre-Raphaelite to Michelangeloesque (the Evangelists in the south aisle).

Spelsbury, Oxon 690 C3, The church was largely rebuilt by the earls of Lichfield and contains some excellent monuments to the family.

Speke Hall
Top: The exterior timberwork has many different patterns. **Centre:** The Oak Drawing Room.

Below: Spofforth Castle, the domestic range with stair turret to the left.

Spetchley Park, Worcs 690 B3, A dignified Regency house of Bath stone built for the Berkeley family, with a large garden and deer park open to the public. The most important phase of the gardens was the late 19th- and early 20th-century period when Rose Berkeley, neé Willmott, and her sister Ellen worked here. Ellen Willmott's fountain garden, with 36 beds, was arranged on the botanical principle that each bed should contain a different family of plants. The unusual Root House, with its eight knobbly elm pillars, is modelled on an 18th-century design by Thomas Wright.

Spofforth Castle, N York 697 H5, One of the famous Percy family's strongholds [EH]. Built very early in the 14th century in an attractive pinkish sandstone, it is partly hewn out of the rock from which the stone was quarried. Access to the upper floors and the roof was by a stair turret which has a fine spired top. In Spofforth churchyard can be seen the tombstone of 'Blind Jack' Metcalf (*see* Knaresborough*) with details of his talents and his overcoming of disability.

Spynie, Moray 702 C4, James Ramsay MacDonald, Britain's first Labour Party prime minister, is buried in Spynie churchyard. To the north of the village a keep with 10-foot (3m) walls stands above the ruins of the Spynie Palace (13th–15th century), which was the palace of the bishops of Moray until it was abandoned after the death of Elgin's last bishop in 1686.

Stackpole, Pembks 692 C7, Although the great castellated house of the Cawdor family (built by Sir Jeffry Wyattville, 1821, and incorporating an 18th-century house) was demolished in the early 1960s, the legacy of its enlightened landscaping can still be enjoyed. Stackpole Quay, once a limestone quarry, is used for aquatic sports, and the area provides an excellent centre for exploring the coast. Barafundle Bay, once the private beach of the Cawdors, can only be reached on foot.

Stacks, North and South, IOA 692 C1, Although Holyhead Mountain gains its prominence because the rest of Anglesey is so flat, it still offers expansive views not only of Snowdon*, but also of the Irish coast and the Isle of Man*. Particularly striking are the cliffs of North and South Stacks, the latter with its lighthouse of 1809, connected to the mainland of Holy Island by a bridge. The area, a vast breeding ground for colonies of sea-birds, is a nature reserve under the surveillance of the Royal Society for the Protection of Birds.

Staffa, *see* **Fingal's Cave*.**

Stafford, Staffs 693 H3, An ancient town which has been a manufacturing centre since the late Middle Ages: first wool, then shoes, then engineering. It is an attractive place with fine public buildings, including the handsome Shire Hall of 1795, and

Top: South Stack lighthouse, built in 1809, and open to the public. Nearby is the South Stack Seabird Centre.

Left: Stafford Shire Hall, the handsome 1790s main front by John Harvey.

Bottom centre: Stamford St Mary's Church, the great west tower and 14th-century spire.

Bottom right: Stamford, Broad Street with its mixture of handsome Georgian houses and the Roman Catholic church of St Augustine by George Goldie, 1864.

plenty of 17th- and 18th-century houses. The tiny church of St Chad has superb Norman stonework. Izaak Walton's Cottage is a small timber-framed and whitewashed cottage. Walton (d. 1683) is best known as the author of *The Compleat Angler*, with its reflections on the pleasures of fishing; the cottage is devoted to his memory.

Stamford, Lincs 694 E5, A perfect small Georgian town which has been used for countless film locations, although the church steeples that punctuate the skyline serve as a reminder that it has an older past still visible in many places. All Saints Church is the hub of the town and much more conspicuous than the 18th-century Town Hall in St Mary's Street. Most of Stamford is constructed with the excellent local building stone, and a large part of it is still owned by the Cecil family from nearby Burghley House*. Many of the 18th-century houses that line the streets have ornamental door and window surrounds copied out of the pattern books of the time.

Stanford Hall
Top left: The Palladian ballroom of 1745 with Victorian ceilng paintings. This was originally an entrance hall.
Right: The panelled library contains 5,000 books.

Stanford in the Vale, Oxon 690 C4, The church has a 17th-century hexagonal font and cover, and a piscina with a shelf and pyx canopy (which was originally a reliquary).

Stanford on Avon, Nhants 694 D7, St Nicholas's church is outstanding both for its stained glass and its monuments, which provide a mini-history of the 15th to the 16th centuries. The monuments continue on into the 18th and 19th, with pieces by Thorneycroft. **Stanford Hall**, just over the border into Leicestershire, is a large and gracious William and Mary house with the hipped roof and heavy quoins of the period. It stands on low ground in an ample park next to the River Avon (which frequently floods in winter), near Lutterworth*. The house was begun in 1697, for the Smiths of Warwick, and finished about 30 years later. The interior, with its panelled rooms, has changed little since the 1730s. Percy Pilcher, the first man in England to fly an aeroplane, was tragically killed when his machine crashed at Stanford; a replica of his plane can be seen in the handsome 1730s stable block.

Stanstead Abbotts, Herts 691 F4, An attractive village and a popular place of retirement, thanks chiefly to the diversions offered by the River Lea, the marina, and the walks along the New River. Nearly a mile to the southeast is the village's late medieval church of St James, containing a good brass to Sir Edward Baeshe (d. 1587), his wife and children.

Stanstead Park, W Susx 690 E7, The Talman mansion was largely destroyed by fire in 1900, but some 18th-century parts remain in the present house by AC Blomfield. There is a Dutch Garden and Ivan Hicks' 'Garden of the Mind'. The little chapel in

Bottom: Stanton Drew, stone circles dating from the Bronze Age.

the grounds has some unusual early 19th-century stained glass illustrating Jewish Old Testament scenes which John Keats saw and remembered when he wrote 'The Eve of St Agnes'.

Stansted Mountfitchet, Essex 691 G3, Named after the Norman family whose castle earthworks are just discernible in this attractive thoroughfare village in the Cam Valley. Its baroque cast-iron drinking fountain, more at home in the British Raj, is matched by late 20th-century ingenuity. Stansted Airport, rising from the fields like a glass cathedral in the mid-1980s, is one of Sir Norman Foster's most successful buildings. (Environmentalists

Top left: Stansted Airport, designed by Sir Norman Foster.

Top right: Stanton Drew, a roadside cottage.

Above: The Gardens and Pope's Tower seen from the roof of the medieval kitchen.

remain unmoved.) With the constant roar of jumbo-jets overhead, the stony repose of Hester Salusbury (d. 1614), in the church on the edge of the park, points a surer way to heaven.

Stanton Drew, Somset 689 H4, The stone circles here are the most important prehistoric monument in Somerset, dating from the Bronze Age. A small version of the more famous site at Stonehenge*, it has 44 stones arranged in three circles, the largest 120 yards across [EH]. The church of St Mary has a good monument of 1717 by Bristol sculptor Michael Sidnell, dedicated to the memory of Cornelius Lyde.

Stanton Harcourt, Oxon 690 D4, This delightful village is focused upon an outstanding group of buildings consisting of manor house, church and parsonage. The Great Kitchen and Pope's Tower are all that remains of the great medieval manor of the Harcourt family, which was largely demolished in c1750 to provide stone for the family's new house at Nuneham Courtenay. The Harcourts were a Norman family who came to England at the time of the Conquest. They acquired the manor of Stanton in the mid-12th century as a wedding gift from Henry I's wife, who was a cousin of the bride. The family returned to the house in 1948.

The gatehouse dates from 1540, but was remodelled in 1868 and 1953. The kitchen was a detached building and is a truly majestic example of its type, dating from the late 14th century. The building is a square, with an octagonal pyramid roof, remodelled in 1485. Looking up at the inside of the roof is like contemplating an idealized spider's web, or a kaleidoscope pattern that at any moment will twist into a new formation. Eight principal beams, linked by wind braces, soar from the points of the octagon up to the apex. There are two open fireplaces and three ovens, but no chimney – the smoke would have escaped through louvered shutters, now replaced by windows. Pope's Tower acquired its name after Alexander Pope stayed here while working on his translation of *The Iliad* in 1717–18. The Chapel on the ground floor retains its original roof and stained glass.

The Norman church of St Michael was richly remodelled in the 13th century, when the chancel was lengthened; note the beautiful east window and the rare rood screen. The Harcourt Chapel may be by William Orchard who designed the vault of the Oxford* Divinity School. It is filled with Harcourt tombs. The stately parsonage, next to the medieval fish ponds, is a little-altered house of c1675.

Stanway
Top right: The detached gateway with the church in the background.

Centre: Starcross pumping house on the banks of the River Exe. The Italianate engine house has a tower disguising the chimney.

Stanway, Gloucs 690 C3, The ensemble of manor house, barns, church and gatehouse renders this a jewel of a place. The gatehouse to the garden, designed like a triumphal arch, writhes with joyous decoration from the 1630s. The main house, built in the early 17th century by Sir Paul Tracy, has an odd plan: a long, south-facing range with the Hall at one side. This means, however, that the main rooms now look over the newly restored 1750s gardens behind the house with pyramid and cascade. Another part of the harmonious grouping of buildings at Stanway is the 14th-century Tithe Barn that is sometimes used as a concert hall. The church of St Peter's is Norman, through extensively rebuilt in Victorian times. Stanway House was once lived in by Sir James Barrie, author of *Peter Pan*.

Stapleford, Leics, 694 E5, Stapleford Park, formerly the home of the Sherard family, is now a hotel. The main house dates from the 1680s with a big Jacobean-style addition of the 1890s, but there is also a small earlier wing of *c*1500; in the 1630s it

Bottom: Staunton Harold, the mansion and church grouped together in the park.

was covered in statues and ornaments by Lady Abigail Sherard. A short distance from the house is the church of St Mary. It was designed in 1783 by George Richardson and is an early example of Gothic Revival. The interior, which has hardly been touched since the 18th century, is arranged like a college chapel, with the seats facing inwards and a gallery for the family at the west end. In the north transept is a very grand monument by Rysbrack to the 1st Earl of Harborough, who died in 1732.

Staplehurst, Kent 691 H6, The hinge of the church door merits particular attention. The metal has been shaped to resemble fishes, snakes and sea monsters.

Starcross, Devon 689 G6, Isambard Kingdom Brunel pioneered a short-lived 'atmospheric' railway in 1844 which ran from Exeter* to Newton Abbot, with the intention that it should then continue over the steep gradients to Plymouth*. The passenger carriages were to be pushed along the track by compressed air produced by pumping

houses at 3-mile (5km) intervals. Only the one at Starcross survives; it is in the Italian style and stands on the bank of the Exe overlooking the departure point for the passenger ferry to Exmouth*.

Staunton Harold, Leics 694 D5 The house and church stand next to each other by a lake within the park. The house has a handsome 18th-century exterior that conceals a complicated building dating back to the 15th century. The church [NT] is exceptionally unusual in that it was built during the Commonwealth. Over the west door is an inscription which begins 'In the yeare: 1653 when all things sacred were throughout ye nation Either demollisht or profaned Sir Richard Shirley Barronet Founded

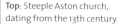

Top: Steeple Aston church, dating from the 13th century.

Left: Staunton Harold Church, an almost complete 17th-century interior.

Right: Stevington St Mary's Church.

Stembridge Tower Mill, Somset 689 H5, The little village of High Ham preserves the last thatched windmill in England. Stembridge Tower Mill [NT] dates from 1822, and was in use until 1910.

Stenness Standing Stones, *see* **Orkney***.

Stevenage, Herts 691 F3, Although it looks perfectly commonplace today, the new town was made famous in the 1940s and 1950s by the creation of a completely pedestrianized centre, one of Europe's first. In Old Stevenage is St Nicholas's Church, with its Norman west tower and some 15th-century choir seats with misericords.

Stevenstone, Devon 688 E5, The Rolles were one of the great families of Devon, and this was their principal seat. The Victorian house in the French style is now in ruins, but the Landmark Trust has preserved the detached 18th-century Orangery and Library. The latter is of red brick with Ionic pilasters of stone rising through to the first floor above the arcade below.

Steventon, Oxon 690 D4, An unusual, roughly paved causeway runs from the medieval church to the Green. Fronting on to it by Mill Street are the timber-framed priory cottages, former monastic buildings which contain the medieval Great Hall of the original priory.

Stevington, Beds 690 E3, East of the village is a wooden post-mill, erected in 1783. Inside St Mary's Church are surviving early 16th-century bench ends: two men kneeling and drinking, two semi-reclining, one writing, and three animals.

Stewkley, Bucks, St Michael's is the most complete Norman church in the county, and was built probably in c1150–80. The vista from west to east, with zig-zag arches, will not soon be forgotten. *See* **Leighton Buzzard* 690 E3.**

this Church whose singular praise it is to have done the best things in ye worst times, and hoped them in the most callamitous [*sic*].' The church is entirely gothic in style; inside, all the original woodwork survives, along with a sumptuous wrought-iron screen by the Derbyshire blacksmith Robert Bakewell, under a handsome painted ceiling of the 1650s.

Steeple Ashton, Wilts 690 B5, A fine church, with a vaulted interior. The tower originally possessed a spire which was blown down in 1670. It remains impressive, however, with pinnacles and buttresses in profusion. The village has some attractive Georgian houses.

Steeple Aston, Oxon 690 D3, The church has been much restored but contains a very grand monument (1730) to Sir Francis and Lady Page by the Fleming Henry Scheemakers. The figures recline against a dark marble pyramid set in a pedimented frame. The handling of the drapery is particularly accomplished.

Above: Steeple Ashton. Its picturesque High Street has timber-framed houses with brick infilling. The four-staged tower of St Mary's rises overall.

Bottom: Steyning, St Andrew's, arcade of the nave.

Steyning, W Susx 691 F7, St Andrew's is reckoned to be the best Norman church in a county rich in Norman churches. It has a nave with spacious arcades of cylindrical pillars and arches covered with zig-zag and other ornament. The legend of its foundation by St Cuthman is the subject of Christopher Fry's play *Boy with a Cart.*

Stirling

Stirling, Stirlg 698 E4, This town, with its former royal residence and historic centre, is one of Scotland's leading tourist destinations. Steep cobbled streets lined with 17th-, 18th- and early 19th-century houses lead to the castle, which stands on a 250-foot (76m) volcanic outcrop above the best crossing on the River Forth, a strategic position which explains its turbulent past. Although some parts date from the 12th century, most of the buildings were constructed in the 15th

and 16th centuries, when James IV and James V transformed the fortress into a comfortable Renaissance palace. The castle was converted into a barracks after 1745, but since it was vacated by the army in 1964 there have been a series of restoration campaigns. Beyond the defensive outworks (1708–17), a ramp climbs to the entrance in the centre of the early 16th-century Gatehouse, past Queen Anne's Garden on the left, and leads on to the Lower Square. On the left of the square is the elegant east façade of the palace, with its alternate windows and statue niches, and, opposite, the south gable of the Great Hall. The palace, built in the 1540s, houses the royal apartments, which are almost bare except for the magnificent carved oak heads ('Stirling Heads') that originally decorated the ceiling of the King's Apartments. Today the heads are displayed on the walls of the Queen's Apartments. The Great Hall, built in 1500 in late gothic style and converted into a barracks in the 18th century, has now been splendidly restored. The Lower Square also gives access to the vaults that housed the kitchens. The archway between the Great Hall and the Palace opens on to the Upper Square. On the far side of the square stands the Chapel Royal, built in 1594 by James VI for the baptism of his son, Prince Henry. Visitors can still admire the ceiling and wall paintings executed by Valentine Jenkin in 1628. On the west side of the square the King's Old Buildings, refurbished as

officers' quarters in the 18th century, today house the Museum of the Argyll and Sutherland Highlanders (there are collections of silverware, memorabilia and military medals).

The old town: In Castle Wynd, the street leading down from the castle, is Argyll's Lodging, an impressive town house built in 1632 by Sir William Alexander of Menstrie, a poet, statesman and courtier under James VI. In the 1620s Menstrie founded and

Top right: Stirling, Church of the Holy Rude, the nave and western tower seen from the garden of Cowane's Hospital.

Far left: Stirling Castle's Chapel Royal.

Centre: The Great Hall.

Bottom: *Stirling in the Time of the Stuarts*, by Johannes Vorsterman, late 17th century.

colonized Nova Scotia. On his death the mansion passed to the Argyll family who extended it in 1674. The apartments that lie behind the beautiful renaissance façade have been entirely restored and furnished in 17th-century style. A little further down the street is the beautifully worked façade of Mar's Wark, all that remains of the renaissance palace commissioned in 1569 by John Erskine, 1st Earl of Mar and Regent of Scotland, but never finished. In the Church of the Holy Rude, on the corner of St John Street, the infant James VI was crowned king in 1567. The 15th-century nave has a remarkable oak roof and vaulted aisles dating from the same period, while the choir and apse date from the 16th century. To the southwest of the church is Cowane's Hospital, a charitable hospice built between 1634 and 1649 by John Cowane, a member of the Scottish Parliament. The Tolbooth, by Sir William Bruce, 1703, is now the Arts Centre. Old Town Jail, at the top of St John Street, dates from 1847.

Wallace Monument: This 220-foot (67m) crown tower by JT Rochead was erected on Abbey Craig hill in 1869 in memory of William Wallace. It houses an exhibition which includes Wallace's two-handed sword and battle tent. The top of the tower (246 steps) offers sweeping views of the Ochil Hills to the east, Stirling to the south and The Trossachs* to the west.

Stockeld Park, N York 697 H6, An intriguing synthesis of Vanbrughian and Palladian architecture, designed by James Paine 1758–63. Its pedimented three-storey centrepiece is flanked by wings with broken pediments. Inside there is an impressive staircase.

Centre and above: Stockeld Park, the garden front and the library. The house contains a fine collection of 18th- and 19th-century paintings and furniture.

Stockport, Gt Man 697 F7, A prosperous market town with the River Mersey, the historic frontier between Lancashire and Cheshire, running through it. The river valley is marked by the dramatic railway viaduct striding across the town and the steep streets and steps which lead up to the historic market place on the hill to the south of the river. Here are St Mary's Church, medieval in origin but largely rebuilt by Lewis Wyatt in 1813 and with some good monuments; Staircase House, a remarkable cruck-framed timber town house, much battered and currently being restored; and an iron and glass Market Hall. The main road south, just to the west of the market, has Stockport Town Hall, one of the grandest of Edwardian civic buildings, by Sir Alfred Brumwell Thomas, an architect who specialized in the building type after his success in winning the Belfast City Hall competition. Further south along the road are George Basevi's classical St Thomas's Church, one of the finest of the early Commissioners' churches, and further south again St George's Church, by Paley and Austin in 1896, and perhaps their finest large town church with a 230-foot (70-metre) spire and excellent detail in both stone and wood. To the north of the town centre, at Reddish, is one of the best examples of a settlement owing all to a mill and its owner. Houldsworth's Mill is a large double mill by AH Stott, a mill specialist; it comprises two large factories set on either side of a central boilerhouse with lofty chimney. Surrounding the mill are streets of worker's houses and buildings provided by Sir William Houldsworth for his employees, including a school and working men's club, designed by Alfred Waterhouse. St Elisabeth's Church, also by Waterhouse, is one of his finest, with an expressive use of brick in a bold composition, an almost detached tower and an excellent spacious interior, plain in the nave and richly detailed with ironwork and marble in the chancel. See also Bramhall Hall*, which is in the suburbs south of Stockport.

Stoke D'Abernon, Surrey, By the River Mole is the poorly restored church of St Mary, which contains the brass of John D'Abernon (d. 1277), supposedly the oldest in England. See **Cobham*** 691 F5.

Stoke Park, Bucks, Begun in 1789 for John Penn, grandson of William, founder of Pennsylvania, on his return from America. The house was remodelled by James Wyatt between 1793 and 1813, and further alterations were made in the second half of the 19th century. It is a commanding building with an ornate interior containing a particularly grand staircase. Humphrey Repton was employed to work on the landscape throughout the 1790s. The house and grounds are now a golf club. *See* **Stoke Poges* 690 E5.**

Stoke Park Pavilions, Northants 690 E3, The lodges are all that survive of a 17th-century house built for Sir Francis Crane, owner of the famous Mortlake tapestry works. Their height, delicate pilasters and subtle colouring show that an

Top: Stoke Park Pavilions, all that remains of the 17th-century house.

Bottom left: Stoke-on-Trent's pottery museum.

Bottom right: Stoke Poges, church of St Giles and the churchyard that inspired Gray's poem.

architect of great skill was involved, possibly Inigo Jones. The locks, narrowboats and canal museum at Stoke Bruerne nearby are also interesting. Odd chimneys rising from the countryside to the north mark the passage of the canal into a tunnel.

Stoke Poges, Bucks 690 E5, It is easy to be put off by the proximity of busy modern Slough*, but Stoke Poges remains a characterful village with interesting connections. The handsome medieval church of St Giles boasts fine stained glass and monuments. One of two lychgates leads to the old churchyard that inspired Thomas Gray to write his 'Elegy in a Country Churchyard'. The Gray Monument to the east was erected in 1799 to designs by James Wyatt and is adorned with quotations from the poem.

Stoke Prior, Worcs 693 H5, The church contains unusual columns with carefully delineated leaves for capitals, but the main attraction here is the Avoncroft Museum of Buildings. It displays buildings relocated from elsewhere, which include a 1940s pre-fab, a working windmill and the national collection of telephone booths.

Stoke Row, Oxon 690 D5, The little village contains the obscure Maharajah's Well, presented in 1863 by the Maharajah of Benares. Exotic features include the onion dome and cast-iron elephant.

Stoke-by-Nayland, Suffk 691 H3, One of several finely preserved villages on a ridge between the Stour and its tributary, the Box. The huge Perpendicular church has a soaring tower with enriched west face, an arcaded Tudor porch with a 17th-century library above, brasses to the Tendring family and alabaster tombs. In the village are the 16th-century Guildhall and Maltings, oak-framed cottages and the popular Angel Hotel. Outside the village **Thorington Hall** is a romantic timber-framed, plastered, gabled and colour-washed Elizabethan house with ornate chimney stacks and oriel window.

Stoke-on-Trent, Staffs 693 H2, The church of St Peter has memorials to Josiah Wedgwood and Josiah Spoke, reflecting the town's status as one of the Potteries*. There is a good museum displaying local pottery in the Minton works in London Road.

Stokesay Castle, Shrops 693 G4, A romantic fortified manor house built just when the English were turning from castles to houses. Attached to a small 12th-century stone tower is a great hall built for Laurence de Ludlow, a cloth merchant who bought Stokesay in 1281. He also added a solar and a second

Stokesay Castle
Top: The hall with Lawrence de Ludlow's south tower added in the 1290s.
Right: A detail of his additions to the top of the north tower.

Centre: Stoke Row, the Maharajah's Well.

tower, but since then the only addition has been the decorative little gatehouse built in 1590 [EH].

Stoke sub Hamdon Priory, Somset, This was built in the 14th century for the priests of the chantry chapel of St Nicholas, now destroyed. The church of St Mary was restored in 1862, but there is a Norman nave and chancel, and a puzzling north door tympanum with a tree of life, three large birds, the lamb and the cross, and many inscriptions. Nearby is Ham Hill, the source of much of the good biscuit-coloured building stone, used throughout the southwest. *See* **Martock* 689 H5.**

Stone, Kent 691 G5, St Mary is a particularly fine 13th-century church, so sophisticated in its details that it seems certain to have been built by the same

Top left: Stonehaven harbour from the south. The new harbour, constructed by Robert Stevenson 1825–6 is in the foreground, with the 16th-century harbour beyond.

masons as Westminster Abbey*. The chancel, higher than the nave, is rib-vaulted (the present vault is an accurate restoration by GE Street) and has trefoil wall-arcading with very fine foliage

Bottom: Stonehenge, the ancient stone circle.

carving. As in Westminster, there is plenty of black Purbeck marble. The nave is equally rich, but has a wooden roof. In the 14th century it was lengthened by one bay, but interestingly the masons tried to match the earlier work, except for the capitals, which feature realistic oak and maple. In the north aisle are two medieval wall-paintings showing the Virgin and Child and the murder of Becket [EH].

Stonehaven, Abers 702 D7, This delightful port founded by George Keith (1553–1623), 5th Earl-Marischal of Scotland, was the county town of Kincardineshire. At the harbour stands the late 16th-century toll booth where episcopalian ministers were imprisoned in 1748–9, although this did not prevent them baptizing children through the bars of their cells. Today the building houses a museum of fishing, cooperage and local history. Stonehaven celebrates Hogmanay (New Year's Eve) with a huge firework display that lights up the port.

Stonehenge, Wilts 690 C6, Some 8 miles (13km) north of Salisbury* stands what is probably the best-known prehistoric monument in western Europe, assumed by most to be part of some great astronomical calendar erected about 5,000 years ago. Its unique circle of stones is oriented on the rising and setting sun, but the origin and placing of the stones themselves remain mysterious, for they seem to match outcrops in north Pembrokeshire in Wales.

The stones need to be seen (most dramatically at sunset) as part of a remote landscape. English Heritage, which owns the site, has at last been given permission to relandscape it. The busy A303 road will be diverted, with stretches hidden in a tunnel, and visitor resources more discreetly sited. The visitor centre provides a three-part audio tour in nine languages, as befits a unique attraction, designated a World Heritage Site by UNESCO.

Stoneleigh Abbey, Warwks 694 C6, Just north of Kenilworth*, Francis Smith of Warwick's majestic mansion is now partially open to the public again after many years. Rising from the remains of a Cistercian Abbey, the 18th-century rebuilding was never completed and more than half of the building remains monastic in character. It has recently been converted into private flats and houses, with the kitchen gardens as a shared but private outdoor space. The state rooms of the piano nobile, the elaborate chapel, the orangery and Repton's landscaped grounds are open to visitors.

Stonor Park, Oxon 690 E4, A substantial house set in a remote valley at the Oxfordshire edge of the Chiltern Hills*. The building's sash-windowed, Georgian appearance conceals some fine medieval features, for the house has belonged to the Stonor family since the 12th century. The simple detached Roman Catholic chapel dates from the 1300s and was remodelled internally between 1796 and 1800. In 1581 it provided a hiding place for the Jesuit Edmund Campion, who was executed at Tyburn later the same year.

Stonyhurst, Lancs 697 F6, This is now a major Roman Catholic public school. Parts of an ancient house survive but what is seen from the front is largely the work of Sir Richard Shireburne in the 1590s, with a bold frontispiece of four superimposed orders, topped by baroque cupolas added in the early 18th century. This was the time of major new work, especially to the setting: the house is now approached by a drive between two straight canals. The Shireburnes were staunch Catholics; after they died out, the property passed to the equally Catholic Welds, who in 1794 gave the property to the Jesuits to establish their English school. The first additional school building is known as Shirk, but the largest and most dramatic addition was

Stonor Park

Top right: The earliest part of the house dates from the 12th century, but most was built in the 14th. It is surrounded by woodland and an extensive deer park.
Left: The Dining Room, with 18th-century gothic decoration and French scenic wallpaper. There is rare furniture, tapestries, sculptures and paintings.

Bottom right: Stott Park Bobbin Mill, a working factory where the machinery and techniques of the Industrial Revolution are demonstrated.

made to the west by Dunn and Hansom in the late 1870s in a free, almost licentious, style that contrasts strongly with the small square pavilions of the early-18th-century garden which it faces. Next to the school is the church added in the 1830s by JJ Scoles, turreted in the manner of King's College Chapel, Cambridge*, with an interior decorated by Goodhart-Rendel in 1954. Stonyhurst is approached via Hurst Green, where the Shireburne Almshouses, built 1706, were transferred to their present site in 1936. The best monuments to the Shireburnes, however, are not their buildings but the family tombs in their chapel at Great Mitton Church, including one to Sir Richard, builder of the gatehouse, and others – by the London mason William Stanton – to those who had overseen the works to house and garden c1700.

Stornoway, *see* **Lewis*.**
Stott Park Bobbin Mill, Cumb 696 E4, Set in the woodland between Windermere* and Coniston. The woods were coppiced for the timber from which bobbins were turned. Bobbins were essential to the textile revolution that took place 60 miles (96 km) to the south in industrial Lancashire. The factory, still working, was built in 1835 [EH]. Nearby is the picturesque village of Finsthwaite where St Peter's Church is perhaps the best of the village churches designed by the Lancaster architects Paley and Austin.

Stourhead

Stourhead, Wilts 689 J4, One of the greatest English landscape gardens, laid out from 1741 for Henry Hoare, a member of the London banking family. It lies 30 miles (48km) east of Salisbury on the western edge of Wiltshire. At the head of the park is the Palladian house designed by Colen Campbell in 1721–4. Walk around the lake from the five-arched bridge, passing the Temple of Flora, and you come to the dark, celebrated Grotto and John Cheere's statue of Neptune (1751). From here there is a splendid view back through the stone-framed opening across the tranquil lake to the bridge and church. At the most distant point from the house is the Pantheon (1753), with its iron gates enclosing a Rotunda. There are statues in niches, the principal of which is Rysbrack's *Flora* (1762). The house contains notable collections of pictures, sculpture, and furniture by Chippendale the Younger, put together by Henry Hoare 'the Magnificent' – notably a great *pietra dura* cabinet, on a stand by Boson, and paintings by Poussin, Cigoli, Maratta and Mengs – and by the historian and antiquary Sir Richard Colt Hoare. In the shadow of the great Palladian house and park [both NT] are Stourton House Flower Gardens.

Right: Pastel portrait of Anne, first wife of Sir Richard Hoare (1735–87), with spinning wheel, *c*1756, by Francis Cotes.

Above: *Flight into Egypt*, by Carlo Maratta.

Left: The splendid pedimented east front to Stourhead, which was designed by Colen Campbell, 1721–5 and based on a villa by Palladio. Four great stone basins flank the entrance, with eagles perching on them – the Hoare family emblem. The portico was part of the original design but only built in 1738.

Centre left: View across the lake to the Pantheon, 1753.

Bottom left: A 17th-century German jewelled and silver-gilt double-headed eagle centrepiece in the Little Dining Room. Made as an Imperial symbol, it was, conveniently, also the heraldic emblem of the Hoares.

Bottom centre: The Convent in the Wood, with its three turrets above a thatched stone cottage.

Top right: The view across the lake to Henry Flitcroft's 'Temple of the Sun', 1767.

Bottom right: The Bristol High Cross, dating from 1373, and placed at Stourhead in 1780. The bottom of it has recently been reopened for the first time since its move.

597

Stow, Lincs 694 E3, This large village boasts St Mary's Church, one of the best early parish churches in England. The nave and the crossing with its narrow transepts are a mixture of late Saxon and early Norman work, all from the 11th century; the complicated history of building and rebuilding can be read in the stonework of the walls. The chancel is a very grand example of Norman church architecture, accurately restored to its original glory in the 1850s.

Stow-on-the-Wold, Gloucs 690 C3, Once an important staging post for coach travellers which possessed no less than 27 inns. The enormous Market Place was used for selling sheep, of which as many as 20,000 could be sold at a single fair.

Stow St Mary
Top left: The early Norman nave and crossing tower.
Top centre: The impressive interior with vaulted ceiling and small Norman windows.

Right: Stowe Landscape Gardens, Palladian Bridge, 1738, probably by Gibbs.

Below centre: Stow-on-the-Wold Church of St Edward, restored in the 1680s and again in the 19th century.

Stowe, Cnwll 688 E5, The house built by John Grenville, Earl of Bath, and completed in 1680, stood in a windswept spot above the cliffs near Kilkhampton. Akin to Belton House* in Lincolnshire, it was a two-storey brick house with a hipped roof crowned with a cupola. Its elaborately decorated rooms and staircases were removed to other houses in the area (such as Prideaux Place* and South Molton* Town Hall) when it was demolished in 1739. All that remains on the site are the distinct lay-outs of the different gardens and two brick buildings that may have been the kitchen block and the Real Tennis court.

Stowe Landscape Gardens, Bucks 690 D3, The beautiful and extensive landscape garden at Stowe

is one of the great creations of the 18th century [NT]. It was fashioned by the Temple-Grenvilles, one of the richest and most powerful Whig families. Three successive generations commissioned some of the most important architects and landscape designers of the day, and the design and evolution illustrate the move away from formal gardens following the pattern of Versailles to the artfully naturalistic landscape of Capability Brown. It is the most important landscape garden in the country, and its influence has spread across the globe as far as Russia and America.

(There is still a horse fair held here twice a year.) The animals would be funnelled into the square along the narrow alleys or 'tunes' around it. Many of them were of the famous and productive breed of 'Cotswold Lions'. Interesting breeds can be seen at the Cotswold Farm Park nearby at Guiting Power. Stow's church of St Edward, built in various periods, was used as a prison by Oliver Cromwell to hold a thousand Royalists after the nearby Battle of Stow in 1646.

Stowe Landscape Gardens
Centre right: The Gothic Temple by Gibbs, 1741–8, built on a triangular plan.
Bottom right: The extensive south front by Thomas Pitt, Lord Camelford, 1771–9.

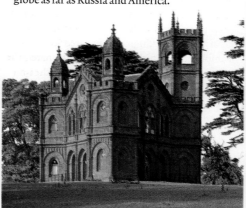

The history of the garden begins with the 3rd Baronet, Sir Richard Temple, who constructed a new house on the present site, complemented by formal gardens of terraces and avenues, the central axis aligned to the spire of Buckingham parish church. His son, the 1st Viscount Cobham, employed the leading garden designer of the time, Charles Bridgeman. He worked in the area to the west of the house where Vanbrugh's Rotunda now stands. It is in Bridgeman's designs that we see the first evidence of a move away from rigid formality. The basic structure remained geometrical, but the garden was surrounded by a ha-ha, blurring the distinction between the man-made garden and the wider landscape. The formal elements were softened in the 1740s and 1750s.

By the 1730s William Kent and James Gibbs were also working at Stowe. Their work survives largely intact to the east of the house: a classical landscape with allegorical structures reflecting the political, historical, literary and philosophic allegiances of Lord Cobham. The Elysian Fields run either side of the stream; here can be found the Temple of Ancient Virtue and the Temple of British Worthies, including busts of Shakespeare, Drake and Milton. Hawkwell Meadow was designed as a *ferme ornée*, the delightful Gothic Temple by James Gibbs, dedicated to 'the Liberty of our Ancestors', sits at the top of the hill. The Grecian Valley is a more naturalistic landscape with belts of trees. It is likely that Capability Brown had a hand in this – the style was to become his trademark.

After Cobham's death in 1749 his nephew, Earl Temple, continued the work on the garden removing the formal elements, naturalizing the Octagon Lake and main avenue and erecting new structures. In turn Earl Temple's nephew, the Marquess of Buckingham, inherited Stowe and completed the finishing touches. Fortunately the garden remained virtually unaltered in the 19th century and, together with the house, was acquired by the public school after World War I. When much of the landscape was passed to the National Trust in 1989, it embarked on a massive restoration programme. The old 17th-century house, which had been extended earlier in the century, was redesigned by Earl Temple. He commissioned designs for the south front from Borra and Blondel, but it was the design by Robert Adam that formed the basis for Thomas Pitt, Lord Camelford's executed scheme. It is a stunning centrepiece stretching across the main vista, a central block linked by low wings terminated by pavilions. Inside are beautiful neoclassical interiors, including the Marble Saloon of 1775–88.

Strata Florida (Ystrad Fflur), Cerdgn 692 E5, The Cistercian abbey was founded by Rhys ap Gruffudd of Dinefwr, the 'Lord Rhys', in 1164. The remarkably well-preserved west doorway is the

Top right: Strata Florida, stone carving of a griffin.

Bottom right: Stratfield Saye, given to the Duke of Wellington c1630, after the Battle of Waterloo. His favourite horse, Copenhagen, is buried in the grounds. The bronze group of the horse and dragon in front of the house was commissioned from Matthew Cotes Wyatt by George IV as a St George and the Dragon, but the king died before the rider was cast. It was bought as it is from the sculptor's son for Apsley House* in 1865, and only brought down here in 1950.

principal structure to survive. Llywelyn ap Iorwerth (Llywelyn the Great) acknowledged the abbey's national significance by making it the meeting place in 1238 of all the princes of Wales to swear allegiance to his son and heir, Dafydd. Dafydd ap Gwilym (fl. 1320–70), the greatest of all Welsh medieval poets, is buried here.

Stratfield Mortimer, Berks, The church of St John (1882) has a reredos painting of Christ at Emmaus by Nathaniel Westlake. *See* **Stratfield Saye* 690 D5.**

Stratfield Saye, Hants 690 D5, The 17th- to 19th-century house was bought by the government and presented to the Duke of Wellington after the battle of Waterloo; it contains some fine relics of the Iron Duke – who is commemorated by a statue on a tall column – and much of Napoleon's library.

Stratford-upon-Avon

Stratford-upon-Avon, Warwks 694 C7, Stratford is principally visited because it was the birthplace of Shakespeare (1564–1616). Although he seems to have escaped from Warwickshire – and his wife and children – to London in a company of travelling players after he was prosecuted for poaching Sir Thomas Lucy's deer at Charlecote Park*, he returned to Stratford in 1597, purchasing the house known as New Place for £60, and lived there from 1610 until his death.

Anne Hathaway's Cottage: Situated a mile (1.6km) west of Stratford at Shottery, the thatched cottage is a substantial building with 16th- and 17th-century additions. The main room was formerly an open hall, and contains an inglenook fireplace. The whole house is fitted out with 17th-century furniture, mostly belonging to the Hathaway family, but its association with Shakespeare is far more important to visitors. Anne Hathaway married Shakespeare in 1582, although she was abandoned soon after when he fled to London. Its situation, which was formerly on the fringes of the Forest of Arden, has been thought to have inspired Celia's home in *As You Like It*. The cottage is owned by the Shakespeare Birthplace Trust, and has a pretty garden.

Hall's Croft: A pleasant half-timbered house, is another property of the Shakespeare Birthplace Trust; it was lived in by Shakespeare's daughter Susanna and her husband John Hall.

Harvard House: Stratford's busy high street contains many 17th-century buildings. Two fires, in 1594 and 1595, meant that many houses were rebuilt shortly afterwards, and the best is Harvard House. Very narrow and very ornate, it is a carver's confection dated 1596. Its builder, a butcher named Thomas Rogers, had a grandson named John Harvard who was one of the founders of Harvard University, and the house is owned by the Harvard Memorial Trust.

Holy Trinity: No visit is complete without walking along the river from the theatres towards the oldest part of town and the church, a spacious, mainly Perpendicular structure. Gerard Johnson's alabaster figure of Shakespeare, dating from his death in 1616, shows him pretentiously adopting the pose and Latin inscription of a scholar. The parish register for 1616 records the death of 'Will. Shakespeare gent.' on 25 April.

Mary Arden's House: Another of the Birthplace Trust's properties at Wilmcote, 3 miles (4.8km) out of town: a Tudor farmstead where Shakespeare's mother once lived. Its outbuildings contain a display of historic farming tools.

New Place: The Shakespeare Memorial Gardens, consisting of the Knott Garden and Great Garden, mark the site of William's own house, New Place. It was demolished in 1759, reputedly because its owner could no longer bear the stream of pilgrims. (He had previously taken the step of cutting down a mulberry tree which Shakespeare was supposed to have planted in an effort to stem the tide.) Shakespeare retired to New Place in old age and died here. The gardens are entered today through the neighbouring Nash's House, once lived in by his grand-daughter Elizabeth and her husband Thomas Nash.

Royal Shakespeare Theatre: The cult of Shakespeare did not develop until the later 18th century, and there was probably no official theatre at all in Stratford in his own time beyond inn courtyards. The theatre that now looms over the Avon won a competition to replace the one burnt down in 1926. Elisabeth Scott was the designer, making it the first important public building in the country to be designed by a woman. In a spare brick design with Art Deco echoes, it was thought locally to be very avant-garde in 1932. The burnt theatre that it replaced had been built in 1879. It still exists, remodelled, as the 'Swan' auditorium, a smaller theatre-in-the-round at the back of the Main House. It gives the more intimate experience of round Elizabethan theatres like the now-reconstructed Globe in London. More experimental plays are put on at a third theatre called 'The Other Place.'

Shakespeare's Birthplace: A half-timbered building, heavily restored, in which Shakespeare's father lived and worked. He was a glover or wool-merchant, and William may well have been born here. The building's frame is constructed from Forest of Arden oak, filled in with wattle and daub. It is entered today from the adjacent modern visitor centre. One of the upper rooms, traditionally where Shakespeare was born, contains a window signed by such well-known tourists as Sir Walter Scott, Thomas Carlyle and Henry Irving.

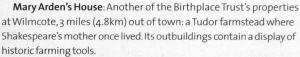

Street, Somset 689 H4, Much of the town was given over to Clark's shoe manufacture. This goes on, though on a much reduced scale, and part of the old shoe factory has been turned into an attractive 'shopping village'. The church of Holy Trinity has a 14th-century tower, and a chancel of about 1330, derived architecturally from the Lady Chapel of Wells* Cathedral.

Strelley, Notts 694 D4, Next to Strelley Hall stands the medieval church of All Saints. The chancel was endowed in the mid-14th century by Samson de Strelley. He and his wife (d. 1405) are buried in a splendid alabaster tomb in the centre of the chancel, and there are other monuments of the Strelley family in the form of floor slabs and wall monuments. The chancel is divided from the nave by the best rood screen in Nottinghamshire.

Studland, Dorset 690 C8, A little seaside village 5 miles (8km) south of Poole*, on a sheltered bay above Swanage*. The surrounding land, dotted with round barrows, reveals its history of ancient occupation, and the unspoiled heathland and countryside is a haven for rare birds. The church is a fine Norman survival of the 11th and 12th centuries, with heavy arches.

Studley Royal, N York, John Aislabie, MP for Ripon* and Chancellor of the Exchequer, was a prominent figure in the South Sea Company when its Bubble dramatically burst in 1720, and he was dismissed from Parliament in 1721. Retiring in disgrace to the local seat he had inherited from his mother, he devoted himself for the rest of his life to creating a

Above: Studland, Old Harry Rocks jut into Poole Bay.

Below: Studley Royal, the Moon Pond with the statue of Neptune and the Temple of Piety.

spectacular water garden, a project he had begun in 1718. Inspired by formal French gardens, he created axes along vistas of water, but his design was innovative in utilizing a natural feature, the River Skell, to make a canal. Blending water and greenery harmoniously but in contrasting forms – horizontal ponds and lawns, vertical cascades, trees and hedges – he 'painted' kinetic pictures. The landscape is dotted with temples, including a Banqueting House by Colen Campbell, a Gothic temple and the Temple of Piety, best seen across the circular moon pond, which is flanked by crescent ponds. A high-level 'surprise view'

Top left: Styal Quarry Bank
Mill. The huge waterwheel is
in working order.

1994. It still retains its wooden machinery, though this is too delicate to operate. **Styal Quarry Bank Mill, Ches 696 F8,** Built in the wooded valley of the River Bollin by Samuel Gregg in 1784. The river drove the massive wheel, and labour was supplied by pauper children, who lived in the apprentice house. The mill was enlarged several times, but the original building still survives. The whole complex has been restored to working order by the National Trust, and is displayed to explain the growth of the textile industry.

Sudbury, Suffk 691 H3, On higher ground above the Stour this wool-turned-silk weaving and market town, whose poverty shocked Daniel Defoe, became the corrupt borough of Eatanswill in Charles Dickens' *The Pickwick Papers* (1837). Of three medieval churches, redundant St Peter's on Market Hill now hosts concerts; ancient St Gregory's, with its remarkable medieval tapering font cover, was rebuilt in 1365 by Simon Sudbury who, when Archbishop of Canterbury, was beheaded in the 1381 Peasants' Revolt (his skull is preserved in the vestry – the teeth long since sold off as holy relics). Gainsborough Street contains

provided a glimpse of the ruins of Fountains Abbey, which was outside his ownership but was acquired by his son William, who also extended the garden downstream into the more romantic Valley of the Seven Bridges. The National Trust's Visitor Centre by Edward Cullinan attempts to use the tower of Fountains Abbey and other features of the estate in a manner complementary to the Aislabies' designs. In the grounds also is St Mary's Church [EH], a magnificent and highly decorative creation by William Burges of the 1870s, and an interesting contrast with his related church at Newby Hall*. *See* **Fountains Abbey* 697 G5.**

Sturminster Marshall, Dorset 690 B7, The White Mill was rebuilt on a site marked as a mill in the Domesday Book. The corn mill [NT] was restored in

Above left: Sudbury Hall, one of the spectacular Grinling Gibbons wood carvings.

Right: Sudbury, Gainsborough's birthplace, painting by Peter Jones, 1991.

Bottom left: Sudbury Hall, begun by George Vernon c1662.

Bottom right: Sudeley Castle. Henry VIII, Ann Boleyn, Lady Jane Grey, Katherine Parr, Elizabeth I and Charles I all stayed there.

which have oriel windows and ornate carving. HE Kendall's Italianate Corn Exchange of 1841 has been brilliantly converted into a skylit library and information centre. There are fine riverside and meadow walks out into Gainsborough country. Always more anonymous than Constable's, downstream in Dedham Vale*, it lies hidden in the woods, fields and churches around Sudbury and Hadleigh, in the cottages and country houses whose owners helped make Gainsborough's name as a portrait painter.

Sudbury Hall, Derbys 694 C4, A comfortable red-brick house whose rooms have some of the richest Charles II decoration in England [NT]. Building started in about 1662 and was finished by 1700. The exterior is an odd mixture of Jacobean features (mullioned windows and a two-storey porch) with the tall roof typical of the post-Civil War period. The rooms follow the familiar Jacobean arrangement of Great Hall, several parlours and first-floor Long Gallery, but the plasterwork by Bradbury and Pettifer and woodcarving by Edward Pierce (with an overmantel and drawing room panelling by Grinling Gibbons) are exceptional.

Sudeley Castle, Gloucs, The overwhelming impression given at Sudeley Castle is of a suave 1930s version of Elizabethan grandeur. Built for JH Dent-Brocklehurst, the house is surrounded by recent gardens. The first buildings on the site date

back to the early to mid-15th century, when Ralph Boteler, Baron Sudeley, remodelled a medieval castle. He was forced to give it up to the Crown, and it was used both by Henry VIII and – in her childhood – by Elizabeth I. The Banqueting Hall, Tithe Barn and Portmore Tower do survive from Boteler's time, beneath later additions. Dolls, toys and needlework are all features of its collections today; among the best known items are the 18th-century bedhangings formerly belonging to Marie Antoinette. *See* **Winchcombe* 690 C3.**

Sulgrave Manor, Nhants 690 D3, The home of George Washington's ancestors is a pleasant 17th-century wool-stapler's manor house with a wing added in the early 18th century. Sir Reginald Blomfield reconstructed a large part of the central block in 1921.

the painter's birthplace, now a museum and gallery in his honour. The imposing red-brick façade was added by his father, who also admired the mulberry tree in the walled garden. Gainsborough's life-size bronze statue of 1913 stands before St Peter's Church. Among timber-framed houses, two 15th-century survivals are of special note: the Old Moot Hall and the merchant's house, Salters Hall, down by the river,

Sudeley Castle
Top left: Jan Steen's *Saying Grace before the Meal*, 1660.
Centre left: Flower painting by Jean-Baptiste Monnoyer.
Centre right: Sudeley Castle, *Landscape with the Rape of Europa,* by Claude Lorraine.

Top left: Sunderland, the Wearmouth Bridge linking the city with the older settlement of Monkwearmouth.

Below centre: Sutton Park, the south front, a good example of Georgian architecture.

Bottom: Sutton Scarsdale Hall, the shell of a baroque mansion designed by Francis Smith in 1724.

Sulhamstead, Berks 690 D5, Lutyens extended the existing timber-framed cottage at Folly Farm on two occasions: initially in 1906 in a classical style, and again in 1912, for new owners, in an early Arts and Crafts manner. The garden is by Gertrude Jekyll.

Sunderland, T & W 697 H2, Situated at the mouth of the Wear, once a major shipbuilding and glass-manufacturing town, in 1992 elevated to the status of city. The old town centre was based around Holy Trinity Church, designed in 1718 by William Etty of York. Prosperity resulting from the Industrial Revolution resulted in a westward expansion with some good terraces and squares in late Georgian style, vestiges of which remain (the neo-Greek John Street, for example). At the corner of Bridge Street and Fawcett Street is a Moorish-style extravaganza, the former Elephant Tea House in red and white terracotta, with elephants in the roof gablets, the projecting corner roof oriel attributing it to 'Doulton & Co.' and 'Henry Hooper Builder', with the date 1873. The original 19th-century Winter Gardens were destroyed by enemy action in 1941, and not replaced until 2000–1, with an impressive modern glazed structure, circular and domed, linked to the Museum and Art Gallery. The glazing is significant, for Sunderland claims to be the 'Living Home of Glass'. Its National Glass Centre is an imaginative building where one can walk on the glass roof. The descent down the ramp from the car park level to the entrance offers a view through to the Wear, along which coal was brought from Newcastle-upon-Tyne*. Sunderland was the first place to use coal for glass-making, which began here in the 1690s with bottles and crown window glass, moving on in the 19th century to elaborate decorative artefacts, often resembling cut glass. Manufacture had peaked by 1877; Pyrex is the town's best-known 20th-century product. The exhibition displays most effectively the wide range of products that incorporate glass, such as microscopes, endoscopes, mirrors and cat's eyes. Twin industrial chimney stacks rising from the famous glass roof reflect the building's purpose, which is not only manufacturing: there are kilns for craftsworkers too. Monkwearmouth lies across the river from Sunderland city centre. The y are linked by the Wearmouth Bridge (1796), an early triumph of cast-iron bridge construction, replaced in 1929 by the present bridge. Monkwearmouth Church was founded in AD 674 by Benedict Biscop, and is a sister monastery to that at Jarrow*. The industrial housing that surrounded the little church in the 19th century has been replaced by the various modern buildings of Sunderland University. The former Monkwearmouth Station of 1848, now a transport museum, is of a highly intellectual Greek Ionic design, with a handsome portico. Further north is Roker, where St Andrew's Church (1906–7) is particularly impressive internally, the parabolic stone arches making it look appropriately like the inside of an upturned ship. To the west, in a somewhat unprepossessing setting, is the square keep of Hylton Castle, built c1400.

Sutton Park
Above: The Drawing Room.
Left: The Library. The interiors were redecorated by John Fowler for Mrs Nancy Sheffield, with chimneypieces from Normanby*.

Bottom: Swaffham's spacious Market Place, with its handsome domed Market Cross surrounded by prosperous Georgian townhouses.

South of Sunderland itself is the former colliery village of Ryhope, where Sunderland and South Shields Water Company's Pumping Station is an impressive complex of 1866–70. Some of the ornate brick buildings, which have stone dressings and are set in landscaped grounds, have Dutch gables and very tall chimneys. The original engines and 1908 boilers are regularly steamed.

Sunningwell, Oxon 690 D4, The church of St Leonard has a delightful seven-sided west porch. It was reputedly given to the church by the Bishop Jewel of Salisbury, who was rector here c1551. The beautifully leaded east window depicts the Adoration of the Shepherds and the Magi; it was designed by JP Seddon, who restored the church in 1877 and was a friend of William Morris and the Pre-Raphaelites.

Sutton at Hone, Kent 691 G5, A rare survival, a 'commandery' of the Knights Hospitallers of St John of Jerusalem, going back to the 13th century. It was adapted as a Georgian house in the 18th century.

Sutton Courtenay, Oxon, A large, pleasant village with some fine medieval domestic buildings. Most interesting is the Norman Hall, a rare surviving manor house of c1190–1200. To the south is another manor house incorporating the 13th-century hall range of the Courtenays amid 15th- and 17th-century additions. Lastly, there is the abbey, not what the name suggests but in fact a

14th-century grange of Abingdon Abbey with a later west front. *See* **Long Wittenham* 690 D4.**

Sutton Hoo, Suffk 691 J3, A hillside above the Deben is contoured with burial mounds, Suffolk's diminutive pyramids. In 1939 one yielded a treasure ship, almost certainly of Raedwald, pagan king of the East Angles, who died in AD 625 and whose Wuffinga dynasty set up their Great Hall in what is now Rendlesham Forest. The astonishing Sutton Hoo treasure, containing magnificent jewellery, silverware and weapons, including the famous warrior helmet, remains Europe's greatest Saxon find. Much of the hoard, kept for years in the British Museum, is now back in Suffolk in a major new on-site interpretation centre [NT].

Sutton Park, N York 697 H5, A mid-18th century Georgian brick house with surprisingly rich plasterwork by Cortese.

Sutton Scarsdale, Derbys 694 D3, A dramatic ruin facing a slope that was once an open-cast coal mine. The remaining shell is mostly the house built in the 1720s for the Earl of Scarsdale [EH]. Shreds of decoration cling to the walls, but some of the rooms were exported to the Philadelphia Museum of Fine Art in the United States.

Swaffham, Norfk 695 H5, An aristocratic retreat for the local gentry in the 18th century, complete with assembly rooms and theatre patronized by Lady Hamilton. The large triangular Market Place is overlooked by elegant brick and knapped flint town houses, notably Montpelier House and Hammond's School House. Symbol of its former prosperity and patronage is the elegant Palladian Market Cross, a domed rotunda surmounted by Ceres and erected by the Earl of Orford in 1793. The town's museum has an exhibition devoted to local boy Howard Carter, who discovered Tutankhamun's tomb, but the town is best known for its medieval legend. Lured to London by a dream, the Pedlar of Swaffham met a stranger who told him to return home, where he struck gold

enough in his garden to build the north aisle of Swaffham's grand church (note too the magnificent double hammerbeam roof, held aloft by 192 angels). The pedlar and his dog are portayed on the prayer desk in the chancel.

Swalcliffe, Oxon 690 D3, Swalcliffe Barn is a handsome, 15th-century half-cruck tithe barn. It now houses agricultural and trade vehicles. The church contains 14th-century wall paintings, including one of Saint Michael holding his scales.

Swallowfield Park, Berks 690 E5, An H-plan house rebuilt in 1689–91 by William Talman for the 2nd Earl of Clarendon, and substantially remodelled again in 1820. John Evelyn wrote that the gardens were 'as elegant as 'tis possible to make a flat by art and industrie and no mean expense'. Note especially the rich, re-erected doorway by Talman.

Swanage, Dorset 690 C8, This coastal town, with its long high street, prospered from its stone-exporting during the 19th century, but gradually developed into a resort town. Curiously, the 1883 Town Hall was given the 1660s façade of the Mercers' Hall in London, which had been salvaged by George Burt, a local contractor. Its wondrous riot of carving is by John Young, working for Edward Jarman and John Oliver. Burt believed that the holiday public coming to Swanage needed instruction, and he gave nearby Durlston Castle (c1890) to the town: its walls reveal many geographical facts about the locality, placed there by George Burt, its owner.

Swansea, Swans 689 F3, Most of the town centre was rebuilt after merciless air bombardment in 1941, and has since suffered from a great deal of civic indecision, with piecemeal development and improvements rather than a comprehensive planning strategy. The area around the mainline station has been woefully abandoned in favour of the Maritime Quarter, where enterprising development has seen the restoration of some early 19th-century buildings in recent years, notably the Old Guildhall in Somerset Place. In 1994 it became

Swallowfield Park
Top: The entrance front, with porte-cochère added in 1820.
Above: The Drawing Room.

Bottom right: Swinbrook church, one of the striking monuments to the Fettiplace family, memorably described by Sir John Betjeman as looking like so many salmon, laid out on a fishmonger's slab.

Ty Llen, the National Literature Centre for Wales, with lecture rooms, a bookshop café and an exhibition of Dylan Thomas's Swansea life. A close neighbour in the much-restored Cambrian Place is the handsome Greek Revival building designed in 1839 to house the Royal Institution of South Wales, now Swansea's official museum.

The town's art gallery, the **Glynn Vivian,** in Alexandra Road – one of the most dignified of its thoroughfares – has a comprehensive collection of the works of the two Swansea artists, Ceri Richards and the lesser-known Evan Walters, whose portrait *The Cockle Woman* is most memorable. Cockle women travel every week from Penclawdd in North Gower to their stalls in Swansea's covered market, which heaves with humorous exchange and banter, the true spirit of the town.

Brangwyn Hall, a great municipal all-purpose space occupying a third of the Civic Centre, is so named because of its wall-paintings by Frank Brangwyn (1867–1956). The murals were originally commissioned to decorate the Royal Gallery of the House of the Lords as a War Memorial to the peers who had lost their lives in battle; they were rejected, however, and were subsequently offered by the artist to Swansea's new Guildhall of the mid-1930s. They have since be become known as the British Empire Panels. They create a powerful setting for the events that are held here, particularly the concerts of international stature that form part of the Swansea Festival of Music (one of the first music festivals to have been established after World War II).

Swarkeston Tower, Derbys 694 D4, A Jacobean tower in a meadow by the River Trent, doubtless connected with the long-demolished mansion of the Harpur family. The tower stands near an enclosure known as the Cuttle; both may have been used for outdoor sports.

and the Technical College (1956–8) by Charles Pike and Partners. The long railway station is of 1841.

Swinton Park, N Yorks 697 G5, A Georgian country mansion, belonging to the Danby family, transformed into a castellated gothic castle by architects James Wyatt and John Foss of Richmond. It has recently been converted into a country house hotel by members of the Cunliffe-Lister family, whose seat it became in the 19th century. Among the interesting parkland features is the Druid's Temple, a miniature Stonehenge folly constructed *c*1820, a time of economic depression, to create work for William Danby's labourers.

Sycharth, Powys 693 F3, A mound is all that remains of Owain Glyndwr's principal residence near Llansilin, where his renowned hospitality was celebrated by the bards.

Swindon, the Great Western Railway Museum
Top left: One of the locomotives, '2516', still recalling the days of steam.
Left: A reconstructed railway-worker's sitting room.

Symonds Yat
Right: The Wye Gorge near Symonds Yat precipice.
Bottom right: The maze in Jubilee Park in the village of Symonds Yat.

Sweetheart Abbey, *see* **New Abbey*.**

Swimbridge, Devon 689 F5, Parson Jack Russell (of terrier fame) was the incumbent here from 1833 until his death in 1881, and his church of St James has one of the most lavish interiors in Devon. Of note are the elaborate screen, some 44 feet (13.4m) long, and the unusual 18th-century font set in a cupboard with a folding cover. Russell and his wife (a local heiress) lived at Dennington Hill.

Swinbrook, Oxon 690 C4, This small village was the home of the Fettiplace family until the early 19th century. In the church are two splendid family monuments. The earlier is of *c*1613 and the later dates from *c*1686, but both follow the same design with near-identical reclining effigies arranged bunk-fashion against the wall. Nancy Mitford and her family are buried in the churchyard.

Swindon, Wilts 690 C5, The great locomotive workshops of this old railway town are now, alas, silent and partly transformed into a 'shopping village'. However, it is still possible to see historic locomotives made here, along with other railway memorabilia, in the Great Western Railway Museum in Faringdon Road. The Art Gallery contains paintings by Graham Sutherland, Ben Nicholson and others. Swindon has the usual combination of 19th-century and later buildings, characterized by the Town Hall in Market Square (a Grecian affair of 1853 with a tower added ten years later), the parish church of St Mark (1843),

Symonds Yat, Herefs 693 G6, The 500-foot (150m) high promontory was one of the picturesque highlights of 18th-century tours of the Welsh Borders (the tourists' steamboats made their way along the Wye as a cheaper alternative to the Italian Lakes). The river's course, largely following the division between England and Wales, is lined by the castles of the Marcher barons. Symonds Yat is a natural fortress, suffering from some erosion, but surrounded by pleasant walks through the woody gorge.

Tabley House, Ches 693 H2, A Palladian mansion designed by John Carr of York for the Leicester family (later the Lords de Tabley), built in 1761–7 to replace Tabley Old Hall, which stood on an island in the lake. It is a handsome red-brick building with fine rooms containing furniture by Gillow and Chippendale. The 17th-century chapel was rebuilt on a new site in 1927, but its Oxbridge-like interior was carefully reinstated.

Tain, Highld 701 H4, This small town on the south shore of Dornoch* Firth is Scotland's oldest royal burgh. Its patron is St Duthus (c1000–65), Bishop of Ross, who was born in the town and whose relics were returned here in 1253. The first two chapels built for pilgrims are now in ruins, but St Duthus Church, built c1360 and now restored, has some beautiful stained-glass windows and a pulpit that was a gift from the Earl of Moray, Regent of Scotland, in the 16th century. Tain Through Time, the museum of local history, is situated near the elegant toll booth (1707). Another local attraction is the Glenmorangie Distillery.

Talley (Tal-y-Llychau), Carmth 692 D6, A peaceful village dominated by the stark remains of the abbey. Belonging to the austere order of the Premonstratensian Canons, the abbey was founded in the 12th century by Rhys ap Gruffudd, 'The Lord Rhys' (1132–97) of Dinefwr*, and is the only one of its kind in Wales. The two lakes, skirted by a road and encircled by rounded hills, were a life-line to an order that was denied meat. In the churchyard are the imposing graves of the Williams-Drummond family of Edwinsford

Top right: Taplow Court. The hall pre-dates William Burn's work, executed c1830. The architect is not known but may have been Thomas Hopper.

Below: Tantallon Castle and Bass Rock, by Alexander Nasmyth, 1816, and (bottom) a photograph of the same view.

(Rhydodyn), a house much praised by the bards. It was a boarding school during World War II, and after that its main rooms, with their fine plaster ceilings, were used for cultivating mushrooms. It is now a forlorn backcloth to a fishing syndicate.

Tantallon Castle, E Loth 699 H4, The ruins of this red sandstone castle stand on a rocky promontory opposite Bass Rock. It was built in 1375 by the Earl of Douglas and reinforced in the 16th century to withstand artillery attacks. The only landward access was defended by a double moat and a 50-foot (15m) rampart wall. It was besieged many

times by the English before finally being destroyed by Cromwell's troops in 1651, after 12 days of bombardment.

Tapeley Court, Devon 688 E5, The home of the Christies of Glyndebourne enjoys a magnificent position above the River Torridge looking across to Appledore* and the sea. The largely Edwardian house overlooks the beautiful gardens with their Italian terraces, a circular grotto, an ice house and a large walled kitchen garden.

Taplow Court, Berks 690 E5, The exterior of the much remodelled Taplow Court is largely the work of William Burn, carried out between 1855 and 1860. The house boasts a rich hall at its centre, built in the neo-Norman style and supposedly modelled on Kirkwall Cathedral, Orkney*. Taplow Court became well known in the early 1900s as its owners, Lord and Lady Desborough, entertained an elite group known as 'The Souls' here. The house is set high above the Thames and offers beautiful views and gardens. Southwest of Taplow Court, in the old churchyard, is a fascinating and important Anglo-Saxon burial mound, which was opened in 1883. The grave finds can be seen in the British Museum*. The old church was demolished in 1828 and rebuilt on a new site in Boundary Road. It contains a brass to Nichole de Aumberdere of c1350, thought to be the earliest surviving civilian example in England. The fine Maidenhead Bridge, by Sir Robert Taylor, was built in 1772–7.

Tarbert, Ag & B 698 C4, This little fishing port and marina stands on East Loch Tarbert, at the northern end of Kintyre. Its name, derived from *an tairbeart*, meaning 'isthmus' in Gaelic, is associated with the memory of the Norse king, Magnus Barfor (or Barelegs). Legend has it that in 1098, when he was trying to persuade the king of Scotland to cede all the islands he could circumnavigate, Magnus Barfor had a galley hauled across the isthmus between East and West Loch Tarbert in order to lay claim to Kintyre. Tarbert, which has always been a herring fishing port, has five processing factories. The

Top left: Taplow Court, entrance front as remodelled by Burn, with chimneys and gables piercing the skyline, and a Coade stone statue of George III in front.

Top right: Tattershall Castle, Ralph Cromwell's great brick keep of c1440.

Bottom: Tarbert, on the shores of East Loch Tarbert.

photographs and archeological remains on display in the An Tairbeart Heritage Centre trace the everyday life of this small community over the centuries. The Castle, whose ruins dominate the port, was built by Alexander II or his son Alexander III in the 13th century, and refurbished by Robert Bruce in 1325. In 1494 James IV built the keep (complete with dungeon) which faced east so that its cannons were aimed at the entrance to the port. The Earl of Argyll was appointed hereditary

keeper in 1505. After serving as the headquarters of the pirate Alan-nan-Sop Maclean, the castle fell into the hands of Cromwell's troops in 1652. The inhabitants are said to have taken advantage of the absence of the garrison, which had gone to gather nuts, to regain possession.

Tattershall Castle, Lincs 695 F3, The great red-brick tower keep [NT] was built by Ralph Cromwell, Treasurer of England between 1430 and 1450, and contained the state rooms that he added to an earlier castle. Only the keep and a small gatehouse survive, surrounded by a water-filled moat. Cromwell also paid for the building of the magnificent Church of the Holy Trinity, which stands next to the castle, as well as some almshouses and a college for priests.

Tatton Park, Ches 696 F8, Owned until 1958 by the Egertons, a branch of the family headed by the earls and dukes of Bridgwater, who became extremely wealthy in the mid-18th century and spent a great deal of money on building and furnishing the present house [NT]. Tatton has a calm, elegant stone exterior that yields no clue to the fact that the western half was built in the 1790s by the architect Samuel Wyatt and the eastern half 20 years later by his nephew Lewis Wyatt. The house also incorporates a rococo dining room which was part of an earlier house built in c1760. The entrance hall and staircase in the centre of the house, with an unusual domed vestibule, are perhaps the best spaces, though all the rooms on the ground floor are impressive. The interior is richly decorated and full of fine furniture. The furniture is predominantly of the late-18th and early-19th century and was made for the house by Gillows of Lancaster, the leading furniture-makers of northern England (and later part of Waring and Gillow). It contains an important collection of old masters, including Chardin's *La Gouvernante*, and three versions of BW Leader's *Manchester Ship Canal*. Outside stretch 60 acres (25ha) of pleasure gardens, including an orangery that still grows oranges and lemons, a fernery and a Japanese garden. There is also a 1,000-acre (400ha) deer park.

Tatton Park
Top left: Samuel Wyatt's portico of the 1780s.
Top right: One of Lewis Wyatt's rich Regency interiors.

Left and below left: Taunton, church of St Mary Magdalene, stained glass and roof details.

Bottom: Tavistock. The medieval abbey gatehouse lies to the right of the early 19th-century civic buildings in the heart of the town.

Taunton, Somset 689 G5, The county town of Somerset, with Georgian architecture in abundance. One of the most interesting buildings, in Fore Street in the town centre, is the Elizabethan town house of the Portman family (1578). Nearby is the Market House (1770–2), which has a pediment over a five-bay front. The church of St Mary Magdalene is a remodelling of the 15th-century church by Benjamin Ferrey and Sir George Gilbert Scott (1862), and has an imposing Perpendicular tower of red Quantock sandstone. The local museum at Taunton Castle has collections from the whole county.

Tavistock, Devon 688 E6, At one end of the main street is a statue of Sir Francis Drake, the famous son of the town, and at the other is a statue (1864) of the 7th Duke of Bedford, whose family had accrued great wealth from the area since the Dissolution of the powerful Tavistock Abbey in 1539. From the Tudor-style 19th-century civic buildings in the centre of the town (some by John Foulston of Plymouth*) to the modest terraces of miners' houses in various suburbs, the influence of the Bedfords is obviously strong. Their wealth came from the copper mines along the Tamar near heir home at Endsleigh Cottage*.

Tawstock, Devon 689 F5, Set high above the river, the large castellated house of the Bourchiers was rebuilt after a fire in 1787, to designs by Sir John Soane. It is now a school. Set not far from the house is the magnificent church of St Peter,

with its abundance of elaborate tombs and monuments to the Bourchiers, earls of Bath; the Wreys, their successors at Tawstock; and members of other local families. The memorials are among the finest in the county, dating from the 14th to the 19th centuries.

Teigh, Rutlnd 694 E5, The delightful small church of Holy Trinity was rebuilt in 1782 under the direction of George Richardson for the Earl of Harborough. Richardson kept the medieval tower and added to it a small Georgian Gothic box. The interior has college-style pews, and a highly unusual west end with reading desks and a central pulpit in front of a painted mock window. There is also an elegant small font designed to be attached to the communion rail.

Teignmouth, Devon 689 G6, The town's many villas and terraced houses, whose visitors included Fanny Burney and John Keats, are the result of the town's prosperity in the later 18th and early 19th century. The largest terrace, Den Crescent, with its central Assembly Rooms, was laid out overlooking the sea to the front, and the estuary of the Teign to the rear. A handsome house set back from Teign Street was the home of the marine artist Thomas Luny for many years. The quays at the mouth of

Top right: Teignmouth, the sheltered waters of the estuary of the River Teign.

Temple Newsam
Centre left: Gothick Room.
Centre: Long Gallery.
Bottom: The 17th-century exterior.

the Teign were built to export local products; granite from Dartmoor* (used for the building of London Bridge) and ball clay from Bovey Tracey*, used in pottery manufacture. The octagonal church of St James (1817–21) lies to the north of the railway station and is not far from Bitton House (now council offices), set in its own small park with an orangery of 1821.

Temple Newsam, W Yorks 697 H6, Set in parkland only 4 miles (6.4km) east of Leeds* city centre, the house contains an outstanding museum of English decorative art, furniture and painting, probably the best in the country after the Victoria & Albert* in London. The building, forming three sides of a large courtyard, is in brick, and mainly of the early 17th century, but one range is a century earlier and survives from the house where Henry, Lord Darnley, the second husband of Mary Queen of Scots, was born in 1545. Later internal alterations include an impressive Georgian remodelling of the Long Gallery by the architect Daniel Garrett in 1738–45, with magnificent Italianate plasterwork, and handsome fireplaces and door-cases in the style of William Kent. Much of the original furniture is on display.

Tenby
Top left: The late-15th-century Tudor Merchant's House.
Bottom: Regency buildings climbing down to the harbour, with Castle Hill in the background.

Centre right: Tenterden, Smallhythe, an early 16th-century half-timbered house, where the actress Ellen Terry lived from 1899 to 1928.

St Catherine's Fort, built in the 1860s to guard the approaches to Milford Haven.

The handsome parish church of St Mary's indicates the medieval prosperity of the town, and reflects the importance of figures of national significance as well as those of a more local curiosity. The Tudor **Merchant's House** [NT] of the late 15th century, the oldest surviving evidence of the town's domestic architecture, conveys the prestigious social standing of its owner. Fresco-paintings, contemporary with the building but not uncovered until the 2000s, have survived remarkably well. Tenby is noted for its attractive early-19th-century buildings, many of them overlooking the harbour. They were the result of the attempt of Sir William Paxton, aided by his architect SP Cockerell, to convert the town into a fashionable resort. The expansive north and south beaches are to this day enormous attractions.

Tenby (Dinbych y Pysgod),
Pembks 692 C7, The town's perennial appeal lies in the haphazard layout of its lanes and alleys, as each domestic and commercial development obeyed the contours of coast, hill and walled defences. It was also noted for its impressive 14th-century west gateway, known as the Five Arches, though much of the enceinte was strengthened in the 16th century with the threat of the Spanish Armada. Part of the masonry fortress on Castle Hill has been adapted to accommodate the Town Museum and Art Gallery, displaying the works of Augustus John and his sister, Gwen John, who spent their early years here. On the opposite promontory stands

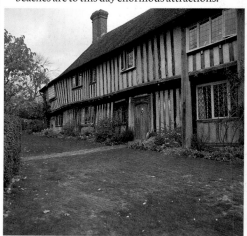

Top left: Tenterden, Smallhythe. The kitchen retains many 16th- and 17th-century features, such as the settle, the big open fireplace and Jacobean chairs.

Top right: Tewkesbury Abbey's massive tower. It survived the Dissolution as a parish church.

Tenterden, Kent 691 H6, An unusual village of considerable character. It consists of one long street with the church near the middle. To the east of the church are the Town Hall of 1790, several half-timbered and jettied houses, Hales Place (with the remains of an Elizabethan garden), and two fine 18th-century houses, East Hill House and Craigthorne House. West of the church the road widens to become a broad expanse of grass and trees. There are more good Georgian homes here: Westwell, dated 1711, is the best. Smallhythe Place [NT], a 16th-century half-timbered house, was the home of Ellen Terry and is now a museum.

Tetbury, Gloucs 690 B4, In 1777 work began on rebuilding the demolished medieval church of St Mary's to a supremely elegant and soaring Gothic design. The high box pews are accessible only from the aisle or from the unusual passages that run around the outside of the church. According to Gloucestershire historian David Verey, entering your pew from the side is like entering a box at the Opera House at Covent Garden*.

Tewkesbury, Gloucs 690 B3, Tewkesbury appears to be full of timbered inns, including the 'Hop Pole' where Mr Pickwick famously warmed his rear and told tales. There are many tempting alleys running down to the Severn and the island of Severn Ham; indeed the town was once an inland port, centred on the waterfront. Landmarks

include the Baptist Meeting House behind the Abbey with 17th-century fittings and the public park known as the Bloody Meadow, site of the Battle of Tewkesbury in 1471, the last battle of the Wars of the Roses. In 1826 the town acquired a cast-iron bridge designed by Thomas Telford. The many large upper windows evident in the town buildings were the result of the 19th-century stocking-makers' need for light. The Abbey's massive tower dominates the town. Inside 14 stout Norman pillars bear down on the nave. The most grotesque feature of the Abbey, in the ambulatory, is the 15th-century carving of a grisly *memento mori*: a decaying corpse being eaten by snakes. The Abbey survived the Dissolution as a parish church. A dramatic restoration was proposed in 1875 by Sir George Gilbert Scott, and aroused the opposition of William Morris. Fired by his objection to this and similar schemes, Morris founded the Society for the Protection of Ancient Buildings.

Thame, Oxon 690 E4, A historic market town with good 15th- to 17th-century buildings and inns. Note the Spread Eagle of *c*1740, which was made famous by John Fothergill's *Innkeeper's Diary* (1931). The large church of St Mary is imposingly set beside the River Thame, a tributary of the Thames. To the west can be seen the interesting medieval Prebendal House with a fine chapel of *c*1250. One mile (1.6km) south is **Thame Park** , an impressive house of *c*1745 by william Smith, son of Francis Smith, which incorporates the important early 16th-century abbot's lodgings of a Cistercian abbey founded here in 1138.

Thaxted, Essex 691 G3, A small medieval wool town in the Chelmer valley, clustered about a grand oversailing Guildhall below a huge Perpendicular church. The timbers of the cutlers' Guildhall were stripped of panelled plasterwork in 1910, creating a trend which spread rapidly (*see* Lavenham*) and has enraged conservationists ever since. Despite this the town is a harmonious mix of brick and plaster lovingly maintained. Two rows of

Bottom: Thaxted, Easton Lodge, home of Edward VII's mistress, the Countess of Warwick, who helped transform Thaxted Church into a centre for Christian socialists.

almshouses beside the churchyard with the 1804 windmill as a backdrop are especially picturesque. Gustav Holst wrote 'The Planets' in a cottage behind the church (now gone) and his 'Carols for Thaxted' are still performed here. Daisy, Countess of Warwick* and mistress of Edward VII, who lived at Easton Lodge, hired Harold Peto to design Italianate and Japanese gardens and, with the help of incumbent Conrad Noel, made the grandest church in Essex a Christian Socialist centre that attracted, among others, her friend HG Wells, who moved to Easton Glebe in 1912.

Theale, Berks 690 D5, The church, commissioned in 1820 by Mrs Sophia Sheppard, the sister of the rector Dr Routh, was built by Edward Garbett in the style of Salisbury* Cathedral.

Theobalds Park, Herts 691 F4, Sir William Cecil, Lord Burghley and Lord Treasurer to Elizabeth I, built the original Theobalds here between 1564 and

Above: Thorney Abbey, one of the great Fenland monastic centres.

Below: Thetford, Thomas Paine's gilded statue in King Street, modelled by Sir Charles Wheeler in 1964.

1585. One of the greatest houses of its age, it was visited by Queen Elizabeth 13 times and became a royal palace under James I, but the Parliamentarians were savage in their destruction during the Civil War and only fragments of walling remain, within what is now an enchanting public park off Theobalds Lane. The surviving Theobalds, a mansion of 1763, was recently used as a college, and is now home to Wren's Temple Bar, moved there from London.

Thetford, Norfk 695 H6, The scattered remains of this important medieval town are well worth investigating. A Saxon settlement developed on the south bank of the Little Ouse and grew rapidly to become the sixth largest town in England, with its own mint and 14 pre-conquest churches. Sacked twice by the Danes it became, briefly, the cathedral city of East Anglia in the late 11th century. The Normans left more tangible evidence in the shape of Roger Bigod's massive Castle Hill – only Silbury Hill* in Wiltshire is higher. Sightings of the Virgin Mary and the discovery of holy relics at the Cluniac priory, founded in 1104, confirmed Thetford's importance as a pilgrimage centre. By the 15th century it could boast 22 churches and 6 religious houses. Among the most impressive ruins are the Cluniac gatehouse and prior's lodgings; the nave of St George's Benedictine nunnery, now home to the British Trust for Ornithology; and the 14th-century Dominican friary in Bridge Street on the old cathedral site. After the Dissolution a new seat of learning rose from the ruins of monastic scholarship when Sir Richard Fulmerstone founded the school that still thrives here. For over two centuries the town refused to recognize its most famous pupil, the radical author Thomas Paine, born in White Hart Street. His gilded statue in King Street was paid for by grateful Americans. Of the three medieval churches that survive, St Peter's, or 'The Black Church', distinguished by knapped flintwork, is the most prominent, on the corner of White Hart Street. Nearby are some of the town's best secular buildings: the Bell Hotel, a half-timbered coaching

inn, handsome Georgian King's House incorporating remains of James I's hunting lodge, and the Ancient House, a richly carved 15th-century merchant's house.

The most attractive streets are lined by rows of early 19th-century flint cottages, some distinguished with fragments of carved stone from the town's ecclesiastical ruins. There are tree-lined paths beside the rivers Thet and Little Ouse, where Spring Walk and the Pump House (1818) are reminders of Thetford's short-lived attempt to become a spa. In 1921 Prince Duleep Singh, monarchist antiquarian and son of the Indian Maharaja who enlarged nearby Elveden Hall into an oriental extravaganza, gave the Ancient House to the town as a museum where Victorian pulpware, Paine memorabilia and replicas of the magnificent Roman treasure discovered on Gallows Hill in 1979 are displayed.

Thirlestane Castle, Border 699 H5, In 1672 the Duke of Lauderdale gave William Bruce the task of extending the castle built in 1590 by his grandfather, John Maitland, Lord Chancellor of Scotland. Further extensions were carried out by David Bryce in 1840. The castle boasts some of the finest 17th-century plasterwork ceilings in Scotland in its state apartments. In one wing of the building the Border Country Life Museum traces the rural history of the Borders.

Thompson, Norfk 695 H5, Mercifully ignored by Victorian restorers, the church has an intensely atmospheric interior, originally collegiate, which may explain its outstanding medieval woodwork. Most notable is the beautiful rood screen, c1330, and misericords alongside 17th-century poppy-head bench ends and a double-decker Jacobean pulpit. Thompson Common, grazed by Shetland ponies, is dotted with pingos, shallow ponds left by the last glaciation. Nearby Wayland ('Wailing') Wood, also managed by Norfolk Wildlife Trust, is a remnant of the original oak forest and the setting of 'The Babes in the Wood' legend.

Thoresby Hall, Notts 694 D3, This great house, once the home of the Duke of Kingston, has been rebuilt three times, most recently when the architect Anthony Salvin pulled down the huge Palladian house and replaced it with the present tall and rather pompous Elizabethan-style mansion in 1865–75. After a spell under the ownership of the National Coal Board, it lay empty for most of the 1980s and 1990s. Appropriately the mansion, which always looked like a large Victorian hotel, has now been converted into one.

Thorney, Cambs 695 F5, St Mary and St Botolph incorporates a slit-windowed stump of Thorney Abbey – the Norman nave of an otherwise demolished cathedral-sized building, founded in 657. Before its dissolution, when stones were carted off to build Cambridge*'s Corpus Christi

Top centre: Thirlestane Castle, Border Country Life Museum, where children can dress up in historic costumes.

Top right: Thoresby Hall, the library fireplace with Robin Hood, Little John and the Sherwood Forest* Oak, by a carver from Mansfield*.

Below: Thornton Abbey, the remains of the octagonal chapter house, completed in 1308.

College, it was one of the great Fenland religious houses, alongside Crowland* and Ramsey* abbeys.

Thornham Parva, Suffk 695 J6, Discovered in 1927 in Lord Henniker's stables, the retable (c1300) in this pretty thatched church is one of the great treasures of English gothic art. Made probably for the Dominican priory in Thetford*, it displays workmanship of the highest quality, with the Crucifixion flanked by slim, swaying saints against a gesso-patterned background. Less accomplished but equally rare are the early 14th-century murals depicting scenes from the Life of St Edmund.

Thornton Abbey, Lincs 697 K6, The Augustinian Abbey church and most of the buildings of the monastic community are now ruins or lumps in the ground, but the massive and forbidding gatehouse still survives almost intact [EH]. The largest of all English abbey gatehouses, it looks like a serious work of fortification, despite the religious sculpture on the outside wall. A proportion of the gate was built in the 1360s but owes its present appearance to an enlargement of the 1380s. The walls are partly faced in stone and partly built of red brick, which would originally have been faced with lime mortar. The main entrance is approached between 15th-century brick walls which form part of a barbican outwork. Inside the gatehouse are two rooms of substantial size, one of which may have been a chapel, and a number of smaller rooms and passages. Beyond is the precinct of the abbey church itself and its conventual buildings, which include two bays of the elaborate chapterhouse built in the 1290s [EH].

Thorpe Hall, Cambs , A rare example of a Commonwealth great house, by Peter Mills, 1653; now a Sue Ryder home. Its Dutch profile, richly carved staircases and ornate plaster ceilings reflect the taste of its Puritan founder, Oliver St John

– a former ambassador to Holland and husband of Cromwell's beloved cousin, Elizabeth.
See **Longthorpe Tower* 695 F5.**

Thorpeness, Suffk 695 K6, North along the shingle beach from Aldeburgh*, hiding Sizewell nuclear power station (sole blot on the Suffolk Heritage Coast), is this bizarre half-timbered holiday village begun in 1910 by estate owner Glencairn Stuart Ogilvie and architect WG Wilson for the London middle classes. Looming over a pleasure lake, the 'House in the Clouds' is both dwelling and water-tower. An 1803 post-mill was moved here from Aldringham in the 1920s.

Threave Castle and Garden, D & G 696 C2, About 1¼ miles (2km) west of Castle Douglas*, lies Threave Garden, first planted in 1871 by the Liverpool merchant William Gordon when he built the baronial house there. The estate comprises just under 120 acres (48ha) of woodland and a 60-acre (24ha) park with 200 varieties of daffodils. The ruins of Threave Castle, the seat of the powerful Black Douglas clan in the 14th and 15th centuries, stand on an island in the River Dee. All that remains of the stronghold, dismantled in 1640, is the impressive 14th-century tower and one of the angle towers of the ramparts.

Three Castles, Mons 693 G6, William Fitzosbern, Earl of Hereford, established three wood-and-timber strongholds in the 12th century, which constituted a powerful unified defence system at assailable river crossings near the English–Welsh border. These became known as 'The Three Castles', or 'The Trilateral'. Each had its own identity, however: **Grosmont**, as its name suggests, occupied a high position on a mound above the Monnow; **Skenfrith** was built on a stretch of

water-edged land; while **White Castle** took its name from the colouring of its walkways, after being refortified in stone by Hubert de Burgh in the early 13th century (who also improved Grosmont and Skenfrith).

Three Castles
Top left: Grosmont Castle, the inner face of the south-western tower.
Top centre: White Castle. Its stern military aspect was never put to the test.
Top right: Skenfrith, the free-standing round keep at Hubert de Burgh's castle. The walls rise to their original height in many places.

Bottom left: Thorpeness, House in the Clouds, a holiday home and a water tower.

Thrumpton Hall
Below centre: The Jacobean house, built in 1607.
Bottom: The panelled Saloon.

Thrumpton Hall, Notts 694 D4, The Jacobean home of the Pigot family, situated by a lake that was once a stretch of the River Trent. It was modernized by Gervase Pigot in the 1660s, when it acquired its curving gables and handsome staircase.

Thursley, Surrey 690 E6, The central belfry was added to the church in the 15th century and is supported on a massive timber cage in the nave.

Thurso, Highld 702 B1, This former Viking outpost enjoyed its golden age in the Middle Ages as the principal trading port between Scotland and Scandinavia. It reverted to fishing in the 17th and 18th centuries and owes its present activity to the ferry service between Scrabster and the Orkney* and Shetland* islands. The British surfing championships are held on Thurso beach.

Tickencote, Rutlnd 694 E5, The church of St Peter and St Paul is a rich and unusual combination of two periods. The Norman church had fallen into decay by the end of the 18th century and was rebuilt in 1792 by the architect Samuel Pepys Cockerell. He repaired the chancel and completely rebuilt the nave. Cockerell's work is a late Georgian version of the Norman style and is therefore a very early example of Norman revival. It is madly fanciful and the architect obviously enjoyed using massive Norman ornament. Inside the church is a truly spectacular Norman chancel arch, extremely elaborate with the crown of the

Top left: Thurso, the old parish church of St Peter, built in the 16th and 17th centuries, behind some fishing boats.

Centre and bottom: Tintagel Castle looking towards Barras Nose, one of the first of the National Trust's properties, acquired in 1896.

arch sunk out of shape. The chancel roof is a stone rib-vault, possibly dating from c1110 and one of the earliest examples of its kind in England.

Tideswell, Derbys 694 C3, The 14th-century church of St John the Baptist is often called the 'Cathedral of the Peak'. The nave and aisles date from c1350, but the chancel was rebuilt in c1370 and is now a very fine example of the Decorated style. The latest part of the church is the west tower, perhaps of c1380. Its little town sits snugly in a valley.

Tidmarsh, Berks 690 D5, The rather unprepossessing exterior hides a magnificently rich Norman south doorway, with an unusual plaited rope pattern and stylized face over the centre. Excellent 13th-century work survives inside the church.

Tilsworth, Beds 690 E3, All Saints Church dates from the 13th century and contains a monument (without effigy) to Gabriel Fowler of 1582.

Tilty, Essex 691 G3, This secluded little valley is the site of a Cistercian abbey approached through fields from its only survivor, the Chapel-outside-the-Gates, now the parish church. Its graceful Decorated chancel is a reminder of past glory.

Tintagel, Cnwll 688 D6, A tourist-orientated village, dominated by the Arthurian myths popularized by the poems of Lord Tennyson. The ancient castle, on the steep headland of Tintagel Island, has long been a defensive site, and traditionally the setting of King Arthur's Court; there is also an Iron Age enclosure, a Roman signal station and a Celtic monastery [NT + EH]. Approached on a misty day across a narrow neck of land and through 13th-century fortifications, the open space of the castle is easily peopled with chivalrous figures, especially as the sea thunders into Merlin's cave, far below. There are Roman remains in the Norman church of St Merteriana, which is set in flower-strewn fields high above the village, and whose tower is visible for many miles around. In Fore Street the Old Post Office is a 15th-century manor house in miniature that was used in the mid-19th century as a Letter Receiving Office for the area.

Tintinhull
Far left: The façade of c1720.
Left: A lily pond in the
20th-century gardens.

Tintern, Mons 693 G7, This great Cistercian abbey – the first in Wales – was founded in 1131 by Walter Fitz-Richard, who had been granted the castle and lordship of Chepstow by Henry I. The building's extraordinary state of preservation sets it apart from most other monastic foundations in England and Wales. A great deal of the tracery remains unharmed, and that of the west window is exquisite. To come to Tintern is not merely to come to a holy place, but also to wander round the ruins and beech woods that remain very much as Wordsworth described them and as Turner painted them.

Tintinhull Garden, Somset 689 H5, A formal garden near Montacute*, which is in fact a 20th-century creation surrounding a perfect 17th-century manor house [NT]. It is enclosed within walls and clipped hedges.

Above and above right: Tintern, one of the country's best-preserved medieval abbeys, situated in the serene Wye Valley.

Right: Tisbury, Place Farm, a survival of a monastic grange, with its buttressed outer gatehouse, dating in part from the 14th century.

Bottom: Tissington Hall has been the home of the FitzHerbert family for over 500 years.

Tiree, Ag & B 700 C8, In the time of St Columba the island, whose Gaelic name means 'land lower than the waves', was the granary of the Inner Hebrides*. Today Tiree and Coll are farmed by smallholders. Scarinish, the main village, is on the northeast coast.

In summer surfers and windsurfers come to try their skill on the Atlantic rollers that break on the island's long, sandy beaches. On the north coast, west of Vaul Bay, are the remains of a broch, Dun Mor Vaul, dating from the 1st century BC. Excavations have revealed pottery shards from the 5th century BC. At the southern tip of the island,

the harbour of Hynish was built by Alan Stevenson in the 1830s to service the construction of the Skerryvore Lighthouse on an island off the coast of Tiree. A group of enthusiasts from the Hebridean Trust has restored the harbour and converted its former signal station into the Skerryvore Museum which traces the history of the lighthouse. The Trust has also reconstructed the interiors of several cottages in Sandaig, on the west coast of Tiree, to reflect the everyday life of the island in days gone by.

Tisbury, Wilts 690 B6, The large church of St John has a wide interior that delights, and splendid timber roofs. The nave has a wagon roof dating to about 1470, and horizontal angels adorn its hammer beams. The ceiled aisle roofs are later, and have moulded and decorated beams, as well as St Andrew's crosses in the panels. Close by this small town is Place Farm, the survival of a nunnery at Shaftesbury, with the largest barn in England. The stone building, nearly 200 feet (60m) long, has a thatched roof.

Tissington, Derbys 694 C4, A secluded and charming village of classic form, with houses, a church and a big house, all of stone and arranged round a green. Tissington Hall is a sturdy square Jacobean mansion with little outside ornament. Inside is the panelled Great Hall; on the first floor the Great Chamber – now called the Drawing Room – has more handsome panelling, with fluted pilasters.

Titchfield, Hants 690 D7, An amazingly well-preserved village with Tudor timber-framed houses, and others fronted in 17th- or 18th-century brick. The lower part of the church tower dates from around 800, originally a porch; inside is fine 15th-century work and the sumptuous monument to the 1st Earl and Countess, and 2nd Earl, of Southampton; the 3rd Earl (commemorated among the family's children on the side of the monument) was Shakespeare's patron. They lived at Titchfield Abbey (north of the village, across the busy A27) which the 1st Earl converted into his mansion at the Reformation; he built the magnificent gatehouse, now a shell, across the former nave [EH]. Fragments remain of the 13th-century abbey, and nearby is a fine monastic barn, now a farm shop.

Titsey, Surrey 691 G5 Situated on the Kent border, this little village contains a church by the Victorian architect JL Pearson. Opposite it are the Church Cottages, a 16th-century timber-framed range with a later brick and flint wing. Titsey Place has been the property of the Gresham and Leveson Gower family since the 15th century. The appearance of the present house dates from a heavy remodelling of 1832. The gardens are extensive and include a Victorian walled garden, lakes, fountains and rose gardens. The Roman Villa within the park was excavated in 1864.

Tittleshall, Norfk 695 H5, St Mary's Church has the most remarkable collection of monuments to the Coke family – including the 1st Earl of Leicester, who built Holkham Hall*, and 'Coke of Norfolk',

Top: Titchfield Abbey. The Elizabethan mansion built on the site (and called by the same name) was mostly demolished in the 18th century, leaving only the magnificent gatehouse.

Right: Titchfield church. The old Saxon west porch was heightened to form a tower and given a low shingled spire.

Bottom left: Tiverton Castle, the southeast tower and the largely 14th-century domestic range. Many styles of architecture can be seen together, from medieval to modern.

the agricultural pioneer. **Godwick**, the best preserved and most atmospheric deserted medieval village in Norfolk, lies to the northeast . In 1585 Sir Edward Coke, Attorney General to Elizabeth I and founder of the great Norfolk dynasty, built a fine brick manor house here. The large barn and ruined church tower, rebuilt as a 17th-century folly, are all that remain among the humps and hollows.

Tiverton, Devon 689 G5, Made prosperous by the Devon wool trade, this small but busy town on the River Exe boasts the handsome church of St Peter, enriched by John Greenway, a merchant whose sailing vessels are represented on the outside of the south porch and aisle. The interior of the porch has an elaborate vault, and above the entrance door an Assumption of the Virgin flanked by John Greenway and his wife. Other town benefactors included George Slee, whose almshouses lie next to his Great House of St George (in St Peters Street), and Peter Blundell, who founded a school that still flourishes on the outskirts of the town. The school building of 1604 is set behind a large yard and was built to accommodate 150 boys, an unusually large foundation for its date. **Tiverton Castle**, built by Richard de Redvers in 1106, long belonged to the Courtenays. At the time of the Restoration it was bought by Peter West, a wealthy merchant and relative of Peter Blundell, who added a new wing and made it into a convenient dwelling. Armour and items relating to Joan of Arc are of interest.

Toddington, Beds 690 E3, St George is a large Perpendicular church of the early 16th century. The south elevation is decorated with a rather charming frieze of animals and grotesques, including an otter, a hawk, a mermaid, a wyvern and peacocks. It has weathered badly but is gradually being

Below left: Tolquhon Castle, the 1580s house with the old tower house on the left.

Below right: One of the many Victorian villas that swarm over the seaward-facing slopes of the town.

Torquay

restored. Traces of wall paintings are visible in the arcades. In the north transept there is a good monument to Maria Wentworth (1632), showing her frontally seated beneath a *baldacchino* with two *putti*. It is now contained within the church vestry, and may be viewed only by appointment.

Tolpuddle, Dorset, The church of St John at Tolpuddle, with its 14th-century roof, has a headstone (1934) by Eric Gill dedicated to the memory of one of the Tolpuddle Martyrs. The Martyrs, six farm labourers from the village, attempted in 1834 to form a union. They were sentenced to seven years' transportation, but after public protest in 1836 their sentences were remitted. *See* **Affpuddle* 690 B7.**

Tolquhon Castle, Abers 702 D5, Although ruined, the castle is a fine example of the development from the medieval castle to the Renaissance mansion. In the 1580s William Forbes had the tower-house incorporated into a much larger building with thinner walls and larger windows. The work was

supervised by Thomas Leiper, who also built the elaborately decorated tomb (1589) of the Forbes family in Tarves churchyard.

Tonbridge, Kent 691 G6, A busy town on the Medway, dominated by its Norman castle, with a shell keep standing on a mound and a well-preserved gatehouse of about 1300. The school, founded 1553, repays a visit, with its fine chapel of 1900.

Topsham, Devon 689 G6, An ancient port on the River Exe. The construction of quays in the 17th century and the expansion of the wool trade account for the large number of Dutch-style houses that face end-on to the Strand. One of these, at No. 25, is the local Museum, which elegantly shows how these gracious houses with attached offices were lived in during the late 17th century.

Torksey, Lincs 694 E3, Here the Roman Fosse Dyke joins the River Trent and links it to the River Witham; by this means the Romans were able to reach the Midlands. Torksey was once second only to Lincoln*, with wharves all along the river bank, but it has shrunk almost to nothing. Isolated on the edge of the Trent are the impressive remains of Sir Robert Jermyn's Elizabethan mansion, Torksey Castle.

Torquay, Devon 689 G7, The English Riviera has long been a popular holiday resort, overlooking the wide and protected waters of Torbay, where even today vessels take refuge and moor for several days. Rapid expansion took place during the early 19th century, when war made it impossible for tourists and invalids seeking balmy climates to travel to Europe. A further impetus to growth came with the arrival of the railways in the middle of the century, and villas and terraces began to climb the wooded valleys and the seven hills of the area looking south over the sea. It became a favourite resort for those in need of recuperation – Elizabeth Barrett and John Keats both came here for their health, and Charles Kingsley brought his wife. When Tennyson visited in 1838, he called it 'the loveliest sea-village in England'; Disraeli also fell victim to its charms. The finest of the terraces is the 1840s Hesketh Crescent at Meadfoot. The villas, of every conceivable style but largely Italianate, mostly stand in modest grounds with winding drives.

On the seafront are the remains of **Torre Abbey**, a Premonstratensian abbey, which was founded in 1196 by William de Brewer. It grew in prosperity, as can be seen by the massive size of the gatehouse beside the old kitchens. The 120-foot (36.5m) long tithe barn of the 13th century is sometimes called the Spanish Barn, after the 400 prisoners who were kept here at the time of the Armada. After the Dissolution, however, the church, chapterhouse and other buildings fell into a ruinous state while other buildings were converted into a home for the Ridgeways and then the Careys. The latter owned it until the 1930s, when the Corporation of Torquay converted the Abbey House into a fine local art gallery and museum. It has a room devoted to the local novelist Agatha Christie, and an interesting collection of the pottery made in fine terracotta or decorated with amusing mottoes in South Devon in the late 19th century. A similar range of this Torquay speciality can be found at the Torquay Natural History Museum in Babbacombe Road, where there are also displays devoted to **Kents Cavern**. Here Paleolithic remains were excavated in the 1860s and contributed much to the debate about the origins of the species.

Torridon, Highld 701 F5, In this small village at
Upper Loch Torridon, the Torridon Countryside
Centre provides information on walks and climbs
in the region, as well as the flora and fauna.
Beyond Torridon, the road enters the steep-sided
valley of Glen Torridon, dominated by Liathach
(3,458 feet/1,054m) and the Beinn Eighe* massif
(3,313 feet/1,010m), whose red sandstone peaks (up
to 800 million years old) are overlaid by white
quartzite (510–550 million years old).

Totnes, Devon 689 F7, One of the most complete early
towns in the country. The main street winds up
the hill from the River Dart, past 16th- and 17th-
century merchants' houses, through the town
walls at the East Gate, past the church, with the

Totnes

Top: Aerial view of the castle.
Above left: East Gate,
remodelled in 1837, straddles
the main (Fore) Street.
Above: Guildhall interior.
Built in c1553, it houses both a
council chamber and a court
room.

Bottom: Towneley Hall
entrance front. The medieval
building has been much
altered and overlaid.

medieval Guildhall behind it, and eventually
reaches the **Castle** [EH]. Judhael of Brittany,
Lord of Totnes, was probably the founder of
the large motte-and-bailey castle. The remains
of the shell keep, dating from the 14th century,
are remarkable. Its builders took advantage of a
naturally defensive site, with views across the rich
farming lands of the Dart Valley. The Guildhall
was built on the site of the refectory of the
Benedictine Priory and incorporates a fine council
chamber, a court room and the associated cells.
The school that was once part of this complex
counted among its pupils Charles Babbage, who is
credited with being the father of the computer.
Displays on his work are to be seen in the
Elizabethan House Museum. The church of St
Mary, with its unusually fine tower (modelled
upon that at Ashburton), was built by subscription
in the mid-15th century. The central figure in the
niches facing south is thought to be Bishop Lacy of
Exeter, who 'made this tore'. The many town
houses date from the 15th to the mid-17th century,
when Totnes was very prosperous – for long
periods one of the 15 largest provincial English
towns. Most of the houses are of two or three
storeys, only one room wide but perhaps two deep.
At the rear, across the courtyard from the ground-
floor shop, was a detached kitchen block. Many of
the upper rooms are elaborately decorated with
panelling and plasterwork ceilings, for which the
West Country was noted at this time.

Totternhoe, Beds 690 E3, St Giles is one of the
county's many delightful churches, here retaining
an excellent late-medieval nave roof with carved
beams and bosses. There are remains of a castle at
the end of a promontory site.

Towneley Hall, Lancs 697 F6, The Hall sits in a
somewhat municipalized setting on the outskirts

of Burnley. Its architectural history is complex, its medieval origins now overlaid by later work, especially extensive alterations of 1817 by Sir Jeffry Wyatville, best known for his work at Windsor Castle*. Most striking, however, is the refitting of the Hall in the 1720s with beautiful plasterwork by the Italian *stuccatori* Vasalli and Quadri, with medallions of Roman emperors. The Townleys were an ancient Catholic family, noted on Lord Burghley's list of recusants as 'of more than ordinary perversity'; they were also cultured and Charles Townley's collection of classical marbles now forms a core collection at the British

vernacular houses in the Lake District* where it is possible to understand the nature of the building and the life lived within it, unobstructed by the literary fame of a previous inhabitant. The house was built in 1626 and remained the home of the Browne family until 1943. It retains many of the traditional domestic arrangements and the furniture [NT]. Here you get a sense of the remoteness of Lake District life that so appealed to romantics like Wordsworth and the Lake poets.

Traquair House, Border 699 G5, This 12th-century royal hunting lodge, fortified in the 13th and extended in the 16th and 17th centuries, has welcomed a number of English and Scottish sovereigns, including Mary Stuart in 1566, and also the Young Pretender in 1745. The chapel in the north wing has a dozen 16th-century paintings on wood, while the library contains more than

Museum*. He is seen in a famous portrait by Zoffany, sitting in his library surrounded by antiquities. Nearby, at Cliviger, is The Holme, an ancient house typical of the larger Pennine stone houses and notable as the house in the early 19th century of Reverend TD Whitaker, local historian and patron of Turner, on whose researches so much of our knowledge of the north is based.

Townend, Cumb 696 E4, Set between Windermere and Ambleside, this is one of the few accessible

3,500 works. The outbuildings include an 18th-century brewhouse which still produces excellent ales. The great iron gates, closed after the departure of Bonnie Prince Charlie, will not be opened again until a Stuart returns to the throne.

Trebah Garden, Cnwll 688 C8, A steep sub-tropical garden descending to a beach on the Helford River. There are waterfalls, fish pools, huge tree ferns and acres of exotic plants. Like Glendurgan*, this was created by the Quaker Fox family.

Trelissick Garden
Top right: The rustic bridge
over the main road to King
Harry Ferry leads to the area
of the garden known as
Carcadden.

Below centre: The
thatched summer house
in Carcasson (NT).

Tredegar House, Newpt 689 H3, The greatest 17th-century house in Wales was built around an earlier stone house in the late 1660s with all the Restoration swagger and optimism of a landowner whose fortune had been established in the Tudor period. The choice of red brick as building material indicated the Morgan wealth, and the extent and quality of the stone embellishments were further tokens of rank and prestige. With the establishment of the 19th-century docks at Newport* and the rapid development of the town, the family became one of the richest in Wales. The interior of the house consists of a sequence of highly ornate rooms, some with intricate panelling, reaching a climax in the Gilt Room, which still has its original opulent decoration. One of the most remarkable things about Tredegar now is that so many of the rooms have been furnished with pieces that belonged to the family. The result is a vivid picture of life with the Morgans and their household. Built a generation after the house, the stable block is one of the most handsome in Wales; abutting it is the Orangery, both buildings forming a focal point for the parterres and geometric gardens. The recently restored wrought-iron 18th-century screen and gates by Edney of Bristol were designed to enclose the principal entrance court, beyond which stretched one of the avenues of the original layout, now bisected by the M4.

Trefignath, IOA 692 C1, A neolithic burial chamber of the 4th or 3rd millennium BC [EH], on the road to Trearddur, a bay popular for generations with English summer settlers.

Trelawnyd, Flints 693 F1, Gop Cairn is probably the largest artificial neolithic mound in Wales. The caves below it were discovered by accident and excavated in the 1880s.

Trelissick Garden, Cnwll 688 C7, A lightly wooded garden largely established by Mr and Mrs Ronald Copeland of the china-making family. With its glorious views out across the water the garden is famed for its early shrubs, the fine dell garden and its extensive herbaceous borders [NT].

Below centre: Tremadog.

Bottom left: Tre'r Ceiri.

Bottom right:
Trengwaignton Garden
tree ferns.

Tremadog, Gwynd, A small planned town created by William Madocks (1773–1828) as part of his scheme to forge a new route from London to Dublin via Porth Dinllaen, a sheltered bay, mercifully still undeveloped. *See* **Porthmadog* 692 D3.**

Trengwainton Garden, Cnwll 688 B8, In the unusual and extensive early 19th-century walled gardens [NT], with their raised beds, Sir Edward Bolitho planted a wide range of exotic plants in the 1930s and later created an outstanding stream garden that has colour all year. The terrace at the top of the garden, near the house, has a panoramic view back across Mount's Bay to Lizard* Point.

Tre'r Ceiri, Gwynd 692 D2, Of all the ancient sites in northwest Wales this hill fort, crowning one of the peaks of Yr Eifl ('The Forks', corrupted to 'The Rivals') above Llanaelhaern, is the most impressive. Surrounded by a formidable protective rampart, it consisted of 150 or more closely packed stone huts of varying shapes and sizes, dating from between 400 and 150 BC, and considered by a Welsh 18th-century traveller and naturalist 'the most perfect, magnificent and artful of any British post I have beheld'. He might have added that no ancient site in Wales has a

Trerice
Above: The east front, constructed of local elvan stone.
Left: The Great Hall, completed in 1572.

Bottom right: Tretower Court, one of the most important early gentry houses in Wales.

better view. The local church is dedicated to St Aelhaearn ('Iron Brow'), who was closely associated with St Beuno (see Lleyn*). Although much restored at the end of the 19th century, it has retained its medieval rood screen and its striking spindle-backed box pews. Like Clynnog Fawr*, it was a stopping-place on the way to Bardsey Island off the Lleyn peninsula.

Trerice, Cnwll 688 C7, An Elizabethan manor house with Dutch-inspired gables built by Sir John Arundell [NT]. Several of the rooms have elaborate plasterwork ceilings and overmantels, and contain fine collections of furniture, pictures (some by John Opie, 'The Cornish Wonder', who was born nearby), and clocks. In the grounds stands a small museum devoted to the history of the lawnmower.

Tresco Abbey Garden, see **Scilly, Isles of***.

Tretower Court and Castle, Powys 693 F6, The name 'Tretower' comes from the Norman military settlement established at the end of the 11th century on the plain where the Rhiangoll flows into the Usk. The original timber was replaced by stone in the mid-12th century, and the next generation introduced one of the most up-to-date innovations of military architecture: the cylindrical keep. Within another generation, the family – in search of space and comfort – started to work on the Court, with a splendid Great Hall. The subsequent ambitious additions to the building were the work of Sir Roger Vaughan, whose family had purchased the property in the 1420s. Insecurity caused by the Wars of the Roses (as well as a wish to show off his status) accounted for Sir Roger's son Thomas' addition of a gatehouse and a battlemented wall-walk. In recent years the sensitive development of the garden around this once-prestigious house recreates the horticultural tastes of Sir Roger's time. Tretower is unique.

Trevarno Estate, Cnwll 688 C8, Many rare trees and shrubs surround the lake, with its charming Victorian boathouse, on this ancient estate near Helston*. Also in the grounds is the National Museum of Gardening, with a huge collection of garden antiques.

Trethevy Quoit, Cnwll 688 C8, A large megalithic chamber tomb of standing stones, built c3200–2500 BC. The area is rich in ancient monuments [all EH]: others include King Doniert's Stone (probably a 9th-century memorial stone), the Hurlers (three circles of c2200–1400 BC) and the Cheesewring (a 30-foot-/9m-high pile of granite slabs).

Trewithen, Cnwll 688 D7, A fine 18th-century house set in magnificent gardens, created at the beginning of the 20th century by George Johnstone. Rhododendrons and magnolias were

Above: Trevethy Quoit, on the edge of Bodmin moor, built c3200–2500 BC. It is 7 feet (2.1m) high and 9 feet (2.7m) wide.

Below: The Trossachs, Loch Katrine. The area is known as Scotland's Lake District.

brought from Asia in the 1920s. There is a formal walled garden and a wide collection of flowering shrubs, many of them rare.

Tring, Herts 690 E4, The late 19th-century character of Tring is mainly attributable to the wealthy Rothschild family, who acquired Tring Park in 1873. The Walter Rothschild Zoological Museum in Akeman Street opened to the public in 1892 to display the remarkable collections of Lionel Walter, 2nd Baron Rothschild (d. 1937), and was bequeathed to the British Museum in 1938. The museum is an extraordinary survival, brimming with stuffed creatures of every possible variety. These include mounted birds, butterflies, monkeys, dogs, reptiles and even sponges.

Trossachs, The, Stirlg 698 E3, The Trossachs, which means the 'bristly country' in Gaelic, is a wild gorge that links Loch Achray and Loch Katrine*. Its idyllic landscapes are described by Walter Scott in *The Lady of the Lake* (1810). Today, the name of this wooded gorge is used to refer to the region that lies between Loch Venachar, to the northwest of Stirling*, and Loch Lomond*. These hills and lochs, which have attracted tourists since the 18th century, are associated with Rob Roy MacGregor, the outlaw whose exploits inspired a number of writers in his lifetime, and who was immortalized by Walter Scott in his novel *Rob Roy* (1818).

Trottiscliffe, Kent 691 G5, The church contains an amazing pulpit with the sounding-board resting on a palm tree. It was made for Westminster Abbey* in 1775 by Henry Keene and was moved here in 1826.

Trotton, W Susx 690 E6, The 13th-century church has a fine collection of brasses.

Trowbridge, Wilts 690 B5, This county town was the centre of the weaving trade from the 14th century. It is now an excellent base from which to tour the Wiltshire Downs. Fore Street and Roundstone Street have fine houses built by prosperous merchants, and the church of St James, restored in 1847, is a copy of an earlier church endowed by the clothier John Terumber (d. 1483). Once the location of the castle, Castle Street was developed in the early 19th century, and opens to a view of at least three of Trowbridge's mill buildings.

Trumpington, Cambs 695 G7, The church of St Mary and St Michael on the southern outskirts of Cambridge has one of the earliest (1298) and most impressive military brasses in England, dedicated to Sir Roger de Trumpington, who is depicted life-

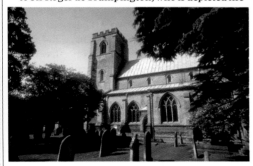

sized and cross-legged. Also of interest is Eric Gill's 1914 inscribed tablet and four reliefs, which grace the village war memorial.

Trunch, Norfk 695 J4, The church of St Botolph has a good hammerbeam roof and one outstanding feature: the columns of its hexagonal font cover (*c*1500), one of only four in England, are a breathtaking menagerie of richly carved birds and animals crawling through luxuriant foliage.

Truro, Cnwll 688 C7, Cornwall's county town is set in a deep valley, with the three spires of the cathedral at its centre, rising above the clustered roofs of the shops and houses. Its foundation stone was laid in 1880. The architect was John Loughborough Pearson, whose son Frank oversaw its completion in 1920. It is Early English in style, with the transept spirelet covered in copper (one of Cornwall's principal industries). The nave appears to be twisted, thanks to the retention of the ancient parish church of St Mary, but rises magnificently to a range of stone vaults. The Baptistery on the south side is unusually rich and complex, with a highly decorative mosaic floor. The **Royal Cornwall Museum** in River Street houses the county's collection of archaeology, with many items relating to the history of the area. They include silver and coins; Plymouth* porcelain made from the locally mined china clay; a fine collection of pictures of the county and its inhabitants; and others by artists such as

Top right: Truro Cathedral. The nave and chancel become more elaborate towards the east.

Centre right: Tunbridge Wells, the Pantiles, a charming arcaded walk where visitors taking the waters in the 18th century could stroll.

Left: Trumpington church of St Mary and St Michael has a square tower and a buff Bath stone surface.

Bottom: Truro's Early-English-style Cathedral is at the bottom of a valley and still dominates the town.

Stanhope Forbes and Patrick Heron, who made their homes here. It also houses the exceptionally fine Rashleigh collection of geological specimens. Boscawen and Lemon streets still have handsome Georgian buildings; the latter is dominated by the Lander Column, in memory of Richard Lander, who discovered the source of the Niger in 1835.

Tudeley, Kent 691 G6, The church belongs to the 18th century but was largely rebuilt in the 19th. It is unusual in that it contains the only piece of Chagall stained glass in England, a memorial to a girl drowned in a sailing accident.

Tunbridge Wells, Kent 691 G6, An attractive town, which developed as a spa in the late 17th century. Of that date is the church of King Charles the Martyr (a rare dedication) which has splendid plasterwork by craftsmen who probably worked on Wren's churches in the City of London. Of the 18th and 19th centuries are the Pantiles (rows of

shops behind raised arcades next to the medicinal spring) and Calverley Park, a semi-circle of 19 Regency villas by Decimus Burton. Near the town is the strange area known as High Rocks, the remains of a hill fort of the 1st century BC.

Turton Tower, Lancs 697 F7, A Lancashire pele tower, which has been much extended, partly in the late 16th century and partly by the antiquarian-minded James Kay who bought it in 1835.

Turvey, Beds 690 E3, In an alcove in the south aisle of All Saints' Church is a beautiful early 14th-century depiction of the Crucifixion, with Christ set against a backdrop of small flowers. The early Elizabethan monument to the 1st Lord Mordaunt is one of the most important in the county. By T Kirby in 1560, it takes the form of a recumbent alabaster effigy with a stone surround of paired and fluted columns, above which caryatids support a crowning pediment. Two fine houses in the village are Turvey Abbey (Jacobean), and Turvey House (1794).

Twyford, Bucks 690 D3, The church has a wonderful Norman south doorway with a frieze of heads, seven stars and fighting lions on the capitals of the columns. Note the kingposts in the Perpendicular timber roof.

Turton Tower

Top: The 16th-, 17th- and 19th-century extensions are built in the traditional Lancashire mixture of stone and timber-framing.
Bottom: The medieval pele tower, surrounded by moorland and woods. It now houses a museum.

Left: Turvey All Saints' Church is of Anglo-Danish origin.

Ty Mawr Wybrnant, Conwy 692 E2, The name 'Ty Mawr' ('Great House') is distinguished among other houses of the same name as the birthplace of William Morgan (1545–1604), the translator of the Bible into Welsh (completed 1588) who was regarded as the saviour of the language. Morgan's phenomenal achievement as a young man from such a remote area – gaining a place at St John's College, Cambridge* – probably had much to do with the patronage of the Wynns of Gwydir* who recognized the talent of one of their tenants' sons.

Tynemouth, T & W 697 H2, This impressive headland was the site of a Christian monastery established in the 7th century, which had links with Durham*. Its sanctity was such that it was to be the burial place of three kings – Oswin of Deira in 651, whose saintly bones were credited with miracles, Osred of Northumbria in 792 and Malcolm III of Scotland in 1093. The promontory made it vulnerable to attack by Danish raiders: it was plundered in the year 800 and destroyed by 875. In 1085 it was refounded as a daughter house of the Benedictine Priory at St Albans in Hertfordshire, which displeased Durham.

Tynemouth Priory, despite its inhospitable site, was to be of considerable financial benefit to St Albans through its export of coal, as well as being a useful posting for any of its recalcitrant members. The founder of the early Norman Priory, Robert de Mowbray, Earl of Northumberland, seems to have built a motte here for his castle, and over the centuries the whole site was fortified against a succession of opponents, including the Norman William Rufus, several bishops of Durham and mayors of Newcastle, and the inevitable Scottish incursions. The result was a priory within a defended site [EH]. Entry is by the gatehouse of the 1390s, a sophisticated tower house that formed the principal accommodation of the castle, its Great Chamber on the top floor. What remains of the priory is mainly Early English in style, but with a small Perpendicular chapel at the east end of the church. This is complete and still offers visitors some sanctuary on this bleak site. Known as the Percy Chantry, it is entered through a doorway with multi-rolled moulding. The vault is low and heavily ribbed, with large bosses that can be studied more easily than most, the subjects carved on them described in English inscriptions in black-letter style. The site defences remained in use long after medieval times. They were improved for Elizabethan artillery and again during the Civil War, after the Restoration, for the Napoleonic Wars, and several times in the 19th and 20th centuries (concrete gun-emplacements and underground magazines representing defences against recent threats). The site has also played a prominent part in the history of navigational aids,

and the ancient monuments share their impressive promontory site with the former coastguard station, a pleasing modern building. Despite its continuous military use, the area around the priory continued to be used as a secular burial ground. Of the 700 or so tombstones, the most interesting is that of Corporal Alexander Rollo, who had the distinction of holding the lantern for the burial of Sir John Moore at Corunna during the Peninsular War in 1809. From the site can also be seen the immense monument erected in 1845 to another heroic figure, Admiral Lord Collingwood. Designed by the Newcastle* architect John Dobson, the 23-foot (7m) high statue is by John Graham Lough.

Tynet, Moray 702 C4, St Ninian's Chapel, built (1755) after the Battle of Culloden* and during the repression of Catholicism, is a modest structure

Tynemouth Priory
Top left: The Percy Chantry.
Bottom: The church viewed from the west.

Above right: Tywyn Railway Museum contains one of the best collections of narrow-gauge relics in Britain.

on the main road. By contrast, the Chapel of St Gregory of Presholme, built in 1788, is a baroque reaffirmation of the Catholic faith.

Tyringham, Bucks 690 E3, The church and house are all that remains of the village. Tyringham House, with its monumental screen gateway and bridge, is by Sir John Soane. The house was much altered in the early 20th century; the central bow with its attached giant columns, incised Greek decoration and balustrade are probably all that Soane would recognize. Lutyens designed the gardens.

Tyttenhanger, Herts 691 F4, A house of similar date (1650) and artisan mannerist eccentricity as nearby Balls Park*. Externally, oversized pediments vie with the second-floor windows for space. The interior boasts an elaborately carved staircase

and there is a small chapel on the second floor.

Tywyn, Gwynd 692 D4, The parish church of St Cadfan contains ample evidence of the antiquity of Tywyn (although it is now more strongly associated with family holidays, for which its extensive stretch of sand is ideal). Tywyn is built on the site of a *clas* (monastery). Its lineage is indicated by 'Cadfan's Stone', which bears the earliest known written Welsh. The town's railway museum is devoted to the history of the narrow-gauge line of Tal-y-Llyn, opened in 1865 and in operation since then, although its original function of carrying people as well as slate from Abergynolwyn is now confined to the efforts of railway preservationists.

Uffculme, Devon 689 G5, In the 17th and 18th centuries, the Exe and Culm valleys were famous for their wool industries. The women of the area would wear red woollen cloaks. One of the last textile mills to be erected (in 1797) was built at Coldharbour by the Quaker merchant Thomas Fox, to utilize the strong and reliable water power. He produced flannel and, later, large quantities of khaki puttees for British soldiers. In a typically philanthropic gesture, the Fox family provided good cottages for their spinners and weavers, which can still be seen close by. The Mill is now open to the public as a working wool museum.

Uffington, Oxon 690 C4, A small village with chalk-built cottages and a fine cruciform church built in c1250. The church retains its original piscina and sedilia. On nearby White Horse Hill is Uffington Castle, a fort probably dating from the Iron Age. It is one of many camps built along the ancient Ridgeway. The stylized hill figure probably dates from the 1st century [EH].

Ufford, Suffk 691 J3, The church has many beautiful fittings, including a rood screen of female saints and intricately carved poppy-head bench ends, eclipsed only by the magnificent font cover, an

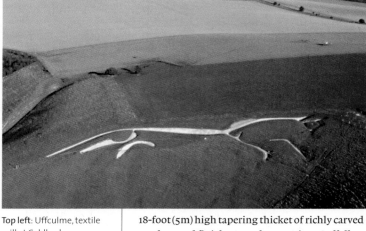

Top left: Uffculme, textile mill at Coldharbour.

Top right: Uffington White Horse.

Below centre: Ugbrooke House, the Adam drawing room.

Bottom: Ullapool, late-Georgian and early Victorian houses on the waterfront.

18-foot (5m) high tapering thicket of richly carved crockets and finials. Even the notorious Suffolk iconoclast William Dowsing left it alone.

Ugbrooke House, Devon 689 F6, Set within a Capability Brown parkland, the plain but castellated house of the Cliffords was built by Robert Adam for the 4th Lord Clifford (d. 1783). His ancestor was Charles II's Lord Chancellor, and this office had done much to improve the family's fortunes. A magnificent silver-gilt bowl and ewer connected with this Lord Clifford (the first member of the Cabal) is still on show in the house. Other treasures include magnificent 18th-century embroideries executed by the Cliffords or their kinswomen, the Howards (they were Catholics and rigidly stuck to the old ways). The chapel wing has a plain Adam exterior which does not prepare the visitor for the exuberance of the mid-19th-century marble-lined Italian interior.

Ullapool, Highld 701 F3, Ullapool was founded in 1788, and then developed by Thomas Telford to

Top left: Upnor Castle, built to defend Chatham Dockyard from attack from the sea.

Top right: Uppark exterior.
Centre: The Saloon.
Bottom: *Meekness* by Pompeo Batoni.

exploit the rich shoals of herring in Loch Broom. Today this rich natural resource is virtually exhausted and a much-reduced fleet fishes mainly for shrimps, which are sold by the pint in local bars or exported to Europe in huge refrigerated containers. The delightful village with its whitewashed houses has become a popular summer tourist resort. Ferries leave the harbour for the isle of Lewis* and boats run trips to the Summer Isles. The church built by Telford (1829) houses a museum of local history.

Unst, Shet 703 J2 , With its green hills and attractive sandy beaches, the most northerly island in Shetland* is not lacking in charm. Its serpentine (ophite) deposits, the garnet that litters the beautiful bay of Woodwick, and the soapstone from the quarries of Clibberswick and Quoys are of great interest to amateur geologists. Ferries from Gutcher (Yell*) land at Belmont.

Baltasound: The island's main settlement enjoyed its golden age between 1880 and 1925, when its population increased from 500 to 10,000 at the beginning of the herring-fishing season.

Haroldswick: The village is named after the Norse king Harald I Hárfagri (c860–940), whose fleet dropped anchor here in the 10th century. Unst Boat Haven, on the beach, has a collection of ancient boats, and Unst Heritage Centre, to the north of the village, traces the history of the herring industry.

Hermaness National Nature Reserve: This nature reserve, to the north of Burrafirth, provides sanctuary for hundreds of thousands of birds. A long walk takes you to the northern tip of the island, opposite the lighthouse (1858) on the islet of Muckle Flugga, the most northerly point of the British Isles.

Lunda Wick: On the Westing road, near Loch Bordastubble, stands the largest megalith in Shetland. To the southwest of the bay of Lunda Wick are the ruins of St Olaf's Church (12th century) and, at Underhoull, to the northwest, the remains of an Iron Age broch and a 9th-century Viking long house.

Uyeasound: To the southeast of this former Hanseatic trading post are Uyea Breck, a 10-foot (3m) standing stone, and Muness Castle (1598), built by Laurence Bruce, the half-brother of Robert Stewart; its first and second floors are virtually intact. The remains of a Viking settlement dominate Sandwick beach, to the north of Muness.

Upnor Castle, Kent 691 H5, At the mouth of the Medway stands the Elizabethan Upnor Castle (1559–67), built to guard the new Dockyard at Chatham*. Unlike Henry VIII's forts at Deal* and Walmer* and the new Italian type of fortification introduced at Berwick-upon-Tweed*, it consists of a two-storeyed block in the centre flanked by towers at either side [EH].

Uppark, W Susx 690 E7, A house of 1685–90 by William Talman. Square, plain, brick-built, it has the quiet dignity of the age of William and Mary. The interior was mostly decorated in the 18th and early 19th centuries, the Saloon being its grandest room, with an elegant stucco ceiling and classical fireplace. Uppark was gutted by a disastrous fire in 1989, but the contents were saved and it has since been restored by the National Trust to the highest possible standard. It is now more popular than before it was burnt.

Upton House
Top: The Hall, with Kentian fireplace from alterations made in 1735.
Below centre: *The Disrobing of Christ*, by El Greco.

Centre right: *Morning*, from *The Four Times of the Day*, by William Hogarth, set in Covent Garden*.

Uppingham, Rutlnd 694 E5, Best known for its school; the original school building of 1584 still survives next to the church, while the 19th- and 20th-century buildings are grouped together on the edge of this pleasant little town, which is very like Oxbridge colleges.

Upton Cresset Hall, Shrops 693 G4, This large medieval timber-framed house is enclosed in a brick skin and with a pretty brick gatehouse. The Hall and parish church lie isolated high on a hill.

Upton House, Warwks 690 D3, A rather dull 17th-century house extended in the 1920s by Walter, 2nd Viscount Bearsted, but with a marvellous art collection. Walter was the son of a 'modern-day Dick Whittington', Marcus Samuel, 1st Viscount Bearsted, who was born in London's East End but finished up as the city's Lord Mayor. His son bought Upton principally to display his pictures, and his changes to the house made it notoriously uncomfortable to live in, especially the double-height picture gallery that was intended to be used as a drawing room. But it serves admirably for displaying his astonishing picture collection, which includes works by Bosch, El Greco,

Left: Urquhart Castle on the shores of Loch Ness. The foundations date from the 13th century.

Hogarth, Bruegel, Guardi, Canaletto and Reynolds. The lawn outside, complete with plutocrat's swimming pool, has a deceptively gentle slope: immediately below, the sunny hillside falls away as an immense steep kitchen garden leads down to the lake. The water gardens continue to the east, where there is a classical temple built to the designs of Sanderson Miller.

Urchfont, Wilts 690 C5, The long church, dedicated to St Michael, culminates in a high and imposing chancel. This is in the Decorated style of about 1320, and its roof is a complex array of ribs and vaults. It is worth seeking out the monument to Robert Tothill (d. 1753) by Peter Scheemakers.

Urquhart Castle, Highld 701 G5, The castle, built on a promontory at the south end of Urquhart Bay to monitor ships moving up and down Loch Ness*, stands on the remains of an Iron Age broch. Its foundations date from the 13th century and the tower-house, defended by a curtain wall and drawbridge, from the 16th century. To prevent the castle falling into the hands of the Jacobite, it was demolished by government troops in 1692.

Valle Crucis, Denbgs , Glyn y Groes, the 'Vale of the Cross', takes its name from the 9th-century Pillar of Eliseg, a cross that once symbolized the royal house of Powys Fadog – although it has long since lost its significance. The 13th-century Cistercian Abbey of Vale Crucis is North Wales's best-preserved medieval monastery, complete with monastic fish pond. *See* **Llangolen* 693 F3.**

Vindolanda, Nthumb 697 F2, Just south of Hadrian's Wall, on the Stanegate, is Chesterholm or Vindolanda [EH], which has in recent years produced some of the most exciting finds ever discovered on Hadrian's Wall*. The wet ground conditions here have preserved organic material, including leather shoes and, most exciting of all, thousands of small wooden tablets still containing traces of cursive ink writing, many of which are displayed in the site museum. A full-scale turret and a length of Hadrian's Wall have been reconstructed on part of this extensive site. The fort seems to have had even more phases of rebuilding and realigning than usual, many

Centre left: Vindolanda, the regimental clerks' room at the back of the headquarters building.

The Vyne
Top right: Exterior view, showing the classical portico.
Centre right: An 18th-century Florentine gilt-bronze and pietra dura casket in the anteroom.
Bottom left: The antecapel, redecorated in the 18th century, but with the ceiling retained from the house of 1520.
Bottom right: The Tomb Chamber of the chapel, built in the mid-18th century to house the monument to Speaker Chaloner Chute by Thomas Carter, one of the finest classical monuments in England.

visible walls sagging over earlier ones underneath. Although the fort outline, gates and headquarters building are discernible, some of the most interesting of the exposed buildings are situated in the *vicus*, or civilian settlement, outside the fort. Here is a *mansio*, or motel-type building, and a bath-house, which still retains some of its original wall-plaster and from which some of the best jewellery finds have come. On the Stanegate can be

seen a Roman milestone in its original position. **Vyne, The, Hants 690 D5,** A magnificent house of brick built by one of Henry VIII's courtiers, with one of the earliest classical porticos in England (added 1655), much superb internal detail and furnishings of the 16th to 18th centuries, in a landscaped park with a lake. There is a Tudor chapel with Renaissance glass and tiles.

Waddesdon Manor, Bucks 690 E4, This opulent French château [NT] is an unlikely sight in the Buckinghamshire countryside. It was built for Baron Ferdinand de Rothschild by Destailleur between 1874 and 1889. It was a mammoth undertaking: the hill was levelled off, fully grown trees were hauled to the site by teams of horses and a railway was specially constructed to extend the line from Quainton Road station to Westcott for the transportation of materials for the house. The Baron's account of the building of the Manor, which included notes of many of the sources which inspired its decoration, was recorded in his *Red Book*, privately printed in 1897.

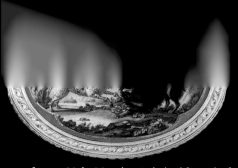

Rodin Museum, which Destailleur worked on in the 1860s. The gardens were laid out between 1874 and 1881 by Monsieur Lainé, with a strict formality around the house which was relaxed further away. The formal gardens contain many statues and ornaments, mostly 18th-century Italian works, or copies from the antique. These include figures from a fountain designed by Giuliano Mozani for the Colorno palace of the dukes of Parma, used to form two separate fountains. The charming rococo aviary (1889) of metal trelliswork cages flanking a central pavilion with a tufa and shell grotto was based on that at the Baron's childhood home at Grüneburg. The contents of Waddesdon astound visitors by their exceptional quality and number; it would take several visits to absorb all that there is to see. Baron Ferdinand, who had inherited part of his father's collection of 16th- and 17th-century works of art (which he left to the British Museum*), made his own collection of 18th-century French decorative art. To this he also added English 18th-century portraits and works of the Dutch and Flemish masters. The collection was expanded by his sister Alice and her great nephew, James. He inherited his father's superb collection, making the Waddesdon collection one of the foremost in the world. It includes 18th-century furniture made for the French royal palaces, a unique group of Savonnerie carpets and a large collection of Sèvres and Meissen china.

Top : Top of a gold box made for Madame de Pompadour, with a Sèvres plaque of two of her favourite dogs, Mimi and Inès.

Destailleur worked in this style for several projects, including the house of Albert de Rothschild in Vienna, and was aided by his restoration work on genuine châteaux. Waddesdon was designed to look as if older François I and Louis XI elements had been incorporated in a new early-17th-century château. The composition is a mixture of elements, with turrets, pediments, dormers and chimneys breaking the skyline; and the decoration is elaborate, culminating in the centrepiece of the garden front (signed 'Destailleur Architecte Paris 1875; Doussamy Sculpteur Paris 1879'), and derived from Lemercier's *Tour de l'Horloge* in the Louvre. Inside are original fittings from great Parisian mansions, including 18th-century *boiseries* (wood panelling) from the Hôtel de Biron, now the

Centre left: An aerial view of the house and formal gardens.

Right: Reisener writing table, an excellent example of 18th-century French craftsmanship, inlaid with marquetry and with gilt bronze mounts. It belonged to Marie-Antoinette.

with the table set for an 18th-century Palace Dessert. All the porcelain is Sèvres.

Bedroom with some authentic and some re-created mid-18th-century panelling .

Bottom: The Grey Drawing Room with rococo panelling from the Paris house of the Duchesse du Maine. The room contains three portraits by Reynolds.

Wadebridge, Cnwll 688 D6, The River Camel is crossed here by a medieval bridge whose original foundations were said to be on wool packs. Wadebridge is now a pleasant shopping town; its John Betjeman Centre in the old railway station commemorates the life and work of the late Poet Laureate, who holidayed and then lived at Daymer Bay a little to the northeast for many years.

Wakefield, W York 697 G6, A rare town with a distinctive skyline. Particularly when approaching from the M1, the eye is drawn to the spire of the Cathedral, the highest in Yorkshire. The 14th-century parish church became a cathedral in 1888 following heavy restoration in the Perpendicular style. Other features of the skyline are the Town Hall, a fine example of the Victorian Queen Anne style with a tower by TE Colcutt, 1877. Also in Wood street are the County Hall and other fine civic buildings. There is a restored Victorian opera house by frank marcham, 1894; and the Bridge Chapel, one of only four surviving in Britain, was a chantry chapel built on the medieval bridge – once the main route out of the town.

Wakehurst Place, W Susx 691 F6, An Elizabethan mansion at Ardingly dating from 1590. The present south front is only one wing, containing the hall, of an original courtyard house of four wings. The grounds have different areas – water gardens, a winter garden, a rock garden – planted with exotic trees and plants [RHS + NT].

Walberswick, Suffk 695 K6, Cross by the summer ferry from Southwold or circumnavigate the Blythe estuary to arrive in this attractive coastal village. Like Covehithe* to the north, Walberswick dismantled its noble church on the western approach in the 17th century and set a humbler structure in the ruins. A single street running through the green leads inexorably to the sea, the dunes and the tarred fishermen's huts by the harbour that fascinated Charles Rennie Macintosh in 1915. Following Wilson Steer's series

Top left and right: Wakehurst Place is the surviving wing of a much larger Elizabethan house. It has typically picturesque gables with lavish ornamentation. The garden is noted for its exotic trees.

Right: Wallington Hall, the Portico House overlooking the pond in the garden.

of Impressionistic beach scenes in the 1880s, the place has been transformed into an artists' colony and holiday retreat for the discerning.

Walcot Hall, Shrops 693 F4, A substantial red-brick house standing in splendid grounds with a large lake in front. Walcot was built for Clive of India in the 1760s to designs by Sir William Chambers.

Wall, Staffs 694 C5, The curious modern name for the Roman settlement of Letocetum, which was an important staging post on the Roman military route to North Wales. The site has been excavated and there is an interesting little museum [EH].

Wallingford, Oxon 690 D4, A riverside town of ancient origins, the last to surrender to the Parliamentarians in the English Civil War. Wallingford has several good 18th-century buildings, including the church of St Peter (1760–9). Note especially the spire built in 1777 to designs by Sir Robert Taylor. At the northeast section of the town are the earthworks and fragmentary remains of the castle. The 17-arched Wallingford Bridge dates mainly from 1751.

Wallington Hall, Nthub 699 J7, In core a late 17th-century courtyard house, much altered in the early 18th century, notably by Daniel Garrett [NT]. The exterior is rather austere, but inside there is some

delightful rococo plasterwork created by Italian *stuccatori*. In the 19th century, after the house had been inherited by the Trevelyans, the family of noted historians, the central court was roofed in to form a two-storeyed hall, around which historical scenes of Northumberland life, now somewhat dated in their interpretation of the past, were painted by William Bell Scott, with contributions

from visiting artists including John Ruskin. The 18th-century kitchen garden, some distance to the south, was converted into an enchanting flower garden in the 1930s. From it can be seen the Owl House – the owl was the crest of the Fenwick family who lived at Wallington in the 17th century. Kirkharle, near the village of Cambo, just north of Wallington, was the birthplace of Lancelot 'Capability' Brown in 1716.

Walmer Castle, Kent 691 J6, One of Henry VIII's forts, built between 1534 and 1540 [EH]. It was once very similar to Deal Castle*, but the interior was remodelled to make it a comfortable residence for the Lord Wardens of the Cinque Ports. The Duke of Wellington died here in 1852. The gardens were laid out about 1800 and extended by the last Warden, Queen Elizabeth the Queen Mother.

Top left: Wallington Hall, the Central Hall, once an open court, with paintings of Northumberland history by William Bell Scott.

Walmer Castle
Top right: The centre of the old fort, lit by a skylight.
Left: *The Duke of Wellington's Study*, by Thomas Shotter Boys.

Bottom: Walpole Old Chapel, the unspoilt and atmospheric interior.

Walpole, Suffk 695 J6, East Anglia is dotted with Nonconformist chapels. One of the finest and earliest rural survivals is Walpole Old Chapel, south of Halesworth. An Elizabethan farmhouse converted by Congregationalists in the mid-17th century, it retains original high-backed benches, lamps and galleries. *See also* **Fens***.

Walsall, W Mids 693 H4, Formerly the centre of the leather industry, the town has a surprisingly good art collection (Jacob Epsteins in particular). The New Art Gallery has attracted much praise as a clean, modern design displaying an interesting use of materials with tactile qualities, such as wood and leather. It has also given new life to a deprived area.

Top left and left:
Walsingham, the Slipper Chapel at Houghton St Giles, restored by Thomas Garner from 1896.

Waltham Abbey
Above right: The Victorian east end, flanked by massive Norman pillars in the nave.
Below: The gatehouse.

Walsingham, Norfk 695 H4, A small atmospheric town in the Stiffkey Valley, stuffed full of monastic remains, gabled timber-framed buildings and Georgian architecture, a rich legacy from its origins as a renowned centre of pilgrimage. Here, in 1061, the Virgin Mary told Richeldis de Fauvraches to build a replica of the Holy House at Nazareth. Augustinian guardians of the shrine built a church whose great east window can be seen in the abbey gardens, entered through a 15th-century gateway. As pilgrimages revived, a red-brick church arose in the 1930s on the shrine's original site. Throughout the Middle Ages paupers, prelates and kings from all over Europe flocked to Walsingham, stopping at shrines along the way. The last was at Houghton St Giles from where, at the Slipper Chapel, now a large Catholic shrine, pilgrims walked the last mile barefoot. Off the Friday Market, the Great and Little Cloisters and Pilgrims Hall of a ruined Franciscan Friary are still visible and the old railway station, with added gold dome, is now a Russian Orthodox monastery.

The long main street with its 15th-century Guildhall opens out into Common Place, where the focal point is a 16th-century octagonal conduit. To one side is the Shirehall, with well-preserved Georgian courthouse and cells.

Waltham Abbey, Essex 691 F4, Once a church founded by Canute's standard bearer, Tofig the Proud, on the banks of the River Lee, it is steeped in history. King Harold is said to have left here for the Battle of Hastings, his body returning for burial. Henry II endowed and expanded the Abbey in penance for Thomas à Becket's murder. It was last of the 600 monasteries Henry VIII dissolved (when Thomas Tallis was organist); but demolition spared part of the Norman nave, one of the finest

pieces of Norman work in England [EH]. Striking zig-zag and spiral-patterned columns supporting gallery and clerestory are reminiscent of Durham* Cathedral. Reduced to a parish church, it has a new east end embellished in Victorian Gothic by William Burges, and Burne-Jones stained glass. The painted ceiling, with the signs of the zodiac, is a 19th-century version of Peterborough*'s Romanesque original.

Walton-on-Thames, Surrey, Inside the church there is a monument by Roubiliac to Viscount Shannon of 1740. The Swimming Pool, by Arup Associates, is a good example of 1960s architecture. *See* **Weybridge* 691 F5.**

Walton on the Hill, Surrey, The lead font in St Peter has been dated 1150–60, making it the oldest lead font in Britain. *See* **Lower Kingswood* 691 F5.**

Wantage, Oxon 690 D4, King Alfred the Great was born in Wantage in the year 849, a fact commemorated by his statue in the Market Place. Another figure connected with the town is great Victorian architect GE Street, who lived at Wantage in 1850–2. Street was responsible for the Vicarage, the original part of St Mary's Convent, and for restoring the church.

Ware, Herts 691 F4, Despite having been badly affected by road schemes, the town has some interesting attractions. Foremost is St Mary's, an imposing 14th- and 15th-century parish church with a five-stage west tower and transepts; its

sumptuous late 14th-century font is carved with figures of saints and angels. Just over the road is The Priory, a large building incorporating remains of the medieval Franciscan friary, with charming gardens and a museum just outside in the High Street. Place House in Bluecoat Yard (commemorating the use of the building as a bluecoat school between 1674 and 1761) was Ware's former manor house, in essence a mid-14th-century building. Scott's Grotto of the 1760s is a miniature labyrinth of passages and rooms lined with flints, shell, quartz and glass.

Wareham, Dorset 690 B8, The town dates back to King Alfred's fight against the Danes, but it suffered a tragic fire in 1762 and there was little local talent available for rebuilding. The best is in a simple brick style, particularly the Red Lion Hotel. Unusually, the town stands partly within a green rectangle of earthworks, made more prominent during World War II, when its banks were raised against tank attack. There is a monument to TE Lawrence in the church.

Warfield, Berks 690 E5, The church of St Michael has admirable cusped tracery in the north chapel and chancel; the charm of the chancel has survived the Victorian alterations. At this time the screen was erected, reportedly to an original design. Parts of the rood loft survive, and there is an interesting monument of 1825: a life-size female figure standing by an urn, in front of an obelisk and holding an extinguished torch.

Warkworth Castle, Nthumb 699 K6, A stronghold of the Percy family, built in a loop of the River Coquet. The Lion Tower, which formed the porch to the Great Hall, takes its name from the Percy lion carved on a boss of the ground-floor vault.

Warkworth Castle
Above: The magnificent 15th-century keep built as a fortified aristocratic residence.
Right: The vaults on the ground floor.

The three-storey keep, ingeniously constructed on a Norman motte, is a superb example of military architecture. In plan a square over which is superimposed a Greek cross, all the outer corners are chamfered, and from its centre rises a taller turret. Built c1400, it provided tower-house accommodation on a very grand scale [EH]. The village was a planned borough in the 12th century. Spanning the Coquet is a rare example of a fortified bridge.

Warleggan, Cnwll 688 D6, The village is famous for its 20th-century rector who alienated his congregation but still preached to a full church of cardboard cutouts.

Warminster, Wilts 690 B6, A bustling army town, near firing ranges and tank courses. The large church of St Denys was rebuilt in the latter half of the 19th century. There are early-Georgian buildings in Silver Street, and an obelisk of 1781. Teddington House in Church Street is dated to c1700, and Lady Weymouth's Grammar School is a fine block of buildings of 1707.

Warwick

Top right: Jousting events are staged at the Castle.

Left: The Great Hall, restored in 1871 following a fire. It contains Oliver Cromwell's death mask.

Opposite page: Aerial view of the castle with a country house between its towers.

Warwick, Warwks 694 C6, The great fire of 1694, about which there is a video in the Warwickshire Museum, destroyed most of medieval Warwick. The result was a new, neat Georgian town which would be attractive even without its castle. There are many splendid post-fire houses from the turn of the 18th century with hearty pilasters and hipped roofs.

Warwick Castle's Norman remains are now swamped by a substantial Victorian country house sandwiched between 14th-century towers, but its skyline is still a dramatic turreted mass, perched over the river with a working watermill below. Warwick Castle was a real pioneer of the heritage industry: the earls of Warwick gave up treating their house as a home long before World War I and welcomed the visitors in. The 5th Earl of Warwick and his wife Daisy first staged a historical 'pageant' in 1893, and the castle now contains a series of themed attractions. The waxworks in the Victorian suite, which tell the story of a 'Royal Weekend Party' which included the 5th Earl and Daisy, are excellent and disconcertingly lifelike – especially as living people in costume mingle among them. The display about Richard 'Kingmaker' Neville, 1st Earl of Warwick, with neighing horses, smells and even 'wenches', is good fun.

Above: Waxwork of Daisy, Countess of Warwick, and her maid, in the Victorian Suite.

Left: Okens House, originally home of Warwick's 16th-century bailiff and benefactor Thomas Oken, and now a museum of dolls.

The church of **St Mary** towards the Market Place is worth visiting, particularly for the Beauchamp chapel. The main body of the church was rebuilt in 1694, but the Perpendicular chapel survived the fire, along with its splendid Renaissance tombs. They include that of Robert Dudley, Earl of Leicester, who welcomed Elizabeth I so extravagantly to his Castle at Kenilworth. His tomb is topped by his family's 'bear and ragged staff' – possibly a dancing bear chained to a log to prevent escape – which has been widely adopted as the town's symbol. Dudley's little son is also buried here, sweetly described in his inscription as the 'noble Imp'.

The **Lord Leycester Hospital** at the other end of the town is a medieval building consisting of a well-preserved domestic interior, Great Hall and courtyard with galleries like a coaching inn. Originally the guilds' hall, it was established by the Earl of Leicester as a home for old soldiers. Eight of the 'Brethren' still live here, and can be spotted by their uniforms of black cloaks, silver chains, and medals depicting Leicester's bear.

Okens House, a tiny half-timbered building in Castle Street, contains the town's eccentric and interesting doll museum.

Warwick Bridge, Cumb 696 E2, West of Carlisle, this village has the church of Our Lady and St Wilfrid, by Pugin, 1841; it is small, with an offset tower and architecturally correct detailing and glass by Hardman. The church ought to be better known; it is a key monument in the Gothic Revival and the Puginian revolution that overtook church architecture in the 1840s.

Washington Old Hall, T & W 697 G2, An unpretentious 17th-century manor house, incorporating 12th-century remains, this was the home of the ancestors of George Washington, who took their name from here. There is a recreated Jacobean garden [NT].

Washington Old Hall
Top left: Exterior view of the 17th-century house with 12th-century remnants. **Centre, left and right:** The staircase and Great Hall.

Watchet, Somset 689 G4, Many north Somerset towns face the Bristol Channel where it enters the sea, and there is a small harbour here. The church of St Decumen has impressive monuments in the Wyndham Chapel, and excellent woodcarvings around the Wyndham Pew of 1688. These could be by the creators of the fine staircase at Dunster Castle* 8 miles (13km) away.

Water Stratford, Bucks 690 D3, The church of St Giles is notable for its admirable Norman sculpture. The tympanum over the south door depicts Christ

Bottom: Wayland Smithy, the neolithic chambered tomb with two types of grave built on top of each other.

in Majesty, and that over the north chancel door, the Lamb and the Cross.

Waterford, Herts, For Victorian and Edwardian fittings, the church of St Michael should not be missed. They include Art Nouveau altar candlesticks and vases, coloured chancel mosaics and a wonderful range of stained glass by artists working for Morris & Co. See **Hertford* 691 F4.**

Waterperry, Oxon 690 D4, The church contains a moving monument by Sir Francis Chantry, 1819, to Anna Maria Graves. She cradles her child on her death-bed while her husband kneels at her feet.

Watford, Herts 691 F4, The flint church of St Mary contains two sumptuous monuments of 1599 and 1628 to Sir Charles Morrison and his son, by Nicolas Stone. The Church of the Holy Rood is by JF Bentley, who also designed the Roman Catholic Westminster Cathedral*, and is an excellent example of the scholarly Gothic Revival with some Arts and Crafts influence. The interior is richly decorated.

Waverley Abbey, Surrey 690 E6, Two miles (3.2km) southeast of Farnham are the mainly 13th-century ruins of Waverley Abbey, England's first Cistercian monastery, founded in 1128 [EH].

Waxham, Norfk 695 J4, The Wodehouse family once lived at the hall, encircled by a garden wall with corner turrets and 15th-century gatehouses. Equally impressive is the huge thatched barn built just after the Dissolution with stone from nearby priories at Broomholm and Hickling.

Wayland's Smithy Cave, Oxon, Just north of the Ridgeway near Uffington* is this neolithic chambered tomb surrounded by a circle of beech trees. The site is atmospheric, and unusual in having two types of graves built upon one another. Its name probably derives from a Scandinavian myth telling of Wayland the Smith and his white horse, although the nearby White Horse is later in date. Legend has it that if you leave your horse here overnight, with a coin, it will be shod by morning [EH]. See **Compton Beauchamp* 690 C5.**

Weald and Downland Open Air Museum, W Susx 690 E7, A collection of historic vernacular buildings brought from other sites in Sussex and assembled into a quite convincing artificial village at Singleton [EH].

Weir, Herefs 693 G6, Old Weir Cottage was built for estate workers at Swainshill in the Victorian era. It is surrounded by wonderful gardens, offering good views of the Wye [NT].

Welbeck Abbey, Notts 694 D3, One of the great mansions of the Dukeries, still partly occupied by the family, who share the building with a school run by the armed forces. Security is tight and the house is seldom open. Welbeck is now a rambling building, with 17th- and 18th-century buildings mostly constructed for the Cavendish family, all

remodelled by Sir Ernest George in 1902 after a fire. The oddest feature is the huge mid-Victorian complex of underground rooms and tunnels constructed for the reclusive 5th Duke of Portland, who also constructed water closets in the corners of many of the main rooms. The vast estate of 3,000 acres (1,221 ha), with hundreds of estate buildings and walled gardens, is largely intact.

Weldon, Nhants 694 E6, As the A43 passes the village, the quarries which provided one of England's most famous building stones can be seen in the fields. The village, formerly known as Weldon-in-the-Woods, stood in Rockingham Forest. The church of St Mary dates from the 13th century, and the 18th-century village lock-up or roundhouse survives.

Welford Park, Berks 690 D5, This good Queen Anne house has lovely grounds, gardens and peaceful riverside walks. The house is open by prior arrangement only.

Well, Lincs 695 G3, The sweet little church of St Margaret was built in 1733 as an eye-catcher in the newly landscaped park of nearby Well Hall. The church has a Tuscan portico copied from that of St Paul's, Covent Garden*, and the interior is in classic 18th-century style with original fittings: pews ranged college-fashion, a three-decker pulpit, royal arms and font. The plaster ceiling is probably late 18th century.

Wellingham, Norfk 695 H5, The church has some of the best medieval figure painting in a county renowned for

Above: The gardens at the Weir offer attractive walks.

Below: Old Weir Cottage was built in the Victorian era for local estate workers.

its rood screens: the martyrdom of St Sebastian, St Michael weighing Souls, St George dispatching the dragon watched by courtiers, and a remarkable Resurrection scene.

Wellington, Somset 689 G5, The church of St John the Baptist, with its red sandstone tower, has a fine monument to Sir John Popham (d. 1607), the Chief Justice in the case against Sir Walter Raleigh. Most of the other buildings in the town are 19th century.

Wellington College, Berks 690 E5, Founded as a memorial to the Duke in 1853, the building is a lively mixture inspired by Wren's baroque and Louis XIII-style French architecture. An important landmark in the history of Victorian architecture, the college was designed by John Shaw. The building is arranged around a series of courtyards and is built of red brick with stone dressings.

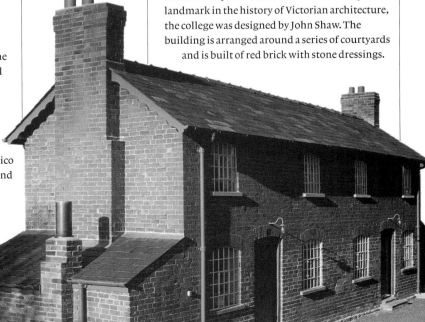

Wells, Somset 689 H4, England's smallest city, but with the most magnificent of cathedrals dominating its narrow streets. The west front forms a vast and amazing backdrop for some 400 figures of saints, prophets and angels. Many were defaced in the Civil War, but they have all benefited from the recent extensive restoration. Within, the great strainer arches of interlocked ogee curves, erected about 1340, straddle each side of the crossing and help to bear the crossing tower's great weight. The two west towers were built *c*1386. There is a famous astronomical clock in the north transept, dating from about 1390. The 36 ribs of the Chapter House rise from a fluted pier to support the centre vault of its roof,

one of the finest examples in England of the tierceron style. You reach it by a memorable flight of bifurcating steps of about 1270. Outside, on the northwest side of the cathedral, is a similarly astounding view: that of the Vicars' Close, a street nearly 500 feet (152m) long, lined on both sides with precise early houses and their walled gardens, and ending in a small chapel of about 1470.

Top left and right: The carved stone examples of medieval life on the Cathedral's exterior include a man pulling a thorn and another with toothache.

Centre left: The view to the strainer arches at Wells is one of the most dramatic in English architecture. They were erected about 1340 to take the weight of the structure above, and come at the end of a series of connecting vaults.

Centre right: Details of the stone figures on the mighty west front, placed there about 1235. They are set in niches with a wide variety of Purbeck shafts and trefoiled arches, and are the richest display in England. Christ in Majesty, the seated Virgin with angels to left and right, the Apostles – they are all there, amid other scenes from the Old and New Testaments.

Right: The astronomical clock, made in about 1390, probably by Peter Lightfoot. On its dial, showing the day of the month, the minute and hour, are the heavenly bodies which move around the earth. A procession of carved figures on horseback prance round above. There is always a crowd waiting to see the hour commemorated in whirring action.

Above centre: The west front, begun in about 1230, although the towers were added later, after 1386, and the north one after 1424. The front demonstrates not only the strength of stone figure-carving, but the long period over which cathedrals were built. High in the towers are the bell-openings, above long blank 'windows'; the uprights are stressed with vigour to give a vertical emphasis.

Top right: Vicars' Close, a street dating from the mid 14th century. The houses were built later (although the street gives a medieval impression), and are still reserved for the use of the choir.

Bottom right: Wells is famous for the excellence of its carved stonework. Notice in particular the stiff-leaf decoration on the capitals and elsewhere. Notice too the monuments of the early bishops, their vestments brilliantly modelled and their features instantly recognizable.

West Dean Gardens
Top left: The pergola is 300 feet (90m) long.
Top right: The walled kitchen garden.

Wells-next-the-sea, Norfk 695 H4, A few fishing boats still dock alongside the quay but the front is now alive with seaside entertainment. Charming narrow streets lined with cobble-fronted fishermen's cottages run inland to The Buttland, a pretty tree-lined green with handsome Georgian houses. Whalebone Lane, a reminder of the town's Icelandic trade, leads through to the High Street and church, rebuilt after a fire in 1875.

Welshpool, Powys 693 F4, On the banks of the Severn is Glansevern Hall Gardens, a Greek revival house set in 15 acres (6ha) of stunning gardens. There are unusual tree species, a rose garden and walks by the lake and through woodland. Trewern Hall is an attractive timber-framed house with a porch beam inscribed 'RF1610', though it is thought that parts of the house may be earlier than this date. Nearby are Powis Castle and Garden*.

Welwyn Garden City, Herts 691 F4, Founded in 1920 under the direction of Ebenezer Howard, this was a more successful attempt to create his vision of a Garden City than Letchworth* and Hampstead (London*) had proved, as the planners were able to learn from past mistakes. Of note are the industrial factory buildings such as the Shredded Wheat Company and Roche Products.

Wenhaston, Suffk 695 J6, The church in the Blyth valley has a famous Doom painting of c1520: a robust composition with Christ in judgement on a rainbow, St Michael weighing souls and naked figures entering hell through the mouth of a monstrous fish. Probably the work of local Blythburgh monks, it once hung above the chancel arch, and was discovered in 1892 under layers of whitewash.

Weobley, Herefs 693 G5, A pretty village crammed with timbered houses, many of them very early,

Centre: West Kennet Long Barrow, the finest in Wiltshire, is over 340 feet (103m) long. The upright sarsen stones at its entrance have been restored.

Bottom: Welshpool, Glansevern Hall Gardens. These important gardens have been carefully restored and sensitively extended in recent years.

and many with the cruck beams of their roofs visible from the outside. The Red Lion Inn is one of the best.

Weobley Castle, Swans 688 E3, The only castle on the north coast of the Gower peninsula, built on a site that has its own natural defences, with views across the Llwchwr estuary to the 19th-century development of Llanelli*. Dating from the late-13th century, it is a fortified manor house built around a small courtyard, and far more austere than Oxwich*.

West Chiltington, W Susx 691 F7, A pretty village with an interesting church containing wall-paintings dating from the 12th to the 14th centuries, not all in very good condition. They show angels and apostles, scenes from the Passion and from the life of the Virgin.

West Dean Gardens, W Susx, A 19th-century layout, with walled kitchen garden, greenhouses, pergola, arboretum and 35 acres (14ha) of ornamental grounds. *See* **Weald and Downland* 690 E7.**

West Green House, Hants 690 E5, A mid-18th-century house with a spectacular garden, in part open with classical features beside a lake, in part densely planted [NT].

West Highland Way 698 D2-4, This 95-mile (152km) footpath runs from Milngavie, in the north of Glasgow*, to Fort William*, at the foot of Ben Nevis. It follows the east shore of Loch Lomond* into the Highlands, where it passes through Glencoe* and crosses Rannoch Moor.

West Kennett, Wilts 690 C5, This splendid
prehistoric long barrow, over 100 yards (91m) long,
has the burial chamber at its east end [EH].

West Lavington, W Susx 690 E7, One of William
Butterfield's best country churches (1850): strong
but not showy. The vicarage is by him too.

West Pennard Court Barn, Somset 689 H4, Near
Glastonbury, a 15th-century barn of five bays, with
an interesting timber roof, which was repaired in
1938 by the Society for the Protection of Ancient
Buildings and then given to the National Trust.

West Stow, Suffk 695 H6, The Saxon village is a

unique and authentic
reconstruction of the
original agricultural
settlement, excavated in
1960, that flourished here
AD 400–650. There were
several large halls, each
central to a group of
thatched wooden huts with sunken rooms.

West Wycombe, Bucks 690 E4, The focus of this
pretty village is West Wycombe House and Park.
The spectacular neoclassical appearance of the
mansion is largely the result of additions made
between c1750 and 1764 by Sir Francis Dashwood
MP, best known as creator of the infamous Hell-
Fire Club. It features a two-storey colonnade on
the south front and superb frescoed interiors.
Surrounding it is an exquisite and perfectly

West Wycombe Park
Top: The landscaped park.
Left: A Roman revival ceiling
in the Tapestry Room.
Centre: Temple of Venus.
Bottom right: The two-storey
colonnade.

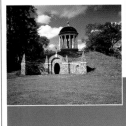

preserved 18th-century landscaped park with
lakes, temples and buildings, some designed by
Nicholas Revett. On the nearby hill stand the
Dashwood Museum and the medieval church,
sumptuously remodelled in the mid-1700s. The
church tower is finished with a golden ball, which
contained seats for ten people. Halfway down the
hill are the West Wycombe Caves, made by
Dashwood in 1750–2. Their chambers have names
such as Inner Temple, XXII, and The Labyrinth, as
they were supposedly used by Sir Francis' Club.

Westbury, Wilts 690 B6, The White Horse, cut in the chalk, is 166 feet (50.6m) long and 163 feet (49.7m) high (*see also* Pewsey* and Preshute*). It was apparently made in the early 18th century, but in 1873 it was alas 'rectified', and now it looks a 'moderately correct, dispirited animal' (Sir Nikolaus Pevsner).

Westbury Court Gardens, Gloucs 693 G6, Down by the Severn, 9 miles (14km) southwest of Gloucester, lie some of the most interesting 17th-century gardens in England [NT]. They are rare

Top left: Westbury White Horse.
Top right: Westbury Court Gardens.

Below left: Westerham, Squerryes Court.

Below right: Westerham, the Drawing Room of Quebec House, the birthplace of General Wolfe.

not because of their design – which is common in pictures of houses in the 1690s – but because of their survival almost unchanged. Two long canals in the Dutch style were made between 1690 and 1715. A tall pavilion (now reconstructed by the National Trust) provides views over the long lines of the canals, and the rows of yew pyramids and holly balls reflected in them. The gardens were created by Maynard Colchester, whose careful account books proved useful in the restoration, as did an engraving by Kip and Knyff.

Westerham, Kent 691 G6, There are two houses of note. Quebec House [NT] is the 17th-century home of General Wolfe, conqueror of Quebec, whose statue stands on Westerham Green; it is a square brick-built house with a fine staircase. Squerryes Court is of the same date, a fine gentry house of brick with stone dressings.

Westleton, Suffk 695 J6, A pretty village gathered around its green, in a huge parish with nature reserves of national importance. Westleton Heath is, along with Dunwich* Heath, one of the best-preserved areas of the lowland heath that once covered much of coastal Suffolk.

Westley Waterless, Cambs 695 G6, The church in this dry chalkland hamlet has an exquisite life-size brass to Sir John de Creke, c1325, in chainmail and surcoat, alongside the robed figure of wife Alyne.

Weston, Herts 691 F3, The church is notable for its Norman crossing, with four crossing arches.

Weston Park, Staffs 693 H4, The house, together with its stables, the parish church and impressive Home Farm buildings, stands on the edge of the enormous park. It was built for the Wilbrahams in 1671, probably to the designs of Lady Wilbraham herself; she also designed the stables and church. In the 18th century the Bridgeman family made numerous alterations, and there has been much redecoration in recent years. There are good furnishings and many superb paintings.

Westonzoyland, Somset 689 H4, In the church of St Mary, a mile or so from Bridgwater*, the

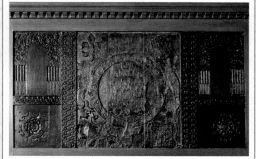

initials of Richard Bere, abbot of Glastonbury* (1493–1524), are carved on one of the buttresses. Of particular interest is the timber ceiling, with its pierced horizontal tie-beams and the large angels holding the central king-posts that rise to the ridge of the roof.

Westonbirt Arboretum, Gloucs 690 B4, Sir Robert Holford liked trees. As well as commissioning a flamboyant 19th-century version of Wollaton Hall* from Louis Vulliamy for his house, now a boarding school, he developed an arboretum on the other side of the road. In 1829, he started to manage a patch of ancient woodland dating from the last Ice Age, and gradually other woods were added as trees were collected. Robert's son cut long rides through the woodland, which are now used by the many walkers who enjoy the 600 acres (243ha) of trees, rhododendroms and azaleas. The Arboretum, looked after by the Forestry Commission, is particularly popular in autumn when the colours are spectacular.

Westward Ho!, Devon 688 E5, This small resort set behind the Pebble Ridge took its name from Charles Kingsley's novel of 1855. Rudyard Kipling attended the United Services College here from 1878 until 1882 and described the place in his *Stalky and Co.* (1899). The 12 houses of the school still survive as Kipling Terrace.

Westwell, Oxon 690 C4, This little village has an idyllic and almost timeless quality, hidden amongst the narrow country lanes to the southwest of Burford*. The church is Norman and contains a handsome Jacobean tomb of one of the former rectors, Richard Thorneton. The grouping

Above left: Westerham, Quebec House, overmantel to the parlour fireplace, re-used from an earlier house.

Above right: Westonbirt Arboretum, a display of rhododendrons. There are 18,000 catalogued trees.

Bottom: Westwood Manor has a modern topiary garden.

of houses around the village pond is singularly attractive. The gardens to the Manor House are occasionally open to the public.

Westwood Manor, Wilts 690 B5, A 15th-century stone manor house, altered in the early 17th century, with late-gothic and Jacobean windows and rich plaster ceilings. The house is administered for the National Trust by its tenant. It has a modern topiary garden.

Weybridge, Surrey 691 F5, This suburban town is named after the River Wey, which joins the Thames here. Weybridge has been pressed upon by London since the 1930s but retains an open, leafy character. It is of mixed architectural merit but does have some historic features. The Tudor walling in Thames Street formerly belonged to Oatlands Palace, an important royal residence rebuilt by Henry VIII from 1538.

Weymouth

Top: The Esplanade is a riot of attractively-sited houses, facing the bustle of the harbour.
Left: The statue of King George III, made of Coade stone and put in place in 1809, stands at the head of the Esplanade.

Below: Whalley Abbey, the ruined nave. The layout of the 14th-century abbey is marked on the grass.

Dormitory of 1415, a long hall built above a storehouse. The stalls from the Abbey are now in Whalley parish church nearby, a fine medieval building; the stalls have very good misericords with all the usual folk and mythical stories. There are some very good pews and benches, including one delightfully named St Anton's Cage [EH].

Whalsay, Shet 703 J3, This island in Shetland* has a long history of fishing and today has a modern and active fleet. The ferry from Laxo lands at Symbister, a broad roadstead used in the 16th century by merchants of the Hanseatic League who came to trade salt, tobacco and clothing for smoked fish. Bremen Böd, a 17th-century

Weymouth, Dorset 689 J6, This ancient port became a flourishing seaside resort after a visit (the first of many) by George III in 1789. A row of handsome Georgian and early Victorian houses, some with ornate ironwork balconies or bow windows, stretches from the harbour to the end of the promenade. The church of St Mary has a fine reredos painting of the Last Supper (1721) by Sir James Thornhill. Of public buildings, the Guildhall and the Portwey Hospital are of 1836 but, alas, a fine 16th-century house was pulled down to erect the undistinguished municipal buildings in 1968.

Whalley, Lancs 697 F6, A rambling small town with attractive buildings along the main street. The principal monument is the former Cistercian Abbey, started in the early 14th century, of which significant parts survive. The plan of most of the church is marked out in the grass. The best upstanding parts are the gatehouse, leading to a courtyard surrounded by the former Abbot's Lodging; the Chapter House; the undercroft of the Monks' Dormitory; and the Lay Brothers'

Hanseatic store, has been transformed into a museum. The island's archeological sites include the Standing Stones of Yoxie – two houses and a megalithic tomb c2000 BC on the east coast. There are also the remains of a broch on an island in the Loch of Huxter, at the south end of the island.

Wharram Percy Deserted Medieval Village, N Yorks 697 J5, Excavations over 41 seasons have produced evidence of a Yorkshire Wolds community's 5,000-year stratified history [EH].

Top: Whipsnade Wild Animal Park, the elephant enclosure. The Park was established to breed endangered species in captivity.

Bottom right: Wharram Percy Deserted Medieval Village, a ruined church.

White Ladies

W

Whipsnade, Beds 690 E4, One of the county's busier places, with a steady stream of visitors arriving at Whipsnade Wild Animal Park, which opened in 1931. It is home to over 2,500 animals, many endangered, and there are 1930s buildings by Lubetkin and Tecton [NT].

Bottom left: Whitby Abbey, the graceful silhouette of the ruined church on a windswept cliff-top.

Whitchurch, Hants 690 D6, Beside the upper reaches of the River Test is the Whitchurch Silk Mill, built in 1815; it produced fine silk fabrics until recently and is now a working museum, continuing production with the original machinery.

Whitby, N York 697 J4, A cliff-side town, with fishing harbour below, and many fascinating nooks and crannies to explore. The town's most famous sailor was Captain James Cook, who explored the Pacific Ocean in the 1760s and 1770s. Jewellery carved from local jet became very fashionable as mourning wear in Victorian times. The ruins of Whitby Abbey [EH] are mainly Early English, and give little evidence of an earlier period of monasticism, when a community for both monks and nuns was founded by St Hilda in AD 657. In 664 a synod met here which debated many contentious issues of the Early Christian Church, and decided on the method of calculating the date of Easter that still appertains. This early monastery was destroyed by a Danish invasion in 867. A post-Reformation building nearby, the late 17th-century Banqueting House, has become a new visitor centre called Cholmley's House. Also on the headland is the 12th-century St Mary's Church, its interior still Georgian, full of galleries and box pews, with a splendid three-decker pulpit of 1778.

Whitchurch, Shrops 693 G3, A pleasant little town with a catholic mixture of timber-framed and Georgian buildings. The parish church of St Alkmund is the largest Georgian church in Shropshire, built in 1713. It has handsome Tuscan columns, galleries, an early Georgian organ case and great brass chandeliers.

White Castle, *see* **Three Castles*.**

Whitehaven, Cumb 696 D3, This was the creation of the Lowther family in the 17th and 18th centuries, who grew rich on a trade based on coal and tobacco. Its street plan rises from the harbour, and many of its houses are essentially still intact. The most important monument is St James's Church, 1752, built by Sir William Lowther's steward, Carlisle Spedding. It is an excellent example of the Georgian church; galleries are supported on Tuscan columns with full entablature and these in turn support Corinthian columns to the fine plasterwork of the ceiling.

White Ladies, Shrops 693 H4, The ruins of a small priory of Augustinian canonesses [EH], just south of Boscobel*.

Whithorn, D & G 696 B3, It was here that St Ninian (c360–432) founded the first Christian mission in Scotland, in 397. Whithorn remained a bishopric of the Celtic and then the Northumbrian church until the Viking invasions, while the saint's tomb continued to be a place of pilgrimage until the 16th century. The priory built on the ruins of the first church by Fergus, Lord of Galloway, c1125, was occupied by Premonstratensian monks up to the Reformation. All that remains today are the nave, two chapels and the crypt of the medieval foundations. A nearby visitor centre presents artefacts discovered and models of the different phases of occupation since the 5th century. The

Top left: Whitmore Hall, a family crest over the fireplace. It has been the seat of the Cavenagh-Mainwarings for over 900 years, although most of the present house is 17th-century.

Whittington Court
Top right: The Dining Room.
Bottom: The Elizabethan manor house.

Museum, in the main street, houses a remarkable collection of early Christian crosses and stones, including the Latinus Stone (c450), the earliest Christian memorial in Scotland. The Isle of Whithorn is the site of the ruins of St Ninian's Chapel (13th century) and St Ninian's Cave, which was a place of pilgrimage until the 11th century.

Whitmore Hall, Staffs 693 H3, The brick exterior is of the 1670s and is an excellent example of Artisan Mannerism – the non-courtly style of this time. Under the brick skin is a large timber-framed house, which contains a fine series of family portraits from the 1630s. Whitmore Hall also has excellent stables with original fittings dating to the 1620s.

Whittington, Glos 690 C4, Whittington Court is a 16th-century manor house furnished with the possessions of the owners over the centuries. The local church has 14th-century effigies.

Whittlesey, Cambs 695 F5, Rescued from Peterborough* by clay pits, Whittlesey survives with its spacious Market Place intact, presided over by a handsome butter cross and St Mary's celebrated stone tower. Surmounted by a slender, crocketed spire, it remains an elegant landmark in a landscape of brickyard chimneys.

Whitton Court, Shrops 693 G5, A very attractive and interesting house, enlarged in Tudor times and again in the 17th century. The interior has much fine 17th-century panelling and a handsome Tudor screen in the Great Hall.

Wichenford Court Dovecote, Worcs 693 H5, A remote but attractive timbered dovecote surrounded by apple trees. Dovecotes often provide an architectural mini-history of an area's building styles, and here indeed is a typical little black-and-white timbered tower, containing 57 nesting boxes. The birds entered through doors in the lantern, and provided the owners with the fresh meat that was so scarce in winter before enough fodder could be grown to keep livestock alive.

Wick, Highld 702 C2, The name of this town on the Wick estuary, derived from the Norse *vik* meaning 'bay', attests to its history of Scandinavian occupation. Thomas Telford designed a model village and new harbour installations in 1808, when Wick became a major fishing and commercial herring port, a period of prosperity evoked in the Wick Heritage Centre (Bank Street).

Bottom left: Wicken Fen, a remnant of undrained fen, complete with restored windpump, managed by the National Trust.

Bottom right: Wichenford Court Dovecote, dating from the 17th century.

Today the town is well served by communication links and is renowned for its production of Caithness glass. To the south of Wick are a number of prehistoric remains, the most remarkable of which are on the Hill o' Many Stanes, near Mid Clyth, to the northwest of Blackness*. Here, some 200 standing stones, dating from *c*1800 BC, are arranged in 22 rows to form a fan shape that may have had astrological significance. Further south, at Occumster, a minor road leads to the Grey Cairns of Camster, two well-preserved neolithic burials dating from between 4000 and 1800 BC.

Wicken Fen, Cambs 695 G6, The Fen [NT] is Britain's oldest nature reserve, a unique and evocative fragment of the vast watery wilderness from which Hereward the Wake harried Norman warlords. Complete with restored windpump and fen cottage it harbours rarities such as the eel-pout, fen violet and swallowtail butterfly. There are shades here, too, of Graham Swift's acclaimed novel *Waterland* (1983). *See also* **Fens***.

Wickham, Berks 690 D5, The church of St Swithin displays two interesting architectural styles, genuine Anglo-Saxon and 19th-century neo-medieval. The chief early survival is the projecting southwest tower. Of the later period (1845–9 by Benjamin Ferrey) are the ornate interiors of nave and chancel. Note the completely out-of-context papier-mâché elephants supporting the aisle roof. They were shown at the Paris Exhibition of 1862.

Wickham, Hants 690 D7, The splendid rectangular Square has Georgian houses built in the distinctive local tradition using grey brick headers with red brick quoins and dressings.

Widecombe in the Moor, Devon 689 F6, A deservedly popular tourist centre, the 'Cathedral of the Moor' has a 120-foot (36.5m) tower with great pinnacles. In October 1638 part of the tower fell, killing four parishioners and injuring many more; inside, painted boards record the details of this tragic accident. The nearby Church House, built about 1500, is now owned by the National Trust. The annual fair to which Uncle Tom Cobley and all were travelling is still held on the second Tuesday in September.

Widford, Oxon, The lovely little church at Widford, once a remote village in the Windrush Valley, now stands alone in the fields. It was built in the 13th

Wigan
Top left: The Leeds and Liverpool Canal.
Top right: The Trencherfield Mill.

.

Bottom: Widecombe in the Moor. The Church of St Pancras lies beneath the open moor.

century on the site of a Roman villa. In the chancel can be seen an exposed section of mosaic flooring. *See* **Swinbrook* 690 C4.**

Wigan, Gt Man 696 E7, An old market town whose pier is a music-hall joke made famous by the title of George Orwell's novel. The pier is, in fact, a wharf on the Leeds and Liverpool Canal from which the local coal trade made the town prosperous in the 19th century. Around the canal are warehouses; Trencherfield Mill contains one of the largest (3000hp) stationary steam engines still working. The old Technical College in the town centre, by Briggs and Wolstenholme of 1901, is an excellent example of the red brick and terracotta

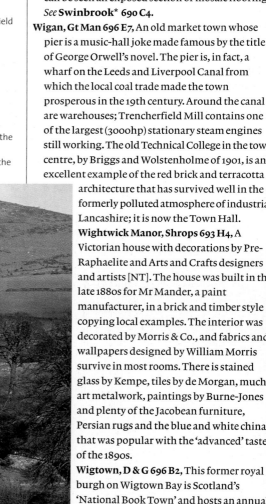

architecture that has survived well in the formerly polluted atmosphere of industrial Lancashire; it is now the Town Hall.

Wightwick Manor, Shrops 693 H4, A Victorian house with decorations by Pre-Raphaelite and Arts and Crafts designers and artists [NT]. The house was built in the late 1880s for Mr Mander, a paint manufacturer, in a brick and timber style copying local examples. The interior was decorated by Morris & Co., and fabrics and wallpapers designed by William Morris survive in most rooms. There is stained glass by Kempe, tiles by de Morgan, much art metalwork, paintings by Burne-Jones and plenty of the Jacobean furniture, Persian rugs and the blue and white china that was popular with the 'advanced' taste of the 1890s.

Wigtown, D & G 696 B2, This former royal burgh on Wigtown Bay is Scotland's 'National Book Town' and hosts an annual book festival. Below the town the Martyrs' Stake commemorates the Wigtown Martyrs, Margaret McLachlan (aged 62) and Margaret Wilson (aged 18), two Covenanters who, in 1685, were tied to a stake in the estuary and left to drown in the rising tide.

Wightwick Manor
Top left: Eduard Ould's red brick and timber 1880s exterior.
Right: One of the William Morris wallpapers inside.

Wilderhope Manor, Shrops 693 G4, A grey stone Tudor house hidden away in the Corvedale Valley, and now a youth hostel. The interior is still of interest: it retains its original wooden spiral staircase, and plasterwork bearing the initials of the builders, Francis and Ellen Smallman.

Willen, Bucks 690 E3, Willen has a simple but powerful church designed by Robert Hooke, 1678–82; it still retains the box pews and wall panelling.

Willesborough, Kent 691 H6, An octagonal windmill dating from 1869.

Top right: Wilmington, the Long Man, 226 feet (69m) tall and holding a staff or spear in each hand.

Bottom: Wilderhope Manor, the back of the house with its great chimneys and the staircase tower.

Willington, Beds 691 F3, Henry VIII's Treasurer of the First Fruits and Tenths, Sir John Gostwick, was probably responsible for the church of St Lawrence. This is unusual in that it was built in a single phase, *c*1530–40. It contains the helmet worn by Gostwick at the Field of the Cloth of Gold.

Wilmington, E Susx 691 G7, The remains of the Benedictine priory are rather confusing. Overlooking the village on the hillside is the Long Man of Wilmington, a quaint figure cut into the chalk. No one knows how old it is.

Wilton House, Wilts 690 C6 The seat of the earls of Pembroke and Montgomery, 2 miles (3.2km) northwest of Salisbury. Its history as a private house begins with the Dissolution, when in 1544 Wilton Abbey and its lands were given by Henry VIII to Sir William Herbert, who had married Anne Parr, sister of Catherine, the King's sixth wife. Of the Tudor building, the Clock Tower (east front) remains, having survived a tragic fire in 1647.

In the 1980s the Royal Commission on Historic Monuments published the results of its long examination of Wilton, revealing that over the years Inigo Jones, John Webb and Isaac de Caux had all played a part in its present-day appearance. De Caux rebuilt the south front of the house from 1636 for the 4th Earl, while Webb (with advice from the aged Jones, who died in 1652) supervised the 1649 rebuilding. The chief architectural features are the great State Apartments, including the Single and Double Cube rooms, with their painted coves and ceilings. In the Double Cube Room is Van Dyck's large and famous canvas of the 4th Earl's family, but contrary to general assumption the room was not built to house it. Its present hanging dates from 1826 at the earliest.

The house is surrounded by 21 acres (8.5ha) of parkland, landscaped for the 9th Earl in 1737 with Roger Morris's precise Palladian Bridge (copied later at Stowe* and Prior Park*). It spans the River Nadder, and is near the four gardens that were created in 1969 by the present Lord Pembroke. In the village of Wilton stands the most remarkable church of St Mary and St Nicholas, built in 1843 in the Italian Romanesque style and with an isolated campanile. There are monuments within to the 9th, 10th and 11th earls of Pembroke.

Top left: A view into one of the four new gardens Lord Pembroke has established at Wilton since 1969. Here the visitor can admire Japanese features or old English roses.

Centre: Van Dyck's Great Family Piece of the 4th Earl of Pembroke and his family. The Earl was Lord Chamberlain to Charles I, and holds his wand of office.

Bottom centre: Richard Wilson's view of the house and bridge at Wilton, c1765.

Bottom right: Roger Morris's Palladian bridge of about 1737 may only straddle an insignificant stretch of water, the River Nadder, but it is sited dramatically, as an eye-catcher, in front of the majestic façade of the 17th-century house.

Top centre: Wimborne
Minster is notable for its two
towers and the variegated
colours of the stonework.

Wimborne Minster, Dorset 690 C7, The two-towered church of St Cuthberga, girdled by busy streets, dominates this small market town. Within the largely Norman building (11th century) is a fine nave that has later (13th century) Purbeck shafts at the transept entrances. There are good heraldic stained-glass windows (1838) by Thomas Willement. South of the Minster are the attractive gardens of Dean's Court, spreading over 13 acres (5.3ha). The Priest's House Museum contains a collection of antiques and some of the best horse brasses in the country. Also worth seeing is Wimborne in miniature, a charming model village close to the church.

Wimpole Hall, Cambs 695 F7, The 18th-century Hall is the largest house in Cambridgeshire, even after

Centre: Wimpole Hall, the main façade, a blend of 17th- and 18th-century architectural styles, looks out across a huge parkland laid out by Repton and Capability Brown.

Elsie Bambridge used her father Rudyard Kipling's royalties to fell two wings before leaving it to the National Trust in 1976. The original central block was built in c1640 for Sir Thomas Chicheley, with various additions culminating in Flitcroft's 1740 work for the Lord Chancellor, the Earl of Hardwicke. The long pedimented front looks out across the park to Sanderson Miller's gothic eyecatcher. Its abiding glories are the James Gibbs Library and Chapel (the latter with *trompe l'oeil* painting by Sir James Thornhill) and Sir John Soane's domed Yellow Drawing Room. Leading landscape gardeners Charles Bridgeman, Capability Brown and Humphry Repton all had a hand in reshaping formal grounds into a picturesque 3,000-acre (1,200 ha) park, which as well as its ruined gothic tower has a Chinese bridge

Wimpole Hall
Centre left: The Great Staircase.
Centre: Sir John Soane's Yellow Drawing Room.
Bottom left: *The Crack Shot*, by James Tissot.

Centre right: Winchcombe, a gargoyle on St Peter's Church.

and 2-mile (3.2km) Great Avenue. Soane also designed Wimpole Home Farm, a model farm of 1794, now home to rare animal breeds. Close by St Andrew's Victorian rebuilt church is a family mausoleum with good monuments by Flaxman and Westmacott.

Wincanton, Somset 689 J5, The town lies in the east of the county near the borders with Wiltshire and Dorset. It has many Georgian buildings, most notably the White Hart Hotel of 1733, a typical coaching inn. These, however, give pride of place to the church of St Peter and St Paul, with its Perpendicular west tower and Georgian south porch. The church was rebuilt (1887–9) by JD Sedding. In the churchyard is a monument (1769) to the Warwickshire architect Nathaniel Ireson, who moved to Wincanton from Stourhead* in 1726.

Winchcombe, Gloucs 690 C3, This little town near Sudeley Castle* contains a street called 'Tobacco Row', a last vestige of the English tobacco industry, which was crushed in order to give the colony of Virginia a monopoly. The town has a 'wool' church and plenty of Tudor buildings. In the main street are the dinky Chandos

Almshouses of 1573. They are complemented by another row nearby, that of the multi-coloured brick Sudeley Almshouses designed by Sir George Gilbert Scott in 1865. St Peter's Church features 40 gargoyles, said to be modelled on local dignitaries.

Winchelsea, E Susx 691 H7, A medieval planned town founded by Edward I in 1283 on a grid pattern. It was never completed but the plan can be easily traced. It became one of the Cinque Ports in 1191. The very ambitious early 14th-century church, of which only the chancel remains, contains five amazing 14th-century tombs with ogee canopies. To the south are the remains of Greyfriars, a 14th-century Franciscan priory.

Winchester

Winchester, Hants 690 D6, The old capital of Wessex, which became the dominant Anglo-Saxon kingdom under King Alfred (871–901), and was later considered the capital of England until, by the 12th century, London assumed that status. It has several outstanding medieval buildings and many pleasant ones of later date.

The **cathedral** was built from 1079 on a site slightly overlapping its Saxon predecessor (whose outlines are indicated in the ground). The north transept remains as built, in strong Norman style with little ornament; the tower was rebuilt after a fall in 1107. The delicately formed retrochoir was added after 1200 in contrasting gothic style, and is filled with a series of richly detailed tomb-chapels, or chantries, of later medieval bishops. The nave was remodelled under Bishop William of Wykeham before 1500 in the newly established Perpendicular style, with William Wynford as master mason. The cathedral is austere externally, but inside it is full of fine details, including medieval wall-paintings of outstanding quality, and delicate 14th-century choir stalls (although the screen in the same style is of 1875 by Sir George Gilbert Scott). Jane Austen is buried under a stone slab in the north aisle.

The **Close**, mainly to the south of the cathedral, developed after the Reformation on the site of the former monastery as the home of the Anglican canons, who were allowed to marry – giving it, like other English cathedral closes, a domestic-clerical quality. The Deanery was converted from the medieval prior's house, with fine original work; other houses set round the irregular green spaces are of varied dates, often with 17th- or 18th-century fronts. One, now Pilgrims' School, has in the small Pilgrims' Hall the earliest hammerbeam roof, dating from c1290. One leaves the Close at its southern end through an arch, then passes through another arch, Kingsgate (with a small church above), into an ancient suburb outside the city wall. In No. 8 College Street, Jane Austen died in 1817; she had come to stay here from her home in Chawton* in order to consult her doctor.

Winchester College was founded in 1382 by Bishop William of Wykeham for boys whom he intended to go on to New College, Oxford*, already founded by him. Little comparable education was then available outside monasteries, so this was a pioneer institution in secular schooling. Most of the original buildings survive, little altered outwardly, with two gateways, a complete courtyard and chapel, together with numerous later accretions to serve what has always been one of the most prestigious boarding schools in Britain.

Wolvesey, east of the college, is the traditional home of the bishop, who now lives in the classical wing of a palace of 1684, otherwise demolished. Behind are the conserved ruins of the medieval palace, built in several stages, most notably by Bishop Henry of Blois in the 12th century. There is a marvellous walk from Kingsgate past the College and Wolvesey, then beside a surviving stretch of the city wall (much restored) and the small River Itchen, to the bridge at the bottom of the High Street.

The High Street follows the line of the main thoroughfare of the Roman town of Venta Belgarum – which declined after the Romans left Britain and was re-established as a town under King Alfred. (His statue of 1901 stands in the middle of the street.) Past the ornate Guildhall (1873) the street narrows between shops, often

Top right: The Perpendicular style east front of the Old Minster.
Centre left: A view from the Old Minster through to the Cathedral's Norman north transept.

Above: Winchester College, founded in 1382 to help boys get into New College, Oxford.

Bottom left: Cathedral Close, established after the Reformation for Anglican canons to live with their families.

Top: Detail of the roof vaulting in the nave of Winchester Cathedral.

Centre left: The stained-glass window shows Bishop William of Wykeham, who was responsible for the nave, although he died in 1404 before it was completed.

Centre right: The nave contains Jane Austen's grave and William of Wykeham's Chantry.

Bottom right: St Cross almshouses, c1445.

under old upper storeys – especially in The Pentice, where the top storeys, supported by pillars, project over the pavement. Nos. 33–4 have 16th-century decorative wooden bargeboards on their gables. The Butter Cross is a rare survival of a civic 'cross'; the top is restored but the lower part is 15th century with later statues. Behind it is a timber-framed building of about the same date, altered but showing what many of the houses were like in late-medieval Winchester. The High Street climbs past 'God Begot', whose elaborate timbered front of 1903 conceals a genuine medieval house, and many interesting Georgian and Victorian frontages (including a delightful Georgian paned shop front, now the offices of the *Hampshire Chronicle*), to end at the medieval Westgate (upstairs is a small museum). Nearby was the site of the great medieval castle. Not much remains except for the Great Hall, internally one of the finest secular medieval buildings of its kind surviving – with arcades of c1230, partly in Purbeck marble. Its great feature is the top of the so-called 'King Arthur's Round Table' hanging on a wall and dating from the later 13th century when the romantic stories of the legendary figure were highly fashionable; the painting, including representations of the knights' seating, was added later. The small Queen Eleanor's Garden nearby was formed in 1986, using plants known to have been characteristic of gardens in the 13th century.

Nearby are several military museums, commemorating the Gurkhas, the King's Royal Hussars, the Light Infantry and the Royal Green Jackets. Another museum, of the Royal Hampshire Regiment, is housed in Serles House, an early 18th-century baroque house, possibly by Thomas Archer, in Southgate Street.

On the southern outskirts of the city is St Cross Hospital, a medieval charity home founded by Bishop Henry of Blois in 1136 and augmented by another bishop in 1445. The magnificent chapel is largely 12th century and illustrates the transition from Norman to gothic. The 15th-century hospital buildings include residents' lodgings and hall. The residents wear distinctive robes or gowns.

Windermere, Cumb 696 E4, This is the largest of England's lakes. Its waters are still crossed by traditional steamers, the oldest being the *Tern* of 1891, and the historic launches of the Windermere Steamboat Centre. This museum contains many outstanding boats including the *Esperance*, which was the inspiration for Captain Flint's houseboat in Arthur Ransome's children's classic, *Swallows and Amazons*. These lake cruises leave from Bowness, now a small town of shops and hotels centering on the historic church of St Martin, which has 15th-century stained glass in its east window. In the middle of the lake on Belle Isle is one of the earliest buildings designed to take advantage of a picturesque site – the remarkable round house designed by John Plaw in 1774 for Thomas English, recently restored after fire damage. The island is now wooded thanks to landscaping carried out for the Curwen family, whose home it was for many years. The house is best seen from cruises on the lake. On the shore are the houses and villas of those whose money was made elsewhere. The two most prominent are of radically contrasting architectural character.

Storrs Hall, south of Bowness and now a hotel, was remodelled by Sir John Soane's protégé Joseph Gandy in 1808. A temple, standing at the end of a causeway into the lake, had been built in 1804 to commemorate admirals Nelson, Duncan, Howe and St Vincent. North of Bowness, and on the west side of the lake, is **Wray Castle**, a romantic silhouette of turrets designed in 1840 by the Liverpool architect Henry Horner for the Liverpool surgeon James Dawson.

Windmill Hill, Wilts 690 C5, The hill is encircled by three concentric neolithic causeways, built *c*3400 BC and probably used until *c*2000 [EH].

Windsor, Berks 690 E5, The bustling town of Windsor is dominated by the massive bulk of the castle (*see* next page), around whose walls it clings and whose development and fortunes have had a direct influence on its growth. Before it was built, there was no settlement on the site; the name Windsor is thought to have come from a settlement further downstream, known as Windlesora (the word indicates a place on the riverbank where there was a windlass). This part

Top: Windermere, England's largest lake. It is busy around Bowness, and more tranquil at its northern and southern ends.

Centre: Windmill Hill. This neolithic camp consists of three ditches of chalk, and was a gathering place for sheep, goats and pigs to be prepared for slaughter.

Below right: Windsor Guildhall, by Sir Thomas Fitch *c*1687 and Wren 1689–90.

of the country has long been associated with the rulers of England, for Windlesora occupied the strategic border position between the Saxon kingdoms of Mercia and Sussex and was the site of a royal palace. The medieval town of Windsor sprang up around the castle in order to supply the goods and services needed. Its narrow streets can still be seen in the area between the High Street and the castle wall. Until fairly recently the street names reflected the functions of the area (Butcher Row, Fish Street, King's Market Place). Queen Charlotte Street, at 51 feet 10 inches (15.8m), must be the shortest street in England. Gradually the town expanded and developed its importance as a river port. An appealing array of 17th-century properties, with many Georgian and Victorian houses, can be seen in Thames Street, High Street and Park Street. Park Street, Georgian with a handful of neo-Georgian properties, was the start of the route to London; the gates were erected in 1851. The town did not expand noticeably until the mid-19th century.

The **Guildhall** is a wonderfully handsome building designed by Sir Thomas Fitch and executed by Sir Christopher Wren in 1690. It is boldly classical, but the Tuscan columns and

arcades only pretend to support the meeting rooms above – Wren left a tiny gap above them, to prove that they are merely decorative. The end elevations are divided by pilasters, and the statues are of Queen Anne and Prince George of Denmark.

Holy Trinity was the nucleus of the early Victorian development of the town. It was designed by Edward Blore, who had remodelled Buckingham Palace* for Prince Albert. Straight avenues lead out from the church. Although **St John the Baptist** dates only from 1820, there has been a church on this site since the 12th century. The present building was designed by Charles Hollis and Jeffry Wyatville. Inside, the use of cast iron for the columns and roof trusses creates a feeling of airy elegance. The south chapel railings, taken from the Chapel at the castle, are by Grinling Gibbons.

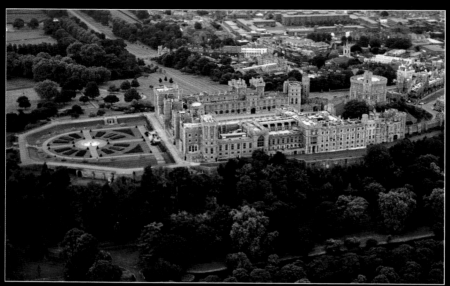

James Wyatt and his nephew Jeffry Wyatville. The latter was responsible for heightening the Round Tower, enhancing the battlements and towers, the Waterloo Chamber and St George's Hall. The contents of the Royal Palace are among the greatest treasures in the land. There are porcelain services from factories such as Sèvres, Meissen and Worcester, and paintings by Rubens and his school hang in the King's Drawing Room, formerly known as the Rubens Room. Other works of art include paintings by Canaletto, Gainsborough, Van Dyck, Holbein and Rembrandt. You will also find three painted ceilings by Verrio and carvings by Grinling Gibbons, commissioned by Charles II.

Windsor Castle, Berks 690 E5, The castle, with its picturesque battlements, is an unforgettable sight. Its location, perched dramatically on the chalk cliff, was chosen by William the Conqueror, c1080, as the one defensible site on the Thames between London and Wallingford, which benefited from commanding views of the surrounding countryside. This is England's premier castle. It has been a royal residence since 1110 when Henry I established domestic quarters here. It contains the royal palace, a spectacular collegiate church, workplaces and residences of people associated with the castle and college. Here, the wealth and glory of the country's monarchs is everywhere demonstrated with sumptuous interiors, and carving and craftsmanship of the highest quality. A serious fire in 1992 did considerable damage, but all has now been comprehensively and beautifully restored.

The motte of William the Conqueror's castle is at the centre of the site and forms the base of the Round Tower built by Henry II. Major building works were undertaken by Henry III, Edward III (the associated College of St George occupies the lower ward), Edward IV, who built St George's Chapel, and Charles II. But the appearance of the Castle today dates from the early 19th century, when changes were made for George III and George IV by

A rare suite of silver furniture dates from the 17th century, a fashion inspired by Louis XIV. There is a bed with the original hangings made for the State Visit of Emperor Napoleon III and Empress Eugénie in 1855.

The Lower Ward contains the Albert Memorial Chapel, St George's Chapel, the Henry VIII Gate and the Horseshoe Cloister. St George's Chapel was begun by Edward IV in 1475 and

finished by his son-in-law Henry VII. It is one of the best examples of Perpendicular Gothic in the country. The Chapel, with its south front of repeated battlements, pinnacles, flying buttresses and polygonal transept, and the west end with a vast 15-light window between two towers, dominates the Lower Ward. Within are the tombs of ten monarchs.

Top left: An aerial view of the Castle and park.

Centre left: Curfew Tower, in the perimeter wall.

Centre right: St George's Chapel, begun by King Edward IV in 1475 and finally completed by Henry VIII in 1528. It is a fine example of Perpendicular Gothic.

Bottom left: The massive King Henry VIII Gate, the entrance to the Lower Ward.

Left: The choir stalls in St George's Chapel, hung with banners of the Knights of the Garter. The chapel is the spiritual home of the Order of the Garter, of which Saint George is the patron saint. The east window is by Clayton and Bell.

Bottom left: The Garter Throne Room, with a state portrait of Her Majesty the Queen by Sir James Gunn, 1954–6, over the fireplace. Both this and the Queen's Bedroom were remodelled by Wyatt for William IV.

Bottom right: The Queen's Ballroom, entirely hung with portraits by Van Dyck, contains a rare collection of silver furniture from the 17th century.

Top left and above:
Wingfield, church of St
Andrew. The vaults contain
interesting tombs.

Opposite page, main picture:
Wisbech, Peckover House,
built in 1722 facing the
River Nene.

Wing, Bucks, All Saints is a well-known church and rightly so, for it retains a 9th-century crypt and nave, and a beautiful 10th-century polygonal apse. Such an ambitious design indicates that the church probably housed the relics of an important saint. Note also the 15th-century hammerbeam roof, rood screen and fine Dormer monuments. *See* **Ascott* 690 E3.**

Wingfield, Suffk 695 J6, Within the creamy limestone interior of St Andrew's ambitious church are beautiful medieval tombs to the de la Poles, who built the moated castle with its impressive gatehouse in 1384, and to the Wingfields who, in 1361, founded the priests' college now hidden behind the pedimented façade of nearby Wingfield College, centre of a celebrated rural arts festival [EH].

Wingfield Manor, Derbys 694 D4, The ruined mansion of Ralph, Lord Cromwell, Treasurer of England, at South Wingfield. It was constructed in 1440–55 round two courtyards, and is of the highest quality. In the 1770s the house was abandoned but in the last century it was absorbed into a farm, which is still functioning.

Winkworth Arboretum, Surrey 690 E6, Southeast of Godalming* is this interesting arboretum, created in the early-20th century and now displaying over 1,000 different shrubs and trees, many of them rare. The spring show of azaleas and bluebells is particularly spectacular.

Winslow, Bucks 690 E3, A small but historic town, the Winslow Estate having been granted by King Offa to St Albans in 795. The church of St Lawrence has good wall-paintings of c1500 but the town's main attraction is Winslow Hall (1700–4), a perfect example of a William and Mary house convincingly attributed to Christopher Wren.

Winterbourne Bassett, Wilts 690 C5, The church of St Katherine has an early English font and 17th-century furniture and fittings. A 13th-century tomb cover has a carving of a man and woman holding hands.

Wirksworth, Derbys 694 C4, The centre of the English lead-mining industry from Roman times;

Above: Winslow Hall, the
wonderfully proportioned
façade.

Bottom: Winkworth
Arboretum. The azaleas are
renowned.

part of the town is made up of a maze of narrow streets lined with small houses, which were presumably occupied by lead miners. Like many of Derbyshire's small towns, Wirksworth gains added interest from its different levels and mixture of buildings. St Mary's Church is large, with a crossing tower. Much of the fabric is 13th century, though there was a grand church here in Norman times, and there has also been a lot of 19th-century restoration. It contains an important Saxon coffin lid of about AD 800, which is covered with figure carving.

Wisbech, Cambs 695 G5, The splendid sequence of Georgian residences and warehouses on either side of the Nene at North and South Brink give this market town and port a distinctly Dutch flavour and a fragile beauty – although it is now at the mercy of flooding and the vagaries of post-war traffic planning. Social reformer Octavia Hill was born at No. 7 South Brink (now a museum) in 1838. She also co-founded the National Trust, which now owns the early 18th-century **Peckover House** on North Brink, former home of Quaker banker Jonathan Peckover. This elegant town house has outstanding plaster and wood rococo decoration and a Victorian walled garden with an orangery and fernery. Nearby a Sir George Gilbert Scott memorial, with Wedgwood bas-reliefs, salutes local hero Thomas Clarkson, who recruited William Wilberforce to his crusade against the slave trade. Wisbech also has a good museum in an atmospheric little square, Joseph Medworth's handsome Georgian circus and a 1793 theatre restored to working order. The church, surrounded by beautiful early 19th-century headstones, has unusual twin naves and aisles, an elaborate 16th-century tower and a huge brass to Sir Thomas de Braunstone, c1400, former constable of the castle.

Wisley Royal Horticultural Society Gardens, Surrey 690 E5, The famed gardens extend to 240 acres (97ha). It is a wonderful place to explore and observe the countless varieties of plants. The spring-flowering azaleas and rhododendrons are especially fine.

Wistman's Wood, Devon 689 F6, A wild place with contorted, lichen-festooned trees that may be a rare remainder of a primeval forest.

Witham, Essex 691 H4, This thoroughfare town is lined with old coaching inns and Georgian brick-fronted houses, including No. 26 Newland Street, home of Dorothy L Sayers from 1926 to 1957. From here she created sleuth Lord Peter Wimsey – and the slogan 'Guinness is Good for You'.

Wisbech, Peckover House
Above: The Dining Room.

18th-century carving on the
Morning Room fireplace.

The summerhouse with
circular pool.

Spring, one of *The Four Seasons*
after Rosalba Carriera.

The Victorian garden covers
2 acres (0.8ha).

Witley Court, Worcs 693 H5, William Ward, 1st Earl of Dudley, was one of the richest men in the world when his trustees purchased Witley Court for him in 1837; visitors later remembered the family Christmas tree being hung with real jewels for the ladies to choose from. An earlier house had been completely remodelled in the 18th century before the Earl of Dudley's confident Italian palace by Samuel Daukes, 1855–9, emerged in Bath stone cladding. He employed the garden-designer WA Nesfield to lay out the grand parterres, but the best features are the stupendous fountains of Perseus and Flora. Perseus was played only twice a week, as the reservoir that powered it needed to be pumped full. At 8pm on 7 September 1937 there began a fire which was to ruin Witley, and coachloads came out from Birmingham* to watch it burn. The gigantic ruins of the house are now a melancholy monument to the industrialist's immense extravagance [EH]. The church of **St Michael** stands very near to the house. Its 18th-century shell was fitted out in 1747 in a remarkable manner: the second Lord Foley, then the house's owner, purchased the contents of the chapel at Canons, including Bellucci's paintings, and brought them to Witley. The stuccowork by Giovanni Bagutti at Canons was also copied, and reproduced in papier-mâché, creating a complete copy of a baroque interior.

Witney, Oxon 690 D4, Witney is an interesting town with a 17th-century butter cross in its Market

Witley Court
Top left: The south front, with John Nash's portico.
Top right: James Forsyth's fountain of Perseus and Andromeda, which was driven by a 40-horse-power steam engine. The family used to row on its pool.
Below: Domed pavillion in the South Parterre garden.

Place. It has long been known for its blanket-making industry, and in the High Street stands the historic Blanket Hall of 1721. The large and handsome church of St Mary dates from the 13th to 15th centuries. The wide expanse of Church Green is lined with attractive Georgian and Victorian houses. The Hermitage includes 16th-century work and was apparently used by the Oxford* Colleges of Merton, St John's and Corpus Christi as a retreat from the plague.

Witley Court
Bottom left: The Orangery, by Samuel Daukes, still contains a camellia that survived the fire.
Bottom right: The spectacular ruins.

Woburn Abbey
Top left: *Valkhof at Nijmegen on the Waal*, by Aelbert Cuyp.

Centre: The Venetian Room contains 21 views of Venice by Canaletto, including *Entrance to the Arsenal*.
Bottom right: The west front.

Woburn Abbey

W

collections of paintings, furniture, porcelain, gold and silver. The number and quality of the portraits in the house is breathtaking; the collection includes works by the finest painters from the 16th century to the present day. The State Dining Room is hung with full-length portraits by Van Dyck. This adjoins the Breakfast Room where, amongst the Reynolds paintings on display is the exquisite picture of Lady Elizabeth Keppel wearing the bridesmaid's dress she wore to Queen Charlotte's wedding. Queen Victoria's Dressing Room contains the collection of 17th-century Dutch and Flemish works, and the Venetian Room houses 21 Venetian views by Canaletto commissioned by the 4th Duke while on the Grand Tour in 1731.

Woburn Abbey, Beds 690 E3, Beautifully situated within 3,000 acres (1,200ha) of rolling parkland, this is one of the great treasure houses of Britain. When the 13th Duke of Bedford opened Woburn Abbey to the public in 1955 in order to fund the repair and maintenance costs, he effectively founded the stately-home business. Today the abbey offers a number of attractions with which to lure the public: the historic house and its collections, the gardens, antiques centre, deer park and safari park. Woburn was granted to the Russell family by Edward VI in 1547, following the Dissolution of the Monasteries. It has been the home of the earls and dukes of Bedford since 1619, when the 4th Earl built the first mansion (he was also responsible for the development of London's Covent Garden*).

Built on the site of the monastic courtyard, the house, with its handsome Palladian appearance, is largely the work of Henry Flitcroft. He was commissioned in 1747 by the 4th Duke to build the stable courts and rebuild the west wing to house the state rooms. The 5th Duke employed Henry Holland to build the east wing, Sculpture Gallery, Chinese Dairy, riding school and tennis court, and to re-model the Dining Room and Library. (Owing to escalating costs and rampant dry rot, the east wing, riding school and tennis court were demolished in 1949.) The grand interiors provide a perfect setting for the rich

In the crypt are the porcelain, gold and silver collections. These include pieces and services from the Sèvres, Meissen and Davenport factories, and masterly work by silversmiths over the centuries. On the ground floor of the north wing the 17th-century grotto survives, now glassed in. The stone is carved in imitation of stalactites and seaweed and inlaid with shells. The furniture carved with shells and dolphins dates from the 18th century. The 6th Duke commissioned Humphry Repton to improve the park and pleasure gardens; Repton's *Red Book*, dated 1804, depicting before and after views, is in the Library. Nine species of deer roam the park, including the rare Père David Chinese deer. This species was saved from extinction by the 11th Duke, and in 1985 was successfully re-introduced to China.

The village of Woburn is very attractive, having retained much of its Georgian character. The church of St Mary was built for the 8th Duke of Bedford by Henry Clutton in 1865–8.

Wolfeton House
Top left: The medieval gatehouse has two unmatched towers.
Top right: The late-16th-century staircase. Underneath it, the plaster ceiling and panelling date from c1580.

Bottom: Wollaton Hall, the fantastic main front of the 1580s.

example of Norman Shaw's work. Lucas Hospital is a very impressive building of 1665, surprisingly early for its design. Two wings project forward from the main block, the central three bays of which are marked with a pediment and coat of arms, with an octagonal cupola above.

Wolfeton House, Dorset 689 J6, Near to the county town of Dorchester*, a medieval and Elizabethan house, which lies in the water meadows near the confluence of the rivers Cerne and Frome. It has a splendid stone chimneypiece in the Long Gallery (c1600), reminiscent of much of the West Country work seen in houses such as Montacute* and Winterborne Herringston, and contains fine paintings and furniture.

Wollaton Hall, Notts 694 D4, One of the most spectacular Elizabethan houses in England, built for Sir Francis Willoughby in the 1580s to parade the wealth he derived from his coal mines. It stands on a hill to the west of Nottingham*, and has four great corner towers; its tower room soars up in the middle. The house is now a natural history museum and its grounds, which include a great stable block and the spectacular Camellia House, are a public

Wokingham, Berks 690 E5, All Saints is a medieval building, now largely obscured by Victorian restoration work. St Paul's is a High Victorian church, given to the town by John Walter of Bearwood. It is worth visiting for the unusual font, which is an early anticipation of the Art Nouveau movement. It is decorated with water lilies with intertwined stalks. Broad Street and Shute End contain many fine Georgian houses. St Crispin's School, built between 1950 and 1953 by the Ministry of Education, is a lightweight steel construction. At Holme Green is Lock's House, a good early 18th-century house with blue headers and red dressings. Nearby is Holme Grange, a fine

park. The parish church in the attractive village is mostly 14th century and contains a large number of monuments to the Willoughby family. There is also a simple monument to Robert Smythson, designer of the Hall and indeed the best-known Elizabethan architect, who was also responsible for Hardwick Hall*.

Wolterton, Norfk 695 J4, The village was swept away to make room for Baron Horatio Walpole's country house; only the round tower of its church survives, now a folly in Repton's park. Horatio, younger brother of Britain's first prime minister, commissioned Thomas Ripley, architect at Houghton*, to design his Palladian mansion in

1726, but before its completion purchased the moated Mannington Hall (dating from 1460) 2 miles (3.2km) away.

Wolverhampton, W Mids 693 H4, The town's gallery houses a surprisingly good collection of art, focusing on Pop Art in particular.

Woodbridge, Suffk 691 J3, This medieval port turned marina on the Deben, best approached either up the estuary or by train down the Finn valley from Ipswich*, has a rare 17th-century tide mill driven from a pond filled twice daily. Wind-powered Buttrum's Mill of 1835 is also restored. This delightful town proudly displays its Tudor and Georgian prosperity in winding streets that radiate out from Market Hill, where Shire Hall is dominant. Reshaped with Dutch gables and an external staircase, c1700, it was given to the town by Thomas Seckford, Elizabethan Master of the Rolls, whose ghost is said to haunt nearby Seckford Hall (now a hotel). He lies in St Mary's, tucked away off Church Street, and entered through the north porch which, like its massive tower, has elaborate flushwork. Edward Fitzgerald, who translated *The Rubaiyat of Omar Khayyam* in 1859 and is buried in Boulge churchyard, joined the Woodbridge Wits, a group of intellectuals who met in The Bull to relieve the boredom of provincial life.

Woodchester Park Mansion, Gloucs 690 B4, Sheltering below the heights of Minchinhampton Common, this shell of a Victorian mansion was never completed and now provides an intriguing

Left: Woodhenge. The position of the original post holes of the large Henge monument are now marked by concrete pillars, spreading over hundreds of feet.

Bottom right: Woodchester Park Mansion, which was never completed. The National Trust run courses on stone masonry and building conservation at the site.

skeleton of a house where work was abandoned in the late 1860s after 14 years of effort. It is sometimes used for training courses in historic building techniques. It was designed by Benjamin Bucknall, Viollet-le-duc's English translator, in homage to that 19th-century French gothicist, with gargoyles copied from those he added to Notre-Dame in Paris. The mansion is a mile's walk along the National Trust's valley with its chain of five 18th-century lakes. Woodchester is also famous for its Roman mosaic. It shows Orpheus playing his lyre, and formed part of a 60-room villa discovered and excavated by Samuel Lysons in the late 18th century. Because of the damage that the mosaic suffered once exposed, it has since been covered up again.

Woodhall Park, Herts 691 F4, This house, built for Thomas Rumbold of the East India Company by Thomas Leverton in 1777, has been much altered over the years, but still contains some fine interiors. The staircase hall is the most memorable space, the cantilevered stair sweeping upwards while the walls are enlivened with delicate grisaille decoration.

Woodhenge, Wilts 690 C6, Six Bronze Age concentric rings of wooden posts, now replaced by concrete, inside a mound and a ditch [EH].

Woodstock, Oxon 690 D4, The main street of this small town is also the principal approach to Blenheim Palace*, whose huge estate dominates

the surrounding area. Woodstock once had a fine medieval royal palace where the young Princess Elizabeth was imprisoned in 1554. This was finally demolished in c1710 despite protests from Vanbrugh, who wanted to retain it as a romantic ruin.

Perpendicular porch, its delicately parapeted freestone face a symmetry of canopied niches. Inside is a magnificent double hammerbeam roof, large grotesque faces and an unusual canopy of honour over the chancel arch. Creamy yellow bricks made locally helped build the White House in Washington, DC.

Woolsthorpe Manor, Lincs 694 E4, A modest limestone house of about 1620 [NT], where Isaac Newton was born and where, in 1665, he discovered the principles of differential calculus. Besides inventing calculus, he solved some of the mysteries of light and, most importantly of all, evolved the theory of gravity. He was educated 7 miles (11km) away, at Grantham* Grammar School, and then at Trinity College, Cambridge*.

Wootton Wawen, Warwks 694 C6, A pretty black-and-white village that is home to a dipper colony which possesses special nesting boxes in the River Alne. St Peter's Church is an interesting puzzle for church-enthusiasts to unravel. A Perpendicular tower is combined with 17th-century windows, a Norman wall to the nave, and another tower at the crossing with Saxon long-and-short work.

Wookey Hole, Somset 689 H4, The caves, a mile (1.6km) north of Wells*, have produced evidence of human occupation dating back to 35,000 BC. They are now owned by Madame Tussaud's*, who have added, among other things, a museum.

Woolpit, Suffk 695 H6, The church has a graceful Victorian spire and masterful

Worcester

Worcester, Worcs 690 B2, Ornate bone china has been manufactured in the city since 1751, and it gained a royal warrant in 1789, so it is unsurprising that it now has its own museums of porcelain – the Museum of Worcester Porcelain and the Worcester Spode Works . There are several interesting buildings here, such as the splendid red-brick 1720s Guildhall and the Royal Worcester factory.

St Wulstan founded the cathedral in 1084, and the earliest surviving part of the building is the Norman vaulted crypt, one of the largest in the country. It originally had a one-way system for the crowds of pilgrims who were visiting the shrine of St Oswald. The later highlights of Worcester Cathedral are the two royal tombs. Before the high altar lies the unpopular King John. He is positioned, as he himself commanded, between the tombs of St Wulstan and St Oswald; the story is that he knew he had little chance of entering the kingdom of Heaven, so he tried to disguise himself as a monk. His beard and hair are neatly combed, as they have been since his monument was made in the 1230s. To his right is Prince Arthur's Chantry, where Henry VIII's elder brother lies. The chantry is a confection of delicate vaulting and 88 tiny sculpted figures, many alas decapitated during the Reformation. Queen Elizabeth I visited the tombs in 1575. She entered the cathedral 'with great and solemn singing and music with cornetts and sackbutts', then 'diligently viewed the tomb of King John, together with the chapel and tomb of her dear uncle late Prince Arthur, all richly and beautifully adorned'. The rest of the interior is consistently and harmoniously 13th- and 14th-century in character, while most of the exterior is Victorian.

Worcester was the first town to declare itself for King Charles in the Civil War, and the very last to surrender. It was after defeat in the final battle of Worcester in 1651 that Charles II had to flee and hide from Cromwell. He planned his final campaign from the **Commandery** – a timber-framed house near the Cathedral. Originally the 11th-century Hospital of St Wulfstan, it has a lofty open-roofed Great Hall dating from around 1500 and some stained glass; it now contains a Civil War exhibition.

Down on the main shopping street, the **Guildhall**, a rosy red-brick monument to civic pride was built in 1721–3 and features statues of Charles I, Charles II and Queen Anne. It has fortunately escaped the demolition that has spoiled much of the historic centre of Worcester. Friar Street has some good Tudor and Elizabethan buildings, including The Greyfriars [NT], which exhibits furniture and textiles. The Tudor House Museum has exhibits on the domestic and social history of the city, and the Worcester City Museum and Art Gallery on Foregate Street features an exhibition on the River Severn.

See also Elgar's Birthplace Museum*, just 3 miles (5km) west of the city.

Top left: Statue of Charles I outside the Guildhall.

Top right: Worcester Cathedral, founded in 1084.

Centre: The Crypt was built by the Normans on the site of the earlier Saxon monastery founded by St Oswald, whose remains are still in the cathedral.

.

Worksop, Notts 694 D3, A little town with a schizophrenic past: it was the centre of a coal field but also part of the Dukeries (*see* Sherwood Forest*). Both the coal and the private estates are much less in evidence now. Medieval Worksop clustered round Worksop Priory, a splendid late 12th-century church that now stands on the eastern edge of the town. On the southern edge are the fragments of the Duke of Newcastle's great mansion, Worksop Manor. Across the road down a track is a hidden architectural gem: Worksop Manor Lodge – a tall mansion of about 1600. Built as some kind of

Top left: Worksop Manor, the triumphal arch of the Doric screen by James Paine.

Wraxall, church of All Saints
Top centre: The stained glass is Victorian, set in Perpendicular tracery.
Right: The 15th-century octagonal font.

dependancy of the 16th-century Worksop Manor and probably designed by Robert Smythson, the lodge is a cross-shaped house. Originally it was two storeys taller and many of the great windows that are now blocked were glazed. Inside are two enormous rooms and a host of smaller ones, all linked by a stone spiral stair.

Worstead, Norfk 695 J4, This attractive village gave its name to the famous woollen cloth that paid for St Mary's late 14th-century church, its west tower over 100 feet (30m) high. Inside, a saintly screen depicts the infant William of Norwich and Saint Uncumber – the original bearded lady.

Worthenbury, Wrexhm 693 G2, St Deiniol's is probably the finest 18th-century church in Wales (built in the late 1730s by Richard Trubshaw). The sophisticated red brick with the stone quoins, together with the quality of the fittings and furnishings all indicate considerable gentry patronage, borne out by box pews, bearing illustrious family crests, with the two largest having their own fireplaces.

Above centre: Wraxall church's grey and buff stones are striped on the Perpendicular church tower, topped by its parapet.

Bottom: Wrest Park, the formal gardens. They include marble fountains, a bath house, parterre and orangery.

Wotton House, Bucks 690 D4, An imposing house at Wotton Underwood, built between 1704 and 1714 for Richard Grenville and given Sir John Soane's characteristic mark in 1821–2. The drastic 18th-century landscaping of the grounds by Capability Brown involved the removal of an entire village.

Wraxall, Somset 689 H3, The fine Perpendicular church of All Saints contains a preponderance of Victorian stained glass by CE Kempe. The windows afford almost too little light to permit a proper examination of the 15th-century tomb, with recumbent effigies, of Sir Edmund and Lady Gorges. Tyntesfield [NT], a great Victorian gothic

house built for the Gibbs family out of the profits of guano, lies within the parish.

Wreay, Cumb 696 E3, One of England's most improbable churches, designed by Sarah Losh as a memorial to her sister who died in 1835. It is in an eclectic neo-Norman/Lombardic style reflecting her extensive travels. The church is decorated with wild carvings of plants and animals. The woodwork has parts of the bark left on and the glass contains fragments from the Archbishop's Palace at Sens. The individuality and eccentricity of the church is maintained in the sisters' tomb in the church, built in random, cyclopean masonry.

Wrest Park, Beds 691 F3, The house (1834–9) was built by Earl de Grey to his own designs in mid-18th-century French château-style [EH]. The gardens cover over 90 acres (36ha) and include a parterre and orangery. The de Grey family mausoleum is at nearby Flitton*.

Wrexham

Wrexham, Wrexhm 693 F2, North Wales' largest town, equidistant from Offa's Dyke* and the English border, developed from a market town into a substantial commercial centre to meet the demands of a growing population dependent on the expanding coal and iron industries. The High Street, with the 18th-century Wynnstay Hotel at its head, has kept most of its varied 19th-century buildings. The turn-of-the-century boom in house-building resulted in the profusion of the locally produced Ruabon red brick.

The parish church of **St Giles** has the grandeur of a cathedral. Its intricately and richly ornamental tower (1506) is extolled in a popular rhyme as one of the 'Seven Wonders of Wales'. A replica of it was built in the 1920s at Yale, Connecticut. The University itself was named after Elihu Yale, its greatest benefactor, whose ancestors were members of a Denbighshire family, and whose father emigrated to America in the 1640s. On Elihu's retirement, after a successful career that included serving as Governor of the East India Company in Madras, he divided his time between London and an estate near Wrexham. The church interior is full of interest: a fine timber roof, enigmatic wall paintings, an impressive early-16th-century brass eagle lectern, and among the many monuments, a very theatrical one by Louis Roubiliac to May Myddelton (d. 1747) of Chirk Castle*. Although much restored in 1900, the churchyard gates of 1720 still bear testimony to the innovative talent of the Davies brothers of Croes Foel, 2 miles (3.2km) away, whose work was sought in the important churches and houses of northeast Wales.

Top: St Giles Church. The tower, 'one of the Seven Wonders of Wales', dominates the town.

Centre: A timber-framed shop in the town centre, formerly the Talbot Hotel of 1904–5. The old library is in the background on the right.

Wroxeter, Shrops 693 G4, The fourth-largest Roman city in Britain [EH]. Much of it has now been excavated and the remains are impressive, especially those of the Bath House. Finds from the excavations are displayed in a museum.

Wroxton Abbey, Oxon, A house begun in the early 17th century incorporating fragments of an early priory. The abbey was worked on by Sanderson Miller and contains some exquisite carved woodwork. *See* **Alkerton* 690 D3.**

Wyddial, Herts 691 F3, The church exhibits a fine example of Tudor brickwork in the north aisle and north chancel. The screen to the chancel dates from the early 17th century.

Wye Valley 693 G6, The Wye (from the Welsh 'gwy' or water) rises on Plynlimon and flows past Ross-on-Wye* and Monmouth* before joining the Severn just south of Chepstow*. The wooded river valley has spectacular scenery, much lauded by 18th-century poets, including Wordsworth and Coleridge. It is dotted with border castles like Goodrich* and Chepstow, and the romantic Tintern Abbey*.

Wylam, Nthumb 697 G2, This small village on the River Tyne was the birthplace on 9 June 1781 of one of the founding fathers of the railway age,

Wroxeter
Opposite page: The bath house and hypocaust.
Top left: An elaborately carved capital.

Top right and right: Wylam, George Stephenson's Birthplace. The whole family occupied one room in the tenement block.

Bottom: Wye Valley. The 'tour', much enjoyed by tourists in the 18th and 19th centuries, is still popular.

George Stephenson, who developed the concept of steam-powered locomotives for the drawing of coal waggons. Appropriately, the half-mile (0.8km) walk to George Stephenson's Birthplace [NT] is along the cinder trackbed of a colliery horse-drawn waggonway. The whitewashed two-storey tenement property, cottage-like in scale, accommodated several mining families.

Wymington, Beds 694 E6, St Lawrence is a late 14th-century church, executed in the slightly outdated Decorated style. Inside is the tomb of the patron, wool merchant John Curteys.

Wymondham, Norfk 695 J5, A small, prosperous wool town of long winding streets lined with an attractive mixture of Georgian town houses and timber-framed buildings that survived the fire of 1615. Centrepiece of its triangular Market Hill is an octagonal market cross on stilts, early 17th century; but Wymondham's chief glory is its twin-towered abbey church rising from the Tiffey watermeadows. The chancel has gone but the massive nave is part of William d'Albini's 1107 foundation. Townsfolk built a second west tower in 1450 after a dispute with a predecessor of Abbott Ferrers whose elaborate terracotta tomb, *c*1525, stands near the high altar.

Wymondley Hall, Herts 691 F3 A handsome early 17th-century house in Little Wymondley, on the road to the early 13th-century Wymondley Priory, which was converted into a dwelling in the mid-1500s by James Nedeham, Surveyor of the King's Works.

Wynnstay, Wrexhm 693 F3, This estate once represented patronage at its most extravagant. The 1858 French château replacement (by Benjamin Ferrey) was built after fire gutted the original house.

Wythenshawe, Gt Man 697 F7, Substantial areas of south Manchester* were covered by the laying out

Top left: Wymondham's distinctive market cross, erected in the early 17th century and repaired several times since.

Right: Wythenshawe Hall, set in the midst of a large suburban park in the south of Manchester.

Below: Yell, a fisherman's memorial.

of the vast Manchester housing estates by Barry Parker in 1931, following the garden city/suburb principles established at Letchworth or Hampstead* in London. There is a great feeling of spaciousness, though the architecture is disappointing. In the park is **Wythenshawe Hall,**

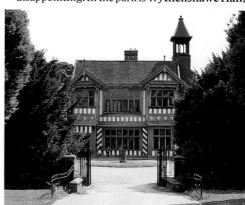

a 16th-century house now much restored, one of the first examples of a hall not open to the roof and with a good 18th-century staircase. Less fortunate in its setting is **Baguley Hall,** a more important and less altered house. Its 14th-century open hall roof is one of the finest in England, with timbers of heroic size, heavily cusped bracing, a spere truss and good examples of the triple doorways to buttery, pantry and kitchen at the service end. These south Manchester suburbs contain a clutch of 20th-century churches of the greatest interest. Outstanding among these are George Pace's William Temple Memorial Church (1964), a brick-clad concrete structure with a dramatic steel roof, almost square in plan but with the liturgical planning on the diagonal; and Cachemaille-Day's St Michael and All Angels (1937) on a plan of intersecting squares that makes the church a fascinating exercise in geometry. Not far away is another Cachemaille-Day church, St Nicholas Burnage, 1931–2, a little formidable from the outside but dramatic inside with staircases leading up and behind the high altar to a Lady Chapel and a lofty Baptistry; a major internal intervention at the west by Antony Grimshaw (2001) provides a circular glazed meeting room.

Yarnton, Oxon 690 D4, The church contains some good 17th-century monuments to the Spencers in the family chapel. The Jacobean screen with strapwork and bosses is very fine.

Yate, Gloucs 689 J3, The low-built church of St Mary is dominated by its impressive Perpendicular west tower, buttressed and pinnacled, with a large stair turret. The font is 14th century.

Yatton, Somset 689 H4, The early 14th-century church of St Mary has the finest decorated (south) porch in Somerset. Thin Perpendicular stone lines rise up over the ogee-curved doorway to the crocketed and pierced balustrade.

Yell, Shet 703 H2, The largest of Shetland*'s northern islands is also the least fertile of the inhabited islands. The road linking Ulsta (ferries from Toft) with Gutcher (ferries to Unst* and Fetlar*) crosses peat bogs and moorland incised by deep fjords.

Aywick: A walk across the moors to the hills above the Bay of Aywick takes you past an Iron Age fort on the islet of Brough of Stoal.

Burravoe: Old Haa Visitor Centre, a small museum housed in a 17th-century manor, provides an introduction to local history. In the same street St Colman's Church (1900) is a delightful example of Arts and Crafts architecture.

Cullivoe: The northeast tip of Yell is less austere, with meadows dotted with haystacks in summer and greenhouses filled with early vegetables. To the west of Breckon beach, seasoned walkers can follow the path that skirts round Gloup Voe, at the north end of the island, crosses the moorland to the southwest and leads to the spectacular ruins of the Burgi Geos broch.

Left: Yatton, the church of St Mary has Norman origins. It was built in the 13th century and enlarged in the 17th.

Right: Yell, the Old Haa Visitor Centre in Burravoe, which has exhibits detailing local history.

Bottom: Yeovilton, the Fleet Air Arm Museum, Concorde, alongside a British jet aircraft.

Mid Yell: About 1 mile (0.8km) to the west of Mid Yell, near the ruins of a haunted manor, Windhouse (1880), are an unexcavated broch, the remains of a Viking farm and a well-preserved megalithic tomb. The RSPB reserve of Lumbister, to the north of Windhouse, provides sanctuary for otters and a number of species of birds, including skuas, merlins, plovers and red-throated divers.

Yeovilton, Somset 689 H5, The Fleet Air Museum was opened at the Royal Naval Air Station in 1964, to celebrate 50 years of naval flying. As well as

displays charting its history and development, there are also over 50 aircraft on show, including the Sea Vampire, the craft that made the first jet deck-landing in 1945, and Concorde 002.

Ynyspandy, Gwynd 692 D3, One of the most unusual reminders of the great North Wales slate industry. Even in ruins, Ynyspandy Slate Mills are impressive and impart the faith that its builders had in the possibility of sawing slate from the Gorseddau quarries by means of water-power. Begun in 1864, the enterprise had failed by 1870.

York

York, N York 697 H5, The Roman city of Eboracum; there was a large military fortress and a high-ranking civilian *colonia* here. It became Eoforwic to the Anglo-Saxons, and Jorvik to the Danes – hence its modern name. York was medieval England's second city, and to this day the Lord Mayor of York gives precedence only to the Lord Mayor of London at national events, just as the Archbishop of York yields only to the Archbishop of Canterbury in church affairs. There are almost 2 miles (3.2km) of city walls surviving, with four gateways or 'bars', and 18 churches remain of the 40 which served the medieval city, in addition to its great Minster and numerous monastic houses. York has preserved many timber-framed houses and shops, such as the famous Shambles. Trade was regulated by craft guilds, the scale of the Merchant Adventurers' Hall giving some idea of their importance. When the great Royalist city fell to the Parliamentarians after a lengthy siege in 1644, Charles I knew that his crown was lost.

The Mansion House, where the Lord Mayor still lives during his or her year of office, was built in 1725, and the splendid Assembly Rooms of 1730 by Lord Burlington provided a venue for elegant Georgian balls. Eighteenth-century elegance is well preserved in Fairfax House, a handsome town house furnished with an outstanding collection of Georgian antiques, especially clocks. Nearby is the castle, with the shell-keep Clifford's Tower [EH] set on a Norman motte. The Castle Museum, with its famous recreated streets, occupies adjacent Georgian prison buildings.

Not far away is the superb Jorvik Viking Centre, recapturing the sights and smells of 10th-century York. The city boasts a wide variety of museums and galleries, including Roman and natural history collections in the Yorkshire Museum in the Museum Gardens next to the medieval ruins of St Mary's Abbey, and the York City Art Gallery, which has a fine collection of pots as well as excellent pictures.

York Minster stands on the site of several earlier minsters – the word is an Old English contraction of the Latin *monasterium* – and the Crypt has evidence of Roman and Norman buildings on the site. By cubic measurement, this is England's largest cathedral. Here, on Easter Day 627, King Edwin of Northumbria was baptized by Saint Paulinus. The mid-13th-century transepts were built by Archbishop Walter de Gray, and the north transept's tall lancets, the 'Five Sisters', have original grisaille glass. The Geometric-traceried windows of the Chapter House occupy the entire width of its eight sides: there is no central column, despite the large span, because the vault here, as in the rest of the Minster, is of wood, hence its susceptibility to major fires. The immense Nave was begun in 1291, the Perpendicular Choir and Lady Chapel completed in 1405. The twin west towers, finished in 1472, were the last medieval addition. The Treasurer's House (NT), substantially rebuilt in the 17th and 18th centuries, was originally home to the Minster's treasures but now houses a fine collection of 18th-century furniture.

The **National Railway Museum** on Leeman Road is one of the biggest in the world, and includes Queen Victoria's saloon carriage, plus the record-breaking locomotive *Mallard*.

Top right: The Rose Window in the south transept of York Minster, rare glass commemorating the ending of the Wars of the Roses by the marriage of Henry VII and Elizabeth of York. It was miraculously saved after the fire of 1984, caused by a lightning strike.

Left: A panel in the Great East Window of 1405.

Right: Micklegate Bar, the main south-facing gateway in the city's walls. The monarch is greeted here on state occasions.

  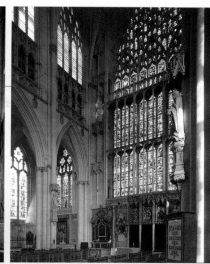

York Minster

Top left: The immense Nave, with William Kent's geometric pavement.

Below: A view of York Minster across the rooftops of streets that still follow the pattern laid down for the Roman fortress of Eboracum in ad 71.

Top centre: The choir stalls, replaced after a disastrous fire started by the painter John Martin's brother in 1829.

Top right: The Great East Window, with original medieval glazing of an area larger than a tennis court.

Yorkshire Dales, N York 697 F5, A series of valleys running west to east, from Swaledale southwards to Wharfedale; their rivers eventually form the River Ouse. Most of the dales take their name from their river, but Wensleydale is the dale of the Ure. Each dale is V-shaped, with relatively steep sides and little flat bottom land, so they are unsuitable for arable agriculture; but the meadows produce a

Yorkshire Dales
Above: Swaledale.
Below: Kilney Crag.

crop of herb-rich hay. The field barns that so characterize the landscape were built to store it, as well as to house cattle. The Dales, the habitat of the red grouse, are home also to more sheep than humans, and are of great beauty. Among the many spectacular natural features of this large area are Malham Cove, a massive vertical limestone cliff that was created during the Ice Age, and White Scar Caves near Ingleton, a series of caves discovered in 1932, stretching for nearly ⅝ of a mile (1km), with underground waterfalls.

Zennor, Cnwll 688 B7, Here is the Wayside Museum, displaying artefacts from the area, and the church of St Senar (or Senner), with its famous pew carved with a mermaid. Pendeen and St Just were two of the main mining centres of the far west, of which remains can be seen at Geevor and Levant.

City Index

Picture credits

Abbreviations:

AA	AA World Travel Library
AH	Angelo Hornak Library, London
BAL	The Bridgeman Art Library, London
CADW	Welsh Historic Monuments, Cardiff
DC	Douglas Corrance, Edinburgh
EH	English Heritage Photographic Library, London
NT	National Trust Photographic Library, London
NGS	National Gallery of Scotland
NTS	National Trust for Scotland
PA	Peter Ashley
RM	Richard Muir
SMPC	The Still Moving Picture Company, Edinburgh
SNPG	Scottish National Portrait Gallery

Pictures are credited as they appear top to bottom from the left to the right of the page.

2-3 © AH
4 © NT/Matthew Antrobus. © NT/Oliver Benn. © CADW. © EH/Nigel Corrie. © CJB Photography, Hagley. © Lindsay Evans.
6 © AA. © Misha Anikst.
8 © NT/Andrew Butler.
9 © The Museum of London. © David Levenson.
10 © NT/J.Whitaker. © NT/Andreas von Einsiedel.
11 © Holkham Estate.
12 © NT/Nick Meers.
13 © AH.
14 © RM. © Lewis-Darley/ Edifice.
15 © AH.
16-23 © RM.
24-39 All pictures by International Artworks © Everyman Publishers.
40 © Victoria & Albert Museum, London/BAL. © National Gallery, London/BAL. © NGS. © Courtesy of the Vicar and Churchwardens of St Mary's Priory Church, Abergavenny.
41 © Coram Foundation, Foundling Museum, London/BAL. © NGS/BAL. © SNPG/BAL. © EH.
42 © Manchester City Art Galleries/BAL. © Leeds Museums and Galleries (City Art Gallery)/BAL. © Ipswich Borough Council Museums and Galleries, Suffolk/BAL. © Dulwich Picture Gallery, London/BAL.
43 © British Museum, London/BAL. © The Barber Institute of Fine Arts, University of Birmingham/ BAL. © Tate, London 2002. © NGS/BAL. © NGS.
44 © Birmingham Museums and Art Gallery/BAL. © Laing Art Gallery, Tyne & Wear/BAL. © Royal Holloway and Bedford New College, Surrey/BAL. © Blackburn Museum & Art Galleries, Lancashire.
45 *Mr and Mrs Clark and Percy*, David Hockney, 1970-71, acrylic on canvas, 84 x 120" © David Hockney/Tate, London 2002. © Whitworth Art Gallery, The University of Manchester/BAL. *Furnaces*, Stanley Spencer © Estate of Stanley Spencer 2002. All Rights Reserved, DACS/Imperial War Museum, London. *Figure Study II*, 1945-46 (oil on canvas), Francis Bacon, Kirkless Metropolitan Council, Huddersfield, Yorkshire/BAL © Estate of Francis Bacon 2002. All rights reserved, DACS. © Reproduced by permission of the Henry Moore Foundation/BAL.
47 © Lewis-Darley/Edifice. © Abbey Dore Court. © AA. © *idem*. © *idem*.
48 © Collections/R. Scruton. © Collections/C. Inch. © DC. © Collections/C. Inch. © AA.
49 © AA. © *idem*.
50 © NT/Andrew Butler. © AA. © *idem*.
51 © SMPC. © Lindsay Evans. © Emily Lane.
52 © A. Johnston/SMPC. © The Friend's School, Ackworth. © NT/ Clive Boursnell. © The Friend's School, Ackworth.
53 © St Mary's Church, Acton. © Adlington Hall Estate. © English Life/Adlington Hall Estate. © NT/ Clive Boursnell.
54 © PA. © Gillian Darley/Edifice. © PA.
55 © NT/Rob Matheson. © Emily Lane. © Museum of Scotland. © Private collection.
56 © English Life/Alnwick Castle. © Graeme Peacock/Alnwick Castle. © *idem*. © Lewis/Edifice. © Althorp Estate.
57 © Althorp Estate. © *idem*. © Alton Towers.
58 © Eddie Ryle-Hodges, Co. Durham. © NT/J. Whitaker. © NT/Derek Croucher.
59 © NT/Derek Croucher. © NT/John Bethell. © Arbeia Roman Fort and Museum/Tyne & Wear Museums. © Appleby Castle.
60 © Lewis-Darley/Edifice. © Arbeia Roman Fort and Museum/Tyne & Wear Museums. © Lewis-Darley/Edifice. © AA.
61 © Arley Hall and Gardens. © *idem*.
62 © Arley Hall and Gardens. © NT/Matthew Antrobus. © DC. © NT/Andreas von Einsiedel.
63 © CADW. © Arundel Castle.
64 © NT/Vera Collingwood. © NT/John Hammond.
65 © NT/John Hammond. © NT/Angelo Hornak. © NT/John Hammond.
66 © EH. © NT/John Blake.
67 © Athelhampton House. © NT/Mike Williams. © NT/James Mortimer.
68 © Phil Nixon, Durham. © *idem*. © Aubourn Hall.
69 © EH. © EH/Jeremy Richards. © EH. © *idem*.
70 © Skyscan Balloon Photography/EH. © EH.
71 ©Lewis-Darley/Edifice. © NT/Matthew Antrobus. © Darley/Edifice. © NT. © NT/John Hammond.
72 © AH. © NT/Rod J. Edwards. © NT/John Hammond. © NT/Andreas von Einsiedel. © NT/Oliver Benn.
73 © AA. © *idem*. © *idem*.
74 © AA. © Sayer/Edifice. © RM.
75 © Charles Coulson. © Emily Lane. © Bowes Museum.
76 © Barnsley House. © *idem*.
77 © NT/Neil Campbell-Sharp. © NT.
78 © AA. © Mary Evans Picture Library, London. © Basildon Park. © NT/John Blake.
79 © Simon McBride/Bath and North East Somerset Council. © Emily Lane.
80 © Bath and North East Somerset Council.
81 © AA. © *idem*. © *idem*. © *idem*.
82 © NT/Joe Cornish. © NT/David Noton. © The Holburne Museum of Art, Bath. © *idem*.
83 © AA. © *idem*.
84 © EH. © *idem*. © *idem*.
85 © CADW. © National Motor Museum, Beaulieu. © *idem*. © RM. © CADW.
86 © Sutton Heritage Service. © CADW. © Roos Hall, Beccles. © PA. © Gillian Darley/Edifice.
87 © PA. © Sayer/Edifice. © Skyscan Balloon Photography/EH. © Andrew Tryner/EH.
88 © EH. © EH/Paul Highnam. © EH.
89 © NT/Mark Fiennes. © *idem*. © NT/Christopher Hurst. © NT/Nick Meers.
90 © Belvoir Castle. © Arthur Pickett. © Belvoir Castle.
91 © NT/Andreas von Einsiedel. © NT. © Malcolm Hill/Bengeo, St Leonards.
92 © NT/Mark Fiennes. © NT/Tim Imrie. © *idem*. © Berkeley Castle.
93 © NT/Nadia McKenzie. © AA. © EH.
94 © AH. © Emily Lane. © EH.
95 © NT/Michael Walters. © NT/Nick Meers. © AA.
96 © RM. © EH.
97 © AA. © Lewis-Darley/Edifice. © Birmingham Museums and Art Gallery. © AA.
98 © AA. © *idem*. © *idem*.
99 © EH. © *idem*. © Blackburn Museum and Art Galleries, Lancashire.
100 © AA. © Lakeland Arts Trust & Jonathan Lynch. © *idem*.
101 © Blair Castle. © *idem*. © AH. © Nick Swallow.
102 © AH. © BAL.
103 Reproduced by kind permission of His Grace the Duke of Marlborough. © NT/John Hammond. © AH.
104 © PA. © Clews Architects.
105 © NT/Alasdair Ogilvie. © NT/Mike Warren. © NT/Christopher Gallagher. © *idem*. © Emily Lane.
106 © Paula Weideger/Edifice. © Lewis-Darley/Edifice. © Paula Weideger/Edifice. © John Morrison. © Bolton Abbey Photo Library.
107 © Cole/Edifice. © *idem*. © *idem*.
108 © EH. © *idem*. © Cornish Picture Library/Paul Watts. © Lewis-Darley/Edifice.
109 © By kind permission of His Grace the Duke of Buccleuch and Queensbury, KT. © *idem*. © *idem*.
110 © AA. © Boughton Monchelsea Place. © AA.
111 © The Bowood Estate. © *idem*. © NT/Andrew Butler. © EH.
112 © Christopher Phillips © *idem*. © Kim Sayer/Edifice.
113 © AA. © *idem*. © Christopher Phillips. © Stockport Metropolitan Borough Council.
114 © AA.
115 © Christopher Phillips. © RM. © Christopher Phillips. © Breamore House.
116 © AA. © RM. © PA. © AA.
117 © AA. © *idem*.
118 © AA. © AH.
119 © AA. © The Royal Pavilion. © AA. © EH/Graeme Peacock.
120 © Nick Swallow. © St Mary Redcliffe Church. © Kim Sayer/Edifice. © Nick Swallow. © *idem*.
121 © Nick Swallow. © AH.
122 © Lord Romsey/Broadlands. © C. Jansen. © AA.
123 © PA. © NT/Nick Meers.
124 © EH. © *idem*. © CADW.
125 © Broughton Castle. © *idem*. © *idem*. © Skyscan Balloon Photography/EH.
126 © Browsholme Hall. © NT/BKS Surveys Ltd.
127 © Christina Jansen. © *idem*. © NT/George Wright. © National Maritime Museum. © NT/George Wright.
128 © Burford House. © EH. © AA. © *idem*.
129 © AA. © *idem*. © Christina Jansen.
130 © English Life Publications Ltd. © *idem*. © *idem*.
131 © Gillian Darley/Edifice. © AA. © Lewis-Darley/Edifice. © AA.
132 © Sayer/Edifice. © Burton Agnes Hall. © *idem*.
133 © Burton Constable Foundation. © *idem*. © *idem*.
134 © St Mary's Church, Bury St Edmunds. © NT/Vera Collingwood.
135 © High Peak Borough Council. © EH. © Flora and Charlotte Wood/Mount Stuart Trust. © Butley Priory. © EH/Andrew Tryner. © Flora and Charlotte Wood/Mount Stuart Trust.
136 © CADW. © Y. Travert/Photo Non Stop.
137 © CADW. © J. Chevallier, F. Desbordes/Gallimard. © CADW. © DC. © A.Wright/SMPC.
138 © NT/Nick Meers. © Pinhole Productions/SMPC. © NT/Rupert Truman. © NT/Christopher Hurst.
139 © RM. © EH.
140 © Emily Lane. © AA. © Angela Edwards. © AA. © *idem*.
141 © Aerofilms, Herts.
142 © AA. © *idem*. © *idem*. © *idem*.
143 © AA. © The Fitzwilliam Museum, University of Cambridge. © *idem*. © *idem*. © *idem*.
144 © NT/Andrew Butler. © NT/Andrew Haslam.
145 © AA. © *idem*. © *idem*.
146 © Scala Publishers. © AH. © Scala Publishers.
147 © Scala Publishers. © AH.
148 © Capesthorne Hall. © *idem*. © The City and County of Cardiff. © AA.
149 © National Museum and Gallery of Wales, Cardiff. © AA. © *idem*. © *idem*. © *idem*.
150 © EH. © Carew Castle. © AA. © *idem*.
151 © AA. © EH.
152 © Lewis-Darley/Edifice. © CADW.
153 © John Morrison. © CADW. © *idem*.
154 © RM. © CADW. © AH. © EH.
155 © AA. © AH. © *idem*. © *idem*.
156 © AH. © G. Simeone/PHOTONONSTOP.
157 © EH. © Cawdor Castle (Tourism) Ltd. © *idem*.
158 © Woodmansterne Ltd, Watford. © AH. © Woodmansterne Ltd, Watford. © PA.
159 © NT/Andreas von Einsiedel. © Verity Welstead, courtesy of Charleston Trust. © Charleston Trust. © NT/Matthew Antrobus.
160 © Roger Smeeton. © Charterhouse. © NT/Derrick E.Witty.
161 © Chartham Church. © Darley/Edifice. © Emily Lane.
162 © AH. © AA.
163 © Chatsworth. © *idem*.
164 © Emily Lane. © Chawton. © Cheltenham Tourism.
165 © **Cheltenham Tourism.** © CADW. © NT/Matthew Antrobus.
166 © AA. © *idem*. © Christine Hinze.
167 © Edifice. © Skyscan Balloon Photography/EH. © Chettle House.
168 © AH. © Chillingham Castle. © Chiddingstone Castle.
169 © Chillington Hall. © Photoair. © Steve Norris/Chiltern Open Air Museum. © PA. © *idem*.
170 © AH. © AA.
171 © AA. © EH/Paul Highnam. © CADW.
172 © Lewis-Darley/Edifice. © *idem*. © AA. Lewis-Darley/Edifice.
173 © NT/John Bethell. © NT/Andy Williams. © NT.
174 © NT/John Hammond. © NT/Andreas von Einsiedel. © NT/Andrew Butler. © NT/John Hammond. © *idem*.
175 AH. © NT/John Blake. © AH.
176 © NT/Nick Meers.
177 © NT/Oliver Benn. © NT. © Cornish Picture Library/Paul Watts. © EH. © NT/John Hammond.
178 © NT/Mike Williams. © Cobham Hall. © NT/John Hammond. © Cobham Hall.
179 © NT/F.A.H. Bloemendal. © NT/Nick Meers. © NT/Andrew Butler.
180 NT/Andrew Butler. © NT/S.Greenwell.
181 © AA. © EH. © *idem*. © NT/Jason Ingram. © Heritage Cards and Souvenirs Ltd. © DC.
182 © NT/Francesco Venturi. © AA.
183 © Lewis-Darley/Edifice. © AA. NT/John Blake. © AA.
184 © RM. © Nick Swallow. © *idem*. © Manjushri Mahayana Buddhist Centre. © EH.
185 © NT/Matthew Antrobus. © RM.
186 © NT/Matthew Antrobus. © EH. © NT/Matthew Antrobus.
187 © Corsham Court Collection. © *idem*. © RM. © NT/ Andreas von Einsiedel. © *idem*.
188 © AA. © Steve Dovey/Gloucestershire County Council. © AA.
189 © Steve Dovey/Gloucestershire County Council. © AA. © *idem*.
190 © NT/ A. F. Kersling. © Cottesbrooke Hall. © Emily Lane. © Cottesbrooke Hall. © NT/George Wright. © *idem*.
191 © Judges Postcards Ltd/Coventry Cathedral. © AA. © The Laurence Sterne Trust.
192 © AH. © NT/Derrick E.Witty. © NTS.
193 © P.Somelet/PHOTONONSTOP. © Robert Lees/SMPC. © NTS. © DC.
194 © NT/Michael Allwood-Coppin. © CADW. © NT. © AA.
195 © Lewis-Darley/Edifice. © PA. © AA. © NT/David Noton.
196 © AA. © Phillipa Lewis/Edifice.
197 © AA. © DC. ©SNPG/BAL. © *idem*. © DC.
198 © Christopher Simon Sykes/The Interior Archive. © NTS. © DC.
199 © Cyfartha Castle. © *idem*. © CADW.
200 © AA. © NT/Roger Hickman. © Kim Sayer/Edifice. © DC.
201 © C. Jansen. © *idem*. © AA. © *idem*.
202 © RM. © EH. © PA.
203 © St Marys church. © Lewis-Darley/Edifice. © CADW.
204 © PA. © *idem*. © EH. © *idem*.
205 © John Morrison. © RM. © PA.
206 © NT/Andrew Butler. © *idem*. © Trevor Burrows Photography. © CADW. © NT.
207 © Lewis-Darley/Edifice. © Doddington Hall. © Lewis-Darley/Edifice. © Doddington Hall.
208 © Doncaster Metropolitan Borough Council. © *idem*. © *idem*.
209 © AA. © *idem*. © Frank Blackwell Photography, Oxfordshire. © AA.
210 © Dorney Court. © NT/Joe Cornish. © NT/John Miller. © Crown Copyright Reserved, Historic Scotland.
211 © EH. © NT/Stuart Chorley. © EH. © *idem*. © Downside Abbey.
212 © Christopher Simon Sykes-The Interior Archive. © B. Lenormand/Gallimard. © P.Taylor.
213 © AA. © DC. © NT/Michael Caldwell. © AA.
214 © B. Lenormand/Gallimard. © Duncombe Park Estate. © D. Robertson/SMPC. © STB/SMPC. © Mika/SMPC.
215 © Duncombe Park Estate. © *idem*. © *idem*. © *idem*.
216 © AA. © *idem*. © *idem*. Bob West/SMPC.
217 © NT/Mike Williams. © G. Reid/City Art Centre, Edinburgh.
218 © NT/Lee Frost. © AA. © NT/Magnus Rew. © AA.
219 © PA. © *idem*. © Nick Swallow. © NT/Bill Batten.
220 © AA. © AH. © *idem*. © *idem*.
221 © AH. © AA.
222 © NT/Andreas von Einsiedel. © idem. © EH. © Earls Barton Church. © NT/Rupert Truman. © EH.
223 © NT. © *idem*. © *idem*.
224 © NT/Matthew Antrobus. © Eastnor Castle. © *idem*.
225 © Eddie Ryle-Hodges/Edifice. © Apex News & Pictures, 2002. © *idem*.
226 © A. Lorgnier/Côtés Vues. © City Art Centre, Edinburgh. © *idem*. © DC.
227 © DC. © Lenormand/Gallimard.
228 © AA. © *idem*. © *idem*.
229 © AA. © DC. © AA. © S. Bosman. © Royal Museum of Scotland.
230 © AA. © *idem*. © *idem*.
231 © AA. © *idem*.
232 © S. Bosman. © Y.Travert/PHOTONONSTOP. © DC. © AA. © *idem*.
233 © AA. © NGS.
234 © EH. © EH/Jonathan Bailey.
235 © Royal Holloway College. © Emily Lane. © DC.
236 © Elstow Moot Hall Museum. © D. Robertson/SMPC. © *idem*.

© Gloucestershire County Council. © Elstow Moot Hall Museum.
237 © Elton Hall. © AA. © Elton Hall.
238 © AH. © *idem*. © RM.
239 © AH. © Christopher Phillips. © RM.
240 © NT/Rupert Truman. © NT/Jerry Harpur. © NT/Andreas von Einsiedel. © *idem*. © NT/Jerry Harpur. © NT/John Hammond.
241 © EH/Jonathan Bailey. © Eton College.
242 © Euston Hall. © *idem*. © Emily Lane.
243 © CADW. © Exbury Gardens. © Richard Greenly Photography/Exbury Gardens. © CADW.
244 © AA. © *idem*. © *idem*.
245 © AA. © Emily Lane. © AA.
246 © Henry Wilson, London/Eyam Hall. © Emily Lane. © Eyam Hall. © Henry Wilson, London/Eyam Hall. © Christopher Phillips.
247 © Geoff Hayworth. © PA. © City Art Centre, Edinburgh. © AA.
248 © Crown Copyright/National Monuments Records, Swindon. © EH. © *idem*.
249 © NT/Joe Cornish. © AA. © Downing Street Studios, Surrey. © Emily Lane.
250 © NT/John Hammond. © PA. © NT/Nadia MacKenzie. © Cole/Edifice. © NT/Nadia MacKenzie.
251 © PA. © *idem*. © M. Duquet/Gallimard.
252 © DC. © EH/Jonathan Bailey. © EH.
253 © AA. © Fishbourne Roman Palace/Sussex Archaeological Society. © AA. © *idem*.
254 © AH. © NT/Colin R. Chalmers.
255 © AA. © EH. © AH. © CADW. © AA.
256 © Forde Abbey. © AA. © *idem*. © *idem*.
257 © AA. © PA. © K. Fergubon/SMPC. © AA.
258 © NT/Joe Cornish.
259 © NT/Matthew Antrobus. © *idem*. © NT/Oliver Benn.
260 © AA. © Skyscan Balloon Photography/EH. © AA. © *idem*. © Emily Lane. © Frampton Court.
261 © EH. © DC. © AA.
262 © Gants Mill. © Carl Wallace/Royal National Rose Society. © EH. © Gaulden Manor.
263 © Gaulden Manor. © Gawsworth Hall. © David Kimbor/Gawsworth Hall.
264 © NT/Nick Meers. © *idem*.
265 © EH. © Glamis Castle. © AA. © *idem*. © Glamis Castle.
266 © Collections/G. Wright. © Glasgow Museums. © AA. © Glasgow Museums.
267 © AA. © Collections/ M. Fife. © Collections.
268 © A. Lorgnier/Côtés Vues. © Collections/D. Dobbie. © AA. © *idem*.
269 © Collections/C. J. Smith. © P. Tompkins/SMPC. © DC.
270 © DC. © *idem*. © AA.
271 © DC. © *idem*. Hunterian Art Gallery, University of Glasgow. © *idem*. © Courtesy of Sotheby's, London.
272 © DC. © K. Paterson/SMPC. © S. Bosman/Gallimard. © Collections/G. Wright. © AA.
273 © Glasgow Museums. © AA. © *idem*. © *idem*.
274 © Glastonbury Abbey Church. © DC. © NT/William R. Davis. © DC. © NT/Jerry Harpur. © R. Beattie/SMPC.
275 © AA. © AH. © *idem*. © Gloucester City Museum.
276 © NT/Andy Williams. © Lindsay Evans.
277 © Godinton House. © Godolphin House. © *idem*. © Country Life Picture Library/Tom Leighton.
278 © EH. © Skyscan Balloon Photography/EH. © Courtesy of the Trustees of the Goodwood Collection/Christopher Simon Sykes.
279 © Gorhambury. © EH. © Gorhambury. © *idem*. © AA.
280 © EH. © A. Black/Dove Cottage, The Wordsworth Trust. © *idem*.
281 © NT. © Emily Lane. © Great Comp Charitable Trust. © NT/John Bethell.
282 © Larraine Walpole/Edifice. © AA. © Lewis-Darley/Edifice. © Darley/Edifice. © AA. © *idem*.
283 © PA. © *idem*. © *idem*. © EH/Nigel Corrie.
284 © AA. © PA. © Gregynog.
285 © All Saints Church, Gresford. © Lindsay Evans. © Skyscan Balloon Photography/EH.
286 © Grimsthorpe Estate. © *idem*. © Guildford House Gallery. © Groombridge Place Gardens.
287 © AA. © NT. © *idem*. © Lewis-Darley/Edifice.
288 © CADW. © NTS. © AA.
289 © Haddon Hall. © *idem*. © *idem*.
290 © RM. © *idem*. © *idem*. © CJB Photography, Hagley. © NT/Mike Williams.
291 © PA. © John Morrison. © Hall Place.
292 © Hamptworth Lodge. © Hammerwood Park. © *idem*. © *idem*. © NT/John Miller.
293 © NT/Alasdair Ogilvie. © RM.
294 © NT/Nick Meers. © NT/Hawkley Studios.
295 © NT/Andreas von Einsiedel. © NT/Nadia MacKenzie. © NT/John Hammond. © NT/Nadia MacKenzie.
296 © Emily Lane. © NT/Geoff Morgan. © NT/Eric Crichton. © Harlaxton Manor. © NT/John Blake.
297 © AA. © CADW.
298 © AA. © Hartland Abbey. © Worcestershire County Council.
299 © Ivanhoe Photography, Stourbridge. © AA. © St Mary in the Castle, Hastings.
300 © NT/Rob Talbot/Talbot & Whiteman. © NT/Bill Batten. © *idem*. © NT/Alan North. © PA. © AA.
301 © Sayer/Edifice. © AA. © AH.
302 © Haughley Park. © NT/John Hannavy. © Hawkstone Park. © EH/Paul Highnam.
303 © Cole/Edifice. © Emily Lane. © *idem*.
304 © AA. © Helmingham Estate. © *idem*. © DC. © NTS.
305 © AA. © PA. © EH.
306 © Hemingford Grey Manor. © AA. © *idem*.
307 © PA. © Hereford Cathedral. © PA. © *idem*.
308 © Hergest Croft Gardens. © AH.
309 © Hever Castle Ltd. © *idem*.
310 © Lewis-Darley/Edifice. © NT/Andrew Lawson. © *idem*. © Highcliffe Castle.
311 © NT/Christopher Hurst. © EH/Jonathan Bailey. © PA. © Simon Ellis. © Weideger/Edifice.
312 © Jarrold Publishing. © Hodnet Hall Gardens. © Jarrold Publishing. © Hoghton Tower Preservation Trust.
313 © Holdenby House. © Peter Marshall/Holdenby House. © AA.
314 © Holkham Estate. © RM. © Holkham Estate.
315 © Holkham Estate. © *idem*.
316 © Emily Lane. © NT/Andreas von Einsiedel. © Skyscan Balloon Photography/EH. © AA.
317 © Arthur Pickett/Honington Hall. © AA. © Arthur Pickett/Honington Hall. © AA.
318 © DC. © NT/John Blake. © NT/Jason Ingram.
319 © Jarrold Publishing/Neil Jinkerson. © *idem*. © Jarrold Publishing. © *idem*. © AA.
320 © EH. © EH/Paul Highnam.
321 © R. Welsby/SMPC. © NT/John Hammond. © NT/John Bethell. © AA. © John Morrison.
322 © Hull City Council/Ferens Art Gallery. © AA. © *idem*.
323 © DC. © C. Pemberton-Piggott. © Hyde Hall. © *idem*.
324 © NT/John Hammond. © NT/Rupert Truman. © NT/Andreas von Einsiedel. © RM.
325 © NT/Rob Matheson. © AH. © Emily Lane. © Bradford Economic Development Unit.
326 © Ingatestone Hall. © Simon Jauncey/Argyll Estate. © DC. © Interior Archive.
327 © Sotheby's Transparency Library. © AA. © *idem*. © *idem*.
328 © Museum of Scotland, Edinburgh. © G. Burns/SMPC. © Trinity College Library, Dublin. © AA.
329 © AA. © *idem*. © Gillian Maddison-Oke, Ipswich Borough Council. © Ironbridge Gorge Museum, Telford/BAL.
330 © Emily Lane. © *idem*.
331 © Brading Villa. © Chis Wormald. © NT/Joe Cornish. © EH. © Brading Villa.
332 © NT/Nick Carter. © EH.
333 © Don French/Quarr Abbey. © NT/Joe Cornish. © Don French/Quarr Abbey. © EH/Paul Highnam.
334 © Ford End Watermill. © EH.
335 © Towneley Hall Art Gallery and Museum, Burnley, Lancs/BAL. © AA. © *idem*. © *idem*. © *idem*.
336 © Emily Lane. © NT/Nadia MacKenzie. © NT/John Hammond. © AA. © NT/Mike Williams.
337 © AA. © EH. © *idem*.
338 © AH.
339 © CADW. © AA. © Kiftsgate Court. © *idem*.
340 © G. Simeone/PHOTONONSTOP. © AA. © AH. © NT/Andreas von Einsiedel. © Kimbolton School, Cambs.
341 © DC. © All Saints Church.
342 © PA. © RM.
343 © PA. © RM. © PA. © *idem*.
344 © PA. © NT/Rupert Truman.
345 © NT/Derrick E. Witty. © NT/James Mortimer. © NT/Roy Fox. © P. Taylor.
346 © Kirkby Lonsdale Church. © EH/Nigel Corrie. © *idem*. © Kirkby Lonsdale Church.
347 © EH. © *idem*. © Hart-Davis/Edifice. © EH.
348 © RM. © Knebworth House. © *idem*. © NT/Rupert Truman.
349 © NT/Andreas von Einsiedel. © *idem*. © NT/John Hammond. © NT/Rupert Truman. © NT/Andreas von Einsiedel.
350 © RM. © NT/Andrew Butler. © NT/Nick Carter. © CADW.
351 © DC. © Lampton Hall Trust. © Lancaster City Museums.
352 © Sayer/Edifice. © Jon Sparks ARPS. © Lancaster Maritime Museum.
353 © Williamson Park. © Lewis-Darley/Edifice. © Darley/Edifice. © Lewis-Darley/Edifice. © Ruskin Museum, Coniston, Cumbria/BAL.
354 © Skyscan Balloon Photography/EH.
355 © NT/Rupert Truman. © NT/Andreas von Einsiedel.
356 © Larmer Tree Gardens. © CADW. © Skyscan Balloon Photography/EH.
357 © NT/John Bethell. © RM. © *idem*. © Layer Marney Tower.
358 © AA. © *idem*. © *idem*.
359 © Leicester City Council. © AA. © Leicester City Council. © AH.
360 © DC. © Leighton Hall. © Collections/M. Fife.
361 © Leonardslee Gardens.
362 © Levens Hall. © AA.
363 © DC. © EH. © Emily Lane. © Museum of Scotland.
364 © PA. © The Usher Gallery, Lincoln. © *idem*. © *idem*. © *idem*.
365 © AH. © EH/Nigel Corrie.
366 © Christopher Phillips.
367 © AH. © NT/Rupert Truman. © DC.
368 © AA. © *idem*. © National Museums and Galleries on Merseyside. © Emily Lane.
369 © Lewis-Darley/Edifice. © Kim Sayer/Edifice.
370 © Emily Lane. © Kim Sayer/Edifice.
371 © Emily Lane. © *idem*. © *idem*. © Lewis-Darley/Edifice.
372 © Walker Art Gallery/National Museums & Galleries on Merseyside. © *idem*. © Walker Art Gallery, Merseyside/Board of Trustees: National Museums & Galleries on Merseyside/BAL. © *idem*. © *idem*. © *idem*. © National Museums & Galleries on Merseyside.
373 © NT/Dennis Gilbert. © *idem*. © Emily Lane. © Lewis-Darley/Edifice.
374 © AA. © *idem*. © *idem*. © *idem*.
375 © AA. © *idem*. © *idem*.
376 © NT/Chris King. © *idem*. © *idem*.
377 © Llanfihangel Court. © *idem*. © CADW.
378 © DC. © A. Johnston/SMPC. © H. Woods/SMPC.
379 © DC. © *idem*. © Sotheby's Transparency Library. © Glasgow Museums.
380 © Nick Swallow. © AA. © Nick Swallow. © EH. © Apsley House. © *idem*.
381 © AH. © Nick Swallow. © *idem*. © Crown Copyright.
382 © Lewis-Darley/Edifice. © AA. © *idem*.
383 © **not in E+W**. © Irene Rhoden. © Anthony Harris/Bevis Marks Synagogue.
384 © The British Museum. © *idem*. © *idem*. © *idem*. © *idem*. © *idem*.
385 © The British Museum. © *idem*. © *idem*. © *idem*. © *idem*.
386 The Royal Collection © 2002, HM Queen Elizabeth II (photo: Derry Moore). © *idem*. © Nick Swallow. © *idem*.
387 © Nick Swallow. © *idem*. © AH. © NT/Rob Matheson.
388 © AH. © Nick Swallow. © AA. © EH.
389 © EH/Paul Highnam. © Emily Lane.
390 © AH. © Phillipa Lewis/Edifice. © AH.
391 © AH. © Lewis-Darley/Edifice. © *idem*. © AH.
392 © Darley/Edifice. © College of Arms. © Museum of London, UK/BAL.
393 © Jefferson Smith. © Dickens House Museum. © By permission of the Trustees, Dulwich Picture Gallery. © Dickens House Museum. © By permission of the Trustees, Dulwich Picture Gallery.
394 © EH/Jonathan Bailey. © *idem*. © *idem*.
395 © Freud Museum, London. © Chris Ridley/Geffrye Museum. © Nick Swallow. © Lewis-Darley/Edifice.
396 © National Maritime Museum, Greenwich. © *idem*. © Flamsteed House. © The Maritime Trust, London. © *idem*.
397 © AH © National Maritime Museum, Greenwich. © AH.
398 © Lewis-Darley/Edifice. © Corporation of London. © NT/Nick Meers. © NT/Bill Batten.
399 © AA. © NT/Vera Collingwood. © NT/Jonathan Gibson.
400 © Crown Copyright: Historic Royal Palaces. © *idem*. © AA.
401 © Crown Copyright: Historic Royal Palaces. © *idem*.
402 © PA. © Darley/Edifice. © AH.
403 © AH. © Houses of Parliament, Westminster, London/BAL. © AH.
404 © Lewis/Darley/Edifice. © Imperial War Museum.
405 © AH. © Lewis-Darley/Edifice. © Fitzwilliam Museum of Cambridge/BAL. © Emily Lane. © Lewis-Darley/Edifice.
406 © 2002 Board of Trustees, Royal Botanic Gardens, Kew. © EH. © *idem*. © *idem*. © *idem*.
407 © 2002 Board of Trustees, Royal Botanic Gardens, Kew. © AH. © Lewis-Darley/Edifice. © AH
408 © AH. © Lewis-Darley/Edifice.
409 © AH. © EH. © AH.
410 © AH. © Museum of Garden History.
411 © AH. © Museum of London. © *idem*.
412 © The National Gallery, London. © *idem*.
413 © The National Gallery, London. © *idem*. © *idem*.
414 © AH. © *idem*.
415 © NT/Bill Batten. © NT/Rupert Truman. © AA. © NT/Dennis Gilbert.
416 © **Petrie Museum of Egyptian Archaeology, University College London. © Lewis-Darley/Edifice. © AA. © AH. © Nick Swallow.**
417 © AA. © *idem*. © Nick Swallow. © Martin Jones.
418 © AA. © *idem*. © Nick Swallow.
419 © Birmingham Museums & Art Gallery/BAL. © Nick Swallow. © British Museum, London/BAL.
420 © Royal Academy of Arts, London/BAL. © AH. © Emily Lane. © Thistlethwaite/Edifice. © Nick Swallow.
421 © AA. © Nick Swallow. © AA. © *idem*.
422 © Lewis-Darley/Edifice. © Nick Swallow. © AH. © Lewis-Darley/Edifice.
423 © AH. © AH. © Nick Swallow.
424 © Nick Swallow. © AH. © Nick Swallow.
425 © PA. © AH. © AH.
426 © Yale Center for British Art, Paul Mellon Collection, USA/BAL. © AH. © *idem*.
427 © AH © *idem*.
428 © AH. © AA. © Martin Charles. © *idem*.
429 © AA. © AH. © Dennis Gilbert/View/Southwark Cathedral.
430 © Spencer House/Mark Fiennes. © Spencer House. © AH. © Nick Swallow.
431 © AH. © NT/Geoffrey Frosh. © AA. © Nick Swallow.
432 © Tate, London 2002. © *idem*. © *idem*.
433 © 2002 Georg Baselitz/Tate, London 2002. © Courtesy the artists/Tate, London 2002. © Succession H. Matisse/DACS 2002/Tate, London 2002.
434 © Misha Anikst. © *idem*. © *idem*.
435 © AH.
436 © AA. © Nick Swallow. © AA.
437 © Nick Swallow. © *idem*. © AA.
438 © AA. © Wallace Collection, London/BAL.
439 © Victoria & Albert Museum/BAL. © AA. © Wesley's Chapel. © Phillipa Lewis/Edifice.
440 © AH. © Nick Swallow. © AH.
441 © AH. © *idem*.
442 © Nick Swallow. © *idem*. © AH. © *idem*.
443 © Richmond House. © William Morris Art Gallery, London. © NT.
444 © AH. © NT/Martin Charles. © AH. © NT/John Blake. © A. H. West.
445 © EH. © *idem*. © NT/Joe Cornish.
446 Loseley Park. © Leeds City Council. © Darley/Edifice. © Leeds City Council.
447 © Ludlow Castle. © L. Dunnell/Edifice.
448 © EH. © NT. © EH. © *idem*. © Cornish Picture Library/Paul Watts.
449 © Luton Borough Council. © Cornish Picture Library/Paul Watts. © NT. © EH.
450 © NT/Andreas von Einsiedel. © NT/Nick Meers. © *idem*.
451 © PA. © *idem*. © NT/Nick Meers.
452 © Lewis-Darley/Edifice. © Darley/Edifice. © CADW. © *idem*.
453 © AH. © Emily Lane. © *idem*.
454 © PA. © Lewis-Darley/Edifice.
455 © Kim Sayer/Edifice.
456 © PA. © *idem*. © *idem*. © Cole/Edifice. © PA.
457 © Lewis-Darley/Edifice. © Kim Sayer/Edifice.
458 © Lewis-Darley/Edifice. © *idem*. © PA.
459 © Emily Cole/Edifice. © AA.
460 © Manderston. © *idem*. © Mapperton Estate.

map pages

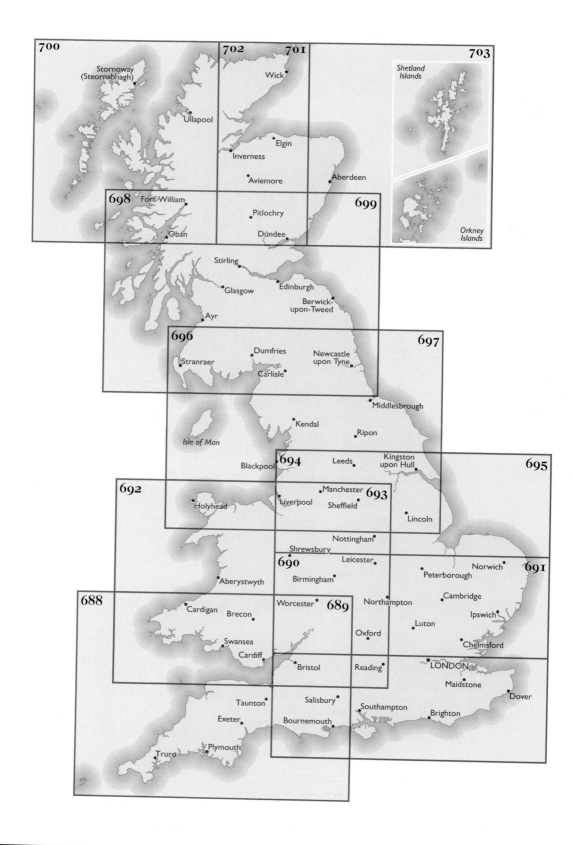

map symbols

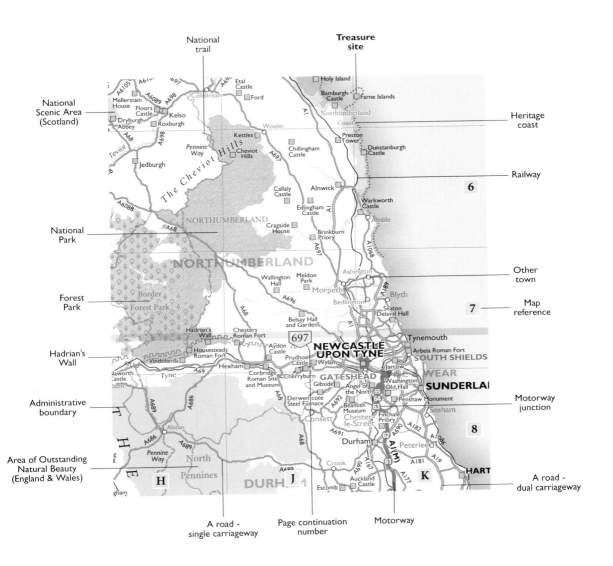

National trail

Treasure site

National Scenic Area (Scotland)

Heritage coast

Railway

National Park

Other town

Map reference

Forest Park

Hadrian's Wall

Administrative boundary

Motorway junction

Area of Outstanding Natural Beauty (England & Wales)

A road - dual carriageway

A road - single carriageway

Page continuation number

Motorway

Scale of mapping pages 688 - 703   1:1,000,000

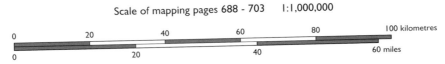

0   20   40   60   80   100 kilometres

0   20   40   60 miles

Certain county, county borough or council area names are abbreviated on the maps as follows:

Aber C	Aberdeen City	*C Glas*	City of Glasgow	*Herts*	Hertfordshire
Beds	Bedfordshire	*Clacks*	Clackmannanshire	*Myr Td*	Merthyr Tydfil
Berks	Berkshire	*Dund C*	Dundee City	*Oxon*	Oxfordshire
Bucks	Buckinghamshire	*E Duns*	East Dunbartonshire	*Warwks*	Warwickshire
C Edin	City of Edinburgh	*E Rens*	East Renfrewshire	*W Duns*	West Dunbartonshire

London entry map references
The locations of most of the London entries are referenced to 'London' on the mapping, 691 F5.

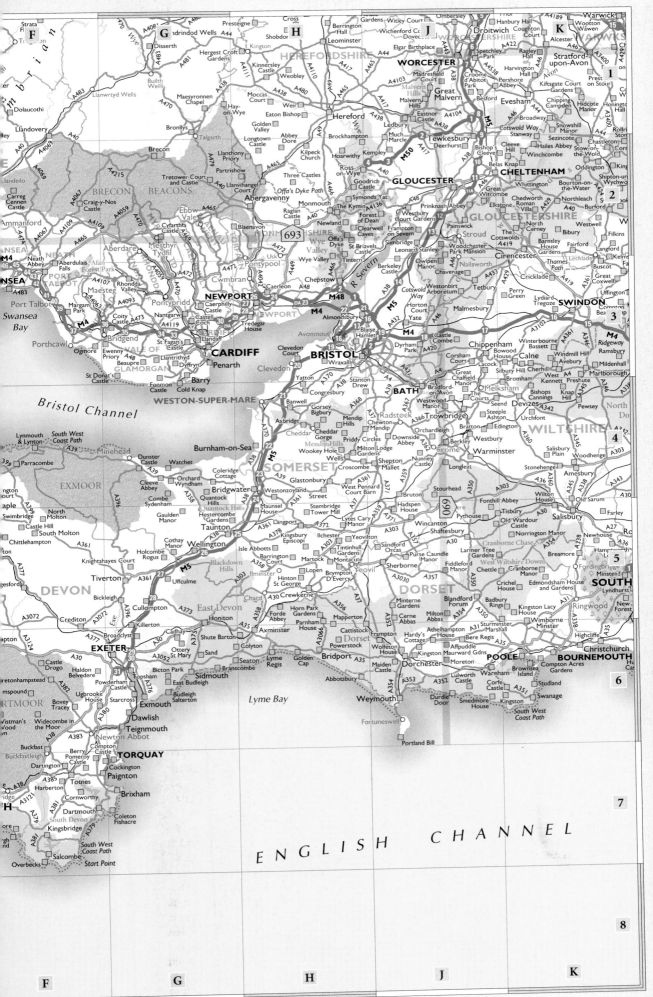

ENGLISH CHANNEL

689

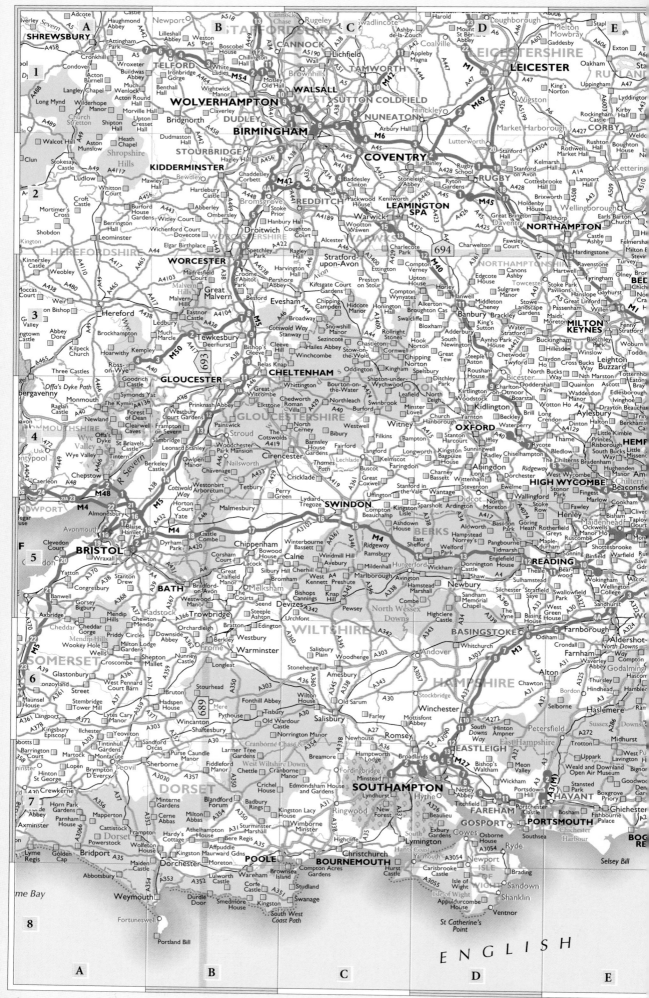

London entry map references

The locations of most of the London entries are referenced to 'London' on the mapping, 691 F5.

A
B
C
D
E
1
2
3
4
5
6
7
8
Llaneilian
Amlwch
Carreglwyd
North and South Stacks
Holyhead
Trefignath
Holy Island
ISLE OF ANGLESEY
A5025
Benllech
Penmon
Great Ormes Head
Llandudno
Colwyn Bay
69
Bodysgallen
Conwy
Abergele
A5
Llangefni
A55
A4080
Rhosneigr
Anglesey
Llanfair P G
Bangor
Beaumaris
Penrhyn Castle
Plas Newydd
Menai Bridge
Cochwillan
Bethesda
Bodnant Gardens
A548
A470
CONWY
Caernarfon
Dolbadarn Castle
A4086
Llanrwst
Caernarfon Bay
Glynllifon
A4085
Snowdon
Pen-y-Gwryd
Betws-y-coed
Capel Garmon
Clynnog-fawr
A487
A498
Dolwyddelan Castle
Ty Mawr Wybrnant
Gwydyr Forest Park
Nant Gwrtheyrn
Tre'r Ceiri
Ynyspandy
Plas Brondanw
Blaenau Ffestiniog
Nefyn
A499
Ffynnon Gybi
Ffestiniog Railway
Bodfuan
Porthmadog
A4212
Lleyn
Llyn
Criccieth Castle
Portmeirion
Pwllheli
Llandegwning
Nanhoron
Lasynys
GWYNEDD
SNOWDONIA
Harlech
Plas-yn-Rhiw
Abersoch
Llanengan
Coed-y-Brenin Forest Park
A494
Bardsey Island
Carneddau Hengwm
A496
Cymer Abbey
Dolgellau
Barmouth
A470
A493
Castell y Bere
A458
Craig yr Aderyn
Peniarth
Dyfi
Tywyn
Machynlleth
Cardigan Bay
Aberystwyth
Pen Dinas
A44
Llanidloes
Nanteos
A4120
CEREDIGION
Rhayader
Strata Florida
Aberaeron
Llanerchaeron
Tregaron
A485
A482
Teifi
Cambrian Mountains
A475
Lampeter
Cardigan
PEMBROKESHIRE COAST
Strumble Head
A484
Cilgerran Castle
A486
Llanwrtyd
A483
Nevern
Newcastle Emlyn
Dolaucothi
Fishguard
Pentre Ifan
Llandovery
Mynydd Preseli
Talley
St David's Head
St David's
PEMBROKESHIRE
A478
CARMARTHENSHIRE
Cwmdu
A4069
Pembrokeshire Coast Path
Aberglasney
Llandeilo
Carmarthen
A40
Dinefwr
Towy
St Brides Bay
Haverfordwest
A4076
Narberth
St Clears
Carreg Cennen Castle
BRECON
Craig-y-Nos Castle
Skomer
Picton Castle
Colby Woodland Garden
A477
Laugharne
A48
Milford Haven
Carew Castle
A4075
Pendine
Ammanford
A4067
A4109
688
Pembroke
Lamphey
Tenby
Pembrokeshire Coast Path
Kidwelly
A476
A474
A465
PEMBROKESHIRE COAST
Carmarthen Bay
Llanelli
SWANSEA
M4
Neath Abbey
Aberdulais Falls
Afan Forest Park
Stackpole
Manorbier Castle
A4139
Weobley Castle
NEATH PORT TALBOT
St Govan's Chapel
Gower Peninsula
SWANSEA
A483
Arthur's Stone
Parc le Breos
A4118
Port Talbot
Maesteg
Gower
Paviland Cave
Oxwich
Port Eynon
Swansea Bay
Margam Park
Porthcawl
Ogmore
Ewenny Priory
St Donat's Castle
Bristol Channel
Lynmouth & Lynton
South West Coast Path
Combe Martin
Ilfracombe
Lundy
Minehead
Parracombe

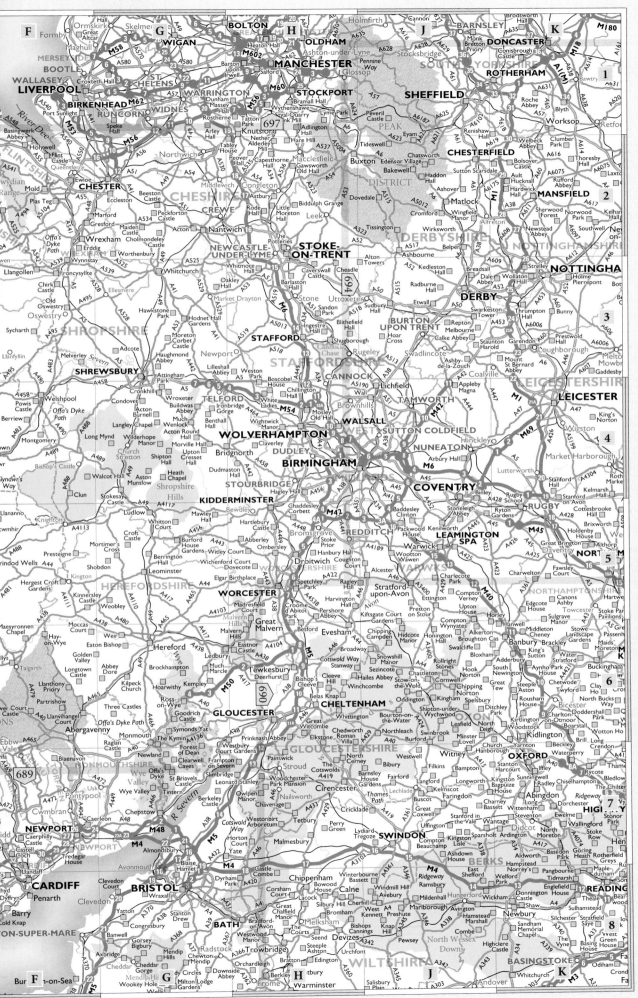

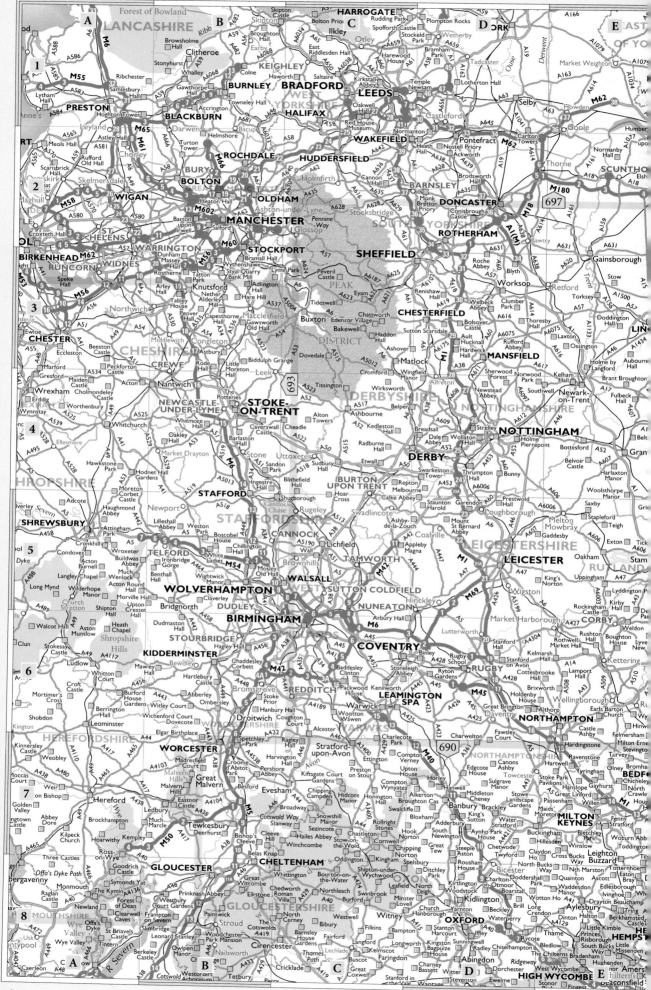

694

A   **B**   AYRSHIRE   **C**   **D**   **E**

1
Electric Brae
Ailsa Craig
Culzean Castle
Crossraguel Abbey
Maybole
Girvan
SOUTH AYRSHIRE
A76
Sanquhar
Nith
Southern Upland Way
Drumlanrig Castle
Thornhill
Moffat
15
Southern Upland Way
Hawick
A7

2
Ballantrae
Loch Ryan
Galloway Forest Park
698
New Galloway
Southern Upland Way
A702
A76
A709
Lochmaben
Lockerbie
Langholm
DUMFRIES & GALLOWAY
16
Annan
18
19
20
Gretna Green
Longtown
Lanercost Priory
A6071
Stranraer
Newton Stewart
A75
A711
Dumfries
Sweetheart Abbey
Nith Estuary
Ruthwell
Caerlaverock Castle
Annan
Gretna
21
44
43
CARLISLE
A7
A689
Bran
Portpatrick
A77 A716
Castle Kennedy Gardens
Wigtown
Fleet Valley
Gatehouse of Fleet
Castle Douglas
New Abbey
Dalbeattie
A710
Solway Coast
Holme Cultram Abbey
Wigton
42
Wreay
A69
Warwick Bridge
A595
M6
Eden
Lo

3
Luce Bay
A747 A746
Wigtown Bay
Kirkcudbright
A711
Threave Castle and Garden
East Stewartry Coast
Dundrennan Abbey
Solway Firth
Maryport
Workington
Whitehaven
A596
A595
A594
A66
A597
A5086
A591
Cockermouth
Keswick
Castlerigg Stone Circle
CUMBRIA
LAKE
A66
Hutton-in-the-Forest
A6
A592
Dalemain
41
Penrith
40
Brou
A66
Lowther Castle
Whithorn
Drummore
Mull of Galloway
Burrow Head

4
Point of Ayre
A10
Isle of Man
Ramsey
A14
A18
Millennium Way
Isle of Man
A18
A3
A4
Peel
A1
Egremont
Calder Abbey
Hardknott Roman Fort
Ravenglass
Muncaster Castle
DISTRICT
Grasmere
Rydal Mount
Ambleside
Hawkshead
Brantwood
Lake District
Hill Top
Grizedale Forest Park
Townend
Windermere
Blackwell
A592
A593
A5074
A591
Kendal
Sizergh Castle
A6

5
Calf of Man
A26
A5
Port Erin
A25
DOUGLAS
Castletown
Broughton-in-Furness
Millom
Ulverston
A595
A5093
Stott Park Bobbin Mill
Dalton-in-Furness
Conishead Priory
Furness
Isle of Walney
BARROW-IN-FURNESS
Holker Hall
Cartmel
Leighton Hall
Levens Hall
A590
A5074
Arnside & Silverdale
Carnforth
36
35
Kirk
Lonsda
A65
Morecambe
Heysham
Lancaster
A588
A6
34
33
M6

6
IRISH
SEA
Fleetwood
Cleveleys
BLACKPOOL
A588
A585
A586
M55
32
Ribcl
Lytham Hall
Lytham St Anne's
A584
A583
PRESTON
Samles
Houghton To

7
SOUTHPORT
A565
A570
Meols Hall
Leyland
Astley Hall
A581
Rufford Old Hall
Scarisbrick Hall
Ormskirk
Great Altcar
Formby
A59
Skelmersdale
Maghull
M58
A570
A580
WI
MERSEYSIDE
BOOTLE
M58

8
North and South Stacks
Holyhead
Trefignath
Holy Island
Rhosneigr
Carreglwyd
Amlwch
Llaneilian
A5025
ISLE OF ANGLESEY
Benllech
692
Penmon
Beaumaris
Llangefni
Llanfair P G
A5
A4080
A55
Bangor
Penrhyn Castle
Cochwillan
Bethesda
Great Ormes Head
Llandudno
Bodysgallen
Colwyn Bay
Conwy
A470
Bodnant Gardens
A547
Rhyl
Abergele
A548
Trelawnyd
Bodelwyddan Castle
Gyrn Castle
St Asaph's Cathedral
A525
Denbigh
A543
CONWY
Pentre Llanrhaeadr
DENBIGH
Clwydian Range
Mold
A494
A541
Plas Teg
Ruthin
Basingwerk Abbey
Holywell
Flint Castle
Queensferry
A548
FLINTSHIRE
Ewloe
CHESTER
A51
A55
Beeston Castle
Eccleston
Peckfort Castle
Marford
Gresford
534
WALLASEY
LIVERPOOL
BIRKENHEAD
M62
Croxteth Hall
ST HELENS
Port Sunlight
A41
RUNCORN
Speke Hall
M53
Hooton
693
M56
WIDN
North
River Dee
A540

Caernarfon Bay
Caernarfon
A499
Plas Newydd
Menai Bridge
A4086
Dolbadarn Castle
Snowdon
Pen-y-Gwryd
A4085
A498
Dolwyddelan
Berwe
Mawr
Wybrant
Capel Garmon
Llanrwst
A548
A543
Llanfair
Offa's

A   **B**   **C**   **D**   **E**

697

A   B   C   D   E

1

2

Butt of Lewis

Port of Ness (Port Nis)

A857

A858

Carloway (Carlabhagh)

Stornoway (Steornabhagh)

Broad Bay

A857

A866

Callanish
Standing Stones

A858

Isle of Lewis

A859

The Min

Lewis (Leodhais) and
Harris (Hearadh)

3

Scarp

WESTERN ISLES
South Lewis,
Harris &
North Uist

A859

St Kilda

St Kilda

Taransay

Tarbert
(Tairbeart)

Shiant
Islands

Outer Hebrides

Sound of Harris

A859

Harris
(Hearadh)

4

Pabbay

Berneray
(Bearnaraigh)

Lochmaddy (Loch nam Madadh)

North Uist

A867

North Uist
(Uibhist a Tuath)

A865

The Little Minch

Trotternish

Uig

Rona

Inver
Gar

5

Benbecula
(Beinn Na Faoghla)

A865

Dunvegan

A850

A855

Skye

Portree

Sound of Raasay

Raasay

Inner Sound

Raasay

A863

Scalpay

South Uist
Machair

South Uist

A865

South Uist
(Uibhist a Deas)

A87

Drynoch

A863

Kyle of Lochalsh

Eilean I
Cas

Lochboisdale (Loch Baghasdail)

Isle
of
Skye

The Cuillin Hills

A87

6

Eriskay (Eiriosgaigh)

Soay

Cuillin

Ardvasar

Sound of Sleat

Knoy

Barra

Sound of Barra

Barra (Barraigh)

Castlebay (Bagh a Chaisteil)

Canna

Cuillin
Sound

Rum, Eigg,
Canna and Muck

Rum

Mallaig

Loch
Morar

Mingulay

The Small Isles

Eigg

A830

A86

7

Inner Hebrides

Muck

Sound of Arisaig

Morar, Moidart &
Ardnamurchan

Acharacle

Loch S

Coll

Ardnamurchan
Peninsula

6

Arinagour

Coll

Tobermory

8

Tiree

Tiree

Scarinish

Sound of Mull

Lochaline

Isle of Mull

Lynn o

Fingal's
Cave

Ulva

Loch na Keal,
Isle of Mull

Mull

A849

Dunstaff
Ca

Iona

Ii

Errera

A   B   C   D   E

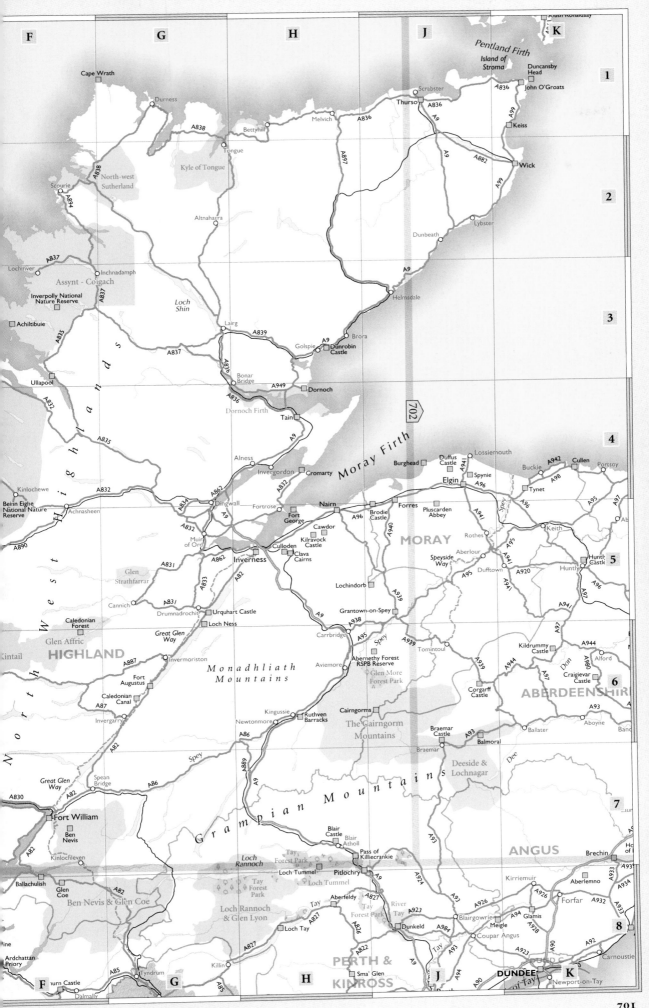

1

Unst
Unst
A968

2

Fetlar
Yell
Yell

Shetland
(North)

A970

A968

St Magnus
Bay

Whalsay

Shetlands
Mainland
A971

3

Foula

Scalloway
Lerwick

Brassay

Shetland
(South)

SHETLAND
ISLANDS

A970

4

Mousa

Jarlshof

Sumburgh Roost

Fair Isle

5

The North Sound

Westray Firth

Sanday Sound

A966

Stromsay Firth

6

A967

Mainland

Skara Brae
Ring of
Brodgar
A965
Kirkwall

Hoy &
West Mainland
Stromness
Maes
Howe
A964
A960

A961

Hoy
Orkneys
ORKNEY
ISLANDS

7

Hoy

A961
South Ronaldsay

Pentland Firth

Island of
Stroma
Duncansby
Head

Scrabster
A836
John O'Groats

8

Membership of English Heritage

We currently have around 470,000 members, people who join because they see their membership as a direct and tangible way of supporting our work as well as enabling them to visit our sites free of charge.

To find out more, or to join, please contact:
 English Heritage Membership Department
PO Box 570
Swindon SN2 2YR
Tel. 0870 333 1181
e-mail: members@english-heritage.org.uk
The catalogue of our wide range of publications
 is available from the same address, or e-mail
customers@english-heritage.org.uk

English Heritage Members' and Visitors' Handbook 2002: Published annually in February, this full-colour guide to over 400 English Heritage properties gives full details of opening hours, prices (where applicable – many of the properties are free), and how to get there. £7.95, but free to members.

Guidebooks to English Heritage properties can be purchased on site, but are also available by mail order from our postal sales service. New for 2002 is a guide to the free sites in the north-west. Details are in the catalogue, or contact:
English Heritage Postal Sales
c/o Gillards
Trident Works
Temple Cloud
Bristol BS39 5AZ
tel: 01761 452966
e-mail: ehsales@gillards.com

Membership of the National Trust

As a charity independent of government, the Trust has depended on voluntary help and the financial contributions of its members and many others since it was founded in 1895. Today, nearly 3 million people are members. Almost 40,000 members and volunteers give generously of their time each year to further its objectives.

Membership of the National Trust gives free entry to all sites plus a free copy of the handbook. Adult membership costs £30* a year; family membership is £57.*

The National Trust
36 Queen Anne's Gate, London SW1H 9AS
Tel. 0870 458 4000
e-mail: enquiries@thenationaltrust.org.uk
www.nationaltrust.org.uk

* Rates correct at time of going to press.

The National Trust publishes a wide range of books, from general interest to gardening, cookery and titles for children. Readers of *Treasures of Britain* will find the following titles invaluable in making visits to Trust properties.

The National Trust Handbook: Published annually, approx. 400 pages of detailed information on places to visit, their opening arrangements, facilities and how to get there. Published in March each year, price approx. £6.95.

Gardens Handbook: A visitors guide to over 140 great gardens of the National Trust, with descriptions of special features and good times to visit. £7.99.

The National Trust Guide: Fully comprehensive and lavishly illustrated guide giving detailed information on National Trust properties, from world-famous gardens such as Sissinghurst to the last water-driven Spade Mill in Ireland. £24.99.

All these books and more can be viewed and purchased online at www.nationaltrust.org.uk/bookshop